HANDBOOK
of
PSYCHOLOGY

HANDBOOK
of
PSYCHOLOGY

VOLUME 6
DEVELOPMENTAL PSYCHOLOGY

Richard M. Lerner
M. Ann Easterbrooks
Jayanthi Mistry

Volume Editors

Irving B. Weiner

Editor-in-Chief

John Wiley & Sons, Inc.

Copyright © 2003 by John Wiley & Sons, Inc., Hoboken, New Jersey. All rights reserved.

Published simultaneously in Canada.

Library of Congress Cataloging-in-Publication Data:

Handbook of psychology / Irving B. Weiner, editor-in-chief.
     p.   cm.
    Includes bibliographical references and indexes.
    Contents: v. 1. History of psychology / edited by Donald K. Freedheim — v. 2. Research methods in psychology / edited by John A. Schinka, Wayne F. Velicer — v. 3. Biological psychology / edited by Michela Gallagher, Randy J. Nelson — v. 4. Experimental psychology / edited by Alice F. Healy, Robert W. Proctor — v. 5. Personality and social psychology / edited by Theodore Millon, Melvin J. Lerner — v. 6. Developmental psychology / edited by Richard M. Lerner, M. Ann Easterbrooks, Jayanthi Mistry — v. 7. Educational psychology / edited by William M. Reynolds, Gloria E. Miller — v. 8. Clinical psychology / edited by George Stricker, Thomas A. Widiger — v. 9. Health psychology / edited by Arthur M. Nezu, Christine Maguth Nezu, Pamela A. Geller — v. 10. Assessment psychology / edited by John R. Graham, Jack A. Naglieri — v. 11. Forensic psychology / edited by Alan M. Goldstein — v. 12. Industrial and organizational psychology / edited by Walter C. Borman, Daniel R. Ilgen, Richard J. Klimoski.
    ISBN 0-471-17669-9 (set) — ISBN 0-471-38320-1 (cloth : alk. paper : v. 1)
— ISBN 0-471-38513-1 (cloth : alk. paper : v. 2) — ISBN 0-471-38403-8 (cloth : alk. paper : v. 3)
— ISBN 0-471-39262-6 (cloth : alk. paper : v. 4) — ISBN 0-471-38404-6 (cloth : alk. paper : v. 5)
— ISBN 0-471-38405-4 (cloth : alk. paper : v. 6) — ISBN 0-471-38406-2 (cloth : alk. paper : v. 7)
— ISBN 0-471-39263-4 (cloth : alk. paper : v. 8) — ISBN 0-471-38514-X (cloth : alk. paper : v. 9)
— ISBN 0-471-38407-0 (cloth : alk. paper : v. 10) — ISBN 0-471-38321-X (cloth : alk. paper : v. 11)
— ISBN 0-471-38408-9 (cloth : alk. paper : v. 12)
    1. Psychology. I. Weiner, Irving B.

BF121.H1955 2003
150—dc21

2002066380

Printed in the United States of America.

10 9 8 7 6 5 4 3 2 1

Editorial Board

Handbook of Psychology Preface

Psychology at the beginning of the twenty-first century has become a highly diverse field of scientific study and applied technology. Psychologists commonly regard their discipline as the science of behavior, and the American Psychological Association has formally designated 2000 to 2010 as the "Decade of Behavior." The pursuits of behavioral scientists range from the natural sciences to the social sciences and embrace a wide variety of objects of investigation. Some psychologists have more in common with biologists than with most other psychologists, and some have more in common with sociologists than with most of their psychological colleagues. Some psychologists are interested primarily in the behavior of animals, some in the behavior of people, and others in the behavior of organizations. These and other dimensions of difference among psychological scientists are matched by equal if not greater heterogeneity among psychological practitioners, who currently apply a vast array of methods in many different settings to achieve highly varied purposes.

Psychology has been rich in comprehensive encyclopedias and in handbooks devoted to specific topics in the field. However, there has not previously been any single handbook designed to cover the broad scope of psychological science and practice. The present 12-volume *Handbook of Psychology* was conceived to occupy this place in the literature. Leading national and international scholars and practitioners have collaborated to produce 297 authoritative and detailed chapters covering all fundamental facets of the discipline, and the *Handbook* has been organized to capture the breadth and diversity of psychology and to encompass interests and concerns shared by psychologists in all branches of the field.

Two unifying threads run through the science of behavior. The first is a common history rooted in conceptual and empirical approaches to understanding the nature of behavior. The specific histories of all specialty areas in psychology trace their origins to the formulations of the classical philosophers and the methodology of the early experimentalists, and appreciation for the historical evolution of psychology in all of its variations transcends individual identities as being one kind of psychologist or another. Accordingly, Volume 1 in the *Handbook* is devoted to the history of psychology as it emerged in many areas of scientific study and applied technology.

A second unifying thread in psychology is a commitment to the development and utilization of research methods suitable for collecting and analyzing behavioral data. With attention both to specific procedures and their application in particular settings, Volume 2 addresses research methods in psychology.

Volumes 3 through 7 of the *Handbook* present the substantive content of psychological knowledge in five broad areas of study: biological psychology (Volume 3), experimental psychology (Volume 4), personality and social psychology (Volume 5), developmental psychology (Volume 6), and educational psychology (Volume 7). Volumes 8 through 12 address the application of psychological knowledge in five broad areas of professional practice: clinical psychology (Volume 8), health psychology (Volume 9), assessment psychology (Volume 10), forensic psychology (Volume 11), and industrial and organizational psychology (Volume 12). Each of these volumes reviews what is currently known in these areas of study and application and identifies pertinent sources of information in the literature. Each discusses unresolved issues and unanswered questions and proposes future directions in conceptualization, research, and practice. Each of the volumes also reflects the investment of scientific psychologists in practical applications of their findings and the attention of applied psychologists to the scientific basis of their methods.

The *Handbook of Psychology* was prepared for the purpose of educating and informing readers about the present state of psychological knowledge and about anticipated advances in behavioral science research and practice. With this purpose in mind, the individual *Handbook* volumes address the needs and interests of three groups. First, for graduate students in behavioral science, the volumes provide advanced instruction in the basic concepts and methods that define the fields they cover, together with a review of current knowledge, core literature, and likely future developments. Second, in addition to serving as graduate textbooks, the volumes offer professional psychologists an opportunity to read and contemplate the views of distinguished colleagues concerning the central thrusts of research and leading edges of practice in their respective fields. Third, for psychologists seeking to become conversant with fields outside their own specialty and for persons outside of psychology seeking information about psychological matters, the *Handbook* volumes serve as a reference source for expanding their knowledge and directing them to additional sources in the literature.

The preparation of this *Handbook* was made possible by the diligence and scholarly sophistication of the 25 volume editors and co-editors who constituted the Editorial Board. As Editor-in-Chief, I want to thank each of them for the pleasure of their collaboration in this project. I compliment them for having recruited an outstanding cast of contributors to their volumes and then working closely with these authors to achieve chapters that will stand each in their own right as valuable contributions to the literature. I would like finally to express my appreciation to the editorial staff of John Wiley and Sons for the opportunity to share in the development of this project and its pursuit to fruition, most particularly to Jennifer Simon, Senior Editor, and her two assistants, Mary Porterfield and Isabel Pratt. Without Jennifer's vision of the *Handbook* and her keen judgment and unflagging support in producing it, the occasion to write this preface would not have arrived.

IRVING B. WEINER
Tampa, Florida

Volume Preface

At this writing, at the beginning of the twenty-first century, the study of human development is framed by theoretical models that stress that dynamic, integrated relations across all the distinct but fused levels of organization involved in human life. The relations among these levels constitute the basic process of development. The levels include biology, individual psychological and behavioral functioning, social relationships and institutions, the natural and designed physical ecology, culture, and history.

Indeed, from the beginning of the last century to the present one, the history of developmental psychology has been marked by an increasing interest in the role of history. Scholars have been concerned with how temporal changes in the familial, social, and cultural contexts of life shape the quality of the trajectories of change that individuals traverse across their life spans. Scholars of human development have incorporated into their causal schemas about ontogenetic change a nonreductionistic and synthetic conception about the influence of context—of culture and history—on ontogenetic change. In contrast to models framed by a Cartesian split view of the causes of change, cutting-edge thinking in the field of human development has altered its essential ontology. The relational view of being that now predominates the field has required epistemological revisions in the field as well. Both qualitative understanding and quantitative understanding have been legitimized as scholars have sought an integrated understanding of the multiple levels of organization comprising the ecology of human development.

The integrated relations studied in contemporary scholarship are embedded in the actual ecology of human development. As a consequence, policies and programs represent both features of the cultural context of this ecology and methodological tools for understanding how variations in individual-context relations may impact the trajectory of human life. As such, the application of developmental science (through policy and program innovations and evaluations) is part of—synthesized with—the study of the basic, relational processes of human development.

In essence, then, as we pursue our scholarship about human development at this early part of a new century, we do so with an orientation to the human life span that is characterized by (a) integrated, relational models of human life,

perspectives synthesizing biological-through-physical ecological influences on human development in nonreductionistic manners; (b) a broad array of qualitative and quantitative methodologies necessary for attaining knowledge about these fused, biopsychoecological relations; (c) a growing appreciation of the importance of the cultural and historical influences on the quality and trajectory of human development across the course of life; and (d) a synthesis of basic and applied developmental science.

These four defining themes in the study of human development are represented in contemporary developmental systems theories, perspectives that constitute the overarching conceptual frames of modern scholarship in the study of human development. We believe that the chapters in this volume reflect and extend this integrative systems view of basic and applied developmental scholarship.

Part I of this volume, "Foundations of Development Across the Life Span," describes the ontological and epistemological features of this synthetic approach to developmental science. The following four parts of the volume provide evidence, within and across successive portions of the life span, of the rich scholarship conducted to describe and explain dynamic relations between developing individuals and their complex contexts. The final part of the volume, "Applied Developmental Psychology Across the Life Span," extends the age-specific discussions of basic person-context relational processes to multiple portions of the life span. Chapters in this section focus on the use of concepts and research associated with developmental systems thinking in applied efforts aimed at enhancing relational processes and promoting positive, healthy developmental trajectories across life.

In sum, by focusing on the four themes of contemporary human development theory and research just described, chapters in this volume reflect and offer a foundation for continued contributions to developmental scholarship aimed at understanding the dynamic relations between individuals and contexts. As we believe is persuasively demonstrated by the chapters in this volume, contemporary human developmental science provides rigorous and important scholarship about the process of human development and applications across the life span. Together, these advances in the scholarship of knowledge generation and knowledge application serve as an invaluable means for advancing science and service pertinent to people across the breadth of their lives.

There are numerous people to thank in regard to the preparation of this book. First and foremost we are indebted to the volume's contributors. Their scholarship and dedication to excellence and social relevance in developmental science and its application enabled this work to be produced. The contributions serve as models of how scholarship may contribute both to knowledge and to the positive development of people across their life spans. We also owe a great debt to editor-in-chief Irving Weiner, both for giving us the opportunity to edit this volume of the Handbook and for his unflagging support and superb scholarly advice and direction throughout the entire project. We are especially indebted to our colleague in the Eliot-Pearson Department of Child Development at Tufts University, Professor David Elkind, for his generous and insightful foreword to this volume.

Our colleagues and students in Eliot-Pearson were great resources to us in the development of this volume. We thank Karyn Lu, managing editor of the Applied Developmental Science Publications Program in Eliot-Pearson, for her expert editorial support and guidance. Jennifer Simon, our publisher at Wiley, was a constant source of excellent advice, encouragement, and collegial support, and we are pleased to acknowledge our gratitude to her.

Finally, we deeply appreciate the love and support given to us by our families during our work on this volume. They remain our most cherished developmental assets, and we gratefully dedicate this book to them.

RICHARD M. LERNER
M. ANN EASTERBROOKS
JAYANTHI MISTRY

Foreword

Longevity within a discipline carries with it certain advantages. Not the least of these is the luxury of a historical perspective. I was increasingly drawn to this perspective as I read over the topics of this sixth volume of the *Handbook of Psychology: Developmental Psychology*. What impressed me, from a perspective of 40 years, was both how much had changed and how much had remained the same. Accordingly, in this foreword I want to take the opportunity to reflect briefly, for each of the major domains covered by the text, both on the progress that has been made and on what remains to be accomplished.

If I were to use one concept to describe the difference between the developmental psychology of today and that of 40 years ago, it would be the movement from *simplicity* to *complexity*. When I was going to school, positivism was in vogue. One facet was the belief in Occam's razor: "Simplify, simplify" was the dictum—that is, reduce everything to the simplest, most basic formulation. Today, in our postmodern world, we recognize that the goal of simplicity was misguided. In all domains of psychological investigation the further we progress, the more we discover the multiplicity, and intricacy, of variables and factors that must be taken into account in the understanding and prediction of human behavior. Complexity, moreover, also entails the breakdown of disciplinary boundaries and the rapid rise of interdisciplinary research and theory.

In their introductory chapter Lerner, Easterbrooks, and Mistry give a comprehensive overview of the multifaceted nature of human development. Development has to be historically situated and connected to the social, cultural, political, and economic forces that are in play at that time in history. Complexity is at play in the psychological processes themselves. Learning, perception, and cognition, as well as other psychological dispositions, are all much more involved than we once supposed them to be. Indeed, each of the chapters in this book is a testament to this new respect for complexity.

Our discipline is also much broader than it was in the past. A case in point is the relatively new interest in human development across the life span. Today, we take this extension of our area of research and theory across the whole life cycle as a given. However, it was not always so. As late as 1954 David Wechsler could still write that intelligence peaked at the age of 18 years and declined thereafter. This psychometric view contributed to a neglect of the psychology of adulthood. Likewise, the prevalence of Freudian psychology contributed to the view that adult personality could be understood completely in terms of childhood experience. Human development after adolescence, in and of itself, was generally regarded as uninteresting if not boring. Erikson's work on the human life cycle was one of the major impetuses to studying adulthood in all of its psychological vicissitudes. In addition, the fact that people live longer and healthier lives has contributed to the concern with development across the whole life cycle.

Today, as Overton describes it, the field is rich in both research and theory. The life-span approach to development has raised a whole new set of questions and theoretical issues that will act back on what we know and think about development from infancy to adolescence. Although developmental psychology has always had an applied dimension, given its close association with both pediatrics and education, that dimension was always subordinate to purely disciplinary concerns. In his chapter, Donald Wertlieb makes clear that that situation has changed and that applied concerns now dictate a great deal of developmental research. This applied emphasis is illustrated not only by Wertlieb's examples but also by a great many chapters in the book wherein the authors draw implication for policy and practice.

Infancy has been one of the most intensely studied and conceptualized fields of developmental psychology. Again, our knowledge in this domain, as in so many others, continues to grow and to demonstrate the complexity of behavior at the infancy level. The chapter titled "Infant Perception and Cognition," by Cohen and Cashon, describes the many contemporary research technologies and theoretical models employed in the study of infants' progress in cognitive ability and conceptual understanding. In the next chapter, titled "Social and Emotional Development in Infancy," Thompson, Easterbrooks, and Padilla-Walker emphasize the contextual variables that have to be considered in understanding attachment and the evolution of self-other understanding.

The interdisciplinary nature of much of today's developmental psychology is nicely evidenced by the Gunnar and Davis chapter titled "Stress and Emotion in Early

Childhood." Workers in this area are bringing together psychological, biological, and neurological concepts to provide a deeper understanding of the dynamics of stress. The next chapter in this section, "Diversity in Caregiving Contexts," by Fitzgerald, Mann, Cabrera, and Wong, is yet another example of the emergence of applied studies. With more than 85% of young children in one or another form of child care, the need to assess the effects of amount and quality of early child care is imperative. This chapter not only reviews the few longitudinal studies in this field but also suggests important caveats in the interpretation of data from such investigations.

In the third part of the book, which deals with childhood proper (ages 6–12), we again see how the study of this stage of development has grown in both breadth and complexity. The first chapter in this section, by Hoff, summarizes contemporary research and theory on language development in childhood. In so doing, Hoff highlights the biological, linguistic, social, and cognitive approaches to this topic as well as the many questions that still remain in the attempts to discover how children learn to talk. In his chapter titled "Cognitive Development in Childhood," Feldman summarizes the many changes undergone in a field that was once dominated by Piagetian research and theory. Neo-Piagetian approaches, information theory models, the individualization of normative development, and the use of brain imaging to study the development of mental processes are but some of the innovations that have transformed this area of investigation over the last few decades.

Likewise, the chapter "Emotion and Personality Development in Childhood," by Cummings, Braungart-Rieker, and Du Rocher-Schudlich, goes well beyond the identification of the primary emotions and their differentiation with age, which once characterized this field. Now researchers look at emotion in connection with many other facets of development from psychobiology to personality. Social-cultural variables are taken into account as well. What is striking with respect to emotions, as with so many other topics covered in this book, is how contextualized the treatment of this topic now is in contrast to the isolated way in which it was once approached.

The following chapter, "Social Development and Social Relationships in Middle Childhood," by McHale, Dariotis, and Kauh, is quite striking in its break with the past. For many decades childhood was a relatively neglected stage except perhaps for cognitive and moral development. But these authors make a strong case for the crucial importance of this period for the development of independence, work habits, self-regulation, and social skills. In their chapter titled

"The Cultural Context of Child Development," Mistry and Saraswathi give evidence that the road to cross-disciplinary research is not always smooth. They illustrate how the fields of cross-cultural psychology, cultural psychology, and developmental psychology do not always map easily on to one another. They give challenging examples of the kinds of research paradigms that might ease the integration of culture and development.

Part IV of the text deals with adolescence. The first chapter, "Puberty, Sexuality, and Health," by Susman, Dorn, and Schiefelbein, is a testament to the complexity with which we now view development. In addition to biopsychosocial models, the paper also includes the perspectives of developmental contextualism and holistic interactionism. It also reflects the new applied emphasis by suggesting some of the policy, and educational implications, of current research on pubertal timing. In their chapter titled "Cognitive Development in Adolescence," Eccles, Wigfield, and Byrnes focus upon the relation of cognitive growth and achievement as this relationship is mediated by gender and ethnic group differences. Again we see that cognitive development, once considered pretty much in isolation, is now placed in a much broader personal-social context.

Galambos and Costigan also demonstrate the new multivariate approach to developmental issues in their chapter titled "Emotion and Personality Development in Adolescence." Among the new themes emerging from this contextual approach are a focus on optimal development, cultural variations, the relation of emotion to temperament, and the person approach. The applied dimension is reflected in the author's suggestions for intervention and prevention programs. In their chapter titled "Positive Behaviors, Problem Behaviors, and Resiliency in Adolescence," Perkins and Borden give the lie to the naive notion that educational curricula are the panacea for all of adolescent problem behaviors. On the contrary, this chapter reflects our current understanding that the real issue is why young people take risks. Perkins and Borden detail the risk factors revealed by contemporary research. They also provide a brief history of the development of resiliency research. In this review they highlight the many forms of social capital that support invulnerability. Authors Kerr, Stattin, Biesecker, and Ferrer-Wreder provide a groundbreaking integration of the parenting and the peer interaction literature in their chapter titled "Relationships with Parents and Peers in Adolescence." Up until very recently these two topics were dealt with as independent issues. This chapter provides a fine example of the integrative work going on both within and between disciplines.

Part V of the text looks at research and theory on adulthood and aging. In their chapter titled "Disease, Health, and Aging," Siegler, Bosworth, and Poon look at the variables coming into play in the study of aging during this new century. These variables include the input from multiple disciplines, a focus on Alzheimer's, the social context of aging, and the impact of new discoveries in medicine and genetics. Dixon and Cohen, in their chapter titled "Cognitive Development in Adulthood," summarize findings from a very active field of research. Both studies dealing with classical and emerging issues are reviewed. One of the classical issues is the study of patterns of intellectual aging. Among the emerging issues are the study of metamemory and social interactive memory.

A major issue of personality research in adulthood is the stability and change of attitudes and traits over time. In their chapter titled "Personality Development in Adulthood and Old Age," Bertrand and Lachman review several approaches, theories, and models that have been put forward to address this issue. They also review findings regarding the relation of identity, self-efficacy, and other variables on the development of adult personality. A novel approach to the study of aging is introduced by Pruchno and Rosenbaum in their chapter titled "Social Relationships in Adulthood and Old Age." These authors focus on research on adult social relations in which at least one of the participants is elderly. They look at relations among spouses, parents and children, siblings, and friends. Their aim is not only to discern patterns but also to identify key research questions that have yet to be addressed.

Part VI of the book is devoted to applied issues. Hauser-Cram and Howell, in their chapter titled "Disabilities and Development," review the history and current state or research on children with disabilities. Although the authors welcome the research relating disabilities to family influences and family health, they cite the lack of research relating disabilities to cultural conceptions of challenged children. The next chapter, "Applied Developmental Science of Positive Human Development," by Lerner, Anderson, Balsano, Dowling, and Bobek, is conceptual and theoretical rather than empirical. A number of different person-context models are reviewed, and the authors use the youth charter model as an example of how the person-context approach can be employed to promote adolescent health. In his chapter titled "Child Development and the Law," Lamb illustrates how developmental research and theory can be invaluable in making legal decisions affecting the family. As cases in point he reviews the research regarding child witness testimony and divorce and custody. This review makes his case that the legal system might well look to developmental science for important information and guidance.

A very interesting approach to life-span development is offered by Connell and Janevic in their chapter titled "Health and Human Development." These authors look at the important issue of how health habits, social involvement, and attitudes at one age period affect health at later periods. A telling example is the relation between a relative lack of physical activity in the early adult years and the contraction of diabetes at middle age. The authors suggest important contextual issues such as socioeconomic status, race, culture, and gender as other variables that enter into the health-aging connection. The final chapter, "Successful Aging," ends on a positive note. In this chapter Freund and Riediger deal with models that have been suggested for successful aging. These models emphasize the importance of actively taking charge of one's life and of continued engagement with the world. In so doing, older people can maintain high-level functioning and well-being. Further research in this area will be especially important as the proportion of our aging population increases with the entrance of the baby boomers into the senior citizen category.

The review of these chapters thus gives evidence of the vigorous growth of child development as a discipline. Complexity of conceptualization and research design, interdisciplinary research, and an applied emphasis all characterize the field today. Although there is so much to admire in the progress we have made, it is perhaps a bit unappreciative to remark on an area that I feel continues to be neglected. This neglected area is education. Child development has so much to contribute to education, yet we continue to remain on the sidelines and limit our involvement to such issues as disabilities or reading problems. The reason may be that there is a whole field of educational research that purportedly is the science of education. But much of educational research is uninformed by developmental psychology. This is particularly true in the domain of content, where educational psychology is particularly remiss. Developmental psychology has a tremendous role to play. We need to explore how children learn different subject matters and look at this learning in the contextual framework that has become so prominent in so many other areas. It is sad to see so much fine developmental research with such clear implications for education, to never be employed in this way. I believe it is time to make education an important field for applied developmental science.

The foregoing remarks are in no way a criticism of this remarkable volume. Rather, they are addressed to the field as a whole. What is so satisfying about this Handbook is how so much of what is new and invigorating in the field is now a part of our conventional wisdom. We are no longer bound by the early constraints of psychology that identified science with experimentation and quantification and operationally defined variables. Observation, ethnographic studies and narrative, and other qualitative methodologies are now part of the developmentalist's tool kit. And we no longer have only the grand theories of Freud, Piaget, and Erikson; we also appreciate the domain specificity of so much of human thought and behavior. This book is not only a solid summary of where we stand with regard to our knowledge of human development today, but also a powerful witness for the readiness of the field itself to grow and to mature.

DAVID ELKIND

Contents

PART SIX
APPLIED DEVELOPMENTAL PSYCHOLOGY ACROSS THE LIFE SPAN

Contributors

Pamela M. Anderson, MS
Eliot-Pearson Department of Child Development
Tufts University
Medford, Massachusetts

Aida Bilalbegović Balsano, MS
Eliot-Pearson Department of Child Development
Tufts University
Medford, Massachusetts

Rosanna M. Bertrand, PhD
Department of Psychology
Brandeis University
Waltham, Massachusetts

Gretchen Biesecker, PhD
Department of Social Science
Örebro University
Örebro, Sweden

Deborah L. Bobek, MS
Eliot-Pearson Department of Child Development
Tufts University
Medford, Massachusetts

Lynne M. Borden, PhD
Children, Youth, and Family Programs
Michigan State University
East Lansing, Michigan

Hayden B. Bosworth, PhD
Duke University Medical Center
Durham, North Carolina

Julia M. Braungart-Rieker, PhD
Department of Psychology
University of Notre Dame
Notre Dame, Indiana

James Byrnes, PhD
Department of Human Development/
    Institute for Child Study
University of Maryland
College Park, Maryland

Natasha Cabrera, PhD
National Institute of Child Health and Development
Bethesda, Maryland

Cara H. Cashon, BS
Department of Psychology
University of Texas
Austin, Texas

Anna-Lisa Cohen, MS
Department of Psychology
University of Victoria
Victoria, British Columbia
Canada

Leslie B. Cohen, PhD
Department of Psychology
University of Texas
Austin, Texas

Cathleen M. Connell, PhD
School of Public Health
University of Michigan
Ann Arbor, Michigan

Catherine L. Costigan, PhD
Department of Psychology
University of Victoria
Victoria, British Columbia
Canada

E. Mark Cummings, PhD
Department of Psychology
University of Notre Dame
Notre Dame, Indiana

Jacinda K. Dariotis, MA
Human Development and Family Studies
Pennsylvania State University
University Park, Pennsylvania

Elysia Poggi Davis, BA
Institute of Child Development
University of Minnesota
Minneapolis, Minnesota

Roger A. Dixon, PhD
Department of Psychology
University of Victoria
Victoria, British Columbia
Canada

Lorah D. Dorn, PhD
School of Nursing
University of Pittsburgh
Pittsburgh, Pennsylvania

Elizabeth M. Dowling, MS
Eliot-Pearson Department of Child Development
Tufts University
Medford, Massachusetts

M. Ann Easterbrooks, PhD
Eliot-Pearson Department of Child Development
Tufts University
Medford, Massachusetts

Jacquelynne Eccles, PhD
Department of Human Development and Social Policy
University of Michigan
Ann Arbor, Michigan

David Elkind, PhD
Eliot-Pearson Department of Child Development
Tufts University
Medford, Massachusetts

David Henry Feldman, PhD
Eliot-Pearson Department of Child Development
Tufts University
Medford, Massachusetts

Laura Ferrer-Wreder, PhD
Department of Social Science
Örebro University
Örebro, Sweden

Hiram Fitzgerald, PhD
Department of Psychology
Michigan State University
East Lansing, Michigan

Alexandra M. Freund, PhD
Max Planck Institute for Human Development
Berlin, Germany

Nancy L. Galambos, PhD
Department of Psychology
University of Victoria
Victoria, British Columbia
Canada

Megan R. Gunnar, PhD
Institute of Child Development
University of Minnesota
Minneapolis, Minnesota

Penny Hauser-Cram, PhD
Lynch School of Education
Boston College
Chestnut Hill, Massachusetts

Erika Hoff, PhD
Department of Psychology
Florida Atlantic University
Davie, Florida

Angela Howell, MA
Lynch School of Education
Boston College
Chestnut Hill, Massachusetts

Mary R. Janevic, MPH
School of Public Health
University of Michigan
Ann Arbor, Michigan

Tina J. Kauh, BA
Human Development and Family Studies
Pennsylvania State University
University Park, Pennsylvania

Margaret Kerr, PhD
Department of Social Science
Örebro University
Örebro, Sweden

Margie E. Lachman, PhD
Department of Psychology
Brandeis University
Waltham, Massachusetts

Michael E. Lamb, PhD
National Institute of Child Health and
    Human Development
Bethesda, Maryland

Richard M. Lerner, PhD
Eliot-Pearson Department of
    Child Development
Tufts University
Medford, Massachusetts

Tammy Mann, PhD
Zero to Three
Washington, DC

Susan M. McHale, PhD
Human Development and Family Studies
Pennsylvania State University
University Park, Pennsylvania

Jayanthi Mistry, PhD
Eliot-Pearson Department of Child Development
Tufts University
Medford, Massachusetts

Willis F. Overton, PhD
Department of Psychology
Temple University
Philadelphia, Pennsylvania

Laura M. Padilla-Walker, PhD
Department of Psychology
University of Nebraska
Lincoln, Nebraska

Daniel F. Perkins, PhD
Department of Agricultural and Extension Education
Pennsylvania State University
University Park, Pennsylvania

Leonard W. Poon, PhD
Department of Psychology
University of Georgia
Athens, Georgia

Rachel Pruchno, PhD
The Center for Work and Family
Boston College
Newton Centre, Massachusetts

Michaela Riediger, PhD
Max Planck Institute for Human Development
Berlin, Germany

Tina Du Rocher-Schudlich, MA
Department of Psychology
University of Notre Dame
Notre Dame, Indiana

Jennifer Rosenbaum, MA
The Center for Work and Family
Boston College
Newton Centre, Massachusetts

T. S. Saraswathi, PhD
Department of Human Development and Family Relations
MS University of Baroda
Gujarat, India

Virginia L. Schiefelbein, BS
Department of Biobehavioral Health
Pennsylvania State University
University Park, Pennsylvania

Ilene Siegler, PhD
Duke University Medical Center
Durham, North Carolina

Håkan Stattin, PhD
Department of Social Science
Örebro University
Örebro, Sweden

Elizabeth J. Susman, PhD
Health and Human Development
The Pennsylvania State University
University Park, Pennsylvania

Ross A. Thompson, PhD
Department of Psychology
University of Nebraska
Lincoln, Nebraska

Donald Wertlieb, PhD
Eliot-Pearson Department of Child Development
Tufts University
Medford, Massachusetts

Allan Wigfield, PhD
Department of Human Development/
    Institute for Child Study
University of Maryland
College Park, Maryland

Maria M. Wong, PhD
Alcohol Research Center
University of Michigan
Ann Arbor, Michigan

Introduction: Dimensions of Developmental Psychology

RICHARD M. LERNER, M. ANN EASTERBROOKS, AND JAYANTHI MISTRY

Wilhelm Wundt labeled the science he is typically credited with launching as *physiological psychology* (Boring, 1950). In turn, at the end of his career Wundt sought to understand the science he had launched within the frame of cultural anthropology (Misiak & Sexton, 1966). Even in its early history, then, psychology has been a field whose individual-level scholarship has been linked to phenomena at levels of organization either more micro or more macro than its own.

Often, however, mechanistic and reductionist models were used to conceptualize the relations among levels. For example, Homans's (1961) social exchange theory used principles of operant learning to reduce dyadic relationships to psychogenic terms. Wilson (1975), in turn, reduced instances of (seemingly) moral behaviors (labeled as altruistic) to purported biogenic explanations (involving the concepts of gametic potential and inclusive fitness).

The field of developmental psychology has been an instance of this general approach in psychology, that is, of the orientation to explain the phenomena of one level of organization by reductive reference to terms associated with another level. Bijou and Baer (1961) attempted to explain all phenomena associated with psychological and behavioral development during infancy and childhood by reduction to the principles of classical and operant conditioning. Rowe (1994) sought to reduce parent-child relations and, in fact, all socialization experiences of childhood by reference to genetic inheritance, as represented by estimates of heritability.

The attempts by such developmental psychologists to portray the phenomena of one level of organization as primary, or "real," and others as derivative, or epiphenomenal, were representative of a more general tendency among developmentalists to split apart the components of the ecology of human life and to treat the bases of development as residing in one or another component, for example, nature or nurture (Overton, 1973, 1998). Indeed, theoretical controversies and associated empirical activity revolved around whether nativist concepts or experiences associated with learning could explain the development of perception, cognition, language, intelligence, or personality (Cairns, 1998; Dixon & Lerner, 1999). This split also is illustrated by the tendency to reduce human relationships to interactions among members of dyads, or individual interaction sequences. In addition, split conceptions of development framed debates about whether continuity or discontinuity characterized the course of life; for instance, a key issue was whether early experience, split off from subsequent periods of life, was integral in shaping the context of the person's psychological-behavioral repertoire across ontogeny (Brim & Kagan, 1980).

LEVELS OF INTEGRATION IN HUMAN DEVELOPMENT

An old adage says that "standing on the shoulders of giants we can see forever." For scholars of human development—especially contemporary developmentalists who eschew the split conceptions of the past—many of these giants came from the fields of biological-comparative psychology (e.g., Gottlieb, 1983, 1997; Gottlieb, Wahlsten, & Lickliter, 1998; Kuo, 1976; Lehrman, 1953; Maier & Schneirla, 1935; Novikoff, 1945a, 1945b; Schneirla, 1957; Tobach, 1981; von Bertalanffy, 1933). Through the cumulative impact of the theory and research of such scholars, by the early years of the twenty-first century scientists studying human development have come to view the reductionist and split conceptions that dominated conceptual debates in developmental psychology during the first seven to eight decades of the twentieth century as almost quaint historical artifacts. The few contemporary remnants of these split conceptions (e.g., Plomin, 2000; Rushton, 2000; Spelke & Newport, 1998) are regarded as theoretically atavistic and as conceptually and methodologically flawed (e.g., see Hirsch, 1997; Lerner, 2002).

Within the context of the contemporary understanding of the theoretical flaws of past and, in some cases, present (e.g., Plomin, 2000; Rowe, 1994; Rushton, 2000), contemporary contributions to the literature of human development derive from ideas that stress that an integrative, reciprocal relation, fusion, or dynamic interaction of variables from multiple levels of organization provides the core process of development. These relational ideas—summarized in the concepts associated with developmental systems models of human development (Ford & Lerner, 1992; Sameroff, 1983; Thelen & Smith, 1998)—are found in the theoretical ideas associated with the work of the comparative psychologists just noted.

To illustrate, the comparative work of Gilbert Gottlieb (1983, 1997; Gottlieb et al., 1998) has been a central influence on contemporary developmental psychology, providing a rigorous, compelling theoretical and empirical basis for viewing human development as involving changes in a person-context developmental system across the life span. Gottlieb's scholarship has documented the probabilistic epigenetic character of developmental changes, that is, alterations that result from variation in the timing of the integrated or fused relations—or the coactions—among levels of organization ranging from biology through the macroecological influences of culture and history. Using examples drawn from a variety of species— and involving, for instance, variation in morphological outcomes of development in the minute parasitic wasp, the emergence of enameled molar teeth resulting from chick oral epithelial cells being placed in contact with mouse cell mesenchyme, dominant frequencies in the vocalizations of mallard duck embryos and hatchlings, phenotypic variation in the body builds of human monozygotic twins reared apart, and secular trends from 1860 to 1970 in the age at menarche of European and United States females—Gottlieb (1997, 1999) provided evidence of a probabilistic epigenetic view of bidirectional structure-function development. This view (Gottlieb, 1997, 1999) may be summarized as

$$\text{Genetic activity (DNA} \leftarrow \rightarrow \text{RNA} \leftarrow \rightarrow \text{Protein)}$$
$$\leftarrow \rightarrow \text{Structural Maturation} \leftarrow \rightarrow$$
$$\text{Function, Activity, or Experience}$$

Thus, Gottlieb's (1983) theoretical work is coupled with rich and convincing empirical documentation that biology-ecology coactions provide a basis of plasticity—of the potential for systematic change—across the course of life (e.g., see Gottlieb, 1997).

Gottlieb's (1997, 1999; Gottlieb et al., 1998) scholarship underscores the importance of focusing developmental analysis on the multilevel, integrated matrix of covariation— on the dynamic developmental system—that constitutes

human development. Moreover, in forwarding a systems view of human development, this scholarship necessitates that developmental psychologists transcend a psychogenic view of their field. This scholarship leads developmentalists to embrace a perspective that includes contributions from the multiple—biological, behavioral, and social—sciences that afford understanding of the several coacting levels of organization integrated in the developmental system.

In a similar vein, scholars building on Vygotsky's (1978) sociocultural perspective on human development also emphasized the need to transcend the boundaries of psychological science. Cole (1990, 1996) and Werstch (1985, 1991) explicated Vygotsky's description of the genetic method for the study of human development, stating that a complete theory of human development for the study of human development must be able to explain development at the phylogenetic, sociohistorical, ontogenetic, and microgenetic levels. The assumption is that such an endeavor requires the integration of perspectives from biology, sociology, anthropology, history, and psychology.

In short, to understand human development, developmental psychologists must become developmental scientists. They must become multidisciplinary collaborators seeking to describe, explain, and optimize the changing interlevel relations that constitute the basic process of development within a developmental systems perspective (Lerner, 1998a, 1998b, 2002).

SCHOLARLY PRODUCTS AND PRODUCERS OF DEVELOPMENTAL SYSTEMS MODELS

The work of Gottlieb and other comparative psychologists found a ready audience among many developmentalists across the last three decades of the twentieth century. This period was a teachable moment in the field of developmental psychology because many scholars were struggling to find a theoretically sound means to frame what were anomalous findings by the then-current split theoretical models (e.g., associated with either nature or nurture, mechanistic conceptions or predetermined epigenetic models; see Gottlieb, 1997; Lerner, 2002; Overton, 1973, 1998; and chapter by Overton in this volume, for discussion of these split approaches).

For example, these findings pertained to cohort or time-of-testing effects on human ontogenetic change, to the role of later life events in altering (creating discontinuities with) the trajectories of individual development, and to the presence of plasticity across life—even in the aged years— regarding biological, psychological, and social functioning (e.g., see Baltes, Lindenberger, & Staudinger, 1998; Baltes,

Staudinger, & Lindenberger, 1999; Brim & Kagan, 1980; Elder, 1998, 1999; Lerner, 2002). These findings demonstrated that dynamic relations between individual characteristics and critical contextual events or nonnormative historical episodes shaped the character of change across the life span.

Several different developmental systems theories were developed in regard to such findings (e.g., Brandtstädter, 1998; Bronfenbrenner & Morris, 1998; Csikszentmihalyi & Rathunde, 1998; Elder, 1998; Feldman, 2000; Fischer & Bidell, 1998; Ford & Lerner, 1992; Gottlieb, 1997, 1998, 1999; Lerner, 2002; Magnusson & Stattin, 1998; Overton, 1998; Thelen & Smith, 1998; Wapner & Demick, 1998). Across these different formulations there is a common emphasis on fused person-context relations and on the need to embed the study of human development within the actual settings of human life.

Such embeddedness may involve tests of theoretically predicated ideas that appraise whether changes in the relations within the system result in alterations in developmental trajectories that coincide with model-based predictions. Depending on their target level of organization, these changes may be construed as policies or programs, and the evaluation of these actions provides information about both the efficacy of these interventions in promoting positive human development and the basic, relational process of human development emphasized within developmental systems models.

As such, within contemporary developmental systems theory, there is a synthesis of basic and applied developmental science. That is, by studying integrated person-context relations as embedded in the actual ecology of human development, policies and programs represent both features of the cultural context of this ecology and methodological tools for understanding how variations in individual-context relations may impact the trajectory of human life. Thus, the application of developmental science (through policy and program innovations and evaluations) is part of—is synthesized with—the study of the basic relational processes of human development.

THE CONTEMPORARY FEATURES OF DEVELOPMENTAL SCIENCE

As the decade of the 1980s ended, the view of developmental science that Paul Mussen (1970) had forwarded at the beginning of the 1970s—that the field placed its emphasis on explanations of the process of development—was both validated and extended. Mussen alerted developmentalists to the burgeoning interest not in structure, function, or content per

se but to change, to the processes through which change occurs, and thus to the means through which structures transform and functions evolve over the course of human life. His vision of and for the field presaged what emerged in the 1990s to be at the cutting edge of contemporary developmental theory: a focus on the process through which the individual's engagement with his or her context constitutes the basic process of human development.

The interest that had emerged by the end of the 1980s in understanding the dynamic relation between individual and context was, during the 1990s, brought to a more abstract level, one concerned with understanding the character of the integration of the levels of organization comprising the context, or bioecology, of human development (Lerner, 1998a, 1998b). This concern was represented by reciprocal or dynamic conceptions of process and by the elaboration of theoretical models that were not tied necessarily to a particular content domain but rather were focused on understanding the broader developmental system within which all dimensions of individual development emerged (e.g., Brandtstädter, 1998; Bronfenbrenner, 2001; Bronfenbrenner & Morris, 1998; Ford & Lerner, 1992; Gottlieb, 1997; Magnusson, 1999a, 1999b; Sameroff, 1983; Thelen & Smith, 1994, 1998). In other words, although particular empirical issues or substantive foci (e.g., motor development, the self, psychological complexity, or concept formation) lent themselves readily as exemplary sample cases of the processes depicted in a given theory (Lerner, 1998a), the theoretical models that were forwarded within the 1990s were superordinately concerned with elucidating the character of the individual-context (relational, integrative) developmental systems (Lerner, 1998b).

During the 1980s and 1990s similar concerns with understanding the nature of the integration between individual development and cultural context led to the development of sociocultural perspectives on human development. As already noted, some scholars extended Vygotsky's (1978) sociohistorical theory to emphasize the study of human development as it is constituted in sociocultural context (Cole, 1990, 1996; Rogoff, 1990; Wertsch, 1985, 1995). Others conceptualized culture as the meaning systems, symbols, activities, and practices through which people interpret experience (Bruner, 1990; Goodnow, Miller, & Kessel, 1995; Greenfield & Cocking, 1994; Markus & Kitayama, 1991; Shweder, 1990).

By the end of the twentieth century, then, the conceptually split, mechanistic, and atomistic views, which had been involved in so much of the history of concepts and theories of human development, had been replaced by theoretical models that stressed relationism and integration across all the distinct but fused levels of organization involved in human life. This dynamic synthesis of multiple levels of analysis is a perspective having its roots in systems theories of biological development (Cairns, 1998; Gottlieb, 1992; Kuo, 1976; Novikoff, 1945a, 1945b; Schneirla, 1957; von Bertalanffy, 1933); in addition, as noted by Cairns (1998), the interest in understanding person-context relations within an integrative, or systems, perspective has a rich history within the study of human development.

For example, James Mark Baldwin (1897) expressed interest in studying development in context, and thus in understanding integrated, multilevel, and hence interdisciplinary scholarship (Cairns, 1998). These interests were shared as well by Lightner Witmer, the founder in 1896 of the first psychological clinic in the United States (Cairns, 1998; Lerner, 1977). Moreover, Cairns describes the conception of developmental processes—as involving reciprocal interaction, bidirectionality, plasticity, and biobehavioral organization (all quite modern emphases)—as integral in the thinking of the founders of the field of human development. For instance, Wilhelm Stern (1914; see Kreppner, 1994) stressed the holism that is associated with a developmental systems perspective about these features of developmental processes. In addition, other contributors to the foundations and early progress of the field of human development (e.g., John Dewey, 1916; Kurt Lewin, 1935, 1954; and even John B. Watson, 1928) stressed the importance of linking child development research with application and child advocacy—a theme of very contemporary relevance (Lerner, Fisher, & Weinberg, 2000a, 2000b; Zigler, 1999).

The field of human development has in a sense come full circle in the course of a century. From the beginning of the last century to the beginning of the present one, the history of developmental psychology has been marked by an increasing interest in the role of history—of temporal changes in the familial, social, and cultural contexts of life—in shaping the quality of the trajectories of change that individuals traverse across their life spans. As a consequence of incorporating into its causal schemas about ontogenetic change a nonreductionistic and a synthetic conception about (as compared to a Cartesian split view of) the influence of context—of culture and history—the field of human development has altered its essential ontology. The relational view of being that now predominates in the field has required epistemological revisions in the field as well. Qualitative as well as quantitative understanding has been legitimated as scholars have sought an integrated understanding of the multiple levels of organization comprising the ecology of human development. In fact, relational perspectives embracing the developmental system stress the methodological importance of triangulation across quantitative and qualitative appraisals of multilevel

developmental phenomena (Lerner, Chaudhuri, & Dowling, in press).

In essence, then, as we pursue our scholarship about human development at this early part of a new century, we do so with an orientation to the human life span that is characterized by (a) integrated, relational models of human life, perspectives synthesizing biological-through-physical ecological influences on human development in nonreductionistic manners; (b) a broad array of qualitative and quantitative methodologies requisite for attaining knowledge about these fused, biopsychoecological relations; (c) a growing appreciation of the importance of the cultural and historical influences on the quality and trajectory of human development across the course of life; and (d) a synthesis of basic and applied developmental science.

These four defining themes in the study of human development are represented in contemporary developmental systems theories, perspectives that constitute the overarching conceptual frames of modern scholarship in the study of human development. We believe as well that across the rest of this century the field will advance through the coordinated emphasis on a culturally and historically sensitive science that triangulates quantitative and qualitative appraisals of the relations among the multiple levels of organization fused within the developmental system.

In short, there has been a history of visionary scholars interested in exploring the use of ideas associated with developmental systems theory for understanding the basic process of human development and for applying this knowledge within the actual contexts of people to enhance their paths across life. For instance, scholars building on Vygotsky's (1978) sociohistorical perspective have explored promising conceptual frameworks to explicate the integration between the individual and cultural context in the process of development (Cole, 1996; Wertsch, 1995). Accordingly, the chapters in this volume reflect and extend the diverse theoretical perspectives that emphasize understanding dynamic and integrated developmental processes as they are situated in the varying contexts of people's lives and circumstances.

THE PLAN OF THIS VOLUME

Developmental science at the beginning of the twenty-first century is marked by an explicit integration of philosophy, theory, and method, on the one hand, and a synthetic understanding of basic developmental processes and applications designed to promote positive human development on the other (Lerner, 2002). Part I of this volume, "Foundations of Development Across the Life Span," presents these integrations in chapters by Overton and by Wertlieb, respectively. The former chapter contrasts relational perspectives with models that were based on philosophically and methodologically problematic, as well as empirically counterfactual, attempts to split the components of development, for instance, into sources related to separate nature or nurture influences. In turn, Overton explains the past and contemporary philosophical and theoretical bases of relational models of human development. The integrative vision he provides for theory and research frames the cutting edge of contemporary basic and applied scholarship in developmental science.

Wertlieb discusses how relational models associated with developmental systems theory are used in applications of developmental science aimed at promoting healthy development across life. Drawing on examples from the literatures of parenting, early care and education, developmental psychopathology, and developmental assets, Wertlieb explains that developmental science is well poised to enhance the well-being of children, adolescents, and their families.

The next four parts of the volume provide evidence, within and across successive portions of the life span, of the rich scholarship conducted to describe and explain dynamic relations between developing individuals and their complex contexts. In Part II of the volume, titled "Infancy," Cohen and Cashon review the explosion of research on infant perception and cognition in the latter half of the twentieth century. The authors' goal is to lend coherence to the sometimes-contradictory evidence regarding the abilities of infants. They adopt an information-processing view as an organizational tool in understanding how infants of different ages and experiences perceive and understand their worlds.

In the chapter by Thompson, Easterbrooks, and Padilla-Walker, the authors examine the dynamics of individual and context in key constructs of early socioemotional development: attachment relationships, self-understanding, and emotional regulation. The ways in which these constructs and developmental processes emerge and take character are examined from a relational context (primarily that of the infant and close caregivers).

Gunnar and Davis apply a dynamic systems approach to the study of the stress and emotion in the early years of life. The chapter emphasizes the biological roots of developing emotion systems and the scope and limitations of developmental plasticity. The authors navigate the fundamental tenets of the psychobiology of stress and emotion, outlining developmental integration across infancy. In addition, Gunnar and Davis place these developmental systems in the context of the relationships between infants and their caregiving environments.

Issues of caregiving environments are at the center of the chapter by Fitzgerald, Mann, Cabrera, and Wong. The authors use a systems approach to understand the role of child care in the lives of very young children and their families. They argue that this field of study needs to include key mediating or moderating factors (temperament, parent-child relationships, family risk load) in order to understand the way in which child care impacts family development.

The chapters in Part III, "Childhood," present current perspectives on the dynamic processes of development and multiple influences of context in various domains of children's development. In the chapter on language acquisition, Hoff focuses on the current state of the scientific effort to explain how children acquire language, presenting the biological, linguistic, social, and domain-general cognitive approaches to the study of language development. Arguing that no approach is sufficient, Hoff emphasizes dynamic and interactive nature of language acquisition.

Similarly, Feldman, in the chapter on cognitive development, presents the broad theories of the past 50 years that have attempted to explain the growth and transformation of the mind. With a focus on the Piagetian revolution, Feldman presents a systematic and logically organized discussion of the emergence, prominence, and subsequent evolution of Piagetian perspectives, leading to more contemporary theoretical frameworks and conceptual issues that are driving current research and theory development.

Cummings, Braungart-Rieker, and Du Rocher-Schudlich take a comprehensive approach in their review of the development of emotion and personality. These authors begin with a focus on individual development of emotion and personality, leading to a discussion of relational influences on development, followed by a review of developmental psychopathology perspectives.

Similarly, McHale, Dariotis, and Kauh provide a comprehensive review of social development and social relationships in middle childhood. Their chapter represents a particularly broad and culturally inclusive account of social development because they begin with a focus on the social ecology of middle childhood, before highlighting individual processes, thus situating individual processes in a larger socioecological context.

Finally, in the chapter on culture and child development, Mistry and Saraswathi describe current understanding of the interface between culture and child development by integrating literature from three subfields of psychology—cultural psychology, cross-cultural psychology, and developmental psychology. They illustrate the complementary contributions of the three subfields in unraveling the culture-individual interface by presenting selective overviews of three topic areas of development: development of self, development of children's narratives, and development of remembering.

The dynamics of person-context relations, and the integrated influence of the multiple levels of the developmental system, frame also the several chapters in Part IV, "Adolescence." For example, the chapter on puberty, sexuality, and health, by Susman, Dorn, and Schiefelbein, examines puberty from the perspective of biopsychosocial models of development. The authors note that the behavioral covariates of pubertal change are influenced by the interrelation of hormones, bodily constitution, and social relationships.

Similarly, in their discussion of cognitive development and achievement during adolescence, Eccles, Wigfield, and Byrnes use relational ideas pertinent of developmental stage-environment fit to discuss current patterns of school achievement and recent changes in both school completion and differential performance on standardized tests of achievement. In addition, their relational theoretical frame is used to understand gender and ethnic group differences in achievement motivation.

In turn, Galambos and Costigan discuss emotional and personality development in adolescence through reference to research areas (e.g., emotion regulation, temperament, and cultural influences on emotion and personality) that draw on integrative understandings of the person and his or her context. The authors stress that their approach to conceptualizing emotion and personality aids in the design of intervention and prevention programs that may result in the promotion of healthy youth development.

Similarly, in their chapter on parental and peer influences on development, Kerr, Stattin, Biesecker, and Ferrer-Wreder emphasize the importance of models of bidirectional relationship between adolescents and their parents or peers for understanding the role of these social groups for adolescent behavior and development. Moreover, the authors emphasize that adolescents act as active agents in their own development and that they integrate their parental and peer contexts across their development.

Finally, in their discussion of positive behaviors, problem behaviors, and resiliency, Perkins and Borden emphasize the interrelation of the behaviors and contents of youth development. They stress that to understand the bases of both risk actualization and resiliency, theory and research must adopt an integrative systems perspective about the multiple individual and contextual influences on adolescent development.

Part V, "Adulthood and Aging," reflects a stress on developmental systems. For instance, in their discussion of disease, health, and aging, Siegler, Bosworth, and Poon conceptualize health as a contextual variable that exists in a bidirectional relationship with personological processes such as personality and cognition. They explain how changes in health may precede changes in individual and social functioning and, as well, how changes in health status may result from changes in these functions.

Similarly, in their chapter on cognitive development in adulthood, Dixon and Cohen explain that cognitive aging involves integrative developmental processes that range from the neurological, through individual, to social levels of analysis. Cognitive developmental processes are used in different ways to accomplish different goals throughout adulthood, but it is always a central component of one's concept of self and of one's adjustment to the challenges of everyday life.

In turn, Bertrand and Lachman emphasize that the key focus of contemporary personality development research in adulthood and old age is on assessment of the multidirectional paths of personality and on the impact of individual differences throughout the life span. The authors discuss the role of contextual models, which incorporate person-environment interactions, in understanding these features of personality development.

Similarly, Pruchno and Rosenbaum explain that individual change in adulthood and old age is linked to the people with whom adults and the aged maintain close relationships. These social relationships involve spouses, children, siblings, and friends.

Across the infancy, childhood, adolescence, and adulthood and aging sections of this volume, the contributing scholars make clear that the basic process of human development involves dynamic interactions among variables from individual and contextual levels of organization. These authors stress that within any focal period of development these integrative relations afford understanding of extant and potential instances of person-context relations. As such, focus on these relations is central both for appreciation of basic features of developmental change and for efforts aimed at enhancing the character and course of human development. The final section of the volume, "Applied Developmental Psychology Across the Life Span," extends the age specific discussions of basic person-context relational processes to multiple portions of the life span, and does so with a focus on the use of concepts and research associated with developmental systems thinking in applied efforts aimed at enhancing relational processes and promoting positive, healthy developmental trajectories across life.

The sample cases included in this section involve, first, disabilities and development. Hauser-Cram and Howell emphasize the importance of longitudinal and contextually sensitive research in attempting to understand the development of young children with biologically based developmental disabilities. They stress the importance of assessing how the strengths of the family system may positively influence the development of these children.

Similar systems effects are discussed by Lerner, Anderson, Balsano, Dowling, and Bobek in their presentation of the key emphases on person-context relations associated with the attempts of applied developmental scientists to promote positive youth development. The authors discuss how the diversity of person-context relations may be capitalized on to provide a frame for policy and program innovations seeking to increase the probability of such development.

The importance of understanding the links between the developing child and the features of his or her context are stressed as well by Lamb, who discusses how knowledge of such relational developmental processes can assist legal authorities. Lamb illustrates this domain of application by discussing the importance of developmental scholarship in the areas of child witness testimony and the resolution of divorce and child custody cases.

A comparable conceptual frame is used in the chapter by Connell and Janevic on health and human development. The authors emphasize the importance of adopting an integrated understanding of biological, cognitive, and social developmental influences on health behaviors from infancy through older adulthood. Connell and Janevic stress the importance of understanding the interaction between developmental phenomena and extrinsic factors such as socioeconomic status and culture in studying health across the life span.

Similarly, Freund and Riediger use dynamic, developmental systems theories to understand the bases of positive, successful aging. By reference to the model of selection, optimization, and compensation; the model of assimilative and accommodative coping; and the model of primary and secondary control, the authors explain how integrated relations between aged people and their contexts can result in the maintenance of high levels of functioning and of well-being.

In sum, the chapters in this volume contribute significantly to extending a quarter century or more of scholarship aimed at understanding the dynamic relations between individuals and contexts. The present volume brings this scholarship to both an empirically richer and a more theoretically nuanced level, one depicting—for multiple substantive foci of human development and both within and across the major developmental epochs of life—the nature of the reciprocal or dynamic processes of human ontogenetic change, of how structures function and how functions are structured over time.

The consistency across chapters in the demonstration of the usefulness of developmental systems thinking for theory, research, and application indicates that this frame for contemporary developmental scholarship is not tied necessarily to a particular content domain, but rather is useful for understanding the broader developmental system within which all dimensions of individual development emerge (e.g., Ford & Lerner, 1992; Gottlieb, 1997; Sameroff, 1983; Thelen & Smith, 1998). In other words, although particular empirical issues or substantive topics (e.g., perceptual development, successful aging, cognition and achievement, emotional behaviors, or complex social relationships) may lend themselves readily as emphases of developmental scholarship within or across developmental periods, the chapters in this volume attest to the importance of focusing on relational, integrative individual-context dynamics to understand the human developmental system.

CONCLUSIONS

The power of contemporary developmental scholarship lies in its integrative character—across substantive domains of individual functioning (e.g., biology, emotional, cognition, and social behaviors), across developmental periods, across levels of organization (from biology through culture and history), and across basic and applied interests in regard to understanding and enhancing human life. As represented by the scholarship in this volume, contemporary developmental science is not limited by (or, perhaps better, confounded by) an inextricable association with a unidimensional portrayal of the developing person (e.g., the person seen from the vantage point of only cognitions, emotions, or stimulus-response connections). Today, the developing person is neither biologized, psychologized, nor sociologized. Rather, the individual is systemized; that is, his or her development is conceptualized and studied as embedded within an integrated matrix of variables derived from multiple levels of organization.

This integrative, systems-oriented approach to developmental science is certainly more complex than its organismic or mechanistic predecessors (Lerner, 2002; Overton, 1998; chapter by Overton in this volume). However, a developmental systems approach is also more nuanced, more flexible, more balanced, and less susceptible to extravagant, or even absurd, claims (e.g., that nature, split from nurture, can shape the course of human development). Moreover, as elegantly demonstrated by the chapters in this volume, developmental systems offer a productive frame for rigorous and important scholarship about the process of human development and applications across the life span. Together, these advances in the scholarship of knowledge generation and knowledge application serve as an invaluable means for advancing science and service pertinent to people across the breadth of their lives.

REFERENCES

Baldwin, J. M. (1897). *Mental development in the child and the race.* New York: Macmillan.

Baltes, P. B., Lindenberger, U., & Staudinger, U. M. (1998). Life-span theory in developmental psychology. In W. Damon (Series Ed.) & R. M. Lerner (Vol. Ed.), *Handbook of child psychology: Vol. 1. Theoretical models of human development* (5th ed., pp. 1029–1144). New York: Wiley.

Baltes, P. B., Staudinger, U. M., & Lindenberger, U. (1999). Life span psychology: Theory and application to intellectual functioning. In J. T. Spence, J. M. Darley, & D. J. Foss (Eds.), *Annual review of psychology: Vol. 50* (pp. 471–507). Palo Alto, CA: Annual Reviews.

Bijou, S. W., & Baer, D. M. (Eds.). (1961). *Child development: A systematic and empirical theory.* New York: Appleton-Century-Crofts.

Boring, E. G. (1950). *A history of experimental psychology* (2nd ed.). New York: Appleton-Century-Crofts.

Brandtstädter, J. (1998). Action perspectives on human development. In W. Damon (Series Ed.) & R. M. Lerner (Vol. Ed.), *Handbook of child psychology: Vol. 1. Theoretical models of human development* (5th ed., pp. 807–863). New York: Wiley.

Brim, O. G., Jr., & Kagan, J. (Ed.). (1980). *Constancy and change in human development.* Cambridge, MA: Harvard University Press.

Bronfenbrenner, U. (2001). Human development, bioecological theory of. In N. J. Smelser & P. B. Baltes (Eds.), *International encyclopedia of the social and behavioral sciences* (pp. 6963–6970). Oxford: Elsevier.

Bronfenbrenner, U., & Morris, P. A. (1998). The ecology of developmental process. In W. Damon (Series Ed.) & R. M. Lerner (Vol. Ed.), *Handbook of child psychology: Vol. 1. Theoretical models of human development* (5th ed., pp. 993–1028). New York: Wiley.

Bruner, J. (1990). Culture and human development: A new look. *Human Development, 33,* 344–355.

Cairns, R. B. (1998). The making of developmental psychology. In W. Damon (Series Ed.) & R. M. Lerner (Vol. Ed.), *Theoretical models of human development: Vol. 1. The handbook of child psychology* (5th ed., pp. 25–106). New York: Wiley.

Cole, M. (1990). Cognitive development and formal schooling: The evidence from cross-cultural research. In L. Moll (Ed.), *Vygotsky and education: Instructional implications and applications of sociohistorical psychology* (pp. 89–110). New York: Cambridge University Press.

Cole, M. (1996). *Cultural psychology: A once and future discipline.* Cambridge, MA: Belknap/Harvard.

Csikszentmihalyi, M., & Rathunde, K. (1998). The development of the person: An experiential perspective on the ontogenesis of psychological complexity. In W. Damon (Series Ed.) & R. M. Lerner (Ed.), *Handbook of child psychology: Vol. 1. Theoretical models of human development* (5th ed., pp. 635–684). New York: Wiley.

Dewey, J. (1916). *Democracy and education: An introduction to the philosophy of education.* New York: Macmillan.

Dixon, R. A., & Lerner, R. M. (1999). History and systems in developmental psychology. In M. Bornstein & M. Lamb (Eds.), *Developmental psychology: An advanced textbook* (4th ed., pp. 3–45). XXXX: Erlbaum.

Elder, G. H., Jr. (1998). The life course and human development. In W. Damon (Series Ed.) & R. M. Lerner (Vol. Ed.), *Handbook of child psychology: Vol. 1. Theoretical models of human development* (5th ed., pp. 939–991). New York: Wiley.

Elder, G. H., Jr. (1999). *Children of the Great Depression: Social change in life experience* (25th anniversary ed.). Boulder, CO: Westview Press.

Feldman, D. H. (2000). Figurative and operative processes in the development of artistic talent. *Human Development, 43,* 60–64.

Fischer, K. W., & Bidell, T. (1998). Dynamic development of psychological structures in action and thought. In W. Damon (Series Ed.) & R. M. Lerner (Vol. Ed.), *Handbook of child psychology: Vol. 1. Theoretical models of human development* (5th ed., pp. 467–561). New York: Wiley.

Ford, D. L., & Lerner, R. M. (1992). *Developmental systems theory: An integrative approach.* Newbury Park, CA: Sage.

Goodnow, J. J., Miller, P., & Kessel, F. (Eds.). (1995). *Cultural practices as contexts for development.* San Francisco: Jossey-Bass.

Gottlieb, G. (1983). The psychobiological approach to developmental issues. In M. M. Haith & J. Campos (Eds.), *Handbook of child psychology: Vol. 2. Infancy and biological bases* (pp. 1–26). New York: Wiley.

Gottlieb, G. (1992). *Individual development and evolution: The genesis of novel behavior.* New York: Oxford University Press.

Gottlieb, G. (1997). *Synthesizing nature-nurture: Prenatal roots of instinctive behavior.* Mahwah, NJ: Erlbaum.

Gottlieb, G. (1998). Normally occurring environmental and behavioral influences on gene activity: From central dogma to probabilistic epigenesis. *Psychological Review, 105,* 792–802.

Gottlieb, G. (1999). *Probabilistic epigenesis and evolution. Heinz Werner Lecture Series* (Vol. 23). Worchester, MA: Clark University Press.

Gottlieb, G., Wahlsten, D., & Lickliter, R. (1998). The significance of biology for human development: A developmental psychobiological systems view. In W. Damon (Series Ed.) & R. M. Lerner (Vol. Ed.), *Handbook of child psychology: Vol. 1. Theoretical models of human development* (5th ed., pp. 233–273). New York: Wiley.

Greenfield, P. M., & Cocking, R. R. (Eds.) (1994). *Cross-cultural roots of minority child development.* Hillsdale, NJ: Erlbaum.

Hirsch, J. (1997). Some history of heredity-vs.-environment, genetic inferiority at Harvard (?), and *The* (incredible) *Bell Curve. Genetica, 99,* 207–224.

Homans, G. C. (1961). *Social behavior: Its elementary forms.* New York: Harcourt, Brace, & World.

Kreppner, K. (1994). William L. Stern: A neglected founder of developmental psychology. In R. D. Parke, P. A. Ornstein, J. J. Rieser, & C. Zahn-Waxler (Eds.), *A century of developmental psychology* (pp. 311–331). Washington DC: American Psychological Association.

Kuo, Z.-Y. (1976). *The dynamics of behavior development: An epigenetic view.* New York: Plenum.

Lehrman, D. S. (1953). A critique of Konrad Lorenz's theory of instinctive behavior. *Quarterly Review of Biology, 28,* 337–363.

Lerner, R. M. (1977). [Biographies of DeSanctis, S., Dewey, J., Gesell, A., Goodenough, F., Locke, J., Terman, L. M., Werner, H., and Witmer, L]. In B. B. Wolman (Ed.), *International encyclopedia of neurology, psychiatry, psychoanalysis, and psychology.* New York: Van Nostrand Reinhold.

Lerner, R. M. (Ed.). (1998a). *Handbook of child psychology: Vol. 1. Theoretical models of human development* (5th ed.). Editor-in-Chief: William Damon. New York: Wiley.

Lerner, R. M. (1998b). Theories of human development: Contemporary perspectives. In R. M. Lerner (Ed.), *Handbook of child psychology: Vol. 1. Theoretical models of human development* (5th ed., pp. 1–24). Editor-in-Chief: William Damon. New York: Wiley.

Lerner, R. M. (2002). *Concepts and theories of human development* (3rd ed.). Mahwah, NJ: Erlbaum.

Lerner, R. M., Chaudhuri, J., & Dowling, E. (in press). Methods of contextual assessment and assessing contextual methods: A developmental contextual perspective. In D. M. Teti (Ed.), *Handbook of research methods in developmental psychology.* Cambridge, MA: Blackwell.

Lerner, R. M., Fisher, C. B., & Weinberg, R. A. (2000a). Toward a science for and of the people: Promoting civil society through the application of developmental science. *Child Development, 71,* 11–20.

Lerner, R. M., Fisher, C. B., & Weinberg, R. A. (2000b). Applying developmental science in the twenty-first century: International scholarship for our times. *International Journal of Behavioral Development, 24,* 24–29.

Lewin, K. (1935). *A dynamic theory of personality.* New York: McGraw-Hill.

Lewin, K. (1954). Behavior and development as a function of the total situation. In L. Carmichael (Ed.), *Manual of child psychology* (2nd ed., pp. 791–844). New York: Wiley.

Magnusson, D., & Stattin, H. (1998). Person-context interaction theories. In W. Damon (Series Ed.) & R. M. Lerner (Vol. Ed.), *Handbook of child psychology: Vol. 1. Theoretical models of human development* (5th ed., pp. 685–759). New York: Wiley.

Magnusson, D. (1999a). On the individual: A person-oriented approach to developmental research. *European Psychologist, 4,* 205–218.

Magnusson, D. (1999b). Holistic interactionism: A perspective for research on personality development. In L. A. Pervin & O. P. John (Eds.), *Handbook of personality: Theory and research* (2nd ed., pp. 219–247). New York: Guilford Press.

Maier, N. R. F., & Schneirla, T. C. (1935). *Principles of animal behavior.* New York: McGraw-Hill.

Markus, H., & Kitayama, S. (1991). Culture and the self: Implications for cognition, emotion, and motivation. *Psychological Review, 98,* 224–253.

Misiak, H., & Sexton, V. S. (1966). *History of psychology in overview.* New York: Grune & Stratton.

Mussen, P. H. (Ed.). (1970). *Carmichael's manual of child psychology* (3rd ed.). New York: Wiley.

Novikoff, A. B. (1945a). The concept of integrative levels of biology. *Science, 62,* 209–215.

Novikoff, A. B. (1945b). Continuity and discontinuity in evolution. *Science, 101,* 405–406.

Overton, W. F. (1973). On the assumptive base of the nature-nurture controversy: Additive versus interactive conceptions. *Human Development, 16,* 74–89.

Overton, W. F. (1998). Developmental psychology: Philosophy, concepts, and methodology. In W. Damon (Series Ed.) & R. M. Lerner (Vol. Ed.), *Handbook of child psychology: Vol. 1. Theoretical models of human development* (5th ed., pp. 107–189). New York: Wiley.

Plomin, R. (2000). Behavioural genetics in the 21st century. *International Journal of Behavioral Development, 24,* 30–34.

Rogoff, B. (1990). *Apprenticeship in thinking.* New York, NY: Oxford University Press.

Rowe, D. C. (1994). *The limits of family influence: Genes, experience, and behavior.* New York: Guilford Press.

Rushton, J. P. (2000). *Race, evolution, and behavior* (special abridged edition). New Brunswick, NJ: Transaction.

Sameroff, A. J. (1983). Developmental systems: Contexts and evolution. In W. Kessen (Ed.), *Handbook of child psychology: Vol. 1. History, theory, and methods* (pp. 237–294). New York: Wiley.

Schneirla, T. C. (1957). The concept of development in comparative psychology. In D. B. Harris (Ed.), *The concept of development* (pp. 78–108). Minneapolis, MN: University of Minnesota.

Shweder, R. A. (1990). Cultural psychology: What is it? In J. W. Stigler & G. Herdt (Eds.), *Cultural psychology: Essays on comparative human development* (pp. 1–43). Cambridge, MA: Cambridge University Press.

Spelke, E. S., & Newport, E. L. (1998). Nativism, empiricism, and the development of knowledge. In W. Damon (Series Ed.) & R. M. Lerner (Vol. Ed.), *Handbook of child psychology: Vol. 1. Theoretical models of human development* (5th ed., pp. 275–340). New York: Wiley.

Stern, W. (1914). *Psychologie der frühen Kindheit bis zum sechsten Lebensjahr.* Leipzig: Quelle & Meyer.

Thelen, E., & Smith, L. B. (1994). *A dynamic systems approach to the development of cognition and action.* Cambridge: MIT Press.

Thelen, E., & Smith, L. B. (1998). Dynamic systems theories. In W. Damon (Series Ed.) & R. M. Lerner (Vol. Ed.), *Handbook of child psychology: Vol. 1. Theoretical models of human development* (5th ed., pp. 563–633). New York: Wiley.

Tobach, E. (1981). Evolutionary aspects of the activity of the organism and its development. In R. M. Lerner & N. A. Busch-Rossnagel (Eds.), *Individuals as producers of their development: A life-span perspective* (pp. 37–68). New York: Academic Press.

von Bertalanffy, L. (1933). *Modern theories of development.* London: Oxford University Press.

Vygotsky, L. S. (1978). *Mind in society: The development of higher psychological processes.* Cambridge, MA: Harvard University Press.

Wapner, S., & Demick, J. (1998). Developmental analysis: A holistic, developmental, systems-oriented perspective. In W. Damon (Series Ed.) & R. M. Lerner (Vol. Ed.), *Handbook of child psychology: Vol. 1. Theoretical models of human development* (5th ed., pp. 761–805). New York: Wiley.

Watson, J. B. (1928). *Psychological care of infant and child.* New York: Norton.

Wertsch, J. V. (1985). *Culture, communication, and cognition: Vygotskian perspectives.* New York: Cambridge University Press.

Wertsch, J. V. (1991). *Voices of the mind.* Cambridge: Harvard University Press.

Wertsch, J. V. (1995). Introduction. In J. V. Wertsch, P. del Rio, & A. Alvarez (Eds.), *Sociocultural studies of the mind.* New York: Cambridge University Press.

Wilson, E. O. (1975). *Sociobiology: The new synthesis.* Cambridge: Harvard University Press.

Zigler, E. (1999). A place of value for applied and policy studies. *Child Development, 69,* 532–542.

PART ONE

FOUNDATIONS OF DEVELOPMENT ACROSS THE LIFE SPAN

CHAPTER 1

Development Across the Life Span

WILLIS F. OVERTON

In this chapter I focus on some ideas that usually rest quietly in the background when development is explored. Background ideas are not unlike the foundation of a house. A foundation grounds, constrains, and sustains the nature and style of the building that can ultimately be constructed. So, too, do background ideas ground, constrain, and sustain both theory and methods of investigation in any area of inquiry. A foundation is usually ignored by those who live and work in the house; at least until something goes wrong—for example, when cracks appear in walls or the house begins to sink into the ground. So, too, are background ideas often ignored by investigators, at least until something goes wrong with theoretical or empirical efforts in the field of study. In this chapter I try to bring these ideas from background to foreground; I also examine how they form the basis for—and constraints of—both theory and research in developmental psychology.

In scientific discussions background ideas are often termed *metatheoretical* or *metatheories*. They transcend (i.e., *meta-*) theories in the sense that they define the context in which theoretical concepts are constructed, just as a foundation defines the context in which a house can be constructed. Further, metatheory functions not only to ground, constrain,

and sustain theoretical concepts, but also to do the same thing with respect to methods of investigation. For convenience, when specifically discussing background ideas that ground methods, these will be termed *metamethods. Methodology* would also be an appropriate term here if this were understood in its broad sense as a set of principles that guide empirical inquiry (Asendorpf & Valsiner, 1992; Overton, 1998).

The primary function of metatheory—including metamethod—is to provide a rich source of concepts out of which theories and methods emerge. Metatheory also provides guidelines that help to avoid conceptual confusions—and consequently, help to avoid what may ultimately be unproductive ideas and unproductive methods.

Theories and methods refer directly to the empirical world, whereas metatheories and metamethods refer to the theories and methods themselves. More specifically, a *metatheory* is a set of rules and principles or a story (narrative) that both describes and prescribes what is acceptable and unacceptable as theory—the means of conceptual exploration of any scientific domain. A *metamethod* is also a set of rules and principles or a story, but this story describes and prescribes the nature of acceptable methods—the means of observational exploration—in a scientific discipline. When metatheoretical ideas—including metamethod—are tightly interrelated and form a coherent set of concepts, the set is often termed a *model* or *paradigm*. These coherent sets can form a hierarchy in terms of increasing generality of application. Thus, for example, a model that contains the basic concepts from which a theory of memory will be constructed is a relatively low-level model because it applies only to memory. A model such as *dynamic systems* applies to a number of domains, including social, cognitive, and emotional domains; hence, it functions at a higher hierarchical level. The hierarchical dimension of any given set of metatheoretical ideas also forms a coherently interrelated system of ideas, and the model operating at the pinnacle of this hierarchy is termed a *worldview* (Overton, 1984). Worldviews are composed of coherent sets of *epistemological* (i.e., issues of knowing) and *ontological* (i.e., issues of reality) principles. In this chapter, most of the discussion concerns ideas that have a very high range of application.

Metatheories and metamethods are closely interrelated and intertwined. For example (as we will see shortly), when considering the very nature of development, a prevailing metatheory may assert the claim that change of form (transformational change) is a legitimate and important part of the understanding of developmental change. If a prevailing metatheory asserts the legitimacy of transformational change, then theories of development will include some type of stage concept, because *stage* is the theoretical concept that is used to describe transformational change. Further, if transformational change and stage are a part of one's metatheory, then the related metamethod will prescribe the significance of methods that assess patterns and sequences of patterns that are appropriate to empirically examining the stage concept in any given specific empirical domain. On the other hand, if a metatheory asserts that transformational change is unimportant to our understanding of development, then any theoretical concept of stage will be viewed negatively, and methods of pattern and sequential assessment will be understood to be of marginal interest.

Broadly, a metatheory presents a vision of the nature of the world and the objects of that world (e.g., a metatheory might present a picture of the child as an active agent constructing his/her known world, and another metatheory might picture the child as a "recording device" that processes information). A metamethod presents a vision of the tools that will be most adequate to explore the world described by the metatheory.

Any rich understanding of the impact of the metatheoretical requires an historical appreciation of the emergence of specific alternative metatheoretical approaches to knowledge. Developmental psychology was born and spent its early years in a curious metatheoretical world. This world, which began in the seventeenth century, has been called the modern world or *modernity*. In the past century, the modern world has undergone major crises; these form the context for alternative contemporary metatheories. Before describing this history, a brief examination of the broad ways that metatheory colors an understanding of the nature of development deserves some attention. This discussion will establish a developmental framework serving as a general context for the remainder of the chapter.

DEVELOPMENTAL INQUIRY AND THE METATHEORETICAL

How should we understand the field of developmental inquiry? Although it is clear that *change* is central in any definition of development, the process of identifying the specific nature of this change and identifying what it is that changes in development is shaped by metatheoretical principles. The most popular current text definition of development is some variation of the idea of *age changes in observed behavior*. Any reflection, however, reveals that serious problems arise when *development* is shaped by this definition. Age has no unique qualities that differentiate it from time; age is simply one index of time. There is also nothing unique or novel about units of age-time, such as years, months, weeks, minutes, and so on (see Lerner, 2002). Thus, this definition merely states that development is about changes that occur in time. The difficulty with this is that all change occurs "in" time, and—as a consequence—the definition is an empty one, merely restating that development is about change. At a minimum the definition omits what some would consider to be critical features of development, including the idea that developmental change concerns change that has a directional quality to it, change that is relatively permanent and irreversible, and change that entails orderly sequences. However, making a judgment that direction and sequence are central concerns—or making the judgment that they are of marginal interest—is a direct product of the metatheoretical platform from which the definition is launched.

Similar problems arise when the definition of 'what' develops is limited to observed behavior. Although observed behavior is clearly central to empirical investigations—the dependent variable of psychological research efforts—whether it is the ultimate goal of inquiry is an issue defined by metatheory. Except in a metatheoretical world identified with behaviorism, observed behavior may be primarily a jumping-off point—a point of inference—for an exploration of unseen processes and patterns of processes that identify mental life. Again, however, making the judgment that mental events are central to understanding—or the judgment that mental events are marginal—is a metatheoretically motivated judgment.

The Nature of Developmental Change: Transformations and Variations

Perhaps the broadest conceptualization of developmental entails the recognition of two fundamental types of change, transformational and variational (see Figure 1.1). *Transformational change* is change in the form, organization, or struc-

ture of any system. The caterpillar transforms into the butterfly, water transforms into ice and gas, the seed transforms into the plant, cells transform into the organism. All nonlinear dynamic systems, including the human psyche, undergo transformation change. Transformational change results in the *emergence of novelty*. As forms change, they become increasingly complex. This increased complexity is a complexity of pattern rather than a linear, additive complexity of elements. As a consequence, new patterns exhibit novel characteristics that cannot be reduced to (i.e., completely explained by) or predicted from earlier components (indicated

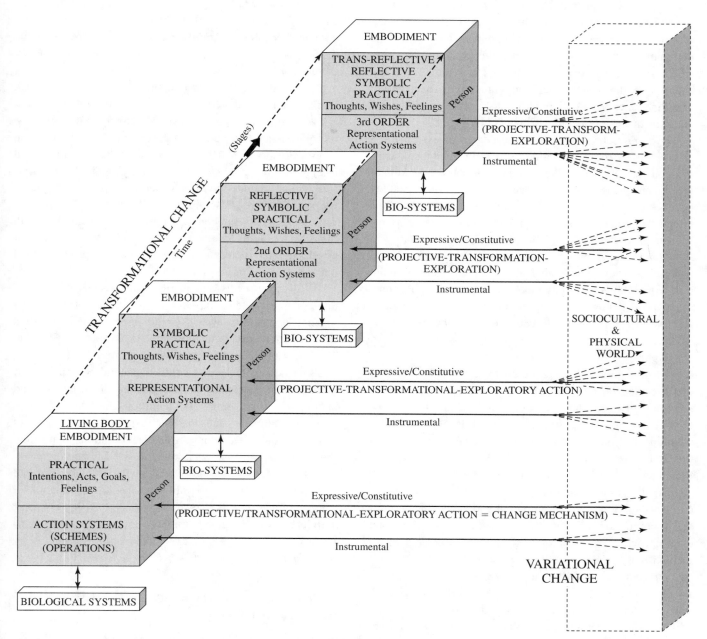

Figure 1.1   The development of the person: levels of transformational and variational change emerging through embodied action in a sociocultural and physical world.

by the four "person" cubes on the left side of Figure 1.1). This emergence of novelty is commonly referred to as *qualitative* change in the sense that it is change that cannot be represented as purely additive. Similarly, reference to *discontinuity* in development is simply the acknowledgment of emergent novelty and qualitative change (Overton & Reese, 1981). Recognizing these features of transformational change is quite important when one considers various notions of stages or levels of development, as these are theoretical concepts that refer to transformational change with the associated emergent novelty, qualitative change, and discontinuity. The philosopher E. Nagel well captured the nature of transformational change when he suggested that the concept of development implies two fundamental features: (a) "the notion of a system, possessing a definite structure [i.e., organization] . . ."; and (b) "the notion of a set of sequential changes in the system yielding relatively permanent but novel increments not only in its structures [i.e., organization] but in its modes of operation as well" (1957, p. 17).

Variational change refers to the degree or extent that a change varies from a standard, norm, or average (see the arrows on the right side of Figure 1.1). Consider the pecking of the pigeon; changes in where, when, and how rapidly pecking occurs are variational changes. The reaching behavior of the infant, the toddler's improvements in walking precision, the growth of vocabulary, and the receipt of better grades in school are all examples of variational change. From an adaptive point of view, developmental variational change is about a skill or ability's becoming more precise and more accurate. This type of change can be represented as linear—completely additive in nature. As a consequence, this change is understood as *quantitative* and *continuous*.

Given these two types of change, there have been three metatheoretical solutions proposed for the problem of how they are related in development. The first and most prominent solution—given the history to be described later—has been to treat variation as the bedrock reality of development. This solution marginalizes transformational change by claiming that it is mere description, which itself requires explanation. Essentially this claim embodies the promise that all "apparent" transformational change will ultimately be explained—perhaps as our empirical knowledge increases—as the product of variation and only variation. An important consequence of this solution is that the associated meta-method will prescribe methods that can assess linear additive processes, but will marginalize methods that assess nonlinear processes. A classic example of this general solution was the Skinnerian demonstration that given only variations in pecking and reinforcement, it was possible to train pigeons to hit ping-pong balls back and forth over a net. Thus, it was claimed that the "apparent" developmental

novelty of playing ping-pong was in reality *nothing but* the continuous additive modifications in variation. This solution is also adopted by those who portray cognitive development as either a simple increase in representational content (see Scholnick & Cookson, 1994) or as an increase in the efficiency with which this content is processed (Siegler, 1989, 1996; Sternberg, 1984; Valsiner, 1994).

The second metatheoretical solution treats transformational change as the bedrock reality and marginalizes the significance of variation. Here, variation is seen as rather irrelevant noise in a transformational system. Although this solution is seldom actually articulated, some stage theories, such as Erik Erikson's (1968) theory of psychosocial development, have elevated transformational change to a point that the importance of the variational seems to disappear below the horizon.

The third metatheoretical approach does not approach transformation and variation as competing alternative, but rather it understands them as fundamentally real, necessary, and interrelated features of development. This solution asserts a reality in which each assumes a different functional role, but each explains and is explained by the other. Transformational systems produce variation, and variation transforms the system (this solution is illustrated in Figure 1.1). This relational metatheoretical posture is discussed later in this chapter as a "take on reality" that resolves many of developmental inquiry's most controversial problems and opens new paths of investigation.

In relation to this and to other discussions of systems and dynamic systems explored in this chapter, it should be noted that the term *systems* is ambiguous unless clarified through articulation of its metatheoretical roots (see Overton, 1975). As pointed out by Ludwig von Bertalanffy (1968a, 1968b), the acknowledged father of general systems theory, *systems* has different meanings, depending on the background assumptions that frame its definition. Bertalanffy's own systems approach—and the one explored in the present chapter—begins from background assumptions that stress the central significance of irreducible activity and organization. Other definitions, however, emerge from background assumptions that stress an ultimate absolute foundation of static uniform objects and a reductionism of any apparent activity and organization to this foundation. Bertalanffy himself referred to these alternative approaches to systems as the *organismic* and *mechanistic* respectively.

What Changes in Development? The Expressive and the Instrumental

As with development itself, the *what* of development has classically entailed two alternatives. Any action, at any level from the neuronal to the molar, can be considered from the perspective of what it expresses or from the perspective of the instrumental value of the behavior. The *expressive-constitutive* function refers to the fact any action may be considered the reflection of some underlying organization or dynamic system. For example, in human ontogenesis we speak of cognitive systems, affective systems, and motivational systems (see the systems described in the cubes on the left of Figure 1.1). These systems have characteristic forms of activity that are expressed as actions and patterns of action in the world (center horizontal lines of Figure 1.1). A verbalization may reflect the nature of the child's system of thought, a cry in a particular context may reflect the status of the child's attachment system, and a series of behaviors may reflect the child's intentional system. The expressive function is *constitutive* in the sense that it reflects the creative function of human action. It reflects the base from which new behaviors, new intentions, and new meanings are constituted. When inquiry is directed toward the assessment or diagnosis of the nature, status, or change of the underlying psychological system, the expressive function is central. It can also be central when explanations are presented from the perspective of biological systems. When exploring the expressive function of an action, the *what* that changes in development is the dynamic system that is reflected in the action expression. Dynamic systems become transformed (left cubes of Figure 1.1) through their action (center horizontal lines of Figure 1.1). Thus, dynamic systems as a *what* of change and transformation as a *type of change* are closely related.

The *instrumental* function of an action is understood as a means of attaining some outcome; it is the pragmatic and adaptive dimension of action (see center horizontal lines of Figure 1.1). For example, in human ontogenesis a cognition or thought may be the means to solve a problem, the emotion of crying may lead to acquiring a caregiver, or walking around may be instrumental in acquiring nourishment. Communicative actions are instrumental actions that extend into the domain of the intersubjective (relation of the person cubes at the left and social world at the right of Figure 1.1). When inquiry is directed toward the adaptive or communicative value of an action, the instrumental function is central. What changes when the instrumental is focal is the behavior itself, but the new behavior is some variation of the original. Thus, instrumental behaviors as a *what* of change and variation as a *type of change* are also closely related.

In a fashion analogous to the earlier discussion of types of developmental change, solutions to the relation of the expressive and instrumental functions of change emerge from three different metatheoretical postures. The first takes the instrumental-communicative as bedrock and marginalizes the expressive. This, for example, is the solution of any

perspective that advocates an exclusively functional approach to a topic of inquiry (e.g., see the work on the functional theory of emotions, Saarni, Mumme, & Campos, 1998), of any theory that advocates an exclusively adaptationist view of a domain of interest, and of any theory that explicitly denies or marginalizes the status of mental structures, mental organization, or biological systems as legitimate—if partial—explanations of behavior.

The second metatheoretical solution reverses the bedrock-marginalization process. It establishes the expressive as bedrock and the instrumental as the marginal. Approaches that offer biological systems, mental systems, or both as both necessary and sufficient for the explanation of behavior represent examples of this solution.

The third metatheoretical solution again—as in the case of the nature of change itself—presents the expressive and the instrumental as realities that operate within a relational matrix. The expressive and the instrumental are accepted not as dichotomous competing alternatives, but rather as different perspectives on the same whole (this solution is illustrated in Figure 1.1). Like the famous ambiguous figure that appears to be a vase from one line of sight and the faces of two people from another line of sight, the expressive and instrumental represent two lines of sight, not independent processes. System and adaptation, like structure and function, are separable only as analytic points of view. Focusing inquiry on the diagnosis of underlying dynamic biological and psychological systems in no way denies that behaviors have an adaptive value; focusing on adaptive value in no way denies that the behaviors originate from some dynamic system.

With this introduction to the impact of the metatheoretical on our understanding of the nature of development and our understanding of the nature of what changes in development, we can proceed to examine the details of various metatheoretical postures as they emerged historically and as they currently operate.

A BRIEF HISTORY OF METATHEORETICAL WORLDS AND THE BIRTH OF DEVELOPMENTAL PSYCHOLOGY

The Modern Period

Modernity was defined both by a quest for absolute certainty of knowledge (Toulmin, 1990) and by an effort to expand individual freedom, especially freedom of thought. Building knowledge on rational and reasoned grounds rather than on the grounds of authority and dogma was understood as the key to each of these goals. The early protagonists who developed the basic tenets of this metatheoretical story line were Galileo Galilei and his physics of a natural world disconnected from mind; René Descartes, whose epistemology elevated disconnection or splitting to a first principle; and Thomas Hobbes, who saw both mind and nature in a vision of atomistic materialism. Of the three, Descartes was to have the greatest and most lasting impact on the text and subtexts of this particular metatheoretical story.

Descartes' major contributions entailed the insertion and articulation of splitting and foundationalism as key interrelated themes into the story of scientific knowledge. *Splitting* is the formation of a conceptual dichotomy—an exclusive either-or relationship—and *foundationalism* is a claim that one or the other elements of the dichotomy constitutes the ultimate Reality or bedrock of certainty. Nature and nurture, idealism and materialism (form and matter), reason and observation, subject and object, constancy and change, biology and culture, and so on all can be—and under the influence of Cartesian epistemology are—presented as split-off competing alternatives. Choose a background principle as the "Real"—as the *foundation*—and it follows, under a split metatheory, that the other is mere appearance or epiphenomenal. It must be cautioned at this point that there is a critical distinction between the use of the term *real* in everyday commonsense life and the Real of foundationalism. No one argues—or has ever argued—that there is a lack of reality or realness in the experienced everyday world. This is commonsense realism. Commonsense realism accepts the material existence of a real, actual, or manifest world and all metatheoretical perspectives treat people, animals, and physical objects as having such a real existence. The metatheoretical issue of the Real with a capital *R* (Putnam, 1987) is a very different issue. It concerns the current issue of having an absolute base or foundation from which everything else emerges. In this limited sense, the Real is defined as that which is not dependent on something else—that which cannot be reduced to something else.

Modernity's foundationalism is identified with a final achievement of absolute certainty and the end of doubt. In this story even probable knowledge is knowledge on its way to certainty (i.e., 100% probable). This foundation is not simply a grounding or a vantage point, standpoint, or point of view, and certainty and doubt are not dialectically related. Descartes' foundationalism describes *the* final, fixed, secure base. It constitutes an absolute, fixed, unchanging bedrock—a final Archimedes point (Descartes, 1969).

Cartesian splitting and foundationalism came to operate as a permanent background frame for modernity's scientific story. However, the specification of the *nature* of the ultimate

foundation remained at issue. It was left to the empiricist branch of modernity to locate the Real within a dichotomy of observation split off from interpretation. Hobbs and later empiricists operated within this frame, in which subject became split from object, mind split from body, ideas split from matter; they built into it a *materialist* identification of *atomistic matter* as the ultimate ontological foundational Real. Further, the epistemological rhetoric of Locke, Berkeley, and Hume operated to suppress subjectivity, mind, or ideas, thereby creating *objectivism,* or the belief that the ultimate material reality exists as an absolute—independent of mind or knower (Searle, 1992). This constituted, as Putnam (1990) has said, the idea of a "God's eye view" that would be independent of the mind of the investigator.

Objectivist matter thus came to constitute the ontological Real to which all of commonsense experience would be reduced to arrive at the goal of science: a systematized body of *certain* empirical knowledge. Support for the materialist foundation arose and was further defined by Newton's contributions. Central among these was the redefinition of the nature of matter in a way that conceived of all bodies as *fundamentally* inactive. Prior to Newton, matter was understood as inherently active. Matter had been conceived in terms of the *relation* of *being* (the static, fixed) and *becoming* (the active, changing). Newton, however—through his concept of inertia—split activity and matter and redefined matter as inactivity (Prosch, 1964).

The redefinition of bodies as inert matter and the assumption of the *atomicity* of matter (i.e., bodies as ultimately aggregates of elemental matter that is uniform in nature, and in combination yields the things of the world), were basic for Newton's formulation of his laws of motion. However, they were also ideas that a later generation generalized into a metaphysical worldview (i.e., a metatheory at the highest level of generality). This worldview identified the nature of the Real as fixed inert matter and *only* fixed inert matter. This worldview has been called the "billiard ball" notion of the universe—"the notion that basically everything . . . was made up of small, solid particles, in themselves inert, but always in motion and elasticitly rebounding from each other, . . . and operating mechanically" (Prosch, 1964, p. 66).

With these metatheoretical themes at hand—splitting, foundationalism, materialism, empiricism, and objectivism—it was a short step to the formulation of a completely exclusive scientific metamethod termed *mechanical explanation* that with relatively minor modifications has extended to the present day as the metamethod of empiricism. This metamethod has gone under various names, including neopositivism and later instrumentalism, conventionalism, and functionalism (Overton, 1998).

Mechanical Explanation

The mechanical explanation metamethod continues the splitting process by dichotomizing science into two airtight compartments, *description* and *explanation*. There are three steps to mechanical explanation. The first is considered descriptive and the second two are considered explanatory.

Step 1: Reduction-Description. The first step of mechanical explanation entails addressing the commonsense object of inquiry and *reducing* it to the absolute material, objective, fixed, unchanging, foundational elements or atoms. Terms like *reductionism, atomism, elementarism,* and *analytic attitude* all identify this step. In psychology for many years the atoms were *stimuli* and *responses.* Today they tend to be *neurons* and *behaviors,* or *contextual factors* and *behaviors*—the story line changes but the themes remain the same within this metatheory. In keeping with the framework of empiricism and materialism, the broad stricture here is to reduce all phenomena to the visible.

Briefly consider one impact of this first step on developmental inquiry. Immediately the concepts of *transformational change, stages* of development, and the *mental organizations,* or *dynamic systems* that change during development become suspect as being somehow derivative because they are not directly observable. At best under this story line, transformations, stages, and mental organization can only function as summary statements for an underlying more molecular really Real. In fact, the drive throughout this step is toward the ever more molecular in the belief that it is in the realm of the molecular that the Real is directly observed. This is particularly well illustrated in the recent enthusiasm for a microgenetic method (e.g., D. Kuhn, Garcia-Mila, Zohar, & Andersen, 1995; Siegler, 1996) as a method that offers "a *direct* [italics added] means for studying cognitive development" (Siegler & Crowley, 1991, p. 606). In this approach, an intensive trial-by-trial analysis reduces the very notion of development to a molecular bedrock of visible behavioral differences as they appear across learning trials.

It is important to recognize that the aim of Step 1 is to drive out *interpretations* from the commonsense phenomena under investigation. Under the objectivist theme, commonsense observation is error laden, and it is only through ever more careful *neutral* observation that science can eliminate this error and ultimately arrive at the elementary bedrock that constitutes the level of *facts* or *data* (i.e., invariable observations).

Step 2: Causal Explanation. Step 2 of mechanical explanation begins to move inquiry into the second compartment of compartmentalized science—*explanation.* Step 2 consists of the instruction to find the relation among the elements described in Step 1. More specifically, given our objects of study in developmental psychology—behavior and behavior change—this step directs inquiry to locate antecedents. These antecedents, when they meet certain criteria of necessity and sufficiency, are termed *causes;* the discovery of cause defines explanation within this metamethod. The antecedents are also often referred to as *mechanisms,* but the meaning is identical.

This is another point at which to pause and notice an important impact of metatheory. Here, because of the particular metatheoretical principles involved, the word *explanation* comes to be defined as an antecedent-consequent relation, or the efficient-material proximal cause of the object of inquiry. Further, science itself comes to be defined as the (causal) explanation of natural phenomena. It is critically important to remember here that Aristotle had earlier produced a very different metatheoretical story of scientific explanation. Aristotle's schema entailed *complementary relations* among four types of explanation, rather than a splitting. Two of Aristotle's explanations were causal in nature (i.e., antecedent *material* and *efficient* causes). Two, however, were explanations according to the pattern, organization, or form of the object of inquiry. Aristotle's *formal* (i.e., the momentary form or organization of the object of inquiry) and *final* (i.e., the end or goal of the object of inquiry) explanations were explanations that made the object of inquiry *intelligible* and gave *reasons* for the nature and functioning of the object (Randall, 1960; Taylor, 1995). Today, the structure of the atom, the structure of DNA, the structure of the solar system, and the structure of the universe are all familiar examples of formal pattern principles drawn from the natural sciences. Kinship structures, mental structures, mental organization, dynamic systems, attachment behavior system, structures of language, ego and superego, dynamisms, schemes, operations, and cognitive structures are familiar examples of formal pattern principles drawn from the human sciences. Similarly, reference to the sequence and directionality found in the second law of thermodynamics, self-organizing systems, the equilibration process or reflective abstraction, the orthogenetic principle, or a probabilistic epigenetic principle are all examples of final pattern principles (Overton, 1994a).

Both formal and final pattern principles entail interpretations that make the phenomena under investigation intelligible. Both—within the Aristotelian *relational* scheme— constitute legitimate explanations. However, within the *split* story of mechanical explanation, as guided by reductionism and objectivism, formal and final principles completely lose any explanatory status; explanation is limited to *nothing but* observable efficient (i.e., the force that moves the object) and material (i.e., the material composition of the object) causes. At best, within the mechanical story formal and final principles may reappear in the descriptive compartment as mere summary statements of the underlying molecular descriptive Real discussed in Step 1. In this way transformational change and dynamic psychological systems become eliminated or marginalized as necessary features of developmental inquiry.

Step 3: Induction of Interpretation-Free Hypotheses, Theories, and Laws.

Step 3 of mechanical explanation installs *induction* as the foundational logic of science. Step 3 instructs the investigator that ultimate explanations in science must be found in fixed unchanging laws, and these must be inductively derived as *empirical generalizations* from the repeated observation of cause-effect relations found in Step 2. Weak generalizations from Step 2 regularities constitute interpretation-free hypotheses. Stronger generalizations constitute interpretation-free theoretical propositions. Theoretical propositions joined as logical conjunctions (*and* connections) constitute interpretation-free theories. Laws represent the strongest and final inductions.

Deduction later reenters modernity's story of empirical science as a split-off heuristic method of moving from inductively derived hypotheses and theoretical propositions to further empirical observations. When later editions of the story introduced a "hypothetico-deductive method" it was simply more variation on the same theme. The hypothesis of this method has nothing to do with interpretation, but is simply an empirical generalization driven by pristine data; the generalization then serves as a major premise in a formal deductive argument. Similarly, when instrumentalism moved away from the hypothetico-deductive stance to the employment of models, models themselves functioned merely as the same type of interpretation-free heuristic devices.

Another important variation—but a variation nevertheless—on this same theme was the so-called *covering law model* of scientific explanation. This model was introduced by Carl Hempel (1942) and became the prototype of all later explanations formulated within this metatheory. The covering law model was particularly important for developmental inquiry because it treated historical events as analogous to physical events in the sense that earlier events were considered the causal antecedents of later events (Ricoeur, 1984).

Here, then, is the basic outline of the quest for absolute certainty according to the empiricist modernity story of scientific methodology:

- *Step 1.* Reduce to the objective (interpretation-free) observable foundation.
- *Step 2.* Find the causes.
- *Step 3.* Induce the law.

As noted, variations appear throughout history. In fact, it would be misleading not to acknowledge that probability has replaced certainty as the favored lexical item in the story as it is told today. Indeed, induction is itself statistical and probabilistic in nature. However, as mentioned earlier, this change represents much more style than it does substance, because the aim remains to move toward 100% probability, thereby arriving at certainty or its closest approximation. This type of fallibilistic stance continues to pit doubt against certainty as competing alternatives rather than understand doubt and certainty as a dialectical relation framed by the concept of *plausibility*. More generally, all of the variations that have been introduced since the origin of Newtonian explanation—including those formulated under the methodological banners of neopositivism, instrumentalism, conventionalism, and functionalism—have not at all changed the basic themes.

There is scarcely any doubt that modernity's empiricist metatheory of objective certainty has failed. This failure is too long a story to retell here. It has been thoroughly documented in the arena of scientific knowledge by numerous historians and philosophers of science, including Stephen Toulmin (1953), N. R. Hanson (1958), Thomas Kuhn (1962), Imre Lakatos (1978), Larry Laudan (1977), Richard Bernstein (1983), and—most recently—Bruno Latour (1993). Despite this discrediting, ghosts of modernity's mechanistic worldview continue to haunt the scientific study of development. Nature (material cause) and nurture (efficient cause) are still presented as competing alternative explanations. Biology and culture still compete with each other as fundamental explanations of development (see Lerner, 2002). There are still those who argue that emergence of genuine novel behavior is not possible and that any apparent novelty must be completely explained by antecedent causal mechanisms. Indeed, the claim is still put forth that if a causal mechanism is not identified, then there is no real explanation—only *mysticism* (Elman et al., 1996) or *miracles* (Siegler & Munakata, 1993). This is the same mechanistically defined argument that claims there can be no discontinuity or transformational change in development. All change, according to this mechanistic argument, is (i.e., must be) nothing but additive or continuous in nature; all qualitative change must be reduced to nothing but quantitative change. There are also those who still argue that development must be explained by causal mechanisms and only causal mechanisms. And—last but not least—there are still those who argue that all scientific knowledge about development must begin and end in a world of interpretation-free pristine observations of what "the child actually does," a world that exalts the instrumental-communicative and excludes the expressive.

There are probably several reasons for the failure to recognize and accept the demise of modernity's empiricist metatheory. One of these reasons has to do with socialization. For psychologists who were reared in the strictures of mechanical explanation, these strictures are difficult to abandon, and the values tend to be passed from generation to generation without deep reflection. Indeed, because this metatheory is virtually inscribed with the motto *Don't think, find out* (Cohen, 1931), it is not surprising that fledgling investigators are often discouraged from taking the very notion of metatheory seriously; hence, they seldom evaluate the merits and flaws of alternative background assumptions. Another (perhaps more important) reason, however, has been the apparent lack of viable empirical scientific alternatives—and the seeming abyss of uncertainty that is faced when one abandons a secure rock-solid base. The rise of postmodern thought did nothing to assuage this fear.

The Postmodern Period and the Chaos of Absolute Relativity

Like its predecessor, postmodernism is identified with the ideal of achieving individual freedom. However, the proponents of the postmodern agenda have approached this ideal almost exclusively through attacks directed at modernity's rational quest for absolute certainty. This has left in place the splitting of categories. The effect of this continued splitting is that postmodern thought has tended to define itself in terms of categories that reflect the opposite of those that defined modernity. Thus, if modernity was *rational,* the postmodern celebrates the *emotional;* if modernity was objectivist *observational,* the postmodern celebrates subjectivist *interpretation;* and if modernity aimed for the *universal,* the postmodern argues for the *particular.* Despite the fact that advocates of postmodernism explicitly reject foundationalism and explicitly reject the notion of metatheory—"metanarratives," as they are termed in the postmodern vernacular (Overton, 1998)—splitting into oppositional categories of necessity creates a new (if implicit) foundationalism. In this new foundationalism, modernity is turned on its head. The apparent reality of modernity becomes the real foundational reality of postmodernism. The foundational elevation of interpretation over observation in some versions of hermeneutics and deconstructivism is illustrative. When interpretation is valued to the exclusion of observation, the

end result is a complete (i.e., absolute) relativism. If there is no neutral observational territory to help decide between your judgment and my judgment, then all knowledge is purely subjective and (hence) relative. But this situation is chaotic and precludes any stable general base from which to operate; this is complete relativity and uncertainty. Given this chaotic alternative, it is little wonder that the generation of developmental psychologists that followed the destruction of neopositivism and instrumentalism tended to cling for support to the wreckage of modernity's descending narrative. In their split world, the slow death of fading relevance is less terrifying than the prospect of chaotic fragmentation.

Although much of postmodern thought has moved towards the chaotic abyss, one variant has attempted to establish a stable base for knowledge construction by developing a new scientific metamethod. This position emerged from the hermeneutic and phenomenological traditions (Latour, 1999) and has come to operate parallel to and as a reaction against neopositivism's quest for reductionistic causal explanation. This alternative picture champions *understanding* (in contrast to explanation) as the base of scientific knowledge—at least as this scientific knowledge pertains to the behavioral and social sciences, including the humanities.

Broadly, hermeneutics is the theory or philosophy of the interpretation of meaning. Hermeneutics elevates to a heroic role the very concept that mechanical explanation casts as demon error—*interpretation.* For our purposes, we can pass by the periods of classical, biblical, and romantic hermeneutics, as well as Vico's historical hermeneutics. Our brief focus here is on the effort that Dilthey (1972) promoted at the turn of the present century to construct a metamethod for the social sciences; this was *Verstehen* or *understanding.* Within this metamethod, understanding operates as an epistemological rather than a psychological concept. Furthermore, most important is that interpretation operates as the procedure that results in understanding.

As a metamethod of the social and behavioral sciences, understanding is closely related to *action theory.* Action theory is a person-centered approach to inquiry into processes and operations of the meaning-producing, living embodied agent (Brandtstadter, 1998; Brandtstadter & Lerner, 1999; Overton, 1997a, 1997b). Action theory stands in contrast to exclusively variable approaches to human behavior, which are externalist and event oriented in their focus. Paul Ricoeur has clearly outlined—in the context of Wittgenstein's language games, which are themselves metatheoretical background principles—the distinction between variable-centered events and person-centered actions (see also Magnusson & Stattin, 1998), and in the following outline Ricoeur (1991) suggested the distinction between mechanical explanation and hermeneutic understanding:

> It is not the same language game that we speak of events [variables] occurring in nature or of actions performed by people. For, to speak of events [variables], we enter a language game including notions like cause, law, fact, explanation and so on. . . . It is . . . in another language game and in another conceptual network that we can speak of human action [i.e., a person-centered frame]. For, if we have begun to speak in terms of action, we shall continue to speak in terms of projects, intentions, motives, reasons for acting, agents, [interpretation, understanding] and so forth. (pp. 132–133)

Unfortunately, the creation of a *distinct* metamethod for the social sciences is yet another example of proceeding within a split background frame. *Verstehen* is presented as a *competing* account of human functioning to that found in the natural sciences. However, the articulation of this dichotomy may also provide a clue to the possibility of its resolution—the possibility of a rapprochement between the futility of a search for absolute certainty and the chaos of absolute uncertainty. Verstehen as a metamethod—and action theory as an approach to human functioning—are closely related by the intentional quality of action. Intention is never directly observable by a third party. To intend is to do something for the sake of; it involves direction and order. There is a goal toward which action moves, and a sequence of acts lead to that goal. To explain (understand) action, it is necessary to make interpretative inferences about patterns of acts that make the specific behavioral movements intelligible and give a reason for the movements. For example, the act we term *reaching* in the young infant is only that if the inference is made that the infant intends a particular goal object. Under another inference the observed movements might be termed *stretching*. Making inferences about action patterns is in fact identical to Aristotle's formal and final explanations as they were designed to make the object of inquiry intelligible and give reasons for the nature and functioning of the object. Thus, a rapprochement between developmental psychology as an adherent of a so-called *natural science perspective* might view it—and as an adherent of an *action perspective* might view it—may reside in a metatheoretical perspective that can integrate the mechanical causal explanation and action pattern explanation.

RELATIONAL METATHEORY: A SYNTHESIS OF OPPOSITES

The historian of science Bruno Latour (1993) has sketched just such a rapprochement in his analysis of the modern agenda and postmodernism. Latour begins by rejecting both modernity and postmodernism. He refers to the latter as "a symptom, not a fresh solution" (p. 46) to the problems of modernity.

> It [postmodernism] senses that something has gone awry in the modern critique, but it is not able to do anything but prolong that critique, though without believing in its foundations (Lyotard, 1979). . . .
> Postmodernism rejects all empirical work as illusory and deceptively scientistic (Baudrillard, 1992). Disappointed rationalists, its adepts indeed sense that modernism is done for, but they continue to accept its way of dividing up time (p. 46).

Although adversaries, both groups have played on the field of identical background assumptions. Latour's solution is to move from this to another much broader field of play where foundations are groundings, not bedrocks of certainty; and analysis is about creating categories, not about cutting nature at its joints. Viewed historically, Latour calls this approach "amodernism" as a denial of both modernity and postmodernism. Viewed as a metatheoretical background it is termed "relationism" (p. 114) and its basic identity is defined by a move away from the extremes of Cartesian splits to the center or "Middle Kingdom," where entities and ideas are represented not as pure forms, but as forms that flow across fuzzy boundaries.

Rejecting Splits and Bedrocks

A relational metatheory begins by clearing splitting from the field of play. Because splitting and foundationalism go hand in hand, this also eliminates foundationalism. Splitting involves the belief that there are pure forms, but this belief itself springs from the acceptance of the atomistic assumptions that there is a rock bottom to reality and that this rock bottom is composed of elements that preserve their identity, regardless of context. Thus, acceptance of atomism leads directly to the belief that the mental (ideas, mind) and the physical (matter, body) are two absolutely different natural kinds of things. And if nature is composed of such natural kinds, then it is possible to cut nature at its joints. A relational metatheory abandons atomism and replaces it with a more holistic understanding, which proposes that the identity of objects derives from the relational context in which they are embedded. As a consequence of this form of background idea—as the philosopher John Searle (1992) has suggested—"the fact that a feature is mental does not imply that it is not physical; the fact that a feature is physical does not imply that it is not mental" (p. 15). Similarly, the fact that a feature is biological does not suggest that it is not cultural, the fact that a feature is cultural does not suggest that it is not biological, and so forth.

The rejection of pure forms or essences has broad implications for developmental psychology. To briefly give but one example, consider the seemingly never-ending nature-nurture or biology-culture debate. This debate is framed by the modern agenda of splitting and foundationalism. In the debate's current form, virtually no one actually asserts that matter-body-brain-genes or society-culture-environment provides *the* cause of behavior or development; however, the background idea of one or the other as the real determinant remains the silent subtext that continues to shape debate. The overt contemporary claim is that behavior and development are the products of the *interactions* of nature and nurture. But interaction is still thought of as two split-off pure entities that function *independently* in cooperative ways, competitive ways, or both. As a consequence, the debate simply becomes displaced to another level of discourse. At this new level, the contestants agree that behavior and development are determined by both nature and nurture, but they remain embattled over the relative merits of each entity's contribution. Within the split foundationalist agenda, battles continue over *which* of the two is more important for a specific behavior, which of the two determines the origin versus the appearance of a specific behavior, or how much one or the other contributes to that behavior. Thus, despite overt conciliatory declarations to the contrary, the classical *which one* and *how much* questions that have long framed the split debate (see Anastasi, 1958; Schneirla, 1956) continue as potent divisive frames of inquiry. In fact, it would be impossible to cast questions of development as issues of nativism and empiricism (Spelke & Newport, 1998) were it not for the assumption of pure forms (see Lerner, 2002, for a further elaboration).

The Identity of Opposites

Rejecting atomism eliminates the idea of pure forms and consequently makes any notion of natural foundational splits untenable. This in itself destroys the scientific legitimacy of questions such as the *which one* and *how much* questions of nature-nurture. However, the mere rejection of atomism does not in itself offer a positive approach to resolving the many fundamental dichotomies that have framed developmental as well as other fields of inquiry (see Table 1.1). A general positive resolution requires a second component; this component is the generation of a context in which the individual identity of each formerly dichotomous member is maintained while simultaneously it is affirmed that each member constitutes and is constituted by the other. Thus, a general context is needed in which (for example) both nature and nurture maintain their individual identities while simultaneously it is understood that the fact that a behavior is a product of biology does not imply that it is not equally a product of culture, and

TABLE 1.1 Fundamental Categories of Analysis Expressed as Either-Or Dichotomies

Subject	Object
Mind	Body
Biology	Person
Culture	Biology
Person	Culture
Person	Situation
Intrapsychic	Interpersonal
Nature	Nurture
Stability	Change
Expressive	Instrumental
Variation	Transformation
Reason	Emotion
Form	Matter
Universal	Particular
Transcendent	Immanent
Analysis	Synthesis
Unity	Diversity

that the fact that a behavior is a product of culture does not imply that is not equally a product of biology—that is, it must be shown that while there are both biology and culture, there is no biology that is not culture and no culture that is not biology.

Splitting entails casting categories into an exclusive *either-or* form that forces an understanding of the terms as contradictions in the sense that one category *absolutely* excludes the other (i.e., follows the logical law of contradiction that it is never the case that A = not A). The next step in the formulation of a relational metatheory involves replacing this exclusive framework with an inclusive one. The inclusive framework must accomplish the seemingly paradoxical task of simultaneously establishing both an identity between the opposite categories and retaining the opposite quality of the categories; this is accomplished by considering identity and differences as two moments of analysis.

Guided by a more holistic contextual background assumption that assumes that parts and wholes define each other, the identity among categories is found by recasting the previously dichotomous elements not as contradictions, but as differentiated polarities of a unified matrix—as a relation. As differentiations, each pole is defined recursively; each pole defines and is defined by its opposite. In this identity moment of analysis the law of contradiction is suspended and each category contains and in fact *is* its opposite. Further—and centrally—as a differentiation this moment pertains to character, origin, and outcomes. The character of any contemporary behavior, for example, is 100% nature because it is 100% nurture. There is no origin to this behavior that was some other percentage—regardless of whether we climb back into the womb, back into the cell, back into the genome, or back into the DNA—nor can there be a later behavior that will be a different percentage. Similarly, any action is both expressive and instrumental, and any developmental change is both transformational and variational.

In the second or oppositional moment of analysis, the law of contradiction is allowed to operate and each category again asserts its individuality. The parts are opposites and they assert their differences. In this oppositional moment nature is nature, it is not nurture, and, nurture is nurture, it is not nature. This moment of analysis pertains to settings or momentary context. Thus, it is possible to analyze any behavior from the standpoint of either nature or nurture when this either-or is considered as an inclusive rather than an exclusive disjunction. I return to this point in the following section.

Because the idea and implications of suspending the law of contradiction on the one hand and applying it on the other hand is not a familiar idea, some clarifying comments are needed. Here it must be noted that the relational stance owes much to the notion of the *dialectic* as this was articulated by the nineteenth century philosopher G. W. F. Hegel (1807–1830). For Hegel, historical—and by extension developmental—change is a dynamic expressive-transformational process of growth, represented and defined by the dialectic. The essence of Hegel's dialectic is that of a process through which concepts or fundamental features of a dynamic system *differentiate* and move toward *integration*. Any initial concept or any basic feature of a dynamic system—called a *thesis* or an *affirmation*—contains implicit within itself an inherent *contradiction* that, through action of the system, becomes differentiated into a second concept or feature—the *antithesis* or *negation* of the thesis. As a consequence, even in the single unity of thesis there is the implicit contradictory relation of thesis-antithesis, just as in the unity of the single organic cell there is the implicit differentiation into the unity of multiple cells. This points to the fundamental relational character of the dialectic.

As thesis leads to antithesis—thus producing the differentiation of a relational polarity of opposites—a potential space between them is generated, and this becomes the ground for the *coordination* of the two. The coordination that emerges—again through the mechanism of action of the system—constitutes a new unity or integration called the *synthesis*. The coordinating synthesis is itself a system that exhibits novel systemic properties while subsuming the original systems. Thus, a new relational dynamic matrix composed of three realms—thesis-antithesis-synthesis—is formed. The integration that emerges from the differentiation, like all integrations, is incomplete. The synthesis represents a new dynamic action system—a new thesis—and thus begins a new growth cycle of differentiation and integration.

In this relational scheme, the polarity of opposites (i.e., thesis and antithesis) that emerges from the initial relatively undifferentiated matrix (i.e., thesis) does not constitute a cut-off (split) of contradictory categories that *absolutely* exclude each other. Having grown from the same soil as it were, the two, while standing in a contradictory relation of opposites, also share an identity. Hegel, in fact, referred to this relation as the "identity of opposites" (Stace, 1924) and illustrated it in his famous example of the master and slave. In this example Hegel demonstrated that it is impossible to define or understand the freedom of the master without reference to the constraints of slavery; and it is consequently impossible to define the constraints of slavery without the reference to the freedom of the master. Freedom thus contains the idea of constraint as constraint contains the idea of freedom, and in this we see the identity of the opposites freedom and constraint.

The justification for the claim that a law of logic—for example, the law of contradiction—can reasonably both be applied and relaxed depending on the context of inquiry requires a recognition that the laws of logic themselves are not immune to background ideas. In some background traditions, the laws of logic are understood as immutable realities given either by a world cut off from the human mind or by a prewired mind cut off from the world. However, in the background tradition currently under discussion, the traditional laws of logic are themselves ideas that have been constructed through the reciprocal action of human minds and world. The laws of logic are simply pictures that have been drawn or stories that have been told. They may be good pictures or good stories in the sense of bringing a certain quality of order into our lives, but nevertheless they are still pictures or stories, and it is possible that other pictures will serve us even better. The twentieth century philosopher Ludwig Wittgenstein (1958), whose later works focused on the importance of background ideas, made this point quite clearly when he discussed another law of logic—the law of the excluded middle—as being one possible picture of the world among many possible pictures.

> The law of the excluded middle says here: It must either look like this, or like that. So it really . . . says nothing at all, but gives us a picture. . . . And this picture *seems* to determine what we have to do and how—but it does not do so. . . . Here saying 'There is no third possibility' . . . expresses our inability to turn our eyes away from this picture: a picture which looks as if it must already contain both the problem and its solution, while all the time we *feel* that it is not so. (1953, para. 352)

The famous ink sketch by M. C. Escher titled *Drawing Hands* (Figure 1.2) presents a vivid graphic illustration both of the *identity* of opposites that is found when the law of contradiction is relaxed in this second phase of a relational

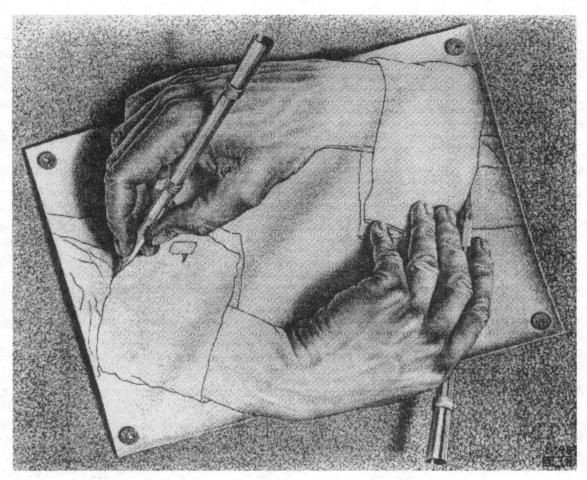

Figure 1.2   M. C. Escher's "Drawing Hands" © Cordon Art B. V.—Baarn—Holland. All rights reserved.

metatheory, and as well as the *opposites* of this identity. In this sketch a left and a right hand assume a relational posture according to which each is simultaneously drawing and being drawn by the other. Each hand is *identical* with the other in the sense of each drawing and each being drawn. This is the relaxed moment of the law of contradiction. Yet they are opposites and contradict each other in that one is a left hand and one is a right hand. Identity is achieved in the context of opposites that define and are defined by each other. It is a useful exercise to write on each hand one term of traditionally split concepts and to explore the resulting effect. Terms that can be written in this fashion range from nature and nurture, biology and culture, transformation and variation, expressive and instrumental to pairs such as subject-object, intrapsychic-interpersonal, interpretation-observation, certainty-doubt, absolute-relative, unity-diversity, stability-change, universal-particular, reason-emotion, ideas-matter, analysis-synthesis, and so on. This exercise is more than merely an illustration of a familiar bidirectionality of effects suggested in many in-

stances by many scientific investigators. The exercise makes tangible the central feature of the relational metatheory; seemingly dichotomous ideas that have often been thought of as competing alternatives can in fact enter into inquiry as complementary supportive partners.

This transformation of competing alternatives into complementary partners is illustrated in a recent exchange of comments concerning research on the topic that social psychology refers to as the *fundamental attribution error.* In this exchange, one group (Gilovich & Eibach, 2001) proceeds from a split position and notes that "human behavior is not easily parsed into situational and dispositional causes" (p. 23) and it is difficult to establish "a precise accounting of how much a given action stems from the impinging stimulus rather than from the faculty or disposition with which it makes contact" (p. 24). The reply to this comment, from a group committed to an identity of opposites (Sabini, Siepmann, & Stein, 2001), asserts that they reject such a position because it reflects confusion between competing and complementary accounts. They argue that the problem with the question of

> How much John's going out with Sue stems from her beauty rather than from his love of beautiful women. . . . is not that it is difficult to answer; it is that it is conceptually incoherent. It is incoherent because it construes two classes of accounts that are in fact complementary as if they were competing. The heart of our argument is that one must take this point seriously. All behavior is jointly a product of environmental stimuli and dispositions. (p. 43)

A similar but subtler example is found in a recently published dialogue on spatial development. Uttal begins this dialogue with the seemingly complementary view that his claims about spatial development "are based on the assumption that the relation between maps and the development of spatial cognition is reciprocal in nature" (2000, p. 247). However, in a commentary on Uttal's article, Liben (2000) raises the question of whether Utall is in fact operating within the context of an identity of opposites, which she proposes as her own approach.

> As I read his thesis, Uttal seems to be suggesting an *independent* contribution of maps, positing that exposure to maps can play a *causal* role in leading children to develop basic spatial concepts. My own preference is to propose a more radically *interdependent* [italics added] role of organismic and environmental factors. (p. 272)

The Opposites of Identity

If we think of the identity of opposites as a kind of figure-ground problem then, to this point, the figure has primarily been the proposition that within a relational metatheory, ideas—that in other metatheoretical systems act as bedrock foundational competing alternatives—exhibit an underlying identity. Equally important, but operating as ground to this point, is the already alluded-to fact that this identity is one of *opposites*. To now make these opposites the figure, opens the way to a third component of a relational metatheory: generating relatively stable platforms from which to launch empirical inquiry.

Without the opposites of identity there would be only the identity of identities and this would present little opportunity for serious empirical work. It has already been noted that a relational metatheory rejects splits and bedrocks. If this were the end of the story—as would be the case with an identity of identities—then we would have eliminated the absolute objective realism of modernity, but we would still be in

danger of falling into the absolute relativism of postmodernism. What is needed is some way to introduce a relative relativism or a relative realism—both would mean the same—in order to establish a stability sufficient to make empirical inquiry possible and meaningful. This goal is met by taking the oppositional moment of analysis as figure and the identity moment of analysis as ground. When relational terms are viewed as opposites, each asserts a unique identity that differentiates it from other identities. These unique differential qualities are stable within any general system and thus may form a relatively stable platform for empirical inquiry. These platforms become *standpoints, points of view,* or *lines of sight* in recognition that they do not reflect absolute foundations (Harding, 1986). Again, considering Escher's sketch, when left hand as left hand and right as right are the focus of attention, it then becomes quite clear that—were they large enough—one could stand on either hand and examine the structures and functions of that hand. Thus, to return to the nature-nurture example, while explicitly recognizing that any behavior is 100% nature and 100% nurture, alternative points of view permit the scientist to analyze the behavior from a *biological* or from a *cultural* standpoint. Biology and culture no longer constitute competing alternative explanations; rather, they are two points of view on an object of inquiry that has been both created by and will only be fully understood through multiple viewpoints. To state this more generally, the unity that constitutes human identity and human development becomes discovered only in the diversity of multiple interrelated lines of sight.

Synthesis: The View From the Center

Engaging fundamental bipolar concepts as relatively stable standpoints opens the way and takes an important first step toward establishing a broad stable base for empirical inquiry within a relational metatheory. However, this solution is incomplete because it omits a key relational component. The oppositional quality of the bipolar pairs reminds us that their contradictory nature still remains and still requires a resolution. As suggested earlier, the resolution of this tension between contradictions is not found in the reduction of one of the system polarities to the other. Rather, moving to the middle and above the conflict—and here discovering a novel system that coordinates the two conflicting systems—establishes the resolution. This position is a position of *synthesis* and it constitutes another standpoint.

At this point the Escher sketch fails as a graphic representation. Although *Drawing Hands* illustrates the identity of opposites and shows the middle ground, it does not present a coordination of the two. In fact, the synthesis for this sketch

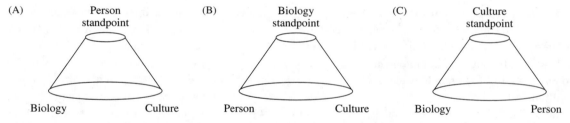

Figure 1.3   Relational standpoints in psychological inquiry: person, biology, and culture.

is the unseen hand that has drawn the drawing hands. The synthesis of interest for the general metatheory would be a system that is a coordination of the most universal bipolarity we can imagine. Undoubtedly there are several candidates for this level of generality, but the polarity between *matter* and *society* seems sufficient for present purposes. What then represents the synthesis of matter and society? Arguably it is the *human organism* (Latour, 1993). Because our specific focus of inquiry is psychology, we can reframe this matter-society polarity as the polarity of *biology* and *culture*. In the context of psychology, then, as an illustration write "biology" on one and "culture" on the other Escher hand, and what is the resulting synthesis?—the human organism, the *person* (see Figure 1.3). Persons—as integrated self-organizing dynamic systems of cognitive, emotional, and motivational processes—represent a novel level or stage of structure and functioning that emerges from and constitutes a coordination of biology and culture (see Magnusson & Stattin, 1998).

At the synthesis, then, there is a standpoint that coordinates and resolves the tension between the other two members of the relation. This provides a particularly broad and stable base for launching empirical inquiry. A *person standpoint* opens the way for the empirical investigation of universal dimensions of psychological structure-function relations (e.g., processes of perception, thought, emotions, values), their individual differences, and their development—(transformational-variational) across the life span. Because universal and particular are themselves relational concepts, no question can arise here about whether the focus on universal processes excludes the particular; it clearly does not, as we already know from the earlier discussion of polarities. The fact that a process is viewed from a universal standpoint in no way suggests that it is not contextualized. The general theories of Jean Piaget, Heinz Werner, James Mark Baldwin, William Stern, attachment theory and object relations theories of John Bowlby, Harry Stack Sullivan, Donald Winnicott all are exemplars of developmentally oriented relational *person standpoints*.

It is important to recognize that one synthesis standpoint is relative to other synthesis standpoints. Human and society

are coordinated by matter, and thus—within psychological inquiry—*biology* represents a *standpoint* as the synthesis of *person* and *culture* (Figure 1.3). The implication of this is that a relational biological approach to psychological processes investigates the biological conditions and settings of psychological structure-function relations. This exploration is quite different from split-foundationalist approaches to biological inquiry that assume an atomistic and reductionistic stance towards the object of study. The neurobiologist Antonio Damasio's (1994, 1999) work on the brain-body basis of a psychological self and emotions is an excellent illustration of this *biological* relational standpoint. And in the context of his biological investigations, Damasio points out

> A task that faces neuroscientists today is to consider the neurobiology supporting adaptive supraregulations [e.g., the psychological subjective experience of self] . . . I am not attempting to reduce social phenomena to biological phenomena, but rather to discuss the powerful connection between them. (1994, p. 124). . . . Realizing that there are biological mechanisms behind the most sublime human behavior does not imply a simplistic reduction to the nuts and bolts of neurobiology (1994, p. 125).

A similar illustration comes from the Nobel laureate neurobiologist Gerald Edelman's (1992; Edelman & Tononi, 2000) work on the brain-body base of consciousness:

> I hope to show that the kind of reductionism that doomed the thinkers of the Enlightenment is confuted by evidence that has emerged both from modern neuroscience and from modern physics. . . . To reduce a theory of an individual's behavior to a theory of molecular interactions is simply silly, a point made clear when one considers how many different levels of physical, biological, and social interactions must be put into place before higher order consciousness emerges. (Edelman, 1992, p. 166)

A third synthesis standpoint recognizes that human and matter are coordinated by society, and again granting that the inquiry is about psychological processes, *culture* represents a standpoint as the synthesis of *person* and *biology* (Figure 1.3). Thus, a relational cultural approach to psychological processes explores the cultural conditions and settings of psychological structure-function relations. From this *cultural standpoint,* the focus is upon cultural differences in the context of psychological functions as complementary to the person standpoint's focus on psychological functions in the context of cultural differences.

This standpoint is illustrated by cultural psychology, or developmentally oriented cultural psychology. However, not all cultural psychologies emerge from standpoint background ideas. When, for example, a cultural psychology makes the social constructivist assertion that social discourse is "prior to and constitutive of the world" (Miller, 1996, p. 99), it becomes clear that this form of cultural psychology has been framed by split-foundationalist background ideas. Similarly, when sociocultural claims are made about the "primacy of social forces," or claims arise suggesting that "mediational means" (i.e., instrumental-communicative acts) constitute the *necessary* focus of psychological interest (e.g., see Wertsch, 1991), the shadows of split-foundationalist metatheoretical principles are clearly in evidence.

A recent example of a relational developmentally oriented cultural standpoint emerges from the work of Jaan Valsiner (1998), which examines the "social nature of human psychology." Focusing on the social nature of the person, Valsiner stresses the importance of avoiding the temptation of trying to reduce person processes to social processes. To this end he explicitly distinguishes between the dualisms of split-foundationalist metatheory and dualities of the relational stance he advocates. Ernst Boesch (1991) and Lutz Eckensberger (1990) have also presented an elaboration of the *cultural standpoint.* Boesch's cultural psychology and Eckensberger's theoretical and empirical extensions of this draw from Piaget's cognitive theory, from Janet's dynamic theory, and from Kurt Lewin's social field theory, and argues that cultural psychology aims at an integration of individual and cultural change, an integration of individual and collective meanings, and a bridging of the gap between subject and object (e.g., see Boesch, 1991).

In a similar vein Damon offers a vision of the *cultural standpoint* in his discussion of "two complementary developmental functions, . . . the social and the personality functions of social development" (1988, p. 3). These are presented by Damon as an identity of opposites. The social function is an act of integration serving to "establish and maintain relations with other, to become an accepted member of society-at-large, to regulate one's behavior according to society's codes and standards" (p. 3). The personality function, on the other hand, is the function of individuation, an act of differentiation serving the formation of the individual's personal identity that requires "distinguishing oneself from others, determin-

ing one's own unique direction in life, and finding within the social network a position uniquely tailored to one's own particular nature, needs, and aspirations" (p. 3). Although others could be mentioned as illustrative (e.g., Grotevant, 1998), it should be noted in conclusion here that Erik Erikson (1968), was operating out of exactly this type of relational standpoint when he described identity as "a process 'located' *in the core of the individual* and yet also *in the core of his communal culture*" (p. 22).

As a final point concerning syntheses and the view from the center, it needs to be recognized that a relational metatheory is not limited to three syntheses. For example, *discourse* or *semiotics* may also be taken as a synthesis of *person* and *culture* (Latour, 1993). In this case biology and person are conflated and the biological-person dialectic represents the opposites of identity that are coordinated by discourse.

As a general summary to this point, the argument has been made that metatheoretical principles form the ground out of which grow the theories and methods of any domain of empirical inquiry. This has been illustrated by exploring several issues that frame the field of developmental psychology. Historically, both the modern and postmodern eras have articulated broad metatheoretical paradigms that have functioned as competing alternatives in the natural and social sciences. The commonality of these paradigms has been that each shares the background assumptions of splitting and foundationalism. A relational paradigm, which begins by rejecting these assumptions, offers a rapprochement of the alternatives through an elaboration of the principles of the identity of opposites, the opposites of identity, and the synthesis of opposites. The question of the specific nature of this rapprochement remains.

A RAPPROCHEMENT: EXPLANATION IN A RELATIONAL CONTEXT

The rapprochement between the natural and social sciences emerges from transforming the historically traditional dichotomies of observation versus interpretation and theory versus data into relational bipolar dimensions. Given this movement in grounding, mechanical explanation and hermeneutic understanding become an integrated metamethod in the following manner.

Step 1: Relational Analysis—Synthesis Replaces Split Reductionism

Clearly the reduction and atomism of mechanical explanation are split principles and they need to be replaced. Simply anointing holism as the guiding principle is not possible because holism, at least as often interpreted, is itself a split principle. Rather, integration requires that analysis and synthesis operate as a relational polarity. Analysis must occur in the context of some integrated whole, and the integrated whole operates in the context of its analytic parts. Because a relational metatheory is sometimes incorrectly viewed as less rigorous than mechanical explanation, a major feature of this first step is the affirmation of the importance of analysis and the analytic tools of any empirical science. The provisos here are that it simultaneously be recognized that the analytic moment always occurs in the context of a moment of synthesis and that the analysis can neither eliminate nor marginalize synthesis.

Step 2: Relational Action Pattern—Conditions Explanation Replaces Split Causes

As noted earlier, the defining marks of mechanical explanation and hermeneutic understanding have been the "nothing but" reliance on causes and action patterns, respectively. By entering into a relational context, these forms of explanation become integrated. In a relational context, causes are transformed from interpretation-free observed objects or events that produce changes in other objects or event into *conditions* that are associated with changes. A cause is interpretation free only when analysis is split from synthesis; in a relational model conditions—as an analytic moment of inquiry—are understood as functioning under some interpretation and some synthesis (Hanson, 1958). A cause can be a *force* that *produces, influences,* or *affects* the status or change of an object only in a model that splits system and activity; in a relational model, system and activity are joined as a structure-function relation. In a relational model, *condition*s are identified as necessary, sufficient, or both to the occurrence of the phenomenon under investigation (von Wright, 1971). Thus, rather than inquiry into the causes of behavior or development, inquiry from a relational perspective examines conditions that are associated with behavior or development. For example, if inquiry concerned the development of a plant, food and water would represent necessary conditions for the plant to grow, but would not cause the plant's development in the sense of producing that development. Similarly, neither nature factors nor nurture factors can be considered the cause of human development; they represent conditions that are associated with that development.

The assertion that causes are best understood as conditions leaves open the question of what in fact does produce behavior and change. The issue here is that of mechanisms. As is the case with other key terms, *mechanism* has several often in-

compatible definitions. In the present case the meaning is closer to "a process, physical or mental, by which something is done or comes into being" than to "the doctrine that all natural phenomena are explicable by material causes and mechanical principles" (American Heritage Dictionary of the English Language, Fourth Edition (2000) online). Hence, for present purposes, mechanism is defined as an active method or process rather than a cause or set of causes. These mechanisms are found in the structure-function relations that identify action patterns. Any active system constitutes a structure-function relation. The system is not a random aggregate of elements; it has a specific organization, an architecture (i.e., a structure). Further, this structure is not randomly active; it has a characteristic activity (i.e., a function). Even computers (structure)—when they are turned on—compute (function). However, computers do not change—at least they do not change in a transformational manner—and for this reason they are rather limited as models of the human mind (Fodor, 2000). The input and output of a computer may change, and this is the basis for traditional and contemporary split functionalist approaches to explanation (Overton, 1994a). However, the organization-activity of the computer itself does not undergo transformational change. Living organisms, on the other hand, are dynamic systems; they are organizations (structures) that are inherently active (function) and exhibit transformational change (dynamic).

When a system is viewed from the standpoint of function, it is the function itself (i.e., the *characteristic* action of the system) that constitutes the mechanism of behavior and change. Systems change through their characteristic action on or in the context of external conditions. Thus, the explanation of behavior and change is given by the function of the system (see Thelen & Smith, 1998). Further, because of the relation of structure and function, when a system is viewed from the standpoint of structure, structure then explains function. Consequently, both structure and function enter centrally into the explanatory process.

Structure and function are central to explanation, but they are also fundamentally interpretative in nature; they are not directly observable. Structure-function relations are patterns of action, but patterns are never directly observed; they must be inferred. When examined from the structural standpoint, the patterns constitute Aristotle's formal and final explanations. From the structural standpoint, action patterns make the object of inquiry *intelligible* and give *reasons* for the nature and functioning of the object. From the functional standpoint, action patterns explain by presenting the mechanism of behavior and development. Action patterns, however, necessarily operate within the context of material conditions both internal to the system and external to it. Thus, the introduction of structure-function relations serves to integrate hermeneutic explanation and natural science conditions explanation. Both types of explanation are necessary, but each operates from a different standpoint.

Developmental psychology offers several illustrations of this explanatory integration. For example, Bowlby's (1958) theory of infant-caregiver attachment posits a behavioral attachment system (structure) in relation to actions that serve the adaptive function of keeping the caregiver in close proximity. Piaget's (1952, 1985) theory presents a more general example. This theory represents an attempt to make sense of (i.e., explain) the development of knowing. Like Bowlby's, Piaget's is a relational theory that takes seriously the background ideas of structure-function and conditions. Because the theoretical goal is to explain the person and the development of the knowing person, Piaget takes a person (and epistemic) standpoint rather than a biological or a cultural standpoint. The theory conceptualizes the person as a dynamic self-organizing action system operating in a world of biological and environmental conditions. Structure and function constitute thesis and antithesis, and the resulting synthesis is transformational change or stages of new structure-function relations. Structures are the mental organizations that are expressed as patterns of action. On the structural side of the equation, Piaget introduces the theoretical concepts *schemes, coordination of schemes, operations, groupings,* and *group.* Each explains (i.e., formal explanation)—at successive novel levels of transformation—the cognitive equipment that the infant, toddler, child, and adolescent come to have available for constructing their known worlds.

Theoretical concepts of *adaptation, assimilation-accommodation, equilibrium, equilibration,* and *reflective abstraction,* constitute the functional side of the equation. Schemes, coordinated schemes, operations, and so forth function; they are active and it is through their action in a world of conditions that they change. Piaget's is an action theory and action is the general mechanism of development. Through the organized actions of the person in the world, the person's mode of knowing the world changes and these changes are adaptive. Action as the mechanism of development becomes more specific through recognition of its biphasic nature. Assimilation is the phase of action that expresses the mental organization. This expression gives meaning to the world; it constitutes the world as known. However, these meanings—including meanings at a presymbolic, preconceptual stage—have an instrumental function as well as the expressive function. When the instrumental function of the action is not completely successful in securing an adaptive goal, *variation* occurs in the action. For example, an infant may intend (assimilate) the side of the breast as a nipple by sucking it, but when the satisfaction of feeding does not

occur, variations arise in the action and this is exemplified by the sucking in various new locations. Variations open new possibilities that both secure a goal and feedback to transform (differentiations and novel coordinations) the system itself. This action phase of variation and organizational modification is the accommodation phase of any action.

Organization explains in the sense of establishing the *form* (structure), and action yields the *explanatory mechanism* (function). This relational polarity operates in the context of *conditions,* such as parents who do or do not provide appropriate opportunities for the adequate exercise of functioning. It is also the case that at the beginning of any stage of novel structure-function relations, the capacity for successful adaptation is limited. This is theoretically expressed in the idea that there is more assimilation than accommodation at the beginning of a stage; hence, there is a lack of balance or *equilibrium* between assimilation and accommodation. Through action this imbalance changes and the two phases of action eventually move into equilibrium within a given stage. Of course, given the relational nature of the theory, equilibrium of assimilation and accommodation also means that the underlying structures have reached a stable state (equilibrium) of differentiation and intercoordination.

The movement toward equilibrium of the action phases of assimilation and accommodation describes the development mechanism *within* a stage. To explain development *across* stages, Piaget introduces a principle that also has both a structural and a functional face. Structurally, this is the *equilibration principle* (Piaget, 1985) and it asserts that development change is directed toward improved states or patterns of the just-described equilibrium. *Improved* here is defined in terms of the adaptive value of one stage of cognitive structures relative to the adaptive value of other stages of cognitive structures. For example, the formal operational structures associated with adolescence represent an improved equilibrium over sensorimotor structures associated with infancy in that the formal structures are more stable, more flexible, and describe a much broader range of potential cognitive experiences than do sensorimotor structures. The equilibration principle introduces hierarchical organization into the theory and explains sequence, order, and direction in the emergence of novel cognitive abilities, just as the second law of thermodynamics explains sequence, order, and direction with respect to the physical world. It reflects Aristotle's metatheoretical final explanation, and it is consistent with the structural final explanations offered in other developmental theories, including Heinz Werner's (1957, 1958) orthogenetic principle and Erik Erikson's (1968) epigenetic principle.

The functional face of the mechanism of development across stages is termed *reflective abstraction.* Reflective abstraction is action, but it is action that has its own biphasic character consisting of reflecting in the sense of projecting something from a lower to a higher level, and *reflexion,* which is the reorganization of what has been projected. The alternation of the reflecting-reflexion phases produces each new stage of cognitive reorganization. Reflection is similar to the act of generalizing; reflexion is acting from the generalized position to consolidate the gains made through generalizing. What is abstracted in this process is the coordination of the differentiated structures of the lower level of organization.

Step 3: Abductive Logic Replaces Split Induction and Deduction

The third step towards a relational metamethod that integrates mechanical explanation and hermeneutic understanding addresses the nature of scientific logic. Modern mechanical explanation split acts of discovery and acts of justification and identified the former with a foundational inductive logic and the latter with a deductive logic. Interpretation-free induction from interpretation-free data was the vehicle for the discovery of hypotheses, theories, laws, and interpretation-free deduction was the vehicle for their justification. A relational metamethod introduces the logic of abduction as the synthesis of the opposite identities of theory (broadly considered, including background ideas) and data. Abduction (also called *retroduction*) was originally described by the pragmatist philosopher Charles Sanders Pierce (1992), and the historian of science N. R. Hanson (1958) has argued that it has long been the fundamental—if often invisible—logic of scientific activity. In a contemporary version, this logic is termed *inference to the best explanation* (Fumerton, 1993; Harman, 1965).

Abduction operates by arranging the observation under consideration and all background ideas (here, including specific theoretical ideas) as two Escherian hands. The possible coordination of the two is explored by asking the question of what must necessarily be assumed in order to have that observation (see Figure 1.4). The inference to—or interpretation of—what must in the context of background ideas necessarily be assumed then comes to constitute the explanation of the phenomenon. The abductive process has also been termed the *transcendental argument.*

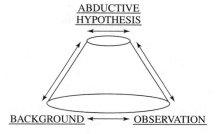

Figure 1.4   The abductive process.

Abductive inference is illustrated in virtually any psychological work that assumes a centrality of emotional, motivational, or cognitive mental organization. Russell (1996), for example, has discussed the significance of abduction to the area of cognition. Chomsky's work in language and Piaget's work in cognitive development are particularly rich in abductive inference. Consider as an illustration of the process the following example drawn from Piaget:

1. There is the phenomenal observation (O) that it is the case that a certain group of people (children around 6–7 years of age) understands that concepts maintain the same quantity despite changes in qualitative appearances (i.e., conservation).

2. Given the relational background ideas discussed in this paper, Piaget forms the abductive inference that the explanation of this observation (E) is that a certain type of action system, having specified features including reversibility (i.e., concrete operations), must be available to these people. This forms the conditional statement "If (E) concrete operational structure, then (O) conservation, is expected."

3. Given (O), the conclusion is, "Therefore, concrete operational structure explains the understanding of conservation."

This, of course, is not the end of the process, as criteria must be established that allow choice among alternative Es—the best E. But this is not a major hurdle, because many of the criteria for theory-explanation *selection* that were articulated within traditional modern science can readily be incorporated here. These criteria include the explanation's depth, coherence, logical consistency, extent to which it reduces the proportion of unsolved to solved conceptual and empirical problems in a domain (Laudan 1977), and last but not least, scope, empirical support, and empirical fruitfulness.

Scope, empirical support, and fruitfulness as part criteria for choice of a best theory-explanation all demand a return to the observational grounds for empirical assessment. Some of the statistical and research strategies associated with this return are described in detail by Rozeboom (1997). *Scope* is assessed through testing the abductive explanation in observational contexts that go beyond the context that generated the explanation. For example, conservation may be assessed in the contexts of number, weight, number, area, volume, or it may be assessed in relation to other skills that should—in the context of the explanation—be associated with it. The assessment of scope also serves the function of establishing that the abductive explanation-observation relation is not viciously circular (i.e., does not constitute an identity of identities).

The *fruitfulness* of an explanation is measured in terms of the extent to which the explanation combines with other

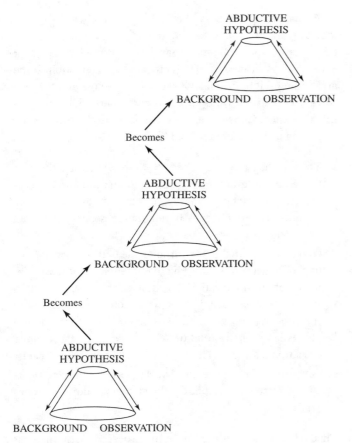

Figure 1.5 Scientific progress through abduction.

abductive hypotheses to generate (predict) new observations. Each new abductive hypothesis in the relational triangle (Figure 1.4) becomes a part of background (background ideas-theory) and thus creates a new enlarged background (see Figure 1.5). The new background generates novel observations, but these too—because they constitute a background-observation relation—yield opposite identities that require further abductive inferences.

Empirical support for an abductive explanation is the outcome of any assessment of scope. Here, another central feature of a relational metamethod needs to be differentiated from the traditional modern split metamethod. Under the rule of split-off induction and deduction, it was assumed that scientific progress moved forward through the *deductive falsification* of theories (Popper, 1959). The criterion of falsification, however, fell into disrepute through demonstrations by several historians and philosophers of science (e.g., Hanson, 1958; T. S. Kuhn, 1962; Lakatos, 1978; Laudan, 1977; Putnam, 1983; Quine, 1953) that although deductive logic, and hence falsification, is applicable to a specific experimental hypothesis, falsification does not reach to the level of rich theories (i.e., background is abductive in character, not

inductive nor deductive). Within a relational metatheory, these demonstrations lead to the principle that falsified experimental hypotheses are important in that they constitute failures of empirical support for the broader abductive explanation, but they are not important in the sense of constituting a refutation of the explanation. T. S. Kuhn, Lakatos, and Luadan describe these failures as *anomalous instances* for the background, and as such they require evaluation; but they do not in and of themselves require abandonment of the abductive explanation (see Overton, 1984, 1994a).

To this point a relational metatheory and an integrative metamethod have been described, and the manner in which these ground, constrain, and sustain various developmentally relevant issues, theories, and methods has been illustrated. The next section of this paper presents a broad illustration of the application of relational metatheory to developmental inquiry.

EMBODIED DEVELOPMENT: A RELATIONAL CONCEPT

This illustration focuses on embodied development. Until recently, the trend of developmental inquiry over the past two decades had been moving towards ever-increasing fragmentation of the object of study. Beginning in the early 1980s the examination of human development aggressively promoted split and foundational approaches to inquiry, including variable-centered, discourse, modular, and domain-specific inquiry. Each of these potentially alternative foci was advanced with claims that it presented the bedrock form of explanation. The result was that inquiry into human development was increasingly split into biologically determined, culturally determined, and bioculturally determined behavior, innate modules of mind, situated cognitions, domain-specific understandings, and communicative and instrumental functioning. What became lost in the exclusivity of these projects was the person as a vital integrated embodied center of agency and action. This is the embodied person—functioning as a self-organizing dynamic action system—expressively projecting onto the world, and instrumentally communicating with self and world, thoughts, feelings, wishes, beliefs, and desires. This is the embodied person who emerges from and transacts with the relational biological-cultural world, thereby developmentally transforming her own expressive and adaptive functioning.

The concept of embodiment was most thoroughly articulated in psychology by Maurice Merleau-Ponty (1962, 1963) and it represents a relational attempt to mend the split understanding of body as exclusively physical and mind as exclusively mental. Embodiment represents the overarching synthesis described earlier between each of the

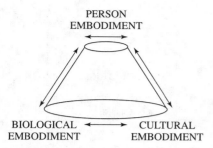

Figure 1.6 Embodiment as synthesis.

biology-person-culture relations (see Figure 1.6); thus, embodiment creates a seamless bridge between the biological, the psychological, and the sociocultural. It has a double meaning, referring both to the body as physical structure, and the body as a form of lived experience, actively engaged with the world of sociocultural and physical objects. As Merleau-Ponty (1963) states with respect to embodiment as the form of life or life form (*Lebensform*),

> One cannot speak of the body and of life in general, but only of the animal body and animal life, of the human body and of human life; . . . the body of the normal subject . . . is not distinct from the psychological. (p. 181)

Embodiment is not the claim that various bodily states have a causal relation to our perceptions, thoughts, and feelings. It would simply be trivial to suggest, for example, that when we close our eyes we perceive differently from when our eyes are open. Rather, embodiment is the claim that perception, thinking, feelings, desires—that is, the *way* we experience or live the world—is contextualized by being an active agent with this *particular kind of body* (Taylor, 1995). In other

words, the kind of body we have is a precondition for the kind of experiences and meanings that we generate.

Ultimately, embodiment is the affirmation that the lived body counts in our psychology. Mental processes of motivation, emotion, and cognition, along with the actions they engender, are not products of a split-off physical and cultural world, nor are they the products of a split-off world of genes and a central nervous systems, nor the products of some additive combination of biology and culture. Mind and actions grow from the embodied person constantly engaged in the world. It is this embodied person that both creates world meaning and is created by the meaning of the world. Embodiment makes our psychological meanings about the world intelligible and hence explains these meanings. Embodied processes and action, so conceived, form a bridge between biological and sociocultural systems.

Person-Centered and Variable Approaches to Developmental Inquiry

As a bridge concept, embodiment can be examined from a biological, a cultural, or a person standpoint. Operating within a relational metatheory, each standpoint on embodiment is complementary to and supports the others (see Figures 1.6 and 1.7). However, for purposes of exposition it is only possible to stand at one place at a time. Thus, the present discussion focuses from a person-centered standpoint and later briefly describes embodiment from both a biological standpoint and a cultural standpoint.

A person-centered approach to inquiry maintains a theoretical and empirical focus on the psychological processes and patterns of psychological processes as these explain the individual's activities in the world (see Figure 1.7). Perhaps

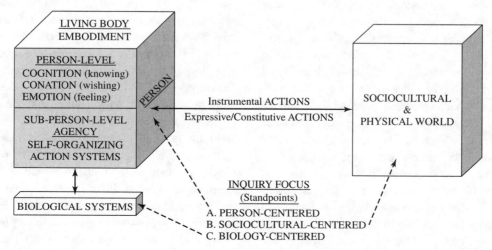

Figure 1.7 Embodied action theory: a relational approach to psychological inquiry.

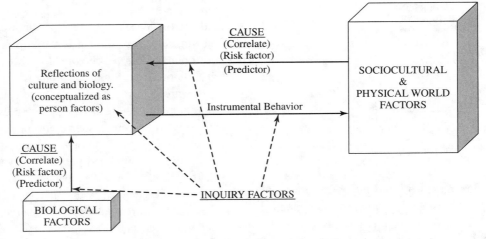

Figure 1.8   A variable approach to psychological inquiry.

this orientation to developmental inquiry is best illustrated by contrast with what has been termed a *variable approach* (see Figure 1.8). In a variable approach, the focus of inquiry is not on the person, nor on the dynamic action systems that characterize the person's functioning. In a variable approach, the focus is on biological, cultural, and individual variables; these are understood to operate as predictors, correlates, risk factors, or antecedent causes of behavior. The distinction being drawn here is similar to that described some time ago by Block (1971) and more recently elaborated by Magnusson (1998; Magnusson & Stattin, 1998). As Magnusson has suggested, from a variable approach, various individual variables (e.g., *child factors*) and contextual variables are understood as the explanatory actors in the processes being studied. From a person-centered standpoint, self-organizing dynamic action systems—which identify psychological mechanisms—operate as the main vehicles of explanation.

Within the context of a relational metatheory a person-centered theoretical orientation (standpoint or point of view; Figures 1.6 and 1.7A) is as necessary to an integrated developmental inquiry as is a relational socioculture-centered standpoint (Figures 1.6 and 1.7B) or a relationally considered biological-centered point of view (Figures 1.6 and 1.7C). In any given inquiry, a focus on the person, or the sociocultural (interpersonal), or the biological is a necessary focus of analysis. However, as suggested earlier, these function as complementary, not alternative competing explanations.

It should also be noted in passing that variable-focused inquiry can be transformed from a split-off exclusivity to yet another necessary point of view of relationally integrated inquiry. Stated briefly, developmental variable-focused inquiry aims at the prediction of events, states, and movements, whereas developmental person-centered inquiry aims

to explain psychological processes and their transformation. There is no necessary conflict in these aims. They are only in conflict in the reductionistic case, in which one or the other is asserted as the exclusive foundational aim of inquiry. In a similar vein, it is important to recognize that the complementarity here is one of aim and not one suggesting that variable inquiry is oriented to research methods and person-centered inquiry is oriented to conceptual context. Both approaches entail the translation of theory into the empirically assessable and the translation of the empirically assessable into theory.

The Person-Centered Point of View

Before detailing a person- or child-centered standpoint or point of view, it is worth noting some of the benefits that accrue to taking this standpoint toward developmental inquiry. First, a person-centered standpoint rescues developmental psychology, as a psychology, from becoming a mere adjunct to biology, to culture, to discourse, to narrative, or to computer science. *Psyche* initially referenced *soul* and later *mind,* and if psychology is not to again lose its mind—as it did in the days of behaviorism—keeping the psychological person as the center of action is a necessary guard against explanatory reduction to biology, culture, discourse, and so on.

Second, a person-centered approach highlights the fact that any act can be profitably understood—again in a complementary bipolar fashion—as both expressive-constitutive and as instrumental-adaptive. Split or dichotomous approaches—especially split-off variable approaches—lead to the illusion that acts exhibit only adaptive-instrumental functions. A person-centered approach argues that any act may also be understood as an expression of an underlying dynamic organization of cognitive, affective, and conative meanings, and this expression operates to constitute the world as known, felt, and desired. Here, Lois Bloom's work (Bloom, 1998; Bloom & Tinker, 2001) on the development of language provides an excellent illustration of the power of conceptualizing language acquisition in the context of the expression of person-centered cognitive, affective, and conative-motivational meanings, rather than exclusively as an instrumental tool operating solely for communicative ends.

A third benefit derived from a person-centered point of view is that it provides the necessary context for the resolution of certain important problems related to our general understanding of psychological meaning. Specifically, a person-centered approach is a necessary frame for solving the so-called symbol-grounding problem. This is the question of how to explain that representational items (e.g., a symbol, an image) come to have psychological meaning (Bickhard, 1993; Smythe, 1992). I return to this problem in a more detailed fashion later in this chapter.

With these examples of some of the benefits of a child- or person-centered approach to developmental inquiry as background, it is possible to turn to a specific description of this approach. A detailed specification of a person-centered approach to developmental inquiry requires the description of four critical interwoven concepts: person, agent, action, and embodiment.

Person-Agent

Person and agent are complementary Escherian levels of analysis of the same whole (see Figure 1.7). The *person* level is constituted by genuine psychological concepts (e.g., thoughts, feelings, desires, wishes) that have intentional qualities, are open to interpretation, and are available to consciousness (Shanon, 1993); or in other words, have psychological meaning. The *agent* level—called the *subpersonal* level by some (Dennett, 1987; Russell, 1996)—here refers to action systems or dynamic self-organizing systems. *Schemes, operations, ego, attachment behavioral system,* and *executive function* are some of the concepts that describe these action systems.

Taken as a whole, the person-agent forms the nucleus of a psychological theory of mind. And in this context mind is defined as a self-organizing dynamic system of cognitive (knowings, beliefs), emotional (feelings), and conative or motivational (wishes, desires) meanings or understandings, along with procedures for maintaining, implementing, and changing these meanings. It is important to note and underline that a person-centered theory of mind is not an encapsulated cognition, but rather a theory that includes emotions,

wishes, and desires, as well as cognition. Further, there is no question about where mind is located. Mind emerges from a relational biosociocultural activity matrix. In the present context, mind is a person-centered concept because the approach being described takes the person standpoint. As a person-centered concept, mind bridges naturally to both the biological and the sociocultural.

Action, Intention, Behavior, and Experience

Person-agency is the source of action. At the agent level, *action* is defined as the characteristic functioning of any dynamic self-organizing system. For example, a plant orients itself towards the sun. Weather systems form high and low pressure areas and move from west to east. Human systems organize and adapt to their biological and sociocultural worlds. At the person level, action is defined as *intentional* activity. Action is often distinguishable from *behavior,* because the action of the person-agent implies a *transformation* in the intended object of action, whereas behavior often simply implies movement and states (von Wright, 1971, p. 199). Thus, when the infant chews (action)—something that from a sociocultural standpoint is called a *basket*—the infant, from a person-centered standpoint, is transforming this part of his or her known world into a practical action *chewable.* Through the intentional act the person projects meaning onto the world.

Action serves at least three major functions in the development of mind (see Figure 1.1). First, action *expresses* cognitive-affective-conative meaning. Here, it is important to recognize that the concept *meaning* itself has a bipolar relational status (Overton, 1994b). "I mean" and "it means" operate in a relational matrix. The former is concerned with person-centered meanings, the latter with sociocultural meanings and reference. From a person-centered standpoint, the focus of analysis is on "I mean" and secondarily on how "I mean" comes to hook up with "it means." Considered in its expressive moment, action entails the projection of person-centered meanings, thus transforming the objective environmental world (i.e., an object point of view) into an actual world as known, felt, and desired.

The second function that action serves is the *instrumental* function of communicating and adjusting person-centered meanings. Communication, dialogue, discourse, and problem solving all call attention to the relational to-and-fro movement between the expression of the self-organizing system and instrumental adaptive changes. Completely adapted action (i.e., successful) entails only projection. Partially adapted (i.e., partially successful) action results in exploratory action, or *variations.* Exploratory action that is adaptive leads to reorganization of the system (transformational change) and hence leads to new meanings.

This general cycle of projected action and exploratory variational action as the accommodation to encountered resistances (see Figure 1.1) constitutes the third and most general function of action: Action defines the *general mechanism of all psychological development*. From a person-centered developmental action standpoint, all development is explained by action. However, action is also identified with *experience*. But caution is necessary here because experience, like meaning and other basic terms, is itself a bipolar relational concept. From a person-centered perspective, experience is the person-agent action of observing, manipulating, and exploring. From a sociocultural and 'objective' environmental point of view, experience is often identified as an event or stimulus that is independent of the person and imposes on or is imposed on the person. For purposes of clarity it would better to retain the former action definition as experience and to redefine the latter as opportunity for experience. Similarly, it should be pointed out that when experience is described as a feeling, the reference here is the person-centered felt meaning of the observational, manipulative, and explorational action.

In defining experience as the developmental action cycle of projecting and transforming the known world while exploring the known world and transforming the system, experience also becomes the psychological bridge between biological and sociocultural systems. There is no sense here of an isolated, cut-off, solitary human psyche. Person-centered experience emerges from a biosociocultural relational activity matrix (e.g., see Gallese, 2000a, 2000b), and this experience both transforms the matrix and is transformed by the matrix. Person development is neither a split-off nativism, nor a split-off environmentalism, nor a split-off additive combination of the two. The neonate is a dynamic system of practical action meanings. These meanings represent the outcome of 9 months of the interpenetrating action (Tobach & Greenberg, 1984) of biology-environment, and this interpenetration stretches all the way down to DNA (Gottlieb, 1997; Lewontin, 1991, 2000).

Person Development

Psychological development of the person-agent entails the epigenetic stance that novel forms emerge through the interpenetrating actions of the system under investigation and the resistances the system encounters in the actual environmental world. It is through interpenetrating actions that the system changes and hence becomes differentiated. But differentiation of parts implies a novel coordination of parts and this

coordination itself identifies the emergence of novelty. Thus, for example, the neurological action system becomes differentiated through the interpenetrating actions of neurological-environmental functioning. This differentiation leads to a novel coordination or reorganization that constitutes the adapted level of conscious practical action found in the neonate. Consciousness is a systemic property of this emergent action system. The initial adapted practical consciousness entails a minimum awareness of the meaning entailed by an act (Zelazo, 1996). Consciousness cannot be reduced to or squeezed, so to speak, out of lower stages; it is the result of a transformation. Similarly, further developmental differentiations and coordinations of actions—described as *higher* levels of consciousness—emerge through the interpenetrations of conscious action and the sociocultural and physical worlds it encounters (Figure 1.1). Symbolic meaning and the symbolic representational level of meanings (Mueller & Overton, 1998a, 1998b) describes forms of consciousness that arise from the coordination of practical actions; reflective and trans-reflective (reflective symbolic understandings of reflective symbolic understandings) meanings describe further developmental advances in the coordination of action systems.

To summarize, to this point I have described the nucleus of a relationally informed person-centered developmental theory of mind, whereby mind is defined as a dynamic self-organizing system of meanings that through projection transforms the world as known and through exploration transforms itself (i.e., develops). However, this remains a nucleus and only a nucleus, because it lacks the critical necessary feature of embodiment.

Embodiment

As discussed earlier, embodiment is the claim that our perception, thinking, feelings, desires—that is, the way we experience or live the world—is contextualized by being an active agent with this particular kind of body (Taylor, 1995). In other words, the kind of body we have is a precondition for the kind of experiences and meanings that we generate.

At the agent level, embodiment specifies the *characteristic* activity of any living system. At the person level, embodiment affirms that—from the beginning—intentionality is a feature of bodily acts (Margolis, 1987). Intentionality is not limited to a symbolic, a reflective, or a trans-reflective system of psychological meanings. Intentionality also extends to a system of psychological meanings that characterize practical embodied actions operating at the most minimum level of consciousness. Thus, psychological meanings are as characteristic of the neonate as they are of the adult person. This in fact solves the symbol-grounding problem described earlier—that is, the explanation for how actual world representational items (e.g., a symbol, an image) come to have psychological meaning resides in the fact that psychological meanings, in the form of practical embodied actions, are present from the beginning. As these become transformed and coordinated, they become available to conventional symbols provided by the sociocultural world.

Embodiment makes our psychological meanings about the world intelligible and hence explains our meanings. Embodied action, so conceived, forms a person-agent bridge between biological and sociocultural systems. Support for the claim that embodiment is central to the explanation of psychological meaning, central to a person-centered developmental action theory of mind, and central as a relational bridge between the several points of view is found in empirical and theoretical work being done from the biological, the cultural, and the person standpoints. The remainder of this chapter reviews some of this evidence.

Embodiment and Biology. If we first consider the biological standpoint of the biology-person-socioculture relational matrix (see Figure 1.7C), it is apparent that biology is increasingly taking embodiment seriously. For example, neurobiologists such as Gerald Edelman (1992), Antonio Damasio (1994, 1999), and Joseph LeDoux (1996) all argue that the cognitive-affective-motivational meanings that constitute mind can no longer be thought of as merely a functionalist piece of software or even merely a function of brain processes, but must be considered in a fully embodied context (see also Gallese, 2000a, 2000b). As Damasio says, "mind is probably not conceivable without some sort of embodiment" (1994, p. 234).

Damasio (1994) comments further on contemporary perspectives on mind:

> This is Descartes' error: the abyssal separation between body and mind. . . . The Cartesian idea of a disembodied mind may well have been the source, by the middle of the twentieth century, for the metaphor of mind as software program. . . . [and] there may be some Cartesian disembodiment also behind the thinking of neuroscientists who insist that the mind can be fully explained in terms of brain events, leaving by the wayside the rest of the organism and the surrounding physical and social environment—and also leaving out the fact that part of the environment is itself a product of the organism's preceding actions. (pp. 249–251)

Similarly, Edelman argues that

> The mind is embodied. It is necessarily the case that certain dictates of the body must be followed by the mind. . . . Symbols do not get assigned meanings by formal means; instead it is assumed that symbolic structures are meaningful *to begin with.* This is so because categories are determined by bodily structure and by adaptive use as a result of evolution and behavior. (p. 239)

Embodiment and the Socioculture Context. On the *sociocultural* side of the biology-person-socioculture relational matrix (see Figure 1.7B), social constructivists such as Harre (1995) and Sampson (1996) have increasingly embraced embodied action as a relational anchoring to the relativism of split-off discourse analysis. Sampson, for example, argues for "embodied discourses" as these "refer to the inherently embodied nature of all human endeavor, including talk, conversation and discourse itself" (p. 609). Csordas (1999) approaches culture and embodiment from an anthropological position. Perhaps the most fully articulated contemporary employment of embodiment in a developmentally oriented cultural psychology is found in the work of the German psychologist Ernest E. Boesch (1991). Boesch's presentation of "the I and the body" is a discussion of the centrality of embodiment for a cultural psychology. Thus, he states that "the body, obviously, is more than just an object with anatomical and physiological properties: *it is the medium of our actions* [italics added], it is with our body that we both conceive and perform actions" (p. 312).

Embodiment and the Person. From the *person-centered* center of the biology-person-socioculture matrix (see Figure 1.7A), Varela, Thompson, and Rosch (1991) have sketched a general outline for an embodied theory of cognition. Sheets-Johnstone (1990) provides an evolutionary anthropological perspective on human embodiment and thought, and Santostefano (1995) has detailed the emotional and cognitive dimensions of practical, symbolic, and reflective embodied meanings. Further, many who have studied psychopathology, from R. D. Laing (1960) to Donald Winnicott (1971) and Thomas Ogden (1986), argue that disruptions in the embodied actions of the person-agent are central to an understanding of the development of severe forms of psychopathology.

At the level of practical actions, Bermudez's (1998) recent work on the development of self-consciousness is central to an understanding of the impact of an embodied person conceptualization. Bermudez's fundamental argument is that late-emerging forms of meaning found in symbolic and reflective consciousness develop from—and are constrained by—embodied self-organizing action systems available to the infant. Most important is that these early systems entail person-level somatic proprioception and exteroception. As these person-centered processes interpenetrate the physical and sociocultural worlds, proprioception operates as the differentiation mechanism for the emergence of a self-consciousness action system, and exteroception operates as the differentiation mechanism for the emergence of an object-consciousness system. Hence, over the first several months of life, a basic practical action associated with *me* and *other* develops, which in turn becomes transformed into the symbolic *me* and *other* of early toddlerhood. Thelen's (2000) work on the role of movement generally, and specifically "body memory" in infant cognitive functioning is another closely related area that illustrates the importance of embodiment at the level of practical actions.

Langer's (1994) empirical studies represent important demonstrations of the *intercoordination* of embodied action systems as these intercoordinations move development from the practical to the symbolic plane of meaning. Earlier work by Held and his colleagues (e.g., Held & Bossom, 1961; Held & Hein, 1958), on the other hand, illustrates the significance of *voluntary* embodied action at all levels of adaptation. Acredolo's research (e.g.,Goodwyn & Acredolo, 1993) on the use of bodily gestures as signs expressing practical meanings in older infants suggests the expressive and instrumental value of embodied practical gesture. Other work has elaborated on the significance of bodily representations at the symbolic and reflective levels of meaning. For example, while the use of fingers for counting is well documented (Gelman & Williams, 1998), Saxe's (1981, 1995) research has shown cross-culturally that other bodily representations enter into counting systems. Further, earlier research by Overton and Jackson (1973) and more recently by Kovacs and Overton (2001) has demonstrated that bodily gestures support emerging symbolic representations at least until the level of reflective meanings.

At the level of symbolic, reflective, and trans-reflective conceptual functioning, the writings of Lakoff and Johnson (1999; see also Lakoff, 1987) are well known for their detailed exploration of the significance of embodiment. For Lakoff and Johnson, embodiment provides the fundamental metaphors that shape meanings at all levels of functioning. In a parallel but distinct approach, Kainz (1988) has described how the basic laws of ordinary logic (i.e., the law of identity, the law of contradictions, and the law of the excluded middle) can be understood as emerging from the early embodied differentiation of self and other. Finally, Liben's (1999) work on the development of the child's symbolic and reflective spatial understanding presents a strong argument for an understanding of this development in the context of an embodied child rather than in the context of the disembodied eye that traditionally has framed this domain.

CONCLUSIONS

This chapter has explored background ideas that ground, constrain, and sustain theories and methods in psychology generally and developmental psychology specifically. An understanding of these backgrounds presents the investigator with a rich set of concepts for the construction and assessment of psychological theories. An understanding of background ideas also helps to prevent conceptual confusions that may ultimately lead to unproductive theories and unproductive methods of empirical inquiry. The importance of this function has recently been forcefully articulated by Robert Hogan (2001) who in an article entitled "Wittgenstein Was Right" notes with approval Wittgenstein's (1958) remark that "in psychology there are empirical methods and conceptual confusions" (p. 27), and then goes on to say that

> Our training and core practices concern research methods; the discipline is . . . deeply skeptical of philosophy. We emphasize methods for the verification of hypotheses and minimize the analysis of the concepts entailed by the hypotheses. [But] all the empiricism in the world can't salvage a bad idea. (p. 27)

REFERENCES

Anastasi, A. (1958). Heredity, environment, and the question "how?" *Psychological Review, 65,* 197–208.

Asendorpf, J. B., & Valsiner, J. (1992). Editors' introduction: Three dimensions of developmental perspectives. In J. B. Asendorpf & J. Valsiner (Eds.), *Stability and change in development: A study of methodological reasoning* (pp. ix–xxii). London: Sage.

Baldwin, J. M. (1895). *Mental development in the child and the race: Methods and process.* New York: Macmillan.

Bernstein, R. J. (1983). *Beyond objectivism and relativism: Science, hermeneutics, and praxis.* Philadelphia: University of Pennsylvania Press.

Bertalanffy, L. von. (1968a). General system theory. New York: George Braziller.

Bertalanffy, L. von. (1968b). Organismic psychology and systems theory. Barre, MA: Barre.

Bickhard, M. H. (1993). Representational content in humans and machines. *Journal of Experimental and Theoretical Artificial Intelligence, 5,* 285–333.

Block, J. (1971). *Lives through time.* Berkeley, CA: Bancroft.

Bloom, L. (1998). Language acquisition in its developmental context. In W. Damon (Series Ed.), D. Kuhn, & R. Siegler (Vol. Eds.), *Handbook of child psychology: Vol. 2. Cognition, perception, and language* (5th ed., pp. 309–370). New York: Wiley.

Bloom, L., & Tinker, E. (2001). The intentionality model and language acquisition. *Monographs of the Society for Research in Child Development, 66* (4 Serial No. 267).

Boesch, E. E. (1991). *Symbolic action theory and cultural psychology*. Berlin: Springer-Verlag.

Bowlby, J. (1958). The nature of the child's tie to his mother. *International Journal of Psychoanalysis, 39,* 350–373.

Brandtstadter, J. (1998). Action perspectives on human development. In W. Damon (Series Ed.) & R. M. Lerner (Vol. Ed.), *Handbook of child psychology: Vol. 1. Theoretical models of human development* (5th ed., pp. 807–864). New York: Wiley.

Brandtstadter, J., & Lerner, R. M. (Eds.). (1999). *Action and self-development: Theory and research through the life span.* London: Sage.

Cohen, M. R. (1931). *Reason and nature: An essay on the meaning of scientific method.* New York: Harcourt, Brace.

Csordas, T. J. (1999). Embodiment and cultural phenomenology. In G. Weiss & H. F. Haber (Eds.), *Perspectives on embodiment* (pp. 143–164). New York: Routledge.

Damasio, A. (1994). *Descartes' error: Emotion, reason, and the human brain.* New York: Avon Books.

Damasio, A. (1999). *The feeling of what happens: Body and emotion in the making of consciousness.* New York: Harcourt, Brace.

Damon, W. (1988). Socialization and individuation. In G. Handel (Ed.), *Childhood socialization* (pp. 3–10). Hawthorne, NY: De Gruyter.

Dennett, D. (1987). *The intentional stance.* Cambridge, MA: MIT Press.

Dilthey, W. (1972*). The rise of hermeneutics* (Fredric Jameson, Trans.). *New Literary History, 3,* 229–244.

Eckensberger, L. H. (1990). On the necessity of the culture concept in psychology: A view from cross-cultural psychology. In F. J. R. van de Vijver & G. J. M. Hutschemaekers (Eds.), *The investigation of culture: Current issues in cultural psychology* (pp. 153–183). Tilburg, Germany: Tilburg University Press.

Edelman, G. M. (1992). *Bright air, brilliant fire: On the matter of the mind.* New York: Basic Books.

Edelman, G. M., & Tononi, G. (2000). *A universe of consciousness: How matter becomes imagination.* New York: Basic Books.

Elman, J. L., Bates, E. A., Johnson, M. H., Karmiloff-Smith, A., Parisi, D., & Plunkett, K. (1996). *Rethinking innateness: A connectionist perspective on development.* Cambridge, MA: MIT Press.

Erikson, E. H. (1968). *Identity youth and crisis.* New York: W. W. Norton.

Fodor, J. (2000). *The mind doesn't work that way: The scope and limits of computational psychology.* Cambridge, MA: MIT Press.

Fumerton, R. (1993). Inference to the best explanation. In J. Dancy & E. Sosa (Eds.), *A companion to epistemology* (pp. 207–209). Cambridge, MA: Basil Blackwell.

Gallese, V. (2000a). The acting subject: Towards the neural basis of social cognition. In T. Metzinger (Ed.), *Neural correlates of consciousness* (pp. 325–334). Cambridge, MA: MIT Press.

Gallese, V. (2000b). The "shared manifold hypothesis": From mirror neurons to empathy. *Journal of Consciousness Studies, 8,* 33–50.

Gelman, R., & Williams, E. M. (1998). Enabling constraints for cognitive development and learning: Domain specificity and epigenesis. In W. Damon (Series Ed.), D. Kuhn, & R. Siegler (Vol. Eds.), *Handbook of child psychology: Vol. 2. Cognition, perception, and language* (5th ed., pp. 575–630). New York: Wiley.

Gilovich, T., & Eibach, R. (2001). The fundamental attribution error where it really counts. *Psychological Inquiry, 12,* 23–26.

Goodwyn, S. W., & Acredolo, L. P. (1993). Symbolic gesture versus word: Is there a modality advantage for onset of symbol use? *Child Development, 64,* 688–701.

Gottlieb, G. (1997). *Synthesizing nature-nurture.* Mahwah, NJ: Erlbaum.

Grotevant, H. D. (1998). Adolescent development in family contexts. In W. Damon (Series Ed.) & N. Eisenberg (Vol. Ed.), *Handbook of child psychology: Vol. 3. Social, emotional, and personality development* (5th ed., pp. 1097–1149). New York: Wiley.

Hanson, N. R. (1958). *Patterns of discovery.* London: Cambridge University Press.

Harding, S. (1986). *The science question in feminism.* Ithaca, NY: Cornell University Press.

Harman, G. H. (1965). Inference to the best explanation. *Philosophical Review, 74,* 88–95.

Harre, R. (1995). The necessity of personhood as embodied being. *Theory and Psychology, 5,* 369–373.

Hegel, G. W. F. (1807). *Phenomenology of spirit* (A. V. Miller, Trans.). New York: Oxford University Press.

Hegel, G. W. F. (1830). *Hegel's logic: Being part one of the encyclopedia of the philosophical sciences* (W. Wallace, Trans.). New York: Oxford University Press.

Held, R., & Bossom, J. (1961). Neonatal deprivation and adult rearrangement: Complementary techniques for analyzing plastic sensory-motor coordinations. *Journal of Comparative Physiological Psychology, 54,* 33–37.

Held, R., & Hein, A. (1958). Adaptation of disarranged hand-eye coordination contingent upon re-afferent stimulation. *Perceptual-Motor Skills, 8,* 87–90.

Hempel, C. G. (1942). The function of general laws in history. *Journal of Philosophy, 39,* 35–48.

Hogan, R. (2001). Wittgenstein was right. *Psychological Inquiry, 12,* 27.

Kainz, H. P. (1988). *Paradox, dialectic, and system: A contemporary reconstruction of the Hegelian problematic.* University Park: Pennsylvania State University Press.

Kovacs, S., & Overton, W. F. (2001, June). *An embodied action theory of mind approach to the development and transformation of symbolic representation in preschoolers.* Paper presented at the 31st annual meeting of the Jean Piaget Society, Berkeley, CA.

Kuhn, D., Garcia-Mila, M., Zohar, A., & Andersen, C. (1995). Strategies of knowledge acquisition. *Monographs of the Society for Research in Child Development, 60* (4, Serial No. 245).

Kuhn, T. S. (1962). *The structure of scientific revolutions.* Chicago: University of Chicago Press.

Laing, R. D. (1960). *The divided self.* New York: Pantheon Books.

Lakatos, I. (1978). *The methodology of scientific research programmes: Philosophical papers* (Vol. 1). New York: Cambridge University Press.

Lakoff, G. (1987). *Women, fire, and dangerous things. What categories reveal about the mind.* Chicago: University of Chicago Press.

Lakoff, G., & Johnson, M. (1999). *Philosophy in the flesh: The embodied mind and its challenge to western thought.* New York: Basic Books.

Langer, J. (1994). From acting to understanding: The comparative development of meaning. In W. Overton & D. Palermo (Eds.), *The nature and ontogenesis of meaning* (pp. 191–214). Hillsdale, NJ: Erlbaum.

Latour, B. (1993). *We have never been modern.* Cambridge, MA: Harvard University Press.

Latour, B. (1999). *Pandora's hope: Essays on the reality of science studies.* Cambridge, MA: Harvard University Press.

Laudan, L. (1977). *Progress and its problems: Towards a theory of scientific growth.* Berkeley: University of California Press.

LeDoux, J. (1996). *The emotional brain: The mysterious underpinnings of emotional life.* New York: Touchstone.

Lerner, R. M. (2002). *Concepts and theories of human development* (3rd ed.). New York: Random House.

Lewontin, R. C. (1991). *Biology as ideology: The doctrine of DNA.* New York: Harper Perennial.

Lewontin, R. C. (2000). *The triple helix: Gene, organism and environment.* Cambridge, MA: Harvard University Press.

Liben, L. S. (1999). Developing an understanding of external spatial representations. In I. E. Sigel (Ed.), *Development of mental representation: Theories and applications* (pp. 297–321). Mahwah, NJ: Erlbaum.

Liben, L. S. (2000). Map use and the development of spatial cognition: Seeing the *bigger* picture. *Developmental Science, 3,* 270–273.

Magnusson, D. (1998). The logic and implications of a person-oriented approach. In R. B. Cairns, L. R. Bergman, & J. Kagan (Eds.), *Methods and models for studying the individual* (pp. 33–63). London: Sage.

Magnusson, D., & Stattin, H. (1998). Person-context interaction theories. In W. Damon (Series Ed.) & R. M. Lerner (Vol. Ed.), *Handbook of child psychology: Vol. 1. Theoretical models of human development* (5th ed., pp. 685–760). New York: Wiley.

Margolis, J. (1987). *Science without unity: Reconciling the human and natural sciences.* New York: Basil Blackwell.

Merleau-Ponty, M. (1962). *Phenomenology of perception* (Colin Smith, Trans.). London: Routledge and Kegan Paul.

Merleau-Ponty, M. (1963). *The structure of behavior* (Alden Fisher, Trans.). Boston: Beacon Press.

Miller, J. G. (1996). Theoretical issues in cultural psychology. In J. W. Berry, Y. H. Poortinga, & J. Pandey (Eds.), *Handbook of Cross-Cultural Psychology: Theory and Method* (pp. 85–128). Boston: Allyn and Bacon.

Mueller, U., & Overton, W. F. (1998a). How to grow a baby. A reevaluation of image-schema and Piagetian action approaches to representation. *Human Development, 41,* 71–111.

Mueller, U., & Overton, W. F. (1998b). Action theory of mind and representational theory of mind: Is dialogue possible? *Human Development, 41,* 127–133.

Nagel, E. (1957). Determinism and development. In D. B. Harris (Ed.), *The concept of development* (pp. 15–24). Minneapolis: University of Minnesota Press.

Ogden, T. H. (1986). *The matrix of the mind: Object relations and the psychoanalytic dialogue.* Northvale, NJ: Jason Aronson.

Overton, W. F. (1975). General system, structure and development. In K. F. Riegel & G. C. Rosenwald (Eds.), *Structure and transformation: Developmental and historical aspects* (pp. 61–81). New York: Wiley-Interscience.

Overton, W. F. (1984). World views and their influence on psychological theory and research: Kuhn-Lakatos-Laudan. In H. W. Reese (Ed.), *Advances in child development and behavior* (Vol. 18, pp. 191–226). New York: Academic Press.

Overton, W. F. (1994a). The arrow of time and cycles of time: Concepts of change, cognition, and embodiment. *Psychological Inquiry, 5,* 215–237.

Overton, W. F. (1994b). Contexts of meaning: The computational and the embodied mind. In W. F. Overton & D. S. Palermo (Eds.), *The nature and ontogenesis of meaning* (pp. 1–18). Hillsdale, NJ: Erlbaum.

Overton, W. F. (1997a). Relational-developmental theory: A psychology perspective. In D. Gorlitz, H. J. Harloff, J. Valsiner, & G. Mey (Eds.), *Children, cities and psychological theories: Developing relationships* (pp. 315–335). Berlin: de Gruyter.

Overton, W. F. (1997b). Beyond dichotomy: An embodied active agent for cultural psychology. *Culture and Psychology, 3,* 315–334.

Overton, W. F. (1998). Developmental psychology: Philosophy, concepts, and methodology. In W. Damon (Series Ed.) & R. M. Lerner (Vol. Ed.), *Handbook of child psychology: Vol. 1. Theoretical models of human development* (5th ed., pp. 107–188). New York: Wiley.

Overton, W. F., & Jackson, J. (1973). The representation of imagined objects in action sequences: A developmental study. *Child Development, 44,* 309–314.

Overton, W. F., & Reese, H. W. (1981). Conceptual prerequisites for an understanding of stability-change and continuity-discontinuity. *International Journal of Behavioral Development, 4,* 99–123.

Piaget, J. (1952). *The origins of intelligence in children*. New York: W. W. Norton.

Piaget, J. (1985). *The equilibration of cognitive structures*. Chicago: University of Chicago Press.

Pierce, C. S. (1992). *Reasoning and the logic of things: The Cambridge conference lectures of 1898*. Cambridge, MA: Harvard University Press.

Popper, K. (1959). *The logic of scientific discovery*. London: Hutchinson.

Prosch, H. (1964). *The genesis of twentieth century philosophy*. New York: Doubleday.

Putnam, H. (1983). *Realism and reason: Philosophical papers*, (Vol. 3). New York: Cambridge University Press.

Putnam, H. (1987). *The many faces of realism*. Cambridge, UK: Cambridge University Press.

Putnam, H. (1990). *Realism with a human face*. Cambridge, MA: Harvard University Press.

Quine, W. V. (1953). *From a logical point of view*. Cambridge, MA: Harvard University Press.

Randall, J. H. (1960). *Aristotle*. New York: Columbia University Press.

Ricoeur, P. (1984). *Time and narrative* (K. McLalughlin & D. Pellauer, Trans.) (Vol. 1). Chicago: University of Chicago Press.

Ricoeur, P. (1991). *From text to action: Essays in hermeneutics* (K. Blamey & J. B. Thompson, Trans.) (Vol. 2). Evanston, IL: Northwestern University Press.

Rozeboom, W. W. (1997). Good science is abductive, not hypothetico-deductive. In L. L. Harlow, S. A. Mulaik, & J. H. Steiger (Eds.), *What if there were no significance tests?* Mahwah, NJ: Erlbaum.

Russell, J. (1996). *Agency: Its role in mental development*. Mahwah, NJ: Taylor and Francis.

Saarni, C., Mumme, D. L., & Campos, J. J. (1998). Emotional development: Action, communication, and understanding. In W. Damon (Series Ed.) & N. Eisenberg (Vol. Ed.), *Handbook of child psychology: Vol. 3. Social, emotional, and personality development* (5th ed., pp. 237–309). New York: Wiley.

Sabini, J., Siepmann, M. & Stein, J. (2001). Authors' response to commentaries. *Psychological Inquiries, 12*, 41–48.

Santostefano, S. (1995). Embodied meanings, cognition and emotion: Pondering how three are one. In D. Cicchetti & S. L. Toth (Eds.), *Rochester Symposium on Developmental Psychopathology: Vol. 6. Emotion, cognition and representation* (pp. 59–132). Rochester, NY: University of Rochester Press.

Sampson, E. E. (1996). Establishing embodiment in psychology. *Theory and Psychology, 6*(4), 601–624.

Saxe, G. B. (1981). Body parts as numerals. A developmental analysis of numeration among the Oksapmin of New Guinea. *Child Development, 52*, 306–316.

Saxe, G. B. (1995, June). *Culture, changes in social practices, and cognitive development*. Paper presented to the annual meeting of the Jean Piaget Society, Berkeley, CA.

Scholnick, E. K., & Cookson, K. (1994). A developmental analysis of cognitive semantics: What is the role of metaphor in the construction of knowledge and reasoning? In W. F. Overton & D. S. Palermo (Eds.), *The nature and ontogenesis of meaning* (pp. 109–128). Hillsdale, NJ: Erlbaum.

Schneirla, T. C. (1956). Interrelationships of the innate and the acquired in instinctive behavior. In P. P. Grasse (Ed.), *L'instinct dans le comportement des animaux et de l'homme* (pp. 387–452). Paris: Mason et Cie.

Searle, J. (1992). *The rediscovery of the mind*. Cambridge, MA: MIT Press.

Shanon, B. (1993). *The representational and the presentational: An essay on cognition and the study of mind*. New York: Harvester Wheatsheaf.

Sheets-Johnstone, M. (1990). *The roots of thinking*. Philadelphia: Temple University Press.

Siegler, R. S. (1989). Mechanisms of cognitive development. *Annual Review of Psychology, 40*, 353–379.

Siegler, R. S. (1996). *Emerging minds: The process of change in children's thinking*. New York: Oxford University Press.

Siegler, R. S., & Crowley, K. (1991). The microgenetic method: A direct means for studying cognitive development. *American Psychologist, 46*, 606–620.

Siegler, R. S., & Munakata, Y. (1993, Winter). Beyond the immaculate transition: Advances in the understanding of change. *SRCD Newsletter*.

Smythe, W. E. (1992). Conception of interpretation in cognitive theories of representation. *Theory and Psychology, 2*, 339–362.

Spelke, E. S., & Newport, E. L. (1998). Nativism, empiricism, and the development of knowledge. In W. Damon (Series Ed.) & R. M. Lerner (Vol. Ed.), *Handbook of child psychology: Vol. 1. Theoretical models of human development* (5th ed., pp. 275–340). New York: Wiley.

Stace, W. T. (1924). *The philosophy of Hegel*. New York: Dover.

Sternberg, R. J. (Ed.) (1984). *Mechanisms of cognitive development*. New York: W. H. Freeman.

Taylor, C. (1995). *Philosophical arguments*. Cambridge, MA: Harvard University Press.

Thelen, E. (2000). Grounded in the world: Developmental origins of the embodied mind. *Infancy, 1*, 3–28.

Thelen, E., & Smith, (1998). Dynamic systems theories. In W. Damon (Series Ed.) & R. M. Lerner (Vol. Ed.), *Handbook of child psychology: Vol. 1. Theoretical models of human development* (5th ed., pp. 563–634). New York: Wiley.

Tobach, E., & Greenberg, G. (1984). The significance of T. C. Schneirla's contribution to the concept of integration. In G. Greenberg & E. Tobach (Eds.), *Behavioral evolution and integrative levels* (pp. 1–7). Hillsdale, NJ: Erlbaum.

Toulmin, S. (1953). *The philosophy of science*. New York: Harper and Row.

Toulmin, S. (1990). *Cosmopolis: The hidden agenda of modernity.* Chicago: The University of Chicago Press.

Uttal, D. H. (2000). Seeing the big picture map use and the development of spatial cognition. *Developmental Science, 3,* 247–264.

Valsiner, J. (1994). Irreversibility of time and the construction of historical developmental psychology. *Mind, Culture, and Activity, 1,* 25–42.

Valsiner, J. (1998). *The guided mind: A sociogenetic approach to personality.* Cambridge, MA: Harvard University Press.

Varela, F. J., Thompson, E., & Rosch, E. (1991). *The embodied mind: Cognitive science and human experience.* Cambridge, MA: MIT Press.

von Wright, G. H. (1971). *Explanation and understanding.* Ithaca, NY: Cornell University Press.

Werner, H. (1957). The concept of development from a comparative and organismic point of view. In D. B. Harris (Ed.), *The concept of development: An issue in the study of human behavior* (pp. 125–148). Minneapolis: University of Minnesota Press.

Werner, H. (1958). *Comparative psychology of mental development.* New York: International Universities Press.

Wertsch, J. V. (1991). *Voices of the mind: A sociocultural approach to mediated action.* Cambridge, MA: Harvard University Press.

Winnicott, D. W. (1971). *Playing and reality.* New York: Basic Books.

Wittgenstein, L. (1958). *Philosophical investigations* (G. E. M. Anscombe, Trans.) (3rd ed.). Englewood Cliffs, NJ: Prentice Hall.

Zelazo, P. D. (1996). Towards a characterization of minimal consciousness. *New Ideas in Psychology, 14*(1), 63–80.

CHAPTER 2

Applied Developmental Science

DONALD WERTLIEB

Developmental psychology's emergent identity as an applied developmental science (ADS) reflects our discipline's rich and complex history and forecasts our discipline's challenges and opportunities as we begin our second century of science and practice. As proponents of a key subdiscipline of psychology, we continue our commitment to advance psychology "as a science, as a profession, and as a means of promoting human welfare" (American Psychological Association, 2000, p. 1) and to "promote, protect, and advance the interests of scientifically oriented psychology in research, application, and the improvement of human welfare" (American Psychological Society, 2000, p. 1). Fulfilling this commitment involves heeding the recent call of a Nobel Foundation symposium for better integrated models of life-span development and for interdisciplinary and international frameworks (Cairns, 1998; Magnusson, 1996).

This chapter provides a brief history of the emergence, or re-emergence, of ADS as a compelling umbrella for advancing developmental psychology, with a particular focus on the first two decades of life, namely, child and adolescent psychology. Consistent with the interdisciplinary and multidisciplinary mandates, consideration of the kindred disciplines that partner to advance knowledge follows. Examples of substantive areas of inquiry and action in ADS are then considered, including articulation of the special methods of ADS, the special ethical imperatives of ADS, and some particular training challenges for ADS.

DEFINING APPLIED DEVELOPMENTAL SCIENCE

Over the last two decades increasing numbers of developmental psychologists have identified themselves professionally as applied developmental scientists. Joining them under this umbrella are colleagues from allied disciplines and specialties in the biological, social, and behavioral sciences and the helping professions, all sharing common goals and visions captured in some of the more formal definitions of the ADS fields. Certainly an early milestone in the staking out of the field's territory occurred with the founding of the *Journal of Applied Developmental Psychology* in 1980, an international multidisciplinary life-span journal. The masthead proclaimed a "forum for communication between researchers and practitioners working in life-span human development fields, a forum for the presentation of the conceptual, methodological, policy, and related issues involved in the application of behavioral science research in developmental psychology to social action and social problem solving" (Sigel & Cocking, 1980, p. i). In welcoming the new journal in an inaugural editorial, Zigler (1980) narrowed the definition of the journal's purview to what he called a "field within a field" (i.e., presumably, applied developmental psychology within developmental psychology) but set high and broad expectations that "these pages shall attest to the synergistic relationship between basic and applied research" (p. 1).

Almost 20 years later, Zigler (1998) issued a similar note of hope, celebration, and welcome in a significant essay called "A Place of Value for Applied and Policy Studies," this time in the pages of *Child Development,* the prestigious archival journal of the Society for Research in Child Development (SRCD). *Child Development* had been singularly devoted to "theory-driven, basic research. Now, after more than six decades of advancing science as a means to expand our understanding of human development, SRCD has formally welcomed into its major journal research that uses this knowledge on children's behalf . . . the result of a very gradual transformation within SRCD from a scientist's science toward a more public science" (Zigler, 1998, p. 532). The continuing vicissitudes of the gaps and synergies between applied and basic research will be a theme of the historical sketch offered in the next section (see also Garner, 1972).

In 1991 a National Task Force on Applied Developmental Science convened representatives from abroad, but not an exhaustive range of professional scientific organizations concerned with the application of the knowledge base of developmental psychology to societal problems. Organizations represented included the American Psychological Association, the Gerontological Society of America, the International Society for Infant Studies, the National Black Child Development Institute, the National Council on Family Relations, the Society for Research on Adolescence, and the Society for Research in Child Development. Goals included the articulation of the definition and scope of ADS along with guidelines for graduate training in this emergent, interdisciplinary field. A consensus process produced a complex four-point definition of ADS, quoted here at length to document the current parameters of content, process, methods, and values:

> 1.1 Applied developmental science involves the programmatic synthesis of research and applications to describe, explain, intervene, and provide preventive and enhancing uses of knowledge about human development. The conceptual base of ADS reflects the view that individual and family functioning is a combined and interactive product of biology and the physical and social environments that continuously evolve and change over time. ADS emphasizes the nature of reciprocal person-environment interactions among people, across settings, and within a multidisciplinary approach stressing individual and cultural diversity. This orientation is defined by three conjoint emphases:
> **Applied:** Direct implications for what individuals, families, practitioners, and policymakers do.
> **Developmental:** Systematic and successive changes within human systems that occur across the life span.
> **Science:** Grounded in a range of research methods designed to collect reliable and objective information systematically that can be used to test the validity of theory and application.

> 1.2 ADS recognizes that valid applications of our knowledge of human development depend upon scientifically based understanding of multilevel normative and atypical processes that continually change and emerge over the life cycle.
> 1.3 ADS reflects an integration of perspectives from relevant biological, social, and behavioral sciences disciplines in the service of promoting development in various populations.
> 1.4 The nature of work in ADS is reciprocal in that science drives application and application drives science. ADS emphasizes the bidirectional relationship between those who generate empirically based knowledge about developmental phenomena and those who pursue professional practices, services, and policies that affect the well-being of members of society. Accordingly, research and theory guide intervention strategies, and evaluations of outcomes of developmental interventions provide the basis for the reformulation of theory and for modification of future interventions. (Fisher et al., 1993, pp. 4–5)

By 1997 these parameters defining ADS were adopted as the editorial scope of a new journal, *Applied Developmental Science,* with further explication of a more inclusive range of methodologies and audiences. The journal publishes

> research employing any of a diverse array of methodologies— multivariate longitudinal studies, demographic analyses, evaluation research, intensive measurement studies, ethnographic analyses, laboratory experiments, analyses of policy and/or policy-engagement studies, or animal comparative studies— when they have important implications for the application of developmental science across the life span. Manuscripts pertinent to the diversity of development throughout the life-span— cross-national and cross-cultural studies; systematic studies of psychopathology; and studies pertinent to gender, ethnic and racial diversity——are particularly welcome. . . . [The audience includes] developmental, clinical, school, counseling, aging, educational, and community psychologists; lifecourse, family and demographic sociologists; health professionals; family and consumer scientists; human evolution and ecological biologists; [and] practitioners in child and youth governmental and nongovernmental organizations. (Lerner, Fisher, & Weinberg, 1997, p. 1)

This amplified definition of ADS postulates a number of hallmarks of ADS key to the discussion of its history, content, and special concerns. Among these hallmarks are

1. A historical context and perspective reflecting the perennial balancing of related constructs such as basic and applied research or science and practice or knowledge generation and utilization. This includes a sensitivity to historical and sociopolitical contexts captured in the notion of ADS as

Scholarship for our times. . . . As we enter the 21st century, there is growing recognition that traditional and artificial distinctions between science and service and between knowledge generation and knowledge application need to be reconceptualized if society is to successfully address the harrowing developmental sequelae of the social, economic, and geo-political legacies of the 20th century. Scholars, practitioners and policymakers are increasingly recognizing the role that developmental science can play in stemming the tide of life-chance destruction caused by poverty, premature births, school failure, child abuse, crime, adolescent pregnancy, substance abuse, unemployment, welfare dependency, discrimination, ethnic conflict, and inadequate health and social resources. (Lerner et al., 1997, p. 2)

2. A broadened and deepened awareness of the ethical challenges and imperatives involved in implementing the scope of ADS. This awareness evolves from challenges in the use of scientific methods in new ways such that protection of the autonomy and well-being research of participants is increasingly complex. Research participants become partners in the inquiry process and new, more complicated collaborations among diverse multidisciplinary professionals and communities become key elements of defining research questions and problems and seeking answers and solutions.

More recently, some leaders have broadened the potential scope of ADS even further, suggesting elements of a blueprint for promoting civil society and social justice, a provocative and compelling elaboration of both the substance and the ethical orientation of the field (Lerner, Fisher, & Weinberg, 2000). Others have focused on more traditional academic or incremental stocktaking for defining ADS with attention to advancing the numerous knowledge bases and methodologies (e.g., Schwebel, Plumert, & Pick, 2000; Shonkoff, 2000; Sigel & Renninger, 1998). ADS is now considered an "established discipline" (Fisher, Murray, & Sigel, 1996), defined with the parameters just outlined. Our survey of this discipline moves now to a more detailed historical analysis, with attention to earlier roots as well as appreciation for the contemporary ferment evident in the definitional emergence of the last few years.

ELEMENTS OF THE HISTORY OF APPLIED DEVELOPMENTAL SCIENCE

From the earliest days of psychology in general and of developmental psychology in particular, tensions and balances basic to the emergence of contemporary ADS as just defined have provided the heat and light for historians of the field.

Observers and analysts are prone to calling upon metaphors such as a swinging pendulum or old wine in new bottles. Indeed, as argued elsewhere, the newness of the ADS orientation "ought not be overemphasized—renewal is perhaps a more accurate frame" (Wertlieb & Feldman, 1996, p. 123). As the definition of ADS just noted emerged, Parke's (1992) Presidential Address to the American Psychological Association Division of Developmental Psychology noted the return of developmental psychologists to "their forerunners' concern for applying science to social problems . . . , and their renewed interest in interdisciplinary work also resembles early developmental psychology" (p. 987). Parke noted that "the applied/nonapplied distinction is an increasingly blurry and perhaps dubious one, as researchers continue to recognize the multifaceted value of social experiments such as Headstart" (p. 987).

Our forerunners were perhaps even bolder in asserting such views. When discussing the case of a chronic bad speller referred to his clinic, Witmer (1907), a founder of clinical psychology, noted that "if psychology was worth anything to me or to others it should be able to assist the efforts of a teacher in a retarded case of this kind. The final test of the value of what is called science is its applicability" (cited in Fagan, 1992, p. 237). Indeed, an elemental challenge in ADS today is overcoming the historical quagmires of scientism versus clinicalism (Perry, 1979) and applied versus scientific acceptability. As evident at psychology's inception, Fagan (1992) reported that "both Hall and Witmer were popular with teacher and parent constituencies, but not always with psychologist colleagues, many of whom viewed their work as less than scientific" (p. 239).

Several extensive histories of the disciplines of developmental psychology and child development have been published, and most include reference to the ebb and flow of interest and priority for what might be termed the applied, practical, or societally oriented issues so central to ADS. Especially relevant are discussions offered by Bronfenbrenner, Kessel, Kessen, and White (1986); Cairns (1998); Davidson and Benjamin (1987); Hetherington (1998); McCall (1996); McCall and Groark (2000); Parke, Ornstein, Reiser, and Zahn-Waxler (1994); Sears (1975); and Siegel and White (1982). Hetherington (1998) framed her analysis by accenting her use of the term "developmental science . . . to emphasize both the scientific and multidisciplinary foundations of the study of development and the recognition that development is not confined to childhood but extends across the lifespan" (p. 93)—emphases lost or diluted in using the too-limiting term *child psychology*. She interpreted and extended Sears's (1975) classic analysis, reaffirming that "unlike many areas in psychology [with their histories documented by Boring (1950) and Koch & Leary (1985)], developmental science originated from the need to solve practical problems and evolved from pressure to improve the education, health, welfare and legal status of children and their families" (p. 93).

The chronology of developmental psychology offered by Cairns (1998) serves as a useful framework in which to specify some of the distinctive or seminal elements of ADS. Cairns delimited the emergence of developmental psychology (1882–1912), the middle period of institutionalization and expansion (1913–1946), and the modern era (1947–1976). His compliance with a convention that 20 years must elapse before qualifying as "historical" leaves much of the significant milestone material mentioned in our earlier definition of ADS outside the realm of his presentation, but he did conclude his account with a clarion call for more integrated interdisciplinary science, quite consistent with what we might term the postmodern or contemporary era (1977–present). Indeed, it is from this most recent period that we draw our substantive examples of ADS, after the conclusion of this historical sketch.

Most accounts, including Cairn's (1998) emergence analysis, portray the dialectic at the base of ADS as pioneered by G. Stanley Hall, the first professor of psychology in America (appointed in 1883 at Johns Hopkins University), the first president of the American Psychological Association (1891), and founder of the first child development research institute (at Clark University) and of the journal *Pedagogical Seminary.*

Hall was a remarkable teacher and catalyst for the field. Some of the most significant areas for developmental study—mental testing, child study, early education, adolescence, life-span psychology, evolutionary influences on development—were stimulated or anticipated by Hall. Because of shortcomings in the methods he employed and the theory he endorsed, few investigators stepped forward to claim Hall as a scientific mentor. His reach exceeded his grasp in the plan to apply the principles of the new science to society. Psychology's principles were too modest, and society's problems too large. Perhaps we should use a fresh accounting to judge Hall's contributions, one that takes into account the multiple facets of his influence on individuals, the discipline, and society. The audit would reveal that all of us who aspire to better the lot of children and adolescents can claim him as a mentor. (Cairns, 1998, p. 43)

White (1992) asserted that

the simple fact is that G. Stanley Hall marched away from experimental psychology toward the study of children because at least six different constituencies existed in American society, basically still our constituencies today—scientists, college administrators, child savers and social workers, mental health workers, teachers, and parents. These constituencies wanted certain kinds of knowledge about children. *Mirabile dictu,* without even being developmental psychologists and before we came into existence, they were all collecting data that look like ours. So if you look at the social history that surrounds the birth of the Child Study Movement, you gradually come to the conclusion that perhaps we represent a professionalization of trends of knowledge gathering and knowledge analysis that existed in our society before our coming. That doesn't completely detach us from the mainstream of the history of psychology, but it certainly throws a very different light on the emergence and evolution of the field and its basic issues. (Bronfenbrenner et al., 1986, p. 1221)

Among Hall's most significant contributions, according to White (1992), were the concern with descriptions of children in their natural contexts and the need "to arrive at a scientific synthesis on the one side and practical recommendations on the other" (cited in Cairns, 1998, p. 43). Contemporary ADS continues in its value in the former and aspires to overcome the too-dichotomous implications of the latter; it emphasizes the reciprocal and mutual interactions of the scientific and practical typical in this earliest era.

The other heroes or giants of history contributing in this foundational period are, of course, Sigmund Freud, Alfred Binet, and John Dewey. Freud's psychoanalytic theories and methods were key forerunners of one of contemporary ADS's most vital arenas, developmental psychopathology. The separate path taken by psychoanalysis in subsequent years is only recently reconverging with developmental psychology. Millennium analyses of the field of developmental psychopathology are intriguing sources of elaboration of the history of ADS, and the reawakened appreciation of psychoanalytic approaches are of special interest (Cicchetti & Sroufe, 2000; Fonagy & Target, 2000).

The measurement and testing of intelligence pioneered by Binet continues to influence extant theories and methods in contemporary ADS, although certainly the scientific revolutions in the ensuing years (e.g., Piagetian psychology), as well as political sensitivities, establish a much more complex and sophisticated set of theories about intelligences, their manifestation and measurement, and their places in a broad array of processes, competencies, or outcomes relevant to developmental status or progress. The abiding links to schooling and education, so basic to the philosophical and scientific contributions of John Dewey, remain core foci in contemporary ADS. Notions of constructivism, of the salience of motivation and everyday experience, and of psychology as a foundational science for applications such as education championed by Dewey pervade contemporary ADS (Cahan, 1992).

The second and third periods of Cairn's (1998) history of developmental psychology emphasize institutionalization, especially of scientific and laboratory-based inquiry, and expansion into a modern behavioral science. Many of the scientific and applied seeds planted in the foundational period grew in the middle of the twentieth century, with what we might term the rise and fall of the then-grand theories being an especially salient process. These grand theories included the elaboration of Freudian psychoanalytic approaches, behaviorism as espoused by Skinnerians and Pavlovians, as well as cognitive theories of Piagetians. Modernism and positivism yielded to postmodernism with the articulations and fragmentations captured by labels such as ego-analytic or neo-Freudian approaches; social-behavioral, social-learning, and cognitive-behavioral approaches; or neo-Piagetian approaches, for example. Bronfenbrenner et al. (1986, p. 1219) described and decried dimensions of this fragmentation process in the middle of the twentieth century, identifying a trend of what they term recurring faddism or, worse, recurrent scientific bias.

The contemporary era in which ADS is now emerging capitalizes on newly grand theoretical formulations. For instance, bioecological theory (Bronfenbrenner & Ceci, 1994), developmental contextualism (Lerner, 1998), and lifespan developmental psychology (Baltes, Lindenberger, & Staudinger, 1998) each represent varying degrees of broadening and integrating (or even reintegrating) consistent with the scope and challenges of ADS. It is useful to consider a historical process somewhat akin to Werner's orthogenetic principle: "Basic and applied aspects of developmental science began as a global unit and became increasingly differentiated. Further maturity now allows for a hierarchical integration of the specialized functions into a synergistic whole" (Zigler, 1998, pp. 533–534).

Substantive challenges or demands inherent in American social policy during the "Great Renaissance" of the 1960s and 1970s (the modern era according to Cairns, 1998) provided the raison d'être for ADS. The War on Poverty, Head Start early education intervention, and the community mental health movements all provided arenas for expectations and conversations between developmental scientists and the society in which they functioned. The newly grand theories were required to guide the generation of research questions, data, interpretation, and application. ADS is providing parameters for advancing with simultaneous and increasingly integrated attention to processes of knowledge generation and knowledge utilization.

As noted earlier, multidisciplinarity and interdisciplinarity are key hallmarks of ADS. Not surprisingly, parallel historical evolution in related subdisciplines and disciplines has been documented such that among the component fields or contemporary renditions of ADS are several emergent integrating or synergizing traditions. This trend has been discussed in kindred subdisciplines of psychology such as clinical psychology (Fox, 1982; Frank, 1984; Kendall, 1984; Levy, 1984; Wertlieb, 1985), community psychology (Marsella, 1998; Masterpasqu, 1981), school psychology (Fagan, 1992, 2000; Ysseldyke, 1982), educational psychology (Bardon, 1983), and pediatric psychology (Brennemann, 1933; Wertlieb, 1999). Other social sciences such as anthropology, policy analysis, social work, home economics/consumer sciences, and public health share some of these elements of differentiation and recent reintegration in interdisciplinary forms consistent with ADS (e.g., Elder, 1998; Featherman & Lerner, 1985; Kaplan, 2000; Nickols, 2001; Schneiderman, Speers, Silva, Tomes, & Gentry, 2001; Winett, 1995).

Within the field of psychology, as well as in the links with kindred disciplines that form ADS, the integrated identity as a "scientist-practitioner" evolves as a basic standard or goal. A similar rubric of reflective practice captures the optimal functioning of a scientist-practitioner (e.g., Schon, 1983). Cultivation of the scientist-practitioner remains an abiding challenge (Belar & Perry, 1992). This bridge between science and practice is requires constant attention, as documented by Kanfer's (1990) articulation of the challenges "to foster and blend the skills, perceptivity and pragmatism of the professional along with training in methods, and exposure to the skeptic-empirical attitude of the researcher" (p. 269). Applied developmental scientists are "translators who a) devote systematic attention to research and dissemination of practical implications and methods derived from various domains of the social sciences and/or b) formulate professional problems in 'basic science' language and collaborate with (or act as) scientists whose expertise encompasses the domain in which these researchable questions are phrased" (p. 265). With definitions of ADS in hand, along with historically significant elements that continue to shape the field, we turn to a selective overview of contemporary domains of inquiry and action in ADS.

DOMAINS OF INQUIRY AND ACTION IN APPLIED DEVELOPMENTAL SCIENCE

At the start of the twenty-first century, scores of applied developmental scientists are actively and productively pursuing hundreds of significant research questions with important implications and applications to the well-being of children, youth, and families. Table 2.1 lists many of these topics of

TABLE 2.1   Areas of Inquiry and Action in Applied Developmental Science

Topic	Sample Study or Review
Early child care & education	Lamb (1998); Ramey & Ramey (1998); Scarr (1998); Zigler & Finn-Stevenson (1999).
Early childhood education	Elkind (2002).
Education reform & schooling	Adelman & Taylor (2000); Fishman (1999); Renninger (1998); Strauss (1998).
Literacy	Adams, Trieman, & Pressley (1998); Lerner, Wolf, Schliemann, & Mistry (2001).
Parenting & parent education	Collins et al. (2000); Cowan et al. (1998).
Poverty	Black & Krishnakumar (1998); McLoyd (1998).
Developmental assets	Benson (1997); Scales & Leffert (1999); Weissberg & Greenberg (1998).
Successful children & families	Masten & Coatsworth (1998); Wertlieb (2001).
Marital disruption & divorce	Hetherington, Bridges, & Insabella (1998); Wertlieb (1997).
Developmental psychopathology	Cicchetti & Sroufe (2000); Cicchetti & Toth (1998b); Richters (1997); Rutter & Sroufe (2000).
Depression	Cicchetti & Toth (1998a).
Domestic violence & maltreatment	Emery & Laumann-Billings (1998).
Adolescent pregnancy	Coley & Chase-Landsdale (1998).
Aggression & violence	Loeber & Stouthamer-Loeber (1998).
Children's eyewitness reports	Bruck, Ceci, & Hembrooke (1998).
Pediatric psychology	Bearison (1998).
Mass media, television, & computers	Huston & Wright (1998); Martland & Rothbaum (1999).
Prevention science	Coie et al. (1993); Kaplan (2000).

inquiry and action to provide a sense of the broad scope of ADS. Recent textbooks (e.g., Fisher & Lerner, 1994), review chapters (e.g., Zigler & Finn-Stevenson, 1999), handbooks (e.g., Lerner, Jacobs & Wertlieb, 2002; Sigel & Renninger, 1998), special issues of journals (e.g., Hetherington, 1998), and regular sections of journals such as the "Applied Developmental Theory" section of *Infants and Young Children* provide ongoing articulation of ADS inquiry. Journals such as the *Journal of Applied Developmental Psychology, Applied Developmental Science,* and *Children's Services: Social Policy, Research and Practice* are among the central outlets for new work in ADS. Each of the chapters that follow in the present volume on developmental psychology reflects, to varying degrees, some influence of ADS in establishing the current state of knowledge, and the final section of this volume includes several chapters specifically focused on ADS-related scholarship across the life span. For the purposes of this chapter's overview of ADS, just two of the many areas of inquiry and action have been selected to illustrate some of the substantive concerns of ADS: (a) parenting and early child care and education, followed by (b) developmental psychopathology and developmental assets. As will be evident, each of these complex areas involves foci of theoretical and methodological concerns, and most link to several of the others listed in Table 2.1, consistent with the highly contextual and interdisciplinary orientation of ADS.

Parenting and Early Child Care and Education

The state of ADS in parenting and early child care education is well summarized in several reviews (e.g., Bornstein, 1995; Collins, Maccoby, Steinberg, Hetherington, & Bornstein,

2000; Cowan, Powell, & Cowan, 1998; Harris, 1998, 2000; Scarr, 1998; Vandell, 2000; Zigler & Finn-Stevenson, 1999) and covers core questions such as

1. How do parenting behaviors influence a child's behavior and development?
2. How do children influence parenting behavior?
3. What are the influences of different forms of child care and early education on children's development?
4. How effective are different interventions for parent education and early education of young children?
5. How do social policies influence the qualities of interventions and programs for children and parents?

Political, philosophical, and scientific controversies permeate many discussions of parenting and early child care and education. In recent years, as challenges to what had become conventional wisdom about the salience of parents' attitudes, beliefs, and behaviors as shapers of their children's development (e.g., Harris, 1998) gained notoriety, applied developmental scientists have acknowledged the shortcomings of extant socialization research (see chapter by Kerr, Stattin, & Ferrer-Wreder in this volume). "Early researchers often overstated conclusions from correlational findings; relied excessively on singular, deterministic views of parental influence; and failed to attend to the potentially confounding effects of biological variation" (Collins et al., 2000, p. 218). Now, with augmented behavior-genetic designs, longitudinal analyses, animal comparative studies, more sophisticated data collection, and analyses and grounding in more comprehensive and contextual biopsychosocial ecological theories, researchers offer more valid and sophisticated accounts of the important influences of parenting on behavior. These accounts are highly nuanced with emphasis on interaction and moderator effects, reciprocal influences, nonfamilial influences, and attention to impacts of macrocontexts such as neighborhoods, policies, and cultures.

As an example, consider the studies of children's temperaments and parenting reviewed by Collins et al. (2000). Children can be characterized in terms of constitutionally based individual differences or styles of reacting to the environment and self-regulating. Developmental research had established modest statistical correlations between "difficult" temperamental profiles in young children and later behavior problems and disorders.

> Bates, Pettit, and Dodge (1995), in a longitudinal study, found that infants' characteristics (e.g., hyperactivity, impulsivity, and difficult temperament) significantly predicted externalizing problems 10 years later. Although this finding at first seems to support the lasting effects of physiologically based characteristics, Bates et al. (1995) also showed that predictive power increased when they added information about parenting to the equation. Infants' early characteristics elicited harsh parenting at age 4, which in turn predicted externalizing problems when the children were young adolescents, over and above the prediction from infant temperament. Similarly, this and other findings imply that even though parenting behavior is influenced by child behavior, parents' actions contribute distinctively to the child's later behavior. (Collins et al., 2000, p. 222)

Coupled with the increasingly sophisticated literature on the development and effectiveness of intervention programs that help parents alter their parenting behavior with infants, young children, or adolescents (e.g., Cowan et al., 1998; Webster-Stratton, 1994), this area of scholarship is a prototypical domain of inquiry and action for ADS, and one that provides theoretical, methodological, and practical contributions.

When care by other than the child's parents is examined, similar advances are evident (Lamb, 1998, 2000; National Institute of Child Health and Human Development Early Child Care Research Network, 2000; Scarr, 1998; Zigler & Finn-Stevenson, 1999). Again, these advances are in the context of political, philosophical, and scientific controversies. The last quarter century has seen a shift away from research aimed at documenting how much damage is done to children who are left in daycare as their mothers enter the work force, to research discovering and describing varieties and qualities of day care and early education experiences for children, and more recently to sophisticated longitudinal studies comparing and contrasting varieties of maternal and nonmaternal care, including in-home, family-based, and center-based

care. These latter studies increasingly include "not only proximal influences on the child but distal influences as well" (Scarr, 1998, p. 101) and adopt conceptual frameworks requiring attention to individual differences in children, in family processes, and contextual issues such as staff training and support, access to care, and related social policies. Attention to the special needs of at-risk populations such as children living in poverty or other disadvantaged conditions shows similarly increasing sophistication as ADS frameworks are employed (e.g., Ramey & Ramey, 1998).

Lamb's (1998) summary of the current state of knowledge on child care reflects the orientation of ADS:

> In general, the quality of care received both at home and in alternative care facilities appears to be important, whereas the specific type of care (exclusive home care, family day care, center day care) appears to be much less significant than was once thought. Poor quality care may be experienced by many children . . . and poor quality care can have harmful effects on child development. Type of care may also have varying effects depending upon the ages at which children enter out-of-home care settings, with the planned curricula of day care centers becoming increasingly advantageous as children get older. Interactions between the type of care and the age of the child must obviously be considered, although claims about the formative importance of the amount of nonparental care and the age of onset have yet to be substantiated empirically. It also appears likely that different children will be affected differently by various day care experiences, although we remain ignorant about most of the factors that modulate these different effects. Child temperament, parental attitudes and values, preenrollment differences in sociability, curiosity and cognitive functioning, sex and birth order may all be influential, but reliable evidence is scanty. . . . We know that extended exposure to nonparental child care indeed has a variety of effects on children, but when asked about specific patterns of effects or even whether such care is good or bad for children we still have to say *It depends.* (pp. 116–117)

Such an analysis of the state of our science becomes a starting point for the ADS professional in pursuing the collaborations with researchers from allied disciplines and community partners to advance knowledge and build and evaluate programs.

Developmental Psychopathology and Developmental Assets

In fostering synergy among disciplines concerned with the understanding and well-being of children, ADS provides a forum for significant scientific cross-fertilization between two powerful new traditions of inquiry and action: developmental psychopathology and developmental assets. An early definition of the science of developmental psychopathology called it "the study of the origins and course of individual patterns of behavioral maladaptation, whatever the age of onset, whatever the causes, whatever the transformations in behavioral manifestation, and however complex the course of the developmental pattern may be" (Sroufe & Rutter, 1984, p. 18). Cicchetti and Toth (1998b) confirmed that

> developmental psychopathologists should investigate function-ing through the assessment of ontogenetic, genetic, biochemical, biological, physiological, societal, cultural, environmental, fam-ily, cognitive, social-cognitive, linguistic, representational, and socioemotional influences on behavior. . . . The field of devel-opmental psychopathology transcends traditional disciplinary boundaries. . . . Rather than competing with existing theories and facts, the developmental psychopathology perspective provides a broad integrative perspective within which the contributions of separate disciplines can be fully realized. . . . The developmental psychopathology framework may challenge assumptions about what constitutes health or pathology and may redefine the man-ner in which the mental health community operationalizes, as-sesses, classifies, communicates about, and treats the adjustment problems and functioning impairments of infants, children, ado-lescents, and adults. . . . Thus, its own potential contribution lies in the heuristic power it holds for translating facts into knowl-edge, understanding and practical application. (p. 482)

As society grasps the challenges and the costs of mental disorder and behavior dysfunction, only a multidisciplinary vision so broad and so bold, with attendant reliance on the newly grand theories noted earlier, especially developmental contextualism and bioecological theory, can suffice. And even with this breadth and boldness evident in developmen-tal psychopathology, vulnerability to the critique of its being illness oriented or deficit oriented limits its scope. Richters's (1997) critique of developmental psychopathology identifies dilemmas and a "distorted lens" (p. 193) that hamper re-search advances. ADS provides a support for the bridges needed by developmental psychopathology by linking to the complementary concepts and methods of the developmental assets approach. When contemporary clinical psychologists or clinical-developmental psychologists (Noam, 1998), for instance, who are increasingly comfortable in claiming their role as developmental psychopathologists, can collaborate with community psychologists, for instance, who are increas-ingly comfortable in cultivating developmental assets, ADS approaches its promise as a framework for understanding and addressing the needs of children in our society.

The developmental assets framework (Benson, Leffert, Scales, & Blyth, 1998; Scales & Leffert, 1999) has some of its roots and branches in developmental psychopathology but contributes its own heuristic power to ADS, especially in

grafting its roots and branches in community psychology and prevention science (e.g., Weissberg & Greenberg, 1998). Although developmental psychopathology may focus more often on outcomes reflecting health and behavior problems or mental disorders or illness, the developmental assets frame-work emphasizes outcomes (or even processes) such as com-petence or thriving, as captured in the "emerging line of inquiry and practice commonly called positive youth devel-opment" (Benson et al., 1998, p. 141; see also Pittman & Irby, 1996). ADS emphasizes the importance of simultaneous consideration of both orientations. In addition, whereas de-velopmental psychopathology is explicitly life-span oriented as noted in the definitions stated earlier, the developmental assets framework, at least to date, is more focused (in deriva-tion though not implication) on the processes boldest in the second decade of life. The empirical and theoretical foun-dations for the framework emphasize "three types of health outcomes: a) the prevention of high risk behaviors (e.g., sub-stance use, violence, sexual intercourse, school dropout); b) the enhancement of thriving outcomes (e.g., school suc-cess, affirmation of diversity, the proactive approach to nutri-tion and exercise); and c) resiliency, or the capacity to rebound in the face of adversity" (p. 143).

Developmental assets theory generates research models that call upon a system or catalog of 40 developmental assets, half of them internal (e.g., commitment to learning, positive values, social competencies, and positive identity) and half of them external (e.g., support, empowerment, boundaries and expectations, and constructive use of time). Assessments of these characteristics and processes in individuals and in com-munities then provide for problem definition, intervention design, and program evaluation. While the developmental psychopathologist might focus on similar constructs and word them only in a negative or deficit manner (e.g., a posi-tive identity is merely the opposite of poor self-esteem), simultaneous consideration of both the assets and psy-chopathology orientations reveals that beyond the overlap-ping or synonymous concept or measure are complementing and augmenting meanings with important implications for both research and practice.

Some features of the synergy obtained with the perspec-tives fostered by developmental psychopathology and devel-opmental assets orientations are evident in theory and research conducted in frameworks termed the *stress and coping paradigm* (e.g., Wertlieb, Jacobson, & Hauser, 1990), or *vulnerability/risk and resiliency/protective factors model* (e.g., Ackerman, Schoff, Levinson, Youngstrom, & Izard, 1999; Hauser, Vieyra, Jacobson, & Wertlieb, 1985; Jes-sor, Turbin & Costa, 1998; Luthar, Cicchetti, & Becker, 2000; Luthar & Zigler, 1991; Masten & Coatsworth, 1998).

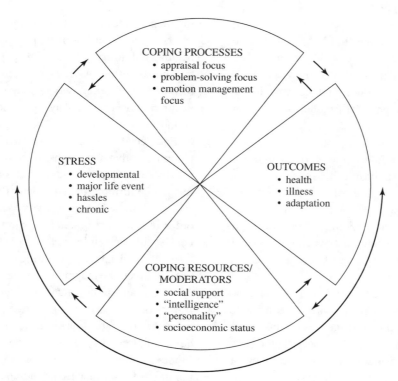

Figure 2.1   The stress and coping paradigm.

To illustrate some dimensions of this synergy that are basic to advancing ADS, we offer an overview of the stress and coping paradigm.

The Stress and Coping Paradigm

An important step toward the integration of emergent approaches to developmental psychopathology and extant stress theories salient to both health and mental health researchers was taken about 20 years ago at a gathering of scholars at the Center for Advanced Study in the Behavioral Sciences. Attendants generated what at the time was a comprehensive state-of-the-art review and compelling research agenda published as *Stress, Coping, and Development in Children* (Garmezy & Rutter, 1983). At a reunion a decade later, many of the same scientists and their younger colleagues now pursuing the agenda took stock of the research to produce *Stress, Risk, and Resilience in Children and Adolescents* (Haggerty, Sherrod, Garmezy, & Rutter, 1994). This latter volume was especially impressive in its articulation of important interventions and prevention applications, reflecting the historical trend noted earlier to be fueling ADS. A comparison of the two titles reveals that the coping construct disappeared—an unfortunate decision in light of present concerns with the promises of coping interventions and developmental assets as elements of overcoming stress, risk, and

poor health outcomes. However, the second title did introduce core biomedical and epidemiological constructs of risk and resiliency, basic conceptual and methodological tools consistent with ADS as defined earlier. In any event, these volumes provide a comprehensive treatment of the stress and coping field as an ADS. Figure 2.1 is a simple schematic that illustrates some basic features.

The stress and coping paradigm depicted in Figure 2.1 juxtaposes four variable domains capturing the complex and dynamic stress process (Pearlin, 1989) as a slice in time and context. The dimensions of time, or developmental progression, and context are those noted earlier as the bioecological framework (Bronfenbrenner & Ceci, 1994) and life-course models (e.g., Clausen, 1995; Elder, 1995); they are the background and foreground absent from, but implicit in, the schematic in Figure 2.1. A common critique of stress research focuses on the circularity of some of its constructs and reasoning. For instance, consider a stressful life event such as the hospitalization of a child and the necessity to consider it both as a stressor in the life of the child and his family and as an outcome of a stress process. As ADS evolves with its more sophisticated longitudinal and nonlinear analytic methodologies, these critiques will be less compelling. For the moment and for the sake of this brief description of the paradigm, a circular form with multiple dual-direction arrows is adopted. The reciprocity of influences and the transactional qualities of relationships among and across domains are signaled by both the intersections of the quadrants and the dual-directed arrows around the circumference. Consideration of each quadrant should convey the substance and form of this developmental stress and coping paradigm and the way it calls upon key variables in developmental psychopathology and developmental assets orientations.

Beginning with the stress quadrant, reference is made to the types of stress that are familiar in the literature and have documented developmental and health consequences. For instance, each child encounters biological, psychological, and social milestones and transitions. Examples include the toddler's first steps, kindergartners entering school, teenagers entering puberty, and young people marrying. These are the developmental stressors, or transitional life events, of development.

Traditional psychosomatic medicine as well as contemporary health psychology and behavioral medicine have focused most heavily on health consequences of major life events. Among these are normative experiences such as entering high school or starting a new job, nonnormative events such as the death of a parent during childhood or getting arrested, and events that do not fit classification by normative life course transitions. Thus, being diagnosed with a serious chronic illness or undergoing a divorce are examples of nonnormative event changes. The horserace between major life events such as these and, in turn, what are termed *hassles,* or the microstressors of everyday life—efforts to quantify one type or the other as more strongly related to particular health outcomes—has been a feature of recent research in developmental psychopathology. This work teaches us the importance of avoiding overly simple variable-centered strategies and striving to capture the richness of conceptualizations that link, for instance, chronic role strain and acute life events, be they major or quotidian (Eckenrode & Gore, 1994; Pearlin, 1989). Notions of chronic stressors allow for consideration of a relatively vast child development literature on the adverse impacts of, for example, poverty (e.g., McLoyd, 1998). The distinction between chronic and acute stressors also serves applied developmental scientists when they can differentiate variables and processes in an acute experience. Thus, for instance, receiving a diagnosis of a chronic illness, such as diabetes, may be considered an acutely stressful event, whereas living with diabetes may be viewed as a chronic stressor (Wertlieb et al., 1990).

Health consequences associated with these stressors appear in the outcomes quadrant of Figure 2.1. Highlighted here are a commitment to multidimensional and multivariate assessments of health outcomes; an appreciation of both physical and mental health indexes, acknowledging both interdependence and unity; an emphasis on a balance among assets, health, and competence indexes; and a context of health as a part of a broader biopsychosocial adaptation. In traditional terms, ADS is concerned with the health and mental health of individuals. In contemporary terms, the health of developmental systems and communities must also be indexed.

For decades, it was these two domains—stressors and outcomes—that alone constituted the field of stress research. Consistent, reliable, and useful relationships were documented confirming the stress and illness correlation. Across scores of studies, statistically consistent relationships on the order of .30 were obtained and replicated. Thus, we could consistently account for close to 10% of the variance shared by stress and health—scientifically compelling, but hardly enough given the magnitude of the decisions that health care providers and policy makers must make. Using the ADS framework, stress and coping researchers pursue a quest for the other 90% of the variance. The expansions and differentiations of stressor types exemplified in the stress quadrant of Figure 2.1 contribute to the cause. In addition, it is the incorporation of the other two quadrants—coping processes and coping resources/moderators—that are the keys to achieving the goal. As these variables are incorporated into our models, explanatory and predictive power increases, and the quest for the other 90% advances.

The present model employs a specific conceptualization and assessment methodology for coping processes as advanced by Lazarus and Folkman (1984) and adapted for children by Wertlieb, Weigel, and Feldstein (1987). This model emphasizes three types or dimensions of coping behavior exhibited by children as well as adults. A focus on the appraisal process, the problem-solving process, or the emotion-management process can be distinguished and measured in the transactions between an individual and the environment as stress is encountered and as developmental or health consequences unfold. Other researchers have employed similar or competing coping theories, and many, perhaps most, are consistent with the broader stress and coping paradigm presented here (e.g., Aldwin, 1994; Basic Behavioral Science Task Force of the National Advisory Mental Health Council, 1996; Bonner & Finney, 1996; Compas, 1987; Fiese & Sameroff, 1989; Luthar & Zigler, 1991; Pellegrini, 1990; Sorensen, 1993; Stokols, 1992; Wallander & Varni, 1992; Wills & Filer, 1996).

Similarly, there is a wide range of coping resources/ moderators investigated in the literature, and Figure 2.1 selects a few examples to illustrate the range and demonstrate the relevance to the developmental psychopathology and developmental assets domains of ADS. Many of the

40 elements of the developmental assets framework reflect various dimensions of social support (e.g., family support, a caring school climate, a religious community, or school engagement). A large and complicated literature documents the manners in which social support in its diverse forms influences the relationships between health and illness. Key discriminations of pathways for such influences in terms of main effects, interactions, buffering effects, and mediation or moderation are elaborated in these studies (Cohen & Syme, 1985; Sarason, Sarason, & Pierce, 1990). Similarly complex, and even controversial, are formulations that call upon constructs and measures of intelligence or cognitive capacities or styles, as resources, moderators, or mediators of the stress-health relationship (Garmezy, 1994; Goleman, 1995). Diverse ranges of personality variables have also been employed in this work, including biologically oriented notions of temperament and psychological control orientations (Wertlieb, Weigel, & Feldstein, 1989).

Socioeconomic status (SES) is depicted in this resource quadrant, reminding us of the problem of redundancy and circularity. In the earlier description of types of stress I noted the manner in which poverty—a level or type of SES—could be modeled. Here, whether the SES is conceived as a factor that psychological researchers too often relegate to the status of background variable in a multivariate model or as a factor that sociologists might emphasize in a social structural analysis, its elements are crucial pieces of the contemporary context for the stress-health linkage. Again, the general stress and coping model in Figure 2.1 can accommodate considerable diversity in this coping resources/moderators domain; success in the quest will reflect the achievement of simplicity and parsimony.

A specific composite case example from our research program in pediatric psychology, or child health psychology, will serve to show the stress and coping paradigm in action. Again, the ADS framework orients us to significant demands for both knowledge generation and knowledge utilization in this example of a child's development, where understanding as well as application in terms of health care intervention and social policy are intertwined (Wertlieb, 1999). The example of Jason Royton involves each of the four domains shown in Figure 2.1.

Twelve-year-old Jason Royton was rushed to the pediatric hospital emergency room by his distraught father the morning after a vociferous battle in their home about whether Jason will get to see the R-rated movies that he contends all his friends are allowed to see. Within hours, the pediatrician emerges with the diagnosis: insulin-dependent diabetes mellitus (IDDM). In this scenario, the applied developmental scientist can quickly document multiple interacting dimensions of stress that potentially impinge on the child: the acute trauma of the health emergency and diagnosis, the parallel stress of the separation and autonomy struggle in the Roytons' lives, the onset of a chronic stressor of living with a life-threatening illness, and the initiation of multiple series of hassles or quotidian stressors associated with the precise regimen of diet, insulin injection, exercise, and medical care. Also immediate are the coping processes and a mélange of challenges and responses—shock, grief, denial, anxiety, appraisal (sizing up the nature of the challenges), problem solving (assessing and marshaling resources to comprehend and meet these challenges)—and for each individual, as well as for the family system, managing the feelings, threats, and disequilibria now introduced into their lives.

Influences of coping resources/moderators can be recognized as well. Mobilization of social support is part of the problem-solving process as we see Jason's grandmother arriving on the scene once they return home. Caring for the other two Royton children will be only a minor worry for Mr. and Mrs. Royton as they get through these initial days of their new status as a family with IDDM. Less minor and more surprising is the extent to which some of the protection offered by their comfortable middle-class lifestyle does not turn out to be what they thought it was. Clarifying their benefits and expenses in their new managed health care plan confirms that health insurance is not what it once was. IDDM, too, is not what it once was. Several decades ago, prior to the 1922 introduction of insulin therapy, the diagnosis was a death sentence. Now, people living with IDDM are part of a large group enjoying productive lives and pioneering novel challenges. The hope for ever-greater advances in biomedical science and technology is part of that life; a cure for IDDM, or a prevention, is an active research area.

Jason, meanwhile, is having his various "intelligences" challenged as his health care team launches him on an education for life with IDDM. Processing complex biomedical and psychosocial information, shifting notions of future threats and complications in and out of awareness, and anticipating how to live with this difference, especially when being different, has little cachet in a young adolescent's social circles. These stressors are moderated and will unfold as elements of the multidimensional health outcomes profile that must be considered in assessing the current or future health of a youngster with IDDM. Most immediate health outcomes focus on maintaining healthy blood glucose levels and some optimal adherence with the medical regimen. Psychological dimensions of accommodation of psychosocial strivings for autonomy and consolidation of a positive sense of competence and self-worth are related developmental processes. Undoubtedly, this set of experiences for Jason and his family engages the applied developmental scientist in an array of conceptual and methodological endeavors guided by frameworks of developmental psychopathology and developmental assets. (A more detailed consideration of IDDM in a stress and coping paradigm can be found in Wertlieb et al., 1990; a comprehensive survey of pediatric psychology is offered by Bearison, 1998.)

In elaborating the stress and coping paradigm as an example of an ADS heuristic, a key point to be made is that although any science can be described by mapping its domains of inquiry, to describe ADS, one must map domains of inquiry *and* action. The synergy and cross-fertilization between inquiry and action are core processes in advancing the ADS field. For instance, in the stress and coping paradigm example, note that each quadrant includes variables that are amenable to some range of intervention, influence, or change. Families, health or social service professionals, communities, or public policies may be among the instigators or agents of such changes. Stressors of various types can be reduced, modified, or ameliorated by individual actions or shifts in public policies. Coping processes can be taught or modified. Resources and moderators can be introduced, altered, strengthened, or weakened. Outcomes can be changed. The design and evaluation of such change processes constitutes key elements of ADS. These foci involve a number of special methods as well as ethical imperatives.

SPECIAL METHODS AND ETHICAL IMPERATIVES OF APPLIED DEVELOPMENTAL SCIENCE

Having sketched key historical and definitional parameters of ADS and having sampled a few of the many substantive domains of inquiry and action in ADS, this section shifts to consideration of some of the special research methods of and ethical issues in ADS. As evident in the sampling of inquiry domains, the ADS parameters are addressed only to a certain extent by traditional research methods and designs. Acknowledgment of the conceptual complexity imposed by the relevant developmental contextual and bioecological theories engages increasingly sophisticated methodological approaches. Orchestration of a researcher's perspectives on a set of problems with a society's perspectives on the problems—be they concerns about how to provide a type of care for children or how to sustain the health and development of an ill child, as considered in this sampling—requires extension and innovation by the applied developmental scientist. Some of the extension and innovation is relatively incremental. For example, study of children's adaptation to illness becomes the province of interdisciplinary teams of

endocrinologists, pediatric psychologists, nurses, and child psychiatrists. Bolder innovation advances ADS when families and communities are recognized and embraced as legitimate partners in the research enterprise, when the audience or "consumer" of research is broadened to include service providers and policy makers, and when traditional institutional structures and functions associated with the ivory tower of the university are challenged or modified. A leading perspective in capturing these extensions and innovations is termed *outreach scholarship* (Chibucos & Lerner, 1999; Lerner & Miller, 1998).

Jensen, Hoagwood, and Trickett (1999) contrast university-based research traditionally supported by the National Institute of Health in an efficacy model with an outreach model that reflects emergent approaches to research consistent with the parameters of ADS and basic to advancement in the numerous domains of inquiry and action listed in Table 2.1. Outreach research or outreach scholarship characterizes the "engaged university" (Kellogg Commission on the Future of State and Land-Grant Colleges, 1999) more so than the traditional ivory tower university (e.g., McCall, Groark, Strauss, & Johnson, 1995). In outreach scholarship, knowledge advances as a function of collaborations and partnerships between universities and communities such that the scientists and the children, families, and communities that they seek to understand and to help are defining problems, methods, and solutions together. Communities include policy makers as well as the families and service providers who both implement and consume interventions and programs. Lerner et al. (2000) properly noted that this involves a "sea change in the way scholars conduct their research" (p. 14) and then noted the principles of outreach scholarship that characterize these special collaborations and methods in ADS. These principles include the following:

(1) an enhanced focus on external validity, on the pertinence of the research to the actual ecology of human development . . . as opposed to contrived, albeit well-designed, laboratory type studies; (2) incorporating the values and needs of community collaborators within research activities; (3) full conceptualization and assessment of outcomes, that is, a commitment to understanding thoroughly both the direct and indirect effects of a research-based intervention program on youth and their context and to measuring these outcomes; (4) flexibility to fit local needs and circumstances, that is, an orientation to adjust the design or procedures . . . to the vicissitudes of the community within which the work is enacted; (5) accordingly, a willingness to make modifications to research methods in order to fit the circumstances of the local community; and (6) the embracing of long term perspectives, that is, the commitment of the university to remain in the community for a time period sufficient to see the realization

of community-valued developmental goals for its youth. . . . [In addition, these principles include] co-learning (between two expert systems—the community and the university); humility on the part of the university and its faculty, so that true co-learning and collaboration among equals can occur; and cultural integration, so that both the university and the community can appreciate each other's perspective. (Lerner et al., 2000, p. 14, italics added)

As articulated in the definitional parameters of ADS that opened this chapter and as reflected in the specific examples of inquiry and action, the extensions and innovations involved in outreach scholarship provide a means to address the conceptual and methodological challenges inherent in attending to the synergy and advancement of science and practice. Along with these tools and potentials comes a series of ethical imperatives reflecting responsibilities of both researchers and practitioners. These complex challenges have been a central concern to ADS from its earliest contemporary renditions, and the frameworks offered by Fisher and Tryon (1990) continue to serve well as an agenda.

Fisher and Tryon (1990) noted that along with the synergy and integration of research and application basic to the advance of the field, the applied developmental scientist is bound by the ethics of research, by the ethics of professional service, and by a complicated admixture that emerges with the acknowledgement of their interdependence. In addition, as the notion of outreach scholarship shifts the applied developmental scientist away from narrow and traditional notions of research subjects, patients, and clients to more appropriate notions of partners, consumers, and collaborators, there emerge areas as yet uncharted by the ethical standards of extant disciplines and professions. Indeed, even the imperative—that ethical behavior in ADS reflects some consensus or amalgam of the applied ethics embraced over time by diverse disciplines or traditions now teaming up in any of the areas of inquiry and action noted earlier—invokes challenge. Distinctive, perhaps even unique, ethical issues arise when the articulation of basic bioecological and contextual theories are parlayed into methods, measures, research designs, interventions, programs, and policies. Further, whether in the traditional disciplines or in emergent ADS, ethical considerations are encumbered and enriched by the mores and pressures of the historical context. Thus, the particular exigencies of our evolving multicultural and global societies that are manifested in concerns about diversity and cultural sensitivity and competence become deep and abiding concerns for the applied developmental scientist as she develops and tests her theories, designs and evaluates her interventions, provides health or social services, or engages policy makers around social programs and policies.

As one example of the special ethical challenges that ADS must master, return to our consideration of the research on early child care and education. As noted then, the sociohistorical shift involving the entry of more women into the workforce fueled the interest and concern of both society and developmental scientists. Hoffman (1990) described the manner in which bias in the scientific process characterized much of the early research on maternal employment. Knowledge was produced and applied with an emphasis on documenting defects or deficits in children left in nonparental day care. As the more sophisticated concepts and methods of ADS were engaged to address the social concern of nonparental care, there were more nuanced and accurate notions of direct and indirect effects of individual differences and quality variables in home-based and center-based care settings. In addition, as dire as were some of the ethical challenges in the conduct of the science aimed at generating understanding about the impacts of different care arrangements, the risks involved in the communication of findings to the public and to policy makers can also be harrowing and daunting. Hoffman (1990) concluded her account with the position that whereas "there is a social responsibility to make findings available for social policy and individual decision, there is also a responsibility to communicate the results accurately, and to educate the public about what the data can and cannot say. The tentative nature of our findings, their susceptibility to different interpretations, and the complications of translating them into individual or policy actions must be communicated to achieve an ethical science" (p. 268).

A second example to capture some of the particular ethical challenges facing ADS pertains especially to this particular historical moment where ADS is gaining recognition as an established discipline (Fisher et al., 1996). Yet, training programs to produce the next generation of applied developmental scientists are only just emerging. Whereas some of the root or allied disciplines may have sophisticated quality-control and credentialing procedures in place to increase the likelihood that ethical standards are met, ADS cannot borrow completely from these traditions. ADS must generate new and appropriate standards reflecting the exigencies of its special methods (e.g., outreach scholarship, university community partnerships) and the special expectations and demands faced by new applied developmental scientists as they pursue work in many, or any, of the domains of inquiry and action listed in Table 2.1.

For instance, traditional developmental psychologists can be trained, and their allegiance to the ethical standards of the American Psychological Association (1992) can be inculcated during their graduate training. Clinical psychologists, as another example, can be educated and held accountable both through their graduate training and later professional career in APA standards and in a variety of state and national licensing and credentialing conventions. Although applied developmental scientists now emerging from traditionally regulated fields such as clinical, school, or counseling psychology will have a starting point in these traditional ethical guidelines, neither they nor their colleagues from diverse disciplinary and multidisciplinary training bases are yet equipped with explicit ethical principles or credentials for the practice of ADS. Indeed, Koocher (1990) alerted the field to this challenge a decade ago, and although the sociopolitical scene has evolved in complex ways since then, the challenge remains for ADS to attend very seriously to issues of graduate training and ethics commensurate with its appropriately broadened scope and deepened mission.

CONCLUSIONS

The tributary of history that was developmental psychology has joined a river that is ADS. This contemporary face of developmental psychology is not really a new focus, but rather a contemporary manifestation of some of the field's earliest roots and priorities. As was originally the case, the understanding of children, their development, and their needs is pursued for the intellectual bounty only in part. It is the use of this knowledge to enhance the quality of life for children that launched the discipline of developmental psychology in the late nineteenth century and that propels ADS in the early twenty-first century.

Recently emerged and sophisticated theoretical frameworks have evolved and are required to address the parameters of ADS. In particular, bioecological theory and developmental contextual theory are useful in capturing the complexities of children's lives over time. As society, including families, caregivers, service providers, and policy makers, as well as youth themselves, convey their awareness of the needs and potentials of today's children, applied developmental scientists can collaborate to generate systematic understandings of how best to meet those needs and achieve those potentials. A large array of substantive areas of inquiry and action is likely to be advanced through such collaboration, and only a few examples were discussed in this chapter. The challenges in many of these areas are considerable—conceptually, methodologically, and ethically. ADS is aware of the challenge and is poised to pursue its potential for enhancing the well-being of children, adolescents, and families across the life span.

REFERENCES

Ackerman, B. P., Schoff, K., Levinson, K., Youngstrom, E., & Izard, C. (1999). The relations between cluster indexes of risk and promotion and the problem behaviors of 6- and 7-year-old children from economically disadvantaged families. *Developmental Psychology, 35,* 1355–1366.

Adams, M. J., Treiman, R., & Pressley, M. (1998). Reading, writing, and literacy. In W. Damon (Series Ed.), I. E. Sigel, & K. A. Renninger (Vol. Eds.), *Handbook of child psychology: Vol. 4. Child psychology in practice* (5th ed., pp. 275–356). New York: Wiley.

Adelman, H. S., & Taylor, L. (2000). Looking at school health and school reform policy through the lens of addressing barriers to learning. *Children's services: Social policy, research, and practice, 3*(2), 117–132.

Aldwin, C. M. (1994). *Stress, coping, and development.* New York: Guilford Press.

American Psychological Association. (1992). Ethical principles of psychologists and code of conduct. *American Psychologist, 47*(12), 1597–1611.

American Psychological Association. (2000). *APA's mission.* Retrieved from http://www.apa.org/about/mission.html, December 10, 2000.

American Psychological Society. (2000). *Our mission.* Retrieved from http://www.psychologicalscience.org/, December 10, 2000.

Baltes, P. B., Lindenberger, U., & Staudinger, U. M. (1998). Life-span theory in developmental psychology. In W. Damon (Series Ed.) & R. M. Lerner (Vol. Ed.), *Handbook of child psychology: Vol. 1. Theoretical models of human development* (5th ed., pp. 1029–1144). New York: Wiley.

Bardon, J. I. (1983). Psychology applied to education: A specialty in search of an identity. *American Psychologist, 38,* 185–196.

Basic Behavioral Science Task Force of the National Advisor Mental Health Council. (1996). Basic behavioral science research for mental health: Vulnerability and resilience. *American Psychologist, 51*(1), 22–28.

Bates, J. E., Pettit, G. S., & Dodge, K. A. (1995). Family and child factors in stability and change in children's aggressiveness in elementary school. In J. McCord (Ed.), *Coercion and punishment in long-term perspectives* (pp. 124–138). New York: Cambridge University Press.

Bearison, D. J. (1998). Pediatric psychology and children's medical problems. In W. Damon (Series Ed.), I. E. Sigel, & K. A. Renninger (Vol. Eds.), *Handbook of child psychology: Vol. 4. Child psychology in practice* (5th ed., pp. 635–712). New York: Wiley.

Belar, C. D., & Perry, N. W. (1992). National conference on scientist-practitioner educational training for the professional practice of psychology. *American Psychologist, 47*(1), 71–75.

Benson, P. L. (1997). *All kids are our kids: What communities must do to raise caring and responsible children and adolescents.* San Francisco: Jossey-Bass.

Benson, P. L., Leffert, N., Scales, P. C., & Blyth, D. A. (1998). Younger and older adults collaborating on retelling everyday stories. *Applied Developmental Science, 2*(3), 138–159.

Black, M. M., & Krishnakumar, A. (1998). Children in low income, urban settings: Interventions to promote mental health and well-being. *American Psychologist, 53,* 635–646.

Bonner, M. J., & Finney, J. W. (1996). A psychosocial model of children's health. In T. H. Ollendick & R. J. Prinz (Eds.), *Advances in child psychology* (Vol. 18). New York: Plenum Press.

Boring, E. G. (1950). *A history of experimental psychology* (2nd ed.). New York: Appleton-Century-Crofts.

Bornstein, M. H. (1995). Introduction to handbook of parenting. In M. Bornstein (Ed.), *Handbook of parenting* (Vol. 1, pp. xxiii–xxiv). Hillsdale, NJ: Erlbaum.

Brennemann, J. (1933). Pediatric psychology and the child guidance movement. *Journal of Pediatrics, 2*(1), 1–26.

Bronfenbrenner, U. (1995). Developmental psychology through space and time: A future perspective. In P. Moen, G. H. Elder, & K. Luscher (Eds.), *Examining lives in context: Perspectives on the ecology of human development* (pp. 619–647). Washington, DC: American Psychological Association.

Bronfenbrenner, U., & Ceci, S. J. (1994). Nature-nurture reconceptualized in developmental perspective: A biological model. *Psychological Review, 101*(4), 568–586.

Bronfenbrenner, U., Kessel, F., Kessen, W., & White, S. (1986). Toward a critical social history of developmental psychology. *American Psychologist, 41*(11), 1218–1230.

Bruck, M., Ceci, S. J., & Hembrooke, H. (1998). Reliability and credibility of young children's reports: From research to policy and practice. *American Psychologist, 53*(2), 136–151.

Cahan, E. D. (1992). John Dewey and human development. *Developmental Psychology, 28*(2), 205–214.

Cairns, R. B. (1998). The making of developmental psychology. In R. M. Lerner (Ed.), *Handbook of child psychology* (5th ed., Vol. 1, pp. 25–105). New York: Wiley.

Chibucos, T., & Lerner, R. M. (1999). *Serving children and families through community-university partnerships: Success stories.* Norwell, MA: Kluwer.

Cicchetti, D., & Sroufe, L. A. (2000). The past as prologue to the future: The times, they've been a-changin' [Editorial]. *Development and Psychopathology, 12*(3), 255–264.

Cicchetti, D., & Toth, S. L. (1998a). The development of depression in children and adolescents. *American Psychologist, 53*(2), 221–243.

Cicchetti, D., & Toth, S. L. (1998b). Perspectives on research and practice in developmental psychopathology. In W. Damon (Series Ed.), I. E. Sigel, & K. A. Renninger (Vol. Eds.), *Handbook of child psychology: Vol. 4. Child psychology in practice* (5th ed., pp. 479–484). New York: Wiley.

Clausen, J. A. (1995). Gender, contexts and turning points in adult's lives. In P. Moen, G. H. Elder, & K. Luscher (Eds.), *Examining lives in context: Perspectives on the ecology of human development* (pp. 365–389). Washington, DC: American Psychological Association.

Cohen, S., & Syme, S. L. (1985). *Social support and health.* Orlando, FL: Academic Press.

Coie, J. D., Watt, N. F., West, S. G., Hawkins, J. D., Asarnow, J. R., Markman, H. J., Ramey, S. L., Shure, M. B., & Long, B. (1993). The science of prevention: A conceptual framework and some directions for a national research program. *American Psychologist, 48*(10), 1013–1022.

Coley, R. L., & Chase-Lansdale, P. L. (1998). Adolescent pregnancy and parenthood: Recent evidence and future directions. *American Psychologist, 53*(2), 152–166.

Collins, W. A., Maccoby, E. E., Steinberg, L., Hetherington, E. M., & Bornstein, M. H. (2000). Contemporary research on parenting: The case for nature and nurture. *American Psychologist, 55*(2), 218–232.

Compas, B. E. (1987). Coping with stress during childhood and adolescence. *Psychological Bulletin, 101*(3), 393–403.

Cowan, P. A., Powell, D., & Cowan, C. P. (1998). Parenting interventions: A family systems perspective. In W. Damon (Series Ed.), I. E. Sigel, & K. A. Renninger (Vol. Eds.), *Handbook of child psychology: Vol. 4. Child psychology in practice* (5th ed., pp. 3–72). New York: Wiley.

Davidson, E. S., & Benjamin, L. T., Jr. (1987). A history of the child study movement in America. In J. A. Glover & Ronning, R. R. (Eds.), *Historical foundations of educational psychology* (pp. 41–60). New York: Plenum Press.

Elder, G. H. (1995). The life course paradigm: Social change and individual development. In P. Moen, G. H. Elder, & K. Luscher (Eds.), *Examining lives in context: Perspectives on the ecology of human development* (pp. 101–139). Washington, DC: American Psychological Association.

Elder, G. H. (1998). The life course and human development. In W. Damon (Series Ed.) & R. M. Lerner (Vol. Ed.), *Handbook of child psychology: Vol. 1. Theoretical models of human development* (5th ed., pp. 939–991). New York: Wiley.

Elkind, D. (in press). Early childhood education. In R. M. Lerner, F. Jacobs, & D. Wertlieb (Eds.), *Promoting positive child, adolescent, and family development.* Thousand Oaks, CA: Sage. Manuscript in preparation.

Emery, R. E., & Laumann-Billings, L. (1998). An overview of the nature, causes, and consequences of abusive family relationships: Toward differentiating maltreatment and violence. *American Psychologist, 53*(2), 121–135.

Fagan, T. K. (1992). Compulsory schooling, child study, clinical psychology, and special education. *American Psychologist, 47*(2), 236–243.

Fagan, T. K. (2000). Practicing school psychology: A turn-of-the-century perspective. *American Psychologist, 55*(7), 754–757.

Featherman, D. L., & Lerner, R. M. (1985). Ontogenesis and sociogenesis: Problematics for theory about development across the lifespans. *American Sociological Review, 50,* 659–676.

Fiese, B. H., & Sameroff, A. J. (1989). Family context in pediatric psychology: A transactional perspective. *Journal of Pediatric Psychology, 14*(2), 293–314.

Fisher, C. B., & Lerner, R. M. (Eds.). (1994). *Applied developmental psychology.* New York: McGraw-Hill.

Fisher, C. B., Murray, J. P., Dill, J. R., Hagen, J. W., Hogan, M. J., Lerner, R. M., Rebok, G. W., Sigel, I., Sostek, A. M., Spencer, M. B., & Wilcox, B. (1993). The national conference on graduate education in the applications of developmental science across the lifespan. *Journal of Applied Developmental Psychology, 14,* 1–10.

Fisher, C. B., Murray, J. P., & Sigel, I. E. (Eds.). (1996). *Applied developmental science: Graduate training for diverse disciplines and educational settings* (Vol. 13) Norwood, NJ: Ablex.

Fisher, C. B., & Tryon, W. W. (Eds.). (1990). *Ethics in applied developmental psychology: Emerging issues in an emerging field* (Vol. 4). Norwood, NJ: Ablex.

Fishman, D. B. (1999). *The case for pragmatic psychology.* New York: New York University Press.

Fonagy, P., & Target, M. (2000). The place of psychodynamic theory in developmental psychopathology. *Development and Psychopathology, 12*(3), 407–426.

Fox, R. E. (1982). The need for a reorientation of clinical psychology. *American Psychologist, 37*(9), 1051–1057.

Frank, G. (1984). The boulder model: History, rationale, and critique. *Professional Psychology: Research and Practice, 15*(3), 417–435.

Garmezy, N. (1994). Reflections and commentary on risk, resilience, and development. In R. J. Haggerty, Sherrod, L., Garmezy, N., & Rutter, M. (Eds.), *Stress, risk, and resilience in children and adolescents: Processes, mechanisms, and interventions* (pp. 1–18). Cambridge, UK: Cambridge University Press.

Garmezy, N., & Rutter, M. (1983). *Stress, coping, and development in children.* New York: McGraw Hill.

Garner, W. R. (1972). The acquisition and application of knowledge: A symbiotic relation. *American Psychologist, 27,* 941–946.

Goleman, D. (1995). *Emotional intelligence.* New York: Bantam Books.

Gore, S., & Eckenrode, J. (1994). Context and process in research on risk and resilience. In R. J. Haggerty, L. R. Sherrod, N. Garmezy, & M. Rutter (Eds.), *Stress, risk, and resilience in children and adolescents: Processes, mechanisms, and interventions* (pp. 19–63). Cambridge, UK: Cambridge University Press.

Haggerty, R. J., Sherrod, L. R., Garmezy, N., & Rutter, M. (Eds.). (1994). *Stress, risk and resilience in children and adolescents: Processes, mechanisms and interventions.* Cambridge, UK: Cambridge University Press.

Harris, J. R. (1998). *The nurture assumption: Why children turn out the way they do.* New York: Free Press.

Harris, J. R. (2000). Socialization, personality development, and the child's environments: Comment on Vandell. *Developmental Psychology, 36*(2), 711–723.

Hauser, S. T., Vieyra, M., Jacobson, A., & Wertlieb, D. (1985). Vulnerability and resilience in adolescence: Views from the family. *Journal of Early Adolescence, 5,* 81–100.

Hetherington, E. M. (1998). Introduction: Relevant issues in developmental science [Special issue]. *American Psychologist, 53*(2), 93–94.

Hetherington, E. M., Bridges, M., & Insabella, G. M. (1998). What matters? What does not? Five perspectives on the association between marital transitions and children's adjustment. *American Psychologist, 53*(2), 167–184.

Hoffman, L. W. (1990). Bias and social responsibility in the study of maternal employment. In C. B. Fisher & W. W. Tyron (Eds.), *Ethics in applied developmental psychology: Emerging issues in an emerging field* (Vol. 4, pp. 253–272). Norwood, NJ: Ablex.

Huston, A. C., & Wright, J. C. (1998). Mass media and children's development. In W. Damon (Series Ed.), I. E. Sigel, & K. A. Renninger (Vol. Eds.), *Handbook of child psychology: Vol. 4. Child psychology in practice* (5th ed., pp. 999–1058). New York: Wiley.

Jensen, P., Hoagwood, K., & Trickett, E. (1999). Ivory towers or earthen trenches? Community collaborations to foster "real world" research. *Applied Developmental Science, 3*(4), 206–212.

Jessor, R., Turbin, M. S., & Costa, F. M. (1998). Risk and protection in successful outcomes among disadvantaged adolescents. *Applied Developmental Science, 2*(4), 194–208.

Kanfer, F. H. (1990). The scientist-practitioner connection: A bridge in need of constant attention. *Professional Psychology: Research and Practice, 21*(4), 264–270.

Kaplan, R. M. (2000). Two pathways to prevention. *American Psychologist, 55*(4), 382–396.

Kellogg Commission on the Future of State and Land-Grant Colleges. (1999). *Returning to our roots: The engaged institution.* Washington, DC: National Association of State Universities and Land-Grant Colleges.

Kendall, P. C. (1984). Social cognition and problem solving: A developmental and child-clinical interface. In B. Gholson & T. L. Rosenthal (Eds.), *Applications of cognitive developmental theory* (pp. 115–148). Orlando, FL: Academic Press.

Koch, S., & Leary, D. E. (Eds.). (1985). *A century of psychology as science.* New York: McGraw-Hill.

Koocher, G. P. (1990). Practicing applied developmental psychology: Playing the game you can't win. In I. E. Sigel (Ed.), *Ethics in applied developmental psychology: Emerging issues in an emerging field* (Vol. 4, pp. 215–225). Norwood, NJ: Ablex.

Lamb, M. E. (1998). Children in poverty: Development, public policy, and practice. In W. Damon (Series Ed.), I. E. Sigel, &

K. A. Renninger (Vol. Eds.), *Handbook of child psychology: Vol. 4. Child psychology in practice* (5th ed., pp. 73–134). New York: Wiley.

Lamb, M. E. (2000). The effects of quality of care on child development. *Applied Developmental Science, 4*(3), 112–115.

Lazarus, R. S., & Folkman, S. (1984). *Stress, appraisal and coping.* New York: Springer.

Lerner, R. M. (1998). Theories of human development: Contemporary perspectives. In R. M. Lerner (Ed.), *Theoretical models of human development* (5th ed., Vol. 1, pp. 1–24). New York: Wiley.

Lerner, R. M., Fisher, C. B., & Weinberg, R. A. (1997). Applied developmental science: Scholarship for our times. *Applied Developmental Science, 1*(1), 2–3.

Lerner, R. M., Fisher, C. B., & Weinberg, R. A. (2000). Toward a science for and of the people: Promoting civil society through the application of developmental science. *Child Development, 71*(1), 11–20.

Lerner, R. M., Jacobs, F, & Wertlieb, D. (Ed.). (2002). *Handbook of applied developmental science: Promoting positive child, adolescent, and family development: A handbook of program and policy innovations.* Manuscript in preparation.

Lerner, R. M., & Miller, J. R. (1998). Developing multidisciplinary institutes to enhance the lives of individuals and families: Academic potentials and pitfalls. *Journal of Public Service and Outreach, 3*(1), 64–73.

Lerner, R. M., Wolf, M., Schliemann, A., & Mistry, J. (2001). Child development and schools. In R. M. Lerner, M. A. Easterbrooks, & J. Mistry (Eds.), *Developmental psychology* (Vol. 6). New York: Wiley.

Levy, L. H. (1984). The metamorphosis of clinical psychology: Toward a new charter as human services psychology. *American Psychologist, 39*(5), 486–494.

Loeber, R., & Stouthamer-Loeber, M. (1998). Development of juvenile aggression and violence: Some common misconceptions and controversies. *American Psychologist, 53*(2), 242–259.

Luthar, S. S., Cicchetti, D., & Becker, B. (2000). The construct of resilience: A critical evaluation and guidelines for future research. *Child Development, 71*, 543–562.

Luthar, S. S., & Zigler, E. (1991). Vulnerability and competence: A review of research on resilience in childhood. *American Journal of Orthopsychiatry, 61*(1), 6–22.

Magnusson, D. (Ed.). (1996). *The lifespan development of individuals: Behavioral, neurobiological, and psychosocial perspectives. A synthesis.* New York: Cambridge University Press.

Marsella, A. J. (1998). Toward a "global-community psychology": Meeting the needs of a changing world. *American Psychologist, 53*(12), 1282–1291.

Martland, N., & Rothbaum, F. (1999). Cameo feature news: University and community partnership disseminates child development information. In T. R. Chibucos & R. M. Lerner (Eds.), *Serving children and families through community-university partnerships: Success stories* (pp. 173–180). Boston: Kluwer.

Masten, A. S., & Coatsworth, J. D. (1998). The development of competence in favorable and unfavorable environments: Lessons from research on successful children. *American Psychologist, 53*(2), 205–220.

Masterpasqua, F. (1981). Toward a synergism of developmental and community psychology. *American Psychology, 36*(7), 782–786.

McCall, R. B. (1996). The concept and practice of education, research, and public service in university psychology departments. *American Psychologist, 51*(4), 379–388.

McCall, R., & Groark, C. (2000). The future of applied child development research and public policy. *Child Development, 71*, 197–204.

McCall, R. B., Groark, C. J., Strauss, M. S., & Johnson, C. N. (1995). The University of Pittsburgh Office of Child Development: An experiment in promoting interdisciplinary applied human development. *Journal of Applied Developmental Psychology, 16*, 593–612.

McLoyd, V. C. (1998). Socioeconomic disadvantage and child development. *American Psychologist, 53*(2), 185–204.

National Institute of Child Health and Human Development Early Child Care Research Network. (2000). Characteristics and quality of child care for toddlers and preschoolers. *Applied Developmental Science, 4*(3), 116–135.

Nickols, S. Y. (2001). Family and consumer sciences in the United States. In N. J. Smelser & P. B. Baltes (Eds.), *International encyclopedia of the social and behavioral sciences* (Vol. 8, pp. 5279–5286). Oxford, UK: Elsevier.

Noam, G. G. (1998). Clinical-developmental psychology: Toward developmentally differentiated interventions. In W. Damon (Series Ed.), I. E. Sigel, & K. A. Renninger (Vol. Eds.), *Handbook of child psychology: Vol. 4. Child psychology in practice* (5th ed., pp. 585–634). New York: Wiley.

Parke, R. D. (1992). A final word: The passing of the editorial mantle and some reflections on the field. *Developmental Psychology, 28*(6), 987–989.

Parke, R. D., Ornstein, P. A., Reiser, J. J., & Zahn-Waxler, C. (Eds.). (1994). *A century of developmental psychology.* Washington, DC: American Psychological Association.

Pearlin, L. I. (1989). The sociological study of stress. *Journal of Health and Social Behavior, 30*, 241–256.

Pellegrini, D. S. (1990). Psychosocial risk and protective factors in childhood. *Developmental and Behavioral Pediatrics, 11*(4), 201–209.

Perry, N. W., Jr. (1979). Why clinical psychology does not need alternative training models. *American Psychologist, 34*(7), 603–611.

Pittman, K., & Irby, M. (1996, January). *Promoting investment in life skills for youth: Beyond indicators for survival and problem prevention.* Paper presented at an interactional workshop, "Monitoring and measuring the state of children: Beyond survival," Jerusalem, Israel.

Ramey, C. T., & Ramey, S. L. (1998). Early intervention and early experience. *American Psychologist, 53*(2), 109–120.

Renninger, K. A. (1998). Developmental psychology and instruction: Issues from and for practice. In W. Damon (Series Ed.), I. E. Sigel, & K. A. Renninger (Vol. Eds.), *Handbook of child psychology: Vol. 4. Child psychology in practice* (5th ed., pp. 211–274). New York: Wiley.

Richters, J. E. (1997). The Hubble hypothesis and the developmentalist's dilemma. *Development and Psychopathology, 9,* 193–229.

Rutter, M., & Sroufe, L. A. (2000). Developmental psychopathology: Concepts and challenges. *Development and Psychopathology, 12*(3), 265–296.

Sarason, B. R., Sarason, I. G., & Pierce, G. R. (1990). *Social support: An interactional view.* New York: Wiley.

Scales, P. C., Benson, P. L., Leffert, N., & Blyth, D. A. (2000). Contribution of developmental assets to the prediction of thriving among adolescents. *Applied Developmental Science, 4*(1), 27–46.

Scales, P., & Leffert, N. (1999). *Developmental assets: A synthesis of the scientific research on adolescent development.* Minneapolis, MN: Search Institute.

Scarr, S. (1998). American child care today. *American Psychologist, 53*(2), 95–108.

Schneiderman, N., Speers, M., Silva, J. M., Tomes, H., & Gentry, J. H. (Ed.). (2001). *Integrating behavioral and social sciences with public health.* Washington, DC: American Psychological Association.

Schon, D. (1983). *The reflective practitioner.* New York: Basic Books.

Schwebel, D. C., Plumert, J. M., & Pick, H. L. (2000). Integrating basic and applied developmental research: A new model for the twenty-first century. *Child Development, 71*(1), 222–230.

Sears, R. R. (1975). Your ancients revisited: A history of child development. In E. M. Hetherington (Ed.), *Review of child development research* (Vol. 5). Chicago: University of Chicago Press.

Siegel, A. W., & White, S. H. (1982). The child study movement: Early growth and development of the symbolized child. In H. W. Reese (Ed.), *Advances in child development and behavior* (Vol. 17, pp. 233–285). New York: Academic Press.

Sigel, I. E., & Cocking, R. R. (1980). Editors' message. *Journal of Applied Developmental Psychology, 1*(1), i–iii.

Sigel, I. E., & Renninger, K. A. (Eds.). (1998). *Handbook of child psychology: Vol. 4. Child psychology in practice* (5th ed.). New York: Wiley.

Sorensen, E. S. (1993). *Children's stress and coping: A family perspective.* New York: Guilford Press.

Sroufe, L. A., & Rutter, M. (1984). The domain of developmental psychopathology. *Child Development, 55,* 17–29.

Stokols, D. (1992). Establishing and maintaining healthy environments: Toward a social ecology of health promotion. *American Psychologist, 47*(1), 6–22.

Strauss, S. (1998). Cognitive development and science education: Toward a middle level model. In W. Damon (Series Ed.), I. E. Sigel, & K. A. Renninger (Vol. Eds.), *Handbook of child psychology: Vol. 4. Child psychology in practice* (5th ed., pp. 357–400). New York: Wiley.

Vandell, D. L. (2000). Parents, peer groups, and other socializing influences. *Developmental Psychology, 36*(6), 699–710.

Wallander, J. L., & Varni, J. W. (1992). Social support and adjustment in chronically ill and handicapped children. *American Journal of Community Psychology, 17*(2), 185–201.

Webster-Stratton, C. (1994). Advancing videotape parent training: A comparison study. *Journal of Consulting and Clinical Psychology, 62*(3), 583–593.

Weissberg, R. P., & Greenberg, M. T. (1998). School and community competence-enhancement and prevention programs. In W. Damon (Series Ed.), I. E. Sigel, & K. A. Renninger (Vol. Eds.), *Handbook of child psychology: Vol. 4. Child psychology in practice* (5th ed., pp. 877–954). New York: Wiley.

Wertlieb, D. L. (1985). Clinical child psychology as an applied developmental psychology: Toward a redefinition of mission and training. In J. Tuma (Ed.), *Proceedings: Conference on training clinical child psychologists* (pp. 64–68). Washington, DC: American Psychological Association.

Wertlieb, D. L. (1997). Children whose parents divorce: Life trajectories and turning points. In I. Gotlieb & B. Wheaton (Eds.), *Stress and adversity over the life course: Trajectories and turning points* (pp. 179–196). Cambridge, UK: Cambridge University Press.

Wertlieb, D. L. (1999). Society of pediatric psychology presidential address, 1997: Calling all collaborators, advancing pediatric psychology. *Journal of Pediatric Psychology, 24*(1), 77–83.

Wertlieb, D. L. (2001). Applied developmental science. In R. M. Lerner, M. A. Easterbrooks, & J. Mistry (Eds.), *Developmental psychology* (Vol. 6). New York: Wiley.

Wertlieb, D. L., & Feldman, D. H. (1996). Doctoral education in applied child development. In C. B. Fisher, J. P. Murray, & I. E. Sigel (Eds.), *Applied developmental science: Graduate training for diverse disciplines and educational settings* (Vol. 13, pp. 121–141). Norwood, NJ: Ablex.

Wertlieb, D. L., Jacobson, A., & Hauser, S. (1990). The child with diabetes: A developmental stress and coping perspective. In P. T. Costa & G. R. VandenBos (Eds.), *Psychological aspects of serious illness: Chronic conditions, fatal diseases, and clinical care* (pp. 65–101). Washington, DC: American Psychological Association.

Wertlieb, D. L., Weigel, C., & Feldstein, M. (1987). Measuring children's coping. *American Journal of Orthopsychiatry, 57,* 548–503.

Wertlieb, D. L., Weigel, C., & Feldstein, M. (1989). Stressful experiences, temperament, and social support: Impact on children's behavior symptoms. *Journal of Applied Developmental Psychology, 10,* 487–503.

Wills, T. A., & Filer, M. (1996). Stress-coping model of adolescent substance use. In T. H. Ollendick & R. J. Prinz (Eds.), *Advances in child psychology* (Vol. 18). New York: Plenum Press.

Winett, R. A. (1995). A framework for health promotion and disease prevention programs. *American Psychologist, 50,* 341–350.

Ysseldyke, J. E. (1982). The spring hill symposium on the future of psychology in the schools. *American Psychologist, 37*(5), 547–552.

Zigler, E. (1980). Welcoming a new journal. *Journal of Applied Developmental Psychology, 1*(1), 1–6.

Zigler, E. (1998). A place of value for applied and policy studies. *Child Development, 69*(2), 532–542.

Zigler, E. F., & Finn-Stevenson, M. (1999). Applied developmental psychology. In M. H. Bornstein & M. E. Lamb (Eds.), *Developmental psychology: An advanced textbook* (4th ed.). Mahwah, NJ: Erlbaum.

PART TWO
INFANCY

CHAPTER 3

Infant Perception and Cognition

LESLIE B. COHEN AND CARA H. CASHON

Research on infant perception and cognition has grown exponentially over the past four decades. In most respects, this explosion of research has led to spectacular advances in knowledge and appreciation of infants and their abilities. However, this same growth has also led to conflicting theoretical views, contradictory conclusions, and even heated exchanges between investigators—all of which seem to make a coherent picture of infant perceptual and cognitive development difficult if not impossible to achieve. One goal of this chapter is to cut through some of the extravagant claims and rhetorical arguments to examine in some detail what the evidence really

indicates. We shall approach this task from an information-processing point of view by continually asking two interrelated questions: (a) How are infants actually processing the information in their environment? and (b) In what way does that processing change with age and experience? Fortunately, when one takes this approach, an organized and reasonably consistent picture of infant perception and cognition emerges. Furthermore, a number of domain-general propositions, such as those mentioned later in this chapter in the section on information processing, seem to help to explain both infants' information processing at a given age and how that processing develops over time. In this chapter we shall both describe these information-processing principles and—when possible—use them as a convenient tool for organizing the many findings on numerous topics within the domain of infant perception and cognition.

Preparation of this chapter was supported in part by NIH grant HD-23397 to the first author from the National Institute of Child Health and Human Development.

INFANT PERCEPTION VERSUS INFANT COGNITION

Before discussing the findings in the area of infant perception and cognition, the first step should be at least to make some crude attempt to define what we mean by *infant perception and cognition*. The reader may have noticed our tendency so far to treat infant perception and cognition as a single domain rather than as two distinct entities. Even that issue is unclear and debatable. Some, such as Mandler (1992, 2000b), overtly assume that infant perception and cognition are two distinct domains with little communication between them. Under this view, *infant perception* may be seen as including lower-level, automatic processes such as noticing the features of objects and responding to those features. *Infant cognition,* on the other hand, may be seen as involving higher-level, conceptual processes such as making inferences about the functions or meanings of objects. Others, such as Quinn and Eimas (2000), argue that both are aspects of a single domain and that they differ more in degree than in kind.

Our opinion falls closer to Quinn and Eimas's than to Mandler's. We also see the difference between perception and cognition to be more a matter of degree than of kind. Whether one is dealing with perceiving size constancy—perceiving the actual size of an object seen at different distances—or understanding the meaning of a complex causal event in which one object pushes another object across a table, it is the nature of the underlying relationship that must be perceived or understood. In size constancy, the underlying relationship is the size of one object relative to the object's distance or to the size of other objects; in the causal event, it is the movement of one object in space and time relative to the movement of the second object. Some relationships may be perceived automatically and effortlessly; others require a more active comparison. But from an information-processing perspective, they all can be understood in terms of sets of relationships. Our task is to describe the nature of these relationships and how they contribute to some overall organization or information-processing hierarchy.

HISTORICAL ANTECEDENTS

We begin by considering some historical antecedents of the current popularity of research on infant perception and cognition. Certainly interest in infants and what they can perceive and understand has existed for centuries. Classic debates by philosophers such as Locke versus Rousseau exist in modified form to this day. Biologists' and psychologists' biographies of their own babies, such as Teidemann, Preyer, Darwin, and Piaget, provided important insights into their

infants' reactions, although they often were less than totally objective accounts (see Kessen, 1965). More objective experiments on infants' responsiveness to stimulation occasionally appeared in the early 1900s. For example, McDougall (1908) reported finding differential infant fixation times to stimuli varying in color. Blanton (1917) was one of the first to find that infants will pursue a moving stimulus visually, and Irwin (1941) found that changes in light intensity produced modifications in an infant's activity.

Somewhat later, in the 1950s and 1960s, studies began to appear that measured heart rate and sucking measures, as well as visual fixation. Both auditory (e.g., Bridger, 1961) and olfactory (Engen, Lipsitt, Lewis, & Kaye, 1963) stimulation were found to produce changes in heart rate in newborn infants. Furthermore, these studies also showed that repeated presentations of these stimuli led to habituation of the response. A group of Russian investigators (Bronshtein, Antonova, Kamentskaya, Luppova, & Sytova, 1958) presented auditory, olfactory, and visual stimuli to infants under 1 month of age. They found suppression of sucking to all three types of stimulation and habituation of the suppression over trials. Often infants were presented with repetitions of a bright light or 90 dB white noise. Many of these studies examined what Sokolov (1963) had referred to as the "orienting reflex," a pattern of physiological and behavioral changes to the presentation of a novel stimulus. There were several reports that infants exhibited both an orienting response and a decline in that response—habituation—with repeated presentations of the same stimulus. According to Sokolov, habituation of the orienting reflex reflected a form of memory, a point that would be picked up in the 1970s when studies of infant memory first became popular.

These studies and many similar ones demonstrated that infants—even very young infants—were sensitive to stimulation from a number of modalities, and perhaps that they even had some memory of that stimulation. Yet these studies did very little to address more interesting questions about how that stimulation was processed or remembered. This may in part be due to the complexity of the methods involved; in order to conduct these experiments, one needed rather elaborate and expensive recording equipment as well as a team of investigators to monitor that equipment and the infant.

MODERN TECHNIQUES FOR ASSESSING INFANT PERCEPTION AND COGNITION

Infant Visual Preference

Two seminal studies, conducted independently on essentially the same topic, both published in 1958, radically reduced the potential complexity of the experimental method and led to a dramatic change in the nature of research on infant perception and cognition. Berlyne (1958) measured the visual fixations of 3- to 9-month-old infants. On each trial, two black and white checkerboard patterns that differed in brightness or complexity were placed on a display board in front of each infant. An observer who could not see the patterns called out the direction of gaze of the infant—a technique that allowed Berlyne to determine to which pattern the infant first fixated. One of Berlyne's findings was that infants first looked at a complex pattern, such as a checkerboard with many squares, more than at a simple pattern, such as a checkerboard with few squares.

At the same time Fantz, known to many as the founder of modern research on infant perception, began a series of studies (Fantz, 1958, 1961, 1963; Fantz, Ordy, & Udelf, 1962) on infants' visual preferences. Patterns, such as checkerboards with differing numbers of squares, vertical stripes of different thicknesses, and drawings of regular versus scrambled faces were shown to infants two at a time. Fantz's procedure was a methodological advance over Berlyne's in that because of the placement of the infant in a testing chamber, the experimenter could actually see a reflection of the stimulus on the infants' cornea. Also, Fantz measured total looking time rather than just the direction of first look. Among Fantz's findings were that infants tend to prefer patterned surfaces to uniform surfaces and complex patterns to simple patterns.

Both Berlyne's and Fantz's studies represented real advances over previous research in the field. Their innovations included demonstration of a simple, reliable, inexpensive technique for measuring infant visual attention, systematic manipulation of the stimuli presented to infants, and examination of differences in the pattern of visual attention over age. Their technique capitalized on what may be considered infants' natural preferences for some stimuli over others; it has come to be called *the visual preference paradigm.*

The visual preference paradigm is still a very popular technique. Numerous studies by many investigators over the past 40 years have used some version of this visual preference paradigm to examine topics ranging from infant visual acuity to pattern perception, preferences for complexity, and even face perception. Several of these topics are discussed in greater detail later in this chapter.

Novelty Preferences and Habituation

The visual preference technique works well when infants have a natural preference for certain stimuli—that is, when from the outset, infants have the tendency to look at some stimuli longer than at others. When this occurs, we can infer not only that infants have a preference for one stimulus over another, but also that infants can discriminate between those

stimuli. However, many cases exist in which infants do not display an initial preference, yet investigators need to know whether the infants can discriminate between the stimuli. In such cases, investigators often rely on a paradigm that combines the visual preference technique with habituation. Once again, the field is indebted to Fantz for leading the way. In 1964, Fantz reported a study in which infants were shown two magazine pictures simultaneously, side by side, and the infants' looking times to the pictures were recorded. As trials progressed, the picture on one side remained the same, but the one on the other side changed from trial to trial. Over the course of the experiment, infants gradually came to look more and more at the side with novel pictures.

This preference for novelty has become the underlying basis of the most widely used research tool for investigating infant perception and cognition—the infant visual habituation paradigm. Although many variations of this paradigm exist, a prototypical example would be to repeatedly present one visual stimulus until an infant's looking time habituates to some criterion level, such as 50% of the infant's initial looking time. Novel and familiar test stimuli would then be presented to see if the infant looks longer at (i.e., recovers to) the novel ones. Doing so indicates that the infant can differentiate between the novel and the familiar stimuli, even though initially the infant may not have had a natural preference for one over the other.

As we shall see later in this chapter, the infant visual habituation paradigm has been used for over three decades to investigate basic and esoteric questions related to infant perception, attention, memory, language acquisition, object knowledge, categorization, and concept formation. Differences in habituation and recovery have been reported between normal and aberrant infants, and both habituation rates and preferences for novelty appear to be moderately correlated with later IQ.

As simple and straightforward as infant preferences for novelty and habituation appear to be, the situation is actually more complicated. Many people assume that infants always have a preference for novelty. In reality, several studies have shown that a preference for familiarity often precedes a preference for novelty. Furthermore, this early preference for familiarity seems to be stronger in younger infants. It is also stronger when the information-processing task is more complex or difficult for the infant.

Hunter and Ames (1988) have summarized these conditions. According to them, the time it takes for an infant to be familiarized to a stimulus—that is, show a novelty preference—depends upon both the age of the infant and the complexity of the stimulus. For example, the familiarity preferences for older infants (e.g., those over 6 months of age) should be very brief compared to those for younger infants (e.g., those under 6 months of age), and within an age group the familiarity preferences should vary according to stimulus complexity. The bottom line is that if younger infants are repeatedly shown very simple stimuli—or if older infants are shown moderately complex stimuli—both groups are likely to produce the classic monotonically decreasing habituation curve. On the other hand, if infants at either age are shown dynamic moving scenes involving multiple objects, they are likely to prefer familiar scenes prior to preferring novel ones. Therefore, it becomes important in such studies to habituate all infants to a relatively stringent criterion and to include both familiar and novel stimuli at the end to test that the infant indeed prefers novelty. Unfortunately, many infant habituation studies today do not adhere to these procedures.

Other Techniques

Several other techniques have also been used to investigate questions related to infant perception and cognition. In some, infants play a more active role, such as crawling, walking, or reaching. In others, physiological indicators—such as heart rate or cortical evoked potentials—rather than behavioral indicators are assessed. Although some of these techniques are unrelated to visual preference and habituation, others are more related than one might first assume. For example, infant operant conditioning is often used and has many similarities to visual habituation (e.g., Bower, 1966a). In these studies, infants are first conditioned to respond to one stimulus and then tested with novel stimuli that vary in some systematic way from the conditioned stimulus. The logic is similar to that in habituation studies. In habituation, responses are artificially decreased to one stimulus. Discrimination is assessed by determining whether that *decrease* generalizes to other stimuli. In conditioning, responses are artificially increased to one stimulus, and discrimination is assessed by determining whether that *increase* generalizes to other stimuli.

A variety of conditioning studies have also been used to investigate infants' perception of speech (e.g., Eimas, Siqueland, Jusczyk, & Vigorito, 1971), all of which relate either to visual preferences, visual habituation, or both. Such studies have frequently used a high-amplitude sucking procedure in which infants first are conditioned to suck in order to hear a sequence of speech sounds. That procedure continues until their sucking habituates, at which time the speech sounds are changed and recovery of sucking is assessed. Many more recent studies of infant speech perception and early language ability have turned to visual attention as the measure (e.g., Jusczyk & Aslin, 1995). For example, infants may learn to look at a specific location to hear a particular sound. Then a new sound is introduced and changes in looking time are assessed. We find it interesting that just as in

the visual perception literature, some disagreement exists as to whether the infants should look longer or shorter when a novel stimulus is presented. We cannot list all possible techniques that can be used to assess infant perception and cognition, but as we have described, many are related either procedurally or logically to two very important techniques—infant visual preferences and visual habituation.

THEORETICAL PERSPECTIVES

Several theoretical perspectives have been influential in directing research on infant perception and cognition over the past forty years. It is impossible to adequately represent any of these viewpoints in just a single chapter. Indeed, some of them require entire books to explain them adequately. Certainly Piagetian theory, Gibsonian theory, dynamical systems, and connectionist modeling fall into this category. Others are more approaches to studying infant development than they are complete theories. They make certain assumptions and predictions and use certain research techniques to investigate those predictions, but they probably do not qualify as formal theories. Nativism, cognitive neuroscience, and information processing tend to fall into this category. Brief descriptions are provided in the following sections for each of these theoretical perspectives. It should be understood that each description is merely a cursory overview. Any real understanding requires reading much more, including the references provided with each description.

Piagetian Theory

The one researcher who has had the longest—and many would say the most profound—impact on the field of infant cognition and perception is Piaget. Originally a biologist, Piaget developed a theory of cognitive development by observing his own children's behavior on certain tasks during infancy and childhood (e.g., Piaget, 1927, 1936/1952, 1937/1954). For many years, psychologists in the United States disregarded Piaget's theory because his research methods were considered imprecise and his ideas about cognition were in conflict with the behaviorist's zeitgeist of the day. However, that position began to change as comprehensive reviews of Piaget's theory became available in English (e.g., Flavell, 1963; Hunt, 1961). As the reader will see, the modern infant cognition researcher often uses Piaget's theory and observations as a springboard for further ideas and research.

Piaget's (1937/1954) view of infant development is that infants develop an understanding of the world—that is, an understanding about objects, space, time, and causality—by interacting with the environment. Borrowing from the field of biology, Piaget (1936/1952, 1937/1954) believed that infants develop through the processes of assimilation and accommodation. Piaget also believed that development is stagelike and discontinuous. Furthermore, the infant, according to Piaget, is as an active learner who is motivated to learn about the world; but cognitive development, like other aspects of development, represents an interaction between maturation and learning.

Piaget specified four major periods corresponding to different ages of the developing child. The first period of Piaget's (1937/1954) theory of cognitive development, the *sensorimotor period,* describes infants from birth to around 18–24 months of age, or about the age that language first appears. During this period, infants are thought to go through six stages, starting from interacting with the world strictly with innate reflexes (Stage 1) to using mental representations for acting on the world (Stage 6). Topics examined by Piaget include the development of infants' understandings of time, space, causality, and the permanence of objects.

Many modern developmental researchers agree with Piaget's view that the child is an active learner, but disagree with his view that development is discontinuous, or stagelike. Theoretical positions, such as information processing and the connectionist view of development, are similar in some ways to Piaget's view in that both emphasize the role of learning and experience to help explain developmental changes and both can be considered constructivist theories. Like Piaget, both assume that developmental change is a building-block process that starts small and gradually becomes more elaborate or sophisticated. Other more nativist views believe that Piaget was much too conservative about infants' developing abilities; they claim he underestimated the ability of the infant. Some modern researchers believe that because Piaget's method of research was not truly experimental, his findings were not generalizable. His findings are sometimes criticized for erroneously focusing too much on the child's competence at a very specific task that may or may not reveal the child's true understanding of the world (e.g., Baillargeon, Spelke, & Wasserman, 1985; Bower, 1974). Nevertheless, Piaget is revered today by many infant cognition and perception researchers and is appreciated for his ingenuity and his insights into the mind of the infant (see Flavell, 1963).

Gibson's Ecological Theory

Not all theories of development rely so much on the developing mind of the infant. For example, Gibson's ecological approach to the study of infant perceptual development places emphasis on the environment and infant's abilities to detect important information from the world. Her view is based primarily on two key issues: (a) the infant's ability to discover new *affordances*—ways upon which an environment lends itself to be acted, and (b) the infant's ability to *differentiate*—parse out invariant information from the world. As infants act in the world, they differentiate information in their environment and discover affordances. With this new understanding of the world around them, their actions in the world change.

According to Gibson, perception and action are closely related for the infant, and much Gibsonian research examines that relationship (Gibson, 1995). For example, it has been found that an infant may tumble down a slope the first couple of times he or she approaches such a surface. Soon the infant begins to understand that one affordance of the slope, compared to other surfaces, is that it may cause tumbling (Adolph, Eppler, & Gibson, 1993a). Another example is Gibson and Walk's (1960) classic work on infants' perception of depth, known as the "visual cliff" experiment. In this study, it was found that infants would not crawl across a table that appeared to have a drop-off, or cliff, in the middle. Gibson and Walk saw this as evidence that infants of crawling age had enough experience with depth to know that it could afford danger. (For a more detailed discussion of this theory and related research, see the review by Adolph, Eppler, & Gibson, 1993b).

Dynamical Systems

Another theoretical view that emphasizes the close relationship between perception, cognition, and action is dynamical systems. In a recent set of books, Smith and Thelen (1993) and Thelen and Smith (1994) attempt to unify recent advances in dynamical systems theory with research in developmental neuroscience and behavioral development. They argue that development can best be understood in terms of complex nonlinear systems that are self-organizing. Developmental changes tend to be described in the language of physical nonlinear systems—that is, *attractor states, phase transitions,* and *stability* versus fluctuations of the system. This view, with its emphasis on mechanisms of change, is clearly opposed to nativist explanations. Although it has been applied most successfully to issues of motor development, its advocates are attempting to apply it to perceptual and cognitive development as well. As we shall see, it also has important elements in common with connectionist modeling.

Nativism

A persistent theoretical debate throughout the entire history of developmental psychology has been nativism versus empiricism. Nowhere is this debate more apparent than in modern-day infant perception and cognition. A chief spokesperson for the nativist position is Spelke. According to Spelke (1985), infants are endowed by nature with capacities to perceive and understand objects and events in the world. This *core knowledge* includes an understanding of partially and fully occluded objects; the ability to reason about physical properties of objects, such as continuity and solidity; an understanding of number; and knowledge of physical causality. Spelke and others, most notably Baillargeon, have argued that human infants are more competent than others (such as Piaget) had believed. To bolster their claims, they have provided considerable evidence based upon ingenious variations of methods involving infant habituation and visual preference. In some of these variations, infants must not only perceive events involving one or more objects, but must also make inferences when a portion of those events is hidden behind an occluder.

Needless to say, this viewpoint has been controversial. Many believe the nativist assumptions about the competencies of young infants are unwarranted. In fact, they question whether such assumptions can even be considered explanations. Recent debates on the pros and cons of nativism have appeared in the literature between Spelke (1998) versus Haith (1998) and Baillargeon (1999) versus Smith (1999). Furthermore, empirical research on some of these topics is beginning to show that simpler explanations can account for the apparent cognitive sophistication proposed by the nativists. Some of the research both for and against the nativist viewpoint is described in later sections of this chapter.

Connectionist Modeling

The connectionist modeling approach stands in sharp contrast to the nativist approach. The most complete description of the application of connectionism to development has been published in a recent book entitled *Rethinking Innateness* (Elman et al., 1996). Whereas nativism assumes infants come prewired with certain core knowledge, connectionists reject this form of innateness. They argue that at all levels—molecular, cellular, and organismic—interactions occur between organisms and the environment. A more appropriate meaning of innateness is that the outcome is constrained to some extent at each of those levels. These constraints operate on the type of representation, the architecture, and the timing of the developmental process that is being considered. Comparisons—sometimes real, sometimes metaphorical—are made between the structure of the brain and computerized connectionist networks. So, for example, just as brains include neuronal synapses and specific areas, connectionist models include patterns of connections and types of units or levels. Connectionist models also include nonlinear learning

rules that may lead to emergent, stagelike properties and thus are quite compatible with a dynamical systems approach. Many early models were developed to counter the prevalent nativism of linguistic theory. Modelers tried to demonstrate that what some assumed were innate rules of language could be approximated by connectionist models through experience. Connectionism has spread to simulations of infant perception and cognition. New models are appearing on infant categorization (Mareschal & French, 2000), object permanence (Munakata, McClelland, Johnson, & Siegler, 1997), speech perception (Schafer & Mareschal, 2001), and rule learning (Shultz & Bale, 2001). The adequacy of these models is still being hotly debated (Marcus, 1999a, 1999b) but there is no doubt that these models are presenting a challenge to the view that infants possess innate knowledge structures.

Cognitive Neuroscience

Developmental neuroscience is an area that has grown substantially over the last 10 to 20 years. Like dynamical systems and connectionist modeling, its users attempt to make links between development of the brain and development of behavior associated with perception and cognition. Whereas previous approaches to ties with brain development have been somewhat metaphorical, developmental neuroscientists attempt to measure brain development directly and then relate it to cognitive development. However, finding the answers to questions about brain development and cognitive development in infants is not such a straightforward business. Procedures that may be useful for studying the link between brain and cognition in older children may not be appropriate for studying this link in infants. For example, PET (positron-emission tomography) and fMRI (functional magnetic resonance imaging) methods may work fairly well with children and adults, but these are considered too intrusive for use with infants (M. H. Johnson, 1997). The methods most often used to study the developing brain in infants are EEGs (electroencephalographs), ERPs (event related potentials), and animal models (for a review of studies on infant perception and attention, see M. H. Johnson, 1996).

Information Processing

The information-processing approach contains elements of some of the other approaches described previously. Like Piaget, proponents of the information-processing approach believe that perceptual and cognitive development is constructive. According to one view, at least, the emphasis is on infants' learning to process the relationship among properties to form the whole (Cohen, 1988, 1991, 1998; Cohen & Cashon, 2001b). Young infants are able to process simple perceptual properties of objects, such as color, form, and shape, before they can process objects as a whole. As in Piagetian theory, development is also hierarchical. From an information-processing perspective, what counts as a unique whole at one age can serve as a property or element of a larger or more complex whole at an older age. Therefore, after infants perceive or organize perceptual properties into unique objects, they can treat objects themselves as properties of larger wholes and look for relationships between objects in dynamic events involving multiple objects. One such relationship is causality; infants can distinguish causal, direct-launching events from noncausal events. At a later point in development, even these causal events can become elements in more elaborate event sequences.

Recently this approach has been summarized by a set of six propositions (Cohen & Cashon, 2001b):

1. Perceptual-cognitive development follows a set of domain-general information-processing principles.
2. Information in the environment can be processed at a number of different levels of organization.
3. Higher (more holistic) levels can be defined in terms of the types of relationships among lower (parts) levels.
4. Development involves progressing to higher and higher levels.
5. There is a bias to initiate processing at the highest level available.
6. If an information overload occurs (such as when movement is added or when the task involves forming a category), the optimal strategy is to fall back to a lower level of processing.

Much like connectionist modeling and dynamical systems and unlike nativism, the information-processing approach emphasizes the role of experience, learning, and nonlinear changes in development. In fact, attempts are currently underway to produce a connectionist model that follows the preceding six propositions (Chaput & Cohen, 2001). Along with other approaches, visual attention and habituation are frequently used to assess infant information-processing. In contrast to other approaches, it also emphasizes changes in attention and memory over age. An information-processing perspective has often been used in studies of individual differences in preterm versus full-term infants or normal versus aberrant infants as well as long-term predictions of later intellectual ability (e.g., Bornstein & Sigman, 1986; Fagan, 1984).

INFANTS' PERCEPTION OF PROPERTIES OF OBJECTS

We begin by considering three classic topics in perception that have also been studied extensively in infants—form perception, color perception, and perceptual constancies. If space permitted, we could have included many other topics that have also been investigated in infants, including the perception of sound, touch, odor, and motion. Although our selections are not exhaustive, they are representative of the type of questions being asked about infant perception and its development. They also serve as a reasonable starting point for our progression from topics that most would agree are clear examples of infant perception to topics which fall more into the category of infant cognition.

Form Perception

Form perception in infants is usually studied with two-dimensional or three-dimensional static figures or shapes that have well-defined contours (Slater, 1995b; Slater & Johnson, 1998). The issue most often investigated in form perception is whether infants will respond to the component parts of a shape or to the figure as a whole (Slater, 1995b; Slater & Johnson, 1998). However, making this distinction experimentally is not always easy. For example, Slater, Morison, and Rose (1983) found that newborn infants can discriminate between the outlines of the shapes of a triangle, a square, and a cross. Is this form perception? Perhaps not. In fact, in one of the earliest form perception studies with infants, Salapatek and Kessen (1966) found that when newborns scanned a large triangle, they only scanned a small portion near the apex. To provide clear evidence of form perception, it is important to show that infants are discriminating between these shapes based upon more than just a portion of their outlines or some other component of the figure. It also must be shown that infants process the figure as a whole. As Banks and Salapatek (1983) discussed (see also Slater, 1995b), it is very difficult to obtain unambiguous evidence of form perception because there are often simpler, perceptual explanations for results with infants. Thus, even topics as basic as form perception must deal with issues about part-versus-whole processing that are central to the information-processing approach mentioned earlier.

Fortunately, there are ways to examine this experimental issue. In one such study, Cohen and Younger (1984) investigated developmental differences in the perception of angles by 14- and 6-week-old infants and were able to get clear evidence of form perception in the older infants. Cohen and Younger (1984) tested whether infants would process the parts of the angle—that is, the orientations of the lines—or whether they would process the whole angle—that is, the relationship between the lines. After habituating infants to one angle, they presented variations that either changed the line orientations but not the angle, or that changed the angle but not the line orientations. Their results indicated a developmental shift in the manner in which infants process angles and perhaps other simple forms. The younger infants seem only able to process the line orientations, or the independent parts of the angle, whereas the older infants are able to process the relationship between the lines and process the angle as a whole form.

Slater, Mattock, Brown, and Bremner (1991) conducted a similar set of experiments with newborns. In the first experiment, newborns were found to behave similarly to the younger, 6-week-old infants in the Cohen and Younger (1984) study. Not surprisingly, the newborns in the Slater et al. (1991) study responded to a change in line orientation and not to a change in the angle. In a second experiment, Slater et al. (1991) investigated whether newborns could process the angle independently of its orientation. In this experiment, newborns were familiarized either to an acute or an obtuse angle presented in six different orientations, much like a category study. Infants were then tested on an acute and an obtuse angle, one of which was familiar and the other novel, both in novel orientations. Slater et al. (1991) found that the newborns showed a novelty preference for the novel angle. Slater (1995b) suggested that this could be evidence of form perception in newborns, although he acknowledged that it may not be unambiguous evidence.

One important alternate interpretation has been referred to as the "blob theory" (Slater et al., 1991). This interpretation rests on the notion that at the apex of an angle a low-frequency "blob" is formed, and the size of the blob varies depending on the size of the angle. When newborns discriminated between the acute and obtuse angles in the Slater et al. (1991) test, they may have been responding to the difference in relative size of the blobs and not actually to the angle itself. If this is the case, then the results would be consistent with a developmental progression in the perception of angles, whereby newborns respond to the size of the apex (the blob), 6-week-olds respond to the independent lines of an angle, and 14-week-olds respond to relationship of the lines of the angle or the form of the angle.

Slater and Morison (as cited in Slater, 1995b) also found evidence for a developmental progression in form perception. In this experiment, newborns, 3-month-olds and 5-month-olds were tested on whether they could extract the general shape from a series of figures that varied only slightly from one another in design or texture. After being familiarized to six exemplars of a shape, infants were tested on a novel exemplar of the familiar shape and a novel shape. By showing infants slight variations of the same shape, the experimenters were able to see whether infants could form a category based on the overall form of the shape. If infants were in fact able to form this category, then one would expect infants to show a novelty preference for the novel shape. This is exactly what the 3- and 5-month-old infants did; however, the newborns did not show the preference. These results fit nicely with an information-processing approach and provide further support that form perception may develop over time.

Color Perception

Our knowledge about infants' color perception has grown considerably in the last 25 years (for a review, see Teller & Bornstein, 1987). Before that time, the results of research conducted on infant color perception were somewhat ambiguous. It was never clear in these early experiments whether infants were discriminating between different hues or some other aspect of color, such as brightness or intensity.

In 1975, several researchers invented clever tasks to show that infants younger than 3 months of age can discriminate between stimuli that vary in hue, not just brightness. For example, Peeples and Teller (1975) tested 2-month-old infants on a hue preference test and found that they could discriminate a red hue from a white hue, independent of brightness. More recently, Adams, Courage, and Mercer (1994) tested infants shortly after birth and found that newborns could discriminate red from white, but not blue, green, or yellow from white. As Kellman and Arterberry (1998) concluded, however, by about 2 to 3 months of age, infants seem to have color vision very similar to that of to adults and can discriminate between many colors.

So, within the first 2 to 3 months of life, infants appear to be sensitive to the same spectrum of color as adults. But do infants view the boundaries between colors in the same way as adults? Adults group a range of colors into *blue* and another range into *green,* and so on. In other words, do infants (like adults) organize colors into distinct categories? Bornstein, Kessen, and Weiskopf (1976) tested this question with 4-month-old infants. They habituated infants to a stimulus of a certain hue, or wavelength. Then the infants were tested with the same stimulus, a stimulus of a different wavelength but from the same color category, and a stimulus of a different wavelength that was considered by adults to be in a different category. If infants dishabituated to both novel stimuli, one would conclude that they must have responded to the wavelength and not the color categories. However, Bornstein et al. (1976) found that infants dishabituated only to the stimulus that adults considered to be in a different color category. Thus, infants not only perceive colors at an early age, they also seem to organize them into roughly the same color categories as adults.

From an information-processing viewpoint, it is interesting that like form perception, even infants' color perception appears to go through a developmental pattern whereby infants begin by processing information at a lower level, and then later they integrate that information and process it at a higher level. In the case of color perception, infants first gain the ability to discriminate between colors (around 2–3 months of age) and then later, building upon that ability, are able categorize colors (around 4 months of age). In the next section, we examine something that looks very much like categorization with infants' perception of shape and size constancy.

Perceptual Constancy

Artists are taught to be conscious of the way they see the world and to create visual illusions such as size, perspective, and distance on the canvas. For example, to create the illusion that an object is farther away, an artist simply draws the object higher and smaller on the page than he or she would draw an object that is meant to be up close. Similarly, adults have little difficulty making sense of the environment and understanding the illusions created on our retina. For example, you would have no trouble recognizing this book as the same book whether you saw it inside on your desk under fluorescent lighting or outside in the bright daylight. You would not be fooled by the different perceptual characteristics of the book due to the different illuminations and would effortlessly understand that it is the same book. Furthermore, you would perceive the book as the same despite its change in location or orientation. This ability to identify an object as the same despite a perceptual transformation is known as perceptual constancy.

One question that researchers have asked is whether young infants see real objects as adults do or retinal images of objects? For example, how would an infant make sense of seeing a teddy bear from across the room and then seeing the same teddy bear up close? Would the infant respond to the objective characteristics of the teddy bear and recognize the two images as the same teddy bear, or would the infant respond to the different-sized images on the retina and perceive the bears as two distinct objects, one much larger than the other? If infants perceived the two images as the same, as adults would, we would say that infants have *size constancy*—that is, despite the fact that the retinal image of the close teddy bear may be twice as large as the retinal

image of the distant teddy bear, the objective size is still preserved.

The notion of constancy can also refer to *shape constancy,* which is the ability to perceive an object as being the same despite changes to its orientation or slant. For example, if an infant saw a rectangular block from the frontal view and then saw it at a 45° angle, would the infant know that it was the same block? In other words, would the infant (like an adult) understand that despite the change in slant, both objects are the same rectangular block? Or would the infant perceive only the retinal image of these two objects and treat these two as different shapes, one as a rectangle and one as a trapezoid?

Size Constancy

Piaget and Inhelder (1969) adhered to the position that infants first respond to the retinal images of objects and believed that infants did not get size constancy until 5 or 6 months of age. They based this belief on the finding that if one taught infants to reach for a large box, the infant would continue to reach for that box even though it projected a smaller image on the retina than did a box that was closer and smaller in real size.

Bower, however, challenged the traditional view of size constancy and was one of the first researchers to test its claims empirically. In several experiments (e.g., Bower, 1966b), he used an operant conditioning paradigm to investigate whether young infants based their responses to an object on that object's real size, retinal size, or distance. Bower (1966b) found that infants generalized their response based upon both the objective size and the object's distance, but not retinal size. Thus, he had evidence that infants younger than 2 months of age do not rely on the retinal size of objects and can respond on the basis of an object's real size and distance.

Day and McKenzie (1981) continued the work on infant size constancy using a habituation paradigm, a completely different technique from Bower's operant conditioning experiments. They also found evidence for size constancy in infants as young as 18 weeks of age. Subsequently, two independent research laboratories tested newborns in a habituation paradigm, and both found evidence of size constancy (Granrud, 1987; Slater, Mattock, & Brown, 1990).

Shape Constancy

In addition to studying size constancy in infants, Bower also used his operant conditioning technique to study shape constancy. In one experiment with 50- to 60-day-olds, he trained infants on a rectangle that was slanted at a 45° angle, which created a retinal image that looked like a trapezoid.

He then looked for a generalized response to (a) a rectangle at a frontal view (new retinal image, same objective shape, new slant); (b) a trapezoid at a frontal view (same retinal image, new objective shape, new slant); and (c) a trapezoid slanted at a 45° angle (new retinal image, new objective shape, same slant). Bower found that infants generalized their responses to the rectangle presented at a frontal view. This result indicates that the infants responded to the objective shape of objects and not the shape of the retinal image or the slant of the objects.

Caron, Caron, and Carlson (1979) also addressed the issue of shape constancy in young infants, but did so in several studies using a habituation paradigm. Their results supported Bower's finding that young infants perceive the objective shape of objects and do not rely solely on the retinal image of those objects. In fact, in a more recent habituation study, Slater and Morison (1985) also found evidence of shape constancy in newborns.

Constancy as a Relationship Between Features

In sum, the evidence suggests that young infants do not rely solely on the retinal image of objects and are capable from birth (or shortly thereafter) of understanding size and shape constancy. How is it that infants are able to understand these constancies and respond to more than the retinal image of objects at birth? The key may be that all constancies require an understanding or appreciation of relational information. To return to the examples in the beginning of this section, the reason this book outdoors is not perceived as brighter is that relative to other objects, it is *not* brighter. Furthermore, the reason that an infant would perceive the teddy bear up close and far away as the same bear is that the size is constant relative to the distance of the object. The up close bear may appear two times as large, but it is also two times as close as the distant bear. Thus, the relationship between size and distance has remained the same. It is these constant relationships to which the infants must be sensitive.

Being sensitive to the relationships among things in the world is a necessary requirement for understanding the world around us. From our information-processing perspective, understanding relationships is the central principle around which infant perceptual and cognitive development proceeds. Throughout this chapter, we demonstrate that as infants get older, the types of relationships they process, understand, and remember become more complex and abstract. In that sense, the abilities to understand size, shape, and other constancies become building blocks from which infants learn about first objects and later events in the world about them.

Even some types of constancies may be more cognitively demanding or require more conscious attention to relationships than do others. One of these constancies may be object

constancy, which is an understanding that despite a significant physical transformation of an object in space, time, or both, it is the same object. An example would be understanding that the bottle now on its side but seen previously standing up is the same bottle—or recognizing the back of mother's head is the same person who is normally seen from the front. One could go a step further. What if the object or person were not visible at all? For example, consider an infant who hears her mother's voice in the other room and is able to identify the voice as that of his or her mother—or an infant who recognizes that the toy under the table is the same toy he or she had in hand before dropping it and losing sight of it. This extension of object constancy has been examined in great detail in the infant cognition literature by Piaget and many other investigators under the heading of object permanence. Because the development of an understanding about objects has played such a prominent role in investigations of infant cognition, we shall devote considerable space to it in the next section of this chapter.

INFANTS' UNDERSTANDING OF OBJECTS

Object Permanence

When people think about what infants know about objects, the concept of *object permanence,* or understanding that an object continues to exist in the world even though it is hidden or cannot be seen, often comes to mind. There is the general misconception that infants acquire this concept at 8 or 9 months of age. The misconception arises in part because most people think of object permanence as a unitary concept that infants have or do not have at a particular age.

Because one of the most dramatic developments in object permanence, reaching for and obtaining an object that is totally hidden, occurs around 8 or 9 months of age, this is when many assume infants acquire object permanence. However, for Piaget, obtaining a hidden object is only one intermediate step in a long sequence of accomplishments that infants must master during their first 2 years of life (Piaget, 1936/1952, 1937/1954). Obtaining a completely hidden object is characteristic of the onset of Piaget's Stage 4 (9 to 12 months). However, infants at Stage 3 (1 and one half to 4 or 5 months), although not yet able to retrieve a completely hidden object, are able to retrieve an object that is only partially hidden. And even though infants in Stage 4 can retrieve a completely hidden object, if an experimenter subsequently hides the object under a second cloth, infants at this stage will commit what is known as the *A not B error.* They will mistakenly go to the first cloth to retrieve the object (for more discussion on the A not B error, see Diamond, 1991; and Haith & Benson, 1998).

Infants at Stage 5 (12–18 months) no longer make this error and will correctly retrieve the hidden object from the correct cloth. However, according to Piaget (1937/1954), Stage 5 infants still do not completely have the concept of object permanence because they are fooled by *invisible displacements*. If an experimenter shows an infant an object and then places the object in a small box before hiding it under a cloth on the table, the Stage 5 infant will not look for the hidden object at its final destination. An infant who does successfully retrieve an object under this circumstance is considered by Piaget to be in Stage 6 (18–24 months) and to have completely mastered the object concept. (For more discussion on the development of the object concept, see Diamond, 1991; and Haith & Benson, 1998)

Object Unity

More recent research has extended the work of Piaget and considered other questions about infants' understanding of objects. Kellman and Spelke (1983), for example, investigated the role of coordinated movement of an object parts in infants' perception of *objectness,* or the perception of *object unity.* In this classic study, they habituated 4-month-old infants to a display in which a partially occluded rod moved back and forth behind an occluder. They were then tested on two displays without the occluder. In one test, infants saw a complete rod that moved back and forth, and in the other they saw just the two rod parts that resembled portions visible during habituation. The infants dishabituated to the two rod parts but not to the solid rod, indicating to Kellman and Spelke (1983) that the parts were novel, and thus that they must have perceived the two moving parts during habituation as a single complete rod. This result, according to Kellman and Spelke, indicates that the infants perceived object unity even under conditions of partial occlusion. It is interesting to note that the perception or inference of an object under conditions of partial occlusion at 4 months of age would be consistent with Piaget's Stage 3 behavior. It therefore would be of interest to test younger infants to see whether this ability to perceive or infer a unified object develops during the first few months of life.

Several researchers have in fact attempted to replicate this object unity study with younger infants. Slater et al. (1990) conducted a similar study with newborns and found a very different set of results from those reported by Kellman and Spelke (1983). Slater et al. found that instead of dishabituating to the two rod parts, newborn infants dishabituated to the complete rod, suggesting that they were perceiving the rod parts as separate items rather than as the top and bottom of a single unified object. More recently, researchers have replicated Kellman and Spelke's findings with 2-month-olds and

have found that they dishabituate to the rod parts display in the test if the occluder is rather narrow (S. P. Johnson & Nañez, 1995). Collectively, research on object unity shows that infants are not born with the ability to perceive two parts of a moving, partially occluded object as one object, but that this ability develops over at least the first 4 months of age.

In fact, such a conclusion fits within an information-processing framework by showing once again a developmental change from processing parts to processing wholes. It seems clear from research on object unity and other related topics that well before 7 months of age, infants are capable of perceiving objectness—that is, of perceiving those characteristics that indicate a single unified object exists. From our earlier discussions on form, color, and constancy, it is equally clear that also well before 7 months of age infants perceive many characteristic features of an object. However, as research described in the next section indicates, young infants still lack the ability to distinguish one object from another. This ability has been called *object individuation* or *object segregation* and estimates about when it develops range widely from 4 or 5 months of age to 12 months of age.

Object Individuation

The ability to distinguish two objects as distinct entities is what researchers refer to as object individuation or object segregation. Depending on the procedure used, there are reports that infants can individuate objects at 12 but not 10 months of age (Xu & Carey, 1996), or in some cases as young as 5 months of age (Needham, 2001; Wilcox, 1999). Xu and Carey (1996) employed an "event-mapping" procedure, as it is referred to by Wilcox and Baillargeon (1998), in which infants were shown an event and then tested on two events—one that was considered consistent and another that was considered inconsistent with the first event. Specifically, infants initially saw one object move behind an occluder from the left, then a different object emerge from behind the occluder and move to the right. The authors reasoned that if infants understood that there were two objects in the original event, then they should look longer at the inconsistent event—that is, the display with one object. They found that the 12-month-olds but not the 10-month-olds, looked longer at the one-object display. Based upon these findings, Xu and Carey concluded that these older infants understood that there were two objects present in the event and had successfully individuated the objects.

However, studies with younger infants suggest that they also—under certain circumstances—can individuate objects. In a very recent set of studies, Needham (2001) gave infants exposure to an object prior to presenting two test events that involved an object similar to the prior-experience–object but varying on some feature such as texture (Experiments 1 and 2), orientation (Experiment 3), and color (Experiments 4, 5, and 6). One test event can be described as *two objects move together*. In this event, the two objects that are touching and move together could be perceived as either one or two separate objects. The second test event can be described as *one object moves*. In this event, the object remains stationary, so it should be obvious that there are two distinct objects. Needham reasoned that if infants attended to the featural characteristics of the prior-experience–object and its equivalent in the test was similar enough, then infants should still show signs of individuating the objects in the move-together test event. If, however, infants did not view the two objects as similar, then presumably that prior experience with the first object would not help the infants to individuate the objects in the test display. In this case, infants would not be expected to show a difference in response to the two test events. Needham (2001) found that 4.5-month-olds could use texture and orientation but not color cues to help them individuate the objects in the test displays.

In addition to these findings a study by Wilcox (1999) showed a developmental progression in what featural information can be used to help infants individuate objects. She found that at 4.5 months of age infants can use shape and size, at 7.5 months of age they can use pattern, and at 11.5 months of age they can use color to individuate objects. From our earlier discussions on form and color perception, it is clear that infants in the first 3 months can perceive these characteristics about objects. Furthermore, as the discussion on object unity shows, infants are also capable of perceiving objectness (i.e., that something is a separate object) by 2 months of age. Given this information, one may ask why infants cannot consistently individuate objects until possibly 5 or even 10 to 12 months of age; we believe the answer may lie in an information-processing perspective. The ability to individuate objects requires attention to and integration of both featural information and objectness. Thus, object individuation represents another example of a developmental progression from processing the independent features of objects to integrating or relating those features and processing the object as a whole.

Core Knowledge About Objects

Some theorists believe that infants have sophisticated knowledge about objects and object permanence much earlier than others such as Piaget had assumed. In fact, in many of their studies investigating infants' understanding of objects, an understanding of object permanence is a prerequisite for the infants. For example, in one experiment on young infants' understanding of object solidity—that is, that one solid object cannot pass through another solid object—Spelke, Breinlinger, Macomber, and Jacobson (1992, Experiment 3) showed 2.5-month-olds' events in which a ball rolled from the left end of the stage to behind an occluder. After about 2 s, the occluder was raised to reveal the ball resting against a wall. In the habituation phase, when the occluder was raised, the ball was shown resting on the left side of a wall on the right end of the stage. In the test phase, lifting the occluder revealed two walls, one in the center of the stage and one on the right. In one test event, the ball was found resting against the center wall, which was considered a consistent outcome because the wall would have obstructed the ball's path. In the other test event, the ball rested against the right wall, which was considered an inconsistent outcome because the ball would have had to go through the center wall to reach the right wall.

Spelke et al. (1992) found that infants looked longer at the inconsistent outcome and interpreted this result to mean that infants as young as 2.5 months of age understand that a ball cannot travel through a solid center wall to get to the right wall. However, given the fact that the action of the ball took place behind an occluder, to make the interpretation that these very young infants understand object solidity, one also has to assume that these infants understand the ball continues to exist when behind an occluder—in other words, one must assume that they are operating at least at Stage 4 of object permanence.

Recent evidence with 8-month-old infants and animated events, however, suggests a simpler explanation for this apparent sophisticated cognitive ability of infants. It is possible the infants were simply responding to changes in the perceptual cues of the events, such as the duration of movement or the presence of a wall to the left of the ball (Bradley & Cohen, 1994). In another, similar set of experiments on infants' understanding of solidity, Cohen, Gilbert, and Brown (1996) tested 4-, 8-, and 10-month-old infants. They found that infants had to be at least 10 months of age before they really understood that one solid object cannot pass through another solid object.

If this conclusion is accurate, once again it fits within the information-processing framework. As we have mentioned, there is evidence that infants first learn about the independent features of objects by about 4 months and then integrate these features into a whole object by about 7 months. The next developmental step would be for infants to understand the relationship between objects—in this case, to understand that one solid object cannot pass through another solid object. It makes sense to us that the ability to understand object solidity may not develop until approximately 10 months of age, given that infants would first have to be able to individuate and segregate individual objects.

Another type of relationship between objects would be a causal relationship, the simplest version of which would occur in what has been called a *direct launching* event. In this type of event, one moving object hits a second moving object, causing the second object to move. Several studies have now been reported on infants' perception or understanding of causality in these types of events. Once again, as predicted by an information-processing view, when realistic objects are being used, infants do not perceive the causality until approximately 10 months of age. See Cohen, Amsel, Redford, and Casasola (1998) for a review of this literature.

In addition to Spelke and her colleagues, Baillargeon has also reported a large body of research suggesting that infants are precocious (for reviews, see Baillargeon, 1995, 1999). In one of her most well-known set of studies, she reported that infants as young as 3.5 months old understand that an object continues to exist when it is out of sight (Baillargeon, 1987; Baillargeon et al., 1985). Her procedure was very different from the traditional Piagetian object permanence task. Instead of relying on an infants' ability to reach for a hidden object, she (like Spelke) relied on infants' looking times at possible and impossible events.

The procedure involved familiarizing infants with a screen that rotated 180° back and forth, from a position of lying flat on the front part of a stage to lying flat on the back part of the stage. Infants were then tested on a possible and an impossible event, both of which involved the presence of an object such as a yellow box placed in the path of the rotating screen. In the possible event, infants saw the box resting on the stage before the start of the first rotation. The screen then rotated back and forth, as it did in the familiarization event. Each time it rotated back, it hid the object from the infant. Furthermore, the screen stopped rotating at 112° when it appeared to make contact with the object and then rotated back toward the infant, once again reexposing the object. The impossible event was similar to the possible event, except that the screen rotated a full 180°, appearing to go magically through the space that should have been occupied by the box. (There was actually an experimenter behind the stage who removed the box so that the screen could complete its rotation. As the screen rotated toward the infant again, the experimenter replaced the box on the stage in time for the infant to see the box once again resting in the screen's path.)

Baillargeon (1987) found that 4.5- and some 3.5-month-old infants looked longer at the impossible event. She interpreted this finding to mean that the infants "understood that (a) the object behind the screen continued to exist after the screen rotated upward and occluded it and (b) the screen could not move through the space occupied by the object" (p. 662). She based these interpretations on several assumptions:

(a) Infants normally have a novelty preference during the test phase, (b) infants would perceive the impossible event as familiar because the amount of rotation in this event is the same as the amount of rotation in the familiarization event, (c) infants would perceive the possible event as novel because the amount of rotation is novel, and (d) if infants looked longer at the impossible event, which should be perceived as familiar, it must be for reasons other than novelty; it must be because they understood object permanence and object solidity and were observing a violation of both concepts.

However, as with Spelke et al. (1992), recent evidence suggests a simpler, perceptual explanation of Baillargeon's so-called drawbridge results (Baillargeon, 1987; Baillargeon et al., 1985). We have already mentioned the problem of a familiarity effect in habituation-familiarization studies. Along those lines, one alternative interpretation is that the infants in Baillargeon's studies were not fully habituated and thus did not have a novelty preference during the test phase, as she assumed. The results of these more recent studies, which varied familiarization time or used more stringent habituation criteria, support the interpretation that infants looked longer at the impossible event because it was familiar, not because it was impossible (Bogartz, Shinskey, & Schilling, 2000; Cashon & Cohen, 2000; Schilling, 2000; see also Bogartz, Cashon, Cohen, Schilling, & Shinskey, 2000).

The findings that 3.5- to 4.5-month-olds understand object permanence (Baillargeon, 1987) and that infants as young as 2.5 months old understand object solidity (Spelke et al., 1992) stand in stark contrast to Piaget's reported ages and stages. Thus, if one assumes that explanations like Baillargeon's (1987) and Spelke et al.'s (1992) are correct regarding infants' early understanding of object permanence, that explanation has to be reconciled with the fact that under standard object permanence techniques, infants do not show evidence that they understand an object exists when completely hidden until at least 8 or 9 months of age.

The prevailing explanation for this discrepancy is that younger infants understand that hidden objects continue to exist, but they fail to reach for those objects in a standard Piagetian task because they have difficulty with means-end actions (Baillargeon, 1987; Baillargeon et al., 1985; Bower, 1974; Diamond, 1991). In other words, infants may have trouble coordinating two actions to obtain a goal—in this case, removing the cloth and then reaching for the object. Once again, however, recent evidence suggests that infants do not have a means-end deficit. A couple of recent studies, for example, have shown that infants do not have the same reaching problem when the object is behind a transparent obstacle versus an opaque obstacle (Munakata et al., 1997; Shinskey, Bogartz, & Poirer, 2000). Taken together, these more recent results uphold previous findings that infants younger than 8 or 9 months of age fail to search for hidden objects not because they lack a means-end skill, but because they have yet to understand that objects continue to exist when they are hidden.

Face Perception

A considerable amount of research has been conducted on infants' perception of faces over the past 40 or so years (see Maurer, 1985, for review). There is no question that faces are important stimuli for infants. Infants see faces often and use them to help identify others, interact with others, and learn about the world. It may seem odd to some that we have included a section of face perception within a section devoted to objects. However, one issue that arises in the study of infants' perception of faces is whether infants view faces as something special or whether they perceive faces in the same way they perceive other complex objects (see Kleiner, 1993, for discussion). Nativists often argue that faces are a unique class of objects and that the way in which newborns process a face is quite different from the way in which newborns process nonface stimuli (e.g., Fantz, 1961; Morton & Johnson, 1991). Empiricists, however, regard face perception quite differently. They argue that the way in which we process a face is brought about through experience; at least in the beginning, faces are no different from other objects (e.g., Banks & Ginsburg, 1985). In this section, we review some of the literature regarding the issue of infants' preference for facelike over nonfacelike stimuli, followed by a discussion of how infants process faces and how that processing may change with age.

Research on infants' perception of faces has produced conflicting results with respect to the question of whether faces are special to infants. Whether newborns have an innate preference to look at faces over other stimuli is still unresolved (for discussions, see Easterbrooks, Kisilevsky, Hains, & Muir, 1999; Maurer, 1985). Visual tracking studies with newborns have shown that neonates will follow (with their eyes) a facelike pattern farther than they will follow a nonfacelike pattern (Goren, Sarty, & Wu, 1975; M. H. Johnson, Dziurawiec, Ellis, & Morton, 1991; Maurer & Young, 1983). However, preferential looking paradigm studies have provided a different picture. Fantz and Nevis (1967) found that in general, newborns preferred to look at patterned stimuli, such as a bull's-eye and a schematic face, to plain stimuli, and preferred a schematic face to a bull's-eye; however, they did not find a preference for a schematic face over a scrambled face. In another preferential looking study, Maurer and Barrera (1981) found a preference for a facelike

pattern over scrambled faces at 2 months of age, but not at 1 month of age. M. H. Johnson et al. (1991, Experiment 2) replicated Maurer and Barrera's findings with 5- and 10-week-old infants in a preferential looking paradigm and Goren et al.'s (1975) with newborns in a visual tracking task.

It may seem odd that the evidence suggests that newborns have a preference for faces but that this preference disappears by 2 months of age. One possible explanation for the discrepancy, posited by Morton and Johnson (1991) and Johnson and Morton (1991), is that two different testing methods were used that may tap into two different processes of face recognition in place at different ages. The first mechanism they describe is CONSPEC, a subcortical device in the brain of the newborn that contains the information about the structure of a face. CONSPEC is believed to attract infants' attention to stimuli with the same structural information as faces, which would account for newborns' preferential tracking of faces. The second mechanism, CONLERN, is thought to take over by the second month. It is assumed to be a cortical structure that is involved in learning about conspecifics of a face. This mechanism is believed to help in the recognition of individual faces.

If Morton and Johnson are correct that infants have an innate representation of the structure of faces, then we could certainly conclude that faces are special. However, evidence from other studies raised doubts about this conclusion. The results of studies on infants' visual scanning patterns of faces and nonface stimuli have revealed similar scanning patterns and developmental trends for faces and nonface stimuli alike, which suggests that faces may not be special to infants (see Salapatek, 1975, for discussion). Several researchers have reported finding that infants tend to scan mostly the external contour of a face in the first month of life, whereas in the second month, infants tend to scan the internal features (Bergman, Haith, & Mann, 1971, as cited in Salapatek, 1975; Maurer & Salapatek, 1976; Salapatek, 1975). This developmental shift in the scanning pattern of faces has also been found in infants' scanning pattern of nonface stimuli (Salapatek, 1975).

A number of investigators have examined the development of infants' face processing over the first year of life and whether that processing is similar to or different from the development of object processing. Previous findings with 4- and 7-month-olds have shown that the younger infants process the independent features of line-drawn animals, but that the older infants are sensitive to the correlations among features (Younger & Cohen, 1986). More recently, we have been investigating whether this developmental shift from parts to whole processing would also be true in 4- and 7-month-old infants' processing of faces as well. It has been found that adults process upright faces as a whole but inverted faces in a piecemeal manner. Therefore, we also examined the effect of orientation. Half of the infants saw all upright faces and the other half saw inverted faces.

Some of the results were expected; others were surprising. The 7-month-olds behaved as expected—that is, they responded to upright faces as a whole but inverted faces in a piecemeal fashion (Cohen & Cashon, 2001a). The 4-month-olds, however, behaved in a totally unexpected manner. In one sense, they appeared to be more advanced than the 7-month-olds—or even adults. Not only did these younger infants process a face as a whole when it was presented upright, but they also processed it as a whole when it was presented in an inverted orientation (Cashon & Cohen, 2001)! One possible explanation for this finding currently under investigation is that an upright facial orientation may not be as important to infants at 4 months of age. They undoubtedly receive a considerable amount of exposure to faces in a variety of orientations, perhaps much more so than at 7 months when they are stronger and tend to view the world from an upright position.

INFANT CATEGORIZATION

Categorization is a fundamental cognitive ability. It allows us to group together objects and events in the world and to respond equivalently to items that may be perceptually quite different. Infants as well as adults must be able to categorize to some degree. Consider what life would be like for infants if they could not: No two experiences would be identical, learning would be nonexistent, and anticipating the regularities in the world would be impossible. As Madole and Oakes (in press) have stated a bit more conservatively,

> The ability to categorize may be especially important in infancy when an enormous amount of new information is encountered every day. By forming groups of similar objects, infants can effectively reduce the amount of information they must process, learn and remember . . . (p. 1)

But how can one determine whether infants—in particular, young, preverbal infants—are able to categorize? Fortunately that problem was at least partially solved in the late 1970s by a modification of the standard habituation paradigm. Instead of habituating infants to repeated presentations of a *single* item, infants could be habituated to a series of perceptually distinct items that all were members of the same category. If in a subsequent test, infants remained habituated to a novel example from that habituated category, but not to a

novel noncategory item, they would be demonstrating the ability to categorize. In other words, they would be responding equivalently to items that were perceptually distinct.

Cohen and Caputo (1978) were among the first to use this procedure. They tested three groups of 7-month-old infants. One group was habituated to a single, repeated presentation of a photograph of a toy stuffed animal. A second group was habituated to pictures of different stuffed animals, and a third group was habituated to pictures of unrelated objects. All three groups were then tested with a picture of a new stuffed animal and a multicolored arrangement of flowers. The first group dishabituated to both test items. They had not formed a category. The third group did not even habituate. But the second group—the one that had seen different members of the *stuffed animal* category—dishabituated to the flowers but remained habituated to the new stuffed animal. They demonstrated that they were responding on the basis of the stuffed animal category.

Early demonstrations, such as the previously described stuffed animal example, have been followed by other attempts to assess categorization in infants, using a variety of techniques—including habituation and novelty preference, sequential touching, operant conditioning, and even imitation—with infants over 1 year of age. In fact, an explosion of research on categorization in infants has occurred in the past two decades, and several reviews of this literature are available. (e.g., Cohen & Younger, 1983; Hayne, 1996; Madole & Oakes, 1999; Quinn & Eimas 1996; Younger & Cohen, 1985). In reviewing this literature, we shall consider three significant questions regarding categorization in infants: At what age can infants categorize; what is the content of infants' categories; and finally, what information-processing changes underlie infant categorization?

The Earliest Age at Which Infants Can Categorize

Considerable evidence is now available that infants can categorize during the second half of the first year of life. In addition to the previously mentioned study with pictures of stuffed animals, several studies report infant categorization of faces (e.g., Cohen & Strauss, 1979; Strauss, 1979) of three-dimensional as well as two-dimensional representations of animals (Younger & Fearing, 1998) and even adult gender categories (Leinbach & Fagot, 1993). Other studies have reported that as early as 3 or 4 months of age, infants can distinguish cats from dogs (Quinn, Eimas, & Rosenkrantz, 1993) and animals from furniture (Behl-Chadha, 1996). In addition, if one assumes that perceptual constancies may actually be a form of categorization, then there is evidence that newborns can categorize.

Consider size constancy as an example. In a newborn size constancy experiment, infants are habituated to the same object at different distances and then are tested with that same object at a new distance versus a different-sized object at an old distance. Assuming that the infant can discriminate among these distances, then the procedure amounts to a typical categorization experiment. The infants have been habituated to multiple examples of discriminably different stimuli (in this case, the same object at different distances) and then do not dishabituate to a new example (the object at a new distance) but do dishabituate to a nonexample (a new object). Of course, as adults we assume a big difference between an instance of perceptual constancy, which we interpret as different views of one item, and categorization, which we interpret as a grouping of similar but different items. It is a totally unexplored question whether infants make that same distinction and if so at what age they do it.

The Content of Infants' Categories

Although many investigators agree that even newborns may be able to categorize, they also agree that the content of those categories changes over age. It is one thing to group together different views of the same object and quite another to group together very different animals into the category of *mammal* or tables and chairs into the category of *furniture*. An important issue in this regard is the level at which infants first categorize objects. The traditional view has been that infants and young children form basic-level categories (such as *dog* or *chair*) and only later form higher-order superordinate categories (such as *animal* or *furniture;* Mervis & Rosch, 1981). Recent evidence with infants (see Quinn & Eimas, 1996, for a review) provides some support for this view. On the other hand, Mandler (2000a) has argued just the opposite. She has reported studies in which infants first appear to respond in terms of global categories (e.g., Mandler, Bauer, & McDonough, 1991). Quinn and others have also reported that infants respond more readily to global categories than to basic categories (Quinn & Eimas, 1998; Quinn & Johnson, 2000; Younger & Fearing, 2000).

To complicate matters further, one might assume Mandler would be pleased to find additional evidence supporting a priority of global categories over basic categories. However, she makes an additional distinction, also in dispute, between perceptually and conceptually based representations (Mandler, 2000b). She believes the evidence cited previously—which is based primarily upon habituation and novelty preference techniques—taps perceptual categories, whereas her studies—which use manipulation and imitation techniques—tap something independent: conceptual categories. Quinn and Eimas (1996), on the other hand, argue that

there is a continuum between the two, with perceptual categories gradually developing into more abstract conceptual categories.

Information-Processing Changes in Categorization

One of the difficulties in deciding between global versus basic levels or perceptual versus conceptual processing is that these distinctions are based upon the presumed content of the categories from the experimenter's point of view. Evidence that infants distinguish between animals and vehicles, for example, does not necessarily mean that the infants are operating at a global or superordinate level. In fact, Rakison and Butterworth (1998) have shown that in the case of toy animals versus toy vehicles, 14- and 18-month-old infants are actually responding to legs versus wheels. Much younger infants can distinguish cats from dogs, but the distinction is based primarily on features located in the face region (Quinn & Eimas, 1996). Consistent with an information-processing viewpoint, there appears to be a developmental progression from processing these features independently to processing the correlation among the features (Younger & Cohen, 1986). In fact, by 10 months of age, attention to correlations among features becomes a major factor both in the formation of categories and in the differentiation of one category versus another (Younger, 1985).

The number and variety of features to which infants attend also increases with age (Madole & Oakes, in press). One nonobvious type of feature that appears to become salient, particularly in the second year of life, is an object's function. For example, Madole, Cohen, and Bradley (1994) found that 14-month-olds but not 10-month-olds used functional information (what an object does) in their formation of categories. Madole, Oakes, and Cohen (1993) also reported a developmental shift from processing form and function information independently at 14 months to processing the relationship between form and function at 18 months, once again a developmental shift that is consistent with an information-processing view of infant perception and cognition. The increased salience of nonobvious features of objects during the second year of life, such as their function or their animacy (Rakison & Poulin-Dubois, 2001), may account at least in part for what appears to be a shift from perceptual to conceptual categorization.

Current Trends in Infant Categorization Research

Research on infant categorization is continuing at a rapid pace. Among the most exciting developments are the ties developing to other related areas of developmental and cognitive psychology. One of these ties is the relationship between infant categorization and infant language development. Lalonde and Werker (1995), for example, have shown the close tie between the use of correlated attributes in categorization and the development of speech perception. Waxman (1999) has also reported the importance of language labels in infant categorization. Close ties are also developing between infant categorization and connectionist modeling. Several attempts recently have been reported to simulate infant categorization (e.g., Mareschal & French, 2000; Quinn & Johnson, 2000). The most popular approach has been the use of simple auto-encoder models, although other more complex models are on the drawing board. These early attempts to model infant behavior in a categorization task have been remarkably successful. Future, more extensive models are likely to lead to interesting predictions as well.

INDIVIDUAL DIFFERENCES

The vast majority of research on infant perception and cognition has been concerned with discovering the abilities of normal infants along with changes in those abilities over age and development. Both theoretical predictions and experimental designs generally have been based upon differences between groups, with the goal of describing and explaining how infants in one condition differ from those in another condition, or how one age group differs from another age group. The average performance of these groups is not even the emphasis. It is the optimal performance of infants at a certain age, so that often the behavior of 25% or more of the infants in a study is discarded for some reason. Perhaps it is because the infants were too irritable, or they were too sleepy, or they did not attend sufficiently, or they did not habituate. In such studies, individual differences traditionally are treated as error variance. They are considered primarily as an indication of the degree of experimental control or the statistical power of the experiment.

This overwhelming emphasis on group differences among normal infants does not mean that investigators of infant perception and cognition have been totally unconcerned about the value of assessing individual differences in normal populations or in discovering what differences exist between normal and aberrant infants. In fact, a frequent argument often made in significance sections of grant proposals is that one must first collect data on normal infants before one can determine the most important ways in which aberrant infants deviate from normal ones. Fagan, a basic researcher of infant attention and memory in the 1970s, has gone considerably further than that. He has developed a clinical screening device—based upon his measure of infant novelty preferences—that he argues should be used to differentiate

those infants truly at risk for some long-term deficit from those who may seem to be at risk, but really are not (Fagan, 1984).

To be accurate, individual differences in infants' functioning have been of interest to some investigators of infant perception and cognition since the 1970s. That research has come primarily from those focused on differences in infant attention, memory, and information processing. As Rose and Feldman (1990) noted, this research on individual differences can be subdivided into two broad categories: differences between normal versus risk groups and measures of predictive validity, primarily in normal infants.

Full-Term Versus Preterm Infants

The term *at risk* usually refers to infants who are born with some difficulty that may or may not lead to a long-term deficit. The most common group of at-risk infants are those who are born prematurely with or without additional symptoms. Much of the early research on individual differences in infant perception and cognition compared full-term versus preterm infants. One of the first such studies was reported by Fagan, Fantz, and Miranda (1971). They tested normal and preterm infants on a novelty preference task from approximately 6 to 20 weeks of age. Their infants were familiarized to one complex black and white pattern and then tested with that pattern versus a novel pattern. A clear difference between the groups was obtained with normal-term infants first showing a novelty preference at 10 weeks of age, but preterm infants not showing a novelty preference until 16 weeks of age. Of more importance from a developmental perspective was that when the two groups were equated for conceptional age (gestational age plus age since birth) the group difference disappeared. Both groups first showed a strong novelty preference at about 52 weeks of conceptional age. Thus, at least on this one task, maturation seemed to play a more important role than that of the total amount or type of external stimulation the infants had received.

Others, however, have found differences between preterm and full-term infants even when conceptional age is equated. Sigman and Parmelee (1974), for example, found that at 59 weeks of conceptional age, full-term infants preferred faces to nonfaces, whereas preterm infants did not. Unlike the results in the Fagan et al. (1971) study, full-term but not preterm infants also displayed a novelty preference. Of course, there are many reasons that preterm infants may be delayed compared to full-term infants. Preterm infants usually have more serious medical complications, they are more isolated from their parents, they stay in the hospital longer, they tend to be disproportionately male and lower class, the parents tend to have received less prenatal care and poorer nutrition, and so on. Any number of these factors in isolation or combination could be responsible for delays in perceptual or cognitive development.

In another study (Cohen, 1981) three groups of infants were compared at 60 weeks conceptional age. The *severe* group had a number of complications, including prematurity and hyaline membrane disease; several had seizures, one had severe hypocalcemia, and one had congenital heart disease. In general these infants had suffered considerable prenatal or perinatal trauma but had survived relatively intact. They all also came from lower-class family backgrounds. A second group included only full-term, healthy infants, also from lower social class backgrounds. Finally, a third group included only full-term infants from middle-class backgrounds. In this study, low and middle SES (socioeconomic status) groups differed in number of two-parent families, years of education, racial background, and place of residence. All three groups were habituated to a picture of a face and then tested with two different novel faces. The middle-class group dishabituated to the novel faces (i.e., showed a novelty preference), but neither of the lower-class groups did so. It appeared that factors associated with class status were more significant than those associated with prematurity or risk status in this particular study.

We find it interesting that Rose, Gottfried, and Bridger (1978) reported a similar finding with one-year-old infants and a cross-modal task. Middle-class full-term infants, lower-class full-term infants, and preterm infants were allowed oral and tactile familiarization with a three-dimensional block. When shown that object and a novel object, only the middle-class infants looked longer at the novel object. In a subsequent study, however, using a visual task with simple geometric shapes presented at 6 months of age, lower-class full-term infants displayed a novelty preference but lower-class preterms did not (Rose et al., 1978). Thus the evidence is mixed with respect to preterm versus full-term differences. Systematic differences between these groups are frequently reported, but the bases for those differences are not always clear. In some cases, the difference appears to be based upon conceptional age or social class. In other cases, risk status seems to be implicated more directly.

The differences discussed so far between full-term and preterm infants have been rather global; full-term infants dishabituate or show a novelty preference, whereas preterm infants do not. But at least one study has gone further to investigate how the two groups differ in their information processing. Caron, Caron, and Glass (1983) tested preterm and full-term infants on a variety of problems that involved processing the relations among the parts of complex facelike drawings and other stimuli that they presented. They then tested to see whether the infants had processed the stimuli on a configural basis (e.g., the overall configuration of a face) and a component basis (e.g., the type of eyes and nose that made up the faces). They found clear evidence that the full-term infants were processing configurations, whereas the preterm infants were processing components.

Infants With an Established Risk Condition

A distinction is sometimes drawn between infants who are "at risk" for later disability and infants who have an "established risk condition," such as Down's syndrome, cerebral palsy, and spina bifida (Tjossem, 1976). Several studies have established that Down's syndrome infants, for example, are delayed relative to normal infants in habituation and novelty preference (e.g., Fantz, Fagan, & Miranda, 1975; Miranda, 1976).

One of the more interesting comparative studies was reported by McDonough (1988). She tested normal 12-month-old infants as well as 12-month-old infants with spina bifida, cerebral palsy, or Down's syndrome. The infants were given a category task similar to the one reported earlier by Cohen and Caputo (1978). Infants were habituated to a series of pictures of stuffed animals and then tested with a novel stuffed animal versus an item that was not a stuffed animal (a chair). The normal infants and the infants with spina bifida or cerebral palsy habituated, but the infants with Down's syndrome did not. Apparently the presentation of multiple distinct objects was too difficult for them to process. However, in the test, only the normal infants and the infants with spina bifida showed evidence of categorization by looking longer at the noncategory item than at the new category member; even though the infants with cerebral palsy habituated, they showed no evidence of forming the category.

These and other studies that have compared normal with at-risk infants provide compelling evidence that the at-risk infants perform more poorly on certain tests of habituation and novelty preference. Additional evidence on these differences is available in edited volumes by Friedman and Sigman (1981) and Vietze and Vaughan (1988). An important question is what these differences mean. Most would assume that habituation, and novelty preference tests are assessing certain aspects of information processing, such as attention, memory, or perceptual organization. But even if some at-risk infants perform more poorly during the first year of life, does this performance predict any long-term deficiency in one or more of these processes? Even if some long-term prediction is possible, does that prediction only apply to group differences, such as those between normal and at-risk or established-risk infants? Or can one also use habituation and novelty preference measures to make long-term predictions of individual differences even among normal infants? This question is addressed in the next section.

Predictive Validity of Habituation and Novelty Preference Measures

An examination of the predictive value of traditional standardized tests of infant development, such as the Bayley or the Gesell scales, has led to the unfortunate but definite conclusion that these tests have dubious long-term predictive validity for normal populations (e.g., McCall, 1979; McCall, Hogarty, & Hurlburt, 1972), as well as for populations that include infants at risk (Kopp & McCall, 1982). This lack of predictive validity of traditional tests was at first considered not to be a failure in the tests themselves but simply a reflection of the discontinuity and qualitative nature of change over age in intellectual development from infancy to childhood (McCall, 1981; McCall, Appelbaum, & Hogarty, 1973).

That view became somewhat suspect in the 1980s as studies appeared demonstrating sizable correlations between infant habituation or novelty preference usually assessed sometime between 3 and 8 months of age and later IQ—usually assessed between 3 and 8 years of age (e.g., Caron et al., 1983; Fagan & McGrath, 1981; Rose & Wallace, 1985). Both Bornstein and Sigman (1986) and McCall and Carriger (1993) provide excellent reviews and analyses of this literature. McCall and Carriger, for example, report that across these studies the median correlation between information-processing measures assessed via habituation or novelty preference tasks and childhood intelligence is approximately .47, whereas it is approximately .09 between standardized infant tests and later intelligence. Furthermore these high correlations between information processing and later IQ tend to occur even in small samples and with normal populations.

Although many specific measures of infant information processing have been tried, three classes of them appear to be the best predictors of later intelligence (Slater, 1995a). One is preference for visual novelty. Following brief exposure to a visual pattern (usually 5–20 s), the familiar and a novel pattern are presented side by side and the percent responding to the novel pattern is recorded. This percent novelty tends to be positively correlated with later IQ. A second is some measure of habituation rate. Various measures of habituation, such as the total looking time until some habituation criterion is reached or the total number of habituation trials prior to criterion are sometimes found to be correlated with later intelligence. In general, those who habituate more rapidly tend to have higher IQs. The third is some measure of fixation duration independent of habituation. The measure may be the duration of a look at the outset of the habituation trials, or the duration of the longest look during habituation, or the average duration of a look during habituation. In general, the shorter the look by the infant, the higher the IQ found later in life. Some have even found systematic individual differences between short and long lookers. For example, it has been found that younger infants tend to look longer at most pictures that they can see clearly than do older infants (Colombo & Mitchell, 1990).

Although most investigators agree that these measures tap some aspect of information processing, it is less clear what the underlying mechanism or mechanisms may be. Most explanations of differences in infants' performances have something to do with differences in encoding or processing speed or the ability to remember old information and compare it to new information. Perhaps the most popular explanation is based upon processing speed. Why speed of processing visual pattern information in infancy should be related to later IQ in childhood is still an open question, although Rose and Feldman (1995) have recently reported that these infancy measures correlate with perceptual speed at 11 years of age, even when IQ was controlled.

Whatever the mechanism, correlations in the .4, .5, or even .6 range between measures of infant attention at around 6 months and later measures of IQ at around 6 years are quite impressive, particularly in light of the failure of standardized IQ tests to predict. But the results are not without controversy; not everyone obtains such high correlations. Both Lecuyer (1989) and Slater (1995a), for example, point out that the so-called 0.05 syndrome makes it difficult to publish a paper if the correlations are not statistically significant. Many studies have probably not found a relationship between infant attention and IQ, but they are not counted in summaries or meta-analyses because no one knows about them. In their meta-analysis of this literature, McCall and Carriger (1993) evaluate three other criticisms that have been raised about the importance of these correlations. First, habituation and novelty preference measures may not reflect any interesting cognitive process. Second, the infancy measures have only moderate test-retest reliabilities. Third, the small sample sizes used may lead to a prediction artifact—that is, the inclusion of a few extreme scores, perhaps by infants who have known disabilities, can inflate correlations when the sample N is small. McCall and Carriger conclude that although these criticisms have some merit, in the end they do not negate the fact that even with normal populations, the ability to make long-term predictions is impressive.

A Specific Information-Processing Explanation

Before leaving this section, it might be worthwhile to try to understand these individual differences by referring to the specific set of information-processing propositions mentioned previously in this chapter (Cohen & Cashon, 2001b). First, it seems a bit odd that previous explanations have assumed that somehow habituation and novelty preferences are tapping infant information processing, but they do not emphasize how infants are actually processing the information or how that processing changes with age. It is not a coincidence that the best predictions seem to result when infants are between about 4 and 7 months of age and they are shown complex, abstract patterns or pictures of faces. That is just the age period when infants should be making a transition from processing those pictures in a piecemeal fashion to processing them holistically. If one makes the additional assumption that processing and remembering something holistically takes less time and fewer resources than processing it one piece at a time, then the following set of results—all of which have been reported—would be predicted.

- Younger infants should look longer at complex patterns than do older infants because the younger ones, who are processing the individual features, in effect have more to process.
- At 4 or 5 months of age, infants with short looking times should be more advanced than are infants with long looking times because the short lookers have made the transition to holistic processing, whereas the long lookers are still processing the stimuli piece by piece.
- Optimal predictions should occur in a novelty preference procedure when familiarization times are short. Obviously if familiarization times are long enough, even piecemeal processors will have sufficient time to process and remember all or most of the pieces.
- Both measures of infant fixation duration in habituation tasks and measures of percent novelty in novelty preference tasks should work equally well; both are essentially testing the same thing in different ways. Short fixation durations imply holistic processing. Therefore, short lookers should be more advanced than long lookers. Novelty preference tasks work when familiarization times are short—in other words, at the end of familiarization the holistic processor will have had time to process and remember the pattern presented, but for the piecemeal processor much about the pattern will still be novel. Therefore, when tested with the familiar versus a novel pattern, the holistic processor should show a greater novelty preference.

Thus, according to this version of the information-processing approach, the correlations with later intelligence occur because the infant tasks are tapping into an important developmental transition in information processing at exactly the right age and with exactly the right stimuli to assess that transition. Those who develop more rapidly as infants will tend to continue that rapid development and become the

children with higher IQs. Whether the developmental progression that is being assessed in infancy is specific to infant perception and cognition or whether it is much more general really has yet to be determined.

Two final points can be derived from this approach. First, it is clear that the piecemeal to holistic transition is hierarchical. It occurs at several different levels at different ages. Therefore, one would predict that if simpler stimuli were presented with younger ages or more complex stimuli such as categories or events involving multiple objects were presented at older ages, one might achieve the same level of prediction that one now finds with complex two-dimensional patterns in the 4- to 7-month age period. At the very least this viewpoint predicts that the most appropriate stimuli for the infants to process will change systematically with age.

The other point is that the information-processing tasks given to infants might be tapping processing or perceptual speed as some assume, but only in an indirect way. More advanced infants may appear to process the items more rapidly because they effectively have fewer items to process in the same stimulus—not because they are processing each item more rapidly. After the manner in which infants process information at a particular age is understood, one can design experiments that equate the effective amount of information at different ages to see whether older and more advanced infants really do process and remember information more rapidly.

CONCLUDING COMMENTS

As we were contemplating topics to include in this chapter, it became obvious that it would be impossible to review all or even most of the research on infant perception and cognition in the space allotted. Instead we decided to concentrate on several areas that not only have been very productive over the years, but also tend to relate to each other in one way or another. The purpose was to provide some overall organization to the field. Admittedly, that organization is based upon an information-processing perspective, the perspective we believe most adequately encompasses most of the findings, both basic and applied. However, we also included other theoretical perspectives and attempted to show how these perspectives are similar or different from one another. It should be obvious that we relied almost exclusively on issues and evidence from infant visual perception and cognition and on techniques designed to address those issues. One could argue that that is where most of the action is these days.

We fully recognize, however—and want the reader to appreciate—that many other topics are equally important and exciting. These topics include but are not limited to auditory and speech perception, the relationship between perception and action, cross-modal perception, the perception of number, the understanding of causality and animacy, the expectation and anticipation of future events, and an understanding of the organization of complex sequences of events. We believe many of the issues addressed in this chapter apply to these topics as well. For example, some of these areas are clearly in the domain of perception and others are much more in cognition; still others fall somewhere in between. Again, the nature versus nurture debate rears its head with respect to these topics as well as to the ones described in more detail in the chapter. Furthermore, traditional theoretical perspectives have been applied to these topics and to the ones covered in this chapter. Like those topics covered in this chapter, we believe more recent theoretical approaches such as connectionist modeling, dynamical systems, and information processing may lead to advances in these topics as well.

One thing is certain. The area of infant perception and cognition is alive and well and making continued progress. Spectacular results and unwarranted assumptions are being replaced by solid evidence. The field is expanding. Topics investigated under the rubric of infant perception and cognition are becoming more and more advanced, and the subjects of previous studies are getting older and older. At the same time, investigators of cognitive processes in children are going younger and younger to find the origins of those processes. In some cases—such as in *theory of mind* research—the two fields have met, and fruitful collaborations are taking place. Collaborations are also beginning between investigators in infant perception and cognition and those in other apparently quite disparate areas such as sensory psychophysics, cognitive neuroscience, language acquisition, and even artificial intelligence and robotics. It is an exciting and dynamic time. Over the past 25 years we have seen exponential growth in research on infant perception and cognition. Given current attempts to apply approaches broad enough to relate basic and applied research—and excursions into collaborations that will add new dimensions to our understanding—continued rapid progress in research on infant perception and cognition is not only likely, it is inevitable.

REFERENCES

Adams, R. J., Courage, M. L., & Mercer, M. E. (1994). Systematic measurement of human neonatal color vision. *Vision Research, 34,* 1691–1701.

Adolph, K. E., Eppler, M. A., & Gibson, E. J. (1993a). Crawling versus walking infants' perception of affordances for locomotion over sloping surfaces. *Child Development, 64,* 1158–1174.

Adolph, K. E., Eppler, M. A., & Gibson, E. J. (1993b). Development of perception of affordances. In C. Rovee-Collier & L. P. Lipsitt (Eds.), *Advances in infancy research* (Vol. 8, pp. 51–98). Norwood, NJ: Ablex.

Baillargeon, R. (1987). Object permanence in 3.5- and 4.5-month-old infants. *Developmental Psychology, 23,* 655–664.

Baillargeon, R. (1995). A model of physical reasoning in infancy. In C. Rovee-Collier & L. P. Lipsitt (Eds.), *Advances in infancy research* (Vol. 9, pp. 305–371). Norwood, NJ: Ablex.

Baillargeon, R. (1999). Young infants' expectations about hidden objects: A reply to three challenges. *Developmental Science, 2,* 115–132.

Baillargeon, R., Spelke, E. S., & Wasserman, S. (1985). Object permanence in five-month-old infants. *Cognition, 20,* 191–208.

Banks, M. S., & Ginsburg, A. P. (1985). Early visual preferences: A review and new theoretical treatment. In H. W. Resse (Ed.), *Advances in child development and behavior* (Vol. 19). New York: Academic Press.

Banks, M. S., & Salapatek, P. (1983). Infant visual perception. In P. H. Mussen (Ed.), *Handbook of child psychology* (pp. 435–571). New York: Wiley.

Behl-Chadha, G. (1996). Basic-level and superordinate-like categorical representations early in infancy. *Cognition, 60,* 343–364.

Berlyne, D. E. (1958). The influence of the albedo and complexity of stimuli on visual fixation in the human infant. *British Journal of Psychology, 49,* 315–318.

Blanton, M. G. (1917). The behavior of the human infant during the first thirty days of life. *Psychological Review, 24,* 456–483.

Bogartz, R. S., Cashon, C. H., Cohen, L. B., Schilling, T. H., & Shinskey, J. L. (2000). Reply to Baillargeon, Aslin, and Munakata. *Infancy, 1,* 479–490.

Bogartz, R. S., Shinskey, J. L., & Schilling, T. H. (2000). Object permanence in 5.5-month-old infants. *Infancy, 1,* 403–428.

Bornstein, M. H., Kessen, W., & Weiskopf, S. (1976). Color vision and hue categorization in young infants. *Journal of Experimental Psychology: Human Perception and Performance, 2,* 115–129.

Bornstein, M. H., & Sigman, M. D. (1986). Continuity in mental development from infancy. *Child Development, 57,* 251–274.

Bower, T. G. R. (1966a). Slant perception and shape constancy in infants. *Science, 151,* 832–834.

Bower, T. G. R. (1966b). The visual world of infants. *Scientific American, 215,* 80–92.

Bower, T. G. R. (1974). *Development in infancy.* San Francisco: W. H. Freeman.

Bradley, K. L., & Cohen, L. B. (1994, May). *The understanding of solidity in 8-month-old infants.* Poster presented at the Midwestern Psychological Association meeting, Chicago.

Bridger, W. H. (1961). Sensory habituation and discrimination in the human neonate. *American Journal of Psychiatry, 117,* 991–996.

Bronshtein, A. I., Antonova, T. G., Kamenetskaya, A. G., Luppova, N. N., & Sytova, V. H. (1958). On the development of the functions of analyzers in infants and some animals at the early stage of ontogenesis. In *Problems of evolution of physiological functions* (PTS Report No. 60-61066). Moscow: Academy of Science.

Caron, A. J., Caron, R. F., & Carlson, V. R. (1979). Infant perception of the invariant shape of objects in slant. *Child Development, 50,* 716–721.

Caron, A. J., Caron, R. F., & Glass, P. (1983). Responsiveness to relational information as a measure of cognitive functioning in non-suspect infants. In T. Field & A. Sostek (Eds.), *Infants born at risk: Physiological, perceptual, and cognitive processes* (pp. 181–209). New York: Grune and Stratton.

Cashon, C. H., & Cohen, L. B. (2000). Eight-month-old infants' perception of possible and impossible events. *Infancy, 1,* 429–446.

Cashon, C. H., & Cohen, L. B. (2001, April). *Developmental changes in infants' processing of faces.* Symposium paper presented at the Society for Research in Child Development Meeting, Minneapolis.

Chaput, H. H., & Cohen, L. B. (2001). *A model of infant causal perception and its development.* J. D. Moore & K. Stenning (Eds.), *Proceedings of the 23rd Annual Conference of the Cognitive Science Society* (pp. 182–187). Mahwah: Erlbaum.

Cohen, L. B. (1981). Examination of habituation as a measure of aberrant infant development. In S. Friedman & S. Sigman (Eds.), *Preterm birth and psychological development* (pp. 241–258). New York: Academic Press.

Cohen, L. B. (1988). An information processing view of infant cognitive development. In L. Weiscrantz (Ed.), *Thought without language* (pp. 211–228). Oxford, UK: Oxford University Press.

Cohen, L. B. (1991). Infant attention: An information processing approach. In M. J. Weiss & P. R. Zalazo (Eds.), *Newborn attention: Biological constraints and the influence of experience* (pp. 1–21). Norwood, NJ: Ablex.

Cohen, L. B. (1998). An information-processing approach to infant perception and cognition. In F. Simion & G. Butterworth (Eds.), *The development of sensory, motor, and cognitive capacities in early infancy* (pp. 277–300). Hove, UK: Psychology Press.

Cohen, L. B., Amsel, G., Redford, M. A., & Casasola, M. (1998). The development of infant causal perception. In A. Slater (Ed.), *Perceptual development: Visual, auditory, and speech perception in infancy* (pp. 167–209). East Sussex, UK: Psychology Press.

Cohen, L. B., & Caputo, N. F. (1978, May). *Instructing infants to respond to perceptual categories.* Presented at the Midwestern Psychological Association Meeting, Chicago.

Cohen, L. B., & Cashon, C. H. (2001a). Do 7-month-old infants process independent features or facial configurations? *Infant and Child Development, 10,* 83–92.

Cohen, L. B., & Cashon, C. H. (2001b). Infant object segregation implies information integration. *Journal of Experimental Child Psychology, 78,* 75–83.

Cohen, L. B., Gilbert, K. M., & Brown, P. S. (1996, April). *Infants' understanding of solidity: Replicating a failure to replicate.* Poster session presented at the International Conference on Infant Studies, Providence, RI.

Cohen, L. B., & Strauss, M. S. (1979). Concept acquisition in the human. *Child Development, 50,* 419–424.

Cohen, L. B., & Younger, B. A. (1983). Perceptual categorization in the infant. In E. Scholnick (Ed.), *New trends in conceptual representation* (pp. 197–220). Hillsdale, NJ: Erlbaum.

Cohen, L. B., & Younger, B. A. (1984). Infant perception of angular relations. *Infant Behavior and Development, 7,* 37–47.

Colombo, J., & Mitchell, D. W. (1990). Individual differences in early visual attention: Fixation time and information processing. In J. Colombo & J. Fagen (Eds.), *Individual differences in infancy* (pp. 193–227). Hillsdale, NJ: Erlbaum.

Day, R. H., & McKenzie, B. E. (1981). Infant perception of the invariant size of approaching and receding objects. *Developmental Psychology, 17,* 181–309.

Diamond, A. (1991). Neuropsychological insights into the meaning of object concept development. In S. Carey & R. Gelman (Eds.), *The epigenesis of mind: Essays of biology and cognition* (pp. 67–110). Hillsdale, NJ: Erlbaum.

Easterbrooks, M. A., Kisilevsky, B. S., Hains, S. M. J., & Muir, D. W. (1999). Faceness or complexity: Evidence from newborn visual tracking of facelike stimuli. *Infant Behavior and Development, 22,* 17–35.

Eimas, P. D., Siqueland, E. R., Jusczyk, P. W., & Vigorito, J. (1971). Speech perception in infants. *Science, 171,* 303–306.

Elman, J., Bates, E., Karmiloff-Smith, A., Johnson, M., Parisi, D., & Plunkett, K. (1996). *Rethinking Innateness: A connectionist perspective on development.* Cambridge, MA: MIT Press.

Engen, T., Lipsitt, L. P., Lewis, P., & Kaye, H. (1963). Olfactory responses and adaptation in the human neonate. *Journal of Comparative and Physiological Psychology, 56,* 73–77.

Fagan, J. F. (1984). The relationship of novelty preferences during infancy to later intelligence and recognition memory. *Intelligence, 8,* 339–346.

Fagan, J. F, Fantz, R. L., & Miranda, S. B. (1971, April). *Infants' attention to normal stimuli as a function of postnatal and conceptional age.* Paper presented at a meeting of the Society for Research in Child Development, Minneapolis, MN.

Fagan, J. F., & McGrath S. K. (1981). Infant recognition memory and later intelligence. *Intelligence, 5,* 121–130.

Fantz, R. L. (1958). Pattern vision in young infants. *Psychological Record, 8,* 43–47.

Fantz, R. L. (1961). The origin of form perception. *Scientific American, 204*(5), 66–72.

Fantz, R. L. (1963). Pattern vision in newborn infants. *Science, 140,* 296–297.

Fantz, R. L. (1964). Visual experience in infants: Decreased attention to familiar patterns relative to novel ones. *Science, 146,* 668–670.

Fantz, R. L., Fagan, J. F., & Miranda, S. B. (1975). Early visual selectivity as a function of pattern variables, previous exposure, age from birth and conception, and expected cognitive deficit. In L. B. Cohen & P. Salapatek (Eds.), *Infant perception: From sensation to cognition: Vol. 1. Basic visual processes* (pp. 249–346). New York: Academic Press.

Fantz, R. L., & Nevis, S. (1967). Perceptual preferences and perceptual-cognitive development in early infancy. *Merrill-Palmer Quarterly, 13,* 77–108.

Fantz, R. L., Ordy, J. M., & Udelf, M. S. (1962). Maturation of pattern vision in infants during the first six months. *Journal of Comparative and Physiological Psychology, 55,* 907–917.

Flavell, J. H. (1963). *The developmental psychology of Jean Piaget.* New York: Van Nostrand.

Friedman, S. L., & Sigman, M. (Eds.). (1981). *Preterm birth and psychological development.* New York: Academic Press.

Gibson, E. J. (1995). Exploratory behavior in the development of perceiving, acting, and the acquiring of knowledge. In L. P. Lipsitt & C. Rovee-Collier (Eds.), *Advances in infancy* (Vol. 9, pp. xxi–lxi). Norwood, NJ: Ablex.

Gibson, E. J., & Walk, R. D. (1960). The "visual cliff." *Scientific American, 202,* 64–71.

Goren, C. C., Sarty, M., & Wu, P. Y. K. (1975). Visual following and pattern discrimination of face-like stimuli by newborn infants. *Pediatrics, 56,* 544–549.

Granrud, C. E. (1987). Size constancy in newborn human infants. *Investigative Ophthalmology and Visual Science, 28*(5, Supplement).

Haith, M. M. (1998). Who put the cog in infant cognition? Is rich interpretation too costly? *Infant Behavior and Development, 21,* 167–179.

Haith, M. M., & Benson, J. B. (1998). Infant cognition. In W. Damon (Series Ed.), D. Kuhn, & R. S. Siegler (Vol. Eds.), *Handbook of child psychology: Vol. 2. Cognition, perception and language* (5th ed., pp. 199–254). New York: Wiley.

Hayne, H. (1996). Categorization in infancy. In C. Rovee-Collier & L. P. Lipsitt (Eds.), *Advances in infancy* (Vol. 10, pp. 79–120). Norwood, NJ: Ablex.

Hunt, J. M. (1961). *Intelligence and experience.* New York: Ronald.

Hunter, M. A., & Ames, E. W. (1988). A multifactor model of infant preferences for novel and familiar stimuli. In C. Rovee-Collier & L. P. Lipsitt (Eds.), *Advances in infancy research* (Vol. 5, pp. 69–95). Norwood, NJ: Ablex.

Irwin, O. C. (1941). Effect of strong light on the body activity of newborns. *Journal of Comparative and Physiological Psychology, 32,* 233–236.

Johnson, M. H. (1996). From cortex to cognition: Cognitive neuroscience studies of infant attention and perception. In C. Rovee-Collier & L. P. Lipsitt (Eds.), *Advances in infancy research* (Vol. 10, pp. 161–217). Norwood, NJ: Ablex.

Johnson, M. H. (1997). *Developmental cognitive neuroscience.* Oxford, UK: Blackwell.

Johnson, M. H., Dziurawiec, S., Ellis, H. D., & Morton, J. (1991). Newborns' preferential tracking of face-like stimuli and its subsequent decline. *Cognition, 40,* 1–19.

Johnson, M. H., & Morton, J. (1991). *Biology and cognitive development: The case of face recognition.* Oxford, UK: Blackwell.

Johnson, S. P., & Nañez, J. E. (1995). Young infants' perception of object unity in two-dimensional displays. *Infant Behavior and Development, 18,* 133–143.

Jusczyk, P. W., & Aslin, R. N. (1995). Infants' detection of sound patterns of words in fluent speech. *Cognitive Psychology, 29,* 1–23.

Kellman, P. J., & Arterberry, M. E. (1998). *The cradle of knowledge: Development of perception in infancy.* Cambridge, MA: MIT Press.

Kellman, P. J., & Spelke, E. S. (1983). Perception of partly occluded objects in infancy. *Cognitive Psychology, 15,* 483–524.

Kessen, W. (1965). *The child.* New York: Wiley.

Kleiner, K. A. (1993). Specific vs. non-specific face recognition device. In B. de Boysson-Bardies, S. de Schonen, P. Jusczyk, P. McNeilage, & J. Morton (Eds.), *Developmental neurocognition: Speech and face processing in the first year of life* (pp. 103–108). Boston: Kluwer.

Kopp, C. B., & McCall, R. B. (1982). Predicting later mental performance for normal, at risk, and handicapped infants. In P. B. Baltes & O. G. Brim, Jr. (Eds.), *Life-span development and behavior* (Vol. 4, pp. 33–61). New York: Academic Press.

Lalonde, C. E., & Werker, J. F. (1995). Cognitive influences on cross-language speech perception in infancy. *Infant Behavior and Development, 18,* 459–475.

Lecuyer, R. (1989). Habituation and attention, novelty and cognition: Where is the continuity? *Human Development, 32,* 148–157.

Leinbach, M. D., & Fagot, B. I. (1993). Categorical habituation to male and female faces: Gender schematic processing in infancy. *Infant Behavior and Development, 16,* 317–332.

Madole, K. L., Cohen, L. B., & Bradley, K. (1994, June). *Ten-month-old infants categorize from but not function.* Presented at the Ninth International Conference on Infant Studies, Paris, France.

Madole, K. L., & Oakes, L. M. (1999). Making sense of infant categorization: Stable processes and changing representations. *Developmental Review, 19,* 263–296.

Madole, K. L., & Oakes, L. M. (in press). Principles of developmental change in infants' category formation. In D. Rakison & L. Oakes (Eds.), *Categories and concepts in early development.* Oxford, UK: Oxford University Press.

Madole, K. L., Oakes, L. M., & Cohen, L. B. (1993). Developmental changes in infants' attention to function and form-function correlations. *Cognitive Development, 8,* 189–209.

Mandler, J. M. (1992). How to build a baby II: Conceptual primitives. *Psychological Review, 99,* 587–604.

Mandler, J. M. (2000a). What-global-before-basic trend. Commentary on perceptually based approaches to early categorization. *Infancy, 1,* 99–110.

Mandler, J. M. (2000b). Perceptual and conceptual processes in infancy. *Journal of Cognition and Development, 1,* 3–36.

Mandler, J. M., Bauer, P. J., & McDonough, L. (1991). Separating the sheep from the goats: Differentiating global categories. *Cognitive Psychology, 23,* 263–298.

Marcus, G. (1999a). Do infants learn grammar with algebra or statistics? *Science, 284,* 433.

Marcus, G. (1999b). Response: Rule learning by seven-month-old infants and neural networks. *Science, 284,* 875.

Mareschal, D., & French, R. (2000). Mechanisms of categorization in infancy. *Infancy, 1,* 59–76.

Maurer, D. (1985). Infants' perception of facedess. In T. M. Field & N. A. Fox (Eds.), *Social perception in infants* (pp. 73–100). Norwood, NJ: Ablex.

Maurer, D., & Barrera, M. (1981). Infants' perception of natural and distorted arrangements of a schematic face. *Child Development, 52,* 196–202.

Maurer, D., & Salapatek, P. (1976). Developmental changes in the scanning of faces by young infants. *Child Development, 47,* 523–527.

Maurer, D., & Young, R. (1983). Newborns' following of natural and distorted arrangements of facial features. *Infant Behavior and Development, 6,* 127–131.

McCall, R. B. (1979). Qualitative transitions in behavioral development in the first two years of life. In M. Bornstein & W. Kessen (Eds.), *Psychological development from infancy* (pp. 183–224). Hillsdale, NJ: Erlbaum.

McCall, R. B. (1981). Toward an epigenetic conception of mental development in the first year of life. In M. Lewis (Ed.), *Origins of intelligence* (pp. 97–122). New York: Plenum Press.

McCall, R. B., Appelbaum, M., & Hogarty, P. (1973). Developmental changes in mental performance. *Monographs of the Society of Research in Child Development, 38*(3, Serial No. 150).

McCall, R. B., & Carriger, M. (1993). A meta-analysis of infant habituation and recognition memory performance as predictors of later IQ. *Child Development, 64,* 57–79.

McCall, R. B., Hogarty, P., & Hurlburt, N. (1972). Transitions in infant sensorimotor development and the prediction of childhood IQ. *American Psychologist, 27,* 728–748.

McDonough, S. C. (1988). Early information processing in aberrant infants. In P. M. Vietze & H. G. Vaughan, Jr. (Eds.), *Early identification of infants with developmental disabilities* (pp. 318–329). Philadelphia: Grune and Stratton.

McDougall, W. (1908). An investigation of the colour sense of two infants. *British Journal of Psychology, 2,* 338–352.

Mervis, C. B., & Rosch, E. (1981). Categorization of natural objects. *Annual Review of Psychology, 32,* 89–115.

Miranda, S. B. (1976). Visual attention in defective and high-risk infants. *Merrill-Palmer Quarterly, 22,* 201–227.

Morton, J., & Johnson, M. H. (1991). CONSPEC and CONLERN: A two-process theory of infant face recognition. *Psychological Review, 98,* 164–181.

Munakata, Y., McClelland, J. L., Johnson, M. H., & Siegler, R. S. (1997). Rethinking infant knowledge: Toward an adaptive process account of successes and failures in object permanence tasks. *Psychological Review, 104,* 686–713.

Needham, A. (2001). Object recognition and object segregation in 4.5-month-old infants. *Journal of Experimental Child Psychology, 78,* 3–24.

Peeples, D. R., & Teller, D. Y. (1975). Color vision and brightness discrimination in human infants. *Science, 189,* 1102–1103.

Piaget, J. (1927). *The child's conception of physical causality* (M. Gabain, Trans.). Atlantic Highland, NJ: Humanities Press.

Piaget, J. (1952). *The origins of intelligence in children* (M. Cook, Trans.). New York: Basic Books. (Original work published 1936)

Piaget, J. (1954). *The construction of reality in the child* (M. Cook, Trans.). New York: Basic Books. (Original work published 1937)

Piaget, J. & Inhelder, B. (1969). *The psychology of the child.* New York: Basic Books.

Quinn, P. C., & Eimas, P. D. (1996). Perceptual organization and categorization in young infants. In C. Rovee-Collier & L. P. Lipsitt (Eds.), *Advances in infancy research* (Vol. 10, pp. 1–36). Norwood, NJ: Ablex.

Quinn, P. C., & Eimas, P. D. (1998). Evidence for a global categorical representation for humans by young infants. *Journal of Experimental Child Psychology, 69,* 151–174.

Quinn, P. C., & Eimas, P. D. (2000). The emergence of category representations during infancy: Are separate perceptual and conceptual processes required? *Journal of Cognition and Development, 1,* 55–61.

Quinn, P. C., Eimas, P. D., & Rosenkrantz, S. L. (1993). Evidence for representations of perceptually similar natural categories by 3-month-old and 4-month-old infants. *Perception, 22,* 463–475.

Quinn, P. C., & Johnson, M. H. (2000). Global before basic object categorization. *Infancy, 1,* 31–46.

Rakison, D. H., & Butterworth, G. E. (1998). Infants' use of object parts in early categorization. *Developmental Psychology, 34,* 49–62.

Rakison, D. H., & Poulin-Dubois, D. (2001). Developmental origin of the animate-inanimate distinction. *Psychological Bulletin, 127,* 209–228.

Rose, S. A., & Feldman, J. F. (1990). Infant cognition: Individual differences and developmental continuities. In J. Colombo & J. F. Fagan (Eds.), *Individual differences in infancy* (pp. 247–270). Hillsdale, NJ: Erlbaum.

Rose, S. A., & Feldman, J. F. (1995). Prediction of IQ and specific cognitive abilities at 11 years from infancy measures. *Developmental Psychology, 31,* 685–696.

Rose, S. A., Gottfried, A. W., & Bridger W. H. (1978). Cross-model transfer in infants: Relationship to prematurity and socioeconomic background. *Developmental Psychology, 14,* 643–652.

Rose, S. A., & Wallace, I. F. (1985). Visual recognition memory: A predictor of later cognitive functioning in preterms. *Child Development, 56,* 843–852.

Salapatek, P. (1975). Pattern perception in early infancy. In L. Cohen & P. Salapatek (Eds.), *Infant perception: From sensation to cognition: Vol. 1. Basic visual processes* (pp. 133–248). New York: Academic Press.

Salapatek, P., & Kessen, W. (1966). Visual scanning of triangles by the human newborn. *Journal of Experimental Child Psychology, 3,* 155–167.

Schafer, G., & Mareschal, D. (2001). Modeling infant speech sound discrimination using simple associative networks. *Infancy, 2,* 7–28.

Schilling, T. H. (2000). Infants' looking at possible and impossible screen rotations: The role of familiarization. *Infancy, 1,* 389–402.

Shinskey, J. L., Bogartz, R. S., & Poirier, C. R. (2000). The effects of graded occlusion on manual search and visual attention in 5- to 8-month-old infants. *Infancy, 1,* 323–346.

Shultz, T. R., & Bale, A. C. (2001). Neural network simulation of infant familiarization to artificial sentences: Rule-like behavior without explicit rules and variables. *Infancy, 2,* 501–536.

Sigman, M., & Parmelee, A. H. (1974). Visual preferences for four-month-old premature and full-term infants. *Child Development, 45,* 959–965.

Slater, A. M. (1995a). Individual differences in infancy and later IQ. *Journal of Child Psychology and Psychiatry, 36,* 69–112.

Slater, A. M. (1995b). Visual perception and memory at birth. In C. Rovee-Collier & L. P. Lipsitt (Eds.), *Advances in infancy research* (Vol. 9, pp. 107–162). Norwood, NJ: Ablex.

Slater, A. M., & Johnson, S. P. (1998). Visual sensory and perceptual abilities of the newborn: Beyond the blooming, buzzing confusion. In F. Simion & G. Butterworth (Eds.), *The development of sensory, motor and cognitive capacities in early infancy* (pp. 121–141). Hove, UK: Psychology Press.

Slater, A. M., Mattock, A., & Brown, E. (1990). Size constancy at birth: Newborn infants' responses to retinal and real size. *Journal of Experimental Child Psychology, 49,* 314–322.

Slater, A. M., Mattock, A., Brown, E., & Bremner, J. G. (1991). Form perception at birth: Cohen and Younger revisited. *Journal of Experimental Child Psychology, 51,* 395–405.

Slater, A. M., & Morison, V. (1985). Shape constancy and slant perception at birth. *Perception, 14,* 337–344.

Slater, A. M., Morison, V., & Rose, D., (1983). Perception of shape by the new-born baby. *British Journal of Developmental Psychology, 1,* 135–142.

Slater, A. M., Morison, V., Somers, M., Mattock, A., Brown, E., & Taylor, D. (1990). Newborn and older infants' perception of partly occluded objects. *Infant Behavior and Development, 13,* 33–49.

Smith, L. B. (1999). Do infants possess innate knowledge structures? The con side. *Developmental Science, 2,* 133–144.

Smith, L. B., & Thelen, E. (1993). *A dynamical systems approach to development: Applications.* Cambridge, MA: MIT Press.

Sokolov, E. N. (1963). *Perception and the conditioned reflex.* Hillsdale, NJ: Erlbaum.

Spelke, E. S. (1985). Preferential-looking methods as tools for the study of cognition in infancy. In G. Gottlieb & N. Krasnegor (Eds.), *Measurement of audition and vision in the first year of postnatal life* (pp. 323–363). Norwood, NJ: Ablex.

Spelke, E. S. (1998). Nativism, empiricism, and the origins of knowledge. *Infant Behavior and Development, 21,* 181–200.

Spelke, E. S., Breinlinger, K., Macomber, J., & Jacobson, K. (1992). Origins of knowledge. *Psychological Review, 99,* 605–632.

Strauss, M. S. (1979). Abstraction of prototypical information in adults and 10-month-old infants. *Journal of Experimental Psychology: Human Learning and Memory, 5,* 618–632.

Teller, D. Y., & Bornstein, M. H. (1987). Infant color vision and color perception: In P. Salapatek & L. Cohen (Eds.), *Handbook of infant perception: Vol. 1. From sensation to perception* (pp. 185–236). Orlando, FL: Academic Press.

Thelen, E., & Smith, L. B. (1994). *A dynamical systems approach to the development of cognition and action.* Cambridge, MA: MIT Press.

Tjossem, T. D. (1976). Early intervention: Issues and approaches. In T. D. Tjossem (Ed.), *Intervention strategies for high risk infants and young children* (pp. 3–33). Baltimore: University Park.

Vietze, P. M., & Vaughan, H. G. (Eds.), (1988). *Early identification of infants with developmental disabilities.* Philadelphia: Grune and Stratton.

Waxman, S. R. (1999). Specifying the scope of 13-month-olds' expectations for novel words. *Cognition, 70,* B35–B50.

Wilcox, T. (1999). Object individuation: Infants' use of shape, size, pattern, and color. *Cognition, 72,* 125–166.

Wilcox, T., & Baillargeon, R. (1998). Object individuation in infancy: The use of featural information in reasoning about occlusion events. *Cognitive Psychology, 37,* 97–155.

Xu, F., & Carey, S. (1996). Infants' metaphysics: The case of numerical identity. *Cognitive Psychology, 30,* 111–153.

Younger, B. A. (1985). The segregation of items into categories by 10-month-old infants. *Child Development, 56,* 1574–1583.

Younger, B. A., & Cohen, L. B. (1985). How infants form categories. In G. Bower (Ed.), *The psychology of learning and motivation: Advances in research and theory* (Vol. 19, pp. 211–247). New York: Academic Press.

Younger, B. A., & Cohen, L. B. (1986). Developmental change in infants' perception of correlations among attributes. *Child Development, 57,* 803–815.

Younger, B. A., & Fearing, D. (1998). Detecting correlations among form attributes: An object-examining test with infants. *Infant Behavior and Development, 21,* 289–297.

Younger, B. A., & Fearing, D. (2000). A global to basic trend in early categorization: Evidence from a dual-category habituation task. *Infancy, 1,* 47–58.

CHAPTER 4

Social and Emotional Development in Infancy

ROSS A. THOMPSON, M. ANN EASTERBROOKS, AND LAURA M. PADILLA-WALKER

Infancy is a period of origins. It is when a child's capabilities, individuality, and first relationships begin to develop. Early social and emotional development is concerned with developing capacities for emotional expression, sociability, self-understanding, social awareness, self-management, and other facets of socioemotional growth. Research in this field is important for understanding these central features of early development and for applying this knowledge to understanding why some young children become anxiously insecure in their attachments, easily dysregulated in their behavior when stressed, or preoccupied with sad affect early in life. By studying the dimensions and contexts of healthy or maladaptive growth, developmental scientists can contribute to preventive and therapeutic interventions and public policies designed to ensure that infancy is a period of growing competence, connection, happiness, and self-confidence.

Because infancy is a period of origins, the study of socioemotional development also addresses some of the most significant questions of contemporary developmental psychology. How are nature and nurture processes fused in shaping developmental pathways (cf. chapter by Overton in this volume)? How may early experiences have an enduring effect on social and emotional growth ("as the twig is bent, so grows the tree"), and under what conditions are their influ-

ences subsumed by subsequent developmental processes? In what ways are early relationships of significance for the growth of social dispositions, self-understanding, and personality? Under what conditions does early temperament provide a foundation for mature personality?

These enduring questions cast the study of early social and emotional development within the broader context of life-span development, and they focus on the early years as a period of potentially formative influences. Although not all developmental scholars concur that infancy may be a foundation for later development (see Kagan, 1984; Lewis, 1997; Scarr, 1992), belief in the enduring effects of early experiences is deeply rooted in Western and Eastern cultures as well as in developmental science. This belief contributes to the concerns of parents, practitioners, and policy makers that young children are afforded a good start in infancy because of the difficulties in later correcting developmental pathways that begin awry. The National Academy of Sciences Committee on Integrating the Science of Early Childhood Development recently highlighted the "fundamental paradox" that "development in the early years is both highly robust and highly vulnerable . . . because it sets either a sturdy or fragile state" for later development (Shonkoff & Phillips, 2000, pp. 4, 5). Although an overemphasis on infancy as a period of formative influences can lead people to perceive the early years primarily as they foreshadow later development—rather than as a developmental period that is significant in itself—this view also highlights the practical and scientific value of understanding social and emotional growth in infancy.

Research on early socioemotional development is important, therefore, because it affords understanding of the growth of emotions, relationships, and self in infancy; provides knowledge enabling parents and practitioners to promote healthy early psychosocial growth; and offers unique opportunities to explore central questions of early development, especially those related to the significance of the early years. Each of these perspectives on early socioemotional development provides a guiding orientation to this chapter.

We begin by placing infancy in context. We consider the psychobiological context of temperamental individuality and neurobiological growth that shape early emotions, individuality, and patterns of relating to others. We also consider the contexts of culture and family that shape, and are shaped by, early experiences. In doing so, the dynamic interplay of nature and nurture is profiled at the outset of the chapter (see, too, chapter by Overton in this volume).

Early emotional development and the growth of sociability are profiled next, with special attention to the importance of emotion to early social interaction and social relationships. This intertwining illustrates the integration of developmental functions, structures, and processes in infancy. In the section that follows, we focus on attachment relationships between infants and their caregivers, a topic of significant research interest during the past 30 years. Two central questions are highlighted: (a) how infants develop different patterns of attachment behavior in these relationships and (b) the controversial question of potentially enduring consequences of variations in attachments during infancy. The importance of relationships for self-awareness, emotional understanding, empathy, and conscience is subsequently discussed with respect to the early representations that are influenced by relational experience. Our focus on the representational features of early relationships constitutes a bridge between infancy and psychosocial development in early childhood, when representations of self, others, and relationships truly flourish. Finally, in a concluding note we consider the implications of research and theory in this field for policy and practice.

SOCIOEMOTIONAL DEVELOPMENT IN CONTEXT

Because the young of the human species cannot thrive outside of a relational context (Tobach & Schnierla, 1968), in order to understand infant socioemotional development, one must understand also the broader caregiving context. This sentiment, illustrated by Winnicott's celebrated statement that "there is no such thing as an infant" (Winnicott, 1965), sets the framework for this chapter. By its very definition socioemotional development invokes relationships. The mother-infant relationship is central to popular and scientific images of social and emotional development in infancy. This emphasis occurs because of cultural and theoretical traditions emphasizing that the sensitivity, warmth, and responsiveness of this first and primary relationship shapes a baby's initial, and in some conceptualizations continuing, social dispositions and expectations for others. Later in this chapter we examine research concerning this relationship, especially within the context of attachment theory. It is important first, however, to establish a broader framework for our discussion of early socioemotional development by considering how social and emotional responding and the very relationships that develop transactionally (Sameroff & Chandler, 1975) are shaped by the psychobiological context of neurological development and temperament, as well as by the broader social contexts of culture and family.

Psychobiological Context

Neurobiological Underpinnings

Infancy is a period of rapid physical and neurological growth, second only to the prenatal months in the scope and pace of development. This has significant implications for the changes that occur in emotional and social responding (see chapter by Gunnar & Davis in this volume). Emotional development is predicated on the growth of richly interconnected brain structures and hormonal influences that organize the arousal-activation and regulatory-recovery interplay of emotional behavior (LeDoux, 1996; Schore, 1994). Because emotions are biologically essential features of human functioning in that they are critical to the very survival of the infant from the earliest postnatal days, they are based on regions of the human nervous system that develop very early, including structures of the limbic system and the brain stem. The capacity of a newborn to exhibit distress, excitement, and rage reflects the early emergence of these deeply biologically rooted emotional brain systems.

Major advances in emotional responding occur during the initial years of life as a result of developmental changes in central neurobiological systems, including maturation in adrenocortical activation and parasympathetic regulation systems, and the slow growth of frontal regions of the neocortex that exert regulatory control over limbic activation (Gunnar, 1986; Porges, Doussard-Roosevelt, & Maiti, 1994;

Thompson, 1994). This development helps to account for the ontogeny of the newborn, whose unpredictable swings of arousal can be disconcerting to neonate and caregivers alike, into the emotionally more nuanced and well-regulated toddler, who is capable of responding emotionally to a wide range of events and whose emotional reactions can be managed by self and others. There are, of course, significant advances in emotional development yet to occur in childhood and adolescence with further growth in these and other brain processes.

For decades we have recognized that caregivers play a role in the infant's psychobiological organization. Sander (1964), for example, proposed that the first role of the caregiver was to aid the infant in achieving physiological regulation. There is intriguing recent evidence that individual differences in the quality of caregiving can influence the development of these neurobiological systems when early experiences are highly stressful (Gunnar, 2000; chapter by Gunnar & Davis in this volume) or when mothers are seriously or chronically depressed (Dawson & Ashman, 2000). This research suggests that development of the physiological systems managing emotion and coping is impaired by experiences of chronic stress when the caregiver is either the source of stress or fails to buffer it.

Although the topic of early brain development and its role in shaping cognitive and emotional development has enjoyed both scientific and popular currency during the last decade, it is important to understand the extent to which findings representing acute or chronic severe deprivation or stressors apply more broadly. At present there is little evidence that more typical variations in early care have a significant impact on individual differences in brain development. Nor is there strong evidence that time-limited critical periods or "windows of opportunity" exist for early socioemotional development during which essential experiential catalysts are required for the young brain to develop normally—this despite widely publicized claims to the contrary (Thompson, 2002; Thompson & Nelson, 2001). In other words, much of early brain development is *experience expectant* rather than *experience dependent*. In most cases, the typical circumstances of early care afford many opportunities for healthy social and emotional development to occur; caregivers who are not abusive or neglectful typically provide these opportunities in the course of their everyday social interactions with the infants in their care (Shonkoff & Phillips, 2000). For development to proceed otherwise would indicate a very fragile system indeed.

Because of these developmental changes in the neurobiological systems governing early social and emotional responding, it is not surprising that temperamental individuality also emerges and flourishes during infancy. The construct of temperament has eluded firm definition. Scientists enumerating the dimensions that comprise the domain of temperament have reported from three to nine dimensions (Chess & Thomas, 1986; Rothbart & Bates, 1998). Some of the most distinctive temperamental attributes that characterize infants at birth are based on emotional response tendencies, whether they concern the baby's dominant mood, adaptability, soothability, or reactions to novelty. In general, most theorists agree that aspects of temperament involve biologically based, heritable, response tendencies that involve emotionality, activity, and attention (see chapter by Cummings, Braungart-Rieker, & Rocher-Schudlich in this volume; Rothbart & Bates, 1998) and that are somewhat stable across time and context.

Temperamental individuality describes not only emotional response tendencies but also self-regulatory qualities (Goldsmith et al., 1987; Kagan, 1998; Rothbart & Bates, 1998); each of these has implications for social interactions and relationships. Young children who are behaviorally shy in response to new people or situations, for example, are displaying a temperamental attribute that is both emotional in quality (i.e., fearful) and self-regulatory (i.e., inhibited), with profound implications for the child's social functioning (Kagan, 1998). Both reactive and self-regulatory aspects of temperament are based on early-emerging biological individuality founded on differences in neuroendocrine functioning, the reactivity of subcortical or sympathetic nervous system structures, variability in parasympathetic regulation, or other nervous system processes (Rothbart & Bates, 1998).

The Construct of Temperament

Because infant socioemotional development is embedded in a relational context, understanding the construct of temperament is key. Because social relationships are influenced by temperament, they also have an effect on the expression of temperamental individuality. A young child's temperamental profile significantly influences how the child interacts with people in at least two ways. Temperamental qualities tend to *evoke* certain reactions from others (e.g., a temperamentally positive infant naturally elicits smiles and interest from others, paving the way for the development of mutually satisfying relationships) as well as *shape* a child's preferences for certain partners, settings, and activities (e.g., a temperamentally shy child tends to withdraw from unfamiliar social situations; Scarr & McCartney, 1983). Thus, temperamental qualities shape social and emotional growth because they channel the young child's early experiences in particular ways.

This interactional stance implies that early socioemotional growth can be significantly affected by how well a young child's temperamental profile accords with the requirements of his or her social settings, a concept known as *goodness of fit* (e.g., Chess & Thomas, 1986; see also chapters by Eccles, Wigfield, & Byrnes and by Lerner, Anderson, Balsano, Dowling, & Bobek in this volume). A temperamentally shy child is likely to be happier and become less withdrawn, for example, when parents are tolerant and accommodating to the child's need for greater support and time with new partners. These parents may want to invite a potential sitter into their home on several occasions while they remain at home, before they leave their infant alone with the new caregiver. By contrast, even a temperamentally easy-going child will have difficulty in settings where social demands are excessive and developmentally inappropriate. Because of this, social experiences can considerably modify the behavioral manifestations of temperamental qualities a baby exhibits at birth. The interactions, or transactions, between the child's constitutional makeup and the social "surround" acknowledge a more dynamic view of temperament than previously recognized (e.g., Lerner, 2002).

In light of this, and in view of the remarkable psychobiological advances of the early years, it is perhaps unsurprising that temperamental characteristics in infancy are only modestly predictive of later temperament, or of other behavior in the years that follow (Rothbart & Bates, 1998). Stronger evidence for enduring associations between temperament and later behavior begins to appear in children after the second birthday (Caspi, 1998; Sanson, Prior, Oberklaid, & Smart, 1998; see also chapter by Cummings, Braungart-Rieker, & Rocher-Schudlich in this volume), perhaps because many of the biological foundations of temperament have consolidated after infancy (although some continue to mature throughout childhood). An additional factor may be measurement artifact, with greater difficulty measuring appropriate manifestations of temperament in the early years. Stronger continuity after infancy also may be advanced by the fact that the 2-year-old is a more self-aware child whose developing self-understanding is likely to incorporate temperamental qualities that cause the child to perceive herself, and to respond to situations, in temperament-consistent ways. Thus, temperamental qualities in infancy may not foreshadow the personality of the adult, although they are significant for shaping the quality of a baby's social interactions with others.

There are, however, notable exceptions to this conclusion, namely the work on temperamental shyness or behavioral inhibition and work involving the construct of temperamental *difficulty*. Behavioral inhibition, associated with a unique physiological pattern including high and stable heart rate, elevated baseline cortisol, right frontal electroencephalograph (EEG) activation, and negative emotional and motor

reactivity to the unfamiliar (e.g., Calkins, Fox, & Marshall, 1996; Kagan, Reznick, & Snidman, 1987; Schmidt, Shahinfar, & Fox, 1996), has been identified early in infancy (Fox, Henderson, Rubin, Calkins, & Schmidt, 2001; Kagan & Snidman, 1991). Some work shows that the extremes of inhibition and the opposite end of the continuum, exuberance or uninhibited behavior, demonstrate considerable continuity from early infancy into toddlerhood and childhood (Fox et al., 2001; Kagan et al., 1987; Kagan & Snidman, 1991; Kagan, Snidman, & Arcus, 1998). Despite the stability, there also is lawful discontinuity in the behavioral manifestations of this pattern, with more early-inhibited children later showing decreased inhibition than early low-reactive or uninhibited children demonstrating later behavioral inhibition. Multiple factors may be implicated by this pattern of findings. Societal norms of desired behavior (e.g., positive affect, independence, sociability) may push for control of negative affect and manifestations of inhibition. Environmental factors may play an additional role. Fox et al. (2001) reported that infants who became less inhibited had significant out-of-home care experiences during the first two years. Whether these experiences with multiple caregivers, peers, and environments contributed to decreases in behavioral inhibition or whether differences among the groups in parent personality or child temperament affected families' decisions to place children in out-of-home care is a question that remains unanswered.

In addition to the intriguing work on behavioral inhibition, temperament research that demonstrates some measure of continuity from infancy into childhood utilizes the construct of temperamental difficulty (Chess & Thomas, 1986). Temperamental difficulty is a constellation of qualities that includes negative mood, frequent and intense negative emotional behavior, irregularity, poor adaptability, and demandingness. As was suggested by the research on temperamental inhibition, the interaction, or transaction, of temperamental characteristics and environmental characteristics aids prediction of long-term continuity or consequences. Difficult temperament in infancy is significantly more prognostic of later psychosocial difficulties because this constellation of characteristics is likely to create and maintain problems in early interactions with others and to color many aspects of early experience compared to other temperamental configurations (Bates, 1987; Rothbart & Bates, 1998).

Relational Context

Contrary to traditional maturationist views (e.g., Gesell, 1940), therefore, the infant is psychobiologically constituted by early experiences as well as heredity. This is one reason for interest in early caregiving relationships that sensitively accommodate to the infant's temperamental qualities and offer support for the unfolding of positive emotional and social dispositions. The research evidence reviewed earlier suggesting that neurobiological systems governing emotion and coping with stress can be affected by abusive or neglectful care, by the caregiver's serious depression, and possibly by other chronic experiences not yet studied contributes further to an appreciation of the importance of these relationships for healthy psychobiological growth.

But the social context of infancy extends far beyond relationships with primary caregivers to include other family members, including fathers and siblings. Although early relationships with these partners have been studied much less, infants develop qualitatively distinct modes of interaction with their fathers and older siblings that arise from the unique social experiences that they have with each (Dunn, 1993; Lamb, 1997). Infant-father interactions are characterized by exuberant, emotionally animated physical play, for example, that helps to account for a baby's excitement in the father's presence (Lamb, 1997; Parke & Tinsley, 1987). These characteristics of many father-infant play interactions may in part account for the importance of the father-child relationship to emotional regulation and control (Gottman, Katz, & Hooven, 1997). Although *style* of paternal involvement (warmth, sensitivity) is linked to positive outcomes for children, *amount* of involvement is not (Easterbrooks & Goldberg, 1985; Elder, Van Nguyen, & Caspi, 1985; Lamb, 1997).

Siblings also are unique sources of social and emotional understanding as young children carefully observe, interpret, and inquire about their behavior directly with the sibling or with others in the family (Dunn, 1998). In fact, sibling relationships may play a very important role in the emotional and social development of infants, given the special nature of the relationships. Sibling relationships, notable for their emotional intensity, provide ample opportunities for observing, experiencing, and interpreting both positive and negative emotions. Although sibling rivalry may be accompanied by intense competition and negative emotions, parents also state that siblings often can most easily induce positive mood in infants. These observations, combined with the role structure of sibling relationships, may serve as a catalyst for developmental growth in infants' social and emotional repertoire. In part, this may be due to the fact that the demands of sibling relationships may encourage infants to stretch emotionally in ways that relationships with parents or other adult caregivers do not.

Whereas the direct interactions between infants and their family members are recognized as important, far less attention has been devoted to the indirect effect of other relationships,

in terms of both their influence *on* infant development and the ways in which they are influenced *by* a developing infant. Positive marital relationships are more likely to be associated with sensitive parent-infant interactions because marital harmony is thought to provide support for the sometimes-difficult tasks of parenting (Gottman et al., 1997; Goldberg & Easterbrooks, 1984). Conversely, marital conflict is associated with less optimal parent-infant interaction and infant adjustment (e.g., attachment, emotion regulation; Cummings & Davies, 1994). In similar fashion, the extent to which fathers become actively involved in caregiving responsibilities significantly affects the extent to which mothers feel stressed or supported in their caregiving role.

The social ecology of infancy extends significantly beyond the family, of course, to include relationships with adults and peers in out-of-home care (see chapter by Fitzgerald, Mann, Cabrera, & Wong in this volume). This means that early social and emotional development is shaped not only by the quality of the relationship with the primary caregiver but also by relationships with a range of partners of varying developmental status and different characteristics who are encountered in widely varying social contexts (Howes, 1999). Zimmerman and McDonald (1995) reported, for example, that infant emotional availability was distinct with mothers and other adult caregivers (e.g., fathers, day care providers).

Research in the 1970s and 1980s established that infant peer relationships develop as early as the first year of life and help to define the structure and content of these interactions (Adamson & Bakeman, 1985; Howes, 1988; Mueller & Vandell, 1979). Although infant peer relationships involve both positive and negative emotions (Adamson & Bakeman, 1985; Hay, Nash, & Pedersen, 1983), positive affect predominates.

Familial and nonfamilial relationships may have overlapping or independent influences on early psychosocial growth. Recognizing these patterns undermines any assumption that, within this broad social ecology, a baby's social and emotional dispositions arise from social encounters with the mother alone. In fact, several studies suggest that relationships with nonparental caregivers are more predictive of later social skills than are relationships with parents (Oppenheim, Sagi, & Lamb, 1988). Indeed, understanding how different social partners have unique and overlapping influences on early socioemotional growth is one of the significant research challenges in this field.

Cultural Context

Uniting these diverse social influences are the values of the culture. Cultural values define the needs and characteristics of infants, the roles and responsibilities of caregivers, and the goals of child development that are based on the mature attributes that are consensually valued (see chapter by Saraswathi & Mistry in this volume). Cultural beliefs and values guide the behavior of caregivers, family members, and others in the community with an interest in young children and, in doing so, shape the ecology of infant care (New, 2001). For example, among the Efe, a foraging community in the forests of Zaire, infants receive care from birth by many adults besides the mother, and this intense social contact leads to strong connections with many people in the community (Morelli & Tronick, 1991; Tronick, Morelli, & Winn, 1987). This cultural pattern of infant care not only ensures that young children are protected by accommodating to the wide-ranging foraging activities of men and women, but also incorporates diverse community members into infant care and socializes infants into the intrinsically interactive, cooperative features of community life.

Culture is not synonymous with nationality. Within the United States and other heterogeneous nations, multiple cultural communities exist with distinct values related to young children and their care. General cultural attitudes are related to specific parental child-rearing beliefs, or ethnotheories, and practices (Small, 1998). One of the most important values related to child care that transcends specific national norms is the emphasis placed on the independence or interdependence of infants with their caregivers (based on Triandis's 1995 distinction between individualist and collectivist cultures). Belief in the importance of infant-caregiver independence or interdependence affects many features of infant care and is influential even before a baby's birth. Korean mothers, for example, are explicitly instructed to view each prenatal event as an experience shared with the fetus, and they are encouraged to avoid unpleasant experiences that might affect the child or the mother-infant relationship (Yu, 1984). The interdependence fostered by cultural beliefs such as these significantly influences subsequent patterns of infant care in Korea and in other cultures.

The extent to which cultural values emphasize the independence or interdependence of infant and caregiver affects early socioemotional growth through its impact on infant care practices. In most families in the United States, for example, infants sleep in their own beds independently of their parents within the first few months after birth, and their parents are extremely concerned about the establishment of reliable sleeping patterns and report a large number of sleeping problems in their offspring (Morelli, Rogoff, Oppenheim, & Goldsmith, 1992). By contrast, Japanese, African, and Mayan infants sleep with their mothers until toddlerhood, and their sleeping patterns are determined by the sleeping rhythms of those around them and are less of a family disturbance

(Small, 1998). Infants who awaken are more easily and quickly comforted, fed, and returned to sleep (Harkness, 1980; Morelli et al., 1992). Likewise, not only does the constant carrying of infants by mothers of the !Kung hunter-gatherers of the Kalahari desert permit reliable contact and regular feeding, but also the baby's fusses receive an immediate response before they escalate, and soothing can occur more quickly (Barr, Bakeman, Konner, & Adamson, 1987; Hunziker & Barr, 1986). By contrast, the cries of infants in the United States often escalate because soothing is delayed by the physical distance between infant and mother or by other demands in a child-care setting. The close physical contact of sleeping and carrying reflects cultural values concerning infant-mother interdependence that reduces the incentives for infants to acquire skills for managing their distress independently (Pomerleau, Malcuit, & Sabatier, 1991).

A cultural emphasis on independence or interdependence also influences other aspects of mother-infant interaction, including feeding practices, verbal stimulation, and provision of play materials. In one observational study, Puerto Rican mothers were found to be more likely to restrain their infants, physically position them, and issue direct commands to them, each of which was consistent with a maternal emphasis on interdependence and the infant's need for guidance. By contrast, American mothers offered more suggestions to their offspring and praised infant behavior much more than Puerto Rican mothers did (Harwood, Scholmerich, & Schulze, 2000). In another study, Japanese mothers were observed to respond in a more animated fashion when the infant's attention was directed toward them, whereas mothers in the United States were more responsive when infants were looking at objects rather than at them (Bornstein, Tal, & Tamis-LeMonda, 1991; Bornstein, Toda, Azuma, Tamis-LeMonda, & Ogino, 1990). This difference is consistent with the close intimacy fostered by Japanese mothers with their offspring, in contrast to the greater emphasis on individualism and independence of mothers in the United States.

Cultural differences in normative patterns of social interaction are important not only because of how they affect early social and emotional responding, but also because they compel developmental scientists' attention to the appropriate assessment of early social interaction and social relationships. Researchers cannot assume that caregiving practices and infant behavior that are normative for middle-class families in the United States are standard worldwide, nor even within different cultural communities inside the United States. Thus, early socioemotional development must be viewed within the context of the specific cultural values and goals that guide child-rearing practices. However, many aspects of early socioemotional growth, such as forming close attachments to caregivers, are broadly observed in different cultural contexts and appear to be universal features of psychosocial development based on human evolutionary adaptation (van IJzendoorn & Sagi, 1999). An important challenge to students of socioemotional development, therefore, is how to study broadly generalizable processes of social and emotional growth while respecting cultural differences in how these processes are realized (see, e.g., Rothbaum, Weisz, Pott, Miyake, & Morelli, 2000).

Summary

Taken together, the psychobiological context of infant development and the contexts of culture and family offer reminders that early socioemotional development occurs within a broader network of influences than is commonly portrayed. Although the majority of the research reviewed in this chapter focuses on developmental influences in the context of close relationships—most commonly mother-infant relationships—these relationships are influenced by the integration of the infant's rapid neurobiological maturation and the values and beliefs of family and cultural members.

DEVELOPING EMOTIONS AND SOCIABILITY

It is difficult to conceive of early social development apart from the emotions that color social interactions in infancy. Emotions have been called the language of infancy, and infants as "emotion detectors" (Tronick, 2001). Infants signal their emerging social discriminations and preferences according to which partners can most readily evoke smiles and cooing, and adults become engaged in social play with babies because of the animated, exuberant responses that they receive. Caregivers attune to the preemptory sound of the infant cry and the hunger, pain, or startled fear it reflects, and the baby's developing sensitivity to the emotional expressions of others reflects achievements in an emerging understanding of people. In short, the study of "socioemotional" development reflects how interwoven are the processes of early social and emotional growth, each of which provides a window into psychological development.

Although it is common to view emotions as disorganizing, unregulated influences on infant behavior, it is more appropriate to regard their influence as both organizing and disorganizing (similar to how emotions affect adults). The image of a 3-month-old in a raging, uncontrollable tantrum must be joined to the image of the same child who has been motivated to learn how to make a crib mobile spin because of the interest and pleasure it evokes. Even a toddler's angry

conflict with a parent can motivate and organize new understanding of another's thoughts, feelings, or motives.

Development of Emotional Expression and Sensitivity

Most conceptualizations of early socioemotional development place the social nature of emotions as a centerpiece of early development. Emotional availability, a relational construct, is considered central to healthy socioemotional development (Easterbrooks & Biringen, 2000). According to Emde (1980), emotional availability refers to responsiveness and attunement to another's signals, goals, and needs. Stern (1985) called it a "dance"—those captivating images of parent and infant immersed in interaction, oblivious to the outside world. Such pictures highlight the extent to which emotions are part of the fabric of complex relationships, not simply sensations to be regulated. Emotions, in fact, "are apt to be a sensitive barometer of early developmental functioning in the child-parent system" (Emde & Easterbrooks, 1985, p. 80).

Face-to-Face Social Interaction

An important early social context in which the organizing influence of emotions is apparent is face-to-face social interaction with an adult partner. This activity becomes prominent by the time infants are 2 to 3 months of age, when they are capable of sustained alertness and display preferential responses to familiar people, and it continues until about 6 or 7 months, after which more active kinds of infant-parent interactions ensue with the baby's developing locomotor skills (Tronick, 1989). Face-to-face play involves short but intense episodes of focused interaction between an infant and an adult (typically the mother) in which each partner entertains the other with smiling, vocalizing, animated facial expressions, and other social initiatives and responses. The goal of this activity is the establishment and maintenance of well-coordinated exchanges that elicit mutual pleasure, although these synchronous exchanges occur only about 30% or less of the time that mothers and infants interact with each other (Tronick, 1989; Tronick & Cohn, 1989). These sequences of affective synchrony and mismatches offer opportunities for infants to learn important lessons about the possibilities of reparation of dyssynchronous states (Kohut, 1977; Lyons-Ruth, Bronfman, & Parson, 1999; Tronick, 2001). For example, rules of communication within and across interactions, preferred interactive tempo and intensity, and ways to convert negative affect into neutral or pleasurable states can be learned. As a consequence, other developmental skills, such as learning to self-regulate (including managing emotional arousal) and to repair dyssynchronous interaction, are also fostered by these intensive social exchanges (Gianino & Tronick, 1988).

Although adults take the lead in face-to-face interaction by sensitively scaffolding their initiatives to accord with the infant's readiness to respond (Kaye, 1982), infants also participate actively through their animated emotional expressions, approach and withdrawal, and patterns of gazing that signal their interest in social play. In this respect, emotions organize early social interaction by structuring the ebb and flow of social activity and by providing signals by which each partner can respond in a coordinated fashion to the other. Moreover, changes in infant behavior during play over the early months also indicate changes in the emerging social expectations that guide the baby's behavior. Infants begin to expect, for example, that others will spontaneously interact with them, and when their mothers are instructed to be impassive and expressionless, their offspring respond with social elicitations (e.g., brief smiles, increased vocalizing and reaching) followed, eventually, by withdrawal (Cohn, Campbell, & Ross, 1991; Cohn & Tronick, 1983). Even more, infants begin to expect to receive responses from their partners that are contingent on their own behavior: They respond with positive animation to responsive partners but turn away from partners who are comparably active but not responsive to the infant's initiatives (Murray & Trevarthen, 1985; Symons & Moran, 1987). Taken together, these behaviors suggest that within the first 6 months, the infant is learning about the rules of social interaction and is developing a rudimentary awareness of her or his own efficacy in evoking responses from other people.

Later in the first year, infants respond differently also to the appearance of their mothers and fathers in social play, reflecting the development of discriminative expectations for specific familiar partners (Lamb, 1981). According to Tronick (2001), two qualities regulate the uniqueness of relationships that infants have with different social partners: *implicit relational knowing* (e.g., "how we interact together") and *thickness*. Implicit relational knowing derives from repeated patterns of affect in interaction with a partner; thickness refers to the number of different time-activity contexts of interactions (e.g., play, feeding, bathing, putting to bed). As infants develop, then, much of implicit relational knowing is increasingly unique to specific relationships, which become more differentiated.

The Role of Distress-Relief Sequences

Face-to-face play is not the only context in which social expectations develop. From repeated experiences of distress and its subsequent relief from a caregiver's nurturant response, infants begin to expect to be soothed after the adult arrives. This is revealed in the baby's anticipatory quieting, after fussing occurs, to the sound of the caregiver's footsteps (Gekoski, Rovee-Collier, & Carulli-Rabinowitz, 1983; Lamb & Malkin, 1986). By the latter part of the first year, therefore, infants have begun to learn about the behavioral propensities of others, as well as the self's efficacy in provoking these behaviors, and this makes the baby a more competent and self-aware social partner. These early social expectations also shape emotional responding because an awareness of the contingency between one's actions and another's response is a highly reliable elicitor of smiling and laughter and can contribute to the alleviation of distress (Watson, 1972, 1979). Consequently, an infant's early experiences of face-to-face play and the relief of distress contribute significantly to the social expectations and positive emotional responses to caregivers that set the stage for the development of attachment relationships.

The Growth of Meaning, Reciprocity, and Competence in Emotional Development

Throughout the first year, infants develop a more acute sensitivity to the emotions of others as they are expressed in vocal intonation, facial expression, and other behavior. Because these various modes of emotional expression typically covary, infants have many opportunities to learn about the behavioral propensities of someone with, say, an angry vocal tone, or the facial expressions that accompany the sound of laughter. By the second half of the first year, the emotions of others have become affectively meaningful to the baby through processes of conditioning, emotion contagion, or of empathy (Saarni et al., 1998). That is, the emotions of others become meaningful to the baby because of the actions with which they are associated and the resonant emotional responses that they evoke in the infant. Equally important, an awareness of the emotions of others in circumstances that evoke emotion in the infant herself contributes to a growing realization that other people, like oneself, are subjective human entities.

Later in the first year, the growth of crawling, creeping, and walking introduces new challenges to parent-infant interaction and socioemotional growth (Bertenthal & Campos, 1990; Biringen, Emde, Campos, & Appelbaum, 1995; Campos et al., 2000; Campos, Kermoian, & Zumbahlen, 1992). On one hand, self-produced locomotion changes the child, who, with the capacity to move independently, becomes more capable of goal attainment, as well as of wandering away from the parent, acting in a dangerous or disapproved manner, and experiencing the varieties of emotion and feelings of self-efficacy that these activities inspire. Parents commonly report that this developmental transition is accompanied by their child's increased expressions of affection but also of anger and frustration, and offspring also become more adept at monitoring the parents' whereabouts (Campos et al., 1992; Campos et al., 2000). On the other hand, self-produced locomotion changes the parent, who must now more actively monitor the child's activity by using prohibitions and sanctions and expecting compliance from offspring. The testing of wills that ensues from self-produced locomotion not only is a challenge to the emotional quality of the parent-child relationship, but also provides a catalyst to the infant's early grasp of mental states in others that are different from the child's own.

This development is important because by 9 to 10 months of age infants begin to show other indications of a dawning awareness of mental states in others. For example, they strive to achieve joint visual attention with those with whom they are communicating, and their protocommunicative acts (e.g., gestures, vocal appeals) and imitative activity each increase in sophistication. Taken together, infants are beginning to understand that others are intentional agents with potentially shared subjective orientations toward objects and events that are worth understanding. This dawning psychological understanding changes how they interact with others and their interpretations of why people act as they do (Bretherton, McNew, & Beeghly-Smith, 1981; Carpenter, Nagell, & Tomasello, 1998; Tomasello, Kruger, & Ratner, 1993).

Social Referencing

Another reflection of the infant's growing realization that others have mental states is the emergence of social referencing, in which infants respond to events (particularly novel or ambiguous events) based on the emotional expressions that they detect in other people (Campos & Stenberg, 1981; Feinman, 1992; Saarni, Mumme, & Campos, 1998). In a manner similar to how adults take their cues from others nearby when responding to unexpected or uncertain situations, the sight of an adult's reassuring smile or terrified gaze (especially if it is accompanied by the appropriate vocalizations and other behavior) can significantly influence whether a young child approaches or withdraws from an unfamiliar person or novel object. Social referencing is commonly believed to arise from the infant's active search for clarifying information from another's emotional reactions, although it may also be derived less deliberately when the child shares a new experience or seeks reassurance from a caregiver (Baldwin & Moses, 1996). In either case, social referencing

is important for socioemotional development because it indicates that infants are competent at obtaining and enlisting emotional information from others into their own responses to events, and it reflects the infant's growing awareness of accessible subjective states in others.

Although its direct effects on an infant's behavior can be modest and transient, social referencing in the first year is the vanguard of the variety of more sophisticated referencing activities that enable young children to acquire social understanding from the experiences that they share with adults. During the second year, for example, social referencing permits toddlers to compare their own evaluation of events with those of others, enabling them to begin to understand conflicting as well as shared mental states. Somewhat later, social referencing becomes an important avenue to conscience development as behavioral standards are conveyed through the parent's nonverbal affective reaction to approved or disapproved activity, which may be referenced by a young child even prior to acting in a disapproved way (such as the toddler who watches the parent's face carefully while reaching sticky fingers into the VCR; Emde & Buchsbaum, 1990; Emde, Johnson, & Easterbrooks, 1987). Social referencing can also be a source of pride and self-confidence as children consult their parents' approving expressions after succeeding at a difficult task (Stipek, 1995). In these ways, the infant's dawning awareness of subjectivity in others, as well as interest in understanding these mental states, transforms the development of social understanding and self-awareness.

As social and emotional capabilities develop in concert, they are mutually influential. Emotional connections to familiar people provide a foundation for developing attachments and social understanding, and early social experiences cause the generalized emotional systems of early infancy to become more discretely and functionally organized (Saarni et al., 1998).

Emotion Regulation

Social development and emotional development are interwoven also in how emotions become enlisted into social competence. One way this occurs is through the growth of skills of emotion regulation (Thompson, 1994). In infancy, of course, parents assume the prominent role in managing the emotions of offspring. They do so by directly intervening to soothe or pacify the child, as well as by regulating the emotional demands of familiar settings like home or child care (e.g., by creating predictable routines), altering how the young child construes an emotionally arousing experience (e.g., by smiling reassuringly when a friendly but unfamiliar adult approaches the child), and later by actively coaching young children on the expectations or strategies of emotion management. Moreover, young children's emotions are managed because of the security or confidence that they derive from their relationships with caregivers, such as in a baby's anticipatory soothing to the sound of the parent's arrival. Infants and toddlers who can anticipate reassurance from the arrival of their caregivers are aided by the belief that, with the adult's assistance, emotions are neither uncontrollable nor unmanageable (Cassidy, 1994; Nachmias, Gunnar, Mangelsdorf, Parritz, & Buss, 1996).

In the early years, however, young children are also developing rudimentary means of managing their own emotions. This can be observed initially in the comfort seeking of a distressed infant or toddler, but young children quickly appreciate that emotions can also be managed by making active efforts to avoid or ignore emotionally arousing situations, through reassuring self-talk, by obtaining further information about the situation, and in other simple ways (Braungart & Stifter, 1991; Calkins & Johnson, 1998; Grolnick, Bridges, & Connell, 1996). Developing skills of emotion regulation are built on slowly maturing brain regions that also contribute to the young child's capacities to inhibit impulsivity and that enable rule-governed behavior (Diamond, Werker, & Lalonde, 1994; Rothbart, Posner, & Boylan, 1990). Moreover, individual differences in temperamental "inhibitory control" emerge early and are related to conscience development (Kochanska, Murray, & Coy, 1997). Not surprisingly, therefore, the growth of emotion regulation is part of a constellation of developing capabilities that are related to social competence and behavioral self-control, and successful emotion regulation, within a cultural framework, is seen as a central developmental task of early childhood.

Summary

Caregivers assume a significant role in supporting the development of these features of socioemotional competence that enable young children to enlist their emotions constructively to accomplish social goals (Saarni, 1999). Unfortunately, for some children temperamental vulnerability combined with poor caregiver support can contribute to the growth of emotion-related difficulties in the early years, including problems related to sad, depressed affect (Cicchetti & Schneider-Rosen, 1986), anxious fear (Thompson, 2002), and angry behavioral problems (Shaw, Keenan, & Vondra, 1994). Often, these are conceptualized as relationship problems rather than difficulties of the individual (Zeanah & Boris, 2000; Zeanah, Boris, Heller, Hinshaw-Fuselier, Larrieu, Lewis, Palomino, Rovaris, & Valliere, 1997), reminiscent of Winnicott's maxim about infants existing within a social system. The presence of clear disturbances in emotion regulation during infancy and toddler years is a reminder of the importance of establishing the social and emotional competencies that are a foundation for psychosocial health in the years that follow.

RELATIONSHIPS: THE DEVELOPMENT OF ATTACHMENTS

Freud (1940/1963) described the infant-mother relationship as "unique, without parallel, established unalterably for a whole lifetime as the first and strongest love-object and as the prototype of all later love-relations." (p. 45) Although the typical conditions of early care in Western cultures have changed significantly since Freud's day (i.e., fathers, child-care providers, babysitters, and extended family members now share infant care with mothers), Freud's famous assertion draws attention to the importance of the initial attachments a baby develops to caregivers and to their potentially enduring significance. An attachment can be described as an enduring affectional bond that unites two or more people across time and context, and the development of attachment relationships between infants and their caregivers is one of the hallmarks of early socioemotional growth (Ainsworth, Blehar, Waters, & Wall, 1978; Bowlby, 1969/1982; Cassidy & Shaver, 1999).

Developmental Aspects of Attachments

Except in highly unusual conditions of neglect or abuse, virtually all infants develop close emotional ties to those who care for them. These initial attachments are as biologically basic as learning to crawl and talk because they have been crucial to the protection, nurturance, and development of infants throughout human evolution (Gould, 1977; Tobach & Schnierla, 1968). Bowlby (1969/1982) placed special emphasis on the role of distress-relief sequences as key interactions for the development of attachments, with attachment behaviors eliciting caregiver proximity and care for a vulnerable, dependent infant.

Attachment theorists believe that these infant-caregiver relationships address two fundamental needs of the infant (see Ainsworth et al., 1978; Cassidy & Shaver, 1999). First, a caregiver's support reduces a young child's fear, distress, or anxiety in novel or challenging situations and enables the child to explore with confidence and to manage negative emotions (Ainsworth, 1967; Emde & Easterbrooks, 1985). This is commonly reflected in *secure base behavior,* by which an infant maintains reassuring psychological contact with the caregiver (through looks and smiles from a distance and occasionally returning to the adult for affection) while exploring and playing. Second, the caregiver's sensitive and prompt responding to the baby's needs and signals strengthens the child's sense of competence and efficacy, especially for obtaining assistance from others. Attachment relationships begin to develop very early on and become consolidated between 6 and 12 months of age as infants become gradually aware of the psychological qualities of other people, acquire expectations for their behavior, and develop trust in certain caregivers upon whom they rely for this kind of assistance and support (Ainsworth et al., 1978; Colin, 1996).

Individual Differences in Attachments

Although virtually all infants become attached to their caregivers, not all attachments exhibit characteristics that attachment theorists define as secure (Ainsworth et al., 1978). Whereas the markers of a secure attachment are the child's confident exploration and secure base behavior in the caregiver's company, as well as ready soothing of distress when the child is upset, infants sometimes develop attachments to caregivers that reflect uncertainty or distrust in the responsiveness of the parent, child-care provider, or other caregiver. Infants with insecure attachments are not so easily soothed by the caregiver, and their exploratory play may be better characterized either by independence or by anxious dependency on the adult (Ainsworth et al., 1978; Colin, 1996; Thompson, 1998). An insecure attachment is not, however, equivalent to no attachment at all. Even a young child who is uncertain about the caregiver's nurturance derives important emotional support from the caregiver's presence that would not be derived from the company of someone to whom the child had no attachment at all. Even so, as we shall see, attachment relationships characterized by insecurity provide young children with a weaker psychological foundation for the growth of sociability, emotion management, and self-understanding than do secure attachments. Insecure attachments do not presage or accompany the development of psychopathology. There is, however, some evidence of an association between one kind of insecure attachment—insecure disorganized attachment—and psychopathology in childhood and adulthood, particularly in the context of high psychosocial risk environments (Dozier, Stovall, & Albus, 1999; Greenberg, 1999; Lyons-Ruth & Jacobvitz, 1999; Sroufe, 1997). Although some of these data are cross-sectional, others are drawn from a handful of longitudinal studies following the development of infants into the childhood or adolescent—and now early adult—years.

Given the importance of secure attachment, what characteristics of care contribute to its creation? Although a child's temperament is influential, the most important determinant of whether an infant develops a secure or insecure attachment is the caregiver's sensitivity to the child's needs and intentions (de Wolf & van IJzendoorn, 1997; Thompson, 1998). Sensitivity can be described as responding promptly and appropriately to the child and being available to help when needed, especially when the child is distressed. The word "appropriately" is key here because the quickest response is not necessarily the most sensitive, particularly beyond early infancy. Appropriate timing of sensitive responsiveness allows older infants opportunities to develop competent self-regulation of emotions and coping strategies. Sensitive responding thus addresses the two fundamental needs of the infant described earlier: It helps to manage the child's distress to permit confident exploration, and it consolidates a young child's sense of efficacy, both in the self and in soliciting the support of others and the expectation of an effective response.

Sensitive care—and its opposite, whether conceptualized as unresponsiveness, uninvolvement, rejection, or psychological unavailability—is influenced by many features of a caregiver's life experiences (Berlin & Cassidy, 1999; George & Solomon, 1999; Isabella, 1995). The amount and nature of social stress and support that an adult experiences; the caregiver's personality and childhood history, including his or her own attachment relationships; competing demands, beliefs, and values; and many other factors can influence the sensitivity shown to a young child at any moment (Bornstein, 1995; Easterbrooks & Graham, 1999; Fonagy, Steele, & Steele, 1991; Holden, 1995). Sensitivity also is undermined by more severe circumstances, such as parental depression or other forms of mental illness (Seifer & Dickstein, 1993). A baby's temperamental difficulty, developmental delay, or other needs influence how sensitivity is expressed in the relationship with the caregiver (e.g., Brazelton, Koslowski, & Main, 1974) and can also affect the child's *perceptions* of the adult's responsiveness (Easterbrooks, 1989; Seifer, Schiller, Sameroff, Resnick, & Riordan, 1996; van den Boom, 1989). Thus, the sensitive care leading to secure attachment is affected by the psychobiological and familial contexts of infant development discussed earlier, reflecting the view that attachment relationships are the product of an integrated developmental system.

Multiple Attachment Relationships

In typical conditions of contemporary care, infants develop attachments to many caregivers, including mothers and fathers at home, child-care providers, preschool teachers, and sometimes also grandparents and other adults (Berlin &

Cassidy, 1999; Howes, 1999). Infants' attachments with these caregivers can be secure or insecure based on their experience with each person, largely independent of the security of their relationships with the other people who care for them. This means that a child can be insecurely attached to the mother but securely attached to the father or a child-care provider, or the reverse may be true. This has important implications for early socioemotional development because it means that young children are affected by relationships with a variety of caregivers, each of whom provides opportunities to develop the social skills, emotional understanding, and self-confidence that are offered by a secure attachment. Secure relationships with each are optimal, but a secure attachment to one may support healthy psychosocial growth even if relationships with others are insecure. Early socioemotional development is, in short, affected by a variety of relationships, not just the mother-infant bond, although the mother-infant relationship remains most significant for most children (Easterbrooks & Goldberg, 1990; Main, Kaplan, & Cassidy, 1985; Suess, Grossman, & Sroufe, 1992; NICHD Early Child Care Research Network, 1997).

Issues of Stability and Continuity in Attachments

Relationships are not static. They change and grow in concert with the developing child and the changing social contexts in which the child lives. Parents and the quality of care that they provide also change over time (Holden & Miller, 1999). This means that the security of attachment can change in the early years when changes occur in the caregiver's sensitivity, in family circumstances, or for other reasons (Thompson, 1998). Longitudinal studies have found, for example, that changes in attachment security occur because of common changes in family circumstances such as alterations in child-care arrangements, the birth of a new sibling, or family stress (like marital discord) that causes a reorganization of familiar patterns of interaction with caregivers (Belsky, Campbell, Cohn, & Moore, 1996; Cummings & Davies, 1994; Teti, Sakin, Kucera, Corns, & Das Eiden, 1996; Vaughn, Egeland, Sroufe, & Waters, 1979). A child with an insecure attachment in infancy, therefore, may later have opportunities to develop greater confidence in the same caregiver, and a child who begins with a secure attachment is not safeguarded against the possibility of later insecurity if the caregiving context and quality should change toward insensitivity. There is no guarantee that the influence of early attachment security will endure, unless that environmental caregiving support and ensuing security are maintained in the years that follow through the continuing sensitivity of parental care and a supportive developmental context.

Therefore, one of the most important long-term consequences of a secure attachment in infancy is that it inaugurates a positive relationship with a caregiver that heightens the child's receptiveness to the adult and that supports, but does not ensure, continuing parental sensitivity (Kochanska & Thompson, 1997; Waters, Kondo-Ikemura, Posada, & Richters, 1991; Thompson, 1999). If this positive relationship is maintained over time, it contributes to the development of mutual trust and responsiveness between parent and child in which young children are motivated to accept and adopt the parent's instruction, guidance, and values. Such a relationship provides not only a secure base for confident exploration in infancy but also support, in early childhood, for a young child's emerging conscience and sense of moral responsibility, emotional understanding, positive sense of self, and motivation to achieve (Kochanska & Thompson, 1997; Laible & Thompson, 1998, 2000; Thompson, 2000a; Waters et al., 1991). A secure attachment in infancy is important, in short, because it reflects a positive parent-child relationship and inaugurates processes of mutual positive regard that can support healthy socioemotional growth in the years that follow.

A secure attachment in infancy also supports other socioemotional competencies (see Thompson, 1998, 1999, for reviews). Longitudinal studies report that children with secure attachments to parents (typically mothers) develop more positive, supportive relationships with teachers, friends, camp counselors, and others whom they come to know well. Their positive social skills and friendly approach to those with whom they develop new relationships seem to evoke closer friendships with others. There is also evidence that securely attached infants have stronger social skills in their initial encounters with unfamiliar adults, perhaps because they generalize the positive sociability that they acquire in their relationships with caregivers.

Attachment relationships are important also because of how they influence young children's emergent understandings of who they are and of what other people are like. Secure or insecure attachments are associated with a child's developing conceptions of self, others, and relationships that constitute some of their earliest representations (or, in the parlance of attachment theory, *internal working models*) of the social world (Bretherton & Munholland, 1999; Thompson, 2000a). Securely attached infants have been found, for example, to have a more complex and sophisticated understanding of themselves and their mothers compared to insecurely attached infants (Pipp, Easterbrooks, & Brown, 1993; Pipp, Easterbrooks, & Harmon, 1992; Pipp-Siegel, Easterbrooks, Brown, & Harmon, 1995; Schneider-Rosen & Cicchetti, 1984).

In early childhood, when representations of self and the social world begin to develop more fully, the influence of secure attachments on the "self" becomes more apparent (Thompson, 2000a). Securely attached young children have been found to have positive views of the self (Cassidy, 1988; Verschueren & Marcoen, 1999), a more easily-accessed or balanced self-concept (Cassidy, 1988; Easterbrooks & Abeles, 2000), a more sophisticated grasp of emotion (Laible & Thompson, 1998), more positive understandings of friendship (Cassidy, Kirsh, Scolton, & Parke, 1996; Kerns, 1996), and more advanced conscience development (Kochanska & Thompson, 1997; Laible & Thompson, 2000) compared with insecurely attached young children (see review by Thompson, 1999). Attachment theorists argue that this arises not only because of the continuing influences of sensitive parental care, but also because attachment security provides important lessons about what people, including the self, are like in close relationships, including how rewarding or painful they might be. Positive notions lend confidence in the self and guide young children's understanding and expectations in their encounters with new relational partners (Sroufe & Fleeson, 1986).

Summary

The body of research just summarized adds credence to traditional views, expressed in Freud's famous maxim, that the mother-infant relationship has enduring effects on early psychosocial development. Especially when the sensitivity that initially led to a secure attachment is maintained into early childhood, attachment security contributes to the growth of a positive orientation toward others, emotional and moral awareness, and self-understanding that are crucial aspects of healthy psychological development. However, the dynamic changes that can occur in the quality of caregiving, and thus attachment security, remind us also that the effects of early attachment are provisional, that is, contingent on the enduring quality of these relationships in the years to come. Moreover, early attachment does not solely determine the course of later socioemotional growth and is only one of the complex influences on early psychological development (Sroufe, Carlson, Levy, & Egeland, 1999; Sroufe, Egeland, & Kreutzer, 1990).

This means that in understanding the course of early development, it is important to take a *developmental contextualist* view (Lerner, 2002; Lerner & Kaufmann, 1985) and to consider, along with the security of attachment, the influences of a child's temperamental attributes, biological characteristics, intellectual capabilities, the parent's stresses and supports, the marital relationship, the demands or opportunities associated with socioeconomic status, and other

influences on early socioemotional growth (Belsky, 1981; Easterbrooks, Davidson, & Chazan, 1993; Lyons-Ruth, Easterbrooks, & Cibelli, 1997). Security of attachment is important for its direct influences on early socioemotional development, but it is also important as it buffers (or heightens) the impact of risk factors that can undermine healthy psychosocial growth, and enhances (or undercuts) the benefits of other supports that exist in the child's world.

RELATIONSHIPS AND REPRESENTATION

The Transitions of Toddlerhood

As attachment theorists have shown, and as developmental scientists concerned with cognitive development also have recognized, early relationships are important for the growth of social representation. From their experiences in close attachment relationships and interactions with others, infants acquire a sense of who they are, what people are like, and the qualities of close relationships in the form of internal working models that encompass provisional understandings of the self and social world. These rudimentary representations are continuously revised in the years after infancy with advances in conceptual understanding and experience in new and different relationships. As infancy evolves into toddlerhood and early childhood, a young child's working models of self and relationships change significantly as parent-child relationships become forums of mutual understanding and disagreement and as the child develops more complex forms of psychological self- and other-awareness.

The Role of Conflict in Relationships

Although the emphasis of attachment theory is on the development of warm, nurturant relationships with parents and other caregivers, we have already noted that conflict and its resolution are also part of these early relationships. In fact, even securely attached dyads experience *affective errors* or mismatches in emotional communication (Lyons-Ruth et al., 1999); the repair of these missed communications is key to successful emotion regulation and secure attachments. From the dyssynchrony experienced in early face-to-face play to the testing of wills evoked by the toddler's independent locomotion, parent-child differences in behavior, goals, intentions, and expectations provide some of the most important early catalysts to the young child's growing awareness of the subjectivity inherent in interpersonal relationships. Nothing focuses a young child's attention on what others are thinking, feeling, and expecting better than the realization that disagreement with that person must be resolved. As a consequence, conflict as well as security in early relationships helps to shape emergent representations of self, others, and relationships. Conflict, then, may be development enhancing (Turiel, 1978, 1997).

The second and third years of life are marked by significant changes in parent-child relationships. Young children are developing the cognitive skills to understand parental expectations and apply them to their own behavior, and they are becoming increasingly capable of regulating their own actions according to internalized standards of conduct (Kopp, 1982; Kopp & Wyer, 1994). At the same time, parents "up the ante" in their expectations for the behavior of offspring to incorporate consideration for others, basic skills at self-care, safety concerns, and compliance with family routines and manners (Campos et al., 2000; Erikson, 1950; Gralinski & Kopp, 1993). The strategies used by parents to elicit compliance also change to build on the young child's maturing capacities for self-control, and they begin to make greater use of explanations, bargaining, indirect guidance, and other nonassertive strategies (Belsky, Woodworth, & Crnic, 1996; Crockenberg & Litman, 1990; Kuczynski, Kochanska, Radke-Yarrow, & Girnius-Brown, 1987). In response, young offspring cooperate but also assert their own independent judgment by refusing before they comply and by negotiating, compromising, and displaying other indicators of self-assertion (Kuczynski & Kochanska, 1990; Kuczynski et al., 1987; Vaughn, Kopp, & Krakow, 1984). As a consequence, parent-child interaction in the toddler period is a psychologically more complex process of mutual understanding than it was in early infancy. This affords young children frequent opportunities to expand and elaborate their understandings of self and social relationships because of their experience of shared and conflicting intentions, feelings, and beliefs in their interactions with caregivers.

Developments in Self and Social Understanding

These changes in parent-child interaction arise because of the growth of psychological self-awareness in the second and third years. Self-understanding grows rapidly in infancy and early childhood (Stern, 1985, 1995). Early in infancy, a rudimentary subjective self-awareness emerges from the infant's experience of the self as a causal agent in social interaction and a volitional agent in play, especially when accompanied by the strong emotions that are often experienced in these situations. Somewhat later in the first year, as noted earlier, a new form of self-awareness arises as infants become aware of subjective states in others that can be

accessed and altered, contributing to the realization that differences exist between another's feelings and intentions and one's own.

By the middle of the second year, another form of self-awareness develops with the growth of physical self-recognition. Toddlers who catch sight of their mirror images after a spot of rouge has been surreptitiously applied to their noses begin to respond with self-referential behavior (e.g., touching their noses) and other self-conscious acts (e.g., smiling, looking away) that indicate that they recognize the mirror image to be themselves (Lewis, 1993). By the end of the second year and during the third year, young children become more psychologically self-aware. They begin to use their names and personal pronouns more frequently, describe themselves and their experiences to others, and assert their competence, independence, and responsibility as autonomous agents by insisting on "doing it myself" (Bullock & Lutkenhaus, 1990; Heckhausen, 1988; Stipek, Gralinski, & Kopp, 1990). This emergent psychological self-awareness also contributes to the defiance and obstinacy that can occur with parents (leading to the charming description of this period as the "terrible twos"); but beneath a young child's assertion of self-will is a newly discovered self-conscious sense inspiring reflection and requiring expression and respect from others.

Because of these changes in the parent-child relationship and the child's psychological self-awareness, the end of infancy and the beginning of early childhood also witness rapid advances in social awareness. The initial, provisional working models of infancy change considerably as the young child acquires growing insight into the feelings, intentions, and (at a somewhat later age) thoughts of other people and into the nature of human relationships. The child's developing sensitivity to the violation of behavioral standards and emerging capacities for self-control, for example, together with the incentives to cooperate with the parent that arise from a secure attachment relationship, provide the foundations for conscience development in early childhood as young children adopt and comply with the expectations of parents (Dunn, 1987; Emde et al., 1987; Kochanska & Thompson, 1997). The emotional repertoire of infancy expands considerably to include self-referential emotions like pride, guilt, shame, and embarrassment that reflect the young child's growing awareness of and sensitivity to the evaluations of others (Lewis, 1993; Tangney & Fischer, 1995). And with a developing understanding of the mental states of others, young children begin to enlist this understanding in more competent social interaction, whether this consists of negotiating with parents, teasing a sibling, or achieving personally meaningful goals (e.g., having dessert after dinner).

Summary

The close of infancy and the beginning of early childhood brings, therefore, remarkable advances in psychological growth that arise, in part, from the flourishing representational capacities of the second and third years of life. As a consequence, young children perceive themselves and regard others much differently and become capable of understanding relationships and interacting with others in ways that take into account the perspectives, emotions, and intentions of other people. Throughout this period, a young child's close relationships with caregivers remain central to the growth of these representational working models through the warmth and sensitivity of adult care. When caregivers focus a young child's attention on the human consequences of misbehavior, exuberantly applaud a child's accomplishments, help a young child understand a sibling's actions, or talk about the child's own emotions, they contribute to the growth and refinement of a young child's early representations of who they are, what other people like, and how relationships are negotiated. These relational catalysts to social and emotional understanding begin to be influential at the same time that children's representational abilities unfold (Thompson, 1998, 2000a), providing a reminder that although caregiving relationships change significantly from infancy to early childhood, the sensitivity of care—expressed in age-appropriate ways—remains important throughout.

CONCLUSIONS: APPLICATIONS TO POLICY AND PRACTICE AND IMPERATIVES FOR A RESEARCH AGENDA

During the past decade or so, we have witnessed an explosion of interest in infancy, within the scientific and popular milieu. Technological advances in understanding the development and functioning of the infant brain have gone hand in hand with public engagement campaigns highlighting the importance of the early years of life for social and emotional, as well as cognitive, development. Very early child development has enjoyed currency in major media outlets and among politicians and entertainers. The market is filled with infant products (T-shirts, toys, videos, music) extolling the amazing skills of infants and is aimed at making babies "more stimulated," "smarter," or "better attached." Researchers and academics now must ask the "so what?" question (Brady, Jacobs, & Lerner, 2002) and consider how best to translate advances in the scientific knowledge base about early social and emotional development into policies and practices that promote positive development (e.g., secure attachments, curiosity, self-confidence, cooperation, conflict resolution).

Although most researchers do not operate acontextually, it is important to bring these issues of dissemination, policy, and practice to the forefront, rather than the recesses, of scientific investigation (Brady et al., 2002; Shonkoff & Phillips, 2000). Thus far, the potential benefits of developmental science have yet to be realized. The reasons are complex, including (a) traditional academic or university structures that do not facilitate dissemination of applied work, (b) the natural tendency of academe toward scientific conservatism based on standards of scientific rigor, and (c) the occasional suspicion of academe by some policy makers and practitioners (Lerner, Fisher, & Weinberg, 2000). Efforts to bridge the divide between research and application may be enhanced by embracing broader definitions of the scientific enterprise, scientific rigor, and the surrounding context of scholarly and public policy endeavors (Easterbrooks, Jacobs, Brady, & Mistry, 2001; Thompson & Nelson, 2001).

The publication of *From Neurons to Neighborhoods: The Science of Early Childhood Development* (Shonkoff & Phillips, 2000) by the Committee on Integrating the Science of Early Childhood Development presents a compelling mandate for policy-makers, employers, and individuals to consider what we know to be the fundamental needs of infants and whether our social policies and practices facilitate positive infant social and emotional development for all infants. Several key questions accompany this directive, including those of the roles of culture and individual differences in biological predispositions and environmental context in shaping individual development.

The bulk of our scientific knowledge in infant social and emotional development is drawn from Western samples (primarily North American) that are not representative of diversity in race or ethnicity, family structure, or economic context. In fact, some have assumed that all infants are the same, echoing a bias that "babies are just babies," not really conscious beings until the onset of language. Although all cultures have traditions that promote competence, in a heterogeneous society it is sometimes difficult to distinguish individual differences in typical social and emotional development from deviations requiring concern and intervention. How does an early intervention home visitor, for example, distinguish culture-bound caution and shy behavior from potentially problematic emotional inhibition? In addition, to what extent can particular individual, relational, or contextual strengths compensate for particular vulnerabilities or risks, particularly in the frequent context of double jeopardy (Parker, Greer, & Zuckerman, 1988) or multiple risks? The fact that we do not have immediate answers to many of the most pressing questions in early social and emotional development does not mitigate the responsibility to use the extant knowledge to ensure the best start for all infants.

The application of scientific research in infant social and emotional development spans disciplinary boundaries (e.g., interdisciplinary or transdisciplinary team approaches to early intervention). Earlier in this chapter we discussed recent significant developments in the knowledge base about infant socioemotional functioning that have emerged from neuroscience. This work in neuroscience crosses traditional notions of disciplinarity but is easily embedded in a developmental framework that includes social relationships. This research calls into question both the limits of developmental plasticity as well as deterministic views of early brain development. Future work needs to map this knowledge of early development onto the actual social ecology of infancy that considers not only the primary caregiving relationship but also the broader social networks and contexts in which infants develop.

Our understanding of the growth of social and emotional capacities in infancy highlights that although infancy is a period of origins, developmental processes early in life are complex and multifaceted. Nature and nurture are in dynamic interplay throughout infancy as caregivers respond to the psychobiological individuality of offspring but also alter temperamental qualities through the quality of care. Early influences can have an enduring effect on young children, but change is also evident. Continuity in early adaptation is apparent primarily when the developmental context is maintained as the child grows so that early influences are actually continuing ones that impact on psychosocial growth. The dispositions, understanding, and relationships of the first two years are important not because they may inaugurate unchanging developmental pathways, but because they provide a foundation for the emergence of new representational capacities and relational capacities in the years that follow. These underpinnings ideally set the stage for the transitions of early childhood to be approached with security, curiosity, and confidence in the self and in relationships.

REFERENCES

Ainsworth, M. D. S. (1967). *Infancy in Uganda: Infant care and the growth of love.* Baltimore: Johns Hopkins University Press.

Ainsworth, M. D. S., Blehar, M. C., Waters, E., & Wall, S. (1978). *Patterns of attachment.* Hillsdale, NJ: Erlbaum.

Baldwin, D. A., & Moses, L. J. (1996). The ontogeny of social information-processing. *Child Development, 67,* 1915–1939.

Barr, R. G., Bakeman, M., Konner, M., & Adamson, L. (1987). Crying in !Kung infants: Distress signals in a responsive context. *American Journal of Diseases of Children, 141,* 486.

Bates, J. E. (1987). Temperament in infancy. In J. D. Osofsky (Ed.), *Handbook of infant development* (2nd ed., pp. 1101–1149). New York: Wiley.

Belsky, J. (1981). Early human experience: A family perspective. *Developmental Psychology, 17,* 3–19.

Belsky, J., Campbell, S. B., Cohn, J. F., & Moore, G. (1996). Instability of infant-parent attachment security. *Developmental Psychology, 32,* 921–924.

Belsky, J., Woodworth, S., & Crnic, K. (1996). Trouble in the second year: Three questions about family interaction. *Child Development, 67,* 556–578.

Berlin, L., & Cassidy, J. (1999). Relations among relationships: Contributions from attachment theory and research. In J. Cassidy & P. R. Shaver (Eds.), *Handbook of attachment* (pp. 688–712). New York: Guilford Press.

Bertenthal, B., & Campos, J. J. (1990). A systems approach to the organizing effects of self-produced locomotion during infancy. In C. Rovee-Collier & L. Lipsitt (Eds.), *Advances in infancy research* (Vol. 6, pp. 1–60). Hillsdale, NJ: Erlbaum.

Biringen, Z., Emde, R. N., Campos, J. J., & Appelbaum, M. I. (1995). Affective reorganization in the infant, the mother, and the dyad: The role of upright locomotion and its timing. *Child Development, 66,* 499–514.

Bornstein, M. H. (1995). Parenting infants. In M. H. Bornstein (Ed.), *Handbook of parenting: Vol. 1. Children and parenting* (pp. 3–39). Hillsdale, NJ: Erlbaum.

Bornstein, M. H., Tal, J., & Tamis-LeMonda, C. S. (1991). Parenting in crosscultural perspective: The United States, France, and Japan. In M. H. Bornstein (Ed.), *Cultural approaches to parenting* (pp. 69–90). Hillsdale, NJ: Erlbaum.

Bornstein, M. H., Toda, S., Azuma, H., Tamis-LeMonda, C. S., & Ogino, M. (1990). Mother and infant activity and interaction in Japan and in the United States: Pt. II. A comparative microanalysis of naturalistic exchanges focused on the organization of infant attention. *International Journal of Behavioral Development, 13,* 289–308.

Bowlby, J. (1982). *Attachment and loss:, Vol. 1. Attachment.* (2nd ed.). New York: Basic Books. (Original work published 1969)

Brady, A. E., Jacobs, F. H., & Lerner, R. M. (2002). Social policy and the enhancement of infant development. In M. Lewis & A. Slater (Eds.), *Introduction to infant development* (pp. 284–299). New York: Oxford University Press.

Braungart, J. M., & Stifter, C. A. (1991). Regulation of negative reactivity during the Strange Situation: Temperament and attachment in 12-month-old infants. *Infant Behavior and Development, 14,* 349–364.

Brazelton, T. B., Koslowski, B., & Main, M. (1974). The origins of reciprocity: The early mother-infant interaction. In M. Lewis & L. Rosenblum (Eds.), *The effect of the infant on its caregiver* (pp. 49–76). New York: Wiley.

Bretherton, I., McNew, S., & Beeghly-Smith, M. (1981). Early person knowledge as expressed in gestural and verbal communication: When do infants acquire a "theory of mind"? In M. Lamb & L. Sherrod (Eds.), *Infant social cognition* (pp. 333–373). Hillsdale, NJ: Erlbaum.

Bretherton, I., & Munholland, K. A. (1999). Internal working models in attachment relationships: A construct revisited. In J. Cassidy & P. R. Shaver (Eds.), *Handbook of attachment* (pp. 89–111). New York: Guilford Press.

Bullock, M., & Lutkenhaus, P. (1990). Who am I? Self-understanding in toddlers. *Merrill-Palmer Quarterly, 36,* 217–238.

Calkins, S. D., Fox, N. A., & Marshall, T. R. (1996). Behavioral and physiological antecedents of inhibition in infancy. *Child Development, 67,* 523–540.

Calkins, S. D., & Johnson, M. C. (1998). Toddler regulation of distress to frustrating events: Temperamental and maternal correlates. *Infant Behavior and Development, 21,* 379–395.

Campos, J. J., Anderson, D. I., Barbu-Roth, M. A., Hubbard, E. M., Hertenstein, M. J., & Witherington, D. (2000). Travel broadens the mind. *Infancy, 1,* 149–219.

Campos, J. J., Kermoian, R., & Zumbahlen, M. R. (1992). Socioemotional transformations in the family system following infant crawling onset. In N. Eisenberg & R. A. Fabes (Eds.), *Emotion and its regulation in early development* (pp. 35–40). San Francisco: Jossey-Bass.

Campos, J. J., & Stenberg, C. R. (1981). Perception, appraisal, and emotion: The onset of social referencing. In M. E. Lamb & L. R. Sherrod (Eds.), *Infant social cognition* (pp. 273–314). Hillsdale, NJ: Erlbaum.

Carpenter, M., Nagell, K., & Tomasello, M. (1998). Social cognition, joint attention, and communicative competence from 9 to 15 months of age. *Monographs of the Society for Research in Child Development, 63*(4, Serial No. 255), 1–176.

Caspi, A. (1998). Personality development across the life course. In W. Damon (Series Ed.) & N. Eisenberg (Vol. Ed.), *Handbook of child psychology: Vol. 3. Social, emotional, and personality development* (5th ed., pp. 311–388). New York: Wiley.

Cassidy, J. (1988). Child-mother attachment and the self in six-year-olds. *Child Development, 59,* 121–134.

Cassidy, J. (1994). Emotion regulation: Influences of attachment relationships. *Monographs of the Society for Research in Child Development, 59*(2–3, Serial No. 240), 228–249.

Cassidy, J., Kirsh, S., Scolton, K. L., & Parke, R. D. (1996). Attachment and representations of peer relationships. *Developmental Psychology, 32,* 892–904.

Cassidy, J., & Shaver, P. R. (Eds.). (1999). *Handbook of attachment: Theory, research, and clinical applications.* New York: Guilford Press.

Chess, S., & Thomas, A. (1986). *Temperament in clinical practice.* New York: Guilford Press.

Cicchetti, D., & Schneider-Rosen, K. (1986). An organizational approach to childhood depression. In M. Rutter, C. Izard, & P. Read (Eds.), *Depression in young people: Clinical and developmental perspectives* (pp. 71–134). New York: Guilford Press.

Cohn, J. F., Campbell, S. B., & Ross, S. (1991). Infant response in the still-face paradigm at 6 months predicts avoidant and secure attachment at 12 months. *Child Development, 54,* 367–376.

Cohn, J. F., & Tronick, E. Z. (1983). Three-month-old infants' reaction to simulated maternal depression. *Child Development, 54,* 185–193.

Colin, V. L. (1996). *Human attachment.* New York: McGraw-Hill.

Crockenberg, S., & Litman, C. (1990). Autonomy as competence in 2-year-olds: Maternal correlates of child defiance, compliance, and self-assertion. *Developmental Psychology, 26,* 961–971.

Cummings, E. M., & Davies, P. (1994). *Children and marital conflict.* New York: Guilford Press.

Dawson, G., & Ashman, S. B. (2000). On the origins of a vulnerability to depression: The influence of the early social environment on the development of psychobiological systems related to risk for affective disorder. In C. A. Nelson (Ed.), *The Minnesota Symposia on Child Psychology:, Vol. 31. The effects of early adversity on neurobehavioral development* (pp. 245–279). Mahwah, NJ: Erlbaum.

de Wolf, M. S., & van IJzendoorn, M. H. (1997). Sensitivity and attachment: A meta-analysis on parental antecedents of infant attachment. *Child Development, 68,* 571–591.

Diamond, A., Werker, J. F., & Lalonde, C. (1994). Toward understanding commonalities in the development of object search, detour navigation, categorization, and speech perception. In G. Dawson & K. W. Fischer (Eds.), *Human behavior and the developing brain* (pp. 380–426). New York: Guilford Press.

Dozier, M., Stovall, K. C., & Albus, K. E. (1999). Attachment and psychopathology in adulthood. In J. Cassidy & P. R. Shaver (Eds.), *Handbook of attachment* (pp. 497–519). New York: Guilford Press.

Dunn, J. (1987). *The beginnings of social understanding.* Cambridge, MA: Harvard University Press.

Dunn, J. (1993). *Young children's close relationships: Beyond attachment.* Newbury Park, CA: Sage.

Dunn, J. (1998). Siblings, emotion, and the development of understanding. In S. Braten (Ed.), *Intersubjective communication and emotion in early ontogeny: Studies in emotion and social interaction* (pp. 158–168). New York: Cambridge University Press.

Easterbrooks, M. A. (1989). Quality of attachment to mother and to father: Effects of perinatal risk status. *Child Development, 60,* 825–830.

Easterbrooks, M. A., & Abeles, R. (2000). Windows to the self in eight-year-olds: Bridges to attachment representation and behavioral adjustment. *Attachment and Human Development, 2,* 85–106.

Easterbrooks, M. A., & Biringen, Z. (2000). Mapping the terrain of emotional availability and attachment. *Attachment and Human Development, 2,* 123–129.

Easterbrooks, M. A., Davidson, C. E., & Chazan, R. (1993). Psychosocial risk, attachment, and behavior problems among school-aged children. *Development and Psychopathology, 5,* 389–402.

Easterbrooks, M. A., & Goldberg, W. A. (1985). Effects of early maternal employment on toddlers, mothers, and fathers. *Developmental Psychology, 21,* 774–783.

Easterbrooks, M. A., & Goldberg, W. A. (1990). Security of toddler-parent attachment: Relation to children's sociopersonality functioning during kindergarten. In M. T. Greenberg, D. Cicchetti, & E. M. Cummings (Eds.), *Attachment in the preschool years* (pp. 221–244). Chicago: University of Chicago Press.

Easterbrooks, M. A., & Graham, C. A. (1999). Security of attachment and parenting: Homeless and low-income housed mothers and infants. *American Journal of Orthopsychiatry, 69,* 337–346.

Easterbrooks, M. A., Jacobs, F. H., Brady, A. E., & Mistry, J. (2001). *Assimilation and accommodation in applied research: The Massachusetts Healthy Families Evaluation.* Manuscript submitted for publication.

Emde, R. N. (1980). Emotional availability: A reciprocal reward system for infants and parents with implications for prevention of psychosocial disorders. In P. M. Taylor (Ed.), *Parent-infant relationships* (pp. 87–115). Orlando, FL: Grune and Stratton.

Emde, R. N., & Buchsbaum, H. K. (1990). "Didn't you hear my Mommy?": Autonomy *with* Iconnectedness in moral self emergence. In D. Cicchetti & M. Beeghly (Eds.), *The self in transition: Infancy to childhood* (pp. 35–60). Chicago: University of Chicago Press.

Emde, R. N., & Easterbrooks, M. A. (1985). Assessing emotional availability in early development. In W. K. Frankenburg, R. N. Emde, & J. W. Sullivan (Eds.), *Early identification of children at risk: An international perspective* (pp. 79–101). New York: Plenum Press.

Emde, R. N., Johnson, W. F., & Easterbrooks, M. A. (1987). The do's and don'ts of early moral development: Psychoanalytic tradition and current research. In J. Kagan & S. Lamb (Eds.), *The emergence of morality in young children* (pp. 245–276). Chicago: University of Chicago Press.

Erikson, E. (1950). *Childhood and society.* New York: W. W. Norton.

Feinman, S. (Ed.). (1992). *Social referencing and the social construction of reality in infancy.* New York: Plenum Press.

Fonagy, P., Steele, H., & Steele, M. (1991). Maternal representations of attachment during pregnancy predict the organization of infant-mother attachment. *Child Development, 62,* 891–905.

Freud, S. (1963). *An outline of psychoanalysis* (J. Strachey, Trans.). New York: W. W. Norton. (Original work published 1940)

Gekoski, M. J., Rovee-Collier, C. K., & Carulli-Rabinowitz, V. (1983). A longitudinal analysis of inhibition of infant distress: The origins of social expectations? *Infant Behavior and Development, 6,* 339–351.

George, C., & Soloman, J. (1999). Attachment and caregiving: The caregiving behavioral system. In J. Cassidy & P. R. Shaver (Eds.), *Handbook of attachment* (pp. 649–670). New York: Guilford Press.

Gesell, A. (1940). *The first five years of life: A guide to the study of the preschool child.* New York: Harper.

Gianino, A., & Tronick, E. Z. (1988). The mutual regulation model: the infant's self and interactive regulation and coping and defensive capacities. In T. Field, P. McCabe, & N. Schneiderman (Eds.), *Stress and coping* (Vol. 2, pp. 47–68). Hillsdale, NJ: Erlbaum.

Goldberg, W. A., & Easterbrooks, M. A. (1984). The role of marital quality in toddler development. *Developmental Psychology, 20,* 504–514.

Goldsmith, H. H., Buss, A. H., Plomin, R., Rothbart, M. K., Thomas, A., Chess, S., Hinde, R. A., & McCall, R. B. (1987). Roundtable: What is temperament? Four approaches. *Child Development, 58,* 505–529.

Gottman, J. M., Katz, L. F., & Hooven, C. (1997). *Meta-emotion: How families communicate emotionally.* Mahwah, NJ: Erlbaum.

Gould, S. J. (1977). *Ontongeny and phylogeny.* Cambridge, MA: Belknap Press.

Gralinski, J. H., & Kopp, C. B. (1993). Everyday rules for behavior: Mothers' requests to young children. *Developmental Psychology, 29,* 573–584.

Greenberg, M. T. (1999). Attachment and psychopathology in childhood. In J. Cassidy & P. R. Shaver (Eds.), *Handbook of attachment* (pp. 469–496). New York: Guilford Press.

Grolnick, W. S., Bridges, L. J., & Connell, J. P. (1996). Emotion regulation in two-year-olds: Strategies and emotional expression in four contexts. *Child Development, 67,* 928–941.

Gunnar, M. R. (1986). Human developmental psychoneuroendocrinology: A review of research on neuroendocrine responses to challenge and threat in infancy and childhood. In M. E. Lamb, A. Brown, & B. Rogoff (Eds.), *Advances in developmental psychology* (Vol. 4, pp. 51–103). Hillsdale, NJ: Erlbaum.

Gunnar, M. R. (2000). Early adversity and the development of stress reactivity and regulation. In C. A. Nelson (Ed.), *Minnesota Symposia on Child Psychology: Vol. 31. The effects of early adversity on neurobehavioral development* (pp. 163–200). Mahwah, NJ: Erlbaum.

Harkness, S. (1980). The cultural context of child development. In C. M. Super & S. Harkness (Eds.), *Anthropological perspectives on child development* (pp. 7–14). San Francisco: Jossey-Bass.

Harwood, R. L., Scholmerich, A., & Schulze, P. A. (2000). Homogeneity and heterogeneity in cultural belief systems. In S. Harkness, C. Raeff, & C. M. Super (Eds.), *Variability in the social construction of the child* (pp. 41–58). San Francisco: Jossey-Bass.

Hay, D. F., Nash, A., & Pedersen, J. (1983). Interaction between six-month-old peers. *Child Development, 54,* 557–612.

Heckhausen, J. (1988). Becoming aware of one's competence in the second year: Developmental progression within the mother-child dyad. *International Journal of Behavioral Development, 11,* 305–326.

Holden, G. W. (1995). Parental attitudes toward childrearing. In M. H. Bornstein (Ed.), *Handbook of parenting: Vol. 3. Status and social conditions of parenting* (pp. 359–392). Hillsdale, NJ: Erlbaum.

Holden, G. W., & Miller, P. C. (1999). Enduring and different: A meta-analysis of the similarity in parents' child rearing. *Psychological Bulletin, 125,* 223–254.

Howes, C. (1988). Peer interaction in young children. *Monographs of the Society for Research in Child Development, 53*(1, Serial No. 217), 1–94.

Howes, C. (1999). Attachment relationships in the context of multiple caregivers. In J. Cassidy & P. R. Shaver (Eds.), *Handbook of attachment* (pp. 671–687). New York: Guilford Press.

Hunziker, U. A., & Barr, R. G. (1986). Increased carrying reduces infant crying: A randomized controlled trial. *Pediatrics, 77,* 641–648.

Isabella, R. A. (1995). The origins of infant-mother attachment: Maternal behavior and infant development. In R. Vasta (Ed.), *Annals of child development* (Vol. 10, pp. 57–82). London: Jessica Kingsley.

Kagan, J. (1984). *The nature of the child.* New York: Basic Books.

Kagan, J. (1998). Biology and the child. In W. Damon (Series Ed.) & N. Eisenberg (Vol. Ed.), *Handbook of child psychology: Vol. 3. Social, emotional, and personality development* (5th ed., pp. 177–235). New York: Wiley.

Kagan, J., Reznick, J. S., & Snidman, N. (1987). The physiology and psychology of behavioral inhibition in children. *Child Development, 58,* 1459–1473.

Kagan, J., & Snidman, N. (1991). Infant predictors of inhibited and uninhibited profiles. *Psychological Science, 2,* 40–44.

Kagan, J., Snidman, N., & Arcus, D. (1998). Childhood derivatives of high and low reactivity in infancy. *Child Development, 69,* 1483–1493.

Kaye, K. (1982). *The mental and social life of babies.* Chicago: University of Chicago Press.

Kerns, K. A. (1996). Individual differences in friendship quality and their links to child-mother attachment. In W. W. Bukowski, A. F. Newcomb, & W. W. Hartup (Eds.), *The company they keep* (pp. 137–157). New York: Cambridge University Press.

Kochanska, G., Murray, K., & Coy, K. C. (1997). Inhibitory control as a contributor to conscience in childhood: From toddler to early school age. *Child Development, 68,* 263–277.

Kochanska, G., & Thompson, R. A. (1997). The emergence and development of conscience in toddlerhood and early childhood. In J. E. Grusec & L. Kuczynski (Eds.), *Parenting strategies and children's internalization of values* (pp. 53–77). New York: Wiley.

Kohut, H. (1977). *The restoration of the self.* New York: International Universities Press.

Kopp, C. B. (1982). Antecedents of self-regulation: A developmental view. *Developmental Psychology, 18,* 199–214.

Kopp, C. B., & Wyer, N. (1994). Self-regulation in normal and atypical development. In D. Cicchetti & S. L. Toth (Eds.), *Rochester Symposium on Developmental Psychopathology: Vol. 5. Disorders and dysfunctions of the self.* (pp. 31–56). Rochester, NY: University of Rochester Press.

Kuczynski, L., & Kochanska, G. (1990). Development of children's noncompliance strategies from toddlerhood to age 5. *Developmental Psychology, 26,* 398–408.

Kuczynski, L., Kochanska, G., Radke-Yarrow, M., & Girnius-Brown, O. (1987). A developmental interpretation of young children's noncompliance. *Developmental Psychology, 23,* 799–806.

Laible, D. J., & Thompson, R. A. (1998). Attachment and emotional understanding in preschool children. *Developmental Psychology, 34,* 1038–1045.

Laible, D. J., & Thompson, R. A. (2000). Mother-child discourse, attachment security, shared positive affect, and early conscience development. *Child Development, 71,* 1424–1440.

Lamb, M. E. (1981). The development of social expectations in the first year of life. In M. E. Lamb & L. R. Sherrod (Eds.), *Infant social cognition* (pp. 155–175). Hillsdale, NJ: Erlbaum.

Lamb, M. E. (1997). The development of father-infant relationships. In M. E. Lamb (Ed.), *The role of the father in child development* (3rd ed., pp. 104–120). New York: Wiley.

Lamb, M. E., & Malkin, C. M. (1986). The development of social expectations in distress-relief sequences: A longitudinal study. *International Journal of Behavioral Development, 9,* 235–249.

LeDoux, J. (1996). *The emotional brain.* New York: Touchstone.

Lerner, R. M. (2002). *Concepts and theories of human development* (3rd ed.). Mahwah, NJ: Erlbaum.

Lerner, R. M., & Kaufmann, M. B. (1985). The concept of development in contextualism. *Developmental Review, 5,* 309–333.

Lerner, R. M., Fisher, C. B., & Weinberg, R. A. (2000). Toward a science for and of the people: Promoting civil society through the application of developmental science. *Child Development, 71,* 11–20.

Lewis, M. (1993). Self-conscious emotions: Embarrassment, pride, shame, and guilt. In M. Lewis & J. M. Haviland (Eds.), *Handbook of emotions* (pp. 563–573). New York: Guilford Press.

Lewis, M. (1997). *Altering fate: Why the past does not predict the future.* New York: Guilford Press.

Lyons-Ruth, K., Bronfman, E., & Parsons, E. (1999). Maternal atypical responsiveness and disorganized infant attachment patterns. *Monographs of the Society for Research in Child Development, 64*(3, Serial No. 258), 67–96.

Lyons-Ruth, K., Easterbrooks, M. A., & Cibelli, C. D. (1997). Infant attachment strategies, infant mental lag, and maternal depressive symptoms: Predictors of internalizing and externalizing problems at age 7. *Developmental Psychology, 33,* 681–692.

Lyons-Ruth, K., & Jacobvitz, D. (1999). Attachment disorganization: Unresolved loss, relational violence, and lapses in behavioral and attentional strategies. In J. Cassidy & P. R. Shaver (Eds.), *Handbook of attachment* (pp. 520–554). New York: Guilford Press.

Main, M., Kaplan, N., & Cassidy, J. (1985). Security in infancy, childhood, and adulthood: A move to the level of representation. *Monographs of the Society for Research in Child Development, 50*(1-2, Serial No. 209), 66–104.

Morelli, G. A., Rogoff, B., Oppenheim, D., & Goldsmith, D. (1992). Cultural variation in infants' sleeping arrangements: Questions of independence. *Developmental Psychology, 28,* 604–613.

Morelli, G. A., & Tronick, E. Z. (1991). Efe multiple caretaking and attachment. In J. L. Gewirtz & W. M. Kurtines (Eds.), *Intersections with attachment* (pp. 41–54). Hillsdale, NJ: Erlbaum.

Mueller, E., & Vandell, D.B. (1979). Infant-infant interaction. In J. D. Osofsky (Ed.). *Handbook of infant development* (pp. 591–622). New York: Wiley.

Murray, L., & Trevarthen, C. (1985). Emotional regulation of interactions between two-month-olds and their mothers. In T. M. Field & N. A. Fox (Eds.), *Social perception in infants* (pp. 177–197). Norwood, NJ: Ablex.

Nachmias, M., Gunnar, M., Mangelsdorf, S., Parritz. R. H., & Buss, K. (1996). Behavioral inhibition and stress reactivity: The moderating role of attachment security. *Child Development, 67,* 508–522.

New, R. (2001). Quando c'e' figli: Observations on Italian early childhood. In L. Gandini & C. Edwards (Eds.), *Infant-toddler centers in Italy: The quality of experience* (pp. 167–194). New York: Teachers College Press.

NICHD Early Child Care Research Network (1997). The effects of infant child care on infant-mother attachment security: Results of the NICHD Study of Early Child Care. *Child Development, 68,* 860–879.

Oppenheim, D., Sagi, A., & Lamb, M. E. (1988). Infant-adult attachments on the kibbutz and their relation to socio-emotional development four years later. *Developmental Psychology, 27,* 727–733.

Parke, R. D., & Tinsley, B. J. (1987). Family interaction in infancy. In J. D. Osofsky (Ed.), *Handbook of infant development* (pp. 579–641). New York: Wiley.

Parker S., Greer, S., & Zuckerman, B. (1988). Double jeopardy: The impact of poverty on early childhood. *The Pediatric Clinics of North America, 35*(6), 1227–1240.

Pipp, S., Easterbrooks, M. A., & Brown, S. R. (1993). Attachment status and complexity of infants' self- and other-knowledge when tested with mother and father. *Social Development, 2,* 1–14.

Pipp, S., Easterbrooks, M. A., & Harmon, R. J. (1992). The relation between attachment and knowledge of self and mother in one- to three-year-old infants. *Child Development, 63,* 738–750.

Pipp-Siegel, S., Easterbrooks, M. A., Brown, S. R., & Harmon, R. J. (1995). The relation between infants' self/mother knowledge and three attachment categories. *Infant Mental Health Journal, 16,* 221–232.

Pomerleau, A., Malcuit, G., & Sabatier, C. (1991). Child-rearing practices and parental beliefs in three cultural groups of Montreal: Quebecois, Vietnamese, Haitian. In M. H. Bornstein (Ed.), *Cultural approaches to parenting* (pp. 45–68). Hillsdale, NJ: Erlbaum.

Porges, S. W., Doussard-Roosevelt, J. A., & Maiti, A. K. (1994). Vagal tone and the physiological regulation of emotion. *Monographs of the Society for Research in Child Development, 59*(2–3, Serial No. 240), 167–196.

Rothbart, M. K., & Bates, J. E. (1998). Temperament. In W. Damon (Series Ed.) & N. Eisenberg (Vol. Ed.), *Handbook of child psychology: Vol. 3. Social, emotional, and personality development* (5th ed., pp. 105–176). New York: Wiley.

Rothbart, M. K., Posner, M. I., & Boylan, A. (1990). Regulatory mechanisms in infant development. In J. T. Enns (Ed.), *The development of attention* (pp. 47–66). Amsterdam: Elsevier.

Rothbaum, F., Weisz, J., Pott, M., Miyake, K., & Morelli, G. (2000). Attachment and culture: Security in the United States and Japan. *American Psychologist, 55,* 1093–1104.

Saarni, C. (1999). *The development of emotional competence.* New York: Guilford Press.

Saarni, C., Mumme, D. L., & Campos, J. J. (1998). Emotional development: Action, communication, and understanding. In W. Damon (Series Ed.) & N. Eisenberg (Vol. Ed.), *Handbook of child psychology: Vol. 3. Social, emotional, and personality development* (5th ed., pp. 237–309). New York: Wiley.

Sameroff, A. J., & Chandler, M. J. (1975). Reproductive risk and the continuum of caretaking casualty. In F. D. Horowitz, M. Hetherington, S. Scarr-Salapatek, & G. Siegel, (Eds.), *Review of child development research* (Vol. 4, pp. 187–244). Chicago: University of Chicago Press.

Sander, L. W. (1964). Adaptive relationships in early mother-child interaction. *Journal of the American Academy of Child Psychiatry, 3,* 231–264.

Sanson, A., Prior, M., Oberklaid, F., & Smart, D. (1998). Temperamental influences on psychosocial adjustment: From infancy to adolescence. *Australian Educational and Developmental Psychologist, 15,* 7–38.

Scarr, S. (1992). Developmental theories for the 1990s: Development and individual differences. *Child Development, 63,* 1–19.

Scarr, S., & McCartney, K. (1983). How people make their own environments: A theory of genotype-environment effects. *Child Development, 54,* 424–435.

Schmidt, L. A., Shahinfar, A., & Fox, N. A. (1996). Frontal EEG correlates of dysregulated social behavior in children [Abstract]. *Psychophysiology, 33,* S8.

Schneider-Rosen, K., & Cichetti, D. (1984). The relationship between affect and cognition in maltreated infants: Quality of attachment and the development of self-recognition. *Child Development, 55,* 648–658.

Schore, A. N. (1994). *Affect regulation and the origin of the self: The neurobiology of emotional development.* Hillsdale, NJ: Erlbaum.

Seifer, R., & Dickstein, S. (1993). Parental mental illness and infant development. In C. H. Zeanah, Jr. (Ed.), *Handbook of infant mental health* (pp. 120–142). New York: Guilford Press.

Seifer, R., Schiller, M., Sameroff, A. J., Resnick, S., & Riordan, K. (1996). Attachment, maternal sensitivity, and temperament during the first year of life. *Developmental Psychology, 32,* 12–25.

Shaw, D. S., Keenan, K., & Vondra, J. I. (1994). Developmental precursors of externalizing behavior: Ages 1 to 3. *Developmental Psychology, 30,* 355–364.

Shonkoff, J., & Phillips, D. (Eds.). (2000). *From neurons to neighborhoods: The science of early childhood development.* Washington, DC: National Academy Press.

Siegel, D. J. (1998). The developing mind: Toward a neurobiology of interpersonal experience. *The Signal, 6,* 1–10.

Small, M. (1988). *Our babies, ourselves: How biology and culture shape the way we parent.* New York: Doubleday.

Sroufe, L. A. (1997). Psychopathology as outcome of development. *Development and Psychopathology, 9,* 251–268.

Sroufe, L. A., Carlson, E. A., Levy, A. K., & Egeland, B. (1999). Implications of attachment theory for developmental psychopathology. *Development and Psychopathology, 11,* 1–13.

Sroufe, L. A., Egeland, B., & Kreutzer, T. (1990). The fate of early experience following developmental change: Longitudinal approaches to individual adaptation in childhood. *Child Development, 61,* 1363–1373.

Sroufe, L. A., & Fleeson, J. (1986). Attachment and the construction of relationships. In W. W. Hartup & Z. Rubin (Eds.), *Relationships and development* (pp. 51–71). Hillsdale, NJ: Erlbaum.

Stern, D. (1985). *The interpersonal world of the infant.* New York: Basic Books.

Stern, D. (1995). *The motherhood constellation.* New York: Basic Books.

Stipek, D. (1995). The development of pride and shame in toddlers. In J. P. Tangney & K. W. Fischer (Eds.), *Self-conscious emotions* (pp. 237–252). New York: Guilford Press.

Stipek, D. J., Gralinski, J. H., & Kopp, C. B. (1990). Self-concept development in the toddler years. *Developmental Psychology, 26,* 972–977.

Symons, D. K., & Moran, G. (1987). The behavioral dynamics of mutual responsiveness in early face-to-face mother-infant interaction. *Child Development, 58,* 1488–1495.

Tangney, J. P., & Fischer, K. W. (Eds.). (1995). *Self-conscious emotions.* New York: Guilford Press.

Teti, D. M., Sakin, J., Kucera, E., Corns, K. M., & Das Eiden, R. (1996). And baby makes four: Predictors of attachment security among preschool-aged firstborns during the transition to siblinghood. *Child Development, 67,* 579–596.

Thompson, R. A. (1994). Emotion regulation: A theme in search of definition. *Monographs of the Society for Research in Child Development, 59*(2–3, Serial No. 240), 25–52.

Thompson, R. A. (1998). Early sociopersonality development. In W. Damon (Series Ed.) & N. Eisenberg (Vol. Ed.), *Handbook of child psychology: Vol. 3. Social, emotional, and personality development* (5th ed., pp. 25–104). New York: Wiley.

Thompson, R. A. (1999). Early attachment and later development. In J. Cassidy & P. R. Shaver (Eds.), *Handbook of attachment* (pp. 265–286). New York: Guilford Press.

Thompson, R. A. (2000a). The legacy of early attachments. *Child Development, 71,* 145–152.

Thompson, R. A. (2000b). Childhood anxiety disorders from the perspective of emotion regulation and attachment. In M. W. Vasey & M. R. Dadds (Eds.), *The developmental psychopathology of anxiety* (pp. 160–182). Oxford, UK: Oxford University Press.

Thompson, R. A. (2002). *Early brain development, the media, and public policy.* Book in preparation.

Thompson, R. A., & Nelson, C. E. (2001). Developmental science and the media: Early brain development. *American Psychologist, 56,* 5–15.

Tobach, E., & Schnierla, T. C. (1968). The biopsychology of social behavior of animals. In R. E. Cooke & S. Levin (Eds.), *Biologic basis of pediatric practice* (pp. 68–82). New York: McGraw-Hill.

Tomasello, M., Kruger, A. C., & Ratner, H. H. (1993). Cultural learning. *Behavioral and Brain Sciences, 16,* 495–511.

Triandis, H. C. (1995). *Individualism and collectivism.* Boulder, CO: Westview.

Tronick, E. Z. (1989). Emotions and emotional communication in infants. *American Psychologist, 44,* 112–119.

Tronick, E. Z. (2001, November). *The process of connecting and disconnecting: Implications for attachment theory.* Paper presented at the meeting of the Boston Institute for the Development of Infants and Parents, Chestnut Hill, MA.

Tronick, E. Z., & Cohn, J. F. (1989). Infant-mother face-to-face interaction: Age and gender differences in coordination and the occurrence of miscoordination. *Child Development, 60,* 85–92.

Tronick, E. Z., Morelli, G. A., & Winn, S. (1987). Multiple caregiving of Efe (Pygmy) infants. *American Anthropologist, 89,* 96–106.

Turiel, E. (1978). Social regulations and domains of social concepts. In W. Damon (Ed.), *New directions for child developmentI: Vol. 1. Social cognition.* San Francisco: Jossey-Bass.

Turiel, E. (1997). The development of morality. In N. Eisenberg (Ed.), *Handbook of child psychology* (5th ed., Vol. 3, pp. 863–932). New York: Wiley.

van den Boom, D. C. (1989). Neonatal irritability and the development of attachment. In G. A. Kohnstamm, J. E. Bates, & M. K. Rothbart (Eds.), Temperament in childhood (pp. 299–318). New York: Wiley.

van IJzendoorn, M. H., & Sagi, A. (1999). Cross-cultural patterns of attachment: Universal and contextual dimensions. In J. Cassidy & P. R. Shaver (Eds.), *Handbook of attachment* (pp. 713–735). New York: Guilford Press.

Vaughn, B. E., Egeland, B., Sroufe, L. A., & Waters, E. (1979). Individual differences in infant-mother attachment at twelve and eighteen months: Stability and change in families under stress. *Child Development, 50,* 971–975.

Vaughn, B. E., Kopp, C. B., & Krakow, J. B. (1984). The emergence and consolidation of self-control from eighteen to thirty months of age: Normative trends and individual differences. *Child Development, 55,* 990–1004.

Verschueren, K., & Marcoen, A. (1999). Representation of self and socioemotional competence in kindergartners: Differentials and combined effects of attachment to mother and to father. *Child Development, 70,* 183–201.

Waters, E., Kondo-Ikemura, K., Posada, G., & Richters, J. E. (1991). Learning to love: Mechanisms and milestones. In M. R. Gunnar & L. A. Sroufe (Eds.), *Minnesota Symposia on Child Psychology, Vol. 23. Self processes and development.* (pp. 217–255). Hillsdale, NJ: Erlbaum.

Watson, J. S. (1972). Smiling, cooing, and "the game." *Merrill-Palmer Quarterly, 18,* 323–339.

Watson, J. S. (1979). Perception of contingency as a determinant of social responsiveness. In E. B. Thoman (Ed.), *Origins of the infant's social responsiveness* (pp. 33–64). Hillsdale, NJ: Erlbaum.

Yu, A. C. (1984). *The child rearing practices in the traditional Korean society.* Seoul, Korea: Jung-Min-Sa.

Zimmerman, L., & McDonald, L. (1995). Emotional availability in infants' relationships with multiple caregivers. *American Journal of Orthopsychiatry, 65,* 147–152.

CHAPTER 5

Stress and Emotion in Early Childhood

MEGAN R. GUNNAR AND ELYSIA POGGI DAVIS

Stress is a fact of life. Even before birth, successful adaptation requires responding to stressors and regulating stress reactions. What causes us to react and how we regulate stress change during development and differ among individuals. These differences affect our physical and emotional health and determine whether we experience events as threats or challenges. In this chapter we adopt a developmental psychobiological approach to the study of stress in early development. Further, we explore the intimate, but not isomorphic, relations among emotions, temperament, and stress.

Developmental psychobiologists approach the study of stress from a systems perspective (e.g., Gottlieb, Whalsten, & Lickliter, 1998). (Note that to reduce the overall length of the chapter, the number of citations had be limited. Whenever possible we have cited review papers rather than original studies. We hope that the interested reader is able to use these reviews to find the original studies supporting the points made in this chapter.) This perspective, with its roots in epigenetic approaches to comparative psychology (e.g., Kuo, 1976), is shared by many developmental frameworks (e.g., Lerner, 1986; Sameroff, 1983). Accordingly, the stress system is viewed as hierarchically organized into reciprocally influencing systems and subsystems. Whereas understanding organization on one level requires understanding the roles played by systems at lower levels of organization, reductionistic explanations are viewed as misleading. Plasticity is seen as an inherent characteristic of living systems; nonetheless, with development, plasticity is expected to narrow. Understanding the boundaries of plasticity and recognizing the processes involved in narrowing the range of likely adaptations as development proceeds are central to research on the developmental psychobiology of stress.

The developmental systems perspective is overwhelmingly complex. Coherence of a sort is achieved by reference to several critical propositions. First, development proceeds through activity-dependent processes. At all levels of the organism, the critical question is how that activity shapes future responses to, creation of, and selection of experiences. Second, activity involves not only responses, but also regulation of responses; thus, no reaction of the organism can be understood without an equal focus on how the reaction is regulated. Finally, the systems that regulate development do not stop at the skin, but extend into the social contexts that are essential for the survival of the developing young.

Work on this manuscript was supported by a National Institute of Mental Health Research Scientist Award (MH00946) to the first author. The authors wish to thank the members of the NIMH-funded, Early Experience and Glucocorticoid Network (MH60766) for insightful discussions of many of the issues contained in this review. Particular thanks are due to Delia Vazquez, Paul Plotsky, and Mar Sanchez of the Network for comments on earlier drafts. In addition, we wish to thank Jonathan Gewirtz, Monica Luciana, and Jay Schulkin for their comments on sections of the manuscript.

The developmental psychobiology of stress is eclectic. Because the neural systems underlying emotions and emotionality influence the activation and regulation of behavioral and physiological responses to stressors, developmental psychobiological research on stress is intimately related to neuroscience research on emotions and temperament. Theory and research in these domains, however, are not always consistent with a developmental systems approach. Temperament theorists, for example, often adopt main effect rather than transactional models in studies of the development of temperament (Kagan, 1994), whereas neuroscience research is often overly reductionist (see discussion by West & King, 2001). Nevertheless, the emphasis on neural plasticity in neuroscience (e.g., Hann, Huffman, Lederhendler, & Meinecke, 1998) and psychobiological models of temperament (Rothbart, Derryberry, & Posner, 1994) provides bridges from these research domains to developmental psychobiological research on stress.

In this chapter we review what is known about the development of activity and regulation of the two arms of the stress system, the limbic-hypothalamic-pituitary-adrenocortical (L-HPA) and brain-stem norepinephrine/sympathetic-adrenomedullary (NE-SAM) systems. We begin with an overview of the neurobiology of the L-HPA system and the autonomic nervous system, emphasizing the SAM system. Next we describe limbic and cortical circuits involved in the ability to anticipate threat and engage in preparatory responses and the way these circuits modulate and may be modulated by the L-HPA and SAM systems. This is followed by a discussion of what is known about the ontogeny of these systems and of the way individual differences in the development of reactivity and regulation of these systems may be related to temperament and caregiving. We conclude with some thoughts about the need for basic research examining the development of stress systems in order to better our understanding of the origins of individual differences in stress reactivity and regulation. We begin, however, with a general discussion of the concept of stress as it is used in the psychobiological literature.

THE PSYCHOBIOLOGY OF STRESS

Stress is difficult to define. Like the terms *motivation* and *emotion,* periodically there are calls to strike *stress* from the scientific lexicon (e.g., Engle, 1985). Stress variously refers to objective events (stressors), subjective psychological states (being stressed), and physiological responses (e.g., increases in cortisol). Following Selye (1975), in this chapter we refer to the events that precipitate stress reactions as

stressors and the responses to those events as stress reactions. Events that have the potential to stimulate stress responses are not stressors for all individuals or at all ages. Intra-individual processes mediate the effect of the event on the response (e.g., Frankenhaeuser, 1979). Stress results when the demands of internal or external events exceed immediately available resources. These demands may be physiological, including being overheated, chilled, and so on. They may also be psychological, including perceived threat, failure of expectation, and social rejection. Such conditions threaten well-being and require a shifting of metabolic resources to fuel the processes needed for self-protection. This shift in metabolic resources favors systems involved in immediate survival and threat-related learning processes. When intense or prolonged, this metabolic shift limits activity in systems performing functions that are future oriented, including functions directed at growth and repair. Shifting resources to maintain organism viability is termed *allostasis* or stability through change (McEwen, 1998). The capacity to respond to stress through allostatic adjustments is necessary for survival. Increasing evidence suggests that when stress responses are limited or acute, they tend to enhance functioning. However, these adjustments have costs that, if frequent or prolonged, may undermine health and development. Thus, as important as activation is in understanding the psychobiology of stress, an understanding of the processes that regulate stress reactions is critical.

Two systems orchestrate stress responses in mammals: the L-HPA and the NE-SAM systems (Johnson, Kamilaris, Chrousos, & Gold, 1992). These systems interact in complex ways at all levels of their organization. In the early 1900s Cannon (1936) argued that the SAM system was responsible for coordinating the physiological and behavioral responses necessary to meet external challenges to the constancy of the internal milieu. Building on Bernard's theory that organisms have evolved complex adaptive mechanisms to stabilize their internal states, Cannon proposed the concept of fight/flight to describe the behavioral functions of the SAM system. Later, when Selye (e.g., 1975) presented his theory of the general adaptation syndrome, attention shifted from the SAM to the L-HPA system. Both Cannon and Selye recognized that thoughts and emotions could produce increases in sympathetic and adrenocortical activity even when there were no physical threats to homeostasis. However, it was not until researchers understood that activity of the pituitary gland was under the regulation of hypothalamic releasing and inhibiting factors that the outlines of our current understanding of stress and its relations to the neurobiology of emotion and cognition began to be discerned. It is now well recognized that the SAM and L-HPA system are regulated in part by forebrain structures and pathways, including regions in the prefrontal cortex (Johnson et al., 1992). As in all areas of neuroscience, most of what we know is based on animal research and, when conducted in humans, generally involves adults. Thus, caution is necessary in extrapolating the information presented here to human infants and children.

Contemporary formulations of stress describe a loosely integrated system consisting of neuroanatomical and functional subsystems. Below the neck, stress biology centers on the regulation of glucocorticoids or CORT (cortisol in primates, corticosterone in rodents) and catecholamines, primarily norepinephrine and epinephrine (NE and EPI) (e.g., Johnson et al., 1992). In the periphery, CORT and catecholamines operate to increase the energy available for action through inhibiting glucose uptake into storage sites and liberating energy from fat and protein stores. Concurrently, they stimulate increases in cardiovascular and pulmonary function to support the increased motor activity needed in times of challenge. Finally, in concert with central components of the stress system, they function to modulate the biology of growth and repair, including digestion, physical growth, immune function, and reproduction. In the brain, the stress system is orchestrated through reciprocal interactions among NE and hypothalamic and extra-hypothalamic corticotropin-releasing hormone (CRH).

Levels of the stress system mature and become organized over the course of development. In humans, the hypothalamic-brain-stem level develops largely during the prenatal period. Development and integration of limbic and hypothalamic-brain-stem circuits likely occur over the course of infancy (Vazquez, 1998). The frontal cortex is also involved in the regulation of limbic and hypothalamic nuclei. The long period of development of the frontal cortex that extends into adolescence (Huttenlocher, 1994) likely means that a protracted period of development of stress reactivity and regulation in humans exists. A prolonged period of postnatal development of the stress system also suggests that postnatal experience may play critical and multiple roles in emerging individual differences in stress reactivity and regulation (e.g., Heim, Owen, Plotsky, & Nemeroff, 1997). Next we describe each level of the stress system in more detail.

The Limbic-Hypothalamic-Pituitary-Adrenocortical System

The L-HPA system orchestrates mammalian stress biology through the activity of CRH (e.g., Nemeroff, 1996). CRH is a neuroactive peptide produced in the hypothalamus and in extra-hypothalamic sites. In the hypothalamus its production begins the cascade of events that culminates in increased

production of CORT by the adrenal glands. Along with several other secretagogues, CRH regulates the production of adrenocorticotropic hormone (ACTH) by the anterior pituitary (for review, see Palkovits, 1987). Released into general circulation, ACTH binds to receptors on adrenocortical cells in the cortex of the adrenal glands and stimulates the biosynthesis and release of CORT into general circulation. Negative feedback regulates L-HPA activation and CORT production. Current evidence suggests that negative feedback is a widely distributed system involving CORT receptors in, but not limited to, the prefrontal cortex, hypothalamus, hippocampus, and the anterior pituitary gland (e.g., de Kloet, Vreugdenhil, Oitzl, & Joels, 1998; Sanchez, Young, Plotsky, & Insel, 2000).

CRH-producing cells in the hypothalamus receive input from other limbic, hypothalamic, and brain-stem nuclei. As discussed later, NE is a major stimulus of CRH activity in response to psychological stressors. However, multiple neurotransmitter and neuropeptide systems, beyond the NE system, are involved in regulating CRH (Palkovits, 1987). Furthermore, hypothalamic CRH-producing cells also receive input from other nuclei in the hypothalamus, particularly those involved in daily energy flow (Dallman et al., 1993). The net result is that the production of cortisol is not a direct reflection of the individual's emotional state. Rather, it reflects the extent to which signals impinging on the hypothalamus from all sources indicate that extraordinary resources can and must be expended in order to meet the demands of the moment.

Balancing internal and external demands is reflected not only in CRH activity at the level of the hypothalamus, but also in CRH activity at extra-hypothalamic sites (Nemeroff, 1996). CRH is produced in many brain structures that are involved in associating fear and anxiety with activation of the stress system, including the amygdala and prefrontal cortex. In addition, one subtype of the CRH receptor, CRH1, appears specifically to mediate fear-related functions, whereas increasing evidence suggests that CRH2 receptors are more involved in anxiety states (Steckler & Holsboer, 1999). The neuroanatomy of the CRH system has lead to the (likely overly simplistic) view of CRH as the central orchestrator of the stress system, both in terms of endocrine and behavioral responses.

CORT has figured prominently in research on the health consequences of chronic stress. One common fallacy about the L-HPA system is that CORT is necessarily bad for one's health and development. In fact, the relationship between CORT and healthy adaptation is an inverted-U function. Although it appears that chronic or frequent high CORT can be detrimental, it is equally apparent that insufficient CORT has negative consequences (McEwen, 1998). One hypothesis is that the basis for this inverted-U function lies in the two receptors for CORT, termed mineralocorticoid receptors (MR) and glucocorticoid receptors (GR), and the different functions they mediate (de Kloet et al., 1998). According to this hypothesis, MRs primarily mediate processes that sustain and promote mental and physical health, whereas GRs mediate effects that shunt metabolic resources from growth and repair to catabolic activities needed to manage immediate threats. MRs tend to be occupied when CORT levels are in the basal range. GRs become occupied as CORT levels rise in response to stressors. As GRs become occupied, CRH activity in the hypothalamus is restrained and the stress response is terminated. Activation of this system and activation of GRs is normal and probably has beneficial effects. However, when GRs are occupied chronically, GR-mediated biochemical events can threaten neuronal viability and downregulate or reduce the GRs available to terminate the stress response, leading to an increase in CORT production. Thus, frequent or prolonged elevations in CORT have been postulated to be one cause of subsequent heightened and prolonged CORT elevations following trauma or chronic adversity. Importantly, early experiences in rodents shape the MR and GR receptor systems (e.g., Caldji et al., 1998; Levine, 1994). Conditions associated with adequate maternal care result in increased MR/GR ratios that allow better containment of the stress response and promotive effects associated with MR occupation to be produced across a wider range of CORT production. Histories of inadequate nurturance result in the opposite pattern of decreased MR/GR ratios.

Autonomic Regulation

Although the L-HPA system now figures prominently in research on stress, the older focus on the SAM system has not been lost (see review by Johnson et al., 1992). Consider the catecholamines EPI and NE. EPI is produced by the adrenal medulla and then released into general circulation. EPI acts as a stress hormone, whereas NE produced at synapses is a neurotransmitter. Both EPI and NE act to energize and mobilize the organism for action. Neurons of the hypothalamus and other cell groups within the brain stem are the central coordinators of the sympathetic nervous system (SNS). In the brain, NE-producing neurons originating in the locus coeruleus (LC) project widely throughout the cortex. Although the LC has often been considered a component of central autonomic control, there is little evidence to support this view. LC projections seem to be involved in arousal (Saper, 1995). In addition, LC neurons project to the CRH-producing cells in the hypothalamus, serving as a primary

stimulus of increased CRH production and sensitization in response to emotional stressors. In a parallel but independent system, CRH-producing neurons in the amygdala project to the LC, bringing activity of the LC under the regulation of extra-hypothalamic CRH. The central nucleus of the amygdala also stimulates activity of the SAM system via projections to the lateral hypothalamus and brain-stem autonomic nuclei. Although the SAM system has long been associated with stress, its activity is not specific to threatening or aversive events. Instead, because of the role of the sympathetic system in supporting rapid energy mobilization, its activity tends to track conditions requiring *effort* and information processing more generally, rather than those involving *distress* and uncertainty about outcomes more specifically (e.g., Frankenhaeuser, 1979). Despite this, frequent mobilization of the sympathetic system, particularly in the presence of elevated CORT, can threaten physical health.

The SAM system forms one arm of the autonomic nervous system (ANS). The other arm of this system is the parasympathetic nervous system (PNS). Unlike the SAM system, which is sometimes referred to as a diffuse or mass-discharge system, the PNS tends to be more fine-tuned, having discrete effects on the organ systems that it innervates (Hugdahl, 1995). Similar to the health-promotive effects of MRs for the L-HPA system, the PNS primarily promotes anabolic activities concerned with the conservation and restoration of energy (Porges, 1995a, 1995b). The presence of PNS terminals on most organs and tissues innervated by the SAM system allows the PNS to serve as a major regulator of sympathetic effects. Furthermore, although both the PNS and SAM systems have been viewed as efferent systems that carry out work dictated by the brain, both systems also have afferent projections to the brain. These afferent projections not only inform the brain about the status of organs and tissues in the periphery but also allow autonomic regulation of the central nervous system.

Parasympathetic neuronal projections leave the brain through several cranial nerves including the 10th cranial, or vagus nerve, which has been the focus of most of the psychophysiological research relating activity of the PNS to stress and emotion (Porges, 1995a, 1995b). In the following description we draw heavily from Porges's work, which has stimulated much of the developmental work on emotion and stress (see also the review by Beauchaine, in press). The primary fibers of the vagus nerve originate in two nuclei in the medulla: the dorsal motor nucleus of the vagus (DMNX), which regulates visceral functions, and the nucleus ambiguus (NA), which regulates functions associated with communication and emotion. In addition, a third medullary nucleus, the nucleus tractus solitarius (NTS) receives many

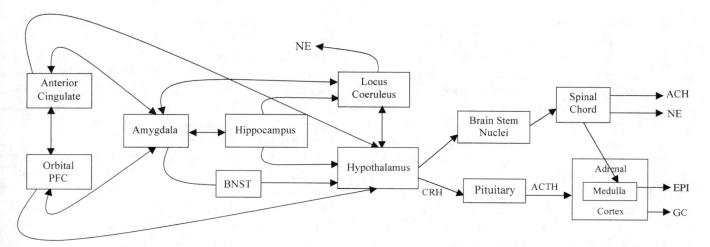

Figure 5.1

of the afferent projections traveling through the vagus from peripheral organs. In his *polyvagal theory,* Porges (1995a) argued that this trinity of nuclei forms the central regulatory component of the vagal system. Efferent projections from the NA, the *smart* vagus (V^na), are the principal vagal component in vagal cardiac and bronchomotor regulation. The intimate associations between V^na and facial and vocal expressions of emotion, in combination with afferent projections through the NTS, provide pathways through which emotion regulation may contribute to stress regulation, and vice versa. Though still speculative, this polyvagal theory offers a number of insights into the potential role of the PNS in regulating stress biology (Porges, 1995b). Specifically, high-baseline V^na should increase the individual's ability to cope effectively with stress by permitting the lifting of what Porges termed the *vagal break,* allowing rapid increases in sympathetic activity to shift metabolic resources quickly in response to challenge. In addition, feedback to the NTS via afferent projections of the vagal system should stimulate CNS containment of both the L-HPA and SAM system reactivity.

Limbic Regulation

The physiology of stress can be activated and regulated with little or no input from limbic or cortical centers. Limbic-cortical involvement provides the opportunity to anticipate threats to homeostasis before they are actualized, allowing for preparatory, defensive responses. Integration of corticolimbic with hypothalamic-brain-stem stress systems also means that feedback and afferent projections of the L-HPA, NE-SAM, and vagal systems influence cognitive-emotional behavior. All attempts to describe the neurobiology of

emotion and stress trace their history to work by Papez as elaborated by MacLean (1952). Accordingly, emotions involve the integration of neural structures that include hypothalamic and brain-stem nuclei, along with structures such as the amygdala, hippocampus, cingulate gyrus, and orbitofrontal cortex (see Figure 5.1).

The amygdala has long been known to mediate adrenocortical responses to psychosocial stressors (Palkovits, 1987). Its role in negative emotion and conditioned fear is also now well established (for review, see Rosen & Schulkin, 1998). The amygdala and the bed nucleus of the stria terminalis (BNST) form the core structures in current views of the neurobiology of fear, anxiety, and emotional activation of the stress system. The amygdala is comprised of multiple nuclei that are richly interconnected with other parts of the brain. The central nucleus of the amygdala (CEA) has widespread influence over the L-HPA, NE-SAM, and vagal systems via amygdalofugal and stria terminalis pathways. Lesions of the amygdala and surrounding cortex in adult animals prevent elevations in stress hormones to psychological stressors such as physical restraint but do not prevent elevations to physical stressors such as illness or surgery. Such lesions also affect negative emotionality and impair fear conditioning. Although some have speculated that the CEA is involved in anxiety (e.g., with regard to behavioral inhibition, see Kagan, 1994), the role of the CEA in anxiety has recently been questioned. Indeed, Davis has argued that the BNST is more centrally involved in regulating anxious affectivity (for discussion, see Rosen & Schulkin, 1998). Nonetheless, although controversy exists regarding the roles of the CEA and BNST in the regulation of fear versus anxiety, both structures and their circuits are involved in the regulation of L-HPA and SAM system responses to events that elicit negative emotionality.

Current views hold that the threshold for activating the CEA and BNST is regulated by extra-hypothalamic CRH. Similar to stimulation of the CEA, microinfusions of CRH into the CEA produce fear behaviors in primates (reviewed by Rosen & Schulkin, 1998). The fear-inducing effects of CRH are mediated by CRH1 receptors, and experiences that increase fearful reactions to events also tend to increase CRH1 receptors in these regions (for review, see Steckler & Holsboer, 1999). There is also increasing evidence that CRF2 receptors may be involved in regulating anxiety and related states. These facts would seem to argue for a close coupling between fear/anxiety and elevations in CORT. As reflected in syndromes such as posttraumatic stress disorder (PTSD), however, this is not always the case. Whereas elevated NE and EPI have been described in PTSD, remarkably, basal cortisol levels are normal or even suppressed and the L-HPA response to stressors is often dampened although levels of CRH are increased (see review by Yehuda, 1998). Nevertheless, emotion-modulated startle responses, which are believed to reflect responsivity of the CEA and BNST, are increased in animal models of PTSD and are further enhanced by infusions of CRH especially in the presence of high CORT (see review by Rosen & Schulkin, 1998). Odd as it may seem, the limbic CRH and hypothalamic CRH systems appear only loosely coupled. It is not uncommon to find dissociations between these levels of the CRH system and, consequently, between activity of the L-HPA and NE-SAM systems. There is some suggestion that these dissociations may be the result of prolonged elevations in CORT (e.g., Rosen & Schulkin, 1998). In animal models, prolonged CORT elevations produce increased activity of CRH-producing cells in the CEA but decreased activity of similar cells in the hypothalamus. Adrenalectomy (i.e., eliminating CORT) has the opposite effect. Dissociations of this sort may contribute to the development of anxiety disorders (see also Cameron & Nesse, 1988).

Frontal Regulation

Frontal regulation of the limbic, hypothalamic, and brain-stem circuits involved in stress and emotion is a comparatively new frontier in stress research. Although it has long been recognized that the orbitofrontal cortex (OFC) and anterior cingulate cortex (ACC) play critical roles in regulating emotional behavior (e.g., MacLean, 1952), their roles in regulating activity of the L-HPA and autonomic systems are increasingly appreciated. Indeed, the degree and breadth of interconnectivity between the amygdala and frontal cortex in primates have been one of the surprising findings of the last two decades (Emery & Amaral, 2000). Perhaps especially in primates, the frontal cortex appears to play a central role in stress reactivity and regulation. In this section we briefly describe OFC and ACC regulation of the stress system. Then we broaden the discussion to current views of the roles played by analytic reasoning and positive affectivity.

The OFC and medial cortex have numerous reciprocal connections to the amygdala and other limbic regions (Price, 1999). These connections support the integration of sensory and affective signals, allowing the organization of behavior in relation to reward and punishment. They are also critically important in organizing and modulating behavior so that it is appropriate to the social context. It has been hypothesized that the OFC and its connections to the amygdala and other limbic regions help to mediate attachment effects on stress reactivity and regulation (Schore, 1996). This argument is supported by evidence that the OFC and medial prefrontal regions have connections with hypothalamic and brain-stem regions that regulate behavioral, neuroendocrine, and autonomic stress responses. Thus, activity in this region may be important in modulating autonomic and neuroendocrine stress responses.

Technically, the ACC is part of the limbic system. However, it has both cortical and limbic functions and serves, in many ways, to balance activity in the prefrontal regions of the brain with activity in the limbic-hypothalamic areas. The ACC long has been associated with emotion. Most critical to this review, dysregulation of autonomic and neuroendocrine stress reactions are produced by lesions of the ACC (e.g., Diorio, Viau, & Meaney, 1993). The ACC also subserves cognition. It has been hypothesized that the cognitive and emotion functions of the ACC involve two subdivisions, a dorsal cognitive and rostral-ventral affective division (Bush, Luu, & Posner, 2000). According to this perspective, the cognitive division is considered part of the anterior attention network, a distributed attentional network that contributes to *executive functioning*. The emotional division, on the other hand, is connected to the OFC and medial prefrontal cortex, to the amygdala, and to hypothalamic and brain-stem regions involved in the regulation of stress physiology (e.g., Price, 1999).

Posner and Rothbart (2000) argued that the anterior attention network forms the basis of the *effortful control* dimension of temperament. Effortful control is believed to contribute importantly to the regulation of social and emotional behavior, particularly when effortful inhibition of actions and emotion are required. Recent evidence that the cognitive and emotional subdivisions of the ACC reciprocally regulate each other may provide one mechanism whereby effortful control exerts inhibitory effects on negative affect and stress physiology (Drevets & Raichle, 1998).

Increases in the size and functional connectivity of the ACC with development may also help explain children's increasing ability to use cognitive coping strategies to regulate emotion, behavior, and stress (e.g., Rothbart, Derryberry, et al., 1994; Wilson & Gottman, 1996).

In addition, affect influences activity of the cognitive and affective subdivisions of the ACC. Positive emotion has been shown to support the cognitive ACC and enhance executive functioning (Ashby, Isen, & Turken, 1999), whereas negative emotion has been shown to decrease activity in the cognitive division (Bush et al., 2000). Thus, conditions that produce anger, fear, and other strong negative affects, if intense, may disrupt children's effortful regulation of their behavior and make it difficult for them to engage in tasks requiring executive function. This ability to dampen negative affects and/or reassert more positive affective states may be critical in regulating stress. Some individuals seem to be able to do this better than others. As discussed in the next section, individual differences may partly reflect asymmetry in neural activity in the prefrontal cortex.

Emotional activity in the prefrontal cortex appears to be lateralized, with activity (for review, see Davidson, 1994; Davidson & Slagter, 2000) in the right prefrontal cortex supporting negative affectivity, while activity in the left supports positive affectivity. It is interesting to note that baseline asymmetry predicts susceptibility to negative and positive emotion-eliciting stimuli and may index the extent of prefrontal-cortex inhibition of limbic-hypothalamic stress circuits. Specifically, greater activity in the right prefrontal cortex may result in disinhibition of the stress system, whereas greater activity in the left prefrontal cortex may help contain and terminate stress reactions. It is not yet clear how this laterality is related to the functioning of specific frontal structures involved in the regulation of the stress response. Nonetheless, the focus on right-frontal asymmetry is consistent with evidence that there is a right bias in the reactive components of the stress system. In rodents there is evidence that the right, not the left, medial frontal cortex mediates neuroendocrine and autonomic responsivity to stressors (Sullivan & Grafton, 1999). Similarly, both sympathetic (Kagan, 1994) and parasympathetic regulation of the heart show a right bias (Porges, 1995a). Hyperactivity in the right frontal regions, then, may reflect a bias not only to negative emotions but also to hyperactivation of the stress system.

Although most of the attention has been on negative emotionality, recently there has been increased attention on positive emotions in stress regulation. Positive affectivity has been associated with problem-focused coping (Folkman & Moskowitz, 2000), perhaps because it supports the engagement of the cognitive ACC and executive functions. Similarly,

positive affectivity as reflected in greater left than right frontal activity has been associated with self-reported preferences for approach-oriented coping strategies (Davidson & Irwin, 1999). This is consistent with Davidson's argument that lateralization of emotion in the frontal lobes reflects differential motor biases, with negative emotions organized to support withdrawal and freezing and positive emotions organized to support approach. Greater left than right frontal activity has also been associated with more rapid termination of CEA-generated fear reactions. Davidson and colleagues have suggested that a left-sided bias in the emotion system may allow individuals to experience negative emotions and produce stress reactions to threat, but then to dampen these responses rapidly once the threat has been removed.

Summary

The physiology of stress and emotions is complex. While we are beginning to develop a much richer understanding of the neurobiological bases of both emotions and stress, most of the work has yet to be conducted with humans. Furthermore, we know the least about infants and young children. Information about neurobiology, however, can serve as a guide in our attempts to construct a psychobiological account of the development of stress and emotion in early childhood. In addition, the information we are accumulating on young children—when *inconsistent* with models based on adults or animals—can challenge researchers in neuroscience to provide explanations that are more congruent with the human developmental data. We turn now to what we know about stress and emotions in early human development.

PSYCHOBIOLOGICAL STUDIES OF STRESS AND EMOTION IN CHILDREN

Psychobiological studies of stress in human infants and children are relatively new. Until the early 1980s, researchers in human development were largely limited to examining heart rate–behavior associations. Only a handful of child studies assessing CORT and catecholamines existed (see review by Gunnar, 1986). After 1980, research on the psychobiology of stress in children burgeoned as the result of the availability of salivary assays for cortisol and theoretical advances in psychophysiology (e.g., Berntson, Cacioppo, & Quigley, 1993; Davidson, 1994; Kirschbaum & Hellhammer, 1989; Porges, 1995a). These technical and theoretical advances corresponded to a heightened interest in the physiological basis of temperament (e.g., Kagan, 1994, 2001). We cover the temperament research later when we discuss individual differences. First we describe what is known at this point about the ontogeny of stress reactivity and regulation in infancy and early childhood.

Developmental Periods of Stress Reactivity and Regulation

Prenatal Origins

The ontogeny of human stress reactivity and regulation begins well before birth. By 18 to 20 weeks gestation, increases in NE and CORT are observed to invasive surgical procedures (e.g., Giannakoulpoulous, Teixeira, Fisk, & Glover, 1999; Giannakoulpoulous, Sepulveda, Kourtis, Glover, & Fisk, 1994). With increased gestational age, basal levels of cortisol and ACTH rise (Economides, Nicolaides, Linton, Perry, & Chard, 1988; Murphy, 1982), and heart rate decreases but becomes more variable and coupled with fetal movement (e.g., DiPietro, Costigan, Shupe, Pressman, & Johnson, 1999). By the latter part of gestation individual differences in fetal movement and heart rate show modest stability and predict maternal reports of infant temperament during the early postnatal months (e.g., DiPietro, Hodgson, Costigan, Hilton, & Johnson, 1996). In general, active fetuses and those with higher heart rates associated with fetal motor movement are described as more difficult, less predictable, and more physically active in early infancy.

Experience begins to shape the infant's stress system before birth. In animal models where maternal stress can be manipulated experimentally, a wide range of environmental (e.g., loud noises) and psychosocial (e.g., entry into new social groups) stressors during pregnancy result in offspring that are more behaviorally and physiologically stress reactive (e.g., Weinstock, 1997). Activity of the maternal L-HPA axis appears to be a mediating factor because controlling maternal CORT levels during these stressors reduces the influence of maternal stress during pregnancy on the offspring's development (e.g., Barbazanges, Piazza, Moal, & Maccari, 1996). One pathway through which maternal CORT may influence the fetus's developing stress system is via effects on placental CRH production (Wadhwa, Garite, & Sandman, 2001). During gestation, the placenta produces a large number of hormones and peptides, including CRH, that maintain the integrity of the fetal-maternal placental unit. As the placenta enlarges during pregnancy, CRH levels increase. Placental CRH binding protein, a molecule that traps CRH, and the anticortisol effects of rising estrogen levels protect both the mother and fetus from activation by stress hormones. CRH binding protein during early pregnancy and the latter part of the third trimester stimulates fetal L-HPA maturation and

contributes to the initiation of labor and delivery. Nonetheless, whereas the CRH molecule is necessary for healthy development of the fetus, it also may provide a mechanism through which maternal stress can influence the development of the infant's stress system.

Proving that maternal stress influences fetal development in humans is hampered by our inability to perform controlled experiments. Nevertheless, evidence now exists that maternal perceptions of high stress and low social support during pregnancy are correlated with higher maternal ACTH and CORT levels, higher maternal CRH levels (which are of placental origin), fetuses with higher and less variable heart rates, and newborns delivered earlier with lower birth weights (e.g., Huizink, de Medina, Mulder, Visser, & Buitelaar, 2000; DiPietro et al., 1996; Wadhwa et al., 2001). Lower versus higher socioeconomic status is also associated with many of these same effects (e.g., DiPietro et al., 1999).

As yet, there are very few prospective studies in humans of the relations between maternal stress during pregnancy and postnatal measures of infant behavior and stress system activity. However, in contrast to one early study that failed to find any association between maternal L-HPA activity and infant temperament (Vaughn, Bradley, Joffe, Seifer, & Barglow, 1987), several recent studies have yielded positive findings (Huizink et al., 2000; Wadhwa et al., 2001). In these latter studies, controlling for a variety of obstetric and psychosocial risk factors, higher maternal CORT and ACTH levels during pregnancy were associated with maternal reports and observational measures of infant negative emotional reactivity and nonadaptability.

Although still preliminary, these studies suggest a transactional view of the fetal origins of infant stress reactivity and regulation. The placenta, which is of fetal origin, expresses genes that both influence and are influenced by maternal hormone levels. Maternal stress hormone levels, in turn, are influenced by obstetric factors and by the mother's reactions to the challenges of her daily life. Impinging on the fetus, these influences may affect the activity of the developing stress system and contribute to the organization of postnatal temperament. Undoubtedly, this is a vast oversimplification of the complex interweaving of organismic and environmental processes that shape the developing stress system prior to birth. Furthermore, birth is not the endpoint of these shaping processes.

Early Postnatal Development

Although it was once thought that the neonatal L-HPA axis was hyporesponsive at birth, this is not the case (for review, see Gunnar, 1992). The newborn displays graded behavioral, endocrine, and autonomic responses to aversive medical procedures. Furthermore, the healthy newborn is remarkably capable of regulating stress. Stressors such as heel-stick blood draws, circumcision, and physical exams produce increases in heart rate, decreases in vagal tone, and elevations in CORT; however, following such stressors the parameters of these systems return rapidly to baseline (e.g., Gunnar, Porter, Wolf, & Rigatuso, 1995).

The healthy neonate has powerful biobehavioral regulatory mechanisms at its disposal. Sleep is one of these mechanisms. Sleep is critical to stress regulation throughout life (Dahl, 1996). Newborns spend the majority of their time asleep, and in the young infant sleep periods are dominated by active or REM sleep as compared to slow-wave or quiet sleep (Anders, 1975). Quiet sleep appears to serve restorative functions in the newborn similar to the restorative functions it serves at later stages of the life cycle. This has been equated with the concept of a *stimulus barrier* in early infancy that protects the newborn from overwhelming stimulation (e.g., Tennes, Emde, Kisley, & Metcalf, 1972). Indeed, stressors alter sleep in the newborn, increasing the ratio of quiet to active sleep (for discussion, see Gunnar, 1992). In animal models the shift into sleep following stress has been shown to be facilitated by the rise in CORT and other stress biochemicals that increase in response to noxious stimulation (e.g., Born, de Kloet, Wenz, Kern, & Fehm, 1991). Thus it may be that stressors stimulate elevations in stress biochemicals that, in turn, facilitate the shift to quiet sleep supporting a return to homeostasis.

In addition to sleep, feeding and tactile stimulation appear to serve stress regulatory functions for the newborn. Blass (e.g., 1996) has recently shown that several components of nursing operate to calm the neonate through opioid- and nonopioid-mediated pathways. Sucking produces calming through nonopioid pathways in both human infants and rat pups. Sucking and swallowing are complex motor acts that engage and are regulated by the vagal system (e.g., Porges, 1995a). Thus, the vagal system may be partially responsible for the behavioral calming produced by nonnutritive sucking. In contrast, the calming and analgesic effects of sweet tastes appear to be opioid mediated. Thus, rat pups given a sucrose-flavored liquid are slower to remove their paws from a hot plate, and this effect is blocked if the pups are first pretreated with an opioid antagonist. Similar calming effects of sucrose have been demonstrated in human newborns. In addition to activating opioid-mediated analgesic pathways, sweet tastes also produce facial expressions of positive affect and increase left-sided anterior EEG activity (Fox & Davidson, 1986). Although it is unlikely that this EEG activity reflects frontal lobe generators in the neonate, it may reflect activity of

deeper structures such as the amygdala that also show asymmetric organization and are rich in opioid receptors (Pitkanen, Savander, & LeDoux, 1997).

Attention and alerting also may be components of the calming effects of sucrose. For example, Barr, Young, Wright, and Hendricks (1997) noted that quinine, an aversive taste, calms crying newborns. They have shown that in response to either sucrose or quinine newborns do not quiet and fall asleep; rather, they enter a sustained calm, alert state. Soothing practices that engage the vestibular and proprioceptive systems (i.e., picking the infant up, rocking) also appear to be most effective when they produce a calm, alert state (e.g., Brackbill, 1975). One interpretation is that these practices disrupt crying by engaging the infant's orienting and attentional mechanisms (Rothbart, Posner, & Rosicky, 1994). As discussed later, attentional mechanisms play a central role in stress regulation.

The regulatory roles for feeding and nonnutritive sucking led Blass (1996) to argue that the mother serves as a shield to buffer the infant from pain and facilitate the restoration of growth processes following periods of stress system activation. Although the concept of mother as shield is attractive, she may not shield all stress-sensitive systems equally (see also Hofer, 1987). Being held, fed, and allowed to suckle appear to have their largest effects on behavioral distress, are less clearly capable of buffering heart rate responses to painful stimulation, and have no apparent impact on CORT responses to either painful or nonpainful stressors (e.g., Gunnar, 1992). Thus, the layers of stress regulation appear to be loosely coupled in the newborn. This is to be expected given the wide range of cultural variation in patterns of holding, carrying, and feeding, and given beliefs about whether and how quickly to respond to infant crying (e.g., Barr, 1990). If soothing practices were tightly coupled to stress regulation, it would seem unlikely that such variations would exist.

Variations in how much the infant is held when not distressed, however, do appear to affect the duration of crying bouts (e.g., Barr, 1990). In addition, breast feeding versus bottle feeding also appears to affect infant irritability and behavioral responsivity to stressors (e.g., Hughes, Townsend, & Branum, 1988). We do not know whether caregiving variations shape differentially responsive stress systems in humans, although in rodent models variations surrounding feeding and contact (licking and grooming) have such effects (e.g., Caldji et al., 1998). Also, there is evidence that activity of the L-HPA system is affected by experience in early life. In newborns, repeated exposure to the same handling stressor results in habituation of the CORT response, although with two exposures at a 24-hour interval, behavioral responses do not habituate (e.g., Gunnar, 1992). Pain, in contrast, may sensitize behavioral and physiological components of the stress system (e.g., Taddio, Katz, Ilarslch, & Koren, 1997).

The First Two Years

It has been suggested that there are two periods of marked change in biobehavioral organization during the first year of life (Emde, Gaensbauer, & Harmon, 1976). The first, between two and four months of age, has been described as the three-month revolution when almost every facet of infant functioning exhibits reorganization. The second is during the later half of the first year, when the emergence of independent locomotion appears to produce dramatic neurobehavioral reorganization (e.g., Campos, Kermoian, & Witherington, 1996; Fox & Bell, 1993). This latter period is also associated with the emergence and organization of secure base behavior (e.g., Bowlby, 1969) and inhibition of approach to novel or strange events and people (e.g., Bronson, 1978). Both of these periods are associated with marked changes in stress reactivity and regulation.

Two to Four Months. Several research groups have used well-baby examinations and childhood immunizations as stressors in developmental studies of stress in infancy (e.g., Gunnar, Brodersen, Krueger, & Rigatuso, 1996; Lewis & Ramsay, 1995). As in the newborn period, CORT increases markedly to exam inoculations at 2 months of age. Heart-rate and vagal-tone changes to inoculations have not been studied, but physical exams elicit significant increases in heart rate and decreases in vagal tone in the 2-month-old infant (White, Gunnar, Larson, Donzella, & Barr, 2000). Both physical exams and inoculations elicit fussing and crying at this age (Gunnar et al., 1996; Lewis & Ramsay, 1995). When facial expressions are coded based on discrete muscle groups, expressions during inoculations at this age reflect generalized distress, rather than more specific negative emotions such as fear or anger, as will be the case by the second year of life (Izard, Hembree, Dougherty, & Spizzirri, 1983). Probing the reasons for the change in CORT response to a physical exam, results showed that it was *not* because the exam produced less behavioral distress in 12-week-old and older infants (as reviewed in Gunnar, 2000). Nor did the change appear to be due to the greater organization of the circadian rhythm in cortisol that emerges around three months. The decreased CORT response to handling around three months could reflect as-yet-unexamined maturation of negative feedback controls of the L-HPA axis. Indeed, feedback regulation of the L-HPA axis changes during early postnatal development in the rodent (Vazquez, 1998).

The L-HPA system is not the only stress-sensitive system to exhibit changes in regulation between 2 and 4 months. Developmental changes in fussing and crying have been well documented (as reviewed in Barr, 1990). The amount of time spent fussing and crying increases from birth to around 6 to 8 weeks and then declines. This developmental pattern in fussing and crying has been described in several cultures with markedly different early child-care practices, suggesting that it may be a universal phenomenon (see Barr, 1990). The basis for this developmental increase and subsequent decline is unknown; however, it raises the question of whether at around 2 months of age the infant might be particularly vulnerable to stress. Certainly, this is the period when some infants develop colic (e.g., Gormally & Barr, 1997), which by definition reflects dysregulation of the behavioral component of the stress system.

If this period of heightened irritability constitutes a stress-vulnerable period, we might expect that infants with colic would be especially vulnerable to hyperresponsivity of the L-HPA and SAM systems. This possibility was recently examined by subjecting 2-month-olds with and without colic to the physical exam stressor paradigm (White, et al., 2000). Remarkably, although the physical exam produced inconsolable crying in many of the infants with colic, changes in CORT, heart rate, and vagal tone were significant but did not differ between groups. These data add to the body of literature indicating that fussing and crying, the primary behavioral measures used to index stress in early infancy, are not always indicative of individual differences in the activity of stress-sensitive physiological systems. Again, the layers of the stress system appear to be only loosely coupled.

Several other systems that are relevant for stress research also undergo developmental shifts during these early months of life. These include sleep, attention, and the parasympathetic nervous system. Changes in sleep emerge gradually, but for most a more mature day-night sleep organization is characteristic of the infant by 3 to 4 months of age (e.g., Coons, 1987). Unfortunately, although sleep and the regulation of the L-HPA and autonomic nervous systems are interrelated (Follenius, Brandenberger, Bandesapt, Libert, & Ehrhart, 1992; Porges, Doussard-Roosevelt, Stifter, McClenny, & Riniolo, 1999), little is known about the relations between stress regulation and the ontogeny of sleep in human infants and children.

Recently, there has been increasing interest in attention and emotion regulation. Early in the first year, between roughly 3 and 4 months, the development of the posterior attention system, which is thought to be involved in the ability to orient attention, may allow increased regulation of infant distress (e.g., Rothbart, Posner, et al., 1994). Development of the posterior attention system also may play a role in the regulation of stress physiology. With the development of this system, gaze aversion and distraction appear to become coping strategies for the infant that are used in increasingly coordinated and sophisticated ways to regulate behavioral arousal and distress over the course of the first year (e.g., Field, 1981).

Attention regulation has been related to ascending influences of the vagal system, particularly the component regulated by the nucleus ambiguus (V^{na}). Porges (1995a) argued that basal V^{na} tone may index the capacity to modulate cardiac-CNS activity to sustain attention to the environment. Maturational increases in basal V^{na} tone can be seen (Porges & Fox, 1986), presumably reflecting myelination of the neural systems underlying vagal regulation. With maturation of the V^{na} system, the infant's capacity to regulate arousal through regulating attention and vice versa is expected to increase. Recently, research on vagal tone has shifted from an exclusive focus on basal tone to an interest in the dynamics of the vagal responses to stimulation. According to Porges's (1995a) polyvagal theory, suppression of V^{na} activity allows increases in sympathetic activity, whereas increases allow the infant to engage in social approach and remain calm. Modulating V^{na} activity thus is viewed as a necessary support for social and attentional regulatory strategies. Huffman et al. (1998) recently argued that not until close to 3 months of age would infants evince the capacity to regulate the V^{na} system to support orienting and soothing. They demonstrated that among 12-week-olds, high basal V^{na} was associated with less irritability, whereas delta V^{na} during testing was related to duration of attention. Both measures were related to measures of soothability.

In sum, the systems influencing stress reactivity and regulation undergo rapid maturation during the early months of life. Three months of age has been described as a qualitative turning point in early infancy from which the infant emerges prepared to engage and sustain a broader range of interactions with the environment. By 3 months the elevations in CORT that have characterized neonatal responses are no longer observed, on average, to handling stressors. Fussing and crying become increasingly dissociated from activity of the HPA system. Vagal tone increases, and some infants show increased competence in using vagal regulation to sustain attention and engagement during challenging stimulation. In addition, more clearly established day-night rhythms may facilitate the regulation of behavioral and physiological responses to potentially stressful stimulation. Unfortunately, we need to know much more about the integration of these various components of the stress system through this developmental period.

Later Infancy. Responsivity of the L-HPA system to stressors appears to undergo another change in the latter part of the first year of life (points below are reviewed in Gunnar, 2000). Elevations in CORT to inoculation procedures are roughly comparable at 4 and 6 months of age; however, by the second year of life (i.e., 12, 15, or 18 months), on average, infants do not exhibit elevations in CORT to these procedures. Similarly, maternal separation, stranger approach, unfamiliar and arousing events, and frustrating tasks do not readily provoke increases in cortisol in children older than 12 months. Whether this decrease in CORT responsivity emerges gradually or abruptly has not been determined, nor have the processes accounting for this change been identified. What has been shown is that there are individual differences in whether the infant exhibits an inhibition of the CORT response to stressors by the end of the first year. Examination of CORT increases at 6 and 15 months using the inoculation paradigm revealed that while most infants failed to elevate CORT at 15 months, some showed increases that were as large or larger than those typically observed at 6 months. These high CORT reactive infants tended to be the ones with an insecure attachment relationship to the parent who accompanied them during the exam-inoculation procedure. The role of relationships in the development of individual differences in stress reactivity and regulation will be discussed more fully below. Here we only note that these data suggest that the organization of secure-base behavior in the latter part of the first year may play a role in the developmental changes in CORT responsivity observed during this age period.

The latter part of the first year is a period of emotional reorganization. In addition to changes in secure-base behavior and distress responses to separation from attachment figures, other developmental changes in negative emotionality are also observed. Given the emphasis on fear-stress relations in neuroscience, the fact that this period is associated with increased behavioral inhibition is of particular interest. In rodents, developmental changes in behavioral inhibition are related to increased CORT responses near the end of the period of relative CORT hyporesponsivity in early development (Takahashi & Rubin, 1993). Administering CORT to the young rat pup speeds up the emergence of behavioral inhibition. This has been taken as evidence that CORT facilitates maturation of fear circuits in the rat brain. There have been too few studies of adrenocortical activity and the development of behavioral inhibition in humans to conclude that a similar pattern does *not* exist in late infancy. However, the correspondence in humans of *increased* fearfulness and *decreased* CORT responsivity over the last part of the first year suggests that the developmental psychobiology of fear and stress may be very different in human infancy.

One reason for the apparent difference may be that fear is rarely the emotion expressed in infant research. More typical is *wariness* or inhibition of approach combined with increased proximity to caregivers, followed by interest and affiliation/exploration (Sroufe, Waters, & Matas, 1974). It is not clear whether wariness is less intense fear or a response that reflects conflict between approach and avoidance (Bronson, 1978). However, wariness in the face of unknown people, objects, and events emerges gradually over the latter part of the first year and is tempered by experience, context, and the controllability of stimulation (e.g., Bronson, 1978; Gunnar, 1980; Sroufe et al., 1974). Many of these same factors are well known to temper physiological responses to threatening stimuli in studies of adults and animals (e.g., Lefcourt, 1973; Maier, Ryan, Barksdale, & Kalin, 1986).

It is important to note that wariness or behavioral inhibition emerges around the same period when infants are increasingly able to control proximity to both safe havens and exciting, new stimulation. Functionalist approaches to emotion argue that in most instances emotions serve to organize, not disorganize, behavior (Campos et al., 1996; Panksepp, 1996). Accordingly, wary responses to the unknown may serve to check the infant's tendency to approach things that are new, foster increased proximity to attachment figures in new situations, and thus provide a window of opportunity for caregivers to warn infants away from situations that are dangerous (Waters, Matas, & Sroufe, 1975). Social referencing, or the infant's tendency near the end of the first year to look to caregivers for their appraisals of unfamiliar or strange events, provides another avenue through which caregivers can curb infant curiosity at a time when infant mobility is increasing (Campos & Stenberg, 1981). Campos et al. (1996) argued that an epigenetic-constructionist perspective on emotional development is helpful in understanding the reorganization of emotions near the end of the first year. This perspective, which is consistent with the developmental psychobiological approach, may also help us understand the organization of fear/wariness and stress in infants near the end of the first year of life.

According to an epigenetic-constructionist perspective, developmental changes in one system can generate experiences that set the stage for widespread biobehavioral changes. In addition, changes in the person bring about bidirectional changes in person-environment relations that set the stage for further development. During the latter part of the first year, learning to crawl and then to walk dramatically alters the infant's relations with the environment. Independent locomotion changes the events and obstacles that the infant encounters daily and requires the development of strategies for managing the environment that are markedly different from those that serve the prelocomotor infant (e.g., Campos et al., 1996). Self-produced locomotion appears to be critical in organizing fear reactions to one particular situation: heights. Infants placed on the deep side of a visual cliff where depth cues indicate they should fall fail to show increases in heart rate prior to the onset of crawling, but they do show such increases after a few weeks of crawling experience. From this epigenetic-constructionist perspective, the critical emotion-organizing feature of motor acquisitions is the increase in agency and intentionality that they allow the infant. Increased experiences of agency and intentionality, in turn, may affect the extent to which the infant appraises events based on his or her certainty of being able to control them (Gunnar, 1980).

Infants are responsive to the contingency of stimulation early in infancy (Watson & Ramey, 1972). Within a few months of birth, infants exhibit positive affect to events that are contingent on their actions, as well as anger or sadness when a previously contingent event begins to occur noncontingently. However, it is not until close to a year of age that the infant's control over producing stimulation determines whether a potentially distressing event produces crying and avoidance or positive affect and approach (for a review, see Gunnar, 1980). Over the course of the second year of life, increases are observed in children's attempts to control directly or alter situations that produce inhibition of approach (e.g., Parritz, 1996). Furthermore, by 12 months of age, approach versus avoidance of strangers reflects the responsiveness of the stranger to the infant's actions, and thus the stranger's controllability (e.g., Mangelsdorf, 1992). Thus, by the first birthday, and increasingly over the second year of life, stress reactivity and regulation may be influenced by the infant's sense of agency or perceived control.

Another approach to understanding changes in emotionality during the latter part of infancy has focused on the development of the frontal lobes (e.g., Bell & Fox, 1992). Many of the social and cognitive accomplishments emerging during the latter part of the first year and throughout the second year depend on the development of the prefrontal cortex and its connections with brain systems involved in motor development and emotion (e.g., Dawson, Panagiotides, Klinger, & Hill, 1992; Diamond, 2000). Maturation of frontal functioning, like other aspects of brain development, is expected to reflect genetically-programmed, activity-dependent neural processes that are supported by the child's interactions with the environment. It is important to note that using 8-month-old infants, Bell and Fox (1997) showed that one to four weeks of independent locomotion was associated with the degree of mass neuronal excitability in the frontal cortex, greater activity over left than right frontal leads, and the ability to tolerate longer delays on a classic frontal lobe task (i.e., the A not B task). These data suggest that as the infant approaches the second year, motor acquisitions that dramatically alter the infant's control over approaching and avoiding stimulation co-occur with maturational changes in anterior regions of the brain. These changes likely underlie the developmental changes in the organization of emotional and physiological responses to stressors that are observed around the first birthday and increasingly over the second year of life (e.g., Campos et al., 1996). Unfortunately, there are no studies as of yet examining the relations between the developmental changes just described and the responsivity of the autonomic or neuroendocrine system to stressors.

The Toddler and Preschool Period

Development of frontal regions of the brain should allow increasing control over emotional behavior and physiological stress responses (Dawson et al., 1992). Indeed, marked increases in self-control of negative emotionality develop between 1 and 3 years (e.g., Kopp, 1989). Studies focusing on individual differences have shown correlations between expressive language development and regulation of negative emotions and social engagement and between both of these domains and cardiac vagal tone (e.g., Bornstein & Suess, 2000). The study of emotion regulation has dominated research on emotional development in the last decade, despite problems in definition and operationalization (Thompson, 1994). The research and theorizing of Posner and Rothbart (e.g., 2000) provided much needed focus in this area. They argued that maturation of the anterior attentional network permits effortful regulation of behavior, including emotional behavior. In line with these predictions, Kochanska, Murray, and Harlan (2000) have shown that children who perform better on tasks designed to assess effortful control also are better at suppressing both positive and negative emotional expressions. Stroop tasks that require inhibition of response to a prepotent stimulus activate the frontal attentional network in imaging studies of adults (Posner & Petersen, 1990). A version of the Stroop that was designed for 2- and 3-year-olds has revealed increases in accuracy over this age period (Gerardi-Caulton, in press). In addition, at 30 months, when some but not all children were able to perform the task, more competent performance was negatively correlated with parent reports of child negative emotionality. Effortful regulation of behavior, nonetheless, undoubtedly involves multiple neural systems; thus, these studies provide only the first insights into the neural bases of self-regulation and its development.

Presumably, as the child develops increasing ability to regulate emotions, she should also become increasingly capable of regulating physiological stress reactions (Stansbury & Gunnar, 1994). This assumption is speculatively based on several arguments. First, with the development of the anterior attentional network, the child should be able to engage the cognitive component of the anterior cingulate cortex, thus suppressing activity of the emotional component (Bush et al., 2000). This should help inhibit and constrain the reactivity of limbic components of the stress system. Second, to the extent that emotion regulation also involves increased activity in the left prefrontal cortical regions, the child should become increasingly capable of using positive affect and approach-oriented behavioral strategies for managing potentially stressful situations (Davidson & Irwin, 1999; Dawson et al., 1992). Third, the ability to regulate negative emotions should foster social competence and better social relationships with peers and adults (e.g., Eisenberg et al., 1993). This ability, in turn, should enhance the child's opportunities to use positive and supportive social relationships to cope with stressful situations. Social competence should also reduce the likelihood that the child's behavior will create stressful interactions with others (for review, Gunnar, 2000). Thus far, no studies examining developmental changes in the presumed neural substrate of emotion regulation and changes in stress reactivity or regulation have been reported. There have been studies of individual differences in effortful control, emotion regulation, and physiology, as reviewed in the next section.

Individual Differences

Questions about the origins of individual differences form the core of developmental research on stress. Most of this research deals with temperament and the argument that some children are biologically predisposed to be more stress reactive than are others. Some research, however, focuses on the importance of early experiences in the shaping of stress reactivity. These research foci come together in arguments about the relations between temperament and attachment and in studies of experience and the continuity of behavioral dispositions. As in other areas of developmental research, main effect arguments based on either nature or nurture explanations are giving way to transactional models that are more consistent with the developmental psychobiological perspective.

Stress and Temperament

Most studies of stress and temperament deal with behavioral inhibition. In this section we draw heavily on several excellent recent summaries of this research (see Fox, Henderson, Rubin, Calkins, & Schmidt, 2001; Kagan, in press; Stevenson-Hinde & Shouldice, 1996). As conceptualized by Kagan (2001), about

10% of children are extremely anxious and inhibited in their reactions to unfamiliar events. Consistent with the neurobiology linking fear and stress, a lower threshold for activation of fear-anxiety circuits in the CEA (or perhaps the BNST) is believed to form the basis of extreme inhibition to the unknown. Kagan argued that extremely negative reactions to stimulation at 4 months of age reflect activity of the CEA and thus predict fearful, anxious reactions to the unknown in later infancy and childhood. With development, behavioral inhibition may be more readily seen to social than to nonsocial stimuli, leading some to talk of social reticence rather than behavioral inhibition when discussing this temperamental disposition in preschoolers and older children. Fox and colleagues (e.g., Schmidt & Fox, 1999) argued that at least two forms of social reticence may have different neurobiological substrates. These forms differ in the extent to which a reticent or shy child is also motivated to be social. Although both patterns reflect a diathesis to be stressed in social situations, children who are both sociable and shy may experience the most conflict between response tendencies and thus may find new social situations to be the most stressful or challenging.

Continuity in extreme inhibition has been examined in several longitudinal studies. Generally speaking, shyness shows modest continuity across childhood, although children selected to be extremely shy often become less so with age (e.g., Kagan, in press; Stevenson-Hinde & Shouldice, 1996). Less continuity has been noted for children selected for high reactivity early in infancy (Fox et al., 2001). Most infants who show extreme negative reactivity at 4 months do not remain behaviorally inhibited into childhood; nevertheless, a small subset does remain so. As discussed later, there is some evidence that consistently inhibited children may be more extreme in their physiological markers of inhibition.

Studies of heart rate and heart rate variability or vagal tone constitute the largest body of literature on physiological differences between extremely inhibited and uninhibited children. In several cohorts, children identified as extremely inhibited during infancy have been shown to have higher and more stable baseline heart rates and lower vagal tone (for a review, see Kagan, in press). Higher and more stable baseline heart rates continue to distinguish behaviorally inhibited children throughout the preschool years. However, with continued development these baseline differences in heart rate become more difficult to find. Thus, several studies of children 7 years and older have failed to obtain differences between shy, inhibited children and uninhibited children using baseline cardiac measures, although heart rate changes in response to social stressors differentiate these groups (e.g., Marshall & Stevenson-Hinde, 1998; Schmidt, Fox, Schulkin, & Gold, 1999). In studies of CORT activity there is also

evidence that between 3 and 7 years of age children become increasingly capable of maintaining the normal diurnal decrease in CORT under normative conditions of social challenge (i.e., a day at daycare; Dettling, Gunnar, & Donzella, 1999). Furthermore, positive correlations between vagal tone and age have been reported over this age period (e.g., Donzella, Gunnar, Krueger, & Alwin, 2000). It may be that by about 7 years of age maturation of these systems allows children, including those who are more fearful or inhibited, to maintain basal functioning even in less protected contexts.

Recently, in attempts to understand the underlying neurobiological differences between extremely inhibited and uninhibited children, researchers have examined more direct indexes of the forebrain systems presumably involved in fearfulness and negative emotionality. To this end, startle amplitude, a measure presumably mediated by the CEA, has been employed in several studies. At 9 months, infants selected at four months for extreme negative reactivity have been shown to exhibit larger startle reactions during stranger approach. Tested again at 4 years, however, larger startle amplitudes were not found for these children, although at this older age only baseline startle was examined, and this might not reflect the same underlying neural circuits (see Schmidt et al., 1997).

Right frontal EEG asymmetry has also been examined in relation to behavioral inhibition. Schmidt and Fox (1999) recently reviewed their studies of EEG asymmetry on 81 children selected at 4 months because they were either high negative, high positive, or low reactive in their behavioral responses to stimulation. At 9 and 24 months, but not at 14 months, high negative infants exhibited greater right frontal activity. At 48 months, the 4-month groupings no longer predicted differences in frontal EEG asymmetry; however, asymmetry scores at 48 months were significantly correlated with concurrent measures of social reticence. When children who were continuously extreme in inhibition were examined separately from those who became less inhibited with age, the continuously inhibited children exhibited greater right frontal asymmetry at 9, 14, and 48 months (Fox et al., 2001).

Consistent with the relative lack of baseline physiological difference between inhibited and uninhibited school-aged children, Schmidt et al. (1999) recently failed to find baseline asymmetry differences in 7-year-olds selected to be extremely shy. However, they did find that these children showed a greater increase in right frontal EEG asymmetry as the social stressor became more intense. Thus, right frontal EEG asymmetry does seem to be associated with behavioral inhibition, although as with other physiological measures, differences are not always obtained, even when extreme groups are chosen. As with other stress-sensitive physiological systems, the capacity to detect baseline differences related to behavioral inhibition may decrease with age.

Dissociations between behavioral and physiological indexes of fear and stress are often noted (e.g., Quas, Hong, Alkon, & Boyce, 2000). Some of these dissociations may reflect the lack of specificity of the physiological measures. Thus, for example, low vagal tone may reflect low emotional expressivity and not just high fearful inhibition (e.g., Cole, Zahn-Waxler, Fox, Usher, & Welsh, 1996; Porges, 1995a). More specific measures of sympathetic activity may help clarify cardiac associations with extremely inhibited behavior (e.g., pre-ejection period; Berntson et al., 1993). Selecting children based on physiological extremes, and not merely behavioral extremes, may also be useful (see Fox, 1989). However, even when all of these analytic choices are made, it is likely that the associations between physiology and behavior will remain elusive. We suggest that this is because context and the resources children need to cope with challenge moderate relations between temperament and the activity of these stress-sensitive physiological systems.

Studies of CORT and temperament make this last point most clearly. While higher CORT levels for shy, inhibited children have been noted in several studies (for review, see Gunnar, 2000), particularly in new social situations, it is often the extroverted children who exhibit greater CORT responsivity (e.g., Davis, Donzella, Krueger, & Gunnar, 1999). At first glance this seems incongruous. Why would extroverted children be *stressed* by meeting other children, an activity that they seem to enjoy? However, activation of the stress system should help children mobilize the resources they need to facilitate adaptation to new situations. Perhaps extroverted children are better at mobilizing to meet social challenge. If so, the critical question may be not whether children react initially, but how rapidly they dampen their reactivity. Indeed, there is evidence that as social situations become familiar, socially competent, outgoing children show reduced CORT activity and associations between high CORT activity and negative, emotional temperament become more likely (see Gunnar, 1994). However, even when young children are familiar with the social situation, higher stress system activity is less often associated with shyness and more often associated with behaviors such as low frustration tolerance and aggression—behaviors that cause preschoolers to be disliked by their peers. In fact, peer rejection appears to be an important predictor of high CORT levels in preschool classrooms (Gunnar, Tout, de Hann, Pierce, & Stansbury, 1997). Combined, these findings strongly suggest that behavioral inhibition is not the only temperamental disposition associated with greater stress reactivity in young children.

Furthermore, they point to the importance of context and relationships in determining how temperamental differences among children impact the activity of stress-sensitive physiological systems. In the following section we deal with caregiver-child interaction. However, it is important to note that the psychobiology of stress in early childhood includes peer- as well as adult-child relations.

Stress and Caregiving Relationships

In work with animals it is well documented that maternal behavior shapes the reactivity of stress-sensitive systems (e.g. Caldji et al., 1998; Levine, 1994). In rats, dams that spend the most time licking and grooming their pups and exhibit well-organized nursing behavior have pups that grow up to be less fearful of novelty, compared to the offspring of mothers low in these behaviors. A number of neurobiological changes accompany these differences in fear reactions, including more rapid containment of the HPA stress response, less evidence of CRH activity in the CEA, BNST, and LC, and decreased NE in response to psychosocial stressors (Caldji et al., 1998). In primates, there is strong evidence that contact with the mother buffers the stress response (e.g., Levine & Weiner, 1988). As long as the infant monkey can gain access to the mother, elevations in CORT to a variety of stressors are reduced, even though the infant may still show agitated, distressed behavior.

In human adults, supportive social relationships moderate the impact of stressful life circumstances on emotional and physical health (Berkman, 1995). In young children, studies of the quality of mother-infant attachment have yielded evidence that secure attachment relationships function to regulate the activity of stress-sensitive systems (see review by Gunnar, 2000). This has been demonstrated during the strange situation task used to assess attachment security, as well as when attachment security is examined as a moderator of temperament-physiology associations in response to other stressful stimuli. Under both kinds of testing situations, both insecure avoidant (A) and insecure resistant (C) infants exhibit larger and more prolonged CORT and heart rate increases (see also Spangler & Grossmann, 1993; Sroufe & Waters, 1979). Furthermore, behavioral indexes of distress or inhibition appear to be associated with heightened CORT responses *only* when infants and toddlers are tested in the presence of a parent with whom they have an insecure attachment relationship (e.g., Spangler & Schieche, 1998). Similar results have been obtained for preschool-aged children. Thus, among 4.5-year-olds, highly inhibited children who were insecurely attached had the highest heart rates during mild social challenges, whereas highly inhibited children who were securely attached had the lowest heart rates (Stevenson-Hinde & Marshall, 1999). Thus, although there is an ongoing debate between attachment and temperament theorists over whether these attachment classifications reflect behavioral inhibition rather than relationship quality (e.g., Belsky & Rovine, 1987), the preponderance of the evidence indicates that differences in stress reactivity between children in secure and insecure relationships are not a reflection of temperament. Rather, they reflect the role of attachment security in moderating relations between temperamental fearfulness and stress system activity.

Attachment theorists argue that infants form secure relationships with caregivers who are sensitive and responsive to their signals. A number of researchers have questioned the strength of these associations (e.g., Goldsmith & Alansky, 1987); however, evidence suggests that these qualities in a caregiver are associated with reduced stress system activity. Infants interacting with an insensitive, unresponsive mother or those randomly assigned to an unresponsive babysitter have been shown to produce increasing levels of CORT during play bouts (e.g., Gunnar, 2000; Spangler, Schieche, Ilg, Maier, & Ackermann, 1994). Furthermore, mothers suffering from clinical depression, who often have trouble being sensitive and responsive, have infants who tend to show right frontal EEG asymmetry and higher CORT levels (e.g., Dawson & Ashman, 2000). Controlling for numerous other factors, it appears that the depressed mothers' unresponsive, intrusive behavior shapes higher CORT and greater right frontal EEG activity (see Dawson & Ashman, 2000). In addition, the timing of maternal periods of clinical depression appears to matter. Periods of depression during the infant's first year have been shown to predict higher CORT levels at age 3, whereas periods of depression during the second and third year predict greater right frontal EEG patterns at three years. Dawson and colleagues speculate that their findings may reflect sensitive periods for the organization of different aspects of the stress system; however, they also note that these data are preliminary and need replication.

Although the results just described strongly suggest that sensitive, responsive parenting regulates the young child's stress system, there is some evidence that overly responsive, overly solicitous parenting may do the opposite. Thomasgard and Metz (1993) argued that from the best of intentions parents may feel that they need to step in to protect their anxious child from upsetting experiences and may intrude into their ongoing activities in ways that are overly protective and overly solicitous. Overly solicitous, intrusive caregiving during threat is associated with larger CORT increases among toddlers and predicts insecure attachment classification (Nachmias, Gunnar, Mangelsdorf, Parritz, & Buss, 1996).

Similarly, parents who are extremely affectionate with and solicitous of infants selected for high negative reactivity at 4 months are more likely to have infants who become extremely inhibited in their second year than are less affectionate and solicitous parents (Arcus, Gardner, & Anderson, 1992). Such parenting might increase fearfulness and stress reactivity because it is insensitive, is organized more around the parent's anxiety about the child than the child's actual needs, and reduces the child's experiences of self-regulation. Regardless, these data suggest that we need more studies of caregiving in stressful circumstances to understand how what the caregiver does during periods of high challenge influences both the parent-child relationship and the child's developing stress system.

Animal studies document that not only normal variations in caregiving but also early maltreatment influence the developing stress system. There are too few studies of early maltreating rearing environments in humans to know whether early experiences shape the stress system in our species (for review, see Gunnar, 2000). In several studies of children who were severely maltreated during their first years of life, elevations in baseline CORT and catecholamine production have been noted several years after removal from their maltreating contexts. Similarly, in a recent study of women who were sexually abused during childhood, heightened ACTH responses to a social stressor were found both for those who were and those who were not clinically depressed. However, the situations that result in maltreatment in humans are complex. Any of a number of factors beyond caregiver-infant interaction, including lack of adequate stimulation, malnutrition, and inadequate medical care might be involved in producing alterations in the development of the stress system. As in other domains of early human experience, proving that maltreatment at the hands of caregivers early in development has permanent effects on the developing stress system will be difficult.

SUMMARY AND CONCLUSIONS

The last several decades have seen tremendous advances in our understanding of the neurobiology of the human stress system. Research on the development of stress reactivity and regulation in infants and children has burgeoned in recent years due largely to the development of noninvasive measurement techniques. However, we are still far from understanding the processes through which individual differences in stress become organized. Repeatedly throughout this review we have noted where basic information is lacking. Much of this information involves normative data on the organization of stress reactivity and regulation at different points during early development. As in the study of emotional development more generally, we have much more information about individual differences in stress reactivity than we do about normative patterns of development and change. However, unless we develop this latter body of knowledge, it will be difficult to explicate the origins of individual differences in stress reactivity and regulation. Research on temperament, especially extremely inhibited temperament, has motivated much of the research on early stress reactivity and regulation. Although this work has been aimed at documenting the stability of temperamental differences among children, the evidence strongly suggests that most children do not remain extremely fearful or inhibited throughout infancy and early childhood. Change is as likely, or even more likely, than stability. Studies of caregiver-child interactions indicate that qualities of care, including sensitivity and responsiveness, are related to reactivity and regulation of the stress system in infants and young children. It seems likely that transactional processes shape the development of the stress system in humans as they appear to in other mammals. These processes, including the child's role in influencing the nature of his or her experiences, remain largely unexplored. We argue that an adequate understanding of the development of stress and emotion in early childhood will require attention both to the transactional nature of the influences that shape differences in stress responsivity among individuals and to the ways these transactions emerge and change during the early years of life.

REFERENCES

Anders, T. (Ed.). (1975). *Maturation of sleep patterns in the newborn infant.* New York: Spectrum.

Arcus, D., Gardner, S., & Anderson, C. (1992). *Infant reactivity, maternal style, and the development of inhibited and uninhibited behavioral profiles.* Paper presented at the International Society for Infant Studies, Miami, FL.

Ashby, F. G., Isen, A. M., & Turken, A. U. (1999). A neuropsychological theory of positive affect and its influence on cognition. *Psychological Review, 106*(3), 529–550.

Barbazanges, A., Piazza, P. V., Moal, M. L., & Maccari, S. (1996). Maternal glucocorticoid secretion mediates long-term effects of prenatal stress. *Journal of Neuroscience, 16*(12), 3943–3949.

Barr, R. G. (1990). The early crying paradox: A modest proposal. *Human Nature, 1*(4), 355–389.

Barr, R. G., Young, S. N., Wright, J. H., & Hendricks, L. A. (1997). Differential response to intraoral sucrose, quinine, and corn oil in crying human newborns. *Physiology and Behavior, 62*(2), 317–325.

Beauchaine, T. (in press). Vagal tone, development, and Gray's motivational theory: Toward an integrative model of autonomic nervous system functioning in psychopathology. *Development and Psychopathology.*

Bell, M. A., & Fox, N. A. (1992). The relations between frontal brain electrical activity and cognitive development during infancy. *Child Development, 63*, 1142–1163.

Bell, M. A., & Fox, N. A. (1997). Individual differences in object permanence performance at 8 months: Locomotor experience and brain electrical activity. *Developmental Psychobiology, 31*(4), 287–297.

Belsky, J., & Rovine, M. (1987). Temperament and attachment security in the strange situation: An empirical rapproachement. *Child Development, 58*(3), 787–795.

Berkman, L. F. (1995). The role of social relations in health promotion. *Psychosomatic Medicine, 57*, 245–254.

Berntson, G. G., Cacioppo, J. T., & Quigley, K. S. (1993). Cardiac psychophysiology and autonomic space in humans: Empirical perspectives and conceptual implications. *Psychological Bulletin, 114*(2), 296–322.

Blass, E. M. (1996). Mothers and their infants: Peptide-mediated physiological, behavioral and affective changes during suckling. *Regulatory Peptides, 66*(1–2), 109–112.

Born, J., de Kloet, E. R., Wenz, H., Kern, W., & Fehm, H. L. (1991). Gluco- and antimineralocorticoid effects on human sleep: A role of central corticosteroid receptors. *American Physiological Society,* E183–E188.

Bornstein, M. H., & Suess, P. E. (2000). Physiological self-regulation and information processing in infancy: Cardiac vagal tone and habituation. *Child Development, 71*(2), 273–287.

Bowlby, J. (1969). *Attachment and Loss: Attachment* (Vol. 1). New York: Basic Books.

Brackbill, Y. (1975). Continuous stimulation and arousal level in infancy: Effects of stimulus intensity and stress. *Child Development, 46*, 364–369.

Bronson, G. (1978). Aversive reactions to strangers: A dual process interpretation. *Child Development, 49*, 495–499.

Bush, G., Luu, P., & Posner, M. I. (2000). Cognitive and emotional influences in anterior cingulate cortex. *Trends in Neuroscience, 4*, 215–222.

Caldji, C., Tannenbaum, B., Sharma, S., Francis, D., Plotsky, P. M., & Meaney, M. J. (1998). Maternal care during infancy regulates the development of neural systems mediating the expression of fearfulness in the rat. *Proceedings of the National Academy of Sciences, USA, 95*(9), 5335–5340.

Cameron, O. G., & Nesse, R. M. (1988). Systematic hormonal and physiological abnormalities in anxiety disorders. *Psychoneuroendocrinology, 13*(2), 287–307.

Campos, J., Kermoian, R., & Witherington, D. (1996). An epigenetic perspective on emotional development. In R. D. Kavanaugh, B. Zimmerberg, & S. Feinman (Eds.), *Emotion: Interdisciplinary perspectives* (pp. 119–138). Mahwah, NJ: Erlbaum.

Campos, J., & Stenberg, C. (1981). Perception, appraisal and emotion: The onset of social referencing. In M. Lamb & L. Sherrod (Eds.), *Infant social cognition: Empirical and theoretical considerations* (pp. 273–314). Hillsdale, NJ: Erlbaum.

Cannon, W. B. (1936). *Bodily changes in pain, hunger, fear and rage.* New York: Appleton-Century-Crofts.

Cole, P., Zahn-Waxler, C., Fox, N. A., Usher, B. A., & Welsh, J. D. (1996). Individual differences in emotion regulation and behavior problems in preschool children. *Journal of Abnormal Psychology, 105,* 518–529.

Coons, S. (1987). Development of sleep and wakefulness during the first six months of life. In C. Guilleminault (Ed.), *Sleep and its disorders in children* (pp. 17–27). New York: Raven Press.

Dahl, R. E. (1996). The regulation of sleep and arousal: Development and psychopathology. *Development and Psychopathology, 8,* 3–27.

Dallman, M. F., Strack, A. M., Akana, S. F., Bradbury, M. J., Hanson, E. S., Scribner, K. A., & Smith, M. (1993). Feast and famine: Critical role of glucocorticoids with insulin in daily energy flow. *Frontiers in Neuroendocrinology, 14,* 303–347.

Davidson, R. J. (1994). Asymmetric brain function, affective style, and psychopathology: The role of early experience and plasticity. *Development and Psychopathology, 6,* 741–758.

Davidson, R. J., & Irwin, W. (1999). The functional neuroanatomy of emotion and affective style. *Trends in Neuroscience, 3,* 11–21.

Davidson, R. J., & Slagter, H. A. (2000). Probing emotion in the developing brain: Functional neuroimaging in the assessment of the neural substrates of emotion in normal and disordered children and adolescents. *Mental Retardation and Developmental Disabilities Research Reviews, 6*(3), 166–170.

Davis, E. P., Donzella, B., Krueger, W. K., & Gunnar, M. R. (1999). The start of a new school year: Individual differences in salivary CORT response in relation to child temperament. *Developmental Psychobiology, 35*(3), 188–196.

Dawson, G., & Ashman, S. (2000). On the origins of a vulnerability to depression: The influence of early social environment on the development of psychobiological systems related to risk for affective disorder. In C. A. Nelson (Ed.), *Minnesota Symposia on Child Psychology: Vol. 31. The effects of adversity on neurobehavioral development* (pp. 245–280). New York: Erlbaum.

Dawson, G., Panagiotides, H., Klinger, L. G., & Hill, D. (1992). The role of frontal lobe functioning in the development of infant self-regulatory behavior. *Brain and Cognition, 20,* 152–175.

de Kloet, R., Vreugdenhil, E., Oitzl, M. S., & Joels, A. (1998). Brain corticosteroid receptor balance in health and disease. *Endocrine Reviews, 19*(3), 269–301.

Dettling, A., Gunnar, M. R., & Donzella, B. (1999). CORT levels of young children in full-day childcare centers: Relations with age and temperament. *Psychoneuroendocrinology, 24*(5), 505–518.

Diamond, A. (2000). Close interrelation of motor development and cognitive development and of the cerebellum and prefrontal cortex. *Child Development, 71*(1), 44–56.

Diorio, D., Viau, V., & Meaney, M. J. (1993). The role of the medial prefrontal cortex (cingulate gyrus) in the regulation of hypothalamic-pituitary-adrenal responses to stress. *Journal of Neuroscience, 13,* 3839–3847.

DiPietro, J. A., Costigan, K. A., Shupe, A. K., Pressman, E. K., & Johnson, T. R. (1999). Fetal neurobehavioral development associated with social class and fetal sex. *Developmental Psychobiology, 33,* 79–81.

DiPietro, J. A., Hodgson, D. M., Costigan, K. A., Hilton, S. C., & Johnson, T. R. (1996). Fetal neurobehavioral development. *Child Development, 67,* 2553–2567.

Donzella, B., Gunnar, M. R., Krueger, W. K., & Alwin, A. (2000). CORT and vagal tone responses to competitive challenge in preschoolers: Associations with temperament. *Developmental Psychobiology, 37*(4), 209–220.

Drevets, W. C., & Raichle, M. E. (1998). Reciprocal suppression of regional cerebral blood flow during emotional versus higher cognitive processes: Implications for interactions between emotion and cognition. *Cognition and Emotion, 12,* 353–385.

Economides, D. L., Nicolaides, K. H., Linton, E. A., Perry, L. A., & Chard, T. (1988). Plasma CORT and adrenocorticotropin in appropriate and small for gestational age fetuses. *Fetal Therapy, 3,* 158–164.

Eisenberg, N., Fabes, R. A., Bernzweig, H., Karbon, M., Poulin, R., & Hanish, L. (1993). The relations of emotionality and regulation to preschoolers' social skills and sociometric status. *Child Development, 64,* 1418–1438.

Emde, R. M., Gaensbauer, T. J., & Harmon, R. J. (1976). *Emotional expressions in infancy: A biobehavioral study.* New York: International University Press.

Emery, N. J., & Amaral, D. G. (2000). The role of the amygdala in primate social cognition. In R. D. Lane & L. Nadel (Eds.), *Cognitive neuroscience of emotion* (pp. 156–191). New York: Oxford University Press.

Engle, B. T. (1985). Stress is a noun! No, a verb! No, an adjective. In T. Field, P. McCabe, & N. Sneiderman (Eds.), *Stress and coping* (Vol. 1, pp. 3–12). Hillsdale, NJ: Erlbaum.

Field, T. (1981). Infant gaze aversion and heart rate during face-to-face interactions. *Infant Behavior and Development, 4,* 307–316.

Folkman, S., & Moskowitz, J. T. (2000). Stress, positive emotion, and coping. *Current Directions in Psychological Science, 9,* 115–118.

Follenius, M., Brandenberger, G., Bandesapt, J. J., Libert, J. P., & Ehrhart, J. (1992). Nocturnal CORT release in relation to sleep structure. *Sleep, 15*(1), 21–27.

Fox, N. A. (1989). Psychophysiological correlates of emotional reactivity during the first year of life. *Developmental Psychology, 25*(3), 364–372.

Fox, N. A., & Bell, M. A. (1993). Frontal function in cognitive and emotional behaviors during infancy: Effects of maturation and experience. In B. de Boysson-Bardies & S. de Schonen (Eds.), *NATO ASI Series D: Behavioural and Social Sciences: Vol. 69.*

Developmental Neurocognition: Speech and Face Processing in the First Year of Life (pp. 199–210). Dordrecht, Netherlands: Kluwer.

Fox, N. A., & Davidson, R. J. (1986). Taste-elicited changes in facial signs of emotion and the asymmetry of brain electrical activity in human newborns. *Neuropsychologia, 24,* 417–422.

Fox, N. A., Henderson, H. A., Rubin, K. H., Calkins, S., & Schmidt, L. A. (2001). Continuity and discontinuity of behavioral inhibition and exuberance: Psychophysiological and behavioral influences across the first four years of life. *Child Development, 72,* 1–21.

Frankenhaeuser, M. (1979). Psychobiological aspects of life stress. In S. Levine & H. Ursin (Eds.), *Coping and health* (pp. 203–224). New York: Plenum Press.

Gerardi-Caulton, G. (in press). Sensitivity to spatial conflict and the development of self-regulation in children 24–36 months of age. *Developmental Science.*

Giannakoulpoulous, X., Sepulveda, W., Kourtis, P., Glover, V., & Fisk, N. M. (1994). Fetal plasma and beta-endorphin response to intrauterine needling. *The Lancet, 344,* 77–81.

Giannakoulpoulous, X., Teixeira, J., Fisk, N. M., & Glover, V. (1999). Human fetal and maternal noradrenaline responses to invasive procedures. *Pediatric Research, 45,* 494–499.

Goldsmith, H. H., & Alansky, J. A. (1987). Maternal and infant temperamental predictors of attachment: A meta-analytic review. *Journal of Consulting and Clinical Psychology, 55*(6), 805–816.

Gormally, S. M., & Barr, R. G. (1997). Of clinical pies and clinical clues: Proposal for a clinical approach to complaints of early crying and colic. *Good Practice Guide, 3,* 137–153.

Gottlieb, G., Wahlsten, D., & Lickliter, R. (1998). A developmental psychobiological systems view. In R. Lerner (Ed.), *Handbook of child psychology: Vol. 1. Theoretical model of human development* (5th ed., pp. 233–274). New York: Wiley.

Gunnar, M. R. (1980). Contingent stimulation: A review of its role in early development. In S. Levine & H. Ursin (Eds.), *Coping and health* (pp. 101–120). New York: Plenum Press.

Gunnar, M. R. (1986). Human developmental psychoendocrinology: A review of research on neuroendocrine responses to challenge and threat in infancy and childhood. In M. Lamb, A. Brown, & B. Rogoff (Eds.), *Advances in developmental psychology* (Vol. 4, pp. 51–103). Hillsdale, NJ: Erlbaum.

Gunnar, M. R. (1992). Reactivity of the hypothalamic-pituitary-adrenocortical system to stressors in normal infants and children. *Pediatrics, 80*(3), 491–497.

Gunnar, M. R. (1994). Psychoendocrine studies of temperament and stress in early childhood: Expanding current models. In J. Bates & T. Wachs (Eds.), *Temperament: Individual differences at the interface of biology and behavior* (pp. 175–198). New York: American Psychological Association Press.

Gunnar, M. R. (2000). Early adversity and the development of stress reactivity and regulation. In C. A. Nelson (Ed.), *The Minnesota Symposia on Child Psychology: Vol. 31. The effects of adversity*

on neurobehavioral development (pp. 163–200). Mahwah, NJ: Erlbaum.

Gunnar, M. R., Brodersen, L., Krueger, K., & Rigatuso, J. (1996). Dampening of adrenocortical responses during infancy: Normative changes and individual differences. *Child Development, 67*(3), 877–889.

Gunnar, M. R., Porter, F., Wolf, C., & Rigatuso, J. (1995). Neonatal stress reactivity: Predictions to later emotional temperament. *Child Development, 66,* 1–14.

Gunnar, M. R., Tout, K., de Haan, M., Pierce, S., & Stansbury, K. (1997). Temperament, social competence, and adrenocortical activity in preschoolers. *Developmental Psychobiology, 31*(1), 65–85.

Hann, D. M., Huffman, L. C., Lederhendler, I. I., & Meinecke, D. (Eds.). (1998). *Advancing research on developmental plasticity: Integrating the behavioral science and neuroscience of mental health* (Vol. 98). Washington, DC: National Institute of Health.

Heim, C., Owen, M. J., Plotsky, P. M., & Nemeroff, C. B. (1997). The role of early adverse life events in the etiology of depression and posttraumatic stress disorder: Focus on corticotropin-releasing factor. *Annals of the New York Academy of Science, 821,* 194–207.

Hofer, M. (1987). Shaping forces within early social relationships. In N. A. Krasnegar (Ed.), *Perinatal development: A psychobiological perspective* (pp. 251–274). Orlando, FL: Academic Press.

Huffman, L., Bryan, Y. E., del Carmen, R., Pedersen, F. A., Doussard-Roosevelt, J., & Porges, S. W. (1998). Infant temperament and cardiac vagal tone: Assessments at twelve weeks of age. *Child Development, 69,* 624–635.

Hugdahl, K. (1995). *Psychophysiology: The mind-body perspective.* Cambridge, MA: Harvard University Press.

Hughes, R. B., Townsend, P. A., & Branum, Q. K. (1988). Relationship between neonatal behavioral responses and lactation outcomes. *Issues in Comprehensive Pediatric Nursing, 11*(5–6), 271–281.

Huizink, A. C., de Medina, P. G. R., Mulder, E. J. H., Visser, G. H. A., & Buitelaar, J. K. (2000). Prenatal psychosocial and endocrinologic predictors of infant temperament. In A. C. Huizink (Ed.), *Prenatal stress and its effects on infant development* (pp. 171–200). Hoorn, Netherlands: Drukkerij van Vliet.

Huttenlocher, P. R. (1994). Synaptogenesis, synapse elimination, and neural plasticity in human cerebral cortex. In C. A. Nelson (Ed.), *Threats to optimal development: Integrating biological, psychological, and social risk factors* (Vol. 27, pp. 35–54). Mahwah, NJ: Erlbaum.

Izard, C. E., Hembree, E. A., Dougherty, L. M., & Spizzirri, C. C. (1983). Changes in facial expressions of 2- to 19-month-old infants following acute pain. *Developmental Psychology, 19*(3), 418–426.

Johnson, E. O., Kamilaris, T. C., Chrousos, G. P., & Gold, P. W. (1992). Mechanisms of stress: A dynamic overview of hormonal and behavioral homeostasis. *Neuroscience and Biobehavioral Reviews, 16,* 115–130.

Kagan, J. (1994). *Galen's prophecy.* New York: Basic Books.

Kagan, J. (2001). Temperamental contributions to affective and behavioral profiles in childhood. In S. G. Hofmann & P. Di Bartolo (Eds.), *Social phobia and social anxiety: An integration.* Boston: Allyn and Bacon.

Kirschbaum, C., & Hellhammer, D. H. (1989). Salivary cortisol in psychobiological research: An overview. *Neuropsychobiology, 22,* 150–169.

Kochanska, G., Murray, K. T., & Harlan, E. T. (2000). Effortful control in early childhood: Continuity and change, antecedents, and implications for social development. *Developmental Psychology, 36*(2), 220–232.

Kopp, C. B. (1989). Regulation of distress and negative emotions: A developmental view. *Developmental Psychology, 25*(3), 343–355.

Kuo, Z. Y. (1976). *The dynamics of behavior development.* New York: Plenum Press.

Lefcourt, H. M. (1973). The functions of the illusions of control and freedom. *American Psychologist, 28,* 417–425.

Lerner, R. M. (1986). *Concepts and theories of human development* (2nd ed.). New York: Cambridge University Press.

Levine, S. (1994). The ontogeny of the hypothalamic-pituitary-adrenal axis: The influence of maternal factors. *Annals of the New York Academy of Sciences, 746,* 275–288.

Levine, S., & Wiener, S. G. (1988). Psychoendocrine aspects of mother-infant relationships in nonhuman primates. *Psychoneuoendocrinology, 13,* 143–154.

Lewis, M., & Ramsay, D. S. (1995). Developmental change in infants' responses to stress. *Child Development, 66*(3), 657–670.

MacLean, P. D. (1952). Some psychiatric implications of physiological studies on frontotemporal portions of limbic system (visceral brain). *Electroencephalography and Clinical Neurophysiology, 4,* 407–418.

Maier, S. F., Ryan, S. M., Barksdale, C. M., & Kalin, N. H. (1986). Stressor controllability and the pituitary-adrenal system. *Behavioral Neuroscience, 100*(5), 669–674.

Mangelsdorf, S. C. (1992). Developmental changes in infant-stranger interaction. *Infant Behavior and Development, 15,* 191–208.

Marshall, P. J., & Stevenson-Hinde, J. (1998). Behavioral inhibition, heart period, and respiratory sinus arrhythmia in young children. *Developmental Psychobiology, 33,* 283–292.

McEwen, B. (1998). Stress, adaptation, and disease: Allostasis and allostatic load. *Annals of the New York Academy of Science, 840,* 33–44.

Murphy, B. P. (1982). Human fetal serum cortisol levels related to gestational age: Evidence of a midgestational fall and a steep late gestational rise, independent of sex or mode of delivery. *American Journal of Obstetrics and Gynecology, 144,* 276–282.

Nachmias, M., Gunnar, M. R., Mangelsdorf, S., Parritz, R., & Buss, K. (1996). Behavioral inhibition and stress reactivity: Moderating role of attachment security. *Child Development, 67*(2), 508–522.

Nemeroff, C. B. (1996). The corticotropin-releasing factor (CRF) hypothesis of depression: New findings and new directions. *Molecular Psychiatry, 1*(4), 336–342.

Palkovits, M. (1987). Organization of the stress response at the anatomical level. In E. R. de Kloet, V. M. Wiegant, & D. de Wied (Eds.), *Progress in brain research* (Vol. 72, pp. 47–55). Amsterdam: Elsevier Science.

Panksepp, J. (1996). Affective neuroscience: A paradigm to study the animate circuits for human emotions. In R. D. Kavanaugh, B. Zimmerberg, & S. Fein (Eds.), *Emotion: Interdisciplinary perspectives* (pp. 29–60). Mahwah, NJ: Erlbaum.

Parritz, R. H. (1996). A descriptive analysis of toddler coping in challenging circumstances. *Infant Behavior and Development, 19,* 171–180.

Pitkanen, A., Savander, V., & LeDoux, J. E. (1997). Organization of intraamygdaloid circuitries in the rat: An emerging framework for understanding function of the amygdala. In J. Smith & G. Schoenwolf (Eds.), *Neurulation* (pp. 517–523). New York: Elsevier Science.

Porges, S. W. (1995a). Orienting in a defensive world: Mammalian modifications of our evolutionary heritage. A poly-vagal theory. *Psychophysiology, 32*(4), 301–318.

Porges, S. W. (1995b). Cardiac vagal tone: A physiological index of stress. *Neuroscience and Biobehavioral Reviews, 19*(2), 225–233.

Porges, S. W., Doussard-Roosevelt, J. A., Stifter, C. A., McClenny, B. D., & Riniolo, T. C. (1999). Sleep state and vagal regulation of heart period patterns in the human newborn: An extension of the polyvagal theory. *Psychophysiology, 36*(1), 14–21.

Porges, S. W., & Fox, N. A. (1986). Developmental psychophysiology. In M. G. H. Coles, E. Donchin, & S. W. Porges (Eds.), *Psychophysiology* (pp. 611–625). New York: Guilford Press.

Posner, M. I., & Petersen, S. E. (1990). The attention system of the human brain. *Annual Review of Neuroscience, 13,* 25–42.

Posner, M. I., & Rothbart, M. (2000). Developing mechanisms of self-regulation. *Development and Psychopathology, 12*(3), 427–442.

Price, J. L. (1999). Prefrontal cortical networks related to visceral function and mood. *Annals of the New York Academy of Sciences, 877,* 383–396.

Quas, J. A., Hong, M., Alkon, A., & Boyce, W. T. (2000). Dissociations between psychobiologic reactivity and emotional expression in children. *Developmental Psychobiology, 37,* 153–175.

Rosen, J. B., & Schulkin, J. (1998). From normal fear to pathological anxiety. *Psychological Review, 105*(2), 325–350.

Rothbart, M. K., Derryberry, D., & Posner, M. I. (1994). A psychobiological approach to the development of temperament. In J. Bates & T. Wachs (Eds.), *Temperament: Individual differences at the interface of biology and behavior* (pp. 83–116). Washington, DC: American Psychological Association.

Rothbart, M. K., Posner, M. I., & Rosicky, J. (1994). Orienting in normal and pathological development. *Development and Psychopathology, 6,* 635–652.

Sameroff, A. (1983). Developmental systems: Contexts and evolution. In W. Kessen (Ed.), *Handbook of child psychology: Vol. 1. History, theory, and methods* (4th ed., pp. 237–294). New York: Wiley.

Sanchez, M. M., Young, L. J., Plotsky, P. M., & Insel, T. R. (2000). Distribution of corticosteroid receptors in the rhesus brain: Relative absence of glucocorticoid receptors in the hippocampal formation. *Journal of Neuroscience, 20*(12), 4657–4668.

Saper, C. B. (1995). Central autonomic system. In G. Paxinos (Ed.), *The Rat Nervous System* (pp. 107–135). New York: Academic Press.

Schmidt, L. A., & Fox, N. A. (1999). Conceptual, biological, and behavioral distinctions among different categories of shy children. In L. A. Schmidt & J. Schulkin (Eds.), *Extreme fear, shyness, and social phobia: Origins, biological mechanisms, and clinical outcomes* (pp. 47–66). New York: Oxford University Press.

Schmidt, L. A., Fox, N. A., Rubin, K. H., Sternberg, E. M., Gold, P. W., Smith, C. C., & Schulkin, J. (1997). Behavioral and neuroendocrine responses in shy children. *Developmental Psychobiology, 30*(2), 127–140.

Schmidt, L. A., Fox, N. A., Schulkin, J., & Gold, P. W. (1999). Behavioral and psychophysiological correlates of self-presentation in temperamentally shy children. *Developmental Psychobiology, 35*(2), 119–135.

Schore, A. N. (1996). The experience-dependent maturation of a regulatory system in the orbital prefrontal cortex and the origin of developmental psychopathology. *Development and Psychopathology, 8,* 59–87.

Selye, H. (1975). Confusion and controversy in the stress field. *Journal of Human Stress, 1*(2), 37–44.

Spangler, G., & Grossmann, K. E. (1993). Biobehavioral organization in securely and insecurely attached infants. *Child Development, 64,* 1439–1450.

Spangler, G., & Schieche, M. (1998). Emotional and adrenocortical responses of infants to the strange situation: The differential function of emotional expression. *International Journal of Behavioral Development, 22*(4), 681–706.

Spangler, G., Schieche, M., Ilg, U., Maier, U., & Ackermann, C. (1994). Maternal sensitivity as an external organizer for biobehavioral regulation in infancy. *Developmental Psychobiology, 27*(7), 425–437.

Sroufe, L. A., & Waters, E. (1979). Heart rate as a convergent measure in clinical and developmental research. *Merrill-Palmer Quarterly, 23*(1), 3–27.

Sroufe, L. A., Waters, E., & Matas, L. (1974). Contextual determinants of infant affective response. In M. Lewis & L. Rosenblum (Eds.), *The origins of fear* (pp. 49–72). New York: Wiley.

Stansbury, K., & Gunnar, M. R. (1994). Adrenocortical activity and emotion regulation. *Monographs of the Society for Research in Child Development, 59*(2–3), 250–283.

Steckler, T., & Holsboer, F. (1999). Corticotropin-releasing hormone receptor subtypes and emotion. *Biological Psychiatry, 46,* 1480–1508.

Stevenson-Hinde, J., & Marshall, P. J. (1999). Behavioral inhibition, heart period, and respiratory sinus arrhythmia: An attachment perspective. *Child Development, 70,* 805–816.

Stevenson-Hinde, J., & Shouldice, A. (1996). Fearfulness: Developmental consistency. In A. J. Sameroff & M. M. Haith (Eds.), *The five to seven year shift: The age of reason and responsibility* (pp. 237–252). Chicago: University of Chicago Press.

Sullivan, R. M., & Grafton, A. (1999). Lateralized effects of medial frontal lesions on neuroendocrine and autonomic stress responses in rats. *Journal of Neuroscience, 19,* 2834–2840.

Taddio, A., Katz, J., Ilarslch, A. L., & Koren, G. (1997). Effects of neonatal circumcision on pain response during subsequent routine vaccination. *The Lancet, 340,* 599–603.

Takahashi, L. K., & Rubin, W. W. (1993). Corticosteroid induction of threat-induced behavior inhibition in preweanling rats. *Behavioral Neuroscience, 107*(5), 860–866.

Tennes, K., Emde, R., Kisley, A., & Metcalf, D. (1972). The stimulus barrier in early infancy: An exploration of some formulations of John Benjamin. In R. R. Holt & E. Peterfreund (Eds.), *Psychoanalysis and contemporary science: An annual of integrative and interdisciplinary studies* (Vol. 1, pp. 206–234). New York: MacMillan.

Thomasgard, M., & Metz, W. P. (1993). Parental overprotection revisited. *Child Psychiatry and Human Development, 24,* 67–80.

Thompson, R. A. (1994). Emotion regulation: A theme in search of definition. In N. A. Fox (Ed.), *The development of emotion regulation: Biological and behavioral considerations* (pp. 25–52). Chicago: University of Chicago Press.

Vaughn, B. E., Bradley, C. F., Joffe, L. S., Seifer, R., & Barglow, P. (1987). Maternal characteristics measured prenatally are predictive ratings of temperamental "difficulty" on the Carey Infant Temperamental Questionnaire. *Developmental Psychology, 23*(1), 152–161.

Vazquez, D. M. (1998). Stress and the developing limbic-hypothalamic-pituitary-adrenal axis. *Psychoneuroendocrinology, 23,* 663–700.

Wadhwa, P. D., Sandman, C. A., & Garite, T. J. (2001). The neurobiology of stress in human pregnancy: Implications for prematurity and development of the fetal central nervous system. *Progress in Brain Research, 133,* 131–142.

Waters, E., Matas, L., & Sroufe, A. (1975). Infants' reactions to an approaching stranger: Description, validation, and functional significance of wariness. *Child Development, 46,* 348–356.

Watson, J., & Ramey, C. (1972). Reactions to response-contingent stimulation in early infancy. *Merrill-Palmer Quarterly, 13,* 219–288.

Weinstock, M. (1997). Does prenatal stress impair coping and regulation of the hypothalamic-pituitary-adrenal axis? *Biobehavioral Review, 21,* 1–10.

West, M. J., & King, A. P. (2001). Science lies its way to the truth . . . really. In E. Blass (Ed.), *Handbook of behavioral neurobiology, Vol. 13: Developmental psychobiology, developmental neurobiology, and behavioral ecology: Mechanisms and early principles.* New York: Plenum.

White, B. P., Gunnar, M. R., Larson, M. C., Donzella, B., & Barr, R. G. (2000). Behavioral and physiological responsivity, and patterns of sleep and daily salivary cortisol in infants with and without colic. *Child Development, 71*(4), 862–877.

Wilson, B. J., & Gottman, J. M. (1996). Attention-The shuttle between emotion and cognition: Risk, resiliency, and physiological bases. In E. M. Hetherington & E. A. Blechman (Eds.), *Stress, coping, and resiliency in children and families* (pp. 189–238). Mahwah, NJ: Erlbaum.

Yehuda R. (1998). Psychoneuroendocrinology of post-traumatic stress disorder. *Psychiatric Clinics of North America, 21*(2), 359–379.

CHAPTER 6

Diversity in Caregiving Contexts

HIRAM E. FITZGERALD, TAMMY MANN, NATASHA CABRERA, AND MARIA M. WONG

Day nurseries and creches have come in for particularly heavy criticism . . . and the World Health Organization actually asserted that their use inevitably caused permanent psychological damage. There is *no* evidence in support of this view. Of course, day nurseries vary greatly in quality and some are quite poor. Bad child care whether in day nurseries or at home is to be deplored but there is no reason to suppose that day nurseries, as such, have a deleterious influence. (Rutter, 1976, p. 160)

A generation ago, infants and toddlers were being described as the new school-age children, in response to what then was an unprecedented demand in the United States for infant and toddler child care (Fitzgerald, Strommen, & McKinney, 1977). In 1940 only 10% of children had mothers in the labor force. By 1970 that percentage had risen to 36%, and today nearly 70% of all children under 5 years of age have mothers who work outside the home (Hernandez, 1997). Impetus for the accelerated demand for child care of very young children that occurred from 1940 to 1970 was fueled by many factors, not the least of which was Franklin Delano Roosevelt's authorization of the Works Progress Administration toward the end of the Depression, which established the first U.S. government-funded child care programs for families in need. In 1944 Congress passed the Lanham Act, thereby authorizing

use of federal funds to support child care for all children, beginning at 2 years of age. By 1945 there were slightly more than 1.5 million children enrolled in full day care centers or nursery schools.

Reviews of the child care literature have described historical trends in the study of nonmaternal child care (Scarr & Eisenberg, 1993; Clarke-Stewart, Allhusen, & Clements, 1995), cross-cultural perspectives on siblings as caregivers (Zukow-Goldring, 1995), kinship care (Wilson & Chipaungu, 1996), contextual setting events and cross-cultural variations in child care (Lamb, 1998), and criteria for selecting child care (Honig, 1995). The extant literature on infant and toddler child care supports the broad conclusion that supplemental nonmaternal child care is not harmful to infants and toddlers—and in fact can be beneficial both to child development and to the quality of the parent-child relationship. Nevertheless, there are many issues that remain unresolved about supplemental child care during the birth-to-three years. There is consensus that quality is the key to success of child care, regardless of where that care takes place. However, the defining features of quality have not been fully articulated—either for parental child rearing or for nonparental child care. There is increasing recognition that fathers play an important role in early child development, but there is not much specificity as to what that role actually is. We know far more about characteristics of children that are correlated with father absence, but we know little about the effects of father presence on child development. Although there is considerable research assessing the impact of nonparental child care on child development, no theoretical or conceptual model currently provides an overarching framework to guide systematic research in this area. Attention is directed to issues related to the physical settings within which nonparental child care takes place, with a distinct focus on health and safety issues, child-to-adult ratios, and training of care providers. In contrast, less attention is given to issues related to the quality of the care provider-child relationship. If the quality of the adult-infant relationship comprises the core of human social-emotional development as attachment theorists would have it, then one would expect that the relationships that infants and toddlers have with their child care providers would contribute to emotion regulation during early childhood.

In this chapter we examine selected aspects of the child care literature to identify streams of research that may best inform efforts to establish benchmarks for quality care of infants and toddlers, particularly in nonparental child care settings. We propose that the study of the impact of early child care would be facilitated by adopting ecological approaches—such as that embodied in systems theory—in order to provide organizational structure to the field. We briefly review several national and local studies of the impact of early child care that have in common use of randomized designs and research designs that provided tracking of children over time. Then we draw attention to four focal issues—infant temperament, caregiver-child relationships, father involvement, family risk load—and suggest that each should be a targeted domain in the overall assessment of the impact of nonparental child care on infant and toddler development. Finally, we close with a discussion of evidence that may be used to establish benchmarks of quality for nonparental care of infants and toddlers.

NONPARENTAL CHILD CARE OF INFANTS AND TODDLERS

Today's demand for supplemental child care for infants and toddlers makes yesterday's reference to new school-age children a gross understatement. According to data from the National Household Survey (1999), 61% of all children 4 years of age or under participated in some form of regularly scheduled child care; this includes 44% of infants younger than 1 year of age, 53% of 1-year-olds, and 57% of 2-year-olds. Today, approximately 12 million children younger than

4 years of age receive some form of partial or full-time non-maternal child care involving as many as 40 or more hours in nonparental care.

Throughout human history, the care of children rarely has been the mother's exclusive responsibility. However, powerful theories of human development emerged during the twentieth century that focused attention to mother as the primary caregiver for infants and toddlers. Early in that century, Freud's (1946) psychoanalytic theory and Piaget's (1952) theory of genetic epistemology drew attention to the first 3 years of life as uniquely important for personality development and cognitive development, respectively. Bowlby (1969) drew heavily from psychoanalytic theory to articulate an extraordinarily influential theory of early personality development as emergent from the quality of the mother-infant relationship. Prior to Bowlby's work, Spitz (1965) focused attention on the impact of maternal and sensory deprivation on infant development. Ainsworth subsequently developed a research procedure, the Strange Situation, that has had a profound impact on the study of the quality of the mother-infant social-emotional relationship (Ainsworth, Bleher, Waters, & Wall, 1978). Although attachment theory and research methods have markedly advanced knowledge of early personality development, affect regulation, and interpersonal relationships, they also created an atmosphere highly suspicious of nonmaternal child care, especially during the first year of life. In addition, they directed such strong attention to the mother-child relationship that the father nearly became a forgotten parent with respect to his parenting role during early childhood development (Coley, 2001). Although few developmental theorists continue to hold onto the view that the events of infancy rigidly determine subsequent outcomes (Rutter, 1995), contemporary brain research asserts that the impact of environmental events on neurobehavioral systems in the early years of development need to be carefully considered (Shonkoff & Phillips, 2001).

There is a tendency in the literature to discuss care of children by individuals other than a parent as *nonmaternal* child care. Although many authors have drawn attention to the fact that throughout human history, "the exclusive care of infants by their mother is an exception rather than a rule" (Werner, 1988, p. 105), supplemental caregivers tend to be other women more often than to be men. Even in cultures that have official policies granting parental leave to men, relatively few men participate equally in the routine care of their infants and toddlers (Mackey, 1996; Salmi, 1994). For example, Finland has one of the highest percentages of women in the workforce of any country of in the world (80%). Parents receive 11 months of parental leave, the first 105 days of which are reserved for mothers. Thereafter, mothers and fathers can choose among a variety of options for allocating the remaining months of parental leave to one or the other parent. However, in relatively few families (4%) do fathers choose to take advantage of the parental leave policy (Salmi, 1994). After 11 postnatal months, families may enroll their toddlers in municipal day care (government-supported child care centers), private day care, or at-home day care. Families choosing options other than municipal child care receive government subsidies to help offset the costs. In Finland (as elsewhere) parental leave policies are associated with lower demand for nonparental infant child care (Kamerman & Kahn, 1995).

The options for nonparental child care in Finland are essentially those found everywhere. Nonparental child care basically takes place in one of two basic settings: in a center or in someone's home. Centers can be located practically anywhere—schools, workplaces, religious institutions, universities, shopping centers, apartment buildings, or independent private buildings. Although center-based care historically involved preschool-aged children, the number of infants and toddlers in such care is increasing. Home-based child care varies, with some infants and toddlers cared for in their own homes (at-home day care) and others cared for in someone else's home, often referred to as family day care or kinship care (Wilson & Chipungu, 1996). Child care that is provided in the child's own home is convenient, but it is also the most expensive type of child care when it is provided by a nonrelative. Kinship care that takes place in the child's own home generally is provided by grandparents, older siblings, or others with the likelihood that services are free or of minimal cost (Wilson & Chipungu, 1996). On the other hand, kinship care often involves low-income families and chosen because it is the only affordable option available to families. When kinship care takes place in the home of a relative, the financial arrangements vary greatly. The issue of financial support to enhance the quality of kinship care is a matter of current policy debate (Hornby, Zeller, & Karraker, 1996). Because kinship care and family care take place in the child care provider's home, it often means that the number of children being cared for is relatively small. When several children are involved, their ages may vary substantially. Multiple age groupings retain a sense of family structure, with older children available as models and teachers for younger children.

Traditional caregiving provided by nonparental persons to infants and toddlers while their parents work is referred to as *child care.* Nonparental caregivers are referred to as *child caregivers, child care providers* or *workers, domestic caregivers, educators* (those providing both education and care), or *teachers.* Although some may also be called *day care*

workers, the term *day care* is used less often as more parents work nontraditional hours, thus requiring child care services evenings, overnight, and on weekends. The term *child care provider* is rapidly becoming the generic descriptor for all child caregiving services provided to infants and toddlers in the absence of their parents. Regardless of the descriptor used to depict nonparental care providers and regardless of where such care takes place, there is a need for some overarching organizational structure to guide the systematic study of the impact of nonparental care on infant and toddler development in all of its cultural complexity and diversity (Cochran, 1993; Kontos, Howes, Shinn, & Galinsky, 1995; Morelli & Verhoef, 1999). For example, studies of the impact of nonparental child care on child development does not yet take into account the full impact of such ecological variables as geographic region, family structure, and maternal characteristics (Singer, Fuller, Keiley, & Wolf, 1998). Singer et al. demonstrated that the type of child care parents choose is influenced by such variables as parental race and ethnicity, geographic location of residence, maternal employment, child age, maternal education, and number of children in the family. We believe that ecological models of human development—especially those that embrace some variant of systems theory—provide the best hope for organizing and directing the systematic study of such diverse sources of impact (see Table 6.1).

SYSTEMS THEORY: AN ORGANIZING FRAMEWORK FOR THE STUDY OF NONPARENTAL CHILD CARE

In the 1930s Ludwig von Bertalanffy, dissatisfied with both mechanistic and vitalist attempts to explain the organization of living things, articulated an alternative organismic position which he subsequently named *general systems theory* (von Bertalanffy, 1950, 1968). Since then a number of investigators have expanded and refined systems theory into a powerful conceptual framework for organizing the study of adaptive behavior and adaptive functioning applicable across the life span. Systems theorists view the organization of all systems as emergent, epigenetic, constructive, hierarchically integrated (Bronfenbrenner, 1979; Ford & Lerner, 1992; Gottlieb, 1991; Miller, 1978; Sameroff, 2000) and potentially chaotic (Thelen & Smith, 1994). Moreover, systems theorists believe that the ecological context within which systems develop plays a key role in the organizational process. Because the components of any system are interdependent, it follows that attempts to understand adaptive functioning at one level require that we understand how that level is embedded

TABLE 6.1   Variables Affecting Family Choice of Child Care

1. *Family demographic and structural variables.*
   Cost of care in relation to family disposable income.
   Cost subsidies available for family.
   Choosing type or mode of care.
   Care by relatives.
   Family geography as a determinant of child care choice.

2. *Family beliefs and cultural variables affecting choice.*
   Parental beliefs about the need for caregiver training.
   Culture and faith preferences for auspices of care.
   Family stress: a determinant of child care choice.

3. *Child variables.*
   Child temperament.
   Child age.
   Number of children needing care.
   Sex of child.
   Child health.
   Children with disabilities.

4. *Caregiver and facility factors.*
   Size of facility and group size.
   Caregiver-child ratios.
   Time during which the facility operates.
   Caregiver characteristics: reliability, stability, and warmth.
   Empathy and positive discipline techniques.
   Curriculum issues: language emphasis.
   The day care provider's family.
   Parent-provider relationships.
   Communication timing and extent.
   Usefulness of a parent handbook of rules and regulations.
   Working conditions for providers.
   Economic viability of provider.

5. *Political, business, and community supports for parental choice.*
   Legislation and regulatory agencies.
   Businesses and unions: supports for family child-care choice.
   Accreditation and referral agencies.

Source. A. S. Honig (1995). Choosing child care for young children. In M. H. Bornstein (Ed.), *Handbook of parenting: Vol 4. Applied and practical parenting* (p. 416), Mahwah, NJ: Erlbaum. With permission.

within the broader system of which it is a part. Moreover, because systems theory posits that all components of a system are interdependent, the parts derive their meaning only in the context of intersystem and intrasystem relationships.

Assessing the impact of any kind of child care on child development requires longitudinal research approaches. One can easily assess proximal impacts with cross-sectional designs, but only through longitudinal designs can one assess changes that occur in relation to events that occur over the life course. From a systems perspective, identifying causal factors related to child care outcomes must take into account intra-individual (within the individual), interindividual (between individuals), contextual (social-historical-temporal events or situations), and organism-environment transaction (ecological, bidirectional) sources of variance. Relying on main effect or direct effect models is unlikely to reveal much about the dynamic changes that occur during the birth-to-three years.

Within this multilevel approach, we focus on four aspects of the child care system: primary system characteristics (characteristics of individual units—child, family, neighborhood—of a system), intrasystem relationships (parent-child, spousal, sibling, kinship interrelationships), adjunctive system influences (ecological contexts that impact the primary system), and intersystem relationships (boundaries, barriers, transitions; Fitzgerald, Zucker, & Yang, 1995). Recent accounts of the impact of neighborhood poverty on child development illustrate the nesting of risk factors in communities (Duncan & Brooks-Gunn, 1997) and support the hypothesis that risky neighborhoods envelop individuals and families within maintenance structures that sustain risk (Zucker et al., 2000). For example, very young children reared in antisocial alcoholic families are more likely to be exposed to parents who themselves had childhood behavior problems, illegal behavior, frequent arrests, chronic lying, relationship disturbances, depression and family violence, neuroticism, poor achievement and cognitive functioning, and low socioeconomic status (SES; Fitzgerald, Puttler, Mun, & Zucker 2000). There is also evidence of assortative mating in such families. This suggests that the nesting environment within which children with a high family history for alcohol are reared also carries a substantially higher risk load (Zucker et al, 2000). Thus, antisocial alcoholic parents provide a high-risk rearing environment that is very likely to be embedded within a high-risk neighborhood (cf. Osofsky & Fenichel, 1994).

All development takes place in a complex environment that consists of the primary system, the transactions that occur within the primary system (Sameroff, 2000), and the transactions that take place between the primary system and all of its adjunctive systems (Carlson & Cassell, 1984; Fitzgerald et al., 1995). Contemporary prevention programs designed to enhance child development during the early years reflect this thinking. They address issues related to child development, parent involvement, consistency of care, and networking to the broader community of human service agencies and to the schools. To the extent that the primary system is embedded in risk, adjunctive child care systems may be the child's best hope for being exposed to individuals and environments that will stretch the boundaries that encapsulate the primary system and will thereby generate resilience structures. The question of specific interest for the current chapter is whether nonparental child care generates resilience, enhances risk, or at the least does no harm. With the exception of large federally funded studies of the impact of child care programs for primarily low-income families, answers to this question will require use of large-representative-sample, multifactorial, interdisciplinary, prospective longitudinal research designs more extensive than has typically characterized research attempting to determine the impact of nonparental child care for infants and toddlers.

EARLY CHILD CARE AND CHILD DEVELOPMENT

During the last third of the twentieth century, many studies of child care programs appeared in the scientific and professional literatures. Often these studies described programs that were narrowly focused—guided by a particular theoretical model. Rarely did studies involve random assignment of participants, use sophisticated quasi-experimental designs, or collect outcome data over time. Moreover, they seldom involved sample sizes sufficient to generate reasonable statistical power. Near the end of the century, however, significant funding from several government agencies established large-scale, longitudinal evaluations of the impact of early child care programs. Nearly all of these studies emphasized child development, parent involvement, and community networking; some utilized random assignment evaluation designs, some were center based, some were home based, and many combined home- and center-based models. Although richly diverse, modestly successful, and collectively limited, when combined with the extant literature these studies provide support for the positive effects of quality supplemental care on early child development, family functioning, and community networking.

During the last decade of the twentieth century, agencies of the United States government provided funding for significant evaluations of the effectiveness of child care programs that involved random assignment, large sample sizes, and repeated assessments over time. For illustrative purposes we describe the National Institute of Child Health and Human Development (NICHD) Study of Early Child Care, the Administration for Children, Youth, and Families national evaluation of Early Head Start, and the Parent-Child Development Centers (which actually were established as long ago as 1969–1970). In addition, we briefly review outcomes from the Carolina Abecedarian Project, for which there are substantive longitudinal findings. For our final example, we describe outcomes from the Goteborg (Sweden) Child Care Study.

NICHD Study of Early Child Care

The NICHD Study of Early Child Care was designed to assess the impact of nonparental caregivers on a broad range of child outcomes, including social-emotional development (interpersonal relationships, self-regulation), cognitive development (reasoning and problem solving), linguistic development (receptive and productive language), achievement performance (literacy, numeracy, school readiness), physical development (height and weight), and health (immunizations, chronic illness, illnesses of childhood). Nonparental caregivers included relatives (kinship care) and nonrelatives. The context for caregiving varied from in-home, in the provider's home, and at child care centers. The NICHD study was guided by ecological (Bronfenbrenner, 1979; Bronfenbrenner & Morris, 1998) and developmental life-course theoretical perspectives. Thus, the study was designed at the outset to examine the impact of contextual influences as well as the interaction between context and age-related experience. Some experiences are normative in that they occur at narrowly circumscribed ages for most people (e.g., school entry). Other experiences are nonnormative in the sense that they are not linked to specific ages (e.g., parental divorce, change in child care arrangement, family relocation). When combined, the ecological and life course perspectives provide a framework for conceptualizing the relations of both normative and individual contextual influences to developmental pathways.

Because the NICHD study is longitudinal, it offers the possibility of tracking the effectiveness of different models (i.e., cumulation, endurance, sleeper, fade) proposed to account for the way in which early care experiences influence later child behavior. The *cumulation model* suggests that child care contributions aggregate over time such that children in child care should show progressively stronger effects over the course of their exposure. The *endurance model* proposes that the effects of child care consolidate and persist over time regardless of changes in the child's educational context. The *sleeper model* predicts that child care effects are least likely to be evident during the time that infants and toddlers are enrolled in child care, but emerge upstream at later points in developmental time. The *fade model* suggests that the effects of child care are transient and so will disappear over time as more proximal events come to exert their influences on child behavior. The NICHD not only provided an opportunity to assess these models, but also allowed investigators to examine the relations between child care experiences and concurrent psychological and health outcomes, the effects of the home environment on child outcomes, and the linkages between demographic and family characteristics and child development (NICHD Early Child Care Research Network, 1994, 1996, 1997, 2000).

Participants in the study were recruited from 24 designated hospitals at 10 data collection sites across the United States. Factors such as location, availability, previous working relations with the site investigators, and the nature of the patient load contributed to the selection of hospitals within sites. A total of 1,364 newborn infants (and their families) were enrolled in the study, with the sample distributed approximately equally over the 10 sites. The enrolled families included mothers who planned to work full time (53%), part time (23%), and not at all (24%) during the child's first year. The enrolled families came from a wide range of socioeconomic and sociocultural backgrounds, as well as from diverse family arrangements (24% ethnic minority children, 11% mothers who did not complete high school, 14% single mothers; these percentages are not mutually exclusive).

On a weekly basis, each site was expected to screen a minimum of 20 newborn infant-mother dyads in the participating hospitals for potential enrollment to the study. The exclusion criteria for the hospital screening included (a) maternal age (<18 years), (b) language proficiency (non-English speakers), (c) family mobility (family planned a move with 12 months), (d) infant medical status (medical complications or maternal substance abuse), (e) maternal illness, (f) adoption placement, (g) lack of maternal cooperation in data collection, (h) family involvement in other research, (i) residence in an neighborhood posing excessive danger for data collectors, (j) maternal failure to complete the hospital interview, and (k) other factors. In addition, researchers collected information about the child's gender, gestational age and weight, the mother's ethnic and racial identification, age, education, employment status, and her partner's residential status and education. Of the original 1,364 families, 1,100 were still participating in the study when most of the children were entering the third grade, yielding an 80.6% retention across the 8 years of study involvement.

Supplemental funding provided by the U. S. Department of Health and Human Services enabled investigators to add direct measures of fathers' attitudes and perceptions in 6 of the 10 sites (Arkansas, California, Kansas, North Carolina, Pittsburgh, and Wisconsin). The fathers' component enabled investigators to examine not only fathers' direct impact on their children, but also the impact of fathers on the quality of the marital relationship and the impact of maternal employment. Experience during early development was assessed through a diverse array of measures designed to capture the child's experience in the context of home and family, in child care, and eventually in school. Measures of social-emotional, cognitive, linguistic, and academic development and physical growth and health were used to assess children's developmental status. Selection of measures was based on (a) the child's developmental level, (b) the psychometric properties of the measure, (c) the applicability of measures to children and families varying in ethnicity and socioeconomic status, (d) the amount of time needed to complete the measure, (e) the relations among the different measures planned for each visit, and (f) the results of pilot

testing. Two criteria were considered in selecting specific child outcomes to be assessed: (a) that the developmental importance of the outcome construct was well documented in previous research and theory, and (b) that there was reason to hypothesize that children's development in a particular domain would be affected by environments of early child rearing.

What have investigators found to date? Reports from the National Institute of Child Health and Human Development (NICHD) Early Child Care Research Network (2000) suggest that during the children's first year of life, there was high reliance on infant care, very rapid entry into care postbirth, and substantial instability in care. By 12 months of age, 84% of the infants in the study had entered some form of nonparental child care, with the majority starting care before the age of 4 months. When they first entered care, 25% of the infants were cared for by their father or their mother's partner, 23% were cared for by other relatives, and only 12% were enrolled in child care centers. Over the first year of life, the majority of children in nonparental care experienced more than two different child care arrangements, and more than one third experienced three or more arrangements.

Economic factors were most consistently associated with the amount and nature of nonmaternal care infants received. For example, mothers with higher incomes and families that were more dependent on the mother's income placed their infants in child care at earlier ages. Maternal personality and beliefs about maternal employment also contributed. For example, mothers who believed that maternal employment has positive effects on children put their children in nonmaternal care for more hours. Poor families were less likely than were affluent families to use child care, but poor children who were in care averaged as many hours as did children from other income groups.

Observations of the quality of care at 6 months indicated that more positive caregiving occurred when children were in smaller groups, child-adult ratios were lower, caregivers held less authoritarian beliefs about child rearing, and physical environments were safe, clean, and stimulating. Observed quality of care for poor children was generally lower than that for nonpoor children when they were cared for by an unrelated caregiver. The single exception was that poor children in centers received better-quality care than near-poor children, perhaps because they were more likely to be in subsidized (and therefore perhaps more regulated) settings. Evaluation of child care centers in relation to guidelines recommended by professional organizations for child-staff ratios, group sizes, teacher training, and teacher education indicated that most classes observed in the study did not meet all four of these guidelines.

Analyses of the effects of family and child care on child outcomes indicated that in general, family characteristics and the quality of the mother's relationship with her child were stronger predictors of child outcomes than were child care factors. Family factors predicted child outcomes even for children who spent many hours in child care, and statistically significant child care effects were relatively small in size. Maternal depressive symptoms comprised one family predictor of child outcomes (in addition to income level, education, attitudes, and behavior). Children whose mothers reported feeling depressed performed more poorly on measures of cognitive-linguistic functioning at 36 months and were rated as less cooperative and more problematic. However, depression effects on expressive language and ratings of cooperation were moderated by maternal sensitivity, with sensitivity predicting better outcomes more strongly among children of depressed mothers.

Analyses controlling for nonrandom use of child care by families of different socioeconomic backgrounds revealed that among the aspects of child care studied, a relatively consistent predictor of child outcomes was the observed quality of care. When observed quality of caregivers' behavior was high, children had better cognitive and linguistic abilities, showed more cooperative behavior with mothers during play, and had fewer behavior problems. For children in center care at 36 months, children had fewer behavior problems and higher scores on language comprehension and school readiness when classes met more of the guidelines recommended by experts for ratios, group sizes, and teacher training and education. Higher-quality child care was also associated with higher-quality mother-child interaction among the families that used nonparental care. Additionally, poor-quality child care was related to an increased incidence of infant insecure attachment to mothers at 15 months, but only when the mother was also relatively low in sensitivity and responsiveness.

Overall, type of child care by itself appeared to have relatively limited impacts on child outcomes. At age 3, greater *cumulative* experience in center care and *early* experience in child care homes were both associated with better performance on cognitive and language measures than were other forms of care, assuming comparable quality of caregiving environment. Experience with group care (settings with at least three other children, not counting siblings), whether in centers or child care homes, made some difference in several social-emotional outcomes at ages 2 and 3. Children with more cumulative experience in group care showed more cooperation with their mothers in the laboratory at age 2, less negative laboratory interaction with their mothers at age 3, and fewer caregiver-reported behavior problems at both ages. However, higher amounts of group experience before

12 months were associated with more mother-reported behavior problems at age 3, suggesting that benefits from group care may begin in the second year of life.

The quantity of nonparental care was also a statistically significant predictor of some child outcomes. When children spent more hours in child care, mothers were less sensitive in their interactions with their children (at 6, 15, 24, and 36 months) and children were less positively engaged with their mother (at 15, 24, and 36 months, the ages at which child engagement was assessed). In addition, analyses of attachment at 15 months show that children who spent more hours in child care *and* had mothers who were relatively insensitive and unresponsive were at heightened risk for insecure mother-infant attachments.

ACYF Study of Early Head Start

In 1994, the United States Congress reauthorized the Head Start Act and stipulated that 4% of the appropriation was to be used to establish Early Head Start. The percentage of funding for Head Start diverted to Early Head Start has increased steadily since 1994, and in 2002 reaches its final authorized level of 10% of the Head Start budget (Raikes & Love, 2002). Designated primarily as a child care program for low-income families, Early Head Start is designed to enhance developmental outcomes for infants and toddlers and to enhance family functioning (Jerald, 2000). The 1994 reauthorization of Head Start stipulated that procedures be established to provide for continuous quality improvement of programs and to monitor the fit between programs and community needs. The reauthorization bill of 1998 affirmed both the continuous quality improvement policy as well as the need to evaluate the extent to which Head Start and Early Head Start were achieving their objectives (Raikes & Love, 2002). In order to monitor program quality, performance standards were adopted in 1996. The standards define the services that must be provided to children and families, although they do not specify how such services must be delivered. The lack of specificity for service delivery allows for greater diversity in programming across communities; it also gives programs greater flexibility to develop community partnerships that are unique to family needs for high-quality child care (Fenichel & Mann, 2001).

The Secretary of the Department of Health and Human Services appointed an Advisory Committee on Services for Families With Infants and Toddlers (1994), which identified four key cornerstones of program quality that must be addressed by every Head Start and Early Head Start program: child development, family development, community development, and staff development (see Administration on

Children, Youth, and Families, 2001; Fenichel & Mann, 2001). Of the four cornerstones, issues related to child development were clearly identified as first among equals (Fenichel & Mann, 2001). Moreover, the performance standards clearly specify that programs must acknowledge the importance of relationships for infant and toddler development, and this includes relationships with all caregivers, including parents. Because parents are considered to be integral to the delivery of quality child care, Early Head Start programs must address issues related to parenting skills, parent-child relationships, and father involvement. In addition, all children must be screened for developmental disabilities within 45 days of enrollment. Ten percent of all openings in EHS must be available for infants and toddlers with defined disabilities. The number of infants and toddlers with established conditions, environmental risks, or combinations of these is substantial, and current EHS funding is insufficient to provide child care programs for all eligible infants and toddlers because of special needs. To achieve the flexibility necessary to fit programming with community needs (Raikes, Kisker, Paulsell, & Love, 2000), Early Head Start child care program services are offered in formats that are designated as (a) home-based, (b) center-based, (c) home-based, center-based combinations, or (d) locally designated options. Currently, there are 635 Early Head Start programs nationwide, serving 45,000 infants and toddlers.

Evaluation of Early Head Start

The Administration for Children, Youth, and Families (ACYF) evaluation of Early Head Start (EHS) involves a partnership among ACYF, Mathematical Policy Research, Columbia University Center for Children and Families at Teachers College, 15 universities, and program staff at 17 sites across the United States. Sixteen sites partnered with university research teams and one site was directly affiliated with Mathematical Policy Research, which also served as the evaluation consultant for the full national study. Each site was also independently funded to conduct local studies. Thus, the evaluation of the impact of Early Head Start consists of analyses of the integrated data from 17 regionally distributed programs (Commissioner's Office of Research and Evaluation, 1999a, 1999b), as well as the independent findings from each of the program sites. In addition, separate studies were conducted to assess the impact of EHS on fathers, child care, health and disabilities, and welfare reform, and a longitudinal follow-up study is currently assessing children as they make the transition from preschool to kindergarten. A similar longitudinal follow-up to track children's transitions to elementary school is being planned.

The EHS research sites were selected to represent geographical and ethnic diversity within the constraints of the income requirements for eligibility. Across the 17 sites, 3,001 families were randomly assigned to either an EHS program or some other child care program that was available in the local community. Randomization resulted in final samples of 1,513 EHS eligible families enrolled in EHS programs and 1,488 EHS eligible families assigned to the control condition. Federal poverty guidelines were used to determine income eligibility for Early Head Start. Families in the control group were able to secure any kind of child care available in their community with the exception of Early Head Start. They were notified that they would have access to Head Start if they continued to be eligible for the program when their child was 4 years old. Originally, seven of the EHS sites were home-based programs, four were center-based programs, and six were mixed programs. In the national evaluation, all programs that were not exclusively home-based or center-based were classified as mixed programs. Center-based programs provided all services to families through the center (which also included a small number of home visits). Home-based programs provided EHS services through home visits, although families were able to use other kinds of child care options as they wished. Mixed programs provided services to some families through centers, home visiting, or some combination of these in addition to local options (Commissioner's Office for Research and Evaluation, 1999a). Initially (1995, 1996), there were five home-based, five center-based, and seven mixed programs. Slightly more than 1 year later, eight programs were home-based, four were center-based, and five were mixed; and by 1999, there were 2 home-based, 4 center-based, and 11 mixed programs (Commissioner's Office for Research and Evaluation, 2001a). As parental needs for nonparental child care increased, EHS programs responded by providing a greater mix of options for parents. Obviously, the evaluation of program effectiveness will have to take into account changes in the type of child care options available to families over the course of the longitudinal evaluation. Regardless of program type, all programs were required to provide child development services, to build family and community partnerships, and to enlist support staff to provide high-quality services for infants, toddlers, and their families. Thus, all EHS programs are conceptualized as seamless systems, with responsibilities for comprehensive child development, family functioning, relationships with program staff, and connections to community resources.

Evaluation data were collected at enrollment (baseline) and at 5, 15, and 26 months after enrollment (parent services interviews) and when children were 14, 24, and 36 months old (parent interviews, child assessments, and videotaped parent-infant interactions). Only summary data from several aspects of the 6–24 month assessment periods has been completed (Commissioner's Office of Research and Evaluation, 2001a, 2001b). Although the findings are only preliminary, they suggest that EHS programs have modest positive influences on child development, particularly with respect to enhancement of cognitive and language skills and reduction of aggression and other behavior problems. No differences were found for toddlers' task-related emotion regulation or their general interactions with mothers during a videotaped free-play interaction. EHS parents were more knowledgeable about infant-toddler development; engaged in more cognitive, language, and literacy activities at home; were generally more positively engaged with their children during free-play interactions; were less likely to have spanked their child (in the past week); and reported less marital conflict than did mothers in the control group (Commissioner's Office of Research and Evaluation, 2001c). Some of the significant differences between EHS and control groups at the 24-month assessment are summarized in Table 6.2.

Center-based programs had their greatest impact on indicators of child development and some parenting behaviors.

Home-based programs had their greatest impact on parenting behaviors, child language, and parent participation in education and job training. The mixed-approach programs were most similar to the center-based programs, but also influenced children's social and language development. EHS participation also seemed to have an energizing effect on participating families because they were more than twice as likely as control families to participate in parent education, parent-child, or parent support group activities, and they were more likely to benefit from key services available in their communities. It will be several years before the national evaluation of EHS reveals the full impact of EHS, but the preliminary analyses of the 24-month data are extremely encouraging. EHS appears to be having a positive impact both on child development and parental competence and self-sufficiency (Robinson & Fitzgerald, 2002).

Early Head Start and Home Visiting

The NICHD and EHS child care and child development programs each involved center-based and home-based components, reflecting the fact that exclusive center-based care during the early years—especially during infancy—is more

TABLE 6.2 National Evaluation of Early Head Start: Selected Global Impacts on Toddlers and Parents at 24 Months

Outcome	EHS Group Mean	Control Group Mean	Effect Size Percent
Bayley Mental Development Index	90.1	88.1	14.9[a]
Percentage with MDI below 85	33.6	40.2	13.5[a]
Percentage combining words	81.0	77.9	7.4
Vocabulary production score (CDI)	56.3	53.9	10.8[a]
Sentence complexity score (CDI)	8.6	7.7	11.4[a]
Aggressive behavior problems	9.9	10.5	10.2[a]
Child negativity toward parent	1.7	1.8	8.0
Child engagement of parent during structured play	4.3	4.2	7.6
Parent supportiveness in structured play	4.1	3.9	13.5[a]
Parent detachment in structured play	1.4	1.5	10.4[a]
Percentage of parents who read to child daily	57.9	52.3	11.3[a]
Percentage of parents who read to child at bedtime	29.4	22.6	16.0[a]
Knowledge of Infant Development Inventory	3.4	3.3	12.3[a]
Parent-child activities	4.6	4.5	11.7[a]
Percentage of parents who spanked child in previous week	47.4	52.1	9.4[a]
PSI parental distress	25.0	25.9	10.2[a]
Percentage of parents who ever participated in an education or job-training program in first 15 months	48.4	43.7	10.7[a]

Items were selected from a list of 41 impacts to illustrate the kinds of statistically significant impacts obtained at the 24 month assessment period.

[a]Commissioner's Office of Research and Evaluation and the Head Start Bureau, Administration on Children, Youth, and Families, Department of Health and Human Services (December–January, 2001). *Building their futures: How Early Head Start programs are enhancing the lives of infants and toddlers in low-income families: Summary report* (pp. 17–18). Washington, DC: U.S. Department of Health and Human Services.

the exception than the rule. For example, approximately 85% of infants receiving nonparental child care do so in their own homes, in the home of a care provider, or the home of a relative. In large measure, our knowledge of the effectiveness of early child care is generated from a database that is not representative of the population (an oversampling of low-income families), or of the contexts within which early child care takes place (an oversampling of center-based child care settings). Although there is great controversy in the literature about the effectiveness of home-visiting programs, the weight of that evidence is slowly shifting to questions of *for whom* and *under what circumstances* rather than whether home visiting is or is not effective in enhancing child development (Tableman, 2001). Moreover, as exemplified by two of the successful national demonstrations of child care for infants and toddlers that spanned low- to middle-class samples (EHS and NICHD), programs that combine some form of home visiting with other types of child care have generated some of the best benchmark guidelines for quality care to date.

However, there is an interesting paradox with respect to home visiting. Most home-visiting programs are designed to have a direct impact on parents and an indirect impact on the child. Of course, in many EHS programs involving home-based–center-based combinations or mixed models, there are both direct and indirect pathways leading to desired outcomes. In any of these cases, the home-based component is designed to enhance parenting skills and knowledge of child development, as well as the parent-infant relationship. Because home visitors work with parents to develop their parenting skills, the quality of their family relationships, and their ability to access human services within their communities, their immersion in child care can be as extensive as that of relatives or nonrelatives if one excludes the direct provision of care. Seldom have such programs been offered to care providers in nonparental child care settings even though infants and toddlers in such settings can have nonparental caregiving for as much as 40–50 hours per week (Smith, 2000). The concept of *home visitor* is implicit in the Head Start/Early Head Start training and technical assistance system designed to provide broad based support for all HS and EHS programs, regardless of the specific mix used by any specific program to deliver high-quality child care. Training and technical assistance staff visit program sites, assist with evaluating needs of program staff, and develop training opportunities related to identified needs (Mann, 2002). Training and technical-assistance on-site visits to programs during the implementation phase of EHS indicated that the time required to establish programs and to coordinate all of the necessary support components to assure quality care was

underestimated. As a result, many programs needed to reorganize their approaches even while they were implementing new child care services (Mann, 2002). Because child care home-visitors help families to develop service delivery plans that are unique to family needs (parental age, parent-child interaction patterns, family resources, family composition) and that are extensions of the child care program, disruptions in the base child care program can have a negative impact on the home-visiting part of the child care service. For example, Gill, Greenberg, and Vazquez (2002) found that changes in program structure negatively affected home-visitor job satisfaction, work motivation, and staff turnover during the transitional period of program reorganization. Because adult-child relationships comprise a critical component of infant-toddler child care regardless of setting, studies of stability of care providers in child care centers reveal essentially the same findings as those found for home visitors (Raikes, 1993; Rubenstein, Pedersen, & Yarrow, 1977). Stability enhances the quality of the care-provider–child relationship and the social-emotional development of the child. Oppenheim, Sagi, and Lamb (1988) found that attachment security was related to personality characteristics of Israeli kindergarten children, but it did not predict specific characteristics such as ego-control, empathy, achievement orientation, or independence. When changes in care provider do occur, infants and toddlers seem more likely to be negatively affected if change occurs during the second year of life (13–18 months) or if changes are frequent (Howes & Hamilton, 1993).

Examples of home visiting programs appear in Table 6.3. Although EHS programs are most likely to use *infant mental health services* or *parents as teachers* home visitor models, the Prenatal Early Infancy Project (PEIP) is one of the best-known home visitor intervention models because of the strong impact it obtained with a high-risk sample. The PEIP was developed to determine whether a home-visiting program could prevent poor developmental outcomes for infants of high-risk mothers (Olds 1988; Olds, Henderson, Chamberlin, & Tatelbaum, 1986; Olds, Henderson, Tatelbaum, & Chamberlin, 1986, 1988). Mothers were low-income, single, or teenage. Like the NICHD and EHS child care evaluations, PEIP families were randomly assigned to a treatment or comparison group. Families in the treatment group received home visits every 2 weeks during pregnancy and every 1–6 weeks for 2 years after birth. During the home visits, nurses provided parent education, helped mothers to develop informal support systems, and connected families with community services. The intervention was related to increased birth weight and gestation length of infants born to teen mothers and to smoking mothers. Throughout the first two postnatal years, mothers in the treatment group were significantly less likely to have verified child

TABLE 6.3   Examples of Home-Visiting Models for Enhancing Developmental Outcomes for Infants and Toddlers

Focus	Purpose	Population Served	Contact
Relationship-based			
Infant mental health services.	Promote positive parent-infant interaction, healthy infant development, and parental competencies.	Parent-infant dyads at risk for or exhibiting disrupted relationships, disorders of infancy, and/or delayed development of the child.	Deborah Weatherson, Ph.D. Merrill-Palmer Institute Wayne State University Detroit, MI aa2233@wayne.edu
Steps toward effective enjoyable parenting.	Promote healthy parent-child relationships and prevent social-emotional problems among children.	Poor, primarily, single, young first-time mothers; most reporting a history of abuse in childhood and/or recent relationships. No more than a high school education.	Martha Erickson, Ph.D. University of Minnesota
Family development project.	Improve child's development and parent's functioning and relationships.	First-time mothers, poor, lacking support, plus other risk factors.	Christoph Heinike, Ph.D. University of California, Los Angeles Department of Psychiatry and Biobehavioral Sciences 760 Westwood Plaza, Los Angeles, CA 90042
Information-based			
Healthy Families America.	Promote positive parenting and prevent child abuse and neglect.	Families with risk factors related to lack of support; low income; less than high school education; history of substance abuse, mental illness, abortions, marital or family problems.	Prevent Child Abuse America 200 South Michigan Ave 17th Floor Chicago, IL 60604 www.preventchildabuse.org
Parents as Teachers.	Educate and empower parents to become active participants in their child's education.	Infants no older than 6 months up to age 4. Intended for any parent.	Parents as Teachers National Center 10176 Corporate Square Drive Suite 230 St. Louis, MO 63132 www.patnc.org
Building Strong Families.	Provide parents and caregivers the knowledge and skills needed to help their children reach their potential.	Parents with limited resources, parents who may or may not have limited literacy, and children age birth to 3 years.	Jodi Spiccer, MSU-E 103 Human Ecology Building Michigan State University East Lansing, MI 48824 *www.msue.msu.edu/msue/* cyffamily/bsfone/html
Behavior-based			
Brief intervention with irritable infants.	Promote secure attachment by enhancing the mother's sense of efficacy in relating with her child.	Normal firstborn infants—from well-functioning low-income families—who were irritable and therefore difficult to care for; at risk of insecure attachment because of irritability and low level of maternal responsiveness characteristic of low-income families.	D. C. van den Boom The Netherlands
Interaction guidance.	Promote infant's well-being through positive change in parent-infant interaction.	Difficult-to-engage families: resistant to other forms of psychotherapy; young, inexperienced, cognitively limited, and infants with failure to thrive, regulation disorders, and organic problems.	Susan C. McDonough, Ph.D. University of Michigan
Adjunct to health care			
Montreal Home Visitation Study.	Promote child's health and development.	Working-class women between 18 and 35 years, no more than high school education, firstborn full-term infants.	C. Larson
Healthy Steps for Young Children Program			

Note. All programs have been evaluated using random assignment or comparison group designs with positive results. Material in this table was adapted from B. Tableman (2000). *Summaries of home visiting models for very young children* (Best Practice Briefs No. 18). East Lansing: Michigan State University, University Outreach Partnerships. Adapted with permission.

abuse than were mothers in the comparison group; they punished their children less, made fewer trips to the emergency room, and provided them with more appropriate toys (Olds, 1988). Mothers in the treatment group had greater increases in their knowledge of community services, use of social supports, and dietary improvements; they also attended more childbirth classes (Olds et al., 1986a, b) and returned to school sooner (Olds et al., 1988) than did mothers in the comparison group. One contributor to the success of PEIP was the relatively low turnover in home-visitor staff.

Carolina Abecedarian Project

The Carolina Abecedarian Project was designed to strengthen the intellectual competence and academic achievement of children from low-income families (Ramey & Campbell, 1984). For this project, 111 infants with single black mothers were randomly assigned either to an intervention group (57) or to a control group (54). Infants in the intervention group attended an educational child care program and the infants in the control group did not. All infants received infant formula, pediatric care, and supportive social services regardless of their assigned group. The preschool intervention provided early childhood education, pediatric care, and family support services beginning in infancy and lasting until the children entered kindergarten. The Abecedarian Project involved families with multiple risks (Ramey & Ramey, 1998), including poor maternal formal education, single-parent families, adolescent mothers, and authoritarian approaches to child rearing (Ramey, 2000; Ramey & Campbell, 1984, 1987; Ramey & Ramey, 1998.

The Abecedarian Project shared common characteristics with other early child care intervention programs, including programming that was connected to other local services for high-risk families, low child-to-teacher ratios, weekday programming available 10 hours per day (7:30–5:30), use of developmentally appropriate practices involving social-emotional and cognitive-language skills, and family support programs including pediatric care and nutritional supplementation. Because children in the control group also received health care assistance, social services, and nutritional supplements, any differences between groups can more readily be attributed to differences in the quality of early child care the children experienced (Ramey, 2000).

At 18, 24, 36, and 48 months of age, children in the intervention group scored higher on measures of cognitive functioning. By 4 years of age, children in the control group were six times more likely to score in the mild mental retardation range of the Stanford-Binet IQ test. When the infants reached preschool age, another randomization took place and children in the original intervention and control groups were assigned to new intervention and control groups. Follow-up studies conducted when the children were 12 indicated that intervention children did significantly better on measures of overall and Verbal IQ, but not Performance IQ. Children in the control group, however, were more likely to have IQ scores in the borderline range for mild mental retardation (F. A. Campbell & Ramey, 1990). Another follow-up performed when the children were 15 indicated that children in the preschool intervention group scored higher on measures of reading and mathematics than did children in the control group. Moreover, more children from the control groups were retained at grade level than were children from the intervention group (F. A. Campbell & Ramey, 1994). By 21 years of age, individuals in the treatment group were more likely to be in school (40% vs. 20%), and three times as many young adults from the treatment group (than from the control group) had either graduated from college or were still pursuing their degrees (35% vs. 12 %). Moreover, only 12% of the children in the treatment group received special education versus 48% of the control group.

Parent-Child Development Centers

The parent-child development centers (PCDCs), first established in 1969–1970, were designed to provide low-income families with support for child development as well as parent education. Mothers were the main targets for educational services, including information on child development, health, nutrition, parenting skills, and how to access community services and build social networks. Sites varied across many dimensions, but most notably in service delivery, ethnic group, program intensity, and home-based versus center-based contexts. A pre- and posttest evaluation strategy was used to evaluate program outcomes. At two of the sites, program participants scored higher than did controls on measures of positive maternal behavior. Dokecki, Hargrove, and Sandler (1983) reported differences in 36-month IQ scores between children in the program groups and those in control groups, with program children scoring significantly higher. PCDCs received negative evaluations for the quality of their facilities, lack of space, high child-staff ratios, low language interactions between parent and child, high dropout rates, and limited health services. Program strengths included positive affective environments, high-quality home-based services, high use of educational services, and organized support for the program. Initial program effects were positive but declined at kindergarten age. Despite these strengths, no differences were found later in IQ or school achievement as a function of the early preschool curriculum.

One of the Parent-Child Development Centers (PCDCs), the Houston Parent-Child Development Center, targeted primarily Mexican-American parents and their 12-month-old children (Johnson, 1988; Johnson & Breckenridge, 1982; Johnson & Walker, 1987, 1991). Emphasis was given to enhancing the positive affective relationships between mothers and their children. During the first year, families received home visits from trained neighborhood peer-educators. Weekend family workshops focused on issues of communication and support. When the children were 24 months of age, they attended a nursery school program while their mothers participated in classes on home management, personal development, and child development. After the 2-year intervention, PCDC mothers had more supportive interactions with the children than did comparison mothers. PCDC children scored better on the Stanford-Binet Intelligence Scale than did the comparison children. Follow-up studies were conducted when children were between 4 and 7 years of age and when they were 8–11 years of age. At the first follow-up, mothers of children in the comparison group reported higher levels of behavior problems—especially for boys—than did mothers of children in the PCDC group. At the second follow-up, teachers rated children in the comparison group—especially boys—as having more behavior problems than did children in the PCDC group.

Goteborg Child Care Study

The Goteborg study involved 140 Swedish 12- to 24-month-old toddlers who were divided into three groups (center-based, family day care, and home cared). Fifty-two of the original sample were followed prospectively through 15 years of age (J. J. Campbell, Lamb, & Hwang, 2000). Over the course of the study, 43 children remained enrolled in family day care (13) or center day care (30), and 9 others changed from family day care to center day care. Data were collected on the quality of the home environment, parent demographics, quality of the supplemental child care setting, and target child peer interactions. Follow-up assessments were made 1 and 2 years after the initial data collection. Social competence was also assessed when the children were 6.5 and 8.5 years old. Final data collection occurred when the children were 15 years old.

Investigators found strong evidence of stability in child behavior over the span of 3–15 years of age as measured by indicators of social competence with peers during early development. However, at both 8.5- and 15-year assessments, neither the quality of home care nor the quality of supplemental child care was associated with social competence. There are striking parallels between stability of social competence

in the Goteborg sample and stability of aggression in Dunedin, New Zealand children over a 20-year span (Caspi, Moffit, Newman, & Silva, 1996) and for externalizing behavior problems over a slightly shorter span for children in Michigan (Wong, Zucker, Puttler, & Fitzgerald, 1999).

Summary: Early Child Care and Child Development

A rich body of evidence has emerged that speaks to the positive effects of quality supplemental care on early child development. These research studies emphasize child development, parent involvement, and community networking. Some use random assignment evaluation designs and focus on different types of nonparental care—center-based, home based, and a combination of the two. Others use designs that allow for comparison of the effects of type of care on development. The most illustrative examples of this work include the NICHD Study of Early Child Care, the Administration for Children, Youth, and Families national evaluation of Early Head Start; the Parent-Child Development Centers, the Carolina Abecedarian Project, and the Goteborg (Sweden) Child Care Study. Collectively, these studies provide information about the type of nonparental care children receive, the quality of that care, and the impact of nonparental care on child outcomes. Additionally, these studies shed light on the effect of comprehensive intervention on child outcomes over time. In general, the majority of infants start some type of nonparental care by the age of 4 months, experience multiple arrangements over the first year of life, and have working parents. More positive caregiving occurs when children are in smaller groups; child-to-adult ratios are lower; caregivers hold less authoritarian beliefs about child rearing; and physical environments are safe, clean, and stimulating. Poor children experience poor-quality family care but good-quality center care. Some studies report that center care has a modest positive effect on cognitive and language skills and reduction of aggression and other behavior problems. Moreover, family characteristics and the quality of mother-child relationships are stronger predictors of child outcomes than are child care factors; hence, interventions—including education and knowledge of child development—that have an effect on parent behaviors are critical in having a positive effect on children.

FACTORS INFLUENCING OUTCOMES IN EARLY CHILD CARE RESEARCH

Regardless of whether supplemental infant care is delivered via home visiting, child care centers, or some mixed model, evaluation of early child care programs must take into account factors beyond those associated only with program components. Recall the conclusion reached by members of the National Research Council and Institute of Medicine (2000) that the question is not whether early preventive-intervention programs work, but for whom and under what circumstances. This clearly was recognized in the national evaluations of the NICHD Child Care Study and EHS, in which considerable effort was devoted to assessing characteristics of children and parents, parent-child interactions, and the ecological contexts within which development takes place. The list of such variables includes community characteristics (violence, community resources), family characteristics (poverty, single parenthood), parent characteristics (education level, substance abuse, depression or other psychopathology, employment), and child characteristics (disabilities, temperament). We believe that there are several critical areas in need of substantive research with respect to their implications for nonparental child care, regardless of whether that care is delivered in centers (including family child care), through home-based programs, or in mixed models. These areas involve child temperament and its impact on the caregiver-child relationship, mother-child social-emotional relationships, and father involvement in child and family development.

Temperament

Temperament refers to individual differences in emotional, motor, and attentional reactivity, as well as differences in self-regulation (see also chapters by Gunnar & Davis and Thompson, Easterbrooks, & Padilla-Walker in this volume). The dominant view expressed in the literature is that such individual differences are biologically based, relatively stable over time and situations, and evident fairly early in infancy (Strelau, 1998). References to variation in temperament date back to the earliest writings of Greek physicians. Although Allport (1937) was among the first to contribute a formal definition of temperament, it was the work of Thomas and Chess (1977) that sparked contemporary research on the role that infant temperament may play in the development of parent-infant relationships. Instead of treating temperament as a characteristic anchored exclusively in biology or personality, Thomas and Chess conceptualized the impact of temperament within the framework of parent-infant interactions, and considered goodness of fit between the child's temperament and the child's parenting environment to be a major influence on the development of normative and atypical behavior (Chess & Thomas, 1986, 1991; Thomas, Chess, & Birch, 1968).

Thomas and Chess began to use the term *temperament*—originally referred to as *individual reaction patterns*—to describe individual differences in behavioral styles in relation

to children's interactions with their environments, particularly their caregiving environments. The impact of temperament resides in the goodness of fit between the child's (perceived) temperament and the demands and expectations of the rearing environment. A good match is more likely to result in minimal conflict and stress between the child and significant adults in the caregiving environment, and a poor match is likely to exacerbate conflict and tension between the child and caregiver (Chess & Thomas, 1991). The bulk of the research has investigated the implications of temperament for mother-child interactions and relationships; little is known about temperament in relation to father or child care provider relationships.

The lack of knowledge about the impact of care-provider–infant goodness of fit is disconcerting when one considers that many infants and toddlers in center-based care spend as many as 50 hours each week in out-of-home settings. This may be especially troublesome for infants who are characterized as having difficult temperaments.

Thomas and Chess (1986) conceptualized difficult temperament as consisting of five components: irregularity, withdrawal from novelty, slow or no adaptation to change, negative mood, and intense emotional reactivity. Since their initial characterization, many investigators have defined *difficult temperament* differently, using a few as one trait and as many as 10 (Windle, 1991). The search for a finite set of operational components of difficult temperament is constrained by the social and perceptual qualities of temperament. Thus, what may be perceived to be difficult by one observer may be perceived to be positive by another. The care provider may be bothered by an assertive or somewhat uninhibited child, whereas the child's father may perceive these traits as positive and in fact reward them. It is possible, however, that children with difficult temperaments actually display more stability across situations. For example, difficult temperament has been linked etiologically to behavioral undercontrol, especially in the context of high family dysfunction (Maziade, Caron, Cote, Boutin, & Thivierge, 1990); alcoholism and substance abuse (Mun, Fitzgerald, Puttler, Zucker, & von Eye, 2001); and poor academic functioning (Martin, 1989). Scarr and McCartney (1983) proposed a Patterson-type coercive model in which infant difficult temperament elicits negative parental responses, which in turn exacerbates the infant's negative behaviors. Specifically, difficult temperament contributed to parental role dissatisfaction, insensitive caregiving, and an insecure infant-caregiver attachment relationship. Studying inner-city, low-income African American mothers and their infants, Ispa, Fine, and Thornberg (in press) found that infant difficult temperament and mother stress reaction were independently and inversely related to attachment security: high difficult temperament was related to low attachment security. Galinsky, Howes, Kontos, and Shinn (1994) found that more than 50 percent of the infants in family day care settings had insecure attachment relationships with their care providers, although this finding is not specifically linked to difficult temperament. Degree of difficulty is not the only aspect of temperament that may affect the quality of the care-provider–infant relationship. Fein (1995) reported that infants who were happy and socially detached received less attention from care providers, suggesting that such infants may fail to provide the normative cues necessary to elicit appropriate caregiver behavior.

Caregiver-Child Social-Emotional Relationships

No issue related to nonparental child care attracts more debate and heated discussion than does attachment (see the chapter by Thompson, Easterbrooks, & Padilla-Walker in this volume). *Attachment* refers to the social-emotional relationship constructed by infants and their primary caregivers during the first year of life that functions to facilitate protection, survival, and reproductive fitness (Berlin & Cassidy, 2000). According to Bowlby (1969), the functional significance of attachment is expressed in proximity seeking (protection, care), avoidance of danger (fear, wariness), connectedness (social and interpersonal behavior), and novelty seeking (exploratory behavior). Attachment relationships during infancy are focused on relatively few individuals, with most infants showing a preference hierarchy when multiple caregivers are available. Typically, the relationship between mothering and the mother-infant attachment relationship is stronger than is the relationship between fathering and the father-infant attachment relationship (van Ijzendoorn & De Wolff, 1997). The set goal of the attachment system is to induce a sense of security and comfort in the infant that will eventually be internalized and expressed as a working model or internal mental representation of self and others (Berlin & Cassidy, 2000).

Because relationships are dynamic and transactional, infants and caregivers are constantly challenged to adjust their behavior as they seek to achieve a secure attachment relationship. Bowlby referred to this as a *goal correcting process.* Everyday observations of infants and toddlers in interaction with their parents, older siblings, and kin readily confirm that they form attachment relationships with many adults. However, as previously indicated, not all attachments are equal! Although infants generally have a preference for mother over father in situations that evoke attachment behaviors, they prefer father over a stranger when mother is not present (Cohen & Campos, 1974). Regardless of who the attachment object is,

infants and adults either successfully negotiate a secure attachment relationship or they fall into one of three variants of insecure attachment: avoidant, ambivalent, or disorganized. Because attachment theory predicts caregiver specificity with respect to attachment relationships, several questions become paramount: Does nonparental child care interfere with the development of secure attachments between mother and infant? Do infants develop attachment relationships with their nonparental caregivers? If so, do nonparental attachments compensate for insecure mother-infant attachment relationships?

Research by Howes and her colleagues clearly illustrates that infants establish attachment relationships with their care providers (Howes & Hamilton, 1992a, 1992b; Howes & Smith, 1995; Howes, Rodning, Galluzzo, & Myers, 1988; Phillips, Howes, & Whitebook, 1992). Moreover, low teacher turnover enhances stability of the attachment relationship (Howes & Hamilton, 1992b). However, the ease of establishing a positive and secure care-provider–infant relationship may depend in part on the degree of preparation care providers have for teaching infants and toddlers. For example, Galinsky, Howes, and Kontos (1995) found that attachment security increased when family day care providers participated in a training program designed to enhance their caregiving skills.

The largest and most comprehensive longitudinal research findings on attachment in relation to child care effects are from the NICHD child care study noted earlier. At 6, 15, 24, and 36 months, 1,364 socially and racially diverse children were assessed after birth and followed to age 6. Positive child caregiving and language stimulation contributed meaningfully to early cognitive and language development. The higher the quality of provider-child interaction, the more positive were the mother-child interactions, and the more sensitive and involved were the mothers over the first 3 years (National Institute of Child Health and Human Development Early Child Care Research Network [NICHD], 1994, 1996, 1997, 2000).

The longer the time that infants and toddlers spent in group care, the fewer positive interactions they had with their mothers at 6 and 15 months of age, and the less affection they showed with their mothers at 2 and 3 years. Family income, mother's vocabulary, home environment, and parental cognitive stimulation were more important than was child care quality in predicting cognitive and language advancements. Children in center care made larger gains than did those in family child care homes. Children from ethnic minority groups were more likely to be cared for in settings that offered fewer opportunities for messy play, reading books, and active explorations than were children from other groups. Children reared in economically disadvantaged homes were more likely to be insecurely attached to their mothers. When mothers strongly endorsed statements supporting the possible benefits of maternal employment for children's development, their infants were more likely to be insecurely attached, and these mothers were also observed to be less sensitive and responsive. Their children were in poorer-quality care at earlier ages and for more hours per week.

Infant child care per se (observed quality of care, amount of care, age of entry, and frequency of care starts) did not appear to be a risk factor for insecure attachment. Maternal sensitivity however, was: Mothers who were least sensitive and responsive had more infants classified insecure avoidant; (16–19%) and fewer secure (53–56%) compared with the most sensitive mothers (9–11% insecure avoidant, 12–14% disorganized, 60–65% secure babies). The lowest proportion of secure attachment was noted when maternal sensitivity and child care quality were both low. For children with less sensitive mothers, attachment security proportions were higher if the children were in high-quality care than if they were in low-quality child care.

Effects of Separation

Separation from parents is a daily event for children of all age levels during early childhood. Putting baby down for a nap or going to the grocery store, to work, for dinner, or to a party are all events that separate parents from children. With the exception of parental employment, the effects of everyday separations on the child's behavior have not been extensively studied. However, everyday separations probably have an overall beneficial influence on the young child, encouraging autonomy, independence, and the development of social competence. This is not to say that toddlers and preschoolers will always accept their parents' departure. In fact, as parents are about to leave, it is quite common for toddlers to protest and to try to stay with parents.

There are separations that can have profoundly disruptive influences on the young child's development. These include the prolonged separations associated with death, divorce, desertion by one parent, or the loss of both parents—as in institutionalization or prolonged absences due to illness or to work. Until recently, the study of the effects of prolonged separation on the child's development has focused on maternal separation involving the institutionalization of illegitimate children. This research raised the basic question of *What are the consequences of prolonged maternal deprivation on the child's development?* To some extent, the hesitancy of American parents to rush into massive group child care for infants and toddlers can be traced to the belief that group care is detrimental to normal growth and development.

This belief is rooted in studies of institutionally reared infants that pointed out the dangers of poor institutional care and deprivation from meaningful relationships with significant caregivers (Goldfarb, 1945; Skeels, 1936; Spitz, 1965).

Prolonged exposure to poor institutional care is associated with apathy, despair, and a pronounced deficit in social responsiveness—what Spitz referred to as *hospitalism.* Moreover, the effects of institutionalization are strongest if the infant is institutionalized during the period when attachment to significant caregivers normally occurs (Spitz, 1965). Rutter (1979) argues that it is not separation per se that causes development of affectionless pathology in children, but rather it is the failure to develop a secure attachment or emotional bond with primary caregivers in the first place that interferes with social competence and personality development.

Institutionalization represents the extreme form of separation from primary caregivers and because it is a rare event in the Western world, relative to the care settings in which most of the world's infants and toddlers are reared, the results of institutionalization may translate poorly to other contexts. The fact is that most infants and toddlers experience frequent separations from their primary caregivers and we know precious little about how infants and their families negotiate these separations. For example, Tronick, Winn, and Morelli (1985) report that by the third week after birth, Efe infants of Zaire are cared for by an average of 3.6 nonmaternal individuals per hour, occupying 39% of daylight hours. By 18 weeks of age, Efe infants experience an average of 4.6 individuals per hour, which occupies 58% of daylight hours. Although when infants are fussy they are more likely to be passed to their mother for comforting, this in fact happens less than half of the time. Among the Loogoli of East Africa, mother's caregiving responsibilities are influenced by such factors as household density. In large households, mothers are less likely to be their infants' caregiver (Munroe & Munroe, 1971). Group size, therefore, may be an important factor for establishing secure infant-caregiver relationships. Infant-caregiver ratio is a standard aspect of all definitions of quality. Presumably, the lower the ratio, the better the care provider-infant relationship should be.

In the United States, Suwalsky, Klein, Zaslow, Rabinovich, and Gist (1987) conducted one of the few studies of naturally occurring mother-infant separations. They tracked mothers of firstborn infants over the course of the first year of life, focusing on six types of separation—three during daytime (nonrecurrent separation for nonreimbursed activities; recurrent separations for employment; recurrent separations for nonreimbursed activities) and three overnight (maternal vacation, maternal employment, maternal illness/hospitalization). The range of separations across the 144 participating families was extraordinary. For example, the number of recurrent separations for employment ranged from 1 to 749; the number of nonrecurrent separations for nonreimbursed activities ranged from 2 to 545. Reasons for separations included work, shopping, education, religious activities, and leisure activities. Excluded are all the instances when infants and caregivers are separated within the household because it is nap time, dinner preparation time, time to work in the yard, or time to clean the house. Suwalsky et al. found that the most frequent location for supplemental care during employment-related separations was the home of the care provider (family child care, neighbor, relative). Fathers and relatives provided 31% of the infant's care. One of the questions of interest to the investigators concerned the effect of changes in maternal employment on everyday separations. We find it interesting that when mothers' employment hours decreased, the likelihood of another type of separation increased because mothers spent more time in nonreimbursed activities outside the home.

Maternal Employment

Some researchers report a slight increase in insecure attachments, aggression, and noncompliance in infants whose mothers were employed full-time during the infant's first year of life (Barglow, Vaughn, & Molitor, 1987; Belsky & Eggebeen, 1991; Belsky & Steinberg, 1978). Others report no relationship between maternal work status and the quality of infants' attachment to their mothers. Lerner and Castellino (2001) suggest that the effects of maternal employment on infant and toddler development are unclear because few investigators adequately account for a wide range of confounding variables, such as the quality and amount of nonparental care, the age at which infants or toddlers enter into nonparental care, the stress load of work and family responsibilities, the degree to which mother receives parenting and housework assistance from other adults in the home, and a variety of characteristics of the infant. Clinical evidence concerning the effects of prolonged maternal deprivation on early development has existed for at least 50 years (Spitz & Wolf, 1946). Moreover, sufficient contemporary evidence exists to support the contention that toddlers' interpersonal competencies flow from their initial relationships with their caregivers and other significant adults (Berlin & Cassidy, 2000). If the quality of the infant's attachment relationship to significant caregivers is damaged, then one would predict difficulties in intrapersonal (self-concept) and interpersonal (self-other) relationships. Therefore, it is reasonable to question whether maternal separations associated with going to work are in any way causally related to negative child outcomes.

Working mothers do seem to provide role models for their children that are different from those provided by working mothers (Lerner & Castellino, 2001). For example, the daughters of working mothers tend to be more independent and more achievement-oriented than do the daughters of nonworking mothers. Both the sons and the daughters of working mothers tend to assume greater responsibility for household chores and to develop more positive attitudes toward maternal employment than do the children of nonworking mothers. In addition, the husbands of working wives tend to become more involved with routine household tasks and with caregiving than do husbands whose wives do not work.

One key determinant of the effects of maternal employment on her children's behavior is the degree to which the mother is satisfied with her work and with the alternative child care arrangements available for her children. In fact, there is some indication that mothers who are satisfied with their personal and work life are more competent mothers than are mothers who either do not work or are not satisfied with their way of life (see Hoffman, 1974; Lerner & Castellino, 2002). Unfortunately, the effects of maternal employment on infant and toddler behavior have not received the research attention they deserve, especially in cultures in which women comprise a substantive portion of the labor force. For example, in the United States and Sweden, substantial numbers of infants and toddlers of working mothers spend 20 to more than 35 hours per week in paid child care (see Table 6.4).

Although working mothers with children under 2 years of age comprise the smallest proportion of working mothers with children under 5 years of age, the numbers are increasing. Not only are more women earning college degrees, but more low-income women are entering the workforce because of welfare-to-work requirements. In the former case, more highly educated women are more likely to be able to afford high-quality child care, whereas more poorly educated women are more dependent upon other family members for child care assistance.

Grandparents have a special role in child care in low-income families (Casper, 1994), and they provide about 30% of the care for all children under 5 years when mothers are at work. Fathers provide about 18% of the care for all children under 5 (Smith, 2000), and low-income fathers are more than twice as likely as nonpoor fathers to be primary caregivers when mothers are at work (Casper, 1997). Nevertheless, in 1995 there were 9,342,000 children under 5 years of age in the United States who received nonparental and nonrelative care (14.8% in day care centers, 13.5% in nursery or preschool, 3.0% in Head Start, and 12.6% in family day care). The average hours in nonparental, nonrelative care ranged from 18.4 to 32.6 hours per week (Smith, 2000).

TABLE 6.4   Rates of Employment Among Mothers of Young Children by the Age of the Youngest Child

Country & Child's Age (years)	Number of Hours of Paid Work per Week			
	None	1–19 Hours	20–34 Hours	35+ Hours
United States				
0–5	48%	8%	10%	33%
Under 1	58%	9%	9%	25%
1	45%	11%	11%	33%
2 or 3	45%	6%	11%	39%
4 or 5	37%	10%	12%	41%
Sweden				
0–5	32%	15%	34%	19%
Under 1	59%	2%	18%	22%
1	20%	27%	43%	10%
2 or 3	24%	20%	40%	17%
4 or 5	25%	13%	35%	27%
The Netherlands				
0–5	73%	20%	3%	6%
Under 1	74%	18%	4%	4%
1	78%	16%	4%	3%
2 or 3	73%	21%	1%	4%
4 or 5	62%	28%	3%	7%

Source. Gustafsson, S., & Stafford, F. (1994). Three regimes of child care: The United States, The Netherlands, and Sweden. In *Social protection versus economic flexibility: Is there a trade-off?* R. Blank (Ed). Chicago and London: University of Chicago Press, pp. 333–361. In *The Future of Children* (1995). Reprinted with permission of the University of Chicago Press.

Honig and Park (1993) found that the longer children experienced out-of-home care, the more likely their teachers were to rate them as instrumentally more aggressive. Moore (1990) reported a link between the number of hours of infant-toddler out-of-home care and teacher reports of behavior problems in school. The relationships pertained to boys but not to girls. Specifically, spending more than 15 hours per week in out-of-home care when the child was between 18 and 21 months of age was associated with more teacher-reported behavior problems in school.

Infant-toddler development is influenced by forces emanating from a broad set of familial and social-cultural sources and is far from being solely an outcome of the mother-infant relationship (Brooks-Gunn, Duncan, & Aber, 1997; Brooks-Gunn, Leventhal, & Duncan, 2000). Historical and cultural factors must be considered with respect to their influence on family life and gender role if the boundaries that bind infants and toddlers to their cultural contexts are to be fully understood (Jordon, 1997). It is culture that in large measure defines the characteristics of family life and defines the nature of gender role—including the role of the father.

Fathers and Nonparental Child Care

Although knowledge of the father's impact on child development lags far behind knowledge of the mother's impact, there is sufficient literature to support a number of working hypotheses related to fathers and their young children (Fitzgerald & Montañez, 2000, 2001). The literature supporting such generalizations disproportionately involves data obtained from white, middle-class fathers. Data from a much more ethnically diverse and economically depressed sample of fathers whose children are participating in the national evaluation of EHS show some interesting parallels (Fitzgerald, Berlin, et al., 2000). The EHS study provided an opportunity to contrast responses from three types of fathers: Residential biological, nonresidential biological, and social fathers (nonbiologically related men who are identified by the mother as having a father role in the life of the child). Preliminary analyses suggest that all fathers in the EHS study were emotionally invested in their children, although the degree of investment was less for social fathers than for biological fathers (see Table 6.5).

Whether such demonstrative signs of investment and involvement reflect deep emotional commitment or are expressions of transitory engrossment (Greenberg & Morris, 1974) remains to be determined.

Thirty Years of Research

The research of the past three decades consistently has demonstrated that fathers' lack of participation in routine

TABLE 6.5 General Findings From National and International Studies of Fathers and Their Impact on Child Development

Men are motivated to have children for psychological reasons, not for social or economic reasons (Mackey, 1996). In short, men like children!

Fathers are not particularly involved with infants, but they become more involved as their children reach the 2–6 age range (Belsky, Rovine, & Fish, 1989).

Fathers can and do perform routine caregiving tasks with their infants (Parke et al., 1979), but when in the presence of mother, fathers yield caregiving management to her (Mackey, 1996).

Across a wide range of cultures, when fathers have access to their children, they take advantage of it (Mackey, 1996).

Physical distance between fathers and their children decreases father involvement (Lerman & Sorensen, 1996).

When father's role as breadwinner is compromised, he is less likely to be involved with his children, and more likely to have mothers limit his access if he is nonresidential (Lerman & Sorensen, 1996; Mackey, 1996).

As mother's economic independence increases, fathers are less likely to be involved with their children (Lerman & Sorensen, 1996).

Source. Adapted from Fitzgerald & Montañez (2000).

caregiving of infants is more a matter of performance than of competence (Parke & Sawin, 1976; Parke, Power, & Gottman, 1979). In the United States the number of fathers who are primary care providers for their children is higher than ever before, and cross-culturally, fathers in dual-parent families are spending more time in routine child care than their fathers did (Burghes, Clarke, & Cronin, 1997; Horn, 2000). However, it is also the case cross-culturally that when fathers are in the presence of mothers and their infants, they tend to yield authority of child care to mothers (Mackey, 1996).

Fathers are invested in their infants and they establish attachment relationships with them. Demonstrating that father-infant attachments occur or that fathers seem to be invested in their children no longer seem to be critical questions. The more important questions and the questions of greater significance concern the circumstances that affect the degree of investment and the quality of the father-infant relationship. Nearly every theory of development assumes that fathers play a key role in the sex role identification of their children. Research attention has been given to fathers' play interactions with infants and toddlers, with the conclusion that fathers are more actively involved in gender role socialization than are mothers, particularly with respect to their playful interactions with their sons and daughters (Fitzgerald, 1977; Power, 1981). Others report that fathers are less likely to differentially interact with their sons and daughters during infancy, but that by the toddler years they have a clear preference for rough-and-tumble play with their sons rather than with their daughters (Yogman, 1982). At least by 20 months

of age, toddlers also respond differently to the play of their mothers and fathers. They are more likely to expect fathers than mothers to initiate play interactions, and by 30 months of age toddlers are more cooperative, involved, excited, and interested in play with their fathers than in play with their mothers (Clarke-Stewart, 1977). Fathers take a more direct role in regulating toddler compliance than mothers do and are particularly directive with demanding compliance from boys (Power, McGrath, Hughes, & Manire, 1994). Finally, fathers are also more likely than are mothers to encourage their children to be competitive, to be independent, and to take risks (Hewlett, 1992).

The most accurate summary statement that can be made at present regarding the effects of paternal deprivation on infants and toddlers is that we have a good sense of what outcomes are correlated with father absence, but that we are a long way from isolating the causal variables that explain the correlations. Cabrera, Tamis-LeMonda, Bradley, Hofferth, and Lamb (2000, p. 128) identified five ways in which father absence may have an impact on child development: (a) without a father there is no coparent, (b) economic loss frequently accompanies single motherhood, (c) social isolation and social disapproval of single or divorced mothers and children may lead to emotional distress and less adaptive functioning, (d) abandonment may cause psychological distress in children, and (e) conflict between parents may negatively influence children's social-emotional development.

What do these findings suggest for infants and toddlers who receive supplemental child care? It may mean that many infants and toddlers spend considerable portions of the nonparental child care day in the presence of women but not in the presence of men. The number of males versus the number of women actively involved in infant and toddler child care is minuscule. Cabrera et al. (2000) note that little is known about how men learn to be fathers. Having been reared in a father-present family seems to be important. Investigators have found that men whose fathers were involved in raising them are more positively involved with their own children (Hofferth, 1999). Regardless of marital status or father presence or absence, it is clear that children reared in dysfunctional family systems or in families characterized by high parental risk loads are more likely to have problems themselves. These risk loads include the presence of intergenerational aggression and antisociality (Shears, Robinson, & Emde, in press). Men who reported high antisocial behavior during their youth had low assessments of themselves as fathers. Conversely, men who reported having positive relationships with their own fathers viewed themselves as good fathers. Some investigators have suggested that sociocultural factors create barriers for male involvement in early child care settings such as Early Head Start (Fitzgerald & Montañez, 2000). Families headed by low-income single mothers might especially benefit by having greater opportunities for men to be actively involved in child care and development. If young children in child care settings rarely interact with men, they may be denied social learning experiences that may be important for learning how to be a father (Cabrera et al., 2000).

Fathers and Family Risk Load

Infant mental health focuses on issues related to emotional development and within that context, the literature suggests that fathers may play a crucial role in helping children learn how to control their emotionality. There is no question that men like children and that fathers are both invested in and involved with their children (Mackey, 1996). Investment and involvement increase dramatically around the toddler years as children's motor and language skills push them into more active, physical, and arousing play interactions, especially with their father or father figure. Outcomes of such activity include enhanced emotional regulation, compliance to rules and authority, and the internalization of rule structures.

Both father absence and father antisocial behavior are linked to behavioral dysregulation in children, especially boys. Antisocial fathers model aggression and provide the context for children to internalize aggressive scripts or schemas as action plans that are linked to specific contexts. This puts children at high risk for poor school performance, poor peer relationships, substance abuse, poor cognitive functioning, and the intergenerational transmission of dysfunctional interpersonal relationships (Carmichel Olsen, O'Connor, & Fitzgerald, 2001; Caspi, Henry, McGee, Moffitt, & Silva, 1995; Dobkin, Tremblay, & Sacchitelle, 1997; Fitzgerald, Puttler et al., 2000; Loukas, Fitzgerald, Zucker, & von Eye, 2001). Evidence suggests that father acceptance-rejection predicts child development outcomes better than does mother acceptance-rejection (Rohner, 1998). The negative effects of father absence or dysfunction are exacerbated by risky rearing environments, including risky neighborhoods (Zucker et al., 2000).

Large-scale child care programs such as Early Head Start that actively promote father involvement appear to be on the right course. Summers et al. (1999) used multiple ethnographic approaches to obtain qualitative responses from low-income fathers of EHS children about their roles as fathers. Fathers identified providing financial support, just being there, caregiving, play, teaching, disciplining, providing love, and protection as key roles. Some evidence suggests that the new perception of fatherhood is one of father as equal coparent (Pleck & Pleck, 1997), and this theme was evident in many of the father interviews. It remains to be determined

whether involvement in EHS programs will be sufficient to offset the gradual distancing that occurs between nonresidential fathers and their children during the time of youth and adolescence (Nord & Zill, 1996). Nevertheless, fathers seem to contribute disproportionately to family risk load, and programs that may help to induce a greater sense of responsibility for fatherhood are likely to assist in the reduction of that load.

Summary: Factors Influencing Outcomes in Early Child Care Research

Several factors influence the outcomes in early child care research. The first factor concerns child temperament and its impact on the caregiver-child relationship. Temperament refers to individual differences in emotional, motor, and attentional reactivity, as well as differences in self-regulation. The impact of temperament resides in the goodness of fit between the child's (perceived) temperament and the demands and expectations of the rearing environment. A good match is likely to result in minimal conflict and stress between the child and significant adults, and a poor match is likely to exacerbate conflict and tension. Much is known about maternal perception of infant temperament and its impact on mother-infant relationships. However, relatively less is known about how perceptions of the father and nonparental caregivers may affect their interactions with infants.

The second factor involves mother-child social-emotional relationships. Attachment refers to the social-emotional relationship constructed by infants and their primary caregivers. Research clearly shows that infants establish attachment relationships with their care providers. The ease of establishing a relationship depends in part on the degree of preparation care providers have for teaching infants and toddlers. In both the United States and other cultures, most infants and toddlers experience frequent separations from their primary caregivers. Yet very little is known about how these separations affect the development of the child. For instance, the effects of maternal employment on child development are still unclear because few investigators control for important confounding variables such as the quality and amount of nonparental care or the age at which children enter into nonparental care.

The third factor concerns father involvement in child and family development. Fathers are more actively involved in gender role socialization than are mothers. They take a more direct role in regulating toddler compliance than mothers do and are more likely than mothers are to encourage their children to be competitive, to be independent, and to take risks. Father absence may have a profound impact on child development. If young children in child care settings rarely interact with men, they may be denied social learning experiences that are important for learning how to be a father. Literature on infant mental health suggests that father absence and father antisocial behavior are linked to adverse outcomes in children, such as behavioral dysregulation, poor school performance, poor peer relationships, poor cognitive functioning, and substance abuse. Fathers seem to contribute disproportionately to family risk load. Programs that induce a greater sense of responsibility for fatherhood are likely to assist in the reduction of that load.

NONPARENTAL CHILD CARE: COST, QUALITY, AND ASSURANCE

Cost and Quality

Cost is a primary concern when choosing child care. Based on the *Children's Defense Fund 2000 Yearbook,* full-time child care costs may range from $4,000 to $10,000 per year per child. In one modest-sized midwestern city, family child care ranges from about $3,000 to $7,000 per year per child. Data from the sites involved with the national evaluation of EHS indicate that $9,646 per year is necessary to provide high-quality care to infants and toddlers in full-year child care. Clearly, nonparental child care is expensive. For some families, approximately one fourth of their income can be consumed by child care. When one considers that half of the families in the United States with young children earn less than $35,000 annually and that families with two full-time working parents, each earning minimum wages, earn less than $22,000 combined, it is clear that access to nonparental child care depends upon the availability of government subsidies. Data from the 1990 National Child Care Survey (Hofferth, 1995) suggest that parental income does not affect the availability of child care. However, the same survey indicated that few programs accept subsidized children. In the final analysis, working poor and working-class families end up paying a greater proportion of their income for child care than do middle-class families. As a result, they often have to depend on kinship care or on informal, low-quality child care.

The pay for child care providers is limited by the income of the families served and is often less than what is considered to be an acceptable wage. The average yearly salary of a child care worker is less than $15,000. There are limited federal subsidies available to assist parents with the costs of licensed child care, but only 1 in 10 eligible children receive the financial support needed. The availability of quality child care is limited by lack of funding subsidies for child care workers and working parents. Making less than a livable wage greatly reduces the number of trained child care providers, the number of available child care slots, and the ability of parents to work, while it simultaneously increases staff turnover.

Benchmarking Quality

In the United States, child care tends to be viewed as a personal issue to be solved at the family level. The minority view is that child care availability and quality are issues of national concern that require extensive government support. According to the *Children's Defense Fund 2000 Yearbook,* approximately 76% of children age birth to 5 years are placed in child care, and 60% of the children are infants. This suggests that quality child care is both a private and public issue; adequate spaces for child care enable working parents to have a placement for their children. Meeting quality standards assures that their children will thrive as well as—or perhaps better than—they might in home care (Phillips, 1992; Phillips, Howes, & Whitebook, 1992; Philips, Lande, & Goldberg, 1990; Phillips & Adams, 2001).

Theoretically, quality child care should be associated with children who are cognitively, linguistically, and socially prepared for preschool and kindergarten—children who are ready to learn. Because of their interactions with peers, they should be as socially skilled as are children who are reared at home with siblings. Initial studies of the effects of infant day care reported that infants reared in day care scored higher on measures of cognitive, linguistic, and social competence than did home-reared infants (Robinson & Robinson, 1971; Fowler, 1972; Lally, 1973; Honig & Brill, 1970; Keister, 1970). Nearly all studies from this era reported that infants in child care formed their strongest attachments to their mother (Caldwell, Wright, Honig, & Tannenbaum, 1970; Ragozin, 1980), thus allaying concerns of critiques that group day care would lead to emotional damage. Some investigators reported that toddlers reared in child care were less attentive to peers than were home-reared toddlers (Kagan, Kearsley, & Zelazo, 1975). Others found no differences between day care and home-reared children with respect to peer relationships. Rubenstein and Howes (1979) note that peers play an important role in child care by serving as models for one another. For example, in their study, infants' positive affect and competence at toy play were higher when they were interacting with peers than when interacting with adults.

The 1970s was also a time when investigators focused on so-called natural experiments in infant-toddler child care that were provided by many countries in the Soviet Union and Western Europe. Child care programs in Hungary, East Germany, Czechoslovakia, Yugoslavia, and the Soviet

Union were described in great detail (Brackbill, 1962; Bronfenbrenner, 1962; Meers & Marans, 1968; Wagner & Wagner, 1971). One lesson learned from these reports was that infant-toddler child care settings and curricula will reflect broader social-cultural values, and therefore might not generalize easily to other cultures.

Because many of these early studies assessed the impact on infants and toddlers enrolled in university demonstration day care centers or in formal state-supported centers, the extent to which findings generalized to the everyday context was compromised. Thus, the basic questions concerning the impact of nonparental child care continue to be raised. Does early nonparental child care have detrimental effects on children's social-emotional and cognitive development? Is there an optimal group size for facilitating the development of competence? Are same-age peer groups more effective than multiple-age peer groups? Are the relationships among children different in day care than in home care, regardless of the nature of the peer group composition? The questions tend to be especially pointed at the group care of infants and toddlers, but they apply equally well to the broad range of caregiving contexts within which very young children are reared by nonparental caregivers.

Some investigators report that infants who experience non-parental center-based child care have poorer social-emotional development and social behavior skills as preschoolers (Belsky, 1986, 1988) and are more likely to score higher on measures of behavioral control than are home-reared children. Other investigators find that consistency in child care may be an important mediator of such outcomes. For example, Ketterlinus, Henderson, and Lamb (1992) found no differences between infants and toddlers reared in nonparental day care and home-reared comparison children. Stability of placement seemed to be a critical component of the lack of differences in outcome; infants or toddlers in the Ketterlinus et al. study experienced two sustained years in stable day care settings. In a retrospective study of maternal reports of their children's behavior, Burchinal, Ramey, Reid, and Jaccard (1995) did not find evidence to support heightened levels of externalizing or internalizing behavior problems in infants reared in day care. Anderson's (1989) study of Swedish 8-year-old children who experienced nonparental child care as infants found similar results from teacher ratings. In fact, teachers rated the children who had experienced day care as more persistent, more independent, less anxious, and more verbal than children who did not have prior day care experience. Of course, one critical variable in studies tracing the effects of infant day care on later developmental outcomes concerns the quality of the child care they experienced. Howes (1990) found that low-quality infant child care predicted poor

peer relationships as kindergartners, whereas high-quality care did not. For example, infants who developed secure relationships with their teachers were gregarious and less aggressive in peer play as 4-year-olds, whereas those who were dependent and socially withdrawn were more aggressive in their play interactions (see also Pianta & Nimetz, 1991).

Publication of optimal standards for high-quality child care occurs frequently, filling newsletters of national child development associations, parenting magazines, state and national agency bulletins, newspaper "living today" sections, and countless web pages. Criteria for high-quality child care include a staff well-trained in child development; a staff that promotes warm, sensitive, and responsive interactions with infants and toddlers; low staff-child ratios and small classroom groups; stability of caregivers over time (Howes & Hamilton, 1992a, 1993); good nutrition and health practices; developmentally appropriate curriculum practices; good provider-parent relationships; and stimulating and safe environments.

Despite almost consensus agreement on these criteria for quality, there have been few systematic efforts to determine whether such factors as group size, child-staff ratios (Belsky, 1990; Hayes, Palmer & Zaslow, 1990), or provider training (Arnett, 1989) actually do define quality care that in turn has positive impacts on child development. Blau (1996) analyzed data from 1,309 teachers from 227 day care centers that participated in the National Child Care Staffing Study. Blau found that in the best-fitting models, conventional benchmarks such as group size, child-staff ratios, and staff training had nearly negligible impacts on quality of child care. Staff training and education had some positive but low-order effects on quality. Child care quality was defined by the Early Childhood Environment Rating Scale (ECERS) for preschool classrooms and the Infant-Toddler Environment Rating Scale (ITERS) for infant-toddler programs (Harms & Clifford, 1980, 1986). Factor analysis of the items in the ECERS and ITERS revealed two aggregate scales, which Blau defined as CARE (Appropriate Caregiving: adult-child interaction, supervision, discipline), and ACTIVITY (Appropriate Activity: materials, schedule, activities as a proxy measure of classroom environment). The Arnett Caregiver Interaction Scale, used to rate teacher's interactions with children, generated three indexes (SENSITIVE, HARSH, DETACHED), which were combined with the ACTIVITY and CARE scales to assess quality of child care. We present this level of detail (a) to specify what Blau defined as quality care and (b) to indicate that none of the variables assessed were linked to child outcome data. Whereas Blau has made an important first step toward a systematic analysis of quality care, the next steps must involve child development outcomes because they represent the ultimate product of interest in the child care system.

Standards for high-quality child care almost always include reference to relationships between parents and care providers. Indeed, in national child care initiatives such as EHS, parents must be an integral component of the operating organization structure. Seldom, however, are parents involved in any systematic way in the evaluation of child care quality. A retrospective study of parents whose infants were enrolled in an infant-toddler child care program attempted to determine whether parent's perceptions of their child's proximal behavior were in any way linked to their attitudes about their child's early child care experience (Ledesma, Fitzgerald, & McGreal, 1980). Parents of all infants who had been enrolled in the child care center over a 9-year period were mailed questionnaires designed to elicit their opinions about their children's past child care experience and their current developmental status.

Nearly all parents reported feeling guilty when first enrolling their infants in the center; most often, this involved parents' concerns about their attachment relationship with their child. We find it interesting that parents reported that they did develop strong attachment relationships with their infants and that their current relationships were also strong. They noted that their infants shared attachments with other caregivers but not to the detriment of the parent-infant relationship. They especially noted that enrollment of their infants in day care resulted in less stress on the family during a time when supplemental care was essential. Ledesma et al. (1980) note that some parents reported that they had to deal with public bias against having their infant in day care:

> . . . and I did feel guilty. Our daughter was only six months old when I went back to school and we had to continuously reassure ourselves that we were doing the right thing. I must have called the center five times a day during her first few months there. Relatives didn't make it any easier. My mother-in-law (as well as one of my professors) kept referring to "mothers who abandon their babies" whenever she could work it into a conversation. (pp. 47–48)

Other concerns frequently expressed involved the degree of parental involvement in center activities, caregiver-infant ratios, maintenance of physical health, and amount of physical space available in the center for play areas. An overwhelming number of parents reported that it was the quality of the center staff that surfaced as the most important factor contributing to parents' perceptions of quality child care. The competent, caring, and knowledgeable senior caregivers (both registered nurses with considerable personal and professional experience with infants and toddlers) seemed to allay any concerns that parents had about physical space, health maintenance, and child development.

We seem to "know" the defining characteristics of child care quality; yet this knowledge faces many contradictions. We know that highly trained staff are essential to quality, yet relatively few states regulate training or have minimal standards for staff competency. We know what quality child care is, yet we continue to conduct research in order to identify the components of optimal child care. In some respects researchers seem to be intent on identifying the just-adequate environment that will do no harm, rather than focusing on the specific individual, familial, and systemic variables that may predict child outcomes independent of or in interaction with particular child care settings.

Although the defining features of high quality nonparental child care have been identified, these features are program and personnel specific—that is to say, child characteristics, family characteristics, and neighborhood characteristics are not typically part of the quality formula. We are a long way from fully understanding how intra-individual and familial variables interact with the child care setting to influence child outcomes, although we have clear pathways marked to guide such research (Anderson, 1989; Howes, 1988; Howes & Hamilton, 1992a, 1992b, 1993; Howes, Hamilton, & Matheson, 1994; Ketterlinus et al., 1992; Lucas, 2001; Pianta & Nimetz, 1991; Raikes, 1993; Ramey, 2000; Ramey & Ramey, 1998; Rubinstein et al., 1977). Do infants with difficult temperaments score higher on measures of aggressive behavior regardless of their child care experiences? Does high-quality child care provide protective factors for children who are reared in low-quality home environments? Does the quality of the teacher-child relationship promote effective social interaction skills? Is high-quality early child care sufficient to facilitate resilience factors and coping skills among children reared in high-risk family or neighborhood environments? One of the strongest conclusions Yoshikawa (1994, 1995) reached in his analysis of the effects of child care was that poor quality is associated with poor outcomes and that high quality is associated with positive outcomes—cooperation with adults, the ability to imitate and sustain positive interactions with adults, and early competence in reading and math.

Assurance: Regulatory Policies and Nonparental Child Care

In the United States, child care centers are rapidly adopting curricula that flow from the principles and practices that constitute developmentally appropriate practices for early childhood

TABLE 6.6 Developmentally Appropriate and Inappropriate Practices (Items From One Research Checklist) from Perspectives of Kindergarten Teachers

Appropriate	Inappropriate
View of growth and development	
Work is individualized.	Work is evaluated against a group norm.
Children move at their own pace.	Everyone is expected to acquire the same narrowly defined skills.
Organization of the curriculum	
Activities center on topics in such areas as science and social studies.	Teacher-directed reading groups. Lecturing to the whole group.
Topic activities include story writing and storytelling, drawing, discussing, listening to stories and informational books, and taking part in cooperative activities.	Paper-and-pencil exercises, workbooks, and worksheets. Projects, learning centers, and play are offered if time permits or as rewards for completing work.
Skills are taught as they are needed to complete a task.	
Teacher preparation and organization of instruction	
Learning centers provide opportunities for writing, reading, math and language games, and dramatic play.	There is little time for enrichment activities. Interest centers are available for children who finish their seatwork early.
Children are encouraged to critique their own work.	Centers are set up so that children must complete a prescribed sequence of teacher-directed activities within an allotted period of time.
Prosocial behavior, perseverance, and industry	
Stimulating, motivating activities that promote student involvement.	Children are lectured about the importance of appropriate social behavior.
Individual choices are encouraged.	Children who become bored and restless with seatwork and whisper, talk, or wander around are punished.
Enough time is allowed to complete work.	Children who dawdle and do not finish work in the allotted time are punished.
Time with friends or teachers is provided.	There is no time for private conversation.
	Only the most able children finish their work in time to visit interest centers or to interact with other students.

Source. Charleswork, R., Hart, C., Burts, D., et al. (1993). Measuring the developmental appropriateness of kindergarten teachers' beliefs and practices. *Early Childhood Research Quarterly, 8,* 255–376.

education (Bredekamp, 1987a, 1987b; see Table 6.6, which outlines an approach to early child development that optimizes individualized instruction.

The developmentally appropriate child-centered approach to early childhood education is not universal (Boocock, 1995). The Maori of New Zealand and residents of many Asian countries view early childhood education as a direct, downward extension of formal schooling. Low child-adult ratios valued in the United States apparently are less meaningful in France and Japan with respect to attainment of high-quality care or positive child development outcomes. Children who attend preschool in developing countries have better cognitive skills and overall school performance when compared with children in the same countries who do not attend preschool

(Boocock, 1995). We find it interesting that countries that report positive outcomes for early childhood education tend to have national policies that support universal preschool and high-quality programs. The United States spends heavily to support a wide variety of prevention programs (EHS, Head Start, Healthy Start, Even Start, Early Start, Success by Six, Early Intervention for Infants and Toddlers) that target children in families whose incomes fit the federal definition of poverty or who for other reasons are at high risk. Currently, 31 states also fund programs that specifically target families with very young children. Only recently have efforts emerged to try to link existing programs into more integrated systems for children of low-income families. For example, performance standards for EHS require programs to build community networks among service providers to facilitate easy access to available services for EHS families.

States with higher levels of child care quality are more likely to report higher economies, safer neighborhoods, and better schools than are states with lower ratings. Young, Marsland, and Zigler (1997) analyzed the regulatory standards for center-based child care in the United States. Noting that a 1980 review reported that no state met federal standards of quality for group composition, staff training, and program of care, Young et al. sought to determine how much change has occurred during the 1980s. Data in Table 6.7 indicate that relatively little progress was made over a 10-year period. With the exception of the number of programs scoring in the *good* category, the majority of states were rated *poor* to *very poor* (or unregulated) on group composition and caregiver qualifications. Indeed, only Minnesota was rated as high as *minimally acceptable* with respect to caregiver qualifications. A more recent analysis of state regulations

(Table 6.8) indicates that the major of states do not have training requirements for either family child care providers or for teachers in child care centers.

Perhaps policies adopted by the United States Department of Defense (DOD) for child care programs available to families in the military should serve as benchmarks for quality assurance (N. D. Campbell, Applebaum, Martinson, & Martin, 2000; N. D. Campbell, 2000; Lucas, 2001). The DOD provides military families with options of full-day care, part-day care, hourly care, occasional care, and long-term care, depending on need. One half of all children in military child care programs are in infant-toddler programs, which provide child care beginning as early as the sixth postnatal week in center programs and the fourth postnatal week in family programs. Regardless of the type of care needed, provision of care and related services is organized in a seamless system with one point of entry for each family. Monitoring for quality assurance requires annual certification of health

TABLE 6.7   Ratings of 1990 State Infant and Toddler Center-Based Child Care Regulation by Domain and Category

Domain	Optimal	Good	Minimally Acceptable	Poor	Very Poor or Unregulated
Overall	(Score = 81) No States	(Range = 65–80) No States	(Range = 49–64) AL, CT, HI, IL, KS, ME, MD, MA, MN, MO, ND, OK, OR, RI, UT, VT, WI	(Range = 33–48) AK, AZ, AR, CA, CO, DE, DC, FL, GA, IN, IA, KY, LA, MI, MT, NE, NV, NH, NJ, NM, NY, NC, OH, PA, SD, TN, TX, VA, WA, WV	(Range = 17–32) ID, MS, SC, WY
Grouping	(Score = 27) No States	(Range = 21–26) CT, DC, MD, MA, OR, VT	(Range = 16–20) AL, CA, HI, KS, MN, MO, WI, UT	(Range = 11–15) CO, IL, IN, IA, ME, MI, MT, NE, NH, NY, ND, OH, OK, PA, SD, TN, WA, WV	(Range = 5–10) AK, AZ, AR, DE, FL, GA, ID, KY, LA, MS, NV, NJ, NM, NC, RI, SC, TX, VA, WY
Caregiver Qualifications	(Score = 81) No States	(Range = 21–26) No States	(Range = 16–20) MN	(Range = 11–15) AK, AZ, AR, CA, DE, IL, IN, ME, MA, MO, NJ, NM, NY, NC, ND, OH, PA, RI, SD, TN, TX, UT, VA, WV, WI	(Range = 5–10) AL, CO, CT, DC, FL, GA, HI, ID, IA, KS, KY, LA, MD, MI, MS, MT, NE, NV, NH, OK, OR, SC, VT, WA, WY
Program	(Score = 27) AK	(Range = 22–26) AL, AZ, DE, HI, IL, ME, MD, MA, MO, MT, NH, NJ, NM, NY, NC, ND, OH, OK, OR, RI, TX, UT, VT, VA, WA, WV, WI	(Range = 17–21) AR, CA, CT, FL, GA, IA, KS, KY, LA, MI, MN, NE, NV, PA, SC, SD, TN	(Range = 12–16) CO, DC, IN, MS	(Range = 7–11) ID, WY

Source. Reprinted with permission from Young, K. T., Marsland, K. W., & Zigler, E. (1997). The regulatory status of center-based infant and toddler child care. *American Journal of Orthopsychiatry, 67,* p. 539.

TABLE 6.8   Training Requirements for Child Care Personnel (1998) for the States and the District of Columbia

	No	Yes	States with Requirements
Training required for family child care providers prior to serving children.	41	10	CO, DE, FL, KT, ME, MD, MN, NE, NV, UT, WI
Training required for teachers in child care center prior to serving children.	33	18	CA, DE, DC, FL, GA, HI, IL, MD, MA, MN, MT, NV, NH, NJ, RI, TX, VT, WI

and safety regulations, developmental programming, child abuse prevention efforts, and staff training. Four unannounced inspections occur annually, one of which involves a multidisciplinary team (Lucas, 2001)! Clearly, the DOD takes seriously its commitment to provide high-quality child care to families serving in the military.

Summary: Nonparental Child Care

Although there continues to be national ambivalence regarding the use of nonparental child care for very young children, it is likely that current employment trends for women of childbearing age are not likely to reverse anytime soon. The simple fact is that many parents—even if they desire to stay at home with their very young children—may not be able to do so for economic reasons. Why should these parents be penalized for making choices that directly affect their ability to contribute to taking care of themselves and their families? More policy options are needed that provide support for families needing to access such care options.

It seems that we have come to recognize this reality as we examine the system established to support those enlisted in the armed forces. The benefits of such a system have been considerable—not only for children who participate in care regulated by the DOD, but also for families and for the government. When parents feel comfortable about the quality and safety of care, it likely has a positive impact on productivity. We need to carefully consider how all aspects of the military child care system (cost, quality, and assurance) can provide a model for what should also be in place in the private sector. Although it is certainly true that federal-, state-, and even foundation-funded efforts have been established, much of this work seems inadequate to sufficiently address the need that presently exists for nonparental child care.

Researchers have an important role to play in this process. As we consider the fact that many families will continue to rely upon nonparental care, we need a generation of research that goes beyond the question of whether child care influences development; more studies are needed that seek to understand the pathways through which these settings exert their influence and how providers can in turn improve their settings as a result of such research.

ENTERING THE TWENTY-FIRST CENTURY

The so-called new school-age child is now around 40 years old, and the realities of the workforce, equality for women, and changing roles for men suggest that the number of infants and toddlers living in supplemental care settings during some significant portion of their lives will continue to increase through the first decade of the twenty-first century. Although it may no longer be meaningful to ask where preventive intervention programs work (e.g, National Research Council and Institute of Medicine, 2000), considerable fine detail needs specification if we are to achieve the quality of child care that will facilitate optimal development of infants and young children. Failure to determine the boundaries of quality and to demand that all nonparental child care experiences fall within those boundaries could have serious neurobiological, psychological, and social consequences for infants and toddlers.

We have suggested several focal domains relevant to specifying the consequences of nonparental child care. The first domain focuses on characteristics of the infant and on the ecological context within which they organize. We suggest that dominant theories of the importance of mother-child relationships fail to adequately address the ecological context within which most parenting takes place, contrasting studies of separation experiences in the laboratory with studies of separations that take place through the normal course of everyday life. Moreover, we suggest that questions raised about the importance of mother-child relationships also be examined with respect to care-provider–infant relationships. The second domain examines the impact of fathers on infant and toddler development. Theory and research on fathers needs to move beyond simple imitation of the vast literature concerning maternal influences on child development. Although many theoretical concepts may prove to apply equally to mothers and fathers, the level of our current knowledge of the impact of fathers on child development will benefit from openness and creativity among developmental researchers. The third domain addresses issues of risk. The dominant questions in child care research have focused as much on a political agenda contrasting at-home rearing with out-of-home rearing as they have on the impact of child care on mother-infant relationships.

Developmentalists need to move beyond these issues and examine the impact of nonparental care on infants who are at biological risk, familial risk, community risk, or any combination. Part of this agenda requires intensive study of the impact of cultural diversity in parenting and child-rearing beliefs, attitudes, and practices as they play out against the realities of needed placements in nonparental care settings (Garcia Coll, 1990). Although research on infants and families defined as ethnic minorities in the United States is increasing, our knowledge of variability in developmental pathways for infants of color is woefully inadequate (Fitzgerald et al., 1999). Finally, we suggested that exemplary models for high-quality care provide a base for setting standards that researchers can use to assess the impact of the child care context on infant and toddler development. Finally, to paraphrase Michael Rutter's observation in 1976, perhaps it is time to consider that the standards that society applies to the consequences of nonparental child care should also be applied to the consequences of parental child care.

REFERENCES

Ainsworth, M. D. S., Blehar, M. C., Waters, E., & Wall, S. (1978). *Patterns of attachment.* Hillsdale, NJ: Erlbaum.

Allport, G. W. (1937). *Personality: A psychological interpretation.* New York: Holt.

Anderson, B.-E. (1989). Effects of public day care: A longitudinal study. *Child Development, 60,* 857–866.

Arnett, J. (1989). Caregivers in day care centers: Does training matter? *Journal of Applied Developmental Psychology, 10,* 541–552.

Barglow, P., Vaughn, B. E., & Molitor, N. (1987). Effects of maternal absence due to employment on the quality of infant-mother attachment in a low-risk sample. *Child Development, 53,* 53–61.

Belsky, J. (1986). Infant day care: A cause for concern? *Zero to Three, 6,* 1–9.

Belsky, J. (1988). The effects of infant day care reconsidered. *Early Childhood Research Quarterly, 3,* 235–272.

Belsky, J. (1990). Parental and nonparental child care and children's socioemotional development: A decade in review. *Journal of Marriage and the Family, 52,* 885–903.

Belsky, J., & Eggebeen, D. (1991). Early and extensive maternal employment and young children's socioemotional development: Children of the National Longitudinal Survey of Youth. *Journal of Marriage and the Family, 53,* 1083–1098.

Belsky, J., & Steinberg, L. D. (1978). The effects of daycare: A critical review. *Child Development, 49,* 929–949.

Berlin, L. J., & Cassidy, J. (2000). Understanding parenting: Contributions of attachment theory and research. In J. D. Osofsky & H. E. Fitzgerald (Eds.), *WAIMH handbook of infant mental health* (pp. 131–170). New York: Wiley.

Bertalanffy, L. von (1950). An outline of General Systems Theory. *British Journal of Philosophy and Science, 1,* 139–164.

Bertalanffy, L. von (1968). *General systems theory.* New York: Braziller.

Blau, D. M. (1996). The production of quality in child care centers. *The Journal of Human Resources, 32,* 334–387.

Boocock, S. S. (1995). Early childhood programs in other nations: Goals and outcomes. *The Future of Children, 5,* 94–114.

Bowlby, J. (1969). *Attachment.* New York: Basic Books.

Brackbill, Y. (1962). Research and clinical work with children. In R. A. Bauer (Ed.), *Some views on Soviet psychology* (pp. 99–164). Washington, DC: American Psychological Association.

Bredekamp, S. (Ed.). (1987a). *Accreditation criteria and procedures of the National Academy of Early Childhood Programs.* Washington, DC: National Association for the Education of Young Children.

Bredekamp, S. (1987b). *Developmentally appropriate practice in early childhood programs serving children from birth through age 8.* Washington, DC: National Association for the Education of Young Children.

Bronfenbrenner, U. (1962). Soviet methods of character education: some implications for research. *American Psychologist, 17,* 550–564.

Bronfenbrenner, U. (1979). *The ecology of human development: Experiments by nature and design.* Cambridge, MA: Harvard University Press.

Bronfenbrenner, U., & Morris, P. (1998). The ecology of developmental processes. In W. Damon (Series Ed.) and R. M. Lerner (Vol. Ed.), *Handbook of child psychology: Vol. 5. Theoretical models of human development* (5th ed., pp. 993–1028). New York: Wiley.

Brooks-Gunn, J., Duncan, G. J., & Aber, J. L. (1997). *Neighborhood poverty* (Vol. 1). New York: Russell Sage.

Brooks-Gunn, J., Leventhal, T., & Duncan, G. J. (2000). Why poverty matters for young children: Implications for policy. In J. D. Osofsky & H. E. Fitzgerald (Eds). *WAIMH handbook of infant mental health: Vol. 3. Parenting and child care* (pp. 89–132). New York: Wiley.

Burghes, L., Clarke, L., & Cronin, N. (1997). *Fathers and fatherhood in Britain.* London: Family Policy Studies Centre.

Burchinal, M. R., Ramey, S. L., Reid, M. K., & Jaccard, J. (1995). Early child care experiences and their association with family and child characteristics during middle childhood. *Early Childhood Research Quarterly, 10,* 33–61.

Cabrera, N. J., Tamis-LeMonda, C. S., Bradley, R. H., Hofferth, S., & Lamb, M. E. (2000). Fatherhood in the twenty-first century. *Child Development, 71,* 127–136.

Caldwell, B. M., Wright, C. M., Honig, A. S., & Tannenbam, J. (1970). Infant day care and attachment. *American Journal of Orthopsychiatry, 40,* 397–412.

Campbell, F. A., & Ramey, C. T. (1990). The relationship between Piagetian cognitive development, mental test performance, and academic achievement in high-risk students with and without early educational experience. *Intelligence, 14,* 293–308.

Campbell, F. A., & Ramey, C. T. (1994). Effects of early intervention on intellectual and academic achievement: A follow-up study of children from low-income families. *Child Development, 65,* 684–698.

Campbell, J. J., Lamb, M. E., & Hwang, C. P. (2000). Early child-care experiences and children's social competence between ½ and 15 years of age. *Applied Developmental Science, 4,* 166–175.

Campbell, N. D. (2000, May). Military provides model for child care reforms. *Department of Defense News Briefing.* Washington, DC: U.S. Department of Defense.

Campbell, N. D., Applebaum, J. C., Martinson, K., & Martin, E. (2000, April). *Be all that we can be: Lessons from the military for improving our nation's child care system.* Washington, DC: National Women's Law Center.

Carlson, N. A., & Cassell, T. Z. (1984). A socio-ecological model of adaptive behavior and functioning. In H. E. Fitzgerald, B. M. Lester, & M. W. Yogman (Eds.). *Theory and research in behavior pediatrics* (Vol. 2, pp. 31–66). New York: Plenum Press.

Carmichael Olson, H., O'Connor, M. J., & Fitzgerald, H. E. (2001). Lessons learned from study of the developmental impact of parental alcoholism. *Infant Mental Health Journal, 22,* 271–290.

Casper, L. M. (1994). Who's minding our preschoolers? Fall 1994 update. *Current Population Reports.* Washington, DC: U.S. Department of Commerce.

Casper, L. M. (1997). My daddy takes care of me! Fathers as care providers. *Current Population Reports.* Washington, DC: U.S. Department of Commerce.

Caspi, A., Henry, B., McGee, R. O., Moffitt, T. E., & Silva, P. A. (1995). Temperamental origins of child and adolescent behavior problems: From age three to age fifteen. *Child Development, 66,* 55–68.

Caspi, A., Moffitt, T. E., Newman, D. L., & Silva, P. A. (1996). Behavioral observations at age 3 years predict adult psychiatric disorders. *Archives of General Psychiatry, 53,* 1034–1039.

Chess, S., & Thomas, A. (1986). *Temperament in clinical practice.* New York: Guilford Press.

Chess, S., & Thomas, A. (1991). Temperament and the concept of goodness of fit. In J. Strelau & A. Angleitner (Eds.). *Explorations in temperament: International perspectives on theory and measurement* (pp. 15–28). New York: Plenum Press.

Clarke-Stewart, K. A. (1977). *Child care in the family: A review of research and some propositions for policy.* New York: Academic Press.

Clarke-Stewart, K. A., Allhusen, V. D., & Clemens, D. C. (1995). Nonparental caregiving. In M. H. Bornstein (Ed.), *Handbook of parenting: Vol. 3. Status and social conditions of parenting* (pp. 151–176). Mahwah, NJ: Erlbaum.

Cochran, M. (Ed.). (1993). *International handbook of child care policies and programs.* Westport, CT: Greenwood Press.

Cohen, L. J., & Campos, J. J. (1974). Father, mother, and stranger as elicitors of attachment behaviors in infancy. *Developmental Psychology, 10,* 146–154.

Coley, R. L. (2001). Emerging research on low-income, unmarried, and minority fathers. *American Psychologist, 56,* 743–753.

Commissioner's Office of Research and Evaluation, Head Start Bureau, Administration on Children, Youth, and Families, & Department of Health and Human Services (1999a, December). *Leading the way: Characteristics and early experiences of selected Early Head Start Programs: Vol. 1. Cross-site perspectives.* Washington, DC: U.S. Department of Health and Human Services.

Commissioner's Office of Research and Evaluation, Head Start Bureau, Administration on Children, Youth, and Families, & Department of Health and Human Services (1999b, December). *Leading the way: Characteristics and early experiences of selected Early Head Start Programs: Vol. 2. Program profiles.* Washington, DC: U.S. Department of Health and Human Services.

Commissioner's Office of Research and Evaluation, Head Start Bureau, Administration on Children, Youth, and Families, & Department of Health and Human Services (2001a, December–June). *Building their futures: How Early Head Start programs are enhancing the lives of infants and toddlers in low-income families: Vol. 1. Technical report.* Washington, DC: U.S. Department of Health and Human Services.

Commissioner's Office of Research and Evaluation, Head Start Bureau, Administration on Children, Youth, and Families, & Department of Health and Human Services (2001b, December–June). *Building their futures: How Early Head Start programs are enhancing the lives of infants and toddlers in low-income families: Vol. 2. Technical report appendices.* Washington, DC: U.S. Department of Health and Human Services.

Commissioner's Office of Research and Evaluation, Head Start Bureau, Administration on Children, Youth, and Families, & Department of Health and Human Services (2001c, December–January). *Building their futures: How Early Head Start programs are enhancing the lives of infants and toddlers in low-income families: Summary report.* Washington, DC: U.S. Department of Health and Human Services.

Dobkin, P. L., Tremblay, R. E., & Sacchitelle, C. (1997). Predicting boys' early-onset substance abuse from father's alcoholism, son's disruptiveness, and mother's parenting behavior. *Journal of Consulting and Clinical Psychology, 65,* 86–92.

Dokecki, P. R., Hargrove, E. C., & Sandler, H. M. (1983). An overview of the Parent Child Development Center social experiment. In R. Haskins & D. Adams (Eds.), *Parent education and public policy.* Norwood, NJ: Ablex.

Duncan, G. J., & Brooks-Gunn, J. (Eds.). (1997). *Consequences of growing up poor.* New York: Russell Sage.

Fein, G. G. (1995). Infants in group care: Patterns of despair and detachment. *Early Childhood Research Quarterly, 10,* 261–275.

Fenichel, E., & Mann, T. L. (2001). Early Head Start for low-income families with infants and toddlers. *The Future of Children, 11,* 135–141.

Fitzgerald, H. E. (1977). Infants and caregivers: Sex differences as determinants of socialization. In E. Donelson & J. Gullahorn (Eds.), *Women: A psychological perspective*. New York: Wiley.

Fitzgerald, H. E., Berlin, L., Cabrara, N., Coker, D., Pan, B., Raikes, H., Roggman, L., Spellman, M., Tamis-LeMonda, C., & Tarrullo, L. (2000, July). *Twenty-four months of fatherhood: Low-income men and their toddlers. Factors affecting paternal involvement in infant and toddler development: insights from early head start*. In symposium (L. Roggman and K. Boller, chairs), *24 months of fatherhood: Low income men and their toddlers*. Presented at the biennial meeting of the International Conference on Infant Studies, Brighton, UK.

Fitzgerald, H. E., Johnson, R. B., Van Eqeren, L. A., Castellino, D. R., Johnson, C. B., & Judge-hawton, M. (1999). *Infancy and culture: An international review and source book*. New York: Falmer Press.

Fitzgerald, H. E., & Montañez, M. (2000, October). *Infant mental health and Early Head Start: Building capacity for father engagement*. Paper presented at the Head Start Infant Mental Health Forum, "Addressing mental health needs of infants, parents, and families in Early Head Start and Migrant Head Start: Lessons from the scientific community," Washington, DC.

Fitzgerald, H. E., & Montañez, M. (2001). Fathers as facilitators of infant mental health: Implications for Early Head Start. *Zero to Three, 22*, 25–28.

Fitzgerald, H. E., Puttler, L. I., Mun, E.-Y., & Zucker, R. A. (2000). Prenatal and postnatal exposure to parental alcohol use and abuse. In J. D. Osofsky & H. E. Fitzgerald (Eds.), *WAIMH handbook of infant mental health: Vol. 4. Infant mental health in groups at high risk* (pp. 124–159). New York: Wiley.

Fitzgerald, H. E., Strommen, E. A., & McKinney, J. P. (1977). *The infant and young child*. Homewood, IL: Dorsey Press.

Fitzgerald, H. E., Zucker, R. A., & Yang, H.-Y. (1995). Developmental systems theory and alcoholism: Analyzing patterns of variation in high risk families. *Psychology of Addictive Behaviors, 11*, 49–58.

Ford, D. H., & Lerner, R. M. (1992). *Developmental systems theory: An integrative approach*. Newbury Park, CA: Sage.

Fowler, W. (1972). A developmental learning approach to infant care in a group setting. *Merrill-Palmer Quarterly, 18*, 145–175.

Freud, S. (1946). *Collected papers* (J. Strachey, Trans.) (Vols. 1, 2, & 3). London: Hogarth Press.

Galinsky, E., Howes, C., & Kontos, S. (1995). *The family child-care training study: Highlights of findings*. New York: Families and Work Institute.

Galinsky, E., Howes, C., Kontos, S., & Shinn, M. (1994). *The study of children in family child care and relative care*. New York: Families and Work Institute.

Gill, S., Greenberg, M. T., & Vazquez, A. (2002). Changes in the service delivery model and home visitors' job satisfaction in an Early Head Start. *Infant Mental Health Journal, 23*, 182–196.

Goldfarb, W. (1945). Effects of psychological privation in infancy and subsequent development. *American Journal of Psychiatry, 102*, 18–33.

Gottlieb, G. (1991). Experiential canalization of behavioral development: Theory. *Developmental Psychology, 27*, 4–13.

Greenberg, M., & Morris, N. (1974). Engrossment: The newborn's impact upon the father. *American Journal of Orthopsychiatry, 44*, 520–531.

Harms, T., & Clifford, R. (1980). *Early Childhood Environment Rating Scale*. New York: Teachers College Press.

Harms, T., & Clifford, R. (1986). *Infant-Toddler Environment Rating Scale*. Chapel Hill: Frank Porter Graham Center.

Hayes, C. D., Palmer, J. L., & Zaslow, M. J. (Eds.). (1990). *Who cares for America's children? Child care policy for the 1990s*. Washington DC: National Academy Press.

Hernandez, D. (1997, June). *Findings about the changing face of childhood: family, economics, and ethnicity*. Paper presented at the Science Writers Workshop, NIH Office of Behavioral and Social Sciences. Washington, DC: American Sociological Association.

Hewlett, B. S. (1992). Husband-wife reciprocity and the father-infant relationship among AKA pygmies. In B. S. Hewlett (Ed.), *Father-child relations: Cultural and biosocial contexts* (pp. 153–176). New York: de Gruyter.

Hofferth, S. L. (1995). Caring for children at the poverty line. *Children and Youth Services Review, 17*, 61–90.

Hoffereth, S. L. (1999). *Race/ethnic differences in father involvement with young children: A conceptual framework and empirical test in two-parent families*. Paper presented at the Urban Seminar on Fatherhood, Harvard University, Cambridge, MA.

Hoffman, J. M. (1994). The fish is in the water and the water is in the fish. *The Signal, 2*, 5–6.

Hoffman, L. W. (1974). Effects of maternal employment on the child: A review of research. *Developmental Psychology, 10*, 204–228.

Honig, A. S. (1995). Choosing child care for young children. In M. H. Bornstein (Ed.), *Handbook of parenting: Vol. 4. Applied and practical parenting* (pp. 411–436). Mahwah, NJ: Erlbaum.

Honig, A. S., & Brill, S. A. (1970, September). *A comparative analysis of the Piagetian development of twelve-year-old disadvantaged infants in an enrichment center with others not in such a center*. Paper presented at the meeting of the American Psychological Association, Miami, FL.

Honig, A. S., & Park, K. (1993). Effects of day care on preschool sex-role development. *American Journal of Orthopsychiatry, 63*, 481–486.

Horn, W. F. (2000). Fathering infants. In J. D. Osofsky & H. E. Fitzgerald (Eds.), *WAIMH handbook of infant mental health: Vol. 3. Parenting and child care* (pp. 269–298). New York: Wiley.

Hornby, H., Zeller, D., & Karraker, D. (1996). Kinship care in America: What outcomes should policy seek? *Child Welfare, LXXV*, 397–418.

Howes, C. (1988). The peer interactions of young children. *Monographs of the Society for Research in Child Development, 53*(1, Serial No. 217).

Howes, C. (1990). Can the age of entry and the quality of infant child care predict adjustment in Kindergarten? *Development Psychology, 26,* 252–303.

Howes, C., & Hamilton, C. E. (1992a). Children's relationships with caregivers: Mothers and child care teachers. *Child Development, 63,* 859–866.

Howes, C., & Hamilton, C. E. (1992b). Children's relationships with child care teachers: Stability and concordance with parental attachments. *Child Development, 63,* 867–878.

Howes, C., & Hamilton, C. E. (1993). The changing experience of child care: Changes in teachers and in teacher-child relationships and children's social competence with peers. *Early Childhood Research Quarterly, 8,* 15–32.

Howes, C., Hamilton, C. E., & Matheson, C. C. (1994). Children's relationships with peers: Differential associations with aspects of the teacher-child relationship. *Child Development, 65,* 253–263.

Howes, C., Rodning, C., Galluzzo, D. C., & Myers, L. (1988). Attachment and child care: Relationships with mother and caregiver. *Early Childhood Research Quarterly, 3,* 403–416.

Howes, C., & Smith, E. W. (1995). Children and their child care caregivers: Profiles of relationships. *Social Development, 4,* 44–61.

Ispa, J. M., Fine, M. A., & Thornberg, K. R. (2002). Maternal personality as a moderator of relations between difficult infant temperament and attachment security in low-income families. *Infant Mental Health Journal, 23,* 130–144.

Jerald, J. (2000). Early Head Start. *National Head Start Bulletin, 69,* 1–3.

Johnson, D. J. (1988). Parental racial socialization strategies of Black parents in three private schools. In D. T. Slaughter & D. J. Johnson (Eds.). Visible now: Blacks in private schools (pp. 251–267). Westport, CT: Greenwood.

Johnson, D. L., & Breckenridge, J. N. (1982). The Houston Parent-child Development Center and the primary prevention of behavior problems in young children. *American Journal of Community Psychology, 10,* 305–316.

Johnson, D. L., & Walker, T. (1987). Primary prevention of behavior problems in Mexican-American children. *American Journal of Community Psychology, 15,* 375–385.

Johnson, D. L., & Walker, T. (1991). A follow-up evaluation of the Houston Parent-Child Development Center: School performance. *Journal of Early Intervention, 15,* 226–236.

Jordan, B. (1997). Gender, politics and infant mental health. *The Signal, 3,* 12–13.

Kagan, J., Kearsley, R. B., & Zelazo, P. R. (1975). The emergence of initial apprehension to unfamiliar peers. In M. Lewis & L. Rosenblum (Eds.), *Friendship and peer relations* (pp. 187–206). New York: Wiley.

Kamerman, S. B., & Kahn, A. J. (1995). Innovations in toddler day care and family support services: An international overview. *Child Welfare, LXXIV,* 1281–1300.

Keister, M. E. (1970). *A demonstration project: Group care of infants and toddlers.* Final report submitted to the Children's Bureau, Office of Child Development. Washington, DC: U.S. Department of Health, Education, and Welfare.

Ketterlinus, R. D., Henderson, S. H., & Lamb, M. E. (1992). Les effets du type de garde de l'emploi maternel et del'estime de soi sur le comportement des enfants [The effect of type of child care and maternal employment on children's behavioral adjustment and self-esteem]. In B. Pierrrehumbert (Ed.), L'accueil du jeune enfant: Politiques et recherches dans les differents pays [Child care in infancy: Policy and research issues in different countries] (pp. 150–163). Paris: Les Editions Sociales.

Lally, R. J. (1973). The family development research program: A program for prenatal, infant, and early childhood enrichment. College for Human Development. Syracuse University, Syracuse, NY.

Lamb, M. E. (1998). Nonparental child care: Context, quality, correlates, and consequences. In I. E. Sigel & K. A. Renninger (Eds.), *Handbook of child psychology: Vol. 4. Child psychology in practice* (pp. 73–133). New York: Wiley.

Ledesma, S., Fitzgerald, H. E., & McGreal, C. E. (1980). Parent's perceptions of the infant's day care experience. *Infant Mental Health Journal, 1,* 42–55.

Lerner, J. V., & Castellino, D. R. (2002). Daycare and maternal employment in the 21st century: Conflicts and consequences for infant development. In H. E. Fitzgerald, K. Karraker, & T. Luster (Eds.), *Infant development: Ecological perspectives* (pp. 143–164). New York: Routledge.

Loukas, A., Fitzgerald, H. E., Zucker, R. A., & von Eye, A. (2001). Parental alcoholism and co-occurring antisocial behavior: Prospective relationships to externalizing behavior problems in their young sons. *Journal of Abnormal Child Psychology, 29,* 91–106.

Lucas, M.-A. (2001). The military child care connection. *The Future of Children, 11,* 129–133.

Mackey, W. C. (1996). *The American father: Biocultural and developmental aspects.* New York: Plenum Press.

Mann, T. L. (2002). Training and technical assistance for Early Head Start. *Infant Mental Health Journal, 23,* 36–47.

Martin, R. P. (1989). Activity level, distractibility and persistence: Critical characteristics in early schooling. In G. A. Kohnstamm, J. E. Bates, & M. K. Rothbart (Eds.), *Temperament in childhood* (pp. 451–461). Chichester, UK: Wiley.

Maziade, M., Caron, C., Cote, R., Boutin, P., & Thivierge, J. (1990). Extreme temperament and diagnosis. *Archives of General Psychiatry, 47,* 447–484.

Meers, D. R., & Marans, A. E. (1968). Group care of infants in other countries. In L. L. Dittmann (Ed.), *Early child care* (pp. 237–282). New York: Atherton Press.

Miller, J. G. (1978). *Living systems*. New York: McGraw-Hill.

Morelli, G. A., & Verhoef, H. (1999). Who should raise my child? A cultural approach to understanding nonmaternal child care decisions. In L. Balter & C. S. Tamis-LeMonda (Eds.), *Child psychology: A handbook of contemporary issues* (pp. 491–509). New York: Taylor and Francis.

Mun, E-Y., Fitzgerald, H. E., Puttler, L. I., Zucker, R. A., & von Eye, A. (2001). Temperamental characteristics as predictors of externalizing and internalizing child behavior problems in the contexts of high and low parental psychopathology. *Infant Mental Health Journal, 22*, 393–415.

Munroe, R. H., & Munroe, R. L. (1971). Household density and infant care in an East African society. *Journal of Social Psychology, 83*, 3–13.

National Research Council and Institute of Medicine (2000). *From Neurons to neighborhoods: The science of early childhood development* (J. P. Shonkoff & D. A. Phillips, Eds.). Washington, DC: Board on Children, Youth, and Families, Commission on Behavioral and Social Sciences and Education.

National Institute of Child Health and Human Development Early Child Care Research Network. (1994). Child care and child development: The NICHD study of early child care. In S. L. Friedman & H. C. Haywood (Eds.), *Developmental follow-up: Concepts, domains and methods* (pp. 377–396). New York: Academic Press.

National Institute of Child Health and Human Development Early Child Care Research Network. (1996). Characteristics of infant child care: Factors contributing to positive caregiving. *Early Childhood Research Quarterly, 11*, 269–306.

National Institute of Child Health and Human Development Early Child Care Research Network. (1997). Familial factors associated with the characteristics of nonmaternal care of infants. *Journal of Marriage and the Family, 59*, 389–408.

NICHD Early Child Care Research Network. (2000). Characteristics and quality of child care for toddlers and preschoolers. *Applied Developmental Science, 4*, 116–135.

Nord, C. W., & Zill, N. (1996). *Non-custodial parents' participation in their children's lives: Evidence from the Survey of Income and Program Participation* (2 vols.). Final report prepared for the office of the Assistant Secretary of Planning and Evaluation. Washington, DC: U.S. Department of Health and Human Services.

Olds, D. L. (1988). The prenatal/early infancy project. In R. H. Price (Ed.), *Fourteen ounces of prevention* (pp. 9–23). Washington, DC: American Psychological Association.

Olds, D. L., Henderson, C. R., Chamberlin, R., & Tatelbaum, R. (1986a). Preventing a child abuse and neglect: A randomized trial of nurse home visitation. *Pediatrics, 78*, 65–78.

Olds, D. L., Henderson, C. R., Tatelbaum, R., & Chamberlin, R. (1986b). Improving the delivery of prenatal care and outcomes of pregnancy: A randomized trial of nurse home visitation. *Pediatrics, 77*, 16–28.

Olds, D. L., Henderson, C. R., Tatelbaum, R., & Chamberlin, R. (1988). Improving the life-course development of socially disadvantaged mothers: A randomized trial of nurse home visitation. *American Journal of Public Health, 78*, 1436–1444.

Oppenheim, D., Sagi, A., & Lamb, M. E. (1988). Infant-adult attachments on the kibbutz and their relation to socioemotional development four years later. *Developmental Psychology, 24*, 427–433.

Osofsky, J. D., & Fenichel, E. (Eds.). (1994). *Caring for infants and toddlers in violent environments*. Arlington, VA: Zero to Three/National Center for Clinical Infant Programs.

Parke, R. D., Power, T. G., & Gottman, J. M. (1979). Conceptualization and quantifying influence patterns in the family triad. In M. E. Lamb, S. J. Suomi, & G. R. Stephenson (Eds.), *Social interaction analysis: Methodological issues* (pp. 231–253). Madison: University of Wisconsin Press.

Parke, R. D., & Sawin, D. B. (1976). The father's role in infancy: A reevaluation. *The Family Coordinator, 25*, 365–371.

Phillips, D. A. (1992). Child care and parental well-being: Bringing quality of care into the picture. In A. Booth (Ed.), *Child care in the 1990s: Trends and consequences* (pp. 172–180). Hillsdale, NJ: Erlbaum.

Phillips, D. A., & Adams, G. (2001). Child care and our youngest children. *The Future of Children, 11*, 35–52.

Phillips, D. A., Howes, C., & Whitebook, M. (1992). Child care as an adult work environment. *Journal of Social Issues, 47*, 49–70.

Phillips, D. A., Lande, J., & Goldberg, M. (1990). The state of child care regulations: A comparative analysis. *Early Child-hood Research Quarterly, 5*, 151–179.

Piaget, J. (1952). *The origins of intelligence in children*. New York: International Universities Press.

Pianta, P. C., & Nimetz, S. L. (1991). Relationship between children and teachers: Associations with classroom and home behavior. *Journal of Applied Developmental Psychology, 12*, 379–393.

Pleck, E. H., & Pleck, J. H. (1997). Fatherhood ideals in the United Sates: Historical dimensions. In M. E. Lamb (Ed.). *The role of the father in child development* (3rd ed., pp. 33–48). New York: Wiley.

Power, T. G. (1981). Sex typing in infancy: The role of the father. *Infant Mental Health Journal, 2*, 226–240.

Power, T. G., McGrath, M. P., Hughes, S. O., & Manire, S. H. (1994). Compliance and self-assertion: Young children's responses to mothers versus fathers. *Developmental Psychology, 30*, 980–989.

Ragozin, A. Z. (1980). Attachment behavior of day-care children: Naturalistic and laboratory observations. *Child Development, 511*, 409–415.

Raikes, H. (1993). Relationship duration in infant care: Time with a high ability teacher and infant-teacher attachment. *Early Childhood Research Quarterly, 8*, 309–325.

Raikes, H., Kisker, E., Paulsell, D., & Love, J. (2000). Early Head Start National Research and Evaluation project: Meeting the child care needs of families. *National Head Start Bulletin, 69*, 7–10.

Raikes, H. H., & Love, J. M. (2002). History and purpose of Early Head Start. *Infant Mental Health Journal, 23,* 1–13.

Ramey, C. T. (2000). Michigan Family Impact Seminars: Child care and education. Michigan State University, East Lansing: Institute for Children, Youth and Families.

Ramey, C. T., & Campbell, F. A. (1984). Preventive education for high-risk children: Cognitive consequences of the Carolina Abecedarian Project. *American Journal of Mental Deficiency, 88,* 515–523.

Ramey, C. T., & Campbell, F. A. (1987). The Carolina Abecedarian Project: An educational experiment concerning human malleability. In S. S. Gallagher & C. T. Ramey (Eds.), *The malleability of children* (pp. 127–139): Baltimore, Brooks.

Ramey, C. T., & Ramey, S. L. (1998). Early intervention and early experience. *American Psychologist, 58,* 109–120.

Rohner, R. P. (1998, October). Father love and child development: History and current evidence. *Current Directions in Psychological Science,* 157–161.

Robinson, H. B., & Robinson, N. M. (1971). Longitudinal development of very young children in a comprehensive day care program: The first two years. *Child Development, 42,* 1673–1684.

Robinson, J. L., & Fitzgerald, H. E. (2002). Early Head Start: Contemporary perspectives and promise. *Infant Mental Health Journal, 23,* 250–257.

Rubenstein, J. L., & Howes, C. (1979). Caregiving and infant behavior in day care an in homes. *Developmental Psychology, 15,* 1–24.

Rubenstein, J. L., Pedersen, F. A., & Yarrow, L. J. (1977). What happens when mothers are away: A comparison of mothers and substitute caregivers. *Developmental Psychology, 13,* 529–530.

Rutter, M. (1976). Parent-child separation: Psychological effects on the children. In A. M. Clarke & A. D. B. Clarke (Eds.), *Early experience: Myth and evidence* (pp. 153–186). New York: Free Press.

Rutter, M. (1979). Maternal deprivation, 1972–1978: New findings, new concepts, new approaches. *Child Development, 50,* 283–305.

Rutter, M. (1995). Maternal deprivation. In M. H. Bornstein (Ed.), *Handbook of parenting: Vol. 4. Applied and practical parenting* (pp. 3–31). Mahwah, NJ: Erlbaum.

Salmi, M. (1994). *The parental leave and day care systems in Finland.* Helsinki, Finland: National Research and Development Centre for Welfare and Health.

Sameroff, A. J. (2000). Ecological perspectives on developmental risk. In J. D. Osofsky & H. E. Fitzgerald (Eds.), *WAIMH handbook of infant mental health: Vol. 4. Infant mental health in groups at high risk* (pp. 1–34). New York: Wiley.

Scarr, S., & Eisenberg, M. (1993). Child care research: Issues, perspectives, and results. *Annual Review of Psychology, 44,* 613–644.

Scarr, S., & McCartney, K. (1983). How people make their own environments: A theory of genotype-environment effects. *Child Development, 54,* 424–435.

Shears, J., Robinson, J. L., & Emde, R. N. (2002). Fathering relationships and their associations with juvenile delinquency. *Infant Mental Health Journal, 23,* 79–87.

Singer, J. D., Fuller, B., Keiley, M. K., & Wolf, A. (1998). Early child-care selection: variation by geographic location, maternal characteristics, and family structure. *Developmental Psychology, 34,* 1129–1144.

Skeels, H. M. (1936). Mental development of children in foster homes. *Journal of Genetic Psychology, 49,* 91–106.

Smith, K. (2000). *Who's minding the kids? Child care arrangements: Fall 1995* (Current Population Reports, P 70-70). Washington, DC: U.S. Census Bureau.

Spitz, R. (1965). *The first year of life.* New York: International Universities Press.

Spitz, R. & Wolf, K. M. (1946). *Anaclitic depression: An inquiry into the genesis of psychiatric conditions in early childhood: Vol. 2. The psychoanalytic study of the child* (pp. 313–342). New York: International Universities Press.

Strelau, J. (1998). *Temperament: A psychological perspective.* New York: Plenum Press.

Summers, J. A., Raikes, H., Butler, J., Spicer, P., Pan, B., Shaw, S., Langager, M., McAllister, C., & Johnson, M. K. (1999). Low-income fathers' and mother's perceptions of the father role: A qualitative study in four Early Head Start communities. *Infant Mental Health Journal, 20,* 291–304.

Suwalsky, J. T. D., Klein, R. P., Zaslow, M. J., Rabinovich, B. A., & Gist, N. F. (1987). Dimensions of naturally occurring mother-infant separations during the first year of life. *Infant Mental Health Journal, 8,* 3–18.

Tableman, B. (2001). *Effective home visiting for very young children* (Best Practice Brief No. 17). East Lansing: Michigan State University, University Outreach Partnerships.

Thelen, E., & Smith, L. B. (1994). *A dynamic systems approach to the development of cognition and action.* Cambridge, MA: MIT Press.

Thomas, A., & Chess, S. (1977). *Temperament and development.* New York: Brunner/Mazel.

Thomas, A., & Chess, S. (1986). The New York Longitudinal Study: from infancy to early adult life. In R. Plomin & J. Dunn (Eds.), *The study of temperament: Changes, continuities, and challenges* (pp. 39–52). Hillsdale, NJ: Erlbaum.

Thomas, A., Chess, S., & Birch, H. G. (1968). *Temperament and behavior disorders in children.* New York: New York University Press.

Tronick, E. Z, Winn, S., & Morelli, G. A. (1985). Multiple caretaking in the context of human evolution: Why don't the Efe know the Western prescription for child care. In M. Reite & T. Field (Eds.), *Psychobiology of attachment* (pp. 293–322). New York: Academic Press.

van Ijzendoorn, M. H., & De Wolff M. (1997). In search of the absent father: Meta-analysis of infant-father attachment. A rejoinder to our discussants. *Child Development, 68,* 604–609.

Wagner, M. G., & Wagner, M. M. (1971). Day care programs in Denmark and Czechoslovakia. In E. H. Grotberg (Ed.), *Day care: Resources for decisions* (pp. 28–37). Washington DC: United States Public Health Service, Office of Economic Opportunity.

Werner, E. E. (1988). A cross-cultural perspective on infancy. *Journal of Cross-Cultural Psychology, 19,* 96–113.

Wilson, D. B., & Chipaungu, S. S. (Eds.). (1996) Kinship care. *Child Welfare, LSSV,* 387–662.

Windle, M. (1991). The difficult temperament in adolescence: Associations with substance use, family support, and problem behaviors. *Journal of Clinical Psychology, 47,* 310–315.

Wong, M. M., Zucker, R. A., Puttler, L. I., & Fitzgerald, H. E. (1999). Heterogeneity of risk aggregation for alcohol problems between early and middle childhood. *Development and Psychopathology, 11,* 727–744.

Young, K. R., Marsland, K. W., & Zigler, E. (1997). The regulatory status of center-based infant and toddler child care. *American Journal of Orthopsychiatry, 67,* 535–544.

Yoshikawa, H. (1994). Prevention as cumulative protection: Effects of early family support and education on chronic delinquency and its risks. *Psychological Bulletin, 115,* 28–54.

Yoshikawa, H. (1995). Long term effects of early childhood programs on social outcomes and delinquency. *The Future of Children, 5,* 51–75.

Yogman, M. W. (1982). Development of the father-infant relationship. In H. E. Fitzgerald, B. M. Lester, & M. W. Yogman (Eds.), *Theory and research in behavioral pediatrics* (pp. 221–279). New York: Garland Press.

Zucker, R. A., Fitzgerald, H. E., Refior, S. K., Puttler, L. I., Pallas, D. M., & Ellis, D. A. (2000). The clinical and social ecology of children of alcoholics: Description of a study and implications for a differentiated social policy. In H. E. Fitzgerald, B. M. Lester, & B. S. Zuckerman (Eds.), *Children of addiction: Research, health and policy issues* (pp. 109–141). New York: Garland Press.

Zukow-Goldring, P. (1995). Sibling caregiving. In. M. H. Bornstein (Ed.), *Handbook of parenting: Vol. 3. Status and social conditions of parenting* (pp. 177–208). Mahwah, NJ: Erlbaum.

PART THREE

CHILDHOOD

CHAPTER 7

Language Development in Childhood

ERIKA HOFF

Somehow in the span of just a few years, newborn infants who neither speak nor understand any language become young children who comment, question, and express their ideas in the language of their community. The transition from the stage of the prelinguistic infant to the linguistically competent 4-year-old follows a predictable developmental course. First, newborns' cries give way to coos and babbles. Then, infants who coo and babble start to show signs of comprehension such as turning when they hear their name. Infants then become toddlers who say *bye-bye* and *all gone* and start to label the people and objects in their environment. As their vocabularies continue to grow, children start to combine words. Children's first word combinations, such as

all gone juice and *read me,* are short and lack parts found in adults' sentences. Gradually, children's immature sentences are replaced by longer and more adult-like sentences. As children master language, they also become masters at using language to serve their needs. One-year-olds, who can only point and fuss to request something, become 2-year-olds who say *please;* later they become 4-year-olds capable of the linguistic and communicative sophistication of the child who excused himself from a boring experiment by saying, "My mother says I have to go home now" (Keller-Cohen, January 1978, personal communication).

This course that language development follows is the result of concurrent processes of development in the several domains that together constitute adult knowledge of language. In acquiring language, children master a system for combining sounds into units of meaning (phonology) and a system for combining units of meaning into well-formed

The author is grateful to the editors and to Iris Berent for comments on earlier versions of this chapter.

words and sentences (morphology and syntax). Together these systems constitute the grammar of language. In addition to grammar, a speaker-hearer of a language has acquired a lexicon—a repository of words with their meanings and grammatical categories. Normally, speaker-hearers of a language use that language to communicate. Thus, adult-like language competence includes pragmatic or communicative competence as well as knowledge of a grammar and lexicon. The goal of this chapter is to describe the current state of the scientific effort to explain how these changes take place and how children end up knowing a language. The content of this chapter is not a description of language development; those are readily available elsewhere (e.g., Hoff, 2001). Rather, this chapter provides a description of the field that takes language development as its topic of study.

This description focuses on research that seeks to describe the nature of the mental capacity that underlies the human ability to acquire language. The fact that language acquisition occurs in a range of social and cultural environments is relevant to constructing such a description, and research aimed at identifying the necessary social conditions for language acquisition to occur is reviewed. A more complete consideration of how culture influences language development falls under the heading of language socialization, that is, the process by which children come to use language in the manner of their social or cultural group. That topic is touched on only briefly in this chapter; in-depth treatments can be found in Ochs and Schieffelin (1979), Schieffelin and Ochs (1986), and Slobin, Gerhardt, Kyratzis, and Guo (1996).

The Question to Which Research on Language Development Is Addressed

The study of language development is marked by serious disagreement with respect to both what the correct explanation of language development will look like and how best to discover that explanation. There is, however, an abstract level at which all researchers in the field are trying to answer the same question: What is the nature of the human capacity to acquire language? This question can be conceptualized in the following manner: The human capacity for language is a device residing in the human brain that takes as its input certain information from the environment and produces as its output the ability to speak and understand a language. Everything that is part of adults' knowledge of language (i.e., the output of the device) must either be in the input, be in the internal device, or somehow result from the way the device operates on the input it receives (see Figure 7.1).

Noam Chomsky (1965) termed this capacity the Language Acquisition Device (LAD), and this particular way of posing

Figure 7.1 A model for studying the nature of the human capacity to acquire language.

the question still tends to be made explicit only by those taking a generative grammar approach to the study of language acquisition. However, this conceptualization makes clear two criteria that must apply to all candidate explanations of how children learn to talk. To wit, any proposed account of the language acquisition process must be consistent with two sets of facts: (a) the input that children receive and (b) the competence that they acquire. It is obvious that language acquisition makes use of input because children quite reliably acquire the particular language to which they are exposed. Yet it is not at all clear—and a matter of great dispute—whether input provides sufficient information to explain how children end up knowing what all adult speakers know. It is also clear that what children acquire is knowledge of a productive system because adults can and do understand and produce sentences that they have never heard before. Just how best to characterize that system is also a topic of dispute. As we review the current work in the study of language development, we will see the sometimes stark differences in the views of input and ultimate competence that guide research in this area. These differing views crucially affect the nature of the debate regarding how language is acquired because the problem of explaining acquisition is different depending on the nature of the input and the nature of what is acquired.

Theoretical Approaches to Discovering How Language Is Acquired

Current research on language development can be usefully organized as being motivated by four different premises regarding the nature of the LAD and the language development it produces. One such premise is that the human capacity for language is best understood as a biological phenomenon and language development as a biological process. This leads to research investigating the degree to which language and language development share the hallmark features of other biological processes, such as universality and heritability, and to the study of the anatomical structures and physiological processes that underlie language development. A second premise, which guides other research in the field, is that language acquisition is best understood and studied as a linguistic phenomenon. On this view, the LAD is essentially a linguistic device. This approach starts with a description of the linguistic competence of adults and seeks an account of the acquisition process that is adequate to explain how that end point is reached. This approach is often referred to as the *learnability approach* because its focus is on explaining how it is that language is learnable. The biological and linguistic approaches share the view that language is innate. For the biological approach, innateness is part of the package—something that is part of human biology is, by definition, innate. For the linguistic approach, innateness is a quickly reached conclusion from the following line of reasoning: The complex, abstract system that is adult linguistic competence simply could not be arrived at by any general learning mechanism operating over the input that children receive. The solution to this problem, known as the logical problem of language acquisition (C. L. Baker & McCarthy, 1981), is to propose that substantial language-specific knowledge and language-specific learning mechanisms are part of the equipment that children bring to the language-learning task. The charge for research is to describe that innate knowledge (Crain, 1991).

There are alternative approaches that resist attributing innate linguistic knowledge to the child and that seek a description of how children could learn language from experience using learning mechanisms that are not specific to language. The chasm between the learnability approach and the developmental approach is such that even labeling the field carries implications of allegiance to one view or the other. The term "language acquistion" is most associated with the learnability approach; the terms "language development" and "child language" are most associated with the developmental approach. Research within this *developmental approach*, as it is termed, begins not with the end point of development, but rather with the starting point—the child's demonstrated competencies. Such work seeks to explain not the fact that language is acquired but the developmental course that language learning follows. Within the developmental approach, two different lines of argument and research exist. One starts from the premise that language is essentially a social phenomenon and that language development is a social process. Such research focuses on social aspects of interaction as the experience relevant to language acquisition and on the social-cognitive abilities of the child as the relevant learning capacities. The other starts from the premise that language acquisition is essentially an asocial learning problem that children solve in the same way they solve other learning problems. Research in this vein seeks an account of how language might be learned by the child's application of domain-general cognitive processes to information available in input.

The goal of this chapter is to present each of these four approaches: the biological, the linguistic, the social, and the domain-general cognitive. None of these presentations is comprehensive. Rather, for each approach the aim is to illustrate the nature of the research and theoretical argument it generates and to evaluate its contribution to explaining how children learn to talk.

LANGUAGE DEVELOPMENT AS A BIOLOGICAL PROCESS

If we begin with the premise that the LAD is a biological entity and its operation a biological process, we are led to investigate the degree to which language acquisition shares hallmark features of other biological processes and to investigate how the anatomical structures and physiological processes that accomplish language acquisition actually do their work. The hallmark features of biologically based characteristics include species universality and species specificity, an invariant course of development that is robust over varying environmental circumstances, a critical period for development, heritability, and an adaptive function that explains its evolution as a characteristic of the species. To the extent that human language and language acquisition meet these criteria, language and the capacity for language acquisition would seem to be part of human biology. That is to say, language would appear to be innate.

The Species Universality and Species Specificity of Language

All humans have language, and no other species has a communication system that shares all the features of human language. In addition, in the absence of a language to learn, humans will create one. For example, it has been widely observed that deaf children in hearing families invent systems of signs with which to communicate. These systems have the equivalent of syntax and morphology and a lexicon in which different words belong to different grammatical categories, and the system as a whole is used for the same sort of purposes as are established languages, thus demonstrating the basic features of all human languages. Because children invented rather than learned these home sign systems, it is argued that these features reflect components of language that are built into the human mind (Goldin-Meadow, 1997).

Other evidence similarly suggests that the necessary and sufficient ingredients for language creation are the opportunity for communication with others and a human mind—particularly a child's mind. Although socially isolated children do not invent languages (Shatz, 1994), whenever people come together, language emerges. Pidgins are languages that emerge when circumstance puts together people who share no common language. Pidgins tend to be morphologically simple languages, lacking markers of subject-verb agreement, tense, and so on. With time, and with the birth of children who acquire these pidgins as their native language, the pidgins evolve into creoles, which have more elaborate grammatical morphology. It has been argued—although not universally accepted (e.g., Jourdan, 1991)—that children play a crucial role in the process of creolization and that the structural similarities among creole languages with independent origins suggest the work of the human capacity that is normally put to language acquisition, but which in the absence of a full-blown language to learn, reveals itself as the human capacity for language creation (Bickerton, 1984, 1988).

More recent evidence for the human capacity—and particularly the human child's capacity—to create language comes from the study of Nicaraguan Sign Language (NSL). This language has emerged in just the last 25 years, following the opening of the first public schools for the deaf in Nicaragua in 1978. When they entered the school, the deaf children typically had only their own idiosyncratic home sign systems and no shared language, but in the school setting a new sign language began to develop. Studies of changes in this language over time reveal that the language has moved from a structurally simpler language to a structurally more complex language (Senghas, 1995, 2000). It also appears that the differences in structural complexity show primarily in the signing of those who begin to learn the language at an early age. For example, the early form of NSL contained few verb inflections; the more recent form has such devices for marking subject-verb agreement. It is particularly those individuals who were exposed to the language at an early age that produce the verb inflections that distinguish the newer from the older form. Older learners of the newer form of the language do not master the verb inflections. Such results suggest that the changes that have occurred in NSL over time depend on young children acquiring the language. In sum, not only is language universal in the species, but the nature of the human mind ensures that wherever there are humans, there will be language. Children seem to play a unique role in creating languages with the complex grammatical systems that characterize fully developed languages. We return to this potentially special role of children when we discuss the critical period hypothesis.

The other side of the species-universality coin is species specificity. The literature on species specificity is large and messy, and there is not the space to adequately review it here. Suffice it to say that neither examination of the naturally occurring communicative systems of other species nor the several attempts to teach a language to another species have found human-like language capacities outside the human mind. The criterion on which most other systems and the most nearly successful training efforts clearly fail is syntax (Kako, 1999; Tomasello, 1994). It has also been suggested that other animals, specifically chimpanzees, lack the social interest in other members of their species that a human-like communication system requires for both invention and acquisition (Premack, 1986; Tomasello, Call, Nagell, Olguin, & Carpenter, 1994).

The Invariance and Robustness of Language Development

All normal children in anything remotely like a normal environment learn to talk. Furthermore, the course of language development is, in broad outline, constant across varying environments. These basic facts suggest to many a maturational process, the course and timing of which is determined by the unfolding of a genetic blueprint (Gilger, 1996; Gleitman, 1981). On the other hand, it could be that the universal acquisition of language is the result of universal features of human environments. A review of the literatures that describe the varied social environments in which children learn to talk suggests that all environments provide two sources of support for language acquisition: They show children that language is used to communicate with other people, and they deliver to children, through speech, data that the children use to figure out the underlying linguistic system (Lieven, 1994). Furthermore, there are differences in the rate and course of language development associated with differences in how children's environments provide these two sources of support and in how much speech children hear. For example, in some environments children are talked to directly from birth; in others children observe and overhear conversations among others but are not engaged participants from an early age. This difference has consequences for language development. Children who are not directly talked to appear particularly precocious in the development of skills for joining the ongoing conversations of others (Bernicot & Roux, 1998; Dunn & Shatz, 1989; Hoff-Ginsberg, 1998). Children whose data is in the form of speech among others appear to begin talking by producing rote-learned chunks of speech, and they only later analyze these chunks into their structural and lexical components. Children who hear more speech addressed directly to them rely less on memorized but unanalyzed wholes (Lieven, 1994). These are effects on the style or course of language development. There are also effects on rate. Although it appears to matter more for lexical development than for grammatical development, children who hear more data develop language more rapidly than do children exposed to fewer data (Hart &

Risley, 1995; Hoff & Naigles, 2002; Huttenlocher, Haight, Bryk, Seltzer, & Lyons, 1991). These demonstrated effects of the nature and amount of environmental support for language acquisition make it clear that the process of language acquisition is not solely a maturational process and, therefore, that linguistic innateness by itself is not sufficient as an explanation.

The Heritability of Language

Among children who acquire language normally, there are individual differences in the rate of language acquisition, and some children acquire language quite slowly and with difficulty. Although some of these individual differences can be attributed to differences in experience, there is also evidence that both normal individual differences and some cases of language impairment have a genetic basis. Twin studies that have looked at children past the age of 3 years using standardized tests of children's verbal IQ, vocabulary, and reading ability find that about 50% of the variance among children on these measures can be attributed to genetics (Stromswold, 2001). Receptive and expressive language skills up to 24 months of age show lower heritability—between 1% and 38% of the variance, depending on the measure (Reznick, Corley, & Robinson, 1997). Ganger, Pinker, Chawla, and Baker (2002) used the twin study method to assess the heritability of individual differences in the timing of the achievement of two milestones of language development: the achievement of a 25-word productive vocabulary and the production of first word combinations. They found, as did earlier studies, that the heritability of vocabulary was low. In this study, 11% of the variance was attributable to genetics. In stark contrast, they found that the timing of syntactic development was highly heritable—82% of the variance was attributable to genetics. A larger scale twin study also found that the heritability of grammatical development was higher than the heritability of lexical development, although that study found lower heritability of grammatical development (39%) and higher heritability of lexical development (25%; Dale, Dionne, Eley, & Plomin, 2000).

Evidence of environmental effects on language development provides converging evidence for the greater heritability of grammatical than of lexical development. Hoff-Ginsberg (1998) found grammar to be minimally susceptible to environmental influence and vocabulary development more so. The method of studying the influence of the environment was, in this case, to investigate the effects of family socioeconomic status (SES) and birth order on language development. It is well established that children in high-SES families hear more speech than do children in middle-SES families (Hoff, Laursen, & Tardif, 2002), and it

is reasonable to assume that firstborn children have more opportunity for one-to-one speech than later born children. Thus, these two variables serve as proxies for language experience. Vocabulary development was strongly affected by both birth order and family SES, with firstborn children and children from high-SES families showing larger vocabularies; grammatical development was affected only by birth order, again with firstborns showing more advanced language (Hoff-Ginsberg, 1998). It appears that grammatical development, more than lexical development, may be the result of the unfolding of a genetic blueprint; vocabulary development is more paced by environmental factors.

Evidence that impairment of the normal ability to acquire language has a genetic basis includes findings that language impairment runs in families, that monozygotic twins are more likely to be concordant for language disorders than are dizygotic twins, and that adopted children with language-impaired biological relatives are more likely to be language impaired than are adopted children with no language impairment among their biological relatives (Eley et al., 1999; Stromswold, 1998). In one well-studied family, 16 out of 30 family members were seriously language impaired, and the inheritance patterns suggest that a single dominant gene is responsible (Gopnik & Crago, 1991).

In sum, although it is clear that differences in the environments that children experience contribute to the observed individual differences in language development, work on the genetics of language development makes a strong case for a genetic contribution as well—both within the normal range of variation and, even more so, in cases of atypical development. Syntax seems to fit the biological model of language better than other aspects of language development do. Although this work establishes that there is something genetically based that determines the pace of syntactic development, it does not clearly reveal what that something is—nor how domain specific it is. We know the LAD is a biological entity, but we still do not know how it works.

The Neurological Underpinnings of Language and Language Development

In making the argument that language is innate, Chomsky has referred to a *language organ* in the brain. If there is such a thing, it would seem to be located in the left cerebral hemisphere. It has been known since the nineteenth century that damage to the left side of the brain disturbs language functions, whereas damage to the right side typically does not. This is true even for deaf signers. Although the right hemisphere is primarily responsible for processing visual-spatial information, if that information is linguistic information, it is handled predominantly by the left hemisphere. A wealth of other sources of data also suggests that language is predominantly a left-hemisphere function. Patients with a split corpus callosum can label objects put in their right hand or presented to their right visual field, but they cannot label objects in their left hand or left visual field (e.g., Gazzaniga, 1983). Dichotic listening tests with normal, intact adults show a consistent right-ear advantage for speech stimuli (Springer & Deutsch, 1981). Research that uses scalp electrodes to measure event-related potentials or brain imaging techniques to measure cortical activity also has found greater left-hemisphere activity associated with language processing (e.g., Mazziotta & Metter, 1988). There are, however, some problems with drawing the conclusion that the language organ resides in the left cerebral hemisphere. Other parts of the brain also contribute to language processing. Patients with right-hemisphere damage have difficulty understanding jokes, sarcasm, figurative language, and indirect requests (Weylman, Brownell, & Gardner, 1988). They have difficulty understanding linguistic units that have more than one meaning, and they fail to use broad contextual information in the interpretation of connected discourse (Chiarello, 1991).

The literature provides a couple of suggestions for describing the contributions of the right and left hemispheres to language. Studies of event-related potentials in intact patients show that the right hemisphere is activated by semantic processing, whereas the left is activated primarily by syntax processing (Neville, Nicol, Barss, Forster, & Garrett, 1991). Studies of the language abilities of patients who have had their left hemispheres entirely removed (because of severe pathology) similarly suggest that the right hemisphere can support many language functions but that the left hemisphere is necessary for normal syntax. Together, the findings suggest that for adults the right hemisphere is involved in semantics and pragmatics but that syntax is the province of the left hemisphere. The story becomes a little more complicated if we look at children. The right hemisphere seems to be more important for language acquisition than for language processing once language is acquired. If brain damage is suffered in infancy, prior to language acquisition, right-hemisphere damage is more detrimental to future language acquisition than is left-hemisphere damage (Stiles, Bates, Thal, Trauner, & Reilly, 1998). Another difficulty with concluding that the left hemisphere is the language organ is that although the left hemisphere is primarily responsible for language, it is not necessarily dedicated specifically to language. It has been suggested that the left hemisphere is specialized for executing well-practiced routines (see Mills, Coffey-Corina, & Neville, 1997). The finding that experienced musicians show a right-ear (i.e., left hemisphere) advantage for music stimuli, whereas naive listeners show a left-ear (i.e., right hemi-

sphere) advantage for music stimuli (Bever & Chiarello, 1974) is consistent with this hypothesis. There is additional evidence that the relation between brain localization and language has to do with practice in the findings from children and adults that the neural representation of a bilingual's two languages differ as a function of language proficiency (Conboy & Mills, 2001; Perani et al., 1998).

The Critical Period Hypothesis

Many examples of species-specific, biologically based learnings have the characteristic that the learning must occur during a biologically determined window if the learning is to be successful. Thus, regarding language development as a biological phenomenon suggests the hypothesis that there is a critical period for language acquisition. Seemingly, supportive evidence is obvious and widely available. When families immigrate to a new language community, it is commonly and reliably observed that the young children in the family acquire the new language well and eventually are indistinguishable from native speakers. Older children and adults acquire the language less well, and they typically never achieve native-like proficiency. Young children recover from aphasia following brain damage more rapidly and more nearly completely than do older children and adults. There is also the case of "Genie," a child who was kept isolated and thus deprived of language until the age of 13 (Curtiss, 1977). Despite both exposure and training after her discovery, Genie never achieved normal language. Finally, there appear to be differences in how and where the brain processes language depending on the age at which the language is acquired (Kim, Relkin, Lee, & Hirsch, 1997; Weber-Fox & Neville, 1996), although differences in proficiency may be an alternative explanation. If such phenomena have a biological explanation, it should be found in some biological event. Puberty is often proposed as that event: The hypothesis is that the onset of puberty closes the window on the period during which the brain is best able to acquire language.

Not all the data fit that hypothesis. First, the advantage of being young is seen only in the level of ultimate language achievement. Older learners actually make more rapid progress than do younger learners during the first year in a new language community—provided that the opportunities are roughly equal (Snow & Hoefnagel-Hohle, 1978). Second, the advantage of younger second-language learners over older second-language learners in ultimately achieving native-like competence does not abruptly end at puberty but continues past age 20 (Birdsong, 1999). Finally, that advantage may not be so much a function of differences between younger and older brains as much as it is a function of differences between the experiences of younger and older arrivals in the new language community. Children attend school in the new language, whereas adults must do work that their limited language skills allow, thus limiting their exposure to the new language. Additionally, older children and adults have stronger first-language skills and are more likely to continue to read material in their first language than are young children. A study of Chinese immigrants to New York City found that younger children were more exposed to English than were older children during their first year in the United States, and by the end of the year Chinese was no longer preferred over and dominant relative to English for those younger children. The older children, in contrast, were exposed to English less, and at the end of their first year their preferred and dominant language was still Chinese (Jia & Aaronson, 1999). This provides an alternative explanation for why the younger children's English proficiency was greater than that of the older children.

Although the data on second-language acquisition seem to provide less conclusive support for the critical period hypothesis on close examination than they do at first blush, other evidence remains. Recovery from aphasia is better at younger ages, and children have made unique contributions to the process of grammatical expansion in NSL. As long as these data hold, it does seem to be the case that maturation affects the way the brain acquires language. However, the strongest sort of critical period hypothesis—that the window of opportunity for language acquisition is shut by a single biological event—is not supported. This is not necessarily telling evidence against the claim that language is biologically based. First, puberty is not a single, well-defined biological event. Second, there is evidence that even in the animal world, biology alone does not determine when biologically prepared learning can occur. In songbirds, for example, access to social interaction, as opposed to mere exposure to mature song, extends the sensitive period for song learning (Nelson, 1997).

Language as an Evolved Adaptation

Consonant with the hypothesis that the capacity for language is domain specific and modular, it has been proposed that this capacity was selected for in the course of human evolution to serve its particular function. According to this view, humans have language because having language gave some of our hominid ancestors an advantage in survival and reproduction over those who did not have language (Bloom, 1998; Pinker & Bloom, 1990). This view puts language in the same category as upright posture and bipedal locomotion as evolutionary achievements writ into the human DNA. Further

arguments have been made for why language would have been useful and why language evolved to have the particular structure that it does. With respect to the value of language, it has been argued that language is useful to humans because of humans' unique social characteristics. Language is useful only to a species whose members are interested in communicating with each other, and a system as complex as human language is more useful than calls and hoots only if the interacting members of the species are interested in exchanges of information more complex than food locations and predator warnings. With respect to why language has its particular structure, it has been argued that this level of complexity is necessary for exchanges of the sort of information that is important for human survival. For example, a mechanism for embedding one clause in another is necessary to communicate the distinction between a region that has animals you can eat and a region that has animals that can eat you (Pinker, 1994). There are also arguments for how the anatomical changes that accompanied upright posture, namely the lowering of the larynx in the throat, gave rise to some of the structural features of human language (Carstairs-McCarthy, 1999).

There is no contrary argument that the human capacity for language is not part of human nature, acquired in the course of human evolution. Rather, the argument has to do with domain specificity. One contrary argument is that language evolved as a result of quantitative changes in several preexisting mental abilities (Bates, Thal, & Marchman, 1991; Lieberman, 1975). That is, the human capacity for language is a "new machine built out of old parts" (Bates et al., 1991, p. 35). Another contrary argument is that language is a by-product of general increases in the computational power of the brain—language is just one more thing that humans do with their great intelligence (Chomsky, 1982; Gould & Lewontin, 1979).

Summary and Conclusions

If we ask to what degree language development demonstrates hallmark features of a biological process, we are led to conclude that language is an intrinsic part of human nature. Just what makes language so, however, is unclear. Language is certainly universal in the species and is species specific, but the rate and course of language acquisition are paced and shaped to a significant degree by environmental influence. Among the several components of language, grammar seems most robust—the rate of development is most heritable, and environmental effects are correspondingly weaker. Vocabulary development appears to be very influenced by access to input. Additional support for the notion that grammar is what is really biologically based about language comes from neurolinguistic research. When we look for a dedicated language organ, we find the left hemisphere carrying out the grammatical functions of language. Meaning and use appear to be less isolable functions. Most of the data that address the critical period hypothesis are inconclusive. If there is a critical period, its boundaries are fuzzy and the mechanism unclear. Yet there does seem to be an advantage to having a left hemisphere available to take on language functions, and the availability of the left hemisphere may decline with age. Furthermore, even accepting the conclusion that grammar is a biologically based human capacity that resides in the left cerebral hemisphere does not quite answer the question about the nature of that capacity. It is possible that the capacity is dedicated specifically to language. The data also fit an account in which the left hemisphere is particularly good at the kind of processing that grammar requires. Finally, the biologically based characteristics of humans on which the human capacity for language depends seem also to include the social nature of humans—although social influences are not typically included in biological models. Language is created or acquired only when there is the opportunity for interaction with other humans. This is not to say that language is entirely a social process—that issue will be taken up in later sections—but that the social nature of humans is a necessary ingredient.

LANGUAGE DEVELOPMENT AS A LINGUISTIC PROCESS

If one starts from the premises that (a) all adults have knowledge of a complex, abstract, formal system that is what allows them to be competent speaker-hearers of a language and that (b) the information available in input and the learning mechanisms available to children are inadequate for achieving that system from an initial state of no linguistic knowledge, one is led to the inescapable conclusion that linguistic knowledge must be innate. This is basically the worldview of the generative grammar approach to language acquisition.

The task for research, then, is to describe just what is innate. This enterprise is led by linguistic analysis of the end state of language acquisition. The resultant description of linguistic knowledge, that is, Universal Grammar (UG), is then attributed wholesale to the child. Two explanatory problems remain, however. One is that children acquire different languages, depending on the language they hear, and accommodating that fact requires some mechanism that allows children to acquire the particular language to which they are exposed. The other is that young children do not demonstrate

the competence that they are posited to possess, requiring some explanation for apparent developmental change.

Universal Grammar

To handle the first problem, UG allows options. It consists of a set of principles that are true for all languages and a set of parameters on which languages vary. For example, in some languages, such as English, sentence subjects must be expressed, whereas in other languages, such as Spanish, they need not be. In Spanish, one can say the equivalent of *Goes to school* whereas in English it would be necessary to say *He goes to school*. Languages that allow pro-drop, as it is called, also allow sentences that are the equivalent of *Raining* whereas in English one would need to say *It's raining*. Because some languages allow pro-drop and others do not, this is a parameter in UG that children must set on the basis of their language experience. The argument is that children learning English must hear sentences such as *It's raining*, and then use that input to set the pro-drop parameter. Less work has been done in applying a universal phonological theory to acquisition, but the structure of the problem is the same: There exists a set of universal rules (in the standard theory) or constraints (in the more recent optimality theory; see Bernhardt & Stemberger, 1998). The function of these rules or constraints is to mediate between the underlying representations of words and the surface form of words, just as syntax mediates between the underlying representation of sentences and the surface form of sentences. As it does for syntax, the linguistic approach assumes that rules or constraints cannot be learned from input. Language variation is handled by positing that a universal set of rules or constraints is provided innately, and children use input to learn which rules apply or to set the rankings of the constraints (Bernhardt & Stemberger, 1998).

This approach has encountered both theoretical and empirical problems. As linguistic theories both Principles and Parameter Theory and Optimality Theory are still in development. As a theory of acquisition, Optimality Theory has been too little tested to judge, as work in this area has only just begun (e.g., Dinnesen & O'Connor, 2001). Work applying Principles and Parameters Theory to explaining the acquisition of syntax has longer tradition, and, thus far, the proposal that children use input to set parameters has not found empirical support in data on language acquisition (Maratsos, 1998). Although future work in linguistic theory may prove more successful at describing language in terms of parametric variation and ranked constraints, Maratsos (1998) pointed out that there is a problem, in principle, with the attendant acquisition theory. The notion that a single instance of input would serve as a trigger for parameter setting requires that input be error free, and it certainly is not. Furthermore, a parameter-setting approach in which the role of input is merely that of a trigger predicts that the amount of input should not matter a great deal to the acquisition of any parameterized aspect of language. Contrary to this prediction, there is evidence that a component of grammatical knowledge that is held to be part of UG, *that*-trace phenomena, is acquired earlier by children with more language experience and later by children with less (Gathercole, 2002). There may also be a solution to this problem if parameter setting is not accomplished on the basis of a single instance of input, but requires an accumulation of evidence. This, however, would be a very different sort of model than the current Principles and Parameters theory.

Turning to the problem of apparent developmental change, we find that two solutions have been proposed. One begins with the Continuity Hypothesis (Pinker, 1984), according to which all of UG is in the child's grammar from the beginning. This requires explaining differences between children's and adults' grammatical performance in terms of factors other than knowledge of the grammar. Lack of lexical or pragmatic knowledge or processing limitations that interfere with performance are often invoked. The other proposed solution is the Maturation Hypothesis, according to which some elements of UG become available only later in development. Like permanent teeth and secondary sexual characteristics, these elements of grammar are provided innately, but they are not manifest until their developmental time arrives (Wexler, 1999).

This manner of reasoning and the research it generates can be illustrated with respect to one of the principles of UG. Among the principles of UG is a set of principles called binding principles, which deal with the relations between elements in a sentence. Binding Principle B pertains to how pronouns are related to nouns. Stated formally, Principle B says that personal pronouns must not be coindexed with a c-commanding noun phrase (NP) in the local domain. C-commanding within the local domain refers to a particular structural relationship between parts of a sentence. What Principle B means is that pronouns such as *he* and *her* cannot refer to a noun that is in the same part of the sentence structure as the pronoun. In the sentence *Grover is patting him, him* cannot mean *Grover.* (This is in contrast to Principle A, which applies to reflexives, with the consequence that in *Grover is patting himself, himself* must refer to Grover.)

The reason that Principle B has generated so much research is that children disobey this principle up to a very advanced age—even at 8 years—and well after they demonstrate knowledge of Principle A (Thorton & Wexler, 1999).

This late adherence to a basic principle of UG contradicts both the basic premise of the UG approach, that universal principles are provided innately, and the Continuity Hypothesis, that all of UG is available from the beginning. In fact, many possible explanations of children's seeming ignorance of Principle B are problematic for the UG view. For example, one explanation is to say that Principle B is not innate after all but must be learned from experience and that the learning process takes time. The UG view rejects this explanation and in general rejects learning sorts of accounts of developmental change on the grounds that there is no way for input to give children the information they need to arrive at Principle B. That is because Principle B, like the other principles of UG, makes reference to notions like binding and c-command, and there is no way for children to get such abstract notions from input (Chien & Wexler, 1990). This is an example of how the formal description of grammatical knowledge defines the acquisition problem differently than another sort of description of grammatical knowledge might.

Another possible explanation of children's late adherence to Principle B is to reject the Continuity Hypothesis but save UG and assert that Principle B simply matures late. The problem with this is that the whole theory requires that Principle B be on line early in order to play a necessary role in guiding other learning (Chien & Wexler, 1990). There have also been a variety of proposals regarding other factors that might interfere with children's demonstrating knowledge of Principle B. It could be that the processing demands of the task make it difficult for children to apply their grammatical knowledge or mislead the children in some way so that children's poor performance is a function of the task, not a lack of knowledge (Grimshaw & Rosen, 1990; Grodzinsky & Reinhart, 1993). Alternatively, it could be that children lack the pragmatic knowledge to recognize when Principle B applies.

The argument that children do know Principle B but violate it for extragrammatical reasons comes from studies in which children demonstrate that they do adhere to Principle B under some circumstances, but not others. For example, if the children interpret a sentence such as *The cow is scratching her* to mean the cow is scratching herself because of ignorance of Principle B, then they also should interpret *Every cow is scratching her* to mean many cows are all scratching themselves. Children do not do that, however. This suggests that the interpretation of the first sentence is not the result of ignorance of Principle B, but the result of some other lack of understanding. There are circumstances in which Principle B does not apply. In the sentence, *She's wearing Alissa's clothes,* Principle B requires that *she* not be *Alissa*. However, if the circumstance is that someone who looks a great deal like Alissa but who has a different haircut walks by and the identity of this person is the topic of conversation, it is possible that *she* does mean *Alissa* in the second sentence in the following sequence: *She must be Alissa; she's wearing Alissa's clothes.* One argument for why relatively old children disobey Principle B is that they have experienced exceptions such as this and they do not know that it is an exception allowed only in certain pragmatic contexts. By this account it is a lack of pragmatic understanding, not a lack of grammatical knowledge, that leads to Principle B violations.

At present there are several proposals for how best to explain the seeming late mastery of Principle B. Resolving the issue is not crucial for the present purpose because the aim of the foregoing summary of work on Principle B was not to explain why 6-year-olds sometimes interpret *Grover is patting him* to mean that Grover is patting himself. Rather, the purpose was to illustrate the kind of research and argument that the UG view of language acquisition generates. Although there is disagreement within the UG approach as to how to explain apparent developmental change, there is consistent agreement with the basic premise that UG must be innate.

The work on Principle B is an example of research within the UG approach that makes very little contact with other approaches to language development. Although a great deal of UG work is of this sort, there are some questions that have been tackled by both UG and other approaches to the study of children's language. Several studies have found that before the age of 3 years children do not use the verbs they know in all their possible syntactic and morphological environments (Bloom, Lifter, & Hafitz, 1980; Tomasello, 1992; Valian, 1991). It is a challenge to the claims of the UG approach that children, who are asserted to have complete knowledge of the grammar, produce only a subset of the constructions the grammar allows. The UG explanation is that performance factors impede the expression of the underlying competence. For example, Valian (1991) (Study 5) found that early in development children produce few verbs with direct objects but that the proportion of verbs used with a direct object increases from $1^1/_2$ to 3 years. Valian (1991) interpreted the effect of age as evidence of the role of capacity limitations. Her argument was that the syntactic knowledge underlying the production of direct objects is there from the beginning, but for very young children it is too cognitively demanding for children to actually produce such sentences. As processing capacity increases with age, such performance constraints lessen. We consider an alternative account of these data in the next section.

Innate Lexical Constraints

There is also a learnability approach to lexical development. It begins, like the argument for innate grammar, with an assertion of the impossibility of learning. This assertion was famously made by the philosopher Quine (1960) and is known as the *Gavagai problem.* Imagine that you are a linguist studying a newly discovered tribe. A rabbit runs across the field, and a tribesman shouts *Gavagai.* How do you decide what *Gavagai* means? It could mean "running thing," "whiteness," "furriness," "dinner if we're lucky," "animal," "mammal," or even "rabbit." The point is that in principle, the possible meanings are infinite. Despite this problem, children are good at learning words. By the time children are 6 years old they have vocabularies of up to 14,000 words. Assuming that word learning begins at about 12 months, that works out to a word learning pace of nearly eight words per day. Furthermore, experimental work has demonstrated that very few exposures to a novel term are sufficient for children to form at least a partial entry in their mental lexicons (Dolloghan, 1985; Woodward, Markman, & Fitzsimmons, 1994). Thus, somehow, the infinite possible meanings of a new word in context that bothered Quine do not bother young, language-learning children.

To solve the problem of how children arrive at meanings readily, when the environment does not clearly indicate those meanings, it has been proposed that children come to the word learning task with innate constraints on the kinds of hypotheses they consider. A great deal of research has been aimed at discovering just what those constraints are. One constraint or principle that appears to guide children's inferences about the meanings of newly encountered words is the whole-object principle. This leads children to assume that words refer to whole objects rather than to a part or property of an object. This eliminates "whiteness" and "furriness" as possible meanings of *Gavagai.* The existence of such an assumption is supported both by evidence from word-learning experiments (Markman & Wachtel, 1988; Taylor & Gelman, 1988; Waxman & Markow, 1995) and by errors that young children make. For example, it is not uncommon for very young children to think that hot is the label for stove, given the common experience of hearing, *Don't touch it; it's hot* in reference to the stove.

Another proposed word-learning principle is the taxonomic principle, according to which words refer to things that are of the same kind. This assumption—it is proposed—helps the child figure out what else, other than the particular whole object being labeled, is included in the meaning of the new word. When the child hears the word *dog* in the presence of a dog (and assumes that the whole dog is being referred to because of the whole-object principle), the taxonomic principle leads the child to think that *dog* will also refer to other dogs, but not to things that are thematically related to dogs, such as collars, leashes, or bones. Again, the evidence for this assumption comes from both the fact that in natural language use children tend correctly to extend the meanings of the words they learn and experimental demonstrations that despite a tendency to form thematically related categories, when children are presented with a new word, *sud* with a picture (e.g., a picture of a dog) and asked to find another one that is the same as this *sud,* children pick another picture of a dog. When simply asked to find another one that is the same—without a new word being introduced—preschool children are more inclined to pick the picture of dog food (Markman & Hutchinson, 1984). Another principle, the mutual exclusivity principle, is the principle that different words refer to different kinds of things. So, for example, members of the category labeled dog do not overlap with members of *the* category labeled *cow.* In word-learning experiments, when presented a novel word and an array of objects that includes several objects for which they have labels and one for which they do not, children will take the new word to mean the object for which they have no label. That is, they appear to assume that the new word cannot be a synonym for any of the words that they already know (Markman & Wachtel, 1988; Mervis & Bertrand, 1994).

These principles work in concert, so that the mutual exclusivity assumption provides a basis for overriding the whole object principle, which children must do in order to learn terms for parts and properties of objects. A child who knows the word *rabbit* and hears the word *furry* will not take furry to be a synonym for rabbit but will look for something else to be the referent of the new term. The alternatives to the proposal that word learning is constrained by innate, linguistic principles are (a) that these principles operate in word learning but are themselves learned (Nelson, 1988) and (b) that the assumptions that guide word learning are not specifically linguistic but have a social-pragmatic basis (Clark, 1997). It has also been argued that the process of word learning involves more than mapping sounds onto referents and that multiple learning procedures are brought to bear on the task of building a lexicon (Hoff & Naigles, 2002).

Summary and Conclusions

It is difficult to evaluate the contribution to the general understanding of language development made by the UG approach to grammatical development. The reason for this difficulty is that this work is so isolated from the rest of the field that one must either buy the UG account or reject it as a whole package. This isolation is not a scientific necessity, but rather a sociological fact. There is very little discussion between linguists and nonlinguists because researchers from the two disciplines do not ask the same questions or even use the same vocabulary. There are, of course, exceptions. The work reviewed on the issue of whether children have the category V is an exception, and there is an interesting and empirically informed debate on this topic. Similarly, in the domain of lexical development, the source of and necessity for constraints on the hypotheses children generate has motivated a great deal of research, and that research has advanced understanding of the process of word learning. For example, mixed accounts of lexical development incorporate some innate principles along with other bases for word learning (Golinkoff, Mervis, & Hirsh-Pasek, 1994; Hollich, Hirsh-Pasek, & Golinkoff, 2000).

Even without such integration, however, the linguistic approach makes a contribution to the overall enterprise of understanding language development by forcefully making two points: (a) Grammar is complex, and it is not so easy to show how some of the more abstract aspects of grammar could be derived from input; and (b) children may have more grammatical knowledge than they demonstrate in their speech, because producing speech requires adjunct competencies such as memory and pragmatic understandings, which may be limited in children.

LANGUAGE DEVELOPMENT AS A SOCIAL PROCESS

The approach that considers language as a social phenomenon and language development as a social process begins with very different assumptions than does the previously discussed generative grammar approach. Whereas the generative grammar position asserts that the output of the LAD is a complex, abstract system whose properties are unrelated to the communicative function of language and are not apparent in the surface form of sentences, the social approach, also termed the social-pragmatic view, asserts that language is much simpler (Tomasello, 1992, 2000). The social-pragmatic approach relies on Cognitive-Functional linguistic theory, according to which grammatical devices are not hidden things like c-command and binding but are things like word order and case marking endings on words. Not only are these grammatical devices directly observable, but their functions are related directly to meaning. That is, word order and case markings indicate notions such as *agent of action* and *object of action* that are part of everybody's cognitive understandings of events.

Second, in the social-pragmatic view, the input is richer than in the generative grammar view. According to the social-pragmatic view, it is crucially important to the process of language development that language is learned in the context of interaction with others, in routines such as feeding and dressing and, in some cultures, interactive games, book reading, and more. The significance of these repeated routines is that they create a shared referential context within which the language of the adult makes sense to the prelinguistic child (Carpenter, Nagell, & Tomasello, 1998). Third, the child's learning mechanisms include the all-important capacity for what Tomasello has termed *cultural learning* (Tomasello, 2000; Tomasello, Kruger, & Ratner, 1993). Cultural learning involves imitating others, but it is not uncomprehending mimicry. Rather, cultural learning consists of learning to reproduce the behavior of others for the purpose of achieving the same goal or performing the same function that the learner understands to have been the goal or intended function when that behavior was produced by another. Cultural learning is possible only after around 9 months of age, when children develop the capacity for secondary intersubjectivity, which allows them to coordinate their attention with both the person who is talking to them and the objects or events that are being talked about. This is prerequisite to cultural learning because only with this capacity can children share another's perspective on the world, thereby gaining nonlinguistic access to the communicative intentions of others. Learning language, on this view, is learning to express one's communicative intentions with sequences of sounds that one has previously heard uttered by others to express those same communicative intentions.

In sum, compared to the generative linguistics approach, the social-pragmatic approach assumes that the infant who acquires language is smarter and that the language system that is acquired is simpler. Viewed this way, language is learnable without recourse to stipulation of innate knowledge. In the next sections we consider what this view has to say more specifically with respect to the acquisition of grammar and the lexicon, and we consider some of the arguments that have been made against those proposals.

A Social-Pragmatic Account of Grammatical Development

The gist of the social pragmatic approach to explaining grammatical development is to redescribe both the nature of the child's syntactic competence and the adult syntactic competence eventually achieved so that they are states of knowledge that can be achieved using information available in social interaction and domain-general mechanisms of learning. (There is no social-pragmatic account of phonological development.) The redescription of children's competence is done through analysis of children's spontaneous speech and performance in experimental tasks. The redescription of adult competence is made by referring to cognitive-functional linguistics.

The crucial point in the redescription of child competence is the claim that children do not have a fully productive system. It is that productivity, or generativity, that motivates the abstract system that is generative grammar. Children, it is argued, have only a repertoire of constructions that they have memorized as a result of hearing them in input. Central to this argument is the claim that children do not have the grammatical category V, because sentences are built around verbs. Without the category children cannot have fully productive rules for sentence generation. Instead, children have verb-specific frames that they use to construct sentences. Children do have a noun-like category, and thus they achieve some limited productivity in their speech by substituting nouns in their memorized, verb-based frames.

Recall from the previous section, the observation that children initially do not use the verbs that they know in the full range of environments that the grammar allows. Rather than explaining this as a reflection of performance limitations, as the UG approach does, the social-pragmatic approach argues that children have limited knowledge about how individual verbs can be used. In essence, children know only what they have heard. In support of this view, there is evidence that children use the same frames with each verb as their mothers use (Theakston, Lieven, Pine, & Rowland, 2001). Additionally, there are findings from several experiments in which children are taught new verbs and then asked questions designed to elicit use of those verbs in different sentence structures. The consistently obtained result is that children under 3 years tend not to use their new verbs in utterances that go beyond the way they have heard those verbs used by adults. This contrasts with the finding for novel nouns, which children do use in new combinatorial structures (Tomasello, 2000).

Eventually, of course, children do use verbs productively, and the social-pragmatic theory must account for that. Part of the social-pragmatic solution is the proposal that children move to a system of more general, productive constructions from an item-based set of constructions by noticing patterns among the item-based constructions and combining them. Consistent with this sort of mechanism is that some measures of productivity increase gradually from 2 years to 8 years (Tomasello, 2000). The social-pragmatic account never gives itself the task of explaining how children achieve the autonomous, abstract grammar of the generative linguistic approach. This is where the redescription of adult competence comes into play. Adult linguistic competence, in this view, is also just an inventory of constructions—the difference is that some of them are quite general and productive. The adult grammar can end up with some of the structural apparatus of standard grammars, provided that those structures relate to specific communicative functions. So, for example, syntactic constituents such as noun phrases can be arrived at from input because noun phrases refer to identifiable referents. To paraphrase an example from Tomasello (2000), *your papers* is a coherent constituent because it serves a single referential function. The importance to acquisition of children's understanding of speakers' communicative intentions is made clear by this analysis. All the units of language structure correspond to communicative functions. Thus, understanding the communicative functions of utterances leads inevitably to understanding structure. In this view, no other route to grammar is necessary.

The counterarguments to the social-pragmatic view of the acquisition of grammar are essentially three: (a) Whereas the social understandings that are argued to be the basis of language development are important and perhaps even necessary for some aspects of development, they are not sufficient to account for acquisition; (b) the social-pragmatic position and Cognitive-Functional linguistics underestimate the complexity and functionally independent nature of morphosyntax (Maratsos, 1998; Shatz, 1992); and (c) the data do not quite support the straightforward input-dependent, limited-productivity account offered by the social-pragmatic view. To elaborate the last point, diary data on the first uses of 34 common verbs by eight different children show that many verbs do in fact appear in multiple structures within children's first 10 uses of those verbs, suggesting some early productivity (Vear, Naigles, Hoff, & Ramos, 2001). In addition, although children do tend to use main verbs in the particular syntactic structures in which they have heard those verbs used (deVilliers, 1985; Theakston et al., 2001), this is not the case for auxiliary verbs. One of the most robust input-acquisition relations in the literature is that the frequency in input of questions that prepose auxiliaries (e.g., *Can you eat your breakfast now?*) is related to children's acquisition of auxiliaries, but when the children use auxiliaries it is first in declarative forms (e.g., *I can do it;* Newport, Gleitman, & Gleitman, 1977; Shatz, Hoff-Ginsberg, & MacIver, 1989). This particular datum and the complexity of what children acquire more generally argue that internal mental processes operate over input and transform it into syntactic knowledge that is used in creating novel productions. The social-pragmatic approach to the acquisition of grammar is mute with respect to what those internal mental processes might be.

Social-Pragmatic Approach to Lexical Development

The gist of the social-pragmatic explanation of lexical development is the assertion that children can figure out what newly encountered words mean because they know what the other speakers' communicative intentions are. Early formulations of the social-pragmatic proposal argued that the recurrent social interactions between mother and child establish each participant's intentions through a given routinized activity, allowing the child to predict "where the adult's attention is currently focused and where it is likely to be focused next. Therefore, any language the adult may use in such a context is likely to be immediately meaningful to the child" (Tomasello & Todd, 1983, p. 199). Additionally, if in nonroutinized interaction, mothers talk about the aspects of the activity that the child is focused on, then the meanings the child is harboring should be consistently expressed. Thus, the social-pragmatic argument is that by virtue of either routinization or maternal attentiveness children know what their mothers are saying without understanding the language, and they can use that nonlinguistically acquired knowledge to figure out the meaning of the language they hear.

More recently, the social-pragmatic proposal has focused on the social cognitive abilities and inclinations of children (Akhtar & Tomasello, 2000; Baldwin, 2000). Children are not at the mercy of adults, following their attentional focus in order for word meaning to be made transparent. Rather, children have the ability to discern their mothers' communicative intentions. According to this view, word learning begins once children understand others as intentional agents, assume some communicative intention behind the vocalizations others make, and successfully figure out what those communicative intentions are. Although the earlier and later formulations differ in whether the mother or the child contributes the requisite social-pragmatic skill, in both formulations mutual engagement or joint attention is prerequisite to word learning.

The sort of empirical findings cited in support of this view include findings that maternal responsiveness is positively associated with child vocabulary development (Tamis-LeMonda, Bornstein, Kahana-Kalman, Baumwell, & Cyphers, 1998), that mothers who follow their child's lead have children with larger vocabularies (Akhtar, Dunham, & Dunham, 1991; Harris, Jones, Brookes, & Grant, 1986; Tomasello & Farrar, 1986), and that the proportion of time mothers and children spend in joint engagement predicts vocabulary growth (Carpenter et al., 1998; Tomasello & Todd, 1983). Another important piece of this argument is evidence that children have the ability to use nonverbal cues such as eye gaze to determine a speaker's focus of attention and that they infer that speakers are talking about their own focus of attention, even when it differs from the child's (Baldwin, 1993).

The foregoing arguments address how children can correctly map a newly encountered word onto its intended referent. There is also a pragmatically based argument for how children learn multiple terms for the same referent (Clark, 1997). That is, the same creature can be *the dog, our pet,* or *Rover,* depending on the purpose for which one is labeling him. Children are disinclined to take these different labels to be exact synonyms because they have the principle of contrast, that is, the pragmatic understanding that if a speaker chooses a different word, it indicates a different meaning. The innate constraints approach explains the same behavior with reference to the mutual exclusivity principle. There is evidence consistent with both views. Absent any pragmatic information, children are reluctant to accept new labels for an already-labeled referent (Merriman & Bowman, 1989); however, very young children can learn multiple labels for the same referent if they understand the multiple communicative purposes or perspectives that lead to different word choices (Clark, 1997). Adults also provide help to the would-be word learner through pragmatic directions. To illustrate, Clark offers a hypothetical example in which some birds are flying overhead and the adult speaker first says *look at the birds* and then points to one bird followed by another, saying *This one is a sparrow; this one here is a crow*. By first not individuating and later individuating the referents, the speaker indicates to the child the perspective shift that accompanies the shift in the hierarchical level of the label provided. Although the foregoing example is hypothetical, there are data to the effect that mothers indicate when they are talking about a group labeled by a superordinate category and that simple labeling tends to be used with basic-level or subordinate categories (Callanan, 1985). There are also spontaneous speech data from very young children attesting to their use of multiple labels for the same item (e.g., *food* and *cereal, animal* and *tiger;* Clark, 1997).

The quarrel some have with the social-pragmatic approach to lexical development is similar to the exception taken with respect to social-pragmatic accounts of grammatical development. The problem is one of sufficiency. Although children may well use their social skills to infer speaker intent in episodes of mutual engagement, analysis of published studies of mother-child interaction suggests that only about 20% of the time mothers and children spend in conversation is characterized by the mutual understandings upon which the social-pragmatic view of acquisition depends (Hoff & Naigles, 2002). Furthermore, there is more to building a lexicon than mapping newly encountered words onto referents. Before that initial mapping words must be identified as such in the speech stream, and after the initial mapping there is still more for children to figure out to complete the lexical entry. The sort of information that would contribute to those other parts of the word-learning task and the

sort of learning abilities that would use that information are ignored in the social-pragmatic account.

Acquiring the Social Uses of Language

Thus far we have been discussing socially based accounts of the acquisition of what are considered the core aspects of language: grammar and the lexicon. The extent to which social processes can explain those developments is very much at issue. In contrast, there are other aspects of language development for which a socially based explanation is the most obvious choice. Language development includes language socialization—learning to use language as do adult members of one's social group. This refers to everything from learning to be polite to learning to tell a coherent story. These learnings must depend on the social context in which language is acquired because what constitutes both politeness and a coherent story vary depending on culture (Clancy, 1986; Minami & McCabe, 1995). More direct evidence for the role of social context in these aspects of language development are findings that within a culture, differences in the environmental support provided by other speakers are related to the rate of development of the ability to produce narratives (Fivush, 1991; McCabe & Peterson, 1991; Reese & Fivush, 1993).

Socially based accounts of development have little competition with respect to explaining the acquisition of communicative competence. While there are requisite and perhaps biologically based cognitive developments, it is clear that acquiring communicative competence depends on social experience. A large body of work describes children's development of communicative competence and seeks explanation in terms of social development, cognitive development, and experience in language interaction (see, e.g., Ninio & Snow, 1999). From a distance, however, this sort of research seems not to be the main-stage event in the search for an explanation of how children learn to talk. The main stage is occupied by the study of grammar and the lexicon.

Summary and Conclusions

There is no quarrel from any quarter that language is used to communicate or that it is acquired in the context of communicative interaction. Thus, there is most certainly a social basis to language development (Shatz, 1992). At issue is the explanatory power of this social basis. The claim made by advocates of the social-pragmatic view—that learning language is merely a matter of learning to produce the sounds to express one's intentions that one has heard others produce to express those intentions—is not particularly revolutionary.

If intentions are meanings, and it seems that they must be, then this statement is simply a paraphrase of a statement in every linguistics textbook: Language is a system for relating sound to meaning. The question is, What is the nature of that system and what does it take to learn it? According to the social-pragmatic approach, the system is fairly simple and based in the communicative functions of language. Thus, learning the system is a natural consequence of children's social-cognitive abilities to understand others' intentions, their desire to communicate their own intentions, and their ability to imitate the means of communicating intentions that they see modeled by others. To the extent that language is complex and has structural properties not grounded in the communicative functions of language, it will require more to be learned than social understandings and a capacity to imitate the goal-directed behavior of others.

LANGUAGE DEVELOPMENT AS DOMAIN-GENERAL LEARNING

It is possible, in principle, that substantial aspects of linguistic knowledge are neither innate nor achieved in the manner described by the social-pragmatic approach. Linguistic knowledge could be learned via the application of asocial and domain-general learning procedures to language input. The work in this vein does not come from a single theoretical orientation but rather comprises a variety of approaches that have in common a rejection of the assumptions that language is too complex, the input too impoverished, and the child's learning mechanisms too weak to account for language acquisition without stipulating innate linguistic knowledge. Some, but not all, domain-general proposals also entail a description of the adult linguistic knowledge that differs from the generative linguistics account. The domain-general learning approach differs also from the social-pragmatic approach in locating the information used by language learners in the speech stream itself and in the nonlinguistic context accompanying speech rather than in socially achieved understandings. Information about utterance or word meaning that children derive through their understandings of other speakers' intentions may be useful, but it has no special status that is different from other sources of information. Furthermore, the mechanisms for learning are more than the mechanisms of cultural learning referred to by the social-pragmatic approach. The argument for a domain-general approach to language development is made primarily with three sources of evidence: (a) studies of infants showing that language learners do indeed have powerful learning mechanisms available to them, (b) computer implementations of connectionist

models of language acquisition demonstrating the sufficiency of some aspects of input for at least some aspects of language development, and (c) developmental data suggesting that children do apply general learning procedures to input in the process of acquiring language.

The Nature of Infants' Learning Mechanisms

Recent attention to infant learning mechanisms began with a study demonstrating that 8-month-old babies can learn the statistical regularities in a stream of sounds presented for only 2 min (Saffran, Aslin, & Newport, 1996). The babies listened to a tape-recording that presented four different three-syllable "words" (e.g., *tupiro, golabu*) combined in random order in an uninterrupted stream. After 2 min of exposure, the babies were tested with stimuli that either recombined the same words in a different order or recombined the same syllables in a different order, violating the integrity of the former "words." Eight-month-old babies could tell the difference. They appeared to have learned the distributional regularities in the first sequence, that is *ro* always follows *pi* which always follow *tu*, whereas *tu* can follow any of three different word final syllables. Although this finding demonstrated that babies were more powerful learners than had previously been thought, there remains substantial disagreement over how much of the burden of explaining language acquisition even this kind of learning can carry. Some have hailed this finding as evidence that babies can learn language (Bates & Elman, 1996), whereas others, including the original authors, have been quick to point out that there is more to learning a language than identifying words in the steam of speech (Pinker, 1996).

There is other evidence that babies are capable of even more sophisticated learning. That is, babies seem able not only to learn the distributional regularities among the particular sounds they hear but also to abstract a pattern that can be applied to other dissimilar sounds (Marcus, Vijayan, Bandi Rao, & Vishton, 1999). Marcus et al. (1999) presented 7-month-olds with 2-min sequences that followed an ABA pattern (e.g., *ga ti ga, li na li*) or an ABB pattern (e.g., *ga ti ti, li na na*). Subsequently, the babies were able to distinguish between the pattern that they had heard and the other pattern, even when those patterns were presented using entirely different syllables. According to Marcus et al. (1999), these babies learned algebraic rules, not just statistical regularities, but there are dissenters from this view (McClelland & Plaut, 1999). The assertion that infants can learn rules has broad implications. Rules capture patterns among abstract variables, and variables can refer to any stimuli, old or new, regardless of their similarity to the stimuli that produced the learning.

Thus, a rule is highly generalizable knowledge. In contrast, statistical learning consists of memorizing the co-occurrence patterns among stimuli actually experienced. These patterns can be generalized, but there must be some physical similarity between the stimuli that produced the learning and the new stimuli to which the learning is applied. The scope of generalization for statistical learning is much narrower than for rule learning, and rule learning is therefore a much more powerful learning mechanism (Marcus, 2001).

The significance of the evidence that babies can learn rules is tied up with one of the central topics of dispute between some domain-general approaches to language acquisition and the generative linguistic approach: Is knowing language knowing a system of rules? According to traditional accounts, it is. The rules are rules for word formation (in phonology and morphology) and sentence formation (in syntax) that operate over symbols. The symbols are variables that stand for abstract categories such as Noun and Verb; the rules apply to anything that is an instance of those categories. This is what allows language to be productive. According to some connectionist accounts, linguistic knowledge is not knowledge of a rule system that operates on variables. Rather, language is a function of the strength of connections among less abstract units—in some models the units are actually sound sequences.

Connectionism as a Domain-General Challenge to Nativism

Connectionism is the main domain-general challenge to linguistic nativism, and there have been computer implementations of connectionist models of aspects of the development of phonology (e.g., Plaut & Kello, 1999), of morphology (e.g., Daugherty & Seidenberg, 1994), of syntax (e.g., Elman, 1993), and of lexical development (e.g., Siskind, 1996; see Brent, 1997; Plunkett, 1998, for comprehensive treatments). The basic learning mechanism is that of establishing connections among units and adjusting the strength of those connections. The strength of the connection between two units increases each time the stimuli that activate those two units are presented together. Thus, like old-fashioned associationism, connectionist learning is a function of the contiguity of stimuli in experience. Unlike older models, however, connectionist models contain a complex internal structure that mediates between experience and learning with the result, it is claimed, that what is learned is greater than the sum of the learner's experiences. The strongest claim of connectionism is that it offers an alternative to the tradeoff between finding the structure of language in the input or building the structure into the acquisition mechanism. Instead, structure emerges from the effect of input on the connectionist network

(Plunkett, 1998; see also MacWhinney, 1999, for a more complete treatment of the notion of emergence). Another attraction of connectionist models is that they seem closer to biology than symbolic models do because we know that the brain is a set of interconnected neurons. If cognitive processing could be modeled in a system that is closer to the "wetware" of the brain, the hope is that the problem of determining how the brain represents symbols and rules could be eliminated.

Although connectionism has generated a great deal of excitement as a potential new way to explain both how language is learned and how the brain accomplishes this feat, there are also naysayers. The success of many connectionist implementations is disputed, as is their relevance to what children actually do. Also, connectionism is not an alternative to a system of symbols and rules if it is merely an implementation of symbols and rules. According to Marcus (1998), many connectionist models—particularly those that successfully mimic some aspect of language acquisition—actually contain within them nodes that stand for variables. If the connectionist model merely implements a symbolic processor, then the problem of explaining symbolic processing and the attendant problems of explaining the acquisition of symbols and rules are not solved. Furthermore, the analogy between connectionist models and the brain has been criticized as illusory. Not only are nodes not neurons, but also no one knows how the neurons in the human brain represent what humans know. For that reason, connectionism does not bring us closer to knowing how the brain represents or acquires linguistic knowledge (Fodor, 1997).

Even if connectionism does not provide an account of how children learn language using domain-general learning procedures, there are other arguments that language development depends on some sort of general learning—that neither innate linguistic knowledge nor solely social processes can be the entire story. We turn now to more specific proposals within the domains of phonological, morphosyntactic, and lexical development and to arguments that have been made on the basis of developmental data.

A Problem-Solving Model of Phonological Development

In contrast to the view of linguistic nativism—that all the universally possible rules or constraints of phonology are provided innately and selected or ranked by input, there is a widely held view that phonological development is the result of the child's problem-solving activity (Ferguson & Farwell, 1975; Macken & Ferguson, 1983). The problem that requires solution by the child is how to match the target language given the child's articulatory constraints. According to the problem-solving model, children figure out how to use their limited articulatory abilities to approximate the target language using their general capacities for perception, production, and problem solving. Initially children do this on a word-by-word basis, with the attested result that sounds may be produced in different ways across words. Later children arrive at a system for mapping individual sounds in the target language onto a set of sounds that they can produce. This results in consistency, but occasionally in regression for sounds that were produced accurately in only some words. Because different children hit upon different solutions to the problem, there will be individual differences among children in the phonological systems achieved. Applications of nativist models in contrast tend to focus on universals of phonological development rather than individual differences, and part of the argument among different approaches concerns how much individual variation exists.

Domain-General Processes in Morphosyntactic Development

The argument that the development of morphology and syntax are the result of general cognitive processes has been made on the basis of analysis of the task itself (Maratsos, 1998) and on the basis of evidence that children make use of information in input in acquiring syntax (Hoff-Ginsberg, 1986; Shatz et al., 1989). The task analysis consists of describing the complexity of morphological systems that are specific to particular languages and thus could not be provided innately. (In fact, the UG position makes no claim in this regard.) The question is how could children acquiring Turkish, to pick an example, learn that a particular suffix, -u, indicates patienthood of the noun to which it is attached (and, according to Maratsos, 1998, this is a simplified example of the problem of learning Turkish morphology). Children will hear sentences in which a noun has -u as a suffix, but they need to figure out from the universe of possibilities what that suffix indicates. Maratsos argued that there must be some innate constraints on the possibilities considered, but languages vary enough in what meanings get grammaticized that even an innately constrained list of possibilities would be quite long. The child would need many examples of the -u suffix in order to figure out what meaning reliably co-occurs with -u. This process of figuring out is a process of sifting through data, and it requires a great deal of data. Thus, although some innate constraints on the problem may be involved, the process is not like the learning process in UG models in which input functions as a trigger. The process is also unlike that proposed by the social-pragmatic view because neither the hypothesizing of candidate meanings nor the sifting

through data has anything to do with social processes. Other speakers do not point out which of the many meanings that co-occur with a particular instance of -u is being encoded by that suffix, and the process of grinding through the data to find the right one is entirely internal to the child. Learning depends on asocial input and internal data-analytic processes operating over that input.

Add to Maratsos's argument for data sifting the facts that languages are not perfectly regular and that speech is not completely error free. This leads to the inevitable conclusion that the internal data-sifting mechanism must be able to detect probabilistic patterns in the environment. In fact, Newport and Aslin (2000) documented children's abilities to detect the regularities in less-than-perfect input, and they argued that this importantly enables language acquisition. The ability to exploit probabilistic information is useful to most species in many domains because, as Kelly and Martin (1994) put it, "the structure of the environment itself is often probabilistic" (p. 105). Thus, we are led to the conclusion that the acquisition of morphology depends on massive language data that feed data-analytic abilities that are domain-general.

The notions that input provides information that requires an internal data-sifting mechanism, that children use that information in learning language, and that the value of that input is independent of its communicative function are also supported by evidence from the study of the relation between properties of mothers' child-directed speech and their children's syntactic development. The frequency with which mothers ask questions with preposed auxiliaries, produce partial expansions of child speech, and produce partial self-repetitions and expansions have all been found to predict the rate at which children develop some aspects of grammar (N. D. Baker & Nelson, 1984; Hoff-Ginsberg, 1985, 1986; Newport et al., 1977). Hoff-Ginsberg (1985) argued that these features of input are useful because they make the phrase structure of language salient to a distributional learning mechanism. Finally, the properties of input that provide this sort of information are unrelated to the functions to which the speech is put. Although the use of question forms is of course related to the expression of questioning as a communicative intent, it is not clear what the functional basis would be of a particular benefit of questions that involve preposed auxiliaries. Mothers' use of partial self-repetitions and expansions has been found to be unrelated to the functions of maternal speech (Hoff-Ginsberg, 1986, 1990, 1999).

Domain-General Processes in Lexical Development

The proposal that domain-general learning processes contribute to lexical development also begins with an analysis of the task itself. Current research and theory suggest that the process of word learning consists of at least the following three, ordered, components: (a) word segmentation, (b) an initial fast mapping of the new word onto a referent, and (c) a longer, extended process of completing the lexical entry. Both the innate constraints view and the social-pragmatic view address only the process of mapping words onto referents. They have nothing to say about word segmentation or the internal data-sifting processes that must be involved in completing a lexical entry. In contrast, there is substantial evidence that the amount and nature of input contribute to the child's lexical development. With respect to word segmentation, there is evidence that stress patterns, prosody, and repetition of words in combination with a variety of different words all contribute (see references in Aslin, Saffran, & Newport, 1999; Morgan & Demuth, 1996). With respect to the word-to-world mapping that the innate constraints and social-pragmatic views address, there is evidence for the potential usefulness and actual use of other information in the content and structure of the utterance in which a new word appears. Computer simulations (Siskind, 1996) have demonstrated that the use of partial linguistic knowledge to constrain hypotheses, combined with the ability to extract commonalities across different situations of use, can result in lexical acquisition by a system that has no access to speaker intentions. To illustrate, knowledge of what the word *ball* means, combined with knowledge about what kinds of entities do what kinds of things, indicates to the learning device that if the word *ball* is in the utterance, then an unknown word in that utterance is more likely to mean "roll" than "eat." Evidence that humans can similarly make inferences about word meaning from information in the utterance containing a novel word comes from Gillette, Gleitman, Gleitman, and Lederer's (1999) simulation of word learning with human (adult) participants. The learners in this case were shown a series of silent video clips of real mother-child interactions during which a specific verb had been spoken by the mother. The participants were provided with various clues to the identity of the verb, including (a) just the video clips, (b) the video clips plus the nouns in the mother's utterance, (c) just the nouns in the utterance, (d) just the sentence frames in which the verb was placed, (e) the sentence frames plus the nouns, or (f) the video clips, the sentence frames, and the nouns. With only the video clip information, the participants made correct identifications of the target verbs only 7.7% of the time. Each additional bit of information raised this level of accuracy significantly, until those with complete information (i.e., Condition f) reached 90.4% correct.

These foregoing studies involve simulations by computer or adult learner. There is also substantial evidence from studies of children's performance in experiments and from studies of input correlates of lexical development that young children find sources of information in the speech they hear and in the nonlinguistic context of that speech. Those findings suggest that neither the innate constraints view nor the social-pragmatic view provides a complete account of the process of word learning. Experimental studies of young children show that they can make use of structural information in figuring out what a newly encountered word means (Goodman, McDonough, & Brown, 1998; Prasada & Choy, 1998; Waxman, 1999; see Woodward & Markman, 1998, for a summary). For example, Naigles (1990) found that given a scene in which multiple interpretations of a novel verb are possible, 2-year-olds make systematically different conjectures depending on whether they hear *The duck is gorping the rabbit* or *The duck and the rabbit are gorping* (see also Naigles, 1996, 1998). Children's ability to use cross-situational information to converge on meaning has also been demonstrated (Akhtar & Montague, 1999), again suggesting an internal process of data sifting.

Evidence that children actually use syntax as a source of information in lexical development comes from studies of correlations between properties of input and measures of lexical development that find, for example, that the diversity of syntactic frames in which a verb appears predicts its order of acquisition (Naigles & Hoff-Ginsberg, 1998) and, more generally, that the syntactic complexity of maternal speech (indexed by mean length of utterance) is positively related to children's vocabulary development (Bornstein, Haynes, & Painter, 1998; Hoff & Naigles, 2002). Evidence that the process of lexical development requires a great deal of data to sift through comes from multiple findings that the amount of input addressed to children is a positive predictor of their vocabulary development. Huttenlocher et al. (1991) found that the amount of speech mothers produced was a significant, positive predictor of their children's rates of vocabulary growth over the course of 10 to 12 months. Studying the vocabulary of bilingual children, Pearson, Fernandez, Lewedeg, and Oller (1997) found that the relative sizes of 1- to 2-year-old children's vocabularies in each of the languages they were acquiring was related to the relative amount of input in each language.

Summary and Conclusions

The evidence reviewed in this section argues that Chomsky may have overstated the case when he said that input was too impoverished and children's learning mechanisms too weak for language to be learnable. The evidence suggests that children's language development is to a nontrivial degree the result of children's general capacities for learning the regularities in their environment applied to information in language input. As was the case for the social-pragmatic approach, the problem of sufficiency remains. None of the demonstrations that input is useful and used in the process of language acquisition constitutes proof that linguistic nativism is unnecessary.

CONCLUSION

In this chapter we reviewed the theoretical and empirical arguments that address the nature of the capacity that underlies language development. We organized those arguments under four headings that refer to four different premises regarding the nature of that capacity: the biological, the linguistic, the social, and the domain-general cognitive approaches to the study of language development. No approach seems sufficient alone, and each approach makes some contribution to the current understanding of how children learn to talk. The implication is that nature has equipped children with innate constraints, social inclinations and abilities, and asocial computational processes, all of which contribute to children's language development. If this is true, then an important goal for researchers in the field of language development must be to specify not only the nature of each source's contribution but also how these factors interact in the course of language development.

REFERENCES

Akhtar, N., Dunham, F., & Dunham, P. J. (1991). Directive interactions and early vocabulary development: the role of joint attentional focus. *Journal of Child Language, 18,* 41–50.

Akhtar, N., & Montague, L. (1999). Early lexical acquisition: The role of cross-situational learning. *First Language, 19,* 347–358.

Akhtar, N., & Tomasello, M. (2000). The social nature of words and word learning. In R. M. Gollinkoff, K. Hirsh-Pasek, L. Bloom, L. B. Smith, A. L. Woodward, N. Akhtar, M. Tomasello, & G. Hollich (Eds.), *Becoming a word learner: A debate on lexical acquisition* (pp. 115–135). Oxford, UK: Oxford University Press.

Aslin, R. N., Saffran, J. R., & Newport, E. L. (1999). Statistical learning in linguistic and nonlinguistic domains. In B. MacWhinney (Ed.), *The emergence of language* (pp. 359–380). Mahwah, NJ: Erlbaum.

Baker, C. L., & McCarthy, J. J. (Eds.). (1981). *The logical problem of language acquisition.* Cambridge, MA: MIT Press.

Baker, N. D., & Nelson, K. E. (1984). Recasting and related conversational techniques for triggering syntactic advances by young children. *First Language, 5,* 3–21.

Baldwin, D. (1993). Infants' ability to consult the speaker for clues to word reference. *Journal of Child Language, 20,* 395–419.

Baldwin, D. (2000). Interpersonal understanding fuels knowledge acquisition. *Current Directions in Psychological Science, 9,* 40–45.

Bates, E., & Elman, J. (1996). Learning rediscovered. *Science, 247,* 1849–1850.

Bates, E., Thal, D., & Marchman, V. (1991). Symbols and syntax: A Darwinian approach to language development. In N. A. Krasnegor, D. M. Rumbaugh, R. L. Schiefelbusch, & M. Studdert-Kennedy (Eds.), *Biological and behavioral determinants of language development* (pp. 29–66). Hillsdale, NJ: Erlbaum.

Bernhardt, B. H., & Stemberger, J. P. (1998). *Handbook of phonological development from the perspective of constraint-based nonlinear phonology.* San Diego, CA: Academic Press.

Bernicot, J., & Roux, M. (1998). La structure et l'usage des enonces: Comparison d'enfants uniques et d'enfants second nes [The structure and use of expressions: Comparing only children and second born children]. In J. Bernicot, H. Marcos, C. Day, M. Guidetti, J. Rabain-Jamin, V. Laval, & G. Babelot (Eds.), *De l'usage des gestes et des mots chez les enfants* [*Children's use of gestures and words*] (pp. 157–178). Paris: Armand Colin.

Bever, T. G., & Chiarello, R. J. (1974). Cerebral dominance in musicians and nonmusicians. *Science, 185,* 537–539.

Bickerton, D. (1984). The language bioprogram hypothesis. *Behavioral and Brain Sciences, 7,* 173–221.

Bickerton, D. (1988). Creole languages and the bioprogram. In F. J. Newmeyer (Ed.), *Linguistics: The Cambridge survey* (Vol. II, pp. 268–284). Cambridge, England: Cambridge University Press.

Birdsong, D. (1999). Introduction: Whys and why nots of the critical period hypothesis for second language acquisition. In D. Birdsong (Ed.), *Second language acquisition and the critical period hypothesis* (pp. 1–22). Mahwah, NJ: Erlbaum.

Bloom, L. (1998). Language acquisition in its developmental context. In D. Kuhn & R. S. Siegler (Eds.), *Handbook of child psychology: Vol. 2. Cognition, perception, and language* (5th ed., pp. 309–370). New York: Wiley.

Bloom, L., Lifter, K., & Hafitz, J. (1980). Semantics of verbs and the development of verb inflection in child language. *Language, 56,* 386–412.

Bornstein, M. H., Haynes, M. O., & Painter, K. M. (1998). Sources of child vocabulary competence: A multivariate model. *Journal of Child Language, 25,* 367–393.

Callanan, M. A. (1985). How parents label objects for young children: The role of input in the acquisition of category hierarchies. *Child Development, 56,* 508–523.

Carpenter, M., Nagell, K., & Tomasello, M. (1998). Social cognition, joint attention, and communicative competence from 9 to 15 months of age. *Monographs of the Society for Research in Child Development, 63*(4, Serial No. 255).

Carstairs-McCarthy, A. (1999). *The origins of complex language: An inquiry into the evolutionary beginnings of sentences, syllables, and truth.* Oxford, UK: Oxford University Press.

Chiarello, C. (1991). Interpretation of word meanings by the cerebral hemispheres: One is not enough. In P. J. Schwanenflugel (Ed.), *The psychology of word meanings* (pp. 251–278). Hillsdale, NJ: Erlbaum.

Chien, Y.-C. & Wexler, K. (1990). Children's knowledge of locality conditions in binding as evidence for the modularity of syntax and pragmatics. *Language Acquisition, 1,* 225–295.

Chomsky, N. (1965). *Aspects of the theory of syntax.* Cambridge, MA: MIT Press.

Chomsky, N. (1982). Discussion of Putnam's comments. In M. Piattelli-Palamarini (Ed.), *Language and learning: The debate between Jean Piaget and Noam Chomsky* (pp. 310–324). Cambridge, MA: Harvard University Press.

Clark, E. V. (1997). Conceptual perspective and lexical choice in acquisition. *Cognition, 64,* 1–37.

Conboy, B. T., & Mills, D. (2001, April 19–22). *Two languages, one developing brain: Effects of vocabulary size on bilingual toddlers' event-related potentials to auditory words.* Poster presented at the meetings of the Society for Research in Child Development, Minneapolis, MN.

Crain, S. (1991). Language acquisition in the absence of experience. *Behavioral and Brain Sciences, 14,* 597–650.

Curtiss, S. (1977). *Genie: A psycholinguistic study of a modern day "wild child."* New York: Academic Press.

Dale, P. S., Dionne, G., Eley, T. C., & Plomin, R. (2000). Lexical and grammatical development: a behavioral genetic perspective. *Journal of Child Language, 27,* 619–642.

deVilliers, J. (1985). Learning how to use verbs: lexical coding and the influence of the input. *Journal of Child Language, 12,* 587–595.

Dinnsen, D. A., & O'Connor, K. M. (2000). Typological predictions in developmental phonology. *Journal of Child Language, 28,* 597–628.

Dollaghan, C. (1985). Child mets word: "Fast mapping" in preschool children. *Journal of Speech and Hearing Research, 28,* 449–454.

Dunn, J., & Shatz, M. (1989). Becoming a conversationalist despite (or because of) having an older sibling. *Child Development, 60,* 399–410.

Eley, T. C., Bishop, D. V. M., Dale, P. S., Oliver, B., Petrill, S. A., Price, T. S., Purcell, S., Saudino, K. J., Simonoff, E., Stevenson, J., & Plomin, R. (1999). Genetic and environmental origins of verbal and performance components of cognitive delay in 2-year-olds. *Developmental Psychology, 35,* 1122–1131.

Elman, J. L. (1993). Learning and development in neural networks: The importance of starting small. *Cognition, 48,* 71–99.

Ferguson, C. A., & Farwell, C. B. (1975). Words and sounds in early language acquisition. *Language, 51,* 439–491.

Fodor, J. (1997, May 16). Do we have it in us? *Times Literary Supplement,* 3–4.

Fivush, R. (1991). The social construction of personal narratives. *Merrill-Palmer Quarterly, 37,* 59–81.

Ganger, J., Pinker, S., Chawla, S., & Baker, A. (2002). Heritability of early milestones of vocabulary and grammar: A twin study. Unpublished manuscript.

Gathercole, V. C. M. (2002). Monolingual and bilingual acquisition: Learning different treatments of *that*-trace phenomena in English and Spanish. In D. K. Oller & R. E. Eilers (Eds.), *Language and literacy in bilingual children* (pp. 220–254). Clevedon, UK: Multilingual Matters.

Gazzaniga, M. S. (1983). Right hemisphere language following brain bisection: A twenty-year perspective. *American Psychologist, 38,* 525–537.

Gilger, J. W. (1996). How can behavioral genetic research help us understand language development and disorders? In Mabel L. Rice (Ed.), *Toward a genetics of language* (pp. 77–110). Mahwah, NJ: Erlbaum.

Gillette, J., Gleitman, H., Gleitman, L., & Lederer, A. (1999). Human simulations of vocabulary learning. *Cognition, 73,* 135–176.

Gleitman, L. R. (1981). Maturational determinants of language growth. *Cognition, 10,* 103–114.

Goldin-Meadow, S. (1997). The resilience of language in humans. In C. Snowdon & M. Hausberger (Eds.), *Social influences on vocal development* (pp. 293–311). Cambridge, UK: Cambridge University Press.

Golinkoff, R. M., Mervis, C. B., & Hirsh-Pasek, K. (1994). Early object labels: The case for a developmental lexical principles framework. *Journal of Child Language, 21,* 125–156.

Goodman, J., McDonough, L., & Brown, N. (1998). The role of semantic context and memory in the acquisition of novel nouns. *Child Development, 69,* 1330–1344.

Gopnik, M., & Crago, M. B. (1991). Familial aggregation of a developmental language disorder. *Cognition, 39,* 1–50.

Gould, S. J., & Lewontin, R. C. (1979). The spandrels of San Marco and the Panglossian paradigm: A critique of the adaptationist programme. *Proceedings of the Royal Society of London, 205,* 581–598.

Grimshaw, J., & Rosen, S. (1990). Knowledge and obedience: The developmental status of the binding theory. *Linguistic Inquiry, 21,* 189–222.

Grodzinsky, Y., & Reinhart, T. (1993). The innateness of binding and development of coreference: A reply to Grimshaw and Rosen. *Linguistic Inquiry, 24,* 69–103.

Harris, M., Jones, D., Brookes, S., & Grant, J. (1986). Relations between the non-verbal context of maternal speech and rate of language development. *British Journal of Developmental Psychology, 4,* 261–268.

Hart, B., & Risley, T. (1995). *Meaningful differences in the everyday experience of young American children.* Baltimore: Brookes.

Hoff, E. (2001). *Language Development.* Wadsworth: Thompson Learning. California.

Hoff, E., Laursen, B., & Tardif, T. (2002). Socioeconomic status and parenting. In M. H. Bornstein (Ed.), *Handbook of parenting* (2nd ed., pp. 231–252). Mahwah, NJ: Erlbaum.

Hoff, E., & Naigles, L. (2002). How children use input to acquire a lexicon. *Child Development, 73,* 418–433.

Hoff-Ginsberg, E. (1985). Some contributions of mothers' speech to their children's syntactic growth. *Journal of Child Language, 12,* 367–385.

Hoff-Ginsberg, E. (1986). Function and structure in maternal speech: Their relation to the child's development of syntax. *Developmental Psychology, 22,* 155–163.

Hoff-Ginsberg, E. (1990). Maternal speech and the child's development of syntax: A further look. *Journal of Child Language, 17,* 85–99.

Hoff-Ginsberg, E. (1994). Influences of mother and child on maternal talkativeness. *Discourse Processes, 18,* 105–117.

Hoff-Ginsberg, E. (1998). The relation of birth order and socioeconomic status to children's language experience and language development. *Applied Psycholinguistics, 19,* 603–630.

Hoff-Ginsberg, E. (1999). Formalism or functionalism? Evidence from the study of language development. In M. Darnell, E. Moravscik, M. Noonan, F. Newmeyer, & K. Wheatley (Eds.), *Functionalism and formalism in linguistics* (pp. 317–340). Amsterdam: John Benjamins.

Hollich, G. J., Hirsh-Pasek, K., & Golinkoff, R. M. (2000). Breaking the language barrier: An emergentist coalition model for the origins of word learning. *Monographs of the Society for Research in Child Development, 65* (3, Serial No. 262).

Huttenlocher, J., Haight, W., Bryk, A., Seltzer, M., & Lyons, T. (1991). Early vocabulary growth: Relation to language input and gender. *Developmental Psychology, 27,* 236–248.

Jia, G., & Aaronson, D. (1999). Age differences in second language acquisition: The dominant language switch and maintenance hypothesis. In A. Greenhill, H. Littlefield, & C. Tano (Eds.), *Proceedings of the 23rd Annual Boston University Conference on Language Development* (pp. 301–312). Somerville, MA: Cascadilla Press.

Jourdan, C. (1991). Pidgins and creoles: The blurring of categories. *Annual Review of Anthropology, 20,* 187–209.

Jusczyk, P. W. (1997). *The discovery of spoken language.* Cambridge, MA: MIT Press.

Kako, E. (1999). Elements of syntax in the systems of three language-trained animals. *Animal Learning and Behavior, 27,* 1–14.

Kelly, M. H., & Martin, S. (1994). Domain-general abilities applied to domain-specific tasks: Sensitivity to probabilities in perception, cognition, and language. In L. Gleitman & B. Landau (Eds.), *The acquisition of the lexicon* (pp. 105–140). Cambridge, MA: MIT Press.

Kim, K. H. S., Relkin, N. R., Lee, K.-M., & Hirsch, J. (1997). Distinct cortical areas associated with native and second languages. *Nature, 388,* 171–174.

Lieberman, P. (1975). *On the origins of language: An introduction to the evolution of human speech.* New York: Macmillan.

Lieven, E. V. M. (1994). Crosslinguistic and crosscultural aspects of language addressed to children. In C. Gallaway & B. J. Richards (Eds.), *Input and interaction in language acquisition* (pp. 56–73). Cambridge, UK: Cambridge University Press.

Macken, M. A., & Ferguson, C. (1983). Cognitive aspects of phonological development: Model, evidence, and issues. In K. E. Nelson (Ed.), *Children's language* (Vol. 4, pp. 256–282). Hillsdale, NJ: Erlbaum.

MacWhinney, B. (1999). *The emergence of language.* Mahwah, NJ: Erlbaum.

Maratsos, M. (1998). The acquisition of grammar. In D. Kuhn & R. S. Siegler (Eds.), *Handbook of child psychology: Vol. 2. Cognition, perception, and language* (5th ed., pp. 421–466). New York: Wiley.

Marcus, G. F. (1998). Rethinking eliminative connectionism. *Cognitive Psychology, 37,* 243–282.

Marcus, G. F. (2001). *The algebraic mind.* Cambridge, MA: MIT Press.

Marcus, G. F., Vijayan, S., Bandi Rao, S., & Vishton, P. M. (1999). Rule learning by seven-month-old infants. *Science, 283,* 77–80.

Markman, E. M., & Hutchinson, J. E. (1984). Children's sensitivity to constraints on word meaning: Taxonomic vs. thematic relations. *Cognitive Psychology, 16,* 1–27.

Markman, E. M., & Wachtel, G. A. (1988). Children's use of mutual exclusivity to constrain the meanings of words. *Cognitive Psychology, 20,* 121–157.

Mazziotta, J. C., & Metter, E. J. (1988). Brain cerebral metabolic mapping of normal and abnormal language and its acquisition during development. In F. Plum (Ed.), *Language, communication, and the brain* (pp. 245–266). New York: Raven Press.

McCabe, A., & Peterson, C. (1991). Getting the story: A longitudinal study of parental styles in eliciting narratives and developing narrative skill. In A. McCabe & C. Peterson (Eds.), *Developing narrative structure* (pp. 217–253). Hillsdale, NJ: Erlbaum.

McClelland, J. L., & Plaut, D. C. (1999). Does generalization in infant learning implicate abstract algebra-like rules? *Trends in Cognitive Sciences, 3,* 166–168.

Merriman, W. E., & Bowman, L. L. (1989). The mutual exclusivity bias in children's word learning. *Monographs of the Society for Research in Child Development, 54* (3–4, No. 220).

Mervis, C., & Bertrand, J. (1994). Acquisition of the novel name-nameless category principle. *Child Development, 65,* 1646–1662.

Mills, D. L., Coffey-Corina, S., & Neville, H. (1997). Language comprehension and cerebral specialization from 13 to 20 months. *Developmental Neuropsychology, 13,* 395–445.

Minami, M., & McCabe, A. (1995). Rice balls and bear hunts: Japanese and North American family narrative patterns. *Journal of Child Language, 22,* 423–446.

Morgan, J., & Demuth, K. (1996). *Signal to syntax: Bootstrapping from speech to grammar in early acquisition.* Hillsdale, NJ: Erlbaum.

Naigles, L. (1990). Children use syntax to learn verb meanings. *Journal of Child Language, 17,* 357–374.

Naigles, L. (1996). The use of multiple frames in verb learning via syntactic bootstrapping. *Cognition, 58,* 221–251.

Naigles, L. (1998). Developmental changes in the use of structure in verb learning. In C. Rovee-Collier, L. Lipsitt, & H. Haynes (Eds.), *Advances in infancy research* (Vol. 12, pp. 298–318). London: Ablex.

Naigles, L. R., & Hoff-Ginsberg, E. (1998). Why are some verbs learned before other verbs? Effects of input frequency and structure on children's early verb use. *Journal of Child Language, 25,* 95–120.

Nelson, D. A. (1997). Social interaction and sensitive phases for song learning: A critical review. In C. T. Snowdon & M. Hausberger (Eds.), *Social influences on vocal development* (pp. 7–23). New York: Cambridge University Press.

Nelson, K. (1988). Constraints on word learning? *Cognitive Development, 3,* 221–246.

Neville, H. J., Nicol, J. L., Barss, A., Forster, K. I., & Garrett, M. (1991). Syntactically based sentence processing classes: Evidence from event-related brain potentials. *Journal of Cognitive Neuroscience, 3,* 151–165.

Newport, E. L., & Aslin, R. N. (2000). Innately constrained learning: Blending old and new approaches to language acquisition. In S. C. Howell, S. A. Fish, & T. Keith-Lucas (Eds.), *Proceedings of the 24th Boston University Conference on Language Development* (pp. 1–21). Somerville, MA: Cascadilla Press.

Newport, E. L., Gleitman, H., & Gleitman, L. R. (1977). Mother, I'd rather do it myself: Some effects and non-effects of maternal speech style. In C. E. Snow & C. A. Ferguson (Eds.), *Talking to children: Language input and acquisition* (pp. 109–150). Cambridge, UK: Cambridge University Press.

Ninio, A., & Snow, C. E. (1999). The development of pragmatics: Learning to use language appropriately. In W. C. Ritchie & T. K. Bhatia (Eds.), *Handbook of child language acquisition* (pp. 347–386). New York: Academic Press.

Ochs, E., & Schieffelin, B. B. (1979). *Developmental pragmatics.* New York: Academic Press.

Pearson, B. Z., Fernandez, S. C., Lewedeg, V., & Oller, D. K. (1997). The relation of input factors to lexical learning by bilingual infants. *Applied Psycholinguistics, 18,* 41–58.

Perani, D., Paulesu, E., Galles, N. S., Dupous, E., Dehaene, S., Bettinardi, V., Cappa, S. F., Fazio, F., & Mehler, J. (1998). The bilingual brain: Proficiency and age of acquisition of the second language. *Brain, 121,* 1841–1852.

Pinker, S. (1984). *Language learnability and language development.* Cambridge, MA: Harvard University Press.

Pinker, S. (1994). *The language instinct: How the mind creates language.* New York: Morrow.

Pinker, S. (1999). *Words and rules.* New York: Basic Books.

Pinker, S., & Bloom, P. (1990). Natural language and natural selection. *Behavioral and Brain Sciences, 13,* 707–784.

Plaut, D., & Kello, C. (1999). The emergence of phonology from the interplay of speech comprehension and production: A distributed connectionist approach. In B. MacWhinney (Ed.), *The emergence of language* (pp. 381–416). Hillsdale, NJ: Erlbaum.

Plunkett, K. (Ed.). (1998). *Language acquisition and connectionism.* East Sussex, UK: Psychology Press.

Prasada, S., & Choy, J. (1998, November). *The role of syntactic structure in the interpretation of proper nouns.* Paper presented at the 23rd Annual Boston University Conference on Language Development, Boston.

Premack, D. (1986). *Gavagai! Or the future history of the animal language controversy.* Cambridge, MA: MIT Press.

Reese, E., & Fivush, R. (1993). Parental styles of talking about the past. *Developmental Psychology, 29,* 596–606.

Reznick, J. S., Corley, R., & Robinson, J. (1997). A longitudinal twin study of intelligence in the second year. *Monographs of the Society for Research in Child Development, 62* (1, Serial No. 249).

Saffran, J. R., Aslin, R. N., & Newport, E. L. (1996). Statistical learning by 8-month-old infants. *Science, 274,* 1926–1928.

Schieffelin, B. B., & Ochs, E. (Eds.). (1986). *Language socialization across cultures.* Cambridge, UK: Cambridge University Press.

Senghas, A. (1995). The development of Nicaraguan Sign Language via the language acquisition process. In D. MacLaughlin & S. McEwen (Eds.), *Proceedings of the 19th Boston University Conference on Language Development* (pp. 543–552). Somerville, MA: Cascadilla Press.

Senghas, A. (2000). The development of early spatial morphology in Nicaraguan Sign Language. In S. C. Howe, S. A. Fish, & T. Keith-Lucas (Eds.), *Proceedings of the 24th Boston University Conference on Language Development* (pp. 696–707). Somerville, MA: Cascadilla Press.

Shatz, M. (1992). A forward or backward step in the search for an adequate theory of language acquisition? *Social Development, 1,* 2.

Shatz, M. (1994). *A toddler's life: Becoming a person.* New York: Oxford University Press.

Shatz, M., Hoff-Ginsberg, E., & MacIver, D. (1989). Induction and the acquisition of English auxiliaries: the effects of differentially enriched input. *Journal of Child Language, 16,* 121–140.

Siskind, J. M. (1996). A computational study of cross-situational techniques for learning word-to-meaning mappings. In M. R.

Brent (Ed.), *Computational approaches to language acquisition* (pp. 39–91). Cambridge, MA: MIT Press.

Slobin, D. I., Gerhardt, J., Kyratzis, & Guo, J. (Eds.). (1996). *Social interaction, social context, and language: Essays in honor of Susan Ervin-Tripp.* Mahwah, NJ: Erlbaum.

Snow, C. E., & Hoefnagel-Hohle, M. (1978). The critical period for language acquisition: Evidence from second language learning. *Child Development, 49,* 1114–1128.

Springer, A., & Deutsch, G. (1981). *Left brain, right brain.* San Francisco: W. H. Freeman.

Stiles, J., Bates, E. A., Thal, D., Trauner, D., & Reilly, J. (1998). Linguistic, cognitive, and affective development in children with pre- and perinatal focal brain injury: A ten-year overview from the San Diego longitudinal project. In C. Rovee-Collier, L. Lipsitt, & H. Hayne (Eds.), *Advances in Infancy Research* (Vol. 12, pp. 131–164). Stamford, CT: Ablex.

Stromswold, K. (1998). The genetics of spoken language disorders. *Human Biology, 70,* 297–324.

Stromswold, K. (2001). The heritability of language: A review and metaanalysis of twin, adoption and linkage studies. *Language, 77,* 647–723.

Tamis-LeMonda, C. S., Bornstein, M. H., Kahan-Kalman, R., Baumwell, L., & Cyphers, L. (1998). Predicting variation in the timing of linguistic milestones in the second year: An events-history approach. *Journal of Child Language, 25,* 675–700.

Theakston, A., Lieven, E., Pine, J., & Rowland, C. (2001). The role of performance limitations in the acquisition of verb-argument structure: an alternative account. *Journal of Child Language, 28,* 127–152.

Tomasello, M. (1992). *First verbs: A case study of early grammatical development.* Cambridge: Cambridge University Press.

Tomasello, M. (1992). The social bases of language acquisition. *Social Development, 1,* 67–87.

Tomasello, M. (1994). Can an ape understand a sentence? A review of *Language comprehension in ape and child* by E. S. Savage-Rumbaugh et al. *Language & Communication, 14,* 377–390.

Tomasello, M. (2000). Do young children have adult syntactic competence? *Cognition, 74,* 209–253.

Tomasello, M., Call, J., Nagell, K., Olguin, R., & Carpenter, M. (1994). The learning and use of gestural signals by young chimpanzees: A trans-generational study. *Primates, 35,* 137–154.

Tomasello, M., & Farrar, M. J. (1986). Joint attention and early language. *Child Development, 57,* 1454–1463.

Tomasello, M., Kruger, A., & Ratner, H. (1993). Cultural learning. *Behavioral and Brain Sciences, 16,* 495–552.

Tomasello, M., & Todd, J. (1983). Joint attention and lexical acquisition style. *First Language, 4,* 197–212.

Valian, V. (1991). Syntactic subjects in the early speech of American and Italian children. *Cognition, 40,* 21–81.

Vear, D., Naigles, L., Hoff, E., & Ramos, E. (2001, December, 5–8). *An investigation of the syntactic flexibility within young children's early verb development: Evidence from a cross-sectional diary study.* Paper presented to the Early Lexicon Acquisition Conference, Lyon, France.

Weber-Fox, C. M., & Neville, H. J. (1996). Maturational constraints on functional specializations for language processing: ERP and behavioral evidence in bilingual speakers. *Journal of Cognitive Neuroscience, 8,* 231–256.

Wexler, K. (1999). Maturation and growth of grammar. In W. C. Ritchie & T. K. Bhatia (Eds.), *Handbook of child language acquisition* (pp. 55–111). San Diego, CA: Academic Press.

Weylman, S. T., Brownell, H. H., & Gardner, H. (1988). "It's what you mean, not what you say": Pragmatic language use in brain-damaged patients. In F. Plum (Ed.), *Language, communication, and the brain* (pp. 229–244). New York: Raven Press.

Woodward, A. L., & Markman, E. M. (1998). Early word learning. In D. Kuhn & R. S. Siegler (Eds.), *Handbook of child psychology: Vol. 2. Cognition, perception, and language* (5th ed., pp. 371–420). New York: Wiley.

Woodward, A. L., Markman, E. M., & Fitzsimmons, C. M. (1994). Rapid word learning in 13- and 18-month-olds. *Developmental Psychology, 30,* 553–556.

CHAPTER 8

Cognitive Development in Childhood

DAVID HENRY FELDMAN

As a distinct subfield of developmental psychology, cognitive development has about a 50-year history. Prior to the 1950s, the field had few specialists in cognitive development. A related area, the study of learning in children, goes back to the beginnings of the field (e.g. see Thorndike, 1914; Watson, 1913), but the theoretical frameworks within which the study of learning was carried out differ sharply from those that came to prominence after about the middle of the twentieth century. Learning was conceptualized primarily in terms of behavioral principles and association processes, whereas cognitive development emerged from the cognitive revolution, the revolution in psycholinguistics, and especially Piaget's work on children's reasoning about a myriad of subjects like space, time, causality, morality, and necessity (Kessen, 1965; Piaget, 1967, 1970). Therefore, although superficially similar, research and theory on learning versus research and theory on cognitive development represent very different histories and very different perspectives.

The present chapter deals mainly with broader theories that have been devised to try to explain how the mind grows and transforms. Its time frame extends from about the middle of the twentieth century to the present time. It does not deal directly with related topics in cognitive psychology such as learning, perception, attention, motivation, and memory; these are seen as more properly belonging to the larger field

of *cognition,* of which cognitive development represents a part of the overall story (Flavell, 1977). The chapter also does not address the topic of *language development,* found in a separate chapter in this Handbook (see the chapter by Hoff in this volume). Language development has emerged as a substantial research topic in its own right, and although closely related to more general issues in cognitive development, it is now a specialty area large enough to merit separate treatment. Its roots are separate as well, springing from the debates between behaviorism and nativism as explanations for language acquisition. Indeed, there are specialists in cognitive development who may not know a great deal about language development, and (although less likely) vice versa.

THREE REVOLUTIONS

The field of cognitive development became a separate area of developmental psychology largely as a consequence of three sets of related events that all occurred around the middle of the last century: the cognitive revolution (Bruner, 1986; Gardner, 1985; Miller, 1983), the language revolution (Chomsky, 1957), and the Piagetian revolution (Flavell, 1963; Piaget, 1970). All three of these revolutions had the quality in common that they opened up the black box, so to speak, of the mind and set as a goal the exploration of the mental processes and mental structures that control thought—particularly human thought. Prior to these revolutions, psychology (at least on the North American continent) was largely dominated by behavioristic and positivistic perspectives that eschewed what they viewed as speculation about the inner workings of the mind (Boring, 1950; Gardner, Kornhaber, & Wake, 1996). As the combined effects of the three new approaches accumulated, the study of mental processes, how they work, and how and why they develop became central to the field of developmental psychology. Thus emerged the new specialty of cognitive development.

Each of the three revolutions had important influences on the form that the field of cognitive development would take. Although there were other influences to be sure, it is fair to say that the end of the 1960s largely set the shape and contour of cognitive development as a field of study. Although any one of the three might have been sufficient to inspire a new specialty in cognitive development, it is the synergistic impact of the three that gives the field its distinctive form.

Because of its central role in the field and because of its continuing influence on all areas of cognitive development, this chapter focuses on Piaget and the Genevan tradition, summarizing its main contributions and the main lines of criticism that have been mounted in recent decades. Although three revolutions gave rise to the field of cognitive development, one of them (the Piagetian revolution) has been so far the most influential and most enduring.

Prior to 1960, few scholars labeled themselves as cognitive developmentalists. From 1960 through the end of the century, hundreds of scholars were trained in and pursued research careers in cognitive development, largely because of the excitement and challenge of the work done in Geneva.

After briefly reviewing some of the main features of the other two primary sources of inspiration for the field of cognitive development, a more detailed review of the Piagetian system and its features are presented.

The Cognitive Revolution

From the newly emerging field of cognition, the assumption that there are important mediating processes that internally organize and direct behavior was integrated into the study of cognitive development from the start. The study of cognition focused on control of motor processes, perception, attention, association, and memory—processes too fine-grained for most cognitive developmentalists. But topics like problem solving strategies, hypothesis formation, skill acquisition, skill sequences, classification, and hierarchical organization processes have been of great interest to researchers and

theorists in the field (e.g., Brainerd, 1978; Case, 1972; Fischer, 1980; Flavell, 1977; Klahr, 1984; Siegler, 1981, 1996). The field rapidly broadened its reach to embrace some more socially and culturally weighted topics like social cognition and moral reasoning (e.g., Ainsworth, 1973; Kohlberg, 1973; Miller, 1983). The hallmark of virtually all research inspired by the study of cognition has been its emphasis on identifying, describing, and explaining the inner workings of thought, the ways in which thought evolves, and how knowledge and understandings are achieved. These more general issues are prominent in most research and theory in cognitive development.

The Revolution in Language Acquisition

The influence of the revolution in language was essentially twofold: It showed that mentalistic approaches to speech were necessary; also, it proposed that linguistic structures were innate and required no special environmental circumstances for them to appear. With Chomsky's publication of *Syntactical Structures* (1957), the identification of a set of mental rules that guide the production of an infinity of speech forms helped transform the study of language from a behaviorally oriented to a mentally oriented enterprise. Chomsky's debates with Skinner and others (e.g., Chomsky, 1972) cracked the hold that behavioral analysis held on the field of research on language and successfully questioned the adequacy of association rules to account for the diversity of speech forms that exist.

The second major influence of cognitive linguistics was less immediate in its impact but no less important. A central assumption of the approach of Chomsky and his followers was that linguistic rules are native and natural to human beings. It assumed that human beings come into the world equipped with a language acquisition device or language module that contains all the information necessary for each individual to become a user of human speech (barring organic deficit, of course; Bruner, 1986; Chomsky, 1957; Piattelli-Palmerini, 1980).

With the nativist assumption as its inspiration, the seeds were planted for two important strains of work to germinate. One attempted to specify the nature of innate modules for various forms of human thought beyond speech (e.g., face recognition, space, music, dance, time, quantity) and the rules that underlie each module (Carey, 1985; Fodor, 1980, 1983; Gardner, 1983; Keil, 1984, 1989). Another strain set out to establish the existence of abilities and skills, including theories and ontological distinctions present even in the earliest months of life (e.g. Gelman, 1998; Gopnik & Meltzoff 1997; Spelke & Newport, 1998). Thus, along with a set of core domains and privileged content areas, the field began to seek a set of core cognitive capabilities, some of which are quite sophisticated, that are natural to human minds from the outset (Bates, Thal, & Meacham, 1991; Gelman, 1998; Greenfield, 2001; Spelke, 2001). These lines of work in turn were challenging to the Piagetian tradition and led to reaction and response from both sides (see Piattelli-Palmerini, 1980).

Intelligence and Artificial Intelligence

Although not quite as influential, two other areas of research—one that predates the field of cognitive development and the other appearing at about the same time—need to be mentioned to complete the picture of the main ingredients of the field during its 50-year history. The study of *intelligence* (usually expressed in IQ or G terms) dates from at least the beginning of the twentieth century and has provided a foil against which other approaches to cognitive development have railed. The effort to simulate cognitive processes using computer programming techniques has in turn provided a demanding criterion against which claims for the adequacy of accounts of cognitive development have often been evaluated.

The field of *artificial intelligence* has added a degree of rigor and precision to many of the efforts to study particular instances of problem solving or skill acquisition (e.g., Siegler, 1981, 1984). Essentially, if a team of researchers is successful in getting a computer to behave in ways that support their claims for a learning process of a particular kind, their claims are supported by the accomplishment. More recently, the study of simulated neural networks has provided a challenge that is (in certain respects) even more demanding than efforts to explain transformation and change in cognitive structures through computer simulation (Elman et al., 1996; J. A. Feldman, 1981; Plunkett & Sinha, 1992).

The Piagetian Revolution

As John Flavell (1998) has written of Piaget (quoting another source), estimating the influence of Piaget on developmental psychology is like trying to estimate the influence of Shakespeare on English literature. In other words, Piaget's impact was (and in many respects still is) incalculable. For the study of cognitive development, three influences have been particularly important for the direction in which the field has gone; these influences are the emphasis on the development of universal cognitive structures, the claim that all cognitive structures are constructed by the individual child (neither taught by others nor innate), and the necessity of

explaining novel structures through processes that account for transitions from earlier and less powerful to later and more powerful forms of reasoning (Beilin, 1985; Piaget, 1963, 1970, 1971b).

Other important influences of Piaget and the Genevan research enterprise include the increasing emphasis on explaining changes in logical reasoning as the central goal of the work, the tendency to study scientific reasoning (space, time, causality, necessity) over other possible topics (e.g., learning school subjects, artistic areas, physical development), and a tendency to de-emphasize the importance of language and thus separate mainstream cognitive development work from work on language acquisition.

When Piaget began his work in the early 1920s, he worked as an assistant in the laboratory of T. H. Simon, the French researcher who was the co-inventor of the standardized intelligence test (Bringuier, 1980; Gardner et al., 1996). Piaget found the psychometric approach to intelligence deeply problematic and quite intentionally set out to define intelligence in a very different way.

Rather than finding out whether children know the right answers to standard questions, Piaget believed that children's reasoning and the ideas that they generated were of greater interest than was the correctness of their responses. And he found the set format of psychometric procedure to be confining and constraining in what could be discovered about the child's mind and how it deals with the challenges of the world (Gardner et al., 1996).

Piaget's efforts to redefine intelligence as the development of cognitive structures of a certain sort has not been completely successful; most people—professional and nonprofessional alike—would still say that intelligence is the quality estimated by IQ tests (Neisser et al., 1996).

Cognitive Development as a Separate Field

The field of cognitive development split off from the field of psychometric intelligence virtually from its beginnings in Geneva. Each approach to intelligence was pursued largely without regard to the other. By the late 1960s or early 1970s, most people in the field of cognitive development would not have considered psychometric studies of intelligence as part of their field of study—and vice versa for those whose work was primarily psychometric; they would have identified themselves as belonging to the field of individual differences or differential psychology. Only during the most recent decades have there been serious efforts to bring the two approaches to intellectual development into a productive relationship (e.g., Elkind, 1976; Fischer & Pipp, 1984; Gardner, 1983, 1993).

Piaget's work and the work of his many colleagues and collaborators was well known before the 1950s. Piaget's first five books, written during the 1920s and 1930s, were widely read and often quoted. It was not until the publication of John Flavell's influential text on Piaget appeared in 1963, however, that a major shift in orientation occurred. Prior to the Piagetian breakthrough, the field of learning was dominated by behaviorally oriented learning paradigms such as those proposed by Pavlov, Thorndike, Watson, and Skinner. Psychometrics was influential in the applied areas of education, business, the military and civil service, but—as mentioned previously—was largely seen as a separate field from the study of learning and problem solving. Although there were no doubt other influences, Flavell's book on Piaget seemed to catalyze a dramatic shift from behavioral theory to cognitive constructivism as the consensus paradigm for the emerging field (Flavell, 1963).

In arguing that Piaget's work deserves the most serious study, Flavell (1963) warned against dismissing the theory too hastily:

> Piaget's system is susceptible to a malignant kind of premature foreclosure. You read his writings, your eye is drawn at once to its surface shortcomings, and the inclination can be very strong to proceed no further, to dwell on these. . . . A case could be made that Piaget's system has suffered precisely such a fate for a long time, and that only recently has there been any sustained effort to resist the siren of criticism in favor of trying to extract underlying contributions. (p. 405)

Partly through efforts like those of Flavell and partly because of the joint influence of the other shifts in fields like linguistics and cognition, the field of child development rushed toward Piaget and the Genevan school with great energy, both positive (e.g., Ginsburg & Opper, 1988; Green, Ford, & Flamer, 1971; Murray, 1972; Tanner & Inhelder, 1971) and negative (e.g., Bereiter, 1970; Brainerd, 1978; Gelman, 1969; Trabasso, Rollins, & Shaughnessy, 1971). The 1960s and 1970s saw a veritable torrent of studies, reviews, books, and articles replicating, extending, challenging, and attempting to apply Piagetian theory and research. In the 1970 edition of *Carmichael's Manual of Child Psychology* (Mussen, 1970), Piaget had his own chapter, the only instance in which a contemporary figure wrote about his or her own work (Piaget, 1970). Piaget was cited 96 times in the index of the volume, with a number of the citations being several pages long—a far greater representation than that for any other single figure; Freud was cited 20 times, all single-page citations, and Erik Erikson was cited twice. Jerome Bruner, who helped establish the influence of Piaget with his own brand of constructivist cognitive development, was cited 60 times in the *Manual*.

By the next edition of the *Handbook of Child Psychology* (Mussen, 1983), an entire volume was devoted to cognitive development (with John Flavell as one of its editors), and Piaget's citations had increased to 113, with the word *passim* added 22 times (compared with none in 1970). Clearly, Piaget's importance in the field of cognitive development was very evident in how the field responded to his work. Six of the 13 chapters in the 1983 *Manual* were directly based on work done in or inspired by Genevan research and theory. A separate field within child development had been established largely based on Piaget's work.

In the most recent edition of the *Handbook of Child Psychology* (Damon, 1998), the number of citations of Piaget is still high, but there are fewer than in the previous edition; this may be for several reasons, but it is fair to say that the place of Piaget's work at the center of the field was shaken from its place until recently. More generally, the field of cognitive development itself has shown some signs of diminished visibility. In the current decade cognitive development has had a tendency to show signs of waning as a major subfield of developmental psychology, perhaps because more specialized areas like brain development, neonativist frameworks, language development, artificial intelligence, and dynamic systems approaches have moved to center stage.

Piaget's enormous influence began to lessen after his death in 1980, when Vygotsky's more sociocultural approach to development began to eclipse Piaget's as the century moved toward its final decade (Bruner, 1986). Although still arguably a cognitive developmentalist, Vygotsky's framework could be equally plausibly thought of as social, cultural, historical, or educational as easily as it could be called cognitive (Glick, 1983; Vygotsky, 1978).

More recently, Genevan work has been gaining attention again in the field as efforts to explain, extend, elaborate and—where necessary—modify Piaget's theory have shown increasing momentum (e.g., Beilin, 1985; Case, 1991; D. H. Feldman, 2000; Fischer, 1980; Flavell, 1998; Gelman, 1979). Examining how the theory has waxed and waned is a productive way to follow the movements of the field of cognitive development.

MAIN FEATURES OF THE PIAGETIAN SYSTEM

The features of Piaget's system that found their way to wide acceptance in the study of cognitive development are too numerous to mention, but five seem particularly important. These are (a) an emphasis on *universals* in the development of cognitive structures; (b) an assumption that there are *invariant sequences* of stages and substages in cognitive development; (c) *transitions* between stages and substages must be explained, particularly given the assumption that there are a number of broad, qualitative advances in reasoning structures; (d) the main goal of cognitive development is to acquire a set of *logical structures* that underlie reasoning in all domains, including space, time, causality, number, and even moral judgment; and (e) that all new structures are *constructed* by the individual child, who seeks to understand the world in which she or he lives, rather than imposed from the outside by the environment or expressed as a direct biological function of growth.

Universals

The study of child development has tended to focus on normative and general qualities of children as they grow up, but that tendency did not extend to intellectual development until Piaget's work became prominent. Partly to develop an antidote to what he considered to be an unhealthy emphasis on differences between and among individual children, Piaget wanted to build a theory of cognitive development that would show the common patterns of intellectual development that are shared—regardless of gender, ethnicity, culture, or history.

By choosing to study universals, Piaget and his group showed that every human being is naturally curious and a naturally active learner, sufficiently well equipped to construct all of the essential cognitive structures that characterize the most powerful mind known. In other words, Piaget sacrificed the ability to shed light on differences between and among individuals (see Bringuier, 1980) in order to shine a beam on those qualities that are distinctive to the growing human mind generally. In Piaget's world, all children are equally blessed with the necessary equipment to build a set of cognitive structures that are the equal of any ever constructed.

Invariant Sequence

The assumption of invariant sequence gives direction and order to cognitive development. The idea that a child must begin with the first set of challenges in a given area and then move in order through to the last step was a powerful claim that generated a great deal of reaction. There are those within the Genevan inner circle who began to back away from the strong form of the claim, especially when data from studies around the world cast doubt on the accuracy of the claim that all children go through a sequence of four large stages from *sensorimotor* (ages 0–18 months), to *preoperational*

(2–6 years), to *concrete operations* (6–12 years), to *formal operations* (about 12 years onward).

Less controversial—but still very important to the theory—are a number of sequences that describe progress of certain more limited concepts such as the object concept, seriation, and many others (Bringuier, 1980; Ginsburg & Opper, 1988; Piaget, 1977). Although some Genevans backed away from the stronger claims of the sequence of stages of the theory (see Cellerier, 1987; Karmiloff-Smith & Inhelder, 1975; Sinclair, 1987), it appears that Piaget never relaxed his claim that all normal children go through the four large-scale stages, reaching the final stage sometime during adolescence (D. H. Feldman, 2000). In a film made a few years before he died, Piaget mentioned stages and sequences more than a dozen times (Piaget, 1977).

Transitions

Perhaps the most controversial feature of Piagetian theory is its mechanism for trying to account for movement from one stage to another (at whatever level of generality the stage is proposed). For this purpose, Piaget borrowed and adapted ideas primarily from the fields of biology and physics. His main goal in proposing the so-called equilibration model was to offer a plausible account of qualitative change in the structures underlying the child's reasoning that were neither empirical nor innate in origin (e.g., see Piattelli-Palmarini, 1980).

For Piaget, the only kind of transition process that made sense was one that put an active, curious, goal-oriented child at the center of the knowledge-seeking enterprise—a child that would make sustained efforts to build representations and interpretations that became ever more veridical and adaptive of the objects in the world (Bringuier, 1980). Piaget assumed that a child seeks to build accurate representations of the objects important to her or him and to build powerful systems of interpretation to better understand these objects and their relationships to one another and to the child him- or herself.

The notions of equilibrium and systems dynamics from physics were integrated with notions of adaptation and organization from biology to form a mechanism for accepting relevant information (*accommodating*) and interpreting it using available categories, rules, hierarchies, and conceptual properties available at the time (*assimilating*). Change in the available instruments for knowing the world come about when existing ways to interpret things are perceived to be inadequate and an apprehension that better ones must be constructed provides needed motivation. The readiness of a growing cognitive system to undergo change is assumed to include some maturational readiness to enable the system to transform, along with sustained efforts on the part of the child to bring about changes perceived to be essential to additional understanding of the world.

Piaget's theory assumed that the equilibration process is a lifelong effort representing more or less stable outcomes of the functional invariants of organization and adaptation that are the inherent goals of all efforts to build cognitive structures. The effort is never complete; rather, moves through a sequence of four systemwide transformations, resulting in a set of formal organizational structures that provide the most powerful means of understanding the world available to human minds.

It should be noted that Piaget was never fully satisfied with his efforts to account for transitions (e.g., see Bringuier, 1980; Piaget, 1975). One of the last projects he took on was his revision of the equilibration model, an indication of just how vital he felt this aspect of the theory was to its success.

Logical Structures

For Piaget, the ability to use the rules and principles of logical reasoning was the hallmark and the highest goal of human cognitive development. He did not necessarily mean by *logical reasoning* the set of formal algorithms and techniques of the professional logician. Closer to his meaning would be to describe the goal of cognitive development to be a mind that functions like a well-trained natural scientist— with widespread use of systematic, hypothetico-deductive reasoning: hypothesis testing, experimental design, appropriate methods for gathering information, and rigorous standards of proof. It is not too great a distortion of Piaget's intent to describe the end of his cognitive developmental model as the mind of a biologist, mathematician, chemist, or physicist.

Later in his career, Piaget began to believe that he had perhaps overly emphasized formal logic as an appropriate reference for the kinds of cognitive structures his last stage represented (see Beilin, 1985; Ginsburg & Opper, 1988). He explored a number of alternative processes and frameworks that might better capture his image of what the formal operations stage is about (e.g., Ginsburg & Opper, 1988; Inhelder, de Caprona, & Cornu-Wells, 1987; Piaget, 1972). Thus the term *logical* for the final stage in Piaget's system may be less adequate than originally thought, but what seems clear is that Piaget never abandoned his belief that all children achieve a version of formal operations. He thought this in spite of the fact that many scholars—including some within his own inner circle—began to doubt this claim (e.g., see Beilin, 1985;

Commons, Richards, & Ammons, 1984; D. H. Feldman, 2000; Inhelder et al., 1987).

Constructivism

If there has been a triumph of the Genevan school, it is no doubt its emphasis on constructivist explanations of cognitive development. Prior to Piaget, most approaches to mind were either empiricist or rationalist in nature. That is to say, either it was assumed that the child's mind was a function of the specific history of experiences that formed it, including systematic events in the environment (e.g., sunrise and sunset), purposeful efforts to shape the mind (e.g., teaching, discipline, etc.), or chance events (e.g., accidents, earthquakes, war, etc.); or it was assumed that the mind was formed through some process, such as genetic endowment, supernatural intervention, reincarnation, and so on, beyond the control of the individual.

Piaget rejected both of these long-standing sources of explanation, and instead he proposed that mind is constructed as an *interaction* between a mind seeking to know and a world with certain inherent *affordances* (Gibson, 1969) that give rise to certain kinds of knowledge. The idea of interaction is intended to go beyond a vacuous invocation that both nature and nurture are involved in development and to try to propose a rigorous set of processes that explain the construction of cognitive structures (see the previous section of this chapter entitled "Transitions") through logical-mathematical and physical-empirical experience (often labeled *operative* and *figurative* in Piagetian theory; see Milbrath, 1998).

Although Piaget's version of constructivism is not universally accepted, there are few major streams of current cognitive developmental research and theory that do not have constructivist assumptions of one sort or another. Piaget's then-revolutionary assumptions of a curious, active, knowledge-seeking child, a child who wants to know and understand the world around her or him, is a feature of virtually all major frameworks in the field of cognitive development (e.g., see Damon, Kuhn, & Siegler, 1998; Liben, 1981).

Taken together, the five features of Piagetian theory just described have transformed the landscape of the study of cognitive development. In addition to these features, many other contributions have had major impact. Two of the more important of these are briefly summarized in the following discussion.

In addition to the major strands of the framework, several other features of Piaget's approach to cognitive development have made their way into the field. Methodologically, Piaget tended to favor small, informal, exploratory forays into new areas. For these purposes Piaget and his colleagues developed what is now called the *clinical method,* based as it is on the one-on-one interviews that are common in clinical psychology. Over time, the clinical method of the Geneva school evolved into a highly subtle and carefully articulated set of flexible techniques for guiding a dialogue between an inquiring researcher and a participating child (Ginsburg & Opper, 1988). Although not without its own limitations, the clinical method has gained considerable credibility within cognitive developmental research. Many studies use a version of the interview method often complemented with other more traditional methods such as experiments, correlational and cross-sectional studies, and longitudinal research. Piaget tended to be skeptical of statistics and large-scale sampling (see Bringuier, 1980), favoring the more interpretive and analytic approach to research.

As part of the effort to reduce the clinical method's dependence on speech and language abilities, the Genevans invented many ingenious activities and tasks designed to reveal the structures being acquired and the processes used to respond to the challenges posed to children without depending upon the child's verbal response. Several of these activities (e.g., the balance beam task) have become almost domains of their own, with dozens and dozens of studies done with them both inside and outside the Genevan framework (e.g., Siegler, 1981, 1996). A task requiring children to take different perspectives on a geographical landscape (the three mountains task; is another example of a clever activity that has been used for many different purposes. As is often the case when an approach to research has great influence, its methodological proclivities and its techniques for gathering special information prove to be as (or more!) important than its broad theoretical or empirical claims.

There are many other influences that emanated from the Genevan school. Some of these have become so well integrated into the field that specific citations for Piaget have lessened. This has been particularly true in the study of infant cognitive development, a specialty area that has exploded since Piaget first showed that babies were active, curious, and surprisingly competent (Gopnik, Meltzoff, & Kuhl, 1999; Piaget, 1967). For someone currently just entering the field, it would be difficult if not impossible to trace the Genevan origin of many of the research topics and techniques.

In spite of the pervasive influence that Piaget and his many followers around the world had from the 1960s to the 1980s, as the century moved into its final decades it appeared that Piaget's central place in the field was waning—perhaps partly because *le patron* himself died in 1980, or perhaps because the field needed to move forward in different directions. Works that criticized Piaget's theory and that questioned the empirical findings of the Genevan school had been

part of the literature for decades, to be sure, but the weight of the criticism seemed heavier after about 1980.

Jerome Bruner, one of the founders of the cognitive revolution, one of the first cognitive developmentalists, and an admirer of Piaget, wrote about the rising influence of the Russian Vygotsky:

> So, while the major developmental thinker of capitalist Western Europe, Jean Piaget, set forth an image of human development as a lone venture for the child, in which others could not help unless the child had already figured things out on his own and in which not even language could provide useful hints about the conceptual matters to be mastered, the major developmentalist of socialist Eastern Europe set forth a view in which growth was a collective responsibility and language one of the major tools of that collectivity. Now, all these years later, Vygotsky's star is rising in the Western sky as Piaget's declines. (in Rogoff & Wertsch, 1984, p. 96).

There are several themes in this quote that we discuss in more detail later in the chapter, but at this point it is sufficient to note that one of the great leaders in the field of cognitive development was announcing the end of one era (Piaget's) and the beginning of another (Vygotsky's). This view was widely accepted at the time.

PROBLEMS WITH PIAGET'S THEORY AND EFFORTS TO RESPOND TO THEM

Criticisms of various aspects of Piaget's theory and research program ranged from outright dismissal (e.g., Atkinson, 1983; Brainerd, 1978) to general acceptance but with a need for modification (e.g., Case, 1984; D. H. Feldman, 1980; Fischer, 1980; Fischer & Pipp, 1984). There were also vigorous defenses of Genevan positions (e.g., Elkind, 1976; Inhelder & Chipman, 1976; Inhelder et al., 1987).

The main problems with the theory can be summarized as follows:

1. The theory claimed that cognitive development was universal but would not specify the role that maturation plays in the process.

2. The theory proposed that each stage of cognitive development was a complete system—a structured whole available to the growing child as she or he moved into that stage. Yet empirical results indicated again and again that children were unable to carry out many of the tasks characteristic of a given stage, leading to charges that the theory invoked an "immaculate transition"

that happened but could not be seen (see Siegler & Munakata, 1993).

3. Related to the previous point is that other than proposing a six-phase substage sequence for sensorimotor behavior, the subsequent three large-scale stages of the theory had little internal order. This problem gets worse with each stage because each stage increases in the number of years it encompasses—from 2, to 4, to 6, to at least 8 (see D. H. Feldman, 2002).

4. Formal operations, the final stage according to the theory, seemed not to be achieved by many adults (see Commons et al., 1984; Piaget, 1972).

5. A number of researchers claimed that stages beyond formal operations exist and needed to be added to the theory (e.g., Commons et al., 1984; Fischer, 1980).

6. There was widespread dissatisfaction with the equilibration process as an explanation for qualitative shifts from stage to stage (e.g., Brainerd, 1978; Case, 1984; Damon, 1980; D. H. Feldman, 1980, 1994; Fischer & Pipp, 1984; Keil, 1984, 1989; Piattelli-Palmarini, 1980; Snyder & Feldman, 1977, 1984).

7. The theory seemed to depend too much on logic as both a framework for describing cognitive structures and as an ideal toward which development was supposed to be aimed (e.g., Atkinson, 1983; Ennis, 1975; Gardner, 1979; Gardner et al., 1996). Areas of development that were not centrally logical (art, music, drama, poetry, spirituality, etc.) seemed to be largely beyond the theory's compass.

8. The methods that the Genevan school favored, although appropriate for exploratory research, lacked the rigor and systematic techniques of traditional experimental science (e.g., see Bringuier, 1980; Gelman, 1969; Ginsburg & Opper, 1988; Klahr, 1984). Its claims were made at such a broad and general level that it was often difficult to put them to rigorous test (Brainerd, 1978, 1980; Case, 1999; Klahr, 1984; Siegler, 1984).

9. The theory did not deal with emotions in any systematic way (Bringuier, 1980; Cowan, 1978 text; Langer, 1969; Loevinger, 1976).

10. The theory did not deal with individual differences, individuality, or variability (Bringuier, 1980; Case, 1984, 1991; Fischer, 1980; Fischer & Pipp, 1984; Siegler, 1996; Turiel, 1966).

11. The theory implied that progress was a natural and inevitable reality of cognitive development, an assumption that seemed to be more and more a relic from the nineteenth century (Kessen, 1984).

12. The theory gave little role to cultural, social, technological, and historical forces as major influences on cognitive development (e.g., Bruner, 1972; Bruner, Olver, & Greenfield, 1966; Cole & Scribner, 1981; Rogoff, 1990; Shweder & LeVine, 1984; Smith, 1995). In particular, it seemed to paradoxically both inspire educational reform and at the same time offer no important role for educators (D. H. Feldman, 1980, 1994).

13. As a theory that aims to be suitable for formal analysis, Piaget's framework was found to have serious flaws conceptually, logically, and philosophically (Atkinson, 1983; Bereiter, 1970; Ennis, 1975; Fodor, 1980, 1983; Lerner, 1986; Oyama, 1985, 1999; Piaget, 1970, 1971b; Piattelli-Palmarini, 1980).

These and other criticisms of Piaget's great edifice eventually weakened its hold on the field and allowed other perspectives to emerge or reemerge. As Case (1999) suggested, Piaget's theory was so powerful that for several decades it seemed to overwhelm everything else. The empiricist-learning tradition that preceded it in influence was all but swept aside, while the cultural-historical-social tradition inspired by the writings of Marx and Engel was unable to gain a foothold in North American scholarly discourse. As the century drew to a close, however, the field began to apply (or in the case of empiricism, reengage) topics raised in these other approaches to the growing young mind.

Neo-Piagetian Contributions

The dilemma facing the field in the post-Piaget period, as Case (1999) pointed out, was to somehow transcend the major weakness of the theory while preserving its considerable strengths. A number of divergent paths were taken to try to achieve these ends, of which the so-called neo-Piagetians were the earliest and closest to the original Genevan approach. The two most prominent neo-Piagetian theories were those of Robbie Case (1984, 1991, 1999) and Kurt Fischer (1980; Fischer & Kennedy, 1997; Fischer & Pipp, 1984). These theories had much in common but also certain distinct features.

Both Case and Fischer tried to preserve a version of Piaget's stages, but added features that made them less problematic. In both theories there is a systematic role for biological maturational processes—processes that prepare the brain and central nervous system for the kinds of changes in structure that the theories propose. Here they were trying to reduce the miraculousness of the stage transition process by invoking a physical enabling change to occur in the central nervous

Figure 8.1 Developmental regions from universal to unique.

system as part of the transition process. Both theories also dropped the *structures as a whole* requirement for stages, making movement from stage to stage both a more gradual and more variable process. The shift from stage to stage could take place in a number of different content domains and in a variety of molecular sequences.

Finally, both Case's and Fischer's theories installed a *recursive* within-stage sequence to help deal with the disorder that was found within Piaget's stages, particularly those beyond Sensorimotor behavior (see Figure 8.1 for an illustration of how Case's and Fischer's theories used recursive sub-stage sequences in the stage architecture).

Although different in detail, both theories proposed a recurring four-phase sequence in each of the major stages (four major stages in Case's theory and three in Fischer's). The final phase of each large-scale stage overlaps with the first phase of its more advanced neighbor, becoming integrated into a new kind of organization as the system proceeds forward. This feature helps make transitions less abrupt by showing how elements from a former stage become integral to a more advanced succeeding stage. Thus two problems in the Piagetian formulation are addressed using recursiveness in phases: the lack of order within the large-scale stages and the lack of plausibility of the explanation of how a child moves from large-scale stage to another large-scale stage (Case, 1984, 1991, 1998, 1999; D. H. Feldman, 2000; Fischer, 1980; Fischer & Bidell, 1998).

In these ways (and others) neo-Piagetian theories demonstrated that some of the most intractable problems of Piaget's formulation could be transcended while still preserving most of the major features of the theory. In order to accomplish these goals, however, both theories focused on more specific contents and narrower sets of processes, losing some of the grandeur and overall sweep of the original. Case's theory dealt primarily with solving ever more complex and challenging problems through a natural ability to process more kinds of information and construct more complex rules for doing so. Fischer's theory prescribed a sequence of more and more complex skills that when acquired would allow the child (or young adult) to deal with more and more challenging situations.

As Case (1999) noted, both his and Fischer's theories explicitly attempted to integrate the broader approach of Piaget with some of the features of the empirical-learning tradition that had been so influential up until the 1960s in North

America, with the result that a more variegated, fine-grained pattern could describe each child's movement through the sequence of broad stages that the theories proposed. Both theories also allowed for greater impact from forces in the child's environment, thus restoring a major role in cognitive development for parents, caregivers, teachers, and technologies that seemed to have been largely lost in Piaget's framework (D. H. Feldman, 1976, 1981).

Vygotsky and Sociocultural Theories

While neo-Piagetians and others identified with the rationalist-structuralist tradition attempted to work from within the Piagetian edifice, others were sufficiently disillusioned with the limitations of Genevan theory that they looked elsewhere for inspiration. Partly in response to broader historical and cultural changes (e.g., the end of the Cold War, the civil rights movement, feminism, reactions to excessive greed in the 1980s, etc.), the works of the great Russian developmentalist Lev Vygotsky began to make their way into the mainstream of the field of cognitive development following the translation and publication of his seminal book *Thought and Language* (sometimes translated as *Thinking and Speech;* Vygotsky, 1962).

Jerome Bruner (1962) wrote a warm and appreciative foreword to *Thought and Language,* and Piaget himself (1962) also wrote a set of comments about the work, a rare tribute from Geneva. Michael Cole, Sylvia Scribner, and other scholars (e.g., Cole, Gay, Glick, & Sharp, 1971; Scribner & Cole, 1973) began to promote the work of Vygotsky and other Russian work as having importance for cross-cultural research on intelligence and other topics. The importance of guided assistance from others and the greater role of the social context in promoting or impeding cognitive development were themes of these works that resonated with greater and greater force in the field.

The combination of increasing impatience with some of the limitations and constraints of Piagetian theory along with the refreshing insights into learning based on the wider circle of influence in the Russian work started a groundswell of interest in that work and also inspired new approaches based on Soviet research and theory. Connections heretofore not easily made began to form across disciplines such as anthropology, comparative linguistics, history of science, and cognitive development (e.g., Cole & Means, 1981; Rogoff & Lave, 1984; Shweder & LeVine, 1984). Everyday activities like counting and tailoring that would have seemed irrelevant were suddenly of intense interest to cognitive developmentalists (e.g., Carraher, Carraher, & Schliemann, 1985; Saxe, Guberman, & Gearhart, 1987). A major new area of research and theory had been launched and would threaten to eclipse the Piagetian hegemony.

The main features of the Vygotskiian-Russian revolution are an emphasis on shared participation in culturally valued activities, recognition that cultures vary in what kinds of skills and abilities are valued, the importance of culturally constructed and preserved tools and technologies as key to cognitive development, and—in striking contrast to Piaget—the absolutely central role in human cognitive development of *language* (Cole & Means, 1981; Rogoff & Lave, 1984; Shweder & LeVine, 1984; Vygotsky, 1962, 1978).

This last feature of the sociocultural revolution—the placement of language in the theoretical center of the study of cognitive development—helped make yet another connection that had been waiting to happen since the earliest days of the cognitive revolution. Chomsky (1957, 1972) had claimed that speech was an innate ability, whereas Piaget had claimed that language was no more important than any other symbolic system to be used in constructing cognitive structures (Bringuier, 1980; Piaget, 1970). According to Piaget, speech structures were constructed using the same principles and processes as other symbol systems and were based on the same general procedures created during the first eighteen months of life.

These two powerful claims were apparently sufficient to keep the study of language development largely separate from the rest of the field of cognitive development during most of 50-year period that it has been systematically studied (Brown, 1973; Tomasello, 1992). It was one of Piaget's strongest convictions that the general procedures for constructing cognitive structures were applied to the challenge of speech as they were applied to the challenge of number, causation, space, time, and many other topics (see Bringuier, 1980). This claim helped support Piaget's view that human cognitive development shared many of its principles and processes of change with those of other creatures, placing human cognitive development as one among many examples of biological adaptation, neither superior to nor fundamentally different from other examples (Piaget, 1971a, 1971b).

Although this view acknowledged that human cognitive development is distinctive in certain respects (including features like the acquisition of speech and logical reasoning), these features did not set our species above the rest of the organic world. The particular forms that adaptation took in human evolution and individual development represent specific examples of general processes: birdsong and echolocation would be other instances found in other species (Bringuier, 1980; Carey & Gelman, 1991; Piaget, 1971a, 1971b).

CONTEMPORARY TRENDS

As a new century begins, there seems to be less need in the field to insist that humans and other species represent fundamentally similar forms of adaptation to the challenges of survival. Neo-Piagetian theories have proposed systematic biological contributions to the processes of cognitive development without compromising the constructivist core of their frameworks (Case, 1999; Fischer, 1980; Gelman, 1998). There is less of an either-or quality to the discussion about the role of nature versus nurture in development (Gottlieb, 1992; Overton, 1998; Sternberg & Grigorenko, 1997). It is also more widely accepted that biological aspects must be understood as vital to the process of cognitive development (Gardner, 1983). At the same time, the Piagetian assumption is ever more widely accepted that humans construct their own systems for representing and understanding the world and their experience of it (Carey & Gelman, 1991; Gelman, 1998). There are increasing numbers of examples of healthy cross-fertilization between the fields of cognitive development and language development (although they still are covered in different chapters in this Handbook).

The acquisition of speech is now understood to be a remarkable human adaptation, the investigation of which is central to understanding human cognitive development. It is also understood that language, with its powerful evolutionary and natural underpinnings, is constructed through a complex set of processes that are individual, social, cultural, and contextual (Cole & Cole, 1993). Contemporary researchers in language development such as Elizabeth Bates (Bates et al., 1991), Michael Tomasello (1992) and Susan Goldin-Meadow (2000) reflect this trend to draw upon several traditions (Piagetian, Vygotskiian, evolutionary, nativist, computational) to build their frameworks for interpreting language development (see also the chapter by Hoff in this volume).

The Universal Versus Individual Cognitive Development

The field of cognitive development for most of its history has been concerned with those sequences of changes that are likely to occur in all children during the course of the first decade or two of life (D. H. Feldman, 1980, 1994; Gelman, 1998; Strauss, 1987). A consequence of this preoccupation with universals is that the variations caused by group or individual differences have tended to be of less interest to the field (Thelen & Smith, 1998). Piaget reflects this view in his response when asked about the individual:

> Generally speaking—and I'm ashamed to say it—I'm not really interested in individuals, in the individual. I'm interested in the development of intelligence and knowledge. (Bringuier, 1980, p. 86)

Efforts at Integration

Two recent theories have tried to integrate the general sequences of large-scale changes in cognitive development with modular approaches to mind. The late Robbie Case (1998, 1999; Case & Okamoto, 1996) proposed that general stagelike structures of the Piagetian sort were part but not all of the story of cognitive development. Playing off these universal structures were a set of more content-specific modules of mind, each of which is particularly sensitive to and built to process specific contents. Following from Chomsky's work in language (1957), a number of modular theories were proposed, usually with several specific kinds of content domains proposed (e.g., Fodor, 1980, 1983; Gardner, 1983, 1993; Karmiloff-Smith, 1992; Keil, 1984, 1989). Examples of proposed modules other than speech that appear in one or more modular theories are music, space, gesture, number, face recognition, and self-other understanding.

In Case's version of an integrated framework, domain-specific knowledge (as it is often labeled) interacts with systemwide principles and constraints to form what are labeled *central conceptual structures*. The content-specific nature of the structures in designed to help explain how broad systemwide structures can be formed without resorting to a radical nativist interpretation (Case & Okamoto, 1996). Rather than formed as a consequence of the interaction of a child's general structures with the objects of the world, central conceptual structures are formed as a consequence of the child's concern with certain content areas like narrative, number, and space, each of which has distinct constraints and distinct opportunities for learning. Because of the many ways in which the central conceptual structures may be assembled, Case and his colleagues argued that their theory includes room for variation and individuality in the actual course of development (Case & Okamoto, 1996).

A second version of an integrated theory is that of Karmiloff-Smith (1992). In Karmiloff-Smith's theory, general, systemwide structures are abandoned altogether in favor of a set of content modules that are universal: language; the physical world and how it works; quantity; thought and emotion; and symbolic representation. What remains constant

across modules, however, is a set of processes of representing and rerepresenting that give the child the ability to bootstrap from level to level, transcending constraints that each module poses to the developing child.

Using concepts from connectionist modeling in artificial intelligence and dynamic systems approaches (e.g., see Thelen & Smith, 1998), Karmiloff-Smith (1992) has proposed a theory that has both general processes for change and specific-content domains within which such changes take place. Her assumptions are that there are natural, content-specific constraints on development, but that children construct their understanding of the world through progressive efforts to represent and reinterpret their representations of the knowledge in each domain:

> One can attribute various innate predispositions to the human neonate without negating the roles of the physical and sociocultural environments and without jeopardizing the deep-seated conviction that we are special . . . (p. 5).

A third approach concerns itself with the range and variety of content domains that have been established by human effort without taking a stand one way or another on the issue of modularity (D. H. Feldman, 1980, 1994, 1995). This approach attempts to specify the distinctive markers for categories of domains ranging from *universal* to *unique* (see Figure 8.1). The main goal of the effort to specify the qualities that mark domains in each region of the universal to unique continuum of domains is to show that there is vast developmental territory that is not universal, but which is nonetheless developmental in an important sense (i.e., important to individuals, groups, societies, and cultures; D. H. Feldman, 1994).

Nonuniversal theory (as Feldman's theory is called) aims to provide a framework for knowledge and knowing that encompasses Piaget's universalist framework and places it into a context of other less universal developmental domains. By describing the levels of various domains in each of the regions of the universal to unique continuum, some of the commonality across domains and some of the distinctiveness of each region and each domain are revealed (van Geert, 1997).

A more recent effort at integration is to be found in the work of Patricia Greenfield (2001). In this framework, the kind of cognitive developmental theory that best explains how children learn and develop is a function of the cultural context within which the processes and activities of learning and development take place. Based on studies in several distinct cultural settings in the United States, Mexico, and Central America, Greenfield and her colleagues have proposed that a more Piagetian framework is most appropriate in cultural context in which economic constraints on learning are minimal, whereas a Vygotskyan framework better captures learning and development when there is pressure to acquire particular skills and techniques to ensure economic well-being.

For Greenfield and her colleagues, there is not a single theory that is a best fit to every cultural context. Rather, different theories will capture the experience of learning and development depending upon the kinds of constraints imposed by the social and cultural contexts that surround them.

The theories just described have in common that they attempt to preserve some of the useful features of approaches like Piaget's that emphasize universals in cognitive development, while at the same time trying to build into their architecture important variations within and across individuals, groups, societies, and cultures. Case's approach focuses on how individuals use modules of specified content to construct universal conceptual structures, with the primary aim to better account for general, systemwide change than do previous frameworks. Karmiloff-Smith abandons general, systemwide change in favor of more domain-specific development, but with sequences of processes of change that can be found across domains. Thus, her theory also aims primarily to account for universals in development, but to do so in ways that reconcile nativist and constructivist perspectives.

Nonuniversal theory is primarily intended to illustrate the diversity in developmental domains that may engage the energies of individuals. While recognizing that there are some domains that are universal or nearly so, as Piaget proposed, the theory proposes that many other domains of knowledge and skill can be conceptualized as developmental in the sense that they are built in sequences of developmental levels and are achieved through change processes that include qualitative shifts in organization and functioning. By drawing attention to common as well as distinct features of various domains, some of which are universally achieved and others of which may be achieved only by members of a species, a culture, a discipline, an avocation, or even an individual, the range of topics of concern to developmentalists is greatly expanded.

Greenfield's approach is intended less to integrate various theoretical frameworks into a single one, but rather to add a set of broader social and cultural considerations to the discussion of learning and development that help guide the selection of one or another existing theoretical explanation. In this respect, theories are less competing explanations for a single truth, but rather exist as possible sources of truth, understanding, enrichment, and guidance, depending upon the context within which they are used (Greenfield, 2001).

Theories like Piaget's and Vygotsky's—in the context of the universal-to-unique continuum of developmental domains—can be better understood as dealing with different kinds of domains: Piaget's theory is about universals, and Vygotsky's is about pancultural and cultural domains (D. H. Feldman & Fowler, 1997). Therefore, trying to determine which theory is right and which is wrong misses the essential point that they are about different aspects of developmental change.

Nonuniversal theory is therefore useful in helping make conceptual and theoretical distinctions between and among various theories of cognitive development, but does not focus as much on how qualitative change occurs as do Case's and Karmiloff-Smith's theories (van Geert, 1997).

FUTURE DIRECTIONS IN COGNITIVE DEVELOPMENTAL THEORY AND RESEARCH

With more than half a century of productive work behind it, the field of cognitive development seems well established as a specialty area within developmental psychology. Although dominated by the Genevan approach for much of its history, the field has recently reengaged some of its traditional areas of emphasis, such as experimental learning studies and sociocultural-historical research (Case, 1999). It has also spawned some cross-disciplinary efforts to better deal with the challenges of explaining systematic, qualitative change, which is the heart of the matter for cognitive developmentalists. Drawing on work done in systems theory or connectionism from artificial intelligence, a number of contemporary researchers have tried to build frameworks that are complex enough to allow for many levels of description to interact with each other to produce major change (Fischer & Bidell, 1998; Thelen & Smith, 1998; van Geert, 1991, 1997). Efforts to model qualitative change using dynamic systems (Lewis, 2000; Thelen & Smith, 1998; van Geert, 1991) and chaos theory (van der Maas & Molenaar, 1992) have shown promise as sources of explanation for stagelike shifts. By working at a fine grain of detail, dynamic systems and other approaches take a further step toward trying to integrate general and specific, universal and unique, commonality and variation, and description and explanation (Lerner, 1998).

Similarly, research and theory from newly emerging disciplines like evolutionary robotics and artificial life simulations have become important sources of ideas for research and theory in cognitive development (D. H. Feldman, 2002; Norman, 1993; Varela, Thompson, & Rosch, 1993; Wilensky & Resnick, 1999). Starting with simple sensorimotor processes, detailed histories of interactions between and among levels of activity provide rich sources of information about change, including large-scale changes that can occur without changing the simple processes that gave rise to the emergent layers of activity in the system and that sustain it (Bedeau, 1997; Thompson & Fine, 1999).

There have also been great strides made in the technologies that permit brain imaging and of studies of the neural basis of brain development and functioning, both of which will no doubt have impact on the field of cognitive development, and perhaps vice versa (Johnson, 1998). The thrust of work in these areas is fully consistent with the direction of other current approaches in being interdisciplinary, systems oriented, interactive, and constructivist (Lerner, 1998). The interactive relations between brain and behavior—each influencing the development of the other within the context of other systems emerging and changing—reflects the growing consensus within the field that all levels of description, from the molecular to the whole organism in context, will be necessary aspects of our efforts to explain cognitive development.

Finally, we may wish to conclude this brief summary of the field of cognitive development by noting that the boundaries and borders between and among aspects of human development have become more permeable (Lerner, 1998). It is increasingly recognized that important influences on cognitive development may come from emotions, motivations, challenges, and environmental events (Bearison & Zimiles, 1986; D. H. Feldman, 1994). Although it seems likely that a field called *cognitive development* is likely to continue to exist within developmental psychology, the range of topics, the variety of phenomena encompassed, and the degree of interaction with other specialties are all likely to increase in the decades to come. There are without doubt sufficient challenges in the study of cognitive development to keep a cadre of researchers and theorists busy for many decades to come.

REFERENCES

Ainsworth, M. D. (1973). The development of infant-mother attachment. In B. M. Caldwell & H. N. Ricciuti (Eds.), *Review of child development research* (Vol. 3, pp. 1–94). Chicago: University of Chicago Press.

Atkinson, C. (1983), *Making sense of Piaget: The philosophical roots*. London: Routledge & Kegan Paul.

Bates, E., Thal, D., & Marchman, B. (1991). Symbols and syntax: A Darwinian approach to language development. In N. Krasnegor, D. Rumbaugh, R. Schiefelbusch, & M. Studdert-Kennedy (Eds.), *Biological and behavioral determinants of language development* (pp. 29–65). Hillsdale, NJ: Erlbaum.

Bearison, D., & Zimiles, H. (Eds.). (1986). *Thought and emotion: Developmental perspectives*. Hillsdale, NJ: Erlbaum.

Bedeau, M. A. (1997). Weak emergence: Philosophical perspectives. *Mind, Causation, and World, 11,* 374–399.

Beilin, H. (1985). Dispensable and nondispensable elements in Piaget's theory. In J. Montangero (Ed.), *Genetic epistemology: Yesterday and today* (pp. 107–125). New York: City University of New York, The Graduate School and University Center.

Bereiter, C. (1970). Educational implications of Kohlberg's cognitive-developmental view. *Interchange, 1,* 25–32.

Boring, E. (1950). *A history of experimental psychology.* New York: Appleton-Century-Crofts.

Brainerd, C. (1978). The stage question in cognitive-developmental theory. *The Behavioral and Brain Sciences, 1,* 173–182.

Bringuier, J.-C. (1980). *Conversations with Jean Piaget.* Chicago: University of Chicago Press.

Brown, R. (1973). *A first language.* Cambridge, MA: Harvard University Press.

Bruner, J. (1962). Introduction. In L. Vygotsky, *Thought and language* (pp. v–x). Cambridge, MA: MIT Press.

Bruner, J. (1972). The nature and uses of immaturity. *American Psychologist, 27,* 1–22.

Bruner, J. (1986). *Actual minds, possible worlds.* Cambridge, MA: Harvard University Press.

Bruner, J., Olver, R., & Greenfield, P. (1966). *Studies in cognitive growth.* New York: Wiley.

Carraher, T. N., Carraher, D. W., & Schliemann, A. D. (1985). Mathematics in the streets and schools. *British Journal of Developmental Psychology, 3,* 21–29.

Carey, S. (1985). *Conceptual change in childhood.* Cambridge, MA: MIT Press.

Carey, S., & Gelman, R. (Eds.). (1991). *The epigenesis of mind: Essays on biology and cognition.* Hillsdale, NJ: Erlbaum.

Case, R. (1972). Learning and development: A neo-Piagetian interpretation. *Human Development, 15,* 339–358.

Case, R. (1984). The process of stage transition: A neo-Piagetian view. In R. Sternberg (Ed.), *Mechanisms of cognitive development* (pp. 19–44). San Francisco: W. H. Freeman.

Case, R. (1985). *Intellectual development: Birth to adulthood.* New York: Academic Press.

Case, R. (1991). *The mind's staircase: Exploring the conceptual underpinnings of children's thought and knowledge.* Mahwah, NJ: Erlbaum.

Case, R. (1998). The development of conceptual structures. In D. Kuhn & R. Siegler (Eds.), *Handbook of child psychology: Vol. 2. Perception, cognition, and language* (5th ed., pp. 745–800). New York: Wiley.

Case, R. (1999). Conceptual development in the child and the field: A personal view of the Piagetian legacy. In E. Scholnick, K. Nelson, S. Gelman, & P. Miller (Eds.), *Conceptual development: Piaget's legacy* (pp. 23–51). Mahwah, NJ: Erlbaum.

Case, R., & Okamoto, Y. (1996). The role of central conceptual structures in the development of children's thought. *Monographs of the Society for Research in Child development, 61* (1–2, Serial No. 246).

Cellerier, G. (1987). Structures and functions. In B. Inhelder, D. de Caprona, & A. Cornu-Wells (Eds.), *Piaget today* (pp. 15–36). Hillsdale, NJ: Erlbaum.

Chomsky, N. (1957). *Syntactic structures.* The Hague, The Netherlands: Mouton.

Chomsky, N. (1972). Psychology and ideology. *Cognition, 1,* 11–46.

Cole, M., & Cole, S. (1993). *The development of children* (2nd ed.). New York: Scientific American Books.

Cole, M., Gay, J., Glick, J., & Sharp, D. (1971) *The cultural context of learning and thinking.* New York: Basic Books.

Cole, M., & Means, B. (1981). *Comparative studies of how people think: An introduction.* Cambridge, MA: Harvard University Press.

Cole, M., & Scribner, S. (1981). *Culture and thought: A psychological introduction.* New York: Wiley.

Commons, M., Richards, F., & Ammons, C. (Eds.). (1984). *Beyond formal operations: Late adolescent and adult development.* New York: Praeger.

Cowan, P. (1978). *Piaget: With feeling.* New York: Holt, Rinehart, & Winston.

Damon, W. (1980). Patterns of change in children's social reasoning. *Child Development, 51,* 101–107.

Damon, W. (1998). Preface. In W. Damon & R. Lerner (Eds.), *Handbook of child psychology: Vol. 1. Theoretical models of human development* (5th ed.). New York: Wiley.

Damon, W., Kuhn, D., & Siegler, R. (Eds.). (1998). *Handbook of child psychology: Vol. 2. Cognition, perception, and language* (5th ed.). New York: Wiley.

Elkind, D. (1976). *Child development and education: A Piagetian perspective.* New York: Oxford University Press.

Elman, J., Bates, E., Johnson, J., Karmiloff-Smith, A., Parisi, D., & Plunkett, K. (1996). *Rethinking innateness: A connectionist perspective on development.* Cambridge, MA: MIT Press.

Ennis, R. (1975). Children's ability to handle Piaget's propositional logic: A conceptual critique. *Review of Educational Research, 45,* 1–41.

Feldman, D. H. (1976). The child as craftsman. *Phi Delta Kappan, 58,* 143–149.

Feldman, D. H. (1980). *Beyond universals in cognitive development.* Norwood, NJ: Ablex.

Feldman, D. H. (1994). *Beyond universals in cognitive development* (2nd ed.). Norwood, NJ: Ablex.

Feldman, D. H. (1995). Learning and development in nonuniversal theory. *Human Development, 38,* 315–321.

Feldman, D. H. (2002, June). *Piaget's stages revisited (and somewhat revised).* Presented at the Annual Meeting of the Jean Piaget Society, Philadelphia, PA.

Feldman, D. H., & Fowler, C. (1997). The nature(s) of developmental change: Piaget, Vygotsky and the transition process. *New Ideas in Psychology, 15,* 195–210.

Feldman, J. A. (1981). A connectionist model of visual memory. In G. Hinton & J. Anderson (Eds.), *Parallel models of associative memory.* Mahwah, NJ: Erlbaum.

Fischer, K. W. (1980). A theory of cognitive development: The control and construction of hierarchies of skills. *Psychological Review, 87,* 477–531.

Fischer, K. W., & Bidell, T. (1998). Dynamic development of psychological structures in action and thought. In W. Damon & R. Lerner (Eds.), *Handbook of child psychology: Vol. 1. Theoretical models of human development* (5th ed., pp. 467–561). New York: Wiley.

Fischer, K. W., & Kennedy, B. (1997). Tools for analyzing the many shapes of development: The case of self-in-relationships in Korea. In K. A. Renninger & E. Amsel (Eds.), *Change and development: Issues of theory, method, application* (pp. 117–152). Mahwah, NJ: Erlbaum.

Fischer, K. W., & Pipp, S. (1984). Processes of cognitive development: Optimal level and skill acquisition. In R. Sternberg (Ed.), *Mechanisms of cognitive development* (pp. 45–80). San Francisco: W. H. Freeman.

Flavell, J. (1963). *The developmental psychology of Jean Piaget.* New York: Van Nostrand.

Flavell, J. (1977). *Cognitive development.* Englewood Cliffs, NJ: Prentice Hall.

Flavell, J. (1998). Piaget's legacy. In A. Woolfolk (Ed.), *Readings in educational psychology* (pp. 31–35). Boston: Allyn and Bacon.

Fodor, J. (1980). On the impossibility of acquiring "more powerful" structures. In M. Piattelli-Palmerini (Ed.), *Language and learning: The debate between Jean Piaget and Noam Chomsky* (pp. 142–149). Cambridge, MA: Harvard University Press.

Fodor, J. (1983). *The modularity of mind.* Cambridge, MA: MIT Press.

Gardner, H. (1979). Developmental psychology after Piaget: An approach in terms of symbolization. *Human Development, 22,* 73–88.

Gardner, H. (1983). *Frames of mind.* New York: Basic Books.

Gardner, H. (1985). *The mind's new science: A history of the cognitive revolution.* New York: Basic Books.

Gardner, H., Kornhaber, M., & Wake, W. (1996). *Intelligence: Multiple perspectives.* Fort Worth, TX: Harcourt Brace.

Gelman, R. (1969). Conservation acquisition: A problem of learning to attend to relevant attributes. *Journal of Experimental Child Psychology, 7,* 167–187.

Gelman, R. (1979). Why we will continue to read Piaget. *The Genetic Epistemologist, 8,* 1–3.

Gelman, R. (1998). Domain specificity in cognitive development: Universals and nonuniversals. In M. Sabourin, F. Craik, & M. Robert (Eds.), *Advances in psychological science: Vol. 2.*

Biological and cognitive aspects (pp. 557–579). East Sussex, UK: Psychology Press.

Gibson, E. J. (1969). *Principles of perceptual learning and development*. New York: Appleton-Century-Crofts.

Ginsburg, H., & Opper, S. (1988). *Piaget's theory of intellectual development* (3rd ed.). New York: Prentice-Hall.

Glick, J. (1983). Piaget, Vygotsky, and Werner. In S. Wapner & B. Kaplan (Eds.), *Toward a holistic developmental psychology* (pp. 51–62). New York: Hudson Hills Press.

Goldin-Meadow, S. (2000). Beyond words: The importance of gestures to researchers and learners. *Child Development, 71,* 231–239.

Gopnik, A., & Meltzoff, A. N. (1997). *Words, thoughts, and theories*. Cambridge, MA: MIT Press.

Gopnik, A., Meltzoff, A., & Kuhl, P. (1999). *The scientist in the crib*. New York: HarperCollins.

Gottlieb, G. (1992). *Individual development and evolution: The genesis of novel behavior*. New York: Oxford University Press.

Green, D., Ford, M., & Flamer, G. (Eds.). (1971). *Measurement and Piaget*. New York: McGraw-Hill.

Greenfield, P. (2001). Culture and universals: Integrating social and cognitive development. In L. Nucci, G. Saxe, & E. Turiel (Eds.), *Culture, thought, and development* (pp. 231–277). Mahwah, NJ: Erlbaum.

Inhelder, B., & Chipman, H. (Eds.). (1976). *Piaget and his school*. New York: Springer-Verlag.

Inhelder, B., de Caprona, D., & Cornu-Wells, A. (Eds.). (1987). *Piaget today*. Mahwah, NJ: Erlbaum.

Johnson, M. (1998). The neural basis of cognitive development. In W. Damon (Series Ed.), D. Kuhn, & R. Siegler (Vol. Eds.), *Handbook of child psychology: Vol. 2. Cognition, perception, and language* (5th ed., pp. 1–49). New York: Wiley.

Karmiloff-Smith, A., & Inhelder, B. (1975). If you want to get ahead, get a theory. *Cognition, 3,* 195–212.

Keil, F. (1984). Mechanisms in cognitive development and the structures of knowledge. In R. Sternberg, (Ed.), *Mechanisms of cognitive development* (pp. 81–100). San Francisco: W. H. Freeman.

Keil, F. (1989). *Concepts, kinds, and cognitive development*. Cambridge, MA: MIT Press.

Kessen, W. (1965). *The child*. New York: Wiley.

Kessen, W. (1984). Introduction: The end of the age of development. In R. Sternberg (Ed.), *Mechanisms of cognitive development* (pp. 1–18). San Francisco: W. H. Freeman.

Klahr, D. (1984). Transition processes in quantitative development. In R. Sternberg (Ed.), *Mechanisms of cognitive development* (pp. 101–139). San Francisco: W. H. Freeman.

Kohlberg, L. (1973). The claim to moral adequacy of the highest stage of moral development. *Journal of Philosophy, 70,* 630–646.

Langer, J. (1969). *Theories of development*. New York: Holt, Rinehart, & Winston.

Lerner, R. (1986). *Concepts and theories of human development* (2nd ed.). New York: Random House.

Lerner, R. (1998). Theories of human development: Contemporary perspectives. In W. Damon & R. Lerner (Eds.), *Handbook of child psychology: Vol. 1. Theoretical models of human development* (5th ed., pp. 1–24). New York: Wiley.

Lewis, M. (2000). The promise of dynamic systems approaches for an integrated account of human development. *Child Development, 71,* 36–43.

Liben, L. (1981). Individuals' contributions to their own development during childhood: A Piagetian perspective. In R. M. Lerner & N. Busch-Rossnagel (Eds.), *Individuals as producers of their development* (pp. 117–153). New York: Academic Press.

Loevinger, J. (1976). *Measuring ego development*. New York: Jossey-Bass.

Milbrath, C. (1998). *Patterns of artistic development in children*. Cambridge, UK: Cambridge University Press.

Miller, P. H. (1983). *Theories of developmental psychology*. San Francisco: W. H. Freeman.

Murray, F. (1972). The acquisition of conservation through social interaction. *Developmental Psychology, 6,* 1–6.

Mussen, P. (Ed.). (1970). *Carmichael's manual of child psychology*. New York: Wiley.

Mussen, P. (Ed.). (1983). *Handbook of child psychology* (4th ed., Vol. IV). New York: Wiley.

Neisser, U., Boodoo, G., Bouchard, T., Boykin, A., Brody, N., Ceci, S., Halpern, D., Loehlin, J., Perloff, R., Sternberg, R., & Urbina, S. (1996). Intelligence: Knowns and unknowns. *American Psychologist, 51,* 77–101.

Norman, D. A. (1993). Cognition in the head and the world: An introduction to the special issue on situated action. *Cognitive Science News, 17,* 1–6.

Overton, W. (1998). Developmental psychology: Philosophy, concepts, and methodology. In W. Damon & R. Lerner (Eds.), *Handbook of child psychology: Vol. 1. Theoretical models of human development* (pp. 107–188). New York: John Wiley.

Oyama, S. (1985). *The ontogeny of information: Developmental systems and evolution*. Cambridge, UK: Cambridge University Press.

Oyama, S. (1999). Locating development: Locating developmental systems. In E. Scholnick, K. Nelson, S. Gelman, & P. Miller (Eds.), *Conceptual development: Piaget's legacy* (pp. 185–208). Mahwah, NJ: Erlbaum.

Piaget, J. (1962). Comments on Vygotsky's critical remarks. Preface. In L. Vygotsky, *Thought and language* (pp. 1–14). Cambridge, MA: MIT Press.

Piaget, J. (1963). *The origins of intelligence in children*. New York: W. W. Norton.

Piaget, J. (1967). *Six psychological studies*. New York: Random House.

Piaget, J. (1970). Piaget's theory. In P. Mussen (Ed.), *Carmiachael's manual of child psychology* (pp. 703–732). New York: Wiley.

Piaget, J. (1971a). *Biology and knowledge.* Chicago: University of Chicago Press.

Piaget, J. (1971b). The theory of stages in cognitive development. In D. Green, M. Ford, & G. Flamer (Eds.), *Measurement and Piaget* (pp. 1–11). New York: McGraw-Hill.

Piaget, J. (1972). Intellectual evolution from adolescence to adulthood. *Human Development, 15,* 1–12.

Piaget, J. (1975). *The development of thought: Equilibration of cognitive structures.* New York: Viking Penguin.

Piaget, J. (1977). *Piaget on Piaget* [Motion picture]. New Haven, CT: Yale University Press. (Distributed by Yale University Media Design Studio, New Haven, CT, 06520).

Piattelli-Palmarini, M. (Ed.). (1980). *Language and learning: The debate between Jean Piaget and Noam Chomsky.* Cambridge, MA: Harvard University Press.

Plunkett, K., & Sinha, C. (1992). Connectionism and developmental theory. *British Journal of Developmental Psychology, 10,* 209–254.

Rogoff, B. (1990). *Apprenticeship in learning.* Cambridge, MA: Harvard University Press.

Rogoff, B., & Lave, J. (Eds.). (1984). *Everyday cognition.* Cambridge, MA: Harvard University Press.

Rogoff, B., & Wertsch, J. (Eds.). (1984). *Children's thinking in the zone of proximal development.* San Francisco: Jossey-Bass.

Saxe, G., Guberman, S., & Gearhart, M. (1987). Social processes in early number development. *Monographs of the Society for Research in Child Development, 52* (2, Serial No. 216).

Scribner, S., & Cole, M. (1973). Cognitive consequences of formal and informal instruction. *Science, 182* (35), 553–559.

Shweder, R., & LeVine, R. (Eds.). (1984). *Culture theory: Essays on mind, self, and emotion.* New York: Cambridge University Press.

Siegler, R. S. (1981). Developmental sequences within and between concepts. *Monographs of the Society for Research in Child Development, 46* (2, Serial No. 189).

Siegler, R. S. (1984). Mechanisms of cognitive growth: Variation and selection. In R. Sternberg (Ed.), *Mechanisms of cognitive development* (pp. 141–162). New York: W. H. Freeman.

Siegler, R. S. (1996). *Emerging minds: The process of change in children's thinking.* New York: Oxford University Press.

Siegler, R. S., & Munakata, Y. (1993, Winter). Beyond the immaculate transition: Advances in the understanding of change. *Newsletter of the Society for Research in Child Development, 3,* 10–13.

Sinclair, H. (1987). Conflict and congruence in development and learning. In L. Liben (Ed.), *Development and learning: Conflict or congruence* (pp. 1–17). Mahwah, NJ: Erlbaum.

Smith, L. (Ed.). (1995). *Sociological studies.* London: Routledge.

Snyder, S. S., & Feldman, D. H. (1977). Internal and external influences on cognitive developmental change. *Child Development, 48,* 937–943.

Snyder, S. S., & Feldman, D. H. (1984). Phases of transition in cognitive development: Evidence from the domain of spatial representation. *Child Development, 55,* 981–989.

Spelke, E. (2001). Core knowledge. *American Psychologist, 55,* 1233–1243.

Spelke, E., & Newport, E. (1998). Nativism, empiricism, and the development of knowledge. In W. Damon & R. Lerner (Eds.), *Handbook of child psychology: Vol. 1. Theoretical models of human development* (5th ed., pp. 181–200). New York: Wiley.

Sternberg, R., & Grigorenko, W. (Eds.). (1997). *Intelligence, heredity, and environment.* New York: Cambridge University Press.

Strauss, S. (1987). Educational-developmental psychology and school learning. In L. Liben (Ed.), *Development and learning: Conflict or congruence* (pp. 133–157). Mahwah, NJ: Erlbaum.

Tanner, J., & Inhelder, B. (Eds.). (1971). *Discussions on child development.* New York: International Universities Press.

Thelen, E., & Smith, L. (1998). Dynamic systems theories. In W. Damon & R. Lerner (Eds.), *Handbook of child psychology: Vol. 1: Theoretical models of human development* (5th ed., pp. 563–634). New York: Wiley.

Thompson, L., & Fine, G. (1999). Socially shared cognition, affect and behavior. *Personality and Social Psychology Review, 3,* 278–302.

Thorndike, E. L. (1914). *The psychology of learning.* New York: Teachers College Press.

Tomasello, M. (1992). The social bases of language development. *Social Development, 1,* 159–162.

Trabasso, T., Rollins, H., & Shaughnessy, E. (1971). Storage and verification stages in processing concepts. *Cognitive Psychology, 2,* 239–289.

Turiel, E. (1966). An experimental test of the sequentiality of developmental stages in the child's moral judgments. *Journal of Personality and Social Psychology, 3,* 611–618.

van der Maas, H., & Molenaar, P. (1992). Stagewise cognitive development: An application of catastrophe theory. *Psychological Review, 99,* 395–417.

van Geert, P. (1991). A dynamic systems model of cognitive and language growth. *Psychological Review, 98,* 3–53.

van Geert, P. (1997). The draughtman's contract. *New Ideas in Psychology, 15,* 227–234.

Varela, F., Thompson, E., & Rosch, R. (1993). *The embodied mind: Cognitive science and human experience.* Cambridge, MA: MIT Press.

Vygotsky, L. (1962). *Thought and language.* Cambridge, MA: MIT Press.

Vygotsky, L. (1978). *Mind in society.* Cambridge, MA: Harvard University Press.

Watson, J. B. (1913). Psychologist as a behaviorist views it. *Psychological Review, 20,* 158–177.

Wilensky, U., & Resnick, M. (1999). Thinking in levels: A dynamic systems approach to making the world. *Journal of Science Education and Technology, 8,* 1–39.

CHAPTER 9

Emotion and Personality Development in Childhood

E. MARK CUMMINGS, JULIA M. BRAUNGART-RIEKER, AND TINA DU ROCHER-SCHUDLICH

A dramatic change in views about the roles of emotions in socioemotional development—including the relations between emotion and personality—has taken place in recent years. The traditional perspective was that emotions were experiential, intrapsychic events that occurred more or less secondarily, as by-products of more significant causal processes and phenomena. Thus, emotions were characterized as feelings or affects primarily limited to intrapersonal experience. Given that emotions were difficult to observe, define, and assess, little impetus therefore existed to include accounts of emotions in explanations of children's social and personality development, and—for some scientific disciplines (e.g., behaviorism)—the study of emotions was even regarded as anathema to a science of behavior (Eisenberg & Fabes, 1998).

The past two decades of research and theory have advanced different perspectives on the role and significance of emotions to child development. Although a consensus on

the definition and functions of emotions is not yet apparent—reflecting the fact that these phenomena remain elusive and difficult to capture—various current directions in the study of emotions place much greater emphasis on the significance and role of emotions in social functioning and personality development.

Support is increasing for the view that emotions play an important role in the appraisal and evaluation of children's experiences and their readiness for action in response to contextual changes and events (Eisenberg, 1998; Oatley & Jenkins, 1996). Emotional expressions and emotional understanding are elements of social communication, and appropriate emotional regulation may be pertinent to children's adaptive versus maladaptive functioning. Emotional expression and regulation are also fundamental to individual differences between children in temperament and personality. Moreover, according to a functionalist perspective on emotions, emotions constitute more than what might be measured as self-reported feelings. Instead, emotions are seen as reflecting processes and configurations of responding pertinent to children's evaluation of the meaning of experiential contexts in relation to their goals (Campos, Campos, & Barrett, 1989; Jenkins, Oatley, & Stein, 1998; Saarni, Mumme, & Campos, 1998). Emotions are understood as part of the child's immediate reactions to person-environment contexts and of the extent to which their goals are met by ongoing events (Lazarus & Folkman, 1984; Stein, Trabasso, & Liwag, 1994). Thus, emotional functioning contributes to processes underlying the individual's dynamic processes of adaptation or—alternatively—risk for the development of psychopathology.

The present chapter aims to provide state-of-the-art coverage of various themes pertaining to the increasing understanding of the role of emotions in children's development, examining what is known, what is currently being done, and in what directions future conceptualizations and research are likely to take. Specifically, the organization of the chapter is divided into three parts, reflecting a progression from (a) an examination of individual development of emotion and personality in children, to (b) a discussion of relational influences, and then to (c) a consideration of emotions and children's adjustment.

Individual Development of Emotions and Personality in Children

Even if one is not yet prepared to accept the assumptions of the functionalist perspective regarding the role of emotions, emerging directions serve to call greater attention to the role of emotions in children's individual development. At the least, children's emotional expressions and regulation are understood to influence—and be influenced by—their social interactions, relationships, and contexts. Moreover, it follows that children's expression and regulation of emotions are reciprocally related to the responses of others to their social functioning.

Emotions and emotionality are also increasingly seen as related to important individual differences between children in social functioning, temperament, and personality. For example, the conceptualization of self is related to emotional processes (Harter, 1998), including the self-conscious emotions of shame, guilt, and embarrassment (Lewis, Sullivan, Stranger, & Weiss, 1989; Denham, 2000). Moreover, emotions are related to fundamental differences between individuals in personal characteristics and styles of social functioning. Thus, attention has been called to the significance of reactivity and self-regulation—each with implications for emotional functioning—as basic dispositions of

temperament (Rothbart & Bates, 1998). Moreover, temperamental differences in infancy have been linked to individual differences in personality as individuals get older (Caspi, 1998; Caspi, Elder, & Bem, 1987).

Relational Influences on Emotional and Personality Development in Children

Increasing emphasis is also being placed on relational influences on emotional and personality development in childhood. A functionalist perspective on emotions is particularly pertinent to emotional processes in social contexts viewed from a relational perspective. Emotional expression and functioning are closely tied to the individual's responses to social contexts, especially the contexts defined by significant categories of social relationships. For example, children's relationships with parents serve as an important foundation for emotional functioning in social situations. Thus, security of attachment pertains to children's emotional regulation in stressful situations (Cassidy, 1994; Thompson & Calkins, 1994). At the same time, the quality of emotional expressions and communications is related to the development of attachments between children and parents. For example, hostile emotional expressions and lack of emotional availability are related to insecure attachment. The quality of emotional relationships has been related to dimensions of parenting pertinent to children's socialization and personality development (Cummings, Davies, & Campbell, 2000). Furthermore, reflecting the significance of emotion to relations between parents and children, attachments are fundamentally defined as emotional bonds that endure over space and time (Colin, 1996).

Relational influences on children's emotional and personality development are also documented in the effects of marital functioning on children's functioning and development (Cummings & Davies, 1994). In particular, marital conflict—including negative emotional expressions of anger and hostility—may induce significant emotional and behavioral dysregulation in the children. Moreover, consistent with a functionalist perspective on emotions, current theory suggests that children's emotions serve an appraisal function with regard to children's responses to marital conflict and serve to organize, guide, and direct children's reactions (Davies & Cummings, 1994). For example, children who appraise marital conflict as distressing are motivated to intervene, whereas children who make the appraisal that parents will be able to work out conflict have little motivation to mediate in parental disputes (Emery, 1989).

Ultimately, these various relational influences on children's emotional functioning do not act in isolation, but are likely to have cumulative effects on children's reactions and behaviors. For example, there is evidence that children's emotional security—which has implications for children's emotional regulation capacities and dispositions in the face of stress—is a function of the influence of multiple family systems, including parent-child relations and the marital system (Cummings & Davies, 1996). Thus, in order to more fully understand effects on personality development, understanding relational influences must ultimately move to the level of including multiple sources of family and extrafamilial influence. With regard to the latter, there is increasing emphasis on the role of culture and diversity as potentially significant sources of differences in responding to emotional events in the family and in children's dispositions towards emotional functioning (Parke & Buriel, 1998).

Normal and Abnormal Emotional and Personality Development: A Developmental Psychopathology Perspective

Finally, although the study of emotional processes as normative influences on development is a relatively recent focus for mainstream developmental research, concern about the implications of disturbances in emotional and personality development can be traced back to Freud and early psychoanalytic theory. In recent years a convergence of emerging themes for process-oriented perspectives on both normal and abnormal development has found articulate expression in research and theory from a developmental psychopathology perspective (Cicchetti & Cohen, 1995). The study of new directions toward advanced understanding of abnormal emotional and personality development adds to the richness and breadth of normative models for child development emerging from the investigation of emotional and personality development.

INDIVIDUAL DEVELOPMENT OF EMOTION AND PERSONALITY

Emotions: Expression, Understanding, and Regulation

This section presents information regarding the development of and individual differences in the emotional system. Topics include emotional expressions and regulation or coping of emotions. In particular, age is examined as a factor in individual differences in emotional functioning. As children's cognitive and language capacities develop, so too does their emotional system. As is shown in the following discussion, changes occur in children's emotional expressions and in their awareness of their own and others' expressions

(Denham, 1998; Mascolo & Fischer, 1995); they are also better able to describe the causes and consequences of various emotions (Stein & Levine, 1999). In addition, children become increasingly savvy about how and when to strategically use emotions (e.g., maximizing or minimizing them) in relevant social situations (Saarni, 1998). They are also better able to regulate their emotions and cope with negative feelings associated with social interactions. Even within age periods, however, substantial individual differences between children in their emotional abilities are apparent.

Emotional Expressions: The Emergence of Self-Conscious Emotions

As children leave the toddler phase and enter into the preschool and school-aged periods, a number of changes in their emotional expressions can be observed. For example, the expression of basic emotions (e.g., anger, sadness, happiness), which are well documented to emerge in infancy (Zahn-Waxler, Cummings, & Cooperman, 1984), starts to become more context-dependent. In peer settings, for example, anger and happiness are expressed more frequently than are sadness or pain and distress (Denham, 1986). In addition, the frequency with which negativity in general is expressed declines with age (Cole, Mischel, & Teti, 1994). Emotional expressions also show more complexity over time. Children's expressions may show blends of various basic emotions. For example, children engaging in rough-and-tumble play show facial expressions of both anger and happiness (Cole, 1985).

However, perhaps the most significant changes in emotional expressivity emerging during early childhood following the infancy and toddler periods are the development of self-conscious emotions. As children's sense of self develops, particularly in the second and third years of life, they show emerging emotional reactions of pride, shame, embarrassment, and guilt (e.g., Lewis, Sullivan, Stanger, & Weiss, 1989; Mascolo, & Fischer, 1995). Self-conscious emotions are important to understand, given that such emotions affect intrapersonal and interpersonal dynamics and functioning (Barrett, 1998). Furthermore, deficits in self-conscious emotions (e.g., inability to experience guilt or excessive feelings of shame) have clinical implications across the entire life span.

According to *differential emotions theory* (DET), self-conscious emotions involve an interplay between affective and cognitive processes (Ackerman, Abe, & Izard, 1998)—that is, self-conscious emotions cannot operate without the sense of self, the ability to discriminate the self and other, the ability to sense the self and other as causal agents, and cognitive evaluations or appraisal processes that enable the ability to form comparisons. DET also argues that self-conscious emotions do not have consistent signatures in expressive behaviors over the life span. In a study comparing younger versus older children during a situation in which they fail a task, children younger than 42 months of age were more likely to look away from the experimenter after failing—perhaps indicating their concern with social evaluation from the experimenter. In contrast, older children were twice as likely to pout or frown (Stipek et al., 1992). Stipek and colleagues suspect that in both cases, younger and older children were experiencing shame, but that shame moves from being more externally to more internally based over time.

From a functionalist's perspective, although self-conscious emotions such as guilt, shame, and embarrassment reflect a more general "feeling-bad-about-performance" category, unique functions characterize each of the negative self-conscious emotions (Barrett, 1998; Denham, 1998). For example, when experiencing guilt, one wishes that one had behaved differently, and one will often seek reparation. When feeling ashamed, on the other hand, the ramifications extend well beyond those of guilt; an offensive self—as well as offensive behavior—is perceived (Denham, 1998). Moreover, feelings of embarrassment result from processes or events different from those involved in the feelings of shame or guilt. Children aged 5 to 8 reported that they would be unlikely to feel embarrassment in the presence of a passive audience, but would feel embarrassment in the presence of a ridiculing audience (Bennett, 1989). Thus, embarrassment—at least during early childhood—appears to result as a function of negative evaluations from others as opposed to the self (Denham, 1998).

Individual differences in the experience and expression of self-conscious emotions as a function of context are also evident. In a study examining 2-year-olds' responses to playing with an experimenter's "favorite doll" that breaks during play, some children showed amending responses by trying to resolve the situation, whereas others showed avoidance by averting their gaze (Barrett, Zahn-Waxler, & Cole, 1993). Barrett et al. (1993) concluded that amenders were experiencing feelings of guilt as evidenced by their approaching and attempts for reparation, whereas avoiders were experiencing shame, given that they were withdrawing from the situation. It would be interesting to examine why some children experience guilt and others experience shame even within the same context.

In a study examining gender differences, Stipek et al. (1992) found that girls show more shame *and* pride compared to boys. This gender difference is interesting, given that girls are more at risk for internalizing disorders, in which feelings of shame and self-loathing are evident. Another interesting

gender difference is that shame and guilt are positively correlated for girls but are distinct emotions in boys (Lewis et al., 1992). Whether such gender differences in self-conscious emotions are a result of socialization or of biological differences remains to be found.

Some evidence suggests that temperament in addition to gender is related to self-conscious emotions. In a study of school-aged children (6–7 years), children rated higher in internalizing components of negative affectivity were higher on prosocial characteristics such as the tendency to experience guilt or shame. In addition, children rated higher in effortful control (e.g., impulse control) were found to be more empathic and higher in guilt and shame (Rothbart et al., 1994). Such findings have implications for the ease with which a child can be socialized, as well as the development of the conscience (Kochanska, 1993), given that emotions such as guilt or shame remind individuals to think about rules and standards. Research related to the association between temperament and conscience is described later.

Emotional Understanding

In addition to undergoing changes between infancy and early childhood in emotional experiences and expressions, children become more sophisticated in their understanding of emotions. Young children not only show increasing awareness of their own emotional states, but they also become more adept at evaluating and appropriately responding to others' feelings and expressions. They become able to describe the causes and consequences of various emotions (Stein & Levine, 1999). In addition, children become increasingly knowledgeable about display rules—the social customs for when and to whom certain emotions are appropriate to express.

Much of what we know about children's understanding of emotions has stemmed from naturalistic research. Dunn and colleagues have frequently reported on observations of children in the family context (e.g., Dunn & Brown, 1994; Youngblade & Dunn, 1995) or peer context (Hughes & Dunn, 1997, 1998) because the "daily lives of young children are full of emotional drama" (p. 230; Dunn, 1999). By age 3, children evidence significant increases in the frequency with which they ask questions about others' feeling states (Dunn, 1988). Children also appear to learn about emotions in situations in which emotions are being experienced. For example, Dunn and Brown (1994) reported that mothers were more than twice as likely to talk about feelings with their children when the children were expressing distress or anger than when they were expressing happy or neutral states. Moreover, children were more likely to have causal discussion of feelings when they were mildly upset. In addition,

Dunn and Brown (1993) found that those children who engaged more frequently in such causal conversations were more advanced in later tests of emotional understanding. In particular, individual differences in children's understanding of emotions are important to understand because children who have difficulty in identifying emotional expressions and talking about the causes and consequences of emotions have been reported to be less accepted by their peers (Cassidy, Parke, Butkovsky, & Braungart, 1992). It is important to keep in mind that research on children's understanding of emotions has generally been conducted on children living in cultures in which emotional expression and discussion are accepted and encouraged. Cultural display rules may vary across cultures; thus, findings in this regard may be moderated by culture contexts.

In addition to gaining a better understanding of emotions, children become more aware of cultural display rules as they move from early to later childhood. In a classic study of children's responses after they received an undesirable gift (e.g., babyish toy), 6-year-olds (especially boys) were openly negative in their expressions, and 8- to 9-year-olds (and younger girls) showed *transitional behavior* in which their arousal level was apparent (e.g., lip biting), but their negativity was not as openly expressed (Saarni, 1984). Children aged 10–11 (especially girls), however, were most likely to exhibit positive behavior. Thus, older children become better able to mask their true feelings when they understand how their expressions might affect others. Individual differences in display rule use may be pertinent to social competence. Recently, McDowell, O'Neil, and Parke (2000) reported that fourth-grade children—especially girls—who used more appropriate display rules during a disappointment task were rated as more socially competent by both teachers and peers.

Emotion Regulation and Coping With Stressful Situations

As Thompson (1994) has pointed out in a monograph devoted to the topic of emotion regulation, there is surprising diversity in the ways in which different researchers conceptualize emotion regulation. Despite such diversity, most definitions of emotion regulation include aspects surrounding a person's ability to modulate, control, or reduce the intensive and temporal features of an emotion (Saarni & Crowly, 1990; Saarni & Mumme, 1998; Thompson, 1994; Thompson, 1998). In addition, regulation can occur at the neurophysiological, hormonal, attentional, and behavioral levels (Calkins, 1994; Fox, 1994; Rothbart & Derryberry, 1981; Stansbury & Gunnar, 1994; Thompson, 1994).

The term *coping* has sometimes been used interchangeably with emotion regulation (Brenner & Salovey, 1997), especially to the extent that effective coping is inseparable from effective emotion regulation and vice versa (Saarni, 1999). In addition, the term *self-regulation* has sometimes been used to mean emotion regulation. Self-regulation, however, may be a broader term that includes the ability to manage not only one's emotions but also one's thoughts and actions in adaptive and flexible ways (Kopp, 1982). As Saarni (1999) recently pointed out, however, self- and emotion regulation seem to be highly related, especially in Western cultures. It is not as clear whether self- and emotion regulation would be intertwined in non-Western societies.

Several researchers have recently attempted to examine the ways in which children attempt to regulate their emotions and cope with stressful situations. Saarni (1997) interviewed children aged 6–8 and 10–12 about the types of strategies that children would use during various stressful situations. The strategies that emerged, with the most adaptive strategy listed first and the least adaptive listed last, were problem solving (attempting to change the situation), support seeking from caregivers or peers (either for seeking solace or help), distancing-avoidance, internalizing, and antisocial behaviors (i.e., externalizing).

Rossman (1992) developed a questionnaire to assess the coping strategies of 6- to 12-year-old children from a diverse sample (children from a university subject pool, those from a battered women's shelter, and those experiencing incest). Children were asked to describe what they did when attempting to feel better and the degree to which they felt that a particular strategy enabled them to effectively reduce negative feelings. Similar to Saarni's (1997) findings, the following factors emerged: use of caregivers, solitary distraction-avoidance, seeking out peers, self-calming behaviors (e.g., taking lots of deep breaths), and distressed-externalizing behaviors (e.g., "it helps to get in a fight or hit someone"). Interesting age and gender effects also emerged from this study: girls were more likely than boys to rely on others (caregivers and peers), and younger children were more likely to rely on caregivers, distraction, and self-calming strategies than were older children. Somewhat surprisingly, age-by-gender effects also indicated that boys were more likely to report using distressed-externalizing techniques than were girls at younger ages, but this pattern reversed for the older ages. Rossman (1992) also examined the degree to which the various coping strategies predicted children's perceptions of self-worth. After controlling for age and gender, Rossman found that seeking help from caregivers and self-calming strategies were positively associated with self-worth, whereas distress-externalizing techniques were negatively related to self-worth. Thus, similar to Saarni's (1997) rank ordering, strategies involving either the self-reliance or seeking help from others were more adaptive than were those involving antisocial behaviors. Such externalizing behaviors may actually reflect the *lack* of managing one's emotions.

Whether certain styles of coping are more adaptive than others may also depend on other factors. In a sample of preschool-aged children, Eisenberg et al. (1993) found that gender was a salient moderator of the effect of coping strategy and social competence. More specifically, greater social competence of boys (but not that of girls) could be predicted by their display of adaptive strategies such as problem solving. Somewhat differently, greater social competence of girls could be predicted from their use of avoidant coping strategies. For both boys and girls, however, high emotional intensity was associated with lower levels of constructive coping and attentional control. In turn, children who showed excessive negative emotionality were regarded by adults as less mature and by their peers as less attractive as playmates. Thus, even by the preschool period, children who are able to manage their negativity in a more adaptive manner seem to fare better socially.

According to Kopp (1989), caregivers play a crucial role in serving as an external support system for the regulation of emotions—particularly when children are very young (i.e., during infancy). As children's cognitive development becomes more sophisticated, changes in the emotion regulation system can be observed. During the second year of life, toddlers begin to develop a more sophisticated sense of the self, as well as the ability to understand causes of distress (Kopp, 1989). Such changes suggest that toddlers become aware of their own distress and begin to realize that their own behavior can help alleviate negative feelings. In a study involving several emotionally laden situations, Grolnick, Bridges, and Connell (1996) found that 2-year-olds most frequently dealt with their distress by using active engagement with substitute objects, regardless of the context of the situation (delay of gratification vs. maternal separations). In addition, toddlers who used more active engagement were less distressed than were those who used other types of strategies (e.g., focusing on the forbidden toy). Thus, focusing ones' attention away from a task appears to help minimize negativity. Furthermore, classic studies by Mischel (e.g., 1974) have demonstrated that children who orient their attention away from a forbidden object are better able to delay their gratification, thus facilitating behavioral control as well as emotion regulation.

However, as Saarni (1999) recently pointed out, we do not have a systematic empirical literature that tells us what coping strategies tend to emerge at what age, especially given

that studies differ substantially on sample and contextual characteristics. Two general patterns have emerged, however: (a) As children get older, they can generate more coping alternatives; and (b) older children are better able to make use of cognitively oriented coping strategies for situations in which they have no control (e.g., Compas, Malcarne, & Fondacaro, 1988).

Although age is one factor related to children's differences in emotion regulation and coping, other factors appear to be important as well. Explaining individual differences in emotion regulation is an important challenge to undertake because older children who appear to have difficulties in managing emotions (e.g., anger) are at risk for developing behavioral disorders (Cole, Michel, & Teti, 1994; Dodge & Garber, 1991). Although psychopathological outcomes may represent extreme deficits in emotion regulation, less than optimal outcomes may also occur for children who struggle with regulating emotions. For example, Calkins (1994) has speculated that children who have trouble managing anger may have difficulties in establishing positive peer relationships.

It has been suggested that parenting contributes a great deal to children's ability to regulate their emotions (Eisenberg et al., 1998). For example, in a study of 9- to 10-year-olds' coping strategies for everyday stressful situations, Hardy, Power, and Jaedicke (1993) found that mothers who were more supportive in moderately low-structured homes had children who generated more coping strategies across situations. In addition, supportive mothers also had children who used fewer aggressive coping strategies and more avoidant coping strategies when children perceive the stressor as uncontrollable. Thus, parenting appears to affect both the breadth and manner in which coping is exhibited.

Temperament and Personality

In this section, we provide definitions of temperament and personality and review recent work related to the structure of each, as well as associations between temperament and personality. In addition, we examine recent research related to biological foundations of temperament and personality, as well as its links with social outcomes.

Definition

Much of the early work on temperament during childhood stemmed from Thomas, Chess, and colleagues' (1963; 1977) seminal studies involving the New York Longitudinal Study (NYLS). At that time, researchers and clinicians were acknowledging the importance of infants' and children's own contributions to their development and the possibility that socialization effects were bidirectional rather than stemming solely from parents to children (Bell, 1968). Current theory proposes that *temperament* is a component of the more general domain of personality and involves individual differences in basic psychological processes such as emotionality, activity, and attention that are relatively stable over situations and time (Goldsmith et al., 1987; Rothbart & Bates, 1998; Thompson, 1999). Although not all temperament researchers have agreed on the specific dimensions that comprise temperament, there is a general consensus that temperament arises at least in part from hereditary differences—and that temperament influences and is influenced by experience (Rothbart, Ahadi, & Evans, 2000).

By contrast, current work proposes that *personality* encompasses much more than temperament does—and that it includes skills, habits, values, perceptions of the self, and the relation of the self to others and events (Rothbart & Bates, 1998). Those significant others who provide physical and emotional support, care, and security are believed to help shape personality (Ainsworth, Blehar, Waters, & Wall, 1978). Furthermore, personality is influenced by broader social experiences involving neighborhood, school, and community contexts (Eccles & Roeser, 1999), as well as children's emerging morality, conscience, and gender identity (Turiel, 1998). Likewise, personality influences how experiences are construed and interpreted and the choices that a person might make (Thompson, 1999). Thus, similar to temperament, personality is influenced by and influences experiences over time. Moreover, some investigators have proposed that temperament might be viewed as early-appearing personality characteristics. Thus, the conceptual borders between temperament and personality as individual difference constructs are to some extent blurred. Despite the conceptual overlap between temperament and personality, however, empirical investigations involving both domains are quite sparse (see Caspi, 1998, for a recent review).

Structure

Compared to the structure of temperament during infancy, it seems that temperament during childhood involves fewer dimensions (Rothbart & Bates, 1998), especially if one considers temperament and personality to be organized hierarchically with broad traits (e.g., *extroversion*) representing the most general dimensions and lower levels including the more specific traits (e.g., *energetic*). Based on factor analyses of maternal report data on items from the NYLS for 3- to 8-year-olds, three higher-order factors were found: Negative Emotionality, Self-Regulation, and Sociability

(Sanson, Smart, Prior, Oberklaid, & Pedlow, 1994). Similarly, Rothbart's Childhood Behavior Questionnaire (which was developed in relation to infant and toddler versions), which is used for children aged 3–8, consistently yields three broad temperament factors (Rothbart, Ahadi, & Hershey, 1994). The first factor is Surgency, which includes approach, high-intensity pleasure, activity level, and shyness (reversed). The second factor, Negative Affectivity, consists of discomfort, fear, anger-frustration, sadness, and soothability (reversed). The third factor has been labeled Effortful Control, and includes scales related to inhibitory control, attentional focusing, low-intensity pleasure, and perceptual sensitivity. Interestingly, the three dimensions from both Sanson et al.'s (1994) and Rothbart et al.'s (1994) research resemble adult personality structures such as the Big Three (Tellegen, 1985)—Extroversion (Sociability and Surgency), Neuroticism (Negative Emotionality and Negative Affectivity), and Constraint (Self-Regulation and Effortful Control). Other child temperament-personality researchers have generally found support for five factors that are equivalent to the adult Big Five (see Halverson, Kohnstamm, & Martin's 1994 book for an extensive review). Thus, in addition to Extroversion, Neuroticism, and Conscientiousness (similar to Constraint), there is also Agreeableness and Openness. Such a structure has been found in child personality research despite differences in sampling and methodology (Caspi, 1998).

Although most theorists have conceptualized and measured temperament or personality on quantitative dimensions, some have argued for a categorical approach. By placing children into categories or typologies, one is able to take an *ipsative,* or a *person-centered* approach to understanding the child (Caspi & Silva, 1995). More typically, however, temperament and personality researchers have used a variable-centered approach, which involves the examination of multiple factors or dimensions, but each dimension is examined separately. In the end, both approaches may be useful. Categories or typologies are helpful because they suggest that a particular constellation of dimensions are greater than the sum of their parts, so to speak. Indeed, Thomas and Chess's (1977) original approach to temperament included both dimensional ratings (e.g., *approach-withdrawal*) and categorical aspects (e.g., *difficult child*).

As pointed out by Aksan et al. (1999), however, one difficulty with using grouping techniques is deciding what to do about cases that are ambiguous. If children are forced into a classification, within-group heterogeneity can be high (even if between-group differences are high). Thus, using the restriction that heterogeneity is minimal, Aksan et al. (1999) found that two typologies emerged for preschool-aged children: *controlled-nonexpressive* and *noncontrolled expressive*. Although these two types show overlap with previous typology work, only 15% of the children satisfied both between-category distinctiveness and within-category homogeneity criteria. Thus, categorical approaches may be helpful in capturing children's general dispositional styles, but also may be limited if within categories, children show wide variability.

Links Between Early Temperament and Later Personality

Despite the limitations of dimensional or categorical approaches, there has been some evidence that temperament and personality are related. However, it is also important to note that the amount of research to date that has examined the stability between temperament over time or between early temperament and later personality is still quite sparse (Caspi, 1998). Challenging questions pertaining to major developmental issues may prevent a simple examination of the stability between early and later dispositional styles. As pointed out by Thompson (1999), for example, can the same temperamental attribute be measured at different ages using age-appropriate measures? Just because we assign the same label to a dimension (e.g., Activity) at two ages, do we necessarily examine the same behaviors at both times or do we expect that there are qualitative changes in how a "trait" is expressed? In the following discussion, we highlight several studies that have examined stability in early temperament and later temperament or stability in early temperament and later personality. See also Caspi (1998), Rothbart and Bates (1998), and Thompson (1999) for more extensive reviews.

Using categorical approaches, Kagan, Resnick, and Gibbons (1989) found that toddlers who were selected at 14 and 20 months because they were highly inhibited were found to be more cautious and fearful at age 4. In a long-term longitudinal study, Caspi and Silva (1995) found significant associations between 3-year temperament groups and 15- to 18-year personality: Young children who were temperamentally undercontrolled were more likely to show higher levels of aggression, danger seeking, and impulsivity during adolescence. Inhibited children at age 3, on the other hand, were more likely to be rated as cautious and restrained during adolescence.

Studies relying on quantitative dimensions have found modest levels of stability over time. For example, Rothbart, Derryberry, and Hershey (2000) found modest stability between infant temperament and 7-year temperament for certain dimensions and a lack of stability for others. In brief, frustration-anger, fear, and approach showed significant stability over time, but activity and smiling-laughter did not.

Rothbart et al. (2000) makes an interesting conclusion that those dimensions showing significant stability are considered to reflect the more psychobiologically rooted dimensions.

Recently, Goldsmith, Lemery, Aksan, and Buss (2000) used both dimensional and categorical approaches in the study of stability of childhood temperament from age 4 to 7. They found evidence for moderate stability (and some change), regardless of how temperament was measured. Children rated by their mothers as higher in fearfulness, anger, positive affect, and emotion regulation at age 4 were rated higher relative to their peers at age 7 on these dimensions (rs ranged from .55 to .77; Goldsmith et al., 2000). Based on behaviors in the lab, children rated as Bold, Intermediate, or Shy at age 4 generally were found to show consistent group classification at age 7. One interesting result, however, was that greater stability in classification was found for the Bold group, suggesting that the Intermediate and Shy groups were more susceptible to change (Goldsmith et al., 2000).

Psychobiological Links With Temperament and Personality

Recent research involving childhood temperament has been examining the extent to which biological indexes map onto temperament characteristics. Studies that apply a psychobiological approach to temperament basically find converging evidence that temperamental attributes are rooted at least in part in biological bases. This convergence occurs despite the wide variety of methods applied and markers examined as potential indicators (Goldsmith et al., 2000). Behavioral genetics is a methodology that examines the extent to which temperament and personality attributes show heritability. Other research has relied more on direct physiological markers. The most common indexes that are used include heart rate and heart rate variability, cortisol, and brain activity as measured by an electroencephalogram (EEG). Several studies of child emotionality have also examined skin conductance.

Behavioral Genetics. Behavioral genetic approaches seek to determine the degree to which individual differences in temperamental or personality characteristics are related to both heritability and environmentality (see Caspi, 1998, and Goldsmith, Buss, & Lemery, 1997, for the most recent reviews of behavioral genetic research on temperament and personality during childhood). In short, behavioral genetic methods compare the degree to which family members' characteristics show resemblance and whether the amount of similarity varies as a function of genetic relatedness.

In general, most temperamental characteristics show some degree of heritability (e.g., around 40%), as well as non-shared environmental effects (e.g., those experiences that make family members different; Daniels & Plomin, 1985), in spite of whether samples involved twins or adoptive siblings, or whether the temperament measure was based on parent ratings or lab observations. We find it interesting, however, that several studies have found an exception to this general pattern. Factors involving positive affect and approach (Plomin et al., 1993)—as well as effortful control (Goldsmith et al., 1997)—have significant effects due to the shared family environment. Such findings suggest that future research should examine what specific types of shared family experiences promote (or impede) the development of positive affect and effortful control. Behavioral genetic findings on heritability also indicate that future research should examine the specific physiological mechanisms that link genotype with phenotype—that is, for traits showing substantial heritability, how do gene systems eventually become manifested in behavior? And what are the environmental conditions that might moderate such biological influences?

Cortisol. Cortisol is the primary product of the hypothalamic-pituitary-adrenocortical system (HPA)—a major stress-sensitive system (Palkovitz, 1987). Under conditions of stress, basal regulation of the HPA system is overridden, causing elevated levels of cortisol. At one time, it was predicted that elevated cortisol levels would be higher for inhibited children compared with uninhibited children (Kagan, Reznick, & Snidman, 1987). However, elevated cortisol levels have not been consistently found among behaviorally inhibited children (Tennes & Kreye, 1985). For example, Nachmias et al. (1996) found elevated cortisol levels during novel situations if toddlers were behaviorally inhibited *and* in an insecure parent-child attachment relationship. It is possible that securely attached inhibited children are better able to rely on their attachment figure, have effective emotional-regulatory skills, or both—any of which could then buffer the stress response. Moreover, Gunnar (1994) has argued that behavioral inhibition may actually reduce the likelihood of an HPA stress response in certain novel situations—that is, behavioral inhibition may serve as a coping response that reduces the child's engagement with overly arousing and unpredictable events. Indeed, a recent study by deHaan, Gunnar, Tout, Hart, and Stansbury (1998) seems to suggest that although cortisol levels were elevated for children showing shy, anxious, and internalizing behavior in the home setting, higher cortisol responses in a new preschool context were associated with aggressive, angry, and assertive styles

of behavior. Thus, HPA responses are complex and may reflect not only certain temperamental attributes, but also the context within which the child is examined.

Heart Rate and Heart Rate Variability. Studies examining relations between heart rate and temperament have been fairly consistent; there has been some disagreement, however, about the interpretation of findings. In a study by Kagan et al. (1987) in which inhibited children showed higher resting heart rates, as well as less variable heart rate patterns, Kagan concluded that such patterns reflected the activation of the sympathetic nervous system. Porges (1992) has argued, however, that cardiac activity in response to novel situations reflects activity in the parasympathetic nervous system (PNS). He has suggested that the increased and less variable heart rate patterns of inhibited children might reflect PNS withdrawal—and thus low vagal tone. Studies examining vagal tone (e.g., as indexed by respiratory sinus arrhythmia; RSA) have shown that increased baseline RSA and greater suppression of RSA following a stressor is generally associated with more positive temperamental characteristics (see Porges & Doussard-Roosevelt, 1997, for a review).

Electroencephalogram (EEG). Fox and Davidson (1984) proposed that the left and right hemispheres were specialized: Activation in the left hemisphere would be associated with positive affect and approach, whereas activation in the right hemisphere would be related to negative affect and avoidance. Some empirical support has been found—particularly with infants, but also with children. For example, Fox, Calkins, and Bell (1994) showed that infants 9–24 months of age with stable right frontal EEG asymmetry exhibited more fearfulness and inhibition to laboratory situations. Similarly, at age 4, children showing right frontal asymmetry also expressed more reticence and social withdrawal.

Skin Conductance. In a study of children in kindergarten and the second grade, Fabes et al. (1994) found a positive correlation at both ages between facial distress (when watching films of children being hurt in an accident) and skin conductance. In addition, skin conductance was inversely related to prosocial behaviors, suggesting that high skin conductance was reflective of a dysregulated state. In a similar study of somewhat older children (third- and sixth-graders), skin conductance was positively related to facial distress and negatively related to mothers' reports of general helpfulness (but only for girls; Fabes et al., 1993).

Early Temperament and Personality and Later Social Outcomes

Much of the work focusing on outcomes of temperament has concentrated on children's adjustment—such as internalizing and externalizing problems and conduct disorders—and other areas of developmental psychopathology (see Rothbart & Bates, 1998, for a review). In this section, we provide a brief overview of the research on long-term predictions of temperament and later adjustment. In addition, other, less widely studied areas—but nonetheless exciting research topics—are covered. More specifically, new research examining temperament's prediction to the development of the conscience, as well as its prediction to peer status, will be covered.

Behavioral Adjustment

Rothbart, Posner, and Hershey (1995) have discussed several ways in which temperament would relate to later adjustment: directly, indirectly, or by moderated linkages (e.g., temperament X environment interactions). Much of the work on temperament and behavioral adjustment has focused on direct linkages, in which a particular trait is associated with the development of an adjustment pattern (Rothbart & Bates, 1998). For example, in the Bloomington Longitudinal Study, infants and toddlers rated high on difficultness (high in frequency and intensity of negative affect) had more externalizing and internalizing problems in the preschool through middle-childhood periods (Bates & Bayles, 1988; Bates et al., 1991).

Temperament might also affect the development of later adjustment in an indirect manner. A child's temperament might elicit certain parenting behaviors, which in turn affect the child's development; in this case, a child's temperament is evoking certain responses from the environment (Scarr & McCartney, 1983). Alternatively, a child's temperament might predispose him or her to seek out certain experiences. In this case, a child is playing a more active role in creating (or niche-picking) his or her environment (Scarr & McCartney, 1983). There is some empirical support for indirect effects of temperament, although it should be noted that relatively few studies have examined indirect effects. In addition, several studies have found that models testing for direct effects fit better than do those including indirect effects (e.g., McClowry et al., 1992). One recent study, however, examining complex relations among concurrent temperament, externalizing problems, social factors, and drug use in sixth-graders, found significant mediation (Wills, Windle, &

Cleary, 1998)—that is, higher activity level and negative emotionality predicted more drug use. Furthermore, externalizing adjustment problems mediated the link between temperament and drug use. Finally, associations between externalizing problems and drug use were mediated by negative life events and by having friends who used drugs.

Temperament might also interact with environmental characteristics. For example, goodness-of-fit models suggest that it is not the child's temperament that will determine later behavioral problems; rather, how that child's temperament fits with his or her environment will affect the development of behavioral outcomes (Thomas & Chess, 1981). Again, however, relatively few studies test these ideas empirically. Moreover, many of the studies examining temperament-environment interactions have not controlled for main effects (Rothbart & Bates, 1998). One study that did examine main effects in conjunction with interaction effects, however, found modest support for temperament X environment effects. Hagekull and Bohlin (1995) found that toddlers who were rated as temperamentally easy and who were in higher-quality child care were less aggressive at age 4 than were easy children in lower-quality care. In contrast, difficult children's aggressiveness was not influenced by quality of care.

Conscience

Kochanska (1993) proposed two temperamental factors likely to be associated with the development of conscience: the child's proneness to distress and inhibitory control. Children prone to distress—particularly fear—may be afraid to commit a wrongful act. In addition, children with high inhibitory control may have an easier time preventing or "putting the brakes on" a behavior that violates rules. In addition, children with low fear, inhibitory control, or both may be harder to socialize. Kochanska found that for highly fearful children, maternal compliance strategies that de-emphasize power are correlated with child compliance—not only concurrently at 3.5 years, but also a year later (Kochanska, 1997).

In a study involving 2.5-year-olds, children rated by their mothers as higher in temperamental negative reactivity were more likely to show noncompliant behavior in the lab (refusing to clean up toys and touching a prohibited objected). Moreover, mothers of more negatively reactive children used more power-assertive methods as a means of controlling their children (Braungart-Rieker, Garwood, & Stifter, 1997). Thus, negative reactivity appears to affect parent behavior as well as children's internalized control abilities.

Peer Status

There are numerous reasons to expect that temperament would predict peer status, especially given that temperament is related to behavioral adjustment (e.g., Bates et al., 1985); in turn, antisocial and prosocial behaviors are related to peer acceptance (e.g., Coie, Dodge, & Kupersmidt, 1990). Surprisingly, however, there is relatively little research examining the extent to which temperament directly or indirectly relates to peer relationships (Maszk, Eisenberg, & Guthrie, 1999). There is some evidence, for example, that the ability to regulate emotions or manage anger contributes to peer sociometric status (Hubbard & Coie, 1994). Children who can regulate their arousal engage in fewer aggressive interactions with peers (Gottman, Katz, & Hooven, 1996). In a recent short-term longitudinal study that controlled for earlier peer status, Maszk et al. found that children aged 4 to 6 years of age who were higher in emotional intensity and lower in regulation (as reported by teachers) were rated as more popular by their peers. An interesting result was that earlier levels of social status did not predict later emotionality or regulation (Maszk et al., 1999).

In summary, research and theory supports the importance to children's socioemotional development of individual differences between children in emotional expression and regulation and the role of emotional processes in broader organizations of temperament and personality. The construct of emotion regulation offers particularly exciting promise for future advances, especially as understood in relation to temperament and personality development. However, more work is needed to further clarify the definitions of these constructs, their interrelations with each other over time and context, and the biological, experiential, and psychological processes that underlie the significance of these constructs to the individual's development in childhood. Moreover, these dimensions of functioning do not operate in isolation from children's social contexts; it is to the matter of the role of social context that we next turn.

RELATIONAL INFLUENCES ON EMOTION AND PERSONALITY DEVELOPMENT

The family is clearly the most important relational influence on children's emotionality and emotional development (Cummings, Davies, & Campbell, 2000). Accordingly, this section focuses on family as a source of relational influences. Traditional research has emphasized the importance of the parent-child subsystem for children's emotional functioning, often to the exclusion of the study of possible effects of other family subsystems. The parent-child subsystem is certainly the most significant single category of family influence on child development. However, the emotional qualities of the marital subsystem in particular may also have pervasive implications for the emotional quality of children's lives, as well as overall emotionality of family functioning (Cowan & Cowan, 2002; Cummings, 1998). In order to more fully account for relational influences on children's emotional and personality development, a familywide perspective is needed that goes beyond considering only the parent-child subsystem. Moreover, one cannot assume that relations found in one cultural context (e.g., race, ethnicity) will necessarily be found for others (Parke & Buriel, 1998)—that is, culture may moderate relations between children's emotional expressions, experiences, and personality development. Accordingly, the importance of appreciating and examining contextual influences on emotionality as a function of culture is indicated.

Accordingly, this chapter examines a variety of relational influences within the family on children's emotional and personality development, including factors associated with the parent-child relationship, the marital relationship, familywide functioning, and cultural contexts. Given their importance to a consideration of family influences, cultural influences as elements of relational influences are also examined. Although other factors (e.g., peers, schools; Crick & Dodge, 1994) also undoubtedly affect children's early emotional and personality development, a consideration of these additional influences is beyond what can be attempted in this relatively brief treatment.

Parent-Child Relationships

This section is concerned with parental emotional influences on children's development. Children have some of their first experiences with internal affective states, including anger, fear, anxiety, and happiness, in the context of their relationships with their parents. Moreover, the quality and intensity of children's emotional experiences are affected by the quality of their relationships with their parents. Parents may be highly influential—especially for young children—in children's regulation of their affect (Kopp, 1982; 1989). Chronic experience with enduring and intense negative emotions can be excessively challenging to the capacities of young children to regulate their emotions, and children with less-than-secure relationships with parents may have more frequent and difficult experiences with fluctuating and unpredictable affective states.

Emotionality is also a significant dimension of parent-child interactions and relationships, including parenting as acceptance, emotional availability, sensitivity, and parent-child emotional bond or attachment (i.e., emotional relationship; Barber, 1997; Cummings & Davies, 1995). Dimensions of parent-child relations pertaining to the emotionality of parenting, parenting styles, and the quality of the parent-child emotional relationship have been found to have substantial implications for children's emotional and personality development.

Emotional Dimensions of Parenting: Parental Acceptance and Emotional Availability

The terms *acceptance* and *emotional availability* have been used to describe a relatively diverse set of behaviors pertaining to the emotional quality of relations between parents and children (e.g., parental support, expressions of warmth or positive emotional tone, sensitivity to children's psychological states) that nonetheless share common ground—relations with demonstrated implications for children's emotional and personality development. Parental acceptance and responsiveness have been shown to predict positive child development outcomes, including greater sociability, self-regulation, prosocial behavior, self-esteem, and constructive play. In contrast, parental behaviors indicative of a lack of responsivity or availability have been prospectively linked with a variety of maladaptive outcomes, including social withdrawal, aggression, and attention deficit disorder (Darling & Steinberg, 1993; Maccoby & Martin, 1983).

Emotional mediators within the child are implicated in the effects of parental emotionality on children's functioning. Observing interactional bouts between parents and children provides one method for understanding the processes that parenting practices induce in children. For example, parental withdrawal and unresponsiveness have been shown to elicit infant protest, distress, and wariness, and children commonly react to parental intrusiveness and hostility by withdrawing and disengaging (Cohn & Tronick, 1989).

As another example of the role of children's emotionality in responding to emotional qualities of parenting, Parke, Cassidy, Burks, Carson, and Boyum (1992) have proposed that various affect management skills of the child mediate relations between parenting style and children's developmental functioning. Specifically, styles of parenting (e.g., stimulation, responsiveness) are seen to influence children's emotion regulation, interpersonal information processing (e.g., encoding, decoding) in social-emotional contexts, and understanding of emotion (e.g., ability to recognize and produce emotional expressions, understanding of the causes and meaning of emotion, understanding one's own history of emotional experiences and others' emotional displays)—which in turn affects children's ability to function competently in other interpersonal contexts (e.g., with peers, in friendship groups).

Thus, to elaborate on one pathway, emotionally negative parenting may foster children's negative attribution styles about parent-child relations, with subsequent effects on children's processing of peer events and relationships. Proclivities toward hostile evaluations and response tendencies in turn may increase children's susceptibility to poor peer relationships, aggression, social isolation, and depression (Crick & Dodge, 1994). On the other hand, parental availability may promote children's capacities for interpersonal connectedness, fostering a general view of the social world as a safe, secure place, and equipping children with the social skills necessary to advance the quality of their relationships with others (Barber, 1997).

Notably, as other examples of relations between parenting and children's emotionality, parental responses to children's emotional expressions may affect children's emotional and social functioning. Fabes, Eisenberg, and Murphy (1996) have hypothesized that children display the most constructive ways of regulating and expressing negative emotion when parents show moderate (rather than high or low) encouragement of emotional expression. However, parental encouragement of emotional expression is only one of the ways in which parents respond to their children's emotions that influence children's functioning. Additional dimensions, such as parental distress, dismissing children's emotions, comforting, and encouraging and helping children to solve distressing problems may also have implications for children's emotional and personality development (Eisenberg, 1996; Eisenberg & Fabes, 1994).

Emotional Dimensions of Parenting and Parenting Styles

Another level of conceptualization of parenting that has had implications in children's emotional and personality development are parenting styles. Baumrind (1967, 1971) proposed that the effectiveness of parenting styles for children's personality development reflects both the quality of the parent-child emotional relationships (e.g., responsiveness, warmth, availability) and parental control (e.g., demandingness, monitoring, consistent discipline). Working from these assumptions, Baumrind distinguished between three qualitatively different types of parenting styles (authoritative, authoritarian, and permissive parenting styles), each with emotional elements and with implications for children's emotional and personality development.

Authoritative parents utilize firm, consistent control, centered around integrating the child into the family and society and insisting that the child meet increasing standards of maturity as he or she gets older. Communication styles with children are characterized by warmth, clarity, reciprocality, and verbal give and take between parent and child. Children of authoritative parents are most likely to exhibit a healthy balance between high levels of agency (i.e., achievement-oriented, high self-esteem, independent) and communion (i.e., sociable, interpersonally cooperative, friendly).

Authoritarian parents are also firm in their control practices. However, their control strategies differ qualitatively from those of authoritative parents. Strict, unquestioned obedience to parental authority is expected, with any assertion of individuality by the child met with swift and severe punishment. Furthermore, authoritarian parents evidence detachment and lack of warmth. These children are at greater risk for internalizing symptoms, self-devaluation, social submissiveness, low self-efficacy, and diminished autonomy (Baumrind, 1967, 1971, 1991).

Permissive parents evidence high acceptance, associated with frequent expressions of warmth and affection by parents; there is also low enforcement of rules and authority. This laxness in monitoring and discipline means that children are left to regulate their own behavior and make decisions concerning their own actions (e.g., bedtime, meals; Maccoby & Martin, 1983). Accordingly, children of permissive parents exhibit high levels of self-worth and self-esteem, but exhibit impairments in maturity, impulse control, social responsibility, and achievement.

Extending Baumrind's work, Maccoby and Martin (1983) proposed that parenting styles can be defined in terms of two parenting characteristics ordered along linear continuums: (a) demandingness and (b) responsiveness. Four parenting styles (authoritative, authoritarian, indulgent, indifferent-uninvolved) emerged from the crossing of these two dimensions, with the first three similar to Baumrind's authoritative, authoritarian, indulgent. The last style was characterized by emotional uninvolvement with the child. For this parenting style, interactions with the children are considered an inconvenience and are dealt with in the way that most quickly and effortlessly terminates the interaction. This style predicts the most maladaptive outcomes of the various parenting styles, including low levels of social and academic competence—and also delinquency, alcohol problems, and drug use (Baumrind, 1991; Patterson, DeBaryshe, & Ramsey, 1989).

Parent-Child Attachment: Emotional Bonds Between Parents and Children

The effects of parental behavior on children's adjustment are more than a matter of the behaviors that parents direct towards their children or even the emotional intensity of

interactions or parenting behavior; rather, they reflect the underlying emotional quality of the relationship between parents and children—that is, interactions between parents and children are influenced by the emotional bond or attachment that has formed between the parent and child. Thus, in deciding how to behave, children not only respond simply to the behaviors directed at them by parents, but also respond as a function of the their emotional relationships with parents.

John Bowlby and Mary Ainsworth's attachment theory provides the most influential conceptualization of the nature of the emotional bonds between parents and children (Bowlby, 1969; Ainsworth, Blehar, Waters, & Wall, 1978). Moreover, the attachment theory tradition provides considerable empirical support for the significance of attachments to children's (and adults') adjustment (Cassidy & Shaver, 1999), although variability in the stability of attachment over time—and in the prediction of later behavior based upon earlier attachment—is evident in the literature (Belsky, Campbell, Cohn, & Moore, 1996; Thompson, 2000).

Parent-Child Attachment Patterns: Secure Versus Insecure Emotional Relationships

Attachment as parenting is neither defined as simply a set of behaviors that are observable at a microscopic level of analysis, nor is it defined as a global trait. Rather, attachment is an organizational construct—that is, goals or plans that serve to organize and motivate behavior that emerges from the functioning of the attachment behavioral system. Moreover, this system functions in a manner that is highly sensitive to context, including the past history of the relationship (e.g., the perceived availability and sensitive responsiveness of the parent) and the circumstances of the immediate situation (e.g., the appraisal of threat).

Attachment is a life-span construct, and a variety of methodologies have been derived to assess attachment security across the life span (Cassidy & Shaver, 1999). At all ages, however, security of attachment is held to have implications for the individual's emotional regulation and emotional functioning, with corresponding implications for personality development.

In infancy and early childhood, individual differences in patterns of attachment security are assessed based on the Strange Situation (Ainsworth et al., 1978), which consists of a sequence of brief contexts for observing the children's functioning—most notably, functioning in relation to the parent's presence, absence, and return. Children's attachment securities are classified to distinguish parent-child relationships in terms of the infant's relative effectiveness in deriving security from the parent in these various contexts and the parent's effectiveness in providing security.

The organization of children with *secure* attachments reflects optimal use of the attachment figure as a secure base and as support in the context of the attachment relationship. The child thus demonstrates a coherent strategy for using the parent as a source of security. For example, upon the return of the parent after separation, the recovery from an overly aroused or distressed state due to separation from the parent is smooth and readily carried to completion—that is, after making connection with the parent, the child rather quickly returns to a nondistressed state and to exploration or play. This pattern is associated with greater responsivity and warmth by the parents towards the children in the home.

The behavioral pattern exhibited by children with *avoidant* attachments indicates less-than-optimal secure base use and secure base support in the context of the attachment relationship. Thus, upon reunion the child conspicuously avoids proximity or contact with the parent. Avoidant infants are not responsive to parental attempts at interaction, may quite demonstratively turn away or look away from the parent and fail to proactively initiate interaction with the parents. These children are more fussy and readily distressed by separation in the home, and may have more difficulty with arousal control at a physiological level in the Strange Situation. Parents of avoidant children are more rejecting, tense, irritable, and avoidant of close bodily contact towards the children in day-to-day interaction in the home; they may also be more intrusive and overstimulating (Belsky, Rovine, & Taylor, 1984), thereby fostering less confidence in the child about the parents as a reliable source of security.

The organization of *anxious, resistant* attachment also reflects relatively ineffective use of the parent as a source of security in times of stress—and reflects the particular strategy of extreme dependence. Prior to separation, these infants are often clingy and uninterested in toys. Upon reunion, resistant children may mix angry behavior (e.g., struggling when held, stiffness, hitting or pushing away) with excessive contact and proximity seeking. Children are not readily reassured by the parents' presence or comforting (e.g., continued fussing and crying), and have considerable difficulty settling and returning to well-regulated emotional functioning. These attachment patterns are also associated with problematic histories of parent-child interaction in the home, including parenting that is relatively inept or inconsistent.

Emotional Dimensions of Parenting and Attachment Security

Attachment research provides evidence for the role of emotional dimensions of parenting practices, in particular, in the formation of attachment relationships. Bowlby's theory (Bowlby, 1969, 1973) proposed the importance of the parent's emotional availability and responsiveness for the development of secure attachments. The work of Ainsworth et al. (1978) provided empirical support for the pertinence of sensitivity, accessibility, acceptance, and cooperation as parenting behaviors relevant to the development of security of attachments to the parents.

A core prediction of attachment theory from its initial formulation thus was that the child's sense of emotional security would derive from the responsiveness, warmth, and emotional availability of the parent. Maternal sensitivity was particularly emphasized and defined by Ainsworth as the parent's ability to accurately perceive the child's signals and to respond appropriately and promptly. Although the size of the relations reported in Ainsworth's pioneering Baltimore study were particularly strong, dozens of published studies have reported that constructs reflecting maternal sensitivity and emotional availability or related constructs significantly predicted the quality of attachment. A meta-analysis suggests that the support for this relation is much more than convincing from a statistical perspective (De Wolff & van IJzendoorn, 1997). Attachment security is also predicted from parent's emotional availability as seen from a relational perspective (i.e., maternal structuring, maternal sensitivity, child responsiveness, child involvement; Easterbrooks, Biesecker, & Lyons-Ruth, 2000).

A Functionalist Perspective on Emotion Regulation, Attachment, and Personality Development

The attachment behavioral system has been hypothesized as organized and directed by children's appraisals of their felt security in specific social situations and contexts (Sroufe & Waters, 1977). Thus, children's emotions are viewed as an aspect of their appraisals of their emotional well-being or felt security in specific contexts, also serving to guide and direct their behavioral responding—for example, their decisions about whether to seek proximity of contact with parents.

Bowlby emphasized the role of self-regulatory processes in the impact of parenting on children's emotional and personality development, including children's emotional and cognitive appraisals of situational and contextual challenges and threats as influencing children's emotional and behavioral responding. In particular, emotional reactions reflecting children's evaluations of events were conceptualized as playing a role in children's organization and motivation of their responses to these events, a point made by Bowlby and subsequently expanded by later theorists (Carlson & Sroufe, 1995; Sroufe & Waters, 1977). Over time, these emotionally based self-regulatory patterns, which reflected the relative security or insecurity afforded by their experiential histories with parents in multiple situations, were seen as characterizing their functioning in response to current experiences. Thus, such responses were one class of processes derived from day-to-day experiences with the parents; over time, these responses served to mediate relations between experiential history and child outcomes—that is, these processes reflected internal self-regulatory structures derived from experience that served to guide current responding. Carlson and Sroufe (1995) articulate this idea:

> From a developmental perspective, these self-regulatory structures and mechanisms are viewed as characteristic modes of affect regulation and associated expectations, attitudes, and beliefs internalized from patterns of dyadic interaction. . . . These processes, or internalized 'models' (Bowlby, 1980), serve not as static traits, but as guides to ongoing social interaction, supporting the maintenance of existing patterns of adaptation. . . . Such processes are of great theoretical and practical importance, not only because they may explain continuity in individual development but also because they may lead to an understanding of pathogenesis itself. (p. 594)

This direction in attachment research and theory is consistent with other research and theory that demonstrate that self-regulatory processes may mediate relations between children's emotional experiences with the parents and developmental outcomes (e.g., Campos, Campos, & Barrett, 1989; Cole, Michel, & Teti, 1994). For example, Eisenberg and her colleagues have stressed the role of children's regulatory capacities in accounting for relations between familial experiences (e.g., parents' positive or negative emotional expressivity towards the child), children's temperament, and children's social competence and risk for adjustment problems (Eisenberg, Spinrad, & Cumberland, 1998; see also Thompson & Calkins, 1996). Increasing evidence also suggests that children's emotional and other self-regulatory capacities are influenced by their relationships with parents (Kochanska, Murray, & Coy, 1997).

Marital Relationships

Marital conflict has proven to be a particularly significant category of emotional event in the family with regard to child, marital, and family functioning (Cummings & Davies, 1994). Family systems researchers (e.g., Easterbrooks & Emde, 1988; Easterbrooks & Goldberg, 1990) have stressed the significance of the marital dyad to parenting and family functioning. When this relationship is distressed, family responsibilities and coping skills suffer (Gilbert, Christensen, & Margolin, 1984). Moreover, links between marital conflict and children's

adjustment problems have long been indicated, including externalizing disorders (e.g., aggression), internalizing difficulties (e.g., anxiety, withdrawal), and academic problems (Cummings & Davies, 1994; Emery, 1989; Grych & Fincham, 1990).

Direct Effects of Exposure to Marital Relations on Children's Emotionality

Emotionality in the marital subsystem—especially during interparental conflict—has direct effects on children's emotions and behaviors (e.g., Cummings, 1987) and indirect effects by influencing the quality of emotional communications in the parent-child subsystem (e.g., Jouriles & Farris, 1992). Furthermore, researchers using a number of different analogue paradigms have isolated the emotional qualities of interparental communications as influential in terms of children's emotions and behaviors (e.g., Shifflett-Simpson & Cummings, 1996).

Observational studies of children's emotional reactions to parents' conflicts are especially informative with regard to the direct effects of interadult emotions on children's emotional functioning. Examinations of children's reactions to naturally occurring marital anger and affection expressions and simulated emotion expressions indicate that marital conflict induced distress and anger in 10- to 20-month-old infants—a reaction that was markedly different from their reaction to marital harmony (Cummings, Zahn-Waxler, & Radke-Yarrow, 1981). In a follow-up study, Cummings, Zahn-Waxler, & Radke-Yarrow (1984) found that children's reactions to expressions of anger and affection in the home changed over time. Children who were 6–7 years old overtly expressed their emotions (e.g., cry, yell, laugh) during interparental anger situations significantly less often than they did as toddlers; they were also much more likely to intervene in marital conflict situations, as evidenced by the significantly higher rate of mediation attempts. O'Hearn, Margolin, and John (1997) also reported on children's reactions to marital conflict based on parents' completions of daily reports of marital conflicts that occurred in front of their child. Children from homes with physical marital conflict were more likely to evidence negative emotions (appear sad or frightened), become hostile (misbehave or appear angry), or attempt to control exposure to marital conflict (leave the room) than were children from nonphysical-conflict or low-conflict families. In addition, children from high-conflict families (physical or nonphysical) were more likely to take sides during marital conflict episodes than were children from the low-conflict homes.

The emotionally stressful effects of exposure to adults' conflicts have been documented in children as young as

6 months of age. Literally dozens of studies—with the findings converging on the same conclusions even when based upon multiple and different types of home- and laboratory-based methodologies—have consistently shown that children react with emotional distress as bystanders to conflict (Cummings & Davies, 1994). Distress responses shown by children include motor inhibition and freezing; self-reported anger, distress, concern, self-blame, and fear; behavioral responses of anger, distress, and hostile aggression; physiological indications of stress reactions (e.g., blood pressure, heart rate elevation, galvanic skin response); and children's concerned mediation in the parents' disputes. Children's reports of negative representations and expectations about interparental relations indicative of emotional distress are also associated with exposure to marital conflict (e.g., Davies & Cummings, 1998; Grych, 1998; Shamir, Du Rocher-Schudlich, & Cummings, 2002). It is notable that children's distressed reactions to marital conflict increase as a function of negative marital conflict histories, and such reactions to marital conflict are associated with adjustment problems (Cummings & Davies, 1994).

Indirect Effects of Marital Relations on Children's Emotionality via Influence on Parenting

A substantial literature supports relations between marital conflict and negative changes in parenting. Relationships marked by the presence of violence or a high frequency of overt conflict have been linked to inconsistent child rearing (Holden & Ritchie, 1991) and disciplinary problems (Stoneman, Brody, & Burke, 1989). Marital conflict has also been associated with increased parental negativity and intrusive control (Belsky, Youngblade, Rovine, & Volling, 1991) and with low levels of parental warmth and responsiveness (Cox, Owen, Lewis, & Henderson, 1989). Conflict between parents may drain them of the necessary emotional resources to operate effectively (Goldberg & Easterbrooks, 1984), or anger between parents may translate directly into angry interactions with children (Kerig, Cowan, & Cowan, 1993).

Marital relations are also predictive of the quality of the emotional bond or attachment that forms between parents and children. Increases in marital conflict during the first 9 months (Isabella & Belsky, 1985)—or even prenatally (Cox & Owen, 1993)—are linked to insecure attachment at 12 months of age. Another study found that high marital conflict when children were 1 year of age predicted insecure attachment at age 3 (Howes & Markman, 1989). Finally, children's relationships with their parents may also change because of the negative effects on their sense of trust or high regard for parents due to watching them behave in mean or hostile ways toward each other (Owen & Cox, 1997).

To synthesize the information from studies of marital relations and parent-child relations, Erel and Burman (1995) performed a meta-analysis of 68 pertinent studies. The results indicated a moderately large relationship between marital conflict and parenting. Furthermore, significant relations were found between marital conflict and multiple forms of problems in parenting. Based on this extensive meta-analysis, the authors concluded that "these findings suggest that, regardless of causality, positive parent-child relations are less likely to exist when the marital relationship is troubled" (pp. 128–129).

More recent observational studies of the emotional functioning of triadic family contexts of marital conflict and children's functioning add to the case for the effects of marital conflict on children's emotional functioning in triadic contexts (i.e., the mother, father, and child are present). In one such study, Easterbrooks, Cummings, and Emde (1994) reported that toddlers showed more positive emotional behaviors than distressed behaviors when their parents demonstrated harmonious or positive expressions during a marital problem-solving task. On the other hand, expressions of distress between the parents were significantly related to children's distress. In another recent study, Kitzman (2000) reported that family emotional processes involving mothers, fathers, and their 6- to 8-year-old sons become disrupted after conflictual marital interactions but not after pleasant marital interactions. Lower levels of family cohesion as well as higher levels of unbalanced alliances were found following marital disagreements. In addition, fathers demonstrated significantly less support and engagement toward their sons following the conflictual discussion compared to the pleasant discussion. Finally, Davis, Hops, Alpert, and Sheeber (1998), using a sequential analysis procedure, found that conflictual mother-father interactions led to children's subsequent hostile aggressiveness during triadic family interactions. Moreover, adolescents' aggressive and dysphoric responses to interparental aggression sequences contributed to the prediction of their overall aggressive and depressive functioning when general marital satisfaction was included as a control variable.

Familywide Perspective

Families are appropriately viewed as relational environments with systems qualities (Cox & Paley, 1997). At this level of analysis, familial influences can be seen to reflect the multiple and mutually influential effects of multiple systems, including interparental, parent-child, sibling, and whole family systems; thus, a systems theory perspective may be usefully applied to outlining the complex patterns of mutual influence of emotional expression and behavior that characterize family functioning. Accordingly, such a perspective in part emphasizes viewing families as organized wholes, with the wholes having influences above and beyond those of its parts. For example, overall family emotional expressiveness may constitute a context for children's reaction to family emotion—beyond effects due to the emotional qualities of specific family subsystems (Cassidy, Parke, Butkovsky, & Braungart, 1992).

At the same time, it also follows from systems theory that the family is appropriately seen as composed of multiple distinct subsystems, with each exercising influence on the others and on the whole. Accordingly, the actions and emotions of family members are necessarily interdependent, having a reciprocal and continuous influence on other family members, with each individual or dyadic unit inextricably embedded within the larger family system. Thus, a family systems model advocates against simple linear models of causality or the assumption that one can adequately understand family influences by focusing exclusively on certain individual subsystems (Emery, Fincham, & Cummings, 1992). Applied to a familywide model of emotions, systems theory predicts that the emotions and behaviors of each subsystem are related to the emotions and behaviors of other subsystems. It is notable that the emotional and social functioning of the sibling subsystem is also affected by marital conflict (Stocker & Youngblade, 1999).

Children and Family Emotionality in the Home

Research based on parental diary reports of emotional expressions in the context of marital interactions indicate pervasive interconnections between emotions and behaviors among family members during everyday interactions. Given that the meaning rather than the specific content of family communications is particularly important in the consideration of effects on both parents and children (Fincham, 1998), the perspective afforded by parental reports of their own emotions and their perceptions of the partners' and children's emotions may be particularly telling about emotionality and family functioning.

Taking the examination of relational influences on family emotionality a step further than in previous research (e.g., Cummings et al., 1981), Cummings, Goeke-Morey, and Papp (in press) examined the interdependence between emotions and behaviors within the marital subsystem and the effects on the emotionality of the marital subsystem on the emotional functioning of children—that is, progress toward a familywide model was achieved to the extent that effects pertaining to the responses of mothers, fathers, and children were

examined, especially in the context of interparental and triadic systems (mother, father, child). Consistent with a familywide perspective on the role of emotions in families, it was expected that the emotions experienced or expressed by one member of the family would be related to emotions experienced or expressed by other members of the family, including mothers, fathers, and children. Moreover, consistent with a functionalist perspective on emotions, it was expected that the apparent meaning of parental emotions—as evidenced by the negativity versus positivity of emotions—would predict the other parent's and children's emotional and behavioral responses.

With regard to interparental communications, substantial reciprocity was found between wives' and husbands' emotional expressions, both for positive and for negative emotional expressions—that is, the emotions of one spouse had a substantial and predictable relation to emotions of the other spouse. Specifically, parents reported that when one partner (either wife or husband) expressed more anger, sadness, fear, or negative emotionality (negativity, i.e., the sum of anger, sadness, and fear), the other partner engaged in more destructive behaviors (such as physical aggression, threats, yelling, giving dirty looks, withdrawing). Moreover, when one partner expressed anger, the other expressed more negative emotionality and engaged in less productive (such as calmly discussing, problem solving, reaching a partial resolution) and less constructive (such as humorous, affectionate, supportive, apologetic, compromising) behaviors. Conversely, when one partner expressed more positive emotionality, the other expressed more positive emotionality and engaged in less destructive behaviors and in more productive and constructive behaviors.

Moreover, Cummings, Goeke-Morey, and Papp (in press) also reported that emotions and behaviors between the parents were linked to children's emotional and behavioral reactions in a manner consistent with a functionalist perspective on the role of emotion in family functioning—that is, children's responses were consistent with the apparent meaning of the parent's emotionality as indicated by the valence of the parent's emotions. Thus, when parents expressed more anger, sadness, fear, and negative emotionality in marital conflict, children were more concerned. Moreover, children generally expressed more negative emotion and less positive emotion when their parents expressed negative emotions during marital conflict. Parents also reported that their and their partners' positive emotionality was related to their children's positive emotionality.

Furthermore, parents reported that children engaged in insecure behaviors (crying, freezing, misbehaving, yelling at parents, being aggressive) when parents were angry or evidenced negative emotionality. Moreover, children's negative emotional appraisals appeared to activate, organize, and motivate behavioral responding to marital conflicts, shown either by their overt avoidance of exposure to marital conflict or by active efforts to ameliorate the parent's marital problems (i.e., children acting as mediators). Parents further reported that children's efforts to act as mediators (involvement in the parents' conflict through such acts as comforting, helping out, taking sides) were related to the parents' expressions of negative emotionality, fear, anger, and sadness. Parents also reported that their negative emotionality, anger, and sadness was related to children's avoidance and that parents' positivity was inversely related to children's avoidance. Similar findings were reported for children's responses to the mothers' and fathers' expressions of emotions during marital conflict, and mothers' and fathers' diary records yielded remarkably similar patterns of findings.

In summary, these data illustrate the intriguing patterns of mutual influence of emotions between and among family members in the everyday context of the home. Moreover, the evidence indicated that individuals' emotions were more closely linked with their own behaviors and the responses of others to these behaviors than were other categories of social expression and behavior (Cummings, Goeke-Morey, & Papp, in press). Thus, although by no means a formal or direct test of the strong assumptions of the functionalist perspective on the role of emotions in family functioning, these results are sufficiently suggestive to support—even encourage—further exploration of the hypotheses of a functionalist perspective.

A Functionalist Perspective on Emotionality, Family Functioning, and Personality Development

Cummings and Davies have proposed a theoretical model for a functionalist perspective on the role of emotions in organizing, regulating, and directing children's responses to marital conflict (Davies & Cummings, 1994) and family functioning (Cummings & Davies, 1996). This theory, called the *emotional security hypothesis,* specifically places considerable emphasis on emotional regulation and reactivity as significant elements of children's appraisals and responses to family events. Moreover, when events are appraised as threatening, emotional reactions are seen as serving to organize and motivate children's responses (e.g., children serving as mediators in marital conflicts) to threatening events (e.g., hostile marital conflict; see also Emery, 1989).

The theory is proposed as an extension of attachment theory to a familywide model of processes that account for children's responses to family events, with these response processes—in particular, emotional regulation and reactivity—seen as having implications for children's personality development over

time. Some tentative evidence to support the model has emerged. Recent empirical tests of the role of emotional regulation as a mediator of children's functioning due to marital conflict histories have been conducted. For example, using a latent variable path analysis, Davies and Cummings (1998) examined whether links between marital relations and children's adjustment were mediated by response processes indicative of emotional security. Analyses supported theoretical pathways whereby emotional reactivity (e.g., vigilance, distress) mediated relations between marital conflict and both externalizing and internalizing symptoms.

More recently, basing their conclusions on tests formulated in terms of structural equation modeling, Harold and Shelton (2000) reported that children's emotional reactivity in response to marital conflict—as well as attachment security—mediated relations between family functioning and child adjustment.

Cultural Contexts

Consistent with the propositions of Bronfenbrenner's (1979) ecological perspective, childhood development is best understood as embedded in a variety of social and other ecological contexts, including community, cultural, and ethnic contexts of child development. Neighborhood and community, socioeconomic status (SES), and ethnicity (including generation and acculturation) are among the contextual-ecological influences that may affect children's emotional and social functioning, including the relative efficacy of different socialization practices (Parke & Buriel, 1998). Each of these factors may exercise influence and may change the relative impact of family events and processes on child development. Thus, it is critical that attention be paid to whether the socialization models developed on middle-class Caucasian samples are appropriate to other, often-neglected samples (Cowan, Powell, & Cowan, 1998).

Research directions that examine influences of culture and ethnicity are essential to understand the full range of variation in family functioning and child development, including the determination of whether family practices and their effects are culture-specific or culture-universal (Bornstein, 1991). There is an emerging consensus that innovative approaches are needed to advance substantially the cross-cultural study of psychological processes (van de Vijver & Leung, 2000). For example, in cross-cultural psychology, culture typically is treated as an independent variable. New directions in the study of culture conceptualize culture as process (Keller & Greenfield, 2000), with the effects of culture seen in terms of dynamic response processes occurring in individuals due to transactions between the individual and environment over time (Cummings, Davies, & Campbell, 2000).

For example, in contrast to much of the research in development psychology, an impressive body of attachment research has been conducted across cultures. In fact, an interest in cross-cultural perspectives has characterized attachment research from the beginning (Bowlby, 1969, 1973). Moreover, observational study of attachment security in naturalistic contexts and initial exploration of the tripartite classification of attachment (i.e., secure, avoidant, resistant) began with Ainsworth's work among the Ganda in Africa (van IJzendoorn & Sagi, 1999). In addition to the extensive research based on European samples, a substantial body of work has been based on cultures from other parts of the world, including Japan, Israel, China, Columbia, Chile, and several African cultures. This cross-cultural database is an admirable contribution, although the number of cultures that have been studied must be regarded as relatively modest in relation to the worldwide domain of different cultures (van IJzendoorn & Sagi, 1999).

Furthermore, cross-cultural research can be seen as generally supporting the validity of the basic propositions of attachment theory. Attachment phenomena—for example, the child's use of the parents as a secure base—are readily observed across cultures. Moreover, the different patterns of attachment found in Western cultures are generally found elsewhere and appear to describe the domain of attachments as adequately in non-Western cultures as they do in Western cultures. It would also appear that secure attachments are not just a Western ideal, but are normative and preferred across cultures.

However, cross-cultural research can also been interpreted as raising challenges for attachment theory. For example, the distributions of insecure attachments (i.e., avoidant, resistant) in particular have been reported to vary across cultures. We wish to note, however, that the more significant question for attachment theory is whether variations in attachment patterns follow from variations in parenting, especially emotional dimensions of parenting (e.g., parental sensitivity, emotional availability, and responsiveness), consistent with the predictions of attachment theory. This question exemplifies the process-oriented level of analysis that is a needed next step in the study of cultural influences on attachment. This level of analysis has been explored only in a limited number of cultures, especially with regard to the prediction of different patterns of attachment following from variations in the emotional dimensions of parenting (Waters & Cummings, 2000). On the other hand, although the evidence to date is relatively scant, emotional dimensions of parent-child relationships—especially parental sensitivity—have been linked with secure attachment in virtually all cultures in which statistically significant results are found (van IJzendoorn & Sagi, 1999).

Consider another example: As we have seen, a substantial body of evidence indicates that marital conflict and discord has negative effects on children's functioning and adjustment (Grych & Fincham, 1990). However, understanding of the pervasiveness of these relations is limited because most research has been based upon children and families from American or other Western cultures (e.g., British samples; Rutter & Quinton, 1984). Put another way, the study of families in other cultures or non-White ethnic groups has rarely considered marital functioning as an influence on children's functioning (Parke & Buriel, 1998).

To address this gap, Cummings, Wilson, and Shamir (2000) recently reported that children's exposure to marital hostility and other indexes of marital discord were related to adjustment among Chilean children, with effects at least as evident as those found among American children. Moreover, reflecting a process-oriented level of analysis, the qualities of marital conflict behavior were found to be related to children's processes of emotional responding to marital conflict across cultures, with Chilean children making distinctions in emotional responding between unresolved and resolved conflict similar to (or even greater than) those of American children.

In summary, research and theory are emerging to support a familywide perspective on emotions from a systems perspective; moreover, specific process models are being developed that emphasize the function of emotions in organizing and directing children's reactions to family interactions. Consistent with the move to process-level explanation of relations between emotions and personality, research has begun also to articulate cultural contexts as influences on relations between emotional functioning and relationships, family contexts, and children's personality development. However, more research is needed to further explore interrelations between family, especially the significance of sibling relationships and the effects of extended family members (e.g., grandparents), culture, and children's emotions and behaviors, with ongoing prospective longitudinal studies especially significant for further understanding the causal role of children's emotional functioning in their personality development across cultural contexts.

NORMAL AND ABNORMAL EMOTIONAL AND PERSONALITY DEVELOPMENT: A DEVELOPMENTAL PSYCHOPATHOLOGY PERSPECTIVE

The study of emotional and personality disorders in childhood has a long history in psychology. However, increasing emphasis is being placed on moving beyond simply documenting correlations between childhood factors and later development to advanced understanding of the processes underlying children's emotional and personality development. In particular, the developmental psychopathology perspective has underscored the importance of understanding the processes that underlie normal and abnormal development (Cicchetti & Cohen, 1995; Cummings, Davies, & Campbell, 2000). The purpose of this last section is to briefly review the themes that characterize these emerging directions for conceptualizing emotional and personality development.

Conceptualizing Personality Disorders as Processes, Not Outcomes

Childhood psychopathology was long viewed from the perspective of a static model of development (e.g., something that a person "has")—that is, disorders were treated as discrete, enduring, and having linear trajectories in terms of causes and outcomes (Sroufe, 1997), with the focus on symptom description and the classification of disorders rather than on etiological processes (Sroufe & Rutter, 1984). Precursors to disorders were expected to be single pathogens (e.g., biologically based pathogens) or early forms of the disorder, and psychopathology was assumed to be qualitatively different from normality (Rutter, 1986).

In addition, the focus was on decidedly on abnormality and risk vulnerability. For example, marital conflict was assumed to be a homogeneous stimulus with uniformly negative and distressing effects on children. Recent work—consistent with a developmental psychopathology perspective—has shown that distinctions can be made between constructive and destructive marital conflict behaviors from the perspective of effects on children; with some forms actually beneficial for children to witness and with possibly protective effects (Cummings, 1998; Cummings & Davies, 1994).

Moreover, the developmental psychopathology approach calls attention to the importance of understanding the multiplicity of individual, biological, social, familial, and other processes that underlie the development of childhood problems. For example, multiple emotional, cognitive, and physiological processes have been implicated as mediators of relations between marital conflict and children's adjustment and social competence (Cummings & Davies, 2002). Additionally, a focus is on an in-depth understanding of the developmental processes and pathways that precede and account for the development of clinical disorders. A developmental psychopathology approach also advocates simultaneously examining both abnormal and normal and risk and resiliency to provide a more accurate, appropriately complex, and complete picture of the processes that account for the risk for—and emergence of—psychopathology in children.

Accordingly, developmental psychopathology can best be defined in terms of its primary goal: achieving a science that can unravel the dynamic-process relations underlying pathways of normal development and the development of psychopathology (Cummings, Davies, & Campbell, 2000). Given the process-oriented focus, it follows that children's adjustment and functioning ultimately must be assessed using a multidisciplinary, multidomain, multicontextual, and multimethod strategies (Cicchetti & Cohen, 1995). It is notable that the developmental psychopathology perspective assumes a contextualistic worldview, in which development is viewed as emerging from ongoing interactions involving an active, changing organism in a dynamic, changing context (Cummings, Davies, & Campbell, 2000). A transactional model of developmental process is adopted, whereby reciprocal interactions occur between children's intraorganismic characteristics, their adaptational history, and the current context (Sroufe, 1997). Thus, psychopathology is not due to a single pathogen's acting on the child, but rather is the end result of complex interactions between risk and protective factors over time.

The aim is to uncover dynamic-process relations, including moderators and mediators of childhood outcomes. Psychopathology is viewed as reflecting deviations from normative patterns over time (Sroufe, 1997). Inherent in this concept are the notions of *multifinality,* in which the same pathways lead to different outcomes, and *equifinality,* in which more than one pathway leads to the same outcome. The development of disorder is understood from a probabilistic perspective (i.e., change is possible at any point in time), although change is constrained by prior adaptation. Furthermore, emphasis is placed on the significance of context for interpreting developmental patterns: What may be dysfunctional or harmful in one context may be adaptive in another.

Although the focus of developmental psychopathology is not on describing and identifying specific disorders in children, this perspective advocates for fuller conceptualization by emphasizing the importance of taking into account both the context and the developmental level of the child in nosological systems. For example, this approach to defining disorders is pertinent to understanding the comorbidity of disorders. Note that children often have behaviors that fit into two or more diagnostic categories. Although some approaches may attempt to assign only one or the other diagnosis or may assume that multiple disorders are present, the developmental psychopathology perspective considers the possibility that underlying processes do not necessarily fit into standard nosological classifications (Sroufe, 1997)—that is, the concept of static diagnostic categories may be not be an optimal heuristic for capturing the dynamic patterns of processes of psychological functioning, nor for capturing the current and historical contexts that underlie children's functioning. For example, diagnoses of attention-deficit/hyperactivity disorder and oppositional defiance disorder often go hand in hand, but children fitting both classifications may have family histories, developmental courses, and prognoses different from those of children with one or the other problem (Cummings, Davies, & Campbell, 2000). For example, children fitting both classifications are more likely than are other groups to have dysfunctional families with high rates of psychopathology; they are also more likely to have poorer outcomes in adolescence (Layhey et al., 1988) and adulthood (Weiss & Hechtman, 1993). In sum, focusing on the child, familial, social, and developmental factors occurring and changing over time provides avenues for greater understanding of how and why maladjustment occurred and how to best treat it.

As can be seen, the dynamic process-oriented approach of developmental psychopathology provides a powerful theoretical framework for charting new directions for studying and understanding child adjustment problems. This approach encourages directions towards determining more precisely which factors pose risks for children's development over time and which are protective or compensatory in nature. The goal of process-oriented research is to "describe the specific responses and patterns in the context of specific histories or developmental periods that account over time for normal versus clinically significant outcomes" (Cummings, Davies, & Campbell, 2000). In other words, the goal is to be able to characterize how and why the psychological, physiological, and other factors function over time as dynamic processes.

Children of Depressed Parents

Children of depressed parents provide an example of the pertinence of such an approach toward examining processes underlying adjustment. Children of depressed parents are at heightened risk for a full range of adjustment problems—including emotional and personality problems—and are at specific risk for clinical depression (Downey & Coyne, 1990). Biological and cognitive models are important in accounting for the relationship between parental depression and child adjustment problems, but they only partially account for this relationship. Many children with depressed parents do not develop adjustment problems, and not all children develop problems at the same point in their development—evidence that other environmental factors must be considered. The heterogeneity of outcomes in children demands further explication of the processes that account for and modify children's adjustment (Cummings & Davies, 1994).

Children may be affected by parental depression through direct exposure, altered patterns of parent-child interactions and attachment, and associated increases in conflict and discord within the family (Cummings, DeArth-Pendley, Du Rocher Schudlich, & Smith, 2000). The importance of examining several contexts is further exemplified by findings that marital conflict is an even better predictor than is depression of adjustment problems in children when there is parental depression. Thus, Downey and Coyne (1990) comment that "marital discord is a viable alternative explanation for the general adjustment difficulties of children with a depressed parent" (p. 68).

This example makes evident the need for a complex, flexible theoretical model that can incorporate these diverse findings and yield a viable explanation of the multiple potential pathways of development. Thus, it is not as simple as just a genetic predisposition's causing maladjustment in children of depressed parents, and it is not just the presence or absence of certain factors that can lead to adjustment or maladjustment; rather, it is the way in which these factors transpire that helps account for children's adjustment at any given time.

Resilience

The fact that children from adverse circumstances may evidence nonadverse personality outcomes has been characterized in terms of the concept of resilience. The treatment of resilience in the developmental psychopathology approach provides an example of how the developmental psychopathology approach treats relatively complex personality outcomes that may sometimes be oversimplified.

Defining and operationalizing the terms *resilience* and *adversity* have varied greatly across theorists and researchers. Although diverse empirical methodology is essential to expand understanding of the resilience construct, it can lead to a host of unrelated findings, questions as to whether it is even the same entity being studied, and varying estimates of rates of resilience among similar risk groups (Luthar, Cicchetti, & Becker, 2000). In contemporary research on children, *resilience* has typically been used to refer to the ability of children to function well in the face of adversity.

Resilience is currently conceptualized in two ways that reflect different usages of the construct. The first conceptualization of it refers to resilience as a positive psychological outcome in the face of adversity. This notion reflects the extent to which diagnostic outcomes of greater competence and fewer adjustment problems (e.g., internalizing or externalizing disorders) are found despite exposure to negative influences (e.g., parental mental illness, poverty; Cummings, Davies, & Campbell, 2000). This is a static notion under protective factors foster resilient outcomes, which is not consistent with the cutting-edge conceptualizations of developmental psychopathology. The second way of conceptualizing resilience refers to the dynamic processes of psychological functioning that foster greater positive and diminished negative outcomes in the face of adversity, both at the present time and in the future (Cummings, Davies, & Campbell, 2000). In this sense, resilience refers to the various protective factors that foster processes of resilience that promote adaptation rather than just resilient outcomes. This conceptualization assumes that processes of resilience operate in opposition to the processes of vulnerability to adversity.

More specifically, "resilience refers to the process of, capacity for, or outcome of successful adaptation despite challenging or threatening circumstances" (Masten, Best, & Garmezy, 1990, p. 425). Two conditions are inherent within this definition: exposure to threat or adversity and positive adaptation despite these threats or adverse conditions. From a process model, maladaptive and adaptive trajectories result from dynamic, bidirectional relations between experiential and organismic factors; accordingly, notions of risk, resilience, and protective factors must be considered in such terms (Cummings, Davies, & Campbell, 2000).

A key tenet of the developmental psychopathology perspective is the study of risk and resilience, taking into account prior adaptation and its relation to current risk—and defining and finding relations between those developmental pathways leading to psychopathology and those leading away (Sroufe, 1997). Accordingly, risk and resiliency or stress and coping are mutually defining and informing in charting processes affecting children's development. For example, examining how and why protective factors serve as buffers of risk for resilient children from high-conflict homes is just as informative as looking at risk factors leading to psychopathology (Cummings, 1998).

Until recently, researchers assumed resilience was homogenous and was either present or not present. In fact, risk and resilience are not all-or-none phenomena and are heterogeneous. Resilience can be present in certain contexts and domains but not in others, just as certain behaviors can be adaptive in some contexts but not in others (Luthar, Doernberger, & Zigler, 1993). For example, studies of children of depressed parents reveal that although some children seem to be coping relatively well (e.g., in academics), even these well-coping children showed considerable vulnerability for developing depression (Radke-Yarrow & Sherman,

1990). Other studies on at-risk inner-city children found that high-stress children who demonstrated considerable behavioral competence were highly vulnerable to emotional distress over time (Luthar, Doernberger, & Zigler, 1993).

Research in the area of marital conflict and children's adjustment also highlights the importance of examining different types of children's competence. For example, children's intervening behaviors during their parents' disagreements may lead one to think that such children are unusually well-behaved, well-adjusted, and mature. However, examining other responses of the children (physiological responses and self-reported emotions) and their adjustment outside of their family context would yield completely different interpretations. This more complex analysis would suggest that the children are quite distressed and have an increased risk for dysfunction later on as a result of their taking on too much responsibility for their parents' relationship (Cummings & Davies, 1994).

These findings indicate a considerable lack of consistency in the difficulties children experience across domains of competence; they also point to the importance of examining different types of children's functioning (physiological, emotional, and behavioral) in different domains (e.g., academic, emotional, social). Given the multiple outcomes and the particular risks some children may face, some outcomes may need to be accorded more importance than others as the most critical indicators of resilience (Luthar, Cicchetti, & Becker, 2000). For example, in children at risk for a mood disorder, their emotional functioning logically would appear to be more critical than their academic functioning would.

Masten and Coatsworth (1998) reviewed research on resilience over the past 25 years to understand the development of competence in children who are faced with unfavorable or highly adverse situations such as living with severely mentally ill parents, family violence, poverty, natural disasters, and other high-risk situations. Results of the studies were remarkably consistent in pointing to qualities of child and context that are associated with better psychological functioning following adversity. Child characteristics associated with resilience were good intellectual functioning; appealing, sociable, easygoing disposition; self-efficacy, self-confidence, high self-esteem; talents; and faith. Characteristics of the family that were associated with resilience were having a close relationship to a caring parent figure, authoritative parenting (e.g., warmth, structure, high expectations), socioeconomic advantages, and connections to extended supportive family networks. Finally, characteristics of the extrafamilial context associated with resilience were having bonds to prosocial adults outside the family, having connections to prosocial organizations, and attending effective schools.

Just as resilience is purported not to be an all-or-none phenomenon, it is also is posited to not be static (Luthar, Cicchetti, & Becker, 2000). In other words, it is unstable; a child who is not resilient at one point in time can later develop resilience, and one who has been resilient can later falter and subsequently deteriorate. Additionally, the meaning of competency and resilience may change across contexts and people. For these reasons it is important to focus on the *how* and *why* questions (i.e., mediators) of risk and resilience—as well as on the *who* and *when* questions (i.e., moderators)—after the *what* questions have been answered. In other words, the next step is to delineate the protective factors and processes that account for children's adaptation under adverse circumstances.

Similarly, inconsistency is evident in the field regarding what constitutes a protective factor. One commonality across many researchers, however, has been a focus on inherently positive characteristics. Protective factors, however, are not restricted to pleasant, positive, desirable things; in fact, they can often be quite adverse and stressful. Challenge models posit that small amounts of adversity have so-called steeling effects—much like those produced by immunizations—that serve to enhance coping, facilitate adjustment, and inoculate children against future psychological trauma. For example, Cummings and Davies (1994b) suggest that children of depressed parents may learn particularly adaptive interpersonal skills—such as sensitivity and empathy—as a result of their exposure to their parents' depression and to moderate negative affect in the home.

Thus, just as it is important to examine the underlying processes of child maladjustment, it is equally important to examine the underlying processes of resilience that account for their effects rather than simply identify a factor associated with positive outcome. The processes by which protective factors may lead to resilient outcomes include (a) mitigating the riskiness of the stressor or adverse situation, (b) decreasing exposure to the stressor, (c) breaking adverse cycles or chains of bad luck brought about by a stressor, (d) fostering positive self-esteem and confidence, (e) increasing the range of positive opportunities and options, and (f) facilitating emotion regulation and coping skills (Cummings, Davies, & Campbell, 2000).

Future Directions

Many promising directions for future research toward better understanding of emotional and personality development from this perspective can be identified. However, it is challenging to adequately measure children's psychological functioning at the level of dynamic processes and to integrate such microscopic levels of analysis into more macroscopic models that convey the big picture, so to speak, with regard to children's patterns of adaptation and maladaptation over time in context. Additionally, it is challenging to conduct multimethod research and still make good sense of the results of patterns of information that may diverge on the picture provided (Cummings, Davies, & Campbell, 2000). Finally, it remains a future goal to more fully incorporate context and developmental history into a diagnostic system, such that a nosology or heuristic integrates the different types of information pertinent to the appraisal of the child's level of adjustment (Cummings, Davies, & Campbell, 2000).

CONCLUSION

This chapter thus documents the widely ranging research directions concerned with emotional and personality development that have emerged in recent years and promise to continue to develop in the future. As we have shown, the increased emphasis placed on the complexity of emotional processes, the role of emotions in characterizing individual differences between children, and the dynamic effects of emotions in children's functioning and development over time are among the most significant emerging directions in research. It will be exciting in the future to determine the extent to which a functionalist perspective on the role of emotions in children's socioemotional development can be further articulated. Relatedly, emerging perspectives—notably as advanced in the emerging work from a developmental psychopathology perspective—call attention to the promise for future conceptual and clinical advances of investigating emotional and personality development from a process-oriented perspective. Moreover, this work has served to call further attention to the significance of emotional processes to normal development and the development of psychopathology. Thus, an exciting prospect is that the next two decades will see advances as substantial as those found in the past two decades in our understanding of these vital processes underlying socioemotional development and adjustment in children.

REFERENCES

Ackerman, B. P., Abe, J. A., & Izard, C. E. (1998). Differential emotions theory and emotional development: Mindful and modularity. In M. F. Mascolo & S. Griffin (Eds.), *What develops in emotional development?* (pp. 85–108). New York: Plenum Press.

Ainsworth, M. D. S., Blehar, M., Waters, E., & Wall, S. (1978). *Patterns of attachment.* Hillsdale, NJ: Erlbaum.

Aksan, N., Goldsmith, H. H., Smider, N. A., Essex, M. J., Clark, R., Hyde, J. S., Klein, M. H., & Vandell, D. L. (1999). Derivation and prediction of temperamental types among preschoolers. *Developmental Psychology, 35,* 958–971.

Barber, B. K. (1997). Introduction: Adolescent socialization in context: The role of connection, regulation, and autonomy in the family. *Journal of Adolescent Research, 12,* 5–11.

Barrett, K. C. (1998). A functionalist perspective to the development of emotions. In M. F. Mascolo & S. Griffin (Eds.), *What develops in emotional development?* (pp. 109–134). New York: Plenum Press.

Barrett, K. C., Zahn-Waxler, C., & Cole, P. M. (1993). Avoiders versus amenders-Implications for the investigation of guilt and shame during toddlerhood? *Cognition and Emotion, 7,* 481–505.

Bates, J. E., & Bayles, K. (1988). The role of attachment in the development of behavior problems. In J. Belsky & T. Nezworski (Eds.), *Clinical implications of attachment* (pp. 253–299). Hillsdale, NJ: Erlbaum.

Bates, J. E., Bayles, K., Bennett, D. S., Ridge, B., & Brown, M. M. (1991). Origins of externalizing behavior problems at eight years of age. In D. Pepler & K. Rubin (Eds.), *Development and treatment of childhood aggression* (pp. 93–120). Hillsdale, NJ: Erlbaum.

Bates, J. E., Maslin, C. A., & Frankel, K. A. (1985). Attachment security, mother-child interaction, and temperament as predictors of behavior problem ratings at age three years. *Society for Research in Child Development Monographs, 50* (1/2, Serial No. 209), 167–193.

Baumrind, D. (1967). Child care practices anteceding three patterns of preschool behavior. *Genetic Psychology Monographs, 75,* 43–88.

Baumrind, D. (1971). Current patterns of parental authority. *Developmental Psychology Monograph, 41* (1, Pt. 2), 101–103.

Baumrind, D. (1991). The influence of parenting style on adolescent competence and substance use. *Journal of Early Adolescence, 11,* 56–95.

Bell, R. Q. (1968). A reinterpretation of the direction of effects in studies of socialization. *Psychological Review, 75,* 81–95.

Belsky, J., Campbell, S. B., Cohn, J. F., & Moore, G. (1996). Instability of infant-parent attachment security. *Developmental Psychology, 32,* 921–924.

Belsky, J., & Isabella, R. A. (1985). Marital and parent-child relationships in family of origin and marital change following the birth of a baby: A retrospective analysis. *Child Development, 56,* 342–349.

Belsky, J., Rovine, M., & Taylor, D. G. (1984). The Pennsylvania Infant and Family Development Project: Pt. 3. The origins of individual differences in infant-mother attachment: Maternal and infant contributions. *Child Development, 55,* 718–728.

Belsky, J., Youngblade, L., Rovine, M., & Volling, B. (1991). Patterns of marital change and parent-child interaction. *Journal of Marriage and the Family, 53,* 487–498.

Bennett, M. (1989). Children's self-attributions of embarrassment. *British Journal of Developmental Psychology, 7,* 207–217.

Bornstein, M. C. (1991). Approaches to parenting in culture. In M. C. Bornstein (Ed.), *Cultural approaches to parenting* (pp. 3–22). Hillsdale, NJ: Erlbaum.

Bowlby, J. (1969). *Attachment and loss: Vol. 1. Attachment.* New York: Basic Books.

Bowlby, J. (1980). *Attachment and loss: Vol. 3. Loss: Sadness and depression.* New York: Basic Books.

Braungart-Rieker, J. M., Garwood, M. M., & Stifter, C. S. (1997). Compliance and noncompliance: The roles of maternal control and child temperament. *Journal of Applied Developmental Psychology, 18,* 411–428.

Brenner, E., & Salovey, P. (1997). Emotion regulation during childhood: Developmental, interpersonal, and individual considerations. In P. Salovey & D. Sluyter (Eds.), *Emotional literacy and emotional development* (pp. 168–192). New York: Basic Books.

Brofenbrenner, U. (1979). *The ecology of human development: Experiments by nature and design.* Cambridge, MA: Harvard University Press.

Calkins, S. D. (1994). Origins and outcomes of individual differences in emotion regulation. *Monographs for the Society of Research in Child Development, 59* (1–2, Serial No. 240), 53–72.

Campbell, S. B. (1990). *Behavior problems in preschool children: Clinical and developmental issues.* New York: Guilford Press.

Campos, J. J., Campos, R. G., & Barrett, K. C. (1989). Emergent themes in the study of emotional development and emotion regulation. *Developmental Psychology, 25,* 394–402.

Carlson, E. A., & Sroufe, L. A. (1995). Contribution of attachment theory to developmental psychopathology. In D. Cicchetti & D. Cohen (Eds.), *Developmental psychopathology: Theory and methods* (Vol. 1, pp. 581–617). New York: Wiley.

Caspi, A. (1998). Personality development across the life course. In W. Damon (Series Ed.) & N. Eisenberg (Vol. Ed.) *Handbook of Child Psychology: Vol. 3. Social, emotional, and personality development* (5th ed., pp. 311–388). New York: Wiley.

Caspi, A., & Silva, P. A. (1995). Temperamental qualities at age 3 predict personality traits in adulthood: Longitudinal evidence from a birth cohort. *Child Development, 66,* 486–498.

Cassidy, J., Parke, R. D., Butkovsky, L., & Braungart, J. M. (1992). Family-peer connections: The roles of emotional expressiveness within the family and children's understanding of emotions. *Child Development, 63,* 603–618.

Cassidy, J., & Shaver, P. R. (Eds.). (1999). *Handbook of attachment: Theory, research, and clinical applications.* New York: Guilford Press.

Cicchetti, D., & Cohen, D. J. (1995). Perspectives of developmental psychopathology. In D. Cicchetti & D. J. Coehn (Eds.), *Developmental psychopathology: Vol. 1. Theory and methods* (pp. 3–20). New York: Wiley.

Cohn, J. F., & Tronick, E. Z. (1989). Specificity of infants' response to mothers' affective behavior. *Journal of the American Academy of Child and Adolescent Psychiatry, 28,* 242–248.

Coie, J. D., Dodge, K., & Kupersmidt, J. B. (1990). Peer group behavior and social status. In S. R. Asher & J. D. Coie (Eds.), *Peer rejection in childhood.* Cambridge, UK: Cambridge University Press.

Cole, P. M. (1985). Display rules and the socialization of affective displays. In G. Zivin (Ed.), *The development of expressive behavior* (pp. 269–290). New York: Academic Press.

Cole, P. M., Michel, M. K., & Teti, L. O. (1994). The development of emotion regulation and dysregulation: A clinical perspective. *Monographs for the Society of Research in Child Development, 59* (1–2, Serial No. 240), 73–100.

Compas, B., Malcarne, V., & Fondacaro, K. I. (1988). Coping with stressful events in older children and young adolescents. *Journal of Consulting and Clinical Psychology, 56,* 405–411.

Cowan, P. A., & Cowan, C. P. (2002). What an intervention design reveals about how parents affect their children's academic achievement and behavior problems. In J. G. Borkowski, M. M. Bristol-Power, & S. L. Ramey (Eds.), *Parenting and the child's world: Influences on academic, intellectual, and social emotional development* (pp. 75–97). Hillside, NJ: Erlbaum.

Cowan, P. A., Powell, D., & Cowan, C. P. (1998). Parenting interventions: A family systems perspective. In W. Damon (Series Ed.), I. E. Sigel, & K. A. Renninger (Vol. Eds.), *Handbook of child psychology: Vol. 4. Child psychology in practice* (5th ed., pp. 3–72). New York: Wiley.

Cox, M. J., & Owen, M. T. (1993, March). *Marital conflict and conflict negotiation: Effects on infant-mother and infant-father relationships.* In M. Cox & J. Brooks-Gunn (Chairs), *Conflict in families: Causes and consequences.* Symposium conducted at the meeting of the Society for Research in Child Development, New Orleans, LA.

Cox, M. J., Owen, M. T., Lewis, J. M., & Henderson, V. K. (1989). Marriage, adult adjustment, and early parenting. *Child Development, 60,* 1015–1024.

Cox, M. J., & Paley, B. (1997). Families as systems. *Annual Review of Psychology, 48,* 243–267.

Crick, N. R., & Dodge, K. A. (1994). A review and reformulation of social information-processing mechanisms in children's social adjustment. *Psychological Bulletin, 155,* 74–101.

Cummings, E. M. (1987). Coping with background anger in early childhood. *Child Development, 58,* 976–984.

Cummings, E. M. (1995). The usefulness of experiments for the study of the family. *Journal of Family Psychology, 9,* 175–185.

Cummings, E. M. (1997). Marital conflict, abuse, and adversity in the family and child adjustment: A developmental psychopathology perspective. In D. Wolfe (Ed.), *Child abuse: New directions in prevention and treatment across the lifespan* (pp. 3–26). Newbury Park, CA: Sage.

Cummings, E. M. (1998a). Children exposed to marital conflict and violence: Conceptual and theoretical directions. In G. Holdern, B. Geffner, & E. Jouriles (Eds.), *Children exposed to marital violence: Theory, research, and applied issues* (pp. 55–94). Washington, DC: American Psychological Association.

Cummings, E. M., & Davies, P. T. (1994a). *Children and marital conflict: The impact of family dispute and resolution.* New York: Guilford Press.

Cummings, E. M., & Davies, P. T. (1994b). Maternal depression and child development. *Journal of Child Psychology and Psychiatry, 35,* 73–112.

Cummings, E. M., & Davies, P. T. (1995). The impact of parents on their: An emotional security hypothesis. *Annals of Child Development, 10,* 167–208.

Cummings, E. M., & Davies, P. T. (1996). Emotional security as a regulatory process in normal development and the development of psychopathology. *Development and Psychopathology, 8,* 123–139.

Cummings, E. M., & Davies, P. T. (2002). Effects of marital conflict on children: Recent advances and emerging themes in process-oriented research. *Journal of Child Psychology and Psychiatry, 43,* 31–63.

Cummings, E. M., Davies, P. T., & Campbell, S. B. (2000). *Developmental psychopathology and family processes: Theory, research, and clinical implications.* New York: Guilford Press.

Cummings, E. M., DeArth-Pendley, G., Du Rocher Schudlich, T., & Smith, D. A. (2000). Parental depression and family functioning: Towards a process-oriented model of children's adjustment. In S. Beach (Ed.), *Marital and family processes in depression* (pp. 89–110). Washington, DC: American Psychological Association.

Cummings, E. M., Goeke-Morey, M. C., & Papp, L. M. (in press). A family-wide model for the role of emotion in family functioning. *Marriage and Family Review.*

Cummings, E. M., Wilson, J., & Shamir, H. (2001). *Reactions of Chilean and American children to marital conflict and marital conflict resolution.* Manuscript submitted for publication.

Cummings, E. M., Zahn-Waxler, C., & Radke-Yarrow, M. (1981). Young children's responses to expressions of anger and affection by others in the family. *Child Development, 52,* 1274–1282.

Cummings, E. M., Zahn-Waxler, C., & Radke-Yarrow, M. (1984). Developmental changes in children's reactions to anger in the home. *Journal of Child Psychology and Psychiatry, 25,* 63–75.

Daniels, D., & Plomin, R. (1985). Differential experience of siblings in the same family. *Developmental Psychology, 21,* 747–760.

Darling, N., & Steinberg, L. (1993). Parenting style as context: An integrative model. *Psychological Bulletin, 113,* 487–496.

Davies, P. T., & Cummings, E. M. (1998). Exploring children's emotional security as a mediator of the link between marital relations and child adjustment. *Child Development, 69,* 124–139.

Davis, B. T., Hops, H. Alpert, A., & Sheeber, L. (1998). Child responses to parental conflict and their effect on adjustment:

A study of triadic relations. *Journal of Family Psychology, 12,* 163–177.

DeHaan, M., Gunnar, M. R., Tout, K., Hart, J., & Stansbury, K. (1998). Familiar and novel contexts yield different associations between cortisol and behavior among 2-year-old children. *Developmental Psychobiology, 33,* 93–101.

Denham, S. A. (1986). Social cognition, social behavior, and emotion in pre-schoolers: Contextual validation. *Child Development, 57,* 194–201.

Denham, S. A. (1998). *Emotional development in young children.* New York: Guilford Press.

De Wolff, M., & van Ijzendoorn, M. H. (1997). Sensitivity and attachment: A meta-analysis on parental antecedents of infant attachment. *Child Development, 68,* 571–591.

Dodge, K. A., & Garber, J. (1991). Domains of emotion regulation. In J. Garber & K. A. Dodge (Eds.), *The development of emotion regulation and dysregulation* (pp. 159–181). Cambridge, UK: Cambridge University Press.

Downey, G., & Coyne, J. C. (1990). Children of depressed parents: An integrative review. *Psychological Bulletin, 108,* 50–76.

Dunn, J. (1988). *The beginnings of social understanding.* Cambridge, MA: Harvard University Press.

Dunn, J. (1999). Making sense of the social world: Mindreading, emotion, and relationships. In P. D. Zelazo, J. W. Astington, & D. R. Olson (Eds.), *Developing theories of intention: Social understanding and self-control* (pp. 229–242). Hillsdale, NJ: Erlbaum.

Dunn, J., & Brown, J. (1993). Early conversations about causality: Content, pragmatics, and developmental change. *British Journal of Developmental Psychology, 11,* 107–123.

Dunn, J., & Brown, J. (1994). Affect expression in the family, children's understanding of emotions, and their interactions with others. *Merrill-Palmer Quarterly, 40,* 120–137.

Easterbrooks, M. A., Biesecker, G., & Lyons-Ruth, K. (2000). Infancy predictors of emotional availability in middle childhood: The role of attachment security & maternal depressive symptomatology. *Attachment and Human Development, 2,* 170–187.

Easterbrooks, M. A., Cummings, E. M., & Emde, R. N. (1994). Young children's responses to constructive marital disputes. *Journal of Family Psychology, 8,* 160–169.

Easterbrooks, M. A., & Emde, R. N. (1988). Marital and parent-child relationships: The role of affect in the family system. In R. A. Hinde & J. Stevenson-Hinde (Eds.), *Relationships within families: Mutual influences* (pp. 83–103). London: Oxford University Press.

Easterbrooks, M. A., & Goldberg, W. A. (1990). Security of toddler-parent attachment: Relation to children's sociopersonality functioning during kindergarten. In M. T. Greenberg & D. Cicchetti (Eds.), *Attachment in the preschool years: Theory, research, and intervention* (pp. 221–244). Chicago: University of Chicago Press.

Eccles, J. S., & Roeser, R. W. (1999). School and community influences on human development. In M. H. Bornstein & M. E. Lamb (Eds.), *Developmental psychology: An advanced textbook* (4th ed., pp. 503–554). Mahwah, NJ: Erlbaum.

Eisenberg, N. (1996). Meta-emotion and socialization of emotion in the family: A topic whose time has come: Comment on Gottman et al. (1996). *Journal of Family Psychology, 10,* 269–276.

Eisenberg, N., & Fabes, R. A. (1994). Mothers' reactions to children's negative outcomes: Relations to children's temperament and anger behavior. *Merrill-Palmer Quarterly, 40,* 138–156.

Eisenberg, N., Spinrad, T. L., & Cumberland, A. (1998). Parental socialization of emotion. *Psychological Inquiry, 9,* 241–273.

Eisenberg, N., Fabes, R., Bernzweig, J., Karbon, M., Poulin, R., & Hanish, L. (1993). The relations of emotionality and regulation to preschoolers: Social skills and sociometric status. *Child Development, 64,* 1418–1438.

Emery, R. E. (1989). Family violence. *American Psychologist, 44,* 321–328.

Emery, R. E., Fincham, F. D., & Cummings, E. M. (1992). Parenting in context: Systemic thinking about parental conflict and its influence on children. *Journal of Consulting and Clinical Psychology, 60,* 909–912.

Erel, O., & Burman, B. (1995). Interrelations of marital relations and parent-child relations: A meta-analytic review. *Psychological Bulletin, 188,* 108–132.

Fabes, R. A., Eisenberg, N., & Eisenbud, L. (1993). Behavioral and physiological correlates of children's reactions to others in distress. *Developmental Psychology, 29,* 655–663.

Fabes, R. A., Eisenberg, N., Karbon, M., & Troyer, D. (1994). The relations of children's emotion regulation to their vicarious emotional responses and comforting behaviors. *Child Development, 65,* 1678–1693.

Fabes, R. A., Eisenberg, N., Smith, M. C., & Murphy, B. C. (1996). Getting angry at peers: Associations with liking of the provocateur. *Child Development, 67,* 942–956.

Fincham, F. D. (1998). Child development and marital relations. *Child Development, 69,* 543–574.

Fox, N. A. (1994). Dynamic cerebral processes underlying emotion regulation. *Monographs for the Society of Research in Child Development, 59* (1–2, Serial No. 240), 152–166.

Fox, N. A., Calkins, S. D., & Bell, M. A. (1994). Neural plasticity and development in the first two years of life: Evidence from cognitive and socioemotional domains of research. *Development and Psychopathology, 6,* 677–696.

Fox, N. A., & Davidson, R. J. (1984). Hemispheric substrates of affect: A developmental model. In N. A. Fox & R. J. Davidson (Ed.), *The psychology of affective development* (pp. 353–382). Hillsdale, NJ: Erlbaum.

Gilbert, R., Christensen, A., & Margolin, G. (1984). Patterns of alliances in non-distressed and multiproblem families. *Family Processes, 23,* 75–87.

Goldberg, W. A., & Easterbrooks, M. A. (1984). The role of marital quality in toddler development. *Developmental Psychology, 20,* 504–514.

Goldsmith, H. H., Buss, K. A., & Lemery, K. S. (1997). Toddler and childhood temperament: Expanded content, stronger genetic evidence, new evidence for the importance of environment. *Developmental Psychology, 33,* 891–905.

Goldsmith, H. H., Buss, A. H., Plomin, R., Rothbart, M. K., Thomas, A., Chess, S., Hinde, R. A., & McCall, R. B. (1987). Roundtable: What is temperament? Four approaches. *Child Development, 59,* 505–529.

Goldsmith, H. H., Lemery, K. S., Aksan, N., & Buss, K. A. (2000). Temperamental substrates of personality development. In V. J. Molfese & D. L. Molfese (Eds.), *Temperament and personality development across the lifespan* (pp. 1–32). Mahwah, NJ: Erlbaum.

Gottman, J. M., Katz, L. F., & Hooven, C. (1996). Meta-emotion and socialization of emotion in the family? A topic whose time has come: Comment on Gottman et al. (1996). *Family Psychology, 10,* 269–276.

Grolnick, W. W., Bridges, L. J., & Connell, J. P. (1996). Emotion regulation in two-year-olds: Strategies and emotional expression in four contexts. *Child Development, 67,* 928–941.

Grych, J. H. (1998). Children's appraisals of interparental conflict: situational and contextual influences. *Journal of Family Psychology, 12,* 437–453.

Grych, J. H., & Fincham, F. (1990). Marital conflict and children's adjustment: A cognitive-contextual framework. *Psychological Bulletin, 108,* 267–290.

Gunnar, M. R. (1994). Psychoendocrine studies of temperament and stress in early childhood: Expanding current models. In J. E. Bates & T. D. Wachs (Ed.), *Temperament: Individual differences at the interface of biology and behavior* (pp. 175–198). Washington, DC: American Psychological Association.

Hagekull, B., & Bohlin, G. (1995). Day care quality, family and child characteristics, and socioemotional development. *Early Childhood Research Quarterly, 10,* 505–526.

Halverson, C. F., Jr., Kohnstamm, G. A., & Martin, R. P. (1994). *The developing structure of temperament and personality from infancy to adulthood.* Hillsdale, NJ: Erlbaum.

Hardy, D., Power, T., & Jaedicke, S. (1993). Examining the relation of parenting to children's coping with everyday stress. *Child Development, 64,* 1829–1841.

Harold, G. T., & Shelton, K. (2000, April). Testing the emotional security hypothesis: An analysis across, time, gender and culture. In G. T. Harold (Chair), *Marital conflict, emotional security and adolescent adjustment: A cross-site investigation.* Symposium conducted at the Eighth Biennial Meeting of the Society for Research on Adolescence, Chicago, IL.

Holden, G. W., & Ritchie, K. L. (1991). Linking extreme marital discord, child rearing, and child behavior problems: Evidence from battered women. *Child Development, 62,* 311–327.

Howes, P., & Markman, H. J. (1989). Marital quality and child functioning: A longitudinal investigation. *Child Development, 60,* 1044–1051.

Hubbard, J. A., & Coie, J. D. (1994). Emotional correlates of social competence in children's peer relationships. *Merrill-Palmer Quarterly, 40,* 1–20.

Hughes, C., & Dunn, J. (1995). Understanding mind and emotion: Longitudinal associations with mental-state talk between young friends. *Developmental Psychology, 34,* 1026–1037.

Hughes, C., & Dunn, J. (1997). "Pretend you don't know": Preschoolers' talk about mental states in pretend play. *Cognitive Development, 12,* 381–403.

Jensen, P. S., & Hoagwood, K. (1997). The book of names: DSM-IV in context. *Development and Psychopathology, 9,* 231–250.

Jouriles, E. N., & Farris, A. M. (1992). Effects of marital conflict on subsequent parent-son interactions. *Behavior Therapy, 23,* 355–374.

Kagan, J., Reznick, J. S., & Gibbons, J. (1989). Inhibited and uninhibited types of children. *Child Development, 60,* 838–845.

Kagan, J., Reznick, J. S., & Snidman, N. (1987). The physiology and psychology of behavioral inhibition. *Child Development, 58,* 1459–1473.

Keller, H., & Greenfield, P. M. (2000). History & future of development in cross-cultural psychology. *Journal of Cross-Cultural Psychology, 31,* 52–62.

Kerig, P. K., Cowan, P. A., & Cowan, C. P. (1993). Marital quality and gender differences in parent-child interaction. *Developmental Psychology, 29,* 931–939.

Kitzman, K. M. (2000). Effect of marital conflict on subsequent triadic family interactions and parenting. *Developmental Psychology, 36,* 3–13.

Kochanaksa, G. (1993). Towards a synthesis of parental socialization and child temperament in the development of guilt and conscience. *Child Development, 64,* 325–347.

Kochanska, G. (1997). Multiple pathways to conscience for children with different temperaments: From toddlerhood to age 5. *Developmental Psychology, 3,* 228–240.

Kochanska, G., Murray, K., & Coy, K. C. (1997). Inhibitory control as a contributor to conscience in childhood: From toddler to early school age. *Child Development, 68,* 263–277.

Kopp, C. B. (1982). Antecedents of self-regulation: A developmental perspective. *Developmental Psychology, 18,* 199–214.

Kopp, C. B. (1989). Regulation of distress and negative emotions: A developmental view. *Developmental Psychology, 25,* 343–354.

Layhey, B. B., Pelham, W. E., Stein, M. A., Loney, J., Trapani, C., Nugent, K., Kipp, H., Schmidt, E., Lee, S., Cale, M., Gold, E., Hartung, C. M., Willcutt, E., & Bauman, B. (1998). Validity of DSM-IV attention-deficit/hyperactivity disorder for younger children. *Journal of the American Academy of Child and Adolescent Psychiatry, 37,* 695–702.

Lewis, M., Alessandri, S. M., & Sullivan, M. (1992). Differences in shame and pride as a function of children's gender and task difficulty. *Child Development, 63*, 630–638.

Lewis, M., Sullivan, M., Stanger, C., & Weiss, M. (1989). Self-development and self-conscious emotions. *Child Development, 60*, 146–156.

Luthar, S. S., Cicchetti, D., & Becker, B. (2000). The construct of resilience: A critical evaluation and guidelines for future work. *Child Development, 71*, 543–562.

Luthar, S. S., Doernberger, C. H., & Zigler, E. (1993). Resilience is not a unidimensional construct: Insights from a prospective study of inner-city adolescence. *Development and Psychopathology, 5*, 703–717.

Maccoby, E., & Martin, J. (1983). Socialization in contexts of the family: Parent-child interaction. In E. M. Hetherington (Ed.), *Handbook of child psychology: Vol. 4. Socialization, personality, and social development* (4th ed., pp. 1–101). New York: Wiley.

Mascolo, M., & Fischer, K. (1995). Developmental transformations in appraisals for pride, shame, and guilt. In J. Tangney & K. Fischer (Eds.), *Self-conscious emotions: The psychology of shame, guilt, embarrassment and pride* (pp. 64–113). New York: Guilford Press.

Masten, A. S., Best, K., & Garmezy, N. (1990). Resilience and development: Contributions from the study of children who overcame adversity. *Development and Psychopathology, 2*, 425–444.

Masten, A. S., & Coatsworth, J. D. (1998). The development of competence in favorable and unfavorable environments: Lessons from research on successful children. *American Psychologist, 53*, 205–220.

Maszk, P., Eisenberg, N., & Guthrie, I. K. (1999). Relations of children's social status to their emotionality and regulation: A short-term longitudinal study. *Merrill-Palmer Quarterly, 45*, 468–492.

McClowry, S. G., Giangrande, S. K., Tommasini, N. R., Clinton, W., Foreman, N. S., Lynch, K., & Ferketich, S. L. (1994). The effects of child temperament, maternal characteristic, and family circumstances on the maladjustment of school-age children. *Research in Nursing and Health, 17*, 25–35.

McDowell, D. J., O'Neil, R., & Parke, R. D. (2000). Display rule application in a disappointing situation and children's emotional reactivity: Relations with social competence. *Merrill-Palmer Quarterly, 46*, 306–324.

Mischel, W. (1974). Processes in delay of gratification. In L. Berkowitz (Ed.), *Progress in experimental personality research* (Vol. 3, pp. 249–292). New York: Academic Press.

Nachmias, M., Gunnar, M., Mangelsdorf, S., Parritz, R. H., & Buss, K. (1996). Behavioral inhibition and stress reactivity: The moderating role of attachment security. *Child Development, 67*, 508–522.

O'Hearn, H. G., Margolin, G., & John, R. S. (1997). Mothers' and fathers' reports of children's reactions to naturalistic marital conflict. *Journal of the American Academy of Child and Adolescent Psychiatry, 36*, 1366–1373.

Owen, M. T., & Cox, M. J. (1997). Marital conflict and the development of infant-parent attachment relationships. *Journal of Family Psychology, 11*, 152–164.

Palkovitz, M. (1987). Organization of the stress response at the anatomical level. *Progress in Brain Research, 72*, 47–55.

Parke, R. D., & Buriel, R. (1998). Socialization in the family: Ethnic and ecological perspectives. In W. Damon (Series Ed.) & N. Eisenberg (Vol. Ed.), *Handbook of child psychology: Vol. 3. Social, emotional, and personality development* (pp. 463–552). New York: Wiley.

Parke, R. D., Cassidy, J., Burks, V. M., Carson, J. L., & Boyum, L. (1992). Familial contribution to peer competence among young children: The role of interactive and affective processes. In R. D. Parke & G. W. Ladd (Eds.), *Family-peer relationships: Model of linkage* (pp. 107–134). Hillsdale, NJ: Erlbaum.

Patterson, G. R., DeBaryshe, B., & Ramsey, E. (1989). A developmental perspective on antisocial behavior. *American Psychologist, 44*, 329–335.

Radke-Yarrow, M., & Sherman, T. (1990). Hard growing: children who survive. In J. Rolf, A. S. Masten, D. Cicchetti, K. H. Nuechterlein, & S. Weintraub (Eds.), *Risk and protective factors in the development of psychopathology* (pp. 97–119). New York: Cambridge University Press.

Ramey, C. T., & Ramey, S. L. (1998). Early intervention and experience. *American Psychologist, 53*, 109–120.

Rutter, M. (1986). The developmental psychopathology of depression: Issues and perspectives. In M. Rutter, C. E. Izard, & P. B. Read (Eds.), *Depression in young people: Developmental and clinical perspectives* (pp. 3–30). New York: Guilford Press.

Rutter, M., & Quinton, D. (1984). Parental psychiatric disorder: Effects on children. *Psychological Medicine, 14*, 853–880.

Shamir, H., Du Rocher-Schudlich, T., & Cummings, E. M. (2002). Marital conflict, parenting styles, and children's representations of family relationships. *Parenting: Science and Practice, 1–2*, 123–151.

Shifflett-Simpson, K., & Cummings, E, M. (1996). Mixed message resolution and children's responses to interadult conflict. *Child Development, 67*, 437–448.

Sroufe, L. A. (1997). Psychopathology as an outcome of development. *Development and Psychopathology, 9*, 251–268.

Sroufe, L. A., & Rutter, M. (1984). The domain of developmental psychopathology. *Child Development, 55*, 17–29.

Sroufe, L. A., & Waters, E. (1977). Attachment as an organizational construct. *Child Development, 48*, 1184–1199.

Stocker, C. M., & Youngblade, L. (1999). Marital conflict and parental hostility: Links with children's sibling and peer relationships. *Journal of Family Psychology, 13*, 598–609.

Stoneman, Z., Brody, G. H., & Burke, M. (1989). Marital quality, depression, and inconsistent parenting: Relationship with observed mother-child conflict. *American Journal of Orthopsychiatry, 59,* 105–117.

Thompson, R. A. (2000). Legacy of early attachment. *Child Development, 59* (2–3, Serial No. 240), 25–52.

Thompson, R. A., & Calkins, S. D. (1996). The double-edged sword: Emotional regulation for children at risk. *Development and Psychopathology, 8,* 163–182.

van de Vijver, F. J. R., & Leung, K. (2000). Methodological issues on psychological research on culture. *Journal of Cross-Cultural Psychology, 31,* 33–51.

van Ijzendoorn, M. H., & Sagi, A. (1999). Cross-cultural patters of attachment: Universal and contextual dimensions. In J. Cassidy & P. R. Shaver (Eds.), *Handbook of attachment: Theory, research, and clinical applications* (pp. 713–734). New York: Guilford Press.

Wakefield, J. C. (1997). When in development disordered? Developmental psychopathology and the harmful dysfunction analysis of mental disorder. *Development and Psychopathology, 9,* 269–290.

Waters, E., & Cummings, E. M. (2000). A secure based from which to explore close relationships. *Child Development, 49,* 164–172.

Weiss, G., & Hechtman, L. T. (1993). *Hyperactive children grown up: ADHD in children, adolescents, and adults* (2nd ed.). New York: Guilford Press.

Willett, J. B., Singer, J. D., & Martin, N. C. (1998). The design and analysis of longitudinal studies of development and psychopathology in context: Statistical models and methodological recommendations. *Development and Psychopathology, 10,* 395–426.

CHAPTER 10

Social Development and Social Relationships in Middle Childhood

SUSAN M. McHALE, JACINDA K. DARIOTIS, AND TINA J. KAUH

Middle childhood is a time of considerable change in children's social competencies and interpersonal relationships. Descriptions of the salient features of this developmental period highlight an expansion of the social world as children spend increasing amounts of time outside their homes, away from their families, at school, with peers, and in extracurricular activities (Collins, 1984; Eccles, 1999). Learning to interact effectively in these new and diverse social settings is at the core of social development in middle childhood. Building on conceptual models that emphasize adaptation to interpersonal and setting demands as fundamental to social behavior and social competence (Cairns & Cairns, 1994; Ogbu, 1995; Rose-Krasnor, 1997), in this chapter we describe the nature of and influences on social development between ages 6 and 12 years.

Although middle childhood is often viewed as a period of consolidation between two periods of striking change (i.e., infancy and early childhood on the one hand and adolescence on the other), both theoretical accounts and empirical evidence highlight the unique developmental tasks that children confront during the school-age years. From the realm of ego psychology, the writings of Erik Erikson (1963) and Harry Stack Sullivan (1953) stress the significance of experiences in middle childhood for later healthful development. Erikson portrayed this period as one focused on the development of a *sense of industry* as children become competent at a range of activities valued by the societies in which they live. Middle childhood is a time when children become immersed in work: schoolwork in the case of children living in industrialized countries and paid labor in the case of children in developing countries. In the context of new work roles, social behaviors emerge, are practiced, and change, and their emerging social competencies are an important component of children's successful task performance.

Sullivan (1953) described the importance of what he termed the *juvenile era* (the early part of middle childhood) as "the actual time for becoming social" (p. 227). Key to making the transition into this developmental period are declines in egocentrism and increasing awareness of others' perspectives brought about through association with age-mates. The social developmental process continues in the *preadolescent era* through the development of an intimate and egalitarian relationship with a particular same-sex age-mate, or *chum*. According to Sullivan, the chum relationship is central to both the development of self-understanding and the individual's later involvement in mature, close relationships. From

Sullivan's perspective, adaptations children make in the context of their social interactions with a best friend define social development in middle childhood.

A second perspective on development in middle childhood targets changes in children's cognitive abilities. Jean Piaget's theory (Piaget, 1932) highlights advances in logical reasoning, problem solving, and the ability to think about abstract representations. Metacognitive skills—which allow children to step back and think about their thoughts, plans, and activities—also develop at this time (Flavell, 1976). Piaget, like Sullivan, highlighted the accommodations children make in the course of social exchanges with peers as an important impetus for cognitive growth. Later in this chapter we consider how children's emerging understandings of self, other, and the social world have implications for their social behavior and relationships.

In contemporary research, the work of Robert Cairns and colleagues (Cairns, 1991; Cairns & Cairns, 1994; Cairns, Gariepy, & Hood, 1990) has contributed conceptually and empirically to our understanding of social behavior and development. Basing their ideas on a series of human and comparative studies, Cairns and colleagues argue that adaptations in social behavior arise out of a tension between forces for continuity and forces that promote novelty and change (Cairns et al., 1990). With respect to the experiences of the individual in the context of interpersonal interactions, for example, Cairns (1991) explains that "a special feature of social behavior is the ability to adapt to changing circumstances while simultaneously maintaining internal coherence and dyadic organization in action. Social behaviors are jointly determined from within and without, yet there is both intrapersonal synchrony and interpersonal integration. Despite having to serve two masters simultaneously—or because of it—the system is kept reasonably stable as well as reasonably plastic" (p. 25). One reason that the study of social behavior is important is that external influences on individual development can be directly observed in the behavioral accommodations that appear during the course of social exchange.

Stepping back to consider the larger picture of development and change, Cairns et al. (1990) highlight a second set of tensions that control the emergence of novelties in the development of the individual and in the evolution of the species. Although evolution and development are conservative processes, these authors argue that "... there must be avenues for rapid change both in ontogeny and in microevolution if behavioral systems are to be functional in time and space" (p. 62). From this perspective, the study of social behavior also is important because its inherently accommodating function makes social behavior the leading edge of the adaptations that constitute individual development and microevolution.

These ideas—core to a psychobiological approach to the study of development—imply several challenges for an analysis of social development in middle childhood. The psychobiological concept of development not only directs attention to understanding *continuities* in development, but also emphasizes the search for *novelty* and *change*. We therefore ask the following question: In the face of the consolidation of earlier skills and abilities that characterizes middle childhood, what are the emergent features of social development that also define this developmental period? A psychobiological framework also highlights the web of coacting influences that guide the course of social development—influences ranging from the biological to the contextual and including the active, mediating role of children's own constructions of their social worlds and their social experiences (Cairns & Cairns, 1994; Lerner, 1982). In this chapter we review factors that influence developmental and individual differences in children's social behavior and social experiences; in the face of models that highlight coacting influences on children's social functioning, documenting the workings of these processes is a complex effort whose goal remains elusive.

Eisenberg (1998) recently provided an insightful analysis of emerging themes in research within the broad domain of social, emotional and personality development. First, Eisenberg noted the attention paid in recent research to external influences on children's social development, particularly in studies of the ways in which features of the larger social context influence children's social experiences. Reflecting the field's increasing appreciation of the network of influences on children's social development, Eisenberg also highlighted a focus on *within-individual processes,* including biological, emotional, and cognitive factors in children's social behavior and development. With respect to these within-individual developmental processes, another research emphasis noted by Eisenberg pertains to self-regulation processes—specifically, developmental changes in the integration of external and self-control across the course of childhood. Studies of regulatory processes provide a window on changes during middle childhood in the nature and significance of children's active role in their own experiences and development. Yet another important theme in recent literature is the importance of the role of interpersonal relationships in children's social development. Finally, Eisenberg stressed the importance of questions of process—that is, the delineation of mechanisms through which internal and external influences operate together to produce individual differences and developmental changes in children.

A discussion of the complete range of social developmental phenomena is beyond the scope of this chapter; readers are directed to the recent review chapters on topics ranging from emotion and prosocial development (Eisenburg & Fabes, 1998; Saarni, Mumme, & Campos, 1998), to peer relationships (Rubin, Bukowski, & Parker, 1998) and family influences (Bugental & Goodnow, 1998; Parke & Buriel, 1998) in the *Handbook on Child Psychology* for in-depth analyses of issues in children's social development. In reviewing research on social development here, we have chosen topics relevant to many of the themes of contemporary research on social development highlighted in Eisenberg's analysis of the field. We begin broadly with a picture of the social ecology of middle childhood; one goal of this discussion is to direct attention to the diversity of settings in which children spend their lives. Specifically, we consider models for conceptualizing and measuring children's social ecologies, and we review research on children's everyday activities as one instantiation of an ecological perspective on children's social development. We then turn our attention to studies of individual developmental processes that constitute the bulk of extant research on social development, focusing on two domains—social cognitive development and emotion regulation—as examples of such developmental processes. Our review highlights how these processes unfold during middle childhood, what factors influence individual differences in these domains, and how these processes are tied to children's social experiences and competencies. Our survey of ecological and individual factors in social development provides a grounding for a discussion of children's interpersonal relationships—specifically, their parent-child, peer, and sibling relationships—in the final section of this chapter. A focus on children's social development implies an analysis of the emerging social competencies and behaviors of the individual child, but the study of social relationships also demands a dyadic level of conceptualization and analysis (Hinde, 1979). As we note, studying children's individual development in the context of their interpersonal relationships is not the same as studying the development of children's interpersonal relationships. Furthermore, as our review reveals, we know somewhat more about the former than about the latter.

THE SOCIAL ECOLOGY OF MIDDLE CHILDHOOD

The contexts of children's social development are as diverse as they are dynamic. For example, in the space of a generation or two, the family setting for European-American middle-class children (the focus of most extant research on social development) has changed dramatically in at least two important ways: the involvement of their mothers in the labor force and the likelihood that youth will spend at least some of their

childhood in a single-parent or stepfamily. For U.S. children as a whole, between 1940 and the mid-1990s the rate of maternal employment went from less than 10% to greater than 70% (L. W. Hoffman & Youngblade, 1999). Furthermore, whereas fewer than 10% of children were living in a single-parent family in 1960, by the mid-1990s that figure reached almost 35% (Hernandez, 1997). Changing family demographics make for changes in the socialization agents and institutions of childhood: stepparents and siblings, after-school child care programs, and caregivers figure in the social experiences of greater numbers of U.S. children, thereby increasing the diversity and complexity of their social ecologies.

Possibly even more significant are analyses that have alerted researchers to large populations of children in the United States who traditionally have been neglected in child development research—including children living in poverty, who constitute more than 20% of children in the United States, and children of ethnic minority status, who constitute almost 45% of children in the United States (Hernandez, 1997). In the face of recent efforts directed at their study, we still know very little about the social ecologies of these children's lives. When one considers that children in developed countries—where most child development research has been conducted—constitute less than a fifth of the world's population of children, it becomes evident that our field faces an important challenge as researchers seek to document the range of social development experiences that characterize middle childhood.

Models of the Social Ecology of Childhood

In his 1979 volume, *The Ecology of Human Development,* Urie Bronfenbrenner laid out his influential model of contextual influences on the developing child, a model that highlighted contexts ranging from the everyday settings in which children spend their time—such as the family, peer group, or school—to larger cultural-societal systems that exert their impact by virtue of the structure, expectations, and meanings they impose on children's everyday settings and experiences. From the field of cultural anthropology come theoretical constructs such as the *ecological niche* (Weisner, 1984), which provide a framework for operationalizing and measuring the ecologies of middle childhood. According to Weisner, the ecological niche refers to the social and cultural environment within which a child and his or her family are embedded. The term *niche* highlights the *dynamic* and *adaptive* nature of the social-cultural environment. The evolution of the niche comes about as a function of subsistence demands that operate within a given physical, political, and social setting; children and their families adapt to the demands of the setting but also act on their settings to effect change. Furthermore, the ecological niche includes not only the physical environment, but also the goals, motivations, and scripts of the individuals within that setting.

Weisner (1984) defined five categories or clusters of niche characteristics that provide challenges to and supports for children's development; the everyday behavioral adaptations children make to these setting demands are at the heart of their social development. The first includes factors related to the *health and mortality* of the child's social group. Features of the context, ranging from health care availability to dangers in the community—in forms ranging from predators, to warfare, to traffic laws, to the availability of bicycle helmets—fall into this category; learning the social rules and scripts a society has developed to negotiate these setting features is an important component of social development in middle childhood. The second category has to do with the *provision of food and shelter*. What kinds of work parents do and when they do it, parents' expectations for their children's future roles as workers, and—as we shortly consider later in some detail—children's own role in the family economy are context characteristics with implications for children's social experiences and development. A third set of niche characteristics highlights the *"personnel" involved in children's everyday activities* and the kinds of caregiving activities those individuals undertake. The extent to which children spend time with adults, other children, or both, in relative isolation or in groups are some of the ways in which niches can be distinguished. Such a focus highlights the different social opportunities of children in different ecologies. Related to the issue of personnel present is the *role of women* in the community and the extent to which distinctions are made in the opportunities and expectations for males versus females in a society; such patterns will be central to children's everyday social experiences, as well as to their images of their future roles in adulthood. A final category has to do with the *availability of alternative cultural models*—that is, the extent to which variations in the characteristics previously outlined exist within a community or are evident from without; children's experiences vis à vis alternative models affect the way they interpret the social demands of their own settings, as well as their ideas about their own developing roles and competencies.

The elements of children's social ecologies outlined by Weisner define a broader range of life circumstances for children than is common in most accounts by developmental scholars who study children's social development. Efforts to capture variation in children's life circumstances often have relied on global indexes such as social class or ethnic background—what Bronfenbrenner and Crouter (1983) refer to as "social address variables." As Weisner (1984) argued,

measuring features of the ecological niche directly allows the researcher to "decompose global descriptors like socioeconomic level into much more complex set of measures. In addition, measures derived from ecocultural niche domains are more likely to reveal the mechanisms by which class or education produce their effects on children." This is because elements of the ecological niche have direct implications for children's everyday experiences including (a) the activities and tasks in which children spend their time each day, (b) children's companions in their everyday activities, and (c) the cultural scripts that provide the meaning and motivation for children's everyday experiences.

Children's Daily Activities

In research on cross-cultural differences in children's time use, we see how features of the ecocultural niche shape children's everyday activities in ways that are likely both to reflect and to have important implications for children's social development (Bronfenbrenner, 1979; Larson & Verma, 1999). Reviewing the literature on how children and adolescents spend their time, Larson and Verma highlight as foremost in importance differences in the relative amounts of time children spend on work and leisure that distinguish children and youth from industrial, preindustrial, and transitional societies. Cross-cultural analysis of the nature of and balance between children's work and leisure shows how these areas change between early childhood and adolescence and how they are tied to the subsistence demands and associated material conditions of families and communities. Societies also differ markedly in the extent to which children's work and leisure—and the balance between the time spent in each—are sex-typed.

Within the sphere of work, children's activities can be divided into work activities that contribute to economy of their families, including unpaid domestic work (household chores, sibling caregiving), wage-earning activities (which usually take place outside the home), and "work" activities that are designed to promote children's individual development and skills such as schoolwork (Larson & Verma, 1999). In industrialized societies, where making a living requires specialized skills, children's work comes predominantly in the form of schoolwork. Data from a range of cultures reveal that children in nonindustrial societies—girls in particular—may spend half their waking hours doing housework; however, among children in industrial societies who attend school, the average child spends less than half an hour a day on household chores (Goodnow, 1988; Larson & Verma, 1999; Medrich, Roizen, Rubin, & Buckley, 1982). These differences in time use have implications in such areas as the kinds of social rules and scripts children learn, their everyday social partners, their family roles as economic contributors versus "ornaments" (Zelizer, 1985), and their expectations regarding their future roles as adults. In turn, their social competencies will be an important element in children's success in their everyday work activities. Sex differences in children's work are striking: Whereas girls tend to spend more time than boys do in housework, boys tend to be more involved than girls are in wage-earning jobs. In the United States, common paid jobs during middle childhood are paper routes and babysitting (Medrich et al., 1982), but elsewhere around the world, middle childhood is the time when children begin working for pay in factories, in agriculture, and on the street (Larson & Verma, 1999). Despite variations in the form work takes, across diverse settings, middle childhood is the time at which children's work responsibilities begin to comprise a significant portion of their waking hours: By this metric, middle childhood can indeed be described as a period of industry (Erikson, 1963).

On the other hand, the meanings attributed to children's work—both their schoolwork and their labor—vary considerably within and across cultures. Moreover, it is in the meaning of children's work that cultural values—particularly those of individualism versus collectivism—inhere. Recently researchers have given more attention to the meanings and motivations for work—both household work and schoolwork—undertaken by children in Western societies. The results of this research suggest that the developmental implications of children's work vary considerably as a function of whether work is seen as directed at fulfilling personal versus family needs and goals. When differences emerge, it appears that a collectivist (as opposed to an individualistic) orientation promotes developmental advantages in the form of prosocial development and individual well-being and achievement (Goodnow, 1988; Weisner, 1984).

The amount of free time available for children to spend in play and leisure activities also varies considerably around the world. Larson and Verma (1999) suggest that among some nonindustrialized societies, availability of free time is sex-typed, with boys having up to twice as much free time as girls. Subsistence opportunities and demands are probably the most important factor in explaining children's free time in nonindustrialized societies; when employment and economically productive opportunities for children's relatively unskilled labor are available, children have less time for play and leisure. Children in the United States are notable for the sizable quantity of their free time—up to 50% of their waking hours (Larson & Verma, 1999). Across middle childhood, the nature of children's leisure changes in potentially important ways, from more time spent in relatively unstructured play (e.g., sociodramatic play, play with toys) to more time spent in organized activities away from home, for example, in the

form of clubs or team sports (Medrich et al., 1982; Newson & Newson, 1976; Posner & Vandell, 1999; Timmer, Eccles, & O'Brien, 1985). Despite its significance in the ecology of everyday life, however, we know little about the implications of free time use during middle childhood for children's social development. Free time may be a source of stress to the extent that children are hurried by frenetic schedules of extracurricular activities (Elkind, 1981)—a missed opportunity for cognitive development to the extent that it takes children away from schoolwork (Stevenson & Lee, 1990), or free time may present an opportunity to develop social competencies and interpersonal ties (Larson & Verma, 1999; Werner, 1993).

Along with changes in what children do with their free time and where they spend it come changes in the social contexts of children's leisure activities. As children move toward adolescence, an increasing amount of their time is spent with peers, outside the direct supervision of parents (Collins, Harris, & Susman, 1995; Parke & Buriel, 1998). Consequently, parenting from a distance by acquiring information about children's activities and companions and helping to organize children's involvement in social activities outside the home becomes an increasingly important component of child-rearing activities for parents during middle childhood. Children who spend their free time in sports and organized activities are likely to do so in the company of nonparental adults who can play an important role as mentors and sources of support; these social opportunities may be particularly important for children in troubled family circumstances (Werner, 1993). One of the most dramatic features of middle childhood—and one that distinguishes this period from early childhood on the one hand and adolescence on the other—is the extent to which peer experiences are sex-segregated (Maccoby, 1990). As we note in our discussion of peer relationships later in this chapter, sex segregation in the peer group during middle childhood is a phenomenon that has been observed in cultures around the world. The social contexts of children's everyday activities both reflect and have implications for an important domain of social-psychological functioning—children's gender role development (Maccoby, 1998).

In sum, in contrast to what we have learned in recent decades about normative (within-individual) social developmental processes, we know much less about the everyday lives of children—including what they do, where they go, and with whom they spend their time. Furthermore, even less is understood about the social developmental implications of children's everyday activities (see McHale, Crouter, & Tucker, 2001; Posner & Vandell, 1999, for some exceptions). An important direction for future research will be to describe how the ecologically grounded meanings and motives for children's activities mediate the links between children's time use and their social functioning and adjustment. Also needed is research on how patterns of everyday activities develop in different ecological niches.

Children's everyday activities, including their task and interpersonal demands are a forum within which children's social behavior emerges, is practiced, and changes. Within the individual, however, developmental processes also shape and set constraints on social behavior and relationship experiences, and these processes provide a foundation for the development of social competence. Indeed, as we have noted, most of the research on children's social development highlights this latter focus on within-individual processes. It is to these developmental processes—specifically children's social cognitive development, their emotion regulation abilities, and these abilities' role in the development of social competence—to which we now turn.

SOCIAL DEVELOPMENTAL PROCESSES IN MIDDLE CHILDHOOD

Social Cognition and Social Competence During Middle Childhood

Middle childhood is a period during which children become better able to reason and think logically, no longer relying on superficial qualities or characteristics as the basis for their problem solving (Piaget, 1932). The emergence of logical reasoning abilities coincides with a decline in egocentrism and with the development of social perspective-taking abilities (Grusec & Lytton, 1988); these changes have implications for children's self-awareness, self-understanding, and self-evaluation abilities (Harter, 1999). Children's social understanding—in combination with their emerging sense of self—undergird the social comparison skills that also develop during middle childhood. Indeed, one skill that coalesces in middle childhood is children's ability to use information from social comparisons in self-evaluations (Harter, 1999; Ruble, 1983). The array of social cognitive abilities that emerges in middle childhood is both cause and consequence of children's involvement in an expanding and increasingly complex social world.

Research on how cognitive developmental changes are linked to children's social understanding is one area in which researchers have focused almost exclusively on European-American children; except in the domain of moral development, we know little about how the nature of or the demands on children's social understanding vary across age in diverse cultural settings. Furthermore, although Piagetian ideas

served as a basis for early empirical studies of social cognitive development in middle childhood, contemporary researchers have moved away from such broad developmental models in order to examine developmental processes within specific areas of functioning (e.g., perspective taking, moral development). In addition, researchers have incorporated new frameworks of cognitive development—specifically, information processing models—into their conceptualization and study of social cognitive development. In the following discussion we consider three areas of study highlighted in work on children's social cognitive development: the development of children's perspective-taking abilities, their prosocial dispositions, and their social information-processing skills.

Development of Perspective-Taking Skills

Selman (1980) described social development in terms of qualitative changes in children's ability to understand the perspectives of others. Specifically, he argued that children's social understanding progresses through an invariant sequence of stages marked by distinct and universal patterns of thinking. In contrast to cognitive developmental changes as outlined by Piaget, however, Selman emphasized that "social perspective taking involves a developing understanding of the intrinsic psychological characteristics and capacities of individuals, not just the complex coordination of decentered cognitive operations, that is, it has an intrinsically social component . . . the social or psychological content is inextricable and equally as important as the logical or operational structure which may in turn be its basis" (Selman, 1980, p. 22). Likewise, according to Selman, shifts in perspective-taking abilities result as a function of the interaction between children's cognitive development and their interactions in their social environments. By middle childhood—through the role-playing of familiar social roles, for example, in play—children gain skills that allow them to realize that two individuals can have different interpretations of the same event. By around age 10, when children tend to be immersed in more coordinated and organized activities such as games, clubs, or sports, they are able to understand others' perspectives as well as their own. By the end of middle childhood, Selman argues, children have the ability to simultaneously consider multiple social perspectives and abstract societal norms.

Changes in perspective-taking ability have implications across multiple domains, including the development of the self system and experiences in close friendships, peer-group relations, and parent-child relations (see Selman, 1980, for a detailed discussion of these domains). For instance, Selman suggests that shifts in perspective-taking ability during middle childhood allow for more elaborated understanding of the internal and external selves; such understanding has important implications for self-consciousness, including notions of an imaginary audience and personal fable that emerge in adolescence (Vartanian & Powlishta, 1996). As with other research on children's social cognitive development, however, research on perspective taking generally has been limited to a focus on White, middle-class children in the United States. Moreover, although a number of studies have provided empirical support for Selman's model of progressive sophistication in perspective-taking ability (e.g., Gurucharri, Phelps, & Selman, 1984), some recent research suggests that perspective-taking abilities may emerge in particular domains (e.g., visual or spatial) earlier than Selman had originally suggested (Miller, Holmes, Gitten, & Danbury, 1998; Taylor, 1988), and that child-specific characteristics may play an important role in the development of these abilities (e.g., Miletic, 1996). Furthermore, intervention-oriented studies suggest that training and practice can improve perspective-taking abilities (Chalmers & Townsend, 1990; Lane-Garon, 1998). Researchers have begun to examine the implications of perspective-taking ability for ethnic identity development as a way to enhance exploration opportunities that minority children need for identity achievement later in adolescence (Markstrom-Adams & Spencer, 1994; Quintana, Castaneda-English, & Ybarra, 1999).

Development of Prosocial Cognition and Behavior

Children can use their social cognitive abilities in more or less positive ways; they may direct their abilities to achieve self-, other-, or mutual goals. The study of children's prosocial dispositions—which define the goals and motivations for children's social behavior—encompasses research on the development of moral judgment and moral behavior in children. Although they are conceptually related, research in these two areas has been conducted within two distinct traditions.

The study of moral development has focused on children's moral judgments and cognitive developmentally based changes in children's understanding of right and wrong. Based on his early studies, Piaget (1932) argued that middle childhood marks shifts from an heteronomous stage, in which children's moral values develop out of a unilateral respect for authority, to an autonomous stage, in which conceptions of reciprocity and equality emerge. Consequently, during middle childhood, rules previously perceived as fixed are now seen as more fluid and based on internalized standards. These changes are associated with children's cooperation and perspective-taking skills and are brought about by increased

peer interaction in an expanding social world (Piaget, 1932). Kohlberg (1976) built on Piaget's ideas, proposing a three-level model of the development of moral judgment directed toward the achievement of a *postconventional* moral orientation, in which individual, self-chosen principles prevail. In outlining his developmental model, Kohlberg claimed that members of all cultures follow the same universal, invariant sequence of stages moving toward the same universal ethical principles. Kohlberg and Kramer (1969) also suggested that females were less likely than were males to reach the highest level of moral development, although few studies have found substantial sex differences.

Reviewing research that has tested Kohlberg's model, Snarey (1985) found evidence substantiating Kohlberg's model across diverse cultures ranging from tribal villages to industrialized cities. Snarey found, however, that cultural groups that value collective solidarity rather than individual rights and justice were significantly less likely to achieve Kohlberg's postconventional moral level. Similarly, Gilligan (1982) argued that Kohlberg inadequately described female moral development, which—in contrast to Kohlberg's focus on *moral justice*—follows an alternate path focusing on the *morality of care and responsibility for others*. Gilligan suggested that these differential paths emerge as a result of the greater concern females give to relationships, caregiving, and intimacy. Eisenberg et al. (1987) found evidence supporting Gilligan's assertions in a longitudinal study following children from middle childhood into adolescence.

Gilligan's work was one impetus for a reinterpretation of moral development among some theorists who view moral values as consisting of distinct domains that research has often mistakenly lumped together (Turiel, 1994). In some cultures, for instance, the moral domain consists of justice-related issues involving individuals' rights or welfare, whereas the societal domain consists of rules dictating social conventions or norms, such as gender roles. Research suggests, however, that welfare and the law may not be culturally universal principles for basing evaluations in the moral domain (Nisan, 1987). In the United States, Smetana and Braeges (1990) found that children can distinguish between these two domains by early childhood, but their distinctions become more consistent across criteria with increasing age. Arsenio and Ford (1985) suggest further that children come to distinguish between these two domains via the greater affect related to moral transgressions relative to that associated with social norm violations.

Studies of empathy move analyses from a focus on children's prosocial cognitions to the study of their prosocial feelings and behavior, which Eisenberg et al. (1999) suggest may reflect personality dispositions formed during childhood that remain relatively stable into adulthood. Empathy represents an individual's emotional response to another's emotional state and has been the focal point of studies examining prosocial behavior during childhood (Bengtsson & Johnson, 1992; Eisenberg et al., 1999; Litvack-Miller, McDougall, & Romney, 1997). Some studies suggest that empathy tends to be stronger in girls than in boys (Zahn-Waxler, Friedman, & Cummings, 1983), and this work shows that empathic responses include multiple reactions, such as personal distress and sympathy (Eisenberg et al., 1999). M. L. Hoffman (1982) proposed that social cognitive development and emotion processes interact to explain empathic reactions; emotional and social perspective-taking skills—which more fully develop during middle childhood—mediate affective arousal and thus influence the intensity of the empathic response. Therefore, children who are better able to see others' points of view experience greater empathy and are more likely to help others out of sympathy rather than as an attempt to alleviate personal distress (Eisenberg et al., 1999). Numerous studies have documented links between perspective-taking skills, empathy, and prosocial behavior among school-aged children across cultures and socioeconomic levels (Bengtsson & Johnson, 1992; Carlo, Knight, Eisenberg, & Rotenberg, 1991; Garner, 1996; Litvack-Miller et al., 1997).

Although the relationship between empathy and prosocial behaviors becomes stronger with age (e.g., Eisenberg et al., 1999), Blasi (1980) argued that a variety of situation-specific factors—such as the genuineness and urgency of the other's needs—mediate the relationship between moral judgment and moral behavior and become increasingly important with age. Blasi (1980) also suggested that developmental changes in middle childhood have significant implications for the extent to which children enact their moral cognitions and feelings. For instance, children who lack perspective-taking abilities will be less likely to behave prosocially when self-needs compete with others' needs. Grusec (1983) proposed that children's socializing agents can play an important role by establishing social scripts or schemas of prosocial behavior and by encouraging children's use of those scripts during social interactions. It is important that children learn to adapt their social scripts to the needs and expectations of their social partners and to the demands of their immediate settings within a larger system of social values and beliefs.

Development of Social Information-Processing Skills

An information-processing approach to explaining children's social development differs from a cognitive developmental approach in several important ways. Researchers in this tradition begin with a precise analysis of particular social tasks facing a child; these investigators' primary goal is to learn how children use the information available to them in responding to task demands. Changes in children's behavior—due to intervention efforts or to everyday experiences—are thought to be a function of changes in children's content knowledge about a task and their strategies for using task-related information.

Several social information-processing (SIP) models of social cognitive development have been proposed to explain the links between the ways in which children interpret or understand social behaviors and cues, children's resulting social behaviors, and—in turn—their social adjustment. Crick and Dodge (1994), for example, outlined one SIP model that suggests that children, whose abilities at any given age are limited by biologically based constraints, enter social situations with a database of past experiences, including memories, rules, social schemas, and social knowledge. During social interactions, children go through a series of steps including encoding and interpreting social cues, clarifying their goals for social interaction, accessing possible behavioral responses, choosing a response from their pool of choices, and then enacting their chosen response. When children search their database for previously applied responses, the database conversely stores information regarding the current situation for future use.

SIP models such as the one just described have been used extensively in the study of socially maladjusted children, particularly those who are highly aggressive. The results from a series of studies of U.S. children suggest that those with poor social adjustment and skills may suffer from distortions or deficits in their information-processing skills at one or more of the steps of information processing (Crick & Dodge, 1994). For instance, researchers have identified attributional biases in rejected and/or aggressive children who exhibit a greater tendency to see hostile intentions as the cause of others' behaviors toward them (Dodge, 1980; Quiggle, Garber, Panak, & Dodge, 1992). Other evidence suggests that these kinds of inaccurate attributions may be specific to children who display reactive or retaliatory aggression (Crick & Dodge, 1996). Here, children's strategies for interpreting social cues are perceived to be faulty, and thus intervention efforts should be directed at changing the way children understand others' behaviors.

In contrast to the idea that deficits in social cognitive abilities give rise to social adjustment problems, recent research suggests that some aggressive children might actually be manipulative experts in social situations. Sutton, Smith, and Swettenham (1999), for example, found that 7- to 10-year-old "ringleader bullies" scored higher on tests of perspective-taking than did "follower bullies" (bully-supporters), victims, or even children who defended victims. These ringleaders were essentially best at understanding the mental states, beliefs, and emotions of others, suggesting that this particular group of aggressive children may be advanced in some elements of their social knowledge. Thus, whereas social information processing models provide an account of how children's social understanding may be linked to their ability to negotiate social interactions effectively, other kinds of models are needed to explain individual differences in children's motivations and goals for their social interactions and relationships. Furthermore, although information processing models make assumptions that cognitive abilities and skills are maturationally constrained and improve across development, explanation of the sources of such developmental changes awaits further study. An important direction for SIP research is to examine the applicability of these kinds of models across a range of cultural and subcultural contexts.

Emotional and Social Development: Self-Regulation and Self-Control in Middle Childhood

Emotion is commonly conceived as a motivational force underlying social behaviors, and expression of emotion is a central component of social interaction (Eisenberg, 1998; Saarni et al., 1998). According to Sarni et al., emotion is "the person's attempt or readiness to establish, maintain, or change the relation between the person and the environment on matters of significance to that person" (p. 238). Emotion regulation in turn involves a dynamic process of matching intrinsic reactive tendencies and coping strategies with environmental stressors and coping resources on the one hand, and norms about appropriate emotional expression on the other (Eisenberg, 1998; Saarni et al., 1998). A body of studies on the development of emotion regulation documents that children who effectively regulate their emotions and their emotion-related behaviors via a diverse and flexible repertoire of responses—tailored to contextually grounded demands and motives—are more socially competent (Eisenberg, 1998; Parke, Burks, Carson, Neville, & Boyum, 1994; Saarni et al., 1998).

Changing patterns of everyday activities during middle childhood—including spending more time outside the home and away from direct parental supervision—mean that children must learn to manage their own emotions. In childhood, effective emotion regulation is reflected in children's control over when and how they express their emotions, as well as in children's expanding opportunities and abilities to pick niches—including particular activities or specific social settings—whose demands fall within the range of their coping and self-control abilities (Eisenberg, 1998; Skinner &

Wellborn, 1994). A larger social world also means that children confront increasingly varied behavioral repertoires in their social partners and encounter new requirements for emotion expression and regulation. As children move into new and more varied settings, they learn that they must adapt their emotion expression to contextual demands.

In the following pages we describe factors that influence emotion regulation during middle childhood; we also highlight the implications of emotion regulation processes for children's social competence and adjustment. Characteristics of the individual that have implications for emotion regulation include developing cognitive abilities, which, for example, allow children to recognize emotions in themselves and others or anticipate reactions by others (Dodge, 1989; Parke et al., 1994; Saarni et al., 1998). Individual differences in temperament also play a role, for example, in the intensity of a child's reactions to social experiences or the degree to which children attend to and learn from socialization efforts (Skinner & Wellborn, 1994). Factors from without or *extrinsic factors* range from the emotional climate, to the demands of proximate environments, to the availability of role models of appropriate emotional expression (Dunsmore & Halberstadt, 1997; Sarni et al., 1998). Such factors also include the behavior of the social partners who elicit emotional reactions from children, children's experience of stressful life events, and circumstances that may place extra demands on children's regulation capacities (Skinner & Wellborn, 1994). These personal and interpersonal processes in turn take place within contexts (family, peer group, school) that define specific but potentially very different ranges of appropriate emotional expression. This area of study is a broad and burgeoning one with a heavy emphasis on the study of infants and young children (detailed analyses of development in this domain can be found in reviews by Eisenberg 1998; Fox, 1994; Saarni et al., 1998; Thompson, 1991).

Intrinsic Factors in Emotion Development

Intrinsic factors that underlie emotion and emotion regulation help to establish children's social interaction styles and thresholds for social stressors. Some of these factors have documented biological substrates and include genetic factors undergirding individual differences in temperament, sex differences in boys' versus girls' emotion behavior, and maturational factors that govern cognitive developmental changes in self-understanding, -regulation and -control.

Temperament can be defined as differences in reactivity, including children's disposition toward impulsivity or inhibition; temperamental characteristics contribute to individual differences in self-regulatory behaviors, such as arousal threshold and reaction duration and intensity (Eisenberg, 1998; Saarni et al., 1998). Children with high emotional intensity may be inclined toward less effective coping strategies and less attention control, and those who are easily distracted or prone to arousal may be less successful at attending to and processing signals from others (Eisenberg, 1998). Of significance is that individual differences in children's dispositions toward emotional expression—grounded in temperament—mean that the effects of socialization efforts or contextual demands will vary considerably across children. The goodness of fit between a child's temperament and environmental demands (e.g., expectations, stressors) determines how much tailoring a child must do to accommodate successfully to a given social context (e.g., Lerner, 1982).

Sex differences in children's emotion-related social cognitive abilities are not widely apparent; girls and boys are equally capable of encoding and decoding emotion and of developing emotion-coping repertoires. Nonetheless, girls and boys may evoke contrasting gender socialization efforts regarding their emotionality and emotion expression. With respect to their strategies for coping with stress, girls are more likely to use emotion-focused coping strategies, whereas boys are more likely to use problem-solving strategies (Saarni et al., 1998). Sex differences in adjustment that have emotion-related components are also widely evident and become more pronounced toward the end of middle childhood, with girls more inclined to exhibit internalizing problems such as low self-esteem or depression, and boys more inclined to exhibit externalizing problems such as physical aggression or thrill-seeking behavior.

Cognitive developmental processes constitute an additional set of intrinsic factors that undergird emotional regulation. For example, during early childhood cognitive advances allow children to recognize their emotional states; perspective-taking skills, consolidated in middle childhood, mean that children become better able to anticipate and understand the expectations, reactions, and behaviors of others. Cognitive advances also provide for more sophisticated social cue recognition and interpretation and greater sensitivity to both person and situation signals. Children also become better able to anticipate others' emotional reactions and the consequences for their own emotional displays and to understand the causes of their own and others' emotions (Eisenberg, 1998; Saarni et al., 1998; Selman, 1980). Drawing upon their developing meta-understanding of emotion, children expand their repertoires of coping strategies to include introspection (e.g., reinterpreting negative situations more positively), redirecting attention, and arousal avoidance (Saarni et al., 1998; Skinner &

Wellborn, 1994). Children also recognize that their own and others' overt reactions are not always consistent with felt emotions. As a result of knowing that emotions and reactions are sometimes disassociated, children learn to change their reactions—despite feeling the same emotion—to conform to situational demands and experience social approval. For example, children bullied at school may exhibit courage, while experiencing fear; in the face of failure and disappointment, children learn to keep smiles on their faces.

Extrinsic Factors in Emotion Development

Between early and middle childhood, adult regulation of children's emotions and emotional expression transforms into adult-child coregulation, and ultimately to children's self-regulation of their emotion experiences (Collins, 1984). Some researchers have targeted the family—in particular, parent-child interactions—as the root of emotion and emotion regulation (Dunsmore & Halberstadt, 1997; Eisenberg, 1998; Thompson, 1991). For example, children's expectations regarding their own and others' emotional displays and reactions may be influenced by their exposure to models of emotional expressiveness within the family. In the family context, children learn values and norms about appropriate emotional displays and about their own responsibility for their emotional expression (Dunsmore & Halberstadt, 1997; Saarni et al., 1998). Some work suggests that when parents are overly restrictive of their children's emotional displays, children's social competence may be impaired (e.g., Gottman, Katz, & Hooven, 1997). In addition, family interactions provide children with practice at controlling and expressing their emotions and at reading the emotions of others (Dunsmore & Halberstadt, 1997; Gottman et al., 1997; Parke et al., 1994; Saarni et al., 1998). Finally, parents can help children learn to avoid uncontrollable stressors by orchestrating their involvement in everyday activities and social contexts outside the home (Parke et al., 1994; Saarni et al., 1998).

Whereas infants and young children require sensitive adults to read and respond to their cues, by middle childhood children can play a more active role in directing their everyday experiences, such as by choosing activities, contexts, and social partners that better support their emotional styles and needs (Saarni et al., 1998). The expanding social world of middle childhood, however, means that children must learn and apply norms of emotion expression that vary across context: What is permissible in the context of the family may differ markedly from what is appropriate in the peer group or at school. Increasing autonomy and time spent outside of direct parental supervision also means that greater *self*-control is required from children. The school setting is marked by pressure for children to conform to behavioral expectations, serving as a major motivation for self-regulation and constructive coping of emotion during the middle childhood years (Saarni et al., 1998). The peer group is also an important context for emotional development, and a number of studies have documented that appropriate emotion regulation in the peer group is linked to greater social competence and more positive peer relationships (Rubin et al., 1998; Parker & Seal, 1996). An important consideration is that differences across settings in what constitutes appropriate emotional expression may be more pronounced for some children than for others; likewise, the demands for self-control and constraints on emotion expression in particular settings may or may not be compatible with a child's dispositions. For instance, children reared by depressed parents or those who experience coercive parent-child relationships may develop emotion expression dispositions that involve withdrawal in the former case or escalation of negative emotion in the latter (Saarni et al., 1998; Thompson, 1991). These types of emotion regulation, however, do not translate well to the school environment or to the peer group and may result in social rejection or isolation. In turn, rejected and isolated children miss opportunities to learn different and adaptive social-emotional interaction styles (Dunsmore & Halberstadt, 1994; Saarni et al., 1998).

Personal Characteristics, Socialization Influences, and Contextual Demands: Interacting Influences on Emotion Regulation

Developmental models highlight interactive processes involving individual characteristics, learning and experience, and the demands of the immediate setting in explaining social behavior (Cairns, 1991). Because it is a period marked by increased opportunities for independence and involvement in new social settings, middle childhood may present a challenge for children's emotion regulation in the form of potential inconsistencies between personal dispositions and past learning on the one hand and the demands of new and immediate settings on the other. Dunsmore and Halberstadt (1997) propose that the match between familial emotional style of expression, child predispositions, and extrafamilial contextual demands will be an important determinant of effective emotion regulation in children. Although Collins (1984) suggests that a certain degree of inconsistency may enable children to develop a more differentiated understanding of the social world, children who experience less consistency may have more difficulty regulating their emotions and may

require more resources—in the forms of social support or coping strategies—to do so. Extant research provides scant evidence about how to support children in their response to the diverse and sometimes inconsistent demands for emotion expression and regulation in their everyday experiences. Such information would enhance our understanding of individual differences in emotional regulation and provide insights about potential avenues for intervention.

Summary

Research on children's everyday social experiences and social competencies during middle childhood highlights the challenges children face as—with ever-increasing autonomy—they navigate a more diverse and complex social world. Maturing cognitive and physical abilities allow children to undertake new and different kinds of activities in their work and in their play; novel activity settings in turn place demands on children's social competencies; and it is in the behavioral accommodations children make in adapting to new settings that social development is manifested (Cairns, 1991). As such, an agenda for researchers studying social development is to explore just how the demands of their activity settings first elicit and then support adaptations in children's social behavior.

Recent theoretical efforts directed at defining social competence highlight the importance of understanding children's social behavior in its larger context. Rose-Krasnor (1997), for example, argues that social competence should be defined as *effectiveness in social interaction;* competence can not be evaluated independent of the social context because (a) the context-dependent nature of social competence means that behaviors that are effective in one context may not be so in another; (b) children's everyday social behaviors are influenced in part by factors such as emotional arousal or motivation level, which are affected by setting conditions; (c) children's social behaviors are goal directed, and their goals are tied to the demands and constraints of their social settings; and (d) children's social behaviors emerge in their interactions with particular social partners and therefore must be evaluated in terms of the responses of others. Rose-Krasnor's focus on effectiveness as fundamental to social competence is congruent with John Ogbu's (1995) argument, framed within a broader, cultural-ecological perspective, that human competencies must be understood in terms of the adaptation requirements of a given ecology. For children this means that socialization experiences will be directed at developing different kinds of social knowledge and self-regulation abilities in different social and cultural settings.

A challenge for social development researchers is to expand the scope of their studies to examine the array of settings around the world in where children spend their time in which they develop and practice novel social behaviors.

SOCIAL RELATIONSHIPS AND DEVELOPMENT IN MIDDLE CHILDHOOD

Children's interpersonal relationships provide a context for their social development. Social behaviors emerge, are practiced, and change in the context of interactions with significant others, casual acquaintances, and strangers. The "personnel present" is one important component of children's activity settings (Weisner, 1984); the everyday lives of children in different cultures and in different historical eras can be distinguished by whom they spend their time with and also by the nature of the relationships they form with their companions.

Children develop as individuals in the context of their relationships, and their relationships also undergo development and change. Changes in dyadic relationships are a function of the development of both partners as individuals as well as the history of the relationship partners' shared experiences (Hinde, 1979). As should become evident, research on how children's individual development is affected by their relationship experiences represents the bulk of the literature in this domain; focusing on change at the level of the dyad adds an element of complexity to the study of social development but is an important focus for researchers interested in children's social development. In this section we consider three kinds of relationships that are central in the lives of children: relationships with parents, with peers, and with siblings. We begin each section with an overview of how these relationships change during middle childhood, and then we discuss research on how their relationship experiences have implications for children's individual growth and competencies.

Children and Their Parents

During middle childhood, parent-child relationships evolve in the direction of greater mutuality, with adult regulation increasingly supplanted by coregulation and reciprocal exchange between parent and child (Collins et al., 1995; Collins & Russell, 1991). The nature of parents' involvement with their children also changes. Time spent during infancy and early childhood in shared activities focused on caregiving and play is supplanted by parenting from a distance, as when parents observe or supervise their children's activities or learn about their children's experiences second-

hand. Finally, children's emerging social cognitive skills mean that they are developing a more differentiated perspective on their parents: all-knowing and powerful parental figures may be increasingly perceived as individuals with needs and interests that go beyond their parenting roles, and this recognition may alter children's and parents' behaviors and emotions in their shared relationship. Despite these many changes, however, relatively few studies have studied parent-child *relationships* during middle childhood; instead, much of the focus on developmental changes in parent-child relationship focuses on adolescence (see Collins & Russell, 1991; Russell & Saebel, 1997, for reviews of research on parent-child relationships).

What is evident in the literature on children's relationships with their parents are the important differences between their experiences with their mothers versus their fathers. A thorough review of issues of gender and parent-child relationships is beyond the scope of this chapter; at the most general level, this literature suggests that children's relationships with their mothers and fathers generally take distinct forms, with mothers being more involved overall and children feeling closer to their mothers; fathers' involvement, in contrast, tends to center on play and leisure activities, with conversations focusing on instrumental topics. In addition, probably because of their more extensive contact and closeness, children's relationships with their mothers involve more conflict, whereas in their relationships with their fathers, children are more deferential (see Collins & Russell, 1991; Maccoby, 1998; Russell & Saebel, 1997, for reviews).

As we have suggested, the majority of research on parents and children has been devoted to studying how the quality of parenting is linked to children's social development and well-being. In the face of increasingly diverse and changing family forms (Hernandez, 1997), however researchers are becoming more focused on the family contexts of children's experiences with their parents. Families are not limited to maritally intact, biological mothers and fathers with children; in fact, this traditional family form is becoming increasingly rare in Western societies. An ecological perspective highlights that parent-child relationship dynamics—as well as the effects of parent-child relationships on children's social development—are likely to vary as a function of family structure and as a function of the larger cultural context in which the family is embedded. A discussion of the range of parent socialization and parent-child relationship experiences in diverse family settings is beyond the scope of this chapter (interested readers are directed to overviews by Parke & Buriel, 1998, on differences in parenting across ethnic groups, Arendell, 1997, on parenting in divorced and remarried families, Allen, 1997, on lesbian and gay parents).

We limit our discussion to an overview of models of parental influence, highlighting what may be the special features of family experiences that are connected to social development during middle childhood.

Most of the research on parental influences on children's social development focuses on parents' role as interaction partners with their children (Parke & Buriel, 1998). By virtue of their level of warmth and responsiveness and by the ways in which they attempt to control their children's behavior, parents provide children with social interactional experiences that shape children's expectations about, understandings of, and behaviors in other interpersonal relationships. Research that focuses on children's emotional attachments to their parents (e.g., Ainsworth, Blehar, Waters, & Wall, 1978) and research that examines the links between parental style and children's social functioning (e.g., Baumrind, 1971, 1991) fall within this tradition.

Recent analyses of parents' role in the socialization process have noted limitations of these early, more deterministic models, directing attention, for example, to contextual moderators of parent socialization influences, to the impact of children's characteristics and behaviors on parental activities, and to the cognitive and affective processes that underlie observed parenting practices (e.g., Bugental & Goodnow, 1998; Collins, Maccoby, Steinberg, Hetherington, & Bornstein, 2000). These accounts highlight the complexities of parental socialization processes and suggest new directions for research. As one example of an expanded model of parental socialization, the tripartite model of parenting proposed by Parke and colleagues (Parke et al., 1994) focuses on parents' activities as "direct instructors" and "providers of opportunities" along with their role as interaction partners. Whereas the influence of parent-child interactions on children's social development is *indirect* (as when children develop expectations for experiences in close relationships that are generalized to new social partners), parents may *directly influence* their children's social development by giving their children advice about negotiating new social experiences and inculcating values about appropriate ways of relating toward relatives, friends, or strangers (i.e., direct instruction) or by engineering social opportunities for their children such as by picking the community where their children will reside or providing funds for and transportation to school and extracurricular activities. Relative to research on parents' indirect role in children's social development, we know much less about parents' direct role in children's social experiences. Yet when one considers the broad range of circumstances in which children's lives unfold and the corresponding goals for social competence that parents hold (Ogbu, 1995), parents' directive activities are clearly a central component of parental

roles. In the following pages we review the limited research on parents' direct influence and highlight key areas of study focused on parents' indirect influences on children's social development.

Parents' Role in Children's Social Development: Direct Influences

Within the context of the parent-child relationship, parents directly influence their children's social development in a variety of ways. Of fundamental significance is the parents' choice of the *environment*s in which their children are reared (Parke et al., 1994; Super & Harkness, 1986). Aspects of the environment include the social and physical characteristics of the child's immediate setting, such as the home, neighborhood, and school; but as Weisner (1984) suggested, elements of the broader social setting—including its political, economic, and cultural components—also have important implications for children's development. The range of choices available to parents is necessarily limited, but within this range children may develop ideas about their parents as powerful and competent adults and about their own significance in their parents' lives based on parents' ability and willingness to make choices that are advantageous to children's well-being.

Parents also are responsible for *transmitting values and attitudes*—both their own and those of the larger community in which they live—to their children. Parents serve as role models and educators for children, they construct their home environments in ways that convey parental values, and they engineer children's out-of-home activities in ways that will promote their goals for their children's development. For instance, parents who value education may make it a priority in children's lives by limiting the amount of television viewing or by encouraging children to read (Stevenson & Lee, 1992). Parents also create and maintain a home environment that teaches children about acceptable interaction styles. For example, parents demonstrate their values about appropriate social behavior by how they behave toward other family members; a body of studies has established links between parents' experiences in other dyadic relationships in the family (such as with their spouse or with a child's siblings) and children's social development and well-being (Davies & Cummings, 1994; Gottman et al., 1997; Perlman & Ross, 1997). Additionally, parents teach children values by the kinds of activities they assign or support. Gender socialization may be fostered, for example, by how parents allocate household tasks to their daughters and sons or by the kinds of extracurricular activities they encourage (McHale, Crouter, & Tucker, 1999). Finally, explicitly through instruction or implicitly through their own reactions and behaviors, parents teach children how to decode the meaning of others' social behavior and how to respond in kind (Parke et al., 1994).

Another important element of parents' directive role involves their efforts to *scaffold* their children's development (Rogoff, 1990). The process of scaffolding includes sensitivity to children's current ability level coupled with stepwise advising and training to foster new skill acquisition. Parents usher children on to their next level of social functioning by choosing new developmentally appropriate social activities that challenge but do not overwhelm, by practicing new scripts (e.g., riding the bus on the first day of school) before they actually are needed, or by intervention in an ongoing interaction when a child appears to be floundering (Palacios, Gonzalez, & Moreno, 1992).

Parenting from a distance becomes increasingly prominent in middle childhood with children's burgeoning autonomy and involvement in a new array of social settings. Parents actively select children's activities, set rules concerning children's whereabouts and companions, and monitor their children's behavior from afar. This places a new burden on the children, who must adjust to new routines and social scripts and to parental expectations for conduct and disclosure. A body of work on parental monitoring and knowledge of their children's activities highlights the importance of this domain of parenting activities for children's well-being (Crouter & Head, 2002).

Although research on parents' directive role focuses on parents as socialization agents, the active role of the child should not be dismissed. Within their family and community contexts, children evoke reactions from others by virtue of their personal characteristics, and they seek increasing opportunities to select their own niches (Scarr & McCartney, 1983). Furthermore, the success of parents' directive socialization efforts is dependent in part on children's willingness to be socialized. Darling and Steinberg (1993) argue that warmth and closeness in the parent-child relationship, developed through parent-child interaction experiences, is an important determinant of whether parents' socialization practices will be effective.

Parents' Role in Children's Social Development: Indirect Influences

The bulk of research on the role of parent-child relationships in children's development highlights how interactions within the parent-child relationship have broader implications for children's social development and well-being. Such indirect influences of parent-child relationships have been studied by researchers focused on parent- (particularly mother-) child

attachment and by those focused on parental style. Although these perspectives traditionally de-emphasized the active role of the child in the socialization process, the theoretical orientation to socialization has shifted in past decades from a parent-to-child model to a greater appreciation for the reciprocal nature of influences between parents and children. Characteristics such as children's sex, temperament, and cognitive sophistication are important factors in determining the kinds of parenting strategies parents employ as well as the effectiveness of those strategies (Collins et al., 1995; Deater-Deckard & Dodge, 1997; McGillicuddy-DeLisi, 1992).

Research on parent-infant attachment links sensitive responsiveness by caregivers early in children's lives to later social and relationship competence. The importance of early experience derives from children's sense of security that their needs will be met within the context of their first social relationships (which usually are with parents). As a result of interpreting and internalizing their early parent-child relationship experiences, children are thought to develop internal working models or expectations about future relationships with others. Sroufe and Fleeson (1986) argue further that these early parent-child relationship experiences underlie personality development, where personality is defined as the "organization of attitudes, feelings, expectations, and behaviors of the individual across contexts" (p. 52). From this perspective, continuity in personality organization should be evident across age, although the manifestations of individual differences will change with development. In middle childhood, attachment researchers have documented links between early parent-infant attachment and children's social competence with peers (Rubin et al., 1998; Sroufe, 1979).

A second line of study has examined the significance of parental style for children's social development and well-being. Baumrind (1973) proposed one of the most influential models in this regard, documenting the significance of *authoritative parenting,* a style characterized by high warmth, democratic discipline, and developmentally appropriate limit-setting, for the development of social competence from early childhood through adolescence. Expanding on Baumrind's typology, Maccoby and Martin (1983) identified four patterns of parenting that vary along two dimensions: the extent of parent control and the degree to which parents are responsive and child centered. As in Baumrind's typology, in addition to the authoritative style (appropriate control and high in responsiveness) Maccoby and Martin identified a group labeled *authoritarian,* which refers to a parental style characterized by high levels of restrictiveness in combination with low levels of responsiveness and warmth. Baumrind (1991) found that this style was associated with especially poor outcomes for boys. In contrast, *indulgent* or *permissive* parents are high in responsiveness but low in control and tend to have children who have poor impulse control. Finally, *neglectful* or *uninvolved* parents are low in both warmth and control and are focused more on their own needs than on those of their children.

Parental style is connected to the broader circumstances of family life. McLoyd and others (McLoyd, 1990; McLoyd & Wilson, 1990), for example, describe how the stresses that accompany poverty may give rise to emotional distress and decreased responsiveness and involvement on the parts of parents. Stressors such as marital separation and divorce also negatively affect parenting style (Hetherington, 1989), with implications for children's social competence and adjustment. Equally important influences on parental style are parents' child-rearing goals and values. For example, Kohn (1977) argued that the more authoritarian style of working-class fathers in the United States arises out of men's belief that obedience and conformity are important attributes for success in the workplace and that a harsher and more restrictive discipline style best promotes such qualities. Other writers suggest that context characteristics ranging from the level of violence and danger in the neighborhood to cultural norms within the wider ecology that highlight collectivist versus individualistic values will have implications for parents' choice of child-rearing style as well as for how a particular style is associated with social competence and adjustment in children (Ogbu, 1995; Parke & Buriel, 1998). Finally, a burgeoning literature stresses that parents' beliefs about how children develop and their attributions about the causes of child behaviors highlight some of the processes through which the larger social ecology may exert an impact on parental behavior (Bugental & Goodnow, 1998; McGuillicuddy-DeLisi, 1992). These kinds of analyses highlight that parent-child relationships and their implications for children's development are best understood when they are examined within their larger social ecology.

Children and Their Peers

Middle childhood is a developmental period when children turn from parents to peers for companionship in their everyday activities; this change is part of a pattern of children's increasingly active role in choosing where and with whom they spend their time. Research suggests that children's interest in their peers, together with their increasingly sophisticated social cognitive and emotion regulation abilities, are tied to newly emerging characteristics of children's peer experiences. These emerging characteristics involve quantitative changes in peer group size and qualitative changes in the bases of friendships. A body of work examines how children's

experiences with their friends and in their peer social networks have implications for their current and future social competence and adjustment. Our discussion in the following pages provides an overview of the predominant areas of research on peer relationships in middle childhood.

The Development of Peer Relationships in Middle Childhood

Several important changes characterize peer experiences and friendships during middle childhood; like other elements of children's social development, these changes reflect both children's developing cognitive abilities and their expanding social worlds. With respect to peer experiences more generally, increased exposure to a world outside of the family context means that children spend their time with a more diverse set of same-age peers. Children also begin to spend their time with peers outside the direct supervision of parents or other adults. A striking element of peer interaction during middle childhood is its sex-segregated quality, which has been documented in cultures around the world (Cairns & Cairns, 1994; Fagot, 1994; Maccoby, 1994). In early childhood, mixed-sex peer groups play together. Later in adolescence, boys and girls develop dyadic romantic relationships, and larger social groups may include both sexes. In middle childhood, however, cross-sex friendships and activities are quite rare within the *visible* peer group, such as on the school playground (Adler, Kless, & Adler, 1992; Maccoby, 1998), although some findings show that same-sex friendships occur in more private settings (e.g., Gottman, 1994). Maccoby (1990) suggests that gender segregation may be based in boys' and girls' distinct and sometimes incompatible interaction and play styles; sex segregation in peer and friendship groups in turn exacerbates sex differences in social interaction styles. Other investigators (e.g., Fagot, 1994; Leaper, 1994) concur that the tendency for sex segregation in the peer group may both reflect and have important implications for gender role socialization. Fagot (1977), for example, found that girls who attempt to join male peer groups and who participate in cross-sex behaviors are ignored whereas boys' feminine activities and behaviors instigate negative feedback from both male and female peers.

Groups or cliques—which consist of stable, voluntary friendships, typically of three to nine same-sex, same-race children—also form for the first time during middle childhood. These social groups provide a reference point for social comparisons and self-evaluations; only later in development will adolescents begin to use absolute and personal standards (Harter, 1999). The emergence of cliques also leads to the organization of popularity hierarchies. In middle childhood, boys' place in the social hierarchy tends to be based on social dominance, athletic ability, coolness, and toughness (Adler et al., 1992; Hartup, 1992). In contrast, girls' social status depends on family background and socioeconomic status (SES) and physical appearance (Adler et al., 1992; Thorne, 1994). For both boys and girls, social skillfulness is an important factor in social dominance.

Children's awareness of and concern for their popularity status greatly increases during middle childhood and may be related in part to their social cognitive development, which provides for an increasing appreciation of the perspectives of others. Consistent with such changes is the increasing prominence of gossiping (Parker & Gottman, 1989). Gossip is one basis for a child's social reputation with peers (Hartup, 1992; Hymel, Wagner, & Butler, 1990) and can serve other social functions, including the communication of social norms and expectations to group members; such communications often take place through negative evaluations of others (Eder & Enke, 1991; Gottman & Mettetal, 1986). Because direct confrontation is inappropriate within their peer culture, gossip constitutes an important form of communication among girls, in particular (Corsaro & Eder, 1990).

Children's increased autonomy during middle childhood coincides with their greater control over the types of activities in which they participate. Rough-and-tumble play is replaced by games with or without formal rules, and peer interactions become increasingly coordinated (Corsaro & Eder, 1990). Although the activity settings of children's peer interactions during middle childhood have not been well described, Zarbatany, Hartmann, and Rankin (1990) found that peer involvement most often occurred during conversation (both in person and over the telephone), while children were "hanging out," and when they were playing sports. The only sex difference in peer interactions that emerged in this study of peer activities was that girls interacted with their peers more through telephone conversations than did boys.

In addition to developmental changes in orientations toward the peer group, middle childhood also is a time of change in friendships. Among the U.S. children who have been the primary focus of study, friendships in middle childhood tend to be age- and sex-homogeneous (Hartup, 1992; Rubin et al., 1998). In a biracial southern community, Shrum, Cheek, and Hunter (1988) found that during middle childhood, gender homophily peaks and then begins to fall in adolescence, whereas race homophily first appears and then begins to increase during middle childhood, plateauing in adolescence—a pattern that may reflect children's initial awareness of racial identity. Children's friendships in middle childhood are also characterized by greater reciprocity, commitment, and affectional bonds compared to those at younger ages. As mentioned earlier, Sullivan (1953) suggested that

the development of friends, or chumships, is predicated on decreasing egocentrism and increasing perspective-taking ability; these changes provide the potential for greater reciprocity in peer interactions (Selman, 1980). In addition to sharing the view that middle childhood coincides with loss of egocentrism, Piaget (1932) suggested that middle childhood brings about the ability for greater abstract thinking. Consequently, the basis of friendships evolves from participation in common activities and the satisfaction of instrumental needs (e.g., for a play partner) at the start of middle childhood to the satisfaction of more abstract relational needs and goals, such as trust, honesty, and loyalty, in adolescence and beyond (Cairns & Cairns, 1994). Parker and Asher (1993) found that validation, help, and companionship are associated with greater satisfaction with friendships during childhood, whereas conflict is related to decreased satisfaction. They also noted that boys characterized their friendships as having less intimacy, validation, and help than did girls. Similarly, Cairns and Cairns (1994) reported that honesty and loyalty were more important to girls than to boys possibly, as self-protection against the relational aggression that is manifested, in gossip and social manipulation (Crick & Grotpeter, 1995). In contrast to the greater prevalence of verbal or physical aggression in boys' interactions relative to those of girls, Crick and Grotpeter (1995) found that such relational aggression strategies were more common among third- through sixth-grade girls than boys.

Children's friendships have been characterized as having stability—that is, as showing continuity over time, distance, and events, but empirical data on this issue are equivocal (Rubin et al., 1998). For example, although relationship stability was greater for children in middle childhood than for those at earlier ages, based on their longitudinal study, Cairns and Cairns (1994) reported a high degree of long-term volatility in children's friendships. During middle childhood, relationship change was at least partially attributed to limited opportunities for maintaining friendships—for example, when children moved to another community or were assigned to a different classroom at school. Although middle childhood marks a time of development in which children gain greater autonomy and greater control over their activities, their lives are still constrained. In the face of forces toward instability, however, behavioral characteristics of children do make a difference in children's tendencies to establish and maintain friendships and in their social status, an issue we further consider in the next section.

Peer Influences on Children's Social Development

A body of work examines the connections between children's experiences with peers and their social competencies and adjustment; as with studies of friendship, most of this work focuses on U.S. children. One set of studies focuses on children's sociometric status, examining children's social skills and adjustment as both cause and consequence of their popularity with peers. Using peer nominations, researchers in this tradition classify children into one of several categories: (a) Children who receive a high number of positive nominations (i.e., expressions of liking) and few negative nominations (i.e., expressions of disliking) are labeled *popular;* (b) those with many negative nominations and few positive nominations are labeled *rejected;* (c) children are labeled *neglected* if they receive few negative and few positive nominations; (d) they are labeled *average* when they receive an average number of both negative and positive nominations; and (e) children are considered *controversial* if they are given a high number of both negative and positive nominations. Although popular and rejected statuses seem relatively stable over time (Hymel, Rubin, Rowden, & LeMare, 1990; Roff, Sells, & Golden, 1972) neglected, average, and controversial statuses are less so (Ladd, 1999; Rubin et al., 1998).

A number of studies have shown that socially competent behaviors—including the ability to enter groups, initiate relationships, and maintain those relationships over time—are linked to sociometric status (Putallaz & Wasserman, 1990) as are children's abilities to regulate their emotions (Eisenberg et al., 1987). Indeed, consistent manifestation of either positive or negative social behaviors is predictive of acceptance or rejection by the peer group (Coie, Dodge, & Kupersmidt, 1990; Dodge, Coie, Pettit, & Price, 1990; Harrist, Zaia, Bates, Dodge, & Pettit, 1997; Parker & Seal, 1996).

Moving away from a focus on social skill deficits of the rejected or neglected child, Hymel, Wagner et al. (1990) focused on the ways in which the *social structure* within the child's environment can negatively influence a child's peer acceptance. They suggest that—due to biases formed by previously established reputations—members of the peer group may be more likely to shun rejected children's attempts to enter groups or initiate interactions.

In turn, substantial evidence links problematic childhood peer relationships to both current and future adjustment. Much of this work is premised on one of two models (Parker & Asher, 1987). The *causal* model suggests that low-accepted children are limited in their normal peer interactions and are thus excluded from normal socialization experiences and social support networks; such low involvement further perpetuates unacceptable patterns of social cognition, emotion, and behavior. In contrast to the assumption that problematic peer relationships *cause* maladjustment, the *incidental* model suggests that early forms of a disorder, which will later develop into maladjustment, inhibit positive peer relationships during

childhood (see Parker & Asher, 1987, for limitations of these models).

Most research on the implications of social status for social adjustment has focused on popular and rejected statuses. As noted, *popular* children tend to be socially competent at entering new situations and are viewed as cooperative, friendly, sociable, and sensitive by peers, teachers, and observers (Dodge, Coie, & Brakke, 1982; Dodge, McClaskey, & Feldman, 1985; Putallaz, 1983; Newcomb, Bukowski, & Pattee, 1993). Although neglected- and average-statuses during childhood are not closely tied to later well-being outcomes, peer group *rejection* is associated with adjustment problems such as depression, aggression, poor grade retention, and poor academic competence over time (Coie, Lochman, Terry, & Hyman, 1992; Panak & Garber, 1992). Most sociometric research has focused on short-term correlational studies linking children's peer acceptance to their concurrent or future adjustment, but some longitudinal analyses have documented the predictive power of peer acceptance (e.g., Hymel, Rubin et al., 1990; Kupersmidt & Coie, 1990). Based on their review of risk research, Parker and Asher (1987) concluded that low acceptance and aggressiveness predicted later maladjustment (criminality and early school dropout), but that there was insufficient evidence linking shyness and social withdrawal to poor outcomes. This may be in part because current research highlights overtly negative behaviors and externalizing problems rather than the mental health and relationship problems that may be more common in the development of children who are socially withdrawn and neglected by their peers.

In sum, an array of empirical evidence supports the proposition that peer acceptance has significant implications for children's social development. Future research in this area should move beyond a focus on the number of children's friends to examine the *qualities of children's relationships* and the *characteristics of the peer group* (Hartup, 1996). Research on "deviancy training" (Dishion, Andrews, & Crosby, 1995) suggests, for example, that a child may have many friends, but that if all are antisocial, children's well-being may be at risk. How children's peer experiences are linked to the values and expectations of the larger social ecology is another topic for future study.

Children and Their Siblings

Like peer relationships, sibling relationships are an important part of life in middle childhood. These relationships have received less empirical scrutiny than have parent-child and peer relationships, but a body of work documents the unique role that siblings play in one another's development (Dunn, 1998; Dunn & Plomin, 1990; Brody & Stoneman, 1995).

Through their everyday interactions, siblings can affect one another when they serve as models, teachers, and social partners. Siblings also influence one another indirectly by virtue of their impact on roles and relationship dynamics in the larger family system. In this final section, we describe the special properties of sibling relationships, highlighting the experiences of children in middle childhood. We then review research that exemplifies the mechanisms through which siblings may influence one another's social development.

The Development of Sibling Relationships in Middle Childhood

Most children grow up in households that include one or more siblings. In the United States, demographic changes in fertility rates and divorce-remarriage mean that the size and structure of sibships have been undergoing striking change (Eggebeen, 1992). For example, U.S. census data show that among White families in 1950, over half of children of preschool age were living in households with more than two siblings; by 1980 this figure had declined to 30%. Among African Americans, the percent of young children with more than two siblings declined from almost 80% in 1950 to about 40% in 1980 (Eggebeen, 1992). More recent census data indicate that family size among all segments of the U.S. population continues to fall (Hernandez, 1997).

In the face of such statistics, cross-cultural analyses highlight the ubiquity of siblings in children's everyday lives as companions and caregivers; from these analyses comes the observation that what varies across cultures is *who else besides siblings* will be an important part of the child's social world (Weisner, 1989). Documenting the centrality of siblings in the everyday lives of working- and middle-class White children in the United States, daily diary reports show that during middle childhood, siblings are children's most common out-of-school companions (McHale & Crouter, 1996). The companionship that siblings experience in childhood provides a foundation for what is one of the few *lifelong relationships* that most individuals will experience.

In addition to their centrality in children's everyday lives, another important feature of sibling relationships in middle childhood is emotional intensity (Dunn, 1998). In fact, the emotional intensity of the sibling relationship may be what gives this relationship its developmental significance (Dunn, 1998). The sibling relationship has been described as a love-hate relationship to reflect a common observation that playful companions can turn very quickly into bitter enemies; indeed, conflict between siblings is one of the most common child-rearing problems reported by parents (Perlman & Ross, 1997). The nature and level of negativity between siblings are

likely to be quite different from what occurs between children and their friends; because friendships are a voluntary relationship, children are likely to be more invested in maintaining harmony (Updegraff, McHale, & Crouter, 2001). Theories of the origins of sibling conflict that highlight the significance of sibling rivalry (e.g., for parents' attention and family resources) underscore that the origins of sibling conflict also are different from the sources of conflict within other social dyads (Ansbacher & Ansbacher, 1956).

A third feature that distinguishes sibling relationships from other kinds of dyadic relationships pertains to the nature of sibling roles. Parent-child and peer relationships in childhood are distinguished by their degree of role asymmetry, with the former characterized by complementarity and the latter by more equalitarian or reciprocal exchanges. In contrast, sibling relationships involve both kinds of roles (Dunn, 1998). Although in some ways sibling relationships are peer-like, age and birth order differences mean that older siblings may assume the role of caregiver, teacher, or model. Indeed, in middle childhood and adolescence, as children spend increasing amounts of time outside the family, older siblings are often looked to as sources of information and advice (e.g., on peer experiences, school) in areas in which parents are seen as having less expertise (Tucker, McHale, & Crouter, in press).

Sibling Influences on Children's Social Development

Siblings' role in children's social development is both direct— siblings have an impact on one another in the course of their everyday interactions—and indirect, to the extent that siblings affect the daily activities, roles, and relationships in the broader family system. Early work on sibling influences highlighted sibling interaction experiences as a source of social development. Based on a series of studies in which interactions of young siblings were observed, Dunn (1998) argued that the emotional intensity of the sibling relationship motivates children's development and use of increasingly sophisticated social skills and problem-solving strategies; in their efforts to prevail in the context of sibling exchanges, young siblings are likely to display more sophisticated social abilities than they might need in the context of interactions with either parents or peers. These ideas are based largely on studies of children during early childhood, however, and we know less about the kinds of social competencies children learn and practice with their siblings in middle childhood and beyond.

Cross-cultural work on siblings' role as caregivers has likewise highlighted the importance of sibling experiences for positive social development. Describing the organization of agricultural and pastoral societies, Weisner (1989), for example, points out that older siblings—girls in particular—have a larger role in direct caregiving of children than do mothers. In such societies, mothers are likely to spend their time in subsistence activities (e.g., work close to home in the fields) while groups of young children, including neighbors and kin, are in the direct care of older girls, usually girls of middle childhood age. The organization of such societies, Weisner (1984) argues, promotes "attachment to community, early expectations of prosocial, mature behaviors, strong compliance and deference expectations, work and responsibility expectations . . ." (p. 346). These sibling caregiving experiences in turn are linked to social empathy, a focus on affiliation and cooperation (as opposed to competition), and a focus on age-mates—rather than adults—as a source of help and guidance (Weisner, 1984).

Not all of what children learn from their experiences with siblings promotes positive development. Work by Patterson (1986), for example, highlights sibling exchanges as a breeding ground for aggression. Studying sibling interactions within a social learning framework, Patterson found evidence of conflict escalation in sibling exchanges; these coercive cycles of escalating conflict practiced in the context of the sibling relationship can be generalized to parent-child and peer interactions. Such findings are echoed in research showing the sometimes deleterious impact of older, adolescent-age siblings on their younger sisters and brothers (e.g., Rowe, Rodgers, & Meseck-Bushey, 1992). Adolescent-age siblings may introduce their younger sisters and brothers to older peers and invite their involvement in risky behaviors such as substance use or early sexual activity. Some work suggests that younger sisters of older adolescent-age brothers are particularly vulnerable to these kinds of negative influences (Bank, Patterson, & Reid, 1996).

Another line of investigation—one of the earliest areas of research on sibling influences on social development—examined siblings' role in gender socialization. Operating within a social learning framework that emphasized the significance of older siblings as role models, early investigators tested the hypothesis that sisters and brothers would model and reinforce their own qualities in their siblings, and thus that girls with brothers would develop more masculine qualities and boys with sisters more feminine ones (e.g., Koch, 1956; Sutton-Smith & Rosenberg, 1970). Although some support was found for this social learning hypothesis, results overall were equivocal, and the early studies suffered from a number of methodological shortcomings. More recently, researchers have attempted to study some of the dyadic and family processes through which siblings may affect one another's gender development. Observational research on school-age children with opposite-sex siblings,

for example, revealed that boys and girls with older brothers engaged in relatively more stereotypically masculine play activities and girls with older sisters engaged in relatively more feminine ones (Stoneman, Brody, & MacKinnon, 1986). More generally, the sex constellation of sibships has important implications for family patterns of activities, roles, and relationships (McHale et al., 1999).

What children learn from making comparisons between their own versus their siblings' family experiences is an important means through which siblings indirectly influence one another's social development. Following on the writings of Alfred Adler, who highlighted the role of sibling rivalry in personality development (Ansbacher & Ansbacher, 1956), researchers have devoted substantial attention to the role of parents' differential treatment—specifically, favoritism directed at one child. A body of research links differential treatment to children's social emotional well-being (e.g., Dunn, Stocker, & Plomin, 1990). Recently, investigators have suggested that the links between differential treatment and child functioning are not direct. Rather, the meanings children attribute to their parents' differential treatment—including children's understanding of their parents' reasons for treating their offspring differently and children's perceptions of the legitimacy of their parents' differential treatment—are important moderating factors (Kowal & Kramer, 1997; McHale & Pawletko, 1992). More generally, the study of siblings' differential treatment exemplifies what can be learned about children's development from studying the family system of relationships; the significance of parents' differential treatment for children's individual adjustment highlights the ways in which dyadic family relationships may be mutually influential.

Summary

Research on children's interpersonal relationships suggests that as children move through middle childhood, their developing social-emotional and cognitive abilities give rise to changes in their relationships with important people in their lives. Children's relationships in turn are a forum within which new social competencies emerge, are practiced, and change. Substantial effort has been directed at studying children's social competencies in the context of their relationships, particularly their peer relationships (Eisenberg, 1998), and important new lines of study involve examination of the connections between children's experiences in different social relationships and explorations of how children's relationships operate within larger social systems such as the family (e.g., Easterbrooks & Emde, 1988; Parke & Buriel, 1998; Parke & Ladd, 1992). A direction for future work is to learn more about how children's relationships change over time.

Also important are studies of how the social roles children assume in their relationships—as well as the scripts they employ and the behaviors they exhibit—are tied to the values and expectations of the larger social ecology.

CONCLUSIONS

Our goal in this chapter was to provide an overview of social development and social relationships in middle childhood. Middle childhood has been described as a period of skill consolidation between two periods of striking developmental change; our review underscores that important social competencies, including social cognitive skills and emotion regulation strategies, are practiced and refined during this period and have implications for children's relationships with significant others in their lives. As we have suggested, an important limitation of work on developmental processes is its heavy focus on European American samples of children. Given the inherently adaptive nature of social behavior, it will be important to examine how social developmental processes unfold across a wider range of settings.

Stepping back from a focus on within-individual developmental processes to consider the larger context of children's everyday lives, we see that middle childhood is also a time of *new* demands and expectations for social competencies as children enter new social settings and spend their time in a diverse array of social contexts. Task demands are one important new component of the activity settings of middle childhood in cultures around the world; this developmental period is a time when children first become seriously involved in work and when children must learn to adapt their social behaviors to instrumental demands (Erikson, 1963). The activities of middle childhood—at school, in the context of paid labor, and even during free time—are ones in which children can succeed or fail, and children's social competencies are central to their ability to succeed in many of their endeavors.

Middle childhood also is notable for the extent to which children spend time with other children—both siblings and friends—outside of the direct supervision and involvement of adults. Children's self-regulation and social problem-solving skills are essential in the absence of parents or other authority figures; sanctions for inept or inappropriate social behavior may be absolute and harsh in the context of the peer group. On the other hand, shared experiences with peers that take place outside the company of adults may give rise to the feelings of intimacy and mutual understanding that first emerge in middle childhood and that are hallmarks of close friendships and group solidarity (Sullivan, 1952; Weisner; 1989).

Finally, middle childhood marks an expansion in children's social worlds: Children spend their time in an increasingly diverse array of social contexts where they assume different roles, adapt to the expectations of different social partners, and conform to different setting demands—often without adults to scaffold their behavior. The expansion of the social world requires an ability to read and respond flexibly to setting demands and is linked in a reciprocal fashion to the metacognitive skills (i.e., children's ability to think about their own social behavior and its implications) that first emerge in middle childhood. The kinds of behavioral adaptations that children make as they enter the novel roles, relationships, and activities of middle childhood are social developmental phenomena worthy of continued study.

REFERENCES

Adler, P. A., Kless, S. J., & Adler, P. (1992). Socialization to gender roles: Popularity among elementary school boys and girls. *Sociology of Education, 65*(3), 169–187.

Ainsworth, M., Blehar, M., Waters, E., & Wall, S. (1978). *Patterns of attachment*. Hillsdale, NJ: Erlbaum.

Allen, K. R. (1997). Lesbian and gay families. In T. Arendell (Ed.), *Contemporary parenting* (pp. 154–195). Thousand Oaks, CA: Sage.

Ansbacher, H. L., & Ansbacher, R. R. (1956). *The individual psychology of Alfred Adler*. New York: Basic Books.

Arsenio, W. F., & Ford, M. E. (1985). The role of affective information in social-cognitive development: Children's differentiation of moral and conventional events. *Merrill-Palmer Quarterly, 31*, 1–17.

Bank, L., Patterson, G. R., & Reid, J. B. (1996). Negative sibling interaction patterns as predictors of later adjustment problems in adolescent and young adult males. In G. H. Broad (Ed.), *Sibling relationships: Their causes and consequences* (pp. 197–229). Norwood, NJ: Ablex.

Baumrind, D. (1971). Current patterns of parental authority. *Developmental Psychology Monograph*, 1971, 4(1, Pt 2).

Baumrind, D. (1991). Parenting styles and adolescent development. In J. Brooks-Gunn, R. Lerner, & A. C. Peterson (Eds.), *The encyclopedia of adolescence* (pp. 746–758). New York: Garland Press.

Bengtsson, H., & Johnson, L. (1992). Perspective taking, empathy, and prosocial behavior in late childhood. *Child Study Journal, 22*(1), 11–22.

Blasi, A. (1980). Bridging moral cognition and moral action: A critical review of the literature. *Psychology Bulletin, 88*, 1–45.

Brody, G., & Stoneman, Z. (1995). Sibling relationships in middle childhood. In R. Vasta (Ed.), *Annals of child development* (Vol. 11, pp. 73–93). London: Jessica Kingsley.

Bronfenbrenner, U. (1979). *The ecology of human development.* Cambridge, MA: Harvard University Press.

Bronfenbrenner, U., & Crouter, A. C. (1983). The evolution of environmental models in developmental research. In P. Musen (Ed.), *The handbook of child psychology* (Vol. 1, pp. 358–414). New York: Wiley.

Bugental, D. B., & Goodnow, J. J. (1998). Socialization processes. In W. Damon (Series Ed.) & N. Eisenberg (Vol. Ed.), *Handbook of child psychology: Vol. 3. Social emotional and personality development* (pp. 389–462). New York: Wiley.

Cairns, R. B. (1991). Multiple metaphors for a singular idea. *Development Psychology, 27,* 23–26.

Cairns, R. B., & Cairns, B. D. (1994). *Lifelines and risks: Pathways of youth in our time.* New York: Cambridge University Press.

Cairns, R. B., Gariepy, J. L., & Hood, K. E. (1990). Development, microevolution, and social behavior. *Psychological Review, 97,* 49–65.

Carlo, G., Knight, G. P., Eisenberg, N., & Rotenberg, K. J. (1991). Cognitive processes and prosocial behaviors among children: The role of affective attributions and reconciliations. *Developmental Psychology, 27*(3), 456–461.

Chalmers, J. B., & Townsend, M. A. (1990). The effects of training in social perspective taking on socially maladjusted girls. *Child Development, 61,* 178–190.

Coie, J. D., Dodge, K., & Kupersmidt, J. B. (1990). Peer group behavior and social status. In S. R. Asher & J. D. Coie (Eds.), *Peer rejection in childhood* (pp. 17–59). New York: Cambridge University Press.

Coie, J. D., Lochman, J. E., Terry, R., & Hyman, C. (1992). Predicting early adolescent disorder from childhood aggression. *Journal of Consulting and Clinical Psychology, 60,* 783–792.

Collins, W. A. (1984). Conclusion: The status of basic research on middle childhood. In W. A. Collins (Ed.), *Development during middle childhood: The years from six to twelve* (pp. 398–421). Washington, DC: National Academy Press.

Collins, W. A., Harris, M., & Susman, A. (1995). Parenting during middle childhood. In M. Bornstein (Ed.), *Handbook of parenting: Vol. 1. Children and parenting* (pp. 65–89). Mahwah, NJ: Erlbaum.

Collins, W. A., Maccoby, E. E., Steinberg, L., Hetherington, E. M., & Bornstein, M. H. (2000). Contemporary research on parenting: The case for nature and nurture. *American Psychologist, 55,* 218–232.

Collins, W. A., & Russell, G. (1991). Mother-child and father-child relationships in middle childhood and adolescence: A developmental analysis. *Developmental Review, 11,* 99–136.

Corsaro, W. A., & Eder, D. (1990). Children's peer cultures. *Annual Review of Sociology, 16,* 197–220.

Crick, N. R., & Dodge, K. A. (1994). A review and reformulation of social information processing mechanisms in children's social adjustment. *Psychological Bulletin, 115,* 74–101.

Crick, N. R., & Dodge, K. A. (1996). Social information-processing mechanisms in reactive and proactive aggression. *Child Development, 67,* 993–1002.

Crick, N. R., & Grotpeter, J. K. (1995). Relational aggression, gender, and social-psychological adjustment. *Child Development, 66,* 710–722.

Crouter, A. C., & Head, M. R. (2002). Parental monitoring: What are we really measuring and what does it mean? In M. H. Bornstein (Ed.), *The handbook on parenting* (pp. 461–484). Mahwah, NJ: Erlbaum.

Darling, N., & Steinberg, L. (1993). Parenting style as context: An integrative model. *Psychological Bulletin, 113,* 487–496.

Davies, P., & Cummings, M. (1994). Marital conflict and child adjustment: An emotion security hypothesis. *Psychological Bulletin, 116,* 387–411.

Deater-Deckard, K., & Dodge, K. (1997). Externalizing behavior problems and discipline revisited: Nonlinear effects and variation by culture, context, and gender. *Psychological Inquiry, 8,* 161–175.

Dishion, T. J., Andrews, D. W., & Crosby, L. (1995). Antisocial boys and their friends in early adolescence: Relationship characteristics, quality, and interactional process. *Child Development, 66,* 139–151.

Dodge, K. A. (1980). Social cognition and children's aggressive behavior. *Child Development, 51*(1), 162–170.

Dodge, K. A. (1989). Coordinating responses to aversive stimuli: Introduction to a special section on the development of emotion regulation. *Developmental Psychology, 25,* 339–342.

Dodge, K. A., Coie, J. D., & Brakke, N. P. (1982). Behavior patterns of socially rejected and neglected preadolescents: The role of social approach and aggression. *Journal of Abnormal Child Psychology, 10,* 389–410.

Dodge, K. A., Coie, J. D., Pettit, G. S., & Price, J. M. (1990). Peer status and aggression in boys' groups: Developmental and contextual analyses. *Child Development, 61,* 1289–1309.

Dodge, K. A., McClaskey, C. L., & Feldman, E. (1985). A situational approach to the assessment of social competence in children. *Journal of Consulting and Clinical Psychology, 53,* 344–353.

Dunn, J. (1998). Siblings, emotion, and development of understanding. In S. Braten (Ed.), *Intersubjective communication and emotion in early ontogeny: Studies in emotion and social interaction* (pp. 158–168). New York: Cambridge University Press.

Dunn, J., & Plomin, R. (1990). *Separate lives: Why siblings are so different.* New York: Basic Books.

Dunn, J., Stocker, C., & Plomin, R. (1990). Non-shared experiences within the family: Correlates of behavioral problems in middle childhood. *Development and Psychopathology, 2,* 113–126.

Dunsmore, J. C., & Halberstadt, A. G. (1997). How does family emotional expressiveness affect children's schemas? *New Directions for Child Development, 77,* 45–68.

Easterbrooks, M. A., & Emde, R. N. (1988). Marital and parent-child relationships: The role of affect in the family system. In R. Hinde & J. Stevenson-Hinde (Eds.), *Relationships within families* (pp. 83–103). Oxford, UK: Clarendon Press.

Eccles, J. S. (1999). The development of children ages 6 to 14. *Future of Children, 9,* 30–44.

Eder, D., & Enke, J. L. (1991). The structure of gossip: Opportunities and constraints on collective expression among adolescents. *American Sociological Review, 56*(4), 494–508.

Eggebeen, D. J. (1992). Changes in sibling configurations in American preschool children. *Social Biology, 39,* 27–44.

Eisenberg, N. (1998). Introduction. In W. Damon (Series Ed.) & N. Eisenberg (Vol. Ed.), *Handbook of child psychology: Vol. 3. Social, emotional, and personality development* (pp. 1–24). New York: Wiley.

Eisenberg, N., & Fabes, R. (1998). Prosocial development. In W. Damon (Series Ed.) & N. Eisenberg (Vol. Ed.), *Handbook of child psychology: Vol. 3. Social, emotional, and personality development* (pp. 701–778). New York: Wiley.

Eisenberg, N., Guthrie, I. K., Murphy, B. C., Shepard, S. A., Cumberland, A., & Carlo, G. (1999). Consistency and development of prosocial dispositions: A longitudinal study. *Child Development, 70*(6), 1360–1372.

Eisenberg, N., Shell, R., Pasternack, J., Beller, R., Lennon, R., & Mathy, R. M. (1987). Prosocial development in middle childhood: A longitudinal study. *Developmental Psychology, 23*(5), 712–718.

Elkind, D. (1981). *The hurried child.* Reading, MA: Addison-Wesley.

Erikson, E. H. (1963). *Childhood and society* (2nd ed.). New York: W. W. Norton.

Fagot, B. (1977). Consequences of moderate cross-gender behavior in preschool children. *Child Development, 4,* 902–907.

Fagot, B. I. (1994). Peer relations and the development of competence in boys and girls. *New Directions for Child Development, 65,* 53–66.

Flavell, J. H. (1976). Metacognitive aspects of problem solving. In L. B. Resnick (Ed.), *The nature of intelligence* (pp. 231–235). Hillsdale, NJ: Erlbaum.

Fox, N. (1994). The development of emotion regulation: Biological and behavioral considerations. *Monographs of the Society for Research in Child Development, 58*(2/3, Serial No. 240), 152–166.

Garner, P. W. (1996). The relations of emotional role taking affective/moral attributions, and emotional display rule knowledge to low-income school-age children's social competence. *Journal of Applied Developmental Psychology, 17,* 19–36.

Gilligan, C. (1982). *In a different voice: Psychological theory and women's development.* Cambridge, MA: Harvard University Press.

Goodnow, J. (1988). Children's housework: Its nature and functions. *Psychological Bulletin, 103,* 5–26.

Gottman, J. M. (1994). Why can't men and women get along? In D. Canary & L. Stafford (Eds.), *Communication and relational maintenance* (pp. 203–229). San Diego, CA: Academic Press.

Gottman, J. M., Katz, L. F., & Hooven, C. (1997). *Meta-emotion: How families communicate.* Mahwah, NJ: Erlbaum.

Gottman, J. M., & Mettetal, G. (1986). Speculations about social and affective development: Friendship and acquaintanceship through adolescence. In J. Gottman & J. Parker (Eds.), *Conversations of friends: Speculations on affective development* (pp. 192–237). New York: Cambridge University Press.

Grusec, J. E. (1983). The internalization of altruistic dispositions: A cognitive analysis. In E. T. Higgins, D. N. Ruble, & W. W. Hartup (Eds.), *Social cognitive and social development: A sociocultural perspective* (pp. 275–293). New York: Cambridge University Press.

Grusec, J. E., & Lytton, H. (1988). *Social development: History, theory, and research.* New York: Springer-Verlag.

Grucharri, C., Phelps, R., & Selman, R. (1984). Development of interpersonal understanding: A longitudinal and comparative study of normal and disturbed youths. *Journal of Consulting and Clinical Psychology, 52*(1), 26–36.

Harrist, A. W., Zaia, A. F., Bates, J. E., Dodge, K. A., & Pettit, G. S. (1997). Subtypes of social-withdrawal in early childhood: Sociometric status and social-cognitive differences across four years. *Child Development, 68,* 278–294.

Harter, S. (1999). *The construction of the self: A developmental perspective.* New York: Guilford Press.

Hartup, W. W. (1992). Peer relations in early and middle childhood. In V. B. Van Hasselt & M. Hersen (Eds.), *Handbook of social development: A lifespan perspective* (pp. 257–281). New York: Plenum Press.

Hartup, W. W. (1996). The company they keep: Friendships and their developmental significance. *Child Development, 67,* 1–13.

Hernandez, D. J. (1997). Child development and the social demography of childhood. *Child Development, 68,* 149–169.

Hetherington, E. M. (1989). Coping with family transitions: Winners, losers and survivors. *Child Development, 60,* 1–14.

Hinde, R. (1979). *Toward understanding relationships.* New York: Academic Press.

Hoffman, L. W., & Youngblade, L. M. (1999). *Mothers at work: Effects on children's well-being.* Cambridge: Cambridge University Press.

Hoffman, M. L. (1982). The contribution of empathy to justice and moral judgment. In N. Eisenberg & J. Strayer (Eds.), *Empathy and its development: Cambridge studies in social and emotional development* (pp. 47–80). New York: Cambridge University Press.

Hymel, S., Rubin, K. H., Rowden, L., & LeMare, L. (1990). Children's peer relationships: Longitudinal prediction of internalizing and externalizing problems from middle to later childhood. *Child Development, 61,* 2004–2021.

Hymel, S., Wagner, E., & Butler, L. (1990). Reputational bias: View from the peer group. In S. R. Asher & J. Coie (Eds.), *Peer rejection in childhood* (pp. 156–186). New York: Cambridge University Press.

Koch, H. L. (1956). Sissiness and tomboyishness in relation to sibling characteristics. *Journal of Genetic Psychology, 88,* 231–244.

Kohlberg, L. (1976). Moral stages and moralization. In T. Lickona (Ed.), *Moral development and behavior: Theory, research and social issues* (pp. 31–53). New York: Holt, Rinehart, & Winston.

Kohlberg, L., & Kramer, R. (1969). Continuities and discontinuities in childhood moral development. *Human Development, 12,* 93–120.

Kohn, M. (1977). *Class and conformity: A study of values* (2nd ed.). Chicago: University of Chicago Press.

Kowal, A., & Kramer, L. (1997). Children's understanding of parental differential treatment. *Child Development, 68,* 113–126.

Kupersmidt, J. B., & Coie, J. D. (1990). Preadolescent peer status, aggression, and school adjustment as predictors of externalizing problems in adolescence. *Child Development, 61.*

Ladd, G. W. (1999). Peer relationships and social competence during early and middle childhood. *Annual Review of Psychology, 50,* 333–359.

Lane-Garon, P. S. (1998). Developmental considerations: Encouraging perspective taking in student mediators. *Mediation Quarterly, 16*(2), 201–217.

Larson, R., & Verma, S. (1999). How children and adolescents spend time across the world: Work, play and developmental opportunities. *Psychological Bulletin, 126,* 701–735.

Leaper, C. (1994). Exploring the consequences of gender segregation on social relationships. *New Directions for Child Development, 65,* 67–86.

Lerner, R. M. (1982). Children and adolescents as producers of their own development. *Developmental Review, 2,* 342–370.

Litvack-Miller, W., McDougall, D., & Romney, D. M. (1997). The structure of empathy during middle childhood and its relationship to prosocial behavior. *Genetic, Social, and General Psychology Monographs, 123*(3), 303–324.

Maccoby, E. E. (1990). Gender and relationships: A developmental account. *American Psychologist, 45,* 513–520.

Maccoby, E. E. (1994). Commentary: Gender segregation in childhood. *New Directions for Child Development, 65,* 87–98.

Maccoby, E. E. (1998). *The two sexes: Growing up apart, coming together.* Cambridge, MA: Harvard University Press.

Maccoby, E. E., & Martin, J. A. (1983). Socialization in the context of the family: Parent-child interaction. In P. H. Mussen (Series Ed.) & E. M. Hetherington (Vol. Ed.), *Handbook of child psychology: Vol. 4. Socialization, personality and social development* (pp. 1–101), New York: Wiley.

Markstrom-Adams, C. M., & Spencer, M. B. (1994). A model for identity intervention with minority adolescents. In S. L. Archer (Ed.), *Interventions for adolescents* (pp. 84–102). Thousand Oaks, CA: Sage.

McGillicuddy-DeLisi, A. V. (1992). Parents' beliefs and children's personal social development. In A. V. McGillicuddy-DeLisi & J. J. Goodnow (Eds.), *Parental belief systems: The psychological consequences for children* (pp. 115–142), Hillsdale, NJ: Erlbaum.

McHale, S. M., & Crouter, A. C. (1996). The family contexts of sibling relationships. In G. Brody (Ed.), *Sibling relationships: Their causes and consequences* (pp. 173–196). Norwood, NJ: Ablex.

McHale, S. M., Crouter, A. C., & Tucker, C. J. (1999). Family context and gender role socialization in middle childhood: Comparing girls to boys and sisters to brothers. *Child Development, 70,* 990–1004.

McHale, S. M., Crouter, A. C., & Tucker, C. J. (2001). Free time activities in middle childhood: Links with adjustment in early adolescence. *Child Development, 72,* 1764–1778.

McHale, S. M., & Pawletko, T. (1992). Differential treatment of siblings in two family contexts. *Child Development, 63,* 68–81.

McLoyd, V. (1990). The impact of economic hardship on Black families and children: Psychological distress, parenting, and socioemotional development. *Child Development, 61,* 311–346.

McLoyd, V. C., & Wilson, L. (1990). Maternal behavior, social support, and economic conditions as predictors of distress in children. *New Directions for Child Development, 46,* 49–69.

Medrich, E. A., Roizen, J. A., Rubin, V., & Buckley, S. (1982). *The serious business of growing up: A study of children's lives outside school.* Berkeley, CA: University of California Press.

Miletic, G. (1996). Perspective taking: Knowledge of level 1 and level 2 rules by congenitally blind, low vision, and sighted children. *Journal of Visual Impairment and Blindness, 89*(6), 513–523.

Miller, S. A., Holmes, H. A., Gitten, J., & Danbury, J. (1998). Children's understanding of false beliefs that result from developmental misconceptions. *Cognitive Development, 12*(1), 21–51.

Newcomb, A. F., Bukowski, W. M., & Pattee, L. (1993). Children's peer relations: A meta analytic review of popular, rejected, neglected, controversial and average sociometric status. *Psychological Bulletin, 113,* 99–128.

Newson, J., & Newson, E. (1976). *Seven years old in the home environment.* New York: Wiley.

Nisan, M. (1987). Moral norms and social conventions: A cross-cultural comparison. *Developmental Psychology, 23*(5), 719–725.

Ogbu, J. U. (1995). Origins of human competence: A cultural-ecological perspective. In N. R. Goldberger & J. B. Veroff (Eds.), *The culture and psychology reader* (pp. 245–275). New York: New York University Press.

Palacios, J., Gonzalez, M., & Moreno, M. (1992). Stimulating the child in the zone of proximal development: The role of parents' ideas. In I. E. Sigel, A. V. McGillicuddy-DeLisi, & J. J. Goodnow (Eds.), *Parental belief systems: The psychological consequences for children* (pp. 71–94). Hillsdale, NJ: Erlbaum.

Panak, W. F., & Garber, J. (1992). Role of aggression, rejection, and attributions in the prediction of aggression in children. *Developmental Psychopathology, 4,* 145–165.

Parke, R. D., & Buriel, R. (1998). Socialization in the family: Ethnic and ecological perspectives. In W. Damon (Series Ed.) & N. Eisenberg (Vol. Ed.), *Handbook of child psychology: Vol. 3. Social, emotional, and personality development* (pp. 463–552). New York: Wiley.

Parke, R. D., Burks, V., Carson, J., Neville, B., & Boyum, L. (1994). Family-peer relationships: A tripartite model. In R. D. Parke & S. Kellam (Eds.), *Advances in family research: Vol. 4. Family relationships with other social systems* (pp. 115–145). Hillsdale, NJ: Erlbaum.

Parke, R. D., & Ladd, G. W. (1992). *Family-peer relationships: Modes of linkage.* Hillsdale, NJ: Erlbaum.

Parker, J. G., & Asher, S. R. (1987). Peer relations and later personal adjustment: Are low-accepted children at risk? *Psychological Bulletin, 102,* 357–389.

Parker, J. G., & Asher, S. R. (1993). Friendship and friendship quality in middle childhood: Links with peer group acceptance and feelings of loneliness and social dissatisfaction. *Developmental Psychology, 29,* 611–621.

Parker, J. G., & Gottman, J. M. (1989). Social and emotional development in a relational context: Friendship interaction from early childhood to adolescence. In T. J. Berndt & G. W. Ladd (Eds.), *Peer relations in child development* (pp. 95–131). New York: Wiley.

Parker, J. G., & Seal, J. (1996). Forming, losing, renewing, and replacing friendships: Applying temporal parameters to the assessment of children's friendship experiences. *Child Development, 67,* 2248–2268.

Patterson, G. (1986). The contribution of siblings to training for fighting: A microsocial analysis. In D. Olweus, J. Block, & M. Radke-Yarrow (Eds.), *Development of antisocial and prosocial behavior: Research, theories, and issues* (pp. 235–261). New York: Academic Press.

Perlman, M., & Ross, H. (1997). The benefits of parent intervention in children's disputes: An examination of concurrent changes in children's fighting styles. *Child Development, 64,* 690–700.

Piaget, J. (1932). *The moral judgment of the child.* New York: Harcourt, Brace, and World.

Posner, J. K., & Vandell, D. L. (1999). After school activities and the development of low-income children: A longitudinal study. *Developmental Psychology, 35,* 868–879.

Putallaz, M. (1983). Predicting children's sociometric status from their behavior. *Child Development, 54,* 1417–1426.

Putallaz, M., & Wasserman, A. (1990). Children's entry behaviors. In S. R. Asher & J. Coie (Eds.), *Peer rejection in childhood* (pp. 60–89). New York: Cambridge University Press.

Quiggle, N. L., Garber, J., Panak, W. F., & Dodge, K. A. (1992). Social information processing in aggressive and depressed children. *Child Development, 63*(6), 1305–1320.

Quintana, S. M., Castaneda-English, P., & Ybarra, V. C. (1999). Role of perspective-taking abilities and ethnic socialization in development of adolescent ethnic identity. *Journal of Research on Adolescence, 9*(2), 161–184.

Roff, M., Sells, B. B., & Golden, M. M. (1972). *Social adjustment and personality development.* Minneapolis: University of Minnesota Press.

Rogoff, B. (1990). *Apprenticeship in thinking: Cognitive development in a social context.* New York: Oxford University Press.

Rose-Krasnor, L. (1997). The nature of social competence: A theoretical review. *Social Development, 6,* 111–135.

Rowe, D. C., Rodgers, J. L., & Meseck-Bushey, S. (1992). Sibling delinquency and the family environment: Shared and unshared influences. *Child Development, 63,* 59–67.

Rubin, K. H., Bukowski, W., & Parker, J. G. (1998). Peer interactions, relationships, and groups. In W. Damon (Series Ed.) & N. Eisenberg (Vol. Ed.), *Handbook of child psychology: Vol. 3. Social emotional and personality development* (pp. 619–700). New York: Wiley.

Ruble, D. N. (1983). The development of social-comparison processes and their role in achievement-related self-socialization. In E. T. Higgins, D. N. Ruble, & W. W. Hartup (Eds.), *Social cognition and social development: A sociocultural perspective* (pp. 134–157). New York: Cambridge University Press.

Russell, A., & Saebel, J. (1997). Mother-son, mother-daughter, father-son, and father-daughter: Are they distinct relationships? *Developmental Review, 17,* 111–147.

Saarni, C., Mumme, D. L., & Campos, J. J. (1998). Emotional development: Action, communication and understanding. In W. Damon (Series Ed.) & N. Eisenberg (Vol. Ed.), *Handbook of child psychology: Vol. 3. Social, emotional, and personality development* (pp. 238–295). New York: Wiley.

Scarr, S., & McCartney, K. (1983). How people make their own environments: A theory of genotype-environment effects. *Child Development, 54,* 424–435.

Selman, R. L. (1980). *The growth of interpersonal understanding: Developmental and clinical analyses.* New York: Academic Press.

Shrum, W., Cheek, N. H., & Hunter, S. M. (1988). Friendship in school: Gender and racial homophily. *Sociology of Education, 61*(4), 227–239.

Skinner, E., & Wellborn, J. (1994). Coping during childhood and adolescence: A motivational perspective. In R. Lerner (Ed.), *Lifespan development and behavior* (pp. 91–133). Hillsdale, NJ: Erlbaum.

Smetana, J. G., & Braeges, J. L. (1990). The development of toddlers' moral and conventional judgments. *Merrill-Palmer Quarterly, 36,* 329–346.

Snarey, J. R. (1985). Cross-cultural universality of social-moral development: A critical review of Kohlbergian research. *Psychological Bulletin, 97*(2), 202–232.

Sroufe, L. A. (1979). The coherence of individual development: Early care attachment and subsequent developmental issues. *American Psychologist, 34,* 834–841.

Sroufe, L. A., & Fleeson, J. (1986). Attachment and the construction of relationships. In W. W. Hartup & Z. Rubin (Eds.), *Relationships and development* (pp. 52–71). Hillsdale, NJ: Erlbaum.

Stevenson, H. W., & Lee, S. (1990). Contexts of achievement. *Monographs of the Society for Research in Child Development, 55*(1–2, Serial No. 221).

Stoneman, Z., Brody, G., & MacKinnon, C. (1986). Same-sex and cross-sex siblings: Activity choices, roles, behavior, and gender stereotypes. *Sex Roles, 15,* 495–510.

Sullivan, H. S. (1953). *The interpersonal theory of psychiatry.* New York: W. W. Norton.

Super, C. M., & Harkness, S. (1986). The developmental niche: A conceptualization at the interface of child and culture. *International Journal of Behavior Development, 9,* 1–25.

Sutton, J., Smith, P. K., & Swettenham, J. (1999). Social cognition and bullying: Social inadequacy or skilled manipulation? *British Journal of Developmental Psychology, 17,* 435–450.

Sutton-Smith, B., & Rosenberg, B. G. (1970). *The sibling.* New York: Holt, Rinehart, and Winston.

Taylor, M. (1988). Conceptual perspective taking: Children's ability to distinguish what they know from what they see. *Child Development, 59*(3), 703–718.

Thompson, R. A. (1991). Emotional regulation and emotional development. *Educational Psychology Review, 3,* 269–307.

Thorne, B. (1994). *Gender play: Girls and boys in school.* New Brunswick, NJ: Rutgers University Press.

Timmer, S. G., Eccles, J., & O'Brien, K. (1985). How children use time. In F. T. Juster & F. P. Stafford (Eds.), *Time, goods, and well-being* (pp. 353–382). Ann Arbor, MI: Institute for Social Research.

Tucker, C. J., McHale, S. M., & Crouter, A. C. (in press). Conditions of sibling support in adolescence. *Journal of Family Psychology.*

Turiel, E. (1994). The development of social-conventional and moral concepts. In B. Puka (Ed.), *Fundamental research in moral development* (Vol. 2, pp. 255–293). New York: Garland.

Updegraff, K. A., McHale, S. M. & Crouter, A. C. (2001). Adolescents' sex-typed experiences: Does having a sister versus a brother matter? *Child Development, 71,* 1597–1610.

Vartanian, L. R., & Powlishta, K. K. (1996). A longitudinal examination of the social-cognitive foundations of adolescent egocentrism. *Journal of Early Adolescence, 16*(2), 157–178.

Weisner, T. S. (1984). Ecocultural niches of middle childhood: A cross-cultural perspective. In W. A. Collins (Ed.), *Development during middle childhood: The years from six to twelve.* Washington, DC: National Academy of Sciences.

Weisner, T. S. (1989). Comparing sibling relationships across cultures. In P. Goldring Zukow (Ed.), *Sibling interaction across cultures* (pp. 11–25). New York: Springer-Verlag.

Werner, E. E. (1993). Risk, resilience and recovery: Perspectives from the Kawaii Longitudinal Study. *Development and Psychopathology, 5,* 503–515.

Zahn-Waxler, C., Friedman, S. L., & Cummings, E. M. (1983). Children's emotions and behaviors in response to infants' cries. *Child Development, 54,* 1522–1528.

Zarbatany, L., Hartman, D. P., & Rankin, D. B. (1990). The psychological functions of preadolescent peer activities. *Child Development, 61,* 1067–1080.

Zelizer, V. A. (1985). *Pricing the priceless child.* New York: Basic Books.

CHAPTER 11

The Cultural Context of Child Development

JAYANTHI MISTRY AND T. S. SARASWATHI

In the field of developmental psychology the stage is set for a gradual yet profound change in the conceptualization of children's development. Culture and context are becoming increasingly significant constructs in the study of child development for several reasons. Forces from outside the field, such as trends toward globalization (economic, political, and social) with concomitant increase in the interface between the diverse communities of the world, bring to the fore the multiple realities of humanity. The Western world can no longer ignore the multiple realities of the human condition within its own countries and those countries that Kagitçibasi (1996b) claimed constitute the "majority world" (p. 3). In addition, change in the conceptualization of development is being wrought also from within the field. Be it "rumble or revolution" (Kessen, 1993, p. 272), calls for putting culture at the core of developmental psychology (Cole, 1996; Hatano,

1999) and for paradigm shifts abound in the recent literature (Garcia-Coll & Magnuson, 1999; Saraswathi & Dasen, 1997).

The changes in conceptualization that are being demanded are not minor. They may well require a shaking of the foundations and a need to look outside the field for theoretical insights. Emphasizing the need for a global-community psychology, Marsella (1998) suggested that emerging social, cultural, political, and environmental problems around the world are placing increasing demands on the field. "Psychology can assist in addressing and resolving these problems, especially if it is willing to reconsider some of its fundamental premises, methods, and practices that are rooted within Western cultural traditions and to expand its appreciation and use of other psychologies" (Marsella, 1998, p. 1282). In a similar vein, Kessen (1993) claimed that "it is imperative that developmental psychology loosen its tie to the dream of the one best system, be it theoretical or methodological" (p. 272). Toward these ends of broadening the vision and charge of developmental psychology, we undertake the task of integrating perspectives from within and without the field.

Acknowledgments: We appreciate comments made by Ranjana Dulta, Barbara Rogoff, and Pierre R. Dasen on a previous version of this chapter.

Our primary goal in this chapter is to represent current understanding of the interface between culture and child development by drawing on three subfields of psychology: cultural psychology, cross-cultural psychology, and developmental psychology. In the first half of the chapter we provide a brief overview of these three subfields of psychology, highlighting how the interface between culture and development is explained in each. We end this part of the chapter emphasizing the increasing convergence and parallels between the three subfields while delineating the differences and debates that persist.

In the second half of the chapter we present an integrative framework that synthesizes the complementary foci of the various approaches to the study of culture and child development and then use this framework to organize an integrative overview of three selected topics in child development. Our exemplars include development of self, development of children's narratives, and the development of remembering. Because a comprehensive review of all potential domains of development is beyond the scope of this chapter, we have selected only three exemplars to illustrate the possibility of integrating literature from cultural, cross-cultural, and developmental psychology. We have selected these three exemplars from domains of development within which we believe sufficient inroads have been made to develop theories that are culturally based and broad enough to encompass the database of mainstream developmental patterns and cultural variations in a coherent manner.

MAJOR APPROACHES TO THE STUDY OF CULTURE AND CHILD DEVELOPMENT

In the discipline of psychology three subfields have made significant contributions to our current knowledge about the cultural context of child development. We highlight major approaches to the study of culture and development from each subfield, focusing on the core assumptions or defining elements of each stream of knowledge. We do not provide an overview of each subfield, as there are handbooks or full-length books devoted to that task in each field (Berry et al., 1997; Damon, 1998; J. G. Miller, 1997; Shweder et al., 1998; Triandis, 1980).

Cross-Cultural Psychology

Although culture has been the focus of study in anthropology since E. B. Tylor wrote *Primitive Culture* in 1871 (Tylor, 1871/1958), the interest in culture is much more recent in the discipline of psychology. Tracing the origins of culture-related psychology, several historical overviews of the field

of cross-cultural psychology emphasize its relatively recent institutionalization as a subdiscipline of psychology during the 1960s (Jahoda, 1990; Segall, Dasen, Berry, & Poortinga, 1999; Jahoda & Krewer, 1997). As these reviews highlight, several publication outlets and organizations devoted to cross-cultural and cross-national research were established at this time.

Understanding the origins of this field is important because the essential defining characteristics of cross-cultural psychology as a field are rooted in the reasons for its emergence. It is critical to remember that cross-cultural psychology emerged as a subdiscipline of psychology in reaction to the tendency in psychology to ignore cultural variations and to consider them nuisance variables or error (Kagitçibasi & Poortinga, 2000). Thus, cross-cultural psychology is often defined primarily by its method of comparative cross-cultural research aimed at exploring similarities and differences of human psychological functioning (Berry, 1980; Berry, Poortinga, Segall, & Dasen, 1992; Brislin, 1983; Jahoda, 1992; Jahoda & Krewer, 1997). It has functioned as a particular methodological strategy of mainstream psychology rather than as a subfield with a specific epistemological, theoretical, or content-related emphasis (Brislin, 1983).

The centrality of the culture-comparative approach is clearly reflected in statements of the overall goals of the field from early deliberations of the emerging area of research (Berry & Dasen, 1974) to more recent discussions of cross-cultural psychology as a scholarly discipline (Segall, Lonner, & Berry, 1998; Segall et al., 1999). The three primary goals of cross-cultural psychology have remained the following: (a) to test or extend the generalizability of existing theories and findings in psychology; (b) to use naturalistic variations provided by various cultures to test or discover range of variation in behaviors; and (c) to integrate findings to generate a more universal psychology applicable to a wider range of cultural settings.

In addition to its characteristic methodological approach, the culture-comparative approach of cross-cultural psychology is rooted also in assumptions about the universality of psychic functioning (J. G. Miller, 1997; Poortinga, 1997). As suggested by the goals just delineated, cross-cultural research is designed to test emerging theories in a broader range of cultural contexts and lead to the identification of psychological universals. Whereas the first goal specifically focuses on the search for psychological universals, the second emphasizes the documentation of diversity. However, both goals are always complementary and ultimately aimed at generating a more universal psychology (Segall, Dasen, Berry, & Poortinga, 1999). The centrality of assumptions of universality of psychic functioning in culture-comparative approaches is particularly well highlighted by Kagitçibasi and Poortinga (2000). They argued that assumptions of cultural relativism or universalism have important implications for methodology: "In so far as there is non-identity of psychological processes cross-culturally, there is non-comparability of data. Insistence on the uniqueness of phenomena defies comparison and makes the use of common methods and instruments inappropriate. Thus, the entire enterprise of culture comparative research collapses if the assumption of psychic unity of human kind is rejected" (p. 131).

Much of the cross-cultural research undertaken during the first half of the twentieth century reflected the goals of establishing universal laws of human behavior and examining how psychological processes are affected by different aspects of cultural context. For example, more than half of the studies carried out in the African continent during the early 1900s were concerned with IQ testing—reflecting the primary goal of testing existing theories and constructs in psychology (Jahoda & Krewer, 1997). This focus on testing existing theories (essentially those developed in the West) led to a large body of cross-cultural research that was primarily replicative in nature. Much of this work was fraught with indiscriminate use of tests and procedures developed in Western settings and used without concern for their ecological validity in very different settings.

Fortunately, the rapid growth of comparative cross-national research following the institutionalization of cross-cultural psychology in the 1960s generated far more promising trends. Concerns about the validity of constructs, instruments, and procedures developed by mainstream psychology became highlighted by significant lines of cross-cultural research in the two decades following the 1960s (Cole, Gay, Glick, & Sharp, 1971; Dasen, 1974; Dasen & Heron, 1984; Laboratory of Comparative Human Cognition [LCHC], 1983; Lancy, 1978; Serpell, 1977). These researchers went beyond documenting differences between Western and non-Western groups. Their research reflected deep insights about the particular non-Western groups and communities being studied, primarily gained through extended periods of residence and work within the communities and culturally sensitive and systematic attempts to revise procedures, instruments, and even constructs to understand better the phenomenon being studied from an insider's perspective.

During this period of rapid growth in cross-cultural research, there was also a shift toward a more substantive and theory-building approach. This was a particularly significant trend for a field primarily characterized by its methodological approach. For example, Segall, Campbell, and Herskovits's (1966) study of cross-cultural differences in illusion susceptibility Berry's (1966) study of cross-cultural differences in

psychological differentiation, and Whiting and Whiting's (1975) study of child-rearing in six cultures not only stimulated significant bodies of research but also generated substantive theorizing about the links between ecological contexts, modes of subsistence, socialization processes, and individual psychological functioning.

Another promising trend resulted from the efforts of psychologists working in developing countries who began to question the validity of theories developed in the Western world. Rather than accepting existing psychological theories as objective, value-free, and universal, indigenous psychologists claimed that these were deeply enmeshed with Euro-American values that champion liberal, individualistic ideals (Kim & Berry, 1993; Kim, Park, & Park, 2000). Psychologists in East and Southeast Asia have been particularly vocal since the late 1970s in advocating the need to develop psychological constructs and frameworks rooted in local cultural and philosophical traditions, rather than relying on imported ones (Enriques, 1977; Ho, 1988, 1993; D. Sinha, 1986, 1997). For example, in Confucian heritage cultures, constructs that depict the fundamental relatedness between individuals played a particularly important role in promoting the role of indigenous psychological frameworks (Ho, 1976, 1988; Kim & Choi, 1994; Lebra, 1976). In modern Indian psychology, context-sensitivity, multidimensionality, and adult-child continuity (Kakar, 1978; Kumar, 1993; Marriott, 1989; A. K. Ramanujam, 1989) are examples of indigenously derived psychological concepts that are rooted in assumptions and orientations that are fundamentally different from Western approaches to knowledge about psychological functioning (Kao & Sinha, 1997; Mishra, 1997; D. Sinha, 1997).

Thus, whereas the subfield of cross-cultural psychology may initially have been defined primarily in terms of its comparative approach, the past 30 years of cross-cultural research in psychology have led to a critical discussion of the initial approach and a rediscovery of a more socioculturally oriented tradition in psychology (Jahoda & Krewer, 1997; Poortinga, 1997; Segall et al., 1999). Although the comparative approach and the search for a culturally inclusive yet universal psychology remain hallmarks of cross-cultural psychology, recent trends indicate promising areas of convergence with other subfields of psychology that also examine the interface of culture with human development.

Cultural Psychology

Although cross-cultural psychology as just presented proceeds from the perspective of the search for universals in psychological functioning, cultural psychology has often been viewed as representing the perspective of cultural relativism.

However, we suggest that to portray cultural psychology as primarily representing a cultural-relativist stance is inaccurate and glosses over more significant defining features of this approach to the study of culture and human development. We highlight three core features of cultural psychology in this section.

In recent discussions of the cultural psychology approach to the study of human development (Harwood, Miller, & Irizarry, 1995; J. G. Miller, 1997; Shweder et al., 1998), numerous approaches have been categorized under this overarching label. The most common examples include extensions of Vygotsky's (1978) sociohistorical theory, which emphasizes the study of human development as it is constituted in sociocultural context (Cole, 1990, 1996; Rogoff, 1990; Wertsch, 1985, 1991), and theories that emphasize culture as the meaning systems, symbols, and practices through which people interpret experience (Bruner, 1990; Goodnow, Miller, & Kessel, 1995; Greenfield & Cocking, 1994; Markus & Kitayama, 1991; Shweder, 1990). Models that incorporate ecological constructs with those from the culture and personality school of thought (D'Andrade, 1984; LeVine, 1973; LeVine et al., 1994; Super & Harkness, 1986; Whiting & Whiting, 1975) and models based on activity theory (Eckensberger, 1996) are also included under the umbrella of cultural psychology.

Although cultural psychology does not have a unifying definition or theoretical perspective, all these approaches share a common focus on understanding culturally constituted meaning systems. Thus, the first core feature of all these approaches is the common assumption that human beings construct meaning through the cultural symbol systems available to them in the context of social interactions. Thus, cultural psychologists view human psychological functioning as an emergent property that results from symbolically mediated experiences with the behavioral practices and historically accumulated ideas and understandings (meanings) of particular cultural communities (Shweder et al., 1998).

Along with the emphasis on the cultural meanings, a *second* unifying theme across various cultural psychology approaches is the assumption that culture and individual psychological functioning are mutually constitutive. It is assumed that culture and individual behavior cannot be understood in isolation, yet they are also not reducible to each other (Cole, 1996; J. G. Miller, 1997; Rogoff, 1990). In such a view, culture and individual development are not separated into independent and dependent variables. In addition, the assumption that culture and individual functioning are mutually constitutive goes beyond an emphasis on the bidirectionality

of influence. Cultural psychologists argue that to define the relation between culture and individual development as mutually constitutive requires a fundamental reconceptualization of the nature of the relationship between culture and individual development (Cole, 1996; J. G. Miller, 1997; Shweder et al., 1998). Sociocultural perspectives offer such a reconceptualization of the relation between mind and culture in the central assumption that human development—conceptualized as particular modes of thinking, speaking, behaving—is assumed to arise from and remain integrally tied to concrete forms of social practice (Cole, 1990; Vygotsky, 1978; Wertsch, 1985): "Mind, cognition, memory, and so forth are understood not as attributes or properties of the individual, but as functions that may be carried out intermentally or intramentally" (Wertsch & Tulviste, 1992, p. 549). Thus, instead of conceptualizing individuals as "having abilities and skills," the focus is on the "person-acting-with-mediation-means" as the appropriate unit of analysis (Wertsch, 1991, p. 119). In other words, individual "ability" or "tendency" is not separated from the contexts in which they are used. The argument is that when the focus is on human actions, we are immediately forced to account for the context of the actions and therefore cannot separate context from human functioning.

A third unifying theme in approaches to cultural psychology lies in the interpretive methodology preferred by these various approaches. Because the basic assumption is that culture and behavior are essentially inseparable, psychological functioning tends to be described in terms of the understanding of behavior and experience by the members of a cultural group themselves. Hence, the focus is on representing the meaning that behavior has for the behaving person. The roots of this preferred methodology have been traced to hermeneutics, or the theory of interpretation derived from the Greeks. W. Dilthey is credited with translating hermeneutic tradition to a historic methodology in which general validity is established through seeking objectified meanings within a coherence of contexts (Harwood et al., 1995; Jahoda, 1992; Jahoda & Krewer, 1997; Shweder et al., 1998).

Although cultural psychology is not a dominant perspective in mainstream psychology, it has stimulated attempts to develop more culturally inclusive theories of human development in the field of cross-cultural psychology (Dasen, 1993; Jahoda & Krewer, 1997) and in the field of developmental psychology (Cole, 1995, 1996; LCHC, 1983; Rogoff, 1990; Rogoff & Chavajay, 1995; Valsiner, 1989). Such cross-disciplinary contributions are the focus of a later section, so we now turn our attention to major approaches to the study of culture and human development within the field of developmental psychology.

Developmental Psychology

The primary focus in the field of developmental psychology has been to describe and explain development and developmental processes in all domains of human physical and psychological functioning. In the study of human development, defined as "changes in physical, psychological, and social behavior as experienced by individuals across the lifespan from conception to death" (Gardiner et al., 1998, p. 3), developmental change necessarily becomes the focus of inquiry. During the twentieth century much of the theoretical and empirical focus on the bases of developmental change centered on establishing the significance of nature versus nurture. However, contemporary developmental psychologists, going beyond prior debates between the proponents of nature versus nurture, stress that the dynamic relations between individual and context represent the basic processes of human development (Lerner, 1991, 1998, 2002; Sameroff, 1983; Thelen & Smith, 1998).

Historically, concerns about following the traditions of established science and assumptions about universality as a defining characteristic of human development have discouraged attention to the diversity and influence of varied developmental contexts. Recently, however, there has been increasing focus on the contexts of psychological functioning. This attention to the contexts of development has been prompted by several intersecting trends in the past couple decades. Theoretical models and perspectives that have been developed from within the field, particularly the ecological model (Bronfenbrenner, 1979, 1986), developmental contextualism (Lerner, 1991, 1996), and the life-span approaches (Baltes, Lindenberger, & Staudinger, 1998; Baltes, Reese, & Lipsitt, 1980), have been particularly influential in focusing attention on the contexts of individual development. In most of the ecologically based theories (with origins in the ecological sciences that examine the interrelationships between organisms and their environments), context is viewed as one of the major environmental variables that facilitate or constrain individual development. Similarly, life-span psychologists also emphasize social context, based on the central assumption that changes in the individual's social context across the life span interact with the individual's unique history of experiences, roles, and biology to produce an individualized developmental pathway. More recently, theorizing on the dynamic relation between individual and context has been brought to a more abstract and complex level through the concepts associated with developmental-systems models of human development (Dixon & Lerner, 1999; Lerner, 2002). In such models, integrative, reciprocal, and dynamic relations

and interactions among variables from multiple levels of organization constitute the core processes of developmental change (Ford & Lerner, 1992; Gottlieb, 1997; Lerner, 1998; Thelen & Smith, 1998).

It is not surprising that the models and perspectives just listed have been credited for the increasing amounts of research on the diversity of social contexts and life experiences. In summarizing state-of-the-art reviews of conceptual and empirical work on social, emotional, and personality development, Eisenberg (1998) identified increasing focus on contextual and environmental inputs to development as a key theme: "Burgeoning interest in context in developmental psychology is reflected in the study of many levels of influence, including diversity in culture and subculture, race and ethnicity, sex and gender, and types of families and groups" (p. 20). Similarly, Eisenberg noted that conceptual frameworks are becoming more conditional, multifaceted, and complex and that there is an increasing tendency to view development as a consequence of "social interactions that are shaped by contextual factors and characteristics of all participants in the interaction" (p. 20). Thus, investigation of the diversity of contexts of individual development has become a major research agenda in most domains of psychological functioning (Damon, 1998; Eisenberg, 1998; Maasten, 1999; Wozniak & Fischer, 1993).

Applied and problem-oriented research has also contributed to the increasing relevance of context in human development. Context has been the specific focus of research aimed at understanding the particular circumstances of children growing up in poverty or adverse socioeconomic conditions (McLloyd, 1990, 1998). Similarly, research that examines children's environments to enable the design of intervention programs to improve their welfare have focused specifically on context variables (Kagitçibasi, 1996b) because it is assumed that these mediating contextual factors can be addressed by programs.

Despite the increasingly more sophisticated conceptualizations of developmental processes and contexts of children's development just noted, there appears to be a common underlying tendency to treat culture and context as synonymous in developmental psychology. Culture is operationalized as context variables and treated as an independent variable. Even when investigated as a transactional or interactional relationship, it is treated as separate from the individual developmental outcomes with which it interacts. This focus on culture as context may reflect the field's continued reliance on the methods of experimental psychology and the concern with establishing universal relationships between context and behavior. Having highlighted essential dimensions of each field's approach to the study of culture, we now turn our attention to the convergence between major approaches followed by an emphasis on the continuing differences and debates.

Emerging Convergence Between the Major Approaches

Recent calls for paradigm shifts to enable the integrated study of culture and human development are emerging from within all three fields—cross-cultural psychology, cultural psychology, and developmental psychology. Within cross-cultural psychology there is a current shift toward more socioculturally oriented theorizing and empirical work, representing the inroads made by cultural psychology approaches. Further, there are increasing attempts to integrate knowledge generated by indigenous psychologies (Kim et al., 2000). Taking a stance similar to that of cultural psychology, indigenous psychologists advocate a paradigm shift in which constructs and theories are developed inductively from within the culture and culture is not treated as an independent variable. Although theory development within indigenous psychology is not far advanced, it appears to hold promise for integrating the concerns of cultural psychology and cross-cultural psychology (Saraswathi & Dasen, 1997).

Cultural psychology approaches also have had significant influence within developmental psychology, more so in some areas than in others, for example, in infancy research, adolescence, and cognitive development (Kagitçibasi & Poortinga, 2000). For example, Rogoff and Chavajay (1995) described the transformation of research on culture and cognitive development. They described the shift from the cross-cultural comparisons approach of the 1960s and 1970s to the more substantive, socioculturally based theorizing and research that became a significant tradition of research in cognitive development within mainstream developmental psychology by the beginning of the 1990s. Interestingly, Rogoff and Chavajay documented this transformation by following the trajectories of a number of researchers and scholars whose initial research began within the traditions of cross-cultural psychology, became increasingly sociocultural in orientation, and eventually became an integral part of developmental psychology (e.g., Cole, 1996; Miller, 1997; Rogoff, 1998).

Convergence between cross-cultural psychology and developmental psychology has been evident primarily in the use of culture-comparative approaches to test developmental theories and constructs. Examples of such research include studies that tested the universality of Piagetian stages (Dasen, 1972; Dasen & Heron, 1981) and the cross-cultural applicability of developmental differences in cognitive competencies (Cole et al., 1971; LCHC, 1983) and that examined the universality of secure patterns of attachment (Sagi, 1990; Thompson, 1998; Van Ijzendoorn & Kroonenberg, 1988).

However, developmental psychology has had much less influence on the field of cross-cultural psychology. The volume of culture-comparative research on developmental issues published in cross-cultural publications is small (Keller & Greenfield, 2000). One reason for this within the domain of cross-cultural psychology is intellectual: Developmentalists are interested in documenting the developmental trajectory in different domains of development, and in the socialization and enculturation processes, that is, the processes by which children are taught and acquire competencies as they grow up (Kagitiçibasi & Poortinga, 2000). Cross-cultural psychologists, however, are interested primarily in examining cultural variability and establishing universally applicable lawful relations between cultural and ecological contexts and individual behavior. Much of cross-cultural psychology focuses on cultural variability of adult behavior, and therefore intersects more with social psychology than developmental psychology. Although this has been useful for developmental psychologists because the culturally constructed behavior of adults can be viewed as an endpoint along a developmental pathway, lack of comparative research on ontogenetic development suggests that questions of central importance to developmental psychologists have not influenced the agenda of cross-cultural psychologists. However, recent shifts indicating more convergence between the aims of cross-cultural, cultural, and developmental psychology suggest a promising future for integrative approaches. Increasing culture-comparative research in international journals of behavioral development reflect such convergence. Keller and Greenfield (2000) outlined their vision for the future of cross-cultural psychology, in which "developmental issues and methods will be theoretically, methodologically, and empirically integrated into cross-cultural psychology, thus enabling our field to make significant advance in research and theory" (p. 60).

Continuing Issues and Debates

Despite the cross-disciplinary convergences and contributions just highlighted, critical differences and debates between the major approaches persist. Although there has been increasing agreement in the field of developmental psychology on the need to situate psychological phenomena in cultural context, answering the question of how to integrate culture into developmental or psychological analysis has been difficult (Kagitçibasi, 1996b). Issues in addressing this question are both conceptual and methodological. These are perhaps best exemplified in the debates that have been ongoing between cultural and cross-cultural psychologists and are now also being debated within the field of developmental psychology—between those influenced by ecological and contextualist approaches to development and those influenced by cultural and sociohistorical perspectives. Often, the difference is oversimplified by assuming that cross-cultural psychology proceeds from the perspective of the search for universals, while cultural psychology proceeds from the perspective of cultural relativism. Arguing that this distinction is misleading, we summarize recent discussions of the differences between cultural and cross-cultural psychology that delve into the issues in more depth (Harwood et al., 1995; Kagitçibasi, 1996; Poortinga, 1997; Saraswathi & Dasen, 1997; Shweder et al., 1998). We highlight some of the more important issues because these continue to be debated in the field of developmental psychology and need to be resolved if we are serious in our goal to generate more culturally inclusive theories of human development.

Debates on conceptual issues often focus on the question of how culture or cultural context should be conceptualized and operationalized in psychological research. Most of the research examining cross-cultural differences can be criticized for not clarifying the conceptual frameworks or the explicit theoretical models of culture within which cross-cultural findings are examined and understood (Harwood et al., 1995). In recent debates between cross-cultural psychologists and cultural psychologists on this issue of how to conceptualize culture, some cross-cultural psychologists suggested that culture can be operationalized as a set of conditions (Poortinga, 1992, 1997; Segall, 1984). In such a view, cultural variables are conceptualized as independent and antecedent variables influencing human behavior. In this endeavor "there is a tendency to take cultural context, including ecological as well as sociocultural variables, as a set of antecedent conditions, while behavior phenomena, including attitudes and meanings as well as observed behaviors, are seen as the outcomes or consequents of these antecedent influences" (Poortinga, 1997, p. 350).

Similarly, in the ecological model (Bronfenbrenner, 1979, 1986) or the developmental contextualist (Lerner, 1991, 1996) approaches that have been particularly influential in development psychology research, cultural context is operationalized in terms of various levels of children's ecological context, and research in this area attempts to document the interplay between historical, cultural, biological, and psychological influences on behavior in a systems approach to understanding influences on development.

In contrast, cultural psychologists maintain that in studying culture, the focus should be on understanding culturally constituted meaning systems. Thus, the study of the individual behavior must involve an examination of culturally constituted psychological processes, including culturally shared cognitive models and meaning systems (Harwood et al., 1995). Contrary to the ecological or contextualist perspectives, in cultural psychological approaches cultural context is not conceptualized as an independent variable or influence on behavior (LCHC, 1983; Rogoff, 1990; Rogoff & Mistry, 1985). As Shweder et al. (1998) claimed, "This insistence in cultural psychology that contexts and meanings are to be theoretically represented as part and parcel of the psychological system and not simply as influences, factors, or conditions external to the psychological system distinguishes cultural psychology from other forms of psychology which also think of themselves as contextual (or situated)" (p. 871).

A related conceptual issue that distinguishes cross-cultural and cultural psychology relates to the primary goals of each approach. A primary goal of cross-cultural psychology is to test the generalizability of psychological theories and establish universalities and differences in human functioning. In cultural psychology the attention shifts from finding lawful relationships between environmental variables (as culture and context are often operationalized) and behavioral outcomes to understanding the directive force of shared meaning systems in the lives of individuals and how these meanings are constructed in given contexts (D'Andrade & Strauss, 1992; Harkness & Super, 1992). Whereas cultural psychologists recognize that children grow up within the multiple contexts represented in ecological models, they also argue that contexts cannot be merely conceptualized as environmental influences. Understanding context must include understanding the tacit social and interactional norms of the individuals who exist within those settings, and whose behaviors and expectations both shape and are shaped by the institutional structures of which they are a part (Harwood et al., 1995). This focus on understanding the rule-governed understandings, interpretations, and behaviors in particular contexts, and the processes whereby individuals coconstruct and appropriate these understandings and interpretations through participation in various contexts, is the primary goal of cultural psychologists (Harwood et al., 1995).

The methodological debate between cross-cultural psychology centers on how to study culture. Cross-cultural psychologists emphasize a comparative approach with a focus on using common constructs and common measures across cultural communities, whereas cultural psychologists prefer an emphasis on the uniqueness of constructs in each cultural context because they derive their meanings from these contexts (Kagitçibasi, 1996b). Thus, the debates about the preferred research orientation have been cast in terms of the emic-etic distinction (Berry, 1969; Poortinga, 1997), or the indigenous versus universalist orientation to study phenomenon (D. Sinha, 1997). Behavior is emic—or culture specific—to the extent that it can only be understood within the cultural context in which it occurs; it is etic or universal in as much as it is common to human beings independent of their culture (Kagitçibasi, 1996b; Poortinga, 1997). Thus, the debate centers on the issue of whether a comparative or decontextualizing methodology is preferred or a holistic, contextualized methodology is to be used. Proponents of each view criticize the methodology preferred by the other. The interpretive methodologies that are particularly appropriate to study culturally unique phenomena from an emic perspective are often not acceptable to psychologists using conventional empirical standards of methodological rigor. Similarly, culture-comparative methodologies that utilize etic constructs to establish lawful relationships between cultural variables and psychological phenomenon have been criticized (Greenfield, 1997) as insensitive to cultural context.

Although some discussions of these contrasts between cultural psychology and cross-cultural psychology have taken oppositional stances, more recent discussions have attempted to find areas of convergence in the search for more culturally inclusive theories that can encompass cultural universals as well as differences and uniqueness. Convincing arguments made by cross-cultural psychologists (Poortinga, 1997) and by ecological and developmental contextual models in developmental psychology (Bronfenbrenner, 1986; Lerner, 1991, 1996) emphasize the need to establish lawful relations obtained between cultural, environmental, and behavioral variables. In general agreement with the need to establish lawful relations, cultural psychologists however emphasize that psychological structures and processes can vary fundamentally in different cultural contexts (Miller, 1997) and that there may be multiple, diverse psychologies rather than a single psychology (Shweder et al., 1998).

Arguing that the search for a science of human nature must be concerned with meanings as well as lawful behavior and that no approach can fully explain or account for all behavior (Poortinga, 1997), we suggest that each approach has something unique and complementary to contribute to a comprehensive understanding of human development. Similarly, the contrasting methodological approaches to the study of culture should also be seen as complementary—"a comparative approach does not preclude a contextualist orientation" (Kagitiçibasi, 1996b, p. 12). For example, Rogoff, Mistry, Göncü, and Mosier (1993) specifically use a derived-etic approach in which contextualized constructs are used for comparative analyses. In fact, conceptualizing the context-dependency of psychological phenomena can focus

investigations to uncover causal relations in different contexts that could actually lead to better generalizability. Our next section, and the rest of the chapter, is directed toward this goal of drawing on complementary approaches to build a more comprehensive understanding of human development.

INTERFACE BETWEEN THE STUDY OF CULTURE AND THE STUDY OF CHILD DEVELOPMENT

In this section we focus on the issue of integrating knowledge gained from the literature in cultural psychology and cross-cultural psychology with the rest of developmental psychology. Toward this end we delineate a broad integrative framework that draws on the lessons learned from each of the three subfields and integrates the complementary foci and constructs of various approaches to create culturally based conceptual frameworks that can encompass cultural variations in a coherent manner. Then we utilize this integrative framework to present a selective review of specific topics in child development as exemplars to document how it is possible to integrate the cultural, cross-cultural, and developmental literature. Three topical areas of child development—development of self, children's narrative development, and development of remembering—serve as exemplars for the construction of a culture-sensitive and culture-inclusive developmental psychology.

As discussed earlier, a central conceptual debate (between cultural and cross-cultural psychologists, and between contextualist approaches and sociocultural approaches) focuses on the question of how culture or cultural context should be conceptualized and operationalized in psychological research. Should culture be conceptualized as context and as an independent influence (e.g., set of antecedent conditions) on behavior or development, or should it be conceptualized as culturally constituted meaning systems? Should the focus be on finding lawful relationships between environmental variables (as cultural context is often operationalized) and behavioral outcomes, or should our focus be on understanding how culturally constituted meaning systems are constructed in given contexts?

Perhaps the more important question is this: Should not our focus be on understanding both contexts and the culturally constituted meaning systems embedded in various contexts? When the focus is solely on culturally constituted meaning systems, there is the danger of relying on cultural explanations for variations that often tend to preclude more substantial analyses (Kagitçibasi & Poortinga, 2000). Understanding important social-structural factors such as social-class standing, poverty, and low educational levels is then easily overlooked. On the other hand, focusing on context as social address variables (Bronfenbrenner, 1986) can reinforce past assumptions that causes of development are similar across groups but that variations between groups are caused by differential exposure to causal agents or conditions and biological predispositions. In the following discussion we suggest how each perspective can be viewed as complementary and can be integrated.

Integrative Conceptual Framework

Here we develop a broad integrative framework that we use to synthesize the cultural, cross-cultural, and developmental literature on each of our selected topics. This framework integrates constructs from contextualist approaches (Bronfenbrenner, 1986; Lerner, 1991, 1996), sociocultural theory, and cross-cultural psychology's contribution of promising substantive constructs that are pan-cultural as well as those that are more unique within a culture (Segall et al., 1999; Triandis, 1994).

Ecological context theories (e.g., Bronfenbrenner, 1986; Lerner, 1991, 1996) provide the labels and operationalization for layers of context—for example, macro system as cultural level shared ideology; exo system as the societal level institutions; meso and micro system settings as the closest layer of context for children's development. Sociocultural perspectives (Cole, 1996; Rogoff, 1990; Wertsch, 1991; Vygotsky, 1978) and Super and Harkness's (1986) construct of developmental niche provide the mediating constructs through which broad cultural (macro) level contexts and ideology get instantiated or reflected in the contexts of daily life (e.g., micro and meso systems). Thus, each setting of a child's micro or meso system (e.g., home, school, peer group, neighborhood, religious setting) can be conceptualized as consisting of physical and social activities, practices, and psychology of caregivers (i.e., the constructs that constitute the developmental niche). These then are the more proximal level influences within which individual development is embedded and constituted, and through which broad cultural level contexts and ideology get instantiated in the day-to-day life of individuals in their micro and meso system settings.

Similarly, constructs from sociocultural theory can also complement those from ecological context models, particularly to operationalize context and understand the mechanisms or processes of developmental change. Concepts such as context, activity (Leont'ev, 1981; Wertsch, 1985), cultural practices (P. J. Miller & Goodnow, 1995), and situated practice (Lave, 1990) have been discussed as various means of operationalizing cultural context. Cole (1996) offered a

particularly comprehensive discussion of these concepts as attempts to define a supraindividual sociocultural entity that is the cultural medium within which individual growth and development take place. Cole drew on both the sociohistorical school of thought (represented in the writings of Vygotsky, Lucia, and Leont'ev) and on anthropological theory to offer a conceptualization of such an entity, defining "culture as a medium constituted of artifacts" (p. 31).

Artifacts refer to the tools and objects used in a cultural community that are developed by prior generations and that get institutionalized and privileged in the institutions, practices, and valued activities of that cultural community. Books, calculators, and computers are common examples of physical artifacts or tools of our present-day literate and technological society that mediate how we interact with our social and physical world (and thus are examples of mediation means). Written language, the alphabet, numeral systems, the decimal system (as a way of organizing numbers), and the calendar (organizing time into years, months, days) are examples of conceptual artifacts (or mediation tools) that also regulate human functioning and behavior.

This notion of culture as a medium constituted of historically developed artifacts that are organized to accomplish human growth highlights the study of culture as central to understanding the processes or mechanisms of human development (Cole, 1995). But this begs the next question: What is the appropriate unit of analysis that will enable us to focus on both individual functioning and the supraindividual context within which it is situated? From a sociocultural perspective the appropriate mode of research is to analyze the way in which human thinking occurs within culturally organized forms of activity. Based on the assumption that human functioning cannot be separated from the context of activities through which development takes place, it follows that rather than focusing on individuals as entities, the aim should be to examine individuals as participants in culturally valued activities.

In fact, sociocultural theory posits that the integration of individual, social, and cultural-sociohistorical levels takes place within the analytic unit of activity (Cole, 1985, 1995; Leont'ev, 1981; Tharp & Gallimore, 1988; Wertsch, 1985, 1991). Thus, the assumption is that activities mediate the impact of the broader sociocultural system on the lives of individuals and groups (Gallimore & Goldenburg, 1993). Using activity as the unit of analysis contrasts with the independent-dependent variable approach that separates individual responses from environmental stimuli as the units of analysis. Rather, activity as the unit of analysis consists of individuals (as active agents) engaged in goal-directed behavior, carrying out actions and using culturally valued tools and mediation means within a framework of shared cultural assumptions and expectations (Cole, 1985; Leont'ev, 1981; Tharp & Gallimore, 1988; Wertsch, 1985).

In the rest of the chapter we use this integrative framework to organize a selective review of three topics in child development, including key publications from cultural and cross-cultural psychology and developmental psychology. We hope to document the inroads that have been made in unraveling the culture-individual interface, ranging from delineating the larger context, institutional mechanisms, and specific situation contexts and their embedded meaning that result in the individual's construction and acquisition of culture, as well as a precipitation of social-cultural change. We emphasize how the complementary contributions from three subfields of psychology enable a rich understanding of the interface between culture and individual development.

Within each topic area we begin with contributions from developmental psychology that often focus on descriptions of "normative" development as well as cultural variations on the "normal" outcomes of development. Then we highlight contributions from cross-cultural psychology that identify cultural or societal variations that have emerged from the culture-comparative approach. Finally, we utilize the integrative approach just delineated to integrate or link together societal-level cultural variations and individual development. We highlight the possibility of multiple normal developmental pathways that exist in varying cultural contexts.

DEVELOPMENT OF SELF

We include the development of self as an exemplar to document the interface between culture and development because there has been much research generated on this topic within all three subfields (developmental, cross-cultural, and cultural psychology). Studies on the development of self (Greenfield, 1994; Kagitçibasi, 1996a; Markus & Kitayama, 1991, 1994; Shweder, 1991) provide a rich source of information regarding the significance of culture as a context for development. From the moment of birth, or even before, every individual is immersed in a complex cultural context that provides the settings, meanings, and expectations that enable the growing child to become an acceptable member of a given culture. Whether viewed from the perspective of social construction (J. G. Miller, 1997; Shweder & Bourne, 1991), which implies that both culture and individuals constitute each other, or from the perspective of culture as an independent variable (Triandis, 1989; Kagitçibasi, 1996b), the total immersion of the individual child in culture is clearly recognized: "Theorists, psychologists, anthropologists, and

sociologists alike generally acknowledge that the self is a social phenomenon" (Markus, Mullally & Kitayama, 1997, p. 14).

Developmental Trends: Contributions From Developmental Psychology

In the developmental psychology literature, theories and empirical work on the development of self have concentrated on documenting developmental differences and the chronology of the development of self-representations from infancy through adolescence, as well as on determining the factors that influence individual differences in self-evaluations (Harter, 1998). Harter noted that the integration of research in cognitive, affective, and social domains in the past 15 years has contributed to a more comprehensive understanding of the basis and development of self-awareness, self-representation, and self-evaluations through normative developmental shifts and transitions. Although the developmental progression is primarily descriptive at this point, Harter underscores increasing theoretical emphasis on the role of interactions with caregivers and socialization agents in influencing normative progression, not just in creating individual differences. Developmental researchers also have focused on numerous issues—such as discrepancies between real and ideal self-concepts, multidimensional selves versus the unified self, the relation to self-esteem, stability of self-representations—leading to better understanding of the complexities of developmental processes and how individual differences emerge.

Most of the theorizing and research in developmental psychology has been based on a Western view of the self that emphasizes separateness, autonomy, individualism, and distinctness. In contrast, the cross-cultural literature provides a much richer and in-depth analysis of alternate constructions of the self that exist among different cultural communities and are considered appropriate and mature within these communities. Our discussion now turns to this literature.

Alternate Definitions of Self: Contributions from Cross-Cultural and Cultural Psychology

Review of the rich culture-comparative literature indicates a general consensus regarding predominance of two major alternate views of the self. These two alternate frameworks have been variously referred to as independence versus interdependence (Greenfield, 1994; Markus & Kitayama, 1994), individualist versus collectivist orientations (Kim & Choi, 1994; Triandis, 1989), autonomous versus relational self (Kagitçibasi, 1996a), and cultural themes promoting the referential versus indexical selves (Landrine, 1992).

Based on the ideology of individualism, the Western definitions of the self emphasize it as an independent, self-contained entity. The self is viewed as comprising of a unique configuration of internal attributes (including traits, emotions, motives, values, and rights) and behaving primarily to meet the demands of these attributes (Markus & Kitayama, 1994). The self in this perspective is seen as "bounded, unique, singular, encapsulated, noncorporeal" (Landrine, 1992, p. 747). The autonomous self is seen as an active agent that promotes selective abstraction of information from the environment (Triandis, 1989), as stable over time and across contexts, and as using environmental resources and all relationships instrumentally in the service of the self. The normal, healthy, independent self is expected to be assertive, confident, and goal oriented toward self-fulfillment, enhancement, and actualization (Landrine, 1992).

In contrast to the autonomous self, the interdependent or indexical self is not discrete, bounded, separate, or unique and is constituted (created and recreated) through social interactions, contexts, and relationships (Landrine, 1992). The self is viewed as embedded in relationships and the social context and has no existence independent of the same (Markus & Kitayama, 1994). In fact, "experiencing interdependence entails seeing oneself as part of an encompassing social relationship and recognizing that one's behavior is determined by, contingent on, and to a large extent, organized by what the actor perceives to be the thoughts, feelings, and actions of others in the relationships" (Markus et al., 1997, p. 26). Further, the boundaries of the individual self are permeable with fusion between self and others, self and social roles, and in some cultures such as the NSO of Cameroon in Africa (Nsamenang & Lamb, 1994) and Hindu India (Marriott, 1989; Shweder & Bourne, 1991) include the supernatural and ancestral spirits.

Cross-cultural literature has also emphasized the culture-bounded nature of what is considered the appropriate goal or endpoint of development. Contrasting the Western worldview of the place of the individual self in society with the socially and contextually embedded Indian self, Marriott (1989) commented that in the former worldview, "individuals are seen as indivisible, integrated, self-developing units, not normally subject to disjunction or reconstitution" (p. 17). These same characteristics that denote positive features when viewed from the independence-autonomy dimension may be perceived as immodest, arrogant, and aggressive when viewed from the perspective of the interdependent or indexical self: "To members of socio-centric organic cultures the concept of the autonomous individual, free to choose and mind his or her own business, must feel alien, a bizarre idea cutting the self off from the interdependent whole, dooming it to a life of isolation and loneliness" (Kakar, 1978, p. 86). Parallel to the contrasting perceptions of desirable self-ways (discussed later) of the referential self, the indexical or interdependent self is viewed as passive, weak, and unstable from the cultural framework that fosters autonomy, even while it is viewed as socially sensitive, harmonious, and unselfish from the sociocentric perspective (Landrine, 1992; B. K. Ramanujam, 1979).

Integrated Perspectives: Multiple Developmental Models and Pathways

Several researchers have emphasized the coexistence of alternative definitions of self within a culture, as well as within individuals across developmental stages and across contexts. Markus, Mullally, and Kitayama (1997), in introducing their comprehensive review of literature from contrasting cultural contexts, suggested that "taken together, this work reveals that there are multiple ways to construct interdependence and independence and that constructions of both can be found in all cultural contexts" (p. 13). The coexistence of the private and public self (Triandis, 1989), the integration of autonomy and relational orientations (Kagitçibasi, 1996b), and the variations in expressions of independence and interdependence (Kim & Choi, 1994) have received focused attention in the cross-cultural literature. Similarly, developmental psychologists criticize the sharp dichotomy between autonomy and connectedness. Harter (1998) argued that the recent trend toward incorporating both concepts of autonomy and connectedness in theories of self, rather than treating them as competing orientations, is leading to promising lines of research within developmental psychology.

Although cross-cultural research that documents the existence of alternate conceptualizations of self has been a significant contribution, it is not enough for a comprehensive theory of self. Such a theory must be able to explain the process of social construction whereby these alternate conceptualizations of self are appropriated by individuals, describe the multiple developmental pathways for the appropriation of these different concepts of self, document the source of individual variations in developmental pathways, and explain how individuals collectively bring about macro- or societal-level changes. The conceptual framework we delineated earlier that integrates cultural psychology perspectives and ecological-contextual models of development is utilized here to synthesize the contributions of cross-cultural and developmental research in such an endeavor.

Role of Social and Cultural Institutions

We suggest that sociocultural perspectives enable us to understand the role of cultural and social institutions of the macro system and exo system in institutionalizing culturally idealized notions of self and society, as well as the processes whereby individuals collectively bring about change in institutions and in cultural values or macro-level ideology. Societal institutions and macro-level ideology may create the conditions and contexts for the social construction of self at the individual level, but they themselves are constructed and institutionalized by collective individual actions. Individuals confronted by conflicting demands arising from changes within a society or brought about by interacting societal contexts can also become the impetus for creating and institutionalizing new cultural patterns of behavior. For example, Kumar (1993) drew attention to the contradictory forces that impinge on the urban middle-class child in India today. On the one hand, the competitive settings of institutions such as the school and the aggressive commercial media call for individuation, but the continued emotional hold of the family on the child's decision making necessitates developing sociocentricism. The resulting tendency on the part of individuals to respond to both needs and appropriate a model of self that integrates individuation and sociocentricism eventually becomes the culturally valued norm.

Similarly, Kagitçibasi (1996b) suggested that increasing urbanization and nucleation of families in traditional societies, along with the introduction of the institutions of information technology and the market economy, have created a context in which individuals have constructed valued notions of self in which both independence and dependence are integrated. Families have responded to the shift from agrarian economies to market economies by weakening intergenerational material interdependencies while maintaining the emotional interdependency, thus creating new cultural patterns and norms.

Individual Social Construction and Development of Self in Context

When the focus of attention shifts to the individual level as we address questions of developmental pathways and processes, it is essential to reiterate a basic assumption about the social construction of the self. Although cultural psychologists have always viewed the self as a social construction and its development as a social coconstructive process, there appears to be increasing agreement among developmental psychologists about the critical role of social interactive processes. However, this is often conceptualized as the variable of caregiver's role or style (Harter, 1998; Neisser & Jopling, 1997). In highlighting notable advances in research on the development of self-representation, Harter (1998) commented that while in earlier research "care giving styles

were related to *individual differences* in child self-related behaviors, recent conceptualizations and supporting evidence point to the major role that caregiver-infant interactions play in influencing the *normative* progression of self-development" (p. 566).

While there remains much to be done, recent attempts in the literature to describe different developmental pathways for the appropriation of alternate conceptualizations of self and for accounting for individual differences are also emerging (Neisser & Jopling, 1997). Markus, Mullally, and Kitayama (1997) used the term *self-ways* to include broader cultural connotations than that of the individual self. They define self-ways as including "key cultural ideas and values, including understandings of what a person is, as well as senses of how to be a 'good,' 'appropriate,' or 'moral' person" (p. 16). This connotation assumes special significance because it provides for distinction between the modal cultural pattern and individual differences within a culture that may be shaped by a complex set of cultural dimensions including social class, gender, and age.

Recent theorizing to consider the developmental implications of alternate conceptualizations of the self has led to the generation of hypotheses and some empirical support about alternate developmental pathways related to distinctions between individualistic and sociocentric concepts of self. Development of self-consistency and stability of self-concepts and emphasis on uniqueness are important developmental milestones representing increasing maturity when the individualistic self is the culturally valued goal of development (Harter, 1998; Neisser & Jopling, 1997).

However, contrasting the Western worldview of individualism and autonomy with the Hindu world view of sociocentricism, Marriott (1989) commented that in Hindu postulations "persons are in various degrees nonreflexive (not necessarily consistent) in their relations" (p. 16). Interpersonal relations are viewed as irregular and fluid. It follows that such a self would exhibit little stability across contexts and time, and the individual self's attributes, values, and needs emerge from or reflect the needs of the relationships and contexts (Greenfield, 1994; Kim & Choi, 1994; Shweder & Bourne, 1991). Thus, in cultures like India, context sensitivity is the preferred formulation (J. G. Shweder & Miller, 1991; A. K. Ramanujam, 1990; Shweder & Bourne, 1991) and, one might extrapolate, the preferred indicator of increasing maturity.

There is some evidence to support the notion of different developmental pathways. When asked to describe themselves in 20 statements, Japanese youths' responses indicated a predominance of contextualized responses, in contrast to American youths' responses emphasizing personal attributes. In a similar vein, Shweder and Miller (1991) presented developmental data documenting increasing context sensitivity with age among Indian children and adolescents, compared to the increasing proportion with age of statements about general dispositions of the agent among American children. Similarly, Hart and Fegley (1995) documented African American children's relatively more sophisticated self-descriptions compared to children tested in Iceland and explained the difference in terms of the cultural heterogeneity of life experiences, suggesting that children who encounter a variety of perspectives are better able to articulate their varying self-concepts.

We conclude this section with a specific example of the social construction of self in Hindu India, a culture in which one of us (Saraswathi) is deeply embedded. We use this specific example to highlight the different developmental outcomes and trajectories that are possible for the development of self. The development of self in the Indian context can make a case study by itself for several reasons. First, India has a sociohistorical context with a philosophical tradition that is thousands of years old and rooted in the belief of harmony, multiplicity (e.g., many deities, one God), and context sensitivity. Second, India has a prescriptive religious philosophy deeply embedded in the psyche of the average Hindu (see Kakar, 1978; Marriott, 1989; D. Sinha & Tripathi, 1994) that details the acceptable code of conduct for each stage of life and includes the engagement and disengagement of the self in relationships and social bonds. Third, India has a fast-paced rate of social change due to urbanization, industrialization, and a market economy that coexists with a rural India still deeply rooted in tradition.

A. K. Ramanujam (1989) illustrated this coexistence of contradictions in Indians who learn, quite expertly, modern science, business, or technology. However, this "scientific temper" and the new ways of thought and behavior do not replace older religious ways but live among them. Ramanujam's own father, who was a well-known mathematician and astronomer, also specialized in astrology and hosted with ease both astronomers and astrologers, never finding it paradoxical. In a similar vein J. B. P. Sinha (1980) presented the idea of the nurturant task leader, who is authoritarian but effective as a benevolent patriarch in an Indian organizational setting that competes in modern global trade.

The Hindu *ashramadharma* theory describes the code of conduct for each life stage (Kakar, 1978). In the context of the development of self, what is noteworthy is that whereas marriage and procreation and the fulfillment of the duties of the householder are considered imperative for personhood from emerging adulthood to late adulthood, the process of disengagement from social bonds is expected to be initiated from early old age (*vanavas*), leading to complete renunciation

(*sanyas*) in late old age. In fact the ritualistic ceremonies of the completion of the 60th and 80th birthdays provide formal recognition to the expected (idealized) shift. This shift is from the sociocentric self embedded in worldly relationships and duties to a individualized self leading to the path of inward search and self actualization to ultimate salvation or Nirvana. Thus, both the sociocentric and individualistic self are valued, but at different stages of life. Here lies the challenge for developmental theory "to devise organizing frameworks that can account for developmental change, cultural diversity, and contextual variation in a model that presents development as multi-determined" (Cocking, 1994, p. 394) and, we would add, multidimensional.

DEVELOPMENT OF CHILDREN'S NARRATIVES

We select a topic in language and communication as our second exemplar because this is another domain of development in which the integration between developmental and cross-cultural research has been promising, if not achieved. When language is viewed primarily as code acquisition, the tendency is to focus on the underlying universal processes and theories of language acquisition (chapter by Hoff in this volume). However, in cross-cultural psychology there has been a shift away from attempts to validate linguistic models and toward the notion of language and communication as socially embedded cultural phenomenon (Mohanty & Perregaux, 1997; Schieffelin & Ochs, 1986). The bulk of cross-cultural research on language development consists of cross-linguistic studies that focus on the formal structure and rules of different languages and document that different grammatical structures create different types of problems for a child's acquisition of language (Slobin, 1992). However, there is also increasing interest in language socialization and the various socially embedded cultural devices used to socialize children in the pragmatics of language use (Mohanty & Perregaux, 1997).

The interface between individual development and culture becomes particularly critical when language is viewed as involving social action and the creation of meaning, rather than as merely code acquisition. In light of this, we select the topic of narratives from the broad domain of language development because development of narrative skills involves meaning making and communication that are culturally embedded and not merely the acquisition of linguistic codes. In addition, significant inroads have been made in unraveling the interface between individual development and culture in this body of literature.

Developmental Trends: Contributions From Developmental Psychology

Research from a developmental psychology perspective has focused on documenting developmental trends in the nature of children's narratives and the acquisition of narrative skills, including the social-interactive processes whereby children learn to produce narratives. Much of the research examining the development of children's narratives has used definitions of narratives based on the types of narratives valued in formal school settings. Skills and knowledge that allow for the understanding and production of narratives have been delineated based on definitions and characterizations of what constitutes such school-based narrative styles (Feagans, 1982). These include knowledge of such information as introductions, setting, character descriptions, themes, event sequences, reactive events, and conclusions (Rumelhart, 1975; Stein, 1988), as well as knowledge of how to sequence information to form a coherent and cohesive narrative.

Age-related progression in the production of narratives has also been documented, beginning with the rudimentary narratives produced between the ages of 2 to 3 years of age (Sachs, 1983; Snow & Goldfield, 1982), to the personal narratives produced by 6- to 9-year-olds that include most of the basic elements that are typical in the narratives told by adults in the community, such as orienting information and evaluations and resolutions of climactic events (Peterson & McCabe, 1983). The social-interactive processes through which children learn to tell the type of narratives valued by adults have also been the focus of research on children's narratives. Some examples of the social-interactive activities that were common in early research on the development of narratives are joint book reading activities (Snow & Goldfield, 1982), dialogues with adults around storybooks (Cazden, 1988), talking about personal experiences and stories (Heath, 1982), school tasks and activities related to comprehension, and processing of information from written narratives and texts (Stein, 1988).

Cultural Variations in Narratives: Contributions From Cross-Cultural and Cultural Psychology

The main contribution of culture comparative research has been to emphasize that conceptions of normative narratives are themselves culturally constructed and culture bound. The models of story structure, such as the story grammar models derived from research in the United States (Mandler & Johnson, 1977; Stein, 1988), cannot always be applied to narratives from other cultures. Based on an analysis of 150 Japanese folktales,

Matsuyama (1983) concluded that story grammar models were difficult to apply to the folktales because these often did not have the goal structure (a goal for the main character to achieve) that is common in Western folktales.

Similarly, Heath's (1983) landmark research on different cultural communities in the United States described how three communities differed in their definition of stories—even though telling stories was a valued activity in all the communities. In one community (a White mill community of Appalachian origin), culturally valued stories were factual and chronological, included a lesson to be learned, and were used to reinforce behavioral norms. In contrast, in another community (an African American mill community of rural origin), stories were highly creative and fictionalized and were used to entertain and assert individual strengths.

Distinctive structural patterns also have been delineated for narratives generated by Hispanic American and Japanese children (Minami & McCabe, 1991; Rodino, Gimbert, Perez, & McCabe, 1991), in African-American children's narratives (Gee, 1989; Michaels, 1991; Nichols, 1989), and in Hawaiian children's narratives (Watson, 1975). In fact, the difficulty in applying story grammar structures to narratives from various cultures led to the development of other types of structural analysis, such as verse analysis and stanza analysis (Gee, 1986; Hymes, 1974).

Integrative Perspectives: Toward Multiple Models of Narrative Development

Whereas developmental research attempts to delineate normative trends in the development of children's narratives, cross-cultural research emphasizes variations in the structure and form of culturally valued narratives. However, merely documenting variations is not enough to explain the process whereby these differences in what is culturally valued are generated and maintained by becoming institutionalized in cultural institutions and ideology. Similarly, delineating developmental differences, or the factors that lead to individual differences, is not enough to understand how individuals appropriate the narrative forms and styles valued in their cultural communities and in turn collectively create, institutionalize, and privilege particular forms of narratives in their communities.

We argue that it is essential to integrate research from all three subfields (cross-cultural, developmental, and cultural psychology) to benefit from their complementary foci and develop a more comprehensive understanding of the interface between culture and narrative development. An example of such integration of various bodies of literature is offered by Mistry (1993) and is briefly summarized here.

Using the sociocultural perspective to facilitate the integration of empirical work on the development of children's narratives, Mistry (1993) organized her literature review to document how sociocultural context is an integral part of children's narrative development at both an institutional and an interpersonal level. At the institutional level, cultural history creates and establishes institutions (e.g., schools, literary organizations) that value, foster, and reward (through tools such as grades, awards, and other means of formal or informal recognition) particular types of narratives and narrative practices. At the interpersonal level, the cultural basis of narrative practices is manifested in the nature of the task that the narrator and listener seek to accomplish, the values involved in determining the appropriate goals and means, the intellectual tools available (e.g., language system and conventions), and the institutional structures within which interactions take place (e.g., schools, social organizations, economic systems).

Role of Social and Cultural Institutions

To understand development in any domain, it is first essential to identify goals of development or culturally accepted endpoints of development within that domain. At the broadest level, cultural institutions serve to establish these norms and goals of development. In a literate and technologically oriented society, social and cultural institutions privilege particular forms of narratives and narrative practices, which then become the desired norms that determine what is considered normal progression toward mature and developmentally sophisticated forms. Sociolinguists have pointed to the existence of a literate bias in contemporary approaches to narratives (Gee, 1991; Michaels, 1991). Similarly, cross-cultural literature has emphasized that the unidirectional focus and value placed on academic and literate contexts of development must be questioned, as the goals of literacy and academic discourse are not universal. To understand the development of children in the context of their own communities requires study of the local goals and means of approaching life (Rogoff, Mistry, Göncü, & Mosier, 1993). Each community's valued skills, institutionalized in cultural ideology and institutions (the macro and exo systems), constitute the local goals of development.

In addition to privileging particular forms of narratives and narrative practices, cultural institutions also provide the context and structure the situations and activities of the micro and meso systems within which children hear narratives and gain practice in producing them. For example, in European American middle-class communities, the dominant interactional contexts within which narrative activities take place are related to the institutions of formal schooling and the socioeconomic systems that call for literate means of communication (Mistry, 1993). Hence, young children's narrative skills develop within the interactional contexts of school-like learning activities. The occurrence of school-like narrative activities, such as story reading and recounting of events during parent-child conversations (Feitelson & Goldstein, 1986; Fivush, 1991; Haight, 1991; Heath, 1989; Snow, 1989) have been well documented in the developmental psychology literature on European American middle-class children. Parallels and continuity in the patterns of narrative discourse between home and school in middle-class, school-oriented communities occur because the cultural and social institutions that serve as a dominant context for development are similar in each case.

The consistency between children's narrative patterns and those apparent in the discourse patterns of adults participating in several institutional contexts of community life, such as the church, has been documented by Heath (1983) for an African American mill town community: "Throughout the sermons, prayers, and raised hymns of the church, there appears a familiar pattern which marks many other features of Trackton life: the learning of language, telling of stories, and composing of hand-clap and jump-rope songs" (p. 211). Patterns of language use that were apparent in children's and adult's storytelling were also evident in other institutional contexts in the community, such as in parts of the church service (sermons, hymns, personal testimonials), in the music, in community events, and in children's games and play.

Links between children's narrative patterns and culturally institutionalized discourse patterns are also evident in Minami and McCabe's (1991) research on Japanese children's narratives. They link the short length of Japanese children's conversational narratives to culturally valued literary forms in which the emphasis is on brevity, such as haiku (a literary form that combines narrative and poetry and has strict length limitations) and *karuta* (a game that displays three lines of written discourse). Thus, within any cultural community there is continuity in the patterns of narrative discourse used at home and the discourse patterns utilized and privileged by the cultural institutions controlled by people in the communities (Mistry, 1993). However, the fact that the narrative patterns and the cultural institutions that support them can be very different across cultural communities underscores the importance of recognizing multiple goals and pathways of development. Having emphasized the role of cultural institutions in privileging particular forms of narratives and structuring the settings and activities in which children appropriate these forms, we now turn our attention to the role of individual social construction.

Individual Social Construction and Development of Narratives

As we pointed out earlier, much of the research examining children's development of narrative skills delineates the mature skills of storytelling based on definitions of narratives valued in schools and other institutions in a literate society. Developmental trends in how children acquire and appropriate school-based narrative styles and conventions through their dialogues and joint activity with adults in school-like learning activities and conversations have been well documented in the developmental psychology literature (Cochran-Smith, 1983; Snow, 1989). However, less is known about the social-interactional contexts and processes through which narrative practices valued in other cultural communities are acquired and appropriated.

Some cultural differences in aspects of joint conversational or narrative activity have been documented through culture-comparative approaches. Blum-Kulka and Snow (1992) found variation in the amount of assistance and the degree of independence given children during dinner-time conversations in working-class, middle-class American and middle-class Israeli homes. Similarly, Minami and McCabe (1991) reported differences in the length of time children are given the floor during mother-child conversations in Canadian and Japanese homes. Canadian mothers encouraged lengthy turns by asking many extending questions, whereas Japanese mothers regularly capped the length of their children's turns at three utterances.

To summarize our integration of the literature on the development of children's narrative from developmental, cross-cultural, and cultural psychology perspectives, we emphasize the contributions from each subfield of psychology in building a more comprehensive and culturally inclusive theoretical and empirical knowledge base. Research within developmental psychology has delineated normative trends in the development of children's narratives in communities in which the institutions of schooling and literacy are dominant contexts for this development. By documenting variations in the structure and form of culturally valued narratives, cross-cultural research has enabled us to recognize the culture-bounded nature of what might be construed as normative developmental trends and acknowledge these as situated in particular communities, specifically those dominated by the institutions of schooling and literacy. Finally, sociocultural perspectives have elucidated the processes whereby differences in what is culturally valued are generated and maintained by becoming institutionalized in cultural institutions and ideology. Such perspectives also offer theoretical conceptualizations of how individuals appropriate the narrative forms and styles valued in their cultural communities, and in turn collectively create, institutionalize, and privilege particular forms of narratives in their communities.

DEVELOPMENT OF REMEMBERING

In the cross-cultural psychology literature, cognitive development has been identified as by far the most frequently studied topic of cultural-comparative research. Whereas cross-cultural researchers in the first half of the twentieth century focused on testing the applicability of the IQ construct (Jahoda & Krewer, 1997), after the 1960s researchers concentrated on studying cognitive processes such as memory, mathematical thinking, and categorization (Cole et al., 1971; Dasen, 1972; Dasen & Heron, 1981; Wagner, 1981). Since the 1970s several scholars have provided detailed accounts of cross-cultural research on cognition (Altaribba, 1993; Berry & Dasen, 1974; Mishra, 1997; Rogoff, 1981; Segall, Dasen, Berry, & Poortinga, 1999; Wagner, 1981). Research carried out during the last half of the twentieth century has also led to significant shifts in understanding the interface between culture and human development. Therefore, we considered it important to include a topic in cognitive development as an exemplar of the integration of research from various subfields of psychology. However, to delimit our task, we have chosen to focus on the topic of remembering.

Developmental Trends: Contributions From Developmental Psychology

Although research on the development of memory has a long history, there has been a shift in emphasis from describing developmental differences in memory performance to identifying the underlying mechanisms of developmental change. This shift may have been a result of the increasing prominence of information processing and neuroscience approaches in the 1960s (Schneider & Bjorklund, 1998). Although developmental differences on working memory capacity was a significant line of research, developmental differences in the use of mnemonic strategies became a particularly important area of research in this attempt to explain developmental differences.

Several reviews of research (Paris, Newman, & Jacobs, 1985; Perlmutter, 1988; Schneider & Pressley, 1989; Weinert & Perlmutter, 1988) documented early attempts to explain memory development as the development of increasingly flexible and more general memory strategies between 5 and 11 years of age. Age-related changes in operative knowledge (knowing how to use mnemonic strategies), epistemic (content) knowledge, and metacognitive knowledge were assumed to contribute to age-related improvements in memory performance (Perlmutter, 1988). However, research within developmental psychology itself, such as evidence of strategic remembering among young children in familiar contexts (Wellman, 1988) and the role of prior knowledge in facilitating better recall (Chi, 1978), highlighted the problems with decontextualized generalizations about memory development.

In a recent review Schneider and Bjorklund (1998) underscored the heterogeneity and variability in different aspects of memory and the expectation that different types of memory abilities will have different developmental functions and trajectories. Some dimensions of memory are assumed to develop slowly over childhood and to be influenced by environmental context, whereas others are viewed as developmentally invariant and relatively impervious to environmental factors (Schneider & Bjorklund, 1998). Noting the shift away from research on conscious and strategic remembering to a focus on basic-level unconscious and nondeliberate micro processes, Schneider and Bjorklund placed particular emphasis on the need to study memory at multiple levels and from multiple perspectives, including perspectives that focus on the social construction of remembering.

Variability in Remembering: Lessons From Cross-Cultural Research

Reviews of cross-cultural research on remembering (Mistry, 1997; Rogoff & Mistry, 1985) characterize much of this research as based on a model in which culture and memory were conceived of as separate variables. The influence of culture on individual performance or development was typically studied by comparing the memory performance of individuals from two or more cultures. Evidence from such research in the 1960s and 1970s indicated that individuals from non-Western cultures did not use the type of mnemonic strategies that were assumed to facilitate better recall among individuals from Western cultures and to be responsible for developmental differences (Cole & Scribner, 1977; Rogoff, 1981; Rogoff & Mistry, 1985; Wagner, 1981).

Despite the predominance of research focused on testing psychological theories using constructs and procedures developed in the West, important lessons were learned from such culture-comparative research (Mistry, 1997). Cross-cultural studies conducted by Cole and his colleagues in the 1970s (Cole et al., 1971; Cole & Scribner, 1977; Sharp, Cole, & Lave, 1979) were particularly notable for their insightful use of ethnographic methods. These researchers combined ethnographic methods to gain a deep understanding of cultural context with experimental procedures to elaborate features of the memory tasks and materials that mediated cultural differences in performance on remembering tasks. Along with evidence from descriptions of non-Western people's memory in their everyday life (Bartlett, 1932; Lord, 1965), such research emphasized the variability of remembering as a function of familiarity and practice with specific materials, tasks, mediational means, and the modality of remembering (Mistry, 1997).

Cross-cultural research also highlighted another important lesson for research on memory in general. It enabled researchers to separate variables that vary simultaneously in the United States but are separable in other cultures. For example, in many nontechnological societies, formal schooling is not yet universal, so the relative independence of age and amount of schooling provides investigators with a natural laboratory for investigating effects of age and schooling separately. Cross-cultural comparisons of memory performance by individuals varying in schooling experience allowed consideration of whether developmental changes in remembering were due to experience with school rather than maturation (Rogoff, 1981, 1990; Sharp, Cole, & Lave, 1979). Western children enter school at about age 5, and there is high correlation between age and grade in school thereafter. Thus, cross-cultural research facilitated awareness of the fact that "cognitive-developmental research has been measuring years of schooling, using age as its proxy variable" (LCHC, 1979, p. 830). This evidence from cross-cultural studies, along with recent research on the impact of training on use of mnemonic strategies, has led developmental psychologists to recognize the social construction of memory (Schneider & Bjorklund, 1998).

Integrated Perspectives: Multiple Dimensions of Remembering

Although the variability of memory has been well documented in cross-cultural research, it is essential to go beyond merely documenting differences to developing a theory or conceptual framework that describes and explains the multidimensional complexity of the development of remembering in diverse contexts. If the notion of culture is to be integral to a theory of memory development, it must take into account contemporary ideas and findings in the field (Wertsch & Tulviste, 1992). Therefore, we emphasize the need for an integrative perspective that will enable us to interpret research at many levels, examining the larger social context to institutional mechanisms and the specific situation contexts and the embedded meaning that results in the individual's construction and acquisition of remembering.

Role of Social and Cultural Institutions

Although much of the cross-cultural research in the study of memory has not been conducted from a sociocultural or cultural-psychology perspective, this body of research is reviewed to examine how it elucidates a theory of memory development in which the interface between culture and individual development is integral.

Early cross-cultural research focused on testing constructs and procedures for assessing memory performance among people from different cultural communities. On classic memory tasks developed by developmental psychologists (e.g., free or serial recall of lists of words or series of pictures), people in non-Western communities were widely observed to perform poorly (see reviews by Cole & Scribner, 1977; Rogoff, 1981; Rogoff & Mistry, 1985; Wagner, 1981). Furthermore, following the prevalent approach in cross-cultural psychology, researchers typically examined characteristics that commonly varied between cultures (e.g., the amount of formal schooling, degree of modernity, urban vs. rural residence) as an explanation for these differences in remembering. However, the research that documented differences in remembering as a function of these variables did not elaborate the cultural context of remembering because it did not *unpackage* (Whiting, 1976) specific aspects of the environmental or experiential context that differentiated the groups.

Toward the goal of elaborating the cultural context of remembering, we draw on sociocultural perspectives to facilitate the development of a conceptual framework of remembering in which culture is integral. In such a conceptual framework, it is essential to consider how remembering is coconstructed in the context of specific institutions that privilege particular goals for remembering, particular forms of remembering, and particular modalities and particular mnemonic strategies (or mediational tools) for remembering. From this perspective, differences in recall performance between schooled and nonschooled people can be interpreted as reflecting the significant role of schools as a social institution in privileging particular goals and mediational means for remembering.

Research has documented that people with schooling tend to use organizational strategies (e.g., mediational means) that enhance their recall, whereas people not exposed to Western schooling tend not to use such mnemonic strategies. Discussing these findings from a cultural perspective, Rogoff and Mistry (1985; Mistry, 1997) pointed out that school is one of the few places in which a person has to remember information deliberately, as a goal in itself, and make initially meaningless, unrelated pieces of information fit together sensibly. Many of the organizational strategies that facilitate recall of classic laboratory memory tasks (which impose some organization on meaningless material) are valued and therefore learned in school because they serve a valued purpose in school learning.

Similarly, research documenting different outcomes for learning and memory for varied forms of schooling or other institutions for literacy (Mishra, 1997; Serpell & Hatano, 1997) emphasize the significance of the institution of schooling, albeit different forms of schooling. The rote memory–based learning valued in Koranic schools, which is well suited to remembering long Koranic verses, has been linked to the superior performance of Muslim children in Morocco schooled in these schools compared to nonschooled children (Wagner, 1993). In their classic work to examine how institutions of literacy structure and organize the way individuals remember, Scribner and Cole (1981) compared the performance of Vai people who varied in the use of several types of literacy: Arabic literacy gained through the study of religious script in traditional Koranic schools, literacy in the indigenous Vai script learned through informal means for practical correspondence in trade, and literacy in English learned in Western-style schools. The Arabic literates had a great advantage over the other groups on recall of words when the preservation of word order was required, consistent with the incremental method of learning the Koran (adding a new word to a series at each attempt). Thus, each form of literacy training, each embedded in different institutions of learning, privileged and facilitated particular ways of remembering.

Cross-cultural findings of outstanding memory performance by non-Western people can also be interpreted and understood as instances of how cultural, social, and economic institutions and their valued goals facilitate particular ways of remembering. The extraordinary skills in memory, inference, and calculation for navigation among Micronesian sailors (Gladwin, 1970) and the exceptional ability to recall genealogy and family history among oral historians of clans in Africa who serve a critical function in resolving disputes (D'Azevedo, 1982) are just a few examples among many that have been discussed elsewhere (Mistry, 1997; Mistry & Rogoff, 1994; Rogoff & Mistry, 1985).

Individual Social Construction of Remembering

As evident from the discussion thus far, once research on remembering is contextualized by situating it in particular institutional and sociocultural contexts, cross-cultural differences are better understood and can be integrated into a more comprehensive theoretical perspective that provides a coherent explanation for such differences. For example, much of the research on remembering represented in the field of developmental psychology occurs in situations in schools, homes, and laboratories that are structured and influenced by institutions such as schooling and literacy, which are dominant in Western society. Remembering in these contexts will naturally be different from remembering in cultural contexts in which institutions other than schooling are dominant. Although explanations of such differences at the cultural level are now better understood, an integrated perspective on remembering must also be able to interpret individual differences and the social-interactional and individual processes whereby remembering is socially constructed in culturally specific situation contexts with their embedded meaning.

At the level of individual processes, cross-disciplinary contributions can also be particularly valuable. Cross-cultural research that situates variability in remembering as a function of different aspects of the activity in which remembering takes place, such as differential familiarity with materials, mediational means, modalities, and motivations for remembering, can be useful to developmental psychologists in their attempt to understand individual differences in remembering. On the other hand, research from developmental psychology that delineates how children learn to use mnemonic tools or approach memory problems more skillfully through supportive interaction with more skilled partners can serve as models for culture comparative research.

Several studies of remembering in U.S. contexts have specifically focused on the question of whether and how social interaction supports memory development. Building on Vygotsky's (1978) emphasis on the role of joint interaction, some have suggested that adults may serve as children's *auxiliary metamemory* (Wertsch, 1978). Studies have documented such parental roles and the consequences for remembering. For example, McNamee (1987) suggested that memory for connected text develops between adults and children as they converse; DeLoache (1984) noted the supportive role of mothers' memory questions in picture book reading; and Fivush (1991) documented the social construction of narratives by young children. Similarly, guided participation in remembering with adults has been documented to facilitate children's performance on categorization and remembering tasks (Ellis & Rogoff, 1982; Rogoff & Gardner, 1984; Rogoff & Mistry, 1990).

However, culture-comparative studies of the individual construction and appropriation of culturally valued means for remembering are lacking in the cross-cultural literature. This gap in the cross-cultural literature must be addressed if we are to build a theoretically and empirically integrated

knowledge base on the development of remembering. For the development of such a knowledge base, we reiterate the need for an integrative perspective that will enable us to interpret research at many levels, examining the larger social context to institutional mechanisms and the specific situation contexts and their embedded meaning that results in the individual's construction and acquisition of remembering.

CONCLUDING COMMENTS

As a final thought, we underscore the importance of drawing on multiple streams of knowledge to build more comprehensive and culturally inclusive theories and empirical databases on children's development. Despite the fact that cross-cultural, cultural, and developmental psychology approach the study of culture and human development from different perspectives, we document how it is possible to integrate literature from all three subfields to build more culturally inclusive understandings of any domain of development. Building on Kessen's (1993) commentary that the elevation of context in developmental psychology represents a shaking of its foundations, we reiterate that in the reconstruction of the field, we must be willing to incorporate perspectives from cultural and cross-cultural psychology as well.

In focusing on the interface between culture and human development, developmental psychology has not been at the forefront in looking outside its discipline for theoretical insights or research. As Kessen (1993) suggested, this may be due to the tensions between the emerging intentions of developmental psychologists and the traditions of experimental science. However, there are promising signs of changes being wrought from within the field. The work of developmental psychologists who are able to blend the methodologies valued in developmental psychology with the concerns voiced by cultural psychologists on the need to incorporate a focus on cultural meaning systems represent the most promising approaches to bringing about the reconstruction that Kessen suggests is now underway.

Studies of children's cognition and learning as situated in the contexts of activities and interactional processes (Wozniak & Fischer, 1993) are examples of changes in conceptualization being wrought from within the field. Attempts to unpackage culture in ways that go beyond treating it as a social address variable, and instead to operationalize it in concrete variables constructed from emic perspectives, are all examples of promising research that bridges the concerns of both developmental and cultural psychology (Garcia-Coll & Magnuson, 1999; Rogoff et al., 1993; Harwood et al., 1995). To continue the process of bringing about change from within and meeting the challenge of developing theories and empirical databases that can account for developmental change and cultural and contextual variation, it is essential for developmental psychology to push the boundaries of the field.

REFERENCES

Altaribba, J. (Ed.). (1993). *Cognition and culture: A cross-cultural approach to cognitive psychology.* Amsterdam, The Netherlands: Elsevier Press.

Baltes, P. B., Lindenberger, U., & Staudinger, U. M. (1998). Life-span theory in developmental psychology. In R. L. Lerner (Ed.), *Handbook of child psychology: Vol. 1. Theoretical models of human development* (pp. 1029–1144). New York: Wiley.

Baltes, P. B., Reese, H. W., & Lipsitt, L. P. (1980). Life-span developmental psychology. *Annual Review of Psychology, 31,* 65–110.

Bartlett, F. C. (1932). *Remembering.* Cambridge, UK: Cambridge University Press.

Berry, J. W. (1966). Temne and Eskimo perceptual skills. *International Journal of Psychology, 1,* 207–229.

Berry, J. W. (1969). On cross-cultural comparability. *International Journal of Psychology, 4,* 119–128.

Berry, J. W. (1980). Introduction to methodology. In H. C. Triandis & J. W. Berry (Eds.), *Handbook of cross-cultural psychology: Vol. 2. Methodology* (pp. 1–28). Boston: Allyn and Bacon.

Berry, J. W., & Dasen, P. R. (1974). *Culture and cognition: Readings in cross-cultural psychology.* London: Methuen.

Berry, J. W., Poortinga, Y. H., Pandey, J., Dasen, P. R., Saraswathi, T. S., Segall, M. H., & Kagitçibasi, C. (Eds.). (1997). *Handbook of cross-cultural psychology* (2nd ed., Vols. 1–3). Needham Heights, MA: Allyn and Bacon.

Berry, J. W., Poortinga, Y. H., Segall, M., & Dasen, P. R. (1992). *Cross-cultural psychology: Research and applications.* Cambridge, UK: Cambridge University Press.

Blum-Kulka, S., & Snow, C. E. (1992). Developing autonomy for tellers, tales, and telling in family narrative events. *Journal of Narrative and Life History, 2,* 187–217.

Brislin, R. W. (1983). Cross-cultural research psychology. *Annual Review of Psychology, 3,* 363–400.

Bronfenbrenner, U. (1979). *The ecology of human development.* Cambridge, MA: Harvard University Press.

Bronfenbrenner, U. (1986). Ecology of the family as a context for human development. *Developmental Psychology, 22*(6), 723–742.

Bruner, J. (1990). Culture and human development: A new look. *Human Development, 33,* 344–355.

Cazden, C. (1988). *Classroom discourse: The language of teaching and learning.* Portsmouth, NH: Heinemann.

Chi, M. (1978). Knowledge structure and memory development. In R. S. Siegler (Ed.), *Children's thinking: What develops?* (pp. 73–96). Hillsdale, NJ: Erlbaum.

Cochran-Smith, M. (1983). Reading stories to children: A review critique. In B. Hutson (Ed.), *Advances in reading/language research* (pp. 197–229). Greenwich, CT: Jai Press.

Cocking, R. R. (1994). Ecologically valid frameworks of development: Accounting for continuities and discontinuities across contexts. In P. M. Greenfield & R. R.Cocking (Eds.), *Cross-cultural roots of minority child development* (pp. 393–409). Hillsdale, NJ: Erlbaum.

Cole, M. (1985). The zone of proximal development: Where culture and cognition create each other. In J. W. Werstch (Ed.), *Culture, communication, and cognition* (pp. 146–162). Cambridge, UK: Cambridge University Press.

Cole, M. (1990). Cognitive development and formal schooling. In L. Moll (Ed.), *Vygotsky and education* (pp. 89–110). New York: Cambridge University Press.

Cole, M. (1995). Culture and cognition development: From cross-cultural research to creating systems of cultural mediation. *Culture and Psychology, 1*(1), 25–54.

Cole, M. (1996). *Cultural psychology: A once and future discipline.* Cambridge, MA: Belknap/Harvard.

Cole, M., Gay, J., Glick, J., & Sharp, D. W. (1971). *The cultural context of learning and thinking.* New York: Basic Books.

Cole, M., & Scribner, S. (1977). Cross-cultural studies of memory and cognition. In R. V. Kail & J. W. Hagen (Eds.), *Perspectives on the development of memory and cognition* (pp. 239–271). Hillsdale, NJ: Erlbaum.

Damon, W. (Series Ed.). (1998). *Handbook of child psychology* (Vols. 1–4). New York: Wiley.

D'Andrade, R. G. (1984). Cultural meaning systems. In R. A. Shweder & R. A. LeVine (Eds.), *Culture theory: Essays on mind, self, and emotion* (pp. 88–119). New York: Cambridge University Press.

D'Andrade, R. G., & Strauss, C. (1992). *Cultural models and human motives.* Cambridge, UK: Cambridge University Press.

Dasen, P. R. (1972). Cross-cultural Piagetian research: A summary. *Journal of Cross-Cultural Psychology, 7,* 75–85.

Dasen, P. R. (1974). The influence of ecology, culture and European contact on cognitive development in Australian aboriginies. In J. W. Berry & P. R. Dasen (Eds.), *Culture and cognition* (pp. 381–408). London, UK: Methuen.

Dasen, P. R. (1984). The cross-cultural study of intelligence: Piaget and the Baole. In P. S. Fry (Ed.), *Changing conceptions of intelligence & intelligence functioning: Current theory and research* (pp. 107–134). Amsterdam, North-Holland.

Dasen, P. R. (1993). What's in a name? *Cross-cultural Psychology Bulletin, 27*(2), 1–2.

Dasen, P. R., & Heron, A. (1981). Cross-cultural tests of Piaget's theory. In H. C. Triandis & A. Heron (Eds.), *Handbook of cross-cultural psychology: Vol. 4. Developmental Psychology* (pp. 295–341). Boston: Allyn and Bacon.

D'Azevedo, W. A. (1982). Tribal history in Liberia. In U. Neisser (Ed.), *Memory observed: Remembering in natural contexts* (pp. 274–292). San Francisco: Freeman.

DeLoache, J. (1984). What's this? Maternal questions in joint picture book reading with toddlers. *Quarterly Newsletter of the Laboratory for Comparative Human Cognition, 6,* 87–95.

Dixon, R. A., & Lerner, R. M. (1999). History and systems in developmental psychology. In M. Bornstein & M. Lamb (Eds.), *Developmental psychology: An advanced textbook* (4th ed., pp. 3–45). Mahwah, NJ: Erlbaum.

Eckensberger, L. H. (1996). Agency, action and culture: Three basic concepts for cross-cultural psychology. In J. Pandey & D. Sinha (Eds.), *Asian contributions to cross-cultural psychology* (pp. 72–102). Thousand Oaks, CA: Sage.

Eisenberg, N. (1998). Introduction. In W. Damon (Series Ed.) & N. Eisenberg (Vol. Ed.), *Handbook of child psychology: Vol. 1. Theoretical models of human development* (5th ed., pp. 1–24). New York: Wiley.

Ellis, S., & Rogoff, B. (1982). The strategies and efficacy of child versus adult teachers. *Child Development, 53,* 730–735.

Enriques, V. G. (1977). Filipino psychology in the Third World. *Phillipine Journal of Pyschology, 10,* 3–18.

Feagans, L. (1982). The development and importance of narrative for school adaptation. In L. Feagans & D. C. Farran (Eds.), *The language of children reared in poverty* (pp. 25–36). New York: Academic Press.

Feitelson, D., & Goldstein, Z. (1986). Patterns of book ownership and reading to young children in Israeli school-oriented and non-school-oriented families. *Reading Teacher, 39,* 924–930.

Fivush, R. (1991). The social construction of personal narratives. *Merrill-Palmer Quarterly, 37,* 59–82.

Ford, D. L., & Lerner, R. M. (1992). *Developmental systems theory: An integrative approach.* Newbury Park, CA: Sage.

Gallimore, R., & Goldenburg, C. (1993). Activity settings of early literacy: Home and school factors in children's emergent literacy. In E. A. Forman, N. Minick, & C. A. Stone (Eds.), *Contexts for learning: Sociocultural dynamics in children's development* (pp. 313–335). New York: Oxford University Press.

Garcia-Coll, C., & Magnuson, G. (1999). Cultural influences on child development: Are we ready for a paradigm shift? In A. Masten (Ed.), *Cultural processes in child development: The Minnesota symposia on child psychology* (Vol. 29, pp. 1–24). Hillsdale, NJ: Erlbaum.

Gardiner, H. W., Mutter, J. D., & Kosmitzki, C. (1998). *Lives across cultures: Cross-cultural human development.* Boston: Allyn and Bacon.

Gee, J. P. (1986). Units in the production of narrative discourse. *Discourse Processes, 9,* 391–422.

Gee, J. P. (1989). Commonalities and differences in narrative construction. *Discourse Processes, 12,* 287–307.

Gee, J. P. (1991). Memory and myth: A perspective on narrative. In A. McCabe & C. Peterson (Eds.), *Developing narrative structure* (pp. 83–98). Hillsdale, NJ: Erlbaum.

Gladwin, T. (1970). *East is a big bird.* Cambridge, MA: Belknap.

Goodnow, J. J., Miller, P., & Kessel, F. (Eds.). (1995). *Cultural practices as contexts for development.* San Francisco: Jossey-Bass.

Gottlieb, G. (1997). *Synthesizing nature-nurture: Prenatal roots of instinctive behavior.* Mahwah, NJ: Erlbaum.

Greenfield, P. M. (1994). Independence and interdependence as developmental scripts: Implications for theory, research, and practice. In P. M. Greenfield & R. R. Cocking (Eds.), *Cross-cultural roots of minority child development* (pp. 1–40). Hillsdale, NJ: Erlbaum.

Greenfield, P. M. (1997). Culture as process: Empirical methods for cultural psychology. In J. W. Berry, Y. H. Poortinga, J. Pandey, P. R. Dasen, T. S. Saraswathi, M. H. Segall, & C. Kagitçibasi (Series Eds.) & J. W. Berry, Y. H. Poortinga, & J. Pandey (Vol. Eds.), *Handbook of cross-cultural psychology: Vol. 1. Theory and method* (2nd ed., pp. 301–346). Needham Heights, MA: Allyn and Bacon.

Greenfield, P. M., & Cocking, R. R. (Eds.). (1994). *Cross-cultural roots of minority child development.* Hillsdale, NJ: Erlbaum.

Haight, W. (1991). *Parents' ideas about pretend play.* Paper presented at the meetings of the Society for Research in Child Development, Seattle, WA.

Harkness, S., & Super, C. M. (1992). Parental ethnotheories inaction. In I. E. Sigel, A. V. McGillicuddy-DeLisi, & J. J. Goodnow (Eds.), *Parental belief systems* (pp. 373–391). Hillsdale, NJ: Erlbaum.

Hart, D., & Fegley, S. (1995). Prosocial behavior and caring in adolescence: Relations to self-understanding and social judgment. *Child Development, 66,* 1346–1359.

Harter, S. (1998). The development of self-representations. In W. Damon (Series Ed.) & N. Eisenberg (Vol. Ed.), *Handbook of child psychology: Vol. 1. Theoretical models of human development* (5th ed., pp. 553–617). New York: Wiley.

Harwood, R. L., Miller, J. G., & Irizarry, N. L. (1995). *Culture and attachment: Perceptions of the child in context.* New York: The Guildford Press.

Hatano, G. (1999). Is cultural psychology on the middle ground or farther? *Human Development, 42*(2), 83–86.

Heath, S. B. (1982). What no bedtime story means: Narrative skills at home and school. *Language in Society, 11*(1), 49–76.

Heath, S. B. (1983). *Ways with words: Language, life, and work in communities and classrooms.* New York: Cambridge University Press.

Heath, S. B. (1989). The learner as cultural member. In M. L. Rice & R. L. Schiefelbusch (Eds.), *The teachability of language* (pp. 333–350). Baltimore: Paul H. Brookes.

Ho, D. Y. F. (1976). On the concept of face. *American Journal of Sociology, 81,* 867–884.

Ho, D. Y. F. (1988). Asian psychology: A dialogue on indigenization and beyond. In A. C. Paranjpe, D. Y. F. Ho, & R. W. Reiber (Eds.), *Asian contributions to psychology* (pp. 53–77). New York: Praeger.

Ho, D. Y. F. (1993). Relational orientation in Asian social psychology. In U. Kim & J. W. Berry (Eds.), *Indigenous psychologies: Research and experience in cultural context* (pp. 240–259). Newbury Park, CA: Sage.

Hymes, D. (1974). Foundations in sociolinguistics: An ethnographic approach. Philadelphia, Pennsylvania: University of Pennsylvania Press.

Jahoda, G. (1990). Our forgotten ancestors. In J. Berman (Ed.), *Cross-cultural perspectives* (pp. 1–40). Nebraska Symposium on Motivation, 1989. Lincoln: University of Nebraska Press.

Jahoda, G. (1992). *Crossroads between culture and mind.* Cambridge, MA: Harvard University Press.

Jahoda, G., & Krewer, B. (1997). History of cross-cultural and cultural psychology. In J. W. Berry, Y. H. Poortinga, J. Pandey, P. R. Dasen, T. S. Saraswathi, M. H. Segall, & C. Kagitçibasi (Series Eds.) & J. W. Berry, Y. H. Poortinga, & J. Pandey (Vol. Eds.), *Handbook of cross-cultural psychology: Vol. 1. Theory and method* (2nd ed., pp. 1–42). Needham Heights, MA: Allyn and Bacon.

Kagitçibasi, C. (1996a). The autonomous-relational self: A new synthesis. *European Psychologist, 1*(3), 180–186.

Kagitçibasi, C. (1996b). *Family and human development across cultures: A view from the other side.* Mahwah, NJ: LEA.

Kagitçibasi, C., & Poortinga, Y. (2000). Cross-cultural psychology: Issues and overarching themes. *Journal of Cross-Cultural Psychology, 31*(1), 129–147.

Kakar, S. (1978). *The inner world: A psycho-analytic study of childhood and society in India.* London: Oxford University Press.

Kao, H. S. R., & Sinha, D. (Eds.). (1997). *Asian perspectives on psychology.* New Delhi, India: Sage.

Keller, H., & Greenfield, P. M. (2000). History and future of development in cross-cultural psychology. *Journal of Cross Cultural Psychology, 31*(1), 52–62.

Kessen, W. (1993). Rumble or revolution: A commentary. In R. H. Wozniak & F. W. Fischer (Eds.), *Development in context: Acting and thinking in specific environments* (pp. 269–279). Hillsdale, NJ: Erlbaum.

Kim, U., & Berry, J. W. (Eds.). (1993). *Indigenous psychologies: Research and experience in cultural context.* Newbury Park, CA: Sage.

Kim, U., & Choi, S. H. (1994). Individualism, collectivism, and child development: A Korean perspective. In P. M. Greenfield & R. R. Cocking (Eds.), *Cross-cultural roots of minority child development* (pp. 227–256). Hillsdale, NJ: Erlbaum.

Kim, U., Park, Y. S., & Park, D. (2000). The challenge of cross-cultural psychology: The role of the indigenous psychologies. *Journal of Cross-Cultural Psychology, 31*(1), 63–75.

Kumar, K. (1993). Study of childhood and family. In T. S. Saraswathi (Ed.), *Human development and family studies in India: An agenda for research and policy* (pp. 67–76). New Delhi, India: Sage.

Laboratory of Comparative Human Cognition. (1979). What's cultural about cross-cultural psychology? *Annual Review of Psychology, 30,* 145–172.

Laboratory of Comparative Human Cognition. (1983). Culture and cognitive development. In W. Kessen (Vol. Ed.), *Handbook of child psychology: Vol. 1. History, theory, and methods* (4th ed., pp. 295–356). New York: Wiley.

Lancy, D. (1978). The indigenous mathematics project [Special issue]. *Journal of Education, 14.*

Landrine, H. (1992). Clinical implications of cultural differences: The referential versus the indexical self. *Clinical Psychology Review, 12,* 401–415.

Lave, J. (1990). The culture of acquisition and the practice of understanding. In J. W. Stigler, R. A. Shweder, G. Herdt (Eds.), *Cultural psychology* (pp. 309–327). New York: Cambridge University Press.

Lebra, T. S. (1976). *Japanese patterns of behavior.* Honolulu, HI: University of Hawaii Press.

Leont'ev, A. N. (1981). The problem of activity in psychology. In J. V. Wertsch (Ed.), *The concept of activity in Soviet psychology* (pp. 37–71). Armonk: Sharpe.

Lerner, R. M. (1991). Changing organism-context relation as the basic process of development: A developmental-contextual perspective. *Developmental Psychology, 27,* 27–32.

Lerner, R. M. (1996). Relative plasticity, integration, temporality, and diversity in human development: A developmental contextual perspective about theory, process, and method. *Developmental Psychology, 32,* 781–786.

Lerner, R. M. (1998). Theories of human development: Contemporary perspectives. In R. M. Lerner (Ed.), *The handbook of child psychology: Vol. 1. Theoretical models of human development* (5th ed., pp. 1–24). New York: Wiley.

Lerner, R. M. (2002). *Concepts and theories of human development* (3rd ed.). Mahwah, NJ: Erlbaum.

LeVine, R. A. (1973). *Culture, behavior, and personality.* Chicago: Aldine.

LeVine, R. A., Dixon, S., LeVine, S., Richman, A., Leiderman, P. H., Keefer, C., & Brazelton, T. B. (1994). *Child care and culture: Lessons from Africa.* Cambridge, UK: Cambridge University Press.

Lord, A. B. (1965). *Singer of tales.* New York: Methuen.

Maasten, A. (Ed.). (1999). *Cultural processes in child development: The Minnesota symposia on child psychology: Vol. 29.* Mahwah, NJ: Erlbaum.

Mandler, J., & Johnson, N. (1977). Remembrance of things parsed: Story structure and recall. *Cognitive Psychology, 9,* 111–151.

Markus, H. R., & Kitayama, S. (1991). Culture and the self: Implications for cognition, emotion, and motivation. *Psychological Review, 98,* 224–253.

Markus, H. R., & Kitayama, S. (1994). The cultural construction of self and emotion: Implications for social behavior. In S. Kitayama & H. R. Markus (Eds.), *Emotion and culture: Empirical studies of mutual influence* (pp. 89–130). Washington, DC: American Psychological Association.

Markus, H. R., Mullally, P. R., & Kitayama, S. (1997). Self ways: Diversity in modes of cultural participation. In U. Neisser & D. A. Jopling (Eds.), *The conceptual self in context: Culture, experience, self-understanding* (pp. 13–61). Cambridge: Cambridge University Press.

Marriott, M. (1989). Constructing an Indian ethnosociology. In M. Marriott (Ed.), *India through Hindu categories* (pp. 1–39). New Delhi, India: Sage.

Marsella, A. J. (1998). Toward a "global-community psychology": Meeting the needs of a changing world. *American Psychologist, 53*(2), 1282–1291.

Matsuyama, U. K. (1983). Can story grammar speak Japanese? *The Reading Teacher, 36,* 666–669.

McLloyd, V. C. (1990). Minority children: Introduction to the special issue. *Child Development, 61*(2), 263–266.

McLloyd, V. C. (1998). Children in poverty: Development, public policy, and practice. In W. Damon (Series Ed.) & I. E. Sigel & K. A. Renninger (Vol. Eds.), *Handbook of child psychology: Vol. 4. Child psychology in practice* (pp. 135–210). New York, NY: Wiley.

McNamee, G. (1987). The social origins of narrative skills. In M. Hickman (Ed.), *Social and functional approaches to language and thought* (pp. 287–304). San Diego: Academic Press.

Michaels, S. (1991). The dismantling of narrative. In A. McCabe & C. Peterson's (Eds.), *Developing narrative structure* (pp. 303–351). Hillsdale, NJ: Erlbaum.

Miller, J. G. (1997). Theoretical issues in cultural psychology. In J. W. Berry, Y. H. Poortinga, J. Pandey, P. R. Dasen, T. S. Saraswathi, M. H. Segall, & C. Kagitçibasi, (Series Eds.) & J. W. Berry, Y. H. Poortinga, & J. Pandey (Vol. Eds.), *Handbook of cross-cultural psychology: Vol. 1. Theory and method* (2nd ed., pp. 85–128). Needham Heights, MA: Allyn and Bacon.

Miller, P. J., & Goodnow, J. J. (1995). Cultural practices: Toward an integration of culture and development. In J. J. Goodnow, P. J. Miller, & F. Kessel (Eds.), *Cultural practices as contexts for development* (pp. 5–16). San Francisco: Jossey-Bass.

Minami, M., & McCabe, A. (1991). Haiku as a discourse regulation device: A stanza analysis of Japanese children's personal narratives. *Language in Society, 20,* 577–599.

Mishra, R. C. (1997). Cognition and cognitive development. In J. W. Berry, Y. H. Poortinga, J. Pandey, P. R. Dasen, T. S. Saraswathi, M. H. Segall, & C. Kagitçibasi (Series Eds.) & J. W. Berry, P. R. Dasen, & T. S. Saraswathi (Vol. Eds.), *Handbook of cross-cultural psychology: Vol. 2. Basic processes and human development* (2nd ed., pp. 143–175). Needham Heights, MA: Allyn and Bacon.

Mistry, J. (1993). Cultural context in the development of children's narratives. In J. Altaribba (Ed.), *Cognition and culture: A cross-cultural approach to cognitive psychology* (pp. 207–228). Amsterdam, The Netherlands: Elsevier Press.

Mistry, J. (1997). The development of remembering in cultural context. In N. Cowan (Ed.), *The development of memory in children* (pp. 343–368). Sussex, UK: Pyschology Press.

Mistry, J., & Rogoff, B. (1994). Remembering in cultural context. In W. Lonner & R. Malpass (Eds.), *Psychology and culture* (pp. 139–144). Needham Heights, MA: Allyn and Bacon.

Mohanty, A. K., & Perregaux, C. (1997). Language acquisition and bilingualism. In J. W. Berry, Y. H. Poortinga, J. Pandey, P. R. Dasen, T. S. Saraswathi, M. H. Segall, & C. Kagitçibasi (Series Eds.) & J. W. Berry, P. R. Dasen, & T. S. Saraswathi (Vol. Eds.), *Handbook of cross-cultural psychology: Vol. 2. Basic processes and human development* (2nd ed., pp. 217–253). Needham Heights, MA: Allyn and Bacon.

Neisser, U., & Jopling, D. A. (Eds.). (1997). *The conceptual self in context: Culture, experience, self-understanding* (pp. 13–61). Cambridge: Cambridge University Press.

Nichols, P. C. (1989). Storytelling in Carolina: Continuities and contrasts. *Anthropology and Education Quarterly, 20,* 232–245.

Nsamenang, B. A., & Lamb, M. E. (1994). Socialization of Nso children in the Bamenda grassfields of northwest Cameroon. In P. M. Greenfield & R. R. Cocking (Eds.), *Cross-cultural roots of minority child development* (pp. 133–146). Hillsdale, NJ: Erlbaum.

Paris, S. G., Newman, D. R., & Jacobs, J. E. (1985). Social contexts and functions of children's remembering. In C. J. Brainerd & M. Pressley (Eds.), *Cognitive learning and memory in children* (pp. 81–115). New York: Springer-Verlag.

Perlmutter, M. (1988). Research on memory and its development: Past, present and future. In F. E. Weinert & M. Perlmutter (Eds.), *Memory development: Universal changes and individual differences* (pp. 353–380). Hillsdale, NJ: Erlbaum.

Peterson, C., & McCabe, A. (1983). *Developmental psycholinguistics: Three ways of looking at a child's narrative.* New York: Plenum.

Poortinga, Y. H. (1992). Towards a conceptualization of culture for psychology. *Cross-Cultural Psychology Bulletin, 24*(3), 2–10.

Poortinga, Y. H. (1997). Towards convergence. In J. W. Berry, Y. H. Poortinga, J. Pandey, P. R. Dasen, T. S. Saraswathi, M. H. Segall, & C. Kagitçibasi (Series Eds.) & J. W. Berry, Y. H. Poortinga, J. Pandey (Vol. Eds.), *Handbook of cross-cultural psychology: Vol. 1. Theory and method* (2nd ed., pp. 347–387). Needham Heights, MA: Allyn and Bacon.

Ramanujam, A. K. (1989). Is there an Indian way of thinking? An informal essay. In M. Marriott (Ed.), *India through Hindu categories* (pp. 41–58). New Delhi, India: Sage Publications.

Ramanujam, B. K. (1979). Toward maturity: Problems of identity seen in the Indian clinical setting. In S. Kakar (Ed.), *Identity and adulthood* (pp. 37–55). Delhi, India: Oxford University Press.

Rodino, A., Gimbert, C., Perez, C., & McCabe, A. (1991). *Getting your point across: Contrastive sequencing in low-income African-American and Latino children's personal narratives.* Paper presented at the Boston University Conference on Language Development, Boston, MA.

Rogoff, B. (1981). Schooling and the development of cognitive skills. In H. C. Triandis & A. Heron (Eds.), *Handbook of cross-cultural psychology: Vol. 4: Developmental Psychology.* (pp. 233–294). Rockleigh, NJ: Allyn and Bacon.

Rogoff, B. (1990). *Apprenticeship in thinking.* New York: Oxford University Press.

Rogoff, B. (1998). Cognition as a collaborative process. In W. Damon (Series Ed.) & D. Kuhn & R. S. Siegler (Vol. Eds.), *Handbook of child psychology: Vol. 2. Cognition, perception, and language* (pp. 679–744). New York: Wiley.

Rogoff, B., & Chavajay, P. (1995). What's become of research on the cultural basis of cognitive development? *American Psychologist, 50* (10), 859–877.

Rogoff, B., & Gardner, W. P. (1984). Adult guidance of cognitive development. In B. Rogoff & J. Lave (Eds.), *Everyday cognition: Its development in social context* (pp. 95–116). Cambridge, MA: Harvard University Press.

Rogoff, B., & Mistry, J. (1985). Memory development in cultural context. In M. Pressley & C. Brainerd (Eds.), *Cognitive learning and memory in children* (pp. 117–142). New York: Springer-Verlag.

Rogoff, B., & Mistry, J. (1990). The social and functional context of children's memory skills. In R. Fivush, J. Hudson, & U. Neisser (Eds.), *Knowing and remembering in young children* (pp. 197–222). New York: Cambridge University Press.

Rogoff, B., Mistry, J., Göncü, A., & Mosier, C. (1993). Guided participation in cultural activity by toddlers and caregivers. *Monographs of the Society for Research in Child Development, 58* (8, Serial No. 236).

Rumelhart, D. E. (1975). Notes on a schema for stories. In D. G. Bobrow & A. Collins (Eds.), *Representation and understanding: Studies in cognitive science* (pp. 211–237). New York: Academic Press.

Sachs, J. (1983). Talking about the there and then: The emergence of displaced reference in parent-child discourse. In K. Nelson (Ed.), *Children's language: Vol. 4* (pp. 1–28). Hillsdale, NJ: Erlbaum.

Sagi, A. (1990). Attachment theory and research from a cross-cultural perspective. *Human Development, 33,* 10–22.

Sameroff, A. J. (1983). Developmental systems: Contexts and evolution. In W. Kessen (Ed.), *Handbook of child psychology: Vol. 1. History, theory, and methods* (pp. 237–294). New York: Wiley.

Saraswathi, T. S., & Dasen, P. R. (1997). Introduction. In J. W. Berry, Y. H. Poortinga, J. Panday, P. R. Dasen, & T. S. Saraswathi, M. Segall, & C. Kagitçibasi (Series Eds.) & J. W. Berry, P. R. Dasen, & T. S. Saraswathi (Vol. Eds.), *Handbook of cross-cultural psychology: Vol. 2. Basic processes and human development* (pp. 1–28). Needham Heights, MA: Allyn and Bacon.

Schieffelin, B. B., & Ochs, E. (Eds.). (1986). *Language socialization across cultures.* Cambridge, UK: Cambridge University Press.

Schneider, W., & Bjorklund, D. F. (1998). Memory. In W. Damon (Series Ed.) & D. Kuhn & R.S. Siegler (Vol. Eds.), *Handbook of child psychology: Vol. 2. Cognition, perception, and language* (5th ed., pp. 467–). New York: Wiley.

Schneider, W., & Pressley, M. (1989). *Memory development between 2 and 20.* New York: Springer-Verlag.

Scribner, S., & Cole, M. (1981). *The psychology of literacy.* Cambridge, MA: Harvard University Press.

Segall, M. H. (1984). More than we need to know about culture, but are afraid to ask. *Journal of Cross-cultural Psychology, 15* (2), 153–162.

Segall, M. H., Campbell, D. T., & Herskovits, M. J. (1966). *The influence of culture on visual perception.* Indianapolis, IN: Bobbs-Merrill.

Segall, M. H., Dasen, P. R., Berry, J. W., & Poortinga, Y. H. (1999). *Human behavior in global perspective.* New York: Elmsford.

Segall, M. H., Lonner, W. J., & Berry, J. W. (1998). Cross-cultural psychology as a scholarly discipline: On the flowering of culture in behavioral research. *American Psychologist, 53* (10), 1101–1110.

Serpell, R. (1977). Strategies for investigating intelligence in its cultural context. *The Quarterly Newsletter of the Laboratory for Comparative Human Development, 1,* 11–15.

Serpell, R., & Hatano, G. (1997). Education, schooling, and literacy. In J. W. Berry, Y. H. Poortinga, J. Panday, P. R. Dasen, T. S. Saraswathi, M. Segall, & C. Kagitçibasi (Series Eds.) & J. W. Berry, P. R. Dasen, & T. S. Saraswathi (Vol. Eds.), *Handbook of cross-cultural psychology: Vol. 2. Basic processes and human development* (pp. 339–376). Needham Heights, MA: Allyn and Bacon.

Sharp, D., Cole, M., & Lave, J. (1979). Education and cognitive development: The evidence from experimental research. *Monographs of the Society for Research in Child Development, 44* (1–2, Serial No. 178).

Shweder, R. A. (1990). Cultural psychology: What is it? In J. W. Stigler & G. Herdt (Eds.), *Cultural psychology: Essays on comparative human development* (pp. 1–43). Cambridge, MA: Cambridge University Press.

Shweder, R. A. (1991). *Thinking through cultures: Expeditions in cultural psychology.* Cambridge, MA: Harvard University Press.

Shweder, R. A., & Bourne, E. J. (1991). Does the concept of the person vary cross-culturally? In R. A. Shweder (Ed.), *Thinking through cultures: Expeditions in cultural psychology* (pp. 113–155). Cambridge, MA: Harvard University Press.

Shweder, R. A., Goodnow, J., Hatano, G., LeVine, R. A., Markus, H., & Miller, P. (1998). The cultural psychology of development: One mind, many mentalities. In R. L. Lerner (Ed.), *Handbook of child psychology: Vol. 1. Theoretical models of human development* (pp. 865–938). New York: Wiley.

Shweder, R. A., & Miller, J. G. (1991). The social construction of the person: How is it possible? In R. A. Shweder (Ed.), *Thinking through cultures: Expeditions in cultural psychology* (pp. 156–185). Cambridge, MA: Harvard University Press.

Sinha, D. (1986). *Psychology in a third world country: The Indian experience.* New Delhi, India: Sage.

Sinha, D. (1997). Indigenizing psychology. In J. W. Berry, Y. H. Poortinga, J. Panday, P. R. Dasen, T. S. Saraswathi, M. Segall, & C. Kagitçibasi (Series Eds.) & J. W. Berry, Y. H. Poortinga, & J. Pandey (Vol. Eds.), *Handbook of cross-cultural psychology: Vol. 1. Theory and method* (2nd ed., pp. 129–170.) Needham Heights, MA: Allyn and Bacon.

Sinha, D., & Tripathi, R. C. (1994). Individualism in a collectivist culture: A case of coexistence of opposites. In U. Kim, H. C. Triandis, C. Kagitçibasi, S. C. Choi, & G. Yoon (Eds.), *Individualism and collectivism: Theory, method and applications* (pp. 123–136). London: Sage.

Sinha, J. B. P. (1980). *The nurturant task leader.* New Delhi, India: Concept Publishing House.

Slobin, D. I. (Ed.). (1992). *The cross-linguistic study of language acquisition.* Hillsdale, NJ: Erlbaum.

Snow, C. E. (1989). Understanding social interaction and language acquisition; sentences are not enough. In M. H. Bornstein & J. S. Bruner (Eds.), *Interaction in human development* (pp. 83–103). New Jersey: LEA.

Snow, C. E., & Goldfield, B. A. (1983). Turn the page please: Situation-specific language acquisition. *Journal of child language, 10*(3), 551–569.

Stein, N. L. (1988). The development of children's storytelling skill. In M. B. Franklin & S. S. Barten (Eds.), *Child language: A reader* (pp. 282–297). New York: Oxford University Press.

Super, C., & Harkness, S. (1986). Developmental niche: A conceptualization at the interface of child and culture. *International Journal of Behavioral Development, 9,* 545–569.

Tharp, R., & Gallimore, R. (1988). *Rousing minds to life: Teaching, learning, and schooling in social context.* Cambridge, UK: Cambridge University Press.

Thelen, E., & Smith, L. B. (1998). Dynamic systems theories. In W. Damon (Series Ed.) & R. M. Lerner (Vol. Ed.), *Handbook of child psychology: Vol. 1. Theoretical models of human development* (5th ed., pp. 563–633). New York: Wiley.

Thompson, R. (1998). Early sociopersonality development. In W. Damon (Series Ed.) & N. Eisenberg (Vol. Ed.), *Handbook of child psychology: Vol. 3. Social, emotional, and personality development* (5th ed., pp. 25–104). New York: Wiley.

Triandis, H. C. (1980). Introduction to handbook of cross-cultural psychology. In H. C. Triandis & W. W. Lambert (Eds.), *Handbook of cross-cultural psychology: Vol. 1. Perspectives* (pp. 1–14). Boston, MA: Allyn and Bacon.

Triandis, H. C. (1989). The self and social behavior in differing cultural contexts. *Psychological Review, 96*(3), 506–520.

Triandis, H. C. (1994). Culture and social behavior. In W. J. Lonner & R. Malpass (Eds.), *Psychology and culture* (pp. 169–174). Needham Heights, MA: Allyn and Bacon.

Tylor, E. B. (1958). *The origins of culture.* New York: Harper and Row. (Original work published 1871)

Valsiner, J. (1989). *Human development and culture.* Toronto: Lexington Books.

Van Ijzendoorn, M. H., & Kroonenberg, P. M. (1988). Cross-cultural patterns of attachment: A meta-analysis of the Strange Situation. *Child Development, 59,* 147–156.

Vygotsky, L. S. (1978). *Mind in society: The development of higher psychological processes.* Cambridge, MA: Harvard University Press.

Wagner, D. (1981). Culture and memory development. In H. C. Triandis & A. Heron (Eds.), *Handbook of cross-cultural psychology: Vol. 4. Developmental Psychology* (pp. 187–232). Boston, MA: Allyn and Bacon.

Wagner, D. (1993). *Literacy, culture, and development: Becoming literate in Morocco.* Cambridge: Cambridge University Press.

Watson, K. (1975). Transferable communicative routines: Strategies and group identity in two speech events. *Language in Society, 4*(1), 53–72.

Weinert, F. E., & Perlmutter, M. (Eds.). (1988). *Memory development: Universal changes and individual differences.* Hillsdale, NJ: Erlbaum.

Wellman, H. M. (1988). The early development of memory strategies. In F. E. Weinert & M. Perlmutter (Eds.), *Memory development: Universal changes and individual differences* (pp. 3–30). Hillsdale, NJ: Erlbaum.

Wertsch, J. V. (1978). Adult-child interaction and the roots of metacognition. *Quarterly Newsletter of the Institute for Comparative Human Development, 2,* 15–18.

Wertsch, J. V. (1985). *Culture, communication, and cognition: Vygotskian perspectives.* New York: Cambridge University Press.

Wertsch, J. V. (1991). *Voices of the mind.* Cambridge, MA: Harvard University Press.

Wertsch, J. V. (1995). The need for action in sociocultural research. In J. V. Werstch, P. del Rio, & A. Alvarez (Eds.), *Sociocultural studies of the mind* (pp. 56–74). New York: Cambridge University Press.

Wertsch, J. V., & Tulviste, P. (1992). L. S. Vygotsky and contemporary developmental psychology. *Developmental Psychology, 28*(4), 548–557.

Whiting, B. B. (1976). The problem of the packaged variable. In K. F. Riegel & J. A. Meacham (Eds.), *The developing individual in a changing world.* Chicago, IL: Aldine.

Whiting, B. B., & Whiting, J. W. (1975). *Children of six cultures: A psycho-cultural analysis.* Cambridge, MA: Harvard University Press.

Wozniak, R. H., & Fischer, K. W. (1993). *Development in context: Acting and thinking in specific environments.* Hillsdale, NJ: Erlbaum.

PART FOUR

ADOLESCENCE

CHAPTER 12

Puberty, Sexuality, and Health

ELIZABETH J. SUSMAN, LORAH D. DORN, AND VIRGINIA L. SCHIEFELBEIN

Puberty, the passage from childhood to adulthood, fascinates scientists, parents, and adolescents alike. This fascination originates from its complexity, rapid and pervasive physical growth, profound psychological changes, and sexual awakening. Puberty is perceived to contribute to the turbulence and stress experienced by some adolescents.

Fortunately, over the last few decades, the conception of adolescence as a period of storm and stress (Blos, 1962; Hall, 1904) is being replaced by a more balanced view of adolescence as a period when biological, cognitive, emotional, and social functioning becomes reorganized. The majority of adolescents are viewed as experiencing neither maladjustment nor grossly undesirable behaviors.

Along with the reconceptualization of adolescence great strides have been made in developing interdisciplinary models of puberty that realistically portray the diversity of pathways through which adolescents progress from childhood to adulthood. Because of the myriad biological and psychological changes that characterize it, puberty engenders scientific interests that span the social, behavioral, medical and life sciences. Research foci include the biological and social

mechanisms that initiate puberty, the timing of puberty, and the interactive influences among hormones, physical growth changes, emotions, problem behavior, cognition, and sexual activity. This chapter presents a summary of two predominant models of development at puberty as well as current perspectives on the biological processes of puberty, timing of puberty and psychological development, secular trends in timing of puberty, puberty and sexuality, and implications for theory, research, and social policy.

THEORIES AND MODELS OF PUBERTY
AND ADJUSTMENT

The biological processes of puberty historically were integrated with the psychological processes at a conceptual level. In fact, in the early twentieth century perspectives on adolescent development featured the centrality of biological processes in psychological development. In contrast, at an empirical level, research tended to focus either on biological and health issues or on social, emotional, and contextual processes in adolescent development but seldom on the interactions between biological, psychological, and contextual processes. Contextualism, behaviorism, and learning theory supplanted theories of development and evolution that dominated the early twentieth century (S. T. Parker, 2000). The empirical research reflected the predominant interest in contextual influences on development.

A turning point in the integration of puberty with biological, psychological, and contextual processes was the publication of *Girls at Puberty* (Brooks-Gunn & Petersen, 1983), followed shortly thereafter by models that incorporated the reciprocal interactions among biological, psychological, and contextual processes that contribute to the experience of puberty (Lerner & Foch, 1987; D. Magnusson, 1981; D. Magnusson, Stattin, & Allen, 1985). Subsequent to the articulation of these theories, empirical studies linking puberty-related hormones and psychological development began to appear in the literature. These studies addressed issues of aggressive behavior (Susman et al., 1985, 1987), adjustment (Nottelmann et al., 1987), depressed mood (Brooks-Gunn & Warren, 1989), and sexuality (Udry, Billy, & Morris, 1986; Udry, Billy, Morris, Groff, & Raj, 1985; Udry & Talbert, 1988). These studies integrated rather than compartmentalized psychological, biological, and contextual influences on development.

An early example of this integration was the recognition of the interdependence of family interactions and the adolescent's stage of pubertal development (e.g., Steinberg, 1988; Steinberg & Hill, 1978). In later theoretical perspectives integrating biological and psychological processes, no single level of functioning is viewed as primary or as the ultimate causal influence on development. Rather, development is characterized by reciprocal interaction, bidirectionality, plasticity, and organization (Cairns, 1997; Cairns & Rodkin, 1998; Lerner, 1998; D. Magnusson & Stattin, 1998). Systems or configural views of development are considered paramount with processes from different levels viewed as equal forces in development (Ford & Lerner, 1992; Susman, 1998). Within this perspective, the physical maturational, hormonal, and psychological processes of puberty interact to create the diversity of changes at adolescence.

Two compatible and overlapping theoretical perspectives exemplify the integration of biological, psychological, and contextual influences on adolescent development: developmental contextualism and holistic interactionism.

Developmental Contextualism

The developmental contextualism model of adolescence, proposed by Lerner (1998), parallels modern life-span developmental theories. The life-span perspective is a set of ideas about the nature of human development and change from birth to death. This perspective is concerned with issues of the embeddedness of evolution and ontogeny, of consistency and change, of human plasticity, and of the role the developing person plays in his or her own development (Lerner, 1987). Within the developmental contextual perspective, individuals are viewed as producers of their own development (Brandtstaedter & Lerner, 1999): The theory embodies the notion of the dynamic interactions between individuals and the multiple contexts within which they live. With reference to adolescence, the biological changes of puberty both influence and reciprocally are influenced by psychological, behavioral, and social influences (Lerner, 1987; Lerner & Foch, 1987). Key concepts of the developmental contextualism perspective relevant to puberty are embeddedness, dynamic interactionism, and plasticity.

Embeddedness encompasses the notion that the phenomena of human life exist at multiple levels of being: inner-biological, individual-psychological, social network, community, societal, cultural, and the larger physical ecology and historical contexts. The biological, psychological, and social aspects of change are embedded in the contexts of development. Contexts of development include family, peers, and the multiple social institutions that surround the developing individual. The levels are not interdependent; rather, the processes at one level influence and are influenced by the processes at the other levels.

Dynamic interactionism refers to the dynamic interaction among the levels of analysis. This concept is especially central to integrating the biological and social contextual aspects of pubertal development. In contrast to a previous view that biological processes are deterministic or causal, dynamic interaction concepts embody the notion that biological processes and substances are dynamic and simultaneously influence and are influenced by the psychological and social contextual levels of analysis. For instance, genes no longer are considered purely deterministic influences on development. Instead, they are viewed as requiring a specific environment to be expressed. Furthermore, genetic influences are not static but shift with development (Rowe, 1999). Genes responsible for pubertal development, such as genes related to gonadotropin releasing hormone (GnRH), begin to express mRNA in late childhood, leading to a cascade of hormonal growth and psychological changes. Genes, the individual, and the environment consistently are in a state of dynamic interaction.

Plasticity evolves from the notion that the potential for change exists across the life span in the multiple levels of organization that characterize the developing human (Lerner,

1998). Contemporary theorists emphasize *relative* plasticity throughout the life span (Lerner, 1998). Relative plasticity implies that across the lifetime, intra-individual development is constrained. All developmental modifications are not possible, and all possible variations are not desirable (Brandtstaedter, 1998). Development and systematic change have constraints imposed both from endogenous (e.g., genetic) and exogenous (e.g., legal sanctions) constraints.

With regard to puberty, social and nutritional circumstances affect the timing of puberty, yet the normal age range for the onset of puberty is constrained by genetic influences. The normative current age range varies from 9 to 15 years for girls and 10 to 16 for boys, although this range may be broadening (see the section titled "Phases of Puberty: Adrenarche and Gonadarche"). Beyond this age range, plasticity in the timing of puberty becomes replaced by an abnormal or pathophysiological condition that requires evaluation and intervention. In brief, only a subset of variations in puberty is compatible with the natural laws of development.

Plasticity is influenced by the individual's experiential history in interaction with the multiple contexts of development. Behaviors, social contexts, and nutrition are hypothesized to affect the relative plasticity of timing of puberty. For instance, boys with a history of aggressive, disruptive behavior with peers and family were later in their pubertal development and were lower on testosterone than were their nondisruptive peers (Schaal, Tremblay, Soussignan, & Susman, 1996). Overall, the study of plasticity involves scrutiny of the history of dynamic organism-context interactions or the fusion of nature and nurture (Lerner, 1998). Plasticity is a feature neither of nature nor of nurture but rather the fusion of the dynamic interactions between nature and nurture.

Viewed from the developmental contextualism perspective, development at puberty is the product of the dynamic interactions among psychological, biological, and contextual processes. These processes reciprocally and bidirectionally influence each other (Lerner & Foch, 1987). Processes at different levels of functioning are not independent but are merged throughout puberty. The physical and hormonal manifestations of puberty are a product of a species genotype. Yet the experiential history of adolescents and the contexts for social interactions can interact with genes to change the timing and tempo of puberty. Puberty is, then, a process of change and the product of a complex interaction among genotype, brain-behavior, and context. No one research project can test these multiple reciprocal influences on adolescent development. Rather, the developmental contextual model acts as a guide for selecting constructs and measures to

be considered in the conceptual framework and design of a specific study.

Holistic Interactionism

A basic proposition of holistic interactionism's theoretical framework is that the individual is an active, intentional part of an integrated complex, dynamic, and adaptive person-environment system who develops in that context from the fetal period until death (D. Magnusson, 1999). The holistic interactionism model of development can be summarized in a set of fundamental principles (D. Magnusson & Cairns, 1996): An individual (a) develops as an integrated organism (b) in a dynamic, continuous, and reciprocal process of interaction with the environment. This functioning (c) depends on and influences the reciprocal interaction among subsystems within the individual (perceptual, cognitive, emotional, physiological, morphological, and neurobiological). (d) Novel patterns of functioning arise during ontogeny, and (e) differences in the rates of development, such as differences in timing of puberty, may produce differences in the organization and configuration of psychological functions that are (f) extremely sensitive to the environmental circumstances in which they are formed, particularly the environment as it is perceived and interpreted by the individual. It follows that an individual is viewed as an active, intentional part of an integrated complex, dynamic, and adaptive person-environment system.

Furthermore, within this person-environment system, the individual functions and develops as an integrated organism in which biological, psychological, and behavioral factors operate in reciprocal interaction and dependency within integrated multidetermined, dynamic, and adaptive processes (Magnusson, 1999). Each aspect of the structures and processes that are operating in the individual (perceptions, plans, values, goals, motives, biological factors, and conduct), as well as each aspect of the environment, takes on meaning from its role in the total functioning of the individual. A specific element derives its significance not from its structure or function per se, but from its role in the system of which it forms a part. From a holistic interactionism perspective, development at puberty takes on meaning not from physical change per se but from its meaning to the adolescent in relation to psychological attributes, experiences, the timing of the change relative to peers, and its role as a social signal. Physical development is a signal that a child is becoming an adolescent, and this new status implies new social roles and responsibilities in the societal and cultural system in which the individual develops.

The holistic nature of the functioning of the integrated organism is that normally a psychological-biological process cannot be determined by a single factor. As a consequence of the holistic nature of humans, the processes cannot be subdivided into independent parts in the analysis of the integrated organism's way of functioning. To understand and explain the role of a specific element in the functioning and development of an individual, it has to be analyzed in the context of the relevant system to which it belongs. Applied to the current instance, psychological and behavioral processes at puberty (e.g., aggressive behavior) cannot be understood without an awareness of the biological and contextual processes that simultaneously influence the adolescent. These processes range from the molecular and cellular levels to the level of the individual as an active, intentional part of an integrated sociocultural person-environment system.

Within a holistic interactionist view, developmental processes are accessible to systematic, scientific inquiry because they occur in a specific way within organized structures and are guided by specific principles. The claim for a holistic view on individual development implies that any theoretical or empirical analysis of developmental processes has to be performed with reference to a complex set of phenomena. This view does not imply that all aspects of puberty need to be considered simultaneously. Rather, the interpretation of findings at one level of functioning should be made by integrating the findings to levels above and below the level of empirical verification. An investigation of hormones at the physiological level and emotions at the psychological level can more meaningfully be interpreted by simultaneously considering the social (peer or family) levels of analysis.

WHAT IS PUBERTY?

Puberty encompasses a wide variety of phenomena, as reflected in the following definition: "Puberty is a transitional period between childhood and adulthood, during which a growth spurt occurs, secondary sexual characteristics appear, fertility is achieved, and profound psychological changes take place" (National Research Council, 1999, p. 1).

Phases of Puberty: Adrenarche and Gonadarche

Historically, puberty refers to the stage of development characterized by maturation of the reproductive system. Puberty now is considered to have two components, adrenarche and gonadarche, which are thought to be independent events controlled by separate mechanisms (Counts et al., 1987), although the mechanisms separating these periods remain controversial.

The first component of puberty, *adrenarche* (awakening of the adrenal glands), begins between the ages of 6 and 9 years. At adrenarche, the adrenal androgen concentrations begin to rise (Forest, 1989; Grumbach & Styne, 1992), but hormones of the hypothalamic-pituitary-gonadal (HPG) axis, testosterone and estrogen, are initially quiescent. The adrenal androgens continue to increase throughout gonadarche and include dehydroepiandrosterone (DHEA), dehydroepiandrosterone sulphate (DHEAS) and androstenedione (Δ4-A). The initial hormonal increases in adrenal androgen secretion occur prior to external physical changes, such as pubic hair development. The exact mechanism responsible for the onset of adrenarche is controversial, although recent evidence suggests that adrenocorticotropic hormone (ACTH; Weber, Clark, Perry, Honour, & Savage, 1997) or 3-hydroxysteroid dehydrogenase plays a significant role in the regulation of adrenarche (Gell et al., 1998). Adrenarche is severely understudied in relation to emotions and behavior change, an unfortunate happenstance given findings linking adrenarche and behavior (Brooks-Gunn & Warren, 1989; Susman et al., 1987). In addition, a recent study showed that premature-adrenarche children have significantly more behavior problems and psychopathology than do age-matched peers (Dorn, Hitt, & Rotenstein, 1999). (Findings relating adrenal androgens to behavior are discussed later.)

The second component of puberty, *gonadarche,* is the reactivation of the hypothalamic-pituitary gonadotropin-gonadal system, which initially had been activated during fetal and early infant development. Gonadarche begins at approximately age 9 to 10 years in White girls and at 8 to 9 years in African American girls (Herman-Giddens et al., 1997) and at 10 to 11 years in boys (Grumbach & Styne, 1992). Gonadarche is what most individuals refer to as "puberty" and entails sexual maturation and reproductive maturity. At gonadarche, HPG-axis activation and physical maturation result in the development of the primary sexual characteristics (testes and ovaries) and secondary sexual characteristics (pubic hair, body hair, and genital and breast growth). The culmination of gonadarche and reproductive function is menarche for girls and spermarche for boys.

Mechanisms Controlling the Onset of Puberty

Neural Control of Puberty

In the last two decades major advances have been made in explaining the physiology of puberty from the molecular level to the whole-organism level. Given that puberty (gonadarche) marks the development of reproductive capability, the physiology of puberty becomes synonymous with that of reproductive maturation. Gonadarche occurs when the

GnRH pulse generator (neurons in the medial basal hypothalamus) is reactivated or reaugmented (Knobil, 1988; Medhamurthy, Gay, & Plant, 1990; Tersawa, Bridson, Nass, Noonan, & Dierschke, 1984) and gonadal sex steroid hormone secretion increases. The mechanism for understanding the control system that defines timing of puberty and the neurobiological basis of this reaugmentation of the GnRH pulse generator continues to be speculative (Plant, 1995; Suter, Pohl, & Plant, 1998). Much of what we do know about puberty is based on a nonhuman primate model. In humans, research on the onset of puberty is much more difficult to carry out because frequent serial sampling of blood at night in prepubertal children is required as gonadotropin pulsatile secretion first occurs at night. In addition, very sensitive assays are required for detection of low concentrations of gonadotropins and gonadal steroids. Thus, few human studies are available on the onset of puberty, and in those that do exist, the sample size is small and not likely to be representative of the general population.

Hormone and growth changes at puberty are the consequence of complicated neuroendocrine processes. In the early days of research on the endocrine component of puberty, the emphasis was on specific releasing hormones or specific hormones such as testosterone and estrogen. The emphasis now is on the neural (Plant, 1998) and genetic control of puberty. Specifically, the identification of specific genes and the expression of genes responsible for the onset and progression of puberty now are the focus of study. Given these advances, the most widely accepted explanation of the onset of puberty is the expression of genes controlling the GnRH pulse generator and the reactivation of the HPG axis. In addition, the cortex, limbic system, and neurotransmitter systems modulate hypothalamic function (Brooks-Gunn & Reiter, 1990) and thus puberty.

Weight, Body Fat, and the Onset of Puberty

Various theories posit additional factors contributing to the onset of puberty in combination with programmed genetic influences. One earlier theory posits that critical body mass must be attained before puberty (specifically, menarche as an index of puberty) will occur (Frisch, 1984). The findings indicated that menarche is dependent on the maintenance of a minimum weight for height, likely representing a critical fat storage level (Frisch & McArthur, 1974). Undernutrition also delays puberty in boys. Fat may influence reproductive ability in girls through two mechanisms: (a) Fat converts androgens to estrogens that are critical to regular menstrual cycles and the maintenance of pregnancy, and (b) relative fatness influences the direction of estrogen metabolism from its least

to most potent form (Frisch, 1984). It was hypothesized that absolute and relative amounts of fat are important because the individual must be large enough to reproduce successfully. This theory largely fell from wide acceptance. Somatic growth and maturation at puberty are now considered to be influenced by several additional factors that act interdependently to influence the onset of puberty.

Leptin and Puberty

Discovery of the hormone leptin led to the theory that it may be a signal allowing for the initiation of and progression toward puberty (Mantzoros, Flier, & Rogol, 1997). An alternative perspective is that leptin is implicated in the onset of puberty but may not be the cause of the onset. Leptin is a 16-kDa adipocyte-secreted protein, a product of the obesity gene. Serum leptin levels reflect mainly the amount of energy stores but are also influenced by short-term energy imbalance as well as several cytokines (indexes of immune system function) and hormones (Mantzoros, 2000). Leptin is implicated in the initiation of puberty, energy expenditure, normal menstrual cycles, fertility, maintenance of pregnancy, and nutrition. Specifically, leptin may well be one of the messenger molecules signaling the adequacy of the fat stores for reproduction and maintenance of pregnancy at puberty (Kiess et al., 1999). The possible mechanism involves leptin as a hormone that serves to signal the brain with information on the critical amount of fat stores that are necessary for luteinizing hormone-releasing hormone (LHRH) secretion and activation of the hypothalamic-pituitary-adrenal (HPA) axis. Moreover, circadian and ultradian variations of leptin levels are also associated with minute-to-minute variations of LH and estradiol in normal women (Mantzoros, 2000). The mechanisms whereby leptin regulates body weight, adiposity, and the hormones that increase at puberty (e.g., testosterone and estrogen) are not yet known.

Controlling for adiposity, leptin is higher in girls than in boys (Blum et al., 1997). At the initiation of puberty, circulating leptin concentrations diverge in boys and girls. In boys leptin concentrations increase and then markedly decrease to prepubertal concentration levels in late puberty. In contrast, in girls there are increasing concentrations at puberty (Roemmich & Rogol, 1999). The increase in leptin is believed to result from alterations in the regional distribution of body fat in boys and girls at puberty. Overall, sex differences in leptin concentrations are accountable to differences in the amounts of subcutaneous fat in girls and greater androgen concentrations in boys (Roemmich et al., 1998).

The biological effects of leptin in adult humans are still to be determined, but reports show that congenital leptin deficiency leads to hyperphagia and excessive weight gain from early infancy onward as well as failure of pubertal onset in adolescence (Ong, Ahmed, & Dunger, 1999). Leptin concentrations also are higher in girls with premature adrenarche than in girls with on-time adrenarche (Cizza et al., 2001). Leptin concentrations have not yet been examined in relation to behavior changes at puberty, but leptin provides a promising biological probe for understanding physiological pubertal processes and issues of body image, self-esteem, and behavior at puberty.

Growth at Puberty

It is well known that pubertal growth includes a significant increase in height, or linear growth, as well as changes in body size and proportions. Puberty brings on the most rapid rate of linear growth since infancy (Rogol, Roemmich, & Clark, 1998). Rate of linear growth slows throughout childhood and reaches a low point just before the growth spurt (Tanner, 1989). The growth spurt refers to a rapid increase in linear growth at puberty. The timing and magnitude of the growth spurt is different for girls and boys. Girls grow an average of 25 cm with a peak rate of 9 cm per year at about age 12 (Marshall & Tanner, 1969). Boys grow more than girls, but their growth occurs later than in girls because they grow at an average of 28 cm with a peak rate of 10.3 cm per year at about age 14 (Marshall & Tanner, 1970). Tanner (1989) described much of what is known about growth and changes in physical proportions. The rapid increase in height in boys is largely due to faster growth in trunk length than in leg length, particularly since leg length peaks about 6 to 9 months before trunk length does (Tanner, 1989). However, the legs and trunk are not the only parts of the body that are growing. Adolescents show some increase in head diameter, an aspect of growth that has otherwise been basically dormant since the first few years of age. The skull bones also demonstrate an increase in thickness of about 15% (Tanner, 1989). Growth arrest occurs as a result of epiphyseal fusion (Cohen & Rosenfeld, 1996) or ossification (hardening) of the ends of long bones.

The main regulator of growth is growth hormone (GH), a hormone produced in the anterior pituitary. GH is secreted at puberty, first at night, followed by surges during the day in later stages of puberty. The hypothalamic hormones, growth hormone releasing hormone (GHRH) and somatostatin, stimulate and inhibit GH secretion, respectively (Cohen & Rosenfeld, 1996). The increase in GH at puberty parallels the growth spurt. Other endocrine factors influence growth, such as thyroid hormone and glucocorticoids. Sex steroids, primarily testosterone and estrogen, also facilitate growth at puberty. Many nonendocrine growth factors are implicated in

growth, the largest of which are genetic influences that control the growth rate, age of puberty, and adult height (Cohen & Rosenfeld, 1996). Growth also can be affected by nutrition, physical activity, and stressors.

In addition to height and other linear measurements, body weight increases dramatically during puberty. Fifty percent of adult body weight is gained during adolescence (Rogol et al., 1998). As with height, girls reach their peak growth in weight earlier than boys, but boys show a greater increase in weight than girls. Girls' average rate of weight gain peaks at 8.3 kg per year at about 12.5 years of age and about 6 months after their peak height increase (Barnes, 1975; Tanner, 1965). Boys' peak weight gain of 9 kg per year occurs at about the same time (14 years) as their peak increase in height (Barnes, 1975; Tanner, 1965).

Along with the increase in body weight, body composition also changes at puberty. The changes in body composition are quite different for boys and girls. Girls reach the fat-free mass of a young woman by about 15 to 16 years of age (Rogol et al., 1998). Fat mass also increases by about 1.14 kg per year, and it increases to a greater extent than the fat-free mass, meaning that girls have a net increase in percentage of body fat (Rogol et al., 1998). Girls' body fat is redistributed during puberty in a female-specific pattern. The deposition rate of subcutaneous fat on girls' limbs decreases (Tanner, 1989), while estrogens promote fat deposition at the breasts, thighs, and buttocks (Sherwood, 1993). Another source of the body mass increase in girls is a deposition of skeletal minerals. Girls accumulate almost one third of their total bone mineral within 3 to 4 years after beginning puberty (Bonjour, Theintz, Buchs, Slosman, & Rizzoli, 1991; Slemeda et al., 1994). The importance of emphasizing good nutrition and exercise in fostering bone accretion during puberty has not been public health policy. Therefore, an important opportunity to prevent osteoporosis later in development may have been missed by many women.

Body composition in boys follows a very different pattern. Boys' fat-free mass increases faster and for a longer period of time than in girls, and boys reach the fat-free mass of a young man at about 19 to 20 years of age (Rogol et al., 1998). During this time of increase in fat-free mass, boys maintain a fairly constant fat mass, so they show a net decrease in percentage of body fat (Rogol et al., 1998). The skeletal mineral accumulation in boys also differs from that of girls. Boys accumulate bone mineral content for a longer period of time after the pubertal growth spurt, and they have substantial increases in mineralization between 15 and 18 years of age (Rogol et al., 1998), which may explain the lower incidence of osteoporosis in men than in women.

The sex differences in growth and especially in body-composition changes during puberty result in the typical female and male body types (Rogol et al., 1998). There are other sex differences in how body and facial structure change during puberty in addition to the previously discussed differences in height, weight, fat-free mass, body fat and its distribution, and skeletal mineralization. Adolescent girls experience a large spurt in hip width, a spurt that is quantitatively as great as boys' growth even though girls' growth is less in almost all other dimensions (Tanner, 1989). Boys demonstrate a large increase in shoulder width (Tanner, 1989). The differences in these body proportions are due to the responsiveness of cartilage cells in the hip to estrogens and of the shoulder cartilage cells to androgens, particularly testosterone (Tanner, 1989). Another sex difference is that the later growth spurt of boys results in the greater leg length typical of males (Tanner, 1989): boys' legs grow for a longer period of time than do girls'. Finally, facial features change over the course of puberty, with the forehead becoming more prominent, the jaws growing forward, and facial muscles developing, although these changes tend to be much more pronounced in boys than in girls (Tanner, 1989). Facial structure in girls is rounder and softer than it is angular.

Secondary Sexual Characteristics

Secondary sexual characteristics refer to breast and pubic hair development in girls and genital and pubic hair development in boys. These changes have been carefully described and fall into five stages (Marshall & Tanner, 1969, 1970; pictures of these five stages appear in these references; see also Brooks-Gunn & Reiter, 1990). However, the description of stages of puberty has been done only for White adolescents; therefore, little information exists regarding pubertal changes in populations throughout the world. Adolescent, parent, or health-professional ratings of the five stages are frequently used in research assessing the relationship between pubertal development and psychological development, although the most well-accepted rating is that of a trained health care professional. Important to note is that there is wide variability in the timing and rate of pubertal development. This variability is normal yet may be distressful from the perspective of individual adolescents as their early or late maturation renders them different from same-age peers.

PUBERTY AND CHANGES IN EMOTIONS AND BEHAVIOR

Puberty long has been considered a progenitor of changes in moods and behavior. Until the last two decades, studies of behavior change at puberty considered only physical morphological characteristics in assessing biological change. These physical changes were considered in relation to

psychological processes and the various ecological contexts of development that included family, peers, neighborhood, and socioeconomic factors. This perspective now has been enriched by studies that include actual biological substances, such as hormones, that are essential for establishing the direct effects of biological changes at puberty, as well as physical characteristics and contextual factors in development. Overall, hormones have a stronger relationship to emotions and behavior than does pubertal stage.

Contemporary biopsychosocial theories reflect the theoretical perspectives discussed earlier: developmental contextualism and holistic interactionism. "A biobehavioral science recognizes that behaviors are simultaneously determined by processes within the individual, in the social ecology, and in interactions between the two. A focus on either social or biological factors can yield only part of the story of aggressive and violent behaviors: integrative investigations are essential to complete the picture" (Cairns & Stoff, 1996, p. 338). In the last decade the empirical research on hormones and behavior during adolescence reflects this integrated perspective.

Adolescent increases in depression, aggressive and delinquent behavior, and sexual activity have been attributed to changes in hormones and physical morphological changes, brain changes (Giedd et al., 1999; Lange, Giedd, Castellanos, Vaituzis, & Rapoport, 1997; Zijdenbos et al., 1999), altered reactivity to stressors (e.g., life events), and cognitive changes (Bebbington et al., 1998; Nolen-Hoeksema & Girgus, 1994). The links between the biological changes at puberty and changes in affective qualities and aggressive behavior have been extensively reviewed (Brain, 1994; Brain & Susman, 1997; Petersen, 1988; Susman & Finkelstein, 2001; Susman & Petersen, 1992). Given these comprehensive reviews, a brief summary of changes in behavior and affective qualities will be considered in relation to the two groups of hormones most often examined at puberty: sex steroids (testosterone and estrogen) and adrenal androgens (4-A, DHEA, and DHEAS).

Testosterone and Behavior

Products of the endocrine system, principally the steroid hormone testosterone, are implicated in physical aggression in animals and antisocial behavior in adolescents and adults, but the findings are not entirely consistent across human model studies (see Archer, 1991; Brain, 1994, for extensive reviews of both animal and human model studies). The effects of steroid hormones like testosterone on antisocial behavior are hypothesized to derive from the regulatory functions of hormones on brain development that occur during pre- and postnatal periods (organizational influences) as well as in later development (activational influences). Because males are exposed to higher concentrations of androgens than females during pre- and postnatal development and because males tend to express greater physical aggression, androgens are implicated in the higher incidence of physical aggression and dominance in boys than in girls. Because testosterone rises at puberty and antisocial behavior also rises at puberty, testosterone is assumed to affect antisocial behavior at puberty.

Evidence for the relationship between testosterone and aggressive behavior is derived from both correlational and experimental studies. Olweus, Mattson, Schalling, and Low (1988) examined the causal role of testosterone in older adolescents on provoked and unprovoked aggression. Based on path analysis, the findings showed that at Grade 9 testosterone exerts a direct causal influence on provoked aggressive behavior. Testosterone appeared to lower the boys' frustration tolerance at Grade 9. A higher level of testosterone appears to lead to an increased readiness to respond with vigor and assertion to provocation and threat. For unprovoked aggressive behavior (starting fights and verbal aggression) at Grade 9, the findings were somewhat different. Testosterone had no direct effects on unprovoked aggressive behavior. There was an indirect effect of testosterone with low frustration tolerance as the mediating variable. The authors conclude that higher levels of testosterone made the boys more impatient and irritable, in turn increasing readiness to engage in unprovoked aggressive behavior. The findings of the Olweus et al. studies are consistent with a study of midadolescent boys. Adolescents higher in testosterone levels did exhibit behaviors that are distinguishable from behavior in boys with lower concentrations of testosterone. Adolescent boys' perceptions of peer dominance were reflected in testosterone concentrations (Schaal et al., 1996; Tremblay et al., 1997). Testosterone was significantly higher in perceived leaders than in nonleaders.

A negative relationship between testosterone and behavior problems was reported in healthy young boys (Susman et al., 1987). In contrast, there was no relationship between diagnoses of conduct disorder problems and testosterone (Constantino et al., 1993). The low concentration of testosterone in 4- to 10-year-old children in combination with the older relatively insensitive assays made the measurement of testosterone difficult in young boys.

In girls, testosterone was not related to aggressive behavior in two studies (Brooks-Gunn & Warren, 1989; Susman et al., 1987). Furthermore, testosterone was not related to dominance behaviors when young adolescent boys and girls interacted with their parents (Inoff-Germain et al., 1988). It is noteworthy that the associations between antisocial behavior and testosterone are less apparent in girls and in male children and younger adolescents (Brooks-Gunn & Warren,

1989; Constantino et al., 1993; Nottelmann et al., 1987) than in the associations in older adolescents (Olweus, 1986; Olweus et al., 1988) and adults (see review by Archer, 1991). These inconsistencies should be expected given the different constructs and measures used in the studies. Questionnaires that assess aggressive behavior may not have adequate sensitivity for capturing subtle differences in the behavior of adolescents that covary with testosterone levels. The developmental differences in findings between children, adolescents, and adults indicate that elevated testosterone and antisocial behavior may be a consequence as opposed to a cause of aggressive behavior during adulthood (Constantino et al., 1993; Susman, Worrall, Murowchick, Frobose, & Schwab, 1996). Boys who consistently displayed disruptive behavior problems across 6 years were significantly lower on testosterone than were boys who were not disruptive and who were later in pubertal maturation (Schaal et al., 1996). The effect of antisocial behavior on suppression of gonadal steroids may result from higher concentrations of stress-related products of the HPA axis (corticotropin releasing hormone [CRH], ACTH, and cortisol; Susman, Nottelmann, Dorn, Gold & Chrousos, 1989).

Given the dynamic interactive process models discussed earlier, it is likely that biological characteristics, ongoing behaviors, and characteristics of the environment interact to predispose an individual toward certain levels of sex steroids. In an animal model, Sapolsky (1991) showed that the dynamic interactions between one's place in the dominance hierarchy affected both cortisol and testosterone. As dominance increased, testosterone rose and cortisol decreased. In contrast, as dominance decreased, testosterone fell and cortisol increased, suggesting the importance of social interactions as influences on testosterone. High dominance was related to higher concentrations of testosterone, but this relationship was not stable over time. In an extensive review of the literature on testosterone and dominance, Mazur and Booth (1998) concluded that dominance is more closely linked to testosterone than is physical aggression. Dominance sometimes does entail physical aggression with the intent of inflicting harm on another person, but dominance also can be expressed nonaggressively such as in rebellion, competitiveness, and illegal behavior.

Testosterone is related to depression as well as to aggressive behavior at puberty. Earlier research assessed the indirect effect of hormone change on depression as reflected in the relationship between depression and pubertal stage. Transition to Tanner stage III was associated with a sharp increase in rates of unipolar depression (defined by the *Diagnostic and Statistical Manual of Mental Disorders–Fourth Edition*) in girls, but neither the timing of puberty nor menarche had any effect on depression (Angold & Worthman,

1993). Tanner stage had a bigger effect on depression than did age, suggesting that biological change rather than merely a period in development had an effect on depression. A later study found an effect of Tanner stage on depression but a larger effect for testosterone (Angold, Costello, Erkanli, & Worthman, 1999). When Tanner stage and hormones were entered simultaneously, the effect for Tanner stage became nonsignificant, but the effect for testosterone and estradiol remained unchanged.

Experimental studies are the preferred method for establishing the cause-effect relationship between hormones and behavior at puberty. A unique experiment was carried out to examine this cause-effect relationship. Testosterone or estrogen was administered to boys and girls in a placebo-controlled, randomized, double-blind, cross-over design study. The boys and girls had delayed puberty and were being treated with physiological doses of testosterone (boys) or conjugated estrogens (girls; Finkelstein et al., 1997; Kulin et al., 1997; Susman et al., 1998). Each 3-month treatment period was preceded and followed by a 3-month placebo period. The doses of gonadal steroids were calculated to simulate the concentrations of gonadal steroids in blood in normal early (low dose), middle (middle dose), and late (high dose) pubertal adolescents. Aggressive behaviors, problem behavior, and sexual activity were measured by self-reports. In boys who were treated with testosterone, aggressive behaviors were measured by self-reports about physical and verbal aggression against peers and adults, aggressive impulses, and aggressive inhibitory behaviors. Significant increases in aggressive impulses and physical aggression against peers and adults were seen in boys but only at the middle dose. (Findings for estrogen are discussed later.) There were no effects for testosterone treatment on behavior problems (Susman et al., 1998). Administering midpubertal levels of testosterone to hypogonadal boys resulted in significantly increased self-reports of nocturnal emissions, touching girls, and being touched by girls (Finkelstein et al., 1998). (See also the section titled "Puberty and Sexual Activity.") In brief, testosterone levels are related to aggressive behavior, but the results are not consistent across studies.

Estrogen and Behavior

The effects of estrogen, the other major sex steroid that increases rapidly at puberty, are less frequently examined in relation to behavior than is testosterone. In the few studies that have examined estrogens in relation to emotions and antisocial behavior, the relationship between estrogen and moods and behavior at puberty in girls may be as strong, or stronger in some instances, than the relationship between testosterone and moods and behavior in boys. The lack of

progression of research on estrogen and behavior reflects two issues. First, only males are included in the majority of studies on hormones and antisocial behavior as physical aggression and violence occur more frequently in men and violence in women rarely comes to the attention of the judicial system or the media. Second, testosterone was considered the major hormone associated with antisocial behavior until recently.

The relationship between estrogen and behavior in girls may parallel that of testosterone in boys. In adolescents, correlational studies and a recent clinical trial study show a connection between estrogen and self-reports of aggressive tendencies. Of note is that in 9- to 14-year-olds, girls with higher concentrations of estradiol were more dominant while interacting with their parents than were girls with lower levels of estradiol (Inoff-Germain et al., 1988). In the same study, estrogen was not related to aggressive or delinquent behavior problems (Susman et al., 1987). In both sets of findings, pubertal stage did not contribute to the findings. In a parallel study girls were grouped by pubertal breast stages and four stages of estradiol secretion (Brooks-Gunn & Warren, 1985; Warren & Brooks-Gunn, 1989). No significant mood or behavior changes were reported as a function of pubertal stages. The hormonal stages revealed a significant curvilinear trend for depressive affect (increase, then decrease), impulse control (decrease, then increase), and psychopathology (increase, then decrease; Warren & Brooks-Gunn, 1989), indicating significant differences in these indexes during times of rapid increases in hormone levels.

In the placebo-controlled, randomized, double-blind, cross-over design study just described, girls with delayed puberty were treated with physiological doses of estrogen. Significant increases in self-reported aggressive impulses and in physical aggression against both peers and adults were seen in girls at the low and middle doses but not at the high dose (Finkelstein et al., 1997). In contrast, in boys, significant increases in aggressive impulses and physical aggression against peers and adults were seen but only at the middle dose of testosterone. Problem behaviors also were assessed using the Child Behavior Checklist (CBCL; Achenbach, 1991). In girls, only withdrawn behavior increased with estrogen treatment and only after the low dose (Susman et al., 1998). Unfortunately, there were no objective measures of reports (arrests, school or police reports) of dangerous behaviors in these adolescents.

In a recent study, the relationship between depression and estradiol was linear, with depression increasing with increases in estrogen (Angold et al., 1999) as opposed to the nonlinear relationship in the Warren and Brooks-Gunn study. Slight differences in the manner in which estradiol was categorized may have led to the different findings in these two studies. Collectively, these results demonstrate a clear relationship between estrogen and depression. Given the lack of relation-ships between physical maturation based on pubertal stage and emotions or behavior, hormonal changes appear to be more important than the physical changes as correlates of mood and behavior patterns at puberty.

Even though physical maturational changes at puberty were not directly related to depression, underlying hormone changes appear to have indirect effects on behavior, princi-pally in girls. Stattin and Magnusson (1989) showed that morphological estrogen-related changes apparent in physical development, such as breast development, have life-long im-plications for development. Early maturation in girls was re-lated to engaging in interactions with older peers and norm violation in midadolescence. In adulthood, the earlier matur-ers were likely to bear children earlier, have more children and more abortions, hold lower position employment, and have fewer years of education than were later maturers. In brief, the timing of physical maturational influences at puberty were potent predictors of later social development.

In summary, there is a significant relationship among sex roles, steroid hormones and depression symptoms, aggres-sive behavior, and mood in adolescents. Physical matura-tional status is related to emotions and aggressive behavior as well as to hormones. Adding hormones to a statistical model tends to account for variance above and beyond physical maturational status or to eliminate the relationship between physical maturation and behavior and emotions. Nonethe-less, the relationships between physical maturation and ado-lescent behavior may be latent until adulthood, as evidenced by the outcome of early maturers (Stattin & Magnusson, 1989). When considering maturational influences, attention must be given to the contextual processes that may moderate or mediate maturation and emotions and behavior. Family and peer interactions are likely candidates as moderators of maturational effects as evidenced by the associations between high problem behavior and lack of parental monitor-ing and adolescent associations with deviant peers (Ary et al., 1999). In keeping with the developmental contextualism (Lerner, 1998) and holistic interaction (D. Magnusson, 1999) models described earlier, simultaneous consideration of emo-tions and individual behavior, biological influences, and the social context of development are essential for explaining individual development.

Adrenal Androgens

The adrenal androgens traditionally receive little attention in relation to behavior. The adrenal androgens are considered weak bonding androgens relative to testosterone (Bondy, 1985). Nonetheless, adrenal androgens are associated with

aggressive behavior, affect, psychiatric disorder symptoms, and sexual behavior (Brooks-Gunn & Warren, 1989; Susman et al., 1987; Udry et al., 1985; Udry & Talbert, 1988). Higher levels of DHEA also predicted the onset of the first episode of major depression (Goodyer, Herbert, Tamplin, & Altham, 2000). Adrenal androgen actions may parallel those of testos-terone and behavior because one of the adrenal androgens, Δ4-A, is a precursor of both testosterone and estrogens. The rationale for examining the connections between behavior and adrenal androgens stems from findings from both animal and human model studies. In the female spotted hyena, the adrenal androgen Δ4-A is present in high concentrations, and the fe-males of the species are highly aggressive and highly anatom-ically masculinized (Glickman, Frank, Davidson, Smith, & Siiteri, 1987). High Δ4-A concentrations during pregnancy may organize or activate sex-reversed traits in female spotted hyenas (Yalcinkaya et al., 1993). The roles of Δ4-A and other adrenal androgens (DHEA, DHEAS) in humans are not as clear as in hyenas beyond their roles in the development of pubic hair, body odor, and acne during puberty.

In the last decade several studies of adolescents report rela-tionships between adrenal androgens and antisocial behavior in adolescents. In healthy puberty-age girls (Brooks-Gunn & Warren, 1989), higher DHEAS correlated negatively with ag-gressive affect. The interaction between negative life events and DHEAS and aggressive affect also was significant. Girls with lower concentrations of DHEAS who experienced nega-tive life events had more aggressive affect than did girls with fewer negative life events. The second study included 9- to 14-year-old healthy boys and girls. Reports from this study show a relatively consistent pattern of high adrenal androgens and low gonadal steroids associated with problem behaviors and negative affect (Nottelmann et al., 1987; Nottelmann, Inoff-Germain, Susman, & Chrousos, 1990; Susman et al., 1987; Susman, Dorn, & Chrousos, 1991). Adrenal androgens also correlate with dominance in interactions with parents (Inoff-Germain et al., 1988). This interaction supports the per-spective of Raine, Brennan, and Farrington (1997) that bio-logical factors interact with social factors to predispose an individual to antisocial behavior.

The third study demonstrates the contribution of adrenal androgens to sexual behavior and activities (Udry et al., 1985; Udry & Talbert, 1988). A fourth study with boys with conduct disorder reported significantly higher levels of DHEA and DHEAS and the intensity of aggression and delinquency (van Goozen, Matthys, Cohen-Kettenis, Thijssen, & van Engeland, 1998). Finally, DHEAS levels interact with timing of puberty and depression in girls. Girls with high levels of DHEAS and early maturation had the highest emotional arousal and depressive affect scores (Graber, Brooks-Gunn, &

Warren, in press). In brief, although adrenal androgens have a lower (weaker) binding affinity compared to testosterone, the relationship between adrenal androgens and antisocial behavior parallels the relationships between testosterone and antisocial behavior in adults.

TIMING OF PUBERTY AND PSYCHOSOCIAL DEVELOPMENT

Wide variation exists among individuals in the timing of the onset of activation of the HPG axis and pubertal growth spurt; therefore, there is a wide range of physiologic variations in sexual reproduction capability and normal growth at puberty. These variations are a result of genetic influences and nutritional status, resulting from self-induced restriction of energy intake and heavy exercise training (Rogol, Clark, & Roemmich, 2000). The variation in timing of puberty and psychological development constitutes one of the most often examined topics in the entire field of adolescent development.

Early and Late Pubertal Timing

The classic studies of the effects of timing of puberty were first reported in the 1930s (H. E. Jones, 1938; M. C. Jones, 1958; M. C. Jones & Bayley, 1950). Psychological consequences of timing of puberty continue to be of sustained interest. In general, for boys in the early studies, early maturation tended to be advantageous, particularly with respect to social development. In contrast, early maturation for girls often tended to be disadvantageous (Faust, 1969; Jones, Bayley, & Jones, 1948; Stolz & Stolz, 1944), although the results were not always consistent across studies.

With the rise of interest in biobehavioral research, beginning in the 1980s, two predominant hypotheses were formulated to explain the influence of physical maturation on primarily negative psychological outcomes. First, the *maturational deviance hypothesis* (e.g., Brooks-Gunn, Petersen, & Eichorn, 1985; Caspi, Henry, McGee, Moffitt, & Silva, 1995; Caspi & Moffitt, 1991; Petersen & Taylor, 1980; Tschann et al., 1994; Williams & Dunlop, 1999) suggested that adolescents who are off time (earlier or later) in their pubertal development, with respect to peers, experience more stress than on-time adolescents. Being an off-time maturer may result in an adolescent's lacking the usual coping resources and social support that characterize being on time in pubertal development. The added stress and lack of resources may increase vulnerability to adjustment problems. In brief, a maturational-deviance hypothesis predicts that early-maturing girls and late-maturing boys experience

heightened emotional distress, which influences the initiation of antisocial behavior including use of illegal substances, sexual activity, and delinquent behavior.

The second hypothesis, the *early-maturational* or *early timing hypothesis* (e.g., Brooks-Gunn et al., 1985; Caspi & Moffitt, 1991; Petersen & Taylor, 1980; Tschann et al., 1994) posited that being an early developer is especially disadvantageous for girls (Stattin & Magnusson, 1990). The disadvantage may result from the missed opportunity for completion of normal psychosocial developmental tasks of middle childhood (Brooks-Gunn et al., 1985). Early maturers may face greater social pressure to conform to adult norms and, importantly, to engage in adult behaviors. Earlier maturing adolescents look more physically mature than their chronological age, and hence society may view them as older and more socially, emotionally, and cognitively advanced (Brooks-Gunn et al., 1985; Caspi & Moffitt, 1991). However, the cognitive and social development of early maturers may lag far behind their seemingly adult status. With this mismatch, expectations are high for more adult-like behaviors and actions, yet the physically early maturing girls may not be ready for adult behaviors and roles. Thus, an early-maturation hypothesis predicts that early-maturing girls engage in more acting-out behavior or negative emotions than all other groups, independent of emotional distress.

Although not always consistent, the results from the early timing of maturation studies report that early maturation for boys appears to be positive, particularly with respect to social development, whereas for girls early maturation is related to more negative moods and behaviors (Faust, 1969; Ge, Conger, & Elder, 2001a; Jones & Bayley, 1938; Stolz & Stolz, 1944). For instance, early-maturing girls experienced significantly higher levels of psychosocial distress and were more vulnerable to prior psychological problems, deviant peer pressures, and fathers' hostile feelings when compared to on-time and late-maturing peers (Ge, Conger, & Elder, 1996). However, early-maturing boys also report more hostile feelings and internalizing behavior problems than do their later maturing peers (Ge, Conger, & Elder, 2001b). Other studies show that early timing is negative for both boys and girls. This finding was supported in studies of African American children as well (Ge, Brody, Conger, & Simons, in press). Tschann et al. (1994) reported that boys and girls who are earlier maturers reported more substance abuse compared to later maturers.

Earlier maturing boys and girls were more sexually active and participated in more antisocial behavior (Flannery, Row, & Gulley, 1993), and early-timing boys reported more antisocial behavior than on-time boys (Williams & Dunlop, 1999) compared to late maturers. Early-maturing boys also engaged in more health risk behaviors (Orr & Ingersoll, 1995). In other studies, early-maturing girls were least satisfied with their height and weight, had poorer body image, or were less happy (Blyth, Simmons, & Zakin, 1985; Brooks-Gunn et al., 1985; Brooks-Gunn & Warren, 1989; Duncan, Ritter, Dornbusch, Gross, & Carlsmith, 1985; Petersen & Crockett, 1985) and had more internalizing problems (Hayward et al., 1997), more behavioral and emotional problems (Caspi & Moffitt, 1991), and more interactions with peers who were deviant (Silbereisen, Petersen, Albrecht, & Kracke, 1989).

Timing of puberty is related to a variety of health and risk behaviors. Eating problems were reported by 9th-, 10th-, and 11th-grade girls who perceived their pubertal timing to be earlier than that of peers (Swarr & Richards, 1996). Moreover, they report that interactions between pubertal timing and various experiences or perceptions of parents are related to eating problems. Similarly, early-maturing girls engaged in risk behaviors such as drinking, smoking, and sexual activity at an earlier age (D. Magnusson et al., 1985). In another study, girls with earlier puberty had their first alcohol experience and drank moderate amounts of alcohol sooner than those with later pubertal timing did (Wilson et al., 1994). Finally, the perception of earlier pubertal timing was a statistical predictor for future suicide attempts in Norwegian adolescents, and this relationship was stronger in girls than in boys (Wichstrom, 2000).

Other studies show that early timing in girls and late timing in boys are related to affective and behavior problems. For example, early timing of puberty in girls and late timing in boys were related to a higher incidence of psychopathology and depressed mood (Graber, Lewisohn, Seeley, & Brooks-Gunn, 1997), and poor body image was evident in boys (Siegel, Yancey, Aneshensel, & Schuler, 1999). Similarly, Andersson and Magnusson (1990) reported that both early- and late-maturing boys may be more likely to be alcohol users. Using hormone concentrations standardized for age as an index of timing of puberty, earlier maturing adolescents, based on adrenal androgen levels, tended to have poor adjustment; however, the findings varied depending on the hormone under consideration (Susman et al., 1985). Later maturing adolescents, based on sex steroids, tended to have poorer adjustment. The findings were more pronounced for boys than for girls.

Later maturation is not as consistently related to negative emotions and behavior problems as is earlier maturation. Later maturation in boys was related to lower achievement (Dubas, Graber, & Petersen, 1991), lower self-esteem or confidence, and less happiness (Crockett & Petersen, 1987; Simmons, Blyth, Van Cleave, & Bush, 1979). Other studies showed no effects of pubertal timing, either earlier or later, in relation to mood and behavioral outcomes. For example, Brooks-Gunn and Warren (1989) reported no relationship between pubertal timing and negative emotions in girls, and Angold, Costello, and Worthman (1998) reported no relationship between pubertal timing and the rates of depression in boys and girls.

In summary, there is support for both the maturational deviance hypothesis and the early-maturational hypothesis. Adolescents who are off time in pubertal timing generally report more adjustment problems, supporting the maturational deviance hypothesis. Early timing of puberty does appear to be more disadvantageous for girls than for boys (the early-maturational hypothesis), but boys are negatively affected by early timing as well. Nonetheless, there also is evidence that timing of puberty has no effect on adjustment and that earlier puberty is neither consistently disadvantageous for girls nor advantageous for boys. The effects of timing of puberty on adjustment and deviant behavior are made even more difficult to unravel by imprecise definitions and measurement of puberty and the inclusion of a wide age group of adolescents.

Theoretical and Methodological Issues

The studies just reviewed show both consistencies and major inconsistencies regarding the relationship among timing of puberty and behavior, adjustment, and psychopathology. Nonetheless, it is legitimate to conclude that both earlier and later timing of puberty has a major impact on multiple dimensions of psychological functioning in boys and girls. Of note is that timing of puberty has long-term implications. Later in adolescence or adulthood, early-maturing girls reported more psychopathology (Graber et al., 1997) and less educational achievement and career success than did later maturing girls (Stattin & Magnusson, 1990). The inconsistencies across studies of earlier and later puberty emerge from conceptual and methodological differences. The major theoretical interest appears to be on earlier timing of puberty given societal concerns regarding potential consequences of early maturation: precocious sexuality, substance use, and deviance. With some exceptions, few studies examine the longer term effects associated with earlier maturation. Earlier or later maturation has been theorized to be a stable characteristic of individuals rather than a dynamic concept that changes with changing age and contextual factors. The behaviors that are related to timing of puberty during adolescence, such as risky sexual behavior and other forms of externalizing problems, may disappear in late adolescence and adulthood. Nonetheless, the longer term implications of timing of puberty will emerge as transformed manifestations of these early behaviors as described by Stattin and Magnusson (1990). Specifically, early maturers may become affiliated with older and deviant peers for a limited time period and engage in deviant behaviors that cease in late adolescence. The expense of engaging in these behaviors is reduced achievement and educational and occupational success.

Although the findings regarding early and late puberty seem inconsistent, there is consistency across studies. The consistency of findings showing earlier maturation and problems in adjustment suggests that adolescents are exquisitely sensitive to their early pubertal status. Such is not the case for later maturers. The fewer findings relating later maturation and psychological functioning indicate the ability of adolescents to adapt to differences between themselves and same-age peers as puberty progresses. Less theorizing has taken place regarding developmental implications of later maturation.

Methodological differences also contribute to the inconsistencies in findings. The chronological age when adolescents are assessed for effects of timing, the measure of timing (age of menarche, pubertal stage, or other measure) and the construct assessed (antisocial behavior, depression, parent-adolescent interactions) all may contribute to the discrepancies in how timing of puberty and psychological functioning co-occur. The method used to assess timing of puberty likely plays a major role in the discrepancies across studies. To a large degree, timing of puberty has been assessed utilizing a self-report measure of puberty (e.g., pubertal stage, age at menarche, appearance of body hair). Other studies use objective measures of physical development such as pubertal stage by physical examination (Tanner criteria; Marshall & Tanner, 1969, 1970) or hormone concentrations. The lack of reliability in self-reports of pubertal status (Dorn, Susman, Nottelmann, Inoff-Germain, & Chrousos, 1990) and age of menarche (Dorn et al., 1999) is likely a major source of error variance in assessing the multiple connections between timing of puberty and psychological functioning.

PUBERTY AND ADOLESCENT HEALTH: CULTURAL SIGNIFICANCE AND SECULAR CHANGE

Secular Changes in Timing of Puberty

Timing of puberty currently captures the interest of the public as well as the scientific community. *Time* (October 2000) magazine's front cover and accompanying article featured the problem of early timing of puberty in girls. There has been a decrease in age of menarche over the last century (Blythe & Rosenthal, 2000; Gerver, De Bruin, & Drayer, 1994; Grumbach & Styne, 1992; Tanner & O'Keeffe, 1962;

Wyshak & Frisch, 1982). The secular (generational) trend in age at menarche has been evident from at least the mid 1800s to currently when a decrease in the age of menarche was noted from 15 years to 12.7 years (Garn, 1992). Age at menarche decreased by approximately 1 year for those women born from 1900 to 1950. A decrease in the age of menarche also is evident in international studies.

In a nationwide growth study in the Netherlands, age of menarche was assessed in two cohorts. The first cohort was enrolled in 1952–1956, and the most recent cohort was enrolled in 1996–1997. Age at menarche decreased to 13.15 years, which was a 6-month decline over four decades (Fredriks et al., 2000). Similarly, in two cohorts of American girls 14 years apart, age at menarche was found to decrease (Wattigney, Srinivasan, Chen, Greenlund, & Berenson, 1999). Cohort 1 included 1,190 girls (64% White) who were examined in 1978–1979. The second cohort was examined in 1992–1994 and included 1,164 girls (57% White). In Cohort 2 more than twice as many girls reached menarche before age 12 years than did in Cohort 1. Menarche occurred earlier in Cohort 2 for both Black and White girls. Furthermore, in both cohorts all of the obesity measures used in the study were correlated with age at menarche. The decrease in timing of menarche has generally been attributed to cultural factors, specifically, improved nutrition and socioeconomic conditions evident in the United States and numerous developing countries.

In 1997 a large-scale study of pubertal development in American girls received widespread attention in the media as well as in the health care and research arenas. Herman-Giddens et al. (1997) studied over 17,000 pre- and peripubertal-age girls (90.4% White) to determine age at onset of pubertal changes. They reported that African American girls began puberty on average between age 8 and 9 whereas White girls began puberty by age 10. For example, at age 9, 62.6% of African American girls had breast development at stage 2 or higher (indicative of puberty) compared to 32.1% of White girls. Similarly, age at menarche was 12.16 years for African American girls and 12.88 years for White girls (Herman-Giddens et al., 1997). In a follow-up article (Kaplowitz, Oberfield, & the Drug and Therapeutics and Executive Committees, 1999), based on the Herman-Giddens study, the suggestion was that breast or pubic hair development is not precocious unless under age 7 in White girls and 6 in African American girls. Thus, girls beginning puberty above that range need no medical follow-up. However, they further stress that no follow-up is needed only if other factors are not present (e.g., bone age >2 years ahead of chronological age and predicted height of 2 SD or more below target height or <59 inches, underlying neurological finding, etc.; Kaplowitz et al., 1999). It appears prudent to seek medical advice in all instances of suspected early puberty.

Although, the Herman-Giddens et al. (1997) study is unique and important in that it includes a large number of girls, a number of important methodological considerations may have affected the findings and interpretations of secular trends in timing of puberty. These methodological considerations include the method of conducting the physical examination. Breast stage was determined by visual inspection and not palpation. Even with palpation conducted by an experienced clinician, it is difficult to distinguish between breasts and adipose tissue. Thus, some girls could have been classified as pubertal at Stage 2 when the actual cause of apparent breast development was obesity. Statistically controlling for body mass could have partially addressed the problem of overestimating the extent of breast development although the problem would not have been eliminated. Additionally, characteristics of the sample may have contributed to ratings of early puberty. Some of the girls in the sample likely were brought to their primary care provider for the evaluation of early pubertal development. In addition, nearly 7% of the sample had a chronic disease, and 3% were on medication. These percentages were higher in the African American sample. Finally, not all of the girls in the study had reached menarche (Emans & Biro, 1998), thereby possibly decreasing the average age of menarche. The authors are to be commended on the study, but the mean age of menarche reported may not truly be representative of the general population of adolescent girls. In spite of the earlier age of onset of puberty, there was little change in age at menarche noted in the Herman-Giddens et al. report compared to reports in the previous 25 years.

The report by Herman-Giddens et al. (1997) continues to remain controversial. In the fall of 2000, Rosenfield et al. (2000) emphasized that it is premature to state that puberty is occurring earlier in girls based on one study. Rosenfield et al. cited similar criticisms to those expressed earlier (e.g., stage of puberty was based on visual inspection versus palpation) but particularly emphasized the "fatal flaw" (p. 622) of utilizing a nonrandom sample. The authors concluded that regardless of race, when breast development or pubic hair appear before age 8 or 9 years, a diagnostic evaluation should be conducted for bone age and height prediction. Based on these results as well as the physical examination, decisions for further follow-up should then be made.

The exact decrease in the true onset of timing of puberty as opposed to the timing of menarche is difficult to assess as the timing of puberty is often indexed in girls by "age at menarche." Age at menarche is a relatively easy marker to obtain by self-report or parental report but is not an accurate index of timing of onset of puberty. Variability in accuracy of reports of onset of menarche (Dorn et al., 1999) contributes

to the difficulty of estimating secular trends in the onset of puberty. Unfortunately, the data on secular trends in onset of puberty in boys are much less complete than for girls. Theoretically, the first nocturnal emission or spermarche is a comparable timing measure for boys; however, information on spermarche is difficult to obtain. Sanders and Soares (1986) reported that many adult men either had difficulty recalling their first nocturnal emission or were hesitant to reveal the information. Few psychosocial studies include the concept of spermarche as an index of timing of puberty (for exceptions, see Downs & Fuller, 1991; Gaddis & Brooks-Gunn, 1985; Kim & Smith, 1998; Kim, Smith, & Palermiti, 1997). Information regarding secular trends in timing of puberty is not easily gleaned from these studies because they include a wide age range of subjects (up to age 62) or small sample sizes. None provided normative data regarding average age of spermarche or reliability of the measurement of spermarche. In an earlier study, Kulin, Fronera, Demers, Barthlomew, and Lloyd (1989) reported the average age of spermarche to be age 14, and at that age gonadotropins were at adult concentrations. To our knowledge, this is the only study that simultaneously assessed self-reported age at spermarche and gonadotropin levels. Given the lack of information regarding onset of puberty in boys, there is no valid method of estimating secular trends in the onset of puberty in boys. A study of boys that parallels the Herman-Giddens et al. (1997) study of girls in a randomly selected representative sample could make a significant contribution to the literature.

Puberty and Adolescent Health

Puberty implies that an adolescent is becoming an adult. Contemporary culture is ambivalent about the desirability of this transition. On the one hand, puberty implies independence and adult roles and the emergence of a physical morphology and reproductive capability characteristic of adults. On the other hand, for girls the thin prepubertal physique is valued, whereas fat deposition at puberty is viewed as a less desirable characteristic of female adults. These changes in physical size and proportions have definite negative social signaling value. As boys and girls progress in physical development there are societal expectations for moodiness and disruptive behavior and opportunities for risky sexual behavior. With the engagement in sexual activities, there is added risk for sexually transmitted diseases (STDs; e.g., HIV transmission) and teen pregnancy (Udry, 1979; Udry & Cliquet, 1982). Puberty, then, is a period of development ripe for the emergence of major health risk behaviors and health problems. Public health policies tend to focus on preventing the occurrence of the health problems (substance use, risky sex, and accidents) but at the same time ignore the role of puberty as a major factor affecting the onset and trajectory of risky health behaviors. The effects of timing of puberty on adult health are only now beginning to be identified.

Puberty and Adult Health

Health policies to reduce the risk of long-term implications of early timing of puberty are just beginning to be considered. This emphasis, based primarily on observational studies, regards the relationship between reported age of puberty and later health problems. Timing of puberty and later health have been understudied in males, so disorders linked with timing of puberty in males are yet to be identified. The lack of attention to long-term implications of pubertal processes (particularly, timing of puberty) represents a missed opportunity for possible public health prevention efforts.

Research on puberty and later health has focused primarily on cancer, obesity, and reproductive disorders. An increased risk of breast cancer is associated with early puberty based on age at menarche (Kampert, Whittemore, & Paffenbarger, 1988; C. M. Magnusson et al., 1999; Rockhill, Moorman, & Newman, 1998; Vihko & Apter, 1986; for a review, see Key, 1999). The increased risk of cancer in early maturers is attributed to the longer duration of exposure to circulating estrogens across the life span. Women who experience earlier menarche have higher levels of circulating free estrogen into at least the third decade of life compared to later maturers (Apter, Reinila, & Vikho, 1989). An additional indirect measure of estrogen, the timing of the pubertal growth spurt, is also associated with breast cancer risk. Women who attain their adult height at a later age have a lower risk of breast cancer, possibly due to their having lower levels of growth hormone (GH) and insulin-like growth factor (IGF1) during breast development (Li, Malone, White, & Daling, 1997). However, it is important to note that other studies do not show an increased risk of breast cancer with earlier menarche (e.g., R. G. Parker, Rees, Leung, & Legorreta, 1999) and that the cause of breast cancer is no doubt multifactorial.

Early maturing girls are at greater risk for obesity (Lovejoy, 1998; Ness, Laskarzewski, & Price, 1991). Obese girls also have an earlier timing of puberty, so the direction of the relationship between obesity and timing of puberty is unknown. Obesity in adolescence is related to major risk factors for cardiovascular disease (Morrison, Barton, Biro, Daniels, & Sprecher, 1999). In Black and White 10- to 15-year-olds, overweight status was related to lower high-density lipids and higher low-density lipids, a risk-profile for cardiovascular disease. Obesity is also linked to the high incidence of Type II diabetes mellitus in adolescents.

Reproductive disorders related to timing of puberty are evident primarily in ovarian pathophysiology. Polycystic ovarian syndrome (PCOS) is a disorder in adulthood reported to be related to early puberty. PCOS is a heterogenous disorder characterized by oligo/amenorrhea (few or no menstrual periods), insulin resistance or high insulin, and hyperandrogenism, which is associated with an increased risk of developing impaired glucose tolerance and Type II diabetes (Ibáñez et al., 1993). PCOS is reported in 5% to 10% of women of reproductive age. PCOS can begin to express itself during puberty and continue into the adult reproductive years with ensuing infertility.

One possible mechanism linking PCOS and early puberty is premature adrenarche. During adrenarche the adrenal androgens, DHEA and DHEAS, and Δ-4A begin to rise. When adrenarche occurs prior to age 8 in girls and 9.5 in boys, it is considered premature (Siegel, Finegold, Urban, McVie, & Lee, 1992; Siegel & Lee, 1992; see Reiter & Saenger, 1997, for review). Premature adrenarche is characterized by high adrenal androgen concentrations and pubic hair development with no evidence of breast development. Off-time activation of the adrenal glands is presumed to be the cause of premature adrenarche. Premature adrenarche has been considered a benign condition (Kaplowitz, Cockerell, & Young, 1985) representing a variation of puberty; therefore, treatment was deemed unnecessary (Reiter & Saenger, 1997). Recent research suggests that children with premature adrenarche may have long-term sequelae such as PCOS, anovulation in late adolescence (and potentially infertility), and insulin resistance (Ibáñez, de Zegher, & Potau, 1999; Ibáñez et al., 1993; Ibáñez, Potau, Zampolli, Street, & Carrascosa, 1997; Oppenheimer, Linder, Saenger, & DiMartino-Nardi, 1995; Richards et al., 1985). In adulthood, women with PCOS have an increased risk for cardiovascular problems (Birdsall, Farquhar, & White, 1997; Talbott et al., 1995) and complications from diabetes mellitus (Dunaif, 1997, 1999; Dunaif, Futterweit, Segal, & Dobrijansky, 1989). Thus, women with early adrenarche may be at risk for PCOS, resulting in significant physical morbidity. It is unknown if there is continuity of adjustment problems observed in premature adrenarche (Dorn et al., 1999) and severe psychopathology observed in adult women with PCOS.

The timing of puberty is considered to have implication for brain development. Saugstad (1989b) pointed out that the "onset of puberty coincides with the last major step in brain development: the elimination of some 40% of the neuronal synapses" (p. 157) and postulated that synaptic loss may have implications for the development of manic-depressive psychosis and schizophrenia. Secular, social class, and geographic trends in body build and mental disorders suggest that early maturers may be more susceptible to manic-depressive psychosis and that late maturers may be more susceptible to schizophrenia (Saugstad, 1989a, 1989b). These hypotheses remain speculative until longitudinal studies provide more definitive findings.

Timing of Puberty and Stress

One of the most controversial issues regarding timing of puberty is whether stressors accelerate or delay the timing of puberty. Consistent with the theoretical perspectives discussed earlier, timing of puberty and behavior and experiences are considered dynamic and bidirectional processes (Susman, 1997). Experiences as well as genetic factors are speculative influences on the tremendous variations in the timing of puberty. Experiential-based sources of variation include disruptive behavior disorders (Schaal et al., 1996), family relationships (Steinberg, 1987, 1988), participation in intensive physical exercise such as ballet dancing (Warren et al., 1991), negative emotional states (Nottelmann et al., 1990; Susman et al., 1989), and family adversity (Belsky, Steinberg, & Draper, 1991). Interest in the mechanism for explaining the relationship between experience and timing of puberty began to emerge in the last decade.

The concept of stress is hypothesized to play a major role in timing of puberty. There are two opposing views on the relationship between stress and timing of puberty. The first perspective, advocated by Belsky et al. (1991), is based on an evolutionary model of psychosocial influences on the timing of puberty. The premise is that early on children develop an understanding of the availability of resources, the duration of close relationships, and the trustworthiness of adults. Exposure to these different types of resources and caretaking adults in the child's environment are hypothesized to influence the child's reproductive strategies. Environments characterized by stress are hypothesized to contribute to early reproductive development (Belsky et al., 1991). Three possible avenues are proposed whereby early stress accelerates reproductive development and subsequently earlier childbearing: (a) the stress of living in a conflicted family, (b) the stress of being reared in a single family home, especially with a single mother, and (c) exposure to the parental paramours if in a single parent home. Belsky et al. proposed that these early stressful experiences act by changing the child's view of the world in general and the child's view of relationships, in particular, as uncertain, unpredictable, and unstable. The uncertainty of living in a stressful environment has both psychological and physiological consequences. Early stress acts on psychological development via the individual's having adopted a view of the world as being uncertain. If individuals

view the world as uncertain, reproducing early, while they still can, is an adaptive strategy to counteract the uncertainty of the difficult family environment. Uncertainty also leads these individuals to not count on their partners for resources, thereby creating unstable pair bonds. Early stress is proposed to act on physiological systems to accelerate pubertal development, although the exact mechanisms involved in acceleration of puberty are not addressed.

The hypothesis has received mixed support. Conflict in the family at age 7 predicted earlier menarche (Moffitt, Caspi, Belsky, & Silva, 1992). Divorce as a stressor and as a context for girls being raised in father-absent versus father-present homes also has been linked to timing of puberty. Girls in father-absent homes tend to reach puberty earlier than girls reared in father-present homes (Jones, Leeton, McLeod, & Wood, 1972; Moffitt et al., 1992; Surbey, 1990; Wierson, Long, & Forehand, 1993). The stress of living in a conflicted family has been extended to include having a father who is an alcoholic (Malo & Tremblay, 1997). Other studies show that greater marital and family conflict, as well as less marital and family harmony, are associated with pubertal timing in girls (Ellis & Garber, 2000; Ellis, McFadyen-Ketchum, Dodge, Pettit, & Bates, 1999; Graber, Brooks-Gunn, & Warren, 1995; Moffitt et al., 1992; Steinberg, 1988). Absence of positive parent-child relationships, rather than negative relationships, predicted early pubertal timing (Ellis et al., 1999). Positive interactions included greater supportiveness in the parental dyad and more father-daughter and mother-daughter affection.

Absence of positive parent-child relationships, rather than negative relationships, predicted early pubertal timing (Ellis et al., 1999). Positive relationships included greater supportiveness in the parental dyad and more father-daughter and mother-daughter affection. The quality of fathers' investments in the family emerged as the most important feature of the proximal family environment. Presence of fathers in the home, more time spent by fathers in child care, greater supportiveness in the parental dyad, more father-daughter affection, and more mother-daughter affection, as assessed prior to kindergarten, each predicted later pubertal timing by daughters in seventh grade. The positive dimension of family relationships, rather than the negative dimension, accounted for these relations (Ellis et al., 1999). The interpretation was that the findings are consistent with the Belsky model because positive dimensions were related to later timing of puberty. The findings could also be interpreted as inconsistent with the Belsky model because it predicts that negative aspects of the family will predict earlier timing of puberty.

The mechanisms linking earlier onset of puberty and family stress are not articulated in the existing research. In contrast, the effect of father absence as a precipitant of earlier puberty is hypothesized to be mediated by endocrine mechanisms. Biological father absence frequently is replaced by a stepfather or mother's boyfriend. Exposure to pheromones of unrelated males is hypothesized to lead to earlier onset of puberty. Exposure to chemosignals and pheromonal systems in a variety of species, including humans, leads to changes in menstrual cycles (McClintock, 1998; Stern & McClintock, 1998) and timing of puberty (Sanders & Reinisch, 1990). Pheromonal systems and chemosignals may function as modulators or signaling substances that precipitate the onset of puberty.

The relationship between family stress and timing of puberty, as well as the psychobiological perspective, in particular, has generated controversy regarding the validity of theoretical perspectives and the imprecision of defining and assessing family stress. A primary criticism of the stress and early timing hypothesis focuses on the logic of the argument that stress is responsible for early onset of puberty. The physiology of the stress system is such that stress should attenuate timing and progression of puberty. This perspective is based on the physiological principle of adaptation to stressors. Adaptation is accomplished at both the physiological and behavioral levels. At the neuroendocrine and peripheral levels CRH is secreted by the hypothalamus, ACTH by the pituitary, and cortisol from the adrenal glands (Chrousos & Gold, 1992; Stratakis & Chrousos, 1997). These components of the HPA stress system down-regulate the reproductive HPG axis at the level of the hypothalamus, pituitary, and gonads. For instance, cortisol exerts inhibitory effects at the levels of the LHRH neuron, the pituitary gonadotroph (responsible for secreting luteinizing hormone and follicle stimulating hormone), and the gonad itself, thereby suppressing sex steroids (testosterone and estrogen) and maturation of reproductive function. Down-regulation or attenuation of secretion of HPG-axis hormones is accomplished either directly or via endorphin. CRH suppresses the LHRH neuron in the hypothalamus. Adaptation at a behavioral level involves a delay or cessation of sexual reproduction activities to conserve vital metabolic resources (Chrousos, 1998). Based on these physiological and behavioral processes, the onset of reproductive capability will be attenuated in children reared in stressful environments (Nottelman et al., 1990; Susman et al., 1989). Conditions that are physically stressful, such as malnutrition and physical stressors (e.g., intense exercise), also suppress reproduction.

In young adolescents stress reflected in behavior problems and self-image problems was related to later maturation based on hormone levels and stage of pubertal development (Tanner criteria, Marshall & Tanner, 1969, 1970; Nottelmann et al., 1987; Susman et al., 1987). Family stressors related to paternal alcoholism led to a delay of male pubertal onset, supporting the hypothesis that stress activates the HPA axis and inhibits the HPG axis (Malo & Tremblay, 1997). Additional longitudinal studies that include actual indexes of stress hormones, as well as adolescent and family stressors, are needed to explain further the links between stress and timing of puberty.

A set of papers (Hinde, 1991; Maccoby, 1991) that accompanied the publication of Belsky et al. (1991) raised additional criticisms regarding the family stress and evolutionary theory of socialization. Maccoby (1991) evoked the concepts of *quality* and *quantity* to argue against the Belsky et al. perspective. The quantity argument based on the Belsky et al. perspective is that unstable rearing environments will lead to early maturation and sexual activity, and presumably earlier and more frequent childbearing. Maccoby proposed that if males invest less, females must invest more in rearing the young and that if the male is not available, she recruits investment from her mother and sisters. Her basic strategy should be to select a mate who has the resources and the motivation to be a quality parent rather than a quantity parent. Maccoby further suggested that it does not seem plausible that evolution would have shaped psychological and physiological maternal characteristics such that she would have more children in the absence of a supportive family environment as each additional child increases the difficulty of raising each child. Thus, skepticism is warranted regarding the claim that females have evolved so as to take up a quantity reproductive strategy in the face of instability in childhood relationships. Finally, Maccoby suggested that evolutionary concepts are not essential for explaining contemporaneous functioning. Social learning could explain the effects of family functioning on early sexual activity. Girls from disorganized families likely have less surveillance, are more aware of sexual activity (especially if the mother has multiple sexual partners), or have relationships with older men who are viewed as avenues for escaping dysfunctional homes.

The evolutionary approach to timing of maturation brings together rich perspectives on puberty from animal and human models of adaptation and change. Nonetheless, this perspective is at odds with the two predominant theories articulated at the beginning of the chapter, developmental contextualism and holistic interactionism. Both perspectives acknowledge the importance of evolutionary and genetic contributions to development but include the contemporaneous dynamic interaction between psychological, biological, and contextual processes. Family context provides an arena within which parent-adolescent interactions evolve as a result of their past history together as well as current self-organizing properties.

Early maturation at puberty within these frameworks is a product of contextual factors (e.g., nutritional consumption and related obesity) and parent-adolescent interactions characterized by detachment or warmth. The relationship between timing of puberty and family processes is further clouded by the limited research on direction of relationships. Lewontin and Levins (2000) concurred with the contextualism and holistic interactionism developmental models in emphasizing that when considering systems of any complexity there are positive and negative feedback systems. Biological and psychological feedback loops at any time in development. Clear evidence based on models linking sequential and dynamic influences between family stability and instability and timing of puberty is essential to allow for an escape from current controversies regarding timing of puberty and family processes.

Puberty and Sexuality

One of the things that can be stated assuredly is that adolescence "is when most individuals first experience sexual intercourse" (Meschke, Zweig, Barger, & Eccles, 2000, p. 316). The Centers for Disease Control and Prevention (CDC; 1999) reported that in 1999 over 47% of the girls and 52% of the boys surveyed in grades 9 through 12 had had intercourse, and over one third of the sample had been sexually active in the previous three months; 4.4% of girls and 12.2% of boys reported experiencing intercourse before age 13. Trends in sexual activity vary by historical time. Singh and Darroch (1999) examined trends in sexual activity of American women across a 13-year period in three surveys. In the 1980s there was an increase in the proportion of adolescents who had ever had sexual intercourse, but by the mid-1980s and on into the 1990s this increased trajectory stabilized. On average, approximately 40% of adolescents in the 15- to 19-year-old age group had had sexual intercourse in the last three months. These percentages were equal across the three surveys. Kaufmann et al. (1998) reported similar trends.

There is some variation between subpopulations of adolescents. For example, Finkelstein et al. (1998) reported that delayed-puberty boys tended to engage in more advanced sexual behavior than did delayed girls of similar age. Halpern, Udry, and Suchindran (1997) found differences in the self-reported sexual behaviors of Black and White girls, with White girls more likely to report masturbation and Black girls more likely to report petting and coitus.

The influences on adolescent sexuality arise in many spheres: biological, psychological, social, and the media. Biologically, hormones are known to bring about sexual development at puberty and are also considered influences on adolescent sexual behavior. Hormones are thought to have both direct and indirect (e.g., via pubertal physical development) effects on sexuality (Halpern, Udry, & Suchindran, 1998). Androgens, in particular, are considered potent influences on sexuality in both boys and girls. The pubertal increase in male testosterone levels "is thought to provide a biological foundation for the increases in sexual interest and activity that occur during adolescence" (Halpern et al., 1998, p. 446). Studies have examined the relationship between testosterone and sexual activity using both randomized clinical trials and correlational and group difference designs. In a randomized clinical trial of sex hormone replacement therapy, intramuscular administration of mid-pubertal levels of testosterone to hypogonadal boys resulted in significantly increased self-reports of nocturnal emissions, touching girls, and being touched by girls (Finkelstein et al., 1998). Similarly, Halpern et al. (1998) found that adolescent boys with higher levels of salivary testosterone were more likely to initiate coitus and to participate in other partnered sexual behaviors. Within individuals, salivary testosterone increases were also associated with a greater likelihood of partnered sexual activity. Additionally, the study illustrated the importance of physical developmental influences on sexual activity. When the analysis of testosterone and partnered activity controlled for pubertal development, neither testosterone nor pubertal development reached statistical significance. These findings suggest that evaluations of the propensity to engage in sexual activity should consider multiple levels of influence by psychological, biological, and social functioning.

Testosterone and other androgens also have striking effects on sexuality in adolescent girls. Halpern et al. (1997) reviewed several lines of evidence for androgenic effects on female adolescent sexuality, including hormone replacement studies, female behavioral responsiveness to testosterone, and connections between testosterone levels and sexual activity during puberty (see also Hutchinson, 1995). Udry et al. (1986) reported that adolescent girls' androgen levels, namely testosterone and the adrenal androgens DHEA, DHEAS, and Δ-4A, predicted the girls' anticipation of future sex. Halpern et al. examined within-individual changes as well as differences between girls and found that higher plasma testosterone levels were associated with a higher incidence of transition to coitus in both Black and White girls. Frequency of attendance at religious services operated as a social control factor among White females. Testosterone was concluded to be a causal factor in female sexual activity, but biological effects were moderated by relevant social variables. Processes at both the social and biological levels appear to interact to influence sexual activity.

Less research has examined the role of estrogens in adolescent sexuality, but there is some evidence for estrogenic effects on female adolescent sexual behavior. Finkelstein et al. (1998) found that administering oral conjugated estrogen to hypogonadal female adolescents resulted in significantly increased self-reports of necking behavior, but only at the highest dose used (intended to simulate the late stages of puberty). Of note is that when testosterone or estrogen is measured in blood or saliva and related to sexual activity, moods, or behavior, it is not known which of the hormones activates or is permissive of the expression of sexual behavior as testosterone can be converted to estrogen.

A plethora of nonhormonal factors also influences adolescent sexuality, but an additional factor is of note: body fat. Halpern, Udry, Campbell, and Suchindran (1999) examined the dating frequency and sexual behaviors of seventh- and eighth-grade girls in relation to measured body fat. Comparing girls with mean body fat levels to those 1 SD above or below showed that the lower body fat was associated with a greater chance of dating. This pattern was true for both Black and White girls, although the relationship was stronger for White girls. Additionally, this difference in dating frequency explained the relationship between higher body fat and lower incidence of coitus and petting. Halpern et al. warned, however, that these results must be taken in context because synchronous transitions (e.g., when dating begins at the same time as menarche and the transition to middle school) may exert unique pressures (as in Smolak, Levine, & Gralen, 1993). Other factors also influence dating such as late maturation in girls, with later maturers being less likely to date despite their lower levels of body fat.

Peer sexual activity is considered a potent influence on sexual activity. Udry et al. (1986) found that the strongest predictor of sexual behavior in pubertal girls was whether their close friends were sexually active. Meschke et al. (2000) supported these findings in a report showing that timing of first intercourse was associated with peer achievement levels and popularity for boys, along with "dating alone" and pubertal timing for girls. Siblings also influence sexual activity. Based on a social modeling theory, East and Shi (1997) proposed a sibling interaction hypothesis to explain sexual activity in pregnant or parenting teens and their younger sisters. Negative sibling relationship qualities, such as rivalry, competition, and conflict, were more closely related to younger sisters engaging in problem behavior and sexual behavior than were positive relationship qualities, such as warmth and closeness. Additionally, a shared friendship network with the older sister was found to be associated with extensive younger sister problem behavior and sexual behavior. Compared with the younger siblings of never-pregnant teenagers, the younger sisters of pregnant teenagers viewed school and career as less important, were more accepting of adolescent childbearing, perceived younger ages as appropriate for first intercourse, marriage, and childbearing, and engaged in more problem behavior (East, 1996). These attitudes are conducive to increasing the probability of early sexual activity and early childbearing. Collectively, these studies aptly demonstrate that a biopsychosocial model had greater statistical power for both boys and girls than do models that take fewer factors into account. In summary, hormones and pubertal development appear to impact strongly adolescents' sexual development, but sexuality occurs within the context of the adolescent's social development that incorporates peers and siblings.

Sexual Risk Taking

Sexual activity beginning sometime during puberty might be considered normative given the high number of adolescents engaging in early sexual activity. The danger inherent in considering sexual activity normative is that risky sexual behaviors are linked to high rates of morbidity and even mortality in adolescents. In a national survey of 10,645 youth, engaging in multiple health risk behaviors (including sexual behavior) increased across age in youth (Brener & Collins, 1998). For those in the 12–13 year age group, 1 in 12 engaged in two or more sexual behaviors, whereas one third of 14- to 17-year-olds and 50% of the 18- to 21-year-olds engaged in multiple sexual behaviors. There was a greater likelihood for males to engage in multiple health-risk behaviors. The predictive stability of early sexual behavior with regard to later mental and physical health problems is not well known. In one of the few longitudinal studies addressing this issue, women's reproductive experiences during adolescence had repercussions in adult life with regard to sexuality, self-image, and state of gynecological health (C. M. Magnusson et al., 1999). Women who had gynecological problems during adolescence experienced their adolescent sexual experiences as generally negative. In early adulthood these women had more recurrent and varied gynecological illnesses than did their comparison-group counterparts. Women's early sexual experience was also linked to an increase in norm-breaking behavior, lower educational attainment, and a younger age of adult responsibilities compared with the control women. These findings are unique in that they document long-term consequences of early sexual activity in diverse domains: health, adjustment, achievement, and socially sanctioned behavior. The lack of longitudinal information does not allow for sorting out whether early sexual activity is reflective of a constellation of behavior problems that persist over time or whether sexual activity, per se, leads to unique mental health and gynecological problems that persist into adulthood.

Limitations of self-report of sexual debut are acknowledged and likely result in an overestimate in the age of onset as well as the frequency of sexual activity during adolescence. In the National Youth Survey (Lauritsen & Swicegood, 1997) there were inconsistencies in age at first intercourse from reports as an adolescent to reports as an adult by 28% to 32% of subjects. Those most likely to have consistent reporting across time were females (70%), whereas only 27% of Black males were consistent in reporting. Given the seriousness of risky sexual behavior it seem prudent to continue to press for programs to reduce risky sexual behavior even in the absence of quality statistics on onset and progression of sexual activity during adolescence.

IMPLICATIONS FOR RESEARCH AND SOCIAL POLICY

The rapid increase in research findings in the last two decades relating puberty to various domains of functioning provides an exceptionally strong platform for planning interventions to improve the well-being of adolescents and to prevent problems. Findings from basic and applied research have implications for the content of prevention and intervention programs, the timing and type of interventions, and the modalities for delivering the program message. In addition, in the past several decades the importance of adolescence has been the focus of attention of various organized groups, which have, in turn, directed programs or policy issues toward that age group. For example, the American Academy of Pediatrics (www.aap.org) has a section on adolescent health, founded in 1978. Additionally, the Society of Adolescent Medicine offers specialized health services to adolescents (www.adolescenthealth.org). These services include not only the assessment of normal growth and physical health problems of adolescents but also psychosocial issues, health promotion, disease prevention, and anticipatory guidance. Unfortunately, the problem of maldistribution of health professionals specializing in adolescent health is significant. Many practitioners of adolescent health are in academic medical centers located in urban areas. Rural areas of the country continue to lack support services for adolescents. A parallel scenario is noted for psychiatrists specializing in adolescent development.

Policy-related goals for adolescent health and development also have been articulated. In 1998 Brindis et al. reviewed 36 national documents that emerged over the last decade and focused on or pertained to the health of adolescents. Through the synthesis of these documents, the committee determined the following six policy-related goals for the health of adolescents: (a) improve access to health care for adolescents, (b) improve the adolescent environment, (c) increase the role of schools in improving adolescent health, (d) promote positive adolescent health, (e) improve adolescent transitions to adulthood, and (f) improve collaborative relationships. In addition to the six policies, the committee also provided several cross-cutting themes that emerged from their recommendations. Most germane to this chapter is the theme that a "greater programmatic focus on primary prevention and early intervention, which is substantiated and shaped by rigorous research, is needed" (p. 183). Currently, adolescent health care focuses on secondary rather than primary prevention, and there is a dearth of research that characterizes the effect of providing counseling or anticipatory guidance services in the health care visits of youth or the effect of content and quality of primary care visits.

Content of Programs on Puberty

Public health policy lags behind the sophisticated knowledge that is accumulating regarding puberty, especially with regard to the notion that puberty signals the onset of reproductive competence, sexual activity, and risky sexual behavior. The majority of citizens in the United States are unaware of the recent advances in understanding the physiological aspects of puberty as well as the positive dimensions of psychological development during puberty. The sexual reproductive aspects of puberty receive disproportional attention compared to the normative and positive aspects of development during adolescence. The result is that normative health and developmental concerns receive little attention from major social institutions: health care, education, and family. A public health focus on puberty might profitably be based on the following questions: What do parents, educators, and the public need to know about puberty? What do adolescents want to know? Research initiatives and prevention programs arise almost exclusively from adults with virtually no consultation from adolescents. Therefore, a wide gap may exist between what information is presented to adolescents and what they want to know. In a rare study on what adolescents want to know, a majority of the questions reflected biological topics (88%), such as genital physiology (26%) and sexuality and reproduction (26%). Only 6% addressed psychosocial questions (Ryan, Millstein, & Irwin, 1996). Both females and Asians (compared with other ethnic or racial groups) expressed greater interest in the differences between male and female development. Prepubertal males were more concerned about general puberty than were boys in later Tanner stages.

In North America the study of puberty and reproduction is confused with sexual activity and the breaking of religious and social norms. Puberty and emerging sexuality take on negative societal connotations and thereby become shunned by the family and educational institutions. Adolescent sexuality is rarely viewed in the broader perspective as involving a social and cultural component. The interactions between boys and girls do not necessarily lead to sexual activity. Rather, these interactions reflect an arena whereby the social- and culture-based roles of males and females are learned and practiced.

Those entrusted with the care of adolescents should be cognizant of the broad range of emotional, behavioral, and even sexual activities that characterize the pubertal transition. Along with this awareness, those same persons should recognize that the diversity of acceptance or rejection of such functioning is often dictated by gender, ethnicity, age, and life history. Those involved in the health care system are in a prime position to educate the public and adolescents themselves about the range of new emotions and behaviors that will emerge by late puberty.

In addition to innovative content, positive attitudes about adolescents are critical elements of an effective program. Health care providers must recognize the specific challenges and rewards of providing services for adolescents. Quality care begins with the establishment of trust, respect, and confidentiality between the caregiver and the adolescent. Especially when providing care for the younger teen, caregivers must focus on involving a member of the family or another significant adult to provide needed support and guidance.

Anticipatory guidance for parents should focus on assessing their parenting styles and promoting supervision and monitoring. Although parents should strive to maintain open communication with their adolescents, they may estimate neither the depression and anxiety of their adolescents nor the sexual activity and the sexual risk experienced by their teenage children accurately. Most adolescents want to discuss sexual-related issues with health care providers and others and will welcome direct questions about sexual behaviors and possible risks when posed in a confidential and nonmoralistic manner. Discussion of the physical, emotional, familial, and social changes related to adolescence will encourage healthy sexual development.

Timing of Puberty and Prevention

A goal of prevention is to find a point in development when prevention efforts have some hope of success (Coie et al.,

1993). With regard to puberty, the goal is to initiate interventions before or simultaneously with the biological changes. Puberty may be occurring at earlier ages than anticipated in girls (Herman-Giddens et al., 1997), which has important health care, educational, and social policy implications. Programs to improve adolescent mental and physical health problems should correspondingly begin earlier in ontogeny than in the past. All individuals responsible for any aspect of the well-being of adolescents—parents, teachers, and health system personnel—should be aware that puberty may be occurring earlier in American girls than it did a few decades ago. In earlier maturing adolescents, the effects of hormone changes can occur two to three years before they are anticipated by parents and teachers. Important to note is that much less is known about boys than girls and timing of puberty. Given that boys and girls find themselves together in multiple contexts, programs to prevent mental and physical health problems should be introduced simultaneously for boys and girls.

Prevention efforts to reduce early risky sexual behaviors and mental health problems, like depression, are likely to have a higher probability of success if initiated at a younger age than in the past, given the earlier age of puberty. Social policy with regard to the cognitive abilities of adolescents, parent training, and school health and sex education and guidance programs will need to be modified to take into account the early onset of puberty (Reider & Coupey, 1999). Body self-awareness and emotion recognition programs are especially important to implement early in gonadarche; otherwise, adolescents will be confused by body changes that accompany puberty. Similarly, parental monitoring in sexual possibility situations, as well as in other situations (e.g., when alcohol or drugs may be present), will need to occur earlier than in the past. In all cases, programs to prevent early sexual activity will present a challenge to program planners given the cognitive developmental status of the adolescents and the complexities of presenting information about the physiology and psychology of sexuality.

Research and Theory Development

Scholars of adolescent development have accepted the importance of the integration of biological, psychological, and contextual processes long before it was fashionable in other areas of developmental science. The theoretical frameworks discussed earlier (developmental contextualism and holistic interactionism) are hallmarks for the acknowledgment of the importance of integrated biological, psychological, and social perspectives on development. These theoretical perspectives are consistent with the emerging perspective that processes of development can only be understood by considering the multiple systems that function at multiple levels of development, from the genetic, molecular, and cellular levels to the societal level (Susman, 1998). Given these complexities, the following principles might guide research in the future.

First, models that consider multiple biological, psychological, and contextual levels of functioning will be interdisciplinary, bringing together the expertise of multiple professionals. An example of such interdisciplinary research in the future is that offered by the Human Genome Project, which offers a myriad of possibilities for linking individual genes or patterns of genes to specific behaviors in specific contexts. Given that experiences affect the timing of puberty and that genes are responsible for the initiation of puberty, future interdisciplinary studies have the potential of identifying genes that link experience and the onset of puberty.

Second, the complexity of integrating multiple levels of analysis necessarily implies that the scale and scope of investigations will be larger than in the past. Nonetheless, hypothesis-driven, small-scale studies at specific levels of analysis are critically important to continue as well. If studies focus on one level of analysis, such as the biological level, it is critical to acknowledge the contribution of mediators and moderators at other levels as well.

Third, methodological innovations and the integration of biology and behavior are possible given the advances in statistical models in the last decade. In addition, theoretical innovations act in concert with methodological innovations. This premise is nowhere more apparent than in the new methodologies for considering the dynamic interplay between hormones and behavior. The dynamic and changing nature of physical maturation, hormones, and psychological characteristics at puberty now can be captured in longitudinal statistical models using estimates of how changes in one domain (hormones) can lead to changes in another domain (behavior). Additionally, perspectives like the holistic interaction model proposed by D. Magnusson (1999) capture dynamic holistic processes through related methodological strategies (e.g., longitudinal cluster analysis) developed by Bergman and Magnusson (1997). These methodological strategies look for patterns or configurations in developmental processes.

REFERENCES

Achenbach, T. M. (1991). *Manual for Child Behavior Checklist/4-18 and 1991 Profile*. Burlington: University of Vermont.

Andersson, T., & Magnusson, D. (1990). Biological maturation in adolescence and the development of drinking habits and alcohol abuse among young males: A prospective longitudinal study. *Journal of Youth and Adolescence, 19,* 33–42.

Angold, A., Costello, E. J., Erkanli, A., & Worthman, C. (1999). Pubertal changes in hormone levels and depression in girls. *Psychological Medicine, 29,* 1043–1053.

Angold, A., Costello, E. J., & Worthman, C. M. (1998). Puberty and depression: The roles of age, pubertal status and pubertal timing. *Psychological Medicine, 28,* 51–61.

Angold, A., & Worthman, C. (1993). Puberty onset of gender differences in rates of depression: A developmental, epidemiologic and neuroendocrine perspective. *Journal of Affective Disorders, 29,* 145–158.

Apter, D., Reinila, M., & Vikho, R. (1989). Some endocrine characteristics of early menarche, a risk factor for breast cancer, are preserved into adulthood. *International Journal of Cancer, 44,* 783–787.

Archer, J. (1991). The influence of testosterone on human aggression. *British Journal of Psychology, 82,* 1–28.

Ary, D. V., Duncan, T. E., Biglan, A., Metzler, C. W., Noell, J. W., & Smolkowski, K. (1999). Development of adolescent problem behavior. *Journal of Abnormal Child Psychology, 27,* 141–150.

Barnes, H. V. (1975). Physical growth and development during puberty. *Medical Clinics of North America, 59,* 1305–1317.

Bebbington, P. E., Dunn, G., Jenkins, R., Lewis, G., Brugha, T., Farrell, M., & Meltzer, H. (1998). The influence of age and sex on the prevalence of depressive conditions: Report from the National Survey of Psychiatric Morbidity. *Psychological Medicine, 28,* 9–19.

Belsky, J., Steinberg, L., & Draper, P. (1991). Childhood experience, interpersonal development, and reproductive strategy: An evolutionary theory of socialization. *Child Development, 62,* 647–670.

Bergman, L. R., & Magnusson, D. (1997). A person-oriented approach in research on developmental psychopathology. *Development and Psychopathology, 9,* 291–319.

Birdsall, M. A., Farquhar, C. M., & White, H. D. (1997). Association between polycystic ovaries and extent of coronary artery disease in women having cardiac catheterization. *Annals of Internal Medicine, 126,* 32–35.

Blos, P. (1962). *On adolescence: A psychoanalytical interpretation.* New York: Free Press.

Blum, W. F., Englaro, P., Hanitsch, S., Juul, A., Hertel, N. T., Muller, J., Skakkebaek, M. L., Heinman, M., Birkett, A. M., Attanasio, W., Kiess, W., & Rascher, W. (1997). Plasma leptin levels in healthy children and adolescents: Dependence on body mass index, body fat mass, gender, pubertal stage, and testosterone. *Journal of Clinical Endocrinology and Metabolism, 82,* 2904–2910.

Blyth, D. A., Simmons, R. G., & Zakin, D. F. (1985). Satisfaction with body image for early adolescent females: The impact of pubertal timing within different school environments. *Journal of Youth and Adolescence, 14,* 207–225.

Blythe, M. J., & Rosenthal, S. L. (2000). Female adolescent sexuality. Promoting healthy sexual development. *Obstetrics and Gynecology in Clinics of North America, 27,* 125–141.

Bondy, P. K. (1985). Disorders of the adrenal cortex. In J. D. Wilson & D. W. Foster (Eds.), *Williams textbook of endocrinology* (pp. 816–890). Philadelphia: Saunders.

Bonjour, J., Theintz, G., Buchs, B., Slosman, D., & Rizzoli, R. (1991). Critical years and stages of puberty for spinal and femoral bone mass accumulation during adolescence. *Journal of Clinical Endocrinology and Metabolism, 73,* 555–563.

Brain, P. F. (1994). Hormonal aspects of aggression and violence. In A. J. Reiss Jr., K. A. Miczek, & J. I. Roth (Eds.), *Understanding and preventing violence: Vol. 2. Biobehavioral influences* (pp. 173–244). Washington, DC: National Academy Press.

Brain, P. F., & Susman, E. J. (1997). Hormonal aspects of antisocial behavior and violence. In D. M. Stoff, J. Breiling, & J. Maser (Eds.), *Handbook of antisocial behavior* (pp. 314–323). New York: Wiley.

Brandtstaedter, J. (1998). Action perspectives on human development. In W. Damon (Series Ed.) & R. M. Lerner (Vol. Ed.), *Handbook of child psychology: Vol. 1. Theoretical models of human development* (pp. 807–863). New York: Wiley.

Brandstaedter, J., & Lerner, R. M. (1999). *Action and self-development: Theory and research through the life span.* Thousand Oaks, CA: Sage.

Brener, N. D., & Collins, J. L. (1998). Co-occurrence of health-risk behaviors among adolescents in the United States. *Journal of Adolescent Health, 22,* 209–213.

Brindis, C. D., Ozer, E. M., Handley, M., Knopf, D. K., Millstein, S. G., & Irwin, C. E. (1998). *Improving adolescent health: An analysis and synthesis of health policy recommendations, full report.* San Francisco: University of California, San Francisco.

Brooks-Gunn, J., & Petersen, A. C. (1983). *Girls at puberty: Biological and psychosocial perspectives.* New York : Plenum Press.

Brooks-Gunn, J., Petersen, A. C., & Eichorn, D. (1985). The study of maturational timing effects in adolescence [Special issue]. *Journal of Youth and Adolescence, 14,* 149–161.

Brooks-Gunn, J., & Reiter, E. O. (1990). The role of pubertal processes. In S. S. Feldman & G. R. Elliott (Eds.), *At the threshold: The developing adolescent* (pp. 16–53). Cambridge, MA: Harvard University Press.

Brooks-Gunn, J., & Warren, M. P. (1985). Measuring physical status and timing in early adolescence: A developmental perspective. *Journal of Youth and Adolescence, 14,* 163–189.

Brooks-Gunn, J., & Warren, M. P. (1989). Biological and social contributions to negative affect in young adolescent girls. *Child Development, 60,* 40–55.

Cairns, R. B. (1997). Socialization and sociogenesis. In D. Magnusson (Ed.), *The lifespan development of individuals: Behavioral, neurobiological and psychosocial perspectives: A synthesis* (pp. 277–295). New York: Cambridge University Press.

Cairns, R. B., & Rodkin, P. C. (1998). Phenomena regained: From configurations to pathways. In R. B. Cairns & L. R. Bergman (Eds.), *Methods and models for studying the individual* (pp. 245–265). Thousand Oaks, CA: Sage.

Cairns, R. B., & Stoff, D. M. (1996). Conclusion: A synthesis of studies on the biology of aggression and violence. In D. M. Stoff & R. B. Cairns (Eds.), *Aggression and violence: Genetic, neurobiological and biosocial perspectives.* Mahwah, NJ: Erlbaum.

Caspi, A., Henry, B., McGee, R. O., Moffitt, T. E., & Silva, P. A. (1995). Temperamental origins of child and adolescent behavior problems: From age three to fifteen. *Child Development, 66,* 55–68.

Caspi, A., & Moffitt, T. E. (1991). Individual differences are accentuated during periods of social change: Sample case of girls at puberty. *Journal of Personality and Social Psychology, 61,* 157–168.

Centers for Disease Control and Prevention (1999). *Youth Risk Behavior Survey* [On-line]. Available at www.cdc.gov/epo/mmwr/preview/mmwr.html/ss4905a1.htm.

Chrousos, G. P. (1998). Stressors, stress, and neuroendocrine integration of the adaptive response. *Stress of Life: From Molecules to Man, Annals of the New York Academy of Sciences, 851,* 311–335.

Chrousos, G. P., & Gold, P. W. (1992). The concepts of stress and stress system disorders. *Journal of the American Medical Association, 267,* 244–1252.

Cizza, G., Dorn, L. D., Lotsikas, A., Sereika, S., Rotenstein, D., & Chrousos, G. P. (2001). Circulating plasma leptin and IGF-1 levels in girls with premature adrenarche: Potential implications of preliminary study. *Hormone and Metabolic Research, 33,* 138–143.

Cohen, R., & Rosenfeld, R. G. (1996). Growth regulation. In J. E. Griffin & S. R. Agate (Eds.), *Textbook of endocrine physiology* (pp. 244–259), New York: Oxford University Press.

Coie, J. D., Watt, N. F., West, S. G., Hawkins, J. D., Asarnow, J. R., Marksman, H. J., Ramee, S. L., Shure, M. D., & Long, B. (1993). The science of prevention: A conceptual framework and some directions for a national research program. *American Psychologist, 48,* 1013–1022.

Constantino, J. N., Grosz, D., Saenger, P., Chandler, D. W., Nardi, R., & Earls, F. J. (1993). Testosterone and aggression in children. *Journal of the American Academy of Child and Adolescent Psychiatry, 32,* 1217–1222.

Counts, D. R., Pescovitz, O. H., Barnes, K. M., Hench, K. D., Chrousos, G. P., Sherins, R. J., Comite, F., Loriaux, D. L., & Cutler, G. B., Jr. (1987). Dissociation of adrenarche and gonadarche in precocious puberty and in isolated hypogonadotropic hypogonadism. *Journal of Clinical Endocrinology and Metabolism, 64,* 1174–1178.

Crockett, L. J., & Petersen, A. C. (1987). Pubertal status and psychosocial development: Findings from the Early Adolescence

Study. In R. M. Lerner & T. T. Foch (Eds.), *Biological-psychosocial interactions in early adolescence: Child psychology* (pp. 173–188). Hillsdale, NJ: Erlbaum.

Dorn, L. D., Hitt, S., & Rotenstein, D. (1999). Psychological and cognitive differences in children with premature vs. on-time adrenarche. *Archives of Pediatrics and Adolescent Medicine, 153,* 137–145.

Dorn, L. D., Susman, E. J., Nottelmann, E. D., Inoff-Germain, G., & Chrousos, G. P. (1990). Perceptions of puberty: Adolescent, parent, and health care personnel ratings of pubertal stage. *Developmental Psychology, 28,* 322–329.

Downs, A., & Fuller, M. J. (1991). Recollections of spermarche: An exploratory investigation. *Current Psychology: Research and Reviews, 10,* 93–102.

Dubas, J. S., Graber, J. A., & Petersen, A. C. (1991). The effects of pubertal development on achievement during adolescence. *American Journal of Education, 99,* 444–460.

Dunaif, A. (1997). Insulin resistance and the polycystic ovary syndrome: Mechanism and implications for pathogenesis. *Endocrine Review, 18,* 774–800.

Dunaif, A. (1999). Insulin action in the polycystic ovary syndrome. *Endocrinology and Metabolism Clinics of North America, 28,* 341–359.

Dunaif, A., Futterweit, W., Segal, K. R., & Dobrijansky, A. (1989). Profound peripheral insulin resistance independent of obesity in the polycystic ovary syndrome. *Diabetes, 38,* 1165–1174.

Duncan, P. D., Ritter, P. L., Dornbusch, S. M., Gross, R. T., & Carlsmith, J. M. (1985). The effects of pubertal timing on body image, school behavior, and deviance. *Journal of Youth and Adolescence, 14,* 227–235.

East, P. L. (1996). The younger sisters of childbearing adolescents: Their attitudes, expectations, and behaviors. *Child Development, 67,* 267–282.

East, P. L., & Shi, C. R. (1997). Pregnant and parenting adolescents and their younger sisters: The influence of relationship qualities for younger sister outcomes. *Journal of Development and Behavioral Pediatrics, 18,* 84–90.

Ellis, B. J., & Garber, J. (2000). Psychosocial antecedents of variation in girls' pubertal timing: Maternal depression, stepfather presence, and marital and family stress. *Child Development, 71,* 485–501.

Ellis, B. J., McFadyen-Ketchum, S., Dodge, K. A., Pettit, G. S., & Bates, J. E. (1999). Quality of early family relationships and individual differences in the timing of pubertal maturation in girls: A longitudinal test of an evolutionary model. *Journal of Personality and Social Psychology, 77,* 387–401.

Emans, S. J., & Biro, F. (1998). Secondary sexual characteristics and menses in young girls (Letter to the editor). *Pediatrics, 101,* 949–950.

Faust, M. S. (1969). Developmental maturity as a determinant of prestige in adolescent girls. *Child Development, 38,* 1025–1034.

Finkelstein, J. W., Susman, E. J., Chinchilli, V., Kunselman, S. J., D'Arcangelo, M. R., Schwab, J., Demers, L. M., Liben, L., Lookingbill, M. S., & Kulin, H. E. (1997). Estrogen or testosterone increases self-reported aggressive behavior in hypogonadal adolescents. *Journal of Clinical Endocrinology and Metabolism, 82,* 2433–2438.

Finkelstein, J. W., Susman, E. J., Chinchilli, V. M., D'Arcangelo, M. R., Kunselman, S. J., Schwab, J., Demers, L. M., Liben, L. S., & Kulin, H. E. (1998). Effects of estrogen or testosterone on self-reported sexual responses and behaviors in hypogonadal adolescents. *Journal of Clinical Endocrinology and Metabolism, 83,* 2281–2285.

Flannery, D. J., Rowe, D. C., & Gulley, B. L. (1993). Impact of pubertal status, timing and age on adolescent sexual experience and delinquency. *Journal of Adolescent Research, 8,* 21–40.

Ford, D. H., & Lerner, R. M. (1992). *Developmental systems theory: An integrative approach.* Newbury Park, CA: Sage.

Forest, M. G. (1989). Physiological changes in circulating androgens. In M. G. Forest (Ed.), *Androgens in childhood* (pp. 104–129). Basel: Karger.

Fredriks, A. M., Van Buuren, S., Burgmeijer, R. J. F., Muelmeester, J. F., Roelien, J., Brugman, E., Roede, M. J., Verloove-Vanhorick, S. P., & Wit, J. M. (2000). Continuing positive secular growth change in the Netherlands 1955–1997. *Pediatric Research, 47,* 316–323.

Frisch, R. E. (1984). Body fat, puberty and fertility. *Biological Reviews of the Cambridge Philosophical Society, 59,* 161–188.

Frisch, R. E., & MacArthur, J. (1974). Menstrual cycles: Fatness as a determinant of minimum weight for height necessary for their maintenance or onset. *Science, 185,* 949–951.

Gaddis, A., & Brooks-Gunn, J. (1985). The male experience of pubertal change. *Journal of Youth and Adolescence, 14,* 61–69.

Garn, S. M. (1992). Physical growth and development. In S. B. Friedman, M. Fisher, & SK Schonberg (Eds.), *Comprehensive adolescent health care* (pp. 18–23). St. Louis, MO: Quality Medical.

Ge, X., Brody, G. H., Conger, R. D., & Simons, R. L. (in press). Pubertal transition and African American children's internalizing and externalizing symptoms. *Journal of Youth and Adolescence.*

Ge, X., Conger, R. D., & Elder, G. H. (2001a). Pubertal transition, stressful life events, and the emergence of gender differences in adolescent depressive symptoms. *Developmental Psychology, 37,* 404–417.

Ge, X., Conger, R. D., & Elder, G. H. (2001b). The relationship between pubertal status and psychological distress in adolescent boys. *Journal of Research on Adolescence, 11,* 49–70.

Ge, X., Conger, R. D., & Elder, G. H., Jr. (1996). Coming of age too early: Pubertal influences on girls' vulnerability to psychological distress. *Child Development, 67,* 3386–3400.

Gell, J. S., Carr, B. R., Sasano, I. I., Atkins, B., Margarf, L., Mason, J. I., & Rainey, W. E. (1998). Adrenarche results from development of a 3-beta-hydroxysteroid dehydrogenase-deficient adrenal reticularis. *Journal of Clinical Endocrinology and Metabolism, 83,* 3695–3701.

Gerver, W. J., De Bruin, R., & Drayer, N. M. (1994). A persisting secular trend for body measurements in Dutch children: The Oosterwolde II Study. *Acta Paediatrica, 83,* 812–814.

Giedd, J. N., Blumenthal, J., Jeffries, N. O., Rajapakse, J. C., Vaituzis, A. C., Liu, H., Berry, Y. C., Tobin, M., Nelson, J., & Castellanos, F. X. (1999). Development of the human corpus callosum during childhood and adolescence: A longitudinal MRI study. *Progress in Neuro-psychopharmacology and Biological Psychiatry, 21,* 1185–1201.

Glickman, S. E., Frank, L. G., Davidson, J. M., Smith, E. R., & Siiteri, P. K. (1987). Androstenedione may organize or activate sex-reversed traits in female spotted hyenas. *Proceedings of the National Academy of Science, 84,* 3444–3447.

Goodyer, I. M., Herbert, J., Tamplin, A., & Altham, P. M. (2000). First-episode major depression in adolescents: Affective, cognitive and endocrine characteristics of risk status and predictors of onset. *British Journal of Psychiatry, 176,* 142–149.

Graber, J. A., Brooks-Gunn, J., & Warren, M. P. (1995). The antecedents of menarcheal age: Heredity, family environment, and stressful life events. *Child Development, 66,* 346–359.

Graber, J. A., Brooks-Gunn, J., & Warren, M. P. (in press). Pubertal effects on adjustment in girls: Moving from demonstrating effects to identifying pathways. *Journal of Youth and Adolescence.*

Graber, J. A., Lewisohn, P. M., Seeley, J. R., & Brooks-Gunn, J. (1997). Is psychopathology associated with the timing of pubertal development? *Journal of the American Academy of Child and Adolescent Psychiatry, 36,* 1768–1776.

Grumbach, M. M., & Styne, D. M. (1992). Puberty: Ontogeny, neuroendocrinology, physiology, and disorders. In J. D. Wilson & P. W. Foster (Eds.), *Williams textbook of endocrinology* (pp. 1139–1231). Philadelphia: Saunders.

Hall, G. S. (1904). *Adolescence.* New York: Appleton.

Halpern, C. T., Udry, J. R., & Suchindran, C. (1998). Monthly measures of salivary testosterone predict sexual activity in adolescent males. *Archives of Sexual Behavior, 27,* 445–465.

Halpern, C. T., Udry, J. R., & Suchindran, C. (1997). Testosterone predicts initiation of coitus in adolescent females. *Psychosomatic Medicine, 59,* 161–171.

Halpern, C. T., Udry, J. R., Campbell, B., & Suchindran, C. (1999). Effects of body fat on weight concerns, dating, and sexual activity: A longitudinal analysis of Black and White adolescent girls. *Developmental Psychology, 35,* 721–736.

Hayward, C., Killen, J. D., Wilson, D. M., Hammer, L. D., Litt, I. F., Kraemer, H. C., Haydel, F., Varaday, A., & Taylor, C. B. (1997). Psychiatric risk associated with early puberty in adolescent girls. *Journal of the American Academy of Child and Adolescent Psychiatry, 36,* 255–262.

Herman-Giddens, M. E., Slora, E. J., Wasserman, R. C., Bourdony, C. J., Bhapkar, M. V., Koch, G. G., & Hasemeier, C. (1997). Secondary sexual characteristics and menses in young girls seen in office practice: A study from the Pediatric Research in Office Settings Network. *Pediatrics, 99,* 505–512.

Hinde, R. A. (1991). When is an evolutionary approach useful? *Child Development, 62,* 671–675.

Hutchinson, K. A. (1995). Androgens and sexuality. *The American Journal of Medicine, 98,* 111S–115S.

Ibáñez, L., de Zegher, F., & Potau, N. (1999). Anovulation after precocious pubarche: Early markers and time course in adolescence. *Journal of Clinical Endocrinology and Metabolism, 84,* 2691–2695.

Ibáñez, L., Potau, N., Virdis, R., Zampolli, M., Terzi, C., Gussinye, M., Carrascosa, A., & Vicens-Calvet, E. (1993). Postpubertal outcomes in girls diagnosed of premature pubarche during childhood: Increased frequency of functional ovarian hyperandrogenism. *Journal of Clinical Endocrinology and Metabolism, 76,* 1599–1603.

Ibáñez, L., Potau, N., Zampolli, M., Street, M. E., & Carrascosa, A. (1997). Girls diagnosed with premature pubarche show an exaggerated ovarian androgen synthesis from the early stages of puberty: Evidence from gonadotropin-releasing hormone antagonist testing. *Fertility and Sterility, 67,* 849–855.

Inoff-Germain, G., Arnold, G. S., Nottelmann, E. D., Susman, E. J., Cutler, G. B., Jr., & Chrousos, G. P. (1988). Relations between hormone levels and observational measures of aggressive behavior of early adolescents in family interactions. *Developmental Psychology, 24,* 129–139.

Jones, B., Leeton, J., McLeod, I., & Wood, C. (1972). Factors influencing the age of menarche in a lower socio-economic group in Melbourne. *Medical Journal of Australia, 2,* 533–535.

Jones, H. E. (1938). The California adolescent growth study. *Journal of Educational Research, 31,* 561–567.

Jones, M. C. (1958). A study of socialization patterns at the high school level. *Journal of Genetic Psychology, 92,* 87–111.

Jones, M. C., & Bayley, N. (1950). Physical maturing among boys as related to behavior. *Journal of Educational Psychology, 41,* 129–148.

Jones, M. C., Bayley, N., & Jones, H. E. (1948). Physical maturing among boys as related to behavior. *American Psychologist, 3,* 264.

Kampert, J. B., Whittemore, A. S., & Paffenbarger, R. S., Jr. (1988). Combined effect of childbearing, menstrual events, and body size on age-specific breast cancer risk. *American Journal of Epidemiology, 128,* 962–979.

Kaplowitz, P. B., Cockerell, J. L., & Young, R. B. (1985). Premature adrenarche. *Clinical Pediatrics, 25,* 28–34.

Kaplowitz, P. B., Oberfield, S. E., and the Drug and Therapeutics and Executive Committees of the Lawson Wilkins Pediatric Endocrine Society. (1999). Reexamination of the age limit for defining when puberty is precocious in girls in the United States: Implications for evaluation and treatment. *Pediatrics, 104,* 936–941.

Kaufmann, R. B., Spitz, A. M., Strauss, L. T., Morris, L., Santelli, J. S., Koonin, L. M., & Marks, J. S. (1998). The decline in US teen pregnancy rates, 1990–1995. *Pediatrics, 102,* 1141–1147.

Key, T. J. (1999). Serum oestradiol and breast cancer risk. *Endocrine-Related Cancer, 6,* 175–180.

Kiess, W., Reich, A., Meyer, K., Glasow, A., Deutscher, J., Klammt, J., Yang, Y., Muller, G., & Kratzsch, J. (1999). A role for leptin in sexual maturation and puberty? *Hormone Research, 51,* 55–63.

Kim, K., & Smith, P. K. (1998). Retrospective survey of parental marital relations and child reproductive development. *International Journal of Behavioral Development, 22,* 729–751.

Kim, K., Smith, P. K., & Palermiti, A.-L. (1997). Conflict in childhood and reproductive development. *Evolution and Human Behavior, 18,* 109–142.

Knobil, E. (1988). The hypothalamic gonadotrophic hormone releasing hormone (GnRH) pulse generator in the rhesus monkey and its neuroendocrine control. *Human Reproduction, 3,* 29–31.

Kulin, H. E., Frontera, M. A., Demers, L. M., Barthlomew, M. J., & Lloyd, T. A. (1989). The onset of sperm production in pubertal boys: Relationship to gonadotropin excretion. *American Journal of Diseases of Children, 143,* 190–193.

Kulin, H. E., Finkelstein, J. W., D'Arcangelo, R., Susman, E. J., Chinchilli, V., Kunselman, S., Schwab, J., Demers, L., Lookingbill, G. (1997). Diversity of pubertal testosterone changes in boys with constitutional delay in growth and/or adolescence. *Journal of Child Clinical Endocrinology, 10,* 1–6.

Lange, N., Giedd, J. N., Castellanos, F. X., Vaituzis, A. C., & Rapoport, J. L. (1997). Variability of human brain structure size: Ages 4–20. *Psychiatry Research, 74,* 1–12.

Lauritsen, J. L., & Swicegood, C. G. (1997). The consistency of self-reported initiation of sexual activity. *Family Planning Perspectives, 29,* 215–221.

Lerner, R. M. (1987). A life-span perspective for early adolescence. In R. M. Lerner & T. T. Foch (Eds.), *Biological-psychological interactions in early adolescence* (pp. 1–34). Hillsdale, NJ: Erlbaum.

Lerner, R. M. (1998). Theories of human development: Contemporary perspectives. In W. Damon (Series Ed.) & R. M. Lerner (Vol. Ed.), *Handbook of child psychology: Vol. 1. Theoretical models of human development* (pp. 1–24). New York: Wiley.

Lerner, R. M., & Foch, T. T. (Eds.). (1987). *Biological-psychological interactions in early adolescence.* Hillsdale, NJ: Erlbaum.

Lewontin, R., & Levins, R. (2000). Let the numbers speak. *International Journal of Health Services, 30,* 873–877.

Li, C. I., Malone, K. E., White, E., & Daling, J. R. (1997). Age when maximum height is reached as a risk factor for breast cancer among U.S. women. *Epidemiology, 8,* 559–565.

Lovejoy, J. C. (1998). The influence of sex hormones on obesity across the female life span. *Journal of Women's Health, 7,* 1247–1256.

Maccoby, E. E. (1991). Different reproductive strategies in males and females. *Child Development, 62,* 676–681.

Magnusson, C. M., Persson, I. R., Baron, J. A., Ekbom, A., Bergstrom, R., & Adami, H. O. (1999). The role of reproductive factors and use of oral contraceptives in the aetiology of breast cancer in women aged 50 to 74 years. *International Journal of Cancer, 80,* 231–236.

Magnusson, D. (1981). *Toward a psychology of situations: An interactional perspective.* Hillsdale, NJ: Erlbaum.

Magnusson, D. (1999). Holistic interactionism: A perspective for research on personality development. In L. A. Pervin & O. P. John (Eds.), *Handbook of personality: Theory and research* (2nd ed., pp. 219–247). New York: Guilford Press.

Magnusson, D., & Cairns, R. B. (1996). Developmental science: Toward a unified framework. In R. B. Cairns, G. Elder, & J. Costello (Eds.), *Developmental science* (pp. 7–30). New York: Cambridge University Press.

Magnusson, D., & Stattin, H. (1998). Person-context interaction theories. In W. Damon (Series Ed.) & R. M. Lerner (Vol. Ed.), *Handbook of child psychology: Vol. 1. Theoretical models of human development* (pp. 685–759). New York: Wiley.

Magnusson, D., Stattin, H., & Allen, V. (1985). Biological maturation and social development: A longitudinal study of some adjustment processes from mid-adolescence to adulthood. *Journal of Youth and Adolescence, 14,* 267–283.

Malo, J., & Tremblay, R. E. (1997). The impact of paternal alcoholism and maternal social position on boys' school adjustment, pubertal maturation and sexual behavior: A test of two competing hypotheses. *Journal of Child Psychology and Psychiatry and Allied Disciplines, 38,* 187–197.

Mantzoros, C. S. (2000). Role of leptin in reproduction. *Annals of the New York Academy of Sciences, 900,* 174–183.

Mantzoros, C. S., Flier, J. S., & Rogol, A. D. (1997). A longitudinal assessment of hormonal and physical alterations during normal puberty in boys: V. Rising leptin levels may signal the onset of puberty. *Journal of Clinical Endocrinology and Metabolism, 82,* 1066–1070.

Marshall, W. A., & Tanner, J. M. (1969). Variations in patterns of pubertal change in girls. *Archives of Disease in Childhood, 44,* 291–303.

Marshall, W. A., & Tanner, J. M. (1970). Variations in patterns of pubertal changes in boys. *Archives of Disease in Childhood, 45,* 15–23.

Mazur, A., & Booth, A. (1998). Testosterone and dominance in men. *Behavioral and Brain Sciences, 21,* 353–397.

McClintock, M. K. (1998). Whither menstrual synchrony? *Annual Review of Sex Research, 9,* 77–95.

Medhamurthy, R., Gay, V. L., & Plant, T. M. (1990). The prepubertal hiatus in gonadotropin secretion in the male rhesus monkey (Macaca mulatta) does not appear to involve endogenous opioid peptide restraint of hypothalamic gonadotropin-releasing hormone release. *Endocrinology, 126,* 1036–1042.

Meschke, L. L., Zweig, J. M., Barger, B. L., & Eccles, J. S. (2000). Demographic, biological, psychological, and social predictors of the timing of first intercourse. *Journal of Research on Adolescence, 10,* 315–338.

Moffitt, T. E., Caspi, A., Belsky, J., & Silva, P. A. (1992). Childhood experience and the onset of menarche: A test of a sociobiological model. *Child Development, 63,* 47–58.

Morrison, J. A., Barton, B. A., Biro, F. M., Daniels, S. R., & Sprecher, D. L. (1999). Overweight, fat patterning, and cardiovascular disease risk factors in black and white boys. *Journal of Pediatrics, 135,* 451–457.

National Research Council, Board on Children, Youth, and Families. (1999). *Adolescent development and the biology of puberty.* Washington: National Academy Press.

Ness, R., Laskarzewski, P., & Price, R. A. (1991). Inheritance of extreme overweight in black families. *Human Biology, 63,* 39–52.

Nolen-Hoeksema, S., & Girgus, J. S. (1994). The emergence of gender differences in depression during adolescence. *Psychological Bulletin, 115,* 424–443.

Nottelmann, E. D., Inoff-Germain, G., Susman, E. J., & Chrousos, G. P. (1990). Hormones and behavior at puberty. In J. Bancroft & J. M. Reinisch (Eds.), *Adolescence and puberty* (pp. 88–123), New York: Oxford University Press.

Nottelmann, E. D., Susman, E. J., Inoff-Germain, G. E., Cutler, G. B., Jr., Loriaux, D. L., & Chrousos, G. P. (1987). Developmental processes in American early adolescence: Relations between adolescent adjustment problems and chronologic age, pubertal stage and puberty-related serum hormone levels. *Journal of Pediatrics, 110,* 473–480.

Olweus, D. (1986). Aggression and hormones: Behavioral relationships with testosterone and adrenaline. In D. Olweus, J. Block, & M. Radke-Yarrow (Eds.), *Developmental of antisocial and prosocial behavior: Research, theories, and issues* (pp. 51–72). Orlando, FL: Academic Press.

Olweus, D., Mattson, A., Schalling, D., & Low, H. (1988). Circulating testosterone levels and aggression in adolescent males: A causal analysis. *Psychosomatic Medicine, 50,* 261–272.

Ong, K. K., Ahmed, M. L., & Dunger, D. B. (1999). The role of leptin in human growth and puberty. *Acta Paediatr Supplement, 88,* 95–98.

Oppenheimer, E., Linder, B., Saenger, P., & DiMartino-Nardi, J. (1995). Decreased insulin sensitivity in prepubertal girls with premature adrenarche and acanthosis nigricans. *Journal of Clinical Endocrinology and Metabolism, 80,* 614–618.

Orr, D. P., & Ingersoll, G. M. (1995). The contribution of level of cognitive complexity and pubertal timing to behavioral risk in young adolescents. *Pediatrics, 95,* 528–533.

Parker, R. G., Rees, K., Leung, K. M., & Legorreta, A. P. (1999). Expression of risk factors for breast cancer in women younger than 49. *American Journal of Clinical Oncology, 22,* 178–179.

Parker, S. T. (2000). Comparative developmental evolutionary biology, anthropology, and psychology. In S. T. Parker, J. Langer, & L. M. McKinney (Eds.), *Biology, brain, and behavior* (pp. 1–24). Sante Fe, NM: Sar Press.

Petersen, A. C. (1988). Adolescent development. *Annual Review of Psychology, 39,* 583–607.

Petersen, A. C., & Crockett, L. (1985). Pubertal timing and grade effects on adjustment. *Journal of Youth and Adolescence, 14,* 191–206.

Petersen, A. C., & Taylor, B. (1980). The biological approach to adolescence. In J. Adelson (Ed.), *Handbook of adolescent psychology* (pp. 117–155). New York: Wiley.

Plant, T. M. (1995). Concluding remarks: Fourth international conference on the control of the onset of puberty. In T. M. Plant & P. A. Lee (Eds.), *The neurobiology of puberty* (pp. 337–342). Bristol: The Journal of Endocrinology Limited.

Plant, T. M. (1998). *The neurophysiology of puberty.* Paper presented at Physical Development, Health Futures of Youth II: Pathways to Adolescent, Maternal, and Child Health Bureau, Annapolis, MD.

Raine, A., Brennan, P. J., & Farrington, D. P. (1997). Biosocial bases of violence: Conceptual and theoretical issues. In A. Raine, D. Farrington, P. Brennan, & S. A. Mednick (Eds.), *Unlocking crime: The biosocial key* (pp. 1–20). New York: Plenum.

Reider, J., & Coupey, S. M. (1999). Update on pubertal development. *Current Opinion in Obstetrics and Gynecology, 11,* 457–462.

Reiter, E. O., & Saenger, P. (1997). Premature adrenarche. *The Endocrinologist, 7,* 85–88.

Richards, G. E., Cavallo, A., Meyer, W. J., III, Prince, M. J., Peters, E. J., Stuart, C. A., & Smith, E. R. (1985). Obesity, acanthosis nigricans, insulin resistance, and hyperandrogenism: Pediatric perspective and natural history. *Journal of Pediatrics, 107,* 893–897.

Rockhill, B., Moorman, P. G., & Newman, B. (1998). Age at menarche, time to regular cycling, and breast cancer. *Cancer Causes and Control, 9,* 447–453.

Roemmich, J. N., Clark, P. A., Berr, S. S., Mai, V., Mantzoros, C. S., Flier, J. S., Weltman, A., & Rogol, A. D. (1998). Gender differences in leptin levels during puberty are related to the subcutaneous fat depot and sex steroids. *American Journal of Physiology, 275,* E543–E551.

Roemmich, J. N., & Rogol, A. D. (1999). Role of leptin during childhood growth and development. *Endocrinology and Metabolism Clinics of North America, 28,* 749–764.

Rogol, A. D., Clark, P. A., & Roemmich, J. N. (2000). Growth and pubertal development in children and adolescents: Effects of diet and physical activity. *American Journal of Clinical Nutrition, 72,* 521S–528S.

Rogol, A. D., Roemmich, J. N., & Clark, P. A. (1998, September). *Growth at puberty.* Paper presented at a workshop, Physical Development, Health Futures of Youth II: Pathways to Adolescent health, Maternal and Child Health Bureau, Annapolis, MD.

Rosenfield, R. L., Bachrach, L. K., Chernausek, S. D., Gertner, J. M., Gottschalk, M., Hardin, D. S., Pescovitz, O. H., & Saenger, P. (2000). Current age of onset of puberty (Letter to the editor). *Pediatrics, 106,* 622.

Rowe, D. (1999). Introduction to the special section on behavioural genetics. *International Journal of Behavioral Development, 23,* 289–292.

Ryan, S. A., Millstein, S. G., & Irwin, C. E., Jr. (1996). Policy section: Puberty questions asked by early adolescents: What do they want to know? *Adolescent Health, 19,* 145–152.

Sanders, S. A., & Reinisch, J. M. (1990). Biological and social influences on the endocrinology of puberty: Some additional considerations. In J. Bancroft & J. M. Reinisch (Eds.), *Adolescence and puberty* (pp. 50–62). New York: Oxford University Press.

Sanders, B., & Soares, M. P. (1986). Sexual maturation and spatial ability in college students. *Developmental Psychology, 22,* 199–203.

Sapolsky, R. M. (1991). Testicular function, social rank, and personality among wild baboons. *Psychoneuroendocrinology, 16,* 281–293.

Saugstad, L. F. (1989a). Age at puberty and mental illness: Towards a neurodevelopmental aetiology of Kraepelin's endogenous psychoses. *British Journal of psychiatry, 155,* 536–544.

Saugstad, L. F. (1989b). Mental illness and cognition in relation to age at puberty: A hypothesis. *Clinical Genetics, 36,* 156–167.

Schaal, B., Tremblay, R., Soussignan, B., & Susman, E. J. (1996). Male pubertal testosterone linked to high social dominance but low physical aggression: A 7 year longitudinal study. *Journal of the American Academy of Child Psychiatry, 35,* 1322–1330.

Sherwood, L. (1993). *Human physiology: From cells to systems.* St. Paul, MN: West.

Siegel, S. F., Finegold, D. N., Urban, M. D., McVie, R., Lee, P. A. (1992). Premature pubarche: Etiological heterogeneity. *Journal of Clinical Endocrinology and Metabolism, 74,* 239–247.

Siegel, S., & Lee, P. (1992). Adrenal cortex and medulla. In W. Hung (Ed.), *Clinical pediatric endocrinology* (pp. 200–201). St. Louis, MO: Mosby.

Siegel, J. M., Yancey, A. K., Aneshensel, C. S., & Schuler, R. (1999). Body image, perceived pubertal timing, and adolescent mental health. *Journal of Adolescent Health, 25,* 155–165.

Silbereisen, R. K., Petersen, A. C., Albrecht, H. T., & Kracke, B. (1989). Maturational timing and the development of problem behavior: Longitudinal studies in adolescence. *Journal of Early Adolescence, 9,* 247–268.

Simmons, R., Blyth, A., Van Cleave, E., & Bush, D. (1979). Entry into early adolescence: The impact of school structure, puberty, and early dating on self-esteem. *American Sociological Review, 44,* 948–967.

Singh, S., & Darroch, J. E. (1999). Trends in sexual activity among adolescent American women: 1982–1995. *Family Planning Perspectives, 31,* 212–219.

Slemeda, C. W., Reister, T. K., Hui, S. L., Miller, J. Z., Christian, J. C., & Johnston, C. C. (1994). Influence on skeletal mineralization in children and adolescents: Evidence for varying effects of sexual maturation and physical activity. *Journal of Pediatrics, 125,* 201–207.

Smolak, L., Levine, M. P., & Gralen, S. (1993). The impact of puberty and dating on eating problems among middle school girls. *Journal of Youth and Adolescence, 22,* 355–368.

Stattin, H., & Magnusson, D. (1989). The role of early aggressive behavior in the frequency, seriousness, and types of later crime. *Journal of Consulting and Clinical Psychology, 57,* 710–718.

Stattin, H., & Magnusson, D. (1990). *Pubertal maturation in female development.* Hillsdale, NJ: Erlbaum.

Steinberg, L. D. (1987). Single parents, stepparents, and the susceptibility of adolescents to antisocial peer pressure. *Child Development, 58,* 269–275.

Steinberg, L. D. (1988). Reciprocal relations between parent-child distance and pubertal maturation. *Developmental Psychology, 24,* 122–128.

Steinberg, L. D., & Hill, J. P. (1978). Patterns of family interaction as a function of age, the onset of puberty, and formal thinking. *Developmental Psychology, 14,* 683–684.

Stern, K., & McClintock, M. K. (1998). Regulation of ovulation by human pheromones. *Nature, 392,* 177–179.

Stolz, H. R., & Stolz, L. M. (1944). Adolescent problems related to somatic variations. *Yearbook of the National Society for the Study of Education, 43,* 80–99.

Stratakis, C. A., & Chrousos, G. P. (1997). Neuroendocrinology and pathophysiology of the stress system. In G. P. Chrousos, R. McCarty, K. Pacák, G. Cizza, E. Sternberg, P. W. Gold, & R. Kvetńanský (Eds.), *Stress: Basic mechanisms and clinical implications. Annals of the New York Academy of Sciences, 771,* 1–18.

Surbey, M. K. (1990). Family composition, stress, and the timing of human menarche. In T. E. Ziegler & F. B. Bercovitch (Eds.), *Socioendocrinology of primate reproduction* (pp. 11–32). New York: Wiley-Liss.

Susman, E. J. (1997). Modeling developmental complexity in adolescence: Hormones and behavior in context. *Journal of Research on Adolescence, 7,* 283–306.

Susman, E. J. (1998). Biobehavioural development: An integrative perspective. *International Journal of Behavioral Development, 22,* 671–679.

Susman, E. J., Dorn, L. D., & Chrousos, G. P. (1991). Negative affect and hormone levels in young adolescents: Concurrent and longitudinal perspectives. *Journal of Youth and Adolescence, 20,* 167–190.

Susman, E. J., & Finkelstein, J. W. (2001). Biology, development and dangerousness. In L. Pagani & G. F. Pinard (Eds.), *Contributors of clinical assessment of dangerousness: Empirical contributions* (pp. 23–46). New York: Cambridge University Press.

Susman, E. J., Finkelstein, J. W., Chinchilli, V. M., Schwab, J., Liben, L. S., D'Arcangelo, M. R., Meinke, J., Demers, L. M., Lookingbill, G., & Kulin, H. E. (1998). The effect of sex hormone replacement therapy on behavior problems and moods in adolescents with delayed puberty. *Journal of Pediatrics, 133*(4), 521–525.

Susman, E. J., Inoff-Germain, G., Nottelmann, E. D., Cutler, G. B., Loriaux, D. L., & Chrousos, G. P. (1987). Hormones, emotional dispositions, and aggressive attributes in early adolescents. *Child Development, 58,* 1114–1134.

Susman, E. J., Nottelmann, E. D., Dorn, L. D., Gold, P. W., & Chrousos, G. P. (1989). The physiology of stress and behavioral development. In David S. Palermo (Ed.), *Coping with uncertainty: Behavioral and developmental perspectives* (pp. 17–37). Hillsdale, NJ: Erlbaum.

Susman, E. J., Nottelmann, E. D., Inoff, G. E., Dorn, L. D., Cutler, G. B., Loriaux, D. L., & Chrousos, G. P. (1985). The relation of relative hormonal levels and social-emotional behavior in young adolescents. *Journal of Youth and Adolescence, 14,* 245–252.

Susman, E. J., & Petersen, A. C. (1992). Hormones and behavior in adolescence. In E. R. McAnarney, R. E. Kreipe, D. P. Orr, & G. D. Comerci (Eds.), *Textbook of adolescent medicine* (pp. 125–130). New York: Saunders.

Susman, E. J., Worrall, B., Murowchick, E., Frobose, C., & Schwab, J. (1996). Experience and neuroendocrine parameters of development: Aggressive behaviors and competencies. In D. Stoff & R. Cairns (Eds.), *Neurobiological approaches to clinical aggression research* (pp. 267–289). Hillsdale, NJ: Erlbaum.

Suter, K. J., Pohl, C. R., & Plant, T. M. (1998). The pattern and tempo of the pubertal reaugmentation of open-loop pulsatile gonadotropin-releasing hormone release assessed indirectly in the male rhesus monkey (Macaca mulattta). *Endocrinology, 139,* 2447–2483.

Swarr, A. E., & Richards, M. H. (1996). Longitudinal effects of adolescent girls' pubertal development, perceptions of pubertal timing, and parental relations on eating problems. *Developmental Psychology, 32,* 636–646.

Talbott, E., Guzick, D., Clerici, A., Berga, S., Detre, K., Weimer, K., & Kuller, L. (1995). Coronary heart disease risk factors in women with polycystic ovary syndrome. *Arteriosclerosis, Thrombosis, and Vascular Biology, 15,* 821–826.

Tanner, J. M. (1965). The relationship of puberty to other maturity indicators and body composition in man. *Symposia of the Society for the Study of Human Biology, 6,* 211.

Tanner, J. M. (1989). *Foetus into man: Physical growth from conception to maturity.* Cambridge, MA: Harvard University Press.

Tanner, J. M., & O'Keeffe, B. (1962). Age at menarche in Nigerian school girls, with a note on their heights and weights from age 12 to 19. *Human Biology, 34*(3), 187–196.

Tersawa, E., Bridson, W. E., Nass, T. E., Noonan, J. J., & Dierschke, D. J. (1984). Developmental changes in the luteinizing hormone secretory pattern in peripubertal female rhesus monkeys: Comparison between gonadally intact and ovariectomized animals. *Endocrinology, 115,* 2233–2240.

Tremblay, R. E, Schaal, B., Boulerice, B., Arseneault, L., Soussignan, R., & Perusse, D. (1997). Male physical aggression, social dominance, and testosterone levels at puberty: A developmental perspective. In A. Raine, D. Farrington, P. Brennan, & S. A. Mednick

(Eds.), *Biosocial bases of violence* (pp. 271–291). New York: Plenum Press.

Tschann, J. M., Adler, N. E., Irwin, C. E., Jr., Millstein, S. G., Turner, R. A., & Kegeles, S. M. (1994). Initiation of substance use in early adolescence: The roles of pubertal timing and emotional distress. *Health Psychology, 13,* 326–333.

Udry, J. R. (1979). Age at menarche, at first intercourse, and at first pregnancy. *Journal of Biosocial Science, 11*(4), 433–441.

Udry, J. R., Billy, J. O. G., & Morris, N. M. (1986). Biosocial foundation for adolescent female sexuality. *Demography, 23,* 217–227.

Udry, R. J., Billy, J. O. G., Morris, N. M., Groff, T. R., & Raj, M. H. (1985). Serum androgenic hormones motivate sexual behavior in adolescent boys. *Fertility and Sterility, 43,* 90–94.

Udry, R., & Cliquet, R. L. (1982). A cross-cultural examination of the relationship between ages at menarche, marriage and first birth. *Demography, 19,* 53–63.

Udry, R. J., & Talbert, L. M. (1988). Sex hormone effects on personality at puberty. *Journal of Personality and Social Psychology, 54,* 291–295.

Van Goozen, S. H. M., Matthys, W., Cohen-Kettenis, P. T., Thijssen, J. H. H., & van Engeland, H. (1998). Adrenal androgens and aggression in conduct disorder prepubertal boys and normal controls. *Biological Psychiatry, 43,* 156–158.

Vihko, R. K., & Apter, D. L. (1986). The epidemiology and endocrinology of the menarche in relation to breast cancer. *Cancer Surveys, 5,* 561–571.

Warren, M. P., & Brooks-Gunn, J. J. (1989). Mood and behavior at adolescence: evidence for hormonal factors. *Journal of Clinical Endocrinology and Metabolism, 69,* 77–83.

Warren, M. P., Brooks-Gunn, J., Fox, R. P., Lancelot, C., Newman, D., & Hamilton, W. G. (1991). Lack of bone accretion and amenorrhea: Evidence for a relative osteopenia in weight-bearing bones. *Journal of Clinical Endocrinology and Metabolism, 72,* 847–853.

Wattigney, W. A., Srinivasan, S. R., Chen, W., Greenlund, K. J., & Berenson, G. S. (1999). Secular trend of earlier onset of menarche with increasing obesity in black and white girls: The Bogalusa Heart Study. *Ethnicity and Disease, 9,* 181–189.

Weber, A., Clark, A. J. L., Perry, L. A., Honour, J. W., & Savage, M. O. (1997). Diminished adrenal androgen secretion in familial glucocorticoid deficiency implicates a significant role for ACTH in the induction of Adrenarche. *Clinical Endocrinology, 46,* 431–437.

Wichstrom, L. (2000). Psychological and behavioral factors unpredictive of disordered eating: a prospective study of the general adolescent population in Norway. *International Journal of Eating Disorders, 28,* 33–42.

Wierson, M., Long, P. J., & Forehand, R. L. (1993). Toward a new understanding of early menarche: The role of environmental stress in pubertal timing. *Adolescence, 28,* 913–924.

Williams, J. M., & Dunlop, L. C. (1999). Pubertal timing and self-reported delinquency among male adolescents. *Journal of Adolescence, 22,* 157–171.

Wilson, D. M., Killen, J. D., Hayward, C., Robinson, T. N., Hammer, L. D., Kraemer, H. C., Varady, A., & Taylor, C. B. (1994). Timing and rate of sexual maturation and the onset of cigarette and alcohol use among teenage girls. *Archives of Pediatrics and Adolescent Medicine, 148,* 789–795.

Wyshak, G., & Frisch, R. E. (1982). Evidence for a secular trend in age of menarche. *New England Journal of Medicine, 306,* 1033–1035.

Yalcinkaya, T. M., Siiteri, P. K., Vigne, J. L., Licht, P., Pavgi, S., Frank, L. G., & Glickman, S. E. (1993). A mechanism for virilization of female spotted hyenas in utero. *Science, 260,* 1929–1931.

Zijdenbos, P. T., Worsley, A., Collins, K., Blumenthal, J., Giedd, J. N., Rapoport, J. L., & Evans, A. C. (1999). Structural maturation of neural pathways in children and adolescents. *Science, 283,* 1908–1911.

CHAPTER 13

Cognitive Development in Adolescence

JACQUELYNNE S. ECCLES, ALLAN WIGFIELD, AND JAMES BYRNES

In this chapter, we focus on two major aspects of adolescent development: cognitive development and both achievement and achievement motivation. First we discuss cognitive development, pointing out the relevance of recent work for both learning and decision making. Most of the chapter focuses on achievement and achievement motivation. We summarize current patterns of school achievement and recent changes in both school completion and differential performance on standardized tests of achievement. Then we summarize both the positive and negative age-related changes in school motivation and discuss how experiences in school might explain these developmental patterns. Finally, we discuss both gender and ethnic group differences in achievement motivation and link these differences to gender and ethnic group differences in academic achievement and longer-term career aspirations.

COGNITIVE DEVELOPMENT

In this section, we review work related to cognitive development. At a general level, the most important cognitive changes during this period of life relate to the increasing ability of youth to think abstractly, consider the hypothetical as well as the real, engage in more sophisticated and elaborate information-processing strategies, consider multiple dimensions of a problem at once, and reflect on oneself and on complicated problems (see Keating, 1990). Indeed, such abstract and hypothetical thinking is the hallmark of Piaget's formal operations stage assumed to begin during adolescence and to continue through young adulthood (e.g., Piaget & Inhelder, 1973; see the chapter by Feldman in this volume). Although there is still considerable debate about when exactly these kinds of cognitive processes emerge and whether their emergence reflects global stagelike changes in cognitive skills as described by Piaget, most theorists do agree that these kinds of thought processes are more characteristic of youth's cognition than of younger children's cognition.

At a more specific level, along with their implications for learning and problem solving, these kinds of cognitive changes affect individuals' self-concepts, thoughts about their future, and understanding of others. Theorists from Erikson (1968) to Harter (1990), Eccles (Eccles & Barber, 1999), and Youniss (Youniss, McLellan, & Yates, 1997) have suggested that the adolescent and emerging adulthood years are a time of change in youth's self-concepts, as they consider what possibilities are available to them and try to come to a deeper understanding of themselves. These sorts of self-reflections require the kinds of higher-order cognitive processes just discussed.

Finally, during adolescence individuals also become more interested in understanding others' internal psychological characteristics, and friendships become based more on perceived similarity in these characteristics (see Selman, 1980). Again, these sorts of changes in person perception reflect the broader changes in cognition that occur during adolescence. We turn now to a more detailed discussion of cognitive development during the adolescent years.

Are there age changes in the structural and functional aspects of cognition, and do these age-related trajectories in cognitive skills differ across gender and ethnic groups? In this section we summarize the research relevant to these questions. A fuller treatment can be found in sources such as Byrnes (2001a, 2001b), Bjorklund (1999), and Feldman (this volume).

Age Changes in Structural and Functional Aspects

Changes in Structural Aspects

Structural aspects of cognition include the knowledge possessed by an individual as well as the information-processing capacity of that individual. Structuralist researchers often focus on the following two questions: (a) What changes occur in children's knowledge as they progress through the adolescent period? and (b) What changes occur in the information-processing capacities of adolescents?

Knowledge Changes.   The term *knowledge* refers to three kinds of information structures that are stored in long term memory: declarative knowledge, procedural knowledge, and conceptual knowledge (Byrnes, 2001a, 2001b). *Declarative knowledge* or "knowing that" is a compilation of all of the facts an adolescent knows (e.g., knowing that $2 + 2 = 4$; knowing that Harrisburg is the capital of Pennsylvania). *Procedural knowledge* or "knowing how to" is a compilation of all of the skills an adolescent knows (e.g., knowing how to add numbers; knowing how to drive a car). The third kind of knowledge, *conceptual knowledge,* is the representation of adolescents' understanding of their declarative and procedural knowledge. Conceptual knowledge is "knowing why" (e.g., knowing why one should use the least common denominator method to add fractions).

Various sources in the literature suggest that these forms of knowledge increase with age (Byrnes, 2001). The clearest evidence of such changes can be found in the National Assessments of Educational Progress (NAEPs) conducted by the U.S. Department of Education every few years. The NAEP tests measure the declarative, procedural, and conceptual knowledge of fourth, eighth, and 12th graders (N's > 17,000) in seven domains: reading, writing, math, science, history, geography, and civics. In math, for example, NAEP results show that children progress from knowing arithmetic facts and being able to solve simple word problems in Grade 4 to being able to perform algebraic manipulations, create tables, and reason about geometric shapes by Grade 12 (Reese, Miller, Mazzeo, & Dossey, 1997). Although similar gains are evident for each of the domains (Beatty, Reese, Perksy, & Carr, 1996), in no case can it be said that a majority of 12th graders demonstrate a deep conceptual understanding in any of the domains assessed (Byrnes, 2001a, 2001b). One reason for the low level of conceptual knowledge in 12th graders is the abstract, multidimensional, and counterintuitive nature of the most advanced questions in each domain. Even in the best of circumstances, concepts such as scarcity, civil rights, diffusion, limit, and conservation of energy are difficult to grasp and illustrate. Moreover, the scientific definitions of such concepts are often counter to students' preexisting ideas. As a result, there are numerous studies showing misconceptions and faulty information possessed by adolescents and adults (see Byrnes 2001a, 2001b; see also the chapter by Feldman in this volume).

In sum, then, one can summarize the results on knowledge as follows:

- In most school-related subject areas, there are modest, monotonic increases in declarative, procedural, and conceptual knowledge between the fourth grade and college years.

- Misconceptions abound in most school subjects and are evident even in 12th graders and college students.

- The most appropriate answer to the question *"Does knowledge increase during adolescence?"* is the following: It depends on the domain (e.g., math vs. interpersonal relationships) and type of knowledge (e.g., declarative vs. conceptual).

- Although there is little evidence of dramatic and across-domain increases in understanding, there is consistent evidence of incremental increases in within-domain understanding as children move into and through adolescence.

Do these kinds of changes in knowledge influence behavior? For example, do older adolescents make better life decisions because they know more? Are they better employees? Parents? College students? Lifelong learners? At some level, the answer to these questions has to be yes. Certainly expanded domain-specific knowledge makes it easier to solve problems and perform complex tasks in activities very closely linked to the same knowledge domain (Byrnes, 2001a, 2001b; Ericcson, 1996). But does expanded knowledge on its own increase the wisdom of more general life decisions? The answer to this question is less clear because such decisions depend on many other aspects of cognitive as well as motivational and emotional processes that influence the likelihood of accessing and effectively using one's stored knowledge. For example, younger adolescents may have the knowledge needed to make decisions or solve problems (on achievement tests or in social situations) but may lack the processing space needed to consider and combine multiple pieces of information. We turn to these other aspects of cognition now.

Capacity Changes. Are there age-related increases in cognitive processing capacity? Processing space is analogous to random-access memory (RAM) on a computer. A very good software package may not be able to work properly if the RAM on a PC is too small. One key index of processing capacity in humans is working memory—the ability to temporarily hold something in memory (e.g., a phone number). It used to be assumed that working memory capacity changes very little after childhood. In fact, however, until quite recently this assumption had not been adequately tested. Several recent studies suggest that working memory does increase during adolescence. For example, Zald and Iacono (1998) charted the development of spatial working memory in 14- and 20-year-olds by assessing their memory for the location of objects that were no longer visible. They found that the introduction of delays and various forms of cognitive interference produced drops in performance that were sharper in the younger than in the older participants. Similarly, Swanson (1999) found monotonic increases in both verbal and spatial working memory between the ages of 6 and 35 in a large normative sample. Such increases should make it easier for older adolescents and adults to consider multiple pieces of information simultaneously in making important decisions. This hypothesis needs more extensive study.

Changes in Functional Aspects of Cognition

Functionalist aspects of cognition include any mental processes that alter, operate on, or extend incoming or existing information. Examples include learning (getting new information into memory), retrieval (getting information out of memory), reasoning (drawing inferences from single or multiple items of information), and decision making (generating, evaluating, and selecting courses of action). As noted earlier, both structural and functional aspects of cognition are critical to all aspects of learning, decision-making, and cognitive activities. For example, experts in a particular domain learn new, domain-relevant items of information better than novices do. Also, people are more likely to make appropriate inferences and make good decisions when they have relevant knowledge than when they do not have relevant knowledge (Byrnes, 1998; Ericsson, 1996). With this connection in mind, we can consider the findings sampled from several areas of research (i.e., deductive reasoning, decision making, other forms of reasoning) to get a sense of age changes in functional aspects.

Deductive Reasoning. People engage in deductive reasoning whenever they combine premises and derive a logically sound conclusion from these premises (S. L. Ward & Overton, 1990). For example, given the premises (a) *Either the butler or the maid killed the duke* and (b) *The butler could not have killed the duke,* one can conclude *The maid must have killed the duke.* Adolescents are likely to engage in deductive reasoning as they try to make sense of what is going on in a context and what they are allowed to do in that context. Moreover, deductive reasoning is used when they write argumentative essays, test hypotheses, set up algebra and geometry proofs, and engage in debates and other intellectual discussions. It is also critical to decision making and problem solving of all kinds.

Although the issue of age differences in deduction skills is somewhat controversial, most researchers believe that there are identifiable developmental increases in deductive reasoning skills between childhood and early adulthood. Competence is first manifested around age 5 or 6 in the ability to draw some types of conclusions from "if-then" (conditional) premises, especially when these premises refer to fantasy or make-believe content (e.g., Dias & Harris, 1988). Several years later, children begin to understand the difference between conclusions that follow from conditional premises and conclusions that do not (Byrnes & Overton, 1986; Girotto, Gilly, Blaye, & Light, 1989; Haars & Mason, 1986; Janveau-Brennan & Markovits, 1999), especially when the premises refer to familiar content about taxonomic or causal relations. Next, there are monotonic increases during adolescence in the ability to draw appropriate conclusions, explain one's reasoning, and test hypotheses, even when premises refer to unfamiliar, abstract, or contrary-to-fact propositions (Klaczynski, 1993; Markovits & Vachon, 1990; Moshman & Franks, 1986; S. L. Ward & Overton, 1990). Again, however, performance is maximized on familiar content about legal or causal relations (Klaczynski & Narasimham, 1998). However, when the experimental content runs contrary to what is true (e.g., *All elephants are small animals. This is an elephant. Is it small?*) or has no meaningful referent (e.g., *If there is a D on one side of a card, there is a 7 on the other*), less than half of older adolescents or adults do well.

Performance on the latter tasks can, however, be improved in older participants if the abstract problems are presented after exposure to similar but more meaningful problems or if the logic of the task is adequately explained (Klaczynski, 1993; Markovits & Vachon, 1990; S. L. Ward, Byrnes, & Overton, 1990). Even so, such interventions generally have only a weak effect. These findings imply that most of the development after age 10 in deductive reasoning competence is in the ability to suspend one's own beliefs and think objectively about the structure of an argument (e.g., *"Let's assume for the moment that this implausible argument is true . . ."*; Moshman, 1998). Little evidence exists for an abstract, domain-general ability that is spontaneously applied to new and different content.

Decision Making.   When people make decisions, they set a goal (e.g., get something to eat), compile options for attaining that goal (e.g., go out, find something in the refrigerator, etc.), evaluate these options (e.g., eating at home is cheaper and healthier than eating out), and finally implement the best option. Alternatively, they must decide whether to engage in a particular behavior that is made available to them in a specific situation (e.g., they decide whether to have sexual intercourse in an intimate encounter or to accept an offered alcoholic drink or illicit drug). Competent decision making entails the ability to identify the risks and benefits of particular behaviors as well as the ability to identify options likely to lead to positive, health-promoting outcomes (e.g., stable relationships, good jobs, physical health, emotional health, etc.) or promote one's short- and long-term goals. Clearly, good decision-making skills are among the most important cognitive skills adolescents need to acquire.

Given the centrality of decision making, it is surprising that so few developmental studies have been conducted (Byrnes, 1998; Klaczynski, Byrnes, & Jacobs, 2001). Considered together, the widely scattered (and sometimes unreplicated) findings suggest that older adolescents and adults seem to be more likely than are younger adolescents or children to (a) understand the difference between options likely to satisfy multiple goals and options likely to satisfy only a single goal (Byrnes & McClenny, 1994; Byrnes, Miller, & Reynolds, 1999), (b) anticipate a wider range of consequences of their actions (Lewis, 1981; Halpern-Felsher & Cauffman, 2001), and (c) learn from their decision-making successes and failures with age (Byrnes & McClenny, 1994; Byrnes, Miller, & Reynolds, 1999). There is also some suggestion that adolescents are more likely to make good decisions when they have metacognitive insight into the factors that affect the quality of decision making (D. C. Miller & Byrnes, 2001; Ormond, Luszcz, Mann, & Beswick, 1991). However, most of the

studies that support these conclusions involved laboratory tasks, hypothetical scenarios, or self-reports. In real-world contexts, other emotional and motivational factors are likely to seriously affect the quality of adolescents' decisions. For example, adolescents may think they will find a particular outcome enjoyable, only to learn later that it was not, either because they had inadequate self-knowledge or because they failed to use the self-knowledge that they had. High states of emotional arousal or intoxication can also reduce an adolescent's ability and motivation to generate, evaluate, and implement success-producing options and to adequately assess the risks associated with various behavioral options. Hence, adolescents and adults who look good in the lab may nevertheless make poor decisions in the real world if they lack appropriate self-regulatory strategies for dealing with such possibilities (e.g., self-calming techniques, coping with peer pressure to drink, etc.). Additional studies are clearly needed to examine such issues. The recent work by Baltes and his colleagues on the selection-optimization-compensation (SOC) models of adaptive behavior provides one useful approach for such research (see Baltes, Lindenberger, & Staudinger, 1998).

In contrast to the dearth of studies on decision making in adolescents, there are quite a number of developmental studies in a related area of research: risk taking (Byrnes, 1998). If a decision involves options that could lead to negative or harmful consequences (i.e., anything ranging from mild embarrassment to serious injury or death), adolescents who pursue such options are said to have engaged in risk-taking (Byrnes, Miller, & Schaefer, 1999). Although all kinds of risk taking are of interest from scientific standpoint, most studies have focused on age changes in physically harmful behaviors such as smoking, drinking, and unprotected sex. Regrettably, these studies reveal the opposite of what one would expect if decision-making skills improve during adolescence; instead, these studies show that older adolescents are more likely than younger adolescents or preadolescents to engage in these behaviors (DiClemente, Hansen, & Ponton, 1995). Repeatedly, studies have shown that those who take such risks do not differ in their knowledge of possible negative consequences. Given that risk-takers and risk-avoiders do not differ in their knowledge of options and consequences, it is likely that the difference lies in other aspects of competent decision making (e.g., self-regulatory strategies, ability to coordinate health-promoting and social goals, etc.). This hypothesis remains to be tested.

Other Functional Aspects.   In addition to finding age-related increases in deductive reasoning and decision-making skills, researchers have also found increases in mathematical reasoning ability, certain kinds of memory-related processes, the ability to perform spatial reasoning tasks quickly, and certain aspects of scientific reasoning (Byrnes, 2001a). The variables that seem to affect the size of these increases include (a) whether students have to learn information during the experiment or retrieve something known already, and (b) the length of the delay between stimulus presentation and being asked to retrieve information. In the case of scientific reasoning, the ability to consciously construct one's own hypotheses across a wide range of contents, test these hypotheses in controlled experiments, and draw appropriate inferences also increases (Byrnes, 2001a, 2001b; Klaczynski & Narasimham, 1998; Kuhn, Garcia-Mila, Zohar, & Andersen, 1995).

Summary

The literature suggests that there are changes in the intellectual competencies of youth as they progress through the adolescent period. However, there are many ways in which the thinking of young adolescents is similar to that of older adolescents and adults. Thus, before one can predict whether an age difference will manifest itself on any particular measure of intellectual competence, one needs to ask questions such as *"Does exposure to the content of the task continue through adolescence?"*, *"Do many issues have to be held in mind and considered simultaneously?, "Are the ideas consistent with naive conceptions?"*, and *"Does success on the task require one to suspend one's beliefs?"* If the answers to these questions are all *"no,"* then younger adolescents, older adolescents, and adults should perform about the same. However, if one or more *"yes"* answer is given, then one would expect older adolescents and adults to demonstrate more intellectual competence than younger adolescents.

Gender and Ethnic Differences in Cognition

It is not possible to provide a comprehensive summary of the vast literature on gender and ethnic differences in a single chapter or portion of a chapter. One can, however, provide an overview of some of the essential findings (see Byrnes, 2001a, 2001b, for a more complete summary). With respect to gender differences, male and female adolescents perform comparably on measures of math, science, and social studies knowledge (e.g., NAEPs) and also obtain nearly identical scores on measures of intelligence, deductive reasoning, decision making, and working memory. Two areas in which gender differences have appeared are risk taking and Scholastic Achievement Test (SAT) math performance. With regard to risk taking, the pattern is quite mixed: Males are more likely than females to take such risks as driving recklessly or taking intellectual risks; in contrast, females are

more likely than males to take such health risks as smoking. The size of such gender differences, however, varies by age (Byrnes, Miller, & Schaefer, 1999). These findings seem to reflect differences in males' and females' expectations, values, and self-regulatory tendencies.

With regard to gender differences on SAT-math scores, male's scores are routinely slightly higher than are female's scores (De Lisi & McGillicuddy-De Lisi, 2002). It is still not clear why this difference obtains, given the fact that there are no gender differences in math knowledge or gender differences in other kinds of reasoning. Researchers have shown, however, that part of this difference reflects gender differences in test-taking strategies, confidence in one's math ability, ability and motivation to use unconventional problem-solving strategies, mental rotation skills, and anxiety about one's math ability, particularly when one's gender is made salient (see De Lisi & McGillicuddy-De Lisi, 2002, for review).

With respect to ethnic differences, European American and Asian American students perform substantially better than do African American, Hispanic and Native American students on standardized achievement tests, the SAT, and most of the NAEP tests. In contrast, no ethnic differences are found in studies of deductive reasoning, decision-making, or working memory. Moreover, ethnic differences on tests such as the SAT and NAEP are substantially reduced after variables such as parent education and prior course work are controlled (Byrnes, 2001). We know even less about the origins of these ethnic group differences than we know about the origins of gender differences in cognitive performance.

ACHIEVEMENT AND ACHIEVEMENT-RELATED BELIEFS

The picture of achievement for adolescents in the United States is mixed. More youth than ever are graduating from high school, and a large number are enrolled in some form of higher education (National Center for Educational Statistics, 1999; Office of Educational Research and Improvement, 1988). High school dropout rates, although still unacceptably large in some population subgroups, are at all-time lows (National Center for Educational Statistics, 1999; Office of Educational Research and Improvement, 1988). Comparable improvements in educational attainment over the last century characterize all Western industrialized countries as well as many developing countries.

In contrast to these quite positive trends in academic achievement, a substantial minority of America's adolescents are not doing very well in terms of academic achievement and school-related achievement motivation: First and foremost, America's adolescents on average perform much worse on academic achievement tests than do adolescents from many other countries (National Center for Educational Statistics, 1995). Between 15 and 30% of America's adolescents drop out of school before completing high school; and many others are disenchanted with school and education (Kazdin, 1993; Office of Educational Research and Improvement, 1988). Both the rates of dropping out and disengagement are particularly marked among poor youth and both Hispanic and Native American youth.

There are also mean level declines in such motivational constructs as grades (Simmons & Blyth, 1987), interest in school (Epstein & McPartland, 1976), intrinsic motivation (Harter, 1981), and self-concepts (Eccles et al., 1989; Wigfield, Eccles, Mac Iver, & Reuman, 1991; Simmons & Blyth, 1987) in conjunction with the junior high school transition. For example, Simmons and Blyth (1987) found a marked decline in some young adolescents' school grades as they moved into junior high school—the magnitude of which predicted subsequent school failure and dropout (see also Roderick, 1993). Several investigators have also found drops in self-esteem as adolescents make the junior and senior high school transitions—particularly (but not always only) among European American girls (Eccles et al., 1989; Simmons & Blyth, 1987; Wigfield et al., 1991). Finally, there is evidence of similarly timed increases in such negative motivational and behavioral characteristics as focus on self-evaluation rather than task mastery (e.g., Maehr & Anderman, 1993), test anxiety (Hill & Sarason, 1966), and both truancy and school dropout (Rosenbaum, 1976; see Eccles, Wigfield, & Schiefele, 1998, for full review).

Few studies have gathered information on ethnic and social class differences in these declines. However, academic failure and dropout are especially problematic among African American and Hispanic youth and among youth from low-SES (socioeconomic status) communities and families (Finn, 1989). It is probable then that these groups are particularly likely to show these declines in academic motivation and self-perceptions as they move into and through the years of secondary school. We discuss this possibility more later in this chapter.

Although these changes are not extreme for most adolescents, there is sufficient evidence of gradual declines in various indicators to make one wonder what is happening (see Eccles & Midgley, 1989). A variety of explanations have been offered. Some scholars attribute these declines to the intrapsychic upheaval assumed to be associated with early pubertal development (see Arnett, 1999). Others have suggested that they result from the coincidence of multiple life changes. For example, drawing upon cumulative stress theory, Simmons and her colleagues suggest that declines in motivation result from the fact that adolescents making the transition to junior high school at the end of Grade 6 must cope with two major transitions: pubertal change and school change (see Simmons & Blyth, 1987). Because coping with multiple transitions is more difficult than coping with only one, these adolescents are at greater risk of negative outcomes than are adolescents who have to cope with only pubertal change during this developmental period. To test this hypothesis, Simmons and her colleagues compared the pattern of changes on the school-related outcomes of young adolescents who moved from sixth to seventh grade in a K–8, 9–12 system with the pattern of changes for those who made the same grade transition in a K–6, 7–9, 10–12 school system. They found clear evidence, especially among girls, of greater negative changes for those adolescents making the junior high school transition than for those remaining in the same school setting (i.e., those in K–8, 9–12 schools). The fact that the junior high school transition effects were especially marked for girls was interpreted as providing additional support for the cumulative stress theory, because at this age girls are more likely than boys are to be undergoing both a school transition and pubertal change. Further evidence in support of the role of the cumulative stress came from Simmons and Blyth's (1987) analyses comparing adolescents who experienced varying numbers of other life changes in conjunction with the junior high school transition. The negative consequences of the junior high school transition increased in direct proportion to the number of other life changes an adolescent also experienced as he or she made the school transition.

The Junior High School Transition

Eccles and her colleagues have focused on the school transition itself as a possible cause of academic-motivational declines. As noted previously, many of these declines coincide with school transitions. The strongest such evidence comes from work focused on the junior high school transition—for example, the work just discussed by Simmons and Blyth. Eccles and her colleagues have obtained similar results using the data from the National Educational Longitudinal Study. They compared eighth graders in K–8 school systems with eighth graders in either K–6, 7–9 systems or K–5, 6–8 systems. The eighth-grade students in the K–8 systems looked better on such motivational indicators as self-esteem, preparedness, and attendance than did the students in either of the other two types of school systems (Eccles, Lord, & Buchanan, 1996). In addition, the eighth-grade teachers in the K–8 system reported fewer student problems, less truancy, and more student engagement than did the teachers in either of the other two types of school systems. Clearly, both the young adolescents and their teachers fared better in K–8 school systems than did those in the more prevalent junior high school and middle school systems. Why?

Several investigators have suggested that the changing nature of the educational environments experienced by many young adolescents helps explain these types of school system differences as well as the mean level declines in the school-related measures associated with the junior high school transition (e.g., Eccles, Midgley, Buchanan, Wigfield, Reuman & Mac Iver, 1993; Eccles & Midgley, 1989; Lipsitz, 1984; Simmons & Blyth, 1987). Drawing upon person-environment fit theory (see Hunt, 1979), Eccles and Midgley (1989) proposed that these motivational and behavioral declines could result from the fact that junior high schools are not providing appropriate educational environments for many young adolescents. According to person-environment theory, behavior, motivation, and mental health are influenced by the fit between the characteristics individuals bring to their social environments and the characteristics of these social environments (Hunt, 1979; see also the chapter by Lerner, Easterbrooks, and Mistry in this volume). Individuals are not likely to do very well or be very motivated if they are in social environments that do not fit their psychological needs. If the social environments in the typical junior high school do not fit very well with the psychological needs of adolescents, then person-environment fit theory predicts a decline in adolescents' motivation, interest, performance, and behavior as they move into this environment. Furthermore, Eccles and Midgley (1989) argued that this effect should be even more marked if the young adolescents experience a fundamental change in their school environments when they move into a junior high school or middle school—that is, if the school environment of the junior high school or middle school fits less well with their psychological needs than did the school environment of the elementary school.

This analysis suggests several questions. First, what are the developmental needs of the early adolescent? Second, what kinds of educational environment are developmentally appropriate for meeting these needs and stimulating further development? Third, what are the most common school environmental changes before and after the transition to middle or junior high school? Fourth—and most important—are these changes compatible with the physiological, cognitive, and psychological changes early adolescents are experiencing? Or is there a developmental mismatch between maturing early adolescents and the classroom environments they experience before and after the transition to middle or junior high

school that results in a deterioration in academic motivation and performance for some children?

Eccles and Midgley (1989) argued that there are developmentally inappropriate changes at the junior high or middle school in a cluster of classroom organizational, instructional, and climate variables, including task structure, task complexity, grouping practices, evaluation techniques, motivational strategies, locus of responsibility for learning, and quality of teacher-student and student-student relationships. They hypothesized that these changes contribute to the negative change in early adolescents' motivation and achievement-related beliefs.

Is there any evidence that such a negative change in the school environment occurs with the transition to junior high school? Most relevant descriptions have focused on school-level characteristics such as school size, degree of departmentalization, and extent of bureaucratization. For example, Simmons and Blyth (1987) point out that most junior high schools are substantially larger (by several orders of magnitude) than elementary schools, and instruction is more likely to be organized departmentally. As a result, junior high school teachers typically teach several different groups of students, making it very difficult for students to form a close relationship with any school-affiliated adult at precisely the point in development when there is a great need for guidance and support from nonfamilial adults. Such changes in student-teacher relationships are also likely to undermine the sense of community and trust between students and teachers, leading to a lowered sense of efficacy among the teachers, an increased reliance on authoritarian control practices by the teachers, and an increased sense of alienation among the students. Finally, such changes are likely to decrease the probability that any particular student' difficulties will be noticed early enough to get the student the help he or she needs, thus increasing the likelihood that students on the edge will be allowed to slip onto negative motivational and performance trajectories leading to increased school failure and dropout. Recent work by Elder and his colleagues (Elder & Conger, 2000) and classic work on the disadvantages of large schools by Barker and Gump (1964) provide strong support for these suggestions.

These structural changes are also likely to affect classroom dynamics, teacher beliefs and practices, and student alienation and motivation in the ways proposed by Eccles and Midgley (1989). Some support for these predictions is emerging, along with evidence of other motivationally relevant systematic changes (e.g., Maehr & Midgley, 1996; B. A. Ward et al., 1982).

First, despite the increasing maturity of students, junior high school classrooms—as compared to elementary school classrooms—are characterized by a greater emphasis on teacher control and discipline and fewer opportunities for student decision making, choice, and self-management (e.g., Midgley & Feldlaufer, 1987; Moos, 1979). For example, junior high school teachers spend more time maintaining order and less time actually teaching than do elementary school teachers (Brophy & Evertson, 1976).

Similar differences emerge on indicators of student opportunity to participate in decision making regarding their own learning. For example, Midgley and Feldlaufer (1987) reported that both seventh graders and their teachers in the first year of junior high school indicated less opportunity for students to participate in classroom decision making than did these same students and their sixth-grade elementary school teachers 1 year earlier.

Such declines in the opportunity for participation in decision making and self-control are likely to be particularly detrimental at early adolescence. This is a time in development when youth begin to think of themselves as young adults. It is also a time when they increase their exploration of possible identities. They believe they are becoming more responsible and consequently deserving of greater adult respect. Presumably, the adults responsible for their socialization would also like to encourage them to become more responsible for themselves as they move towards adulthood; in fact, this is what typically happens across the elementary school grades (see Eccles & Midgley, 1989). Unfortunately, the evidence suggests this developmentally appropriate progression is disrupted with the transition to junior high school.

In their stage-environment fit theory, Eccles and Midgley (1989) hypothesize that the mismatch between young adolescents' desires for autonomy and control and their perceptions of the opportunities in their learning environments will result in a decline in the adolescents' intrinsic motivation and interest in school. Mac Iver and Reuman (1988) provided some support for this prediction. They compared the changes in intrinsic interest in mathematics for adolescents reporting different patterns of change in their opportunities for participation in classroom decision-making items across the junior high school transition. Those adolescents who perceived their seventh-grade math classrooms as providing fewer opportunities for decision making that had been available in their sixth-grade math classrooms reported the largest declines in their intrinsic interest in math as they moved from the sixth grade into the seventh grade.

Second, junior high school classrooms (as compared to elementary school classrooms) are characterized by less personal and positive teacher-student relationships (Feldlaufer, Midgley, & Eccles, 1988). Furthermore, the transition into a less supportive classroom impacts negatively on early adolescents' interest in the subject matter being taught in that classroom, particularly among low-achieving students (Midgley, Feldlaufer, & Eccles, 1989b).

Such a shift in the quality of student-teacher relationships is likely to be especially detrimental at early adolescence. As adolescents explore their own identities, they are prone to question the values and expectations of their parents. In more stable social groups, young adolescents often have the opportunity to do this questioning with supportive nonparental adults such as religious counselors, neighbors, and relatives. In our highly mobile, culturally diverse society, such opportunities are not as readily available. Teachers are the one stable source of nonparental adults left for many American youth. Unfortunately, the sheer size and bureaucratic nature of most junior high schools—coupled with the stereotypes many adults hold regarding the negative characteristics of adolescents—can lead teachers to distrust their students and to withdraw from them emotionally (see Eccles et al., 1993; C. L. Miller et al., 1990). Consequently, these youth have little choice but to turn to peers as nonparental guides in their exploration of alternative identities. Evidence from a variety of sources suggests that this can be a very risky venture.

The reduced opportunity for close relationships between students and junior high school teachers has another unfortunate consequence for young adolescents: It decreases the likelihood that teachers will be able to identify students on the verge of getting into serious trouble and then to get these students the help they need. In this way, the holes in the safety net may become too big to prevent unnecessary "failures." Successful passage through this period of experimentation requires a tight safety net carefully monitored by caring adults—adults who provide opportunities for experimentation without letting the youth seriously mortgage their futures in the process. Clearly, the large, bureaucratic structure of the typical junior high and middle school is ill suited to such a task.

Third, junior high school teachers (again compared to elementary school teachers) feel less effective as teachers, especially for low-ability students. For example, the seventh-grade junior high teachers studied by Midgley, Feldlaufer, and Eccles (1988) expressed much less confidence in their teaching efficacy than did sixth-grade elementary school teachers in the same school districts. In addition, those students who experienced a decline in their teachers' sense of efficacy as they made the junior high school transition lowered their estimates of their math abilities more than did other students (Midgley, Feldlaufer, & Eccles, 1989a). This decline in teachers' sense of efficacy for teaching less competent students could help explain why it is precisely these students who give up on themselves following the junior high school transition.

Fourth, junior high school teachers are much more likely than elementary school teachers are to use such teaching practices as whole-class task organization, public forms of evaluation, and between-classroom ability grouping (see Eccles & Midgley, 1989). Such practices are likely to increase social comparison, concerns about evaluation, and competitiveness (see Rosenholtz & Simpson, 1984), which in turn are likely to undermine many young adolescents' self-perceptions and motivation. These teaching practices also make aptitude differences more salient to both teachers and students, likely leading to increased teacher expectancy effects and both decreased feelings of efficacy and increased entity rather than incremental views of ability among teachers (Dweck & Elliott, 1983). These predictions need to be tested.

Fifth, junior high school teachers appear to use a more competitive standard in judging students' competence and in grading their performance than do elementary school teachers (see Eccles & Midgley, 1989). There is no predictor of students' self-confidence and sense of personal efficacy for schoolwork stronger than the grades they receive. If grades change, then we would expect to see a concomitant shift in the adolescents' self-perceptions and academic motivation; this is in fact what happens. For example, Simmons and Blyth (1987) found a greater drop in grades between sixth and seventh grade for adolescents making the junior high school transition at this point than for adolescents enrolled in K–8 schools. Furthermore, this decline in grades was not matched by a decline in the adolescents' scores on standardized achievement tests, supporting the conclusion that the decline reflects a change in grading practices rather than a change in the rate of the students' learning (Kavrell & Petersen, 1984). Imagine what this decline in grades could do to young adolescents' self-confidence, especially in light of the fact that the material they are being tested on is not likely to be more intellectually challenging.

Finally, several of the changes noted previously are linked together in goal theory. According to goal theory, individuals have different goal orientations when they engage in achievement tasks, and these orientations influence performance, persistence, and response to difficulty. For example, Nicholls and his colleagues (e.g., Nicholls, 1979b; Nicholls, 1989) defined two major kinds of goal orientations: ego-involved goals and task-involved goals. Individuals with ego-involved goals seek to maximize favorable evaluations of their competence and minimize negative evaluations of competence. Questions like "Will I look smart?" and "Can I outperform others?" reflect ego-involved goals. In contrast, with task-involved goals, individuals focus on mastering tasks and increasing one's competence. Questions such as "How can I do this task?" and "What will I learn?" reflect task-involved goals. Dweck and her colleagues suggested two similar orientations: performance goals (like ego-involved goals), and learning goals (like task-involved goals; e.g., Dweck & Elliott, 1983). Similarly, Ames (1992), Maehr and Midgley (1996), and their students (e.g., Midgley, Anderman, & Hicks, 1995) distinguish between performance goals (like ego-involved goals) and mastery goals (like task-focused goals). With ego-involved (or performance) goals, students try to outperform others and are more likely to do tasks they know they can do. Task-involved (or mastery-oriented) students choose challenging tasks and are more concerned with their own progress than with outperforming others. All of these researchers argue—and have provided some support—that students learn more, persist longer, and select more challenging tasks when they are mastery-oriented and have task-involved goals (see Eccles et al., 1998, for review).

Classroom practices related to grading practices, support for autonomy, and instructional organization affect the relative salience of mastery versus performance goals that students adopt as they engage in the learning tasks at school. The types of changes associated with the middle grades school transition should precipitate greater focus on performance goals. In support of this, in Midgley et al. (1995), both teachers and students reported that performance-focused goals were more prevalent and task-focused goals less prevalent in middle school classrooms than in elementary school classrooms. In addition, the elementary school teachers reported using task-focused instructional strategies more frequently than did the middle school teachers. Finally, at both grade levels the extent to which teachers were task-focused predicted the students' and the teachers' sense of personal efficacy. Not surprisingly, personal efficacy was lower among the middle school participants than among the elementary school participants.

In summary, changes such as those noted in the preceding discussion are likely to have a negative effect on many students' school-related motivation at any grade level. But Eccles and Midgley (1989) argued that these types of changes are particularly harmful during early adolescence, given what is known about psychological development during this stage of life—namely, that early adolescent development is characterized by increases in desire for autonomy, peer orientation, self-focus and self-consciousness, salience of identity issues, concern over heterosexual relationships, and capacity for abstract cognitive activity (see Simmons & Blyth, 1987). Simmons and Blyth (1987) have argued that adolescents need a reasonably safe, as well as an intellectually challenging, environment to adapt to these shifts—an environment that provides a "zone of comfort" as well as challenging new opportunities for growth (see Call & Mortimer, 2001, for expanded discussion of the importance of arenas of comfort during adolescence). In light of these needs, the environmental changes often associated with the transition to junior high school seem especially harmful in that they disrupt the possibility for close personal relationships between youth and non-familial adults at a time when youth have increased need for precisely this type of social support; they emphasize competition, social comparison, and ability self-assessment at a time of heightened self-focus; they decrease decision-making and choice at a time when the desire for self-control and adult respect is growing; and they disrupt peer social networks at a time when adolescents are especially concerned with peer relationships and social acceptance. We believe the nature of these environmental changes—coupled with the normal course of development—is likely to result in a developmental mismatch because the "fit" between the early adolescents' needs and the opportunities provided in the classroom is particularly poor, increasing the risk of negative motivational outcomes, especially for those adolescents who are already having academic difficulties.

Based on these general issues and on the research underlying these conclusions, the Carnegie Foundation funded and helped to coordinate several school reform efforts aimed at making middle schools and junior high schools more developmentally appropriate learning environments. By and large, when well implemented, these reforms were effective at both increasing learning and facilitating engagement and positive motivation (Jackson & Davis, 2000).

Long-Term Consequences of the Junior High School Transition

The work reviewed in the previous section documents the immediate importance of school transitions during the early years of adolescence. Do these effects last? Are there long-term consequences of either a positive or negative experience during this early school transition? There have been very few studies that can answer this question. Some of the work reviewed earlier indicated that a decline in school grades at this point is predictive of subsequent high school dropout. Eccles and her colleagues have gone one step further towards answering this question. First they linked self-esteem change over the junior high school transition to changes in other aspects of

mental health and well-being during the transitional period. Second, they linked changes in self esteem over this transition to indicators of mental health, academic performance, and alcohol and drug use in Grades 10 and 12 (Eccles, Lord, Roeser, Barber, & Jozefowicz, 1997). In both sets of analyses, there was a strong association between self-esteem change and other indicators of well-being.

In their first set of analyses, Eccles et al. (1997) found that those students who showed a decline in their self esteem as they made the junior high school transition also reported higher levels of depression, social self-consciousness, school disengagement, worries about being victimized, and substance abuse at the end of their seventh-grade school year. These same students also showed lower self-esteem and more depression during their 10th- and 12th-grade school years and were slightly less likely to be target for graduating from high school on time.

The High School Transition

Although less work has been performed on the transition to high school, the existing work is suggestive of similar problems (Jencks & Brown, 1975). For example, high schools are typically even larger and more bureaucratic than are junior high schools and middle schools. Bryk, Lee, and Smith (1989) provided numerous examples of how the sense of community among teachers and students is undermined by the size and bureaucratic structure of most high schools. There is little opportunity for students and teachers to get to know each other, and—probably as a consequence—there is distrust between them and little attachment to a common set of goals and values. There is also little opportunity for the students to form mentor-like relationships with a nonfamilial adult, and little effort is made to make instruction relevant to the students. Such environments are likely to further undermine the motivation and involvement of many students, especially those not doing particularly well academically, those not enrolled in the favored classes, and those who are alienated from the values of the adults in the high school. These hypotheses need to be tested.

Recent international comparative work by Hamilton (1990) also points to the importance of strong apprenticeship programs that provide good mentoring and solid links to post–high-school labor markets for maintaining motivation to do well in school for non–college-bound adolescents. By comparing the apprenticeship programs in Germany with those in the United States, Hamilton has documented how the vocational educational programs in the United States often do not serve non–college-bound youth very well, either while they are in high school or after they graduate and try to find jobs.

Most large public high schools also organize instruction around curricular tracks that sort students into different groups. As a result, there is even greater diversity in the educational experiences of high school students than of middle grades students; unfortunately, this diversity is often associated more with the students' social class and ethnic group than with differences in the students' talents and interests (Lee & Bryk, 1989). As a result, curricular tracking has served to reinforce social stratification rather than foster optimal education for all students, particularly in large schools (Dornbusch, 1994; Lee & Bryk, 1989). Lee and Bryk (1989) documented that average school achievement levels do not benefit from this curricular tracking. Quite the contrary—evidence comparing Catholic high schools with public high schools suggests that average school achievement levels are increased when all students are required to take the same challenging curriculum. This conclusion is true even after one has controlled for student selectivity factors. A more thorough examination of how the organization and structure of our high schools influences cognitive, motivational, and achievement outcomes is needed.

GENDER AND ACHIEVEMENT

The relation of gender to achievement is a massive and complex topic. Even defining what is included under the topic of achievement is complex. For this chapter, we limit the discussion to school-related achievement and both educational and career planning during the adolescent and young adult years, focusing on the gendered patterns associated with these objective indicators of achievement. But even within this limited scope, the relation of gender to achievement is complex. The patterns of gender differences are not consistent across ages and there is *always* greater variation within gender than across gender. The relation of gender to achievement is even more complex. To make sense of this heterogeneity, we present the findings in relation to the Eccles et al. "expectancy-value model of achievement-related choices," with a specific focus on the ways in which gender as a social system influences individual's self-perceptions, values, and experiences (see Eccles, 1987).

We also limit the discussion to studies focused primarily on European Americans because they are the most studied population. Studies on gender differences in achievement in other populations are just becoming available, and even these are focused on only a limited range of groups. In addition, none of the existing studies on other populations have the range of constructs we talk about in this entry—making comparisons of findings across groups impossible at this point in time. More

work is desperately needed to determine the generalizability of these patterns to other cultural and ethnic groups.

Gender and Academic Achievement

Over the last 30 years, there have been extensive discussions in both the media and more academic publication outlets regarding gender differences in achievement. Much of this discussion has focused on how girls are being "shortchanged" by the school systems. Recently, the American Association of University Women (AAUW; 1992) published reports on this topic. This perspective on gender inequity in secondary schools has been quite consistent with larger concerns being raised about the negative impact of adolescence on young women's development. For example, in recent reports, the AAUW reported marked declines in girls' self-confidence during the early adolescent years. Similarly, Gilligan and her colleagues (Gilligan, Lyons, & Tammer, 1990) have reported that girls lose confidence in their ability to express their needs and opinions as they move into the early adolescent years—she refers to this process as losing one's voice (see also Pipher, 1994).

However, in the 1960s, the big gender equity concern focused on how schools were "shortchanging" boys. Concerns were raised about how the so-called "feminized culture" in most schools fit very poorly with the behavioral styles of boys—leading many boys to become alienated and then to underachieve. The contrast between these two pictures of gender inequities in school was recently highlighted by Sommers in an article in the May 2000 issue of the *Atlantic Monthly*.

So what is the truth? Like most such situations, the truth is complex. On the one hand, female and male youth (both children and adolescents) on average fare differently in American public schools in terms of both the ways in which they are treated and their actual performance. On the other, it is not the case that one gender is consistently treated less equitably than the other is: Female and male youth appear to be differentially advantaged and disadvantaged on various indicators of treatment and performance. In terms of performance, females earn better grades, as well as graduate from high school, attend and graduate from college, and earn master's degrees at higher rates than males. In contrast, males do slightly better than females do on standardized tests—particularly in math and science—and obtain more advanced degrees than do women in many areas of study, particularly in math-related, computer-related, engineering, and physical science fields. Men also are more likely than are women to obtain advanced graduate degrees in all fields except the social sciences and education. These patterns are more extreme in European American samples than in samples of some other ethnic groups within the United States of America.

In terms of treatment, in most ethnic groups in the United States, boys are more likely than girls are to be assigned to all types of special-remedial education programs, and to either be expelled from or forced to drop out of school before high school graduation (National Center on Educational Statistics, 1999). Low-achieving boys (in both European American and African American samples) receive more negative disciplinary interactions from their teachers than do students in any other group—disproportionately more than their "fair" share. In addition, in most studies of academic underachievers, male youth outnumber female youth two to one (McCall, Evahn, & Kratzer, 1992). In contrast, high-achieving boys (particularly European American high-achieving boys) receive more favorable interactions with their teachers than do students in any other group and are more likely to be encouraged by their teachers to take difficult courses, to apply to top colleges, and to aspire to challenging careers (Sadker & Sadker, 1994).

More consistent gender differences emerge for college major and for enrollment in particular vocational educational programs. Here the story is one of gender-role stereotyping. European American women and men are most likely to specialize or major in content areas that are consistent with their gender-roles—that is, in content areas that are most heavily

populated by members of their own gender. This gendered pattern is especially marked in vocational education programs for non–college-bound youth; for physical science, engineering, and computer science majors; and for professional degrees in nursing, social welfare, and teaching. Again this pattern is less extreme in other ethnic groups. Finally, there has been substantial movement of women into previously male-dominated fields like medicine, law, and business over the last 20 years (Astin & Lindholm, 2001).

Why do these gendered matters in educational and occupational aspirations exist? Discussing all possible mediating variables is beyond the scope of a single chapter. Instead, we focus on a set of social and psychological factors related to the Eccles' "expectancy-value model of achievement-related choices and performance" (see Figure 13.1).

Eccles' Expectancy-Value Model of Achievement-Related Choices and Performance

Over the past 20 years, Eccles and her colleagues have studied the motivational and social factors influencing such achievement goals and behaviors as educational and career choices, recreational activity selection, persistence on difficult tasks, and the allocation of effort across various achievement-related activities. Given the striking gender differences in educational, vocational, and avocational choices, they have been particularly interested in the motivational factors

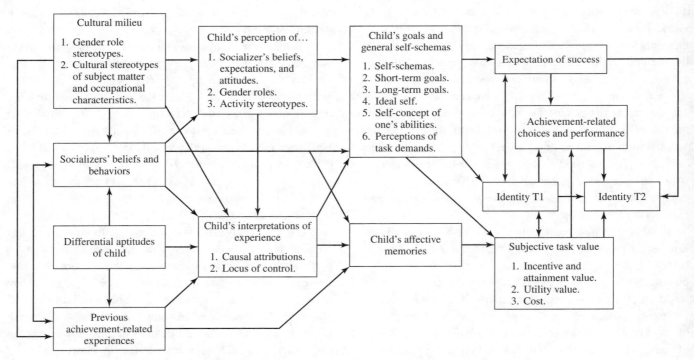

Figure 13.1   General model of achievement choices.

underlying males' and females' achievement-related decisions. Drawing upon the theoretical and empirical work associated with decision-making, achievement theory, and attribution theory, they elaborated a comprehensive theoretical model of achievement-related choices that can be used to guide subsequent research efforts. This model, depicted in Figure 13.1, links achievement-related choices directly to two sets of beliefs: the individual's expectations for success and the importance or value the individual attaches to the various options perceived by the individual as available. The model also specifies the relation of these beliefs to cultural norms, experiences, and aptitudes—and to those personal beliefs and attitudes that are commonly assumed to be associated with achievement-related activities by researchers in this field. In particular, the model links achievement-related beliefs, outcomes, and goals to interpretative systems like causal attributions, to the input of socializers (primarily parents, teachers, and peers), to gender-role beliefs, to self-perceptions and self-concept, to personal and social identities and to one's perceptions of the task itself.

For example, consider course enrollment decisions. The model predicts that people will be most likely to enroll in courses that they think they can master and that have high task value for them. Expectations for success (and a sense of domain-specific personal efficacy) depend on the confidence the individual has in his or her intellectual abilities and on the individual's estimations of the difficulty of the course. These beliefs have been shaped over time by the individual's experiences with the subject matter and by the individual's subjective interpretation of those experiences (e.g., does the person think that her or his successes are a consequence of high ability or lots of hard work?). Likewise, Eccles et al. assume that the value of a particular course to the individual is influenced by several factors. For example, does the person enjoy doing the subject material? Is the course required? Is the course seen as instrumental in meeting one of the individual's long- or short-range goals? Have the individual's parents or counselors insisted that the course be taken, or—conversely—have other people tried to discourage the individual from taking the course? Is the person afraid of the material to be covered in the course? The fact that women and men may differ in their choices is likely to reflect gender differences in a wide range of predictors, mediated primarily by differences in self-perceptions, values, and goals rather than motivational strength, drive, or both.

Competence and Expectancy-Related Self-Perceptions

In the last 30 years, there has been considerable public attention focused on the issue of young women's declining confidence in their academic abilities. In addition, researchers and policy makers interested in young women's educational and occupational choices have stressed the potential role that such declining confidence might play in undermining young women's educational and vocational aspirations, particularly in the technical fields related to math and physical science. For example, these researchers suggested that young women may drop out of math and physical science because they lose confidence in their math abilities as they move into and through adolescence—resulting in women who are less likely than are men to pursue these types of careers. Similarly, these researchers suggest that gender differences in confidence in one's abilities in other areas underlie gender differences across the board in educational and occupational choices. Finally, Eccles and her colleagues suggested that the individual differences in women's educational and occupational choices are related to variations among women in the hierarchy of women's confidence in their abilities across different domains (Eccles, 1994).

But do females and males differ on measures commonly linked to expectations for success, particularly with regard to their academic subjects and various future occupations? And are females more confident of their abilities in female gender-role stereotyped domains? In most studies, the answer is yes. For example, both Kerr (1985) and Subotnik and Arnold (1991) found that gifted European American girls were more likely to underestimate their intellectual skills and their relative class standing than were gifted European American boys—who were more likely to overestimate theirs.

Gender differences in the competence beliefs of more typical samples are also often reported, particularly in gender-role stereotyped domains and on novel tasks. Often these differences favor the males. For example, in the studies of Eccles, Wigfield and their colleagues (see also Crandall, 1969), high-achieving European American girls were more likely than were European American boys to underestimate both their ability level and their class standing; in contrast, the European American boys were more likely than were European American girls to overestimate their likely performance. When asked about specific domains, the gender differences depended on the gender-role stereotyping of the activity. For example, in the work by Eccles and her colleagues, European American boys and young men had higher competence beliefs than did their female peers for math and sports, even after all relevant skill-level differences were controlled; in contrast, the European American girls and young women had higher competence beliefs than did European American boys for reading, instrumental music, and social skills—and the magnitude of differences sometimes increase and sometimes decrease following puberty (Eccles, Adler, & Meece, 1984; Jacobs, Lanza, Osgood, Eccles, & Wigfield, 2002).

Furthermore, in these studies, the young women, on average, had greater confidence in their abilities in reading and social skills than in math, physical science, and athletics; and, when averaged across math and English, the male students had lower confidence than did their female peers in their academic abilities in general. By and large, these gender differences were also evident in preliminary studies of African American adolescents (Eccles, Barber, Jozefowicz, Malanchuk, & Vida, 1999). This could be one explanation for the fact that the young men in these samples—as in the nation more generally—are more likely to drop out of high school than were the young women.

Finally, the European American female and male students in the Eccles and Wigfield studies ranked these skill areas quite differently: for example, the girls rated themselves as most competent in English and social activities and as least competent in sports; the boys rated themselves as most competent by a substantial margin in sports, followed by math, and then social activities; the boys rated themselves as least competent in English (Eccles et al., 1993; Wigfield et al., 1998). Such within-gender, rank-order comparisons are critically important for understanding differences in life choices. In the follow-up studies of these same youths, Jozefowicz, Barber, and Eccles (1993) were able to predict within-gender differences in the young women's and men's occupational goals with the pattern of their confidences across subject domains. The youth who wanted to go into occupations requiring a lot of writing, for example, had higher confidence in their artistic and writing abilities than in their math and science abilities. In contrast, the youth who wanted to go into science and advanced health-related fields (e.g., becoming a physician) had higher confidence in their math and science abilities than in their artistic and social abilities (see Eccles et al., 1997).

One of the most interesting findings from existing studies of academic self-confidence is that the gender differences in self-perceptions are usually much larger than one would expect, given objective measures of actual performance and competence. First, consider mathematics: With the exception of performance on the most anxiety-provoking standardized test, girls do as well as boys do on all measures of math competence throughout primary, secondary, and tertiary education. Furthermore, the few gender differences that do exist have been decreasing in magnitude over the last 20 years and do not appear with great regularity until late in the primary school years. Similarly, the gender difference in perceived sports competence is much larger (accounting for 9% of the variance in one of our studies) than was the gender difference in our measures of actual sport-related skills (which accounted for between 1–3% of the variance on these indicators).

So why do female students rate their math and sports competence so much lower than their male peers do and so much lower than they rate their own English ability and social skills? Some theorists have suggested that female and male students interpret variations in their performance in various academic subjects and leisure activities in a gender-role stereotyped manner. For example, females might be more likely to attribute their math and sports successes to hard work and effort and their failures in these domains to lack of ability than males; in contrast, males might be more likely than females to attribute their successes to natural talent. Similarly, females might be more likely to attribute their English and social successes to natural ability. Such differences in causal attributions would lead to both the between- and within-gender differences in confidence levels reported in the preceding discussion.

The evidence for these differences in causal attributions is mixed (Eccles-Parsons, Meece, Adler, & Kaczala, 1982; see Ruble & Martin, 1998). Some researchers find that European American females are less likely than European American males are to attribute success to ability and more likely to attribute failure to lack of ability. Others have found that this pattern depends on the kind of task used—occurring more with unfamiliar tasks or stereotypically masculine achievement tasks. The most consistent difference occurs for attributions of success to ability versus effort: European American females are less likely than are European American males to stress the relevance of their own ability as a cause of their successes. Instead, European American females tend to rate effort and hard work as a more important determinant of their success than ability. We find it interesting that their parents do also (Yee & Eccles, 1988). There is nothing inherently wrong with attributing one's successes to hard work. In fact, Stevenson and his colleagues stress that this attributional pattern is a major advantage that Japanese students have over American students (Stevenson, Chen, & Uttal, 1990). Nonetheless, it appears that within the context of the United States, this attributional pattern undermines students' confidence in their ability to master increasingly more difficult material—perhaps leading young women to stop taking mathematics courses prematurely.

Gender differences are also sometimes found for locus of control. For example, in Crandall et al. (1965), the girls tended to have higher internal locus of responsibility scores for both positive and negative achievement events, and the older girls had higher internality for negative events than did the younger girls. The boys' internal locus of responsibility scores for positive events decreased from 10th to 12th grade. A result of these two developmental patterns was that older girls accepted more blame for negative events than the older boys did (Dweck & Repucci, 1973). Similarly, Connell (1985) found that boys attributed their (negative) outcomes more than girls did to either powerful others or unknown causes in both the cognitive and social domains.

This greater propensity for girls to take personal responsibility for their failures, coupled with their more frequent attribution of failure to lack of ability (a stable, uncontrollable cause) has been interpreted as evidence of greater learned helplessness in females (see Dweck & Elliott, 1983). However, evidence for gender differences on behavioral indicators of learned helplessness is quite mixed. In most studies of underachievers, boys outnumber girls two to one (see McCall et al., 1992). Similarly, boys are more likely than girls are to be referred by their teachers for motivational problems and are more likely to drop out of school before completing high school. More consistent evidence exists that females (compared to males) select easier laboratory tasks, avoid challenging and competitive situations, lower their expectations more following failure, shift more quickly to a different college major when their grades begin to drop, and perform more poorly than they are capable of on difficult, timed tests (see Dweck & Elliott, 1980; Parsons & Ruble, 1977; Ruble & Martin, 1998; Spencer, Steele, & Quinn, 1995).

Somewhat related to constructs like confidence in one's abilities, personal efficacy, and locus of control, gender differences also emerge regularly in studies of test anxiety (e.g., Douglas & Rice, 1979; Meece, Wigfield, & Eccles, 1990). However, Hill and Sarson (1966) suggested that boys may be more defensive than are girls about admitting anxiety on questionnaires. In support of this suggestion, Lord, Eccles, and McCarthy (1994) found that test anxiety was a stronger predictor of poor adjustment to junior high school for boys, even though the girls reported higher mean levels of anxiety.

Gender-role stereotyping has also been suggested as a cause of the gender differences in academic self-concepts. The extent to which adolescents endorse the European American cultural stereotypes regarding which gender is likely to be most talented in each domain predicts the extent to which European American females and males distort their ability self-concepts and expectations in the gender-stereotypical direction. S. Spencer, Steele, and Quinn (1999) suggested a mechanism linking culturally based gender stereotypes to competence through test anxiety: stereotype vulnerability. They hypothesized that members of social groups (like women) stereotyped as being less competent in a particular subject area (like math) will become anxious when asked to do difficult problems because they are afraid the stereotype may be true of them. This vulnerability is also likely to increase females' vulnerability to failure feedback on male-stereotyped tasks, leading to lowered self-expectations and self-confidence

in their ability to succeed for these types of tasks. To test these hypotheses, S. Spencer, Steele, and Quinn gave college students a difficult math test under two conditions: (a) after being told that men typically do better on this test or (b) after being told that men and women typically do about the same. The women scored lower than the men did only in the first condition. Furthermore, the manipulation's effect was mediated by variations across condition in reported anxiety. Apparently, knowing that one is taking a test on which men typically do better than women do increases young women's anxiety, which in turn undermines their performance. This study also suggests that changing this dynamic is relatively easy if one can change the women's perception of the gender-typing of the test.

In sum, when either gender differences or within-gender individual differences emerge on competence-related measures for academic subjects and other important skill areas, they are consistent with the gender-role stereotypes held by the group being studied (most often European Americans). These differences have also been found to be important mediators of both gender differences and within-gender individual differences in various types of achievement-related behaviors and choices. Such gendered patterns are theoretically important because they point to the power of gender-role socialization processes as key to understanding both girls' and boys' confidence in their various abilities. And to the extent that gender-role socialization is key, it is important to study how and why young women differ in the extent to which they are either exposed to these socialization pressures or resist them when they are so exposed.

But even more important is that all of the relevant studies have documented extensive variation within each gender. Both females and males vary a great deal among themselves in their intellectual confidence for various academic domains. They also vary considerably in their test anxiety, their attributional styles, and their locus of control. Such variations within each gender are a major set of predictors of variation among both young men and young women in their educational and occupational choices. European American adolescent males and females who aspire to careers in math and science and who take advanced courses in math and physical science have greater confidence in their math and science abilities than those who do not. They also have just as much—if not more—confidence in their math and science abilities as in their English abilities (see Eccles et al., 1998).

Gendered Differences in Achievement Values

Achievement values are related to the different purposes or reasons individuals have for engaging in different activities.

Eccles et al. (1983) defined four components of task value: attainment value, intrinsic value, utility value, and cost. They defined attainment value as the personal importance of doing well on the task. They also linked attainment value to the relevance of engaging in a task for confirming or disconfirming salient aspects of one's self-schema or identity. Because tasks provide the opportunity to demonstrate aspects of one's actual or ideal self-schema, such as masculinity, femininity, or competence in various domains, tasks will have higher attainment value to the extent that they allow the individual to confirm salient aspects of these self-schemas (see Eccles, 1984, 1987). *Intrinsic value* is the enjoyment the individual gets from performing the activity or the subjective interest the individual has in the subject. This component of value is similar to the construct of intrinsic motivation as defined by Harter (1981) and by Deci and his colleagues (e.g., Deci & Ryan, 1985; Ryan, Connell, & Deci, 1985). *Utility value* is determined by how well a task relates to current and future goals, such as career goals. A task can have positive value to a person because it facilitates important future goals, even if he or she is not interested in task for its own sake. In one sense, then, this component captures the more "extrinsic" reasons for engaging in a task; but it also relates directly to individuals' internalized short- and long-term goals. Finally, cost is conceptualized in terms of the negative aspects of engaging in the task, such as performance anxiety and fear of both failure and success as well as the amount of effort that is needed to succeed and the lost opportunities that result from making one choice rather than another.

Eccles, Wigfield, and their colleagues have found gender-role stereotypical differences in both children's and adolescents' valuing of sports, social activities, and English (e.g., Eccles et al., 1989; Eccles et al., 1993; Wigfield et al., 1991, Wigfield et al., 1998). Across these studies, boys value sports activities more than girls do, whereas girls value reading, English, and instrumental music more than boys do. It is interesting to note that in the studies they conducted prior to the 1990s, high-school girls valued math less than did high-school boys (Eccles, 1984); this gender difference, however, has disappeared in more recent studies (see Jacobs et al., in press). Although it is encouraging that boys and girls now value math equally, the fact that adolescent girls have less positive views of their math ability is problematic because these differences probably contribute to girls' lower probability of taking optional advanced-level math and physical science courses and of entering math-related scientific and engineering fields, thus contributing to gender-differentiated cognitive outcomes and career choices (see Eccles, 1994). We return to career choice issues later in this chapter.

Values also can be conceived more broadly to include notions of what are appropriate activities for males and females to do. Sometimes such values can conflict with engagement in achievement. The role of conflict between gender roles and achievement in gifted girls' lives is well illustrated by results of an ethnographic study of a group of gifted elementary-school girls. Bell (1989) interviewed a multiethnic group of third- to sixth-grade gifted girls in an urban elementary school regarding the barriers they perceived to their achievement in school. Five gender-role related themes emerged with great regularity: (a) concern about hurting someone else's feelings by winning in achievement contests; (b) concern about seeming to be a braggart if one expressed pride in one's accomplishments; (c) overreaction to nonsuccess experiences (apparently, not being the very best is very painful to these girls); (d) concern over their physical appearance and what it takes to be beautiful; and (e) concern with being overly aggressive in terms of getting the teacher's attention. In each case, the gifted girls felt caught between doing their best and appearing either feminine or caring.

Gender differences have also been found on many of the psychological processes proposed by Eccles and her colleagues to underlie gender differences in subjective task value. For example, Eccles-Parsons et al. (1983) predicted that the attainment value of particular tasks would be linked to (a) conceptions of one's personality and capabilities, (b) long-range goals and plans, (c) schemas regarding the proper roles of men and women, (d) instrumental and terminal values (Rokeach, 1979), (e) ideal images of what one should be like, and (f) social scripts regarding proper behavior in a variety of situations. If gender-role socialization leads males and females to differ on these core self- and role-related beliefs, then related activities will have differential value for males and females. In support, in a study of the link between personal values and college major, Dunteman, Wisenbaker, and Taylor (1978) identified two sets of values that both predicted college major and differentiated the genders: the first set (labeled *thing-orientation*) reflected an interest in manipulating objects and understanding the physical world; the second set (labeled *person-orientation*) reflected an interest in understanding human social interaction and a concern with helping people. Students with high thing-orientation and low person-orientation were more likely than were other students to select a math or a science major. Not surprisingly, the females were more likely than were the males to major in something other than math or science because of their higher person-oriented values. Similarly, the young women in the Jozefowicz et al. (1993; see Eccles, Barber, & Jozefowicz, 1999) study placed more value than did the young men on a variety of female-stereotyped career-related skills and interests, such as doing work that directly helps people and meshes well with child-rearing responsibilities. These values along with ability self-concepts predicted the gender-stereotyped career plans of both males and females (see Eccles & Harold, 1992, for review of the gender-role stereotypical patterns for personal values, occupational values, and personality traits).

Explanations for these gender differences in interests and task values have focused on several things, including adolescents' understanding of what is appropriate for each gender to do. To the extent that adolescents know and have internalized the gender-role stereotypes of their cultures, they are likely to place greater value on activities consistent with their gender's gender role than on activities consistent with the opposite gender's gender role (see Eccles, 1984; Ruble & Martin, 1998).

Gender differences in academic values could also reflect the confluence of both gender-role stereotypes and gender differences in perceived competence. Drawing on the writings of William James (1892/1963), Eccles and her colleagues suggested that children would lower the value they attach to particular activities or subject areas—if they lack confidence in these areas—in order to maintain their self-esteem (Eccles, 1994; Eccles et al., 1998; Harter, 1990). To the extent that girls feel less competent in math than in other subject areas, they may reduce the value they attach to math versus other academic subject areas. This in turn might lead them to be less likely than males to consider future occupations in math-related fields. S. Spencer, Steele, and Quinn (1999) suggested a similar phenomenon related to stereotype vulnerability. They hypothesized that women would disidentify with those subject areas in which females are stereotyped as less competent than males. By disidentifying with these areas, the women will not only lower the value they attach to these subject areas, they will also be less likely to experience pride and positive affect when they are doing well in these subjects. Consequently, these subjects should become less relevant to their self-esteem. These hypotheses remain to be tested. As we noted earlier, girls and young women do not report valuing math less than do boys and young men, at least through the early high-school years. What they do value less than males do are physical science and engineering. Because math is required for both of these fields, this gender difference in values could explain the differential course taking in these fields during both high school and college (Updegraff, Eccles, Barber, & O'Brien, 1996).

In summary, as with competence beliefs, there are gender differences in children's and adolescents' valuing of and interest in different activities. These differences are important for understanding the development of gender differences in cognition and performance. In our research, children's and adolescents' valuing of different activities relates strongly to their choices of whether to continue to pursue the activity (Eccles-Parsons et al., 1983; Meece et al., 1990; Updegraff et al., 1996). Such choices should have an impact on changes in actual competence and subsequent performance, with participation leading to greater increases than nonparticipation.

Gender and Occupational Ability Self-Concepts

Eccles and her colleagues have extended the work on academic and athletic self-concepts by looking at European American and African American adolescents' competence ratings for skills more directly linked to adult occupational choice. As their samples moved into and through high school, these investigators asked the students a series of questions directly related to future job choices. First, they asked them to rate how good they were compared to other students at each of several job-related skills. Second, they asked the students to rate the probability that they would succeed at each of a series of standard careers. On the one hand, the results are quite gender-role stereotyped: The young women (both African American and European American) were less confident of success than were their male peers in both science-related professions and male-typed skilled labor occupations. In contrast, the young men (both African American and European American) were less confident of their success than were their female peers in health-related professions and female-typed skilled labor occupations. On the other hand, there were no gender differences in these 12th graders' ratings of either their confidence of success in business and law or their leadership, independence, intellectual, and computer skills. Furthermore, although the young men were more confident of success in physical science and engineering fields, the young women were more confident than were their male peers of success in health-related fields that involve extensive scientific training (Eccles et al., 1997).

The within-gender patterns were equally interesting. On the average, these young women saw themselves as quite competent in traditionally female-typed jobs and skills related to human service, particularly in comparison to their confidence for science-related jobs and mechanical skills. An interesting finding was that these young women also saw themselves as quite competent in terms of their leadership, intellectual skills, and independence.

Gender and Occupational-Choice–Related Values

Do women and men make gender-role stereotypical life choices because they have gender-role stereotypical values? In most studies, the answer is "yes" for the populations most studied (European Americans and to a lesser extent African Americans). Gender-role stereotypical patterns in adolescents' valuing of sports, social activities, and English have emerged consistently. It is interesting to note that the gendered pattern associated with the value of math does not emerge until high school. Finally, the gendered pattern of valuing math, physics, and computer skills has emerged as the key predictor of both gender differences and individual differences among female students in adolescents' plans to enter math-related scientific and engineering fields (see Eccles et al., 1997).

It is important to note, however, that these gendered patterns have decreased over time for women of most ethnic groups in the United States. Young women today are more likely to aspire to the male-stereotyped fields of medicine, law, and business than were their mothers and grandmothers. And although the numbers are not nearly as large, young women today are also much more likely to seek out occupations related to engineering and physical science. Finally, young women today are also much more involved in athletic activities than were their mothers and grandmothers (see Astin & Lindholm, 2001; Gill, 2001).

Because of their interest in understanding career choice, Eccles and her colleagues asked their African American and European American senior high-school participants to rate how important each of a series of job-related and life-related values and a series of job characteristics were to them (see Eccles et al., 1997). As was true for the job-related skills, they found evidence of both gender-role stereotypical differences and of gender-role transcendence. In keeping with traditional stereotypes, the young women rated family and friends as more important to them than did their male peers; the young women were also more likely than the male peers were to want jobs that were people-oriented. In contrast, but also consistent with traditional stereotypes, the young men placed a higher value on high-risk and competitive activities and wealth; they also were more interested in jobs that allowed for work with machinery, math, or computers. However, counter to traditional stereotypes, there were no gender differences in careerism (focus on career as critical part of one's identity), and the women and men were equally likely to want jobs that allowed flexibility to meet family obligations, that entailed prestige and responsibility, and that provided opportunities for creative and intellectual work.

Evidence of both gender-role typing and transcendence was also evident in the within-gender patterns. Although these young women still, on the average, attached most importance to having a job with sufficient flexibility to meet family obligations and with the opportunity to help people, they also placed great importance on the role of their career

for their personal identity (careerism) and on the importance of both prestige-responsibility and creativity as key components of their future occupations.

Predicting Occupational Choice

Eccles and her colleagues next used these values and ability self-concepts to predict the young men's and women's occupational aspirations (see Eccles et al., 1997). As expected, ability self-concepts were key predictors of both between- and within-gender differences in career aspirations. Also as predicted by the Eccles expectancy-value model of achievement-related choices, the lifestyle and valued job characteristics were significant predictors of career aspirations. The within-gender analyses were especially interesting. Values did an excellent job of discriminating between these young women's occupational plans. Perhaps most interesting was that the value placed on helping other people predicted which women aspired to advanced-level health-related professions (e.g., a physician) and which women aspired to doctoral-level science careers. Both of these groups of women had very high confidence in their math and science abilities. In contrast, they differed dramatically in the value they placed on helping others: The women aspiring to the health-related fields placed more importance on this dimension than on any other value dimension; in contrast, the women aspiring to doctoral-level science careers placed less importance on this dimension than on any other dimension, particularly less than on the value of being able to work with math and computers.

In summary, there is still evidence of gendered patterns in the valuing of different academic subject areas and activities. And although it is encouraging that girls value math during elementary school, the fact that European American young women have less positive views of both their math ability and the value of math is problematic because these differences lead young European American women to be less likely than young European American men to take optional advanced-level math and physical science courses.

Gender and Self-Esteem

Work on gender differences in self-esteem among European Americans also has produced some interesting findings. During the middle childhood years, boys and girls report similar levels of self-esteem. By the early adolescent years, however, European American girls tend to report lower self-esteem than do European American boys. Although self-esteem tends to rise as children move through adolescence (Dusek & Flaherty, 1981), the gender difference remains

(Kling, Hyde, Showers, & Buswell, 1999). Further, young women seem more likely than do young men to develop more serious negative self-evaluations such as depression during the adolescent years (see Eisenberg, Marin, & Fabes, 1996; Harter, 1998; Nolen-Hoeksema & Girigus, 1994).

A variety of explanations have been offered for these gender differences in the self-esteem of European Americans. European American boys have been described as being more likely to handle difficulties by engaging in "externalizing" behavior such as aggression. European Americans girls, by contrast, tend to "internalize" problems to a greater extent (see Eisenberg et al., 1996). Nolen-Hoeksema and Girigus (1994) suggested that females' self esteem is based more on the approval of others and on pleasing others, making it more difficult for them to maintain self-approval, especially when they encounter difficulties.

Physical appearance issues are likely to be central as well, particularly for European American females. Harter (1990, 1998) made three essential points about physical appearance and self-esteem, based on her own work and on that of others. First, as European American boys and girls go through childhood and move into adolescence, the girls (relative to boys) become increasingly less satisfied with their own appearance. Second, society and the media place an incredibly strong emphasis on physical appearance as a basis for self-evaluation, and this is especially true for European American women. There are clear (and often unrealistic) standards for women's appearance that young women strive to attain, often unsuccessfully. Third, Harter's empirical work clearly has shown that for both European American males and females, satisfaction with physical appearance is the strongest predictor of self-esteem. Taking these three points together, European American girls are increasingly unhappy about an aspect of themselves that seems to be the primary predictor of self-esteem. Hence, European American girls are more likely to develop lower self-esteem at this time.

RACIAL AND ETHNIC GROUP DIFFERENCES IN ACHIEVEMENT MOTIVATION

As is the case in many areas of psychology (see Graham, 1992), less is known about the motivation of adolescents from non-European American racial and ethnic groups. However, work in this area is growing quickly, with much of it focusing on the academic achievement difficulties of many African American youth (see Berry & Asamen, 1989; Eccles et al., 1998; Hare, 1985; Jencks & Phillips, 1998; Slaughter-Defoe, Nakagawa, Takanishi, & Johnson, 1990). Recent work has also focused on other minority groups within the

United States and on recent immigrant populations, some of whom are doing much better in school than both European American middle-class children and the third- and fourth-generation members of their same national heritage (e.g., Chen & Stevenson, 1995, Kao & Tienda, 1995; Slaughter-Defoe et al., 1990).

Ethnic Group Differences in Children's Competence, Control, and Attribution Beliefs

Graham (1994) reviewed the literature on differences between African American and European American students on such motivational constructs as need for achievement, locus of control, achievement attributions, and ability beliefs and expectancies; she concluded that these differences are not very large. She also argued that many existing studies have not adequately distinguished between race and SES, making it very difficult to interpret even those differences that did emerge. Cooper and Dorr (1995) did a meta-analysis of some of the same studies reviewed by Graham in order to compare more narrative and more quantitative types of reviews. Although there were some important points of agreement across the two reviews, Cooper and Dorr concluded that there were significant race differences in need for achievement favoring European Americans, especially in lower-SES and younger samples.

In their study of educational opportunity, Coleman et al. (1966) reported that perceived control was a very important predictor of African American children's school achievement. Graham (1994) found some evidence that African Americans are more external than European Americans. However, she also noted that studies looking at relations of locus of control to various achievement outcomes have not shown this greater externality to be a problem; indeed, in some studies greater externality is associated with higher achievement among African Americans.

Research on competence beliefs and expectancies has revealed more optimism among African American children than among European American children, even when the European American children are achieving higher marks (e.g., Stevenson et al., 1990). A more important result, however, was that in Stevenson et al. (1990), the European American children's ratings of their ability were related to their performance, whereas the African American children's were not. Graham (1994) suggested the following explanations: (a) African American and European American children may use different social comparison groups to help judge their own abilities; and (b) African American children may say they are doing well to protect their general self-esteem, and they may also devalue or disidentify academic activities at which they do poorly in order to protect their self-esteem. However, neither of these explanations has been adequately tested, and more work is needed to determine whether and when Stevenson et al.'s results replicate. More recent studies suggest that this ethnic group difference is less extreme than reported by Stevenson et al. (Winston, Eccles, Senior, & Vida, 1997; Winston, 2001).

Ethnic Group Differences in Achievement Values and Goals

There are few ethnic comparative studies specifically focused on the kinds of achievement values measured by Eccles, Wigfield, and their colleagues, or on the kinds of achievement goals measured by Ames, Dweck, Midgley, and their colleagues (see earlier discussion). Researchers studying minority children's achievement values have focused instead on the broader valuing of school by minority children and their parents. In general, these researchers find that minority children and parents highly value school (particularly during the elementary school years) and have high educational aspirations for their children (e.g., Stevenson et al., 1990). However, the many difficulties associated with poverty (see Duncan, Brooks-Gunn, & Klevbanov, 1994; Huston, McLoyd, & Coll, 1994; McLoyd, 1990) make these educational aspirations difficult to attain. It is important for researchers to extend this work to more specific value-related constructs.

Ethnicity and Motivation at the Interface Between Expectancies and Values

Researchers interested in ethnic and racial differences in achievement have proposed models linking social roles, competence-related beliefs, and values. For example, Steele has proposed stereotype vulnerability and disidentification to help explain the underachievement of African American students (e.g., Steele & Aronson, 1995): Confronted throughout their school career with mixed messages about their competence and potential as well as the widespread negative cultural stereotypes about their academic potential and motivation, African American students should find it difficult to concentrate fully on their schoolwork due to the anxiety induced by their stereotype vulnerability (for support, see Steele & Aronson, 1995). In turn, to protect their self-esteem, they should disidentify with academic achievement, leading to both a lowering of the value they attach to academic achievement and a detachment of their self-esteem from both positive and negative academic experiences. In support, several researchers have found that academic self-concept of ability is less predictive of general self-esteem among African-American youth

than among European American youth (Bledsoe, 1967; Winston, Eccles, Senior, & Vida, 1997).

Fordham and Ogbu (1986) made a similar argument linking African American students' perception of limited future job opportunities to lowered academic motivation: Because society and schools give African American youth the dual message that academic achievement is unlikely to lead to positive adult outcomes for them and that they are not valued by the system, some African American youth may create an oppositional culture that rejects the value of academic achievement. Ogbu (1992) argued that this dynamic should be stronger for involuntary minorities who continue to be discriminated against by mainstream American culture (e.g., African Americans) than for voluntary minority immigrant groups (e.g., recent immigrants from Southeast Asia). Although voluntary minorities have initial barriers due to language and cultural differences, these barriers can be overcome somewhat more easily than the racism faced by involuntary minorities, giving voluntary minorities greater access to mainstream culture and its benefits.

Contrary to this view, several investigators have found no evidence of greater disidentification with school among African American students than among other groups including European Americans (e.g., Eccles, 2001; Steinberg, Dornbusch, & Brown, 1992; Taylor, Casten, Flickinger, Roberts, & Fulmore, 1994). Nonetheless, several studies show that disidentification—particularly as a result of inequitable treatment and failure experiences at school—can undermine achievement and academic motivation (e.g., see Finn, 1989; Taylor et al., 1994). It is likely that some students, particularly members of involuntary minority groups, will have these experiences as they pass through the secondary school system. Longitudinal studies of the process of disidentification—and of ameliorating intervention efforts—are badly needed.

Any discussion of performance and motivational differences across different ethnic groups must take into account larger contextual issues. For example, M. B. Spencer and Markstrom-Adams (1990) argued that many minority children—particularly those living in poverty—have to deal with several difficult issues not faced by majority adolescents, such as racist prejudicial attitudes, conflict between the values of their group and those of larger society, and scarcity of high-achieving adults in their group to serve as role models. Such difficulties can impede identity formation in these adolescents, leading to identity diffusion or inadequate exploration of different possible identities (Taylor et al., 1994). Similarly, Cross (1991) argued that one must consider the development of both personal identities and racial group identity. For instance, some African American adolescents may have positive personal identities but be less positive about their racial group as a whole, whereas others may have negative personal identities but have positive orientations toward their group. Cross argued that many researchers have confounded these two constructs, leading to confusion in our understanding of identity development in—and its motivational implications for—African Americans.

Finally, it is critical to consider the quality of the educational institutions that serve many of these youth. Thirty-seven percent of African American youth and 32% of Hispanic youth—compared to 5% of European American and 22% of Asian American youth—are enrolled in the 47 largest city school districts in this country; in addition, African American and Hispanic youth attend some of the poorest school districts in this country. Twenty-eight percent of the youth enrolled in city schools live in poverty, and 55% are eligible for free or reduced-cost lunch, suggesting that class may be as important as (or more important than) race in the differences that emerge. Teachers in these schools report feeling less safe than do teachers in other school districts, dropout rates are highest, and achievement levels at all grades are the lowest (Council of the Great City Schools, 1992). Finally, schools that serve these populations are less likely than schools serving more advantaged populations to offer either high-quality remedial services or advanced courses and courses that facilitate the acquisition of higher-order thinking skills and active learning strategies. Even children who are extremely motivated may find it difficult to perform well under these educational circumstances (Lee & Bryk, 1989).

Graham (1994) made several important recommendations for future work on African American children's motivation. We think these recommendations can be applied more broadly to work on different racial and ethnic groups. Two particularly important recommendations are (a) the need to separate out effects of race and social class; and (b) the need to move beyond race-comparative studies to studies that look at individual differences within different racial and ethnic groups and at the antecedents and processes underlying variations in achievement outcomes among minority youth (e.g., Connell, Spencer, & Aber, 1994; Luster & McAdoo, 1994; Schneider & Coleman, 1993; Steinberg, Lamborn, Dornbusch, & Darling et al., 1992; Kao & Tienda, 1995). Studies of recent immigrant populations and comparative studies of different generations of immigrant populations move in these directions. For example, work by Stevenson and his colleagues, by Tienda and her colleagues, and by Fuligni all demonstrate the power of the types of motivational constructs discussed thus far in explaining both within- and between-group variation in academic achievement (e.g., Chen & Stevenson, 1995; Fuligni, 1997; Kao & Tienda, 1995; Lummis & Stevenson, 1990).

SUMMARY

In this chapter, we focused on two major aspects of adolescent development: cognitive development and both achievement and achievement motivation. First we discussed cognitive development, pointing out the relevance of recent work for both learning and decision making. We pointed out that more research is needed on ethnic group differences and on the link between decision-making skills and actual-decision making behaviors in complex situations. Next we summarized current patterns of school achievement and recent changes in both school completion and differential performance on standardized tests of achievement. We pointed out the educational gains that have been made over the last century as well as the continuing ethnic group and national differences in test performance. We then summarized both the positive and negative age-related changes in school motivation and discussed how experiences in school might explain these developmental patterns. Recent efforts at middle-school reform have supported many of the hypotheses discussed in that section of the paper. More efforts at understanding the difficulty of school reform are badly needed. Finally, we discussed both gender and ethnic group differences in achievement motivation and linked these differences to gender and ethnic group differences in academic achievement and longer-term career aspirations. We now have a very good understanding of the psychological and social origins of gender differences in achievement patterns. More work is desperately needed on the influences on academic performance and both educational and occupational choices of adolescents of color. It is encouraging that the rate of such work has increased dramatically over the last 10 years. We look forward to being able to summarize this new and exciting work in future chapters.

REFERENCES

American Association of University Women. (1990). *Shortchanging girls, shortchanging America: Full data report.* Washington, DC: American Association of University Women Press.

Ames, C. (1992). Classrooms: Goals, structures, and student motivation. *Journal of Educational Psychology, 84,* 261–271.

Arnett, J. J. (1999). Adolescent storm and stress, reconsidered. *American Psychologist, 54,* 317–326.

Astin, H. S., & Lindholm, J. A. (2001). Academic aspirations and degree attainment of women. In J. Worell (Senior Ed.) *Encyclopedia of women and gender* (Vol. 1, pp. 15–28). San Diego, CA: Academic Press.

Baltes, P. B., Linderberger, U., & Staudinger, U. M. (1998). Life-span theory in developmental psychology. In W. Damon &

R. M. Lerner (Eds.), *Handbook of child psychology* (5th ed., Vol. 1, pp. 1029–1145). New York: Wiley.

Barker, R., & Gump, P. (1964). *Big school, small school: High school size and student behavior.* Stanford, CA: Stanford University Press.

Beatty, A. S., Reese, C. M., Perksy, H. R., & Carr, P. (1996). *The NAEP 1994 U.S. History Report Card for the nation and the states.* Washington, DC: U.S. Department of Education, Office of Educational Research and Improvement, National Center for Educational Statistics.

Bell, L. A. (1989). Something's wrong here and it's not me: Challenging the dilemmas that block girls success. *Journal for the Education of the Gifted, 12,* 118–130.

Berry, G. L., & Asamen, J. K. (Eds.). (1989). *Black students: Psychosocial issues and academic achievement.* Newbury Park, CA: Sage.

Bjorklund, D. F. (1999). *Children's thinking: Developmental function and individual differences.* Belmont, CA: Wadsworth.

Bledsoe, J. (1967). Self-concept of children and their intelligence, achievement, interests, and anxiety. *Childhood Education, 43,* 436–438.

Brophy, J. E., & Evertson, C. M. (1976). *Learning for teaching: A developmental perspective.* Boston: Allyn and Bacon.

Bryk, A. S., Lee, V. E., & Smith, J. B. (1989, May). *High school organization and its effects on teachers and students: An interpretative summary of the research.* Paper presented at the invitational conference on "Choice and Control in American Education," Robert M. La Follette Institute of Public Affairs, University of Wisconsin, Madison.

Byrnes, J. P. (1998). *The nature and development of decision-making: A self-regulation perspective.* Mahwah, NJ: Erlbaum.

Byrnes, J. P. (1999). The nature and development of representation: Forging a synthesis of competing approaches. In I. Sigel (Ed.), *Development of representation* (pp. 273–294). Mahwah, NJ: Erlbaum.

Byrnes. J. P. (2001a). *Cognitive development and learning in instructional contexts* (2nd ed.). Needham Heights, MA: Allyn and Bacon.

Byrnes, J. P. (2001b). *Minds, brains, and education: Understanding the psychological and educational relevance of neuroscientific research.* New York: Guilford Press.

Byrnes, J. P., & McClenny, B. (1994). Decision-making in young adolescents and adults. *Journal of Experimental Child Psychology, 58,* 359–388.

Byrnes, J. P., Miller, D. C., & Reynolds, M. (1999). Learning to make good decisions: A self-regulation perspective. *Child Development, 70,* 1121–1140.

Byrnes, J. P., Miller, D. C., & Schaefer, W. D. (1999). Sex-differences in risk-taking: A meta-analysis. *Psychological Bulletin, 125,* 367–383.

Byrnes, J. P., & Overton, W. F. (1986). Reasoning about certainty and uncertainty in concrete, causal, and propositional contexts. *Developmental Psychology, 22,* 793–799.

Call, K. T., & Mortimer, J. T. (2001). *Arenas of comfort in adolescence: A study of adjustment in context.* Mahwah, NJ: Erlbaum.

Chen, C., & Stevenson, H. W. (1995). Motivation and mathematics achievement: A comparative study of Asian-American, Caucasian-American, and East Asian high school students. *Child Development, 66,* 1215–1234.

Coleman, J. S., Campbell, E. Q., Hobson, C. J., McPartland, J., Mood, A., Weinfeld, F. D., & York, R. L. (1966). *Equality of educational opportunity.* Washington, DC: U.S. Government Printing Office.

Connell, J. P. (1985). A new multidimensional measure of children's perception of control. *Child Development, 56,* 1018–1041.

Connell, J. P., Spencer, M. B., & Aber, J. L. (1994). Educational risk and resilience in African American youth: Context, self, and action outcomes in school. *Child Development, 65,* 493–506.

Cooper, H., & Dorr, N. (1995). Race comparisons on need for achievement: A meta-analytic alternative to Graham's narrative review. *Review of Educational Research, 65,* 483–508.

Council of the Great City Schools. (1992). *National urban education goals: Baseline indicators, 1990–91.* Washington, DC: Council of the Great City Schools.

Crandall, V. C. (1969). Sex differences in expectancy of intellectual and academic reinforcement. In C. P. Smith (Ed.), *Achievement-related motives in children* (pp. 11–45). New York: Russell Sage.

Crandall, V. C., Katkousky, W., & Crandall, V. J. (1965). Children's beliefs in their own control of reinforcements in intellectual-academic achievement situations. *Child Development, 36,* 91–109.

Cross, W. E., Jr. (1991). *Shades of black: Diversity in African-American identity.* Philadelphia, PA: Temple University Press.

Deci, E. L., & Ryan, R. M. (1985). *Intrinsic motivation and self-determination in human behavior.* New York: Plenum Press.

De Lisi, R., & McGillicuddy-De Lisi, A. (2002). Sex differences in mathematical ability and achievement. In A. McGillicuddy-De Lisi & R. De Lisi (Eds.), *Biology, society, and behavior: The development of sex differences in cognition* (pp. 155–182). Westport, CT: Ablex.

Dias, M. G., & Harris, P. L. (1988). The effect of make-believe play on deductive reasoning. *British Journal of Developmental Psychology, 6,* 207–221.

DiClemente, R. J., Hansen, W. B., & Ponton, L. E. (1995). *Handbook of adolescent health risk behavior.* New York: Plenum Press.

Douglas, J. D., & Rice, K. M. (1979). Sex differences in children's anxiety and defensiveness measures. *Developmental Psychology, 15,* 223–224.

Duncan, G. J., Brooks-Gunn, J., & Klevbanov, P. K. (1994). Economic deprivation and early childhood development. *Child Development, 65,* 296–318.

Dunteman, G. H., Wisenbaker, J., & Taylor, M. F. (1978). *Race and sex differences in college science program participation.* Report to the National Science Foundation. North Carolina: Research Triangle Park.

Dusek, J. B., & Flaherty, J. (1981). The development of the self during the adolescent years. *Monographs of the Society for Research in Child Development, 46*(4), 1–61.

Dweck, C. S., & Elliott, E. S. (1983). Achievement motivation. In P. H. Mussen (Ed.), *Handbook of child psychology* (3rd ed., Vol. 4, pp. 643–691). New York: Wiley.

Dweck, C. S., & Leggett, E. (1988). A social-cognitive approach to motivation and personality. *Psychological Review, 95,* 256–273.

Dweck, C. S., & Repucci, N. D. (1973). Learned helplessness and reinforcement responsibility in children. *Journal of Personality and Social Psychology, 25,* 109–116.

Eccles, J. S. (1984). Sex differences in achievement patterns. In T. Sonderegger (Ed.), *Nebraska Symposium on Motivation* (Vol. 32, pp. 97–132). Lincoln: University of Nebraska Press.

Eccles, J. S. (1987). Gender roles and women's achievement-related decisions. *Psychology of Women Quarterly, 11,* 135–172.

Eccles, J. S. (1993). School and family effects on the ontogeny of children's interests, self-perceptions, and activity choice. In J. Jacobs (Ed.), *Nebraska Symposium on Motivation, 1992: Developmental perspectives on motivation* (pp. 145–208). Lincoln, NB: University of Nebraska Press.

Eccles, J. S. (1994). Understanding women's educational and occupational choices: Applying the Eccles et al. model of achievement-related choices. *Psychology of Women Quarterly, 18,* 585–609.

Eccles, J. S. (2001, March). *Social identities and adolescent development*. Talk given at the Society for Research on Adolescence, Minneapolis, MN.

Eccles, J. S., Adler, T. F., & Meece, J. L. (1984). Sex differences in achievement: A test of alternate theories. *Journal of Personality and Social Psychology, 46,* 26–43.

Eccles, J. S., & Barber, B. L. (1999). Student council, volunteering, basketball, or marching band: What kind of extracurricular involvement matters? *Journal of Adolescent Research, 14,* 10–43.

Eccles, J. S., Barber, B., & Jozefowicz, D. (1999). Linking gender to educational, occupational, and recreational choices: Applying the Eccles et al. model of achievement-related choices. In W. B. Swann, J. H. Langlois, & L. A. Gilbert (Ed.), *Sexism and stereotypes in modern society: The gender science of Janet Taylor Spence* (pp. 153–192). Washington, DC: American Psychological Association Press.

Eccles, J. S., Barber, B., Jozefowicz, D., Malanchuk, O., & Vida, M. (1999). Self-evaluations of competence, task values and self-esteem. In N. G. Johnson, M. C. Roberts, & J. Worrell (Eds.), *Beyond appearance: A new look at adolescent girls* (pp. 53–84). Washington, DC: American Psychological Association Press.

Eccles, J. S., & Harold, R. D. (1992). Gender differences in educational and occupational patterns among the gifted. In N. Colangelo, S. G. Assouline, & D. L. Amronson (Eds.), *Talent Development: Proceedings form the 1991 Henry B. and Jocelyn Wallace National Research Symposium on Talent Development* (pp. 3–29). Unionville, NY: Trillium Press.

Eccles, J. S., Lord, S., & Buchanan, C. M. (1996). School transitions in early adolescence: What are we doing to our young people. In J. L. Graber, J. Brooks-Gunn, & A. C. Petersen (Eds.), *Transitions through adolescence: Interpersonal domains and context* (pp. 251–284). Hillsdale, NJ: Erlbaum.

Eccles, J. S., Lord, S. E., Roeser, R. W., Barber, B. L., & Jozefowicz, D. M. H. (1997). The association of school transitions in early adolescence with developmental trajectories through high school. In J. Schulenberg, J. Maggs, & K. Hurrelmann, K. (Eds.), *Health risks and developmental transitions during adolescence* (pp. 283–320). New York: Cambridge University Press.

Eccles, J. S., & Midgley, C. (1989). Stage/environment fit: Developmentally appropriate classrooms for early adolescents. In R. Ames & C. Ames (Eds.), *Research on motivation in education* (Vol. 3, pp. 139–181). New York: Academic Press.

Eccles, J. S., Midgley, C., Buchanan, C. M., Wigfield, A., Reuman, D., & Mac Iver, D. (1993). Development during adolescence: The impact of stage/environment fit. *American Psychologist, 48,* 90–101.

Eccles, J. S., Wigfield, A., Flanagan, C., Miller, C., Reuman, D., & Yee, D. (1989). Self-concepts, domain values, and self-esteem: Relations and changes at early adolescence. *Journal of Personality, 57,* 283–310.

Eccles, J. S., Wigfield, A., & Schiefele, U. (1998). Motivation. In N. Eisenberg (Ed.), *Handbook of child psychology* (5th ed., Vol. 3, pp. 1017–1095). New York: Wiley.

Eccles-Parsons, J., Adler, T. F., Futterman, R., Goff, S. B., Kaczala, C. M., Meece, J. L., & Midgley, C. (1983). Expectancies, values, and academic behaviors. In J.T. Spence (Ed.), *Achievement and achievement motivation* (pp. 75–146). San Francisco: W. H. Freeman.

Eccles-Parsons, J., Meece, J. L., Adler, T. F., & Kaczala, C. M. (1982). Sex differences in attributions and learned helplessness. *Sex Roles, 8,* 421–432.

Eisenberg, N., Marin, C. L., & Fabes, R. A. (1996). Gender development and gender effects. In D. C. Berliner & R. C. Calfee (Eds.), *Handbook of educational psychology* (pp 358–396). New York: Macmillan.

Elder, G. H., Jr., & Conger, R. D. (2000). *Children of the land.* Chicago: University of Chicago Press.

Epstein, J. L., & McPartland, J. M. (1976). The concept and measurement of the quality of school life. *American Educational Research Journal, 13,* 15–30.

Ericsson (1996). *The road to excellence: The acquisition of expert performance in the arts, science, sports, and games.* Mahwah, NJ: Erlbaum.

Erikson, E. H. (1968). *Identity, youth and crisis.* New York: W. W. Norton.

Feldlaufer, H., Midgley, C. M., & Eccles, J. S. (1988). Student, teacher, and observer perceptions of the classroom environment before and after the transition to junior high school. *Journal of Early Adolescence, 8,* 133–156.

Finn, J. D. (1989). Withdrawing from school. *Review of Educational Research, 59,* 117–142.

Fordham, S., & Ogbu, J. U. (1986). Black students' school success: Coping with "the burden of 'acting white.'" *The Urban Review, 18,* 176–206.

Fuligni, A. J. (1997). The academic achievement of adolescents from immigrant families: The role of family background, attitudes, and beliefs. *Child Development, 68,* 351–363.

Gill, D. L. (2001). Sport and athletics. In J. Worell (Senior Ed.), *Encyclopedia of women and gender* (Vol. 2, pp. 1091–1100). San Diego, CA: Academic Press.

Gilligan, C., Lyons, N. P., & Tammer, T. J. (1990). *Making connections: The relational world of adolescent girls at the Emma Willard School.* Cambridge, MA: Harvard University Press.

Girotto, V., Gilly, M., Blaye, A., & Light, P. (1989). Children's performance in the selection task: Plausibility and familiarity. *British Journal of Psychology, 80,* 79–95.

Graham, S. (1992). Most of the subjects were European American and middle class: Trends in published research on African Americans in selected APA journals 1970–1989. *American Psychologist, 47,* 629–639.

Graham, S. (1994). Motivation in African Americans. *Review of Educational Research, 64,* 55–117.

Haars, V. J., & Mason, E. J. (1986). Children's understanding of class inclusion and their ability to reason with implication. *International Journal of Behavioral Development, 9,* 45–63.

Halpern-Felsher, B. L., & Cauffman, E. (2001). Costs and benefits of a decision: Decision-making competence in adolescents and adults. *Journal of Applied Developmental Psychology, 22,* 257–276.

Hamilton, S. (1990). *Apprenticeship for adulthood: Preparing youth for the future.* New York: Free Press.

Hare, B. R. (1985). Stability and change in self-perceptions and achievement among African American adolescents: A longitudinal study. *Journal of African American Psychology, 11,* 29–42.

Harter, S. (1981). A new self-report scale of intrinsic versus extrinsic orientation in the classroom: Motivational and informational components. *Developmental Psychology, 17,* 300–312.

Harter, S. (1998). The development of self-representations. In W. Damon (Series Ed.) & N. Eisenberg (Vol. Ed.), *Handbook of child psychology* (5th ed., Vol. 3, pp. 553–618). New York: Wiley.

Harter, S. (1990). Causes, correlates and the functional role of global self-worth: A life-span perspective. In J. Kolligian & R. Sternberg (Eds.), *Perceptions of competence and incompetence across the life-span* (pp. 67–98). New Haven, CT: Yale University Press.

Hill, K. T., & Sarason, S. B. (1966). The relation of test anxiety and defensiveness to test and school performance over the elementary school years: A further longitudinal study. *Monographs for the Society for Research in Child Development, 31*(2, Serial No. 104), 1–76.

Hunt, D. E. (1979). Person-environment interaction: A challenge found wanting before it was tried. *Review of Educational Research, 45,* 209–230.

Huston, A. C., McLoyd, V., & Coll, C. G. (1994). Children and poverty: Issues in contemporary research. *Child Development, 65,* 275–282.

Jackson, A. W., & Davis, G. A. (2000). *Turning points 2000: Educating adolescents in the 21st century.* New York: Teachers College Press.

Jacobs, J. E., Lanza, S., Osgood, W. D., Eccles, J. S., & Wigfield, A. (2002). Changes in children's self-competence and values: Gender and domain differences across grades one through twelve. *Child Development, 73,* 509–527.

James, W. (1963). *Psychology.* New York: Fawcett. (Original work published 1892)

Janveau-Brennan, G., & Markovits, H. (1999). The development of reasoning with causal conditionals. *Developmental Psychology, 35,* 904–911.

Jencks, C. L., & Brown, M. (1975). The effects of high schools on their students. *Harvard Educational Review, 45,* 273–324.

Jencks, C., & Phillips, M. (Eds.). (1998). *The black-white test score gap.* Washington, DC: Brookings Institute Press.

Jozefowicz, D. M., Barber, B. L., & Eccles, J. S. (1993, March). *Adolescent work-related values and beliefs: Gender differences and relation to occupational aspirations.* Paper presented at the Biennial Meeting of the Society for Research in Child Development. New Orleans, LA.

Kao, G., & Tienda, M. (1995). Optimism and achievement: The educational performance of immigrant youth. *Social Science Quarterly, 76,* 1–19.

Kavrell, S. M., & Petersen, A. C. (1984). Patterns of achievement in early adolescence. In M. L. Maehr (Ed.), *Advances in motivation and achievement* (pp. 1–35). Greenwich, CT: JAI Press.

Kazdin, A. E. (1993). Adolescent mental health: Prevention and treatment programs. *American Psychologist, 48,* 127–141.

Keating, D. P. (1990). Adolescent thinking. In S. S. Feldman & G. R. Elliott (Eds.), *At the threshold: The developing adolescent* (pp. 54–89). Cambridge, MA: Harvard University Press.

Kerr, B. A. (1985). *Smart girls, gifted women.* Dayton, OH: Ohio Psychology Publishing.

Klaczynski, P. A. (1993). Reasoning schema effects on adolescent rule acquisition and transfer. *Journal of Educational Psychology, 85,* 679–692.

Klaczynski, P. A., Byrnes, J. E., & Jacobs, J. E. (2001). Introduction to the special issue on the development of decision-making. *Journal of Applied Developmental Psychology, 22,* 225–236.

Klaczynski, P. A., & Narasimham, G. (1998). Representations as mediators of adolescent deductive reasoning. *Developmental Psychology, 34,* 865–881.

Kling, K. C., Hyde, J. S., Showers, C. J., & Buswell, B. N. (1999). Gender differences in self-esteem: A meta-analysis. *Psychological Bulletin, 125,* 470–500.

Kuhn, D., Garcia-Mila, M., Zohar, A., & Andersen, C. (1995). Strategies of knowledge acquisition. *Monographs of the Society for Research in Child Development, 60*(4), 1–128.

Lee, V. E., & Bryk, A. S. (1989). A multilevel model of the social distribution of high school achievement. *Sociology of Education, 62,* 172–192.

Lewis, C. (1981). How do adolescents approach decisions: Changes over grades seven to twelve and policy implications. *Child Development, 52,* 538–544.

Lipsitz, J. (1984). *Successful schools for young adolescents.* New Brunswick, NJ: Transaction Books.

Lord, S., Eccles, J. S., & McCarthy, K. (1994). Risk and protective factors in the transition to junior high school. *Journal of Early Adolescence, 14,* 162–199.

Lummis, M., & Stevenson, H. W. (1990). Gender differences in beliefs and achievement: A cross-cultural study. *Developmental Psychology, 26,* 254–263.

Luster, T., & McAdoo, H. P. (1994). Factors related to the achievement and adjustment of young African American children. *Child Development, 65,* 1080–1094.

Mac Iver, D. J., & Reuman, D. A. (1988, April). *Decision-making in the classroom and early adolescents' valuing of mathematics.* Paper presented at the annual meeting of the American Educational Research Association, New Orleans, LA.

Maehr, M. L., & Anderman, E. M. (1993). Reinventing schools for early adolescents: Emphasizing task goals. *The Elementary School Journal, 93,* 593–610.

Maehr, M. L., & Midgley, C. (1996). *Transforming school cultures.* Boulder, CO: Westview Press.

Markovits, H., & Vachon, R. (1990). Conditional reasoning, representation, and abstraction. *Developmental Psychology, 26,* 942–951.

McCall, R. B., Evahn, C., & Kratzer, L. (1992). *High school underachievers: What do they achieve as adults?* Newbury Park, CA: Sage.

McLoyd, V. C. (1990). The impact of economic hardship on African American families and children: Psychological distress, parenting, and socioemotional development. *Child Development, 61,* 311–346.

Meece, J. L., Wigfield, A., & Eccles, J. S. (1990). Predictors of math anxiety and its consequences for young adolescents' course enrollment intentions and performances in mathematics. *Journal of Educational Psychology, 82,* 60–70.

Midgley, C., Anderman, E., & Hicks, L. (1995). Differences between elementary and middle school teachers and students: A goal theory approach. *Journal of Early Adolescence, 15,* 90–113.

Midgley, C., & Feldlaufer, H. (1987). Students' and teachers' decision-making fit before and after the transition to junior high school. *Journal of Early Adolescence, 7,* 225–241.

Midgley, C., Feldlaufer, H., & Eccles, J. S. (1988). The transition to junior high school: Beliefs of pre- and post-transition teachers. *Journal of Youth and Adolescence, 17,* 543–562.

Midgley, C. M., Feldlaufer, H., & Eccles, J. S. (1989a). Changes in teacher efficacy and student self- and task-related beliefs during the transition to junior high school. *Journal of Educational Psychology, 81,* 247–258.

Midgley, C., Feldlaufer, H., & Eccles, J. S. (1989b). Student/teacher relations and attitudes toward mathematics before and after the transition to junior high school. *Child Development, 60,* 981–992.

Miller, C. L., Eccles, J. S., Flanagan, C., Midgley, C., Feldlaufer, H., & Harold, R. D. (1990). Parents' and teachers' beliefs about adolescents: Effects of sex and experience. *Journal of Youth and Adolescence, 19,* 363–394.

Miller, D. C., & Byrnes, J. P. (2001). Adolescents' decision-making in social situations: A self-regulation perspective. *Journal of Applied Developmental Psychology, 22,* 237–256.

Moos, R. H. (1979). *Evaluating educational environments.* San Francisco: Jossey-Bass.

Moshman, D. (1998). Cognitive development beyond childhood. In W. Damon (Series Ed.), D. Kuhn, & R. S. Siegler (Vol. Eds.), *Handbook of child psychology: Vol. 2. Cognition, language, and perception* (pp. 947–978). New York: Wiley.

Moshman, D., & Franks, B. A. (1986). Development of the concept of inferential validity. *Child Development, 57,* 153–165.

National Center for Education Statistics. (1995). *Overview of TIMSS Project.* Washington, DC: National Center for Educational Statistics.

National Center for Education Statistics. (1999). *On-line reports.* Washington, DC: National Center for Education Statistics.

Nicholls, J. G. (1979a). Development of perception of own attainment and causal attributions for success and failure in reading. *Journal of Educational Psychology, 71,* 94–99.

Nicholls, J. G. (1979b). Quality and equality in intellectual development: The role of motivation in education. *American Psychologist, 34,* 1071–1084.

Nicholls, J. G. (1989). *The competitive ethos and democratic education.* Cambridge MA: Harvard University Press.

Nolen-Hoeksema, S., & Girgus, J. S. (1994). The emergence of gender differences in depression during adolescence. *Psychological Bulletin, 115,* 424–443.

Office of Educational Research and Improvement. (1988). *Youth Indicators 1988.* Washington DC: U.S. Government Printing Office.

Ogbu, J. G. (1992). Understanding cultural diversity and learning. *Educational Researcher, 21,* 5–14.

Ormond, C., Luszcz, M. A., Mann, L., & Beswick, G. (1991). A metacognitive analysis of decision-making in adolescence. *Journal of Adolescence, 14,* 275–291.

Parsons, J. E., & Ruble, D. N. (1977). The development of achievement-related expectancies. *Child Development, 48,* 1075–1079.

Piaget, J., & Inhelder, B. (1973). *Memory and intelligence.* London: Routledge and Kegan Paul.

Pipher, Mary (1994). *Reviving ophelia.* New York: Ballantine Books.

Reese, C. M., Miller, K. E., Mazzeo, J., & Dossey, J. A. (1997). *The NAEP 1996 Mathematics Report Card for the Nation and the States.* Washington, DC: U.S. Department of Education, Office of Educational Research and Improvement, National Center for Educational Statistics.

Roderick, M. (1993). *The path to dropping out: Evidence for intervention.* Westport, CT: Auburn House.

Rokeach, M. (1979). From individual to institutional values with special reference to the values of science. In M. Rokeach (Ed.), *Understanding human values* (pp. 47–70). New York: Free Press.

Rosenbaum, J. E. (1976). *Making inequality: The hidden curriculum of high school tracking.* New York: Wiley.

Rosenholtz, S. J., & Simpson, C. (1984). The formation of ability conceptions: Developmental trend or social construction? *Review of Educational Research, 54,* 31–63.

Ruble, D. N., & Martin, C. L. (1998). Gender development. In N. Eisenberg (Ed.), *Handbook of child psychology* (5th ed., Vol. 3, pp. 933–1016). New York: Wiley.

Ryan, R. M., Connell, J. P., & Deci, E. L. (1985). A motivational analysis of self-determination and self-regulation in education. In C. Ames & R. Ames (Eds.), *Research on motivation in education: Vol. 2. The classroom milieu* (pp. 13–51). London: Academic Press.

Sadker, M., & Sadker, D. (1994). *Failing at fairness: How America's schools cheat girls.* New York: Scribner.

Schneider, B., & Coleman, J. S. (1993). *Parents, their children, and schools.* Boulder, CO: Westview Press.

Selman, R. L. (1980). *The growth of interpersonal understanding.* New York: Academic Press.

Simmons, R. G., & Blyth, D. A. (1987). *Moving into adolescence: The impact of pubertal change and school context.* Hawthorn, NY: de Gruyter.

Slaughter-Defoe, D. T., Nakagawa, K., Takanishi, R., & Johnson, D. J. (1990). Toward cultural/ecological perspectives on schooling and achievement in African- and Asian-American children. *Child Development, 61,* 363–383.

Sommers, C. H. (2000, May). Girls rule! Mythmakers to the contrary, it's boys who are in trouble. *Atlantic Monthly,* 59–74.

Spencer, M. B., & Markstrom-Adams, C. (1990). Identity processes among racial and ethnic minority children in America. *Child Development, 61,* 290–310.

Spencer, S. J., Steele, C. M., & Quinn, D. M. (1999). Stereotype threat and women's math performance. *Journal of Experimental Social Psychology, 35,* 4–28.

Steele, C. M., & Aronson, J. (1995). Stereotype threat and the intellectual test performance of African-Americans. *Journal of Personality and Social Psychology, 69*(5), 797–811.

Steinberg, L., Dornbusch, S., & Brown, B. (1992). Ethnic differences in adolescents achievements: An ecological perspective. *American Psychologist, 47,* 723–729.

Steinberg, L., Lamborn, S. D., Dornbusch, S. M., & Darling, N. (1992). Impact of parenting practices on adolescent achievement: Authoritative parenting, school involvement, and encouragement to succeed. *Child Development, 63,* 1266–1281.

Stevenson, H. W., Chen, C., & Uttal, D. H. (1990). Beliefs and achievement: A study of black, white, and Hispanic children. *Child Development, 61,* 508–523.

Subotnik, R. F., & Arnold, K. D. (1991). *Remarkable women: Perspectives on female talent development.* Cresskill, NJ: Hampton Press.

Swanson, H. L. (1999). What develops in working memory? A life span perspective. *Developmental Psychology, 35,* 986–1000.

Taylor, R. D., Casten, R., Flickinger, S., Roberts, D., & Fulmore, C. D. (1994). Explaining the school performance of African-American adolescents. *Journal of Research on Adolescence, 4,* 21–44.

Updegraff, K. A., Eccles, J. S., Barber, B. L., & O'Brien, K. M. (1996). Course enrollment as self-regulatory behavior: Who takes optional high school math courses. *Learning and Individual Differences, 8,* 239–259.

Ward, B. A., Mergendoller, J. R., Tikunoff, W. J., Rounds, T. S., Dadey, G. J., & Mitman, A. L. (1982). *Junior high school transition study: Executive summary.* San Francisco: Far West Laboratory.

Ward, S. L., Byrnes, J. P., & Overton, W. F. (1990). Organization of knowledge and conditional reasoning. *Journal of Educational Psychology, 82,* 832–837.

Ward, S. L. & Overton, W. F. (1990). Semantic familiarity, relevance, and the development of deductive reasoning. *Developmental Psychology, 26,* 488–493.

Wigfield, A., Eccles, J., Mac Iver, D., Reuman, D., & Midgley, C. (1991). Transitions at early adolescence: Changes in children's domain-specific self-perceptions and general self-esteem across the transition to junior high school. *Developmental Psychology, 27,* 552–565.

Wigfield, A., Eccles, J. S., Yoon, K. S., Harold, R. D., Arbreton, A. J., Freedman-Doan, C. R., & Blumenfeld, P. C. (1997). Changes in children's competence beliefs and subjective task values across the elementary school years: A three year study. *Journal of Educational Psychology, 89,* 451–469.

Winston, C. (2001, November 7). *Towards a better understanding of African Americans' school achievement.* Talk given at University of Michigan. Ann Arbor, MI.

Winston, C., Eccles, J. S., Senior, A. M., & Vida, M. (1997). The utility of an expectancy/value model of achievement for understanding academic performance and self-esteem in African-American and European-American adolescents. *Zeitschrift Fur Padagogische Psychologie [German Journal of Educational Psychology], 11,* 177–186.

Yee, D., & Eccles, J. S. (1988). Parent perceptions and attributions for children's math achievement. *Sex Roles, 19,* 317–333.

Youniss, J., McLellan, J. A., & Yates, M. (1997). What we know about engendering civic identity. *American Behavioral Scientist, 40,* 620–631.

Zald, D. H., & Iacono, W. G. (1998). The development of spatial working memory abilities. *Developmental Neuropsychology, 14,* 563–578.

CHAPTER 14

Emotional and Personality Development in Adolescence

NANCY L. GALAMBOS AND CATHERINE L. COSTIGAN

What is personality? How is temperament related to personality? Where does emotion fit in? What is the significance of emotion, personality, and temperament for understanding behavior and emotional well-being in adolescence? How does culture influence the expression of emotion and personality? These are critical and challenging questions that underlie the study of individual differences in emotional and personality development. Emotional and personality development are complicated, interrelated processes that occur across the life span. The story of emotion and personality in adolescence is essentially a study in identifying indicators and predictors of adolescents' emotional well-being and distress, ascertaining core personality traits seen in adolescence, documenting the evolution of personality characteristics across time, and investigating the links among emotion, emotional well-being and distress, personality, and temperament.

There is a vast array of theory and research on emotion and personality across the life span. This chapter focuses on recent research into the emotional well-being and distress of adolescents, as well as personality and temperament development in adolescence. The examination of emotion and personality in adolescence is interesting for at least two reasons. First, it is in the period of adolescence that we may begin to observe not only the crystallization of emotional and personality styles, but also how emotion and personality will shape the course of individuals' lives. Perhaps for the first time, interested ob-

servers such as parents can be more confident in predicting what kind of adult the individual is likely to become. Continuities in emotional well-being and personality across time are the source for these predictions about future behavior, but to be sure, discontinuities can make those predictions wrong. Second, the field of research on adolescent development that has burgeoned in the last few decades has demonstrated not only that there are significant biological, cognitive, social, and behavioral changes that occur during adolescence, but also that these changes are inextricably linked with one another. It is crucial to understand the role of emotion and personality in producing and affecting these changes.

Given the large amount of research in each of the areas of emotion, personality, and temperament, it is not possible within the confines of this chapter to conduct a comprehensive review of relevant studies. Several excellent books and reviews suit this purpose (e.g., Caspi, 1998; Kagan, 1998; Larson & Richards, 1994; Rothbart & Bates, 1998; Sanson & Rothbart, 1995; Shiner, 1998; van Lieshout, 2000). In this chapter we aim to identify the major issues seen in research on emotional and personality development pertaining specifically to adolescence, to provide examples of illustrative research in these domains, and to explore how future research can increase our understanding of adolescent emotion and personality. In the first section of this chapter we present research on some important issues in emotional development during adolescence. In the second section we discuss some of the key issues related to personality and temperament in adolescence. In the third and final section we identify four emerging themes in research on emotion and personality that will shape the direction of research for some time to come.

EMOTIONAL DEVELOPMENT

Guided by G. Stanley Hall's *storm and stress hypothesis* (the view that adolescence is filled with hormone-induced emotional turmoil), one focus of research on emotions in adolescence has been to examine variability in emotional or mood states (Brooks-Gunn, Graber, & Paikoff, 1994). Larson and Lampman-Petraitis (1989), for example, charted hour-to-hour changes in mood over a week in a sample of preadolescent and adolescent children. It is interesting to note that there was little evidence of variability in the mood states of adolescents compared to preadolescents. The average adolescent, however, was more likely than the average preadolescent to report more mildly negative mood states and fewer extremely positive mood states. Although overall mood may take on a slightly different character in adolescence, rapid mood swings were not evidenced in this research. Another focus of research has examined direct links between hormonal levels in adolescence and emotions such as aggression and depression (Susman, 1997; see chapter by Susman, Dorn, & Schiefelbein in this volume). Some consistent associations have been found between specific hormones and feelings of aggression (particularly among boys) and depression (Brooks-Gunn et al., 1994; Buchanan, Eccles, & Becker, 1992), but only small proportions of variance in emotion (up to 6%) are attributable to hormones (Susman, 1997). More complicated models of hormone-emotion relationships have been proposed, based on research indicating that hormones interact with personality and contextual characteristics to affect emotional states and behavior (Richards & Larson, 1993). These models, which require the use of longitudinal designs, will lead to a better understanding of how hormones are linked to adolescents' emotions indirectly through their impact on the outward physical changes of puberty, the adolescents' responses to these changes and their implications, and others' reactions to the changing adolescent (Brooks-Gunn et al., 1994; Susman, 1997).

Often implicit in the research on the link between hormones and emotion is the assumption that emotions may be something to be feared, that they are linked directly to negative and irrational behavior. Increasingly, though, the conceptualization of emotions in contemporary research has moved away from viewing emotions as sources of negative and irrational behavior toward a view of emotions as adaptive and capable of

organizing behavior in ways that can enhance as well as disrupt functioning (Cole, Michel, & Teti, 1994; Thompson, 1994). A dominant paradigm for studying emotions and emotion-related phenomena is emotion regulation.

Emotion regulation may be broadly defined as the way in which a person uses emotional experiences to provide for adaptive functioning (Thompson, 1994). The construct of emotion regulation has been used to refer to both outcome and process. In terms of outcome, some researchers define emotion regulation as the extent to which an individual shows emotional control versus emotional reactivity (Maedgen & Carlson, 2000). In this view, important components of emotion regulation include emotional lability, maladaptive emotional displays, and negative mood states. Others focus more on process variables such as the coping strategies that individuals employ to modify emotional reactions (Contreras, Kerns, Weimer, Gentzler, & Tomich, 2000; Rossman, 1992; Underwood, 1997). Emotion regulation in this sense refers to how the individual deals with each experience of emotion (Campos, Mumme, Kermoian, & Campos, 1994; Gross & Muñoz, 1995). This view of emotion regulation focuses not only on the modulation of distress but also on attempts to stimulate positive emotions or improve emotional arousal to achieve important interpersonal goals (Calkins, 1994; Thompson, 1994).

A variety of skills are necessary for effective emotion regulation, including flexibility and responsiveness to changing situational demands (Cole et al., 1994; Thompson, 1994). Other skills include an awareness of one's emotional state, the capacity to detect emotions in other people, knowledge of cultural display rules for emotions, and the ability to empathize with others' emotional states (Saarni, 1990; cited in Underwood, 1997). These skills are initially primarily externally supported, such as when a parent helps a child label and talk about their emotions, selectively reinforces adaptive emotional displays, and models effective emotion regulation. With development, socialization influences on emotion regulation give way to more internally mediated emotion regulation processes (Calkins, 1994; Thompson, 1994). By adolescence, individuals are better able to structure their own environment as a way of regulating their emotions, and they are capable of cognitively sophisticated emotion regulation strategies such as reframing and taking another's point of view (Gross & Muñoz, 1995).

This broader view of emotion regulation—that is, as the behavioral strategies one uses to modify, intensify, diminish, or transform emotional reactions—is an integral part of the functionalist perspective on emotion (Campos et al., 1994; Thompson, 1994). The functionalist perspective highlights several characteristics of emotion regulation. For instance, optimal emotion regulation is best conceptualized as context dependent, rather than as a stable feature of individual functioning (Thompson, 1994). Different contexts present diverse emotional challenges, and optimal emotion regulation varies depending on the goals of the individual in specific situations (Thompson, 1994). Accordingly, individuals have different goals depending on the interpersonal context (friend vs. stranger vs. authority figure), and the most adaptive way of dealing with emotions such as anger in each of these situations may differ (Underwood, 1997). Similarly, individuals may show effective emotion regulation in one context (e.g., with peers) but not in another (e.g., with siblings; Thompson, 1994; Whitesell & Harter, 1996). A related emphasis in the functionalist perspective is that emotion regulation is an interpersonal phenomenon more than an intrapsychic phenomenon (Campos et al., 1994). For instance, core emotions such as happiness, guilt, pride, and shame all reflect core relationship themes (Campos et al., 1994). In addition, beliefs about the availability of support and the likely response of others can facilitate or hamper effective emotion regulation (Thompson, 1994). In turn, emotion regulation skills can facilitate or hamper the achievement of important interpersonal developmental tasks, such as forming secure relationships with others (Cole et al., 1994).

Most research on emotion regulation has focused on infants (e.g., Field, 1994) and young children (e.g., Shields & Cicchetti, 1997; Underwood, 1997). Less attention has been directed at how emotion regulation operates in adolescence. Despite this lack of formal theorizing about emotion regulation in adolescence, the emotion regulation framework can be useful for conceptualizing and integrating a variety of constructs that have been the subject of much empirical attention in the literature on adolescence. For instance, indicators of adolescents' psychological well-being (e.g., self-esteem, positive mood) can be interpreted from an emotion regulation perspective as illustrative of the successful regulation of emotions, or adaptive emotional functioning. Likewise, indicators of psychological distress (e.g., depression) can be viewed as capturing emotion dysregulation. In this section we examine research that bears on adaptive emotional regulation, followed by research important to understanding emotion dysregulation.

Indicators of Adaptive Emotion Regulation

How do we know when adolescents are doing well? By what measure can we achieve some level of confidence that teens are successfully negotiating their way around their world, mastering important developmental tasks, and learning to regulate their emotions in ways that will ensure their eventual success in adulthood? Throughout the empirical literature on adolescence, there are a host of constructs and indicators of

emotional well-being, including, but not limited to, a high self-esteem (Haney & Durlak, 1998; Zimmerman, Copeland, Shope, & Dielman, 1997), a positive self-concept and stable sense of identity (Harter, 1990; Nurmi, 1997), a high level of ego development (Allen, Hauser, Bell, & O'Connor, 1994; Hauser & Safyer, 1994), social competence (Bustra, Bosma, & Jackson, 1994; Gullotta, Adams, & Montemayor, 1990), a positive mood or emotional tone (Larson & Richards, 1994; Petersen et al., 1993), school engagement and competence (Sandler, Ayers, Suter, Schultz, & Twohey, in press; Wigfield & Eccles, 1994), and feelings of attachment to parents and friends (Allen, Moore, Kuperminc, & Bell, 1998; Greenberger & McLaughlin, 1998; Paterson, Pryor, & Field, 1995). Although each of these indicators alone is the subject of a large body of research, studies have found that these measures of emotional well-being are typically positively correlated with one another (e.g., DuBois, Bull, Sherman, & Roberts, 1998; Paterson et al., 1995; Petersen et al., 1993). A review of each of these indicators is beyond the scope of this chapter. However, many of these constructs have been generally incorporated into larger integrative models that represent the adolescent's overall level of adaptation. From the perspective of emotion regulation, models of the self-system and psychosocial maturity are particularly appropriate to consider.

The Self-System

In decades of research, many aspects of self have been defined and measured. One of the most common is *self-esteem,* which is typically defined as an affective evaluation of the self, involving feelings of self-worth (DuBois & Hirsch, 2000). A long history of research shows that high levels of global self-esteem are linked with positive adjustment in adolescents, including higher academic achievement and lower levels of internalizing and externalizing problems (DuBois et al., 1998; Haney & Durlak, 1998; Zimmerman et al., 1997). *Self-concept* is typically seen as a cognitive representation of the self, or perceptions of one's personal and interpersonal characteristics (Haney & Durlak, 1998). Although there is no single definition or understanding of self-concept, self-concept is increasingly seen to be multidimensional in nature, incorporating elements of self-evaluation in specific domains, such as the school, peer, and athletic contexts (Harter, 1990; Harter, Bresnick, Bouchey, & Whitesell, 1997).

Self-system is a term recently used to describe in a broad sense the many elements of adolescents' representations of self, including self-esteem, perceived self-efficacy, possible selves, standards for self, values, and motivations (DuBois & Hirsch, 2000; Harter et al., 1997). There is no question that adolescents' positive self-attributions and closer connections between their multiple actual and ideal selves are linked with positive developmental outcomes (DuBois & Hirsch, 2000; Harter et al., 1997). With respect to *identity* development, the establishment of a stable sense of identity (the integration of a coherent sense of self that persists over time) is a key developmental task of adolescence (Erikson, 1968; Harter, 1990). Identity formation requires not only the consolidation of self-attributes into an organized system but also the integration of self with societal roles (Harter, 1990).

Haviland, Davidson, Ruetsch, Gebelt, and Lancelot (1994) have argued that emotion is a central part of identity structures, with adolescents' self-descriptions varying in the extent to which positive and negative emotions are represented. Thus, constructs such as self-esteem, self-concept, and identity fall under the general rubric of the self-system and speak to the issue of successful emotional regulation.

Psychosocial Maturity

Indicators of emotional well-being are also a key feature of psychosocial maturity, as defined by Greenberger and colleagues (Greenberger, Josselson, Knerr, & Knerr, 1975; Greenberger & Sørenson, 1974). This model encompasses three major domains of development, each consisting of multiple dimensions, which must be fostered if the child is to become a productive adult. The first domain is *autonomy,* or the individual's ability to function independently. The achievement of autonomy is characterized by self-reliance (the capacity to take initiative and to have a sense of control over one's life and activities), identity (a coherent self-concept, complete with life goals and internalized values), and work orientation (standards for competence and taking pleasure in work). The second domain is *interpersonal adequacy,* or the individual's ability to communicate and interact well with others. This requires effective communication skills, such as empathy and the ability to understand and receive messages, a sense of trust in others, and knowledge of role-appropriate behavior. The third domain of psychosocial maturity is *social responsibility,* or the individual's capacity to contribute to the well-being of society. This involves a sense of social commitment to the good of the community, an openness to social and political change to achieve higher order goals, and a tolerance and acceptance of individual and cultural differences (Greenberger & Sørenson, 1974). It is easy to observe that specific indicators of emotional well-being (e.g., social competence, attachment to parents and peers, school engagement, strong ego development, and a coherent identity) overlap with elements in this model of psychosocial maturity.

Aside from the fact that various indicators of emotional well-being are contained within larger models of the self and of psychosocial maturity, how can the diverse array of constructs, such as school engagement, self-esteem, identity, positive mood, and attachment to parents and peers, be indicators of "emotional" well-being? What do they have in common? According to Cole et al. (1994), children have a number of emotion-based developmental tasks that they must accomplish, including tolerance for frustration, establishing and enjoying friendships, defending the self, and acquiring interest in learning. In adolescence, major developmental tasks are to search for and establish an identity, pursue and succeed in intimate friendships, accept responsibility for oneself, and prepare for an education and career (Arnett, 2000). Cole et al. argued that the accomplishment of tasks such as these involves the ability to regulate emotions. Emotional regulation, therefore, is a tie that links together and perhaps underlies constructs such as self-esteem, mood, school engagement, identity, social competence, and feelings about parents and peers.

The importance of emotion regulation to the basic task of maturing and becoming an adult is recognizable in adolescents' descriptions of what it means to be "grown up." In a qualitative study (Tilton-Weaver, Vitunski, & Galambos, 2001) examining adolescents' implicit theories of maturity, sixth- and ninth-grade adolescents were told, "Please think of *someone your age* who seems more 'grown up' than most other kids (do not name him or her). What are some words that describe the ways in which this person seems grown up?" Half of the adolescents described what appeared to be genuinely mature adolescents. Incorporated into these adolescents' rich descriptions of genuine maturity were behaviors indicative of emotional regulation: "Doesn't let anger get in the way of good judgment," "if someone wants to fight him, he just walks away," "they are very calm, are helpful, do not get agitated easily," "can control and explain his feelings," and "he talks about feelings instead of hiding them." Not only was control of one's own emotions important in their descriptions of genuinely mature adolescents, but so was the ability to deal with others' strong emotions, as in this description of a peacemaker: "she is very calm when people are fighting, she tries to break it up or get them back together." Tolerance is another feeling that came across in these adolescents' descriptions: "Respects others' feelings, opinions, decisions, character" and "the person doesn't judge people by what they look like . . . which I think is good." Emotion regulation may not be the only hallmark of psychosocial maturity, but it is an important one.

Indicators of Emotion Dysregulation

The construct of emotion regulation not only unites the literature on emotional well-being just reviewed, but it also is central to the study of emotional distress. Emotion-related symptoms are a defining feature of most categories of psychopathology, and the development of emotion regulation is an implied goal of most psychological treatments (Cole et al., 1994). Emotion dysregulation refers to strategies that individuals use to cope with emotions that are maladaptive, such as restricted or inflexible emotional responding (Cole et al., 1994). Examples of emotion dysregulation include not having access to a full range of emotions, an inability to modulate the intensity or duration of emotions, not conforming to cultural display rules for emotions, an inability to integrate mixed emotions, and an inability to think and talk about emotions (Cole et al., 1994).

Emotion dysregulation is not the same as an absence of regulation; dysregulated emotions such as anger or withdrawal serve some adaptive purpose in the short term even though they may interfere with optimal development in the long term (Cole et al., 1994). However, dysregulated emotional styles are considered a vulnerability because maladaptive short-term strategies may become characteristic coping styles and develop into internalizing or externalizing disorders over time (Calkins, 1994; Cole et al., 1994).

Much research into adolescent emotional development has focused implicitly on emotion dysregulation by examining predictors and consequences of internalizing and externalizing disorders. Internalizing problems generally refer to subjective emotions such as depressive feelings and anxiety, whereas externalizing problems refer to more objectively disruptive behaviors such as overt aggressive and antisocial conduct. Although there is a high degree of comorbidity between the two and difficulties such as peer problems and low school motivation may be excluded from the internalizing-externalizing dichotomy (Wångby, Bergman, & Magnusson, 1999), the distinction is still a useful heuristic device for considering maladaptive adjustment patterns in adolescence. Because the development of externalizing problem behaviors is covered elsewhere in this volume (e.g., see chapter by Lerner, Easterbrooks, & Mistry in this volume), we focus our review on the experience of internalizing problems in general and in major depressive disorder (MDD) in particular. An emotion regulation perspective provides a framework for integrating the diverse theoretical orientations related to the experience of depression (see Gross & Muñoz, 1995, for a review).

The Emergence of Internalizing Disorders During Adolescence

Adolescence has traditionally been viewed as a time of increased negative emotions and emotional lability (Arnett, 1999). Reviews of adolescent depression indicate that adolescents report depressed mood at a higher rate than do preadolescents or adults (Petersen et al., 1993). Longitudinal studies of emotion development consistently find that negative affect increases from preadolescence to adolescence (Buchanan et al., 1992) and that depressed mood increases in early adolescence and decreases around late adolescence (Chen, Mechanic, & Hansell, 1998).

Epidemiological studies of the incidence of formal psychiatric disorders also point to adolescence as a time of increased emotional distress relative to later points in the life span. For instance, in the U.S. National Comorbidity Study, the 12-month prevalence of psychiatric disorders was highest in the youngest cohort (ages 15–24 years; Kessler et al., 1994). Similarly, Canada's National Population Health Survey found that major depressive episodes were highest in women ages 12 to 24 compared to males and older women (Beaudet, 1999).

Generally, the point prevalence of psychiatric disturbance in adolescence is about 1 in 4 or 5 (Casper, Belanoff, & Offer, 1996; Offer, Ostrov, Howard, & Atkinson, 1992). Newman et al. (1996) interviewed almost 1,000 adolescents five times over a 10-year period in a nonselected cohort in New Zealand. They found that internalizing disorders were among the most prevalent diagnoses. For instance, at age 21, 16.8% of the sample was diagnosed with MDD. Significantly, they found a sharp increase in depressive disorders during mid- to late adolescence (ages 15 to 18), which suggests that this may be a critical time for studying vulnerability to depression (Hankin et al., 1998).

Similar increases in the rate of depression during adolescence were found in the Oregon Adolescent Depression Project, a longitudinal study of over 1,700 adolescents (Lewinsohn, Rohde, & Seeley, 1998). In this study approximately 28% of adolescents had experienced an episode of MDD by age 19, with a mean age of onset of 14.9 years. Almost half (43%) of adolescents with MDD had a comorbid diagnosis, and in 80% of the cases the MDD was secondary to the comorbid condition. An important finding was that subthreshold levels of depressive symptoms were associated with almost as much psychosocial impairment as clinical levels of depression.

Gender Differences in Internalizing Disorders

Studies of both nonclinical levels of depressed and anxious mood, as well as studies of clinical levels of depression, all report higher rates of distress for females compared with males in adolescence (Chen et al., 1998; Leadbeater, Kuperminc, Blatt, & Hertzog, 1999; Nolen-Hoeksema, 1994). Prospective longitudinal studies indicate that internalizing symptoms remain high or increase for females, whereas they remain at relatively lower levels for males across adolescence (Leadbeater et al., 1999; Scaramella, Conger, & Simons, 1999). Gender differences in clinical levels of depression follow similar patterns. Gender differences in MDD are nonexistent in preadolescence, first emerge in early adolescence (ages 12–14), and increase dramatically in middle to late adolescence (ages 15–18; Hankin et al., 1998; Lewinsohn et al., 1998). By midadolescence the prevalence of MDD among females is more than double that of males; by age 18 approximately 11% of males compared with 24% of females are diagnosed with depression (Hankin et al., 1998; Lewinsohn et al., 1998).

Several explanations for these gender differences have been proposed. According to Nolen-Hoeksema (1994), gender differences in the emotion regulation strategies that males and females use to cope with distress partially account for differential rates of depression. In particular, she argued that females tend to employ passive, ruminative coping styles that place them at greater risk for depression compared with the more active and distracting coping styles of males. Other factors that may be related to gender differences in depression are adolescents' self-representations. For instance, females report lower levels of self-competence than males, and these differences partially account for differences in symptoms of depression and anxiety (Ohannessian, Lerner, Lerner, & von Eye, 1999). In addition, females show more preoccupation with relationships, threats of abandonment, and loss of nurturing compared with males, and these interpersonal vulnerabilities are associated with increased internalizing symptoms (Leadbeater et al., 1999). In general, the quality of relationships with parents and peers shows a stronger relationship to internalizing symptoms in females than males (Leadbeater et al., 1999), and females may feel more pressure to conform to the expectations of parents and peers (Nolen-Hoeksema, 1994). Finally, gender differences in the experience of depression may be related to the finding that females experience greater stress during adolescence (Nolen-Hoeksema, 1994). For instance, the changes in body shape and size that females experience during puberty are generally unwelcome, whereas the pubertal changes to male body shape and size are generally valued. In addition, females experience dramatically greater rates of sexual abuse in early adolescence compared with males, which is associated with elevated rates of depression.

Predictors and Correlates of Internalizing Disorders

Depressed mood has been associated with poor school motivation and performance, marital discord and family conflict,

the experience of stressful life events, low popularity, and, for females, both early- and late-onset puberty (Leadbeater et al., 1999; Lewinsohn et al., 1998; Petersen et al., 1993; Roeser, Eccles, & Sameroff, 1998). Many studies highlight the importance of the interpersonal context of adolescent depressive disorders. For instance, the quality of attachment between parents and adolescents plays a role in internalizing adjustment problems. Adolescents with secure attachments experience fewer symptoms of depression and anxiety, whereas adolescents with preoccupied, anxious, or avoidant attachment relationships experience relatively more psychological distress (Allen et al., 1998; Cooper, Shaver, & Collins, 1998; Marton & Maharaj, 1993; Noom, Dekovic, & Meeus, 1999). Furthermore, interactions in families with a depressed adolescent are observed to be less cohesive and supportive compared with families with well-adjusted adolescents (Sheeber & Sorensen, 1998). In addition, inept and inadequate parenting, characterized by less warmth and acceptance, more hostility, greater psychological control, and less consistent discipline, is associated with increased risk for internalizing symptoms and clinical depression across adolescence (Conger, Conger, & Scaramella, 1997; Ge, Conger, Lorenz, & Simons, 1994; Marton & Maharaj, 1993; Scaramella et al., 1999). For males, greater psychological control by siblings is also associated with increases in internalizing symptoms over time (K. Conger et al., 1997).

These disruptions in parenting and parent-adolescent relationships may affect depressive symptoms through their effects on adolescents' self-representations. For instance, lower maternal acceptance and greater psychological control are associated with lower levels of self-worth, which in turn are associated with elevated levels of depression (Garber, Robinson, & Valentiner, 1997). Similarly, disrupted parent-adolescent relationships (i.e., separation-individuation conflicts, parental rejection, or excessive dependency) are associated with greater self-critical and interpersonal vulnerabilities, which in turn are associated with increased depressed mood (Frank, Poorman, Van Egeren, & Field, 1997). Other intrapsychic variables, such as lower levels of attitudinal and emotional autonomy (Noom et al., 1999) and greater self-awareness (Chen et al., 1998), are also associated with increased depressed mood.

PERSONALITY DEVELOPMENT

Much of what we know about personality development is actually based on research with either young children or adults. These have been largely disconnected lines of inquiry with a long history of research on young children devoted to studying temperament and a great deal of research on adults examining personality. These separate lines of inquiry are now being joined as researchers attempt to understand the overlap and the connections between temperament in childhood and personality in adulthood (Sanson & Rothbart, 1995). As the transition period between childhood and adulthood, adolescence is perhaps an ideal time for considering personality and temperament. In research on adolescent personality and temperament, several key issues have been identified. These issues include (a) the core structure of personality, (b) the origins of personality, (c) continuity in personality across the life span, and (d) the fit between temperament/personality dimensions and the social context. These issues as they pertain to research on adolescence are elaborated in this section.

The Structure of Personality

The search for core features of personality has a long history. In personality research across the twentieth century, a myriad of personality traits has been identified, measured, examined, and linked to each other as well as to the individual's psychosocial adjustment. Given the large array of possible personality constructs, the search for a taxonomy, or descriptive model, of core personality traits has occupied the efforts of many researchers, particularly those examining personality in adults (John, 1990). One taxonomy, the *Big Five,* is a comprehensive model consisting of five broad personality traits or factors under which most if not all other descriptors of personality are subsumed (Goldberg, 1993). This model is based largely on clusters of adjectives that people use to describe themselves. The five factors and examples of adjectives attached to these factors are Extroversion (assertive, enthusiastic, outgoing), Agreeableness (generous, kind, sympathetic), Conscientiousness (organized, planful, responsible), Neuroticism (anxious, self-pitying), and Openness/Intellect (curious, imaginative, wide interests; Caspi, 1998; Goldberg, 1993; John, 1990). Growing support for the Big Five as a meaningful framework for understanding personality dispositions has emerged over the years. This support is based on accumulating empirical evidence that the five-factor structure is robust across many studies and cultures and that it can be used to predict behaviors such as job performance (Goldberg, 1993; McCrae et al., 1999). Nevertheless, there are other models of personality structure, some with two or three factors and some with many more (Church, 1994; Eysenck, 1992; Goldberg, 1993).

Given that most research on the Big Five has been conducted on samples of adults, an important question has been whether these five factors describe the personality structures of children and adolescents. Studies examining this issue in American and Dutch samples have appeared in the last decade, with a five-factor model finding support in samples of individuals ranging in age from early childhood through adolescence, including girls and boys (Digman, 1989; Graziano & Ward, 1992; Havill, Allen, Halverson, & Kohnstamm, 1994; Kohnstamm, Halverson, Havill, & Mervielde, 1996; van Lieshout & Haselager, 1994). One study of 12- to 13-year-old African American and Caucasian boys, rated by their mothers on a set of personality characteristics, found evidence that the Big Five replicated in this ethnically diverse sample (John, Caspi, Robins, Moffitt, & Stouthamer-Loeber, 1994). The results were suggestive also of two additional dimensions of personality at this age: irritability (whines, feelings are easily hurt, has tantrums) and positive activity (energetic, physically active). This research also found that the five factors were linked differentially with indicators of adolescents' emotional well-being. For example, adolescent boys with externalizing problems were less agreeable, less conscientious, and more extroverted than were those not showing externalizing behavior. Boys with internalizing disorders were high on neuroticism and low on conscientiousness. Poorer school performance was seen among boys who scored lower on conscientiousness and lower on openness (e.g., curiosity).

There are several advantages to identifying a comprehensive model of personality. If researchers agree on and measure the same set of core dimensions of personality in their research, the results of their studies are more directly comparable. Essentially, acceptance of a model such as the Big Five ensures that researchers are speaking the same language. A body of research based on a similarly shared understanding of constructs can lead to clearer and more integrated knowledge of the origins, course of development, and implications of personality (John, 1990). Without a common set of constructs that can be measured across the life span, it is more difficult to draw conclusions about how personality develops from infancy through adulthood—a key question in developmental psychology. The field of research on adolescence generally has not been driven by such a model. Rather, there is wide diversity in the personality constructs that have been measured in research on adolescence. Typically, selected personality traits such as self-restraint, aggression, and sensation seeking have been measured, often in isolation from other personality characteristics (Shiner, 1998). These selected characteristics are then related to individual differences in adolescent behaviors such as risk taking, early childbearing, and delinquency (e.g., Black, Ricardo, & Stanton, 1997; Feldman & Weinberger, 1994; Underwood, Kupersmidt, & Coie, 1996). The Big Five is a promising model that could be used by researchers of adolescent development as a way to understand links between adolescents' personalities and their behaviors and emotional well-being.

The Origins of Personality in Temperament

Whereas the study of personality has been located largely in the empirical literature on adults, the study of temperament has been confined mostly to infants and children (for exceptions, see Tubman & Windle, 1995; Wills, DuHamel, & Vaccaro, 1995; Windle, 1992). Only recently has research on personality and temperament begun to be integrated (Sanson & Rothbart, 1995). Although researchers concur neither on a single definition of temperament nor on a core set of temperamental dimensions, it is generally assumed that a child's temperament is composed of multiple behavioral attributes present at birth (Kagan, 1998). Moreover, there is purported evidence from twin and adoption studies of a substantial genetic influence on temperamental and personality attributes in childhood and adolescence, although there are nonshared environmental influences as well (Braungart, Plomin, DeFries, & Fulker, 1992; Caspi, 1998; Rowe, Almeida, & Jacobson, 1999; Saudino, McGuire, Reiss, Hetherington, & Plomin, 1995). Many authors believe that temperament forms the substrate of personality. Specifically, through the influence of the child's increasing capacities and interactions with the environment, temperament evolves or becomes elaborated across childhood into a set of differentiated personality traits (Caspi, 1998; Goldsmith et al., 1987; Sanson & Rothbart, 1995; Shiner, 1998).

The modern study of temperament began with the classic work of Thomas and Chess (1977; see also Chess & Thomas, 1999), who followed a group of infants into adulthood. Based on observations of the behavioral styles of these infants, Thomas and Chess identified nine dimensions of temperament along which infants varied. Among these dimensions were activity level, adaptability, intensity of reaction, quality of mood, rhythmicity, and approach. Thomas and Chess also classified children as having "difficult" or "easy" temperaments on the basis of their patterns on a select set of temperamental dimensions. Their pioneering work recognized that early individual differences in temperament were an influential source of individual differences in parent-child relations and in later emotional well-being.

Other models of temperament followed, most of which identified several core dimensions of temperament (Buss &

Plomin, 1984; Goldsmith & Campos, 1986; Rothbart & Derryberry, 1981). For instance, Buss and Plomin's (1984) *EAS model* identified Emotionality (primarily negative emotions), Activity, and Sociability as basic dimensions of temperament. Rothbart and Derryberry (1981) defined temperament as individual differences in two broad dimensions: reactivity to internal and external stimulation (or the arousability of one's behavioral, emotional, and biological responses) and self-regulation (or processes such as attention, approach, withdrawal, and self-soothing that modulate reactivity). Models of temperament have undergone modifications and development as research has accumulated (Buss & Plomin, 1984; Windle & Lerner, 1986). Rothbart and colleagues have reported that across a number of studies from early childhood to adulthood, three broad factors of temperament emerge (Ahadi & Rothbart, 1994; Capaldi & Rothbart, 1992; Sanson & Rothbart, 1995). The first, labeled Positive Emotionality, Surgency, or Sociability, is captured by higher scores on approach, high-intensity pleasure, and activity subscales. The second, labeled Negative Emotionality or Affectivity, is based on feelings of fear, anger, discomfort, and sadness. A third factor, called Effortful Control or Persistence, is defined by inhibitory control, attentional focusing, low-intensity pleasure, and perceptual sensitivity.

Generally, personality is seen to be broader and more differentiated than temperament, with personality incorporating behavior, motives, emotions, attitudes, and values (Digman, 1994). Because early-emerging temperamental characteristics are believed to mature and become elaborated over time into distinct personality traits (Caspi, 1998), researchers have attempted to delineate how dimensions of temperament converge with the Big Five personality dimensions (Halverson, Kohnstramm, & Martin, 1994). Interestingly, the three factors of Positive Emotionality, Negative Emotionality, and Effortful Control appear to map onto three of the Big Five personality dimensions. Specifically, Positive Emotionality maps onto the Extroversion personality dimension in the Big Five, Negative Emotionality maps onto Neuroticism, and Effortful Control maps onto Conscientiousness (Ahadi & Rothbart, 1994; Sanson & Rothbart, 1995). Other scholars, too, have pointed to the overlap between early emerging dimensions of temperament and adolescent and adult personality structure (Caspi, 1998; Digman, 1994; John et al., 1994; Shiner, 1998).

Continuity in Temperament and Personality

The assumption that temperamental attributes present in childhood are predictive of later temperamental or personality attributes leads us to ask whether there is continuity in these attributes—a question that can only be answered with longitudinal studies following the same individuals from childhood to adulthood. Such studies have examined stability coefficients, that is, correlations between specific temperamental attributes in infancy or childhood and those same aspects of temperament at a later point. Earlier studies of temperamental stability indicated only moderate stability across time, but more recent studies that have controlled for conceptual and methodological problems show relatively high stabilities (in the .70s to .80s) in temperamental characteristics such as sociability and irritability from infancy to age 7 or 8 years (Pedlow, Sanson, Prior, & Oberklaid, 1993; Sanson & Rothbart, 1995). Thus, there is evidence for continuity in temperamental characteristics, although there is also room for change.

Insight into the issue of continuity is also gained by examining how early temperament is linked with later personality traits. One study, conducted in New Zealand, followed individuals from age 3 to young adulthood (Caspi, 2000; Caspi & Silva, 1995). At the age of 3, analyses identified three replicable groups of children based on ratings of their behavior. These groups were labeled as Undercontrolled (e.g., impulsive), Inhibited (e.g., fearful), and Well Adjusted (e.g., coped well, friendly). At the age of 18, these groups were reassessed for personality traits. There were clear and significant associations between temperamental styles at age 3 and personality at age 18. For example, children who were undercontrolled at age 3 had similar characteristics at age 18: They were characterized as impulsive, danger-seeking, high on negative emotionality, and engaged in conflict with others. Inhibited children became rather cautious as young adults, showing a restrained behavioral style: harm-avoidant, not aggressive, and not interpersonally assertive. Well-adjusted children became normal young adults, showing no extreme scores on any personality dimension.

Thus, this study provided evidence for continuity in behavioral styles from early childhood through adolescence. Moreover, in the longer term the early temperamental characteristics of these children were predictive of a wide variety of aspects of functioning, including the quality of interpersonal relations, the availability of social support, unemployment, psychiatric disorders, and criminal behavior (Caspi, 2000). Other studies, too, demonstrate continuities in temperament and personality characteristics such as behavioral inhibition and shyness (Kagan, 1989; Katainen, Räikkönen, & Keltikangas-Järvinen, 1998). Continuities in personality may result from a kind of snowballing effect in which early temperamental styles create consequences, situations, and interactions with others that serve to reinforce natural tendencies (Caspi & Silva, 1995).

The Goodness-of-Fit Model of Temperament

Even though there are clear links between one's early personality and later functioning, some authors assert that the import of temperament is best understood by examining the context in which it takes place. A goodness-of-fit model of temperament posits that the impact of children's temperament on their development is a function of how well their temperamental characteristics fit the demands of the social context (Chess & Thomas, 1999; Thomas & Chess, 1977). When the child's temperament matches those demands, there is a greater likelihood that social interactions will be favorable to the child's development. A poor fit, however, may jeopardize his or her social interactions and subsequent psychosocial adjustment (Chess & Thomas, 1999; Lerner & Lerner, 1983; Nitz, Lerner, Lerner, & Talwar, 1988; Talwar, Nitz, & Lerner, 1990; Thomas & Chess, 1977). In one study (East et al., 1992), young adolescents' fit with their peer group was measured by assessing the difference between adolescents' own temperamental characteristics and their classroom peers' judgments of preferred temperamental characteristics in classmates. These difference or fit scores were then correlated with measures of adolescents' psychosocial competence. As expected, the adolescent's fit with peer group demands for particular temperamental attributes was linked with a variety of measures. For instance, adolescents whose characteristics of adaptability (mood, flexibility, and approach behaviors) matched their peers' demands for adaptability received favorable nominations from peers on sociometric measures. Fit scores for adaptability and rhythmicity also were linked with self- and teacher-rated psychosocial competence. Moreover, some of the relations between fit and psychosocial competence were found consistently across three times of measurement from the beginning to the end of Grade 6. These findings provide evidence that a closer match between the adolescent's temperament and the social context is linked with more desirable psychosocial functioning.

Goodness-of-Fit in Parent and Adolescent Temperaments

One way to conceptualize adolescents' fit with the social context is to consider how adolescents' and parents' temperaments work together. That is, both members of a parent-adolescent dyad bring to their relationship temperamental characteristics that may be complementary—or that may clash. In this sense, one family member's temperament imposes demands on the other, whose own temperament may not fit with those demands (Kawaguchi, Welsh, Powers, & Rostosky, 1998). For example, an adolescent who is rigid with respect to approaching new situations might have a more harmonious relationship with a parent who is flexible than with a parent who is equally rigid. Mismatched temperamental styles might eventuate in conflicted or perhaps even hostile relations. Few researchers have examined parent-adolescent relations as a joint function of the temperaments of parents and adolescents, although there are such studies of younger children (Belsky, 1996; Kawaguchi et al., 1998).

In a test of a goodness-of-fit model in parent and adolescent temperaments, Galambos and Turner (1999) examined in 7th-grade adolescents and their parents whether two broad dimensions of parent and adolescent temperaments (i.e., adaptability and activity level) combined or interacted to predict the quality of parent-adolescent relations. There were significant interactions between parent and adolescent dimensions of temperament in the prediction of some aspects of the parent-adolescent relationship. For example, mother-son conflict was highest in dyads comprised of mothers low on adaptability and their low-activity sons. The authors speculated that low activity levels in sons were not interpreted happily by less adaptable mothers who might have expected boys to be highly active (in keeping with sex stereotypes). On the other hand, mother-daughter conflict was highest in dyads in which mothers were less adaptable and daughters were more active. Again, less adaptable mothers may have had difficulties with girls whose patterns of high activity were not in keeping with traditional sex stereotypes of appropriate female behavior. Another set of results demonstrated that the combination of low adaptability in both fathers and daughters was associated with more psychologically controlling behavior in the fathers. Moreover, less adaptable daughters reported higher levels of conflict with their less adaptable fathers than did other daughters. Low adaptability may be a risk factor for less optimal parent-adolescent relations, particularly when found in both members of the parent-adolescent dyad. Although these results were based on correlational data, they are consistent with a goodness-of-fit model. Selected aspects of parent and adolescent temperaments fit better with each other than do others, as indicated by the quality of parent-adolescent relations.

EMERGING TRENDS AND FUTURE DIRECTIONS

In the previous sections we have reviewed contemporary research related to emotional well-being, emotional distress, personality, and temperament during adolescence. In this final section we would like to highlight four emerging areas of investigation in research on emotions and personality in adolescence. These trends include (a) a more explicit focus on indications of optimal emotional adjustment in

adolescence, (b) an examination of cultural variations in emotions and personality during adolescence, (c) an integration of temperament into the study of adolescent adjustment, and (d) the increasing use of person approaches to studying emotion and personality.

A Focus on Optimal Development

The first emerging theme in research on adolescents' emotional and personality development is a focus on positive adolescent development (Lerner, Fisher, & Weinberg, 2000; Lerner & Galambos, 1998). Adolescent research has been criticized for focusing too much on adolescent problem behaviors and distress, or defining positive development as the absence of difficulties, rather than focusing explicitly on the development of positive, adaptive qualities (Galambos & Leadbeater, 2000; Larson, 2000; Schulenberg, Maggs, & Hurrelmann, 1997; Wagner, 1996). However, research into healthy adolescent development is emerging. Some of this work identifies the protective factors that enable youth in high-risk environments to reach their full potentials. For example, a review of programs designed to promote healthy youth development (Roth, Brooks-Gunn, Murray, & Foster, 1998) highlights the diverse ways in which communities and schools are working to build strengths among adolescents.

Other research in this area explores the development of specific positive qualities among all adolescents. For instance, Wentzel and McNamara (1999) examined the development of prosocial behaviors among early adolescents. Prosocial behaviors, such as cooperation, sharing, and helping, were assessed through peer nominations. They found that prosocial behaviors are facilitated by feelings of peer acceptance. The role of family support in the development of prosocial behaviors was indirect, mediated by emotional distress. Thus, adolescents who are accepted by their peers and who are able to regulate their emotions effectively may have more opportunities to learn prosocial skills. Larson (2000) focused on the development of initiative during adolescence. He defined initiative as the internal motivation to pursue a challenging goal and saw it as a prerequisite for the development of other positive qualities such as leadership and altruism. Adolescents who display initiative feel invested in and excited about their futures. Larson's research highlights the types of contexts that promote initiative and other positive qualities. These contexts consist of structured extracurricular activities, such as sports or organized hobbies, which provide the intrinsic motivation and concentrated attention that are believed to foster initiative.

In order to examine positive adolescent development systematically, a model or definition of the components of optimal development is necessary. Lerner et al. (2000) outlined a model of adolescent development in which five broad features of positive adolescent development are identified. These five characteristics include (a) Caring/Compassion (e.g., empathy), (b) Competence (cognitive, behavioral, and social), (c) Character (e.g., integrity), (d) Connection (e.g., positive bonds with others and with society), and (e) Confidence (e.g., self-efficacy). Similarly, Wagner (1996) developed a model of optimal development in adolescence. He defined aspects of optimal development within six domains: Biological, Cognitive, Emotional, Social, Moral, and Vocational. Within the Emotional domain, for example, optimal development is indicated by qualities such as emotional awareness, self-confidence, optimism, and resilience. Such attention to positive adolescent development holds great promise to increase our understanding of the developmental factors and assets that enable adolescents not just to survive but to thrive (Scales, Benson, Leffert, & Blyth, 2000).

Cultural Variations in Emotional and Personality Development

A second theme that is emerging in research on adolescents' emotional and personality development concerns the role of culture and ethnicity in adolescent development. It is beyond the scope of this chapter to review all of the literature on cultural influences and differences in adolescent development. However, here we survey some of the major areas of inquiry.

The past decade has seen increasing interest in examining the emotional well-being of ethnically diverse adolescents (e.g., Luster & McAdoo, 1994; McAdoo, 1993). Among Asian and Asian American adolescents, researchers have investigated indicators of adjustment such as psychosocial competence (Mantzicopoulos & Oh-Hwang, 1998; Sim, 2000), autonomy (Juang, Lerner, McKinney, & von Eye, 1999), and self-esteem (Watkins, Dong, & Xia, 1997), as well as indicators of maladjustment, such as anxiety (Hishinuma, Miyamoto, Nishimura, & Nahalu, 2000), depression (Ying, Lee, Tsai, Yeh, & Huang, 2000), and psychological distress (Chiu, Feldman, & Rosenthal, 1992). Because most theories of emotional development in adolescence were developed based on research with European American participants, research with ethnically diverse participants is necessary to evaluate whether theories of adolescence generalize to other segments of the population. Some of this literature highlights similarities in the predictors of adolescent emotional development across ethnic groups. Using Chinese adolescents as an example, many aspects of positive parenting, such as warm

parent-child relationships, firm control, monitoring, and the absence of coercive exchanges, are related to higher levels of adolescent emotional well-being in locations such as Hong Kong (Shek, 1997a, 1997b) and Shanghai (Chen, Dong, & Zhou, 1997; Chen, Liu, & Li, 2000; Chen, Rubin, & Li, 1997). However, within North America the evidence is mixed. Some researchers find similar relationships between parenting and adolescents' emotional adjustment across cultural groups (Greenberger & Chen, 1996; Kim & Ge, 2000), whereas others find that these relationships do not replicate in different cultural groups (e.g., Barrett Singer & Weinstein, 2000) or that the specific domains of adolescent adjustment that are affected vary by cultural group (e.g., Bradley & Corwyn, 2000). An important area for future research is to continue to evaluate whether the cultural context within North America moderates the effects of external factors on adolescent's emotional well-being and distress (e.g., Collins, Maccoby, Steinberg, Hetherington, & Bornstein, 2000).

Research with adolescents from ethnically diverse backgrounds also highlights the need to consider emotional development in a cultural context. For instance, Costigan and Cauce (in press) examined developmental changes in adolescent autonomy and parent-adolescent conflict across adolescence among a sample of African American mothers and daughters. Although past literature has described African American mothers as restrictive or authoritarian, findings from this study suggested that mothers were appropriately selective in their willingness to relinquish control and grant autonomy. For example, mothers retained a higher amount of decision-making authority around important safety-related issues, despite a high level of conflict, whereas they allowed greater adolescent autonomy around personal issues such as hairstyles. These findings illustrate the challenge that African American mothers face in balancing the demands of protecting children while also fostering a sense of competence. For African American families such parenting challenges may be met through the assistance of an extended family network that provides goods, services, and emotional support to its members (McAdoo, 1997). Clearly, how the cultural contexts helps shape adolescents' emotional development merits further attention.

Another way in which culture may affect adolescents' emotional development is by influencing adolescents' tendencies to express different emotions and the strategies used to regulate emotions. Emotions are managed in culture-specific ways (Thompson, 1994). First, there are cultural differences in how adolescents construe emotional events. For example, Liem, Lim, and Liem (2000) argued that the emotional responses of Asian Americans are generally more other oriented, focusing on interdependence, whereas European

Americans are generally more self-oriented, focusing on independence. They find that these self-construals change as a result of acculturation. Second, cultures differ in their expectations for emotional displays (Campos et al., 1994). Chinese parents, for example, view dependency, caution, behavioral inhibition, and self-restraint in children more favorably than do parents in Western cultures (Chen, Rubin, & Li, 1997). Finally, cultures have varying emotional baselines and tolerances for the expression of emotions such as support, disagreement, and disapproval (Stillars, 1995). When there is a higher overall baseline for an emotion, there is also a greater tolerance for its expression, so that its expression in any given instance carries less impact. Alternatively, the impact of expressing an emotion for which there is less tolerance is accentuated (Stillars, 1995). This may be one mechanism by which culture moderates the effects of external events, such as parenting, on adolescent adjustment. For example, if lower levels of emotional expressiveness are more normative in Chinese culture, then Chinese parents may not be experienced as less warm by their children (e.g., Chao, 1994). In comparison with Western adolescents, an objectively lower amount of warmth may need to be present before the Chinese adolescents experience it as such.

A consideration of cultural influences also highlights culture-specific predictors of emotional well-being and culture-specific domains of emotional development. For example, for African American adolescents, perceptions of differential treatment based on race are associated with increases in depression and anger over time (Roeser et al., 1998). Furthermore, issues such as family obligations (e.g., Fuligni, Tseng, & Lam, 1999), parental respect (e.g., Chao, 2000), intergenerational value discrepancies (e.g., Phinney, Ong, & Madden, 2000), and acculturative stress are important constructs to examine in order to gain a full understanding of the emotional adjustment of immigrant and minority adolescents (e.g., Fuertes & Westbrook, 1996; Hovey & King, 1996; Kwan & Sodowsky, 1997; Thompson, Anderson, & Bakeman, 2000).

Perhaps the most salient culture-specific domain of emotional adjustment for ethnically diverse adolescents is ethnic identity. Ethnic identity is an important component of overall identity formation, and adolescence is a crucial time for ethnic identity exploration and commitment (Phinney, 1992). Spencer and colleagues (Spencer, Dupree, & Hartmann, 1997) proposed a phenomenological variant of ecological systems theory (PVEST) model to explain the development of stable identities (including ethnic identity) and other aspects of healthy youth development. This model suggests that ethnic identity formation results from an interaction between the stressors that youths encounter in daily life and the subjective understanding or meaning that adolescents ascribe to these experiences.

Ethnic identity is comprised of two primary factors: ethnic identification (e.g., pride in one's ethnic group) and exploration (e.g., trying to find out more about one's ethnic group; Spencer, Icard, Harachi, Catalano, & Oxford, 2000). Adolescence is a key time for ethnic identity development because of advancing cognitive abilities as well as specific ethnic socialization experiences (Quintana, Castañeda-English, & Ybarra, 1999; Spencer et al., 1997). The salience of ethnic identity changes with changes in context, such as moving to a location where one is a minority member (Ichiyama, McQuarrie, & Ching, 1996). However, greater acculturation to a host culture does not necessarily mean a decrease in ethnic identification (Liu, Pope-Davis, Nevitt, & Toporek, 1999). Finally, ethnic identity has implications for adolescents' emotional well-being. In general, a stronger sense of one's ethnic identity is related to higher feelings of self-esteem (Gray-Little & Hafdahl, 2000; Phinney, Cantu, & Kurtz, 1997; Phinney & Chavira, 1992) and self-efficacy (Smith, Walker, Fields, Brookins, & Seay, 1999). However, the relationship between ethnic identity and psychological adjustment is not always consistent and may depend on other factors such as one's identification with the host culture and the ethnic density of one's community (Eyou, Adair, & Dixon, 2000; McAdoo, 1993).

Integration of Temperament Into the Study of Adolescent Adjustment

A third emerging theme in research on adolescents' emotional and personality development concerns integrating the role of temperament into models of adolescent adjustment. Research in this area has accelerated as the construct of emotion regulation has gained prominence in the study of adolescent development. The first step in integrating temperament into this research is to differentiate temperament from related constructs such as mood and emotion regulation. For instance, as outlined by Kagan (1994), the concept of emotion has been used to refer to acute and temporary changes in feeling, more permanent affective states that endure over years, and temperamentally based predispositions to react to events in certain ways. Kagan argues that we need to distinguish between chronic mood states and temperamental characteristics. Individuals with various temperaments differ in the ease with which they experience different emotions, and the emotions experienced may be qualitatively different. Indeed, Kagan (1998) concluded that variation in temperamental characteristics helps to explain why some children do not experience trauma-related symptoms even in the face of major stressors such as kidnapping or divorce. Rothbart and Bates (1998) proposed a number of possible models of the direct, indirect, and interactive effects of multiple temperamental traits on multiple adjustment indicators. Their explication of such linkages provides an abundance of possible processes that can and should be investigated.

Furthermore, we need to differentiate between temperament and emotion regulation skills (Underwood, 1997). Temperament affects the intensity of emotional experience. As a result, an individual who experiences emotions more intensely faces a greater challenge in emotion regulation. Similarly, individuals with different temperaments experience different levels of arousability. Because of differences in arousability, it is difficult to determine whether an adolescent who is apparently effectively managing an emotionally challenging situation is superior at emotion regulation compared with an adolescent who is having more difficulty, or whether that adolescent is simply less reactive (Kagan, 1994). Future research needs to distinguish purposeful emotion regulation from low arousability.

The concept of emotion regulation highlights the role of temperament in socialization processes (e.g., Contreras et al., 2000). Much attention has been directed at the environmental antecedents of different emotional states, positive and negative. For instance, as reviewed earlier, parenting behaviors influence the development of adaptive emotion regulation, such as self-esteem and psychosocial maturity, as well as dysregulated emotions such as depression. However, adolescent adjustment and maladjustment are affected not only by an interpersonal environment that encourages or discourages certain qualities, but also by a person's temperamental dispositions (Kagan, 1994). Future research needs to assess how temperament and socialization work together to influence the development of emotion regulation (Underwood, 1997).

Different models for considering both temperament and socialization in adolescent adjustment are emerging. For instance, Calkins (1994) integrated research on the developmental consequences of temperament and parenting styles in her model of the development of social competence in childhood. She examines the relative contributions of internal and external sources of individual differences in emotion regulation. Internal factors include temperamental characteristics such as physiological regulation (e.g., heart rate) and behavioral tendencies (e.g., soothability, reactivity). External factors include parents' explicit training in emotion regulation skills as well as more global parenting styles (e.g., responsiveness, control). In this model, these internal and external factors independently influence a child's emotion regulation style, which in turn affects subsequent interpersonal functioning such as relationships with peers (Calkins, 1994).

Other models highlight the transactional, bidirectional relationship between temperament and socialization (Collins et al., 2000; Wills et al., 1995). Reciprocal models of parent and child effects (e.g., Bell & Chapman, 1986) are not new to the study of child development. These models consider not only how parenting practices affect child development but also how children's behavioral qualities affect the type of parenting they receive. Some of the research in this area has focused specifically on temperament. For instance, children with impulsive and irritable temperaments elicit more negative parenting than do children with less difficult temperaments (Dix, 1991). A longitudinal study found that parental punitive reactions to children's negative emotions at ages 6 to 8 were linked to increases in these children's problem behaviors and negative emotions by early adolescence (ages 10 to 12; Eisenberg et al., 1999). Such bidirectional models are rare, but much needed, in the study of emotions and socialization in adolescence.

Another model of how temperament can be integrated into studies of adolescent adjustment is emerging from research demonstrating how temperamental traits affect adolescents' susceptibility to parenting and other external events (e.g., Colder, Lochman, & Wells, 1997). What might promote positive adjustment for one adolescent, or most adolescents, may be relatively ineffective with other adolescents. In childhood, evidence is accumulating that different children may require and respond to different levels of structure and support based on their temperamental characteristics (e.g., Belsky, Hsieh, & Crnic, 1998). For example, a hyperactive child may respond well to the type of strict limit setting that would stifle the competence of a shy child. Thus, temperament may moderate the association between parenting practices and adolescent adjustment.

Recent work with youth in late childhood and early adolescence examines these models. For instance, Lengua and colleagues (Lengua & Sandler, 1996; Lengua, Wolchik, Sandler, & West, 2000) have examined the role of temperament in early adolescents' adaptation to parental divorce. In one study the temperamental trait of approach-flexibility (one's orientation toward change and new situations) moderated relationships between adolescents' coping styles and their psychological symptoms. In particular, active coping strategies were related to less anxiety for adolescents with flexible temperaments but was unrelated to adjustment for adolescents with less flexible temperaments. Avoidant coping styles were related to greater anxiety and conduct problems for adolescents with less flexible temperaments but were unrelated to adjustment for adolescents with more flexible temperaments. Thus, certain temperamental styles appear to be protective.

In another study of adolescent adjustment to parental divorce, Lengua et al. (2000) found that early adolescents' temperaments moderated the relationship between parenting practices and their psychological adjustment. Specifically, they found that inconsistent discipline and parental rejection were related to adolescent depression only for adolescents with more difficult temperaments (high on impulsivity and low on positive emotionality). Similarly, inconsistent discipline and parental rejection were related to conduct problems for adolescents low in positive emotionality and high on impulsivity. These parenting styles were unrelated to conduct problems for adolescents with easier temperaments (high on positive emotionality and low on impulsivity).

Finally, in a sample of fourth- and fifth-grade boys, Colder et al. (1997) found that temperament (i.e., fear and activity levels) moderated the relationship between parenting behaviors and children's adjustment. For example, harsh parenting was related to high levels of aggression only for boys with highly fearful temperaments, and poor parental monitoring was related to higher levels of aggression only for boys with highly active temperaments. In addition, both harsh parenting and overinvolved parenting were related to greater symptoms of depression only for boys with highly fearful temperaments.

Overall, the previous studies illustrate some of the challenges faced by researchers who wish to incorporate adolescent temperament into the study of adolescent adjustment, as well as some of the theoretical models that are being used to study these effects. Future research that continues to integrate temperament will likely lead to important advances in our understanding of how to promote healthy adolescent adjustment.

Person Approaches to Understanding Emotion and Personality

A fourth emerging theme is captured by the increasing number of empirical studies of adolescent emotional and personality development that are based on person (or pattern) approaches (e.g., Caspi, 2000; Salmivalli, 1998; Schulenberg, Wadsworth, O'Malley, Bachman, & Johnston, 1996). The person approach considers individuals in a holistic manner, as organisms consisting of multiple attributes (e.g., cognitive, biological, behavioral) that are integrated into an organized system (Block, 1971; Magnusson & Törestad, 1993; see also chapter by Kerr, Stattin, & Ferrer-Wreder in this volume). Advocates of the person approach argue that the individual's pattern or profile across a number of indicators (the total configuration of variables) may carry more meaning for understanding that individual's development than do single variables (Magnusson & Cairns, 1996). The person is the unit of analysis, and individuals who share similar profiles are grouped together (Stattin & Magnusson, 1996). These groups may then be compared on other relevant variables and developmental trajectories.

The person approach can be contrasted with the traditional variable approach, on which most research on adolescence is based. The variable approach examines interrelations among single variables, assuming that these interrelations justify inferences about how variables function in individuals (Magnusson & Cairns, 1996). Magnusson and Törestad (1993) argued, however, that the variable approach masks qualitative differences among people and is limited with respect to delineating how variables operate together within subgroups of individuals. Indeed, in a longitudinal study following individuals from childhood to early adulthood, Stattin and Magnusson (1996) showed that more variance in adult externalizing behaviors was explained by the constellation of characteristics present in adolescence (i.e., a combination of the adolescent's involvement in multiple risk behaviors such as truancy and family background risks such as father's alcoholism) rather than by individual predictor variables.

The person approach can be applied to many phenomena in the study of adolescent emotional and personality development. It may be one way to answer the frequent call for more examination and integration of multiple levels of adolescent development, including the biological, psychological, cognitive, and contextual (e.g., Susman, 1997; chapter by Susman, Dorn, & Schiefelbein in this volume).

Consider a recent study by Galambos and Tilton-Weaver (2000). These authors were intrigued by speculation in the literature on psychosocial maturity that some adolescents, rather than being psychosocially mature, were actually pseudomature: They maintained the appearance of maturity through *behavioral* means (e.g., engagement in problem behaviors such as drinking) without showing genuine *psychological* maturity (e.g., a stable sense of identity, self-reliance, and a strong work ethic; Greenberger & Steinberg, 1986). Galambos and Tilton-Weaver were also intrigued by previous findings showing that adolescents who engaged in higher levels of problem behavior also had older *subjective* ages (i.e., they felt older than their chronological ages), indicating a possible mismatch between their subjective levels of maturity and their actual behavior (Galambos, Kolaric, Sears, & Maggs, 1999). Following a person approach, Galambos and Tilton-Weaver hypothesized that pseudomaturity could be defined by high levels of problem behavior, an older subjective age, and low levels of psychological maturity—a constellation of behavioral, psychological, and subjective attributes. Indeed, in a sample of Canadian adolescents ranging in age from 10 to 17, 13%

emerged as pseudomature (high problem behavior, older subjective age, low psychological maturity). There was also a mature cluster (43% of the sample) who were low on problem behavior, felt slightly older than their chronological ages, and scored high on psychological maturity. The final cluster, immature adolescents, comprised 44% of the sample. They reported low levels of problem behavior, were psychologically immature, and felt relatively young.

The three clusters of adolescents who emerged differed in other ways as well (Galambos & Tilton-Weaver, 2000). Compared to the mature and immature adolescents, the pseudomature adolescents were more advanced with respect to pubertal status, reported a stronger desire to be older and to attain adult privileges, were more socially active, and reported more conflict with mothers (among boys). Compared to mature adolescents, immature adolescents reported a stronger desire to be older, more conflict with mothers, and less acceptance from mothers. The authors concluded that both pseudomature and immature adolescents had a poorer fit with their social environments than did the mature adolescents.

This and similar research speak to the advantages of using person approaches to understand the adolescent as a whole person with multiple, interrelated attributes. Some research questions demand that researchers attempt to integrate biological (including hormonal), cognitive, emotional, psychological, and contextual characteristics in seeking to understand adolescents' lifelong development. The person approach is an exciting paradigm that will add much to our accumulating knowledge of emotional and personality development in adolescence.

SUMMARY

In this chapter we highlighted research on adolescents' emotional development, describing emotion regulation as a useful framework for viewing and uniting broad areas of research on emotional well-being and distress. Theory on adolescents' self-systems and their psychosocial maturity were discussed as models that integrate a variety of indicators of adaptive emotion regulation. The general concepts of internalizing and externalizing problems were discussed as indicative of adolescents' emotional distress and reflective of the experience of emotional dysregulation. Given the significant gender difference in the prevalence of internalizing disorders (with more adolescent girls affected), we reviewed recent research on predictors and correlates of internalizing symptoms.

We also reviewed some recent research on personality and temperament in adolescence, identifying major issues in the structure of personality, the origins of personality, and

continuity in personality and temperament across time. Recent research shows that the Big Five model of personality, based on years of research with adult samples, replicates in samples of adolescents. Moreover, links have been established between dimensions of temperament in childhood and later personality traits. The goodness-of-fit model of temperament was reviewed as a way of understanding how temperament may be shaped, viewed, and responded to differently depending on the social context.

Finally, we identified four exciting themes in recent research on emotion and personality development. The first is a focus on adolescents' optimal development, with a call for better measurement of successful outcomes. The second refers to cultural variations in emotional and personality development, a trend that has burgeoned over the last several years. The third theme involves studies that integrate knowledge of temperament into studies of adolescent adjustment, focusing on the role that temperament may play in emotional expression and regulation. The fourth emerging theme involves increasing interest in conducting studies of adolescents' emotional and personality development from a person approach, which considers intra-individual constellations of multiple attributes in the search for understanding developmental trajectories.

Knowledge emerging from research on these themes has potentially important implications for the targeting, design, and effectiveness of prevention and intervention programs. The identification of emotion regulation as a salient marker of positive youth development means that school- and community-based programs can be designed to help young people regulate and cope with their emotions. Emotion regulation is a strength that consists of a set of skills and strategies, and this asset can be acquired. Teaching effective emotion regulation fits with the goals of prevention programs designed to promote healthy youth development by increasing youth strengths (e.g., Roth et al., 1998).

But do all children and adolescents need training in effective emotion regulation? The research examined here suggests that successful emotion regulation is more of a challenge for some children and adolescents than for others, for example, those with a set of individual risk factors, such as a temperament characterized by negative emotionality and strong reactivity. Thus, in addition to general school- and community-based programs for adolescents at large, some intervention programs could be designed to target at-risk children and adolescents (e.g., those who have been identified as having anger control problems or being easily distressed). If deficits in emotion regulation are caught and addressed early enough, it is likely that the individual will have a more positive developmental trajectory into adulthood.

Prevention and intervention programs should incorporate the important role of parents in promoting positive youth development. Research on the interaction between parenting and temperament is moving toward a clearer understanding of parenting behaviors that are more or less suited to particular temperaments (i.e., goodness of fit). Given the central role of parenting in promoting positive youth development, a wide range of family strengthening and parent-training programs has been developed (for a review, see Kumpfer, 1999). The goals of these programs are to decrease the risk factors associated with developmental problems and increase protective family factors, including supportive parent-child relations. The promotion of emotion regulation strategies and prevention of emotional dysregulation among parents and adolescents could be included as important components of these programs.

In designing effective interventions and social policies, we need to know more about how families, peers, schools, and cultural contexts moderate the relationships among temperament, emotional regulation, and adolescent adjustment. Attention to diverse cultural contexts is particularly important in this regard. For instance, we need to know more about the contexts that promote the achievement of stable ethnic identities, the stressors that challenge ethnic identity development, and the relationship of ethnic identity to other indicators of well being. In addition, we need to identify ways in which models of healthy youth development apply to culturally diverse adolescents (e.g., universal protective factors) and the ways in which they need to be modified to fit unique experiences (e.g., incorporating the experience of racism).

The four emerging themes that we have identified are just beginning to provide the specific empirical knowledge we need to design effective prevention and intervention efforts. To accomplish this, however, it is essential that social policies support (a) the view that the emotion regulation is an issue of health promotion, (b) funding for basic research in the general area of emotion regulation, (c) funding for research and programming that explicitly addresses similarities and differences in the needs and strengths of adolescents from diverse ethnic backgrounds, and (d) funding for applied research that evaluates the effectiveness of prevention and intervention programs designed to increase effective emotion regulation.

As this chapter has shown, researchers have learned a great deal about adolescents' emotional and personality development. The field of research on adolescence is a very active and exciting one, with promising new developments that bring us ever closer to obtaining a more comprehensive understanding of the interacting forces that shape adolescent behavior. With a more complete picture, we will be better able to influence adolescents' lives in ways that will be of benefit to them as they mature into adulthood.

REFERENCES

Ahadi, S. A., & Rothbart, M. K. (1994). Temperament, development, and the Big Five. In C. F. Halverson, Jr., G. A. Kohnstamm, & R. P. Martin (Eds.), *The developing structure of temperament and personality from infancy to adulthood* (pp. 189–207). Hillsdale, NJ: Erlbaum.

Allen, J. P., Hauser, S. T., Bell, K. L., & O'Connor, T. G. (1994). Longitudinal assessment of autonomy and relatedness in adolescent-family interactions as predictors of adolescent ego development and self-esteem. *Child Development, 65,* 179–194.

Allen, J. P., Moore, C., Kuperminc, G., & Bell, K. (1998). Attachment and adolescent psychosocial functioning. *Child Development, 69,* 1406–1419.

Arnett, J. J. (1999). Adolescent storm and stress, reconsidered. *American Psychologist, 54,* 317–326.

Arnett, J. J. (2000). Emerging adulthood: A theory of development from the late teens through the twenties. *American Psychologist, 55,* 469–480.

Barrett Singer, A. T., & Weinstein, R. S. (2000). Differential parental treatment predicts achievement and self-perceptions in two cultural contexts. *Journal of Family Psychology, 14,* 491–509.

Beaudet, M. P. (1999). Psychological health—depression. *Health Reports, 11,* 63–75.

Bell, R. Q., & Chapman, M. (1986). Child effects in studies using experimental or brief longitudinal approaches to socialization. *Developmental Psychology, 22,* 595–603.

Belsky, J. (1996). Parent, infant, and social-contextual antecedents of father-son attachment security. *Developmental Psychology, 32,* 905–913.

Belsky, J., Hsieh, K., & Crnic, K. (1998). Mothering, fathering, and infant negativity as antecedents of boys' externalizing problems and inhibition at age 3 years: Differential susceptibility to rearing experience? *Development and Psychopathology, 10,* 301–319.

Black, M. M., Ricardo, I. B., & Stanton, B. (1997). Social and psychological factors associated with AIDS risk behaviors among low-income, urban, African American adolescents. *Journal of Research on Adolescence, 7,* 173–195.

Block, J. (1971). *Lives through time.* Berkeley, CA: Bancroft.

Bradley, R. H., & Corwyn, R. F. (2000). Moderating effect of perceived amount of family conflict on the relation between home environmental processes and the well-being of adolescents. *Journal of Family Psychology, 14,* 349–364.

Braungart, J. M., Plomin, R., DeFries, J. C., & Fulker, D. W. (1992). Genetic influence on test-rated infant temperament as assessed by Bayley's Infant Behavior Record: Nonadoptive and adoptive siblings and twins. *Developmental Psychology, 28,* 40–47.

Brooks-Gunn, J., Graber, J. A., & Paikoff, R. L. (1994). Studying links between hormones and negative affect: Models and measures. *Journal of Research on Adolescence, 4,* 469–486.

Buchanan, C. M., Eccles, J., & Becker, J. (1992). Are adolescents the victims of raging hormones? Evidence for activational effects of hormones on moods and behavior at adolescence. *Psychological Bulletin, 111,* 62–107.

Buss, A. H., & Plomin, R. (1984). *Temperament: Early developing personality traits.* Hillsdale, NJ: Erlbaum.

Bustra, J. O., Bosma, H. A., & Jackson, S. (1994). The relationship between social skills and psycho-social functioning in early adolescence. *Personality and Individual Differences, 16,* 767–776.

Calkins, S. D. (1994). Origins and outcomes of individual differences in emotion regulation. *Monographs of the Society for Research in Child Development, 59*(2–3, Serial No. 240), 53–72.

Campos, J. J., Mumme, D. L., Kermoian, R., & Campos, R. G. (1994). A functionalist perspective on the nature of emotion. *Monographs of the Society for Research in Child Development, 59*(2–3, Serial No. 240), 284–303.

Capaldi, D. M., & Rothbart, M. K. (1992). Development and validation of an early adolescent temperament measure. *Journal of Early Adolescence, 12,* 153–173.

Casper, R. C., Belanoff, J., & Offer, D. (1996). Gender differences, but no racial group differences, in self-reported psychiatric symptoms in adolescents. *Journal of the American Academy of Child and Adolescent Psychiatry, 35,* 500–508.

Caspi, A. (1998). Personality development across the life course. In W. Damon (Series Ed.) & N. Eisenberg (Vol. Ed.), *Handbook of child psychology: Vol. 3. Social, emotional, and personality development* (5th ed., pp. 311–388). New York: Wiley.

Caspi, A. (2000). The child is father of the man: Personality continuities from childhood to adulthood. *Journal of Personality and Social Psychology, 78,* 158–172.

Caspi, A., & Silva, P. A. (1995). Temperamental qualities at age three predict personality traits in young adulthood: Longitudinal evidence from a birth cohort. *Child Development, 66,* 486–498.

Chao, R. K. (1994). Beyond parental control and authoritarian parenting style: Understanding Chinese parenting through the cultural notion of training. *Child Development, 65,* 1111–1119.

Chao, R. K. (2000, March). *How does the meaning of parenting style differ for Asian immigrants compared to American-born Asians and European Americans?* Paper presented at the meeting of the Society for Research on Adolescence, Chicago, IL.

Chen, H., Mechanic, D., & Hansell, S. (1998). A longitudinal study of self-awareness and depressed mood in adolescence. *Journal of Youth and Adolescence, 27,* 719–734.

Chen, X., Dong, Q., & Zhou, H. (1997). Authoritative and authoritarian parenting practices and social and school performance in Chinese children. *International Journal of Behavioral Development, 21,* 855–873.

Chen, X., Liu, M., & Li, D. (2000). Parental warmth, control, and indulgence and their relations to adjustment in Chinese children: A longitudinal study. *Journal of Family Psychology, 14,* 401–419.

Chen, X., Rubin, K. H., & Li, D. (1997). Relation between academic achievement and social adjustment: Evidence from Chinese children. *Developmental Psychology, 33,* 518–525.

Chess, S., & Thomas, A. (1999). *Goodness of fit: Clinical application from infancy through adult life.* Philadelphia: Bruner/Mazel.

Chiu, M. L., Feldman, S., & Rosenthal, D. A. (1992). The influence of immigration on parental behavior and adolescent distress in Chinese families residing in two Western nations. *Journal of Research on Adolescence, 2,* 205–239.

Church, T. A. (1994). Relating the Tellegen and five factor models of personality structure. *Journal of Personality and Social Psychology, 67,* 898–909.

Colder, C. R., Lochman, J. E., & Wells, K. C. (1997). The moderating effects of children's fear and activity level on relations between parenting practices and childhood symptomatology. *Journal of Abnormal Child Psychology, 25,* 251–263.

Cole, P. M., Michel, M. K., & Teti, L. O. (1994). The development of emotion regulation and dysregulation: A clinical perspective. *Monographs of the Society for Research in Child Development, 59*(2–3, Serial No. 240), 73–100.

Collins, W. A., Maccoby, E. E., Steinberg, L., Hetherington, E. M., & Bornstein, M. H. (2000). Contemporary research on parenting: The case for nature and nurture. *American Psychologist, 55,* 218–232.

Conger, K. J., Conger, R. D., & Scaramella, L. V. (1997). Parents, siblings, psychological control, and adolescent adjustment. *Journal of Adolescent Research, 12,* 113–138.

Contreras, J. M., Kerns, L. A., Weimer, B. L., Gentzler, A. L., & Tomich, P. L. (2000). Emotion regulation as a mediator of associations between mother-child attachment and peer relationships in middle childhood. *Journal of Family Psychology, 14,* 111–124.

Cooper, M. L., Shaver, P. R., & Collins, N. L. (1998). Attachment styles, emotion regulation, and adjustment in adolescence. *Journal of Personality and Social Psychology, 74,* 1380–1397.

Costigan, C. L., & Cauce, A. M. (in press). Changes in African-American mother-daughter relationships during adolescence: Conflict, autonomy, and warmth. In A. M. Cauce & S. Hauser (Eds.), *Adolescence and beyond: Family processes and development.* Mahwah, NJ: Erlbaum.

Digman, J. M. (1989). Five robust trait dimensions: Development, stability, and utility. *Journal of Personality, 57,* 195–214.

Digman, J. M. (1994). Child personality and temperament: Does the five-factor model embrace both domains. In C. F. Halverson, Jr., G. A. Kohnstamm, & R. P. Martin (Eds.), *The developing structure of temperament and personality from infancy to adulthood* (pp. 323–338). Hillsdale, NJ: Erlbaum.

Dix, T. (1991). The affective organization of parenting: Adaptive and maladaptive processes. *Psychological Bulletin, 110,* 3–25.

DuBois, D. L., Bull, C. A., Sherman, M. D., & Roberts, M. (1998). Self-esteem and adjustment in early adolescence: A social-contextual perspective. *Journal of Youth and Adolescence, 27,* 557–583.

DuBois, D. L., & Hirsch, B. J. (2000). Self-esteem in early adolescence: From stock character to marquee attraction. *Journal of Early Adolescence, 20,* 5–11.

East, P. L., Lerner, R. M., Lerner, J. V., Talwar Soni, R., Ohannessian, C. M., & Jacobson, L. P. (1992). Early adolescent-peer group fit, peer relations, and psychosocial competence: A short-term longitudinal study. *Journal of Early Adolescence, 12,* 132–152.

Eisenberg, N., Fabes, R. A., Shepard, S. A., Guthrie, I. K., Murphy, B. C., & Reiser, M. (1999). Parental reactions to children's negative emotions: Longitudinal relations to quality of children's social functioning. *Child Development, 70,* 513–534.

Erikson, E. H. (1968). *Identity: Youth and crisis.* New York: Norton.

Eyou, M. L., Adair, V., & Dixon, R. (2000). Cultural identity and psychological adjustment of adolescent Chinese immigrants in New Zealand. *Journal of Adolescence, 23,* 531–543.

Eysenck, H. J. (1992). Four ways five factors are not basic. *Personality and Individual Differences, 13,* 667–673.

Feldman, S. S., & Weinberger, D. A. (1994). Self-restraint as a mediator of family influences on boys' delinquent behavior: A longitudinal study. *Child Development, 65,* 195–211.

Field, T. (1994). The effects of mother's physical and emotional unavailability on emotion regulation. *Monographs of the Society for Research in Child Development, 59*(2–3, Serial No. 240), 208–227.

Frank, S. J., Poorman, M. O., Van Egeren, L. A., & Field, D. T. (1997). Perceived relationships with parents among adolescent inpatients with depressive preoccupations and depressed mood. *Journal of Clinical Child Psychology, 26,* 205–215.

Fuertes, J. N., & Westbrook, F. D. (1996). Using the Social, Attitudinal, Familial, and Environmental (SAFE) Acculturation Stress Scale to assess the adjustment needs of Hispanic college students. *Measurement and Evaluation in Counseling and Development, 29,* 67–76.

Fuligni, A. J., Tseng, V., & Lam, M. (1999). Attitudes toward family obligations among American adolescents with Asian, Latin American, and European backgrounds. *Child Development, 70,* 1030–1044.

Galambos, N. L., Kolaric, G. C., Sears, H. A., & Maggs, J. L. (1999). Adolescents' subjective age: An indicator of perceived maturity. *Journal of Research on Adolescence, 9,* 309–337.

Galambos, N. L., & Leadbeater, B. J. (2000). Trends in adolescent research for the new millennium. *International Journal of Behavioral Development, 24,* 289–294.

Galambos, N. L., & Tilton-Weaver, L. C. (2000). Adolescents' psychosocial maturity, problem behavior, and subjective age: In search of the adultoid. *Applied Developmental Science, 4,* 178–192.

Galambos, N. L., & Turner, P. K. (1999). Parent and adolescent temperaments and the quality of parent-adolescent relations. *Merrill-Palmer Quarterly, 45,* 493–511.

Garber, J., Robinson, N. S., & Valentiner, D. (1997). The relation between parenting and adolescent depression: Self-worth as a mediator. *Journal of Adolescent Research, 12,* 12–33.

Ge, X., Conger, R. D., Lorenz, F. O., & Simons, R. L. (1994). Parents' stressful life events and adolescent depressed mood. *Journal of Health and Social Behavior, 35,* 28–44.

Goldberg, L. R. (1993). The structure of phenotypic personality traits. *American Psychologist, 48,* 26–34.

Goldsmith, H. H., Buss, A. H., Plomin, R., Rothbart, M. K., Thomas, A., Chess, S., Hinde, R. A., & McCall, R. B. (1987). Roundtable: What is temperament? Four approaches. *Child Development, 58,* 505–529.

Goldsmith, H. H., & Campos, J. J. (1986). Fundamental issues in the study of early temperament: The Denver Twin Study. In M. E. Lamb & A. Brown (Eds.), *Advances in Developmental Psychology* (pp. 231–283). Hillsdale, NJ: Erlbaum.

Gray-Little, B., & Hafdahl, A. R. (2000). Factors influencing racial comparisons of self-esteem: A quantitative review. *Psychological Bulletin, 126,* 26–54.

Graziano, W. G., & Ward, D. (1992). Probing the Big Five in adolescence: Personality and adjustment during a developmental transition. *Journal of Personality, 60,* 425–439.

Greenberger, E., & Chen, C. (1996). Perceived relationships and depressed mood in early and late adolescence: A comparison of European and Asian Americans. *Developmental Psychology, 32,* 707–716.

Greenberger, E., Josselson, R., Knerr, C., & Knerr, B. (1975). The measurement and structure of psychosocial maturity. *Journal of Youth and Adolescence, 4,* 127–143.

Greenberger, E., & McLaughlin, C. S. (1998). Attachment, coping, and explanatory style in late adolescence. *Journal of Youth and Adolescence, 27,* 121–139.

Greenberger, E., & Sørenson, A. B. (1974). Toward a concept of psychosocial maturity. *Journal of Youth and Adolescence, 3,* 329–358.

Greenberger, E., & Steinberg, L. (1986). *When teenagers work: The psychological and social costs of adolescent employment.* New York: Basic.

Gross, J. J., & Muñoz, R. F. (1995). Emotion regulation and mental health. *Clinical Psychology: Science and Practice, 2,* 151–164.

Gullotta, T. P., Adams, G. R., & Montemayor, R. (Eds.). (1990). *Developing social competency in adolescence.* Newbury Park, CA: Sage.

Halverson, C. F., Jr., Kohnstamm, G. A., & Martin, R. P. (1994). *The developing structure of temperament and personality from infancy to adulthood.* Hillsdale, NJ: Erlbaum.

Haney, P., & Durlak, J. A. (1998). Changing self-esteem in children and adolescents: A meta-analytic review. *Journal of Clinical Child Psychology, 27,* 423–433.

Hankin, B. L., Abramson, L. Y., Moffitt, T. E., Silva, P. A., McGee, R., & Angell, K. E. (1998). Development of depression from preadolescence to young adulthood: Emerging gender differences in a 10-year longitudinal study. *Journal of Abnormal Psychology, 107,* 128–140.

Harter, S. (1990). Self and identity development. In S. S. Feldman & G. R. Elliott (Eds.), *At the threshold: The developing adolescent* (pp. 352–387). Cambridge, MA: Harvard University Press.

Harter, S., Bresnick, S., Bouchey, H. A., & Whitesell, N. R. (1997). The development of multiple role-related selves during adolescence. *Development and Psychopathology, 9,* 835–853.

Hauser, S. T., & Safyer, A. W. (1994). Ego development and adolescent emotions. *Journal of Research on Adolescence, 4,* 487–502.

Haviland, J. M., Davidson, R. B., Ruetsch, C., Gebelt, J. L., & Lancelot, C. (1994). The place of emotion in identity. *Journal of Research on Adolescence, 4,* 503–518.

Havill, V. L., Allen, K., Halverson, C. F., & Kohnstamm, G. A. (1994). Parents' use of Big Five categories in their natural language descriptions of children. In C. F. Halverson, Jr., G. A. Kohnstamm, & R. P. Martin (Eds.), *The developing structure of temperament and personality from infancy to adulthood* (pp. 371–386). Hillsdale, NJ: Erlbaum.

Hishinuma, E. S., Miyamoto, S. T., Nishimura, S. T., & Nahulu, L. B. (2000). Differences in state-trait anxiety inventory scores for ethnically diverse adolescents in Hawaii. *Cultural Diversity and Ethnic Minority Psychology, 6,* 73–83.

Hovey, J. D., & King, C. A. (1996). Acculturative stress, depression, and suicidal ideation among immigrant and second-generation Latino adolescents. *Journal of the American Academy of Child and Adolescent Psychiatry, 35,* 1183–1192.

Ichiyama, M. A., McQuarrie, E. F., & Ching, K. L. (1996). Contextual influences on ethnic identity among Hawaiian students in the mainland United States. *Journal of Cross-Cultural Psychology, 27,* 458–475.

John, O. P. (1990). The "Big Five" factor taxonomy: Dimensions of personality in the natural language and in questionnaires. In L. A. Pervin (Ed.), *Handbook of personality: Theory and research* (pp. 66–100). New York: Guilford.

John, O. P., Caspi, A., Robins, R. W., Moffitt, T. E., & Stouthamer-Loeber, M. (1994). The "little five": Exploring the nomological network of the five-factor model of personality in adolescent boys. *Child Development, 65,* 160–178.

Juang, L. P., Lerner, J. V., McKinney, J. P., & von Eye, A. (1999). The goodness of fit in autonomy timetable expectations between Asian-American late adolescents and their parents. *International Journal of Behavioral Development, 23,* 1023–1048.

Kagan, J. (1989). Temperamental contributions to social behavior. *American Psychologist, 44,* 668–674.

Kagan, J. (1994). On the nature of emotion. *Monographs of the Society for Research in Child Development, 59*(2–3, Serial No. 240), 7–24.

Kagan, J. (1998). Biology and the child. In W. Damon (Series Ed.) & N. Eisenberg (Vol. Ed.), *Handbook of child psychology: Vol. 3. Social, emotional, and personality development* (5th ed., pp. 177–235). New York: Wiley.

Katainen, S., Räikkönen, K., & Keltikangas-Järvinen, L. (1998). Development of temperament: Childhood temperament and the mother's childrearing attitudes as predictors of adolescent temperament in a 9-year follow-up study. *Journal of Research on Adolescence, 8,* 485–509.

Kawaguchi, M. C., Welsh, D. P., Powers, S. I., & Rostosky, S. S. (1998). Mothers, fathers, sons, and daughters: Temperament, gender, and adolescent-parent relationships. *Merrill-Palmer Quarterly, 44,* 77–96.

Kessler, R. C., McGonagle, K. A., Zhao, S., Nelson, C. B., Hughes, M., Eshleman, S., Wittchen, H., & Kendler, K. S. (1994). Lifetime and 12-month prevalence of *DSM-III-R* psychiatric disorders in the United States: Results from the National Comorbidity Survey. *Archives of General Psychiatry, 51,* 8–19.

Kim, S. Y., & Ge, X. (2000). Parenting practices and adolescent depressive symptoms in Chinese American families. *Journal of Family Psychology, 14,* 420–435.

Kohnstamm, G. A., Halverson, C. F., Jr., Havill, V. L., & Mervielde, I. (1996). Parents' free descriptions of child characteristics: A cross-cultural search for the developmental antecedents of the Big Five. In S. Harkness & C. M. Super (Eds.), *Parents' cultural belief systems* (pp. 27–55). New York: Guilford.

Kumpfer, K. L. (1999). *Strengthening America's families: Promising parenting and family strategies for delinquency prevention. A User's Guide,* prepared for the U. S. Department of Justice under Grant No. 95-JN-FX-K010 from the Office of Juvenile Justice and Delinquency Prevention, Office of Juvenile Programs, U. S. Department of Justice.

Kwan, K. L. K., & Sodowsky, G. R. (1997). Internal and external ethnic identity and their correlates: A study of Chinese American immigrants. *Journal of Multicultural Counseling and Development, 25,* 51–67.

Larson, R. W. (2000). Toward a psychology of positive youth development. *American Psychologist, 55,* 170–183.

Larson, R., & Lampman-Petraitis, C. (1989). Daily emotional states as reported by children and adolescents. *Child Development, 60,* 1250–1260.

Larson, R., & Richards, M. H. (1994). *Divergent realities: The emotional lives of mothers, fathers, and adolescents.* New York: Basic.

Leadbeater, B. J., Kuperminc, G. P., Blatt, S. J., & Hertzog, C. (1999). A multivariate model of gender differences in adolescents' internalizing and externalizing problems. *Developmental Psychology, 35,* 1268–1282.

Lengua, L. J., & Sandler, I. N. (1996). Self-regulation as a moderator of the relation between coping and symptomatology in children of divorce. *Journal of Abnormal Child Psychology, 24,* 681–701.

Lengua, L. J., Wolchik, S. A., Sandler, I. N., & West, S. G. (2000). The additive and interactive effects of parenting and temperament in predicting adjustment problems of children of divorce. *Journal of Clinical Child Psychology, 29,* 232–244.

Lerner, J. V., & Lerner, R. M. (1983). Temperament and adaptation across life: Theoretical and empirical issues. In P. B. Baltes & O. G. Brim, Jr. (Eds.), *Life-span development and behavior* (Vol. 5, pp. 197–231). New York: Academic Press.

Lerner, R. M., Fisher, C. B., & Weinberg, R. A. (2000). Toward a science for and of the people: Promoting civil society through the application of developmental science. *Child Development, 71,* 11–20.

Lerner, R. M., & Galambos, N. L. (1998). Adolescent development: Challenges and opportunities for research programs and policies. *Annual Review of Psychology, 49,* 413–446.

Lewinsohn, P. M., Rohde, P., & Seeley, J. R. (1998). Major depressive disorder in older adolescents: Prevalence, risk factors, and clinical implications. *Clinical Psychology Review, 18,* 765–794.

Liem, R., Lim, B. A., & Liem, J. H. (2000). Acculturation and emotion among Asian Americans. *Cultural Diversity and Ethnic Minority Psychology, 6,* 13–31.

Liu, W. M., Pope-Davis, D. B., Nevitt, J., & Toporek, R. L. (1999). Understanding the function of acculturation and prejudicial attitudes among Asian Americans. *Cultural Diversity and Ethnic Minority Psychology, 5,* 317–328.

Luster, T., & McAdoo, H. P. (1994). Factors related to the achievement and adjustment of young African American children. *Child Development, 65,* 1080–1094.

Maedgen, J. W., & Carlson, C. L. (2000). Social functioning and emotional regulation in the attention deficit hyperactivity disorder subtypes. *Journal of Clinical Child Psychology, 29,* 30–42.

Magnusson, D., & Cairns, R. B. (1996). Developmental science: Toward a unified framework. In R. B. Cairns, G. H. Elder, Jr., & E. J. Costello (Eds.), *Developmental science* (pp. 7–30). Cambridge, England: Cambridge University Press.

Magnusson, D., & Törestad, B. (1993). A holistic view of personality: A model revisited. *Annual Review of Psychology, 44,* 427–452.

Mantzicopoulos, P. Y., & Oh-Hwang, Y. (1998). The relationship of psychosocial maturity to parenting quality and intellectual ability for American and Korean adolescence. *Contemporary Educational Psychology, 23,* 195–206.

Marton, P., & Maharaj, S. (1993). Family factors in adolescent unipolar depression. *Canadian Journal of Psychiatry, 38,* 373–382.

McAdoo, H. P. (1993). Ethnic families: Strengths that are found in diversity. In H. P. McAdoo (Ed.), *Family ethnicity: Strength in diversity* (pp. 3–14). Newbury Park, CA: Sage.

McAdoo, H. P. (1997). Upward mobility across generations in African American families. In H. P. McAdoo (Ed.), *Black families* (3rd ed., pp. 162). Thousand Oaks, CA: Sage.

McCrae, R. B., Costa, P. T., Jr., de Lima, M. P., Simões, A., Ostendorf, F., Angleitner, A., Maruši, I., Bratko, D., Caprara, G. V., Barbarenelli, C., Chae, J.-H., & Piedmont, R. L. (1999). Age differences in personality across the adult life span: Parallels in five cultures. *Developmental Psychology, 35,* 466–477.

Newman, D. L., Moffitt, T. E., Caspi, A., Magdol, L., Silva, P. A., & Stanton, W. R. (1996). Psychiatric disorder in a birth cohort of young adults: Prevalence, comorbidity, clinical significance, and new case incidence from ages 11 to 21. *Journal of Consulting and Clinical Psychology, 64,* 552–562.

Nitz, K., Lerner, R. M., Lerner, J. V., & Talwar, R. (1988). Parental and peer ethnotheory demands, temperament, and early adolescent adjustment. *Journal of Early Adolescence, 8,* 243–263.

Nolen-Hoeksema, S. (1994). An interactive model for the emergence of gender differences in depression in adolescence. *Journal of Research on Adolescence, 4,* 519–534.

Noom, M. J., Deković, M., & Meeus, W. H. J. (1999). Autonomy, attachment and psychosocial adjustment during adolescence: A double-edged sword? *Journal of Adolescence, 22,* 771–783.

Nurmi, J. E. (1997). Self-definition and mental health during adolescence and young adulthood. In J. Schulenberg, J. L. Maggs, & K. Hurrelmann (Eds.), *Health risks and developmental transitions during adolescence* (pp. 395–419). Cambridge: Cambridge University Press.

Offer, D., Ostrov, E., Howard, K. I., & Atkinson, R. (1992). A study of quietly disturbed and normal adolescents in ten countries. In A. Z. Schwartzberg & A. H. Esman (Eds.), *International Annals of Adolescent Psychiatry* (pp. 285–297). Chicago: University of Chicago.

Ohannessian, C. M., Lerner, R. M., Lerner, J. V., & von Eye, A. (1999). Does self-competence predict gender differences in adolescent depression and anxiety? *Journal of Adolescence, 22,* 397–411.

Paterson, J., Pryor, J., & Field, J. (1995). Adolescent attachment to parents and friends in relation to aspects of self-esteem. *Journal of Youth and Adolescence, 24,* 365–376.

Pedlow, R., Sanson, A. V., Prior, M., & Oberklaid, F. (1993). The stability of temperament from infancy to eight years. *Developmental Psychology, 29,* 998–1007.

Petersen, A. C., Compas, B. E., Brooks-Gunn, J., Stemmler, M., Ey, S., & Grant, K. E. (1993). Depression in adolescence. *American Psychologist, 48,* 155–168.

Phinney, J. S. (1992). The Multigroup Ethnic Identity Measure: A new scale for use with diverse groups. *Journal of Adolescent Research, 7,* 156–176.

Phinney, J. S., Cantu, C. L., & Kurtz, D. A. (1997). Ethnic and American identity as predictors of self-esteem among African American, Latino, and White adolescents. *Journal of Youth and Adolescence, 26,* 165–185.

Phinney, J. S., & Chavira, V. (1992). Ethnic identity and self-esteem: An exploratory longitudinal study. *Journal of Adolescence, 15,* 271–281.

Phinney, J. S., Ong, A., & Madden, T. (2000). Cultural values and intergenerational value discrepancies and non-immigrant families. *Child Development, 71,* 528–539.

Quintana, S. M., Castañeda-English, P., & Ybarra, V. C. (1999). Role of perspective-taking abilities and ethnic socialization in development of adolescent ethnic identity. *Journal of Research on Adolescence, 9,* 161–184.

Richards, M. H., & Larson, R. (1993). Pubertal development and the daily subjective states of young adolescents. *Journal of Research on Adolescence, 3,* 145–169.

Roeser, R. W., Eccles, J. S., & Sameroff, A. J. (1998). Academic and emotional functioning in early adolescence: Longitudinal relations, patterns, and prediction by experiences in middle school. *Development and Psychopathology, 10,* 321–352.

Rossman, B. B. R. (1992). School-age children's perceptions of coping with distress: Strategies for emotion regulation and the moderation of adjustment. *Journal of Child Psychology and Psychiatry, 33,* 1373–1397.

Roth, J., Brooks-Gunn, J., Murray, L., & Foster, W. (1998). Promoting healthy adolescents: Synthesis of youth development program evaluations. *Journal of Research on Adolescence, 8,* 423–460.

Rothbart, M. K., & Bates, J. E. (1998). Temperament. In W. Damon (Series Ed.) & N. Eisenberg (Vol. Ed.), *Handbook of child psychology: Vol. 3. Social, emotional, and personality development* (5th ed., pp. 105–176). New York: Wiley.

Rothbart, M. K., & Derryberry, D. (1981). Development of individual differences in temperament. In M. E. Lamb & A. L. Brown (Eds.), *Advances in developmental psychology* (Vol. 1, pp. 37–86). Hillsdale, NJ: Erlbaum.

Rowe, D. C., Almeida, D. M., & Jacobson, K. C. (1999). School context and genetic influences on aggression in adolescence. *Psychological Science, 10,* 277–280.

Salmivalli, C. (1998). Intelligent, attractive, well-behaving, unhappy: The structure of adolescents' self-concept and its relations to their social behavior. *Journal of Research on Adolescence, 8,* 333–354.

Sandler, I., Ayers, T., Suter, J., Schultz, A., & Twohey, J. (in press). In K. Maton, C. Schellenbach, B. Leadbeater, & A. Solarz (Eds.), *Investing in children, youth, and families: Strengths-based research and policy.* Washington, DC: American Psychological Association.

Sanson, A., & Rothbart, M. K. (1995). Child temperament and parenting. In M. H. Bornstein (Ed.), *Handbook of parenting: Vol. 4. Applied and practical parenting* (pp. 299–321). Mahwah, NJ: Erlbaum.

Saudino, K. J., McGuire, S., Reiss, D., Hetherington, E. M., & Plomin, R. (1995). Parent ratings of EAS temperaments in twins, full siblings, half siblings, and step siblings. *Journal of Personality and Social Psychology, 68,* 723–733.

Scales, P. C., Benson, P. L., Leffert, N., & Blyth, D. A. (2000). Contribution of developmental assets to the prediction of thriving among adolescents. *Applied Developmental Science, 4,* 27–46.

Scaramella, L. V., Conger, R. D., & Simons, R. L. (1999). Parental protective influences and gender-specific increases in adolescent internalizing and externalizing problems. *Journal of Research on Adolescence, 9,* 111–141.

Schulenberg, J., Maggs, J. L., & Hurrelmann, K. (Eds.). (1997). *Health risks and developmental transitions during adolescence.* Cambridge: Cambridge University Press.

Schulenberg, J., Wadsworth, K. N., O'Malley, P. M., Bachman, J. G., & Johnston, L. D. (1996). Adolescent risk factors for binge drinking during the transition to young adulthood: Variable- and pattern-centered approaches to change. *Developmental Psychology, 32,* 659–674.

Sheeber, L., & Sorensen, E. (1998). Family relationships of depressed adolescents: A multimethod assessment. *Journal of Clinical Child Psychology, 27,* 268–277.

Shek, D. T. L. (1997a). Family environment and adolescent psychological well-being, school adjustment, and problem behavior: A pioneer study in a Chinese context. *Journal of Genetic Psychology, 158,* 113–128.

Shek, D. T. L. (1997b). The relation of family functioning to adolescent psychological well-being, school adjustment, and problem behavior. *Journal of Genetic Psychology, 158,* 467–479.

Shields, A., & Cicchetti, D. (1997). Emotion regulation among school-aged children: The development and validation of a new criterion Q-sort scale. *Developmental Psychology, 33,* 906–916.

Shiner, R. L. (1998). How shall we speak of children's personalities in middle childhood? A preliminary taxonomy. *Psychological Bulletin, 124,* 308–332.

Sim, T. N. (2000). Adolescent psychosocial competence: The importance and role of regard for parents. *Journal of Research on Adolescence, 10,* 49–64.

Smith, E. P., Walker, L., Fields, L., Brookins, C. C., & Seay, R. C. (1999). Ethnic identity and its relationship to self-esteem, perceived efficacy and prosocial attitudes in early adolescence. *Journal of Adolescence, 22,* 867–880.

Spencer, M. B., Dupree, D., & Hartmann, T. (1997). A phenomenological variant of ecological systems theory (PVEST): A self-organization perspective in context. *Development and Psychopathology, 9,* 817–833.

Spencer, M. S., Icard, L. D., Harachi, T. W., Catalano, R. F., & Oxford, M. (2000). Ethnic identity among monoracial and multiracial early adolescents. *Journal of Early Adolescence, 20,* 365–387.

Stattin, H., & Magnusson, D. (1996). Antisocial development: A holistic approach. *Development and Psychopathology, 8,* 617–645.

Stillars, A. L. (1995). Communication and family culture. In M. A. Fitzpatrick & A. L. Vangelisti (Eds.), *Explaining family interactions* (pp. 375–399). Thousand Oaks, CA: Sage.

Susman, E. J. (1997). Modeling developmental complexity in adolescence: Hormones and behavior in context. *Journal of Research on Adolescence, 7,* 283–306.

Talwar, R., Nitz, K., & Lerner, R. M. (1990). Relations among early adolescent temperament, parent and peer demands, and adjustment: A test of the goodness of fit model. *Journal of Adolescence, 13,* 279–298.

Thomas, A., & Chess, S. (1977). *Temperament and development.* New York: Bruner/Mazel.

Thompson, C. P., Anderson, L. P., & Bakeman, R. A. (2000). Effects of racial socialization and racial identity on acculturative stress in African American college students. *Cultural Diversity and Ethnic Minority Psychology, 6,* 196–210.

Thompson, R. A. (1994). Emotion regulation: A theme in search of definition. *Monographs of the Society for Research in Child Development, 59*(2–3, Serial No. 240).

Tilton-Weaver, L. C., Vitunski, E. T., & Galambos, N. L. (2001). Five images of maturity in adolescence: What does "grown up" mean? *Journal of Adolescence, 24,* 143–158.

Tubman, J. G., & Windle, M. (1995). Continuity of difficulty temperament in adolescence: Relations with depression, life events, family support, and substance use across a one-year period. *Journal of Youth and Adolescence, 24,* 133–153.

Underwood, M. K. (1997). Top ten pressing questions about the development of emotion regulation. *Motivation and Emotion, 21,* 127–146.

Underwood, M. K. , Kupersmidt, J. B., & Coie, J. D. (1996). Childhood peer sociometric status and aggression as predictors of adolescent childbearing. *Journal of Research on Adolescence, 6,* 201–223.

van Lieshout, C. F. M. (2000). Lifespan personality development: Self-organising goal-oriented agents and developmental outcome. *International Journal of Behavioral Development, 24,* 276–288.

van Lieshout, C. F. M., & Haselager, G. J. T. (1994). The Big Five personality factors in Q-sort descriptions of children and adolescents. In C. F. Halverson, Jr., G. A. Kohnstamm, & R. P. Martin (Eds.), *The developing structure of temperament and personality from infancy to adulthood* (pp. 293–318). Hillsdale, NJ: Erlbaum.

Wagner, W. G. (1996). Optimal development in adolescence: What is it and how can it be encouraged? *Counseling Psychologist, 24,* 360–400.

Wångby, M., Bergman, L. R., & Magnusson, D. (1999). Development of adjustment problems in girls: What syndromes emerge? *Child Development, 70,* 678–699.

Watkins, D., Dong, Q., & Xia, Y. (1997). Age and gender differences in the self-esteem of Chinese children. *The Journal of Social Psychology, 137,* 374–379.

Wentzel, K. R., & McNamara, C. C. (1999). Interpersonal relationships, emotional distress, and prosocial behavior in middle school. *Journal of Early Adolescence, 19,* 114–125.

Whitesell, N. R., & Harter, S. (1996). The interpersonal context of emotion: Anger with close friends and classmates. *Child Development, 67,* 1345–1359.

Wigfield, A., & Eccles, J. S. (1994). Children's competence beliefs, achievement values, and general self-esteem: Change across elementary and middle school. *Journal of Early Adolescence, 14,* 107–138.

Wills, T. A., DuHamel, K., & Vaccaro, D. (1995). Activity and mood temperament as predictors of adolescent substance use: Test of a self-regulation mediational model. *Journal of Personality and Social Psychology, 68,* 901–916.

Windle, M. (1992). Temperament and social support in adolescence: Interrelations with depressive symptoms and delinquent behaviors. *Journal of Youth and Adolescence, 21,* 1–21.

Windler, M., & Lerner, R. M. (1986). Reassessing the dimensions of temperamental individuality across the life span: The Revised Dimensions of Temperament Survey (DOTS-R). *Journal of Adolescent Research, 1,* 213–230.

Ying, Y., Lee, P. A., Tsai, J. L., Yeh, Y., & Huang, J. S. (2000). The conception of depression in Chinese American college students. *Cultural Diversity and Ethnic Minority Psychology, 6,* 183–195.

Zimmerman, M. A., Copeland, L. A., Shope, J. T., & Dielman, T. E. (1997). A longitudinal study of self-esteem: Implications for adolescent development. *Journal of Youth and Adolescence, 26,* 117–141.

CHAPTER 15

Positive Behaviors, Problem Behaviors, and Resiliency in Adolescence

DANIEL F. PERKINS AND LYNNE M. BORDEN

Adolescence is a time of life marked by change and rapid development. In fact, few developmental periods are characterized by so many changes at so many different levels as is adolescence. These changes are associated with pubertal development and the emergence of reproductive sexuality; social role redefinitions; cognitive, emotional, and moral development; and school transitions (e.g., Hamburg, 1974; Lerner, 1995; Simmons & Blyth, 1987).

The purpose of this chapter is to examine risk and protective factors within adolescents and their environments and the manifestation of those factors in terms of risk behaviors or resiliency. Presented first is a detailed exploration of four major risk behaviors in adolescents (i.e., teenage sexual activity, alcohol and substance use/abuse, delinquency and antisocial behavior, and school failure) and the risk factors found to be associated with them. The comorbidity of those behaviors and factors is also discussed. The chapter then investigates the beginning of resiliency research and follows the field's development through to its current status and theoretical understanding of resiliency. Also discussed are the empirical findings related to protective factors and their interaction with risk factors. Finally, directions for future research are presented.

We hope that readers will gain a clearer understanding of the factors that enhance positive development and those factors that inhibit positive development. This chapter strives to provide specific attention to the major risks as well as their comorbidity. Understanding risk behaviors forms a foundation that fosters our understanding of the influence of risk behaviors on the developmental trajectory of young people. Moreover, specific attention to major risk behaviors also offers a basis for understanding the importance of multiple ecological influences, multiple constitutional influences, and the interactions that occur between them. These interactions are critical to the overall development of adolescents, both in positive and negative directions. In addition, understanding why so many are able to overcome adversity provides us with some direction in intervention efforts. Clearly, the ability to intervene within contexts that comprise the adolescents' world is essential if we are to create opportunities that will promote the positive development of young people.

RISK BEHAVIORS AND RISK FACTORS

The term *risk behavior* refers to any behaviors or actions that have the potential to compromise the biological and psychosocial aspects of a developmental period. Involvement in risk behaviors jeopardizes several areas of human development: (a) physical health, physical growth; (b) the accomplishment of normal developmental tasks; (c) the fulfillment of expected social roles; (d) the acquisition of essential skills; (e) the achievement of a sense of adequacy and competence; and (f) the appropriate preparation for the next developmental period of the life span, (i.e., young adulthood for adolescents; e.g., Jessor, Turbin, & Costa, 1998).

The literature provides evidence that risk pertains to the relationship between the individual and the context (e.g., Elliott & Eisdorfer, 1982; Masten, 2001; Werner & Smith, 1992). Moreover, research has found that possession of a particular instance or level of either individual characteristics or embeddedness in a specific context affords different probabilities of experiencing risk (e.g., Dohrenwend, Dohrenwend, Pearlin, Clayton, & Hamburg, 1982; Garbarino, 1994). Risk characteristics refer, then, to those individual and contextual characteristics associated with a decreased likelihood of healthy psychosocial and physical development. Outcome behaviors might include dropping out of high school, delinquency, teen pregnancy, violence, and crime (e.g., Dryfoos, 1990; Masten, 2001; Schorr, 1988); these behaviors may result in outcomes such as unemployability, prolonged welfare dependency, incarceration, and a shortened life span.

Conducting a meta-analysis of the risk behavior research, Dryfoos (1990) found four distinct categories of risk behavior during adolescence: delinquency, crime, and violence; substance use; teenage pregnancy and parenting; and school failure and dropout. Moreover, Irwin and Millstein (1991) provided support for the findings of Dryfoos's research regarding substance use and teenage pregnancy as major risk behaviors.

Social scientists have progressed through several stages in their approach to understanding covariates of risks (e.g., Luthar, Cicchetti, & Becker, 2000; Masten & Coatsworth, 1998; Werner & Smith, 1992). In the initial stage of investigation, researchers emphasized simple bivariate associations, such as a link between factors like low birth weight or a stressful life event (e.g., parental discord) and a single risk behavior (e.g., drug use). Borrowing from the field of epidemiology, several social scientists moved beyond bivariate associations and employed an approach to studying risk behaviors and their covariates that suggested that there are probably many diverse paths that lead to the development of particular risk behaviors (e.g., Irwin & Millstein, 1991; Masten, 2001; Newcomb, Maddahian, Skager, & Bentler, 1987). Indeed, efforts to find a single covariate may not be useful because most behaviors have multiple covariates (e.g., Perry, 2000). Thus, researchers in the social sciences have moved from a bivariate model of risk/vulnerability to a multivariate model,

one that emphasizes the possibility of interactions among variables, such as the co-occurrence of parental addiction (e.g., alcoholism), poverty, and youth problem behaviors (e.g., aggression and school problems; e.g., Masten, 2001; Werner & Smith, 1992).

Although there are variations in the definitions of risk, risk factors, and risk behavior correlates, the research on risk behaviors provides support for the presence of associations among certain individual and contextual characteristics with adolescents' involvement in risk behaviors. These two types of characteristics are examined here in terms of their relationship to the above-mentioned four categories of risk behavior specified by Dryfoos (1990): teenage sexual activity, alcohol and substance use/abuse, delinquency and antisocial behavior, and school failure.

TEENAGE SEXUAL ACTIVITY

The 1970s and 1980s saw a steady increase in the number of teenagers in the United States who were sexually active (Child Trends, 2001). However, the most recent trend data from the National Center for Health Statistics show a steady decline in the teen birthrate (Child Trends, 2001). The 2000 rate of 48.7 births per 1,000 females ages 14 to 19 is 22% lower than the 1991 rate of 61/1,000 (Child Trends, 2001). Despite these declines the United States has one of the highest teen birthrates of all the developed countries (Child Trends, 2001). For example, a recent report concerning the incidence of sexual intercourse among adolescents younger than age 15 reported rates ranging from 12% to 55% (Meschke, Bartholomae, & Zentall, 2000). By age 19 there is a marked increase in these rates: 85% of males and 77% of females have had sexual intercourse at least once (Moore, Driscoll, & Lindberg, 1998).

This increase in sexual experimentation during adolescence has been coupled with adolescents' frequent use of contraception. By 1995 three quarters of teens reported using some form of contraception at *first* sex (Abma, 1999). However, youth who are sexually active fail to engage in safe sex (e.g., sex with a condom). Thus, they are more likely to contract AIDS and other sexually transmitted diseases (STDs) and become pregnant during adolescence (Abma, 1999; Meschke et al., 2000). The number of cases of STDs has been increasing since the 1970s, and adolescents account for one quarter of the estimated 12 million cases of STDs that occur annually (e.g., Meschke et al., 2000). Research has further identified the antecedents and correlates of sexual intercourse during the adolescent years, the onset of sexual intercourse, and the use of contraception (e.g., Brooks-Gunn &

Furstenberg, 1989; Catalano, Bergund, Ryan, Lonczak, & Hawkins, 1999; Dryfoos, 1990; Jessor, 1998; Luster & Small, 1994).

Individual Characteristics

Numerous individual characteristics are associated with adolescent sexual activity. Generally, boys have sexual intercourse at an earlier age than girls (e.g., Dryfoos, 1990; Perry, 2000). Timing of pubertal maturation has also been linked to early sexual activity (e.g., Brooks-Gunn & Furstenberg, 1989; Irwin & Millstein, 1991). Not surprisingly, both males and females who undergo maturation earlier than their peers initiate sexual intercourse earlier than their age-related peers (e.g., Brooks-Gunn & Furstenberg, 1989). The earlier the age of initiation, the more likely it is that an adolescent female will become pregnant or contract an STD. Likewise, the earlier the age of initiation, the more likely an adolescent male is to impregnate a female or contract an STD because both are less likely to use any type of contraception (e.g., Luster & Small, 1994; Ozer, Brindis, Millstein, Knopf, & Irwin, 1998; Perry, 2000).

Ethnicity has also been found to be associated with early sexual activity (Irwin & Millstein, 1991). There is a disproportionate representation of African American adolescents who are sexually active and who experience negative outcomes of sexual activity (e.g., teenage pregnancy or STDs; Ozer et al., 1998). On average, African American and Hispanic male adolescents initiate sexual intercourse earlier than their European American counterparts (e.g., Moore et al., 1998; Perkins, Luster, Villarruel, & Small, 1998; Terry & Manlove, 2000). African American females are the most likely to become teen mothers, followed by Latina adolescents and European American adolescents, respectively (e.g., Ozer et al., 1998). It should be noted that ethnicity and socioeconomic status (SES) covary. When ethnicity is controlled statistically, SES remains associated with adolescent sexual activity. Indeed, low SES is associated with earlier onset of sexual activity (e.g., Brooks-Gunn & Furstenberg, 1989; Perry, 2000).

Several studies have found a linkage between low aspirations or poor school performance and early engagement in sexual activity (e.g., Brooks-Gunn & Furstenberg, 1989; Luster & Small, 1994). In addition, adolescents who lack hope and a positive view of the future are more likely to participate earlier in sexual activity than are those who have a positive view of the future (e.g., Dryfoos, 1990; Perry, 2000). Adherence to conventional religious values is associated with decreased sexual initiation and behavior (e.g., Jessor & Jessor, 1977; Perkins et al., 1998). Some evidence suggests that self-esteem is usually not reported as a significant factor associated with sexual activity in adolescence (Luster & Small, 1994; Perkins, 1995). However, Orr, Wilbrandt, Brack, Rauch, and Ingersoll (1989) found gender differences in regard to the linkage between teenage sexual activity and self-esteem. Adolescent males who had high self-esteem also had the highest levels of sexual activity; however, the opposite was true for females (Orr et al., 1989). Moreover, adolescent sexual behavior is generally associated with or often preceded by other risk behaviors, such as alcohol and drug use and truancy (e.g., Irwin & Millstein, 1991; Jessor, 1998; Jessor & Jessor, 1977; Perry, 2000).

Contextual Characteristics

Research has provided evidence for the association between characteristics of the context and engagement in sexual activity. Adolescents who perceive themselves as having parental support (i.e., communication, accessibility) are less likely to get involved in sexual activity. A similar association has been found between parental monitoring and engagement in sexual activity (e.g., Dryfoos, 1990; Jessor & Jessor, 1977; Meschke et al., 2000). Thus, adolescents who are monitored are less likely to engage in sexual activity (e.g., Dryfoos, 1990; Furstenberg & Hughes, 1995).

Family structure has also been linked with adolescent engagement in sexual activity. Adolescents from single-parent families are more likely to engage in sexual activity and to engage in those activities at an earlier age than are their age-related peers from two-parent homes (e.g., Brooks-Gunn & Furstenberg, 1989; Ketterlinus, Lamb, & Nitz, 1994). However, this association may be confounded by the fact that single-parent families have, on average, considerably lower incomes than two-parent families, as well as the fact that a higher percentage of single-parent families are ethnic minorities than is the case with two-parent families (Calhoun Davis & Friel, 2001). As noted previously, SES (in particular poverty) and ethnicity have been linked to adolescents' engagement in sexual activity. Studying a sample of 8,266 adolescents living in single-parent families, Benson and Roehlkepartain (1993) found that the association between family structure and adolescent sexual activity exists even when income and ethnicity are held constant. Moreover, a history of sexual or physical abuse has also been found to be associated with adolescent engagement in sexual activity (e.g., Benson & Roehlkepartain, 1993; Perkins et al., 1998).

There is some evidence that peer relations are associated with sexual behavior in adolescence (e.g., Masten & Coatsworth, 1998; Perry, 2000; Stättin & Magnusson, 1990).

However, peer influence is more strongly related to perceived sexual behavior than to actual behavior (Perry, 2000). Indeed, adolescents (especially girls) who perceive their best friends as sexually active are more likely to be sexually active themselves (e.g., Billy & Udry, 1985). However, Small and Luster (1994) did not find a significant correlation between peer conformity and sexual behavior in adolescence. They suggested that researchers may overestimate the role that peers play in influencing sexual behavior.

Poor neighborhood characteristics are associated with the increased probability of adolescents' early engagement in sexual activity (e.g., Duncan & Aber, 1997; Kowaleski-Jones, 2000). Adolescents who live in neighborhoods with low monitoring were more likely to become sexually active at an earlier age than were their peers who lived in neighborhoods characterized by high monitoring; thus, nonparental adults in the neighborhood can play an important role in supervising the behavior of adolescents (Small & Luster, 1994).

ALCOHOL AND SUBSTANCE USE/ABUSE

In recent years there have been declines in most alcohol and drug use among adolescents (Johnson, O'Malley, & Bachman, 2001; Kandel, 1991). However, according to data derived from a national sample of high school seniors (Johnson et al., 2001), 52% of 8th graders, 71% of 10th graders, and 80% of 12th graders had tried alcohol, and 15% of 8th graders, 24% of 10th graders, and 31% of 12th graders had smoked cigarettes. Indeed, in that same study over half had tried an illicit drug, and over one third had used an illicit drug other than marijuana. Furthermore, the article stated that "by the end of eighth grade, nearly four in every ten (35%) American eighth graders have tried illicit drugs" (p. 33). Moreover, many adolescents will experiment with cigarettes, chewing tobacco, alcohol, and marijuana (Johnson et al., 2001).

The statistics pertinent to adolescents about frequent or heavy use of alcohol (e.g., having more than two drinks per day or binge drinking, which is five or more drinks in a row three or more times during the past two weeks), about heavy use of cigarettes (smoking five or more cigarettes a day), and about heavy use of illicit drugs (e.g., smoking marijuana 20 times or more in the past 30 days or using cocaine, crack, heroin, or LSD once a week) reflect alarmingly high rates (Johnson et al., 2001). The Centers for Disease Control and Prevention (1998) found that 70.2% of 9th through 12th graders have tried smoking. The Monitoring the Future Study found that "marijuana use rose substantially among secondary school and college students between 1992 and 2000, but somewhat less so among young adults. Nearly one in

seventeen (6.0%) twelfth graders is now a current daily marijuana user" (Johnson et al., 2001, p. 45). As noted previously, the abuse of any one of these substances can have harmful short-term and long-term effects on an individual's physical and mental health (e.g., Hawkins, Catalano, & Miller, 1992; Kandel, 1991).

For adolescents who get heavily involved in drugs (either with one or multiple drugs), the consequences can be devastating, both physically and psychologically. Drug use can severely limit educational, career, and marital success (e.g., Hawkins et al., 1992; Perry, 2000) and has been associated with many societal problems (Dryfoos, 1990; Perry 2000). Indeed, over one third of all automobile fatalities are alcohol related (Perry, 2000). Frequent use of alcohol in the short term is also associated with impaired functioning in school, family problems, depression, and accidental death (e.g., drowning; Perry, 2000).

The heavier the use of a seemingly harmless substance in the early years, the more likely it is that multiple use will occur later (e.g., Johnson et al., 2001; Kandel, 1991). Alcohol and smoking are characterized as gateway drugs because they often lead to more serious substance abuse (e.g., Johnson et al., 2001; Kandel, 1991; Perry, 2000). As with heavy alcohol use, frequent use of marijuana has been linked with the following short-term consequences: impaired psychological functioning, impaired driving ability, and loss of short-term memory.

Over the past 20 years research has identified the antecedents and correlates of alcohol and drug use/abuse during the adolescent years (e.g., Jessor & Jessor, 1977; Johnson et al., 2001; Kandel, 1991). Several studies have identified the individual and contextual characteristics that appear to be associated with alcohol and substance use/abuse in adolescence (e.g., Catalano et al., 1999; Dryfoos, 1990; Jessor & Jessor, 1977; Lerner, 1995; Newcomb et al., 1987).

Individual Characteristics

Several individual characteristics have been associated with adolescents' use of alcohol and drugs. Investigators have presented data suggesting that experimentation at an early age leads to a higher risk of using more dangerous drugs (e.g., Dryfoos, 1990; Johnson et al., 2001; Perry, 2000). The link between ethnicity and alcohol and drug use/abuse is complicated by the underrepresentation of adolescent minorities in empirical research (e.g., African American inner-city youth; Barnes & Farrell, 1994; Dryfoos, 1990). In general, however, European American and Native American adolescents, especially those in urban areas, report the highest rates of alcohol and drug use/abuse, whereas Latino and African American adolescents report intermediate rates of use, and Asian American adolescents report the lowest rates of use (e.g., Barnes & Farrell, 1994; Newcomb et al., 1987; Ozer et al., 1998).

Low grades in school (especially in junior high school) are associated with an increased likelihood of engagement in alcohol and substance use/abuse (e.g., Hawkins et al., 1992; Ketterlinus et al., 1994; Masten, 2001). Indeed, Hundleby and Mercer (1987) found that good school performance reduced the likelihood of frequent drug use in ninth graders.

However, adolescents who have low educational aspirations are more likely to participate in alcohol and substance use/abuse than those youth who are interested in scholastic achievement, such as attending a postsecondary institution (e.g., Catalano et al., 1999; Newcomb et al., 1987). Several studies have found a linkage between low attendance at church services and the likelihood that adolescents will engage in substance use/abuse (e.g., Barnes & Farrell, 1994; Perry, 2000).

Involvement in two specific risk behaviors, school failure and antisocial behavior/delinquency, has been associated with alcohol and substance use/abuse. For instance, adolescents who perform poorly in school and who possess low educational aspirations are more likely to become involved in alcohol and substance use/abuse (Dryfoos, 1990; Hawkins et al., 1992). Not surprisingly, then, school failure (defined as being two or more grades behind in school) has been linked with engagement in alcohol and drug use/abuse (e.g., Hawkins et al., 1992; Ketterlinus et al., 1994; Newcomb et al., 1987). School dropout is also related to alcohol and drug use/abuse (Lerner, 2002).

The relationship between antisocial behavior (delinquency) and alcohol and drug use/abuse has been well established (e.g., Farrington, 1998; Jessor, 1998; Johnson et al., 2001). For example, antisocial behavior that is exhibited through fighting, school misbehavior, and truancy in adolescence is linked to an increased likelihood of alcohol and substance abuse (e.g., Dryfoos, 1990; Farrington, 1998; Jessor & Jessor, 1977). Moreover, several investigators have found that antisocial behavior in the form of lack of law abidance (i.e., delinquency) is associated with alcohol and drug abuse in adolescence (Hawkins et al., 1992).

Contextual Characteristics

A large number of investigations have found evidence for a relationship between the context within which an adolescent is embedded and alcohol and drug use/abuse. Parental-adolescent communication that is characterized by negative patterns (e.g., criticism and lack of praise) has been linked with adolescent engagement in alcohol and drug use/abuse (e.g., Barnes & Farrell, 1994; Hawkins et al., 1992). In addition, lack of parental monitoring and discipline are related to an increased likelihood of adolescent alcohol and substance use/abuse (e.g., Dryfoos, 1990; Hawkins et al., 1992; Scheer, Borden, & Donnermeyer, 2000).

Adolescents who have one or both parents who are addicted to a substance are more likely to engage in alcohol and substance use/abuse than are adolescents who do not have an addicted parent or parents (e.g., Dryfoos, 1990; Masten & Coatsworth, 1998; Resnick et al., 1997). In addition, adolescents who have an older addicted sibling are more likely to get involved in such use than are adolescents who do not have such a sibling (Dryfoos, 1990). There is also a link between parental involvement in a youth's activities and a decrease in the probability that the adolescent will engage in alcohol and drug use/abuse (e.g., Jessor, 1998; Jessor & Jessor, 1977; Resnick et al., 1997).

Consistently, one of the most powerful predictors of adolescent alcohol and drug use/abuse is the behavior of a youth's best friend (e.g., Borden, Donnermeyer, & Scheer, 2001; Jessor & Jessor, 1977; Newcomb et al., 1987). Adolescents whose friends use alcohol and drugs are much more likely to use/abuse them than are those adolescents whose peers do not engage in such behavior. In fact, there is evidence that initiation of alcohol and drug use is through friends rather than strangers (Kandel, 1991).

DELINQUENCY AND ANTISOCIAL BEHAVIOR

The terms *antisocial behavior* and *delinquency* suggest a wide range of behaviors, from socially unacceptable but not necessarily illegal acts to violent and destructive illegal behaviors. Two types of offenses will be presented here in regard to criminal acts. First, status offenses are those offenses that are illegal acts due to the age of the individual who commits them. Status offenses are sometimes classified as juvenile offenses, such as running away, truancy, drinking under age, sexual promiscuity, and uncontrollability. Second, index offenses are offenses that are always illegal and are not dependent on age. Thus, index offenses are criminal acts whether they are committed by juveniles or adults and, as categorized by the Federal Bureau of Investigation, include offenses such as robbery, vandalism, aggravated assault, rape, and homicide (Dryfoos, 1990).

Although most individuals with a history of juvenile delinquency do not go on to become convicted criminals, most convicted criminals do have a history of juvenile delinquency (Dryfoos, 1990). Antisocial behavior has been found to be prevalent in general community samples of adolescents (e.g., Tolan, 1988). For example, the FBI reported that juveniles accounted for 17% of all arrests and 16% of all violent crime arrests in 1999. The substantial growth in juvenile violent crime arrests that began in the late 1980s peaked in 1994. Between 1994 and 1999 the juvenile arrest rate for Violent Crime Index offenses fell by 36% (Snyder, 2000).

Approximately one third of juvenile arrests involved younger juveniles (under age 15). The types of crimes committed included arson (67%), followed by sex offenses (51%), vandalism (44%), and other assaults (43%). "Of all the delinquency cases processed by the Nation's juvenile courts in 1997, 58% involved juveniles younger than 16" (Office of Juvenile Justice and Delinquency Prevention, 2001, p. 22). In fact, in the course of a year, an estimated 500,000 to 1.5 million young people run away from or are forced out of their homes, and an estimated 200,000 are homeless and living on the streets (Administration on Children, Youth, and Families, 2001). Past research suggests that the majority of these youth are female (Dryfoos, 1990). Moreover, "in 1999, 27% juvenile arrests involved female offenders arrested. Between 1990 and 1999, the number of female juvenile offenders arrested increased more or decreased less than the number of male juvenile offenders arrested in most offense categories" (Office of Juvenile Justice and Delinquency Prevention, 2001, p. 22).

The proportion of violent crimes attributed to juveniles has declined in recent years. The proportion of violent crimes that occurred by juvenile arrests grew from 9% in the late 1980s to 14.2% in 1994 and then declined to 12.4% in 1999. Arrest rates are much higher for African American males than for any other group. African American youths experience rates of rape, aggravated assault, and armed robbery that are approximately 25% higher than those for European American adolescents. Rates of motor vehicle theft are about 70% higher for African Americans, rates of robbery victimization are about 150% higher, and rates of African American homicide are typically between 600% and 700% higher (e.g., National Research Council, 1993; Snyder, 2000).

Self-report data by adolescents indicate a wide gap between rates of self-reported antisocial behavior and juvenile arrest and conviction rates (National Research Council, 1993). The rates of self-report are consistently much higher than are the arrest rates (Dryfoos, 1990). Indeed, a review of the literature on self-report surveys concluded that no more than 15% of all delinquent acts result in police contact (Farrington & West, 1982). The majority of adolescents report that they have participated in various forms of delinquent behavior (Dryfoos, 1990). Dryfoos suggested that the number of index offenses committed by adolescents may be 10 times greater than the

number of cases that are discovered and end up in juvenile court. An estimated six million 10- to 17-year-olds reported that within a one-year period they had participated in an act that was against the law; of these, 3.3 million youth were under the age of 14 (Dryfoos, 1990).

Delinquency and antisocial behavior can have harmful short-term and long-term effects on individuals' physical *and* mental health. Antisocial behavior has been linked with psychiatric problems, early and heavy alcohol and drug use/abuse, and school problems. Over the long term, antisocial behavior is associated with an increased likelihood of adult criminal behavior, unemployment, low occupational status and low income, poor marital adjustment and stability, out-of-wedlock parenting, impaired offspring, and reliance on welfare (e.g., Jessor, 1998; Perry, 2000; Werner & Smith, 1992).

Research has identified the antecedents and correlates of antisocial behavior and delinquency during the adolescent years (e.g., Dryfoos, 1990; Glueck & Glueck, 1968; Hawkins et al., 2000; Jessor & Jessor, 1977; Pakiz, Reinherz, & Frost, 1992). These studies identified the individual and contextual characteristics that appear to be associated with antisocial behavior and delinquency during adolescence. Consensus among researchers about these antecedents and correlates is substantial (Hawkins et al., 2000; Herrenkohl, Maguin, Hill, Hawkins, & Abbott, 2001).

Individual Characteristics

Numerous individual characteristics have been associated with antisocial behavior and delinquency during adolescence. Age of initiation in antisocial behaviors has been found to be related to antisocial behavior and delinquency during adolescence. Early onset of adolescent antisocial behavior is associated with high rates of more serious criminal offenses in later adolescence (e.g., Dodge, 2001; Farrington, 1998; Hawkins et al., 2000).

Studies that have utilized self-reports and arrest statistics have consistently demonstrated that there are large gender differences in the prevalence and incidence of most antisocial and delinquent behaviors. Adolescent males engage in considerably more delinquent behaviors than do adolescent females (e.g., Dryfoos, 1990; Farrington, 1998; Hawkins et al., 2000). This difference is more pronounced in serious and violent crimes. Girls, then, are more likely to be involved in status offenses (e.g., running away) than in serious or violent crimes.

Within the studies using arrest statistics, there is a consistent finding that African Americans are disproportionately represented in the arrest data, victimization reports, and incarceration statistics (e.g., Dodge, 2001; Farrington, 1998;

Herrenkohl et al., 2001). However, self-report measures have yielded minimal racial differences in antisocial and delinquent behaviors (National Research Council, 1993).

There is consistent evidence from both cross-sectional and longitudinal research that poor performance in school is associated with antisocial and delinquent behavior (e.g., Dahlberg & Potter, 2001; Hawkins et al., 2000; Herrenkohl et al., 2001). School failure (being two or more years behind in school or dropping out of school) has been found to be associated with antisocial and delinquent behaviors (e.g., Barnes & Farrell, 1994; Hawkins et al., 2000; Herrenkohl et al., 2001). Furthermore, low educational expectations and aspirations have been linked with an increased likelihood of antisocial and delinquent behaviors in youth (e.g., Hawkins et al., 2000; Herrenkohl et al., 2001).

Employment can provide a legitimate means for obtaining material possessions, acquiring status and career paths, and attenuating the negative effects of poor academic achievement (Duster, 1987). Studies have produced inconsistent data on the association of part-time employment and delinquency. Cross-sectional data provide support for an association between employment and lower levels of antisocial and delinquent behaviors during adolescence (e.g., Dodge, 2001; Tolan, 1988). In the longitudinal literature, however, there is little evidence supporting this association, and, in fact, part-time employment may have deleterious effects on adolescent behaviors (e.g., Mortimer & Johnson, 1998; Perry, 2000).

The research findings are mixed with regard to the individual characteristics of self-esteem. Comparison between delinquents and nondelinquents has provided evidence that delinquent adolescents have lower self-esteem (Arbuthnot, Gordon, & Jurkovic, 1987). However, some studies do not provide evidence for the association between self-esteem and delinquency (e.g., Dodge, 2001; Herrenkohl et al., 2001). In his review of the literature, Henggeler (1989) suggested that the association between self-esteem and delinquency is due to association with a third variable (e.g., intelligence quotients, family relations, or school performance).

As noted in the previous section, numerous studies have established the relationship among antisocial and delinquent behaviors and alcohol and drug use/abuse (e.g., Dryfoos, 1990; Hawkins et al., 2000; Herrenkohl et al., 2001; Jessor, 1998). Indeed, antisocial and delinquent behaviors are associated with early and heavy alcohol and substance use/abuse (e.g., Hawkins et al., 2000; Herrenkohl et al., 2001; Jessor & Jessor, 1977; Kandel, 1991).

Contextual Characteristics

Research on antisocial and delinquent behavior has provided support for the association among several contextual characteristics and the presence or development of antisocial or delinquent behavior in adolescence. In general, researchers have found a negative linear relationship between parental support (e.g., positive communication, affection) and adolescent antisocial and delinquent behaviors, such that the more parental support that exists, the less likely the adolescent is to be involved in antisocial or delinquent behaviors (e.g., Barnes & Farrell, 1994; Farrington, 1998; Hawkins et al., 2000; Herrenkohl et al., 2001). In addition, many of the already-noted studies found that a significant relationship exists between parental control (e.g., monitoring, discipline) and antisocial and delinquent behaviors (e.g., Barnes & Farrell, 1994; Dahlberg & Potter, 2001; Farrington, 1998; Henggeler, 1989; Herrenkohl et al., 2001; Mahoney & Stättin, 2000). Higher parental monitoring is associated with low instances of antisocial and delinquent behaviors. Moreover, lax or markedly inconsistent discipline has been linked to high rates of antisocial behavior and delinquency (e.g., Farrington, 1998; Glueck & Glueck, 1968; Herrenkohl et al., 2001; Hirschi & Stark, 1969).

Parental practice of high-risk behaviors is another characteristic of the parent-adolescent relationship that has been linked to antisocial and delinquent behaviors (e.g., Barnes & Farrell, 1994; Farrington, 1998; Glueck & Glueck, 1968; Hawkins et al., 2000). Furthermore, parental physical and sexual abuse of children and adolescents has been found to be associated with antisocial and delinquent behavior (Brown, 1984). Adolescents who are physically or sexually abused by their parent or parents are more likely to participate in delinquent acts (Brown, 1984; Hawkins et al., 2000; Herrenkohl et al., 2001).

In addition to the parent-adolescent relationship, other characteristics of the family have been linked with antisocial behaviors and delinquency. For example, there is an association between adolescent antisocial and delinquent behaviors and family support. Low family support, as measured by low warmth and affection among family members, has been linked with antisocial behaviors during adolescence (e.g., Farrington, 1998; Hawkins et al., 2000; Henggeler, 1989; Herrenkohl et al., 2001). In addition, several studies have found that antisocial and delinquent behavior is associated with low family cohesion and high family conflict (e.g., Farrington, 1998; Herrenkohl et al., 2001; Pakiz et al., 1992; Tolan, 1988).

An association has been found between family structure (whether the household is headed by one or two parents) and antisocial behaviors and delinquency (Barnes & Farrell, 1994; Farrington, 1998). For example, adolescents living in mother-only homes and natural parent-stepparent homes were more susceptible to negative peer pressure and engaged in more antisocial behaviors and delinquent acts than did their age-related peers living in homes with two natural parents (Steinberg, 1987). No data have been presented with regard to father-only homes. However, family structure is not as significant in predicting antisocial behavior and delinquency as is the quality of the parent-adolescent relationship (e.g., Dryfoos, 1990; Farrington, 1998).

For many adolescents, involvement with deviant peers has become a critical aspect of their own delinquent behavior (e.g., Dahlberg & Potter, 2001; Hawkins et al., 2000; Herrenkohl et al., 2001; Mahoney & Stättin, 2000; Perry, 2000). Thus, researchers have found evidence for an association between antisocial behavior and delinquency and engagement with peers who participate in antisocial behaviors and delinquent acts (e.g., Farrington, 1998; Hawkins et al., 2000; Herrenkohl et al., 2001). In fact, there is evidence that a high percentage of antisocial and delinquent behavior is carried out with peers (Emler, Reicher, & Ross, 1987).

Certain types of neighborhoods are linked to adolescent antisocial behaviors, to delinquent behaviors, and to delinquent gang activities (e.g., Dahlberg & Potter, 2001; Duncan & Aber, 1997; Herrenkohl et al., 2001; Taylor, 1990). Neighborhoods that are located in an area with high crime rates, poverty, and dense living conditions are associated with an increased likelihood of adolescent antisocial behavior and delinquent acts, including the emergence of gangs (e.g., Duncan & Aber, 1997; Henggeler, 1989; Taylor, 1990).

Finally, it should be noted that the impact of SES is unclear. Studies have found evidence for a link between low SES and an increased likelihood of adolescent antisocial behavior and delinquency (e.g., Gorman-Smith & Tolan, 1998). However, recent studies have not found SES to be of primary importance in predicting adolescent antisocial and delinquent behavior (e.g., Dahlberg & Potter, 2001; Tolan, 1988).

SCHOOL UNDERACHIEVEMENT AND FAILURE

As noted earlier, low achievement in school has been linked to the three previously mentioned risk behaviors—adolescent sexual activity, alcohol and drug use/abuse, and antisocial behavior and delinquency. In addition, many of the individual and contextual characteristics previously mentioned are linked to school underachievement and failure.

Low school achievement, poor grades, and being overage for grade are often associated with dropping out (e.g., Dryfoos, 1990; Rumberger, 2001). Yet not everyone who has low grades or is overage drops out. The consequences for poorly equipped high school graduates, however, may inhibit their chances of getting into a postsecondary school, and this,

in turn, may limit their chances of getting a well-paying job. High school dropouts are two to three times more likely to be in marginal jobs and to be employed intermittently (Eccles, 1991). Conversely, each added year of secondary education reduces the probability of public welfare dependency in adulthood by 35% (Berlin & Sum, 1988).

School failure here will be defined as possessing poor grades (e.g., half of a student's grades are D or less in regard to academic content areas) and being retained one or more grades. Although some recent studies have suggested that retention may have some positive effects on academic achievement (Roderick, Bryk, Jacob, Easton, & Allensworth, 1999), falling behind one's age-related peers has been found in numerous studies to be strongly predictive of dropping out (e.g., Goldschmidt & Wang, 1999; Jimerson, 1999; Roderick et al., 1999; Rumberger, 2001); even when achievement, SES, and gender are controlled, being held back increases the probability of eventually dropping out of school by 20% to 30% (Smith & Shepard, 1988). Each year, about 5% of all high school students drop out of school (Kaufman, Kwon, Klein, & Chapman, 1999). The majority of adolescents who do eventually drop out of school will encounter long-term employment problems. In 1998 the unemployment rate for dropouts was 75% higher than for high school graduates (United States Department of Education, National Center for Education Statistics, 2000b, Figure 24). Over their lifetimes, each year's class of dropouts will cost $260 billion in lost earnings and foregone taxes (Catterall, 1987). Thus, there are devastating long-term effects of school failure and dropout.

Individual Characteristics

Several individual characteristics have been found to be related to school failure and dropout. Many studies have found that older adolescents who have been retained (held back) from advancing to the next grade level with their age-related peers are more likely to do poorly in school and to drop out (e.g., Eccles, 1991; Powell-Cope & Eggert, 1994; Rumberger, 2001; Wang, Haertel, & Walberg, 1999). Furthermore, in general, adolescents' average course grades decline as they move from primary school into secondary school; that decline is especially marked at each of the school transition points (Simmons & Blyth, 1987).

Females are less likely to be involved in behavior problems in school, and problem behaviors have been linked to school failure and dropout (e.g., Barnes & Farrell, 1994; Hawkins et al., 2001; Jessor, 1998; National Research Council, 1993). For example, in 1995 males were two-thirds more likely to be retained in a grade than were females (United

States Department of Education, National Center for Education Statistics, 1997).

Ethnicity has been linked with trends in achievement, inasmuch as being a member of an ethnic minority increases the probability of school failure and dropout (except for Asian American youth; Eccles, 1991; Kaufman et al., 1999; National Research Council, 1993). Indeed, African American and Latino adolescents have a greater probability of being left behind a grade than do European American students (United States Department of Education, National Center for Education Statistics, 1997; National Research Council, 1993). Simmons and Zhou (1993) obtained similar findings when they examined African American and European American sixth to ninth graders. They found that African American males showed the highest degrees of school problem behavior in general, and probation and suspensions in particular. This higher frequency of minority adolescents failing in school or dropping out may be confounded by the greater incidence of poverty and lower SES among ethnic minorities, especially African Americans and Latinos. Indeed, lower levels of resources and poorer learning environments are more common in high-poverty schools, which are more likely to be attended by minority students (United States Department of Education, National Center for Education Statistics, 1997).

Adolescents who value school less or who have a negative attitude about school are more likely to fail or drop out than are adolescents who value school and possess a positive attitude about school (e.g., Goldschmidt & Wang, 1999; Powell-Cope & Eggert, 1994; Rumberger, 2001; Simmons & Blyth, 1987). Simmons and Zhou (1993), for example, found that at transitions to junior high school and to high school, African Americans' attitudes toward school dropped relatively precipitously. Not surprisingly, adolescents who have low educational aspirations are more likely to fail at school or to drop out of school (e.g., Goldschmidt & Wang, 1999; Rumberger, 2001; Simmons & Blyth, 1987). Moreover, a lack of basic skills and problem-solving abilities has been linked with school failure and dropout; adolescents who are deficient in basic skills and problem-solving skills have an increased probability of failing or dropping out of school (e.g., Dryfoos, 1990; Goldschmidt & Wang, 1999; Rumberger, 2001).

Steinberg and Darling (1993) found that time spent on homework was associated with school failure. They found that adolescents who spent little or no time on their homework were likely to fail at school. However, Dryfoos (1990) did not find lack of time spent on homework to be a significant correlate of school failure or dropout. Thus, more research is needed to test the association between time spent on homework and school failure or dropout. In turn, other investigations have found that potential school failures and

dropouts spend more time socializing, dating, and riding around in cars (e.g., Rumberger, 2001).

An association has been found between self-esteem and school failure and dropout (e.g., Powell-Cope & Eggert, 1994; Simmons & Blyth, 1987). Adolescents who have low self-esteem are more likely to do poorly in school and to drop out. Several researchers have identified an association between involvement in school activities and school failure and dropout. Low interest in school activities and low participation in school activities are linked with an increased likelihood of school failure and dropout (e.g., Eccles, 1991; Eccles & Barber, 1999; Goldschmidt & Wang, 1999; Rumberger, 2001).

Research has also found a link between school failure and dropout and other risk behaviors, such as antisocial behavior and delinquency, alcohol and drug use/abuse, and adolescent sexual activity (e.g., Barnes & Farrell, 1994; Hawkins et al., 1992; Jessor, 1998; Jimerson, 1999; National Research Council, 1993). As noted previously, adolescent pregnancy is a significant antecedent of dropping out. However, dropping out is also an antecedent of teenage childbearing (e.g., Eccles, 1991; Luster & Small, 1994; Perry, 2000). In addition, antisocial behavior and delinquency have been shown to be associated with an increased likelihood of school failure or dropout (e.g., Farrington, 1998; Hawkins et al., 2000; Henggeler, 1989; Herrenkohl et al., 2001). Furthermore, adolescents who frequently use and abuse alcohol and drugs have been found to have a higher probability of failing or dropping out of school (e.g., Dryfoos, 1990; Hawkins et al., 2000; Hawkins et al., 1992). The overlapping of these risk behaviors is discussed in the final section of this literature review.

Contextual Characteristics

Several contextual characteristics have been associated with school failure and dropout. Investigators have found a link between parental support (e.g., positive communication, affection) and school failure and dropout. Adolescents who have parental support and are able to discuss issues with their parents are less likely to fail or drop out of school (e.g., Barnes & Farrell, 1994; Dryfoos, 1990; Goldschmidt & Wang, 1999; Rumberger, 2001). Moreover, authoritatively reared adolescents are less likely to fail or drop out of school (e.g., Simmons & Blyth, 1987; Steinberg & Darling, 1993). Low parental monitoring is associated with failing school and dropping out (Barnes & Farrell, 1994; Rumberger, 2001). Parental education is also strongly related (Rumberger, 2001). Adolescents whose parents have low levels of education have an increased likelihood of school failure and dropout (e.g., Eccles, 1991; McNeal, 1999; Pong & Ju, 2000; Rumberger, 2001).

There has been inconsistent evidence that family structure is associated with school failure and dropout. Adolescents who are from larger families (e.g., more than two siblings) are more likely to fail or drop out of school than are adolescents from smaller families (McNeal, 1997). This association may be related to the consistently low SES of large families. Adolescents who live in single-parent homes have a higher probability of failing or dropping out of school than do adolescents who live in two-parent homes (e.g., Goldschmidt & Wang, 1999; McNeal, 1999; Rumberger, 2001). However, several studies found that the association of family structure with school failure and dropout was minimal when SES was accounted for in the analysis (e.g., National Research Council, 1993; Pong & Ju, 2000). Thus, the relationship between family structure and school failure and dropout is not clear.

Adolescents who have affiliations with peers who have low expectations for school or have friends who have dropped out are more likely to fail or drop out of school than are adolescents whose peers have high expectations and positive attitudes toward school (e.g., Powell-Cope & Eggert, 1994; Rumberger, 2001; Wang et al., 1999). Moreover, Steinberg and Darling (1993) found that, for Asian American, African American, and Latino adolescents, peers are relatively more influential in their academic achievement than are parents. For European American adolescents, parents were a more potent source of influence (Steinberg & Darling, 1993).

Larger schools and larger classrooms are associated with increased likelihood of school failure and dropout (e.g., Rumberger & Thomas, 2000). In addition, school climate has been found to be associated. Schools that emphasize competition, testing, and tracking and have low expectations have a higher number of school failures and dropouts than do schools that have high expectations, encourage cooperation, and have teachers who are supportive (e.g., Powell-Cope & Eggert, 1994; Rumberger & Thomas, 2000; Rutter, 1979). However, McNeal (1997) found no effect of academic or social climate on high school dropout rates after controlling for the background characteristics of students, social composition, school resources, and school structure.

There has been a lack of consensus and consistency of findings regarding the association between adolescents' part-time employment and school failure and dropout (e.g., Steinberg & Darling, 1993). For example, D'Amico's (1984) analysis of the National Longitudinal Study (NLS) youth data demonstrated that employment at low intensity (less than 20 hours per week) lessened dropout rates. However,

Steinberg and Avenevoli (1998) found that those who worked more than 20 hours a week were more likely to become disengaged from school. Furthermore, Mortimer and Johnson (1998) found no association between adolescent employment and school failure or dropout.

A few studies have found some evidence of a positive link between stress/depression and school failure and dropout, such that high stress is associated with school failure and dropout (e.g., Dryfoos, 1990; Eccles, 1991; Rumberger, 2001; Simmons & Blyth, 1987). For example, Brack, Brack, and Orr (1994) found that females who were failing at school had higher levels of reported stress/depression than those females who were doing average or better; however, they did not find a similar relationship for males.

In his extensive review, Rumberger (2001) provided evidence from several studies that communities influence students' withdrawal from school. For example, neighborhood characteristics seemed to predict differences in dropout rates among communities, apart from the influence of families (e.g., Brooks-Gunn, Duncan, Klebanov, & Sealand, 1993).

Neighborhoods that are characterized as urban, high-density, and poverty-stricken are associated with adolescent school failure and dropout (e.g., Brooks-Gunn et al., 1993; Dryfoos, 1990; Eccles, 1991; Schorr, 1988). For example, students in urban areas appeared to drop out at a higher rate than students in rural areas; however, the difference between the rates for these two groups is not statistically significant (United States Department of Education, National Center for Education Statistics, 2000a).

Finally, there is consistent evidence from both cross-sectional and longitudinal research that school failure and dropout are associated with low SES (e.g., Eccles, 1991; National Research Council, 1993; Rumberger, 2001; Schorr, 1988). For example, adolescents from low-income families are three times more likely to drop out of school than are children from middle-income families, and they are nine times more likely to drop out of school than students from high-income families (e.g., United States Department of Education, National Center for Educational Statistics, 2000b).

CO-OCCURRENCE OF RISK BEHAVIORS

As evidenced earlier, risk behaviors do not exist in isolation; they tend to covary (e.g., Dryfoos, 1990; Hawkins et al., 2000; Jessor & Jessor, 1977; Masten, 2001; Perry, 2000). Moreover, among the previously noted risk behaviors there are common individual and contextual characteristics with

TABLE 15.1   Common Individual and Contextual Characteristics Associated With the Four Risk Behaviors

Source	Characteristic
Individual	Age of initiation.
	Gender.
	Ethnicity.
	Poor school performance.
	Low educational aspirations.
	Lack of involvement in activities.
	Negative view of the future.
	Lack of religiosity.
	Low self-esteem.
Family	Poor parent-adolescent communication.
	Poor parental monitoring.
	Parental addiction (e.g., alcohol and drugs).
	Lack of family support.
	Family structure.
Extrafamilial context	Negative peer relations.
	Large school.
	Negative school climate.
	Poor neighborhood quality.
	Low socioeconomic status.
	Nonparental adult relations.

Source. Adapted from Perkins (1995).

which they are associated (e.g., early age of initiation, school underachievement, school misconduct, negative peer behaviors, inadequate parent-adolescent relationships, and low quality neighborhoods). The list of common characteristics has been corroborated by several researchers and is presented in Table 15.1 (e.g., Hawkins et al., 2000; Jessor, 1998; Perry, 2001). In her meta-analysis of the literature on the four risk behaviors noted earlier, Dryfoos (1990), for example, found six overarching characteristics associated with involvement in the four risk behaviors.

First, heavy involvement in risk behaviors and more negative consequences from those behaviors are linked with early initiation or occurrence of any of the risk behaviors. Second, common to all problem behaviors is doing poorly in school and having low expectations of future performance. Third, misconduct in school and other conduct disorders are related to each of the risk behaviors. Fourth, adolescent involvement in any of the risk behaviors is increased when youth have peers that engage in the risk behaviors or when adolescents have a low resistance to peer influence. Fifth, an inadequate parent-adolescent relationship is common to all risk behaviors. Areas that characterize an inadequate relationship are lack of communication, lack of monitoring, inadequate discipline, role modeling of problem behaviors (e.g., exhibiting risk behaviors), and low parental education. Sixth, low quality neighborhoods are associated with involvement in risk behaviors. These neighborhoods are characterized by poverty, violence, urbanization, and high-density conditions.

Several other studies have assessed the co-occurrence of risk behaviors (e.g., Bingham & Crockett, 1996; Farrington & West, 1982; Zucker, Fitzgerald, & Moses, 1995). For instance, in their extensive review of research on alcohol use and alcoholism, Zucker et al. (1995) found that antisocial behavior in adolescence is consistently related to alcoholic behavior. Moreover, findings from the 18-year-long Michigan State University Longitudinal Study have provided evidence that difficulty in achievement-related activity in adolescence is consistently found in youths who later become alcoholics (e.g., Zucker et al., 1995). Bingham and Crockett (1996), who examined adolescent sexual activity longitudinally, have found similar relationships among adolescent sexual activity, antisocial behavior, underachievement, and alcohol use. In addition, they found that the later in ontogeny that adolescents initiated sexual intercourse, the lower was their involvement in other problem behaviors (e.g., antisocial behaviors, alcoholism, and school misconduct).

Clearly, research has found a link between certain characteristics (see Table 15.1), risk factors, and adolescents' participation in risk behaviors. Yet many adolescents exposed to a context containing some or all of the stated risk factors do not engage in risk behaviors and, in fact, appear to adapt well and live successful lives. Moreover, evidence exists demonstrating that some children thrive despite their high-risk status. This phenomenon has been the focus of much research in the last 30 years.

RESILIENCY

Social scientists have gone through several stages in their approach to understanding vulnerability and resiliency (Werner & Smith, 1992). Generally, researchers have studied individuals exposed to biological risk factors and stressful life events as the major focus of vulnerability and resiliency research. In the initial stages of research, investigators emphasized the association between a single risk variable, such as low birth weight or a stressful life event (e.g., parental discord), and negative developmental outcomes. Borrowing from the field of epidemiology, several social scientists have more recently employed an approach suggesting that many diverse paths lead to the development of particular risk behaviors (Newcomb et al., 1987) and that efforts to find a single cause may not be useful because most behaviors have multiple causes (e.g., Small & Luster, 1994). Thus, researchers in the social science field have moved from a "main effect" model of vulnerability research to a model that emphasizes interactional effects among multiple stressors, for example, as in the literature that stresses the co-occurrence of parental psychopathology (e.g., alcoholism or mental illness) and poverty (Masten & Coatsworth, 1998; Werner & Smith, 1992).

Finally, resiliency research has shifted its focus from the emphasis on negative developmental outcomes (e.g., risk behaviors) to an emphasis on successful adaptation in spite of childhood adversity (Luthar, 1991; Masten & Coatsworth, 1998; Werner & Smith, 1992). Indeed, in the last 25 years developmental psychopathologists and other social scientists have increasingly explored the concept of invulnerability rather than focusing predominantly on vulnerability and maladjustment (Luthar et al., 2000). For example, in the mid-1970s, Anthony (1974), a child psychiatrist, introduced the concept of the psychologically invulnerable child into the literature of developmental psychopathology to describe children who, despite a history of severe or prolonged adversity and psychological stress, managed to achieve emotional health and high competence (Werner & Smith, 1992).

However, Rutter (1985) noted that resistance to stress in an individual is relative, not absolute. Thus, an individual's ability to overcome stress is dependent on the level of the stress not exceeding the level of the individual's resiliency characteristics. In addition, the bases of resistance to stress are both environmental and constitutional, and the degree of resistance varies over time according to life circumstances (e.g., Luthar et al., 2000; Masten, 2001; Rutter, 1985). Invulnerability may imply an unbreakable individual, one able to conquer any level of stress. Therefore, the concept of resilience or stress resistance, rather than invulnerability, is preferred by many researchers (e.g., Masten & Garmezy, 1985; Rutter, 1985; Werner & Smith, 1992) because it acknowledges a history of success while also implying the possibility of succumbing to future stressors.

The assumption in these investigations is that resiliency can be displayed or detected only through an individual's response to adversity, whether it is a stressful life event or a situation of continuous stress (e.g., war, abuse; Masten & Coatsworth, 1998). Accordingly, resilient individuals are well adapted despite serious stressors in their lives (Luthar et al., 2000; Masten, 2001). Indeed, resilient individuals are those who cope effectively with stresses arising as consequences of their vulnerability; and a balance, congruence, or fit, among risk, stressful life events, and protective characteristics of the individual and the individual's ecology accounts for the diversity of developmental outcomes (Ford & Lerner, 1992; Kumpfer, 1999). Therefore, studying resiliency involves an examination of the link between the person and the demands of the context in variables, factors, and processes that will either promote or subvert adaptation.

An individual's ability to adapt to the changes within the environment and to alter the environment is basic to that individual's survival. Whether situations are marked by high stress or by low stress found in the challenges of daily life, adaptation is a basic function of human development. Resiliency, then, is the organism's ability to adapt well to its changing environment, an environment that includes stressors (e.g., accidents, death of a loved one, war, and poverty) and daily hassles (e.g., negative peer pressures and grades). Thus, studies of resiliency and risk are investigations about human adaptation to life or about competence. Competence is a generalization about adaptation that implies at the least "good" effectiveness (Masten & Coatsworth, 1998).

Human adaptation or competence is composed of the interplay between the context/ecology and the developing organism (Lerner, 2002; Schneirla, 1957). In resiliency the processes involved in the context/ecology interplay are composed of the interaction over time between the protective factors or risk factors at multiple levels that contributes to the direction of the developmental outcomes, whether positive or negative. This interaction is complex and requires a holistic, comprehensive perspective in order to be adequately examined and understood. Models derived from this perspective posit that there are reciprocal influences between the organism and the context/environment (Schneirla, 1957) and that development occurs through these mutual influences (Bronfenbrenner, 1979; Ford & Lerner, 1992; Kumpfer, 1999; Lerner, 2002). Moreover, these models assert that any single explanation of risk-taking behaviors with regard to protective factors and risk factors is too simplistic, in that such explanations are likely to ignore the importance of multiple ecological influences, multiple constitutional influences, and the interactions that develop among them. In fact, several scholars have suggested that the use of the term *factor* may in fact suggest too static a relationship between risk characteristics, protective characteristics, and risk behaviors (Kumpfer, 1999; Rutter, 1985). *Process* may be a better way to describe the dynamic nature of risk and protective characteristics.

Resiliency involves competence in the face adversity, but more than that, it involves an assessment based on some criteria of the adaptation as "good" or "OK" (Masten, 2001). These assessment criteria are based on specific cultural norms within the historical and social contexts for the behavior of that age and situation (Luthar & Cushing, 1999). Borrowing from Masten (2001), resiliency is defined "as a class of phenomena characterized by good outcomes in spite of serious threats to adaptation or development" (p. 228).

Moreover, resiliency is multidimensional in nature. Thus, one may be resilient in one domain but not exhibit resiliency in another domain. As Luthar et al. (2000) stated, "some high-risk children manifest competence in some domains but exhibit problems in other areas" (p. 548). In a study by Kaufman, Cook, Arny, Jones, and Pittinsky (1994), for example, approximately two thirds of children with histories of maltreatment were academically resilient; however, when examining these same children in the domain of social competence, only 21% exhibited resiliency.

PROTECTIVE FACTORS AND RESILIENCY

Risk and resiliency research provides evidence that specific variables and factors are involved in safeguarding and promoting successful development. That is, research has identified particular variables that are responsible for adolescent resiliency in spite of adverse contexts, while, in turn, other variables have been found to promote failure and to encourage participation in risk behaviors (e.g., Garmezy, 1985; Kumpfer, 1999; Luthar, 1991; Luthar et al., 2000; Masten, 2001; Rutter, 1985; Werner & Smith, 1992). As noted previously in this chapter, risk factors are defined, then, as individual or environmental hazards that increase an individual's vulnerability to negative developmental behaviors, events, or outcomes (e.g., Masten, 2001; Werner & Smith, 1992). However, the presence of risk factors does not guarantee that a negative outcome will occur; rather, it simply increases the probability of its occurrence (e.g., Garmezy, 1985; Masten, 2001; Werner & Smith, 1992).

The probabilities of a negative outcome vary as a consequence of the presence of protective factors. Such factors buffer, modify, or ameliorate an individual's reaction to a situation that, in ordinary circumstances, would lead to maladaptive outcomes (Kumpfer, 1999; Masten, 2001; Werner & Smith, 1992). According to this definition, then, a protective factor is evident only in combination with a risk variable. Thus, a protective factor has no effect in low-risk populations, but its effect is magnified in the presence of the risk variable (e.g., Rutter, 1987; Werner & Smith, 1992). In turn, Rutter (1987) suggested that while protective factors may have effects on their own, such factors have an impact on adjustment by virtue of their interaction with risk variables. However, still another possibility is that protective factors can be defined as variables that are linked with an individual experiencing positive developmental outcomes as compared to negative developmental outcomes.

Although there are variations in the definitions of risk, endangerment, risk factors, and protective factors, the research on resilient or stress-resistant children, adolescents, and young adults provides support for the existence of specific individual and contextual characteristics, namely protective factors (e.g., temperament and social support networks, respectively; Garmezy, 1985; Rutter, 1987; Werner & Smith, 1992). Protective factors are incorporated into adolescents' lives and enable them to overcome adversity. On the other hand, some individual and contextual variables (e.g., difficult temperament, poverty, and lack of adult support) are risk factors that increase the probability of involvement in risk behaviors (e.g., Garmezy, 1985; Luthar et al., 2000; Masten & Coatsworth, 1998; Werner & Smith, 1992).

Models of Protective Factors and Processes

It is not known whether protective variables or protective processes have any effect on low-risk populations because the research has focused on high-risk groups (Masten & Coatsworth, 1998). Rutter (1987) suggested that a protective variable's effect may be magnified in high-risk situations. According to this idea, vulnerability and protection are the negative and positive poles of the same processes. Thus, the potential for involvement in risk behaviors is crucial to this definition because without the risk behavior's presence there is no method of differentiating risk processes from protective processes. Consequently, most resiliency and risk studies have investigated individuals who are living in high-stress situations and life events (e.g., born with low birth weight or living in poverty, war, or economic depression) or who have experienced highly stressful situations (e.g., separation from a parent due to divorce or death, or the experience of physical or sexual abuse; Garmezy, 1985, Masten, 2001). The reason for this focus is that individuals experiencing a lot of stress have a higher probability of involvement in maladaptive behaviors, that is, involvement in risk behaviors (Rutter, 1993). The level of resiliency needed differs depending upon the stressfulness of the ecology of an adolescent. Adolescents who are under severe, multiple stresses (e.g., poverty, parental discord, and maltreatment) will need a higher degree of resiliency or a larger number of protective processes in order to develop positively than would another person who is experiencing mild stress (e.g., difficulty in school). However, the level of stress is also somewhat dependent on the individual's perception of stress (e.g., Kumpfer, 1999).

Using different models, researchers have described several mechanisms through which protective factors help reduce or offset the adverse effects of risk factors (Zimmerman & Arunkumar, 1994). Three models have been developed by Garmezy (1985): (a) the compensatory model, (b) the inoculation model, and (c) the protective factor model. In the compensatory model, the protective factor does not interact with the risk factor; rather, it interacts with the outcome directly and neutralizes the risk factor's influence. In the inoculation model each risk factor is treated as a potential enhancer of successful adaptation provided that it is not excessive (Rutter, 1987). This occurs when there is an optimal level of stress that challenges the individual and, when overcome, strengthens the individual. Thus, the relationship between stress and competence is curvilinear: At low or moderate levels of stress competence increases, but at higher levels of stress it decreases (Wang et al., 1999). In the third model the protective factor interacts with the risk factor in reducing the probability of a negative outcome (Zimmerman & Arunkumar, 1994). Thus, the protective factor is acting as a moderator. Although the protective factor may have a direct effect on an outcome, its effect is stronger in the presence of a risk factor. These three models of interaction describe a process that emphasizes the dynamic nature of the relationship between risk characteristics and protective characteristics. Thus, the term *process* may provide a more adequate description of protective characteristics than the term *factor,* since the latter implies a static condition.

Identified Protective Factors

In their longitudinal study of a cohort of children from the island of Kauai, Werner and Smith (1992) described three types of protective factors that emerge from analyses of the developmental course of high-risk children from infancy to adulthood: (a) dispositional attributes of the individual, such as activity level and social ability, at least average intelligence, competence in communication skills (language and reading), and internal locus of control; (b) affectional ties within the family that provide emotional support in times of stress, whether from a parent, sibling, spouse, or mate; and (c) external support systems, whether in school, at work, or at church, that reward the individual's competencies and determination and provide a belief system by which to live.

Bogenschneider (1998) derived similar conclusions in her review of resiliency literature. She concluded that variables operated as protective factors in adolescence at various levels of the ecosystems of youth: (a) individual level—such as well-developed problem-solving skills and intellectual abilities; (b) familial level—for example, a close relationship with one parent; (c) peer level—a close friend; (d) school level—positive school experiences; and (e) community level—required helpfulness (e.g., as it occurs when the adolescent is needed to bring in extra income or help manage the home), and a positive relationship with a nonparental adult (e.g., neighbor, teacher).

In their extensive review of resiliency research, Masten and Coatsworth (1998) summarized the findings from over 25 years of research. As shown in Table 15.2, they noted that similar protective factors are found across resiliency studies that have been conducted in a wide variety of situations throughout the world (e.g., war, living with parents who have severe mental illness, family violence, poverty, and natural disasters).

TABLE 15.2   Characteristics of Resilient Children and Adolescents

Source	Characteristic
Individual	Good intellectual functioning (e.g., high verbal skills, divergent thinking).
	Appealing, sociable, easygoing disposition.
	Self-efficacy, self-confidence, high self-esteem.
	Talents.
	Faith.
Family	Close relationship to caring parent figure.
	Authoritative parenting: warmth, structure, high expectations.
	Socioeconomic advantages.
	Low family stress.
	Orderly household environment.
	Connections to extended, supportive family networks.
	Prosocial family values.
	Positive role models.
Extrafamilial context	Bonds to prosocial adults outside of the family.
	Connections to prosocial organizations.
	Attending effective schools (see Wang et al., 1999).

Source: Adapted from Kumpfer (1999) and Masten & Coatsworth (1998).

Kumpfer's Resiliency Framework

In her recent examination of resiliency, Kumpfer (1999) integrated the work of others into a resiliency framework that employs a transactional model based on the social ecological model (Bronfenbrenner, 1979) and the person-process-contextual model (Ford & Lerner, 1992). According to Kumpfer (1999), this framework is composed of (a) environmental characteristics that are antecedents (i.e., risk and protective factors), (b) characteristics of the resilient person, and (c) the individual's resilient reintegration or positive outcome after a negative life experience, as well as the dynamic mechanisms that mediate between the person and the environment and the person and the outcome.

Many of the risk factors presented earlier in this chapter reside in the environment. Indeed, high-risk youth are often labeled as such due to a high-risk environment rather than internal high-risk characteristics (Kumpfer, 1999). Protective factors are also found in that same environment. According to Garmezy (1985), microniches of support with adequate growth opportunities for some individuals exist even in these high-risk environments. As noted earlier, protective factors interact with risk factors to act as buffers. The interaction between risk and protective factors describes the first oval of the resiliency framework found in Figure 15.1. Generally, youth adjust reasonably well to one or two risk factors, but beyond two risk factors the likelihood for damage and maladjustment increases rapidly (e.g., Jessor, 1998; Masten, 1999; Rutter, 1993). Conversely, increasing the number of protective processes can help buffer those risk factors (e.g., Masten, 2001; Rutter, 1993, 1997).

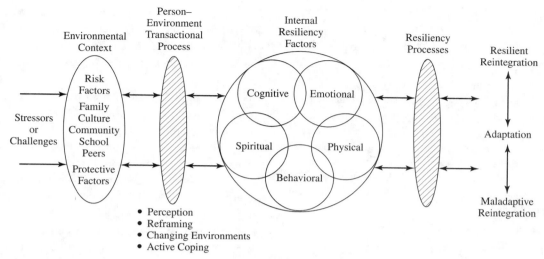

Figure 15.1   Kumpfer's (1999) resiliency framework.

The second oval of the resiliency framework shown in Figure 15.1 involves the transactional processes that mediate between a person and his or her environment. This involves the ways a person consciously or unconsciously modifies his or her environment or selectively perceives the environment. Kumpfer (1999) explains this notion thus:

> Resilient youth living in high drug and crime communities seek ways to reduce environmental risk factors by seeking the prosocial elements in their environment. They maintain close ties with prosocial family members, participate in cultural and community events, seek to be school leaders, and find non-drug using friends and join clubs or youth programs that facilitate friendships with positive role models or mentors. (p. 191)

Kumpfer (1999) identified some transactional processes that help high-risk youth transform a high-risk environment into a more protective environment. These include selective perception, cognitive reframing, planning and dreaming, identification and attachment with prosocial people, active environmental modifications by the youth, and active coping. For example, Kumpfer suggested that resilient youth seek out nurturing adults who facilitate and foster protective processes by positive socialization or caregiving. According to Kumpfer (p. 192), these caring adults provide that positive socialization through "1) role modeling, 2) teaching, 3) advice giving, 4) empathetic and emotionally responsive caregiving, 5) creating opportunities for meaningful involvement, 6) effective supervision and disciplining, 7) reasonable developmental expectations, and 8) other types of psychosocial facilitation or support."

Therefore, a transactional process occurs between the environmental context (risk and protective factors) and internal resiliency factors to create the resiliency process or outcome. Through her review, Kumpfer (1999) found that internal resiliency factors involve the following internal characteristics: cognitive (e.g., academic skills, intrapersonal reflective skills, planning skills, and creativity), emotional (e.g., emotional management skills, humor, ability to restore self-esteem, and happiness), spiritual (e.g., dreams/ goals and purpose in life, religious faith or affiliation, belief in oneself and one's uniqueness, and perseverance), behavioral/social competencies (e.g., interpersonal social skills, problem-solving skills, communication skills, and peer resistant skills), and physical well-being and physical competencies (e.g., good physical status, good health maintenance skills, physical talent development, and physical attractiveness).

The far right of the resiliency framework (Figure 15.1) presents three potential outcomes for the resiliency process (Kumpfer, 1999). Resilient reintegration outcomes involve being made stronger and reaching a higher state of resiliency. Homeostatic reintegration outcomes involve bouncing back to the original state that existed before the stress or crisis occurred. Maladaptive reintegration outcomes involve not demonstrating resiliency, in that the individual functions at a lower state.

The research on resiliency to date has focused on the factors that place individuals at greater risk and the factors that counteract those risk factors. In addition, the insightful criticisms of several scholars (e.g., Masten, 1999; Luthar et al., 2000) have advanced our thinking about the construct, methods, and findings of this work. This research is very useful in that it directs researchers toward potential processes that are worth investigating and toward instruments for analyzing resilience (Masten, 1999). The resiliency research, thus far, also provides us with a greater awareness of the complexity of the concept or resilience (Masten, 2001) because of its integration within the human adaptation system. Indeed, Masten (2001) states,

> The great surprise of resilience research is the ordinariness of the phenomena. Resilience appears to be a common phenomenon that results in most cases from the operation of basic human adaptational systems. If those systems are protected and in good working order, development is robust even in the face of severe adversity; if these major systems are impaired, antecedent or consequent to adversity, then the risk for developmental problems is much greater, particularly if the environmental hazards are prolonged. (p. 227)

FUTURE DIRECTIONS AND CONCLUSIONS

The research being conducted in the area of risk factors, risk behaviors, protective factors, and resiliency points to new directions for future study. According to Rutter (1997), a main topic for future research is to examine the interplay between nature and nurture in development. Thus, future topics include how adolescents' exposure to adversity is related to parent behaviors, peer behaviors, and other significant individuals' behaviors and also how that exposure shapes cognitive and emotional development. These topics include the need for longitudinal studies, interdisciplinary research teams, and robust applied research.

There is a strong need for transactional, cross-lagged longitudinal studies that focus on elucidating the developmental processes underlying the protective and risk factors and the dynamic interactions of those factors, as well as the developmental pathways of individuals. These longitudinal studies and normative samples need to incorporate multifactorial designs and large samples (Masten, 1999). This design and methodology will enable an examination of the individual in the context and an investigation of transactional systems simultaneously. Studies would enable investigators to direct their inquiries toward discovering how assets, moderators, and other mechanisms work, that is, how they confer protective or risk characteristics and how these processes change as a function of development. Through examining mediators and moderators, an investigation could provide insight into the degree to which various mechanisms might influence the effects of a specific risk or protective factor or the interaction of those characteristics (Luthar et al., 2000).

The longitudinal studies proposed previously require integrated teams of researchers that comprise multiple disciplines and address multiple risk factors, protective factors, and outcomes (e.g., prosocial behaviors and risk behaviors).

Research has provided ample evidence of the co-occurrence of risk factors, protective factors, and risk behaviors (Jessor, 1997; Lerner, 1995; Masten, 1999; Perkins, 1995), thus making the notion of single-issue studies seem unwise and inefficient. From the multiple processes (e.g., psychological, sociological, biological), varied pathways to resilience may result in the same effect as well as those that eventuate in multifinality among at-risk individuals (Luthar & Cushing, 1999). Therefore, the complex nature of this research necessitates expertise from various disciplines.

In the short term, comprehensive multivariate studies could be implemented to examine sets of the risk and protective factors simultaneously. These types of studies would enable an investigation of the extent to which one context (e.g., school, peer group, neighborhood) can compensate for another high-risk context or can detract from an enhancing context. Moreover, case studies of adolescents who demonstrate resiliency or engagement in risk behaviors would further elucidate the processes and mechanisms involved in multiple developmental pathways (Wang et al., 1999).

Applied research is needed that employs the accumulated knowledge of basic research to develop and test interventions. Multifaceted and longitudinal interventions need to target multiple risk and protective processes involving various levels of the ecology: micro system (organism, family, peers, schools), macro system (community and culture), and meso system (family and peer interaction; Masten, 1999). Indeed Masten (1999) states,

> Intervention and prevention efforts can be conceptualized as deliberate protective efforts. The key to intervention could lie in triggering or facilitating natural protective systems. A crucial question for the future is whether such efforts are best modeled on naturally occurring resiliency or not. (p. 293)

Experimental designs are required to test intervention and prevention strategies and to further enhance our understanding of the dynamic interactions of risk factors, protective factors, and the outcomes (e.g., engagement in risk behaviors or prosocial behaviors). This research also needs to explore the importance of the timing of the intervention; that is, there may be targeted interventions that will be most efficacious at particular times in an adolescent's life (Perry, 2000). Given the co-occurrence of risk factors, protective factors, and risk behaviors, intervention and prevention efforts must have a triadic focus of increasing multiple protective factors at multiple levels of the ecology, decreasing multiple risk factors at multiple levels of the ecology, and increasing competencies of individuals and systems. Indeed, recent research provides evidence that in communities where the citizens and institutions focus their attention on increasing both competencies of youth and external supports at all levels of the ecology, there is a great likelihood for successfully creating conditions that enable the development of strong and resourceful youth (Furstenberg & Hughes, 1995; Perkins, Haas, & Keith, 1997).

The review of literature on risk factors, risk behaviors, protective factors, and resiliency presented here indicates that we have increased our scientific knowledge and understanding. However, we still have much to learn from the lives of adolescents who succumb to the adverse effects of risk factors, as well as those who do attain normal developmental trajectories despite significant threats to their development.

REFERENCES

Abelson, H., & diSessa, A. (1980). *Turtle geometry. The computer as a medium for exploring mathematics.* Cambridge, MA: MIT Press.

Administration on Children, Youth, and Families. (2001, February). *Youth programs: Runaway and homeless youth program: Fact Sheet.* Washington, DC: Administration on Children, Youth, and Families. Available at http://www.acf.dhhs.gov/programs/opa/facts/youth.htm.

Anthony, E. J. (1974). The syndrome of the psychologically invulnerable child. In E. J. Anthony & C. Koupernik (Eds.), *The child and his family: Children at psychiatric risk* (pp. 529–544). New York: Wiley.

Arbuthnot, J., Gordon, D. A., & Jurkovic, G. J. (1987). Personality. In H. C. Quay (Ed.), *Handbook of juvenile delinquency* (pp. 139–183). New York: Wiley.

Barnes, G. M., & Farrell, M. P. (1994). Parental support and control as predictors of adolescent drinking, delinquency, and related problem behaviors. *Journal of Marriage and the Family, 54,* 763–776.

Benson, P. L., & Roehlkepartain, E. C. (1993). *Youth in single-parent families: Risk and resiliency.* Minneapolis, MN: Search Institute.

Berlin, G., & Sum, A. (1988). *Toward a more perfect union: Basic skills, poor families, and our economic future: Project on social welfare and the American future* (Occasional Paper No. 3). New York: Ford Foundation.

Beyer, J. (1999). *Designing tessellations.* Chicago, IL: Contemporary Books.

Billy, J. O. G., & Udry, J. R. (1985). The influence of male and female best friends on adolescent sexual behavior. *Adolescence, 20,* 21–32.

Bingham, C. R., & Crockett, L. J. (1996). Longitudinal adjustment patterns of boys and girls experiencing early, middle, and late sexual intercourse. *Developmental Psychology, 32,* 647–658.

Bogenschneider, K. (1998). What youth need to succeed: The roots of resiliency. In K. Dogen Schneider (Ed.), *Wisconsin family impact seminars briefing report: Building resiliency and reducing risk: What youth need from families and communities to succeed* (pp. 1–16). Madison: University of Wisconsin.

Borden, L. M., Donnermeyer, J. F., & Scheer, S. D. (2001). Extracurricular activities and peer influence on substance use. *Journal of Adolescent and Family Health, 2*(1), 12–19.

Brack, C. J., Brack, G., & Orr, D. P. (1994). Dimensions underlying problem behaviors, emotions, and related psychosocial factors in early and middle adolescents. *Journal of Early Adolescence, 14,* 345–370.

Bronfenbrenner, U. (1979). *The ecology of human development: Experiments by nature and design.* New York: Cambridge University Press.

Brooks-Gunn, J., Duncan, G. J., Klebanov, P. K., & Sealand, N. (1993). Do neighborhoods influence child and adolescent development? *American Journal of Sociology, 99,* 353–395.

Brooks-Gunn, J., & Furstenburg, F. (1989). Adolescent sexual behavior. *American Psychologist, 44,* 249–257.

Brown, S. E. (1984). Social class, child maltreatment, and delinquent behavior. *Criminology, 22,* 259–278.

Calhoun Davis, E., & Friel, L. V. (2001). Adolescent sexuality: Disentangling the effects of family structure and family context. *Journal of Marriage and Family, 63,* 669–681.

Catalano, R. F., Bergund, M. L., Ryan, J. A. M., Lonczak, H. S., & Hawkins, J. D. (1999). *Positive youth development in the United States: Research findings on evaluations of positive youth development programs.* Washington, DC: U.S. Department of Health and Human Services, National Institute of Child Health and Human Development.

Catterall, J. S. (1987). On the social cost of dropping out of school. *The High School Journal, 71,* 19–30.

Centers for Disease Control and Prevention. (1998). Selected cigarette smoking initiation and quitting behaviors among high school students—United States, 1997. *Morbidity and Mortality Weekly Report, 47,* 386–389.

Child Trends. (2001). *CTS Trends: At a glance.* Washington, DC: Author.

Cramer, K. (in press). Using a translation model for curriculum development and classroom instruction. In R. Lesh & H. M. Doerr (Eds.), *Beyond constructivism: Models and modeling perspectives on mathematics teaching, learning, and problem solving.* Mahwah, NJ: Erlbaum.

Dahlberg, L. L., & Potter, L. B. (2001). Youth violence: Developmental pathways and prevention challenges. *American Journal of Preventive Medicine, 20*(1S), 3–14.

D'Amico, R. J. (1984). Does employment during high school impair academic progress? *Sociology of Education, 57,* 152–164.

Dodge, K. A. (2001). The science of youth violence prevention: Progressing from developmental epidemiology to efficacy to effectiveness to public policy. *American Journal of Preventive Medicine, 20*(1S), 63–70.

Dohrenwend, B. P., Dohrenwend, B. S., Pearlin, L., Clayton, P., & Hamburg, B. (1982). Reports on stress and life events. In G. R. Elliott & C. Elsdorfer (Eds.), *Stress and human health: Analysis and implications of research* (pp. 55–80). New York: Springer.

Dryfoos, J. G. (1990). *Adolescents at risk: Prevalence and prevention.* New York: Oxford University Press.

Duncan, G. J., & Aber, L. (1997). Neighborhood models and measures. In G. Duncan, J. Brooks-Gunn, & L. Aber (Eds.), *Neighborhood poverty: Context and consequences for children* (Vol. 1). New York: Russell Sage Foundation.

Duster, T. (1987). Crime, youth, unemployment, and black urban underclass. *Crime and Delinquency, 33,* 300–316.

Eccles, J. S. (1991). Academic achievement. In R. M. Lerner, A. C. Petersen, & J. Brooks-Gunn (Eds.), *Encyclopedia of adolescence* (pp. 1–5). New York: Garland.

Eccles, J. S., & Barber, B. (1999). Student council, volunteering, basketball, or marching band: What kind of extra-curricular involvement matters? *Journal of Adolescent Research, 14,* 10–43.

Elliott, G. R., & Elsdorfer C. (1982). Conceptual issues in stress research. In G. R. Elliott & C. Elsdorfer (Eds.), *Stress and human health: Analysis and implications of research* (pp. 11–24). New York: Springer.

Emler, N., Reicher, S., & Ross, A. (1987). The social context of delinquent conduct. *Journal of Child Psychology and Psychiatry, 28,* 99–109.

Farrington, D. P. (1998). Predictors, causes, and correlates of male youth violence. In M. Tonry & M. H. Moore (Eds.), *Youth violence, crime, and justice* (Vol. 24; pp. 421–475). Chicago, IL: University of Chicago Press.

Farrington, D. P., & West, D. J. (1982). The Cambridge study in delinquency development, 1980. In F. Dutile, C. Fouste, & D. Webster (Eds.), *Early childhood intervention and juvenile justice* (pp. 11–21). Lexington, MA: D.C. Health.

Ford, D. H., & Lerner, R. M. (1992). *Developmental systems theory: An integrated approach.* Newbury Park, CA: Sage.

Furstenburg, F., Jr., & Hughes, M. E. (1995). Social capital and successful development among at-risk youth. *Journal of Marriage and the Family, 57,* 580–592.

Garbarino, J. (1994, November). *Growing up in a socially toxic environment: Childhood in the 1990's.* Presentation at the National Council on Family Relations, Baltimore, MD.

Garmezy, N. (1985). Stress-resistant children: The search for protective factors. In J. Stevens (Ed.), *Recent research in developmental psychopathology* (pp. 213–233). Oxford, England: Pergamon Press.

Glueck, S., & Glueck, E. (1968). *Delinquents and nondelinquents in perspective.* Cambridge, MA: Harvard University Press.

Goldschmidt, P., & Wang, J. (1999). When can schools affect dropout behavior? A longitudinal multilevel analysis. *American Educational Research Journal, 36,* 715–738.

Goodwin, C. (1996). Transparent vision. In E. Ochs, E. A. Schegloff, & S. A. Thompson (Eds.), *Interaction and grammar* (pp. 370–404). Cambridge: Cambridge University Press.

Gorman-Smith, D., & Tolan, P. (1998). The role of exposure to community violence and developmental problems among inner city youth. *Development and Psychopathology, 10,* 101–116.

Gravemeijer, K. P. (1998). From a different perspective: Building on students' informal knowledge. In R. Lehrere & D. Chazan (Eds.), *Designing learning environments for developing understanding of geometry and space* (pp. 45–66). Mahwah, NJ: Erlbaum.

Gravemeijer, K., Cobb, P., Bowers, J., & Whitenack, J. (2000). Symbolizing, modeling, and instructional design. In P. Cobb, E. Yackel, & K. McClain (Eds.), *Symbolizing and communicating in mathematics classrooms* (pp. 225–273). Mahwah, NJ: Erlbaum.

Grosslight, L., Unger, E. J., & Smith, C. L. (1991). Understanding models and their use in science: Conceptions of middle and high school students and experts. *Journal of Research in Science Teaching, 28,* 799–822.

Hamburg, B. (1974). Early adolescence: A specific and stressful stage of the life cycle. In G. Coelho, D. A. Hamburg, & J. E. Adams (Eds.), *Coping and adaptation* (pp. 101–125). New York: Basic Books.

Hanna, G. (1990). Some pedagogical aspects of proof. *Interchange, 21*(1), 6–13.

Hawkins, J. D., Catalano, R. F., & Miller, J. Y. (1992). Risk and protective factors for alcohol and other drug problems in adolescence and early adulthood: Implications for substance abuse prevention. *Psychological Bulletin, 112,* 64–105.

Hawkins, J. D., Guo, J., Hill, K., Battin-Pearson, S., & Abbott, R. (2001). Long term effects of the Seattle social development intervention on school bonding trajectories. In J. Maggs & J. Schulenberg (Eds.), *Applied Developmental Sciences Special Issue: Prevention or Altering the Course of Development, 5,* 225–236.

Hawkins, J. D., Herrenkohl, T. I., Farrington, D. P., Brewer, D., Catalano, R. F., Harachi, T. W., & Cothern, L. (2000, April). *Predictors of youth violence.* Washington, DC: Office of Juvenile Justice and Delinquency Prevention.

Henggeler, S. W. (1989). *Delinquency in adolescence.* Newbury Park, CA: Sage.

Herrenkohl, T. I., Maguin, E., Hill, K. G., Hawkins, J. D., & Abbott, R. D. (2001). Developmental risk factors for youth violence. *Journal of Adolescent Health, 26,* 176–186.

Hirschi, T., & Stark, R. (1969). Hellfire and delinquency. *Social Problems, 17,* 202–213.

Hundleby, J. D., & Mercer, G. W. (1987). Family and friends as social environments and their relationship to young adolescents' use of alcohol, tobacco, and marijuana. *Journal of Clinical Psychology, 44,* 125–134.

Inhelder, B., & Piaget, J. (1958). *The growth of logical thinking from childhood to adolescence.* New York: Basic Books.

Irwin, C. E., Jr., & Millstein, S. G. (1991). Risk taking behaviors during adolescence. In R. M. Lerner, A. C. Petersen, & J. Brooks-Gunn (Eds.), *Encyclopedia of adolescence* (pp. 934–943). New York: Garland.

Jessor, R. (1998). *New perspectives on adolescent behavior.* Cambridge, UK: Cambridge University Press.

Jessor, R., & Jessor, S. L. (1977). *Problem behavior and psychosocial development: A longitudinal study of youth.* New York: Academic Press.

Jessor, R., Turbin, M. S., & Costa, F. M. (1998). Risk and protection in successful outcomes among disadvantaged adolescents. *Applied Developmental Science, 2,* 194–208.

Jimerson, S. R. (1999). On the failure of failure: Examining the association between early grade retention and education and employment outcomes during late adolescence. *Journal of School Psychology, 37,* 243–272.

Johnson, L. D., O'Malley, P. M., & Bachman, J. G. (2001). *Monitoring the Future national survey results on drug use, 1975–2000: Vol. 1. Secondary school students* (NIH Publication No. 01-4924, pp. 1–226). Bethesda, MD: National Institute on Drug Abuse.

Kandel, D. B. (1991). Epidemiology and developmental stages of involvement in drug use. In R. M. Lerner, A. C. Petersen, & J. Brooks-Gunn (Eds.), *Encyclopedia of adolescence* (pp. 262–264). New York: Garland.

Kaput, J. (1991). Notations and representations as mediators of constructive processes. In E. von Glasersfeld (Ed.), *Radical constructivism in mathematics education* (pp. 53–74). Dordrecht, The Netherlands: Kluwer.

Kaput, J., Roschelle, J., & Stroup, W. (2000). SimCalc: Accelerating students' engagement with the mathematics of change. In M. Jacobson & R. Kozma (Eds.), *Innovations in science and mathematics education: Advanced designs for technologies of learning* (pp. 47–75). Mahwah, NJ: Erlbaum.

Karmiloff-Smith, A. (1979). Micro- and macro-developmental changes in language acquisition and other representation systems. *Cognitive Science, 3,* 91–118.

Kaufman, J., Cook, A., Arny, L., Jones, B., & Pittinsky, T. (1994). Problems defining resiliency: Illustrations from the study of maltreated children. *Development and Psychopathology, 6,* 215–229.

Kaufman, P., Kwon, J. Y., Klein, S., & Chapman, C. D. (1999). *Dropout rates in the United States: 1998.* Washington, DC: U.S. Department of Education.

Kerr, D. R., & Lester, F. K. (1986). An error analysis model for measurement. In D. Nelson & R. E. Reys (Eds.), *Measurement in school mathematics* (pp. 105–122). Reston, VA: National Council of Teachers of Mathematics.

Ketterlinus, R. D., Lamb, M. E., & Nitz, K. A. (1994). Adolescent nonsexual and sex-related problem behaviors: Their prevalence, consequences, and co-occurrence. In R. D. Ketterlinus & M. E. Lamb (Eds.), *Adolescent problem behaviors: Issues and research* (pp. 17–39). Hillsdale, NJ: Erlbaum.

Knuth, E. (2002). Teachers' conceptions of proof in the context of secondary school mathematics. *Journal of Mathematics Teacher Education, 5,* 61–88.

Koellner Clark, K., & Lesh, R. (in press). A modeling approach to describe teacher knowledge. In R. Lesh & H. M. Doerr (Eds.), *Beyond constructivism: Models and modeling perspectives on mathematics teaching, learning, and problem solving.* Mahwah, NJ: Erlbaum.

Kowaleski-Jones, L. (2000). Staying out of trouble: Community resources and problem behavior among high-risk adolescents. *Journal of Marriage and the Family, 62,* 449–464.

Kumpfer, K. L. (1999). Factors and processes contributing to resilience: The resilience framework. In M. D. Glantz & J. L. Johnson (Eds.), *Resiliency and development: Positive life adaptations* (pp. 179–224). New York: Kluwer Academic.

Latour, B. (1990). Drawing things together. In M. Lynch & S. Woolgar (Eds.), *Representation in scientific practice* (pp. 19–68). Cambridge, MA: MIT Press.

Lee, K., & Karmiloff-Smith, A. (1996). Notational development: The use of symbols. In E. C. Carterette & M. P. Friedman (Series Eds.) & R. Gelman & T. Au (Vol. Eds.), *Handbook of perception, Vol. 13, Perceptual and cognitive development* (pp. 185–211). New York: Academic Press.

Lehrer, R., Guckenberg, T., & Sancilio, L. (1988). Influences of Logo on children's intellectual development. In R. E. Meyer (Ed.), *Teaching and learning computer programming: Multiple research perspectives* (pp. 75–110). Hillsdale, NJ: Erlbaum.

Lehrer, R., Jaslow, L., & Curtis, C. (in press). Developing understanding of measurement in the elementary grades. *2003 NCTM Yearbook on Measurement.* Reston, VA: National Council of Teachers of Mathematics.

Lehrer, R., Schauble, L., Strom, D., & Pligge, M. (2001). Similarity of form and substance: Modeling material kind. In S. M. Carver & D. Klahr (Eds.), *Cognition and instruction: Twenty-five years of progress* (pp. 39–74). Mahwah, NJ: Erlbaum.

Lerner, R. M. (1995). *America's youth in crisis: Challenges and options for programs and policies.* Thousand Oaks, CA: Sage.

Lerner, R. M. (2002). *Adolescence: Development, diversity, context, and application.* Upper Saddle River, NJ: Prentice-Hall.

Lesh, R. (2002). Research design in mathematics education: Focusing on design experiments. In L. English (Ed.), *International Handbook of Research Design in Mathematics Education.* Hillsdale, NJ: Erlbaum.

Lesh, R., Cramer, K., Doerr, H. M., Post, T., & Zawojewski, J. S. (in press). Model development sequences. In R. Lesh & H. M. Doerr (Eds.), Mahwah, NJ: Erlbaum. *Beyond constructivism: Models and modeling perspectives on mathematics teaching, learning, and problem solving.*

Lesh, R., & Doerr, H. M. (in press). Foundations of a model and modeling perspective on mathematics teaching, learning, and problem solving. In R. Lesh & H. M. Doerr (Eds.), *Beyond constructivism: Models and modeling perspectives on mathematics teaching, learning, and problem solving.* Mahwah, NJ: Erlbaum.

Lesh, R., Hoover, M., Hole, B., Kelly, A., & Post, T. (2000). Principles for developing thought-revealing activities for students and teachers. In A. Kelly & R. Lesh (Eds.), *Handbook of research design in mathematics and science education* (pp. 591–646). Mahwah, NJ: Erlbaum.

Luster, T., & Small, S. A. (1994). Factors associated with sexual risk-taking behaviors among adolescents. *Journal of Marriage and the Family, 56,* 622–632.

Luthar, S. S. (1991). Vulnerability and resiliency: A study of high risk adolescents. *Child Development, 62,* 600–616.

Luthar, S. S., Cicchetti, D., & Becker, B. (2000). The construct of resilience: A critical evaluation and guidelines for future work. *Child Development, 71,* 543–562.

Luthar, S. S., & Cushing, G. (1999). Measurement issues in the empirical study of resiliency: An overview. In M. D. Glantz & J. L. Johnson (Eds.), *Resiliency and development: Positive life adaptations* (pp. 129–160). New York: Kluwer Academic.

Maher, C. A., & Martino, A. M. (1996). The development of the idea of mathematical proof: A 5-year case study. *Journal for Research in Mathematics Education, 27,* 194–214.

Masten, A. S. (1999). Resilience comes of age: Reflections on the past and outlook for the next generation of research. In M. D. Glantz & J. L. Johnson (Eds.), *Resiliency and development: Positive life adaptations* (pp. 281–295). New York: Kluwer Academic.

Masten, A. S. (2001). Ordinary magic: Resilience processes in development. *American Psychologist, 56,* 227–238.

Masten, A. S., & Coatsworth, J. D. (1998). The development of competence in favorable and unfavorable environments: Lessons from research on successful children. *American Psychologist, 53,* 205–220.

Masten, A. S., & Garmezy, N. (1985). Risk vulnerability and protective factors in developmental psychopathology. In B. B. Lahey & A. E. Kazidin (Eds.), *Advances in clinical child psychology* (Vol. 8, pp. 1–52). New York: Plenum Press.

Mahoney, J. L., & Stättin, H. (2000). Leisure activities and adolescent social behavior: The role of structure and social context. *Journal of Adolescence, 23,* 113–127.

McNeal, R. B. (1997). High school dropouts: A closer examination of school effects. *Social Science Quarterly, 78,* 209–222.

McNeal, R. B. (1999). Parental involvement as social capital: Differential effectiveness on science achievement, truancy, and dropping out. *Social Forces, 78,* 117–144.

Mead, G. H., (1910). Social consciousness and the consciousness of meaning. *Psychological Bulletin, 7,* 397–405.

Meschke, L. L., Bartholomae, S., & Zentall, S. R. (2000). Adolescent sexuality and parent-adolescent processes: Promoting healthy teen choices. *Family Relations, 49,* 143–154.

Moore, K. A., Driscoll, A. K., & Lindberg, L. D. (1998). *A statistical portrait of adolescent sex, contraception, and childbearing.* Washington, DC: National Campaign to Prevent Teenage Pregnancy.

Mortimer, J. T., & Johnson, M. K. (1998). New perspectives on adolescent work and the transition to adulthood. In R. Jessor (Ed.), *New perspectives on adolescent risk taking behaviors* (pp. 425–496). Cambridge, UK: Cambridge University Press.

Moschkovich, J. N. (2002). Bringing together workplace and academic mathematical practices during classroom assessments. In M. E. Brenner & J. N. Moschkovich (Eds.), *Everyday and Academic Mathematics in the Classroom.* Reston, VA: National Council of Teachers of Mathematics.

National Research Council. (1993). *Losing generations: Adolescents in high risk settings.* Washington, DC: National Academy Press.

Newcomb, M. D., Maddahian, E., Skager, E., & Bentler, P. M. (1987). Substance abuse and psychosocial risk factors among teenagers: Associations with sex, age, ethnicity, and type of school. *American Journal of Drug and Alcohol Abuse, 13,* 413–433.

Noss, R. (1987). Children's learning of geometrical concepts through Logo. *Journal for Research in Mathematics Education, 18,* 343–362.

Ochs, E., Gonzales, P., & Jacoby, S. (1996). "When I come down I'm in the domain state": Grammar and graphic representation in the interpretive activity of physicists. In E. Ochs, E. A. Schegloff, & S. A. Thompson (Eds.), *Interaction and grammar* (pp. 328–369). Cambridge: Cambridge University Press.

Office of Juvenile Justice and Delinquency Prevention. (2001). *OJJDP Research 2000.* Washington, DC: U.S. Department of Justice.

Olive, J. (1991). LOGO programming and geometric understanding: An in-depth study. *Journal for Research in Mathematics Education, 22,* 90–111.

Olive, J. (1998). Opportunities to explore and integrate mathematics with the Geometer's Sketchpad. In R. Lehrer & D. Chazan (Eds.), *Designing learning environments for developing understanding of geometry and space* (pp. 395–417). Mahwah, NJ: Erlbaum.

Orr, D. P., Wilbrandt, M. L., Brack, C. J., Rauch, S. P., & Ingersoll, G. M. (1989). Reported sexual behaviors and self esteem among young adolescents. *American Journal of Diseases in Children, 143,* 86–90.

Ozer, E. M., Brindis, C. D. Millstein, S. G., Knop, D. K., & Irwin, C. E. (1998). *America's adolescents: Are they healthy?* San Francisco: University of California.

Pakiz, B., Reinherz, H. Z., & Frost, A. K. (1992). Antisocial behavior in adolescence: A community study. *Journal of Early Adolescence, 12,* 300–313.

Perkins, D. F. (1995). *An examination of the organismic, behavioral, and contextual covariates of risk behaviors among diverse groups of adolescents.* Unpublished doctoral dissertation. University Park, PA: The Pennsylvania State University.

Perkins, D. F., Haas, B., & Keith, J. G. (1997). An integration of positive youth development within the runaway youth and homeless shelter system. *New Designs for Youth Development, 13,* 36–41.

Perkins, D. F., Luster, T., Villarruel, F. A., & Small, S. (1998). An ecological risk-factor examination of adolescents' sexual activity in three ethnic groups. *Journal of Marriage and the Family, 60,* 660–673.

Perry, C. L. (2000). Preadolescent and adolescent influences on health. In B. D. Smedley & S. L. Syme (Eds.), *Promoting health: Intervention strategies from social and behavioral research* (pp. 217–253). Washington, DC: National Academy Press.

Piaget, J. (1970). *Genetic epistemology.* New York: Norton.

Pong, S. L., & Ju, D.-B. (2000). The effects of change in family structure and income on dropping out of middle and high school. *Journal of Family Issues, 21,* 147–169.

Powell-Cope, G. M., & Eggert, L. L. (1994). Psychosocial risk and protective factors: Potential high school dropouts versus typical youth. In R. C. Moss (Ed.), *Using what we know about at-risk youth: Lessons from the field* (pp. 23–51). Lancaster, PA: Technomic.

Reid, D. A. (2002). Conjectures and refutations in grade 5 mathematics. *Journal for Research in Mathematics Education, 33,* 90–111.

Resnick, M. D., Bearman, P. S., Blum, R. W., Bauman, K. E., Harris, K. M., Jones, J., Tabor, J., Beuhring, T., Sieving, R. E., Shew, M., Ireland, M., Bearinger, L. H., & Udry, J. R. (1997). Protecting adolescents from harm: Findings from the National Longitudinal Study on Adolescent Health. *Journal of American Medical Association, 278,* 823–832.

Rips, L. J., & Marcus, S. L. (1976). Suppositions and the analysis of conditional sentences. In M. A. Just & P. A. Carpenter (Eds.), *Cognitive processes in comprehension* (pp. 185–220). Hillsdale, NJ: Erlbaum.

Roderick, M., Bryk, A. S., Jacob, B. A., Easton, J. Q., & Allensworth, E. (1999). *Ending social promotion: Results from the first two years.* Chicago: Consortium on Chicago School Research.

Rosch, E. H. (1973). Natural categories. *Cognitive Psychology, 4,* 328–350.

Rumberger, R. W. (2001, January 13). *Why students drop out of school and what can be done.* A paper prepared for the conference, "Dropouts in America: How Severe is the Problem? What Do We Know About Intervention and Prevention?" Harvard University.

Rumberger, R. W., & Thomas, S. L. (2000). The distribution of dropout and turnover rates among urban and suburban high schools. *Sociology of Education, 73,* 39–67.

Rutter, M. (1979). Protective factors in children's response to stress and disadvantage. In M. W. Kent, & J. E. Rolf (Eds.), *Primary prevention of psychopathology: Vol. 3. Social competence in children* (pp. 49–74). Hanover, NH: University Press of New England.

Rutter, M. (1985). Resilience in the face of adversity: Protective factors and resistance to psychiatric disorder. *British Journal of Psychiatry, 147,* 598–611.

Rutter, M. (1987). Psychosocial resilience and protective factors. *American Journal of Orthopsychiatry, 57,* 316–331.

Rutter, M. (1993). Resilience: Some conceptual considerations. *Journal of Adolescent Health, 14,* 626–631.

Rutter, M. (1997). Nature-nurture integration: The example of anti-social behavior. *American Psychologist, 52,* 390–398.

Schattschneider, D. (1997). Escher's combinatorial patterns. *Electronic Journal of Combinatorics, 4,* 1–31.

Schneirla, T. C. (1957). The concept of development in comparative psychology. In D. B. Harris (Ed.), *The concept of development* (pp. 78–108). Minneapolis, MN: University of Minnesota Press.

Schorr, L. B. (1988). *Within our reach: Breaking the cycle of disadvantage.* New York: Doubleday.

Scheer, S. D., Borden, L. M., & Donnermeyer, J. F. (2000). The relationship between family factors and adolescent substance use in rural, suburban, and urban settings. *Journal of Child and Family Studies, 9*(1), 105–115.

Simmons, R. G., & Blyth, D. A. (1987). *Moving into adolescence: The impact of pubertal change and school context.* New York: Aldine DeGruyter.

Simmons, R. G., & Zhou, Y. (1993). Racial, school, and family context among adolescents. In R. K. Silbereisen & E. Todt (Eds.), *Adolescence in context: The interplay of family, school, peers, and work in adjustment* (pp. 149–175). New York: Springer.

Small, S. A., & Luster, T. (1994). Adolescent sexual activity: An ecological, risk-factor approach. *Journal of Marriage and Family, 56,* 181–192.

Smith, J. P. (1999). Tracking the mathematics of automobile production: Are schools failing to prepare students for work? *American Educational Research Journal, 36,* 835–878.

Smith, M. S., & Shepard, L. (1989). Flunking grades: A recapitulation. In L. Shepard & M. Smith (Eds.), *Flunking grades: Research on policies and retention* (pp. 214–236). Philadelphia, PA: Falmer Press.

Snyder, H. (2000). *Juvenile arrests: 1999. Juvenile Justice Bulletin, December.* Washington, DC: Office of Juvenile Justice and Delinquency Prevention.

Sowder, L. (1994). *University faculty views about mathematics' majors understanding of proof.* San Diego, CA: San Diego State University, Dept. of Math and Computer Science.

Spillane, J. P., & Zeuli, J. S. (1999). Reform and teaching: Exploring patterns of practice in the context of national and state mathematics reforms. *Educational Evaluation and Policy Analysis, 21*, 1–27.

Stättin, H., & Magnusson, D. (1990). *Pubertal maturation in female development.* Hillsdale, NJ: Erlbaum.

Steinberg, L. D. (1987). Single parents, stepparents, and the susceptibility of adolescents to peer pressure. *Child Development, 58,* 269–275.

Steinberg, L., & Avenevoli, S. (1998). Disengagement from school and problem behavior in adolescence: A developmental-contextual analysis of the influences of family and part time work. In R. Jessor (Ed.), *New perspectives on adolescent risk taking behaviors* (pp. 392–424). Cambridge, UK: Cambridge University Press.

Steinberg, L. D., & Darling, N. (1993). The broader context of social influence in adolescence. In R. K. Silbereisen, & E. Todt (Eds.), *Adolescence in context: The interplay of family, school, peers, and work in adjustment* (pp. 25–45). New York: Springer.

Taylor, C. S. (1990). *Dangerous society.* East Lansing: Michigan State University Press.

Terry, E., & Manlove, J. (2000). Trends in sexual activity and contraceptive use among adolescent. *Child Trends Research Brief.* Washington, DC: Child Trends.

Tolan, P. (1988). Socioeconomic, family, and social stress correlates of adolescent antisocial and delinquent behavior. *Journal of Abnormal Child Psychology, 16,* 317–333.

United States Department of Education, National Center for Education Statistics. (1997). *Drop out rates in the United States: 1995.* Washington, DC: U.S. Government Printing Office.

United States Department of Education, National Center for Education Statistics. (2000a). *The condition of education, 2000.* Washington, DC: U.S. Government Printing Office.

United States Department of Education, National Center for Education Statistics. (2000b). *Digest of Education Statistics, 1999.* Washington, DC: U.S. Government Printing Office.

Ventura, S. J., Mosher, W. D., Curtin, S. C., Abma, J. C., Henshaw, S. (1999, December). Highlights of trends in pregnancies and pregnancy rates by outcome: estimates for the United States, 1976–96. *National Vital Statistics Report, 15, 47*(29), 1–9.

Walkerdine, V. (1988). *The mastery of reason.* London: Routledge.

Wang, M. C., Haertel, G. D., & Walberg,, H. J. (1999). Psychological and educational resilience. In A. J. Reynolds, H. J. Walberg, & R. P. Weissberg (Eds.), *Promoting positive outcomes: Issues in children's and families' lives* (pp. 329–365). Washington, DC: Child Welfare League of America.

Washburn, D. K., & Crowe, D. W. (1988). *Symmetries of culture: Theory and practice of plane pattern analysis.* Seattle: University of Washington Press.

Werner, E., & Smith, R. (1992). *Overcoming the odds: High risk children from birth to adulthood.* Ithaca, NY: Cornell University.

Zech, L., Vye, N. J., Baransford, J. D., Goldman, S. R., Barron, B. J., Schwartz, D. L., Kisst-Hackett, R., Mayfield-Stewart, C., & The Cognition and Technology Group (1998). In R. Lehrer & D. Chazan (Eds.), *Designing learning environments for developing understanding of geometry and space* (pp. 439–463). Mahwah, NJ: Erlbaum.

Zimmerman, M. A., & Arunkumar, R. (1994). Resiliency research: Implications for schools and policy. *Social Policy Report, 8,* 1–17.

Zucker, R. A., Fitzgerald, H. E., & Moses, H. D. (1995). Emergence of alcohol problems and the several alcoholisms: A developmental perspective on etiologic theory and life course trajectory. In D. Cicchetti & D. J. Cohen (Eds.), *Developmental psychopathology: Risk, disorder, and adaptation* (pp. 677–711). New York: Wiley.

CHAPTER 16

Relationships With Parents and Peers in Adolescence

MARGARET KERR, HÅKAN STATTIN, GRETCHEN BIESECKER, AND LAURA FERRER-WREDER

How do parents and peers influence adolescent development? At the beginning of the twenty-first century, what is *unknown* about this topic far outweighs what is known; in this chapter, we argue that this is partly because of the question itself. As it is phrased, the question assumes that parents and peers influence adolescent development separately in a unidirectional fashion. These assumptions might actually block the way to a true understanding of the roles of parents and peers in adolescent development; such assumptions ignore the interrelatedness between parent and peer relationships and the roles that adolescents play as active agents in these relationships.

In this chapter, we start with certain assumptions about adolescents' relationships with parents and peers—assumptions that have not necessarily been incorporated into the research in these areas. First, we assume that these relationships are *bidirectional,* meaning that adolescents are not just passively influenced by the important people in their lives; they are active agents in choosing with whom they spend time, and they evoke certain reactions from people. Second, we assume that relationships are not simply related to adjustment but are themselves forms of adjustment. Parenting behaviors and peer relations do not just *produce* adjustment; they are also indicators and results of adjustment. Finally, we assume that parent and peer relationships are linked to each other. The form and quality of relationships with parents will

determine which peer contexts the adolescent chooses, and that choice will evoke reactions from parents that will affect the parent-child relationship. In short, we argue that adolescents play active roles in choosing and shaping their relationships with parents and peers.

CURRENT MODELS AND RESEARCH

There are large bodies of research on both parenting and peer relationships. Several well-defined causal models are currently used in research on parenting, but this is less true in peer research. The peer literature is defined less by clear causal models and more by characteristics of the particular peers that are considered, such as peer groups and best friends. Because these literatures are largely separate, we deal with them separately in the following sections.

Parenting Models

In this section, we discuss several of the most influential theoretical models dealing with parenting of adolescents. We do not endeavor to review all of the research that has been done on parenting of adolescents. Rather, we focus on models that have had the widest influence on the broad conclusions that have been drawn about parenting of adolescents—which parenting strategies are effective and why—and which lie behind the practical advice that parents often receive. In turn, for each model we take the most influential research as representative of the model.

Acknowledgments: Work on this chapter was supported by grants from the Swedish Research Council and The Bank of Sweden Tercentenary Foundation.

The Parenting Styles Model

The parenting styles model has spawned a vast literature related to both child and adolescent development. Different parenting styles instruments have been created, and scores of empirical studies have been done. For the present purposes, we focus on the work that has been the most influential for adolescent research. This, of course, means the theoretical and empirical work of Baumrind and the theoretical work of Maccoby and Martin. We consider, in addition, the empirical work on adolescence that has appeared in flagship developmental journals such as *Child Development* and *Developmental Psychology,* and much of that has come from the Steinberg and Dornbusch research groups.

Background. The parenting styles model is based on the theoretical ideas originally presented by Baumrind (1967) and later revised by Maccoby and Martin (1983). Baumrind grouped nursery-school children according to their social adjustment and then determined how the parents of those groups differed. Her initial results were that (a) "children who were most self-reliant, self-controlled, explorative, and content" had parents who were "controlling and demanding; but they were also warm, rational, and receptive to the child's communication;" (b) "children who . . . were discontent, withdrawn, and distrustful" had parents who were "detached and controlling, and somewhat less warm than other parents;" and (c) "the least self-reliant, explorative, and self-controlled children" had parents who were "noncontrolling, nondemanding, and relatively warm" (Baumrind, 1971, pp. 1–2). Baumrind termed these three groups of parents *authoritative, authoritarian,* and *permissive,* respectively. Believing that parental control was particularly important, she further articulated the qualititative differences between authoritative and authoritarian parents' control strategies (Baumrind, 1968). Authoritative parents, according to Baumrind, communicated with the child about the demands that they placed on the child, whereas authoritarian parents tended to shut down communication about their demands.

Later, Maccoby and Martin (1983) argued that Baumrind's three styles and a wealth of other findings in the parenting literature could be roughly subsumed into a four-field table, with one axis contrasting parents who are controlling and demanding with those who are not and the other contrasting parents who are warm, responsive, and child-centered with those who are not. To their credit, Maccoby and Martin related these constructs more broadly to the psychological literature, and they suggested mechanisms through which such constructs might work. For instance, responsiveness, according to them, meant a willingness to respond to the child's signals. It was closer to the ideas of contingent responsiveness in

attachment theory, to Pulkkinen's (1982) child centeredness, or to the concept of reinforcement in learning theory than it was to warmth in the sense of unconditional, noncontingent expressions of love and support. Based on Seligman's (1975) learned-helplessness studies, they suggested that parents' responsiveness should give the *child* a sense of control that—in authoritative families—would be balanced by the control that parents exerted over the child. Bidirectional communication between parents and child was an essential part of this process.

Yet although the four-field table has been widely used in the parenting styles research that has followed, in conceptual discussions of authoritativeness, communication has faded as an important feature and the concepts of warmth and responsiveness have been blurred. In this body of work, the major conceptual difference between authoritative and authoritarian parents is the presence or absence of warmth along with the high levels of control that both types of parents are thought to exert over their children.

Extensions of the Parenting Styles Model. More recently, parenting styles have been distinguished from parenting practices in an attempt to conceptually refine the model and improve the possibilities for discovering mechanisms (Darling & Steinberg, 1993). The argument was that parenting style should be thought of as the general emotional climate that parents create, whereas practices should be recognized as the goal-directed behaviors in which parents engage in order to change or shape the child's behavior. Practices can be more or less effective depending upon the emotional climate that parents have set up, because the emotional climate will make the child more or less receptive to being shaped by the practices.

In the empirical research that has followed this original, theoretical work, however, the differentiation between styles and practices is unclear. Sometimes, exactly the same full scales as had previously been used to measure styles are used again and labeled *practices* (e.g., Avenevoli, Sessa, & Steinberg, 1999). Other times, the majority of items in the measures of practices are identical or nearly identical to items previously used to measure parenting styles (e.g., B. B. Brown, Mounts, Lamborn, & Steinberg, 1993). Furthermore, it is difficult to look at these measures and determine whether they are conceptually tapping styles or practices.

Limitations of the Parenting Styles Model. We introduce the limitations of the parenting styles model with a history of parenting styles research that might have been. The story is fiction, but we tell it in order to point out how far the actual history of parenting styles research is from ideal. Our story anticipates the critique that follows, but it also points out that the division of that critique into subtopics is somewhat artificial because the different limitations are all interrelated.

A Tale of Parenting Styles Research That We Wish We Could Tell.   Once upon a time, more than 30 years ago, a researcher named Baumrind published her first works on parenting style. During the years that have followed, the original ideas have been refined so much that they are barely recognizable, but they are universally seen as the beginning of what is now a rich understanding of the parent-child interaction processes that are involved in development. These processes used to be called *parenting,* but that term is now recognized as simplistic and misleading because it denotes only part of the process. The search for knowledge in this area proceeded much like one would expect of a scientific endeavor. Baumrind's first studies were somewhat descriptive. She reported that in a small sample of mostly wealthy, white families, there was a covariation between broad patterns of parents' behaviors and broad patterns of children's behaviors. Her explanations of these findings assumed that parents with certain features had shaped certain behaviors in their children, mainly through behavioral mechanisms. Naturally, the untested assumptions and missing links in her logic were immediately pointed out, and researchers began working swiftly to (a) break down the global, conceptually heterogeneous parenting styles into their simplest, most basic elements; (b) develop construct-valid measures of those basic elements and clear, testable explanations of the mechanisms involved; (c) determine whether any of the children's characteristics—or any unrecognized third variables—might be driving Baumrind's correlational findings; and (d) determine whether any causal relations existed between parents' and children's characteristics, what the directions of effects were, whether they should be seen as main effects or interactions, and what mechanisms were involved, including moderating and mediating effects. These efforts helped to build an understanding of the complex links between parents' behaviors and children's adjustment—and everyone lived happily ever after. In the following section we present a detailed discussion of the more serious shortcomings in the parenting styles research. We limit our critique to the major theoretical works and the empirical studies that have been published in major journals. In the vast literature that exists outside of these major works, the same problems exist, often in more extreme forms.

What's Causing What?   Correlation does not prove causality. This is what students learn in their first psychology course. Yet one of the most striking features of the parenting styles literature, from Baumrind's early works to the present, is the assumption that causality is known—parents, through their attitudes and behaviors, shape, mold, or otherwise produce children with certain characteristics. Examples can be found in the introduction and discussion sections of nearly every article on parenting styles—sometimes even in the titles. (Italics ours in these quotations.)

> "*Effects* of Authoritative Parental Control on Child Behavior." (Baumrind, 1966, title)
> "The *Influence* of Parenting Style on Adolescent Competence and Substance Use." (Baumrind, 1991, title)
> "The success of authoritative parents in *protecting* their adolescents from problem drug use and in *generating* competence should be emphasized . . . Unlike any other pattern, authoritative upbringing . . . consistently *generated* competence and *deterred* problem behavior." (Baumrind, 1991, p. 91)

Multiple examples can easily be found in a single article (e.g., Glasgow, Dornbusch, Troyer, Steinberg, & Ritter, 1997):

> "the beneficial *influence* of authoritative parenting does not diminish during adolescence" (p. 508)
> "authoritative parenting *promotes* academic success through a positive effect on adolescents' psychological orientation toward work" (p. 509)
> "Different constellations of parental behaviors and affective expressions *produce* variations in adolescents' perceptions of their own performance capacities . . . Among the four distinct parenting styles, authoritative parenting is the most successful in *fostering* personal and social responsibility in adolescents, without *limiting* their emerging autonomy and individuality" (p. 521)
> "characteristics of authoritative parenting *contribute* to the development of instrumental competence" (p. 511)
> "Indulgent parenting *fosters* instrumental competence . . . but to a lesser degree than authoritative parenting" (p. 511)
> "[this] characteristic of authoritarian parents *thwarts* the development of instrumental competence in adolescents" (p. 511)
> "use of extrinsic reinforcements . . . *undermines* adolescents' perceptions of competence" (p. 511)

The causality assumption began with Baumrind's original identification of parenting styles, because she identified parenting behaviors and child characteristics that covaried and then gave explanations for that covariation that implicitly and explicitly made parents the causal agents (e.g., Baumrind, 1966; Baumrind & Black, 1967). Perhaps this was a reflection of the behaviorist leanings of Baumrind and other parenting styles researchers, or perhaps it was a reflection of the assumptions of the broader culture, as has been suggested earlier (Bell, 1968). At any rate, the assumption that causality is known has continued, and the language seems to have gotten progressively stronger with time, as though the accumulation of correlational results could somehow prove causality.

Although longitudinal studies of parenting styles have been conducted, rarely have the data been used to determine whether causality might be bidirectional. They have instead focused on arguing for parent-to-child effects. For example, a cross-lagged design with parenting and child-behavior measures at two points in time could potentially be used to provide information about whether the correlations between adolescent adjustment and parenting represent unidirectional or bidirectional effects. When only half of this pattern is tested with only parenting as the earlier predictor (e.g., Steinberg, Lamborn, Darling, Mounts, & Dornbusch, 1994), it is impossible to find a bidirectional effect. The use of this design reveals a disinterest in potential bidirectional effects.

Parenting styles researchers have held to a unidirectional, causal interpretation of their correlational findings in spite of growing literatures that present convincing alternative views. For instance, a number of scholars have offered alternative interpretations of the correlations between parents' and children's behaviors that exist in the literature, including—but not limited to—the parenting styles literature (e.g., Bell, 1968; C. Lewis, 1981; Harris, 1995, 1998). At about the same time that Baumrind published her first parenting styles study, Bell (1968) published a review paper questioning the unidirectional interpretations that had been made in socialization studies in general. He cited many examples of experimental findings in which parents' and other adults' behaviors had changed in response to certain children's behaviors; he argued that because of these findings, parent-child correlations should not be interpreted as only parent-to-child effects.

Later, C. Lewis (1981) questioned the directionality assumption in Baumrind's published studies—particularly Baumrind's claim that parental control produced well-adjusted children. She pointed out that in Baumrind's studies it was impossible to tell whether the parental control measures tapped control or simply harmonious relationships, for which the child's temperament could be as important as the parents' ways of dealing with the child (see Baumrind, 1983, for a reply). Furthermore, Lewis pointed out that in Baumrind's published studies the items that really distinguished the parents of competent children from all other groups of parents had nothing to do with the use of control. The strongest predictors were "respect the child's decision," "use reason to obtain compliance," "encourage verbal give and take," and "satisfy child," (C. Lewis, 1981, p. 562), which leaves open the possibility that competence had developed through some process other than parental control. This is especially evident because items such as *respect* and *use reason* may depend on child characteristics.

More recently, Harris (1995, 1998) offered a controversial critique of the assumption that parents influence children in unidirectional fashion. Her critique 'like Bell's and Lewis's, covered the parenting literature more broadly, and was not limited to parenting styles. Concerning the parenting styles findings, however, she offered a reverse-causality explanation for the correlations between authoritative parenting and good child adjustment. She argued that most parents in Western cultures try to be authoritative because they know that is what parents "should" be. If the child behaves well (i.e., is well-adjusted), then parents have no reason to change their strategy. If the child is difficult to manage (i.e., not well-adjusted), however, then they have to become more controlling and less democratic (i.e., more authoritarian). Hence, according to this reinterpretation, parents adjust to the child's behavior rather than producing it, and this adjustment explains the correlation between parenting styles and children's behavior.

In addition, in the parenting literature more broadly there are now numerous experimental and longitudinal studies—from which causality can actually be inferred—that show very clearly that parents and other adults do sometimes react to children's characteristics and adjust their behavior accordingly (e.g., Anderson, Lytton, & Romney, 1986; Bell & Chapman, 1986 for a review; Buss, 1981; Dix, Ruble, Grusec, & Nixon, 1986; Lerner & Spanier, 1978; M. Lewis & Rosenblum, 1974; Mulhern & Passman, 1981; Passman & Blackwelder, 1981) or that show good evidence for bidirectional effects (e.g., Hastings & Rubin, 1999; Kochanska, 1998; Lytton, 1990, 2000; Mink & Nihira, 1986; Stice & Barrera, 1995).

Finally, behavioral genetic studies also cast reasonable doubt on the unidirectional assumption (e.g., Ge et al., 1996; Reiss, Neiderhiser, Hetherington, & Plomin, 2000). They offer evidence that the links between parenting behaviors and children's adjustment are affected by the child's genetic makeup from both directions. First, the child's genetic makeup—expressed in temperament and dispositions—evokes certain parenting behaviors, which then influence the child's adjustment. Second, the child's genetic makeup—again expressed in temperament and dispositions—affects adjustment directly, and that influences how parents react to the child (parenting behaviors). Twin, adoption, and sibling studies also suggest that parents react to their child's unique genetic makeup in that children's unique experiences are more predictive of adjustment than are the experiences they share with their siblings (i.e., parenting factors; Plomin & Daniels, 1987; Plomin, Reiss, Hetherington, & Howe, 1994).

Let us be clear. We are *not* arguing that solely child-to-parent effects are driving the correlations between parenting styles and child adjustment. We do argue, however, that there is enough evidence that child-to-parent effects exist and that they cannot be discounted. In our view, a bidirectional model of parent-adolescent relationships is needed. Any model that takes a unidirectional view—parent-to-child or child-to-parent—is of limited usefulness.

What's Driving the Results?   This is another question that has not been pursued rigorously. Actually, it is a whole complex series of questions about the basic constructs, the measures, and the mechanisms through which the basic constructs are thought to work. Concerning the *basic constructs,* even if one limits oneself to the major publications in this area, one can end up wondering *what* is *authoritative parenting?* Is it as complex as Maccoby and Martin (1983) theorized, involving firm control, demands for mature behavior, emotional warmth, responsiveness to the child's expressed needs and desires, being encouraging of bidirectional communication and devoted to democratic decision-making, and being child- rather than parent-centered? Or is it as simple as warmth-involvement and strictness-supervision (e.g., Lamborn, Mounts, Steinberg, & Dornbusch, 1991; Steinberg et al., 1994)? Concerning the *measures,* if authoritative parenting is as simple as warmth-involvement and strictness-supervision, then why do items that specifically tap communication appear on both types of scales? And why, for example, is knowing a lot about who the child's friends are a warmth-involvement item, whereas knowing a lot about what the child does after school and in his or her free time is a strictness-supervision item (e.g., Lamborn et al., 1991; Steinberg et al., 1994)? Indeed, how is knowing (an end product) a measure of either warmth or strictness? Moreover (although a more detailed discussion of this issue is beyond the scope of this chapter), one gets an even more confusing picture if one looks at the parenting styles literature as a whole—and not just at the major theoretical works and the empirical studies in flagship journals.

Then, concerning *mechanisms,* without having these construct and measurement issues sorted out, it is difficult to begin to sort out the influences of the various elements, how many of the features of the different styles are really important, the direction of effects, and whether they work additively or interactively. Indeed, parenting styles researchers have seemed fairly unconcerned about demonstrating empirically *why* or *how* authoritative parenting might work. The literature abounds with post hoc explanations and untested assumptions. Baumrind clearly favored learning explanations. In her view, authoritative parents modeled desirable behavior through their willingness to communicate; created classically conditioned good feelings through their

warmth and acceptance that would improve their ability to reinforce their children's desirable behavior; and provided appropriate reinforcements and limits through their firm behavioral control (Baumrind, 1971). Still, these explanations remained untested.

The rare studies that have tried to look at mechanisms have been weak in terms of design. For instance, one study tried to test the idea that the connection between authoritative parenting and school performance was due to the fact that authoritative parents foster the right attributional styles in children, which in turn are linked to school performance (Glasgow et al., 1997). But the hypothesized mechanism, *fostering,* was never examined. Only the concurrent correlation between styles and attributions was examined; again, this correlation between a parenting measure and a child behavior was assumed to represent a causal connection in which parents had fostered the attributional style. Hence, this study was not really a test of a mechanism.

Summary.   The parenting styles model is a static, unidirectional view of socialization in the family context. It is static in that it assumes that parents *are* a certain way throughout the child's life, and that their way of being produces—at some undefined point in time—a child with certain characteristics. Furthermore, parents are assumed to have the same style with each child. There is no recognition that parenting might be a developmental process in which parents learn what works and does not work with each child, or in which they develop certain undesirable parenting behaviors through repeated frustrations with a difficult child—as stated by one of the most prominent parenting styles research groups: "Parenting style is a characteristic of the parent (i.e., it is a feature of the child's social environment), independent of characteristics of the developing person" (Darling & Steinberg, 1993, p. 487). Under assumptions such as these, the parenting styles paradigm can bring us no further toward understanding the bidirectional processes operating over time between parents and children that are inextricably linked to the child's adjustment.

The Attachment Model

Attachment theory (Bowlby, 1969/1982) does offer a way of looking at relationships that could be truly dyadic. It views the emotional bond between parents and children as a feedback system, controlling a balance between children's desires for closeness with parents and those for exploring the world. This has been likened to the physiological control systems that maintain physiological measures—such as blood pressure and body temperature—within set limits

(Bowlby, 1988). According to this theory, optimally, during times of stress, infants and adolescents will seek comfort from their caregivers, and parents will give their children a sense of security—a feeling that all is well (Ainsworth, 1990). The need to be close to parents in times of distress—and for parents to respond to their children's distress—are theorized to be biologically based to promote survival of the species. The attachment system draws parents and children together, therefore, to protect children from harm. The positive emotions that can be derived from closeness, such as a sense of security, make attachment behaviors rewarding to both parents and children.

A balance between emerging independence and closeness with parents is a central feature of attachment theory and particularly relevant as children grow into adolescence. Children and parents are increasingly able to take each other's perspectives into consideration and to negotiate in their relationship. Adolescents continue to use parents as a secure base for exploration, using temporary returns to the safe haven of parents to help them, particularly in times of distress, illness, fear, or stress (Marvin & Britner, 1999). The emotional availability of the attachment figure rather than physical proximity becomes the more frequent goal of the attachment system. Attachment experiences not only provide a secure base for adolescents to explore their talents and experiences in a variety of contexts, but such experiences also prepare adolescents to become socially connected with others and to learn how to be caregivers for others (Crittenden, 1992).

Not all attachment relationships, however, provide a truly secure base. The security of attachment relationships can be distinguished by the ways that members of the dyad—such as a parent and child—respond to each other during times of distress. Attachment theory predicts that parents of securely attached children respond consistently and sensitively (Ainsworth, Blehar, Waters, & Wall, 1978). Secure attachments are characterized by open, flexible communication between parents and children around emotion signals, promoting a balance and range of positive and negative emotions (Bowlby, 1988; Cassidy, 1994). Insecure attachments, in contrast, reveal problematic ways of communicating emotions—partners may exhibit a restricted range of emotions or heighten their displays of emotion (Bowlby, 1988; Cassidy, 1994). Parents of insecurely attached children, for example, may respond inconsistently to expressions of distress, ignore them, or act punitively.

Attachment theory suggests that the quality of individuals' interactions with caregivers over time creates a model of how relationships work and of their own value in relationships (Bowlby, 1969/1982; Bretherton, 1985). These cognitive models are thought to guide feelings, behaviors, and how information about the world is processed. Bowlby described these representations of attachment relationships as *working models* because he viewed them as being open to new input and modification as circumstances and relationships change. Individuals are believed to learn both sides of the attachment relationship, and children are motivated to reenact both sides of their attachment relationship in their other relationships with peers, teachers, and others (Sroufe & Fleeson, 1986). Children learn, for instance, whether important people in their lives will come to their aid when they need help and ways of responding to the distress of others.

This aspect of attachment theory offers a perspective to understanding relations among relationships with parents, peers, and other significant people in children's lives. As adolescents begin to spend more time with peers of their own choosing, working models are hypothesized to influence their selection of friends and the quality of their peer interactions. Adolescents are likely to choose friends as attachment figures who fit with their existing working models. The central importance of peers in the lives of adolescents has received a great deal of attention (Allen, Moore, Kuperminc, & Bell, 1998; Csikszenthmihalyi & Larson, 1984), with intimacy in friendships being described as one of the defining characteristics of this age group (Buhrmester, 1990; Sullivan, 1953). The exceptional intensity of adolescent peer relationships has in fact been likened to that of attachment relationships (Ainsworth, 1989; Ainsworth & Marvin, 1995; Allen et al., 1998; Bowlby, 1988).

Furthermore, ways of communicating in attachment relationships appear relevant to understanding adolescents' adjustment (Allen, Aber, & Leadbeater, 1990; Cooper, Shaver, & Collins, 1998; Engels, Finkenauer, Meeus, & Dekovic, 2001) and emotion regulation (Biesecker, 2001; Kobak & Sceery, 1988; Zimmermann, Maier, Winter, & Grossmann, 2001). Adolescents using insecure attachment strategies may have difficulties understanding their own and others' emotions, leaving them more vulnerable to misinterpreting ambiguous situations as hostile and less able to repair disruptions in relationships (Kobak & Cole, 1994). These misinterpretations may lead to hostile or aggressive actions, withdrawal from peers, or other behaviors that undermine the formation of healthy relationships and foster negative feelings about the self. Therefore, understanding the role of these insecure attachment strategies—or ways of communicating and responding to feelings of distress—may shed some light on certain adolescents' "problem behaviors" (Allen et al., 1990) such as substance abuse and conduct disorder.

The attachment model has come further than the other models reviewed here have in portraying the adolescent as an active agent in his or her own adjustment and in trying to explain the links between parent and peer relationships. This model, however, suffers from some of the same limitations as the other parenting models. First, until recently there has been a tendency to view parent relations separately from other relationship experiences. We need more information about how attachment relationships with mothers *and* fathers, siblings, extended family, peers, and romantic partners relate, interact, and possibly modify each other over time.

A second issue is that the different measures used to assess attachment at different ages—particularly after early childhood—have not always demonstrated conceptual equivalence or construct validity. A variety of techniques have been developed to tap attachment in adolescence and adulthood, most of which are based on interviews and self-reports (e.g., Bartholomew & Horowitz, 1991; Brennan, Clark, & Shaver, 1998; Collins & Read, 1990; C. George, Kaplan, & Main, 1985; Hazan & Shaver, 1987; Kenny, 1987), but there is a lack of convergence about a common, reliable method. Although adult measures share theoretical links with measures used in infancy and childhood, the underlying approaches can differ radically between them; little research has been conducted or published to address relations between these different measures. These sorts of psychometric issues make it difficult for attachment researchers to ensure that they are communicating about the same constructs (Brennan et al., 1998). A piece of this problem is an overly broad use of the term *attachment* to encompass more general qualities of the parent-child relationship. Although attachment may be associated with other aspects of parenting, researchers need to make sure that they mean the same thing when they measure it.

Last, attachment researchers are as likely as other parenting researchers are to look almost exclusively at parent effects unless the focus of research is to study certain child influences on the attachment relationship, such as infant temperament (Calkins & Fox, 1992; Crockenberg, 1981; Goldsmith & Alansky, 1987; Susman-Stillman, Kalkose, Egeland, & Waldman, 1996) or Down Syndrome (Ganiban, Barnett, & Cicchetti, 2000; Thompson, Cicchetti, Lamb, & Malkin, 1985). Otherwise, the direction of causality between the quality of attachment relationships and other constructs is almost always examined in one way, suggesting attachment as a predictor of child psychopathology (Greenberg, 1999), for example. The possibility of reverse effects on working models remains largely unknown; for instance, do insecure attachments to parents cause a youth to become delinquent, or do parents who know that their child is delinquent disengage emotionally, perpetuating a pattern of insecurity?

Although the attachment system is said to reside within the individual—the child—considering it as a feedback system makes it reasonable to consider the effects of the child's ways of responding to situations of distress on the parent. How do adolescents, for example, give parents a sense that all is well, and how do they activate their parents' attachment systems? How do parents respond when the stressor activating their attachment system is their own adolescent's behavior? How do parents' attachment histories with their own parents and partners color their reactions to adolescents' behaviors? Who sets the thermostat of the attachment system when?

The Direct Parental Control Model

The main assumption behind this model is that parents need to control their adolescents' behavior and that they will have their influence through direct supervision and control of the adolescents' activities and associations (e.g., Laub & Sampson, 1988; Leibner & Wacker, 1997; Wells & Rankin, 1988). The criterion variables are usually delinquency, drug use, and other problem behaviors. Studies of delinquency in the criminality literature often lean heavily on this model.

There is a problem inherent in the direct control idea, however, which is that parents are seldom physically present when their adolescents are away from home (Csikszentmihalyi & Larson, 1984; Hirschi, 1969; Nye,1958). Therefore, direct control of their behavior is not usually possible. Another problem with this literature lies in the assumptions that are made about intervening processes that are not studied directly. The literature on parental monitoring, which rests on the direct parental control model, provides an illustration. The main idea is that parents' tracking and control efforts are necessary to keep youths from engaging in problem behavior and away from deviant peers who would draw them into problem behavior. A large literature links high parental monitoring to lower levels of (a) delinquency, (b) associations with deviant peers, (c) drug and alcohol use, (d) cigarette smoking, and (e) risky sexual activity (for a review of early work, see Patterson & Stouthamer-Loeber, 1984; for some of the many empirical examples, see Biglan, Duncan, Ary, & Smolkowski, 1995; Cernkovich & Giordano, 1987; Chassin, Pillow, Curran, Molina, & Barrera, 1993; Crouter, MacDermid, McHale, & Perry-Jenkins, 1990; Dishion, Capaldi, Spracklen, & Li, 1995; Flannery, Vazsonyi, Torquati, & Fridrich, 1994; Fletcher, Darling, Steinberg, & Dornbusch, 1995; Fridrich & Flannery, 1995; McCord, 1986; Metzler, Noell, Biglan, Ary, & Smolkowski, 1994; Romer et al., 1994; Sampson & Laub, 1994; Weintraub & Gold, 1991; White & Kaufman, 1997).

This literature involves at least two untested assumptions. The first is that if parents have knowledge, it is because they have done tracking and surveillance to get it. This assumption is inherent in the operationalization of monitoring in this whole literature. Even though monitoring has been conceptualized as tracking and surveillance, which are actions, it has almost universally been operationalized as knowledge, which is not an action but an end result. This literature involves a second untested assumption regarding why parents' knowledge might be important or why it is linked to fewer adolescent problem behaviors and better overall adjustment. The assumption is that if parents have knowledge about their youths' activities and associations, they will be aware if small infractions of rules occur or if dangerous associations with deviant peers start to develop, and they can step in with direct control to stop these small problems before they become large problems. Hence, direct control is an intervening process that is assumed to explain the connection between parents' knowledge and adolescent behavior.

In our research, we have questioned both of these assumptions. We have pointed out this mismatch between the conceptualization of monitoring as tracking and surveillance and its operationalization as parents' knowledge, and we have presented empirical evidence to suggest that parents get most of their information about adolescents' day-to-day activities through the youth's free, spontaneous disclosure of information (Stattin & Kerr, 2000). Parents' active efforts to get information, in contrast, are only weakly related to their knowledge. We have shown, further, that children who tell their parents a lot about their daily activities, rather than those who are strongly controlled by their parents, are better adjusted in a number of different ways (Kerr & Stattin, 2000). In our work, high disclosure of daily activities was linked to less involvement in antisocial behavior, less school maladjustment, less depressed mood, higher self-confidence, better relationships with both parents, and fewer friends with undesirable characteristics. Parents' active efforts showed few links to adjustment. In fact, they were sometimes related to poorer rather than better adjustment. We went on to show that parents' direct control strategies (controlling adolescents' freedom to come and go as they please without informing parents and getting their permission ahead of time or explaining themselves afterward) were correlated with youths' feelings of being overly controlled—which in turn were linked to poor adjustment on all the measures mentioned previously.

These results suggest that the link between parents' knowledge and adolescent adjustment does not exist because surveillance prevents undesirable behavior, as has so often been claimed. Rather, it is because child disclosure is heavily

represented in parents' knowledge, and children who talk openly with their parents tend to be better adjusted. Hence, this raises the larger theoretical question of whether parents' knowledge in and of itself is actually important. Does it play any causal role in adolescent adjustment? If it does, and if that role is not what has been assumed—allowing parents to know when to intervene with direct control—then what is it? Or alternatively, is this just a classic example of an apparent cause-and-effect relation that only appears because there is a third variable that is producing both the apparent cause and the apparent effect? In our research, we have suggested that parents' knowledge *is* important, but not for the reasons that researchers have assumed (so that parents will know when to intervene with direct control). We have theorized instead that knowledge underlies trust, and trust is an important part of a complex, ongoing, bidirectional process within the family in which parents and children react to each other. This process in turn influences the child's adjustment both directly and indirectly through mechanisms that we describe later in this chapter.

Conclusions

The major views of parenting that have dominated research on adolescence during the past 20 years have concentrated on two broad classes of parenting behaviors. One concerns the relational side of parenting—emotional warmth and responsiveness to the youth's needs. The other concerns the regulatory-supervisory side of parenting—active regulation of the youth's activities and associations. Both these classes of parenting behaviors are considered important, particularly the regulatory-supervisory behaviors. All of these models are limited by an assumption that causality resides in parents' behavior, and some models are further limited by measures that have questionable construct validity.

Peer Relationships

In current thinking, the adolescent peer context is regarded as a prime instigator of new behaviors and lifestyles. Friendships are considered more egalitarian than are adult-child relations and are thought to provide young people with approval and support in daily life; experiences of sharing and cooperating; standards for social comparison; opportunities to try out adult roles; leisure time recreation; and forums for personal and intimate disclosure of experiences, thoughts, and ideas (Bagwell, Newcomb, & Bukowski, 1998; Cairns & Cairns, 1994; Hartup, 1983; Parker, Rubin, Price, & DeRosier, 1995).

Friendships are voluntary and self-initiated, but they are also constrained by the broader physical context. Hence, peer networks, cliques, and friendships all describe social associations between individuals of roughly the same age who share about the same ecological conditions, interests, and activities (Kirchler, Palmonari, & Pombeni, 1996; Ladd, 1989; Reisman, 1985). They live in the same neighborhood, are members of the same clubs and associations, and attend the same school or class. They also tend to be of the same sex and ethnicity (Hartup, 1983; Kandel, 1978). These features, however, say more about the physical environment in which adolescents live than about the actual content of the friendships.

Adolescents also tend to choose peers who are attitudinally and behaviorally similar to themselves (Dishion, Patterson, & Griesler, 1994; Hartup, 1983, 1996; Kandel, 1978, 1986). Yet to focus only on similarities is to ignore one of the possible developmental functions of peer association—that it forces youths to understand differences between themselves and others. We should expect that young people choose peers who are different from themselves in certain ways and who satisfy different needs—peers whom they admire for some reason, who have talents they do not have or interests that are different from theirs, and whom they can talk with, learn from, and gain insights from (Eder, 1985; Smith & Inder, 1990).

The theoretical models of peer influences that have been used in research have mainly been the social-cognitive development model and the social learning model. The first rests on the ideas of theorists such as Piaget, Cooley, Mead, Sullivan, and—to some extent—Erikson and Vygotsky. The main idea is that peer relationships help adolescents gain a more sophisticated social understanding and develop cognitively because negotiating relationships and disagreements with peers forces them to take another person's point of view and develop empathy and understanding. Sullivan's clinically derived theory of interpersonal relations was one of the first approaches to directly address the developmental function of peer groups and friendships. From Sullivan's perspective, "chums" or best friends were essential for the evolution of the self-system, cognitive-emotional development, and good adjustment. From a contemporary life span developmental perspective, Youniss (1980) proposed a theory of relationships and self-development that was drawn from the writings of Sullivan and Piaget. The social learning model rests on the ideas of theorists such as Bandura, Cairns, Patterson, Dishion, and colleagues, Coleman, and Bronfenbrenner. The main idea is that peers socialize each other by modeling, imitating, encouraging, and rewarding certain behaviors. This general idea can be seen in much of the research on peer influences.

Research on Peer Relationships

Research on peer relationships addresses questions that derive directly from the particular peers under consideration. Research on dyadic peer relationships examines how friendships develop. Research on groups of peers in predefined settings such as school classrooms looks at how adolescents acquire peer-group status and how that status and the characteristics of the peers influence the individual's behavior. Research on peers in self-chosen settings looks at how peer groups are formed in the natural ecology and how these groups influence individual behavior.

Dyadic Peer Relationships. Many scholars agree that close friends have the potential to serve unique functions in development. Friendships help adolescents build social skills and learn that others think and feel differently from the way they do. Most adolescents have a good friend—often several (Hartup, 1992). A huge literature suggests that intimacy and empathy, self-disclosure, and mutual responsiveness emerge within these friendships. Friendships are self-initiated and are based on openness, affection, empathy, loyalty, and reciprocity, and they make adolescents sensitive to others' perspectives, roles, and feelings (Berndt, 1982; Marcus, 1996; Sullivan, 1953). The behavioral interactions that differentiate friends from nonfriends typically involve positive engagement, conflict management, and ability to engage in tasks together (Hartup, 1996). Similarity and dissimilarity; friendship selection, maintenance, and dissolution; and gender differences in friendships also have all been addressed in the literature on best friends.

Relationships With Groups of Peers: The Peers in Predefined Social Settings. Most studies of peer relations and interactions have been done in the classroom or school, a setting that is predefined for adolescents. During the 1970s and 1980s, hundreds of studies were conducted that examined the relationship between peer status (popular vs. unpopular, neglected, controversial, and rejected) and coping and problem solving, social skills and competence, school adjustment and achievement, personality, emotions, loneliness, prosocial and agonistic behavior, and more (Parker, et al., 1995). These studies showed a strong link between peer status and individual behavior at school and indicated that status and behavior are correlated with later school dropout, delinquency, and mental health problems. These studies present a unidirectional view of causality, however, because they assume that peer status plays a causal role in these correlations.

Relationships With Natural Groups of Peers: The Peers in Self-Chosen Settings. Demographic and ecological investigations have provided insights into how peer groups naturally evolve over time, how broader networks are formed, and how and when cliques and crowds emerge (B. B. Brown et al., 1993; Dunphy, 1963). They have shed light on the role of social networks for adolescents with behavioral problems—and on how deviant peer groups and gangs are formed and maintained (Goldstein, 1994). They have dealt with group processes and behavior stability (Sarnecki, in press). Studies in this domain have shown the close connection between leisure settings and transition behaviors (Silbereisen & Noack, 1988) and between choosing to enter a particular activity such as sports and encountering new friendship experiences (B. B. Brown, 1990; Fine, 1980). These studies have provided some information about properties of peer groups; bases of peer group selection, maintenance, and dissolution; and gender- and age-related differences in peer group configurations.

Peer Associations: Unidirectional Effects?

Historically, adolescents have been portrayed as being receptive to the influence of peers. In view of (a) the number of empirical studies that have claimed to demonstrate that peers influence adolescents' behaviors, (b) existing theoretical models that depict peers as a major socialization influence (cf. differential association, Sutherland & Cressey, 1978; and social control theories, Hirschi, 1969), (c) the many textbooks that support the argument that peers have a pervasive socializing influence on behavior of adolescents, and (d) layman's views, undoubtedly peers should be viewed as having an important steering influence on adolescents' behavior and development. Indeed, one finding that consistently turns up in empirical studies is that peer characteristics are outstanding correlates of individuals' transition behaviors. For smoking, sexuality, delinquency, and drinking or drug use, there is a strong link between individual behavior and peer behavior. In the majority of studies that have looked at the relative roles of parent and peer characteristics in social behavior, peer relationships turn out to be the most predictive.

Factors That Interfere With the Ability to Infer Causality

Researchers refer to peer association with causal terms such as *influence, impact,* or *pressure.* But many studies do not take adequate account of selection factors, do not control

appropriately for relevant individual differences, are not based on independent reports of peers, are ecologically questionable, fail to consider alternative explanations, or suffer from any combination of these problems.

Cross-Sectional Designs. It goes without saying that a correlation between characteristics in subjects and their friends in any cross-sectional study cannot be interpreted causally. The direction of influence may go both ways. For more firm conclusions about causality, longitudinal designs are needed. But causal language—implying a unidirectional peer impact on individual behavior and development—is frequently used in studies that look at concurrent correlates.

Shared Activities. If we focus on behaviors that usually occur in groups, high subject-peer group correlations are not in and of themselves evidence of peer influence. Consider one example: Because delinquent acts are most often performed in groups, one would be very surprised *not* to find an association between delinquency in the adolescent and delinquency in his or her peer group. However, this association does not indicate whether the adolescent was pressured to offend, tended to be the active instigator, or was an active part of planning these offenses (Farrington, 1998).

Perceptual Biases. Many studies deduce peer influences from adolescents' self-reports of peer behavior. For example, many investigations have reported that self-reports of friends' deviance are strongly linked to the subject's own delinquency. Indeed, based on findings from peer perception measures, delinquent peers have been referred to as the best predictor of delinquency (Dishion et al., 1994; Oetting & Donnermeyer, 1998). This raises the old problem of shared method-variance. High correlations between one's own and one's peers' behavior might be partly explained by the fact that adolescents project their own behavior onto friends or justify or rationalize their own behaviors, thereby misreporting their friends' deviance (Conger & Rueter, 1996; Kandel, 1996; Urberg, Degirmencioglu, & Pilgrim, 1997). Studies suggest that self-reports of peers' behaviors are more strongly associated with individuals' own behavior than are independent measures of peers' behaviors (cf. Iannotti, Bush, & Weinfurt, 1996). Hence, data from self-reports of peer behavior are likely to systematically overestimate the role of peer association in individual development (Kandel, 1985).

School as the Analytic Unit. Adolescent peer studies have typically dealt with peer groups in one setting—the school—and the ecological validity of this practice is questionable (Adler & Adler, 1998; Campbell, 1980; T. P. George & Hartmann, 1996; Giordano, Cernkovich, & Pugh, 1986;

Hartup, 1983). A school is an administrative system. Although circumstances can vary with the type of school, students usually have little choice about their classmates and they cannot influence the social environment much. Undoubtedly, the school context should be considered the major breeding ground for peer associations from childhood into late adolescence (Parker & Asher, 1993). But many leisure-time friends are not classmates (T. P. George & Hartmann, 1996; Smith & Inder, 1990). Out-of-school peers are more heterogeneous than in-school peers in both age and gender (cf. Allen, 1989; T. P. George & Hartmann, 1996; Smith & Inder, 1990), and they might have more important implications for individual behavior—concurrently or predictively (Krappmann et al, 1993). It is likely that peers outside of school will be particularly important for adolescents who do not consider school as a valued context or who for reasons such as being rejected by their classmates are not part of the activities of the majority in their class (Ladd, 1983). T. P. George and Hartmann (1996) reported that unpopular 11- to 12-year-olds had more friends outside of school than did average and popular subjects, and the unpopular youths in the class had almost twice as many friends of a different age as the popular youths had. In their investigations of the implications of pubertal maturation on transition behaviors, Stattin and Magnusson (1990) showed that the peers who were most strongly associated with the social behaviors of early-developing females were not conventional types of peers. Most influential were the peers who were chronologically older and those who were in other classes or had quit school—particularly older males. Classroom-based studies would exclude these important peer contacts.

Little is known about leisure-time peer groups or the differences between in-school and out-of-school friends. For example, one of the common questions about deviant peers is the proportion of close friends that the individual has (from none, to half, to all) who engage in delinquent acts (Elliot, Huizinga, & Menard, 1989). This question is standard in research on juvenile delinquency, but it is not informative about who these peers are, where and when they interact with the youth, or what their support or influence is. More research on relationships with peers outside of school is needed for a more accurate picture of how the individual influences and is influenced by his or her peers across contexts.

Peer Selection and Peer Socialization.   Kandel (1978, 1985) first questioned the common practice of interpreting peer association causally and unidirectionally when in studies of homophily, she differentiated peer selection from peer socialization processes. According to a peer socialization interpretation, youths become similar to their peers as they gradually conform to the behaviors, fashions, values, and attitudes that are normative in the peer group. In contrast, according to a peer selection interpretation, similarity exists because youths choose to engage with peers who are similar to themselves. If selection is a major operating factor, then correlations between peer association and individual behavior are spurious (Hartup, 1983, 1992).

Cross-sectional studies cannot possibly differentiate peer selection from peer socialization; this requires longitudinal data. Kandel's studies on juvenile drinking (1978; 1985) were based on best friend nominations at two time points, and they showed that both these processes operated to produce similarities between adolescents and their friends. Other studies have confirmed Kandel's findings. In the domains of drinking and smoking, peer selection is as important as peer socialization (Engels, Knibbe, de Vries, Drop, & van Breukelen, 1999; Engels, Knibbe, Drop, & de Haan, 1997; Ennet & Bauman, 1994; Farrell & Danish, 1993; Fisher & Bauman, 1998; Mounts & Steinberg, 1995; Urberg et al., 1997). These studies clearly show that peer socialization is not the whole story behind the often-found associations between measures of individual and peer behavior.

Other longitudinal studies support this view. For example, they reveal that peer associations change greatly in adolescence, but aggressiveness and antisocial behavior are quite stable (Loeber, 1991; Olweus, 1979; Stattin & Magnusson, 1989), and this pattern of findings argues for selection. Also, several strong longitudinal studies that have looked into complex networks of peer relations over time suggest a reciprocal relationship between peer selection and peer socialization (Patterson, Reid, & Dishion, 1992). Peer association, it appears, is best viewed as a process that includes selection, deselection, and socialization in the peer group (Kandel, 1985, 1986).

In the delinquency literature, studies have looked more closely at the conditions under which selection versus socialization operates. They suggest that the common view that teenagers are drawn into delinquency because of "bad peers" is too simple. Rather, active selection of deviant peers by problem-prone adolescents seems to be particularly pronounced during the early stages of engaging in delinquency and other risk behaviors (Conger & Rueter, 1996; Galambos & Silbereisen, 1987; Kandel, 1985; Maggs & Galambos, 1993; Patterson, DeBaryshe, & Ramsey, 1989). During the later stages, interactions with deviant friends and the mutual reinforcement of common activities accelerate and diversify the criminal activities of adolescents who have a previous history of problematic adjustment (Dishion, French, & Patterson, 1995). According to the *deviancy training hypothesis,* collective antisocial talk among peers in these circles reinforces antisocial talk and antisocial behavior, thereby escalating the level of delinquent behavior for the group members over time (Dishion et al., 1994).

Other studies in the literature show that peer influence is an issue of individual characteristics, youths' prior experiences, and peer characteristics (Agnew, 1991; Fergusson, Lynskey, & Horwood, 1996; Moffitt, 1993; Mounts & Steinberg, 1995; Vitaro, Tremblay, Kerr, Pagani, & Bukowski, 1997). For example, association with deviant friends is considered more likely to predict future delinquency among late starters or transitory delinquents, but it is less likely to affect the behavior of early starters or life-course persistent delinquents. In support of this suggestion, Vitaro et al. (1997) found that having deviant friends was associated with an increase in delinquent behavior among moderately disruptive youths but not among highly disruptive youths.

Still, the general problem of using the school context in peer research prevails. The conclusions about peer selection and peer socialization processes discussed previously were based on data taken from friends at school (Kandel, 1978, 1985). There is little information about peer selection and socialization in out-of-school settings. To our knowledge, a study conducted by Kiesner (2000) is unique in that it included peers in the school context as well as neighborhood friends; this was accomplished by studying an entire community at once. Kiesner's results suggested that in-school and out-of-school peer groups both contribute to the concurrent prediction of individual problem behavior and homework and curfew compliance, whereas only the out-of-school group explained individual involvement in sports (which in Italy take place outside the school) and social activities. Moreover, in-school and out-of-school peer status (defined as the number of nominations received as a member of the other participants' in-school and out-of-school groups) interacted in explaining individual differences in depressed mood, even after controlling for a traditional measure of in-class peer status. Specifically, frequent nominations as an out-of-school group member appeared to buffer individuals from the negative emotional effects of low peer status within the school.

Peer Relations and Community Settings. When parents buy a new house or rent an apartment in a certain area, they mark out the limits of the future life courses of all family members (Barker, 1964; G. W. Brown, Harris, & Peto, 1973; Magnusson & Stattin, 1998). The availability of social situations in a local community determines the possibilities for particular social activities and for the functioning and development of individuals and peer groups. Within these limits, individuals determine their own peer associations by

selecting certain types of leisure settings and recreational contexts over others (Brook, Nomura, & Cohen, 1989). On the group level, the local society to some extent shapes the social activities of peer groups by providing or failing to provide settings that promote prosocial activities.

Adolescent research has only recently started to gain insights into how broader sociocultural influences—as they are represented in the community, the neighborhood, and in particular leisure-time settings—affect peer relations. A few examples of this work in naturalistic settings are Fine and Glassner's (1979) study of baseball little leagues, Mahoney and Stattin's (2000) examination of youth recreation centers, Jackson and Csikszentmihalyi's (1999) studies of the role of sports in adolescent life, and the Berlin Youth Longitudinal Study, which revealed the dual quality of many adolescent behaviors—both compromising momentary or future psychosocial health and being tools in the pursuit of satisfying important personal and social goals of the individual (Silbereisen & Noack, 1988).

A variety of mechanisms have been proposed by which leisure activities may enhance individual competence and protect against adjustment problems. A distinction can be made between structured and unstructured leisure-time activities. A common finding in the literature is that well-adjusted adolescents tend to be more actively involved in structured leisure-time activities and settings such as organized sports, hobbies, religious activities, music, theater, art, and politics. These activities occur during scheduled hours, are often led by an adult, and aim explicitly at skill building. By contrast, adolescents with more problematic personal and social adjustment are more likely to hang out on the streets, attend public drinking places, and be less involved in organized activities (Cochran & Bo, 1987). These more spontaneous or unstructured activities are seldom under direct adult supervision. Although it is likely that different individuals benefit from leisure pursuits for different reasons, high levels of structure, skill-building aims, exposure to conventional values, and the presence of nondeviant peers appear to be particularly strongly linked to lower levels of antisocial behavior (Agnew & Peterson, 1989; Allen, Philliber, Herrling, & Kuperminc, 1997; Csikszentmihayli, 1990; Csikszentmihalyi, Rathunde, Whalen, & Wong, 1993; Fletcher, Elder & Mekos, 2000; Hirschi, 1969; Jones & Offord, 1989; Kinney, 1993; Mahoney, 2000; McCord, 1978).

Studies of Swedish youth recreation centers show that the same principles of selection and socialization that are commonly found in peer research also apply to leisure settings (Mahoney & Stattin, 2000; Mahoney, Stattin, & Magnusson, 2001). These government-supported centers are available to adolescents age 13 and older. The overall philosophy for the youth centers has remained constant across the last three decades—that youths should be allowed to develop their own interests. An explicit aim of centers has been to reduce antisocial activities by keeping adolescents away from certain settings during the evening. The centers are usually accessible every evening of the week, opening around dinnertime and closing as late as 11:30 p.m. on weekends and during the summer. Attendance and activity participation are strictly voluntary. The activities are typically low in structure and do not aim at skill building; they include pool, ping-pong, video games, darts, TV, music, and coffee drinking. Adults are present at the center, but they do not direct or place demands on the youths' activities.

Investigations in different regions have shown that as a group, youths who attended the centers regularly were more antisocial, had more antisocial peers, had more conflicted parent relations, and had parents who knew less about their activities than did those who did not attend the centers (Mahoney & Stattin, 2000). In fact, youths who attended the centers were overrepresented among those with problematic personal and social adjustment on almost all measures studied. Using a longitudinal design, and following 500 boys in a middle-sized Swedish town from ages 10 to 30, clear indications of selection effects for attending these centers were documented (Mahoney et al., 2001). Boys with a multiple problem profile of social and academic deficits at age 10 were most likely to attend the youth centers at age 13. But—even after controlling for relevant factors at age 10 (family and demographic factors and several aspects of child social-academic competence prior to involvement in the centers)— the youths who attended these centers at age 13 had significantly higher rates of criminal offenses up to the age of 30 than did those who did not attend the centers. The findings are consistent with the proposition that the combination of unstructured leisure and socialization influences among problem-oriented peers may promote antisocial behavior, but detailed investigations have not yet addressed the issue of mechanisms: whether these differences are due to low structure of the activities at the centers and associated preference for unstructured leisure pursuits of the youths involved, little or no adult supervision, deviancy training, few opportunities for skill building, and so forth. Such analyses have to be conducted to determine why some leisure activities are associated with criminal behavior. In comparison, North American studies have shown that youth centers can operate in highly effective and potentially beneficial ways for disadvantaged youths (Heath & McLaughlin, 1993; McLaughlin, Irby, & Langman, 1994). However, the Swedish studies suggest that community-sponsored gathering places for youths should not by default be viewed as beneficial.

Conclusions.   The available empirical evidence suggests that peer relations, activities, and contexts are related and considerably self-chosen by the individual within the confines of the existing social milieus in the local community. This view of the adolescent as active and self-determining and this contextualized view of peer relations are in line with recent theoretical discussions in developmental, social, and personality psychology (Bronfenbrenner, 1988; Lerner, 1996; Magnusson & Stattin, 1998). The literature suggests that an agency perspective is needed to understand peer relations in everyday life. Adolescents have much freedom to select their own lifestyles, activities, and interpersonal contexts; peer relations are voluntary and self-chosen.

Empirical data also suggest that to understand adolescent behavior, one must understand the contexts in which adolescents interact with others. A contextual perspective is needed to understand how peer relationships are formed, stabilized, and broken. The choice of peer activities is confounded with the available settings. Attending a particular leisure setting with particular types of activities implies meeting certain (rather than other) kinds of peers. In a *Journal of Adolescent Research* special issue on adolescent socialization in context, Eccles, Early, Frasier, Belansky, and McCarthy (1997) acknowledged the widespread recognition in models of adolescent development that adolescents live their everyday lives in multiple settings, that these contexts are linked to each other, and that each has its special implications for youths. At the same time they noted that almost no systematic research had been done to examine simultaneously the roles of these contexts for personal and social adjustment and for adolescents' social relations. Despite decades of research on the role of peers for individual functioning and development, researchers have only started to clarify how peer relations, activities, and settings are interrelated, and few empirical studies actually test the causal links.

Parent and Peer Models: A Need for Integration

Adolescents have close relationships with parents and peers simultaneously, and certain aspects of both these relationships are linked to adjustment. Most relevant theories have been developed to explain one type of relationship—parents or peers—and they have largely viewed youths as being shaped by parent or peer influences. Thus, they suffer from two weaknesses: a failure to theorize about the possible importance of connections between parent relationships and peer relationships and a failure to consider the active role of youths themselves.

EXPLAINING THE CONNECTIONS BETWEEN PARENT RELATIONSHIPS, PEER ASSOCIATION, AND ADOLESCENT ADJUSTMENT

As revealed in the preceding discussion, adolescent adjustment such as involvement in delinquency has been linked to both parenting factors and peer factors, but the connection between the two has not been adequately explained. The explanation that parents who are effective monitors are able to keep their youths from associating with deviant peers falls apart when one uses construct-valid measures of monitoring rather than relying on parental knowledge measures (Kerr & Stattin, 2000; Stattin & Kerr, 2000). Similarly, authoritative parenting has been said to work by making youths open to their parents' socialization efforts (Darling & Steinberg, 1993), but the effects often seem to be connected more to the neglectful style than to the authoritative style (e.g., Glasgow et al., 1997; Lamborn et al., 1991; Steinberg et al., 1994), and neither the direction of effects nor the mechanisms are clear. The construct validity of these measures can also be questioned. As a theoretical explanation for the findings that delinquent youths have poor emotional bonds to their parents (e.g., Elliot, Huizinga, & Ageton, 1985; Hawkins & Weiss, 1985; Hirschi, 1969), it has been proposed that interactions with parents can undermine youths' self-esteem, which causes them to choose deviant friends who are different from their parents (Kaplan, 1982; Kaplan, Johnson, & Bailey, 1986; Kaplan, Martin, & Johnson, 1986). But there are many missing links in this theoretical chain. For instance, why would youths with low self-esteem choose deviant friends? Why would they not instead choose very nurturing friends who would build up their self-esteem? What kinds of interactions with parents produce low self-esteem? And is self-esteem the really important factor, or could it be a marker for something else?

In what follows, we offer a theoretical explanation for these and other findings that family and parenting factors are linked to youths' choices of friends, such as deviant or delinquent friends. The mechanism that we propose leans on the ideas that (a) adolescents have little choice about their parents, their parent context, or interactions with their parents that evoke strong feelings, but they have much more choice about their peers and peer contexts; (b) peers and peer contexts are inseparably linked; and (c) when adolescents choose certain types of peers and peer activities, they might be choosing the context as much as they are choosing the peers.

Parent and Peer Relationships and Their Contexts

Over the past two decades, person-context models have received much theoretical attention (see Magnusson & Stattin, 1998, for a review). These models advance the ideas that individuals live and develop in multiple settings that change over time and are active agents in their own development. We draw upon these ideas as well.

Relationships Can Evoke Strong Feelings That Are Psychologically Important

Interactions with others can evoke a variety of emotions such as shame, anger, resentment, love, disappointment, and pride. In addition to bringing about these emotions, other people also can give us the sense that we have some degree of control over the environment or can make us feel that we are largely under their control. Whether this is emotional or cognitive is debatable, but the psychological literature—broadly speaking—suggests that individuals experience the loss of personal control negatively. In Rodin and Langer's (1977) classic nursing home study, nursing home patients who were allowed to make their own choices about the details of small privileges such as seeing a weekly movie and having a plant in their rooms were happier and healthier on a whole host of measures than were patients who got the same benefits without being able to exert control over them. In social psychology, reactance theory and other research suggests that when people feel as though someone is trying to control their freedom of action, they react against the threatened loss of control by adopting attitudes or taking actions that are strongly against the would-be controller (Brehm & Brehm, 1981; Heilman, 1976; Nail & Van Leeuwen, 1993). In Seligman's learned-helplessness study (Overmier & Seligman, 1967), dogs who could not control the end of an electrical shock by jumping out of the cage eventually exhibited behavior similar to that of depressed people. The same lack of control over one's circumstances seems to underlie some forms of depression (Klein & Seligman, 1976; Peterson & Seligman, 1984; Seligman, 1975). Interactions with others, then, can evoke emotions that have obvious implications for people's psychological well-being and feelings such as being overly controlled that also have strong implications for well-being.

A Working Model of Parent-Child Interactions and the Feelings They Evoke

In our own recent work, we have developed a model, shown in Figure 16.1, of some of the family interaction processes that are related to parents' knowledge of their youths' daily activities. The model also shows the role of negative and

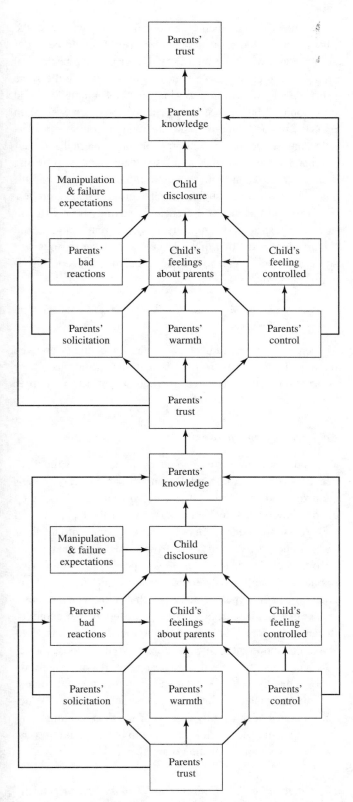

Figure 16.1   A model of bidirectional, ongoing communication and control processes within the family.

positive feelings that interactions with parents can evoke in the child, including the feeling of being overly controlled by parents. We have empirically tested most of the links in this model with cross-sectional and short-term longitudinal data. Hence, this working model has considerable empirical support.

Child disclosure of information about daily activities has a central position in this model, because our studies suggest that parents get most of their information this way and little through their own monitoring efforts (Kerr & Stattin, 2000; Stattin & Kerr, 2000). Because parents' knowledge is strongly linked to adolescent adjustment, explaining why youths do or do not disclose has become a crucial concern for us and for others (Darling, Cumsille, Hames, & Caldwell, 2000; Darling & Dowdy, 2000; Stattin, Kerr, & Ferrer-Wreder, 2000).

As shown in the figure, there is much that we know about adolescents who disclose a lot to their parents about their daily lives. Their parents seldom react negatively (with sarcasm, judgment, or ridicule) to their spontaneous disclosure, and these adolescents do not feel overly controlled by their parents (Kerr & Stattin, 2000). In addition, high-disclosing adolescents expect success on difficult tasks and do not interact with people in deceptive, manipulative ways, whereas secretive adolescents tend to expect failure and to be deceptive and manipulative (Stattin et al., 2000). High-disclosing youths are also low on depression, high on self-esteem, and high on self-reported warm feelings toward parents (Kerr & Stattin, 2000). Taken together, these findings suggest that high-disclosing adolescents have positive experiences in the parent context, and high disclosure could be seen as a marker for positive feelings about the parent context.

As seen in the model, child disclosure provides parents with knowledge, and knowledgeable parents tend to be trusting (Kerr, Stattin, & Trost, 1999). Trusting parents in turn do not react negatively to their adolescents' disclosure (with sarcasm, ridicule, or negative judgments), but untrusting parents do tend to do so (Kerr et al., 1999). The model proposes that parents' trust or mistrust will affect the way they relate to and communicate with the adolescent in the future, and that will affect the adolescent's willingness to disclose his or her feelings and everyday life experiences. Thus, the ongoing process continues, as shown in the upper part of Figure 16.1. The process is bidirectional in that parents act, children react, and parents react back. For the present purposes, it is important to note that the child's feelings—feelings of being overly controlled and positive or negative emotions toward parents—are important links in this chain of actions and reactions.

Structural Features of Parent and Peer Contexts

We argue that over time, children will connect the feelings that interactions with parents evoke with the context in which those interactions take place. Some features of those parent and peer contexts are what we call *structural,* meaning that they are not unique to the particular family or peer group, but they are part of parent or peer contexts themselves.

Structural Features of Parent Contexts Are Fixed

There are some features that are similar across families, regardless of the particular parenting practices or the interactions that take place in the family. We think of them as the structural features of a family context in the same way that walls and windows can be thought of as the structural features of a room. Nearly all rooms have walls and windows, even though they vary in details such as size and shape, and nearly all family contexts have features such as close interactions with adults, the presence of authority figures, the need to share scarce resources, a certain degree of supervision by higher-status others, some rules and structure, and the presence of behavioral values, for want of a better term, or assumptions about how people should behave—in general and in relation to each other. There will of course be individual variations in the expression of these structural features both in degree and in kind (e.g., some families have more rules and structure than others do; some parents believe that they should make all the decisions, whereas others give children a democratic voice in decisions). Nonetheless, these basic structural features still exist in families.

Structural Features of Peer Contexts Vary

There are many different peer contexts, and there are two important ways in which peer contexts differ from each other. First, some peer contexts are not *just* peer contexts because they exist within adult-controlled settings that include structural features that are determined by adults. For instance, the school classroom, extracurricular activities, and other organized activities such as adult-coached sports are usually thought of as peer contexts, but they all have features that are very similar to the family context: interaction with adults, rules and structure, the need to share resources, authority figures, supervision, and behavioral expectations. In contrast, peer settings such as street corners, arcades, cafes, and neighborhood playgrounds have few or none of the same structural features as the parent context.

A second important distinction among peer contexts is that the peers one encounters in different contexts will differ

systematically from each other. For instance, the peers who play an organized sport at school will on average be better adjusted and will have internalized their parents' behavioral values to a greater degree than will those playing the same sport in an unstructured setting such as a neighborhood playground (Mahoney & Stattin, in press; Mahoney et al., in press). Similarly, youths who are hanging out in arcades, cafes, and street corners will probably have internalized their parents' behavioral values to a lesser degree and will be less well adjusted than will those in more structured, adult-supervised situations such as theater groups, bands, orchestras, or choirs. Hence, different peer settings bear different degrees of structural similarity to the parent context, and the different peers that one encounters in those settings will show different degrees of social adjustment, according to adult standards.

Context Choice

The crux of our argument about family contexts and the feelings associated with them is that adolescents use these associations as a basis for gravitating toward some peer contexts and away from others.

Adolescents Can Choose

With adolescence comes increasing freedom and independence. For the first time, adolescents are able to choose their contexts, and they make two types of choices. First, they choose how to divide their time between their parents and their peers—to spend more or less time at home with the family as opposed to being away from home with their peers. Second, they decide *which particular* peers with whom to associate. Although talents, interests, and long- and short-term goals affect the types of activities that adolescents choose, the same activities can be pursued in different peer contexts. Because a variety of behaviors can be socialized in those contexts, it is important to understand why youths choose particular peer contexts over others. We suggest that one important factor is that the feelings that are evoked in the parent context become associated in the child's experience with the structural features of the family context. Then those feelings generalize to some peer contexts and not to others, making some peer contexts more appealing than others.

The Choice of a Peer Context Can Depend Upon Feelings About the Parent Context

Because emotions are easily classically conditioned to contexts, it is reasonable to believe that positive or negative emotions that arise in relationships will become linked, in the child's experience, to parents, peers, and the broad and specific features of the contexts in which interactions with them take place. It is also reasonable to believe that these emotions generalize to similar situations. Most of us can verify this from our own experience, because we have known people with whom we have felt particularly valued and secure (a trusted best friend, perhaps, or a grandparent), and we have noticed that elements of situations in which we spent time with that person (e.g., the smell of a backyard where we used to play or of something that Grandmother used to bake) have the power to evoke those good emotions even years later.

We suggest that the structural features of the parent context that we previously described become linked to specific emotions, and those emotions then generalize to settings with similar features. Thus, a child who has bad experiences such as feeling overly controlled in the parent context connects those negative feelings with contexts that have similar structural features (e.g., close interaction with adults, rules and structure, authority figures, etc.). There are many reasons that negative emotions might arise. Parents might have an authoritarian or parent-centered philosophy that does not lead them to respond well to the child's wishes or demands. The child might have a difficult temperament or be overly active or impulsive, thus leaving parents believing that they have no choice but to exert a lot of control. Or there might be some combination of or interaction between the parents' characteristics and the child's that results in bad feelings. Whatever the cause, the child will undoubtedly end up associating negative feelings with the parents' particular behavioral values and styles of interacting, and we suggest that the child will also associate negative feelings with the broader structural features of the parent context—features such as close interaction with adults, supervision, the presence of authority figures, rules and structure, and the need to share resources.

In our formulation, this association of negative or positive feelings with the parent context becomes important when the child reaches adolescence and is able to choose among different peer contexts. At that time, those who have associated negative experiences with the structural features of the parent context find that those negative feelings generalize to peer contexts that have similar features. Naturally, they gravitate away from such contexts. Avoiding those situations might then become reinforcing in its own right because it could bring a pleasant relief from the negative feelings that are linked to the parent context. In our view, avoiding situations that make one feel bad could be an important reason that some youths choose to hang out on the streets with poorly adjusted peers while others choose to participate in organized activities with better-adjusted peers. It also helps to explain why those who choose to hang out on the streets with poorly

adjusted peers have been found to have poor relationships with their parents.

Context Choice as an Ongoing Process

Through the direct and indirect processes outlined previously, parents can influence an adolescent's *initial engagement* with certain types of peers. Adolescents will choose certain peer groups or leisure settings on the basis of their relationships—good or bad—with parents. After the adolescent is a regular part of a specific setting or peer group, the parents' *reactions* can then maintain, escalate, or inhibit the adolescents' activities. For example, interactions could develop between (even well-meaning) parents and children that leave the child with negative feelings about the parent context. That child might then seek to avoid those feelings in the peer context by gravitating away from school activities and other adult-led, structured activities. In doing so, the child might encounter other peers who are also gravitating away from adult influences.

Our data support this idea in that low child disclosure, negative feelings toward parents, and feelings of being overly controlled by parents are all concurrently linked to higher delinquency, to belonging to deviant peer groups, and to doing poorly in school both socially and academically (Kerr & Stattin, 2000; Stattin & Kerr, 2000). After the child has joined a group of peers who have bad feelings about authority, rules and structure, and adult contact, these peers might coax or reinforce each other into more and more deviant activities, as suggested by the work of Dishion and colleagues (Dishion, McCord, & Poulin, 1999; Dishion, Spracklen, Andrews, & Patterson, 1996; Poulin, Dishion, & Haas, 1999). Parents' disapproving responses to the child's association with deviant peers and the slide into delinquent behavior might make the child feel even more negative about the parent context, thus exaggerating the contrast between the negative feelings that are associated with the parent context and the relief from negative feelings that is associated with the peer context; this could only serve to reinforce the child's ties to those particular peers. This prediction is consistent with Fuligni and Eccles's (1993) finding that what they called "extreme peer orientation" in early adolescence was associated with believing that parents were not loosening their control and not allowing the youth a voice in decision-making.

What is likely to happen next is consistent with past research on parental monitoring (operationalized as parents' knowledge of the youth's activities) and on adolescent life values. If youths become entrenched in a peer context that bears minimal resemblance to the parent context, they will probably avoid telling their parents whom they are with and what they are doing, thus limiting their parents' knowledge of their activities in the peer context—which can help explain why low knowledge is so robustly correlated with delinquency (see Dishion & McMahon, 1998, for a review). Furthermore, these adolescents will probably place greater value and importance on these peer activities and the things that get attention and respect from these peers (Cohen & Cohen, 1996; Stattin & Kerr, in press; see also Bear & Rys, 1994). One can easily imagine that parents' efforts to track or control these adolescents' activities will be ineffective (Kerr & Stattin, 2000; Stattin & Kerr, 2000). In the most extreme scenario, even well-meaning parents might give up on such a child, withdrawing both their emotional support and their communication and control efforts; this provides an interpretation different from that usually offered for the common finding that delinquents tend to have disengaged or uninvolved parents.

Thus, we argue that peers and parents can both contribute to a certain type of behavior at different points in time in ways that do not show up in cross-sectional studies. For many behaviors, peers seem to have more influence than parents do; but parents might have played a critical role in the adolescent's choice of a particular peer context, and parents' reactions to that choice might stabilize a negative trajectory. Longitudinal data are needed to provide a more complete understanding of these processes.

CONCLUSIONS

In a recent presidential address, the president of the Society for Research on Adolescence declared optimistically that "we can stop asking what type of parenting most positively *affects* [italics added] adolescent development. We know the answer to this question." (Steinberg, 2001, p. 13). In this chapter, we too have argued that researchers should stop asking about unidirectional *effects* concerning both parenting and peer relationships, but not because we already know the answers; they were the wrong questions.

What exists in the parent and peer literatures extant are basically snapshot views of parent, peer, and individual characteristics and their correlations with certain aspects of adjustment (or with each other). These views are beneficial in that they have illuminated the global aspects of family and peer relationships that are likely to be linked to behavior problems and psychopathology. They have not, however, provided much knowledge about the mechanisms involved, the processes operating over time, or possible bidirectional effects. Construct validity can be a problem, as can the assumptions that the intervening processes are known. Another problem is that these studies are sometimes based on simplifying assumptions that restrict the generalizability of the findings, such as when studies of friendships are based solely on peers in the classroom.

In this chapter, we have advanced the notion that adolescents are active agents in their own development. Within the constraints of the surrounding physical and social ecology—and based on their personalities, interests, and talents—they choose their different leisure contexts. We argue that this choice has been largely ignored in the literatures on both parenting and peer relationships, and we have offered a theoretical explanation of why youths' choices of peer contexts are not independent of their home environments.

Overall, in order to advance knowledge in this area, researchers must be willing to do the difficult studies. By *difficult studies,* we mean studies that (a) begin with bidirectional or recursive models; (b) take the person-context idea seriously and include it in the design; (c) are longitudinal in order to capture development and experimental in order to test causality and hypothesized mechanisms; (d) specifically measure and study processes and mechanisms rather than rely on assumptions about them; and (e) go to extra lengths to capture the phenomena that actually exist, in ecologically valid contexts, even when that makes data collection difficult (e.g., adolescent peer groups outside of the classroom).

Adolescence is a time of choices. Adolescents are free for the first time to make individual choices that they have never had the freedom to make before, and they face many opportunities to go astray. The ultimate goal of research is to understand why some adolescents do go astray and how that could have been prevented. Undoubtedly, there will be many different answers to the question *why*—each with its own implications for prevention and intervention. But these answers will come from an understanding of adolescents in their complexity as both active and reactive agents who are choosing their contexts for complex reasons. Developing this understanding is the challenge that lies ahead.

REFERENCES

Adler, P. A., & Adler, P. (1998). *Peer power: Preadolescent culture and identity.* New Brunswick, NJ: Rutgers University Press.

Agnew, R. (1991). The interactive effect of peer variables on delinquency. *Criminology, 29,* 47–72.

Agnew, R., & Peterson, D. M. (1989). Leisure and delinquency. *Social Problems, 36,* 332–350.

Ainsworth, M. D. S. (1989). Attachments beyond infancy. *American Psychologist, 44,* 709–716.

Ainsworth, M. D. S. (1990). Some considerations regarding theory and assessment relevant to attachments beyond infancy. In M. T.

Greenberg, D. Cicchetti, & E. M. Cummings (Eds.), *Attachment in the preschool years: Theory, research, and intervention* (pp. 463–487). Chicago: University of Chicago Press.

Ainsworth, M. D. S., Blehar, M. C., Waters, E., & Wall, S. (1978). *Patterns of attachment: A psychological study of the Strange Situation.* Hillsdale, NJ: Erlbaum.

Ainsworth, M. D. S., & Marvin, R. S. (1995). On shaping of attachment theory and research: An interview with Mary D. S. Ainsworth (Fall 1994). In E. Waters, B. E. Vaughn, G. Posada, & K. Kondo-Ikemura (Eds.), Caregiving, cultural, and cognitive perspectives on secure-base behavior and working models. *Monographs of the Society for Research in Child Development, 60*(2–3, Serial No. 244).

Allen, J. P. (1989). Social impact of age mixing and age segregation in school: A context-sensitive investigation. *Journal of Educational Psychology, 81,* 408–416.

Allen, J. P., Aber, L., & Leadbeater, B. (1990). Adolescent problem behaviors: The influence of attachment and autonomy. *Psychiatric Clinics of North America, 13,* 455–467.

Allen, J. P., Moore, C., Kuperminc, G., & Bell, K. (1998). Attachment and adolescent psychosocial functioning. *Child Development, 69*(5), 1406–1419.

Allen, J. P., Philliber, S., Herrling, S., & Kuperminc, G. P. (1997). Preventing teen pregnancy and academic failure: Experimental evaluation of a developmentally based approach. *Child Development, 64,* 729–742.

Anderson, K. E., Lytton, H., & Romney, D. M. (1986). Mothers' interactions with normal and conduct-disordered boys: Who affects whom? *Developmental Psychology, 22,* 604–609.

Avenevoli, S., Sessa, F. M., & Steinberg, L. (1999). Family structure, parenting practices and adolescent adjustment: An ecological examination. In E. M. Hetherington (Ed.), *Coping with divorce, single parenting, and remarriage: A risk and resiliency perspective* (pp. 65–90). Mahwah, NJ: Erlbaum.

Bagwell, C. L., Newcomb, A. F., & Bukowski, W. M. (1998). Preadolescent friendship and peer rejection as predictors of adult adjustment. *Child Development, 69,* 140–153.

Barker, R. G. (1964). *Ecological psychology: Concepts and methods for studying the environment of human behavior.* Stanford, CA: Stanford University Press.

Bartholomew, K., & Horowitz, L. M. (1991). Attachment styles among young adults: A test of a four-category model. *Journal of Personality and Social Psychology, 61*(2), 226–244.

Baumrind, D. (1966). Effects of authoritative parental control on child behavior. *Child Development, 37,* 887–907.

Baumrind, D. (1967). Child care practices anteceding three patterns of preschool behavior. *Genetic Psychology Monographs, 75,* 43–88.

Baumrind, D. (1968). Authoritarian vs. authoritative parental control. *Adolescence, 3,* 255–272.

Baumrind, D. (1971). Current patterns of parental authority. *Developmental Psychology Monographs, 4,* 1–103.

Baumrind, D. (1983). Rejoinder to Lewis's reinterpretation of parental firm control effects: Are authoritative families really harmonious? *Psychological Bulletin, 94,* 132–142.

Baumrind, D. (1991). The influence of parenting style on adolescent competence and substance abuse. *Journal of Early Adolescence, 1,* 56–95.

Baumrind, D., & Black, A. E. (1967). Socialization practices associated with dimensions of competence in preschool boys and girls. *Child Development, 38,* 291–327.

Bear, G. G., & Rys, G. S. (1994). Moral reasoning, classroom behavior, and sociometric status among elementary school children. *Developmental Psychology, 30,* 633–638.

Bell, R. Q. (1968). A reinterpretation of the direction of effects in studies of socialization. *Psychological Review, 75,* 81–95.

Bell, R. Q., & Chapman, M. (1986). Child effects in studies using experimental or brief longitudinal approaches to socialization. *Developmental Psychology, 22,* 595–603.

Berndt, T. J. (1982). The features and effects of friendship in early adolescence. *Child Development, 53,* 1447–1460.

Biesecker, G. (2001). *Attachment to parents and peers and emotion regulation in middle adolescence.* Unpublished doctoral dissertation, Tufts University, Medford, MA.

Biglan, A., Duncan, T. E., Ary, D. V., & Smolkowski, K. (1995). Peer and parental influences on adolescent tobacco use. *Journal of Behavioral Medicine, 18,* 315–330.

Bowlby, J. (1982). *Attachment and loss: Vol. 1. Attachment.* New York: Basic Books. (Original work published 1969)

Bowlby, J. (1988). *A secure base.* New York: Basic Books.

Brehm, S., & Brehm, J. W. (1981). *Psychological reactance: A theory of freedom and control.* New York: Academic Press.

Brennan, K. A., Clark, C. L., & Shaver, P. R. (1998). Self-reported measurement of adult attachment: An integrative overview. In J. A. Simpson & W. S. Rholes (Eds.), *Attachment theory and close relationships* (pp. 46–76). New York: Guilford Press.

Bretherton, I. (1985). Attachment theory: Retrospect and prospect. In I. Bretherton & E. Waters (Eds.), *Growing points in attachment theory and research. Monographs of the Society for Research in Child Development, 50*(1–2, Serial No. 209), 3–35.

Bronfenbrenner, U. (1988). Interacting systems in human development. Research paradigms: Present and future. In N. Bolger, A. Caspi, G. Downey, & M. Moorehouse (Eds.), *Persons in context: Developmental processes* (pp. 217–243). New York: Guilford Press.

Brook, J. S., Nomura, C., & Cohen, P. (1989). A network of influences on adolescent drug involvement: Neighborhood, school, peer, and family. *Genetic, Social, and General Psychology Monographs, 115,* 125–145.

Brown, B. B. (1990). Peer groups and peer cultures. In S. S. Feldman & G. R. Elliott (Eds.), *At the threshold: The developing adolescent* (pp. 171–196). Cambridge, MA: Harvard University Press.

Brown, B. B., Mounts, N., Lamborn, S. D., & Steinberg, L. (1993). Parenting practices and peer group affiliation in adolescence. *Child Development, 64,* 467–482.

Brown, G. W., Harris, T. O., & Peto, J. (1973). Life events and psychiatric disorders: II. Nature of causal link. *Psychological Medicine, 3*(2), 159–176.

Buss, D. M. (1981). Predicting parent-child interactions from children's activity level. *Developmental Psychology, 17,* 59–65.

Cairns, R. B., & Cairns, B. D. (1994). *Lifelines and risks: Pathways of youth in our time.* New York: Cambridge University Press.

Calkins, S. D., & Fox, N. A. (1992). The relations among infant temperament, security of attachment, and behavioral inhibition at twenty-four months. *Child Development, 63,* 1456–1472.

Campbell, A. C. (1980). Friendship as a factor in male and female delinquency. In H. C. Foot, A. J. Chapman, & J. R. Smith (Eds.), *Friendship and social relations in children* (pp. 365–389). New York: Wiley.

Cassidy, J. (1994). Emotion regulation: Influences of attachment relationships. In N. A. Fox (Ed.), *The development of emotion regulation: Biological and behavioral considerations. Monographs of the Society for Research in Child Development, 59*(2–3, Serial No. 240), 228–249.

Cernkovich, S. A., & Giordano, P. C. (1987). Family relationships and delinquency. *Criminology, 24,* 295–321.

Chassin, L., Pillow, D. R., Curran, P. J., Molina, B. S., & Barrera, M. (1993). Relation of parental alcoholism to early adolescent substance use: A test of three mediating mechanisms. *Journal of Abnormal Psychology, 102,* 3–19.

Cochran, M. M., & Bo, I. (1987). *Connections between the social networks, family involvement and behavior of adolescent males in Norway* (Tech. Rep. No. 75). University of Rogaland, Norway.

Cohen, P., & Cohen, J. (1996). *Life values and adolescent mental health.* Mahwah, NJ: Erlbaum.

Coleman, J. C. (1978). Current contradictions in adolescent theory. *Journal of Youth and Adolescence, 7*(1), 1–11.

Collins, N. L., & Read, S. J. (1990). Adult attachment, working models, and relationship quality in dating couples. *Journal of Personality and Social Psychology, 58,* 644–663.

Conger, R. D., & Rueter, M. A. (1996). Siblings, parents, and peers: A longitudinal study of social influences in adolescent risk for alcohol use and abuse. In G. Brody (Ed.), *Sibling relationships: Their causes and consequences* (pp. 1–30). Norwood, NJ: Ablex.

Cooper, M. L., Shaver, P. R., & Collins, N. L. (1998). Attachment styles, emotion regulation, and adjustment in adolescence. *International Journal of Behavioral Development, 25*(4), 331–343.

Crittenden, P. (1992). Attachment in the preschool years. *Development and Psychopathology, 4*(2), 209–241.

Crockenberg, S. B. (1981). Infant irritability, mother responsiveness, and social support influences on the security of mother infant attachment. *Child Development, 52,* 857–868.

Crouter, A. C., MacDermid, S. M., McHale, S. M., & Perry-Jenkins, M. (1990). Parental monitoring and perceptions of children's school performance and conduct in dual- and single-earner families. *Developmental Psychology, 26,* 649–657.

Csikszentmihalyi, M. (1990). *Flow: The psychology of optimal experience.* New York: Harper & Row.

Csikszentmihalyi, M., & Larson, R. (1984). *Being adolescent.* New York: Basic Books.

Csikszentmihalyi, M., Rathunde, K., Whalen, S., & Wong, M. (1993). *Talented teenagers: The roots of success and failure.* New York: Cambridge University Press.

Darling, N., Cumsille, P., Hames, K., & Caldwell, L. L. (2000). Adolescents as active agents in the monitoring process: Disclosure strategies and motivations. Under editorial review.

Darling, N., & Dowdy, B. (2000). *Monitoring, disclosure, and trust: Mothers' and adolescents' perspectives.* Manuscript submitted for publication.

Darling, N., & Steinberg, L. (1993). Parenting style as context: an integrative model. *Psychological Bulletin, 113*(3), 487–496.

Dishion, T. J., Capaldi, D., Spracklen, K. M., & Li, F. (1995). Peer ecology of male adolescent drug use. *Development and Psychopathology, 7,* 803–824.

Dishion, T. J., French, D. C., & Patterson, G. R. (1995). The development and ecology of antisocial behavior. In D. Cicchetti & D. J. Cohen (Eds.), *Developmental psychology: Vol. 2. Risk, disorder, and adaptation: Wiley series on personality processes* (pp. 421–471). New York: Wiley.

Dishion, T. J., McCord, J., & Poulin, F. (1999). When interventions harm: Peer groups and problem behavior. *American Psychologist, 54,* 755–764.

Dishion, T. J., & McMahon, R. J. (1998). Parental monitoring and the prevention of child and adolescent problem behavior: A conceptual and empirical formulation. *Clinical Child and Family Psychology Review, 1,* 61–75.

Dishion, T. J., Patterson, G. R., & Griesler, P. C. (1994). Peer adaptations in the development of antisocial behavior. In L. R. Huesmann (Ed.), *Current perspectives on aggressive behavior* (pp. 61–95). New York: Plenum Press.

Dishion, T. J., Spracklen, K. M., Andrews, D. W., & Patterson, G. R. (1996). Deviancy training in male adolescents friendships. *Behavior Therapy, 27,* 373–390.

Dix, T., Ruble, D. N., Grusec, J. E., & Nixon, S. (1986). Social cognition in parents: Inferential and affective reactions to children of three age levels. *Child Development, 57,* 879–894.

Dunphy, D. C. (1963). The social structure of urban adolescent peer groups. *Society, 26,* 230–246.

Eccles, J. S., Early, D., Frasier, K., Belansky, E., & McCarthy, K. (1997). The relation of connection, regulation, and support for autonomy to adolescents' functioning. *Journal of Adolescent Research, 12,* 263–286.

Eder, D. (1985). The cycle of popularity: Interpersonal relations among female adolescents. *Sociology of Education, 58,* 154–165.

Elliott, D. S., Huizinga, D., & Ageton, S. S. (1985). *Explaining delinquency and drug use.* Beverly Hills, CA: Sage.

Elliott, D. S., Huizinga, D., & Menard, S. (1989). *Multiple problem youth: Delinquency, substance use, and mental health problems.* New York: Springer-Verlag.

Engels, R. C. M. E., Finkenauer, C., Meeus, W., & Dekovic, M. (2001). Parental attachment and adolescents' emotional adjustment: The associations with social skills and relational competence. *Journal of Counseling Psychology, 48*(4), 428–439.

Engels, R. C. M. E., Knibbe, R. A., de Vries, H., Drop, M. J., & van Breukelen, G. J. P. (1999). Influences of parental and best friends' smoking and drinking on adolescent use: A longitudinal study. *Journal of Applied Social Psychology, 29,* 337–361.

Engels, R. C. M. E., Knibbe, R. A., Drop, M. J., & de Haan, J. T. (1997). Homogeneity of smoking behavior in peer groups: Influence or selection? *Health Education and Behavior, 24,* 801–811.

Ennett, S., & Bauman, K. (1994). The contribution of influence and selection to adolescent peer group homogeneity: The case of adolescent cigarette smoking. *Journal of Personality and Social Psychology, 67,* 653–663.

Erikson, E. H. (1959). *Identity and the life cycle.* New York: W. W. Norton.

Farrell, A. D., & Danish, S. J. (1993). Peer drug associations and emotional restraint: Causes or consequences of adolescents' drug use? *Journal of Consulting and Clinical Psychology, 61,* 327–334.

Farrington, D. P. (1998). Youth crime and antisocial behavior. In A. Campbell & S. Muncer (Eds.), *The social child* (pp. 353–392). Hove, UK: Erlbaum.

Fergusson, D. M., Lynskey, M. T., & Horwood, L. J. (1996). Factors associated with continuity and changes in disruptive behavior patterns between childhood and adolescence. *Journal of Abnormal Child Psychology, 24,* 533–553.

Fine, G. A. (1980). The natural history of preadolescent male friendship groups. In H. C. Foot, A. J. Chapman, & J. R. Smith (Eds.), *Friendship and social relations in children* (pp. 293–320). New York: Wiley.

Fine, G. A., & Glassner, B. (1979). The promise and problems of participant observation with children. *Urban Life, 8,* 153–174.

Fisher, L. A., & Bauman, K. E. (1988). Influence and selection in the friendship-adolescent relationship: Findings from studies of adolescent smoking and drinking. *Journal of Applied Social Psychology, 18,* 289–314.

Flannery, D. J., Vazsonyi, A. T., Torquati, J., & Fridrich, A. (1994). Ethnic and gender differences in risk for early adolescent substance use. *Journal of Youth and Adolescence, 23,* 195–213.

Fletcher, A. C., Darling, N. E., Steinberg, L., & Dornbusch, S. (1995). The company they keep: Relation of adolescents' adjustment and behavior to their friends' perceptions of authoritative parenting in the social network. *Developmental Psychology, 31,* 300–310.

Fletcher, A. H., Flannery, D. J., & Mekos, D. (2000). Parental influences on adolescent involvement in community activities. *Journal of Research on Adolescence, 10*(1), 29–48.

Fridrich, A. H., & Flannery, D. J. (1995). The effects of ethnicity and acculturation on early adolescent delinquency. *Journal of Child and Family Studies, 4,* 69–87.

Fuligni, A. J., & Eccles, J. S. (1993). Perceived parent child relationships and early adolescents' orientation toward peers. *Developmental Psychology, 29,* 622–632.

Galambos, N. L., & Silbereisen, R. K. (1987). Substance use in West German youth: A longitudinal study of adolescents' use of alcohol and tobacco. *Journal of Adolescent Research, 2,* 161–174.

Ganiban, J., Barnett, D., & Cicchetti, D. (2000). Negative reactivity and attachment: Down syndrome's contribution to the attachment-temperament debate. *Development and Psychopathology, 12*(1), 1–21.

Ge, X., Conger, R. D., Cadoret, R. J., Neiderhiser, J. M., Yates, W., Troughton, E., & Stewart, M. A. (1996). The developmental interface between nature and nurture: A mutual influence model of child antisocial behavior and parent behaviors. *Developmental Psychology, 32,* 574–589.

George, C., Kaplan, N., & Main, M. (1985). The Berkeley Adult Attachment Interview. Unpublished protocol, Department of Psychology, University of California, Berkeley.

George, T. P., & Hartmann, D. P. (1996). Friendship networks of unpopular average, and popular children. *Child Development, 67,* 2301–2316.

Giordano, P. C., Cernkovich, S. A., & Pugh, M. D. (1986). Friendships and delinquency. *American Journal of Sociology, 91,* 1170–1202.

Glasgow, K. L., Dornbusch, S. M., Troyer, L., Steinberg, L., & Ritter, L. (1997). Parenting styles, adolescents' attributions, and educational outcomes in nine heterogeneous high schools. *Child Development, 68,* 507–529.

Goldsmith, H. H., & Alansky, J. A. (1987). Maternal and infant temperamental predictors of attachment: A meta-analytic review. *Journal of Consulting and Clinical Psychology, 55*(6), 805–816.

Goldstein, A. P. (1994). Delinquent gangs. In L. R. Huesmann (Ed.), *Aggressive behavior: Current perspectives* (pp. 255–273). New York: Plenum Press.

Greenberg, M. T. (1999). Attachment and psychopathology in childhood. In J. Cassidy & P. R. Shaver (Eds.), *Handbook of attachment: Theory, research, and clinical applications* (pp. 469–496). New York: Guilford Press.

Harris, J. R. (1995). Where is the child's environment? A group socialization theory of development. *Psychological Review, 102,* 458–489.

Harris, J. R. (1998). *The nurture assumption: Why children turn out the way they do.* New York: Free Press.

Hartup, W. W. (1983). Peer relations. In E. M. Hetherington (Ed.), *Handbook of child psychology: Vol. 4. Socialization, personality, and social development* (4th ed., pp. 103–196). New York: Wiley.

Hartup, W. W. (1992). Friendships and their developmental significance. In H. McGurk (Ed.), *Childhood social development: Contemporary perspectives* (pp. 175–205). Hillsdale, NJ: Erlbaum.

Hartup, W. W. (1996). The company they keep: Friendships and their developmental significance. *Child Development, 67,* 1–13.

Hastings, P. D., & Rubin, K. H. (1999). Predicting mothers' beliefs about preschool-aged children's social behavior: Evidence for maternal attitudes moderating child effects. *Child Development, 70,* 722–741.

Hawkins, J. D., & Weiss, J. G. (1985). The social development model: An integrated approach to delinquency prevention. *Journal of Primary Prevention, 6,* 73–97.

Hazan, C., & Shaver, P. R. (1987). Romantic love conceptualized as an attachment process. *Journal of Personality and Social Psychology, 52,* 511–524.

Heilman, M. E. (1976). Oppositional behavior as a function of influence attempt intensity and retaliation threat. *Journal of Personality and Social Psychology, 33,* 574–578.

Hirschi, T. (1969). *Causes of delinquency.* Berkeley: University of California Press.

Iannotti, R. J., Bush, P. J., & Weinfurt, K. P. (1996). Perceptions of friends' use of alcohol, cigarettes, and marijuana among urban schoolchildren: A longitudinal analysis. *Addictive Behaviors, 21,* 615–632.

Jackson, S.A., & Csikszentmihalyi, M. (1999). *Flow in sports: The keys to optimal experiences and performances.* Champaign, IL: Human Kinetics Books.

Jones, M. B., & Offord, D. R. (1989). Reduction of antisocial behavior in poor children by nonschool skill-development. *Journal of Child Psychology and Psychiatry, 30,* 737–750.

Kandel, D. B. (1978). Similarity in real-life adolescent friendship pairs. *Journal of Personality and Social Psychology, 36,* 306–312.

Kandel, D. B. (1985). On processes of peer influences in adolescent drug use: A developmental perspective. *Advances in Alcohol and Substance Abuse, 4,* 139–163.

Kandel, D. B. (1996). Processes of peer influences in adolescence. In R. K. Silbereisen, K. Eyferth, & G. Rudinger (Eds.), *Development as action in context: Problem behaviors and normal youth development* (pp. 203–227). Heidelberg, Germany: Springer-Verlag.

Kaplan, H. B. (1982). Self-attitudes and deviant behavior: New directions for theory and research. *Youth and Society, 14,* 185–211.

Kaplan, H. B., Johnson, R. J., & Bailey, C. A. (1986). Self-rejection and the explanation of deviance: Refinement and elaboration of a latent structure. *Social Psychological Quarterly, 49,* 110–128.

Kaplan, H. B., Martin, S. S., & Johnson, R. J. (1986). Self-rejection and the explanation of deviance: Specification of the structure among the latent constructs. *American Journal of Sociology, 92,* 384–411.

Kenny, M. E. (1987). The extent and function of parental attachment among first-year college students. *Journal of Youth and Adolescence, 16,* 17–29.

Kerr, M., & Stattin, H. (2000). What parents know, how they know it, and several forms of adolescent adjustment: Further evidence for a reinterpretation of monitoring. *Developmental Psychology, 36,* 366–380.

Kerr, M., Stattin, H., & Trost, K. (1999). To know you is to trust you: Parents' trust is rooted in child disclosure of information. *Journal of Adolescence, 22,* 737–752.

Kiesner, J. (2000, December). *Peer relations across settings: Measurement issues and relations with individual adjustment.* Paper presented at the Peer Research Workshop, Örebro, Sweden.

Kinney, D. A. (1993). From nerds to normals: The recovery of identity among adolescents from middle school to high school. *Sociology of Education, 66,* 21–40.

Kirchler, E., Palmonari, A., & Pombeni, M. L. (1996). Developmental tasks and adolescents' relationships with their peers and their family. In S. Jackson & H. Rodriguez-Tomé (Eds.), *Adolescence and its social worlds* (pp. 145–167). Hillsdale, NJ: Erlbaum.

Klein, D. C., & Seligman, M. E. P. (1976). Reversal of performance deficits and perceptual deficits in learned helplessness and depression. *Journal of Abnormal Psychology, 85,* 11–26.

Kobak, R., & Cole, H. (1994). Attachment and meta-monitoring: Implications for adolescent autonomy and psychopathology. In D. Cicchetti & S. L. Toth (Eds.), *Rochester Symposium on Developmental Psychopathology: Vol. 5. Disorders and dysfunctions of the self* (pp. 267–297). Rochester, NY: University of Rochester Press.

Kobak, R., & Sceery, A. (1988). Attachment in late adolescence: Working models, affect regulation, and representations of self and others. *Child Development, 59,* 135–146.

Kochanska, G. (1998). Mother-child relationship, child fearfulness, and emerging attachment: A short-term longitudinal study. *Developmental Psychology, 34,* 480–490.

Ladd, G. W. (1983). Social networks of popular, average, and rejected children in school settings. *Merrill-Palmer Quarterly, 29,* 283–307.

Ladd, G. W. (1989). Children's social competence and social supports: Precursors of early school adjustment? In B. H. Schneider, G. Attili, J. Nadel, & R. P. Weissberg (Eds.), *Social competence in developmental perspective. NATO Advanced Science Institutes series: Series D. Behavioural and social sciences* (Vol. 51, pp. 277–291). Norwell, MA: Kluwer.

Lamborn, S. D., Mounts, N. S., Steinberg, L., & Dornbusch, S. M. (1991). Patterns of competence and adjustment among adolescents from authoritative, authoritarian, indulgent and neglectful families. *Child Development, 62,* 1049–1065.

Laub, J. H., & Sampson, R. J. (1988). Unraveling families and delinquency: A reanalysis of the Gluecks' data. *Criminology, 26,* 355–380.

Leibner, M. J., & Wacker, M. E. E. (1997). A theoretical and empirical assessment of power-control theory and single-mother families. *Youth and Society, 28,* 317–350.

Lerner, R. M. (1996). Relative plasticity, integration, temporality, and diversity in human development: A developmental contextual perspective about theory, process, and method. *Developmental Psychology, 32*(4), 781–786.

Lerner, R. M., & Spanier, G. B. (Eds.). (1978). *Child influences on marital and family interaction: A lifespan perspective.* New York: Academic Press.

Lewis, C. (1981). The effects of parental firm control: A reinterpretation of findings. *Psychological Bulletin, 90*(3), 547–563.

Lewis, M., & Rosenblum, L. A. (1974). *The effect of the infant on its caregiver.* New York: Wiley.

Loeber, R. (1991). Antisocial behavior: More enduring than changeable? *Journal of the American Academy of Child and Adolescent Psychiatry, 30,* 383–397.

Lytton, H. (1990). Child and parent effects in boys' conduct disorder: A reinterpretation. *Developmental Psychology, 26,* 683–697.

Lytton, H. (2000). Toward a model of family-environmental and child-biological influences on development. *Developmental Review, 20,* 150–179.

Maccoby, E. E., & Martin, J. A. (1983). Socialization in the context of the family: parent-child interaction. In P. Mussen & E. M. Hetherington (Eds.), *Handbook of Child Psychology* (Vol. 4, pp. 1–101). New York: Wiley.

Maggs, J. L., & Galambos, N. L. (1993). Alternative structural models for understanding adolescent problem behavior in two-earner families. *Journal of Early Adolescence, 13,* 79–101.

Magnusson, D., & Stattin, H. (1998). Person-context interaction theories. In W. Damon & R. M. Lerner (Eds.), *Handbook of child psychology: Vol. 1. Theoretical models of human development* (pp. 685–759). New York: Wiley.

Mahoney, J. L. (2000). Participation in school extracurricular activities as a moderator in the development of antisocial patterns. *Child Development, 71,* 502–516.

Mahoney, J. L., & Stattin, H. (2000). Leisure time activities and adolescent anti-social behavior: The role of structure and social context. *Journal of Adolescence, 23,* 113–127.

Mahoney, J. L., Stattin, H., & Magnusson, D. (2001). Youth recreation centre participation and criminal offending: A 20-year longitudinal study of Swedish boys. *International Journal of Behavioral Development, 25*(6), 509–520.

Marcus, R. F. (1996). The friendships of delinquents. *Adolescence, 31,* 145–158.

Marvin, R. S., & Britner, P. A. (1999). Normative development: The ontogeny of attachment. In J. Cassidy & P. R. Shaver (Eds.), *Handbook of attachment theory, research, and clinical applications* (pp. 44–67). New York: Guilford Press.

McCord, J. (1978). A 30-year follow-up of treatment effects. *American Psychologist, 33,* 284–289.

McCord, J. (1986). Instigation and insulation: How families affect antisocial aggression. In J. Block, D. Olweus, & M. R. Yarrow (Eds.), *Development of antisocial and prosocial behavior* (pp. 343–357). New York: Academic Press.

McLaughlin, M. W., Irby, M. A., & Langman, J. (1994). *Urban sanctuaries: Neighborhood organizations in the lives and futures of inner-city youth.* San Francisco: Jossey-Bass.

Metzler, C. W., Noell, J., Biglan, A., Ary, D., & Smolkowski, K. (1994). The social context for risky sexual behavior among adolescents. *Journal of Behavioral Medicine, 17,* 419–438.

Mink, I. T., & Nihira, K. (1986). Family life-styles and child behaviors: A study of direction of effects. *Developmental Psychology, 22,* 610–616.

Moffitt, T. E. (1993). Adolescence-limited and life-course-persistent antisocial behavior: A developmental taxonomy. *Psychological Review, 100,* 674–701.

Mounts, N. S., & Steinberg, L. (1995). An ecological analysis of peer influence on adolescent grade point average and drug use. *Developmental Psychology, 31,* 915–922.

Mulhern, R. K., Jr., & Passman, R. H. (1981). Parental discipline as affected by the sex of the parent, the sex of the child, and the child's apparent responsiveness to discipline. *Developmental Psychology, 17,* 604–613.

Nail, P. R., & Van Leeuwen, M. D. (1993). An analysis and restructuring of the diamond model of social response. *Personality and Social Psychology Bulletin, 19,* 106–116.

Nye, F. I. (1958). *Family relationships and delinquent behavior.* New York: Wiley.

Oetting. E. R., & Donnermeyer, J. F. (1998). Primary socialization theory: The etiology of drug use and deviance: I. *Substance Use and Misuse, 33,* 995–1026.

Olweus, D. (1979). Stability of aggressive reaction patterns in males: A review. *Psychological Bulletin, 86,* 852–875.

Overmier, J. B., & Seligman, M. E. P. (1967). Effects of inescapable shock upon subsequent escape and avoidance learning. *Journal of Comparative and Physiological Psychology, 63,* 23–33.

Parker, J. G., & Asher, S. R. (1993). Friendship and friendship quality in middle childhood: Links with peer group acceptance and feelings of loneliness and social dissatisfaction. *Developmental Psychology, 29,* 611–621.

Parker, J. G., Rubin, K. H., Price, J. M., & DeRosier, M. E. (1995). Peer relationships, child development, and adjustment: A developmental psychopathology perspective. In D. Cicchetti & D. Cohen (Eds.), *Developmental psychopathology* (Vol. 2, pp. 96–161). New York: Wiley.

Passman, R. H., & Blackwelder, D. E. (1981). Rewarding and punishing by mothers: The influence of progressive changes in the quality of their sons' apparent behavior. *Developmental Psychology, 17,* 614–619.

Patterson, G. R., DeBaryshe, B. D., & Ramsey, E. (1989). A developmental perspective on antisocial behavior. *American Psychologist, 44,* 329–335.

Patterson, G. R., Reid, J. B., & Dishion, T. (1992). *Antisocial boys.* Eugene, OR: Castilia.

Patterson, G. R., & Stouthamer-Loeber, M. (1984). The correlation of family management practices and delinquency. *Child Development, 55,* 1299–1307.

Peterson, C., & Seligman, M. E. P. (1984). Causal explanations as a risk factor for depression: Theory and evidence. *Psychological Review, 91,* 347–374.

Plomin, R., & Daniels, D. (1987). Why are children in the same family so different from one another? *Behavioral and Brain Sciences, 10,* 1–16.

Plomin, R., Reiss, D., Hetherington, E. M., & Howe, G. (1994). Nature and nurture: Genetic influences on measures of family environment. *Developmental Psychology, 30,* 32–43.

Poulin, F., Dishion, T. J., & Haas, E. (1999). The peer influence paradox: Friendship quality and deviancy training within male adolescent friendships. *Merrill-Palmer Quarterly, 45,* 42–51.

Pulkkinen, L. (1982). Self-control and continuity from childhood to adolescence. In P. B. Balter & O. G. Brim (Eds.), *Life-span development and behavior* (Vol. 4). New York: Academic Press.

Reisman, J. M. (1985). Friendship and its implications for mental health or social competence. *Journal of Early Adolescence, 5,* 383–391.

Reiss, D., Neiderhiser, J. M., Hetherington, E. M., & Plomin, R. (2000). *The relationship code: Deciphering genetic and social influences on adolescent development.* Cambridge, MA: Harvard University Press.

Rodin, J., & Langer, E. J. (1977). Long-term effects of a control-relevant intervention with the institutionalized aged. *Journal of Personality and Social Psychology, 35,* 897–902.

Romer, D., Black, M., Ricardo, I., Feigelman, S., Kaljee, L., Galbraith, J., Nesbit, R., Hornik, R. C., & Stanton, B. (1994). Social influences on the sexual behavior of youth at risk for HIV exposure. *American Journal of Public Health, 84,* 977–985.

Sampson, R. J., & Laub, J. H. (1994). Urban poverty and the family context of delinquency: A new look at structure and process in a classic study [Special issue: Children and poverty]. *Child Development, 65,* 523–540.

Sarnecki, J. (in press). *Co-offending youth networks in Stockholm.* Cambridge, UK: Cambridge University Press..

Seligman, M. E. P. (1975). *Helplessness: On depression, development, and death.* San Francisco: W. H. Freeman.

Silbereisen, R. K., & Noack, P. (1988). On the constructuve role of problem behavior in adolescence. In N. Bolger, A. Caspi, G. Downey, & M. Moorehouse (Eds.), *Persons in context:*

Developmental processes (pp. 152–180). Cambridge, UK: Cambridge University Press.

Smith, A. B., & Inder, P. M. (1990). The relationship of classroom organisation to cross-age and cross-sex friendships. *Educational Psychology, 10,* 127–140.

Sroufe, L. A., & Fleeson, J. (1986). Attachment and the construction of relationships. In W. Hartup & Z. Rubin (Eds.), *Relationships and development.* Hillsdale, NJ: Erlbaum.

Stattin, H., & Kerr, M. (2000). Parental monitoring: A reinterpretation. *Child Development, 71,* 1070–1083.

Stattin, H., & Kerr, M. (2001). Values matter. In J.-E. Nurmi (Ed.), *Navigating through adolescence: European perspectives* (pp. 21– 58). London, UK: RoutledgeFalmer.

Stattin, H., Kerr, M., & Ferrer-Wreder, L. (2000). *Two routes to silence: Why nondisclosure to parents is linked to delinquency.* Manuscript in preparation.

Stattin, H., & Magnusson, D. (1989). The role of early aggressive behavior for the frequency, seriousness, and types of later crime. *Journal of Consulting and Clinical Psychology, 57,* 710–718.

Stattin, H., & Magnusson, D. (1990). *Pubertal maturation in female development.* Hillsdale, NJ: Erlbaum.

Steinberg, L. (2001). We know some things: Parent-adolescent relationships in retrospect and prospect. *Journal of Research on Adolescence, 11*(1), 1–19.

Steinberg, L., Lamborn, S., Darling, N., Mounts, N., & Dornbusch, S. M. (1994). Over-time changes in adjustment and competence among adolescents from authoritative, authoritarian, indulgent, and neglectful families. *Child Development, 65,* 754–770.

Stice, E., & Barrera, M., Jr. (1995). A longitudinal examination of the reciprocal relations between perceived parenting and adolescents' substance use and externalizing behaviors. *Developmental Psychology, 31,* 322–334.

Sullivan, H. S. (1953). *The interpersonal theory of psychiatry.* New York: W. W. Norton.

Susman-Stillman, A., Kalkose, M., Egeland, B., & Waldman, I. (1996). Infant temperament and maternal sensitivity as predictors of attachment security. *Infant Behavior and Development, 19*(1), 33–47.

Sutherland, E. H., & Cressey, D. (1978). *Criminology* (8th ed.). New York: Lippincott.

Thompson, R. A., Cicchetti, D., Lamb, M. E., & Malkin, C. (1985). Emotional responses of Down syndrome and normal infants in the Strange Situation: The organization of affective behavior in infants. *Developmental Psychology, 21*(5), 828–841.

Urberg, K. A., Degirmencioglu, S. M., & Pilgrim, C. (1997). Close friend and group influence on adolescent cigarette smoking and alcohol use. *Developmental Psychology, 33,* 834–844.

Vitaro, F., Tremblay, R. E., Kerr, M., Pagani, L., & Bukowski, W. M. (1997). Disruptiveness, friends' characteristics, and delinquency in early adolescence: A test of two competing models of development. *Child Development, 68,* 676–689.

Weintraub, K. J., & Gold, M. (1991). Monitoring and delinquency. *Criminal Behaviour and Mental Health, 1,* 268–281.

Wells, L. E., & Rankin, J. H. (1988). Direct parental controls and delinquency. *Criminology, 26,* 263–285.

White, M. J., & Kaufman, G. (1997). Language usage, social capital, and school completion among immigrants and native-born ethnic groups. *Social Science Quarterly, 78,* 385–398.

Youniss, J. (1980). *Parents and peers in social development: A Sullivan-Piaget perspective.* Chicago: University of Chicago Press.

Zimmermann, P., Maier, M. A., Winter, M., & Grossmann, K. E. (2001). Attachment and adolescents' emotion regulation during a joint problem-solving task with a friend. *International Journal of Behavioral Development, 25*(4), 331–343.

PART FIVE

ADULTHOOD AND AGING

CHAPTER 17

Disease, Health, and Aging

ILENE C. SIEGLER, HAYDEN B. BOSWORTH, AND LEONARD W. POON

Developmental psychology's goal is to describe, predict, and understand the changes that come with age. Developmental psychology is a multidisciplinary field within psychology—a field that cuts across all of the standard areas of psychology. We adopt the conventional terminology for changes, which implies variations in longitudinal measurements on the same persons over time; this is the core of the psychology of aging. We reserve the term *age differences* for cross-sectional age comparisons at a single point in time; such comparisons are the province of experimental aging research or a psychology of the aged. Understanding the variance accounted for by particular health problems or disease statuses requires both approaches. The key term in developmental psychology is age—that is, the age at time of measurement, the age at the

beginning and at the end of the measurement period, the age at the onset of a disorder, and the age at death. Developmental psychology sees age as more than just a marker variable or placeholder. A basic contribution of developmental psychology has been the development of methodological advances to improve ways to assess age changes in the aforementioned contexts. Health and disease are prominent factors that influence changes associated with age; thus, this chapter examines the measurement and meanings of health and disease and their contribution to our understanding of the aging process.

In this chapter we seek to answer the question of what understanding health can add to developmental psychology. It is clear that developmental psychology sees health primarily as a topic of worry and concern to aging persons. It is a source of stress, requires coping, and can start a cascade of life events. It is an extremely important contextual variable whose content can exert considerable impact, depending on the particular area of study.

Disease is an entity physicians treat; it is the province of medicine and—for psychologists—behavioral medicine. Cognition is perhaps the most important aspect of development that is changed when health is compromised. What is important to note here is that the relationships are bidirectional. Not only do changes in health status precede changes in personality, cognition, and social functioning, for example,

Support for this chapter was provided from National Institute on Aging (R01 AG12458; R01 AG19605), National Cancer Institute (P01 CA72099), and National Heart Lung and Blood Institute (R01 HL55356, P01 HL36587) for Ilene C. Siegler. Hayden Bosworth was supported in part by the Department of Veterans Affairs, Veterans Health Administration, HSR&D Service, through Program 824 Funds. Leonard W. Poon was supported in part by the National Institute on Aging (P01-AG17553), National Institute of Mental Health (5R01-MH43435-09), and in part by the AARP Andrus Foundation.

but changes in health status can also be the result of basic developmental changes in other areas of life. Developmental psychology's perspective is closer in this regard to public health concerns about the *global burden of disease*—which seeks to measure the cost in human terms of these parts of the human condition (Murray & Lopez, 1996) rather than as mechanisms for understanding developmental change.

In 1990 a special issue of the *Journal of Gerontology: Psychological Sciences* examined the relationship between health and aging (Siegler, 1990). Confronting the study of aging for the next century are new realities that have developed since that special issue was published over 10 years ago: (a) the explosion of input from other disciplines, (b) the emphasis on Alzheimer's disease and what this has meant for research, (c) changes in the health status of aging populations reflected in demography and centenarian studies, and (d) the genetic revolution. A subtext of these findings is reflected in the samples that are being studied. In the past—when developmental psychology researchers required respondents to be healthy enough to get to the laboratory (see Siegler, Nowlin, & Blumenthal, 1980)—researchers found that selection biases were occurring as the group got older; they simply noted the fact, however, and continued to do research the way they always have. As data have become available from epidemiological studies that include measures of cognition, personality, or both (e.g., see Fried et al., 1998, from the Cardiovascular Health Study; M. F. Elias, Elias, D'Agostino, & Wolf, 2000, from the Framingham Study), we are seeing an explosion of relevant articles in the epidemiological literature that can contribute to our understanding of aging and health. The use of population samples in our research—such as in the Berlin Aging Study (Baltes & Mayer, 1999)—and the addition of measures of cognition to the Asset and Health Dynamics Among the Oldest Old (AHEAD) study (e.g., see Herzog & Wallace, 1997; Zelinski, Crimmins, Reynolds, & Seeman, 1998) have allowed us to better understand estimates of the effects of varying amounts of complete data and to better evaluate the costs and benefits of various sampling approaches.

Some material that might be expected to appear in this chapter is not addressed here because other authors in this volume have integrated health-related issues into their discussions of specific areas of adult development. Clearly, there are important bidirectional relationships between health and cognition (see the chapter by Dixon & Cohen in this volume), personality (see the chapter by Bertrand & Lachman in this volume), social relationships (see the chapter by Pruchno & Rosenbaum in this volume), and—in particular—the very definition of successful aging (see the chapter by Freund & Riediger in this volume). These psychosocial factors have an impact on health status and disease incidence and progression, and specific diseases have major impacts on

cognitive, personality, and social functioning. These relationships were recognized by the National Academy of Science Committee's report on the aging mind (Stern & Carstensen, 2000), and they can be seen in a commissioned chapter by Waldstein (2000) that reviews the findings of medical conditions on cognitive functioning. The regular inclusion of health reflects a major research development in adult development and aging; this development has taken place in the past 5 years and reflects recognition of the centrality of the study of health to the study of aging. Thus, in this chapter we focus on data from newly available data sets not collected by other authors in this volume. Most of the very best new work was done in a multidisciplinary context; we draw our illustrations from these research teams.

BASIC FACTS ABOUT TODAY'S AGING POPULATION

First, what is middle age like now? What is old age like now? In the following discussion we first answer these questions and then discuss how these new realities affect the study of health, behavior, and aging. Finally, we examine the question of which basic issues are important to a study of disease, health, and aging for the future development of this area.

Twenty-First Century Middle Age

An increasing life span is changing the concept of middle age. The ages from 40–60 years are clearly now middle-aged, because many people can reasonably expect to live to 80 to 100 and beyond. In 1995, the age-adjusted death rate for the total population reached an all-time low, and life expectancy at birth increased to 75.8 years, with a high of 79.6 years for White women (R. N. Anderson, Kochanek, & Murphy, 1997); put another way, 70% of people today will live to age 65—the normal retirement age—and 72% of deaths will come from persons over age 65 (Rowe & Kahn, 1998). This makes middle age a potentially different time of life from what it was only 25 years ago. Kaplan, Haan, and Wallace (1999) show how relatively recent this phenomenon is. "Between 1940 and 1995 life expectancy at birth increased 21% for females and 19% for males. Men and women who reach 65 can expect to live 15.7 and 18.9 years more; while life expectancy at age 80 has increased to 8.9 years for women and 7.3 years for men" (p. 90). Individuals now enter middle age under surveillance for diseases and are able to benefit from treatments that allow them to survive with many diagnoses that may not have any impact on their ability to function.

The explosion of interest in middle age is well represented in the collection of chapters in volumes edited by Lachman and James (1997) and Willis and Reid (1999). In terms of health, disease, and aging, the major topic for most middle-aged persons is how to maintain health status as long as possible and how to put off old age. Successful aging really means not aging at all—or not appearing to have aged at all. Health psychology has been very successful at helping to determine the factors that predict disease onset in middle age and premature morbidity and mortality—now defined as below the average population age at death, which in the United States is around 75 years old. In fact, the same set of behavioral risk factors that are related to the onset of major chronic diseases (heart disease, cancer) also predict long-term disability-free survival (Siegler & Bastian, in press).

Bernice Neugarten's (1974) term *young-old* (which divided the aging life cycle into two phases: 55–74 and 75 and older) has now become the expected rite of passage—refusing the *old* part of the young-old label entirely. However, it is important to recognize that successes in disease prevention in middle age make incidence of these same or related diseases higher later in life.

By midlife, health becomes important in definitions of self (Whitbourne & Collins, 1998), and bad health is a major feared possible self. Among middle-aged respondents, 67% versus 49% of the older respondents feared negative health changes (Hooker, 1999). Health threats can have an impact on coping, appraisal risk, and well-being (H. Leventhal et al., 1997). These changes in the boundaries of midlife are also reflected in survival differences that have implications for middle-aged persons—they are increasingly likely to have older parents and in-laws who require help with daily activities. These transfers of help across generations can take the form of time or of money and can have significant impact on both generations (Soldo & Hill, 1995). These experiences also have mental and physical health effects (Hooker, Shifren, & Hutchinson, 1992). Regardless of the relationship of the caregiver to the care recipient or the type of care recipient illness, the vast caregiving literature has shown that caregiving is associated with increased levels of distress, marital strain, and health problems among parents of children with chronic illness (Bristol, Gallagher, & Schopler, 1988; Schulz & Quittner, 1998), family members of organ transplant patients (Buse & Pieper, 1990; Zabora, Smith, Baker, Wingard, & Cubroe, 1992), both children of dementia patients (Haley, Levine, Brown, & Bartolucci, 1987) and spouses of dementia patients (Vitaliano, Russo, Young, Teri, & Maiuro, 1991; Vitaliano et al., 1999; Vitaliano et al., 2002), reflecting the well-known facts that psychological stress is linked to disease (see Baum & Posluszny, 1999).

Decisions about health made in midlife have long-term consequences. Women at around age 50, for example, must make decisions about hormone replacement therapy that may affect their risk of Alzheimer's disease and osteoporosis in the future (Siegler et al., 2002). Furthermore, individual differences in personality predict risk behavior profiles, which also have long-term health consequences (Siegler, Kaplan, Von Dras, & Mark, 1999), personality also predicts just as do screening behaviors such as mammography (Siegler, Feaganes, & Rimer, 1995) and the use of hormone replacement therapy (Bastian, Bosworth, Mark, & Siegler, 1998; Matthews, Owens, Kuller, Sutton-Tyrell, & Jansen-McWilliams, 1998).

A feature of middle age for women is the menopausal transition (Sowers, 2000), and the literature is starting to question endocrine changes in middle-aged men (Morley, 2000). An intriguing developmental question is whether age at menopause is a marker for rates of normal aging in women (Matthews, Wing, Kuller, Meilahn, & Owens, 2000, Perls et al., 2000), such that later menopause is a marker for longevity. Endocrine changes in men are more gradual than in women, but such changes are becoming an area of research interest (Morley, 2000; Tenover, 1999). Like estrogen levels, androgen levels decrease with age and have a broad range of effects on sexual organs and metabolic processes. Androgen deficiency in men older than 65 leads to a decrease in muscle mass, osteoporosis, decrease in sexual activity, and changes in mood and cognitive function—leading us to speculate that there may be at least two phases of chronic diseases related to androgen levels in men. Whether men over 65 would benefit from androgen replacement therapy is not known (Tenover, 1999). Any potential benefits from this therapy would need to be weighed against the possible adverse effects on the prostate and the cardiovascular system. Thus, considering men and women separately may be useful (Siegler et al., 2001).

Twenty-First Century Old Age

Let us remind ourselves of what we know—but that which is not obvious—about those known as "the elderly." A new emphasis on centenarians has meant that national statistics are now available up to age 100 and are often broken down more finely by age than they were before. The age of an older person provides some information about the probability of disability and the probability of living independently in the community; this can be seen in Table 17.1.

Note that until age 80, these indicators are reasonably stable for the older population—that is over 75% with no disability and less than 10% in institutions. We have known for a long time that institutionalization is a marker for the supporting network as much as it is for the functional capacities of the individual, at least until the person is no longer mobile or continent. By age 85, half are disabled. Although these figures vary by gender and other indicators, this is a

TABLE 17.1   What Are Older People Like and How Old Is Old?

Age Group	% No Disability	% in Nursing Home
65–69	83	3
70–74	83	5
80–84	62	10
85–89	45	17
90–94	35	32
95–99	20	42
100+	18	48

Note. From USDHHS (1999). Centenarians in the United States: 1990. See Siegler & Bastian (in press).

reasonable guideline for thinking about current population statistics for today's older population. The great variation in the population makes the design and interpretation of studies increasingly challenging.

Demographic projections suggest that rates of disability are declining (Manton, Corder, & Stallard, 1997) and that the gender ratio may be starting to move towards equalization in countries such as the United States due to efforts at prevention of cardiovascular heart disease (CHD)—benefiting men—and the long-term consequences of smoking in women (Guralnik, Balfour, & Volpato, 2000). However, most older people are women (E. Leventhal, 2000). There is evidence that women have different experiences with health and thus may report symptoms differently (E. Leventhal, 2000). Even when they have the same disease (such as a heart attack), the outcomes may be different (Vaccarino, Berkman, & Krumholz, 2000), and the perceptions of health-related quality of life also differ between men and women with the same disease (Bosworth, Siegler, Brummett, Barefoot, Williams, Clapp-Channing, et al., 1999; Bosworth, Siegler, Brummett, Barefoot, Williams, Vitaliano, et al., 1999).

CHANGES IN OTHER DISCIPLINES

Geriatric medicine is a branch of internal medicine that specializes in the care of older persons—particularly the oldest-old—and differs from developmental psychology in that it is unconcerned with adult development or midlife. Geriatric medicine is now a well-recognized discipline that has regular handbooks that update the new findings on each disease and its presentation in the elderly—with implications for treatment. The *Principles of Geriatric Medicine and Gerontology* (e.g., see Hazzard, Blass, Ettinger, Halter, & Ouslander, 1999) as well as the *Encyclopedia of Aging* (Maddox et al., 2001) have reasonable summaries of each disease and physiological system; the latter is a good reference for developmental psychologists, as are textbooks in gerontology, which provide reviews of physiological systems (e.g., Aldwin & Gilmer, 1999). Epidemiology looks at the

distributions of disease in the population and is starting to consider age as more than a variable to be statistically controlled and a primary risk factor, whereas developmental epidemiology seeks to understand the role of age (see Fried, 2000; NIA Genetic Epidemiology Working Group, 2000). All of these references are good primary sources for developmental psychologists who want to keep up with important developments in health-related fields.

Demographers are way ahead of psychologists in their thinking about the role of behavioral and social variables on survival and the role that age plays in such models. In particular, the detailed discussion—in a chapter by Ewbank (2000)—of the apolipoprotein E (APOE) gene polymorphism, which has implications for both Alzheimer's disease and ischemic heart disease, is particularly useful. The chapter discusses the contributions that genetics will make to demographic studies of aging and is a useful introduction to this complex and important set of issues for psychologists.

THE EMPHASIS ON ALZHEIMER'S DISEASE

One can not overemphasize the importance of the creation of the National Institute on Aging (NIA) in 1974 and the push by NIA to develop the Alzheimer's Centers programs. Research on basic biological mechanisms of the aging process is progressing at such a rate that from the time this chapter is written to the time it is published, this rate of new knowledge generation will have changed significantly what we know. The focus on Alzheimer's disease has also had an impact on understanding cognition and aging so that the age-related and disease-related components can be separated. Progress in developmental psychology does not happen at anywhere near the same rate, but developmental psychology must take into account the developing knowledge base in the biomedical sciences.

This emphasis has also produced some extraordinary studies with multidisciplinary teams of psychological, medical, and epidemiological sophistication; these teams are producing extraordinary data to answer important questions. Even better is that the results are being published in *Psychology and Aging*—our primary journal. Wilson, Gilley, Bennett, Beckett, and Evans (2000) provide an example of the type of research that sets a standard for the future. Their research asks the right questions, has compelling data, and was well-designed to understand the role that age plays in the rate of change in cognitive decline in Alzheimer's disease (AD). Why is this study design so good?

This study (a) was based on a population sample of everyone with AD in the community under study; (b) had state-of-the-art diagnostic measures of the medical condition under study; (c) verified those measures; (d) had state-of-the-art measures of the psychological factors under study; (e) collected repeated-measures data; (f) paid attention to study attrition and reasons for loss to follow-up; (g) used modern statistical methods—growth curve analyses to look at individual patterns of change—that allow for variations in measurement periods, missing data, and multiple measurements; and (h) asked and answered questions about initial level of cognitive functioning and the association of that level with eventual patterns of decline.

Approximately 400 persons with a diagnosis of AD were tested at yearly intervals for up to five repeated measures with a battery of psychometrically validated measures, including 17 key cognitive components of functioning changed in AD. The scales were combined into a composite such that raw scores were transformed to z scores and then averaged if at least eight of the scores were not missing. At the start of the study, individuals were aged 45–95 with a mean of 70.9 years, had graduated from high school, and were primarily female (67%) and White (85%). Mental status scores ranged from 11–29, excluding those with extremely impaired cognitive functioning.

The main results were that cognitive change was large, linear, and progressive (about one half of a standard unit per year). Those with better initial cognitive functioning changed more slowly, and younger persons declined faster than did older persons. Data were presented for estimates of the individuals studied and in 5-year age groups. When the data were reanalyzed substituting changes in mental status with the Mini Mental Status Examination (MMSE; Folstein, Folstein, & McHugh, 1975) a standard screening measure, the basic conclusions were the same: There was an annual loss of 3.26 points per year, with bigger losses for those in their 60s than for those in their 80s. Of individuals who died during the course of the study, autopsy confirmed diagnosis in 96% of the cases.

In their discussion, Wilson et al. (2000) raised important issues that their study was not able to solve. These questions primarily had to do with how to address initial level of cognitive functioning. Everyone in the study had AD at the start of the study as a criterion for selection. Premorbid levels of cognition were not known. Similarly, age at first testing and age of onset of the disease could only be estimated by retrospective accounts of time of first symptoms. One could have started studying a very large population at age 40, conducted a 50-year study, and perhaps have had premorbid estimates of functioning and age at onset. Yet the design employed was an efficient way to help answer some important questions about the age-related nature of cognitive change in patients with AD.

The previously described study is not the only work in the field that meets these criteria—it is just one of the most recent

and available in a single article, and a particular disease was of interest that is not considered a normal part of the aging process. The work of M. F. (Pete) Elias and his colleagues, combining insights from his longitudinal study of hypertension (M. F. Elias, Robbins, Elias, & Streeten, 1998) with work on the Framingham Study population (M. F. Elias et al., 2000; P. K. Elias, Elias, D'Agostino, Cupples, et al., 1997; M. F. Elias, Elias, D'Agostino, & Wolf, 1997; M. F. Elias, Elias, Robbins, Wolf, & D'Agostino, 2000), is also superb. In reviewing the role of age versus particular health conditions in the Framingham population, M. F. Elias et al. (in press) compared the adjusted odds ratios of performing at or below the 25th percentile on the Framingham neuropsychological test measurements controlling for education, occupation, gender, alcohol consumption, previous history of cardiovascular disease, and antihypertensive treatment. They found that age itself was the strongest factor—getting 5 years older increased the odds to 1.61 of performing at or below the 25th percentile on a battery of neuropsychological tests, compared to having Type II diabetes (1.21) or an increase in diastolic blood pressure of 10 mm of mercury (1.30).

The M. F. Elias et al. (2000) data from the Framingham study were reanalyzed to answer two important questions: Does the impact of hypertension interact with age, and what is the practical significance of blood-pressure–related versus age-related changes? In addition, they reviewed findings from their longitudinal study of hypertensive and normotensive individuals (M. F. Elias et al., 1998). Their very careful analyses indicated that increasing age, increasing blood pressure, and chronicity of hypertension were all related to worse neuropsychological performance; there were no age interactions in these cross-sectional analyses of longitudinal data sets. The authors point to the methodological problem with longitudinal studies that do not have groups of non-treated hypertensive participants to follow over time. Thus, although it is clear that increased rates of hypertension are deleterious to cognitive functioning, it is important in future clinical trials that the impact of treatment on cognitive performance of older persons be monitored as well. For additional information, see Siegler, Bosworth, and Elias (in press).

Research examining the factors predicting cognitive decline is not limited to health factors. Fratiglioni, Wang, Ericsson, Maytan, and Winblad (2000) reported that social integration predicted the 3-year incidence of AD in community-dwelling residents of a neighborhood in Stockholm, Sweden. The reason for their finding is unclear but provocative. It will be interesting to follow this cohort until it is depleted and see how many eventually become demented, at what age, and what role social participation plays in understanding the full process.

HEALTH STATUS IN CENTENARIANS

The study of centenarians illustrates many important aspects of how studies of behavior, health, and aging have changed in the past 10 years. Table 17.1 shows the amount of disability that comes with increasing age; thus, longevity does not guarantee good health. This is surprising because most people expect that those who live until 100 should be in excellent physical and mental health. Increased survival does not amount to providing a disease-free old age for everyone.

Research reported in the Georgia and New England Centenarian Studies (Perls & Silver, 1999; Poon, Martin, Clayton, Messner, & Noble, 1992) seemed to indicate that those who survived to extreme old age tended to escape catastrophic disease episodes until they surpassed the average life span. If these findings are generalizable to other long-lived individuals, then the trajectories of health and functioning over the life span would indeed be significantly different from those of the average population. For the long-lived, variations in health and cognition increased for participants in the Georgia Centenarian Study as well as for participants in the Swedish Centenarian Study (Hagberg, Alfredson, Poon, & Homma, 2001). The large within-group variation reflects the diversity and range of health and functioning in the oldest-old.

Estimates are generally that a third of extremely aged individuals are healthy enough to be independent and community dwelling, a third are functionally impaired, and a third are extremely frail and disabled (Forette, 1997). Franceschi et al. (2000) provides similar estimates (within 10%) from all of Italy, with criteria-based disease status and functional ability. The authors point out that the study of centenarians is a type of archeological research that includes social and historical circumstances over the past 100 years. Similar findings were reported by Franke (1977, 1985) on two centenarian samples in Germany. Western Europe has even greater proportions of older persons than does the United States, with 40% of the population expected to be over the age of 60 by 2030 (Giampoli, 2000). Studies of the full centenarian population are more common when measures of cognition are not required for study (see Jeune & Andersen-Ranberg, 2000; Poon et al., 1992); thus, past studies that focused on so-called expert survivors (Poon, Johnson, & Martin, 1997) may have given an overly optimistic picture of this age group.

Study and observation of centenarians are rare in the repertoire of life span researchers and gerontologists. The original data and papers were collected by Belle Boone Beard (1991), and comprehensive interview and testing video tapes of over 140 centenarians from the Georgia Centenarian Study are archived at the Hargrett Library of the University of Georgia. The material is available to all serious researchers who wish to pursue research on this important group of aging persons.

Longitudinal studies of aging can inform studies of the long-lived on predictors of survival. For example, the Alameda County Study (Breslow & Breslow, 1993) isolated seven health practices as risk factors for higher mortality. They are excessive alcohol consumption, smoking cigarettes, being obese, sleeping fewer or more than seven to eight hours per night, having very little physical activity, eating between meals, and skipping breakfast. These findings are very similar to those found in the Harvard College Alumni Study (Paffenbarger et al., 1993). The Dutch Longitudinal Study (Deeg, van Zonneveld, van der Maas, & Habbema, 1989) found that physical, mental, and social indicators of health status are important for predicting the probability of dying.

It is clear that there is strong agreement among longitudinal aging studies that maintenance of health, cognition, and support systems; a positive hereditary predisposition; and an active lifestyle are all influential in prolonging longevity in the general population. An important question is whether these same predictors are equally important for the very long-lived—for example, those whose longevity extends beyond 100 years. There are very limited data that could address this question. Poon et al. (2000) examined survival among a group of 137 centenarians (75.9% women) who participated in the Georgia Centenarian Study, of whom 21 were still alive at the time of the investigation in 1999. They found the following relationships among characteristics of centenarians and length of survival beyond 100 years:

- Women on the average survived 1,020 days after attaining 100 years. Men, on the other hand, survived an average of 781 days. The gender difference in survival in the first 2 years after 100 is not significantly different; however, the difference is quite glaring after 3 years.

- Father's age at death was found to exert a positive effect on the number of days of survival after 100 years. No effect was found for mother's age of death.

- Three variables in social support seem to relate to length of survival among centenarians. They are talking on the phone, having someone to help, and having a caregiver.

- Four anthropometric measures were found to correlate positively to survival. They are triceps skin fold, body mass index, and waist-to-hip ratio.

- Higher level of cognition after 100 was positively related to longer length of survival; this was found for problem solving, learning and memory, and intelligence tests, such as picture arrangement and block design. In this study, gender, family longevity, social support, anthropometry, and cognition all seemed to impact on survivorship after 100 years.

Within centenarians, it is clear that variation is extraordinary in health just as in most other characteristics mentioned. There are special problems associated with studying psychological characteristics in the full centenarian population. Poon et al. (2000) demonstrated the effects of attrition in longitudinal studies of centenarians. If attrition and patterns of attrition are not accounted for in the analyses, the outcome would essentially focus on the survivors—and this would not be representative of the entire population. In this study, attrition seemed to affect different psychological measures differently. In cognition, for example, fluid intelligence seems to be affected more by attrition than is crystallized intelligence.

Data from the Cardiovascular Health Study evaluated 5-year survival from ages 65–101 at baseline (Fried et al., 1998) in almost 6,000 persons, including both White and African American participants. The participants were well-characterized medically for both clinical and subclinical measures of health status and standard CHD risk factors. In addition, depressive symptoms were assessed by the Center for Epidemiologic Study Depression Scale (CES-D; Radloff, 1977), cognition with the MMSE (Folstein et al., 1975), and the Digit Symbol Substitution task of the Wechsler Adult Intelligence Scale (WAIS). Participants were reinterviewed every 6 months and had been followed for 5 years at the time of the article. Individuals from four communities in the United States were identified by random sample from the Health Care Financing Administration, and 57% of the sampled individuals participated. Mortality follow-up was complete for 100% of the sample. There were 646 deaths— 12% of the population had died in 5 years. The effect of age on mortality was greatly reduced by adjusting for other demographic, disease, behavioral, and functional indicators. The effect of age on mortality became substantially weaker with adjustment coded into the prediction equation than when it was analyzed in isolation. Digit Symbol Substitution remained a significant predictor even after adjustment for everything else, including objective measures of both clinical and subclinical disease. Thus, much of the effect of age on mortality is explained by the other disease and personal characteristics. If it were not for the diseases and health habits, people would live longer.

GENETICS REVOLUTION

The genetics revolution affects the study of psychology of aging in two important ways. First, as the source of individual differences, understanding genetic polymorphisms, how they relate to behavior, and how these then change with age becomes critical. Secondly, the genetics of survival and

longevity are a major concern of understanding the biology of aging and of gender differences, which have changed over time and need to be taken into account as the background for theories about life span development and aging.

Although answers to the preceding two sources of genetic influences on behavioral aging are still to be found, McClearn and Heller (2000) provide an interesting explanation of how to assess the literature in this area. They point out that at different ages, the relative contributions of genetic and environmental variance in important characteristics may change— this is a new way of thinking about genetic variation. It is generally assumed that after a genetic marker is known, it will be a stable individual difference characteristic. Although genes are fixed at birth, they can have different effects at different ages, interact with environments differentially at different ages, and behave differentially in different populations. There are age-related changes in *heritability*—that is, the amount of variance in a population due to genetic variance. In addition to age-related changes in heritability, it is quite possible that different genes or different combinations of genes are operative at different parts of the life cycle. Illustrations from the Swedish/Adoption Twin Study of Aging for understanding stability of personality are given by Pederson and Reynolds (1988), and a discussion of patterns for three cholesterol indicators is given by McClearn and Heller (2000).

Together, these data sets illustrate the complex interactions of genes and environment over the adult life cycle. As more and more data become available that attest to the gene-environment interactions across the life cycle, we will be better able to make use of them. To extend this line of thinking further, issues of longitudinal stability and change may be affected or interpreted differently when both genetic and environmental factors are included over time (Pederson & Reynolds, 1998).

The genetic basis of longevity has not been part of developmental psychology. The literature has yet to successfully partial out the influences of genetics and environment on longevity and behavioral aging. However, findings from centenarian studies could begin to shed light on some of these issues. For example, findings from the French Centenarian Study (Robine, Kirkwood, & Allard, 2001) showed a trade-off of fertility and longevity—that is, women who bear no or few children tend to live longer. Does the lower-stress environment of fewer children contribute to longevity, or is there a genetic predisposition to protect women with fewer children in order to decrease stress?

In the Georgia Centenarian Study (Kim, Bramlett, Wright, & Poon, 1998), gender and race were found to combine to influence longevity after 100. African Americans showed longer survival times than did European Americans, and females (as noted earlier) showed increased survivorship in comparison to males. At any given time, the risk of death for women was only 54% of that of men. Likewise, risk of death for African Americans was 57% of that of European Americans at any given time. The order of increasingly longer survival for sex-race subgroups was European American males, African American males, European American females, and African American females. These findings suggest that the differentiation of genetics and environmental influences would help us better understand the impact of race and gender on longevity. Similarly, the Georgia study found that higher levels of cognition are related to longer life—and that among the independent centenarians, everyday problem-solving abilities seemed to be maintained (Poon et al., 1992).

Does experience acquired over one's lifetime help to buffer and maintain problem-solving abilities, which in turn help the individual live longer? These are intriguing questions that could add a new dimension to the study of developmental psychology.

SOME BASIC CONCEPTUAL ISSUES

As our population continues to age, a better understanding of how disease, health, and aging are interrelated becomes all the more important—and more difficult to measure and understand. Health is an odd concept. It does have psychological meaning to individuals and to developmental psychologists. It is not the inverse of disease and it also has a developmental trajectory and importance. How it is defined makes a major differences in the conclusions about health and aging. It is important to remember that *health* is often defined from the research participants' (not the researchers') perspective.

Health-Related Quality of Life (HRQoL)

HRQoL has been defined as a multidimensional concept that includes the physical, mental, and social aspects of health (e.g., Sherbourne, Meredith, & Ware, 1992). HRQoL is important for measuring the impact of chronic disease (Patrick & Erickson, 1993). There is evidence of great individual variation in functional status and well-being that is not accounted for by age or disease condition (Sherbourne et al., 1992). HRQoL is typically conceptualized as an outcome of psychological and functional factors that individuals ascribe to their health.

We have completed a series of studies using a measure of HRQoL using the Short-Form Health Survey (SF-36; Ware, 1993). The specific item that most investigators use to measure health is the question *How do you rate your health? Excellent, very good, good, fair, or poor?* This is also a question on the

SF-36 in the domain of General Health and could be considered the SF-1. The SF-36, the complete HRQoL measure, has proven to be very useful to evaluate a patient's perspective as a medical outcome and is typically scored as eight scales.

The Medical Outcomes Study (MOS) 36-item SF-36 is a Likert-type or forced-choice measure that contains eight brief indexes of general health perceptions, general mental health, physical functioning, role limitations due to emotional problems, limitations in social functioning because of physical health problems, role limitations due to physical problems, bodily pain, and vitality. These indexes have been factored into two overall measures of physical health and mental health.

Our work has been based on a sample of patients referred for coronary angiography; the patients can be separated into those with and those without significant heart disease. Coronary angiography is a surgical procedure used to determine how much stenosis or blockage exists for the major arteries. This group is an interesting sample to study because their actual disease and physiological status have been measured and can be used to control for physical health or disease status. Our work was designed to find out why and how social support can moderate the effects of disease; it followed our report that social support and income predicted mortality from coronary heart disease when actual physical health was accounted for (Williams et al., 1992).

All patients referred to Duke University Medical Center for an evaluation of their symptoms to see whether they had blocked arteries (1992–1996) were invited to be in the study upon admission and given a large battery of psychosocial instruments. Those without coronary artery disease were not studied further. Those with disease were followed for the next 3 years with repeated assessments—including the SF-36—of psychosocial factors. The Duke Cardiovascular Database follows all coronary patients at Duke for assessment of future disease and mortality (Califf et al., 1989). Understanding the characteristics of the sample is important because it allows us to ask some questions from an aging point of view such that we can evaluate younger and older persons with the same disease and see whether psychosocial factors play the same role in younger and older patients.

We looked at the relationship between social support and HRQoL in this sample and observed that a lack of social support was associated with significantly lower levels of HRQoL across all eight SF-36 HRQoL domains after considering disease severity and other demographic factors. We also observed an interesting relationship between age and HRQoL. Older adults were likely to experience lower levels of physical function and physical role function; however, older adults were also more likely to report higher levels of mental health, emotional role function, and vitality compared to younger adults (Bosworth, Siegler, et al., 2000). A possible explanation for this finding is that older patients show mental health better than that of younger patients with similar diseases because the onset of chronic illness in old age is more usual and—subsequently—possibly less disruptive than in younger adults. In addition, older persons may have developed more effective skills with which to manage health deficits (Deeg, Kardaun, & Fozard, 1996). These two points coincide with Neugarten's (1976, 1979) view that the onset of chronic illness in old age is more usual in that part of the life cycle and therefore possibly less disruptive. Subsequently, as individuals lose physical function, they may focus and channel more of their energy and attention on the maintenance of psychological quality of life.

Self-Rated Health (SRH)

After Mossey and Shapiro (1982) found that self-ratings of health (SRH) were predictive of 7-year survival among older adults, there has been an enhanced interest in the use of SRH (usually measured by asking respondents whether they would rate their health as excellent, very good, good, fair, or poor) as a measure of health status. This interest among researchers has grown because this item is easy to administer to large populations, and it captures perceptions of health by using criteria that are as broad and inclusive as the responding individual

chooses to make them (Bosworth, Siegler, Brummett, Barefoot, Williams, Vitaliano, et al., 1999).

SRH is a specific component of HRQoL and reflects more than the individuals' perceptions of their physical health. Psychological well-being also is a relevant factor in SRH (George & Clipp, 1991; Hooker & Siegler, 1992). For example, some researchers have suggested that SRHs reflect a person's integrated perception of his or her health—including its biological, psychological, and social dimensions—that is normally inaccessible to other observers (Mülunpalo, Vuori, Oja, Pasanen, & Urponen, 1997; Parkerson, Broadhead, & Tse, 1992; Ware, 1987)

This sample of patients with coronary artery disease (CAD) has both medically determined and self-perceived ratings of health. It is a particularly interesting group to study because we can help explain the import of SRH measures and how to interpret the single-item index in the context of aging persons who are well-characterized in terms of their actual health-disease status. Some data from this sample are presented in Table 17.2, which shows demographic indicators, the functional scales of the SF-36, and two psychosocial indicators. Table 17.3 shows the other medical conditions present in this population.

The data show that when restricted to the 2,900 persons (ranging in age from 28–93) who had serious and significant coronary artery disease, people rated their health all along the SRH continuum from excellent (3%) to very good (15%) to

TABLE 17.2 Demographic and Psychosocial Characteristics of Study Sample by Self-Rated Health

	Rating				
	Excellent	Very Good	Good	Fair	Poor
Number of subjects	95	442	831	950	544
General health	86.68 (15.8)	75.70 (13.1)	60.77 (14.4)	40.30 (14.4)	26.24 (13.7)
Age	60.3 (11.2)	62.7 (11.1)	61.9 (11.1)	62.8 (11.1)	63.4 (10.4)
% male	86%	78%	74%	62%	61%
% White	84%	88%	84%	79%	78%
Education	13.18 (3.9)	12.87 (3.9)	12.16 (3.6)	10.8 (3.6)	9.87 (3.8)
Income	3.76 (1.9)	3.81 (1.8)	3.34 (1.7)	2.63 (1.6)	2.13 (1.5)
% married	85%	83%	80%	72%	67%
Physical function	82.21 (21.6)	72.25 (24.5)	63.49 (25.4)	44.02 (25.4)	27.70 (22.4)
Physical role	72.80 (37.6)	58.96 (42.0)	47.04 (42.0)	25.31 (36.7)	12.16 (27.2)
Emotional role	89.61 (22.5)	80.02 (35.5)	75.40 (37.7)	60.5 (44.2)	48.67 (44.0)
Social function	87.63 (20.6)	81.81 (22.9)	75.94 (24.0)	61.50 (27.3)	43.94 (27.3)
Bodily pain	66.81 (28.1)	63.91 (25.7)	57.06 (25.1)	45.65 (24.9)	31.75 (23.7)
Mental health	82.67 (16.9)	77.85 (18.0)	74.74 (18.3)	66.47 (21.0)	58.42 (22.0)
Vitality	69.56 (22.9)	59.06 (23.4)	50.20 (22.7)	37.09 (21.4)	24.35 (19.5)
Social support	40.6 (6.8)	41.0 (6.2)	39.6 (6.8)	37.8 (7.2)	35.9 (7.7)
CESD	8.93 (9.3)	9.88 (8.7)	12.47 (10.5)	16.78 (10.7)	21.91 (11.5)

Note. All of the variables except age were significantly related to levels of self-rated health. Standard deviations in parentheses. Significance tests were calculated after adjusting for age, education, and gender. Income on a scale from 1 to 6; 1 = $10,000 or less, 2 = $10,001 − $20,000, 3 = $20,001 − $30,000, 4 = $30,001−$45,000, 5 = $45,001 − $60,000, 6 = $60,001 or greater. CESD = Center for Epidemiological Studies Depression Scale. Social support = Interpersonal Social Evaluation List.

TABLE 17.3   Characteristics of Study Sample by Self-Rated Health and Comorbid Conditions

	Conditions				
	Excellent	Very good	Good	Fair	Poor
Chronic pulmonary	2%	6%	9%	14%	24%
Hypertension	39%	49%	57%	66%	70%
Cerebrovascular	5%	6%	10%	13%	19.5%
Peripheral vascular	5%	9%	11%	14%	23%
Renal insufficiency	2%	6%	10%	16%	24%
Diabetes	1.6%	2%	3%	7%	16%
Depression	0%	1%	4.3%	4.5%	7%

good (29%), to fair (33%), and poor (19%). The average age of each subgroup ranged from 60 to 63.4 years. These findings can be compared to national figures from 1996, in which the percent of the U.S. population that rated their health as fair or poor aged 55–64 was 21.2% and aged 65 and over was 27% (United States Department of Health and Human Services, 1999, p. 211, Table 60). In our sample of a wider age range, with significant heart disease, by comparison, 52% rated their health as fair or poor.

Thus, in a sample with documented serious heart disease, the rate of fair or poor health was twice as high as in a national population sample of the same age. These levels were associated with the *hazard score* (Harrell, Lee, Califf, Pryor, & Rosati, 1984), an index of age and disease severity that captures the probability of 1-year survival (90% at excellent to 75% at poor). For comparison purposes, at baseline, in the University of North Carolina Alumni Heart Study, which started in 1986 (Siegler et al., 1992), among middle-aged persons unselected for health at age 40, 57.3% rated their health as excellent and 39.3% as good. Four years later the ratings were 53.2% excellent and 43.4% good, with 2.8% and 3.4% fair and poor, respectively (Siegler, 1997).

Thus, as a single item, the measure is easy to implement and has predictive validity. It is also predictive of mortality in a wide variety of populations (Bosworth, Siegler, Brummett, Barefoot, Williams, Clapp-Channing, et al., 1999a; Idler & Benyamini, 1997; Idler & Kasl, 1991; Kaplan & Camacho, 1983; Mülunpalo et al., 1997; Mossey & Shapiro, 1982; Wolinsky & Johnson, 1992). Self-rated health captures a lot of summary information about health status, but it does not represent the specific disease status of an individual. Note that even those who say they are in excellent health with major heart disease have comorbid conditions (as shown in Table 17.3), are not clinically depressed, and do not see their disease as affecting their ability to function on a day-to-day basis.

Thus, although the findings reported here do support the importance of assessing SRH, it is not synonymous with

disease. Second, global SRH tends to reflect to a large degree those health problems that are salient for study participants. SRH measures are often used as covariates in examinations of the effect of age. An important question that needs to be answered is what it means to use a single measure of health status as a covariate. Although physical and mental health problems appear to play a major role in shaping an individual's perception of his or her health, a significant proportion of what this single-item indicator explains remains unknown. Treating health status as a covariate reduces the variance associated with age. SRH also reduces the variance due to depression and is differentially associated with gender, race, income, and education. Despite the increased interest among researchers in the use of SRH as a measure of health, it is still unclear how this item relates to health and well-being and how clinicians can use this measure.

One way this item may be used by clinicians is to predict health care utilization. Bosworth, Butterfield, Stechuchak, and Bastian (2000) examined whether SRH predicted health service use among women in an equal-access primary care clinic setting. Women who had poor or fair health were significantly more likely to have more outpatient clinic visits than were women who reported excellent or very good health. Bosworth, Butterfield, et al. (2000) concluded that these findings demonstrate the potential of a single question to provide information about the future needs for health care. The fact that self-rated health was not related to age in our clinical population is an interesting observation that requires some comment. It may reflect the fact than when younger individuals have the same disorder as older individuals, it is generally more serious in younger persons; or it may reflect age-related differences in expectations. The other interesting observation that has not been well documented is a phenomenon referred to as a response shift (Sprangers & Schwartz, 1999). Patients confronted with a life-threatening or chronic disease are faced with the necessity to accommodate to the disease. A *response shift* is potentially an important mediator of this adaptation process; it involves changing internal standards, values, and conceptualizations of quality of life (Sprangers & Schwartz, 1999). Potential age differences in response shifts may explain why it is not uncommon to observe an 80-year-old man who recently underwent coronary bypass surgery as reporting that his health is excellent.

In sum, some guidelines may be proposed for using health measures. First, although the findings reported here do support the importance of assessing SRH, it is not synonymous with disease. Second, global SRH tends to reflect to a large degree those health problems that are salient for study participants. Third, in order to make correct attributions about normal development and behavior change expected under specific conditions and specific ages, developmental psychologists need to learn to verify self-reports of diseases and also include hard disease outcomes such as blood pressure or ejection fraction. Verification of diseases can be very instructive. Medical criteria are not always uniform, which is why epidemiologists obtain actual medical records and code to criteria. As developmental psychologists, we need to know what it is like to age with each disease and each condition, as well as what it is like for those who are fortunate enough to age without them. To accomplish this recommendation, developmental psychologists need to develop long-term collaborative research programs and work with investigators who understand the pathophysiology of the disease process being studied.

In order to better interpret studies that use SRH, it is important to remember that (a) these findings will have an socioeconomic status (SES) gradient related to timing and quality of medical care such that a more severe disease profile will tend to be seen earlier in the life cycle in the disadvantaged (N. A. Anderson & Armstead, 1995; House et al., 1992); (b) the reports will be related to cognitive status because individuals need to remember what the diagnosis is to be able to report it; (c) the reports will be related to psychological symptoms because individuals are more likely to seek medical care if symptomatic (Costa & McCrae, 1995); (d) the self-rated measures will be more highly correlated with psychosocial constructs that are also associated with the same underlying dimensions of personality.

Other Approaches to Measuring Health

Most other approaches used to measure health in psychological research are really measures of disease that require the input of medical colleagues for a diagnosis or an understanding of medical records that can be reviewed and characterized (see E. Leventhal, 2000); in addition, they may be a combination of physiological indicators and medical records reviews (see Vitaliano, Scanlan, Siegler, McCormick, & Knopp, 1998). Zhang, Vitaliano, Scanlan, and Savage (2001) present data on the associations of SRH, biological measures, and medical records in their longitudinal study of caregivers. Self-reports of heart disease were moderately correlated with heart disease diagnoses from the medical records (r = .64), which is significant but not comforting. Self-reports of heart disease and biological indicators (e.g., lipids, blood pressure, insulin, glucose, and obesity) were uncorrelated, whereas these same measured indicators were significantly correlated with the medical record reports of disease. In a principle components analysis, SRH loaded on a component with the other psychosocial measures (anxiety, depression, life

satisfaction), whereas the biological measures loaded on a component with the medical records.

Many developmental psychologists measure disease by simply asking patients whether they have or had a particular disease. Although this information is easy to obtain, it is important to realize the potential for patients to not recall having the particular disease or not wanting to report having had the particular disease. A case in point was recently reported by Desai, Livingstone, Desai, and Druss (2001), who examined the accuracy of self-reported cancer history. The authors compared self-reported responses in the New Haven Epidemiologic Catchment Study and were linked to the Connecticut Tumor Registry—the overall rate of false-negative was 39.2%. Non-European Americans, older adults, increased time since cancer diagnosis, number of previous tumors, and type of cancer treatment received were all related to increased likelihood of not reporting having had a tumor. Thus, despite developmental psychologists' and epidemiologists' using self-reported data about disease, it is important to determine the validity of these reports when possible.

Medical Comorbidity

A relatively unique characteristic of older populations is the coexistence of several chronic conditions. Among persons aged 65–101 at baseline in the Cardiovascular Health Study, 25% had one chronic condition and 61% had two or more chronic conditions (Fried et al., 1998). The tendency has been to construct scales that add up all comorbid conditions (Charlson, Szatrowski, Peterson, & Gold, 1994). This approach may allow a general assessment of chronic disease burden and can be predictive of broad patterns of mortality outcomes; but the process of combining conditions into a single scale obscures considerable pathophysiological detail that may have etiological importance. In addition, simply adding up the number of comorbidities ignores the variability in severity of a particular disease. Patients may vary in the effects of the same disease. For example, patients may have one of four stages of congestive heart failure (New York Heart Classification 1–4) or one of three stages of cancer (local, regional, and distance). In addition, simply adding up the number of comorbidity factors assumes that two diseases have the same impact on patients. For example, most clinicians would argue that experiencing a stroke or a myocardial infarction is more severe than experiencing arthritis, although the resultant disability may vary.

In our own studies in which we examined the relationship between SRH and various comorbid illnesses (see Table 17.3), we observed that various diseases and disorders examined varied in their association with SRH. Stroke, hypertension, diabetes, depression, and chronic obstructive pulmonary disorder were all found to be related to poorer SRH. However, 12 of the other 19 comorbid illnesses were not significantly related, including abdominal aortic aneurysm, thoracic aortic aneurysm, dialysis-dependent renal failure, cancer, substance abuse, depression, arthritis, back pain, peptic ulcer, hepatitis-cirrhosis, and myocardial infarctions. Thus, using a summated comorbidity measure, as commonly used, assumes that each disease is equally influential in affecting whatever the outcome may be. Summation of comorbidities does not consider the variations in prevalence and incidence of diseases, nor does it consider—more important—the severity of diseases (Bosworth, Siegler, Brummett, Barefoot, Williams, Vitaliano et al., 1999b).

Psychiatric Comorbidity and Aging

When considering health, disease, and aging, depression is a particularly important comorbidity that needs to be considered. Medically ill patients often suffer from depression. Depression is common among coronary heart disease patients (Brummett et al., 1998; Carney et al., 1987; Forrester et al., 1992; Hance, Carney, Freeland, & Skala, 1996; Schleifer, Macari-Hinson, & Coyle, 1989) and is predictive of rehospitalization (Levine et al., 1996) and increased disability (Ormel et al., 1994; Steffens et al., 1999). Depression during hospitalization following a myocardial infarction (MI), for example, predicts both long- and short-term survival rates (Barefoot, 1997; Frasure-Smith, Lesperance, & Talajic, 1993).

Depression has consistently been implicated in the causal web of incident disability and of functional decline in population samples (Stuck et al., 1999). Major depressive disorder (MDD), minor depression, and depressive symptoms have each been associated with functional disability. Depression and physical function are intertwined; a feedback loop exists such that depression causes increased disability and increased disability exacerbates depression. Similarly, medication adherence among depressed older persons is poor, and this feedback loop exists such that depression causes nonadherence with medical treatment and nonadherence further exacerbates depression so that a focus on both is essential (DiMatteo, Lepper, & Croghan, 2000). DiMatteo et al. (2000), for example, reported that the relationship between depression and nonadherence was significant and substantial, with an odds ratio of 3.03 (95%; 1.96–4.89).

Depression may increase nonadherence with treatment for multiple reasons. First, positive expectations and beliefs in the benefits and efficacy of treatment have been shown (DiMatteo et al., 1993) to be essential to patient adherence. Depression often involves an appreciable degree of hopelessness, and adherence might be difficult or impossible for a patient who holds little optimism that any action will be worthwhile. Second, considerable research (DiMatteo & DiNicola, 1982; DiMatteo, 1994) underscores the importance of support from the family and social network in a patient's attempts to be compliant with medical treatments. Often accompanying depression are considerable social isolation and withdrawal from the very individuals who would be essential in providing emotional support and assistance. Third, depression might be associated with reductions in the cognitive functioning essential to remembering and following through with treatment recommendations (e.g., taking medication).

Caregiving as a Threat to Health

Depression is often an outcome of studies of stress and aging. This is well represented by the caregiving literature. Two recent special issues (Vitaliano, 1997; Schulz & Quittner, 1998) give an indication of the types of studies that have been done. Work by Vitaliano and colleagues shows that the stress of caregiving also has significant effects on measures of physical health status when indexed with medical records—and with (a) biological indicators of the metabolic syndrome (Vitaliano et al., 1998) and (b) measures of immune system functioning and sleep disturbance (Vitaliano et al., 1999). These relations are found both cross-sectionally and longitudinally. It is also most interesting that women who use hormone replacement therapy (HRT; both caregivers and controls) are better off physiologically than their counterparts who do not use HRT (Vitaliano et al., 2002); Whether this is another example of (a) the so-called healthy woman effect, wherein women who have a risk profile that reduces disease are more likely to take HRT; (b) the effect of estrogen (see Matthews et al., 2000); or (c) the effect of some additional mechanisms is not clear. Nevertheless, this is an observation that should be pursued.

Life tasks are made harder when health problems are present. Multiple problems require more complex management of medications, and increasingly complex decisions about care choices need to be made. Not only are the problems to be solved more complex, the cognitive capacities of the older person may not be operating at peak efficiency (Peters, Finucane, MacGregor, & Slovic, 2000). One solution suggests that there is a greater need for intergenerational collaboration in decision making. When family members are available, this becomes part of the caregiving task. As increasing numbers of older persons have fewer siblings and children than do current older persons, new solutions will need to be found to deal with difficulties in decision making among the elderly.

METHODOLOGICAL CONSIDERATIONS

In the study of health and disease, two particular methodological issues are worthy of note: (a) the role of period effects and (b) selection effects from study designs that sample the actual age distribution of the population versus those that oversample the oldest old.

Period Effects of Disease Detection and Treatments

A *period effect* or *time effect* is a societal or cultural change that may occur between two measurements that presents plausible alternative rival explanations for the outcome of a study (Baltes, Reese, & Nesselroade, 1988; Schaie, 1977). Studies have often focused on cohort and aging effects, but there has been a lack of focus on period effects that may explain observed age changes in longitudinal and age differences in cross-sectional studies that examine the relationship between health, behavior, and aging (Siegler et al., 2001). In addition, period effects may affect the prevalence and incidence of disease.

As discussed elsewhere (Siegler et al., 2001), the introduction of the prostate-specific antigen (PSA) test is an example of the effects of period-time effects accounting for changes in the detection of prostate cancer. A PSA test is a diagnostic tool for identifying prostate cancer, and since its introduction in 1987 there have been increasing numbers of prostate cancers being diagnosed among older adults that would not have been diagnosed based upon previous techniques (Amling et al., 1998). Subsequently, there has been an observed increase in number of prostate cancer diagnoses, and because prostate cancer prevalence rates increase with age, researchers studying longitudinally the relationship between age and onset of prostate cancer would have to account for the introduction of this relatively new diagnostic tool.

Information is being made available more quickly and improvements in diagnostic techniques and treatments are increasing in frequency. This is a benefit for the population, but it makes research more difficult, particularly if an intervention is in process and new information or changes in medical procedure are being made available to the public at large. Subsequently, developmental psychologists and other researchers are going to have to become more aware and flexible in the way they deal with these increasing period-time effects.

An example of researchers who are adapting to historical or period effects is the ongoing Women's Health Initiative Study, in which information on estrogen use is being collected. There have been increased data that suggest the influence of estrogen is related to long-term benefits such as prevention or delay of osteoporosis, heart disease, and Alzheimer's disease (Jacobs & Hillard, 1996), but recent information about raloxifene and tamoxifen have altered women's perception of the use of hormonal replacement medication.

News of health and aging has been gaining more public attention, which also needs to be considered in both cross-sectional and longitudinal studies of aging, health, and disease. Thus, the context in which the study was conducted now must be better characterized. One example comes from our own research, in which we conducted telephone interviews between October 1998 and February 1999 among a random sample of women aged 45–54 residing in Durham County, North Carolina. Women were recruited for a randomized clinical trial to test the efficacy of a decision aid intervention on HRT decision making. One of the factors that determines HRT use and influences HRT decision making has been the cardio-protective effects of HRT. However, an influential publication in the *Journal of the American Medical Association* indicated that women using HRT in the short term were at a increase risk for CHD events (Hulley et al., 1998). Although limited data are available at this time, our study and others looking at HRT decision making are likely to be influenced by these recent results.

Selection Effects

Individuals at higher risk for mortality, morbidity, physical function, and so on may be selected out of the populations at earlier ages. Although this selection applies to any age cohort, the forces of proper selection are much stronger in older populations. The analysis of the consequences of selective survival is complex and can lead to a variety of age-related patterns in differential survival (Vaupel & Yashin, 1985). It is useful to think of three ways in which selective survival might influence age-related trends in risk factor-outcome associations. If those with a particular risk factor experience higher and earlier mortality, then the distribution of risk factors in the survivor population would be altered relative to the original distribution and should reflect lower levels of risk factors (i.e., less likely to smoke, be overweight). This would occur because those with high levels of risk factors are more likely to have been removed from the population. Second, it is possible that there are unmeasured differences in susceptibility to the risk factor among both those previously exposed and those unexposed. Third, the survivors may have other characteristics—genetic or environmental in origin—that prevent or slow the progression of disease, shifting the onset to a later age. Thus, it is important to consider survival effects when conducting research on health and aging.

CONCLUSIONS AND FUTURE DIRECTIONS

There were a series of old questions that were always part of the chapters written about aging and health (e.g., see Eisdorfer & Wilkie, 1977; M. F. Elias, Elias, & Elias, 1990; Siegler & Costa, 1985). These old and current questions and answers include the following:

- Do variations in physical health account for aging effects? Not necessarily; it really depends on the age group studied. New data in centenarians are changing our understanding of these relationships.
- Is there such a thing as normal aging? No. It is a moving target, changing with each new publication.

One explanation for this change is period effects—that is, changes such as improved survival of persons with coronary heart disease influence the definition of normal aging. These changes in survival are due to medical interventions such as angioplasty and coronary artery bypass surgery, which are increasingly made available to older persons with heart disease. How we die is different from what was the case when previous chapters addressing these questions were published. More people now die later in life when the cause may not be due to a specific disease (Fried et al., 1998; Nuland, 1995).

Does this situation mean that there is no longer a need for developmental psychology to be concerned with health? No—we now have new opportunities to consider along with a tremendous base of work on which to stand. Work is underway in all of the following areas.

How should researchers measure the important psychological constructs in everyone who is aging—that is, how they measure psychological constructs for extremely aged persons or those with exceptional longevity? Developmental psychologists know that there is great variation in mental and physical health status and in sensory and motor capacities. Until we can fully measure psychological factors in everyone, we cannot understand these factors completely.

Now that epidemiology and geriatric medicine are measuring disease in the elderly and extreme aging population, we need psychological measures designed to be used in laboratory settings that are associated with disease outcomes and biological indicators. The discussion in Finch, Vaupel, and Kinsella (2000) provides an instructive discussion of this issue.

We also need to continue to develop and validate psychological measures that are appropriate and valid in survey research. Burkhauser and Gertler (1995) describe the Health and Retirement Study, Herzog and Wallace (1997) lay out the issues for the Asset and Health Dynamics of the Oldest-Old Study, while Zelinski et al. (1998) provide an example of the strengths and weaknesses of current approaches. Additional development will require some basic psychometric work for age, content, and size of scales that measure important psychological constructs. This development will require some basic psychometric work for age, content, and size of scale. We know the problems but not the solutions. We also need to conceptualize health in ways that make sense psychologically. Self-rated health is a good single item, but can we do better (Kennedy, Kasl, & Vaccarino, 2001)? How do we measure well-being when health is completely compromised? This is an area of research that Powell Lawton started (1997) and unfortunately did not live long enough to complete. He called for a *valuation of life* that is possible in all health status configuration.

Reevaluate a life span approach. Our life span may have been too conservative, given the data by Kuh and Ben Shlomo (1997) wherein infant and prenatal variables predicted adult onset of disease and adult health, whereas mid-life variables appeared to have no relevance to geriatric syndromes.

Make psychology relevant to important concerns in economics and public policy. Health disparities due to social class, race, and ethnic differences do not disappear with age. The disparity is real and we do not know the causes. How much variability could genetics contribute to resolve the disparity? Is it related to life course exposures? Are there critical periods at various points in the lifecycle? In 1999, *Health, United States* (USDHHS, 1999) picked aging as its special topic for the year, as "older people are major consumers of health care and their numbers are increasing" (p. iii). Some highlights of the report are worth noting: (a) By 2030, 20% of the U.S. population will be over age 65; (b) life expectancy at age 65 and at age 85 has increased over the past 50 years—at age 65 European Americans have a higher life expectancy, whereas at age 85 African Americans have a higher life expectancy; however, health disparities by race are shocking. Mortality rates are 55% higher for African Americans—age-adjusted death rates were 77% higher for stroke, 47% higher for heart disease, and 34% higher for cancer. In an important sense, these mean fundamentally that lower SES persons appear to age faster—that is, things that happen later in the life cycle for those further up the SES ladder happen earlier for those on the bottom of the ladder. Trying to fully understand what this means is a major challenge for our field.

Developmental psychologists know a lot about aging processes and measurement and are interested broadly in all aspects of human development. However, for the study of health and disease to progress, investigators must conduct research in conjunction with research teams expert in all aspects required to solve particular problems. Other disciplines and other countries are well ahead of us on this problem. What can we contribute as developmental psychologists?

Responding to the fears of the public and policy makers about the explosion of aging in the population, Carstensen in a *New York Times* editorial (2001) rightly points out the opportunity to design a new stage of life. She argues that not all aging changes need to be bad. She assumed that medical and psychological science will solve the problems of the elderly today and find a cure for frailty that is not necessarily disease-related. We may have reached Fries's (1980) compression of morbidity, where function is preserved until the final 1, 3, or 5 years of life. After most of the population gets there, what will happen with health maintained until the ninth decade?

We have the knowledge to improve the odds and postpone the deleterious consequences that had previously been attributed to normal aging or even to disease-related aging. Worldwide studies of centenarians and supercentenarians are seeking answers as to what determines the characteristics that lead to 110 years of disability-free life? The simpleminded answer of preventing disease is probably not going to be the correct one. The real future challenge is to figure out how to ask the right questions. Health will play an increasingly important role for developmental psychologists, and—as changes in health care and the demographic revolution continue to occur—we need to be able to include contextual influences and period changes in order to better understand the role of health and disease among older adults.

REFERENCES

Aldwin, C. M., & Gilmer, D. F. (1999). Immunity, disease processes and optimal aging. In J. C. Cavanaugh & S. K. Whitbourne (Eds.), *Gerontology: An interdisciplinary perspective*. New York: Oxford University Press.

Amling, C. L., Blute, M. L., Lerner, S. E., Bergstralh, E. J., Bostwick, D. G., & Zincke, H. (1998). Influence of prostate-specific antigen testing on the spectrum of patients with prostate cancer undergoing radical prostatectomy at a large referral practice. *Mayo Clinic Proceedings, 73*, 401–406.

Anderson, N. A., & Armstead, C. A. (1995). Toward understanding the association of socioeconomic status and health: A new challenge for the bio-psychosocial approach. *Psychosomatic Medicine, 57*, 213–225.

Anderson, R. N., Kochanek, K. D., & Murphy, S. L. (1997, June). Report of final mortality statistics. *Monthly Vital Statistics Report, 45*(11), Supplement 2.

Baltes, P. B., & Mayer, K. U. (Eds.). (1999). *The Berlin Aging Study: Aging from 70–100*. Cambridge UK: Cambridge University Press.

Baltes, P. B., Reese, H. W., & Nesselroade, J. R. (1988). *Introduction to research methods: Life-span developmental psychology.* Hillsdale, NJ: Erlbaum.

Barefoot, J. C. (1997). Depression and coronary heart disease. *Cardiologia, 42*, 1245–1250.

Bastian, L. A., Bosworth, H. B., Mark, D. B., & Siegler, I. C. (1998, November). *Are personality traits associated with the use of Hormone Replacement Therapy in a cohort of middle aged women undergoing cardiac catherization?* Paper presented at the meetings of the Gerontological Society of America, Philadelphia, PA.

Baum, A., & Posluszny, D. M. (1999). Health Psychology: Mapping biobehavioral contributions to health and illness. *Annual Review of Psychology, 50*, 137–163.

Beard, B. B. (1991). *Centenarians: The new generation.* New York: Greenwood Press.

Bosworth, H. B., Butterfield, M. I., Stechuchak, K. M., & Bastian, L. A. (2000). The relationship between self-rated health and health care service use among women veterans in a primary care clinic. *Women's Health Issues, 10*(5), 278–285.

Bosworth, H. B., Siegler, I. C., Brummett, B. H., Barefoot, J. C., Williams, R. B., Clapp-Channing, N., Lytle, B. L., & Mark, D. B. (1999). Self-rated health as a predictor of mortality in a sample of coronary artery disease patients. *Medical Care, 37*(12), 1226–1236.

Bosworth, H. B., Siegler, I. C., Brummett, B. H., Barefoot, J. C., Williams, R. B., Vitaliano, P. P., Clapp-Channing, N., Lytle, B. L., & Mark, D. B. (1999). The relationship between self-rated health and health status among coronary artery patients. *Journal of Aging and Health, 13*(4), 565–584.

Bosworth, H. B., Siegler, I. C., Olsen, M. K., Brummett, B. H., Barefoot, J. C., Williams, R. B., Clapp-Channing, N., & Mark, D. B. (2000). Social support and quality of life in patients with coronary artery disease. *Quality of Life Research, 9*(7), 829–839.

Breslow, L., & Breslow, N. (1993). Health practices and disability: Some evidence from Alameda County. *Preventive Medicine, 22*(1), 86–95.

Bristol, M. M., Gallagher, J. J., & Schopler, E. (1988). Mothers and fathers of young developmentally disabled and non-disabled boys: Adaptation and spousal support. *Developmental Psychology, 24*, 442–445.

Brummett, B. H., Babyak, M. A., Barefoot, J. C., Bosworth, H. B., Clapp-Channing, N. E., Siegler, I. C., Williams, R. B., Jr., & Mark, D. B. (1998). Social support and hostility as predictors of depressive symptoms in cardiac patients one month after hospitalization: A prospective study. *Psychosomatic Medicine, 60*(6), 707–713.

Burkhauser, R. V., & Gertler, P. J. (Eds.). (1995). The health and retirement study. Data quality and early results [Special issue]. *Journal of Human Resources, 30*(Supplement).

Buse, S., & Pieper, B. (1990). Impact of cardiac transplantation on the spouse's life. *Heart and Lung, 19,* 641–648.

Califf, R. M., Harrell, F. E., Jr., Lee, K. L., Rankin, J. S., Hlatky, M. A., Mark, D. B., Jones, R. H., Muhlbaier, L. H., & Oldham, H. N. (1989). The evolution of medical and surgical therapy for coronary artery disease: A 15-year perspective. *Journal of the American Medical Association, 261,* 2077–2086.

Carney, R., Rich, M. W., teVelde, A., Saini, J., Clark, K., & Jaffe, A. S. (1987). Major depressive disorder in coronary artery disease. *American Journal of Cardiology, 60,* 1273–1275.

Carstensen, L. L. (2001). On the brink of a brand-new old age. *New York Times,* p. A19.

Charlson, M., Szatrowski, T. P., Peterson, J., & Gold, J. (1994). Validation of a combined co-morbidity index. *Journal of Clinical Epidemiology, 47,* 1245–1251.

Deeg, D. H. J., Kardaun, J. W. P. F., & Fozard, J. L. (1996). Health, behavior and aging. In J. E. Birren & K. W. Schaie (Eds.), *Handbook of the psychology of aging* (4th ed., pp. 129–149). San Diego, CA: Academic Press.

Deeg, D. H. J., van Zonneveld, R. J., van der Maas, P. J., & Habbema, J. D. (1989). Medical and social predictors of longevity in the elderly: total predictive value and interdependence. *Social Science Medicine, 29*(11), 1271–1280.

Desai, M., Bruce, M. L., Desai, R. A., & Druss, B. G. (2001). Validity of self-reported cancer history: A comparison of health interview data and cancer registry records. *American Journal of Epidemiology, 153*(3), 299–306.

DiMatteo, M. (1994). Enhancing patient adherence to medical recommendations. *Journal of the American Medical Association, 271,* 79–83.

DiMatteo, M., & DiNicola, D. D. (1982). *Achieving patient compliance.* Elmsford, NY: Pergamon Press.

DiMatteo, M., Lepper, H. S., & Croghan, T. W. (2000). Depression is a risk factor for noncompliance with medical treatment: Meta-analysis of the effects of anxiety and depression on patient adherence. *Archives of Internal Medicine, 160*(14), 2101–2107.

DiMatteo, M., Sherbourne, C. D., Hays, R. D., Ordway, L., Kravitz, R. L., McGlynn, E. A., Kaplan, S., & Rogers, W. H. I. (1993). Physicians' characteristics influence patients' adherence to medical treatment: Results from the Medical Outcomes Study. *Health Psychology, 12*(2), 93–102.

Eisdorfer, C., & Wilkie, F. W. (1977). Stress, disease, aging and behavior. In J. E. Birren & K. W. Schaie (Eds.), *Handbook of the psychology of aging* (pp. 251–275). New York: Van Nostrand Reinhold.

Elias, M. F., Elias, J. W., & Elias, P. K. (1990). Biological and health influences on behavior. In J. E. Birren & K. W. Schaie (Eds.), *Handbook of the psychology of aging* (3rd ed., pp. 79–102). San Diego, CA: Academic Press.

Elias, M. F., Elias, P. K., D'Agostino, R. B., & Wolf, P. A. (1997). Role of age, education and gender on cognitive performance in the Framingham Heart Study: Community based norms. *Experimental Aging Research, 23,* 201–235.

Elias, M. F., Elias, P. K., D'Agostino, R. B., & Wolf, P. A. (2000). Comparative effects of age and blood pressure on neuropsychological test performance: The Framingham Study. In S. B. Manuck, R. Jennings, B. S. Rabin, & A. Baum (Eds.), *Behavior, health and aging* (pp. 199–223). Mahwah, NJ: Erlbaum.

Elias, M. F., Elias, P. K., Robbins, M. A., Wolf, P. A., & D'Agostino, R. B. (2000). Cardiovascular risk factors and cognitive functioning: An epidemiological perspective. In S. R. Waldstein & M. F. Elias (Eds.), *Neuropsychology of cardiovascular disease* (pp. 83–104). Hillsdale, NJ: Erlbaum.

Elias, M. F., Robbins, M. A., Elias, P. K., & Streeten, D. H. P. (1998). A longitudinal study of blood pressure in relation to performance on the Wechsler Adult Intelligence Scale. *Health Psychology, 17,* 486–493.

Elias, P. K., Elias, M. F., D'Agostino, R. B., Cupples, L. A., Wilson, P. W., Silbershatz, H., & Wolf, P. A. (1997). NIDDM and blood pressure as risk factors for poor cognitive performance: The Framingham Study. *Diabetes Care, 20,* 1388–1395.

Ewbank, D. (2000). Demography and the age of genomics: A first look at the prospects. In C. E. Finch, J. W. Vaupel, & K. Kinsella (Eds.), *Cells and Surveys* (pp. 64–109). Washington, DC: National Academy Press.

Finch, C. E., Vaupel, J. M., & Kinsella, K. (Eds.). (2000). *Cells and surveys.* Washington, DC: National Academy Press.

Folstein, M., Folstein, S. E., & McHugh, P. R. (1975). "Mini-Mental State": A practical method for grading the cognitive state of patients for the clinical. *Journal of Psychiatric Research, 12,* 189–198.

Forette, B. (1997). Centenarians: Health and frailty. In J.-M. Robine, J. W. Vaupel, B. Jeune, & M. Allard (Eds.), *Longevity: To the limits and beyond* (pp. 105–112). New York: Springer-Verlag.

Forrester, A., Lipsey, J. R., Teitelbaum, M. L., DePaulo, J. R., Andrzekewsli, P. L., & Robinson, R. G. (1992). Depression following myocardial infarction. *International Journal of Psychiatry in Medicine, 22,* 33–46.

Franceschi, C., Motta, L., Valensin, S., Rapisarda, R., Franzone, A., Berardelli, M., Motta, M., Monti, D., Bonafe, M., Ferrucci, L., Deiana, L., Pes, G. M., Carru, C., Desole, M. S., Barbi, C., Sartoni, G., Gemelli, C., Lescai, F., Olivieri, F., Marchegiani, F., Cardelli, M., Cavallone, L., Gueresi, P., Cossarizza, A., Troiano, L., Pini, G., Sansoni, P., Passeri, G., Lisa, R., Spazzafumo, L., Amadio, L., Giunta, S., Stecconi, R., Morresi, R., Viticchi, C., Mattace, R., De Benedictis, G., & Baggio, G. (2000). Do men and women follow different trajectories to reach extreme longevity? *Aging Clinical and Experimental Research, 12,* 93–105.

Franke, H. (1977). Centenarians in the Federal Republic of Germany: State of health and clinical observations. *Schweizerische Rundschau fur Medizin Praxis, 66*(36), 1149–1157.

Franke, H. (1985). *Auf den Spuren der Langlebigkeit.* [Following the paths of longevity] Stuttgart, Germany: Schatthauer.

Frasure-Smith, N., Lesperance, F., & Talajic, M. (1993). Depression following myocardial infarction. *Journal of the American Medical Association, 270,* 1819–1825.

Fratiglioni, L., Wang, H.-X., Ericsson, K., Maytan, M., & Winblad, B. (2000). Influence of social network on occurrence of dementia: A community based longitudinal study. *The Lancet, 355,* 1315–1319.

Fried, L. P. (2000). Epidemiology of aging. *Epidemiologic Reviews, 22,* 77–84.

Fried, L. P., Kronmal, R., Newman, A., Bild, D. E., Mittelmark, M. B., Polak, J. F., Robbins, J. A., & Gardin, J. M. (1998). Risk factors for 5-year mortality in older adults: The Cardiovascular Health Study. *Journal of the American Medical Association, 279,* 585–592.

Fries, J. F. (1980). Aging natural death and the compression of morbidity. *New England Journal of Medicine, 303,* 130–135.

George, L. K., & Clipp, E. C. (1991). Subjective components of aging well. *Generations, 15,* 57–60.

Giampoli, S. (2000). Epidemiology of major age-related diseases in women compared to men. *Aging Clinical and Experimental Research, 12,* 93–105.

Guralnik, J. M., Balfour, J. M., & Volpato, S. (2000). The ratio of older women to men: Historical perspectives and cross-national comparisons. *Aging Clinical and Experimental Research, 12,* 65–76.

Hagberg, B., Alfredson, B., Poon, L. W., & Homma, A. (2001). Cognitive functioning in centenarians: A coordinated analysis of results from three countries. *Journal of Gerontology Series B: Psychological Sciences and Social Sciences, 56,* P141–P151.

Haley, W. E., Levine, E., Brown, S. L., & Bartolucci, A. (1987). Stress, appraisal and social support as predictors of adaptational outcome among dementia caregivers. *Psychology and Aging, 2,* 323–330.

Hance, M., Carney, R. M., Freeland, K. E., & Skala, J. (1996). Depression in patients with coronary heart disease. *General Hospital Psychiatry, 18,* 61–65.

Harrell, F. E., Lee, K. L., Califf, R. M., Pryor, D. B., & Rosati, R. A. (1984). Regression modeling strategies for improved prognostic prediction. *Statistics in Medicine, 3,* 143–152.

Hazzard, W. R., Blass, J. P., Ettinger, W. H., Halter, J. B., & Ouslander, J. G. (1999). *Principles of geriatric medicine and gerontology.* New York: McGraw Hill.

Herzog, A. R., & Wallace, R. B. (1997). Measures of cognitive functioning in the AHEAD study [Special issue]. *Journal of Gerontology: Psychological and Social Sciences, 52B,* 37–48.

Hooker, K. (1999). Possible selves in adulthood. In T. Hess & F. Blanchard-Fields (Eds.), *Social cognition and aging* (pp. 97–122). San Diego, CA: Academic Press.

Hooker, K., Shifren, K., & Hutchinson, C. (1992). Mental and physical health of spouse caregivers: the role of personality. *Psychology and Aging, 7*(3), 367–375.

Hooker, K., & Siegler, I. C. (1992). Separating apples from oranges in health ratings: Perceived health includes psychological well-being. *Behavior, Health, and Aging, 2,* 81–92.

House, J. S., Kessler, R. C., Herzog, A. R., Mero, R. P., Kinney, R. P., & Breslow, M. J. (1992). Social stratification, age and health. In K. W. Schaie, J. House, & D. G. Blazer (Eds.), *Aging, health behaviors and health outcomes* (pp. 1–32). Hillsdale, NJ: Erlbaum.

Hulley, S., Grady, D., Bush, T., Furberg, C., Herrington, D., Riggs, B., & Vittinghoff, E. (1998). Randomized trial of estrogen plus progestin for secondary prevention of coronary heart disease in postmenopausal women. Heart and Estrogen/progestin Replacement Study (HERS) Research Group. *Journal of the American Medical Association, 280*(7), 605–613.

Idler, E. L., & Benyamini, Y. (1997). Self-rated health and mortality: A review of twenty-seven community studies. *Journal of Health and Social Behavior, 38,* 21–37.

Idler, E. L., & Kasl, S. V. (1991). Health perceptions and survival: Do global evaluations of health status really predict morality? *Journal of Gerontology: Social Sciences, 46,* S55–S65.

Jacobs, S., & Hillard, T. C. (1996). Hormone replacement therapy in the aged: A state of the art review. *Drugs Aging, 8*(3), 193–213.

Jeune, B., & Andersen-Ranberg, K. (2000). What can we learn from centenarians? In P. Martin, C. Rott, B. Hagberg, & K. Morgan (Eds.), *Centenarians: Autonomy vs. dependence in the oldest old* (pp. 9–24). Paris: Serdi Edition.

Kaplan, G. A., & Camacho, T. (1983). Perceived health and mortality: A nine-year follow-up of the Human Population Laboratory Cohort. *American Journal of Epidemiology, 117,* 292–304.

Kaplan, G. A., Haan, M. N., & Wallace, R. B. (1999). Understanding changing risk factor associations with increasing age in adults. *Annual Review of Public Health, 20,* 89–108.

Kennedy, B. S., Kasl, S. V., & Vaccarino, V. V. (2001). Repeated hospitalizations and self-rated health among the elderly: A multivariate failure time analysis. *American Journal of Epidemiologic, 153*(3), 232–241.

Kim, J. S., Bramlett, M. H., Wright, L. K., & Poon, L. W., (1998). Racial differences in health status and health behaviors of older adults. *Nursing Research, 47*(4), 243–250.

Kuh, D., & Ben-Shlomo, Y. (Eds.). (1997). *A life-course approach to chronic disease epidemiology.* Oxford, UK: Oxford University Press.

Lachman, M. E., & James, J. (Eds.). (1997). *Multiple paths of midlife development.* Chicago: University of Chicago Press.

Leventhal, E. (2000). Aging women, getting older getting better? In S. B. Manuck, R. Jennings, B. S. Rabin, & A. Baum (Eds.) *Behavior, health and aging* (pp.199–223). Mahwah, NJ: Erlbaum.

Leventhal, H., Benyamini, Y., Brownlee, S., Diefenbach, M., Leventhal, E. A., Patrick-Miller, L., & Robitaille, C. (1997). Illness representations: Theoretical foundations. In K. J. Petrie & J. A. Weinman (Eds.), *Perceptions of health and illness.* Amsterdam: Harwood.

Levine, J., Covino, N. A., Slack, W. V., Safran, C., Safran, D. B., Boro, J. E., Davis, R. B., Buchanan, G. K., Gervino, E. V. (1996). Psychological predictors of subsequent medical care among patients hospitalized with cardiac disease. *Journal of Cardiopulmonary Rehabilitation, 16,* 109–116.

Maddox, G. L., Atchley, R. C., Evans, J. G., Finch, C. E., Kane, R. A., Mezey, M. D., Poon, L. W., & Siegler, I. C. (Eds.). (2001). *Encyclopedia of aging: A comprehensive multidisciplinary review of gerontology and geriatrics* (3rd ed.). New York: Springer.

Manton, K. G., Corder, L., & Stallard, E. (1997). Chronic disability trends in elderly United States populations: 1982–1994. *Proceedings of the National Academy of Sciences, USA, 94,* 2593–2598.

Matthews, K. A., Owens, J. F., Kuller, L. H., Sutton-Tyrell, K., & Jansen-McWilliams, L. (1998). Are hostility and anxiety associated with carotid atherosclerosis in healthy postmenopausal women? *Psychosomatic Medicine, 60,* 633–638.

Matthews, K. A., Wing, R. R., Kuller, L. H., Meilahn, E. N., & Owens, J. F. (2000). Menopause as a turning point in midlife. In S. B. Manuck, R. Jennings, B. S. Rabin, & A. Baum (Eds.), *Behavior, health and aging* (pp. 43–56). Mahwah, NJ: Erlbaum.

McClearn, G. E., & Heller, D. A. (2000). Genetics and aging. In S. B. Manuck, R. Jennings, B. S. Rabin, & A. Baum (Eds.), *Behavior, health and aging* (pp. 1–14). Mahwah, NJ: Erlbaum.

Morley, J. E. (2000). Androgen deficiency in aging males and healthy aging. In J.-M. Robine, T. B. L. Kirkwood, & M. Allard (Eds.), *Sex and longevity: Sexuality, gender, reproduction, parenthood* (pp. 103–115). Berlin: Springer-Verlag.

Mossey, J. M., & Shapiro, E. (1982). Self-rated health: A predictor of mortality among the elderly. *American Journal of Public Health, 72,* 800–808.

Mülunpalo, S., Vuori, I., Oja, P., Pasanen, M., & Urponen, H. (1997). Self-rated health status as a health measure: The predictive value of self-reported health status on the use of physician services and on mortality in the working-age population. *Journal of Clinical Epidemiology, 50,* 517–528.

Murray, C. L. G., & Lopez, A. D. (Eds.). (1996). *The global burden of disease.* Washington, DC: World Health Organization.

National Institute on Aging and Genetic Epidemiology Working Group. (2000). Genetic epidemiologic studies on age-specified traits. *American Journal of Epidemiology, 152,* 1003–1008.

Neugarten, B. L. (1974). Age groups in American society and the rise of the young old. *Annals of the American Academy of Political and Social Science, 415,* 187–198.

Neugarten, B. L. (1976). Adaptation and the life cycle. *The Counseling Psychologist, 6,* 16–20.

Neugarten, B. L. (1979). Time, age, and the life cycle. *American Journal of Psychiatry, 136,* 887–894.

Nuland, S. B. (1995). *How we die: Reflections of life's final chapter.* New York: Random House.

Ormel, J., VonKorff, M., Ustun, T. B., Pini, S., Korten, A., & Oldehinkel, T. (1994). Common mental disorder and disability across cultures: Results from the WHO Collaborative Study on Psychological Problems in General Health Care. *Journal of the American Medical Association, 272,* 1741–1748.

Paffenbarger, R. S., Hyde, R. T., Wing, A. L., Lee, I. M., Jung, D. L., & Kampert, J. B. (1993). The association of changes in physical activity level and other lifestyle characteristics with mortality among men. *New England Journal of Medicine, 328,* 538–545.

Parkerson, G. R., Jr., Broadhead, W. E., & Tse, C. J. (1992). Quality of life and functional health of primary care patients. *Journal of Clinical Epidemiology, 45,* 1303–1313.

Patrick, D., & Erickson, P. (1993). *Health status and health policy: Quality of life in health care evaluation and resources allocation.* New York: Oxford University Press.

Pederson N. L., & Reynolds C. A. (1988). Stability and change in adult personality: Genetic and environmental components. *European Journal of Personality, 12,* 365–386.

Perls, T., Fretts, R., Daly, M., Brewester S., Kunkel, L., & Pucca, A. (2000). Genes and centenarians. In J.-M. Robine, T. B. L. Kirkwood, & M. Allard (Eds.), *Sex and longevity: Sexuality, gender, reproduction, parenthood* (pp. 43–57). Berlin: Springer-Verlag.

Perls, T. T., & Silver, M. H. (1999). Living to 100. Lessons in living to your maximum potential at any age. New York, Basic Books.

Peters, E., Finucane, M. L., MacGregor, D. G., & Slovic, P. (2000). The bearable lightness of aging: Judgment and decision processes in older adults. In P. C. Stern & L. L. Carstensen (Eds.), *The aging mind* (pp. 144–165). Washington, DC: National Academy Press.

Poon, L. W., Johnson, M. A., Davey, A., Dawson, D. V., Siegler, I. C., & Martin, P. (2000). Psychosocial predictors of survival among centenarians. In P. Martin, C. Rott, B. Hagberg, & K. Morgan (Eds.), *Centenarians: Autonomy versus dependence in the oldest old* (pp. 77–90). Paris: Serdi.

Poon, L. W., Johnson, M. A., & Martin, P. (1997). Looking into the crystal ball: Will we ever be able to accurately predict individual differences in longevity? In J. M. Robine, J. W. Vaupel, B. Jeune, & M. Allard (Eds.). *Longevity: To the limits and beyond* (113–119). New York: Springer-Verlag.

Poon, L. W., Martin, P., Clayton, G. M., Messner, S., & Noble, C. A. (1992). The influences of cognitive resources on adaptation and old age. *International Journal of Aging and Human Development, 34*(1), 31–46.

Radloff, L. S. (1977). The CES-D scale: A self report depression scale for research in the general population. *Applied Psychological Measurement, 1,* 385–401.

Robine, J.-M., Kirkwood, T. B. L., & Allard, M. (Eds.). (2001). *Sex and longevity: Sexuality, gender, reproduction and parenthood.* Berlin: Springer-Verlag.

Rowe, J. W., & Kahn, R. L. (1998). *Successful aging.* New York: Pantheon Books.

Schaie, K. W. (1977). Quasi-experimental designs in the psychology of aging. In J. E. Birren & K. W. Schaie (Eds.), *Handbook of the psychology of aging* (pp. 39–58). New York: Van Nostrand Reinhold.

Schleifer, S., Macari-Hinson, M. M., & Coyle, D. A. (1989). The nature and course of depression following myocardial infarction. *Archives of Internal Medicine, 49,* 1785–1789.

Schulz, R., & Quittner, A. L. (1998). Caregiving for children and adults with chronic conditions: introduction to the special issue. *Health Psychology, 17*(2), 107–111.

Sherbourne, C., Meredith, L. S., & Ware, J. E. (1992). Social support and stressful life events: Age differences in their effects on health-related quality of life among the chronically ill. *Quality of Life Research, 1,* 235–246.

Siegler, I. C. (1990). Paradigms in developmental health psychology: From theory to application: Introduction to a special issue. *Journal of Gerontology: Psychological Sciences, 45*(4), P113–P115.

Siegler, I. C. (1997). Promoting health and minimizing stress. In M. E. Lachman & J. James (Eds.), *Multiple paths of midlife development* (pp. 243–255). Chicago: University of Chicago Press.

Siegler, I. C., Bastian L. A., & Bosworth, H. B. (2001). Health, behavior and aging. In A. Baum, T. R. Revenson, & J. E. Singer (Eds.), *Handbook of health psychology* (pp. 469–476). Hillsdale, NJ: Erlbaum.

Siegler, I. C., Bastian, L. A., Steffens, D. C., Bosworth, H. B., & Costa, P. T. (2002). Behavioral medicine and aging: Middle age, aging and the oldest-old. *Journal of Consulting and Clinical Psychology, 70*(3), 843–851.

Siegler, I. C., & Costa, P. T. (1985). Health behavior relationships. In J. E. Birren & K. W. Schaie (Eds.), *Handbook of the psychology of aging* (2nd ed., pp. 144–166). New York: Van Nostrand Reinhold.

Siegler, I. C., Feaganes, J. R., & Rimer, B. K. (1995). Predictors of adoption of mammography in women under age 50. *Health Psychology, 14,* 274–278.

Siegler, I. C., Kaplan, B. H., Von Dras, D. D., & Mark, D. B. (1999). Cardiovascular health: A challenge for midlife. In S. Willis & J. Reid (Eds.), *Life in the middle* (pp. 147–157). San Diego, CA: Academic Press.

Siegler, I. C., Nowlin, J. B., & Blumenthal, J. A. (1980). Health and behavior: Methodological considerations for adult development and aging. In L. W. Poon (Ed.), *Aging in the 1980's: Psychological issues* (pp. 559–612). Washington, DC: American Psychological Association.

Siegler, I. C., Peterson, B. L., Barefoot, J. C., Harvin, S. H., Dahlstrom, W. G., Kaplan, B. H., Costa, P. T. Jr., & Williams, R. B. (1992). Using college alumni populations in epidemiologic research: The UNC Alumni Heart Study. *Journal of Clinical Epidemiology, 45*(11), 1243–1250.

Soldo, B. J., & Hill, M. S. (1995). Family structure and transfer measures in the Health and Retirement Study. *The Journal of Human Resources, 30*(Supplement), S108–S137.

Sowers, M. F. R. (2000). The menopause transition and the aging process: A population perspective. *Aging Clinical and Experimental Research, 12,* 85–92.

Sprangers, M. A., & Schwartz, C. E. (1999). Integrating response shift into health-related quality of life research: A theoretical model. *Social Science and Medicine, 48*(11), 1507–1515.

Steffens, D., O'Connor, C. M., Jiang, W. J., Pieper, C. F., Kuchibhatla, M. N., Arias, R. M., Look, A., Davenport, C., Gonzalez, M. B., & Krishnan, K. R. R. (1999). The effect of major depression on functional status in patients with coronary artery disease. *Journal of the American Geriatrics Society, 47,* 319–322.

Stern, P. C., & Carstensen, L. L. (2000). *The aging mind: Opportunities in cognitive research.* Washington, DC; National Academy Press.

Stuck, A. E., Walthert, J. M., Nikolaus, T., Bula, C. J., Hohmann, C., & Beck, J. C. (1999). Risk factors for functional status decline in community-living elderly people: a systematic literature review. *Social Science and Medicine, 48*(4), 445–469.

Tenover, J. L. (1999). Trophic factors and male hormone replacement. In W. R. Hazzard, J. P. Blass, W. H. Ettinger, J. B. Halter, & J. G. Ouslander (Eds.), *Principles of geriatric medicine and gerontology* (pp. 1029–1040). New York: McGraw Hill.

United States Department of Health and Human Services. (1999). Health, United States, 1999 with Health and Aging Chartbook. Hyattsville, MD: National Center for Health Statistics (PHS No. 99-1232).

Vaccarino, V., Berkman, L. F., & Krumholz, H. M. (2000). Long-term outcome of myocardial infarction in women and men: A population perspective. *American Journal of Epidemiology, 152,* 965–973.

Vaupel, J. W., & Yashin, A. I. (1985). The deviant dynamics of death in heterogeneous populations. In N. B. Tuma (Ed.), *Sociological methodology. Jossey-Bass social and behavioral science series.* (pp. 179–211). San Franciso: Jossey-Bass.

Vitaliano, P. P. (1997). Physiological and physical concomitants of caregiving: Introduction to a special issue. *Annals of Behavioral Medicine, 19,* 75–77.

Vitaliano, P. P., Russo, J., Young, H. M., Teri, L., & Maiuro, R. D. (1991). Predictors of burden in spouse caregivers of individuals with Alzheimer's disease. *Psychology and Aging, 6*(3), 392–402.

Vitaliano, P. P., Scanlan, J. M., Siegler, I. C., McCormick, W. C., & Knopp, R. H. (1998). Coronary heart disease moderates the relationship of chronic stress with the metabolic syndrome. *Health Psychology, 17,* 520–529.

Vitaliano, P. P., Scanlan, J. M., Zhang, J. P., Siegler, I. C., Young, H., & McCormick, W. C. (1999, June). *Associations of caregiving with health outcomes.* National Institute on Aging (NIA) Consensus Conference on Caregiving, Las Vegas, NV.

Vitaliano, P. P., Scanlan, J. M., Zhang, J., Savage, M. V., Hirsch, I. B., & Siegler, I. C. (2002). A path model of chronic stress, the Metabolic Syndrome, and Coronary Heart Disease. *Psychosomatic Medicine, 64,* 418–435.

Waldstein, S. R. (2000). Health effects on cognitive aging. In P. C. Stern & L. L. Carstensen (Eds.), *The aging mind* (pp. 189–217). Washington, DC: National Academy Press.

Ware, J. E., Jr. (1993). *SF-36 Health Survey: Manual and interpretation guide.* Boston, MA: The Health Institute, The New England Medical Center.

Ware, J. E., Jr. (1987). Standards for validating health measures: Definition and content. *Journal of Chronic Diseases, 40,* 473–480.

Williams, R. B., Barefoot, J. C., Califf, R. M., Haney, T. L., Saunders, W. B., Pryor, D. B., Hlatky, M. A., Siegler, I. C., & Mark, D. B. (1992). Prognostic importance of social and economic resources among medically treated patients with angiographically documented coronary artery disease. *Journal of the American Medical Association, 267,* 520–524.

Willis, S. L., & Reid, J. (Eds.). (1999). *Life in the middle: Psychological and social development in the third quarter of life.* San Diego, CA: Academic Press.

Wilson, R. S., Gilley D. W., Bennett, D. A., Beckett, L. A., & Evans, D. A. (2000). Person-specific paths of cognitive decline in Alzheimer's Disease and their relation to age. *Psychology and Aging, 15,* 18–28.

Wolinsky, F. D., & Johnson, R. J. (1992). Perceived health status and mortality among older men and women. *Journal of Gerontology: Social Sciences, 47,* S303–S312.

Zabora, J. R., Smith, E. D., Baker, F., Wingard, J. R., & Cubrow, B. (1992). The family: The other side of bone marrow transplantation. *Journal of Psychosocial Oncology, 10,* 35–46.

Zelinski, E. M., Crimmins, E., Reynolds, S., & Seeman, T. (1998). Do medical conditions affect cognition in older adults? *Health Psychology, 17,* 504–512.

Zhang, J., Vitaliano, P. P., Scanlan, J. M., & Savage, M. V. (2001, March). *Interrelationships of psychological variables, self-reported health, biological measures and medical records in old adults: What goes with what?* Paper presented at the meeting of the Society for Behavioral Medicine, Seattle, Washington.

CHAPTER 18

Cognitive Development in Adulthood

ROGER A. DIXON AND ANNA-LISA COHEN

The area of developmental research focusing on the study of cognitive changes in adulthood is often referred to as the field of cognitive aging. The orienting question for this field is, How does cognition change with aging? Three components of this question may be highlighted initially. First, the term *cognition* is used broadly and inclusively in this chapter to accommodate multiple aspects, dimensions, theories, and measures of a variety of mental activities executed by the brain. These include, but are not limited to, classes of activities known as intelligence, memory, attention, reasoning, problem solving, and wisdom. Second, the term *change* is used broadly and inclusively to accommodate several theories, phenomena, directions, and research designs. Thus, the present approach permits consideration of structural, stage-like, or incremental cognitive changes with aging, as investigated with any of numerous legitimate research designs. No assumptions are made about the nature of cognitive developmental change with aging. Third, the term *aging* is used broadly and inclusively to reflect processes occurring throughout adulthood. It is a neutral term tantamount to "changes with age that occur during adulthood" regardless of the direction or quality of the changes.

Cognitive aging (the field) is a particularly active and vibrant domain of research, one that is at the crossroads of both classic questions and novel trends. Several brief examples of each of the paths leading to this crossroads may be useful. First, classic questions about cognitive aging revolve around core developmental issues such as directionality (i.e., whether adult cognitive changes are gains, losses, or maintenance), universality (i.e., the extent to which there are individual differences in profiles of changes throughout adulthood), and reversibility (i.e., whether experience or intervention may promote recovery or improvement in functioning). For more than a century scholars have wondered about whether the lengthening adult life span would be ineluctably accompanied by diminishing cognitive resources (Dixon, Kramer, & Baltes, 1985). Moreover, because contemporary adulthood represents about 75% of the normal expected life span, few adults would fail to have a vested interest in the cognitive changes they might expect as they grow through their middle and into their later years. Second, novel trends reflect influences that are as easily incorporated into cognitive aging research as into any other developmental area. Recent trends include methodological advances, such as the means of analyzing structure, change, and variability (e.g., Hertzog & Dixon, 1996; Salthouse, 2000). Other novel trends in cognitive aging are often adapted from neighboring disciplines and given new clothing in the context of understanding long-term change. Among recent developments are such new topics as metamemory and memory

Preparation of this chapter was supported by a grant from the U.S. National Institute on Aging (AG08235) to Roger A. Dixon and by a grant from the Swedish STINT foundation to Lars-Göran Nilsson and Roger A. Dixon. Anna-Lisa Cohen was supported by a doctoral fellowship from the Natural Sciences and Engineering Research Council of Canada.

self-efficacy (e.g., Cavanaugh, 1996, 2000), social cognition (Hess & Blanchard-Fields, 1999), practical cognition (e.g., Berg & Klaczynski, 1996; Park, 2000), collaborative cognition (e.g., Dixon, 1999), and brain and cognition (e.g., Raz, 2000; Woodruff-Pak, 1997). How cognition changes with aging is seen as a developmental question, and one that reflects classic developmental issues and relates to numerous neighboring developmental processes.

Issues considered in the study of cognitive aging go to the heart of our view of both the human life course, in general, and of individual aging adults, in particular. Personal expectations about aging are based in part on personal perceptions of cognitive skills—how adaptive they are and how they are believed to change during the adult years (e.g., Cavanaugh, 1996; Hertzog & Hultsch, 2000). Similarly, one of the prominent themes in societal stereotypes of aging is that of cognitive decline (e.g., Hummert, Garstka, Shaner, & Strahm, 1994). Notably, however, some stereotypes of aging include processes believed to improve or grow into and throughout late life (e.g., Heckhausen & Krueger, 1993). Some of these potential growth-like processes have substantial cognitive components (e.g., wisdom). Overall, whether cognitive aging should be characterized as consisting of gains or losses (or both) has been the topic of much debate for many decades (Baltes, 1987; Dixon, 2000; Uttal & Perlmutter, 1989).

Although it may be used in different ways and to accomplish different goals, cognition is no less important in late adulthood than in early adulthood. Not only is it a basis of one's achievements and competence, but it contributes to—or detracts from—one's sense of self-efficacy and the efficiency with which one engages in life planning and life management and pursues life goals. Therefore, it is instructive to compare the basic stories told about cognitive development during the first 20 or so years of life, on the one hand, and during the remaining 40 or 50 (or more) years of life, on the other. Obviously, the stories told of infant, child, adolescent, and even early adult cognitive development are generally optimistic. Cognition during these years is progressing and growing, and cognitive potential is being realized. For normally developing individuals there are some differences in level of performance attained and in the rate at which growth occurs, but virtually no differences in the direction of change. Cognition improves from early infancy.

Around early adulthood, however, the story of cognitive development evidently changes. The word "evidently" is used because there is some controversy about the range and causes of aging-related changes in cognition. There is, however, little remaining controversy regarding the fact that there is substantial and necessary cognitive decline (see, e.g., Craik & Salthouse, 2000). Nevertheless, an important theme in cognitive aging is one of individual differences in profiles, rates, and causes of change. Increasingly, researchers are attending to questions concerning such issues as whether people differ in when they start to decline, whether processes differ in rate of decline, what processes are maintained and for how long, how normal decline differs from that associated with various brain-related diseases (e.g., Alzheimer's disease), and the extent to which this decline affects individuals' everyday lives. A common proposal is that individual differences in cognitive development are greater in late life than in early life. Research in cognitive aging is ideally suited to investigating why such individual differences in change patterns occur.

In this chapter we summarize selected aspects of the field of cognitive aging. Reflecting the breadth of the field, we have elected to focus on several clusters or processes of cognitive functioning. Naturally, this results in numerous unattended processes; interested readers may turn to several recent volumes of collected works in which scholars have reviewed a variety of processes of cognitive aging (e.g., Craik & Salthouse, 2000; Park & Schwartz, 2000). A long-standing area of study in cognitive aging is intelligence; we begin by reviewing scholarship in this area. Perhaps the most commonly researched domain in cognitive aging is memory. Accordingly, we review basic systems and results in this field and indicate several novel directions of research. More recently, numerous researchers have attended to issues of potential or resilience in cognitive aging. Included in this domain are such topics as plasticity and susceptibility to effects of experience, mechanisms of compensating for cognitive impairments, and such intriguing cognitive processes as wisdom and creativity.

INTELLIGENCE

Cognition can be viewed from several related perspectives. From one such perspective, the focus is on cognition as intelligence as an intellectual ability. There is a long tradition of research on intelligence and a surprisingly long history of research on intellectual aging. Research on the aging of intellectual abilities typically uses procedures adapted from research on *psychometric intelligence*. This means that intelligence is measured by one or more tests. These tests may be composed of more than one scale, or subtest. Each subtest measures a relatively unique aspect of intelligence. There are a variety of statistical means through which the uniqueness of the subtests can be evaluated. In addition, however, the subtests typically should be linked both conceptually and empirically.

Contemporary psychometric approaches to adult intellectual development employ multidimensional theories of intelligence. Therefore, they also use intelligence tests in which performance on multiple scales or dimensions may be tested. Using multiple scales of intelligence allows the investigator to examine the extent to which dimensions of intelligence change similarly or differently across adulthood. The psychometric approach to intellectual aging has a long and illustrious history.

Patterns of Intellectual Aging

A typical expectation about intellectual aging is that intelligence increases until early adulthood and then declines through late adulthood. This results in an inverted-U-shaped curve. Botwinick (1977) referred to this curve as a classic pattern, partly because it was so frequently supported in the literature. Interestingly, however, even the earliest theories and research did not lead to the unequivocal conclusion that intelligence inevitably and universally declined after early adulthood. Contemporary research has confirmed the prescient early theorists, who operated without the benefit of modern technology, contemporary theories, or even much research data. Several examples illustrate this point.

Issues of age fairness and late life potential and plasticity were identified early. Kirkpatrick (1903) noted that age-fair intelligence tests were crucial to identifying patterns of intellectual aging. Almost a century ago he also speculated that adults could be trained to perform better on intelligence tests; recently, several researchers (e.g., Schaie, 1996) reported that this was indeed possible. Another important issue raised almost 100 years ago is the potentially close connection between the aging body and the aging mind. For example, Sanford (1902) noted that intellectual decline was likely associated with the inevitable physical decline that accompanies late life. Thus, Sanford anticipated some aspects of contemporary theories focusing on the roles of physiological, neurological, and sensory factors (e.g., Baltes & Lindenberger, 1997). Could older adults overcome such inevitable changes? Sanford speculated that some maintenance of performance levels is possible if aging adults made an effort to maintain them by, for example, continuing challenging activities. This idea, too, has recently been the target of considerable research (e.g., Gold et al., 1995; Hultsch, Hertzog, Small, & Dixon, 1999). Still in the first half of the century, Weisenburg, Roe, and McBride (1936) attended to the questions of whether all adults developed in the same pattern and whether all intellectual abilities changed in the same way. They reported a wide range of ages in adulthood at which performance on intelligence tests peaked. This implies that individuals may differ in peak age, rate of growth and decline, overall degree of decline, and perhaps even final performance level. If some individuals

decline relatively early in adulthood, and if their decline is sharply downward, others may decline relatively late and quite gradually, and perhaps not even noticeably. This prediction, too, proved to be uncannily accurate.

One final similarity between early and recent research on intellectual development may be noted: The study of intellectual aging has long been viewed as a research topic with important and immediate practical implications. That is, how well society understands the characteristics of intellectual aging may have a direct impact on the welfare of individuals and of the society. For example, in the early 1920s, R. M. Yerkes set out to enhance the recruitment and training of excellent military officers. Shortly after World War I it was clear that each side in a war would want people in charge who were intellectually competent, if not intellectually superior. How would the best people be selected and promoted to sensitive and influential positions? How could the best officers be identified and retained? Were older officers less competent than younger officers? Yerkes found that older officers performed worse on an intelligence test than did younger adults. Nevertheless, he argued that many older officers had accumulated valuable experience and had command of specific relevant domains of knowledge. It could take years for younger officers to acquire similar levels of knowledge. Yerkes believed that this actually put older adults at an advantage in the intellectually demanding role of planning and executing war. Thus, even when a great deal is at stake, some observers opted for (older) adults possessing age-related experience and a seasoned mind over (younger) adults who might be able to learn novel information more quickly.

In sum, many early researchers identified remarkably contemporary concerns in the study of intelligence and aging. Moreover, several early leaders commented on the implications of intellectual development for continued cognitive potential throughout life.

Crystallized and Fluid Intelligence

Beginning in the 1960s John Horn and Raymond Cattell began developing an alternative view of the classic aging pattern. Horn and Cattell collected a variety of intelligence-test data from adults of varying ages. Rather than interpreting the scores from each of the tests, or even collapsing across categories of tests (such as Verbal and Performance), Horn and Cattell conducted complicated statistical analyses. In these analyses they sought to assess empirically whether there was indeed more than one category (or factor) of intelligence. If so, this would support the notion that intelligence in adulthood was multidimensional. Empirical support for this fact would then allow Horn and Cattell to investigate three major issues. First, how many and what were the dimensions of intelligence? Second, what were the age-related patterns of performance on these dimensions? Third, to what explanatory processes could these empirically derived dimensions be linked?

In their research, Horn and Cattell (1966; Horn, 1982) identified two major dimensions of intelligence. These dimensions of intellectual abilities were called *fluid intelligence* (Gf) and *crystallized intelligence* (Gc). Fluid intelligence reflected the level of intellectual competence associated with casual learning processes. This learning is assessed by performance on novel, usually nonverbal tests. Crystallized intelligence, on the other hand, reflects intellectual competence associated with intentional learning processes. This variety of learning is assessed by measures of knowledge and skills acquired during school and other cultural learning experiences. Most verbal tests tap processes thought to underlie crystallized intelligence.

How is this perspective an alternative to the classic aging pattern? Because crystallized intelligence indexes life-long accumulation of cultural knowledge, it should show a pattern of maintenance or increase during the adult years. According to the theory, fluid intelligence is more dependent on physiological functioning, including the neurological system. The physiological and neurological base declines with advancing age (e.g., Medina, 1996; Raz, 2000). If this neurological base is impaired, the ability to perform associated intellectual skills is undermined. Horn and Cattell have therefore provided the classic aging pattern with two contributions. First, they provided a firmer empirical basis for the common verbal-performance distinction. Roughly speaking, crystallized intelligence corresponds to verbal intelligence scales, and fluid intelligence corresponds to performance intelligence scales. Second, they have provided potential explanations for the common observation of differential decline across the two dimensions.

Seattle Longitudinal Study

Longitudinal research in intellectual aging has been carried out in a number of locations (Schaie, 1983). Although longitudinal investigations have the advantage of examining age *changes* rather than simply age *differences,* they have their associated limitations as well (see Hultsch, Hertzog, Dixon, & Small, 1998; Schaie, 1983). For example, *selective sampling* and *selective attrition* factors plague longitudinal designs but are now manageable with contemporary design features and statistical techniques (e.g., Hultsch et al., 1998; Schaie, 1996). Individuals who volunteer to participate in longitudinal

studies are committing considerable time and effort over a period of many years. The sample of people who would volunteer for such a long-term commitment are generally positively selected on a number of dimensions that may be relevant to intellectual performance. As well, those who continue in such studies are also positively selected. Indeed, these participants often perform initially on the intelligence tests at a higher level than those who drop out. In this way, a volunteer longitudinal sample is somewhat selective at the outset, and the continuers are more positively selected than the dropouts. Because of this bias, simple longitudinal designs may underestimate the extent of age-related declines.

In 1956 K. Warner Schaie began a carefully designed and exhaustive longitudinal and cohort-sequential study of intelligence in adulthood. Schaie administered the Primary Mental Abilities (PMA) test and additional measures related to intelligence. His initial sample was approximately 500 adults living in the community. This sample was carefully constructed to be representative, and participants ranged in age from 20 to 70 years. Testing was done at seven-year intervals beginning in 1956. At each occasion new participants were added and then followed in subsequent occasions. Thus, there was a sequence of longitudinal studies. Because of the location of all the testing, Schaie's study has become known as the Seattle Longitudinal Study (Schaie, 1996).

Schaie applied special techniques for comparing longitudinal samples to new cross-sectional samples. In doing so, he was able to estimate that until the age of 50 a substantial portion of the age differences observed in cross-sectional studies were not due exclusively to aging-related decline. Instead, much of the observed age differences in cross-sectional studies were due to cohort effects. That is, observed age differences may be related to cultural and historical changes. Indeed, Schaie (1990) reported such a phenomenon when he noted that historical analyses indicate that successive generations have performed at higher levels on intelligence tests. Notably, the patterns suggest that the historical increases may be greater for older than for younger cohorts. If so, future studies may find reduced age differences between younger and older participants. Such a trend can only provide more pressure to utilize the productive potential of older adults.

Throughout his career Schaie (1994, 1996) has emphasized that there are considerable individual differences in degree of decline and age at onset of decline. Indeed, up to age 70 some individuals do not decline at all. Some of these individuals even show modest gains for all of the intellectual abilities that he evaluates. Nevertheless, a prominent conclusion is that the age at which each ability peaks and the patterns of decline thereafter are quite different. For example, those abilities associated with fluid intelligence have earlier peaks and longer declines than those abilities associated with crystallized intelligence. He also pointed out that the patterns vary for women and men. For example, one finding was that women generally decline earlier on fluid intelligence, whereas men generally decline earlier on crystallized intelligence. There is diversity not only in how dimensions of intelligence develop, but also in how men and women develop in different dimensions. Because of this diversity, Schaie (1994, 1996) underscored the warning that an overall index of ability such as the IQ score should not be used in research on intellectual development in adulthood.

Schaie also examined issues of intervention or application. As the Seattle Longitudinal Study progressed, he realized that he could address a unique question with profound implications for both theory and application. The issue is the age at which substantial cognitive decline actually begins. Whether substantial decline begins earlier or later in life could have a profound influence on social policy problems such as mandatory retirement (e.g., Perlmutter, 1990; Schaie, 1994). Schaie's studies suggested that such decline is not observed on average for all dimensions of intelligence until about the late 60s (Schaie, 1996). These results may be surprising to even the most optimistic theorist and practitioner, for they imply that the overall profile of intellectual aging is one of maintenance. In fact, in one analysis Schaie (1990) reported that over 70% of 60-year-olds and over 50% of 81-year-olds declined on only one ability over the previous seven years. Thus, intellectual declines occur with aging, but not appreciably until quite late in life, and then not uniformly across dimensions of intelligence.

Schaie discovered some tentative answers to frequently asked questions about risk and protection factors. Everyone would like to know what they can do to increase the probability that their cognitive aging will by characterized by maintenance and growth and to minimize the probability that it will instead be characterized by decline and decay. By analyzing the differences among individuals in decline versus growth patterns, Schaie (1996) cited several factors that may lead to reducing the risk of cognitive decline in late life. These protective factors include (a) avoiding chronic illnesses, especially cardiovascular disease, or lifestyles that lead to these diseases; (b) pursuing high levels of education and having professions that involve high complexity and higher-than-average incomes; (c) continuing to be active in reading, travel, culture, and further education; (d) being married to a spouse with high and similar cognitive skills; and (e) feeling generally satisfied with life (Schaie, 1996). Of course, these factors were not linked causally or directly to maintenance of intellectual

functioning, so the above list should not be interpreted too literally. Therefore, it is not yet a list of dos and don'ts for maintaining high levels of cognitive performance into late adulthood. Nevertheless, such hypotheses highlight the close link between research on cognitive aging and questions of application to real life. Overall, it can safely be said that the previous factors cannot hurt one's chances of maintaining intellectual functioning; in fact, they may help.

MEMORY

If research on intellectual aging is characterized principally by psychometric assumptions and procedures, research on memory and aging is typically conducted by implementing one or more of a wide range of experimental tasks and techniques in the service of answering a broad range of specific questions. To be sure, all prominent developmental research designs—that is, those that compare age groups (cross-sectionally) or those that follow samples across time (longitudinally)—may be enacted for either psychometric or experimental research. In the case of memory, the bulk of extant research has been cross-sectional and experimental in nature, but there are a growing number of examples of change-oriented, longitudinal studies populating the scholarly literature. Thus, at the most general level the motivating issues of memory and aging research are similar to those propelling scholarship in intelligence and aging. These include (a) whether aging-related changes may be characterized as gains, losses, or both and (b) what accounts for differences in performance as observed across time, age, task, and individuals.

Overall, research on memory and aging is focused on processes through which individuals may recall previously experienced events or information, the extent to which these processes change with advancing age, and the conditions, correlates, or predictors of such changes. Reflecting the sheer volume of research in this field, numerous reviews of memory and aging have been published in recent decades (e.g., Bäckman, Small, Wahlin, & Larsson, 2000; Craik, 2000; Craik & Jennings, 1992; Hultsch & Dixon, 1990; Kausler, 1994; Light, 1992; A. D. Smith & Earles, 1996). Of all aspects of cognitive aging, memory may be the one that has most captivated general human interest and academic attention. Nearly all reviewers begin by noting that (a) memory is viewed as a functional, if not essential, tool of successful development; (b) memory is one of the most frequently mentioned complaints of older adults; (c) memory loss is one of the most feared signs and implications of aging; and (d) many adults believe that, whereas memory abilities improve through childhood, they decline with aging. For these and other reasons, researchers and lay adults are profoundly interested in whether and when their and others' memory abilities change (decline) throughout adulthood (Dixon, 2000).

Systems of Memory

Over the last several decades, research on memory and aging reveals provocative patterns of results. Whereas some tasks are associated with robust findings of age-related deficits, other tasks are associated with less pronounced losses or even equivalent performance by younger and older adults. Tasks typically associated with losses include remembering lists of information, expository texts, picture characteristics, spatial locations, and those that tap the limits of online memory processing. Tasks often associated with relatively unimpaired performance include implicit memory, facts and knowledge, and those that reflect familiar situations with substantial environmental or human support. Although others are available, one well-developed theoretical treatment of memory per se has proven helpful in organizing these disparate results. Specifically, the *memory systems perspective* has been especially influential in research on memory and aging (Bäckman et al., 1999; Craik, 2000; Dixon, 2000; Schacter & Tulving, 1994).

Positing that there are up to five systems of memory, a central goal of this perspective is to explicate the organization of the systems. A memory system is defined as a set of related processes, linked by common brain mechanisms, information processes, and operational principles (Schacter & Tulving, 1994). We define four of the systems briefly and summarize some principal findings with respect to aging. We begin with the two most commonly encountered forms of memory, those to which most people refer when they express their beliefs and fears about the effects of aging on memory functioning (Ryan, 1992).

Episodic Memory

This form refers to memory for personally experienced events or information. Everyday examples are bountiful: trying to remember the names of people one has met at a party, where one parked the car, a conversation or joke one heard, the location of an object in a spatial arrangement, an anecdote one read in a newspaper, or an unwritten list of items to purchase at a store. It is thought to be the latest developing memory system, and some reviewers have suggested that it is correspondingly among the first to begin showing signs of aging-related decline. Indeed, cross-sectional research using a variety of episodic memory tasks (e.g., memory for digits, words, texts,

pictures, objects, faces) and procedures (e.g., free recall, cued recall, recognition) has observed that older adults commonly perform worse than younger adults. Much recent research has targeted potential moderating factors, such as health, lifestyle activities, education, environmental support, collaborative condition, and ecological relevance of the task (e.g., Bäckman et al., 2000; Hultsch et al., 1998). Although no evidence has been marshaled to dispute persuasively the conclusion that episodic memory performance generally declines with advancing age, some cross-sectional (e.g., Nilsson et al., 1997) and longitudinal (Dixon, Wahlin, Maitland, Hertzog, & Bäckman, in press) research has indicated that the magnitude of aging-related change may be more gradual than precipitous for normally aging adults, at least until the mid-70s (Bäckman et al., 2000).

Semantic Memory

This system of memory is expressed through the acquisition and retention of generic facts, knowledge, and beliefs. In research, it is evaluated by administering tests of general world knowledge, facts, words, concepts, and associations. As such, it is similar to the domain represented by crystallized intelligence. The typical finding for semantic memory is that older adults may remember as much information of this sort as do younger adults. For example, normal older adults, through extended cultural and educational experiences, may possess knowledge bases regarding world facts (sports, celebrities, geographical information, political lore) that are superior to those of younger adults. A typical finding in cognitive aging literature is that the vocabulary performance of older adults is similar to or better than that of younger adults. Thus, older adults display similar knowledge structures or associative networks. Nevertheless, some studies have suggested that older adults may access such information more slowly and with more frequent blockages than do younger adults. In a large cross-sectional study, only small differences were observed across the ages of 35 to 80 years (Bäckman & Nilsson, 1996). Moreover, a recent longitudinal study observed modest changes over a 12-year period for adults originally aged 55 to 85 years (Hazlitt, 2000).

Procedural Memory

This form of memory is reflected in the gradual learning (through practice) of a wide variety of cognitive and behavioral skills. Naturally, as one learns a skill, one may acquire information or actions intentionally, deliberately, explicitly, and with awareness. However, other phases and aspects of learning the skill may be accomplished more automatically, implicitly, and without specific awareness. This latter aspect of memory is the one reflected in this system. It is involved in the identification of words, objects, or movements that have been experienced by an individual but about which that individual may have little direct awareness—little episodic memory of having previously encountered the word or object. Memory thus used has been said to be automatic or implicit, as contrasted with intentional or explicit (Howard, 1996). A common expectation is that procedural memory, as evaluated through priming techniques (e.g., Howard, 1996), is relatively unaffected by aging, as long as the involvement of explicit memory is minimized (Craik, 2000; Craik & Jennings, 1992). Although this seems to indicate a beneficial aspect of memory functioning in late life, it may lead unintentionally to a greater propensity to generate and remember false information (see Schacter, Koutsaal, & Norman, 1997).

Primary Memory

Although differing in some respects, this system is also known popularly as working memory and, in some restricted instances, as short-term memory. The terms are selected to convey the fact that some expressions of memory are brief, temporary, not yet (or ever) stored, or still in consciousness. Distinguishing between primary and working memory has proven useful for aging research (Craik, 2000). Specifically, primary memory is observed in conditions in which individuals must repeat minimal information presented immediately prior to the task. For example, primary memory is tapped when an individual must repeat a short list of letters or digits immediately after it is read. For such brief and passive tasks, older adults perform as well as younger adults, or at least not as poorly as in tasks requiring further manipulation of more complex information over a longer duration. Performing working memory tasks requires more active processing and manipulation of incoming information. As such, older adults are typically at a disadvantage as compared to younger adults in performing such tasks. As Craik (2000) noted, this divergent pattern within a memory system implies that aging processes do not adversely affect some everyday memory demands (e.g., copying addresses and numbers as they are read), but it does negatively affect more active aspects of online memory processing.

Emerging Memory Topics

As can be inferred from the preceding summary, memory, like intelligence, is a multidimensional construct. As with other multidimensional constructs of interest in developmental psychology, differentiable dimensions may reveal distinct developmental patterns. Researchers continue to explore with increasing ingenuity each of the clusters of memory phenomena. In addition, many researchers push the boundaries of these memory systems as they apply to aging by considering ever-broader ranges of memory phenomena, as well as correlates and predictors. In this section we briefly note a few trends in memory and aging research, selecting for somewhat more discussion two of these domains.

Biological to the Social

Among the promising new trends in memory and aging research is the ever-increasing attention that biological influences are receiving. This is an entirely logical development, if only because the brain is a crucial site of activation that is representative of memory and other cognitive processing. Structural and functional changes in the brain are related to, if not predictive of, cognitive performance in adults (e.g., Cabeza & Nyberg, 2000; Raz, 2000; Reuter-Lorenz, 2000). Also within a biological level, much current research in memory and aging has focused on the extent to which physiological, sensory, and physical health changes may have an effect on cognitive functioning in late life (e.g., Baltes & Lindenberger, 1997; Waldstein, 2000).

Shifting to a cognitive level of analysis, recent efforts have been made to identify other cognitive factors that influence target cognitive functions. For example, working memory has been identified as a relevant influence on episodic and semantic memory functioning (e.g., Hultsch et al., 1998). Theoretical constructs such as processing resources, inhibitory control, and information-processing speed have, in empirical applications, accounted for age-related variance in memory performance (see Craik, 2000; Salthouse, 1991). At still another level of analysis, recent progress in examining the role of background characteristics such as gender, education, and lifestyle activities on cognitive aging have been made (e.g., Herlitz, Nilsson, & Bäckman, 1997; Hultsch et al., 1999). Finally, social and cultural aspects of memory and aging have been explored with much promise (e.g., Hess & Blanchard-Fields, 1999; Park, Nisbett, & Hedden, 1999). In sum, the goal of understanding memory changes with aging suggests a complex web of changing relationships—among systems of memory, other cognitive influences, and correlates ranging from the neurological to the social-cultural.

Metamemory

Adults of all ages often wonder about their memory—how it works or does not work, why one remembers some things but not others, and whether memory skills will change over the life course. The term *metamemory* refers to such cognitions about memory—thinking about how, why, and whether memory works. Specific aspects of metamemory include knowledge of memory functioning, insight into memory changes or impairment, awareness of current memory processes, beliefs about and interpretations of memory skills and demands, and even memory-related affect. This chapter features an overview of the concept of metamemory and how it applies to aging. The view of metamemory presented here is useful when considering both basic (e.g., how memory and metamemory change and relate to one another in aging) and applied (e.g., the role metamemory may play in compensating for memory impairments and decline) research questions.

Overall, research and theory in metamemory in adulthood incorporate many of the issues raised in the neighboring domains of metamemory research. It does so in part through implementation of an inclusive and multidimensional concept of metamemory (e.g., Dixon, 1989; Hertzog & Hultsch, 2000). Four principal characteristics of this are that (a) it includes a wide variety of behaviors (knowledge, beliefs, evaluations, and estimates), indicating the level, degree, or extent of an individual's metamemory performance or skill; (b) it features a multidimensional concept, in that the multiple facets or behaviors are viewed as separable but linked dimensions of a coherent construct of metamemory; (c) it assumes that multiple operations and dimensions would converge on a higher order construct of metamemory and that metamemory can be discriminated from related constructs; and (d) metamemory is a construct of intrinsic interest in the study of normal cognitive aging, but one that may also have substantial implications for understanding impairments of memory in late life.

Metamemory represents one's knowledge, awareness, and beliefs about the functioning, development, and capacities of one's own memory and of human memory in general (Dixon, 1989). As such, metamemory includes three principal categories (Hertzog & Dixon, 1994). First, declarative knowledge about how memory functions includes knowledge of how the characteristics of memory tasks have an impact on memory performance, whether strategies are required, and which strategies may be usefully applied to particular situations. Second, self-referent beliefs about one's capability to use memory effectively in memory-demanding situations define memory self-efficacy and controllability (e.g., Cavanaugh, 1996, 2000). One's beliefs about one's ability to remember may determine (a) the extent to which one places oneself in memory-demanding situations, (b) the degree of effort one applies to perform the memory task, (c) one's expectation regarding level of memory performance, and (d) one's actual memory performance. Certain aspects of affect regarding

memory (in general) or one's memory performance and change (in particular) may also play a role (e.g., motivation to do well, fear of memory-demanding situations).

Third, awareness of the current, general, and expected state of one's memory performance includes processes of memory insight and memory monitoring. Effective rememberers are able to monitor actively and accurately their performance vis-à-vis the demands of the memory task. A high degree of accuracy in predictions of performance, evaluations of encoding demands, and on-line judgments of learning may indicate an effective and accomplished rememberer (e.g., Hertzog & Hultsch, 2000; Moulin, Perfect, & Jones, 2000). In clinical situations, an awareness of a deficit may be an important precursor to memory compensation (e.g., Dixon & Bäckman, 1995, 1999; Wilson & Watson, 1996).

In aging research, these categories of metamemory have been related to one another theoretically and empirically (see Hertzog & Dixon, 1994; Hertzog & Hultsch, 2000). In principle, for older adults, high performance on given memory tasks should be promoted by the following metamemory profile: (a) a well-structured declarative knowledge base about how memory functions in given tasks, (b) refined knowledge of one's own memory skills, (c) accurate and high memory self-efficacy, and (d) skill at the monitoring and control activities during acquisition, retention, and retrieval. In addition, it could be useful to have (e) stable or low memory-related affect, such that the potential deleterious effects of memory-related anxiety or depression could be avoided. In contrast, some older adults with poorer—and perhaps impaired—performance could be experiencing some components of the following profile: (a) and (b) an ill-structured, incomplete, or erroneous knowledge base pertaining to general memory functioning or one's own memory skills; (c) inaccurate or low memory self-efficacy; (d) an inability to monitor and control the requisite activities of effective remembering; and (e) fluctuant, uncontrolled, or excessive memory-related anxiety or depression. These profiles define two hypothetical ends of a continuum.

Two practical implications of these hypothetical profiles in older adults are evident. First, some aging-related memory disorders or impairments may be remedied through clinical intervention designed to assess and improve selected categories of metamemory. Second, the diagnosis and remediation of some organic memory disorders (e.g., the result of injuries or disease) may be enhanced through the use of metamemory or awareness information. Research on these provocative issues is advancing on a variety of fronts, including cognitive neurorehabilitation (e.g., Prigatano, 2000; Wilson & Watson, 1996), memory compensation in late life (e.g., Dixon, de Frias, & Bäckman, 2001), awareness and insight neuropsy-chological conditions (e.g., Lovelace, 1990; Markova & Berrios, 2000; Schacter, 1990), memory complaints and their origins and implications (e.g., Gilewski & Zelinski, 1986; Grut et al., 1993; G. E. Smith, Petersen, Ivnik, Malec, & Tangalos, 1996), and potential effects of metamemory training on memory (e.g., Lachman, Weaver, Bandura, Elliott, & Lewkowicz, 1992; Verhaeghen, Marcoen, & Goosens, 1992).

Memory in Interactive Situations

For several decades researchers in a surprising variety of fields have addressed aspects of everyday memory activity that appear to operate in the influential context of other individuals. Many observers have noted the frequency with which everyday adult cognitive activity occurs in interactive contexts (e.g., Clancey, 1997; Greeno, 1998). A collaborative context frequently envelops cognitive performance in modern life. Everyday examples of collaborative cognition include (a) family groups or lineages reconstructing stories from their shared past; (b) spouses enlisted to help remember important appointments, duties, or dates; and (c) strangers in unknown cities consulted in order to solve way-finding or map-reading problems (Dixon, 1999; see also Strough & Margrett, 2002). Lurking behind this observation is the contention that collaboration may lead to functional performance outcomes, practical solutions, and improved performance. Of particular importance in cognitive aging research is the possibility that the strategic deployment or use of human cognitive aids (other individuals) may be a means of compensating for individual-level aging-related losses or deficits.

In other literatures the phenomenon has been also called collective (e.g., Middleton & Edwards, 1990), situated (e.g., Greeno, 1998), group (e.g., Clark & Stephenson, 1989), socially shared (e.g., Resnick, Levine, & Teasley, 1991), or interactive (e.g., Baltes & Staudinger, 1996) cognition. In the case of collaborative memory, an assumption is made that two or more individuals attend to the same set of learning or memory tasks and are working cooperatively (although not necessarily effectively) to achieve a recall-related goal. Notably, the members of the collaborating group can be variously passive listeners, conversational interactants, productive collaborators, seasoned tutors, counterproductive or even disruptive influences, or optimally effective partners. Therefore, according to a neutral definition of collaborative memory espoused in this chapter, no a priori assumptions are made about the effectiveness or logical priority of the memory-related interaction. It has long been clear that group *processes* can vary in their effectiveness and thus that group *products*

can vary in their accuracy and completeness (e.g., Steiner, 1972).

The issue of the extent to which collaborative memory is effective has been evaluated from numerous perspectives for several decades. Indeed, much research has focused on this contentious issue (e.g., Dixon, 1999; Hill, 1982), and several key factors appear to play roles in the observations and inferences. These factors include (a) whether the participants are collaborative-interactive experts (e.g., friends or couples), (b) the type of outcome measure observed (i.e., a simple product such as total items recalled or a variety of recall-related products such as elaborations and inferences), (c) the extent to which the actual processes (e.g., strategic negotiations) and byproducts (e.g., affect and sharing) of the collaborative communication are investigated, and (d) the comparison or baseline by which the effectiveness of collaborative performance is evaluated. In general, little extra benefit is observed under conditions in which researchers reduce the dimensionality of the tasks, the familiarity of the interactants, the variety of the memory-related products measured, and the richness of the collaborative communication (e.g., Meudell, Hitch, & Kirby, 1992). In contrast, evidence for notable collaborative benefit may be observed when researchers attend to collaborative expertise, multidimensional outcomes, measurement of actual collaborative processes, and comparisons accommodated to memory-impaired or vulnerable groups (e.g., Dixon & Gould, 1998). In particular, evidence has accumulated that expert older collaborators (long-term married couples) may be able to solve complicated memory problems at levels not otherwise expected for such individuals through cooperative mechanisms that resemble compensatory devices (Dixon, 1999, for review). This is a growing and promising area of both basic and applied research in memory and aging.

Memory for Future Events

The classical sense of memory—and all the examples just noted—refer to remembering events that have occurred in the past. There is, however, a common class of memory activities that refer to future events. Among the plethora of everyday memory experiences are those in which one must remember to carry out an action in the future, such as remembering to take medication, keep an appointment, give a message to a colleague, pick up a loaf of bread on the return trip home, or perform an errand such as mailing a letter. This class of memory has become known as *prospective memory*. Accordingly, it is contrasted with the sizable set of memory activities for past events, which, from this perspective, may be classified as *retrospective memory*. Thus, retrospective memory includes the principal memory systems, such as episodic and semantic memory. Although memory and aging research has been predominantly interested in retrospective memory phenomena, in recent years prospective memory has become a salient research topic (Einstein, McDaniel, Richardson, & Guynn, 1995).

Like retrospective memory, prospective memory and aging have been studied with both naturalistic and experimental procedures. The two classes of memory share also a considerable amount of research examining age-related patterns of performance. In a groundbreaking naturalistic study, Moscovitch (1982) instructed younger and older adults to call an experimenter at prearranged times throughout a period of several days. The intriguing results indicated that older adults' prospective memory performance was actually better than that of the younger adults. Further investigation revealed an unexpected potential explanation; namely, older adults were motivated to perform such tasks and were more likely to use reminders (e.g., written notes) as a way of remembering the intention of phoning the experimenter. Thus, this early study suggested the possibility that older adults may have identified a potential everyday memory deficit as well as an effective compensatory mechanism (see also Dixon, de Frias, et al., 2001).

To investigate such issues further, experimental researchers developed procedures for controlling the strategies that participants might use (e.g., Einstein & McDaniel, 1990). Such laboratory experiments have revealed divergent findings. For example, Dobbs and Rule (1987) asked younger and older adults at the beginning of an experiment to remind the experimenter to give them a red pen at a particular later point in the session. Thus, participants had to monitor this intention over a period of time, without the benefit of external memory aids, while performing other demanding or primary tasks. In this study older adults performed significantly worse than did their younger counterparts.

Einstein et al. (1995) proposed a subdivision of prospective memory tasks. From this analysis, one subset of prospective memory tasks is event-based, as represented in those situations in which an external event acts as a trigger for some previously encoded intention. Theoretically, the occurrence of the event prompts a memory search that will eventually result in the retrieval of the intention. For example, an event could be the sudden meeting of a friend that triggers the memory that one has a message to deliver. In contrast, time-based prospective memory reflects the situation in which the appropriateness of an action or intention is determined by the passage of time. Accordingly, one must remember to take a pill in two hours; in order to do this with no external event,

one must monitor time while performing other (distracting) actions. The provocative hypothesis was that time-based tasks would produce more negative aging-related effects than would event-based tasks because the former require more self-initiated processing (Einstein et al., 1995). The key to older adults' successful performance may be the ability to implement compensatory procedures such as strategic use of environmental cues. Although this idea remains controversial (e.g., Park, Hertzog, Kidder, & Morrell, 1997), the ideas of decomposing this class of memory actions and relating performances to other factors is advancing our understanding of how aging might affect memory for future events.

COGNITIVE POTENTIAL IN ADULTHOOD

Taken together, the bodies of research on intellectual and memory aging reveal that despite robust evidence of gradual decline in performance, there may be some room for slightly optimistic interpretations. To be sure, among the multidimensional constructs and processes considered to be the mechanics of cognitive aging (Park, 2000), intelligence and memory may offer the greatest opportunity to observe even this extent of mixed aging-related patterns. Recent reviews of other more basic processes (e.g., attention, perception) and those more closely linked to biological aging (e.g., those heavily involving sensory, physiological, and neurological functioning) evaluate almost exclusively the magnitude and rate of decline, as well as the extent to which such changes affect other cognitive performances, with little space devoted to maintenance or growth (see Dixon, Bäckman, & Nilsson, in press). Nevertheless, the overall balance between the gains and losses of cognitive aging continues to be an issue of vigorous and compelling debate (e.g., Baltes, 1987; Dixon, 2000; Park, 2000; Salthouse, 1991; Schaie, 1996; Uttal & Perlmutter, 1989). Why is this the case? Perhaps the most compelling reason has been identified by Salthouse (1990), who noted that one of the most vexatious challenges facing cognitive aging researchers is to reconcile what we have learned about cognitive decline from laboratory and psychometric research with the common observation that many older adults are quite competent in cognitively demanding everyday leisure and professional activities into very late life. How can older adults—all of whom will have experienced at least detectable decline in a variety of fundamental cognitive processes—still perform well as world political leaders, CEOs of large corporations, scientists, novelists and poets, expert bridge and chess players, composers and painters, and a variety of other roles? In brief, there must be some aspects or processes of cognitive aging that are not definitively represented or determined by commonly researched domains. In this section we review briefly some of the possible scenarios for observing or optimizing cognitive potential in adulthood, midlife, and beyond.

Concept of Cognitive Gains

With most empirically investigated psychological processes, aging-related changes may follow multiple directions. This is the case, despite the fact that many biologically based processes are in decline for much of middle and late adulthood. In fact, Baltes (1987, p. 613) referred to this idea as one of the principal theoretical propositions of life-span developmental psychology: "Considerable diversity . . . is found in the directionality of changes that constitute ontogenesis, even within the same domain . . . [and] during the same developmental periods." An important implication of this is that the concept of psychological development contains both gains (growth, increases) and losses (decline, decrements). From this perspective, life-span psychological development is not simply or exclusively characterized by incremental growth or structural advances. Instead, development is a concept that contains multiple possible directions—as widely varied as these directions can be (i.e., that between gains and losses). Moreover, as Baltes noted, multiple directions of change can occur within a single multidimensional construct.

Memory is an excellent example. Recall that multiple systems have been posited and that these systems may undergo somewhat different developmental changes with aging (Craik, 2000; Craik & Jennings, 1992). This example is of multiple directions of change across dimensions of a multidimensional construct (e.g., intelligence, personality, memory). It may, as Baltes noted, also apply within a single dimension but across individuals in a single developmental period. That is, a diverse group of adults in their 60s may be at different points, following different trajectories, in the developmental paths of any single psychological process.

Thus, gains and losses have become a key organizing feature of psychological aging (Baltes, 1987; Dixon, 2000). Among the principal challenges for psychologists is not only to describe the cognitive losses that occur with aging and to articulate the mechanisms accounting for those losses. A great deal of evidence pertains to both these descriptive and explanatory undertakings (e.g., Park, 2000). Instead, an important challenge is to articulate classes of examples of gains with psychological aging. In what manner and by what means may there be improvement in psychological functioning with advancing age? Accordingly, several such classes of examples have been identified (e.g., Dixon, 2000).

Specifically, one model proposes that given substantial and unavoidable losses in basic biological and cognitive functioning with aging (Park, 2000), three main categories of gains may still be articulated. These are (a) *gains qua gains,* or the possibility that some gains may emerge and continue independent of the constraints provided by surrounding aging-related losses; (b) *gains as losses of a lesser magnitude,* or the idea that some consolation or adjustment may be made given that some psychological losses occur later than expected (personally or in stereotypes) or to an extent not as devastating as had been feared; and (c) *gains as a function of losses,* or the evident possibility that some psychological gains are linked to specific losses, occasioned by those losses, and that may even compensate partially for such losses, mitigating their detrimental effects (see Dixon, 2000). Interestingly, the latter category includes many examples that operate principally at a basic or neurological level of analysis. In sum, at many levels cognitive aging appears to be multidirectional; this is the case even though much overall loss (decline) occurs with aging.

Plasticity and Experience

Under what circumstances can older adults experience gains in cognitive performance? Whereas early twentieth century researchers only speculated about this matter, recent researchers have produced useful empirical information. Some evidence regarding potential is revealed in intervention research, such as training older adults to perform better on challenging cognitive tasks. For example, this literature supports four principal theses. First, many normal older adults can improve their performance on intelligence tests simply by having the opportunity for some self-directed practice (e.g., Baltes & Willis, 1982). Second, healthy older adults can benefit from specific training on how to perform cognitive tasks (e.g., Verhaeghen, Marcoen, & Goosens, 1992). Third, selected older adults who have experienced severe or pathological decline can benefit from specific and aggressive interventions (e.g., Camp & McKitrick, 1992). Fourth, there may be some conditions in which training higher levels of performance on intelligence tests can lead to better performance in some cognitive tasks of everyday life (e.g., Neely & Bäckman, 1995; Willis, Jay, Diehl, & Marsiske, 1992).

Overall, some interventions work to improve performance or even reverse losses associated with aging. Theoretically, this implies that some degree of normally observed decline in intellectual aging may be due to disuse. Older adults decline partly because they no longer have the experience or the social and cultural context that will help them maintain some intellectual abilities. Recall that several very early observers had produced prescient speculations remarkably consistent with this empirical generalization. The implication is not, however, that there is no real decline, or that simply providing mental exercises or social support will overcome observed decline. Intellectual decline is real, but there is some degree of plasticity available to many older adults. This conclusion supports the contention that the potential for improvement may be present into late life.

The "potential for potential" in late life is of interest not only to theorists and researchers interested in cognitive aging. It is of interest—or should be of interest—also to politicians, policy makers, aging workers, and just about everyone who knows someone who is nearing the retirement years or who plans to reach old age themselves. Why should so many people be interested in the fact that aging individuals retain the potential for cognitive maintenance and growth? One reason is that our population is increasingly an aging one. More people are getting older; more people are reaching retirement age and beyond; and more people may be feeling that they are being closed off from making useful contributions at an age in which they feel quite competent and potentially useful. Many recent books have addressed precisely this issue and its many implications, as the titles of several of them indicate: *Late Life Potential* (Perlmutter, 1990), *Successful Aging* (Baltes & Baltes, 1990), *Promoting Successful and Productive Aging* (Bond, Cutler, & Grams, 1995), and *Compensating for Psychological Deficits and Declines: Managing Losses and Promoting Gains* (Dixon & Bäckman, 1995). These and similar recent contributions explore the possibility that there is considerable cognitive potential in late life, as well as how such potential can be actuated or preserved.

Some authors have focused also on the social policy implications of late life potential. For example, Achenbaum (1990) suggested that North American society may have to place a greater emphasis on adult education. In particular, training and retraining programs may have to be instituted so that potentially competent workers are not placed on the sidelines simply because of their age. A critical issue, however, is how and who will fund such training and retraining programs. Numerous other policy issues can be specified, but most have the same fundamental theme: How do we take advantage of increasing numbers of adults who getting older but not substantially less competent? If this challenge is not addressed soon, the number of individuals who are prematurely discarded or discounted—whose skills and potential contributions will be forever lost—will grow.

Wisdom

The study of wisdom is as old as the study of human thought or philosophy. Although philosophers have struggled with the concept of wisdom for centuries, psychologists and other researchers in human development have addressed it only more recently. In the field of gerontology wisdom is naturally of considerable interest. There are relatively few processes that are generally thought to improve substantially with advancing age. Wisdom is one such process.

Many provocative questions have been addressed. What is wisdom, and how does one know if someone is wise? What are the signs of wisdom, and how might it be recognized? Until the late 1980s only a few researchers had attempted to study the aging of wisdom (e.g., Baltes & Smith, 1990; Baltes & Staudinger, 1993; Clayton & Birren, 1980; Freund & Riediger, this volume; Sternberg, 1990). One early psychologist, G. Stanley Hall (1922), thought that wisdom was one of the desirable characteristics of late adulthood. For Hall, wisdom included taking perspective, synthesizing significant factors of life, and moving toward higher levels. Other observers have portrayed wisdom as good or sound judgment regarding the conduct of life. Good judgment about a life problem would probably involve consideration of a variety of aspects of the situation: personal strengths and weaknesses, talents and emotions, health and physical abilities, as well as social and cultural considerations.

Recent investigators have explored empirically whether wisdom does indeed develop in late life and, if so, whether it is in fact an important aspect of successful aging. The first step is to define wisdom in a way that allows for empirical study. It is clear from common conceptions of wisdom that it involves good judgment about life problems. As pointed out by Kekes (1983), the life problems that bring out wisdom are those for which there may be multiple considerations and even multiple solutions, each with a variety of repercussions. For example, it is likely to require some wisdom to deal with a life problem such as deciding whether to leave college and get a job or whether to marry or divorce somebody. These are everyday problems with many uncertainties associated with them—this is what makes them complex and difficult. Solving such problems well (or wisely) is important because of the significant implications for the individual's (and family's) future.

Wise decisions would therefore involve several ingredients (Baltes & Staudinger, 1993). First, there would be some analysis of the problem. This would include knowledge about (a) the individual and his or her talents and weaknesses, (b) the situation or problem with which they are faced, (c) the context of this problem, especially with respect to the individual's life-span development. In cognitive psychology this kind of knowledge—knowledge about something—is known as *declarative knowledge*. Second, wisdom would involve some knowledge about how to solve the problem. This would include strategies and procedures that typically work for a particular kind of problem. In cognitive psychology this kind of knowledge—knowledge about how to do something—is known as *procedural knowledge*. Third, wisdom would involve good judgment about what to do in particular situations. In this way, the declarative knowledge would be combined with the procedural knowledge and decisions or suggestions would result. Because of the uncertainty associated with many life problems, it is likely that even these judgments would be qualified. That is, good judgments may be characterized less by absolute recommendations than by qualified suggestions. Such tentative suggestions would be dependent on new developments in the life course, new information obtained, or other changing aspects of the context.

Is wise advice therefore inherently indeterminate? Probably not, for the wisest way to solve some life problems could be known with certainty. Solving a problematic life situation by turning to addictive drugs is not a wise decision. A wise person would be unlikely to give a feeble answer to someone seeking advice about whether to begin taking heroin as an escape from a given set of life problems. This fact makes the measurement of wisdom difficult.

How can wisdom be measured? Some researchers have presented a variety of life problems in the form of personal vignettes to adults of all ages (J. Smith & Baltes, 1990). They then asked them to indicate how they would go about giving advice to the character in the vignette. Wisdom is measured by analyzing the responses given to these problems. Two kinds of problems have been used. J. Smith and Baltes (1990) used *life-planning* problems. In these problems individuals learn about a problem in the life of a character and are asked to indicate what the character should do and consider in planning the future. Staudinger, Smith, and Baltes (1992) used *life-review* problems. In these problems a similar vignette is presented in which a character experiences a life event that causes the person to look back over his or her life. The individual solving the problem is asked to describe the aspects of life that the character might remember, as well as how the character might explain or evaluate his or her life.

Would older adults do better at these tasks than younger adults? Or would wise (but not unwise) older adults do better than younger adults? These questions are critical in evaluating the results of the life-planning and life-review wisdom studies. Results from both studies indicate a substantial similarity between young, middle-aged, and older adults in how they respond to these problems. Obviously, an initial expectation would have been that if wisdom is associated with aging, then older adults would do better than younger adults. That this was not found may reflect on (a) the adequacy of the measures of wisdom and (b) the definition of wisdom being used. Future

research will further refine the measures and theories of wisdom and aging (e.g., Simonton, 1990; Sternberg, 1990). One avenue to explore is whether the development of wisdom occurs only for a select few older adults. If this is true, it would be unlikely that a group of normal older adults would perform at a particularly high level. Some results from these studies appear to be promising. For example, middle-aged and older adults who were selected to be tested on the basis of having been nominated by a peer performed slightly better than did comparison groups on some indicators related to wisdom (Baltes & Staudinger, 1993). Wisdom, like intelligence, may require some training and effort to maintain.

Creativity

Creativity is the "ability to innovate, to change the environment rather than merely adjust to it in a more passive sense" (Simonton, 1990, p. 320). If the popular stereotype about wisdom is that it grows with age, the stereotype about creativity may be that it declines during adulthood. Are people more creative in their 20s than in their 60s? Think about all the creative people whom you know—scientists, poets, artists, novelists, actors, musicians, and so forth. Are younger individuals typically better than older individuals in the same field? Are their most creative products generated during their early years in the field? Or are creative people always creative, regardless of their age? Many researchers have investigated these issues. For example, some samples believe that aging is accompanied by an increase in conservatism and cautiousness and a decrease in creative achievement and productivity (e.g., Heckhausen, Dixon, & Baltes, 1989; Hummert et al., 1994). Unlike research on wisdom, there are clear results about the development of creativity during adulthood.

In 1953 Lehman published an influential but controversial volume titled *Age and Achievement,* in which he plotted creative productivity as a function of age. After examining the historical records in numerous domains of productivity, he found that there was an increase in creative output in early adulthood, followed by a decline. Although there were numerous criticisms of his methods and interpretations (e.g., Dennis, 1954, 1956; Lehman, 1956), recent reviewers argue that Lehman's basic results are correct. More recently, Simonton (1990, 1994) noted that across a wide range of studies a robust age-related function can be observed but that there are some important qualifications. For example, in some cases the life-span trajectories have two peaks, one in early adulthood and one in late adulthood. The latter can be thought of as the *second-wind phenomenon.* That is, in some cases there may be a general decline in creative output until a second wind hits about retirement age.

A second important qualification to Lehman's model is that both the age at peak performance and the steepness of the decline in creative productivity vary according to domain. This means that peak creativity in some domains may occur much earlier in life than in other domains. For example, in fields such as pure mathematics, lyric poetry, and theoretical physics, the peaks are in the late 20s or early 30s. In contrast, in fields such as history, philosophy, novel writing, and general scholarship, the peaks are in the 40s or 50s, and the declines are not very steep. For a number of fields—including psychology—the peak of creative output is in the late 30s or early 40s (see Lehman, 1956; Simonton, 1990, 1994).

What about the argument that creativity should not be measured simply by amount of creative output—a quantitative measure? Instead, it should be measured by quality of output—a focus on the truly creative part of productivity. Would this shift in emphasis result in a different profile across the life span? As Simonton (1994) elegantly showed, the answer to this intriguing question is no. Separating the truly creative productions from the less inspired pieces results in virtually identical patterns across the life course. This implies that the quantity of creative output is highly related to the quality of that output. This relationship holds throughout the life course, or the career of an individual. Specifically, those who begin their careers with a great deal of productive output can continue this output throughout their careers. People who are less precocious may also have careers characterized by a stable quality-to-quantity ratio of productivity.

There are several reasons that some careers can be curtailed or become substantially less productive. As Simonton (1990, 1994) noted, these include declining physical health, increasing family responsibilities, and accumulating administrative activities. Declining physical health can, of course, make concentrated effort more laborious or even less frequent. Both increasing family responsibilities and administrative duties can reduce the amount of time available for productive and creative work. Few administrators in universities, for example, are able to maintain full and energetic scholarship programs. However, with seniority some compensatory mechanisms may be available. For example, highly accomplished senior researchers may be called upon to perform full-time administrative duties (e.g., chair of a department at a university), but they may be able to employ several highly qualified and ambitious postdoctoral fellows, as well as numerous graduate students, to carry on their scholarly programs. These younger collaborators become, in this way, human compensatory mechanisms for senior creative scholars.

Overall, Simonton's (1990, 1994) research has generated three general statements about the life course of creativity. First, there is age-related decline in creativity in the late years of life. However, this decline is rarely so substantial as to turn a creative person into a noncreative person. Most creative individuals' lives end before their potential for creative production is exhausted. Second, how creative or productive older adults are depends more on their early-life creativity than on their age. Simonton argued that people who are exceptionally creative in early adulthood are often quite prolific throughout their careers. Indeed, they may continue to produce excellent creative products into very late life. Third, there is no evidence to suggest that the decline in creative output occurs because of a corresponding decline in cognitive skills. Even individuals who enter new arenas of interest in middle or late life have the opportunity to have productive new careers. Creativity, then, may be one area in which potential in late life may be actuated. At the least, it is possible to contend that creative people may continue to be creative across their careers.

Compensation

Compensation is a promising new concept in the field of cognitive aging. It refers to a set of mechanisms through which an individual may continue to perform difficult or complex skills although they are experiencing some loss in relevant abilities required to perform a particular task. As noted earlier, aging involves decline in fundamental sensory, motor, neurological, and cognitive abilities. Many of these abilities are components of higher level skills. Some of these skills may be maintained into late life. One mechanism through which such maintenance can occur is compensation. Adults may be able to compensate for declines that they experience in even very basic components; they may continue to perform even complex skills (composing, writing novels, driving) at competent, if not creative, levels.

Several forms of compensation have been identified (Bäckman & Dixon, 1992; Dixon & Bäckman, 1995, 1999; Salthouse, 1995). For older adults all forms of compensation begin with the experience of a mismatch between their available abilities and the requirements they either place upon themselves (as personal expectations) or accept as given by the community in which they operate. The term *community* can refer to a wide range of environmental demands, such as those accruing as a function of professional requirements, social and interactive obligations, familial responsibilities, sensory and physical contexts, and so forth. The important point is that by using one or more of the forms of compensation, the gap between their ability and their expected level of performance can be closed. In this way, a satisfactory level of performance for a given skill can be attained, and an individual's potential can be maximized. Compensation can occur in normal aging, but also as a form of recovery from brain injury or other pathogenic neurological conditions (e.g., Dixon & Bäckman, 1999; Wilson & Watson, 1996). Compensation is also a viable concept in recovery from a wide range of social and personal deficits and losses, many of which are quite pertinent to the study of cognitive aging (see Dixon & Bäckman, 1995).

What are the forms of compensation applicable to aging in general, and to cognitive aging in particular? Scholars offer somewhat different perspectives on these forms (e.g., Marsiske, Lang, Baltes, & Baltes, 1995; Salthouse, 1995), but the convergence and overlap are impressive (Dixon & Bäckman, 1995). Four forms appear to cover most of the situations in which compensation might occur in late life. The first form is perhaps the simplest. It reflects investing time and effort when there is a deficit in learning or performing a target skill. For example, an individual whose work environment is becoming ever-more computerized, and whose understanding of hardware and specific applications is lagging behind, may compensate for the gap between her environmental demands and skill level by putting more time and effort into acquiring the requisite skills. This deliberate and effortful upgrading of her skill level such that it matches the requirements of her community can result in successful compensation.

The second form of compensation, substitution, originates in a deficit that is the result of important components of skills declining with age, and therefore contributing ineffectively to overall skill performance (e.g., Salthouse, 1995). Compensation as substitution occurs when other components of the skill are correspondingly improved, such that the overall skill performance level is maintained. That is, the global skill is supported by new, emerging components after the original components decline. One well-known example concerns aging typists who can no longer tap their fingers as fast as they might have as younger adults, and who can no longer respond to visual stimuli (e.g., to-be-typed characters) as quickly as they might have in earlier years (Salthouse, 1995). Finger tapping and reaction time are components of the global skill of typing, in that speeded typing cannot be accomplished without some contribution from these abilities. As Salthouse observed, however, some successful older typists compensated for these decrements by possibly developing a substitutable mechanism, namely, eye-hand coordination. That is, they compensated for slower speeds of reaction and tapping by looking further ahead in the to-be-typed text so that their fingers had more time to prepare for the upcoming characters. In this way, their overall performance (typing rate) could be maintained into late life.

A third compensatory process, selection and optimization, involves optimizing one's development overall by selecting different paths or goals when the original one is blocked or unattainable (e.g., chapter by Freund & Riediger in this volume; Marsiske et al., 1995). If the deficit is too great to overcome through investment of time and effort, and if no substitutable components are available, then this form of compensation might be invoked. Essentially, the deficit in the global skill is accepted, and alternative skills and performance domains are emphasized. For example, an aging typist for whom substitution is unavailable might become an office manager, combining "people" or supervisory skills with declarative and procedural knowledge about the office and business. In this way, one has selectively optimized one's development by choosing an alternative path, after the original trajectory was blocked.

A fourth category reflects processes in which one adjusts goals and criteria of success. Specifically, individuals may accommodate deficits by modifying their goals (e.g., Brandtstädter & Wentura, 1995) or lowering their criteria of what constitutes successful performance (Dixon & Bäckman, 1995). For example, older adults may modify their goals or personal expectations of performance such that it is no longer necessary to perform at quite the same level or with quite the same speed as they did when they were younger. Given no other available form of compensation, an older typist might decide that her personally required typing rate can be adjusted downward, focusing perhaps instead on maintaining accuracy. A complication, of course, is that employers or senior colleagues may not concur with the lowered performance goals. For some everyday, social, and life skills, however, such changing expectations may indeed be a viable form of compensating for increasing limitations and performance decrements (Brandtstädter & Wentura, 1995). Managing one's changing resources efficiently may involve devaluing and disengaging from some blocked goals while selecting new and feasible goals. Some aging-related losses may be compensated by rearranging priorities or constructing palliative meanings (i.e., selecting positive interpretations; Baltes, Staudinger, & Lindenberger, 1997; Brandtstädter & Wentura, 1995).

Compensation may be an important mechanism of successful aging, a means of realizing and maintaining cognitive potential into late life (Baltes & Baltes, 1990; Dixon, 1995). It is perhaps not an achievement that will garner awards from historians or critics (as would the creative products of a renowned composer), and it may not be a success that brings the respect accorded to the wise sage. It is, however, a practical and functional process associated with both elite levels of technical and artistic performance and everyday life skills such as driving, working, and leisure activities (Dixon, 1995).

CONCLUSIONS

Cognitive aging is a vibrant field of developmental psychology. The field of cognitive aging has become one of increasing theoretical complexity, methodological sophistication, and practical utility. Theoretical attention is given to diversity, directionality, multidimensionality, context, and (of course) changes with age. Also notable is the fact that the researchable contexts of cognitive aging extend from the biological (especially neurological) to the social (especially interactional) and even to the historical and cultural. This may be one reason that so many large-scale longitudinal studies of cognitive aging are being undertaken in many corners of the globe. These include the Seattle Longitudinal Study, as described in this chapter, as well as the Victoria Longitudinal Study (e.g., Dixon, Wahlin, et al., in press), the Swedish Betula Project (e.g., Nilsson et al., 1997), and the Berlin Aging Study (e.g., Baltes & Smith, 1997).

Because cognitive aging is a complex set of developmental phenomena intrinsically involving processes at many levels of analysis, with methods and techniques originating in disparate disciplines, it is profitably studied from select and complementary perspectives. In this chapter we illustrated some of the main domains of research in cognitive aging, as well as selected emerging trends. Although numerous handbooks and primers are available covering a broader range with more detail, we trust that this brief overview represents principal facets of this growing area of developmental science.

REFERENCES

Achenbaum, W. A. (1990). Policy challenges of late life potential. In M. Perlmutter (Ed.), *Late life potential* (pp. 121–142). Washington, DC: The Gerontological Society of America.

Bäckman, L., & Dixon, R. A. (1992). Psychological compensation: A theoretical framework. *Psychological Bulletin, 112,* 259–283.

Bäckman, L., & Nilsson, L. G. (1996). Semantic memory functioning across the adult life span. *European Psychologist, 1,* 27–33.

Bäckman, L., Small, B. J., Wahlin, A., & Larsson, M. (2000). Cognitive functioning in very old age. In F. I. M. Craik & T. A. Salthouse (Eds.), *The handbook of aging and cognition* (2nd ed., pp. 499–558). Mahwah, NJ: Erlbaum.

Baltes, P. B. (1987). Theoretical propositions of life-span developmental psychology: On the dynamics between growth and decline. *Developmental Psychology, 23,* 611–626.

Baltes, P. B., & Baltes, M. M. (Eds.). (1990). *Successful aging: Perspectives from the behavioral sciences.* New York: Cambridge University Press.

Baltes, P. B., & Lindenberger, U. (1997). Emergence of a powerful connection between sensory and cognitive functions across the adult life span: A new window to the study of cognitive aging? *Psychology and Aging, 12,* 12–21.

Baltes, P. B., & Smith, J. (1990). Toward a psychology of wisdom and its ontogenesis. In R. J. Sternberg (Ed.), *Wisdom: Its nature, origins, and development* (pp. 87–120). New York: Cambridge University Press.

Baltes, P. B., & Smith, J. (1997). Profiles of psychological functioning in the old and oldest old. *Psychology and Aging, 12,* 458–472.

Baltes, P. B., & Staudinger, U. (1993). The search for a psychology of wisdom. *Current Directions in Psychological Science, 2,* 1–6.

Baltes, P. B., & Staudinger, U. M. (Eds.). (1996). *Interactive minds: Life-span perspectives on the social foundation of cognition.* Cambridge, UK: Cambridge University Press.

Baltes, P. B., Staudinger, U. M., & Lindenberger, U. (1997). Life-span psychology: Theory and application to intellectual functioning. *Annual Review of Psychology, 50,* 471–507.

Baltes, P. B., & Willis, S. L. (1982). Enhancement (plasticity) of intellectual functioning in old age: Penn State's Adult Development and Enrichment (ADEPT) Project. In F. I. M. Craik & S. E. Trehub (Eds.), *Aging and cognitive processes* (pp. 353–389). New York: Plenum Press.

Berg, C. A., & Klaczynski, P. A. (1996). Practical intelligence and problem solving: Searching for perspectives. In F. Blanchard-Fields & T. M. Hess (Eds.), *Perspectives on cognitive change in adulthood and aging* (pp. 323–357). New York: McGraw-Hill.

Bond, L. A., Cutler, S. J., & Grams, A. (Eds.). (1995). *Promoting successful and productive aging.* Thousand Oaks, CA: Sage.

Botwinick, J. (1977). Intellectual abilities. In J. E. Birren & K. W. Schaie (Eds.), *Handbook of the psychology of aging* (pp. 580–605). New York: Van Nostrand Reinhold.

Brandtstädter, J., & Wentura, D. (1995). Adjustment to shifting possibility frontiers in later life: Complementary adaptive modes. In R. A. Dixon & L. Bäckman (Eds.), *Compensating for psychological deficits and declines: Managing losses and promoting gains* (pp. 83–106). Mahwah, NJ: Erlbaum.

Cabeza, R., & Nyberg, L. (2000). Imaging cognition: Pt. 2. An empirical review of 275 PET and fMRI studies. *Journal of Cognitive Neuroscience, 12,* 1–47.

Camp, C. J., & McKitrick, L. A. (1992). Memory interventions in Alzheimer's-type dementia populations: Methodological and theoretical issues. In R. L. West & J. D. Sinnott (Eds.), *Everyday memory and aging: Current research and methodology* (pp. 155–172). New York: Springer.

Cavanaugh, J. C. (1996). Memory self-efficacy as a moderator of memory change. In F. Blanchard-Fields & T. M. Hess (Eds.), *Perspectives on cognitive change in adulthood and aging* (pp. 488–507). New York: McGraw-Hill.

Cavanaugh, J. C. (2000). Metamemory from a social-cognitive perspective. In D. C. Park & N. Schwarz (Eds.), *Cognitive aging: A primer* (pp. 115–130). Philadelphia: Taylor & Francis.

Clancey, W. J. (1997). *Situated cognition.* Cambridge, UK: Cambridge University Press.

Clark, N. K., & Stephenson, G. M. (1989). Group remembering. In P. B. Paulus (Ed.), *Psychology of group influence.* Hillsdale, NJ: Erlbaum.

Clayton, V. P., & Birren, J. E. (1980). The development of wisdom across the life span: A re-examination of an ancient topic. In P. B. Baltes & O. G. Brim (Eds.), *Life-span development and behavior* (Vol. 3, pp. 103–135). New York: Academic Press.

Craik, F. I. M. (2000). Age-related changes in human memory. In D. C. Park & N. Schwarz (Eds.), *Cognitive aging: A primer* (pp. 75–92). Philadelphia: Taylor & Francis.

Craik, F. I. M., & Jennings, J. (1992). Human memory. In F. I. M. Craik & T. A. Salthouse (Eds.), *The handbook of aging and cognition* (pp. 51–110). Mahwah, NJ: Erlbaum.

Craik, F. I. M., & Salthouse, T. (Eds.). (2000). *The handbook of aging and cognition* (2nd ed.). Mahwah, NJ: Erlbaum.

Dennis, W. (1954). Review of *Age and achievement. Psychological Bulletin, 51,* 306–308.

Dennis, W. (1956). *Age and achievement:* A critique. *Journal of Gerontology, 9,* 465–467.

Dixon, R. A. (1989). Questionnaire research on metamemory and aging: Issues of structure and function. In L. W. Poon, D. C. Rubin, & B. A. Wilson (Eds.), *Everyday cognition in adulthood and old age* (pp. 394–415). New York: Cambridge University Press.

Dixon, R. A. (1995). Promoting competence through compensation. In L. A. Bond, S. J. Cutler, & A. Grams (Eds.), *Promoting successful and productive aging* (pp. 220–238). Thousand Oaks, CA: Sage.

Dixon, R. A. (1999). Exploring cognition in interactive situations: The aging of N + 1 minds. In T. M. Hess & F. Blanchard-Fields (Eds.), *Social cognition and aging* (pp. 267–290). San Diego, CA: Academic Press.

Dixon, R. A. (2000). Concepts and mechanisms of gains in cognitive aging. In D. Park & N. Schwarz (Eds.), *Cognitive aging: A primer* (pp. 23–42). Philadelphia: Psychology Press.

Dixon, R. A., & Bäckman, L. (Eds.). (1995). *Compensating for psychological deficits and declines: Managing losses and promoting gains.* Mahwah, NJ: Erlbaum.

Dixon, R. A., & Bäckman, L. (1999). Principles of compensation in cognitive neurorehabilitation. In D. T. Stuss, G. Winocur, & I. H. Robertson (Eds.), *Cognitive neurorehabilitation* (pp. 59–72). Cambridge, UK: Cambridge University Press.

Dixon, R. A., Bäckman, L., & Nilsson, L.-G. (in press). (Eds.), *New frontiers in cognitive aging.* Oxford: Oxford University Press.

Dixon, R. A., de Frias, C. M., & Bäckman, L. (2001). Characteristics of self-reported memory compensation in late life. *Journal of Clinical and Experimental Neuropsychology, 23,* 650–661.

Dixon, R. A., & Gould, O. N. (1998). Younger and older adults collaborating on retelling everyday stories. *Applied Developmental Science, 2,* 160–171.

Dixon, R. A., Kramer, D. A., & Baltes, P. B. (1985). Intelligence: A life-span developmental perspective. In B. B. Wolman (Ed.), *Handbook of intelligence: Theories, measurements, and applications* (pp. 301–350). New York: Wiley.

Dixon, R. A., Wahlin, A., Maitland, S., Hultsch, D. F., & Bäckman, L. (in press). Episodic memory change in late adulthood: Generalizability across samples and performance indices. *Memory & Cognition.*

Dobbs, A., & Rule, B. (1987). Prospective memory and self-reports of memory abilities in older adults. *Canadian Journal of Psychology, 41,* 209–222.

Einstein, G. O., & McDaniel, M. A. (1990). Normal aging and prospective memory. *Journal of Experimental Psychology: Learning, Memory, and Cognition, 16,* 717–726.

Einstein, G. O., McDaniel, M. A., Richardson, S. L., & Guynn, M. J. (1995). Aging and prospective memory: Examining the influences of self-initiated retrieval. *Journal of Experimental Psychology: Learning, Memory, and Cognition, 21,* 996–1007.

Gilewski, M. J., & Zelinski, E. M. (1986). Questionnaire assessment of memory complaints. In L. W. Poon (Ed.), *Handbook for clinical memory assessment of older adults* (pp. 93–107). Washington, DC: American Psychological Association.

Gold, D. P., Andres, D., Etezadi, J., Arbuckle, T., Schwartzman, A., & Chaikelson, J. (1995). Structural equation model of intellectual change and continuity and predictors of intelligence in older men. *Psychology and Aging, 10,* 294–303.

Greeno, J. G. (1998). The situativity of knowing, learning, and research. *American Psychologist, 53,* 5–26.

Grut, M., Jorm, A. F., Fratiglioni, L., Forsell, Y., Viitanen, M., & Winblad, B. (1993). Memory complaints of elderly people in a population survey: Variation according to dementia stage and depression. *Journal of the American Geriatrics Society, 41,* 1295–1300.

Hall, G. S. (1922). *Senescence: The last half of life.* New York: Appleton.

Hazlitt, J. E. (2000). *Longitudinal and structural analyses of semantic memory and aging.* Unpublished master's thesis, University of Victoria, Victoria, BC, Canada.

Heckhausen, J., Dixon, R. A., & Baltes, P. B. (1989). Gains and losses in development throughout adulthood as perceived by different adult age groups. *Developmental Psychology, 25,* 109–121.

Heckhausen, J., & Krueger, J. (1993). Developmental expectations for the self and most other people: Age grading in three functions of social comparison. *Developmental Psychology, 29,* 539–548.

Herlitz, A., Nilsson, L. G., & Bäckman, L. (1997). Gender differences in episodic memory. *Memory and Cognition, 25,* 801–811.

Hertzog, C., & Dixon, R. A. (1994). Metacognitive development in adulthood and old age. In J. Metcalfe & A. P. Shimamura (Eds.), *Metacognition: Knowing about knowing* (pp. 227–251). Cambridge, MA: MIT Press.

Hertzog, C., & Dixon, R. A. (1996). Methodological issues in research on cognition and aging. In F. Blanchard-Fields & T. M. Hess (Eds.), *Perspectives on cognitive change in adulthood and aging* (pp. 66–121). New York: McGraw-Hill.

Hertzog, C., & Hultsch, D. F. (2000). Metacognition in adulthood and old age. In F. I. M. Craik & T. A. Salthouse (Eds.), *The handbook of aging and cognition* (2nd ed., pp. 417–466). Mahwah, NJ: Erlbaum.

Hess, T. M., & Blanchard-Fields, F. (1999). *Social cognition and aging*. San Diego, CA: Academic Press.

Hill, G. W. (1982). Group versus individual performance: Are N + 1 heads better than 1? *Psychological Bulletin, 91,* 517–539.

Horn, J. L. (1982). The theory of crystallized and fluid intelligence in relation to concepts of cognitive psychology and aging in adulthood. In F. I. M. Craik & S. Trehub (Eds.), *Aging and cognitive processes* (pp. 237–278). New York: Plenum Press.

Horn, J. L., & Cattell, R. (1966). Refinement and test of a theory of fluid and crystallized intelligence. *Journal of Educational Psychology, 57,* 253–270.

Howard, D. V. (1996). The aging of implicit and explicit memory. In F. Blanchard-Fields & T. M. Hess (Eds.), *Perspectives on cognitive change in adulthood and aging* (pp. 221–254). New York: McGraw-Hill.

Hultsch, D. F., & Dixon, R. A. (1990). Learning and memory in aging. In J. E. Birren & K. W. Schaie (Eds.), *Handbook of the psychology of aging* (3rd ed., pp. 258–274). San Diego, CA: Academic Press.

Hultsch, D. F., Hertzog, C., Dixon, R. A., & Small, B. J. (1998). *Memory change in the aged*. Cambridge, UK: Cambridge University Press.

Hultsch, D. F., Hertzog, C., Small, B. J., & Dixon, R. A. (1999). Use it or lose it: Engaged lifestyle as a buffer of cognitive decline in aging? *Psychology and Aging, 14,* 245–263.

Hummert, M. L., Garstka, T. A., Shaner, J. L., & Strahm, S. (1994). Stereotypes of the elderly held by young, middle-aged, and elderly adults. *Journal of Gerontology: Psychological Sciences, 49,* P40–P49.

Kausler, D. (1994). *Learning and memory in normal aging*. San Diego, CA: Academic Press.

Kekes, J. (1983). Wisdom. *American Philosophical Quarterly, 20,* 277–286.

Kirkpatrick, E. A. (1903). *Fundamentals of child study: A discussion of instincts and other factors in human development with practical applications*. New York: Macmillan.

Lachman, M. E., Weaver, S. L., Bandura, M., Elliott, E., & Lewkowicz, C. J. (1992). Improving memory and control beliefs through cognitive restructuring and self-generated strategies. *Journal of Gerontology: Psychological Sciences, 47,* P293–P299.

Lehman, H. C. (1953). *Age and achievement*. Princeton, NJ: Princeton University Press.

Lehman, H. C. (1956). Reply to Dennis' critique of *Age and achievement*. *Journal of Gerontology, 11,* 128–134.

Light, L. L. (1992). The organization of memory in old age. In F. I. M. Craik & T. A. Salthouse (Eds.), *The handbook of aging and cognition* (pp. 111–165). Mahwah, NJ: Erlbaum.

Lovelace, E. A. (Ed.). (1990). *Aging and cognition: Mental processes, self-awareness, and interventions*. Amsterdam: North-Holland.

Markova, I. S., & Berrios, G. E. (2000). Insight into memory deficits. In G. E. Berrios & J. R. Hodges (Eds.), *Memory disorders in psychiatric practice* (pp. 204–233). Cambridge, UK: Cambridge University Press.

Marsiske, M., Lang, F. R., Baltes, P. B., & Baltes, M. M. (1995). Selective optimization with compensation: Life-span perspectives on successful human development. In R. A. Dixon & L. Bäckman (Eds.), *Compensating for psychological deficits and declines: Managing losses and promoting gains* (pp. 35–79). Mahwah, NJ: Erlbaum.

Medina, J. J. (1996). *The clock of ages*. Cambridge, UK: Cambridge University Press.

Meudell, P. R., Hitch, G. J., & Kirby, P. (1992). Are two heads better than one? Experimental investigations of the social facilitation of memory. *Applied Cognitive Psychology, 6,* 525–543.

Middleton, D., & Edwards, D. (Eds.). (1990). *Collective remembering*. Newbury Park, CA: Sage.

Moscovitch, M. (1982). A neuropsychological approach to memory and perception in normal and pathological aging. In F. I. M. Craik & S. Trehub (Eds.), *Aging and cognitive processes* (pp. 55–78). New York: Plenum Press.

Moulin, C. J. A., Perfect, T. J., & Jones, R. W. (2000). Evidence for intact memory monitoring in Alzheimer's disease: Metamemory sensitivity at encoding. *Neuropsychologia, 38,* 1242–1250.

Neely, A. S., & Bäckman, L. (1995). Effects of multifactorial memory training in old age: Generalizability across tasks and individuals. *Journal of Gerontology: Psychological Sciences, 50,* 134–140.

Nilsson, L. G., Bäckman, L., Erngrund, K., Nyberg, L., Adolfsson, R., Bucht, G., Karlsson, S., Widing, M., & Winblad, B. (1997). The Betula prospective study: Memory, health, and aging. *Aging, Neuropsychology, and Cognition, 4,* 1–32.

Park, D. C. (2000). The basic mechanisms accounting for age-related decline in cognitive function. In D. Park & N. Schwarz (Eds.), *Cognitive aging: A primer* (pp. 3–22). Philadelphia: Psychology Press.

Park, D. C., Hertzog, C., Kidder, D. P., & Morrell, R. W. (1997). Effect of age on event-based and time-based prospective memory. *Psychology and Aging, 12,* 314–327.

Park, D. C., Nisbett, R. E., & Hedden, T. (1999). Aging, culture, and cognition. *Journal of Gerontology: Psychological Sciences, 54B,* 75–84.

Park, D. C., & Schwarz, N. (2000). *Cognitive aging: A primer*. Philadelphia: Psychology Press.

Perlmutter, M. (Ed.). (1990). *Late life potential*. Washington, DC: The Gerontological Society of America.

Prigatano, G. P. (2000). Motivation and awareness in cognitive neurorehabilitation. In D. T. Stuss, G. Winocur, & I. H. Robertson (Eds.), *Cognitive neurorehabilitation* (pp. 240–251). Cambridge, UK: Cambridge University Press.

Prigatano, G. P., & Schacter, D. L. (Eds.). (1991). *Awareness of deficit after brain injury: Clinical and theoretical issues*. New York: Oxford University Press.

Raz, N. (2000). Aging of the brain and its impact on cognitive performance: Integration of structural and functional findings. In F. I. M. Craik & T. A. Salthouse (Eds.), *The handbook of aging and cognition* (2nd ed., pp. 1–90). Mahwah, NJ: Erlbaum.

Resnick, L. B., Levine, J. M., & Teasley, S. D. (Eds.). (1991) *Perspectives on socially shared cognition*. Washington, DC: American Psychological Association.

Reuter-Lorenz, P. A. (2000). Cognitive neuropsychology of the aging brain. In D. Park & N. Schwarz (Eds.), *Cognitive aging: A primer* (pp. 93–114). Philadelphia: Psychology Press.

Ryan, E. B. (1992). Beliefs about memory changes across adulthood. *Journal of Gerontology: Psychological Sciences, 47,* P41–P46.

Salthouse, T. A. (1990). Cognitive competence and expertise in aging. In J. E. Birren & K. W. Schaie (Eds.), *Handbook of the psychology of aging* (pp. 310–319). San Diego, CA: Academic Press.

Salthouse, T. A. (1991). *Theoretical perspectives on cognitive aging*. San Diego, CA: Academic Press.

Salthouse, T. A. (1995). Refining the concept of psychological compensation. In R. A. Dixon & L. Bäckman (Eds.), *Compensating for psychological deficits and declines: Managing losses and promoting gains* (pp. 21–34). Mahwah, NJ: Erlbaum.

Salthouse, T. A. (2000). Pressing issues in cognitive aging. In D. Park & N. Schwarz (Eds.), *Cognitive aging: A primer* (pp. 43– 54). Philadelphia: Psychology Press.

Sanford, E. C. (1902). Mental growth and decay. *American Journal of Psychology, 13,* 426–449.

Schacter, D. L. (1990). Toward a cognitive neuropsychology of awareness: Implicit knowledge and anosognosia. *Journal of Clinical and Experimental Neuropsychology, 12,* 155–178.

Schacter, D. L., Koutsaal, W. E., & Norman, K. A. (1997). False memories and aging. *Trends in Cognitive Sciences, 1,* 229–236.

Schacter, D. L., & Tulving, E. (1994). *Memory systems 1994*. Cambridge, MA: MIT Press.

Schaie, K. W. (1983). The Seattle Longitudinal Study: A twenty-one-year exploration of psychometric intelligence in adulthood. In K. W. Schaie (Ed.), *Longitudinal studies of adult psychological development* (pp. 64–135). New York: Guilford Press.

Schaie, K. W. (1990). Intellectual development in adulthood. In J. E. Birren & K. W. Schaie (Eds.), *Handbook of the psychology and aging* (3rd ed., pp. 291–309). New York: Academic Press.

Schaie, K. W. (1994). The course of adult intellectual development. *American Psychologist, 49,* 304–314.

Schaie, K. W. (1996). *Intellectual development in adulthood: The Seattle Longitudinal Study*. Cambridge, UK: Cambridge University Press.

Simonton, D. K. (1990). Creativity and wisdom in aging. In J. E. Birren & K. W. Schaie (Eds.), *Handbook of the psychology of aging* (3rd ed., pp. 320–329). San Diego, CA: Academic Press.

Simonton, D. K. (1994). *Greatness: Who makes history and why*. New York: Guilford Press.

Smith, A. D., & Earles, J. (1996). Memory changes in normal aging. In F. Blanchard-Fields & T. M. Hess (Eds.), *Perspectives on cognitive change in adulthood and aging* (pp. 192–220). New York: McGraw-Hill.

Smith, G. E., Petersen, R. C., Ivnik, R. J., Malec, J. F., & Tangalos, E. G. (1996). Subjective memory complaints, psychological distress, and longitudinal change in objective memory performance. *Psychology and Aging, 12,* 272–279.

Smith, J., & Baltes, P. B. (1990). Wisdom-related knowledge: Age/cohort differences in response to life-planning problems. *Developmental Psychology, 26,* 494–505.

Staudinger, U. M., Smith, J., & Baltes, P. B. (1992). Wisdom-related knowledge in a life review task: Age differences and the role of professional specialization. *Psychology and Aging, 7,* 271–281.

Steiner, I. D. (1972). *Group Process and Productivity*. New York: Academic Press.

Sternberg, R. J. (Ed.). (1990). *Wisdom: Its nature, origins, and development*. New York: Cambridge University Press.

Strough, J., & Margrett, J. (Eds.). (2002). Special section: Collaborative cognition in later adulthood. *International Journal of Behavioral Development, 26,* 2–59.

Uttal, D. H., & Perlmutter, M. (1989). Toward a broader conceptualization of development: The role of gains and losses across the life span. *Developmental Review, 9,* 101–132.

Verhaeghen, P., Marcoen, A., & Goosens, L. (1992). Improving memory performance in the aged through mnemonic training: A meta-analytic study. *Psychology and Aging, 7,* 242–251.

Waldstein, S. R. (2000). Health effects on cognitive aging. In P. C. Stern & & L. L. Carstensen (Eds.), *The aging mind: Opportunities in cognitive research* (pp. 189–217). Washington, DC: National Academy Press.

Weisenburg, T., Roe, A., & McBride, K. E. (1936). *Adult intelligence: A psychological study of test performance*. London: Commonwealth Fund.

Willis, S. L., Jay, G. M., Diehl, M., & Marsiske, M. (1992). Longitudinal change and prediction of everyday task competence in the elderly. *Research on Aging, 14,* 68–91.

Wilson, B. A., & Watson, P. C. (1996). A practical framework for understanding compensatory behavior in people with organic memory impairment. *Memory, 4,* 456–486.

Woodruff-Pak, D. S. (1997). *The neuropsychology of aging*. Malden, MA: Blackwell.

CHAPTER 19

Personality Development in Adulthood and Old Age

ROSANNA M. BERTRAND AND MARGIE E. LACHMAN

Personality development in adulthood and old age has been the focus of considerable research interest over the last several decades, amassing a body of literature that is richly diverse in its theoretical and methodological approaches. Although some personality research shows that early experiences influence the developmental trajectory (e.g., Caspi, 1987), it is also generally accepted that discontinuity or change in personality makes it possible for individuals to respond appropriately to major, meaningful events as they present themselves later in life (e.g., Haan, Millsap, & Hartka, 1986). Indeed, the primary focus of personality research has turned from questions regarding the stability or susceptibility to change across adulthood to the multidirectional paths of personality and the impact of individual differences throughout the life span (Lachman, 1989; Lachman & Bertrand, 2001; Nesselroade, 1992). For instance, there is increasing evidence that the nature and experiences in adulthood and old age are determined in large part by individual differences in personality. By adopting a life-span approach for the study of personality in adulthood and aging, the impact of variations in personality based on such factors as gender, cohort, and culture can be modeled, and change

over time can be tracked (Baltes, Lindenberger, & Staudinger, 1998).

In this chapter we define and examine the nature of personality in adulthood and old age from multiple perspectives. We first provide a historical overview of theoretical approaches, and then we present the current major theoretical perspectives in the field, including a discussion of relevant findings from key empirical studies. We examine trait approaches (e.g., McCrae & Costa, 1987; Roberts & DelVecchio, 2000) to the study of personality with a focus on rank-order and mean-level consistency, as well as individual differences in personality and how these differences shape the experiences of older adults. We also examine theories with a life-span approach to personality such as stage theories (e.g., Erikson, 1963; Levinson, 1978) and contextual models that incorporate person-environment interactions (e.g., Caspi, 1987; Helson, 1984; Neugarten & Gutmann, 1958). The phenomenological approach to personality is also relevant to the study of adulthood and old age. Some of the major findings regarding subjective personality change (e.g., Fleeson & Baltes, 1998) and personality as a predictor of later life outcomes (e.g., Caspi, 1987) are discussed. We also examine specific aspects of the self-construct such as identity (e.g., Whitbourne, 1987), self-efficacy and control (e.g., Bandura, 1997; Lachman & Weaver, 1998), well-being (e.g., Ryff, 1989), and emotions and coping (e.g., Lazarus & Folkman, 1984). Finally, we summarize the current state of

The authors would like to acknowledge the generous support of the John D. and Catherine T. MacArthur Foundation Research Network on Successful Midlife Development and the National Institute on Aging #AG17920 (ML) and T32 AG 00204 (RB).

the adult personality literature and make suggestions for the direction of future research.

HISTORICAL BACKGROUND

The view of development as a lifelong process can be traced to the eighteenth and nineteenth century philosophers Quetelet, Carus, and Tetens (Baltes, 1983). However, psychological development beyond young adulthood was not embraced by those studying human behavior until much later. Early theorists conceptualized development as a phenomenon unique to the early years of life, suggesting that beyond this point development was virtually nonexistent. This popular sentiment was epitomized in the classic statement by William James when he wrote that by the age of 30, character is "set like plaster, and will never soften again" (W. James, 1890, p. 121). Others, such as Freud, believed that psychological maturity was reached at an even younger age. According to Freud's psychoanalytic theory, personality is determined at some time during middle childhood. Any observation of psychological change after this point in life was seen as the result of early experiences and not of continued development. The child-centric view of development has its roots in the work of Rousseau (1762/1948) and has been reinforced by the writings of Freud (1905) and other preeminent theorists such as Piaget (1936/1974) and Bowlby (1982).

A life-span view of personality development emerged in the early twentieth century with work by C. Jung, C. Buhler, G. Stanley Hall, and E. Erikson. The most well known of these perspectives are Jung's (1933) psychoanalytic theory, which dealt primarily with issues of balancing polarities such as masculinity and femininity throughout adulthood, and Erikson's (1963) psychosocial model of ego development, which expanded Freud's theory to include developmental stages throughout the life-span, including old age.

Advanced primarily by Erikson's psychosocial theory of lifelong development and by early empirical studies conducted by Neugarten and Gutmann (1958), which support the idea of change in later adulthood, research and theory have expanded beyond the child-centric approach to psychological development (e.g., Field & Millsap, 1991; Loevinger, 1976; Vaillant, 1977). A recent surge of theoretical conceptualizations and empirical investigations has culminated in a sizable literature that adopts the view of personality as a lifelong process of development (e.g., Baltes, 1987; Baltes et al., 1998; Featherman & Lerner, 1985; Lachman & Baltes, 1994; R. M. Lerner, 1976). The life-span approach is a useful perspective from which to study personality development in later adulthood. First, through a comprehensive host of theories, the life-span approach represents the dynamic complexities inherent in the experiences of middle-aged and older adults. In addition, this approach integrates sources of variation such as sociocultural, historical, and genetic factors that are especially important to consider when examining the trajectory of development into adulthood and old age.

Furthermore, the advancement of powerful methodological techniques has provided developmentalists with the tools necessary for effectively modeling personality and the self in later years within the context of the life-span perspective (e.g., Schaie, 1996). We are no longer restricted to the investigation of normative individual differences; longitudinal research designs and sophisticated statistical techniques provide the opportunity to model intra-individual change so that complex patterns of development throughout the life span can be explored. With longitudinal designs and state-of-the-art methodological techniques, confounding factors such as age and cohort effects can be teased apart and contextual qualities such as socioeconomic status can be tested for the efficacy of their mediational effects. The adoption of a life-span approach for the study of personality facilitates the investigation of stability and change well into old age.

THEORETICAL PERSPECTIVES ON PERSONALITY

The research on personality development in adulthood and aging has been guided by a variety of theoretical perspectives and conceptual models. For example, some investigations employ contextual models that emphasize the life-span approach. These studies focus on the dynamic interaction between social and historical contexts on personality patterns (Schaie & Hendricks, 2000). Other studies utilize trait and stage theories of development. The underlying premise of trait theory (e.g., Costa & McCrae, 1988; Roberts & DelVeccho, 2000) is that personality attributes are formed early in life and that they exhibit consistency across adulthood. In contrast, stage theories (e.g., Erikson, 1963; Levinson, 1977) are built on the concept that personality continues to evolve throughout adulthood according to the epigenetic principle (see R. M. Lerner, 2002); each stage unfolds from its previous stage in a predetermined, sequential way. Human personality in adulthood and old age is a complex, multifaceted phenomenon that is best represented using multiple perspectives.

Trait Theories

Perhaps the most well-known perspective on personality is the trait view (Costa & McCrae, 1984). A trait is commonly described as an enduring personality characteristic that remains stable over time and is consistent across situations. Purportedly, roots of traits can be traced to genetic components, and their expression is manifested in early temperament (Bouchard, 1997; but see R. M. Lerner, 2002, for a contrasting point of view based on life-span developmental systems theory or Baltes et al., 1998). From the perspective of trait theory, personality can be defined as the expression of these sustaining inherent attributes.

The Big Five

Although several trait taxonomies have been proposed to delineate the structure of personality, the five-factor model known as the Big Five is the most widely applied to adulthood and aging. The five-factor model includes the following dimensions: neuroticism, extroversion, openness to experience, agreeableness, and conscientiousness. There is widespread support for the Big Five using multiple measures including the California Q-Set (McCrae, Costa, & Busch, 1986) and the NEO Personality Inventory (McCrae & Costa, 1987), which have demonstrated convergent and discriminant validity for self-reports and peer and spouse ratings.

Stability and Change

The preponderance of empirical research points to rank-order stability across time on the trait dimensions (e.g., Costa & McCrae, 1988; Haan et al., 1986; Roberts & DelVecchio, 2000). This implies that the ordinal position of individuals within a group remains the same relative to other individuals on trait dimensions over time. For example, using the California Q-sort (see Block, in collaboration with Hann, 1971), Haan et al. (1986) found substantial stability over 50 years (i.e., ages 5–62) in the Oakland Growth and Guidance studies. With one exception occurring in the component of "warm/hostile" during the transition from late adolescence to early adulthood, all test-retest, interval-specific correlations were positive across the life span and into old age.

Support for the stability position comes largely from studies based on the Baltimore Longitudinal Study of Aging. This ongoing, large-sample survey of relatively healthy, highly educated individuals was begun in 1958 and includes individuals from across adulthood ranging in age from the late 20s into the 90s. When analyzed longitudinally, findings from these studies demonstrate remarkable stability on self-reports of personality behavior across approximately 30 years of adulthood (e.g., Costa & McCrae, 1984, 1988; McCrae & Costa, 1985, 1987, 1994). Converging evidence for these findings comes from peer ratings on personality dimensions

(Costa & McCrae, 1988; McCrae & Costa, 1987). Across a 6-year span, consistency in the ratings of personality traits reported by participants' spouses was also revealed.

Meta-analyses conducted by Roberts and DelVecchio (2000) provide a more complicated picture with less definitive answers regarding stability. Their examination of 124 longitudinal studies revealed high levels of rank-order consistency on personality trait dimensions over time, but it was not until the period between middle and older adulthood (i.e., ages 50–59 and 60–73) that trait consistency stabilized, a finding that conflicts with the popular notion that trait stability peaks by the age of 30 (e.g., Costa & McCrae, 1988; W. James, 1890; McCrae & Costa, 1994).

It is important to note that rank order stability does not imply stability at the mean level. Although there is strong evidence for trait consistency when considering rank order, there is also evidence from longitudinal investigations for normative, mean-level changes in some of the traits across time and suggestive support from cross-sectional studies for age differences (e.g., McCrae & Costa, 1994; Haan et al., 1986). For example, Roberts and DelVecchio (2000) reported that although high levels of rank-order stability were found in their meta-analysis, the estimates of between-age-group consistency were not high enough to argue that personality dimensions are impervious to change. This conclusion is supported in the findings from other studies that examine mean-level change in personality traits. For example, McCrae and Costa (1994) reported that compared to younger adults, older adults reported lower levels of extroversion, particularly activity and thrill-seeking, neuroticism, and openness to experience. As a result, older adults were less anxious and self-conscious but also less likely to explore new horizons.

In a 14-year longitudinal study of older adults, Field and Millsap (1991) found an increase in the dimension of agreeableness between ages 69 and 83. Similarly, Haan et al. (1986) noted that in the Oakland Growth and Guidance studies substantial changes in personality continued to occur into later adulthood. Theses authors concluded that with increased age, people confront greater experiential change that, in turn, can lead to a change in the expression of personality. In contrast, other researchers explain consistency in personality dimensions across time as due to fewer novel experiences confronted by the older adult (Glenn, 1980).

Further suggestive evidence for mean-level differences in personality across adulthood comes from the study of Midlife in the United States (MIDUS; John D. and Catherine T. MacArthur Foundation Research Network on Successful Midlife Development) using trait attribute ratings. Findings from this nationally representative cross-sectional study revealed significant mean age-group differences between young, middle-aged, and older adults on some of the Big Five traits (Markus & Lachman, 1996). Specifically, results indicated that scores on agreeableness were highest in the group of older adults, whereas scores on openness to experience and neuroticism were lowest among the older adults. Conscientiousness was highest in the midlife group.

It appears from the discussion of rank-order versus mean-level consistency in trait dimensions that to a large degree the findings vary based on the type of question asked and the type of methodology utilized to answer the question (see Caspi & Roberts, 1999). Specifically, among the studies reported here, those investigating rank order across time by examining test-retest correlations largely demonstrated stability, whereas those interested in between-age-group comparisons revealed mean-level differences on some personality dimensions. Moreover, mean-level differences were revealed in both longitudinal studies that examined intra-individual change in personality dimensions over time and cross-sectional studies that explored differences between age/cohort groups. For example, intra-individual change over time in average agreeableness was demonstrated longitudinally (Field & Millsap, 1991), with supporting cross-sectional evidence revealing age/cohort differences favoring older adults (Markus & Lachman, 1996). Further, between-group differences in neuroticism and openness to experience were found in cross-sectional studies with older adults showing lower levels in these personality traits than younger groups (McCrae & Costa, 1994). Although the issue of stability versus change in personality development across the life span continues to be an interesting topic of study, the focus of personality research has shifted to the potentially more important question of how these stable personality styles impact the course of aging (Lachman, 1989).

Personality Dimensions as Antecedents

Personality attributes are believed to play a major role in the nature and course of development in adulthood and old age (Lachman & Bertrand, 2001). For example, on one hand, it is possible that certain personality styles such as neuroticism may drive individuals toward risk-taking behaviors that could negatively influence their life course and health status in older adulthood. On the other hand, personality styles such as conscientiousness may direct individuals to practice protective health-behaviors that could delay morbidity and mortality in the later adult years (Schwartz et al., 1995; Friedman et al., 1995). Longitudinal evidence from the Terman Life Cycle Study of Children with High Ability supports the hypothesis that childhood personality dispositions predict later life outcomes. Findings demonstrated that certain childhood

and early adult personality traits such as conscientiousness predict increased longevity (Schwartz et al., 1995). The authors concluded that conscientious children were healthier and lived longer because they were more likely to adopt healthy self-care patterns that would prevent or delay illness. In addition, they were more likely to avoid dangerous situations that would put their health at risk. The issue of how the course of aging varies as a function of personality attributes will be addressed in greater detail in a subsequent section of this chapter.

The trait view assumptions of individual differences in personality and stability across adulthood are in direct contrast to stage views of personality development. In the following section we examine some of the predominant stage models of psychological development giving particular attention to the later stages that include adulthood and old age.

Stage Theories

Whereas trait theories assume that personality characteristics are acquired early in life and demonstrate life-long stability (e.g., Costa & McCrae, 1988), stage theories are characterized by the premise of continued development and change across the life span (e.g., Erikson, 1950). In general, stage models divide the life span into periods loosely tied to chronological age to describe normal, sequential patterns of developmental change (Reese & Overton, 1970). According to stage theory, each period is associated with a particular developmental task. When successfully straddled, it provides the foundation from which to confront the challenge of the next stage (Havighurst, Neugarten, & Tobin, 1968). Based on the tenets of stage theory, personality can be defined as a life-long process of maturity in which internal forces interact with external forces through a stepwise series of stages to produce outward behavior.

Erik H. Erikson

Several stage models of development that include adulthood and old age have been theorized (e.g., Erikson, 1950; Vaillant, 1977; Levinson, 1977; Loevinger, 1976); however, perhaps the most preeminent and influential is Erik H. Erikson's (1950) eight-stage psychosocial model of development. An extension of Freud's theory of psychosexual development, Erikson's model has two primary advantages over Freud's. First, it includes a life-span view of development, second, it incorporates societal and cultural influences on development. Freud's theory describes personality as relatively fixed by age 5. Any change in behavior beyond that point is viewed as the result of early childhood influences and not continued development. In addition, Freud assigned primary importance to largely unconscious intrapsychic processes in determining personality development. Erikson expanded on Freud's theory by creating a developmental model in which the ego evolves through the dynamic interaction between internal and external forces throughout the entire life course.

According to Erikson's model, there are eight stages of psychosocial development that are biologically hardwired to unfold in a predetermined, sequential manner. Following his version of the epigenetic principle, Erikson believed that the ego evolves out of this preprogrammed schedule in stages in which different components of the ego have the opportunity to develop during specific times. Erikson proposed that each of the eight stages is marked by a tension or crisis between two opposing challenges (e.g., generativity vs. stagnation). The crises are resolved through a dynamic interaction between inner ego strength that evolves and develops from the previous stage and outer societal and cultural demands. The result of each crisis is a strengthened or weakened ego that, in turn, becomes the basis for resolving the crisis in the next succeeding stage. Development continues to evolve in this manner throughout the life span with later stages built on the foundation of previous ones. The possibility of complete psychosocial maturity is acquired only in later adulthood after all eight stages have been positively resolved (i.e., ego integrity is achieved). Healthy psychosocial development may be comprised, however, if an individual progresses to a stage without the successful resolution of a task at a previous stage. In optimal development the sequence of stages is followed precisely with each respective crisis resolved successfully. However, certain environmental experiences can send an individual off course, thereby changing the timing and pattern of development and hindering the successful resolution of a successive stage. A developmental course influenced in such a way will result in a weakened ego and negatively impact present and future development (Whitbourne, Zuschlag, Elliot, & Waterman, 1992).

Relevant to adulthood, Erikson proposed three distinct stages in which the individual must confront a crisis between opposing forces: intimacy versus isolation in young adulthood, generativity versus stagnation in midlife, and ego integrity versus despair in old age. In young adulthood, after achieving a sense of ego identity, the challenge set forth in Erikson's theory is to establish a relationship with a significant other without losing one's own sense of self. Erikson theorized that middle-aged adults reach a point in their ego development at which they must struggle between assuming a sense of responsibility toward the next generation (i.e., gen-

erativity) and maintaining a position of self-absorption (stagnation). As already discussed, each stage is built on the strength of the ego as it evolves from the resolution of the previous stage. As a result, the midlife adult whose ego was strengthened by successfully achieving intimacy as opposed to isolation as a young adult is more likely to resolve the midlife stage toward generativity. This individual will be trusting and willing to propagate his or her skills and knowledge to the next generation. Although generativity is commonly thought of as the adoption of a parenting role, it can also be carried out via other roles such as a teacher, mentor, or coach. Generativity is reflected in any activity in which the adult assumes the responsibility for guiding the next generation in a productive or creative way (Erikson, 1963; McAdams, 2001). Erikson proposed that the virtues of caring, giving, sharing, and teaching develop out of the need to nurture and direct the next generation.

In contrast, the midlife adult who progressed through the young adult stage with an imbalance toward isolation will have a weakened ego that is likely to inhibit the establishment of generativity. In midlife this adult will be self-centered and self-absorbed and lack interest in training or guiding the next generation. The resultant imbalance toward stagnation will further weaken the ego and render it unable to carry out a successful resolution of the crisis in the final stage of development.

The final stage of psychosocial development proposed by Erikson (1963) is that of ego integrity versus ego despair. As individuals age, there is an increasing awareness of the limits of time—a realization of inevitable, impending death. The effect of this awareness is to inspire older adults to reflect on how they lived their lives. Older adults who look back with satisfaction and contentment and an acceptance of both the negative and positive aspects of their lives are at peace and, in this way, are prepared to accept the inevitability of death. These adults have integrated the past and present and have embraced the importance and meaningfulness of their lives; they have achieved ego integrity. On the other hand, older adults who have not resolved the past, who experience anxiety about making amends for prior mistakes, and who feel the need to complete unfinished business are not ready to accept the inevitability of death. In fact, these adults may fear or dread their impending death and view it as another in a series of failures and disasters that have comprised the quality of their lives. These adults have failed to find purpose and meaning in their lives and have not achieved ego integrity; rather, they are in a state of ego despair (Erikson, 1963; Ryff, 1989).

Although Erikson's theory emphasizes the resolution of tasks that are stage specific and unfold in a preprogrammed sequence, there is also recognition that it is possible to revisit tasks of earlier stages throughout the life span. In adulthood, driven by an urge to establish a sense of integrated wholeness, adults may strive to reconcile earlier unresolved crises. In other words, although the adult has passed through the stages in a preprogrammed, sequential manner, the opportunity to go back to a stage that was not successfully resolved in order to reprocess the crisis exists. The issues associated with each stage are also prevalent throughout life even though they may be most salient at a given time in the life course.

Erikson has been credited for being among the first theorists to propose a model of lifelong development and to integrate both inner forces and external circumstances in determining the fate of ego development. Indeed, his work has inspired the conceptualization and publication of several other stage theories, such as those by Vaillant (1977), Levinson (1977), and Loevinger (1976). However, limitations to Erikson's theory should be addressed. First, it has been criticized for being based on highly educated males and Western cultural norms without an acknowledgment that women and non-Western cultures may have different developmental trajectories (Gilligan, 1982; Kahn, Zimmerman, Cskiszentmihalyi, & Getzels, 1985). Although Erikson's theory should be cautiously applied to more diverse groups, there is some evidence for its generalizability to less privileged samples (Vallaint & Milofsky, 1980).

A second criticism of Erikson's psychosocial theory is that although it is a viable model of development, it is very difficult to quantify and measure. As a result, few empirical studies have been conducted to test the theory. The most comprehensive investigation to date is the Rochester study conducted by Whitbourne and colleagues (Whitbourne & Waterman, 1979; Whitbourne et al., 1992). This cross-sequential, longitudinal study has followed several groups of graduates from the University of Rochester beginning in 1966 with the oldest cohort entering midlife (i.e., age 42) in the most recent analysis (1988). Data that include older adults are not available, nor are they available from a range of ages in midlife. However, based on the sample tested, findings from this study provide moderate support for the validity of Erikson's final stages of development. The college-aged cohort scored lower than the older cohorts on measures of generativity (Stage 7) and ego integrity (Stage 8). In other words, as proposed by Erikson, it appears as though these developmental tasks are not confronted until later adulthood. However, to make such a statement definitively, it will be necessary to follow this sample throughout midlife and into old age. Vaillant and Milofsky (1980) also tested and found support for the invariant sequence of Erikson's stages in adulthood.

Regardless of the limitations of Erikson's theory of psychosocial development, the contribution that it has made to the field of developmental psychology cannot be ignored. In addition to expanding the possibility of development into old age and incorporating societal and cultural influences on development, his model has been the inspiration for the work of many other developmental theorists.

George Vaillant

Similar to Erikson, George Vaillant (1977) believed that the ego evolves and develops as it passes through stages throughout the life span. Based on data collected from the Grant Foundation study of Harvard graduates begun in 1937, Vaillant revised Erikson's eight-stage model by adding two additional stages in adulthood. First, after Stage 6, "intimacy," Vaillant found evidence for a stage that he called "career consolidation versus self-absorption." Individuals who face career consolidation have already established intimacy in the previous stage and are now ready to identify with a career or occupational commitment. These issues seem to preoccupy adults in early adulthood prior to experiencing generativity (Vaillant & Milofsky, 1980). The second additional stage, "keepers of the meaning versus rigidity," was introduced after Stage 7, "generativity." The difference between generativity and keepers of the meaning lies in the basic concepts of caring and wisdom. Generativity includes those who demonstrate the capacity for care, productivity, and guidance for the next generation; however, keepers of the meaning emote a sense of wisdom and cultural preservation. Whereas the earlier generativity stage focuses on more concrete expressions of caring and transmission to the next generation, keepers of the meaning reflects a more abstract exchange of ideology and values.

Although the focus of Vaillant's theory is also the development of the ego, the process is quite different from that in Erikson's model, where each stage is marked by a task that involves resolving a conflict. According to Vaillant's theory, the ego evolves through the process of interpreting the environment and daily experiences through Freudian defense mechanisms. However, unlike Freud's use of defense mechanisms as protectors of the ego, Vaillant utilizes defense mechanisms as central to a lifelong process through which the ego matures and develops by adapting to conflict between the environment and inner consciousness. Findings from the Grant Foundation study (Vaillant, 1977) support this conclusion by demonstrating that throughout adulthood the quality of the defense mechanism matures. In particular, Vaillant noted that immature defenses such as denial and projection were utilized less often and that mature defenses such as intellectualization, sublimation, and humor were used more often as the individual advances through the stages of adulthood. These findings were supported in a study that expanded on the Harvard sample by adding a group of inner-city adults who were interviewed at ages 25, 32, and 47 (Vaillant & Milofsky, 1980). Further, these authors concluded that although their findings demonstrate that personality unfolds in a predetermined sequential manner, ego maturation is open-ended and has no fixed chronological age. In essence, the opportunity for the personality to develop, mature, and change exists throughout adulthood.

The major contribution of Vaillant's work with the Grant Foundation study (Vaillant, 1977; Vaillant & Milofsky, 1980) is the longitudinal nature of the study design. With data collected at multiple time points, changes in the use of defense mechanisms could be identified, and movement through the stages of ego development could be tracked. For instance, results from Vaillant's longitudinal studies cast doubt on Levinson's claim of a midlife crisis by revealing that individuals in midlife are no more likely than individuals at other stages of adulthood to experience significant life events that are often associated with the midlife crisis (Costa & McCrae, 1980; Lachman & Bertrand, 2001).

Despite the positive contributions that Vaillant's work has made to the field, some limitations should be noted. For instance, the Grant Foundation study (1977) was comprised of a group of well-educated, White, middle-class males, therefore restricting the generalizability of the findings to a larger population. A follow-up study conducted by Vaillant and Milofsky (1980) added a group of inner-city men to the sample, thereby broadening the generalizability to include other socioeconomic groups, but still restricting it to males. An additional limitation of the Grant Foundation study is that the data were collected as descriptive narratives. Although they can provide a rich picture, the subjective nature of the data collection and coding methods place some limits on the interpretation of the findings. Finally, although Vaillant has set forth a model of life-span personality development, the studies in which he tested the model did not include adults beyond the age of 47. As a result, the final two stages of the model (keepers of the meaning and integrity) were not empirically tested.

Daniel Levinson

Other theories, such as Daniel Levinson's stage theory (1977), emerged at about the same time as Vaillant's theory and were also inspired by the writings of Erikson. Similar to Erikson's stage theory, Levinson's theory of adult development has a series of distinct, sequential stages that span the

life-course and are each associated with a specific developmental task. In addition, as in Erikson's theory, each stage, when accomplished, becomes the foundation for the next stage. However, rather than a model of ego development as proposed by Erikson, the central theme of Levinson's theory is the life structure. The life structure evolves through five stages (i.e., preadulthood; early adulthood; middle adulthood; late adulthood; and late, late adulthood) by fluctuating between phases of relative stability (life structure) and phases of transition (Levinson, 1978). During the transitional phase the individual reappraises the existing life structure and explores the possibility of change by analyzing his or her internal and external world. The end product of the transitional phase is a committed choice and the beginning of a phase of stability during which a new life structure is built and expanded.

Levinson argues that the transitional phases are universal and necessary aspects of development. As the individual settles into building a life structure around choices that were made during the previous transitional phase, mistakes and regrets come to be realized. The urge to rectify and change these choices eventually becomes paramount and catapults the individual into the next transitional phase (Levinson, Darrow, Kline, Levinson, & McKee, 1978).

Although Levinson's theory spans the entire life course, he is most noted for the midlife transitional phase. According to Levinson et al. (1978), the midlife crisis is the product of the tension and stress caused by resolving the conflict between four opposing forces. Adopted from Jung's theory of opposing polarities, Levinson argued that middle-aged adults struggle between the competing forces of young versus old, destruction versus creation, masculine versus feminine, and attachment versus separation. The tension during the transitional phase is resolved and the next life structure begun when midlife adults have accepted that these opposing forces can coexist within themselves.

Regardless of the notoriety and popularization of the term *midlife crisis,* there is little support for its widespread occurrence (see Lachman & Bertrand, 2001; McCrae & Costa, 1990; Whitbourne, 1986a). Several limitations of Levinson's data from which his theory was derived have been identified. First, the sample was small ($N = 40$) and consisted wholly of well-educated men, three quarters of whom were engaged in professional careers. Subsequently, Levinson conducted a similar study with women (Levinson & Levinson, 1996) and concluded that similar patterns and developmental fluctuations between life structure and transitional phases existed for women.

A second limitation of Levinson's work comes from the fact that the research was based on qualitative clinical interview data that were not statistically analyzed. Qualitative, retrospective reports are inherently biased because of the subjectivity of the respondent and the interpreter. In fact, Levinson acknowledged that "at 46, I wanted to study the transition into middle age in order to understand what I had been through myself" (Levinson et al., 1978, p. x). A final limitation of this descriptive study is that it was a based on a cross-sectional design that captured only one point in time. To understand the nature of the transitions that Levinson describes and to make statements regarding change in behavior from one stage to the next, it is necessary to follow a cohort or group of individuals over time.

Despite its methodological limitations, Levinson's work has made a valuable contribution to the field for underscoring the need for sound scientific research on psychological development in the middle years of adulthood and by adding to the growing body of literature that attempts to describe developmental change throughout the life course and into old age.

Jane Loevinger

Intrigued by the writing of Erikson, Jane Loevinger (1976) conceptualized a theory of ego development that was based on Erikson's psychosocial model, although it was modified theoretically. For both Erikson and Loevinger, the ego was theorized to mature and evolve through stages across the life span as the result of a dynamic interaction between the inner self and the outer environment. However, according to Loevinger, the ego was a more complex structure than described by Erikson. For instance, she placed a strong emphasis on the importance of considering moral development when attempting to understanding personality. She argued that individual differences are central to personality and that by tracing moral stages of development, individual differences in adult personality will be revealed (Loevinger, 1983). Loevinger's theory defines the ego as the organizer, synthesizer, and interpreter of cognition, morality, the self, and other related concepts that encapsulate personality (Loevinger, 1976, 1983). The individual's progression through the stages is motivated by the need to interpret and adjust to changes in the outer social and inner biological environments. During this process, the personality develops slowly as the individual gains an increasingly more precise understanding of him- or herself.

Six of Loevinger's 10 stages or transitional levels of ego development are relevant to adulthood: conformist, conscientious-conformist, conscientious, individualistic, autonomous, and integrated (Loevinger, 1983). Each stage is related to an increasingly differentiated ego that strives toward perfection. The point of ego perfection is reached in the final, integrated stage, when a discrepancy no longer exists between who the individual really is and how the individual

acts. At this stage of development there is a complete acceptance of inner conflict, and outward behavior becomes the expression of the true inner self (Loevinger, 1983). Although Loevinger did not believe that all individuals develop through the final stages of her model, she argued that it is unlikely that they will revert to a prior cognitive level once a higher level has been attained (Loevinger, 1976).

To build the sequential model of ego development, Loevinger used data from the Sentence Completion Test (SCT; Loevinger, Wessler, 1970). Originally designed to measure the ego development of women, the SCT has since been revised to include men (Loevinger, 1985). The measure consists of a series of sentence fragments that respondents are required to complete. Responses are scored according to the developmental stage that they represent. Support for the SCT as a measure of ego development has been demonstrated in studies in which convergent validity was established against tests of similar concepts (e.g., Kohlberg's test of moral maturity; Kohlberg & Kramer, 1969; see Loevinger, 1979). In a more recent study that included adults from diverse racial and socioeconomic backgrounds, the validity of the test items for use with a male population was examined (Loevinger, 1985). Results of these analyses indicate that although the items were more valid for women than for men, when differences in variability were corrected, the resulting estimates were similar, and justification for the use of the SCT with men and women was concluded.

The SCT has been used by many psychologists, particularly those whose research has focused on the interface between cognitive and ego development (e.g., Blanchard-Fields, 1986; Hy & Loevinger, 1996; Labouvie-Vief, Hakim-Larson, & Hobart, 1987). For example, in a study that examined coping strategies across the life span, Labouvie-Vief et al. (1987) found that ego level as measured by the SCT was a strong predictor of the use of coping strategies from childhood to old age.

The advantages of Loevinger's theory of ego development are twofold. First, similar to Erikson's psychosocial theory of ego development, it considers as viable the possibility of development throughout the life span. In addition, the stages postulated by Loevinger are not restricted by chronological age. As a result, individual differences in the pattern of progression through the stages are possible. Second, Loevinger has constructed a measure of ego development that has made it possible to test the model empirically. This is a clear advantage over Erikson's theory, where very little research has been conducted because of the difficulty in quantifying the stages.

Unfortunately, the generalizability of Loevinger's work has a few limitations. One is the lack of longitudinal studies to test this life-span model. Without longitudinal research designs, individual differences in the patterns of sequencing through the stages cannot be addressed, and statements that draw such conclusions cannot be made. A second limitation of Loevinger's work is the fact that the scoring of the ego development instrument is somewhat subjective and difficult to standardize.

In summary, the theories and research just presented that represent stage models of personality development have demonstrated support for the concept of lifelong development. Indeed, the theorists and the models of development that they have proposed that were discussed in this section have served to advance the life-span view of personality and to inspire other researchers in the field. Despite the obvious contributions that have been made by these theorists, limitations have also been identified. For example, most of the data collected to test the theories were gathered from samples that were biased toward highly educated, middle-class White males. As a result, the generalizability of the findings to other populations is limited. A second limitation common to most of the studies is the lack of longitudinal data. With the exception of the Rochester study (Whitbourne & Waterman, 1979; Whitbourne et al., 1992) and the Grant Foundation study (Vaillant, 1977; Vaillant & Milofsky, 1980), most of the work that has been conducted to test the models has utilized cross-sectional data. This is especially problematic for theories that describe development or change across time. To address issues of change confidently, groups of individuals should be followed over time; otherwise, the question becomes one of differences between groups rather than change across time. In addition, although the theories presented cover lifelong development, the studies conducted to test the models did not include older adults. To capture an accurate picture of personality development in older adulthood, individuals of advanced age should be followed as they enter and progress through the final stages presented in the developmental models. The final limitation of the stage models of personality development that will be noted is their focus on internal forces, such as the ego, as the primary motivator of developmental change. Although environmental forces are noted for their interaction effect with internal forces, it is an inner driving force that is central to these theories.

In response to this final point, the following section presents a model that places greater emphasis on the impact of the environmental context on personality development. Contextual models emphasize the importance of the interaction between social and historical conditions and personality characteristics. According to this perspective, a behavior is not carried out in isolation, but is influenced by the continually fluctuating immediate context that was borne out of the past and proliferates into the future. In addition, some contextualists pay particular attention to the impact of cultural age norms and social transitions on development (e.g., Caspi, 1987; Helson & Moane, 1987; Neugarten, 1977).

Contextual Models

The contextual model of personality development is compatible with a life-span developmental perspective. For instance, contextual models view developmental trajectories over an extended period of time; they incorporate multidisciplinary perspectives; and they consider cultural and historical contexts in their models—all tenets of the life-span perspective (Baltes, 1983; Baltes et al., 1998). Personality, as defined by the framework of the contextual model, is the behavioral expression of the dynamic interaction between internal attributes and sociocultural and historical conditions, with a strong influence generated from the timing of transitions relative to socially prescribed age-graded roles, historical period, and nonnormative influences (Baltes, 1983). For researchers who support the contextual model of development, the timing of entry into age-graded roles is important because the meaning of these social transitions can be internalized quite differently depending on the individual's personal life history, socioeconomic resources, and the prevailing historical context. The dynamic interaction among these parameters is theorized to hold lasting developmental implications for the individual and to bring about the effects of stability or change throughout the life course (Elder & Hareven, 1994).

Sociocultural Context

Some of the proponents of the contextual perspective focus their investigations on the impact of sociocultural contexts on personality development (e.g., Caspi, Elder, & Bem, 1987; Kohn & Schooler, 1978; Roberts, 1997; Roberts & Friend, 1998). Caspi and colleagues explored the social context in which childhood personality characteristics predict later life outcomes (e.g., Caspi, 1987; Caspi et al., 1987; Caspi, Elder, & Bem, 1988). An underlying assumption that guides this research is the belief that personality is stable across the life span. With age, the stability of personality characteristics leads to an increasingly congruent, consistent way of responding to experiences across time and across situation (Caspi, 1987). Caspi's work suggests a deterministic view of development, yet he maintains a belief in the dynamic interaction between personality traits and environmental contexts. For Caspi, it is this interaction that reinforces the consistency of personality over time.

To explain and test the sustainability of the dynamic interaction between the environment and personality, Caspi et al. (1987) defined two interactional styles: cumulative continuity and interactional continuity. Cumulative continuity is the result of the process through which the individual's personality attributes systematically select him or her into specific environments that in turn reinforce and sustain those attributes.

For example, "maladaptive behaviors increasingly channel the individual into environments that perpetuate these behaviors; they are sustained by the progressive accumulation of their own consequences" (Caspi et al., 1987, p. 308). Interactional continuity refers to the reciprocal, dynamic interaction between individuals and their environment: "The person acts, the environment reacts, and the person reacts back" (Caspi et al., 1987, p. 308).

Using longitudinal data from the Berkeley Guidance Study, Caspi et al. (1987) determined the impact of early personality dispositions (i.e., explosive, undercontrolled behavior) on the shape of the life course by examining the consistency of interactional styles over a 30-year span; 186 men and women were interviewed at ages 10, 30, and 40. Initial data on childhood temper tantrums were obtained from clinical interviews with the participants and their mothers. Results from these analyses support the hypotheses proposed by Caspi and colleagues that patterns of maladaptive behavior persist over time and have lasting effects on the individual's life trajectory. Findings support the idea that individuals seek out and set up reciprocal person-environment interactions, thus demonstrating a coherent way of approaching and responding to their social world. Children who were reported to display uncontrolled temper tantrums in childhood experienced difficulty across several life tasks such as jobs, marriage, and parenting (Caspi et al., 1987).

For instance, ill-tempered males from middle-class backgrounds demonstrated a progressive deterioration of socioeconomic status that rendered them indistinguishable from their working-class peers by midlife. In addition, they were less likely to receive a formal education and to hold a high-status occupation than were their even-tempered middle-class peers. Ill-tempered women from middle-class backgrounds tended to married men who, into midlife, held and maintained low-status jobs. They were also over twice as likely to be divorced by midlife and more likely to be perceived by their husbands and children as less adequate and more ill-tempered than were their even-tempered peers.

In a related study, Caspi et al. (1988) examined the impact of childhood shyness on the transition to adulthood and explored the cumulative effects of this transitional phase on later life outcomes. Results indicate that men who had demonstrated shyness as children experienced delayed age-graded transitions in adulthood such as marriage, parenthood, and establishing a stable career. As a result of these off-time transitions for shy men, occupational status and stability as well as marital stability were compromised in adulthood. In contrast, women with a history of childhood shyness were more likely than other women to follow a conventional pattern of marriage, childbearing, and homemaking. It is quite interesting to note that the developmental trajectories for individuals with reported childhood shyness were moderated by gender.

In summary, the findings reported by Caspi et al. (1987, 1988) lend support to the concepts of cumulative and interactional continuity; individuals with specific personality styles seek out a context that will support and reinforce personality homeostasis. In turn, the individual reacts to the environment in such a way that further perpetuates sustaining personality dispositions. Children who exhibited explosive, uncontrolled behavior sought and received reciprocal reinforcement from the environment for the maintenance of their maladaptive personality dispositions into adulthood. Similarly, men with a childhood history of shyness delayed engagement in age-graded events such as marriage, parenthood, and career. Instead, they remained in an environment that continued to support their shy dispositions and delayed the transition into an environment in which they would be required to assert themselves and initiate social contacts. In contrast, shy women sought the refuge of conventional marriage patterns, thereby selecting a context that no doubt reinforced their reticent, reserved personality style.

This work also demonstrates that the lives of individuals with similar personality dispositions can follow different developmental trajectories given variance in social contexts. For example, middle-class individuals with an undercontrolled personality style showed a greater downward spiral in socioeconomic status than did their working-class peers. In addition, different life trajectories were revealed for men and women of similar personality dispositions. A final implication of this work is that late entry into age-graded transitions may lead to negative outcomes. As Neugarten (1977) and Helson, Mitchell, and Moane (1984) proposed, being off time on a given social clock can impede psychological adjustment including well-being. Overall, the work of Caspi et al. (1987, 1988) lends support to the idea that interactional styles, formulated early in life, are sustained throughout adulthood and serve as the underlying process through which personality characteristics remain consistent across the life span.

Additional support for the interactional continuity model comes from an investigation conducted by Roberts and Friend (1998) in which data from the Mills Longitudinal Study were prospectively examined for the impact of personality and life context patterns on career momentum (i.e., the perception of mobility in one's career). The ongoing Mills study was begun in 1958 with a group of predominately White, middle-class female seniors from Mills College in Oakland California. Initial assessment was conducted when the women were approximately age 21 with follow-up assessments at ages 43 and 52. Data on career momentum were collected when the women were approximately age 52. Results revealed that the classification of women as exhibiting high, maintaining, or low career momentum could be determined by examining personality dispositions from 30 years earlier. Specifically, women in the high career-momentum group were more confident and independent at age 21 than were women in the maintaining or low-momentum groups. Women who were classified as maintaining career momentum scored high on measures of effective functioning and well-being at initial assessment; however, their trajectories showed a precipitous drop from age 21 to 43. Finally, women in the low-momentum group scored low on measures of self-acceptance, independence, and well-being at each assessment point across adulthood (i.e., ages 21, 43, and 52). The findings from this study also demonstrated that various life structures at age 43 were useful in predicting career momentum at age 52. For example, the high career-momentum women were engaged in higher status occupations at age 43 than were women in the other groups. Taken together, these findings suggest that status in later life on career momentum cannot be reduced to either individual differences in personality traits or variations in life contexts. Rather, they provide support for the concept of interactional continuity by highlighting the importance of the integration of personality characteristics and contextual factors in determining consistency in later life outcomes (Roberts & Friend, 1998).

Other research has also noted the importance of the dynamic interaction between personality dispositions and environmental factors. For example, to assess the relationship between occupational conditions and psychological functioning, Kohn and Schooler (1978) reinterviewed 785 men who were under the age of 65 and who had participated in a 1964 nationally representative study of civil service employees. Results from structural equation analyses demonstrated a reciprocal relationship between occupational conditions and personality characteristics. Furthermore, these analyses indicated high levels of stability on the measures of intellectual flexibility and substantive complexity over a 10-year period. Kohn and Schooler suggested that the consistency in intellectual flexibility across time reflects the stability of the social context in which people live.

Finally, Roberts (1997) found evidence for the importance of the interaction between contextual circumstances and personality dispositions in promoting change, rather than stability. Utilizing the Mills Longitudinal Study, data on women at ages 21, 27, and 43 were analyzed to explore the plaster versus the plasticity hypotheses, that is, whether personality is fixed or malleable (Roberts, 1997). Personality change patterns for each individual were examined via autoregressive latent variable models. This type of analysis allowed for the

examination of interindividual differences in intra-individual change. Results revealed high rank-order consistency across adulthood on the latent personality dimensions of agency and norm adherence. However, individual differences in personality development across time were demonstrated with work experiences explaining a significant amount of variance between individuals on the personality dimensions. Increased participation and success in the work place were predictors of individual differences on the construct of agency (e.g., self-assertion, self-confidence, and independence), and increased job success was a predictor of individual differences on norm adherence. Overall, this study generated support for the plasticity of personality. Under certain contextual circumstances, change in personality is not only possible but also likely, at least into middle adulthood.

Social Clock

Neugarten (1977) and Helson (1984) were among the first to formulate contextual theories of development, basing their models on the concept of the timing of events. Development is marked by the pattern of entry into socially prescribed major life events and transitional phases. Neugarten (1977) theorized that development over the life span may occur on time or off time (early or late) with regard to cultural norms. When individuals confront events at culturally prescribed, age-appropriate times, they are considered on time, and the integrity of personality development is maintained because there is congruence between the societal expectation and the individual's experience. On the other hand, when individuals face these events off time, they are perceived as more stressful to the individual because they are not consistent with societal expectations (Helson et al., 1984). Helson (1984) coined the term *social clock* to represent the phenomenon of the timing of events and argued that the degree to which the individual stays in tune with it throughout the life span determines personality consistency or change (Helson et al., 1984).

Helson et al. (1984) utilized data from the Mills Longitudinal Study to explore the usefulness of the social clock paradigm. Women were categorized into social clock groups according to the path they took to fulfill their family and work roles. The categories included (a) the Feminine Social Clock (FSC), starting a family by the early to middle 20s; (b) the Masculine Occupational Clock (MOC), choosing a career with status potential by age 28; and (c) Neither Social Clock (NSC), adhering to neither social clock by age 28. Findings revealed that personality characteristics measured in young adulthood were effective in distinguishing between social clock patterns. Women who were assessed during their early 20s with high levels of achievement, socialization, intellectual efficiency, and well-being were more likely than their lower scoring peers to adhere to the FSC. In contrast, women who in their early 20s demonstrated greater impulsivity, less awareness and internalization of conventional values, and less motivation to achieve socially structured goals were more likely than their peers to depart from the FSC pattern. Additional findings from this study support the importance of the timing of events. For example, women who by age 28 had either started families or obtained potentially high-status careers demonstrated normative, positive patterns of personality development. These on-time women scored high on scales of well-being and effective functioning in midlife. The off-time women, on the other hand, who had failed to adhere to a social clock (i.e., NSC) by their early 40s reported feeling depressed, alienated, and embittered (Helson et al., 1984).

Helson and Moane (1987) utilized the Mills Longitudinal Study to examine change in personality characteristics with reference to theories of adult development. For example, based on Gutmann's theory (1975), it was hypothesized that femininity would decrease between the ages of 27 and 43. Considerable rank-order stability in personality dispositions was revealed; however, a normative pattern of personality change based on developmental theory was also demonstrated. As predicted, femininity increased in the younger adulthood years but decreased between the ages of 27 and 43. There was also an increase in coping skills, ego development, independence, and confidence for this group of women. This study also revealed that women who were on time in terms of beginning a family or launching a successful career changed on personality dimensions in the normative direction. However, women who were off time on these major life events failed to demonstrate normative change. The authors noted that young adults are confronted with a series of age-graded tasks that direct the developmental trajectory toward normative change if they are met at age-appropriate times.

In more recent work, Helson and colleagues (Mitchell & Helson, 1990; Helson & Wink, 1992) reexamined the Mills graduates and added an additional time of measure (i.e., age of early 50s). Hierarchical regression analyses demonstrated that a sense of well-being in early midlife significantly predicted quality of life among women in their early 50s (Mitchell & Helson, 1990). In a related study, Helson and Wink (1992) examined personality change over time and revealed evidence for inconsistency in personality dispositions in the early 40s followed by a period of stability in the early 50s. Masculinity and femininity scores were among those that resulted in the greatest magnitude of change between the ages of 43 and 52. The women in this sample demonstrated an increase in variables that are associated with masculine traits such as decisiveness and action orientation and a decrease in those associated with feminine characteristics such as vulnerability. This supports the gender-role crossover hypothesis raised by Neugarten and Gutmann (1958), which is discussed next.

In sum, the findings from the studies conducted by Helson and colleagues (Helson et al., 1984; Helson & Moane, 1987; Helson & Wink, 1992; Mitchell & Helson, 1990) illustrate that the social clock serves as a barometer by which individuals evaluate their success in the world. When on time, the individual receives social approval and a positive feeling that comes from being in sync with society. When off time, the individual may experience a lack of social acceptance that results in an unsettled feeling of detachment from society (Helson et al., 1984). The second point based on the findings from these studies is that they confirm the notion that personality dispositions are susceptible to change throughout adulthood. Although this is in contrast to the findings of Caspi et al. (1987), both lines of research emphasize the integral role that context plays in personality development across adulthood.

Gender-Role Crossover Hypothesis

The early work of Neugarten and Gutmann (1958) also supports the existence of change in personality characteristics across adulthood. Utilizing a population of adults between the ages of 40 and 70 from the Kansas City Study of Adult Lives, they explored the use of projective techniques in the study of age-sex roles. Although using a cross-sectional design, the results of this study suggest that, with age, there is a consistent shift in gender-role qualities. Respondents in the Kansas City study were presented with an ambiguous picture of an older and younger adult male and an older and younger adult female. They were then asked to create a story based on the picture. With age, respondents increasingly described the man as passive and no longer symbolizing masculine authority and the woman as assertive and controlling (Neugarten & Gutmann, 1958). These projective data, which demonstrate a cross-over of gendered attributes with older women seen as becoming more agentic and older men as more communal (J. B. James, Lewkowicz, Libhaber, & Lachman, 1995), were interpreted as additional support for the hypothesis that personality has a dynamic quality and is susceptible to over time change.

Person-Environment Fit

Earlier contextual views of personality emerged from the debate over activity (Cavan, Burgess, Havighurst, & Goldhamer,

1949) versus disengagement (Cummings & Henry, 1961) theories. Both the activity and disengagement theories are concerned with the way in which older adults adapt to decreasing roles and societal detachment. The activity theory, on one hand, proposes that detachment is imposed by society and negatively affects the well-being of the older adult unless the older adult is able to "resist the shrinkage of his social world" (Havighurst, Neugarten, & Tobin, 1996, p. 281). Older adults who remain active by finding new roles are expected to fair well. The disengagement theory, on the other hand, suggests that detachment from society is mutual with the older adult withdrawing psychologically from social activities and relationships at the same time that society withdraws support and interest from the older adult. The mutuality of withdrawal results in successful aging according to the disengagement theory.

Research findings from the Kansas City study did not support either view: that the key to well-being is to remain active or to succumb to society's withdrawal. Rather, personality was found to play an integral role in promoting successful adaptation in later life (Havighurst et al., 1968). Achieving a match in later life with one's life-long personal style was associated with the greatest adjustment. This finding led to the formulation of the continuity theory (Atchley, 1989), in which it was argued that either forced disengagement or forced activity leads to a loss of well-being. According to the continuity theory, older adults who are not allowed to maintain their desired level of involvement in society will suffer a loss of well-being. In some ways, this supports more recent findings about personality stability and the need to maximize person-environment fit (J. V. Lerner, Baker, & Lerner, 1985). For some, remaining active was associated with well-being, and for others becoming less involved and withdrawing was adaptive.

In sum, the contextual model provides a rich, complex format from which to view personality development. Contextual models take a life-span approach by viewing development over time in an interdisciplinary, dynamic, interactive framework. From this perspective, it is believed that personality is formed by a continuous reciprocity between the personal style that the individual brings to a situation and the social structure of the prevailing historical time period. The innovative theoretical models of Caspi, Helson, and Neugarten have advanced the field of personality psychology by adopting a life-span view and by bringing to the forefront the importance of the context in which personality evolves.

Ironically, while the advantage of the contextual framework is its multilevel, multidimensional model, it is also a disadvantage. The sophisticated methodological and statistical techniques needed to analyze change over time and to model the complex relationships among antecedents and consequences have only recently become available. Future research that tests contextual models will benefit tremendously from these advances.

Subjective Changes in Personality

As we have seen thus far, there are many methods and measures available to examine personality development across the life span. Another approach is the examination of phenomenological changes—self-perceived changes across time. Studies of subjective change show that individuals typically report more change than they show with objective indexes. In a study by Woodruff and Birren (1972), personality test scores assessed by the California Test of Personality (Kimber, 1947; Woodruff & Birren, 1971) were administered to a group of college graduates in 1944 when they were 21 years old and again in 1969 when they were approximately 46 years old. Participants were asked to complete the personality test two times during the 1969 testing occasion. Instructions given for the first test required that the respondents answer the questions based on their current personality status. Instructions for the second test required that they answer each question the way they thought they had answered in 1944 when they were 21 years old. Findings from this study revealed a high level of stability on the subjective personality ratings across the 25-year period. However, differences were found when the retrospective data were compared with the concurrent data. Results demonstrated that people remembered themselves as less well adjusted 25 years previously than their actual scores indicated. They believed that they had improved across adulthood even though there was no evidence for such a positive change. This finding suggests that adults tend to expect change, especially improvement in personality across adulthood.

Other researchers (Fleeson & Baltes, 1998; Fleeson & Heckhausen, 1997; Lachman, Walen, & Staudinger, 2000; Ryff, 1995) have also found that changes in personality are expected by a large percentage of adults. Participants were asked to rate their personalities in the past, the present, and in the future so that retrospective and prospective comparisons could be made relative to concurrent reports. In a recent study using representative samples from the United States and Germany, Fleeson and Baltes (1998) compared the predictive value of perceived changes relative to concurrent measures. A personality questionnaire (NEO; Costa & McCrae, 1984) was administered to 398 adults between the ages of 26 and 64. In addition, participants were asked to describe their own current personality, their personality when they were 20 to 25 years old, and their projected personality when they will be 65 to

70 years old. Fleeson and Baltes found that many participants anticipated change across adulthood. In addition, although they believed that late adulthood would contain more losses than gains, they expected gains at each life stage including late adulthood. It was also revealed that perceived changes in personality traits accounted for a significant amount of variance beyond the effects of concurrent ratings of personality when predicting health and well-being. This finding suggests that self-ratings of personality dimensions can add meaning when placed within the context of the life course (Fleeson & Baltes, 1998; Fleeson & Heckhausen, 1997).

Lachman et al. (2000) recently conducted a study of individual differences in past, present, and future subjective evaluations of personality characteristics in national samples from the United States and Germany. Although perceived stability of personality was the most prevalent pattern in both countries, 32% of the U.S. and 63% of the German sample showed evidence of perceived change, either incremental or decremental. Based on discriminant function analyses, results revealed that in both samples internal control beliefs were the most important variable in distinguishing between groups of individuals based on perceived change patterns. Participants with high-perceived internal control had more optimistic views of expecting stability or improvements over time, whereas those with a low sense of control remembered the past as better than the present and expected things to get worse in the future.

In general, the findings of subjective personality studies illustrate that adults hold a relatively optimistic view of their developmental trajectory. Except under certain circumstances, such as a low sense of internal control or depression, adults expect to have more positive personality attributes and greater life satisfaction in the future than in the past. The inclusion of subjective reports in the picture of personality adds another dimension to the developmental trajectory and can be useful in predicting patterns of health and well-being in later life.

Personality as a Predictor of Later Life Outcomes

Much of the research on personality development across the life span either tracks the trajectory of personality traits across time in order to assess rank-order stability or explores mean-level change to assess differences between groups. In addition to the empirical questions that can be addressed by these approaches, other interesting developmental issues can be addressed by studying the role that individual differences in personality traits play on later life outcomes (Costa & McCrae, 1988; Lachman, 1989). As discussed earlier, patterns of personality development in adulthood and old age

such as health and mortality, intelligence and wisdom, and adulthood roles (e.g., marital stability/satisfaction, family, work) can be predicted by individual differences in personality attributes assessed earlier in life (e.g., Arbuckle, Gold, Andres, Schwartzman, & Chaikelson, 1992; Baltes, Smith, & Staudinger, 1992; Schwartz et al., 1995). A key issue for personality research is how the course of aging varies as a function of personality attributes.

Health

There is growing evidence that personality characteristics can influence health through a variety of psychosocial mechanisms (Smith & Gallo, 2001; Tucker & Friedman, 1996). For example, certain personality characteristics influence unstable social relationships and initiate the onset of unhealthy behaviors (e.g., smoking and excessive drinking), both potential mechanisms for the link between personality characteristics and later life morbidity and mortality. A study based on the Terman Life Cycle Study of Children with High Ability used archival data to investigate the relationships between childhood personality characteristics and longevity and health outcomes across 70 years (Tucker & Friedman, 1996). Participants in this study had been assessed on a variety of physical health and psychological factors every 5 to 10 years since 1922. A clear link between childhood personality dispositions and longevity was revealed. Specifically, social dependability and lack of impulsivity were the most significant predictors of longevity. In addition, childhood conscientiousness predicted engagement in protective health behaviors that lead to the maintenance of good health in older adulthood. Tucker and Friedman noted that given the multitude of influences on longevity, the strong link to certain personality dispositions suggests that psychological health plays a major role in physical health.

Cognitive Functioning

There is also evidence that early personality patterns are associated with cognitive functioning including intelligence and wisdom in later life. For example, data from the Seattle Longitudinal Study, an ongoing study begun in 1956 (Schaie, 1996), were analyzed to determine whether a flexible personality style was related to intellectual aging. By computing cross-lagged correlations, Schaie revealed that a flexible personality style at midlife was related to the maintenance of higher levels of intellectual performance in old age. This finding implies that a rigid response style will result in earlier declines in intellectual performance in old age. Therefore, older adults need to maintain cognitive flexibility in order to respond to the inevitable changes that are associated with advancing years (Schaie, 1996).

Additional evidence for the relationship between personality dispositions and intellectual outcomes in later life comes from a study of 326 male World War II veterans (Arbuckle et al., 1992) on whom intelligence scores had been obtained when they were young adults. It was found that being less neurotic and more intellectually active predicted reduced intellectual decline and, indirectly, better memory performance. Path models indicated that lower neuroticism scores at an earlier age were associated with higher scores on the M test (a general intelligence test used by the Canadian army) and tests of free recall in later life.

Wisdom

Wisdom has been defined as "expert knowledge in the fundamental pragmatics of life permitting exceptional insight and judgment involving complex and uncertain matters of the human condition" (Baltes et al., 1992, p. 136). In a study that explored the antecedents of wisdom, Staudinger, Lopez, and Baltes (1997) found a relationship between certain personality dimensions and wisdom. In particular, individuals who remained open to experience and interested in understanding and responding to the needs of others (i.e., psychological-mindedness) demonstrated high levels of wisdom-related performance. Indicators of fluid and crystallized intelligence were also related to wisdom. However, after the shared variance between intelligence and personality was considered, only measures of personality-intelligence interface (e.g., judicious, creativity) contributed significant unique variance to the wisdom-related performance measure.

Midlife Crisis

Another example of personality influencing adult outcomes was found in the MIDUS Study (see Lachman & Bertrand, 2001). Those adults who were higher in neuroticism were more likely to report having a midlife crisis. The evidence suggests that it is personality style that predisposes adults to experience crises and that these crises may not be restricted to midlife but may occur at other transitional stages throughout the life course as well.

Adulthood Roles

A final domain that is relevant to the impact of personality dispositions on later life outcomes is adulthood roles such as marriage, family, and work. Kelly and Conley (1987) noted that one of the causes of marital dissatisfaction stems from intrapersonal causes of incompatibility. In other words, the personality characteristics that each partner brings to the relationship, in combination, may inhibit the well-being of the marriage. To examine this hypothesis, Kelly and Conley tested the effectiveness of personality dispositions as antecedents of marital stability and marriage satisfaction. Their longitudinal study consisted of a group of 300 couples assessed from 1930 until 1980. It was found that personality characteristics were significant predictors of both marital satisfaction and marital stability. In particular, neuroticism from the husband or the wife demonstrated the strongest relationship to the marital outcomes. Other studies that explore these phenomena were described in detail in the section in which contextual models were discussed. For example, Caspi et al. (1987, 1988) found that children who displayed explosive dispositions in childhood experienced difficulty across many life tasks such as jobs, marriage, and parenting. Further, in the domain of work and occupational status, Roberts (1997), Roberts and Friend (1998), and Kohn and Schooler (1978) demonstrated the relationship between early life personality patterns and occupational statuses.

The results of the investigations reported here provide evidence that supports the link between early life personality dispositions and later life outcomes across a broad spectrum of domains such as physical health and longevity, cognitive functioning, and the status of work and family. The implications point to the importance of establishing healthy psychological patterns of behavior early in life because they will have lasting effects that may proliferate into multiple domains of adult life.

THE SELF

The self is a multifaceted component at the core of personality (Markus, 1977). It is usually seen as a cognitive dimension that represents the way individuals think about and view themselves. Proponents of the self believe that personality development is an evolving process in which new information from the environment is integrated into existing knowledge structures. These knowledge structures are called schemas and are the guides and regulators of behavior (Crocker & Wolfe, 2001). Schemas are subjective interpretations of past reality that either adjust to new experience or remain the same by filtering out new information that is interpreted as threatening to the self-concept (Markus, 1977). Individuals are continually facing experiences that require the adjustment of existing schemas or the rejection of environmental information. As a result, the self-concept is in a continual state of flux between stability and change

(Whitbourne, 1987). Over long periods of time, however, various aspects of the self-concept remain stable. As a result, they can be used as an anchor or resource for older adults who face later life changes.

Identity

Identity Process Theory

Identity, as defined by Whitbourne and Connolly (1999), is "the individual's self-appraisal of a variety of attributes along the dimensions of physical and cognitive abilities, personal traits and motives, and the multiplicity of social roles including worker, family member, and community citizen" (p. 28). It is flexible and susceptible to change across the life span.

Using data from a study of 94 adults ranging in age from 24 to 61, Whitbourne (1986b) developed a self-concept model based on Piagetian theory. The identity process theory (Whitbourne, 1987; Whitbourne & Connolly, 1999) moves beyond Piaget's view, however, in that it can be used to explain the process of development across the life span. In the identity process model, identity styles are formed when the individual's experiences are interpreted through the processes of assimilation and accommodation. Assimilation occurs by incorporating life events and new experiences into the identity. Assimilation can lead individuals to distort their views of themselves in order to preserve their self-concepts. Although it preserves a positive view of the self, in older adults an imbalance of assimilation has the potential for negative effects. Individuals with a strong assimilative style are seen as rigid and inflexible and deny age-related changes such as physical limitations. For example, they may ignore the advice of a doctor who recommends limiting physical activity. They may react to a difficult situation either by placing blame elsewhere or by avoiding situations in which their physical abilities are challenged.

In contrast to assimilation, accommodation is the process of changing the identity to conform to new experiences. An imbalance of accommodation can also bring about a negative outcome. These individuals have a weak, incoherent identity and overreact to changes. For example, the first sign of gray hair may be the catalyst that causes the adult to take on the identity of an old person. In addition, adults who rely heavily on an accommodative style fail to set goals or to make commitments. Although a balance or equilibrium between the two opposing process styles is desirable, it is the imbalance of one over the other that leads to the formation of different identity styles (Whitbourne & Connolly, 1999). When in balance, the processes produce a healthy approach to new

experiences. When out of balance, however, leaning more heavily toward assimilation or accommodation, the approach is likely to be neurotic or otherwise emotionally unstable.

Whitbourne's model of identity processing is useful for understanding the complexity and dynamic qualities of personality in adulthood and aging. It allows one to grasp the notion of an evolving identity and understand how change can occur across the life span.

Possible Selves

Another important aspect of self-concept relates to the ideas that people have about who they could become, who they would like to become, and who they are afraid of becoming. Markus and Nurius (1986) developed a theory that describes the formation of identity across the life span by addressing these aspects of the self. Their concept of possible selves incorporates hopes and dreams for the self as well as fears and anxieties of undesirable selves. These are integrated into the structure of the self and serve as motivators to achieve their hoped-for selves or to avoid their dreaded selves. When hoped-for selves are realized and feared selves are avoided, positive psychological outcomes occur. However, when the individual perceives that he or she has become the feared or dreaded self at the expense of the hoped for self, the self-concept becomes threatened, and negative outcomes result.

To describe the nature of possible selves across the life span, Cross and Markus (1991) asked a group of respondents between the ages of 18 and 86 to describe their hoped-for and feared possible selves. The groups were compared on the basis of age-related qualities. Across age groups, progressively fewer possible selves (hoped for or feared) were generated. In other words, older adults (i.e., ages 60–86) had fewer expectations of positive choices left in their lives, but they also had fewer fears. However, this should not be taken to imply that the older adults had lost hope. On the contrary, they indicated that hoped-for selves were still important to them. They were also more likely than their younger peers to focus on developing and achieving in their current roles. These personal domains suggest that self-development and growth remain important to the older adult. The fears most frequently reported by older adults were in the physical and personal domains, no doubt reflecting physical and social changes that are associated with aging.

As demonstrated by the work of Cross and Markus (1991), the concept of possible selves facilitates our understanding of the older adult's adaptation to changing roles and losses that are commonly associated with aging. Furthermore, similar to the contextual model, the possible selves framework suggests a reciprocal model where an individual may change or adjust his or her possible selves in response to external influences and personal growth.

The Sense of Control

The sense of control can be understood as the degree to which individuals believe that their behavior will influence outcomes in their lives (Rodin, 1986). The perception that one's behavior will affect outcomes is likely to result in a different response than if one perceives that outcomes are due to chance or other people's actions (Bandura, 1997). Control beliefs have been found to have widespread effects in many different domains of life including work, family, and health. Furthermore, beliefs about control may vary across these different domains (Clarke-Plaskie & Lachman, 1999; Lachman & Weaver, 1998). Research findings provide evidence that control beliefs change in adulthood. For example, based on findings from the MIDUS study, Lachman and Weaver (1998) found that adults increased their sense of control over their work, finances, and marriage. However, in the domains of sex life and children, there was evidence for reduced control. In addition, other studies have found age-related declines in perceived control for health and memory (Lachman, 1991).

Control Beliefs and Health

An indirect link between control beliefs and physical health, including recovery from illness and disability in adulthood and old age, has been found (Bandura, 1997; Lachman & Prenda, in press). Individuals who believe that they are responsible for outcomes in their lives are more likely to engage in effortful and persistent behavior that is goal oriented. They believe that their health is within their own control and are confident in their ability to change. As a result, they will be more likely to act in harmony with the desired outcome by engaging in health-promoting behaviors such as exercise, a healthy diet, and regular physical examinations (Bandura, 1997; Lachman & Prenda, in press). Maintaining a sense of control in adulthood and old age may serve as an important psychosocial resource by fostering preventive and remedial health behaviors (Lachman & Bertrand, 2001). Indeed, there is compelling evidence that factors under personal control (e.g., alcohol use, smoking, mental stability, exercise, body mass index, coping mechanisms, and education) have a strong impact on psychological, physical, and social indicators of successful aging (Vaillant & Mukamal, 2001).

Self-Efficacy

The study of control beliefs has focused on many related constructs including self-efficacy, locus of control, and primary and secondary control beliefs (e.g., Bandura, 1997; Heckhausen & Shulz, 1995). Bandura (1997) argued that as adults age, they will increasingly find themselves in situations in which they will benefit by a strong sense of self-efficacy. For instance, older adults will be faced with the task of establishing new relationships to replace those that have been lost through retirement, relocation, or death. A low sense of social efficacy in these situations will increase the older adult's vulnerability to stress and depression by inhibiting the formation of necessary social supports (Bandura, 1997). In another situation—the routinized, controlled environment in nursing homes and other residential institutions for older adults—there is an undermining of the individual's sense of efficacy. Numerous studies have shown that nursing home residents who have the opportunity to exert control over their environment have better physical and psychological outcomes including a longer life than those residents who do not (see Bandura, 1997).

Primary and Secondary Control

Other forms of control during adulthood and old age such as primary and secondary control beliefs have also been investigated. Heckhausen and Schulz's (1995) model of primary and secondary control is based on the hypothesis that the individual has a strong desire to control his or her interactions with the environment. This control is accomplished by maintaining a balance between the two strategies of control. Primary control strategies involve working toward reaching a goal by changing the situation or the environment. Secondary control strategies focus on changing the self to accommodate the situation or environmental constraints. According to Heckhausen and Schulz (1995), primary and secondary control strategies work in concert to cope with the demands and challenges encountered across the life span. Evidence is provided for the notion that, with aging, there is a shift from the use of primary to secondary control strategies when faced with uncontrollable situations or difficult challenges (Heckhausen & Schulz, 1995). Additional support for age-related shifts in control strategy use comes from a study in which age-related changes in physical, cognitive, and social processes were shown to influence the developmental trajectory and resulted in the older adult's adoption of strategies to compensate for developmental losses (Heckhausen, 1997). Finally, Wrosch, Heckhausen, and Lachman (2000) found that the use of secondary control strategies was more adaptive for older adults, whereas the use of primary control strategies was more adaptive for younger and middle-age adults when faced with health or financial difficulties.

Well-Being

A common myth regarding older adults is to view them as unhappy and depressed. According to Mroczek and Kolarz (1998), this misconception is the result of a belief in the social indicator model, in which social and demographic factors such as gender, income, marital status, and age serve as markers for well-being. Because older adults often experience loss in the physical and social realms, an expectation of depression and low satisfaction could erroneously be made. However, evidence is building to support the argument that regardless of the marked losses as gauged by the social indicator model, older adults are not unhappy or depressed. For example, based on the MIDUS sample, Mroczek and Kolarz (1998) found that the majority of older adults rated themselves as "very" or "pretty" happy. In general, they found that positive emotions increased and negative emotions decreased as adults reached midlife and beyond.

Ryff (1989) defined well-being along six dimensions: positive relations with others, environmental mastery, self-acceptance, having a purpose in life, personal growth, and autonomy. Ryff asked 321 adults to rate themselves along these dimensions. Results demonstrated that adults are more likely to maintain or increase well-being in terms of self-acceptance, positive relations with others, autonomy, and environmental mastery as they reach midlife and beyond. Purpose in life and personal growth was more likely to show declines in later adulthood.

Cross-national data support the findings reported here (Diener & Diener, 1996); world-wide, most adults report being happy. Across the 43 nations that were analyzed, 86% of all studies reported mean happiness and well-being ratings that were above neutral. Among older adults the percentage of participants with positive subjective well-being was between 64% and 97%. These findings suggest that adulthood and old age seem to be periods in which there is a positive sense of well-being. Because well-being can be utilized as an indicator of successful aging, the implication of these findings for older adults is that successful aging is attainable (Rowe & Kahn, 1998).

Emotions and Coping

Emotions have been defined as "the primary forces in organizing human thought and action . . . [namely,] the emotional component of consciousness and experience that gives richness and meaning to individual life and relationships" (Dougherty, Abe, & Izard, 1996, p. 17). Many argue that emotions maintain their salience and expressiveness across the life span (Dougherty et al., 1996).

Socioemotional Selectivity Theory

Carstensen (1995) suggested that, with age, emotions become more important. For example, in a study in which participants were presented with a story narrativeolder people, compared with younger people, had a better recollection of emotional text than they had for neutral text (Carstensen & Turk-Charles, 1994). Carstensen noted that emotions are especially important in the social interactions of older adults, where they serve as the motivating force in the choice and maintenance of relationships. Accordingly, she conceptualized the *socioemotional selectivity theory* (Carstensen, 1993), an organizing conceptual framework that describes the mechanisms involved in the change in social relationships across the life span. The theory posits that there is a fundamental change in quality and quantity of the motives for maintaining social relationships with age. Although similar goals function throughout the life course, there is a change in the importance of the goals, depending on the age of the individual. For adolescents and younger adults, information seeking is the most salient factor in their selection of social relationships. They select new partners frequently because they are seeking to gain information about their social world and their place in it relative to others. In contrast, for infants and older adults emotion regulation is the most important factor in selecting relationships. For example, older individuals are highly selective in their social relationships and generally choose partners with whom they have an established relationship. According to Carstensen (1995) emotion regulation is most salient for older adults for two primary reasons. First, with years of acquired experience, there are fewer individuals who can provide novel information to the older adult; second, as older adults become more aware of their limited time, they tend to base their relationships on the potential for emotional rewards. In this way, older adults cope with the realization that their time is limited by placing more emotional salience on the maintenance of meaningful, long-term relationships and less on relationships that serve to provide novel information.

Coping

Lazarus (1996) noted that an understanding of coping processes is necessary to understand the concept of emotions. He argues that coping is a fundamental aspect of emotion because it incorporates the components of thinking, acting, and action impulses. Lazarus and Folkman (1984, p. 141) defined coping as "constantly changing cognitive and behavioral efforts to manage specific external and/or internal demands that are appraised as taxing or exceeding the resources of the person." They conceptualized two approaches to coping with stress: emotion-focused and problem-focused strategies. In emotion-focused coping individuals attempt to lower their levels of stress by changing the way they view the stressor. In problem-focused coping individuals attempt to lower their levels of stress by altering or confronting the situation head-on. In this type of coping strategy, the individual uses logic and planful solutions.

Several studies have been conducted that examine change in emotion- and problem-focused coping strategies across time. Of particular interest are two studies that revealed discrepant findings. The first is a study by Folkman, Lazarus, Pimley, and Novacek (1987) in which older adults were found to use less problem-focused coping and more emotion-focused (i.e., escape avoidance) styles than younger adults. However, a subsequent study by Aldwin (1991) could not replicate this finding. In fact, older adults in her study reported as many problem-focused strategies as younger adults and fewer emotion-focused strategies. Aldwin (1994) argued that adults learn to distinguish between problems that can be controlled by problem-focused strategies and those that cannot, and they may actually engage in less coping because they are aware of the best strategies that work in a given situation.

Tenacious Goal Pursuit Versus Flexible Adjustment

Related to coping strategies and similar to Heckhausen and Schulz's (1995) primary/secondary control model and Whitbourne's identity process theory (1987) are the concepts of tenacious goal pursuit and flexible adjustment (Brandtstädter & Renner, 1990). This model can account for how older adults cope with obstacles or difficult situations in a way that maintains their sense of well-being and prevents depression. Because adults in old age are increasingly encumbered by physical limitations and disabilities, it becomes more difficult for them to attain their desired goals. Adjustment of goals and expectancies (i.e., flexible goal pursuit) becomes adaptive in order for them to maintain a sense of well-being and avoid depression. Similar to Schaie's (1996) work that demonstrates that a flexible personality style helps to preserve cognitive decline, flexible goal pursuits help to maintain a sense of well-being. In contrast, tenacious goal pursuits in the face of unattainable goals may lead to depression and despair.

CONCLUSIONS AND FUTURE DIRECTIONS

In this chapter we have presented an overview of the field of personality development in adulthood and aging. We summarized theoretical ideas, conceptual models, and empirical research covering over five decades of work. The voluminous body of literature has enriched the field of personality development but has also made it difficult to synthesize in one chapter. An attempt was made, therefore, to present key theoretical and empirical works relevant to personality development in adulthood and old age. As we have seen, researchers continue to conduct research on issues of change and stability in personality dispositions across the life span. Recently, however, the focus has shifted to include the underlying mechanisms involved in the process of personality development. The life-span perspective and the contextual models of development have supported investigations using more complex, multidimensional models. The future of research on personality in adulthood and old age must cut across disciplines to include sociocultural contexts, prevailing historical influences, physical and psychological health, genetics, and other physiological factors.

Furthermore, the trajectory of development is multidirectional and operates as a dynamic process reciprocally interacting between internal and external forces. For example, as a predictor of later life outcomes, personality transcends a particular perspective or a specific domain of later life. Given the demographic swing toward a larger percentage of older adults, a major concern for researchers, practitioners, and laypersons is the delay and prevention of age-related disease and disability. Aspects of the self such as adaptive emotional regulation, coping strategies, and control beliefs may provide an important link between early personality dispositions and later life outcomes.

Research is beginning to focus on understanding the mediators of personality and adaptive outcomes. For example, there is an emerging body of work examining the mechanisms linking aspects of personality and the self with adaptive functioning and health in adulthood and old age (Smith & Gallo, 2001). Specific personality characteristics have been linked with the onset and progression of diseases (e.g., Tucker & Friedman, 1996). Identifying behavioral and physiological factors associated with personality, such as exercise, stress hormones, and immune functioning, can provide useful information for designing interventions to promote successful aging. Such interventions are likely to be most effective if they are tailored to take individual differences in personality into account.

REFERENCES

Arbuckle, T. Y., Gold, D. P., Andres, D., Schwartzman, A., & Chaikelson, J. (1992). The role of psychosocial context, age, and intelligence in memory performance of older men. *Psychology and Aging, 7,* 25–36.

Aldwin, C. (1991). Does age affect the stress and coping process? Implications of age differences in perceived control. *Journal of Gerontology, 46,* 174–180.

Aldwin, C. (1994). *Stress, coping, and development.* New York: Guilford Press.

Atchley, R. C. (1989). A continuity theory of normal aging. *Gerontologist, 29,* 183–190.

Baltes, P. B. (1983). Life-span developmental psychology: Observations on history and theory revisited. In R. M. Lerner (Ed.), *Developmental psychology: Historical and philosophical perspectives* (pp. 79–111). Hillsdale, NJ: Erlbaum.

Baltes, P. B. (1987). Theoretical propositions of life-span developmental psychology: On the dynamics between growth and decline. *Developmental Psychology, 23,* 611–626.

Baltes, P. B., Lindenberger, U., & Staudinger, U. M. (1998). Life-span theory in developmental psychology. In R. M. Lerner (Ed.), *Handbook of child psychology: Vol. 1. Theoretical models of human development* (5th ed., pp. 1029–1143). New York: Wiley.

Baltes, P. B., Smith J., Staudinger, U. M. (1992). Wisdom and successful aging. In Sonderegger, T. B. (Ed.), *Nebraska Symposium on Motivation 1991: Vol. 39. Psychology and aging,* (pp. 123–167). Lincoln: University of Nebraska Press.

Bandura, A. (1997). *Self-efficacy: The exercise of control.* New York: W. H. Freeman.

Blanchard-Fields, F. (1986). Reasoning on social dilemmas varying in emotional saliency: An adult developmental study. *Psychology and Aging, 1,* 325–333.

Block, J. (with Hann, N.). (1971). *Lives through time.* Berkeley, CA: Bancroft Books.

Bouchard, T. J. (1997). The genetics of personality. In K. Blum & E. P. Noble (Eds.), *Handbook of psychiatric genetics* (pp. 273–296). Boca Raton, FL: CRC Press.

Bowlby, J. (1982). *Attachment and loss* (Vol. 1). New York: Basic Books.

Brandtstädter, J., & Renner, G. (1990). Tenacious goal pursuit and flexible goal adjustment: Explication and age-related analysis of assimilative and accommodative strategies of coping. *Psychology and Aging, 5,* 58–67.

Carstensen, L. L. (1993). Motivation for social contact across the life span: A theory of socioemotional selectivity. In J. Jacobs (Ed.), *Nebraska Symposium on Motivation 1992: Vol. 40. Developmental perspectives on motivation* (pp. 209–254). Lincoln: University of Nebraska Press.

Carstensen, L. L. (1995). Evidence for a life-span theory of socioemotional selectivity. *Current Directions in Psychological Science, 4,* 151–156.

Carstensen, L. L., & Turk-Charles, S. (1994). The salience of emotion across the adult life span, *Psychology of Aging, 9,* 259–264.

Caspi, A. (1987). Personality in the life course. *Journal of Personality and Social Psychology, 53*(6), 1203–1213.

Caspi, A., Elder, G., H., & Bem, D. J. (1987). Moving against the world: Life-course patterns of explosive children. *Developmental Psychology, 23,* 308–313.

Caspi, A., Elder, G. H., & Bem, D. J. (1988). Moving against the world: Life-course patterns of shy children. *Developmental Psychology, 24,* 824–831.

Caspi, A., & Roberts, B. W. (1999). Personality continuity and change across the life course. In L. A. Pervin & O. P. John (Eds.), *Handbook of personality: Theory and research* (pp. 300–326). New York: Guilford Press.

Cavan, R. S., Burgess, E. W., Havighurst, R. J., & Goldhamer, H. (1949). *Personal adjustment in old age.* Chicago: Science Research Associates.

Clarke-Plaskie, M., & Lachman, M. E. (1999). The sense of control in midlife. In S. L. Willis & J. D. Reid (Eds.), *Life in the middle: Psychological and social development in middle age* (pp. 182–208). San Diego, CA: Academic Press.

Costa, P. T., & McCrae, R. R. (1980). Still stable after all these years: Personality as a key to some issues in adulthood and old age. *Life Span Development and Behavior, 3,* 65–102.

Costa, P. T., & McCrae, R. R. (1984). Personality as a lifelong determinant of wellbeing. In C. A. Malatesta & C. E. Izard (Eds.), *Emotion in adult development* (pp. 141–157). Beverly Hills, CA: Sage.

Costa, P. T., & McCrae, R. R. (1988). Personality in adulthood: A six-year longitudinal study of self-reports and spouse ratings on the NEO Personality Inventory. *Journal of Personality and Social Psychology, 54,* 853–863.

Crocker, J., & Wolfe, C. T. (2001). Contingencies of self-worth [Special Issue]. *Psychological Review, 108,* 593–623.

Cross, S., & Markus, H. (1991). Possible selves across the life span. *Human Development, 34,* 230–255.

Cummings, E., & Henry, W. (1961). *Growing old.* New York: Basic Books.

Diener, E., & Diener, C. (1996). Most people are happy. *Psychological Science, 7*(3), 181–185.

Dougherty, L. M., Abe, J. A., & Izard, C. E. (1996). Differential emotions theory and emotional development in adulthood and later life. In C. Magai & S. H. McFadden (Eds.), *Handbook of emotion, adult development, and aging* (pp. 27–41). San Diego, CA: Academic Press.

Elder, G. H., & Hareven, T. K. (1994). Rising above life's disadvantage: From the Great Depression to war. In G. H. Elder, J. Modell, & R. D. Parke (Eds.), *Children in time and place: Developmental and historical insights* (pp. 47–72). New York: Cambridge University Press.

Erikson, E. (1950). *Childhood and society.* New York: W. W. Norton.

Erikson, E. (1963). *Childhood and society* (2nd ed.). New York: W. W. Norton.

Featherman, D. L., & Lerner, R. M. (1985). Ontogenesis and socio-genesis: Problematics for theory and research about development and socialization across the lifespan. *American Sociological Review, 50,* 659–676.

Field, D., & Millsap, R. E. (1991). Personality in advanced old age: Continuity or change? *Journal of Gerontology: Psychological Sciences, 46,* 659–676.

Fleeson, W., & Baltes, P. B. (1998). Beyond present-day personality assessment: An encouraging exploration of the measurement properties and predictive power of subjective lifetime personality. *Journal of Research in Personality, 12,* 125–136.

Fleeson, W., & Heckhausen, J. (1997). More or less "me" in past, present, and future: Perceived lifetime personality. *Psychology and Aging, 12,* 125–136.

Folkman, S., Lazarus, R. S., Pimley, S., & Novacek, J. (1987). Age differences in stress and coping processes. *Psychology and Aging, 2,* 171–184.

Freud, S. (1905). Three contributions to the theory of sex (A. A. Brill, Ed. and Trans.). In *The basic writing of Sigmund Freud.* New York: Modern Library.

Friedman, H. S., Tucker, J. S., Schwartz, J. E., Martin, L. R., Tomlinson-Keasy, C., Wingard, D. L., & Criqui, M. H. (1995). Childhood conscientiousness and longevity: Health behaviors and cause of death. *Journal of Personality and Social Psychology, 68,* 696–703.

Gilligan, C. (1982). *In a different voice: Psychological theory and women's development.* Cambridge, MA: Harvard University Press.

Glenn, N. D. (1980). Values, attitudes, and beliefs. In O. G. Brim & J. Kagan (Eds.), *Constancy and change in human development* (pp. 596–640). Cambridge, MA: Harvard University Press.

Gutmann, D. T. (1975). Parenthood: Key to the comparative psychology of the life cycle? In N. Datan & L. Ginsberg (Eds.), *Life-span developmental psychology: Normative life crises* (pp. 167–184). New York: Academic Press.

Haan, N., Millsap, R., & Hartka, E. (1986). As time goes by: Change and stability in personality over fifty years. *Psychology and Aging, 1,* 220–232.

Havighurst, R. J., Neugarten, B. L., & Tobin, S. S. (1968). Personality and patterns of aging. In B. L. Neugarten (Ed.), *Middle age and aging* (pp. 173–177). Chicago: University of Chicago Press.

Havighurst, R. J., Neugarten, B. L., & Tobin, S. S. (1996). Disengagement, personality and life satisfaction in the later years. In D. A. Neugarten (Ed.), *The meaning of age: Selected papers of Bernice L. Neugarten* (pp. 281–287). Chicago: University of Chicago Press.

Heckhausen, J. (1997). Developmental regulation across adulthood: Primary and secondary control of age-related challenges. *Developmental Psychology, 33,* 176–187

Heckhausen, J., & Schulz, R. (1995). A life-span theory of control. *Psychological Review, 102,* 284–304.

Helson, R. (1984). E. Nesbit's 41st year: Her life, times, and symbols of personality growth. *Imagination, Cognition, and Personality, 4,* 53–68.

Helson, R., Mitchell, V., & Moane, G. (1984). Personality and patterns of adherence and nonadherence to the social clock. *Journal of Personality and Social Psychology, 46,* 1079–1096.

Helson, R., & Moane, G. (1987). Personality change in women from college to midlife. *Journal of Personality and Social Psychology, 53,* 176–186.

Helson, R., & Wink, P. (1992). Personality change in women from the early 40s to the early 50s. *Psychology and Aging, 7,* 46–55.

Hy, L. X., & Loevinger, J. (1996). *Measuring ego development* (2nd ed.). Hillsdale, NJ: Erlbaum.

James, W. (1890). *The principles of psychology.* New York: Dover.

James, J. B., Lewkowicz, C., Libhaber, J., & Lachman, M. E. (1995). Rethinking the gender identity crossover hypothesis: A test of a new model. *Sex Roles, 32,* 185–207.

Jung, C. (1933). *Modern man in search of a soul.* New York: Harcourt Press and World.

Kahn, S., Zimmerman, G., Csikszentmihalyi, M., & Getzels, J. W. (1985). Relations between identity in young adulthood and intimacy at midlife. *Journal of Personality and Social Psychology, 49,* 1316–1322.

Kelly, E. L., & Conley, J. J. (1987). Personality and compatibility: A prospective analysis of marital satisfaction. *Journal of Personality and Social Psychology, 52,* 27–40.

Kimber, J. A. M. (1947). The insight of college students into the items of a personality test. *Educational and Psychological Measurement, 7,* 411–420.

Kohlberg, L., & Kramer, R. (1969). Continuities and discontinuities in childhood and adult moral development. *Human Development, 12,* 3–120.

Kohn, M. L., & Schooler, C. (1978). The reciprocal effects of the substantive complexity of work and intellectual flexibility: A longitudinal assessment. *American Journal of Sociology, 84*(1), 24–52.

Labouvie-Vief, G., Hakim-Larson, J., & Hobart, C. J. (1987). Age, ego level, and the life-span development of coping and defense processes. *Psychology and Aging, 2,* 286–293.

Lachman, M. E. (1989). Personality and aging at the crossroads: Beyond stability versus change. In K. W. Schaie & C. Schooler (Eds.), *Social structure and aging: Psychological processes* (pp. 167–190). Hillsdale, NJ: Erlbaum.

Lachman, M. E. (1991). Perceived control over memory aging: Developmental and intervention perspectives. *Journal of Social Issues, 47,* 159–175.

Lachman, M. E., & Baltes, P. B. (1994). Psychological aging in lifespan perspective. In M. Rutter & D. F. Hay (Eds.), *Development through life: A handbook for clinicians* (pp. 583–606). London: Blackwell Scientific.

Lachman, M. E., & Bertrand, R. B. (2001). Personality and the self in midlife. In M. E. Lachman (Ed.), *Handbook on midlife development* (pp. 279–309). New York: Wiley.

Lachman, M. E., & Prenda, K. (in press). The adaptive value of feeling in control in midlife. In C. Ryff, R. Kessler, & O. G. Brim (Eds.), *A portrait of midlife in the United States.* Chicago: University of Chicago Press.

Lachman, M. E., Walen, H., & Staudinger, U. (2000). *Perceived trajectories of subjective well-being: Patterns and predictors in German and American adults.* Manuscript submitted for publication.

Lachman, M. E., & Weaver, S. L. (1998). Sociodemographic variations in the sense of control by domain: Findings from the MacArthur studies of midlife. *Psychology and Aging, 13,* 553–562.

Lazarus, R. S. (1996). The role of coping in the emotions and how coping changes over the life course. In C. Magai & S. H. McFadden (Eds.), *Handbook of emotion, adult development, and aging* (pp. 289–306). San Diego, CA: Academic Press.

Lazarus, R. S., & Folkman, S. (1984). *Stress, appraisal, and coping.* New York: Springer.

Lerner, R. M. (2002). *Concepts and theories of human development* (3rd ed.). Mahwah, NJ: Erlbaum.

Lerner, R. M. (1976). *Concepts and theories of human development.* Reading, MA: Addison-Wesley.

Lerner, J. V., Baker, N., & Lerner, R. M. (1985). A person-context goodness of fit model of adjustment. In P. C. Kendall (Ed.), *Advances in cognitive-behavioral research and therapy* (Vol. 4, pp. 111–136). San Diego, CA: Academic Press.

Levinson, D. J. (1977). The mid-life transition. *Psychiatry, 40,* 99–112.

Levinson, D. J. (1978). Eras: The anatomy of the life cycle. *Psychiatric Opinion, 15*(9), 39–48.

Levinson, D. J., Darrow, C., Kline, E., Levinson, M., & McKee, B. (1978). *The seasons of a man's life.* New York: Knopf.

Levinson, D. J., & Levinson, J. D. (1996). *The seasons of a woman's life.* New York: Ballantine Books.

Loevinger, J. (1976). *Ego development.* San Francisco: Jossey-Bass.

Loevinger, J. (1979). Construct validity of the sentence completion test of ego development. *Applied Psychological Measurement, 3,* 281–311.

Loevinger, J. (1983). Personality: Stages, traits, and the self. *Annual Review of Psychology, 34,* 195–222.

Loevinger, J. (1985). Revision of the sentence completion test for ego development. *Journal of Personality and Social Psychology, 48,* 420–427.

Loevinger, J., & Wessler, R. (1970). *Measuring ego development* (Vol. 1). San Francisco: Jossey-Bass.

Markus, H. R. (1977). Self-schemata and processing information about the self. *Journal of Personality and Social Psychology, 35,* 63–78.

Markus, H. R., & Lachman, M. E. (1996, September). *Attributes and traits: Collective and individual approaches.* Paper presented at (MIDMAC) the John D. and Catherine T. MacArthur Foundation Research Network on Successful Midlife Development meeting, Cambridge, MA.

Markus, H. R., & Nurius, P. (1986). Possible selves. *American Psychologist, 41*(9), 954–969.

McAdams, D. P. (2001). Generativity in midlife. In M. E. Lachman (Ed.), *Handbook on midlife development* (pp. 395–443). New York: Wiley.

McCrae, R. R., & Costa, P. T. (1985). Updating Norman's adequate taxonomy: Intelligence and personality dimensions in natural language and in questionnaires. *Journal of Personality and Social Psychology, 49,* 710–721.

McCrae, R. R., & Costa, P. T. (1987). Validation of the five-factor model of personality across instruments and observers. *Journal of Personality and Social Psychology, 54,* 81–90.

McCrae, R. R., & Costa, P. T. (1990). *Personality in adulthood.* New York: Guilford.

McCrae, R. R., & Costa, P. T. (1994). The stability of personality: Observation and evaluations. *Current Directions in Psychological Science, 3,* 173–175.

McCrae, R. R., Costa, P. T., & Busch, C. M. (1986). Evaluating comprehensiveness in personality systems: The California Q-Set and five factor model. *Journal of Personality, 54*(2), 430–446.

Mitchell, V., & Helson, R. (1990). Women's prime of life: Is it the 50s? *Psychology of Women Quarterly, 14,* 451–470.

Mroczek, D. K., & Kolarz, C. M. (1998). The effect of age on positive and negative affect: A developmental perspective on happiness. *Journal of Personality and Social Psychology, 75,* 1333–1349.

Nesselroade, J. R. (1992). Adult personality development: Issues in assessing constancy and change. In R. A. Zucker, A. I. Rabin, & J. Aronoff (Eds.), *Personality structure in the life course: Essays on personality in the Murray tradition* (pp. 221–275). New York: Springer.

Neugarten, B. T. (1977). Personality and aging. In J. E. Birren & K. W. Schaie (Eds.), *Handbook of the psychology of aging* (pp. 626–649). New York: Van Nostrand Reinhold.

Neugarten, B. T., & Gutmann, D. L. (1958). Age-sex roles and personality in middle age: A thematic apperception study. *Psychological Monographs, 72,* 1–33.

Piaget, J. (1974). *The origins of intelligence in children* (M. Cook, Trans.). New York: International Universities Press. (Original work published 1936)

Reese, H. W., & Overton, W. F. (1970). Models of development and theories of development. In L. R. Goulet & P. B. Baltes (Eds.), *Life-span developmental psychology: Research and theory* (pp. 115–145). New York: Academic Press.

Roberts, B. W. (1997). Plaster or plasticity: Are adult work experiences associated with personality change in women? *Journal of Personality, 65,* 205–232.

Roberts, B. W., & DelVecchio, W. F. (2000). The rank-order consistency of personality traits from childhood to old age: A quantitative review of longitudinal studies. *Psychological Bulletin, 126*(1), 3–25.

Roberts, B. W., & Friend, W. (1998). Career momentum in midlife women: Life context, identity, and personality correlates. *Journal of Occupational Health Psychology, 3*, 195–208.

Rodin, J. (1986). Aging and health: Effects of the sense of control. *Science, 233*, 1271–1276.

Rousseau, J. J. (1948). *Emile or education* (B. Foxley, Trans.). London: J. M. Dent. (Original work published 1762)

Rowe, J. W., & Kahn, R. L. (1998). *Successful aging.* New York: Random House.

Ryff, C. D. (1989). Happiness is everything, or is it? Explorations on the meaning of psychological well-being. *Journal of Personality and Social Psychology, 57*, 1069–1181.

Ryff, C. D. (1995). Psychological well-being in adult life. *Current Directions in Psychological Science, 4*, 99–104.

Schaie, K. W. (1996). *Intellectual development in adulthood: The Seattle Longitudinal Study.* New York: Cambridge University Press.

Schaie, K. W., & Hendricks, J. (Eds.). (2000). *Evolution of the aging self: Societal impact.* New York: Springer.

Schwartz, J. E., Friedman, H. S., Tucker, J. S., Tomlinson-Keasey, C., Wingard, D. L., & Criqui, M. H. (1995). Sociodemographic and psychosocial factors in childhood as predictors of adult mortality. *American Journal of Public Health, 85*(9), 1237–1245.

Smith, T. W., & Gallo, L. C. (2001). Personality traits as risk factors for physical illness. In A. Baum, T. A. Revenson, & J. E. Singer (Eds.), *Handbook of health psychology* (pp. 139–173). Mahwah, NJ: Erlbaum.

Staudinger, U. M., Lopez, D. F., & Baltes, P. B. (1997). The psychometric location of wisdom-related performance: Intelligence, personality, and more? *Personality and Social Psychology Bulletin, 23*(11), 1200–1214.

Tucker, J. S., & Friedman, H. S. (1996). Emotion, personality, and health. In C. Magai & S. H. McFadden (Eds.), *Handbook of emotion, adult development, and aging* (pp. 307–326). San Diego, CA: Academic Press.

Vaillant, G. E. (1977). *Adaptation to life.* Boston: Little, Brown.

Vaillant, G. E., & Milofsky, E. (1980). Natural history of male psychological health: IX. Empirical evidence for Erikson's model of the life cycle. *American Journal of Psychiatry, 137*, 1348–1359.

Vaillant, G. E., & Mukamal, K. (2001). Successful aging. *American Journal of Psychiatry, 158*, 839–847.

Whitbourne, S. K. (1986a). *The me I know: A study of adult identity.* New York: Springer-Verlag.

Whitbourne, S. K. (1986b). Openness to experience, identity flexibility, and life change in adults. *Journal of Personality and Social Psychology, 50*, 163–168.

Whitbourne, S. K. (1987). Personality development in adulthood and old age: Relationships among identity style, health, and well-being. In K. W. Schaie & C. Eisdorfer (Eds.), *Annual review of gerontology and geriatrics* (Vol. 7, pp. 189–216). New York: Springer.

Whitbourne, S. K., & Connolly, L. A. (1999). The developing self in midlife. In S. L. Willis & J. D. Reid (Eds.), *Life in the middle: Psychological and social development in middle age* (pp. 25–45). San Diego, CA: Academic Press.

Whitbourne, S. K., & Waterman, A. S. (1979). Psychosocial development during the adult years: Age and cohort comparisons. *Developmental Psychology, 15*, 373–378.

Whitbourne, S. K., Zuschlag, M. K., Elliot, L. B., & Waterman, A. S. (1992). Psychosocial development in adulthood: A 22-year sequential study. *Journal of Personality and Social Psychology, 63*, 260–271.

Woodruff, D. S., & Birren, J. E. (1971). *Age and personality: A twenty-five year follow-up.* Unpublished manuscript, University of Southern California, Los Angeles.

Woodruff, D. S., & Birren, J. E. (1972). Age changes and cohort differences in personality. *Developmental Psychology, 6*, 252–259.

Wrosch, C., Heckhausen, J., & Lachman, M. E. (2000). Primary and secondary control strategies for managing health and financial stress across adulthood. *Psychology and Aging, 15*, 387–399.

CHAPTER 20

Social Relationships in Adulthood and Old Age

RACHEL PRUCHNO AND JENNIFER ROSENBAUM

Social relationships between adults are complex. They enable people to derive information, affection, and assistance from one another; to learn and convey knowledge about their history; to acquire and maintain self-identity; and to regulate affect (Carstensen, 1992). Most social relationships that include an adult are the product of a lifetime of associations; many have the potential to affect such far-reaching outcomes as physical health and psychological well-being. Virtually all social relationships between adults have the potential to be affected by illness and disability.

In this chapter we review what is known about social relationships between adults. We focus exclusively on social relationships in which all parties are adults and concentrate on those in which at least one person would be considered elderly. Not included, therefore, are relationships between parents and adolescent children and those between grandparents and young grandchildren. We take a life-course perspective on social relationships in this review, meaning that we are concerned with how individuals change over time and how their transitions are linked to the people with whom they maintain close relationships. More specifically, in this chapter we focus on adult social relationships between (a) spouses, (b) parents and their children, (c) siblings, and (d) friends. We examine these bonds both within the context of health and of disability, reviewing conceptual frameworks as well as empirical literature. We concentrate on reviewing critical themes, highlighting recently published literature, and identifying key research questions and findings. On the basis of our review of the state of the art, we conclude by making recommendations for future directions that the next generation of knowledge about social relationships between adults should take.

THEORETICAL PERSPECTIVES

Theories about social relationships between adults generally have sought to predict those aspects of social relationships that are stable over the life course and those that change. They have also been concerned with predicting how social relationships can help to explain psychological well-being.

Convoys of Social Relationships

One of the earliest theoretical frameworks to focus on interpersonal relationships from a life-course perspective was that proposed by Kahn and Antonucci (1980). Their central proposition was that social support is important to individual well-being throughout the life course, both for its direct contributions and for its ability to moderate the effects of stress. They define *social support* as interpersonal transactions that include one or more of the following elements: affect, affirmation, and aid.

Based on theories of attachment and of roles, Kahn and Antonucci developed the concept of *convoys.* They conceptualized an individual as moving through the life cycle surrounded by a set of other people to whom he or she is related by the giving or receiving of social support. An individual's convoy at any point in time, they suggest, consists of the set of people on whom he or she relies for support and those who rely on him or her for support.

Kahn and Antonucci (1980) suggested that relationships between individuals could be symmetrical, with an exchange of approximately equal amounts of support, or asymmetrical, with one individual providing more support to the other. Furthermore, they contended that a person's requirements for social support at any given time are jointly determined by properties of the situation and of the person. They suggested that either too much support or too little support could be detrimental to an individual.

Convoys are conceptualized as being dynamic and lifelong in nature. Although some components will most likely change over time, others will remain stable across time and situations. Kahn and Antonucci suggest that losses and gains in convoys could have a variety of causes, including death, betrayal, changes in role, or location. For additional information about the structure and function of convoys among older Americans, readers are referred to Antonucci and Akiyama (1987).

Socioemotional Selectivity Theory

Consistent with Kahn and Antonucci's theory, Carstensen (1991, 1992) proposed the *socioemotional selectivity theory,* which posits that reduced rates of social interaction in later life are the result of lifelong selection processes by which people strategically and adaptively cultivate their social networks to maximize social and emotional gains and minimize their risks. The theory is rooted in the functions of social contact; it proposes that although these basic functions remain consistent across the life span, one's place in the life cycle influences the salience and effectiveness of specific functions. Carstensen contends that over the life course there is a reduced likelihood that interaction with casual social partners will be rewarding, whereas interaction with a select group of significant others becomes increasingly more valuable.

In an empirical test of the model, Fredrickson and Carstensen (1990) studied the salience of information potential, potential for future contact, and affective rewards from social partners among adolescents, middle-aged people, and healthy and infirm elderly people. They found that adolescents placed the greatest emphasis on the potential for future contact and gathering information about social partners to know them better, whereas elderly people placed the greatest emphasis on the potential for positive rather than negative affect in social interactions. Results provide strong support for the socioemotional selectivity theory, which maintains that reductions in social contacts across the life span reflect increasing selectivity in one's choice of social partners. Although rates of interaction with acquaintances decline steadily from early adulthood on, interactions in significant relationships increase. The findings that interactions with a core group of social partners from whom people derive affective gains become more frequent, satisfying, and emotionally close over the adult life course, while interactions with more casual social contacts provide fewer affective rewards and become less satisfying and frequent support the socioemotional selectivity theory.

In a more recent study Lansford, Sherman, and Antonucci (1998) examined the socioemotional selectivity theory within and across three historical cohorts, from samples interviewed in 1957, 1976, and 1980. Data from three cohorts of national representative samples were analyzed to determine whether respondents' satisfaction with the size of their social networks differed by age, cohort, or both. Results support socioemotional selectivity theory, with more older adults than younger adults reporting feeling satisfied with the current size of their social networks rather than wanting larger networks.

Weiss's Theory of Social Provisions

R. Weiss (1974) developed an elegant theory about provision of support from kin and from nonkin. He maintains that individuals require six key social provisions in order to maintain well-being and to avoid loneliness. These provisions include those that are assistance-related (reliable alliance, guidance) and those that are non–assistance-related (social integration, reassurance or worth, nurturance, attachment). These components, provided by primary group relationships (characterized by closeness, warmth, and commitment), provide the total perceived support to people and supply distinctive benefits to them. People lacking each social provision experience negative effects. For example, a person lacking attachment would experience emotional isolation. Someone lacking so-cial integration would experience social isolation.

R. Weiss (1974) maintains that social relationships tend to become specialized in their provisions. As a result, individuals must maintain a number of different relationships in order to maintain psychological well-being. Some of these provisions typically are provided by family members, and others typi-cally are provided by friends. Reliable alliance or *instrumen-tal support* is most often provided by family members. Weiss states that instrumental support is often provided by family re-gardless of the level of mutual affection or whether one has reciprocated in the past. Guidance—especially important in times of stress—is provided by significant others who are seen as trustworthy and authoritative. Friendships offer provisions associated with a community of interest such as social inte-gration. Reassurance of worth is provided by relationships that support a person's competence in a social role, such as colleagues in the workplace or family members at home. Nur-turance is provided by a relationship in which an individual takes responsibility for the well-being of another. Attachment-providing relationships tend to be an exception where special-ization is concerned. The marital relationship is defined by its sense of attachment, yet attachment can also be provided by relationships with other family members or close friends.

R. Weiss's (1974) model holds that multiple needs must be satisfied by an individual's support network. Moreover, he contends that there is probably an element of almost every relational provision in each supportive relationship. Weiss's theoretical model has received substantial empirical support (Cutrona & Russell, 1987; Felton & Berry, 1992; Mancini & Simon, 1984).

CRITICAL QUESTIONS

Four critical questions have been the focus of scholars of adult social relationships. They are (a) *Do relationships with family and with friends have different effects on people,* (b) *Can social relationships have negative as well as positive effects on people,* (c) *Does the quantity or quality of social support best predict well-being,* and (d) *Can social relation-ships reduce the risk of functional decline and mortality?* Recent literature regarding the status of each question is sum-marized in the following discussions.

Do Relationships With Family and With Friends Have Different Effects on People?

Ties to both family and friends are important. Data consis-tently indicate that although family members are close and

intimate members of most elderly people's network, friends are named as the people with whom they enjoy spending time, engage in leisure activities, and have daily or frequent contact. The proportion of same-sex friends reported does not change across age groups from the teen years through old age. Although the absolute number of social relations is smaller in succeeding age groups, the role of friends remains important throughout life (Davis & Todd, 1985).

There are, however, different roles for family and friends. Friends are expected to provide companionship and short-term crisis intervention, whereas family members are ex-pected to provide more significant resources in areas such as financial matters, health, tasks of daily living, discussion of family problems when necessary, and long-term support for chronic needs (Cantor, 1979; Connidis & Davies, 1990).

Research for two decades has consistently found that friends are more important to the psychological well-being of adults than are family members (Adams & Blieszner, 1995; Antonucci & Akiyama, 1995; Lynch, 1998; Pinquart & Sorensen, 2000). At the same time, adults who have no fam-ily or who have poor relationships with family have much lower levels of general well-being than do others (M. G. Thompson & Heller, 1990).

Several explanations have been offered to explain this empirical finding. One explanation provided by Antonucci (1985) suggests that it is a function of obligatory versus optional relationships. Family relationships are obligatory; friend relationships are optional. Family should be available; thus, their absence is felt as a deficit. Friends do not have to be available; therefore, their presence is so much more a benefit. A second explanation is grounded in the fact that family relationships are ascribed, whereas relationships with friends are chosen. People cannot choose or substitute their parents, siblings, and children, even when these relationships are a constant source of stress. In contrast, people establish and maintain friendships by mutual choice based on a con-sensus of common experiences, interests, values, affection, and reciprocity. The feeling of being desirable elicited by friendship relations enhances well-being and builds self-esteem. A third explanation focuses on the extent to which relationships can be severed. Relationships with family members clearly are more difficult to sever; this—combined with the fact that people of all ages are more likely to report that family members get on their nerves than do friends (Antonucci & Akiyama, 1995)—may make relationships with friends more important to psychological well-being. Fourth, the effect may be a function of the fact that friends are typically members of the same age group and often share personal characteristics, cohort experiences, and lifestyles. Compared with younger family members, higher similarity in values and experiences may promote a higher satisfaction with friendship than with family relationships. Finally, Larson, Mannell, and Zuzanek (1986) suggest that relationships with friends are more likely than relationships with family members to be characterized by positive interactions. Friends are more often a source of enjoyment and socializing; as such, they are a more significant source of satisfaction. Family members, on the other hand, are more likely to be responsible for providing day-to-day physical and emotional assistance and to serve as sources of security and insulation against threats and losses. In this role, family relationships contribute to well-being within a global time frame, as a general state dependent on an individual's overall security and satisfaction. Friends, in contrast, primarily influence immediate well-being.

Can Social Relationships Have Negative as Well as Positive Effects on People?

Although a great deal of research has focused on the positive effects that social support can have on adults, recently researchers have urged greater attention to the negative side of informal social relationships. At issue has been the question of whether positive or negative social exchanges have a greater impact on older adults' health and well-being. Since Rook (1984) demonstrated that social relationships can adversely influence the psychological well-being of older adults, several investigators have examined the effects of both positive and negative social ties in later life (Ingersoll-Dayton, Morgan, & Antonucci, 1997; Okun & Keith, 1998). Rook (1990, 1994), reviewing this literature, concludes that negative and positive social exchanges are unrelated to one another, and that the detrimental effects of negative social exchange are more potent than are the beneficial effects of positive social exchanges. More recently Rook (1997) has shown that negative social exchanges are related to more life stress and less supportive networks. Her findings led her to conclude that both personal characteristics (such as daily mood and self-esteem) and life context (such as the experience of stressful life events) influence older people's vulnerability to negative social exchanges.

Recent results from research by Okun and Keith (1998) suggest that the picture may be more complicated. Among a sample of respondents aged 60–92 years old, they found that positive social exchanges with children cushioned the adverse effects of negative social exchanges with both one's spouse and other relatives and friends. Furthermore, when these older adults experienced negative social exchanges with children, positive social exchanges with other relatives and friends were especially helpful. An interesting result was

that this relationship was not found in a younger sample of respondents.

Does the Quantity or Quality of Social Support Best Predict Well-Being?

Most adults are entrenched in social relationships with people who are important to them. Although social isolation is rare, its effects are devastating in terms of poorer mental and physical health as well as increased likelihood of morbidity and mortality (Berkman & Syme, 1979; Chappell & Badger, 1989).

Extensive research has examined the importance of a single, close, personal relationship. The importance of a confidant as a buffer against decrements that include role loss and reduction of social interaction was first introduced by Lowenthal and Haven (1968). Availability of a confidant has been associated with higher morale and lower levels of loneliness and social isolation in old age (Wenger, Davies, & Shahtahmasebi, 1995). Having someone in whom one can confide seems to be equally important for men and women (Slater, 1995).

Older people who lack confidants report more psychological distress and higher rates of depression (Hays et al., 1998). There is no evidence that widowhood affects levels of confidant support (Dean, Matt, & Wood, 1992). In a study that controlled for health behaviors and other confounders (age, race, education, health conditions), Michael, Colditz, Coakley, and Kawachi (1999) identified elements of a woman's social network as significant predictors of her functional status. Strong predictors of high functioning among older women were having close friends and relatives and the presence of a confidant.

The existence of a special confidant is especially important to unmarried older people without close relatives, who rely on these relationships to satisfy the need for intimacy and emotional security (Gupta & Korte, 1994). Longitudinal research by Wenger and Jerrome (1999) revealed that although marital status and parenthood are important factors in the nature of the confidant relationship, over a 16-year period most older people changed confidants, usually as a result of increased dependency, disability, or death. Daughters are preferred over sons as confidants; sisters are preferred over brothers.

Research indicates that there are differences in the adult friendships of men and women. Women tend to have more intimate friendships than do men; men have a greater tendency to focus their friendships around activities (Antonucci, 1990). In addition, whereas women are more likely to have a female friend as a confidant, men are more likely to rely on their spouse as a confidant (Hess & Soldo, 1985). These gender differences are characteristic throughout the life course (P. H. Wright, 1989).

A great deal of research has examined the number of close ties that adults have. Wellman and Wortley (1989) found that adults have between four and seven close, supportive intimates. In their national sample of men and women over 50 years of age, Antonucci and Akiyama (1987) reported an average of 3.5 very close intimates and 3.5 close intimates. More recently, Antonucci, Akiyama, and Lansford (1998) report that the average number of close relationships named by men and women age 50 and older was 3.65. Women had significantly more close social relations than did men.

The relationship between the number of close ties and psychological well-being is complex. Antonucci et al. (1998) found that for women, the larger the number of close social relations, the less happy they reported being. For men no such association existed. These findings are consistent with Turner and Troll's (1994) caution that the effects on women of having more social ties may not always be positive.

The quality of social relations rather than the structural characteristics of these relations has the most significant effect on well-being (Antonucci & Jackson, 1987; Oxman, Berkman, Kasl, Freeman, & Barrett, 1992). People who are not satisfied with their social relations report higher levels of depressive symptomatology at all ages than do those who are satisfied. This is consistent with Carstensen's (1991) theory of optimization, suggesting that as people age, they are increasingly selective about the relationships in which they choose to invest.

Can Social Relationships Reduce the Risk of Functional Decline and Mortality?

Social relationships have been associated with a host of health outcomes in adults, including a lower risk of mortality, cardiovascular disease, cancer, and functional decline (Berkman, 1995; House, Landis, & Umberson, 1988). These benefits appear to persist into late life (Oxman et al., 1992; Seeman, 1996; Unger, McAvay, Bruce, Berkman, & Seeman, 1999). They have also been shown to improve survival and recovery following acute medical conditions (Berkman, Leo-Summers, & Horwitz, 1992; Glass, Matchar, Belyea & Feussner, 1993; Jenkins, Stanton, & Jono, 1994; Wilcox, Kasl, & Berkman, 1994). Recent research by Mendes de Leon et al. (1999) reveals that being embedded in social relationships reduces the risk of functional disability and enhances recovery from functional disability.

These protective effects of social relationships may result from several processes. They include provision of access to information about health and health care services (Bloom, 1990), encouragement of health behaviors (Bovbjerg et al., 1995; Mermelstein, Cohen, Lichtenstein, Kanmark, & Baer, 1986), provision of tangible aid (Thoits, 1995), provision of emotional support to facilitate coping with life stress (Thoits, 1995), enhancement of feelings of self-esteem and control (Krause & Borawski-Clark, 1994), and influences on neuroendocrine or immune functioning (Seeman et al., 1994; Uchino, Cacioppo, & Kiecolt-Glaser, 1996).

Consistent research indicates that widowhood has more harmful effects on cardiovascular morbidity and mortality for men than for women (Berkman et al., 1993; Seeman, 1996). In a recent study, Unger et al. (1999) found that social relationships had a stronger effect on functional status for men than for women. These investigators also found stronger protective effects of social relationships among respondents with lower levels of physical performance.

SOCIAL RELATIONSHIPS IN THE CONTEXT OF HEALTH

The section that follows presents state-of-the-art information about the social relationships of normal, healthy adults.

Spouse

Although the overwhelming majority of adults marry, significant changes during the past several decades characterize the patterns of marriage, divorce, widowhood, and remarriage. Cherlin and Furstenberg (1994) report that one third of adults can now expect to marry, divorce, and remarry during their lifetimes.

Married men and women have better psychological well-being than do their unmarried peers (Gove, Style, & Hughes, 1990; G. R. Lee, Seccombe, & Shehan, 1991). Research by Marks (1996) suggests that the pattern may in fact be more complex. She found that separated or divorced women, widowed women, and single men were significantly more distressed than were their married counterparts. However, women who had never married by midlife were not significantly different from married women on ratings of psychological distress. Although she concludes that being single at midlife appears to be more problematic for men than for women, she cautions that results are far from conclusive.

For decades cross-sectional research consistently indicated that marital satisfaction changed over the course of time, with satisfaction being high at the beginning of the marriage, lower during the child-raising years, and then high again after the children leave home (Orbuch, House, Mero, &

Webster, 1996). More recently, however, evidence seems to be mounting suggesting that marital satisfaction drops markedly over the first 10 years of marriage and then drops more gradually in the ensuing decades. Analyses by Glenn (1998), for example, fail to support the widespread belief that marriages tend to improve at midterm and that the later years of marriage are the golden ones. Rather, his findings strongly suggest that the differences in marital satisfaction between midterm and long-term marriages are largely a function of cohort differences.

The majority of older adults evaluate their marriages as happy or very happy, and marital adjustment seems to be stable over time in enduring relationships (Huyck, 1995). Levenson, Carstensen, and Gottman (1993) revealed that compared with middle-aged couples, older couples evidenced reduced potential for conflict and greater potential for pleasure. It remains unclear, however, whether this observed change is cohort-specific; due to divorce, which removes those who were unhappy at earlier ages; to the empty nest, which gives couples the opportunity to attend more closely to their relationships; or to characteristics that increase with marital duration, such as shared memories and knowledge of one another. Longitudinal research has shown that over time husbands report greater marital happiness and more affection than do wives (Field, Minkler, Falk, & Leino, 1993).

Much has been learned about marriages by studying those relationships that survive the test of time. One of the first studies of marriages lasting at least 50 years was conducted by Roberts (1979). He reports that significant elements in long-lasting marriages include independence, commitment, companionship, and qualities of caring. In a similar vein, Lauer, Lauer, and Kerr (1990) report that people in long-term marriages identified the following as important to their marriages: being married to someone they liked as a person and enjoyed being with; commitment to the spouse and to the institution of marriage; a sense of humor; and consensus on matters including aims and goals in life, friends, and decision making. Husbands and wives were similar in their views.

Goodman (1999a) reports that spouses in long-term marriages felt that intimacy and avoidance of hostile control were more important than autonomy. Goodman (1999b) also found that spouses in long-term marriages characterized by higher levels of reciprocity rated their marriages as most positive.

Retirement represents a major life transition that has the potential to affect the marriage. Although much of the current literature on retirement has been characterized by its almost exclusive focus on individuals, some recent research has begun to examine the ways in which marital relationships affect retirement as well as the effect that retirement has on marriage (Szinovacz & Ekerdt, 1995). Demographic changes in the past century have created a situation in which more people than ever before make the retirement transition as members of couples (Szinovacz, Ekerdt, & Vinick, 1992). A growing number of couples face the retirement of both spouses. Issues such as how couples time their labor force exits in relation to one another and how they anticipate and adapt to each other's retirement have gained the attention of researchers.

Retirement timing is affected by marital status, spouse's employment, and family obligations. Married men are more likely than are nonmarried men to be employed at all ages. Among women, however, nonmarried and divorced women tend to delay retirement. They are also more likely than are married women to report plans for postponed retirement or plans not to retire at all (Hatch & Thompson, 1992; Morgan, 1992). Married women frequently adjust their retirement to coincide with that of their husbands, thus retiring relatively early (Hurd, 1990). Some literature suggests that spouses time their retirement in relation to one another and tend to opt for joint retirement unless adverse circumstances preclude or render that option too costly (O'Rand, Henretta, & Krecker, 1992). There is some evidence that when a husband retires before his wife does, marital strain may occur (G. R. Lee & Shehan, 1989; Szinovacz, 1989).

Being married at retirement yields more positive retirement attitudes, higher retirement satisfaction, and better post-retirement adaptation than does being unmarried (Atchley, 1992; Seccombe & Lee, 1986). Social and emotional support from spouses is particularly important for married men (Szinovacz, 1992).

The relationship between retirement and division of household work has been well studied. Studies consistently find that retirement does not substantially alter the preretirement division of household work along traditional gender lines. Rather, partners remain responsible for their respective feminine and masculine tasks (Szinovacz, 1989). There is, however, research suggesting that some retired husbands participate more in household work after retirement than they did before retirement. For these couples, the division of labor becomes more egalitarian after retirement (Dorfman, 1992). An egalitarian division of labor seems to be gratifying to couples in retirement (Hill & Dorfman, 1982). Research by Keith and Schafer (1986, 1991) found that too much help from husbands may induce marital tensions. They found that the husband's presence in the wife's domain as well as his increased scrutiny of her housework performance can increase perceptions of conflict and disenchantment among both partners.

A growing body of research discourages the idea that retirement is a serious threat to marital quality (Atchley, 1992;

Szinovacz & Ekerdt, 1995). Rather, it seems that marital quality is stable across the retirement transition. Retirement does, however, have positive as well as negative affects on marriages. Positive changes brought about by retirement include increased freedom to develop joint endeavors, increased companionship, fewer time pressures, and a more relaxed atmosphere at home (Szinovacz & Ekerdt, 1995). Negative changes are evident predominantly from wives' complaints about husbands' being underfoot, a lack of privacy, and too much togetherness (Dorfman & Hill, 1986; Vinick & Ekerdt, 1991).

Parent-Adult Child

Ties between parents and their adult children have been the subject of study of Bengtson and his colleagues at the University of Southern California. Their longitudinal study, begun in 1971, of three-generation families led to the development of a theory of intergenerational family solidarity (Bengtson & Roberts, 1991). According to that theory, intergenerational solidarity is marked by six essential components. They are association or contact, affection or emotional closeness, consensus or agreement, function or instrumental support and source sharing, familism or normative obligations, and opportunity structures for family interaction. Empirical tests of the theory have demonstrated its usefulness for understanding the nature and quality of relationships between parents and adult children (Parrott & Bengtson, 1999; Whitbeck, Hoyt, & Huck, 1994) and the effects of family relationships on the well-being of older adults (Starrels, Ingersoll-Dayton, & Neal, 1995).

Because the lives of parents and their adult children are connected in significant ways for as long as both generations are alive, life-course transitions experienced by members of one generation can have consequences for members of the other generation. Kaufman and Uhlenberg (1998) report that parental divorce and declines in parents' health lead to deteriorating parent-child relationships. Similarly, problems in a child's marriage cause strain in parent-child relationships.

A good deal of research has sought to understand whether the relationships between parents and adult children are more important to the parents or to the children. The developmental stake hypothesis posited by Bengtson and Kuypers (1971) suggests that young adult children and their parents vary in their perception of generational relations based on their location within the family lineage and their developmental stage. Specifically, young adults need to perceive large differences in values and attitudes among family lineage members as they develop an identity separate from that of their parents. At the same time, middle-aged parents have a need to perceive closer ties with their adolescent and young adult children as they strive to achieve generativity and enjoy the fruits of their parenting efforts. Thus, according to the developmental stake hypothesis, members of the older generation should perceive less distance between the generations than do members of the younger generation. The developmental stake hypothesis has been supported by several studies of intergenerational ties (Lynott & Roberts, 1997) More recently, Giarrusso, Stallings, and Bengtson (1995) presented the term *intergenerational stake* to emphasize that the stake refers to relationships between generations. Their analysis of changing perceptions of affectual solidarity among middle-generation parents and their adult children support the concept of an intergenerational stake.

Relationships between parents and their adult children are marked by mutual reliance across the generations (Umberson, 1992). Both generations prefer to live apart from one another; when the generations do live together, however, there has been controversy regarding whether they do so more because of the parent's or the child's needs. Aquilino (1990) and Ward, Logan, and Spitze (1992) present data indicating that parental needs are irrelevant to coresidence and that it is characteristics of adult children that lead to these arrangements. Furthermore, Aquilino (1990) reports that when parents and adult children live together, they usually reside in the parent's rather than the child's home. G. R. Lee and Dwyer (1996), however, caution that these findings may be unique to young-old people and their adult children, while the picture is quite different for very old people. Their analysis, similar to findings by Crimmins and Ingegneri (1990), and Soldo, Wolfe, and Agree (1990), indicates that in addition to children's characteristics (marital status, employment status), the probability of coresiding with adult children is increased by parents' advanced age, failing health, and absence of a spouse.

The accomplishments of adult children have significant effects on the well-being of their parents. Research by Ryff, Schmutte, and Lee (1996) revealed that parents' well-being is linked to assessments of how their children have turned out, how the accomplishments of these children compare with those of their parents, and the extent to which the parents see themselves as responsible for their children. Parents felt better about themselves when they saw their children as doing well. However, parents who felt that their children were doing better than they themselves had done as young adults had lower levels of well-being. Parents who evaluated their children as less successful reported lower levels of responsibility and had the lowest levels of well-being.

Much has been written about filial responsibility. Early research by Seelbach (1984) investigated the extent to which older parents expected their children to assist them in times of need, live near or share a home with them, have contact with them, and provide various forms of emergency assistance. This research found that holding expectations of high filial responsibility was inversely related to morale of the older parents. An interesting analysis contrasting expectations for filial responsibility from the perspective of multiple generations of women by Brody, Johnsen, and Fulcomer (1984) revealed that although each successively younger generation expressed more egalitarian attitudes about the appropriateness of both sons' and daughters' providing parental care than the previous one, all respondents believed that children should be available to help parents when help is needed.

In the United States, parents and their adult children usually have frequent contact with one another (Troll, Miller, & Atchley, 1979), and even where geographic distance is considerable, they usually maintain contact (Dewit, Wister, & Burch, 1988). In addition to being in contact with one another, parents and their adult children are often involved in extensive exchange networks with one another (G. R. Lee & Ellithorpe, 1982). On the whole, older parents continue to provide support of various kinds to their adult children and are more likely to give help to than to receive help from their adult children (Riley & Foner, 1968) until forced by health declines to stop.

Siblings

The sibling bond occupies a unique position among family relationships. It has the potential to last longer than any other human relationship; it includes people who share a common genetic, cultural, and experiential heritage; and because it is an ascribed rather than an achieved role, it remains part of an individual's identity regardless of changes in marital status, place of residence, or financial well-being (Bedford, 1996a, 1996b; Cicirelli, 1995). Yet despite the sibling bond's centrality within an individual's life, research about adult sibling relationships has received little scholarly attention, especially when contrasted with the vast number of studies that have examined spouse and parent-child relationships (Campbell, Connidis, & Davies, 1999; Goetting, 1986).

Sibling relationships vary over the life course. After intense relations in childhood and adolescence, siblings tend to withdraw into families of procreation in adulthood, but come closer together again as their children leave home and their spouses die (Campbell et al., 1999; Goetting, 1986; T. R. Lee, Mancini, & Maxwell, 1990). Research regarding relationships among siblings during middle and old age varies in its conclusions about the strength of ties between siblings.

Most studies of the relationships between adult siblings indicate that these relationships are characterized by supportiveness, concern, and mutual affection (Cicirelli, 1995, 1996; Miner & Uhlenberg, 1997), yet these relationships are expressed differently from the way they were in early childhood (Cicirelli, 1988; Scott, 1990). In terms of exchange, some studies find that adult siblings exchange many services and have frequent contact (e.g., Wellman & Wortley, 1989), whereas other studies find evidence of limited support and contact (Avioli, 1989). When instrumental aid is exchanged between adult siblings, the situation is ordinarily temporary in duration, aid is received reluctantly, and it is accepted only if assistance from a spouse or adult child is not available (Avioli, 1989; Cicirelli, 1991). Both Cicirelli (1995) and Ross and Milgram (1982) found that the frequency of contact and kinds of involvement adult siblings have with one another are volitional and dependent on circumstances. Siblings stand ready to help one another in time of need and provide a sense of companionship and support when there is a crisis or serious family problem (Connidis, 1994).

Sibling support is especially important for unmarried adults, for older people, and for people experiencing short-term crises (Campbell et al., 1999; Connidis, 1989). Nonetheless, direct care by one sibling for another in middle or old age is the exception rather than the rule. Research indicates that most older people have at least one living sibling (Cicirelli, 1996) and that they see their siblings at least several times a year. Very few siblings actually lose contact with one another.

In general, adults express positive feelings about their sibling relationships, with gender (females higher than males) and race (African Americans higher than European Americans) affecting feelings of intimacy, congeniality, and loyalty (Bedford, 1995; Cicirelli, 1995; Miner & Uhlenberg, 1997). Relationships with sisters are particularly important in old age, whether it is a sister-sister or brother-sister relationship (Cicirelli, 1996).

Sibling rivalry is low throughout adulthood and old age. Rivalry is greatest between pairs of brothers and least between cross-sex siblings (Cicirelli, 1985). Research by Bedford (1992) suggests that the sibling relationship waxes and wanes depending on critical events, including marriage or divorce, changing interests, employment change, relocation, illness and death, behavior and achievement of children, and family arguments.

Friends

In contrast to most primary social relationships, those between friends are marked by their voluntary nature. Scholars have been interested in understanding how friendships are formed and maintained. They have also analyzed friendship networks (Blieszner & Adams, 1992). Adams and Blieszner (1994) presented an integrative conceptual framework for studying adult friendships. The framework posits that the social structural and psychological aspects of individual characteristics operate together to shape behavioral motifs, which in turn influence friendship patterns. However, very few empirical studies of adult friendships exist.

Research on friends has focused on describing the effects of various personal characteristics on friendship patterns. Fischer and Oliker (1983) found that middle-aged men tend to have a larger number of friends and middle-aged women tend to have friendships that are more intimate. Friendship patterns are likely to change as people make life-course transitions (Allan & Adams, 1989) or as they mature (Brown, 1991). L. Weiss and Lowenthal (1975) found that older adults—more than middle-aged or younger ones— tended to have complex, multidimensional friendships. Adult friendship networks tend to be homogeneous in terms of occupational status, ethnicity, age, marital status, income, education, gender, and religion (Fischer, 1982; Laumann, 1973).

SOCIAL RELATIONSHIPS IN THE CONTEXT OF ILLNESS AND DISABILITY

As indicated previously, social relationships between adults are marked by varying degrees of reciprocity and interdependence. When an adult suffers from illness or disability, the nature of most of the social relationships in which he or she is engaged changes dramatically. Although a vast literature has focused on the effects that illness and disability have on the mental health of caregivers (Schulz, O'Brien, Bookwala, & Fleissner, 1995), less attention has been paid to the effects that chronic illness and disability have on social relationships. The next section reviews what is known about relationships between spouses, parents and children, siblings, and friends in the context of illness and disability.

When a person becomes ill or disabled and requires assistance, this aid is generally provided by one primary caregiver. Shanas's (1979) observation that caregivers respond following a "principle of substitution" still rings true. The hierarchy of caregivers begins with a spouse. In the absence of a spouse, an adult daughter generally assumes the role of primary caregiver. Sons and daughters-in-law play significant roles when daughters and spouses are not available. Other family members and friends play the role of caregiver when alternatives are not available, although there is evidence

that the caregiving role becomes less intense as the caregiver becomes more removed from the care receiver.

There has been some discussion in the literature about how the quality of the relationship between caregiver and care recipient affects various outcomes. One of the few theoretical perspectives to examine the role that quality of relationship has on outcomes was posited by Lawrence, Tennstedt, and Assmann (1998). Their perspective suggested that quality of the relationship would play a significant role as mediator or moderator of the relationship between primary stressors and caregiver well-being. Empirically they found that relationship quality had a direct effect on outcomes, with higher levels of relationship quality related to lower levels of depression. The mediating and moderating roles of relationship quality were more modest. Relationship quality mediated the linkage between problem behaviors and role captivity, a finding that Lawrence et al. (1998) explain as due to problem behaviors' causing a decrease in relationship quality because of increased role captivity. Townsend and Franks (1995) found evidence that the quality of relationships between adult child caregivers and their elderly parents mediated the impact of the parents' impairment on the adult children's well-being.

Spouse

Chronic illness can affect marital status, marital satisfaction, marital quality, and marital interaction (Burman & Margolin, 1992) by shifting the core relationship. The literature examining a link between the onset of chronic illness and divorce is equivocal, with some studies finding that divorce is more prevalent among individuals with chronic illness, whereas others find that the divorce rates of persons with chronic illness do not differ from those in the general population (Revenson, 1994). Rolland (1994) has suggested that the onset of chronic illness forcefully challenges the emotional and physical boundaries of a couple's relationship. Maintaining emotional connection and knowing how to help one another and how to build the other's self-esteem are important processes in achieving good marital functioning in illness.

Litman (1979) posited that strong marriages become stronger and weak marriages deteriorate in the face of chronic illness. An alternative hypothesis is that close families become severely strained and less enmeshed relationships are better able to adapt to illness. Empirical studies suggest that although some couples report that their marriages become stronger during the course of illness (Fuller & Swensen, 1992), other couples become overwhelmed by the demands of the illness. Wallerstein and Blakeslee (1995) suggest that change of any kind has the potential to strengthen or weaken marriage depending on the transactional patterns developed to meet illness tasks or challenges.

Husbands and wives experience unique stresses as a result of living with a person who is chronically ill. Spouses occupy a dual role when one member has a chronic illness. They are the primary providers of support to the ill person and they are also the family members who need support as they cope with illness-related stressors. Revenson (1994) has suggested that some of the stresses emanate directly from caregiving—spouses are inextricably involved in decision-making about treatment and day-to-day care. Other stresses emerge from the need to restructure family roles and responsibilities as the disease progresses. Still other stresses are filtered through the lens of the individual's experience, as in the case of a spouse who feels helpless at seeing his or her partner in pain.

The chronic illness of a spouse can be particularly challenging when the concomitant role responsibilities lie outside of traditional gender roles. For example, when married women are afflicted with disabling illness such as rheumatoid arthritis or multiple sclerosis, husbands need to take on a greater share of household chores. Similarly, some wives of men whose employment is terminated by disability find that they need to work outside the home.

Spouses are the first line of defense when it comes to caregiving. They provide love and affection as well as tangible assistance with day-to-day responsibilities and special needs created by treatment regimens; validate the patient's emotions or coping choices; help their partners reappraise the meaning of the illness; and share the existential and practical concerns about how the illness may affect the marriage and family in the future. Frail older people who are cared for by spouses are likely to be more impaired and in greater need of long-term care than are those assisted by other informal caregivers (Hess & Soldo, 1985). Studies focusing on spouse caregivers reveal that although women do not necessarily provide more hours of care than do men, they tend to provide more intimate types of care, have more frequent contacts, and more often have to deal with disruptive and aggressive behaviors (L. K. Wright, Clipp, & George, 1993). When men do care for an impaired spouse, they are more likely to receive outside sources of assistance than when women provide care to an impaired spouse (Johnson & Catalano, 1983).

Spouses of individuals with chronic illness often experience depression and anxiety, marital communication difficulties, sleeping disorders, problems at work, and compromised immune system functioning (Coyne & Smith, 1991; Elliot, Trief, & Stein, 1986; Kiecolt-Glaser et al., 1987). Some research has found that spouses of ill persons experience even greater levels of distress than their partners do (Coyne,

Ellard, & Smith, 1990) and that this distress persists over time (Michela, 1987).

Because sexual intimacy is often important within the marital relationship, chronic illness has the potential to dramatically alter this relationship. Research across a number of different illness conditions has documented decreased sexual desire and activity, interference with sexual performance, and increased dissatisfaction with sexual functioning (Andersen, Anderson, & DeProsse, 1989).

Much of the research that has examined changes in the marital relationship in the context of disability has focused on people who are coping with cognitive impairment. These studies reported that significant declines in marital intimacy and quality were associated with the caregiving role (Blieszner & Shifflett, 1990; Morris, Morris, & Britton, 1988; L. K. Wright, 1991). Theories invoked to explain these changes include social exchange, equity theory, and role theory. Social exchange and equity theories suggest that persons who become caregivers will experience less marital happiness than will noncaregivers because of the inequities in benefits and costs associated with the caregiving role (Buunk & Hoorens, 1992). Role theory suggests that marriages coping with chronic illness and caregiving may "suffer a crisis because of the resulting challenge to the established role and myths that maintained the system" (S. C. Thompson & Pitts, 1991, p. 121). Russo and Vitaliano (1995) found that caregiver spouses reported significantly more changes in their marital relationship over time than did noncaregivers. Burman and Margolin (1992) found that spousal illness can affect marital quality and marital interaction. Townsend and Franks (1997) found that greater cognitive impairment of a spouse (but not greater functional impairment) was related to less emotional closeness between spouses. Booth and Johnson (1994) reported that health declines in a spouse were associated with declining marital happiness and with an increase in proneness to divorce.

Tower, Kasl, and Moritz (1997) contend that cognitive impairment can alter the marital relationship in a number of ways. Cognitive decline in a partner can result in changes in personality, mood regulation, behavior, memory, planning, reason, and judgment, all of which have the capacity to interfere with maintenance of empathic connections in close relationships. Cognitive decline can represent the loss of a resource, loss of emotional closeness, and change in the meaning of dependency. Tower et al. (1997) suggest that coping with the cognitive impairment of a spouse may be far more difficult when the couple is emotionally close than when a less intense relationship characterizes the couple. They posit that continuation of mutual closeness in the context of a spouse's severe impairment may represent a failure in adaptation. There is some evidence that close couples are more affected by changes in a spouse than are less close couples (Tower & Kasl, 1996). Tower et al. (1997) found that marital closeness moderated the impact of a wife's cognitive impairment, with husbands in close marriages affected more strongly than husbands in less close marriages. These effects were not found for wives.

The nature and intensity of distress experienced by spouses of persons with chronic illness may be linked to the particular challenges presented by a particular diagnosis (Revenson, 1994). The emotional turmoil experienced by spouses of cancer patients parallels the concerns expressed by patients, focusing on fears of recurrence and death (van der Does & Duyvis, 1989). Spouses of heart disease patients, concerned about a second—possibly fatal—infarction, walk a tightrope between being supportive and protective of their partner, yet not trying to be too controlling and solicitous, and minimizing or hiding their fears and concerns from their spouses (Coyne & Smith, 1991). Studies of patients with rheumatoid arthritis, a highly painful and disabling condition, but one with low life-threat, suggest that the greatest burden is in the areas of social and leisure activities, family activities, sex, and taking on additional household responsibilities as the patient becomes more disabled (Newman & Revenson, 1993).

Cannon and Cavanaugh (1998) describe the changes that ensue for couples when one member develops chronic obstructive pulmonary disease. They find that when illness alters system inputs and increases stress, interpersonal stress and tension may disorganize system functioning. As the patient experiences dyspnea, both partners may limit social activities in order to reduce demands on the patient. As a consequence, opportunities fostering support and self-worth are lost, and feelings of sadness, depression, and guilt can occur. Over time, demands on marital functioning spiral upward as physical functioning declines for the patient and support outside the marital dyad decreases. The physical changes may interfere with each spouse's perceptions and responses to the other's behaviors and expressed feelings, emotions, and thoughts. Over time the health of both spouses as well as their relationship may become jeopardized.

Marital functioning in chronic illness is altered by the increasing demands of illness-related tasks (Cannon & Cavanaugh, 1998). Corbin and Strauss (1984) describe the need for collaboration between partners in the concurrent management of their individual life trajectories and the chronic illness trajectory.

Little is known about how the marital relationship is altered when one member of the couple is dying and the end of the relationship is near. Research on cancer patients and their

spouses describes an increase in the expression of affection (Rait & Lederberg, 1989) and an increase in problems in the relationship caused by the stress of cancer (Knakal, 1988; Pederson & Valanis, 1988). Swensen and Fuller (1992) found that husbands and wives coping with cancer reported expressing more love to each other after the diagnosis of cancer and more love than did a comparison group not coping with a life-threatening health condition. There were no differences in marriage problems reported by the two groups of spouses. Cancer couples reported feeling less committed to one another after the diagnosis of cancer, suggesting that a process of anticipatory grief and "letting go" had begun.

Parent-Adult Child

In the absence of a spouse, an adult daughter usually assumes responsibility for caring for a disabled parent (Horowitz, 1985a). Although sons do participate in parent care, they typically become primary caregivers only when there is not an available female sibling (Horowitz, 1985b). Of the caregiving sons surveyed by Horowitz (1985b), 88% were either only children, had only male siblings, or were the only child geographically available. Moreover, when sons were identified as the primary caregiver, they were more likely than were daughters to rely on their spouses for additional support, less likely to provide as much overall assistance to their parents, and less likely to help with "hands-on" tasks such as bathing and dressing. Dwyer and Coward (1991), in a multivariate analysis, found that even after controlling for a variety of factors known to influence the relationship between gender and the provision of care to impaired elders (age, gender, and level of impairment of the elder; marital status, age, employment status, and proximity of the adult child), daughters were 3.22 times more likely than sons to provide assistance with activities of daily living (ADL) and 2.56 times more likely to provide assistance with instrumental activities of daily living (IADL).

Although the stereotypical model of help for elderly parents is that of one adult daughter who assumes the entire burden of providing help to elderly parents, there is evidence suggesting that in many families adult siblings share parent care responsibilities more equitably. Matthews and her colleagues (Matthews, Delaney, & Adamek, 1989; Matthews & Rosner, 1988) examined the helping behaviors of the entire sibling subsystem. Pairs of sisters in a two-child family tended to share responsibility for both tangible help and moral support to their parents, with an almost equal division when both sisters were employed. In larger families, sisters tended to provide regular, routine help to the parents or to help in a backup capacity, whereas help provided by brothers tended to be limited to a few areas of male expertise, to be sporadic, or to be nonexistent. Coward and Dwyer (1990) also found that brothers from mixed-gender sibling networks provided significantly less help to parents than did their sisters, but that brothers from single-gender siblings provided approximately as much help as did sisters from single-gender sibling relationships. Dwyer, Henretta, Coward, and Barton (1992) found that a given adult child's initiation or cessation of help to an impaired elderly parent was dependent on the helping behaviors of that child's siblings. Cicirelli (1992) reports that in about half the families he studied, all siblings coordinated their efforts in providing care to disabled parents. In about a fourth of the families there was partial coordination of efforts, and in the remaining fourth of the families each sibling helped with care as he or she wished, independently of the others.

Although the overwhelming majority of literature about the effects of disability on parent-child relationships has centered on situations in which the parent becomes ill, there is growing attention to understanding parent-child relationships of adult children with chronic disability. As parents of chronically disabled children enter old age, they face not only the health problems and social changes experienced by their age peers, but they also must confront the challenges associated with the needs of their aging child. As time passes, the situation ensues in which there is increased likelihood that the older adult child may require care from very old parents who themselves may require care. Because of differences in life expectancy between men and women—as well as the tendency for the current cohort of women to have assumed the primary role of lifelong caregiver—mothers of chronically disabled adult children are more likely than fathers are to find themselves in the role of primary caregiver.

The trend towards deinstitutionalization has resulted in parents—especially mothers—having long-term caregiving responsibilities for their severely disabled adult children suffering from developmental disability or from severe mental illness, including schizophrenia (Fujiura & Braddock, 1992; Lefley, 1987). Although the majority of empirical studies have focused on the effects that these caregiving relationships have on the caregiving parents (Greenberg, Seltzer, & Greenley, 1993; Pruchno, Patrick, & Burant, 1996), it is likely that relationship quality and reciprocity between parent and adult play important roles.

Siblings

Although people with disabilities and poor health generally do not turn to their siblings for support, among people who never married and those who are widowed, help from siblings often becomes the first line of defense (Johnson & Catalano, 1981). Gold (1989) reports that sisters both give and receive more help than do brothers. Gold also found that when people stopped providing assistance to their siblings, it was because their own health had declined.

Friends

Although friendships remain important to well-being into late life, certain concomitants of age—especially old age—have been shown to negatively affect friendship relationships. Poor health, especially when it involves functional limitations, has a negative impact on friendships (Allan & Adams, 1989; Mendes de Leon et al., 1999).

Little scholarly research has examined the conditions under which friends become caregivers, the extent to which they provide care, and for whom care is provided. Himes and Reidy (2000) suggest that the role of friends in caregiving is important from two perspectives. First, in some instances friends provide the bulk of care and are an important source of support. Although friends may constitute a small part of the national informal care network, for some individuals they may be a vital source of assistance (Cantor, 1979). Second, the role of friends may increase over time if families become unable or unwilling to provide the level of care needed by frail and disabled family members.

When illness strikes, friends are more likely to provide support when family support is not an option, when short-term assistance is needed, when the need for help is unpredictable, or when it is convenient. Cantor (1979) found that nonrelatives, both friends and neighbors, were a valuable source of care for those without family members. Unmarried older women rely more on their friends for both emotional and instrumental support than do their married peers (Roberto & Scott, 1984). Friends often provide emotional support to one another (Adams & Blieszner, 1989; Roberto, 1996). They generally provide only limited instrumental support, with the most common type of help being transportation (Roberto, 1996; Roberto & Scott, 1984). Furthermore, research indicates that friends help with transportation when they can do so conveniently, or in an emergency when no one else is available. They also help with home repairs, with shopping or errands, and with household tasks. Reinhardt (1996) documented the importance of friendship support independent of family support to people adapting to chronic visual impairment.

Using data from the National Survey of Families and Households, Himes and Reidy (2000) examined the roles that friends play in the provision of care. They found that among caregivers, women providing care to a friend are more likely to be age peers and less likely to be employed or married than were family caregivers. Friends were less likely than were family members to take on care responsibilities when those responsibilities conflicted with other roles. Additionally, when friends do provide care, they provide that care for shorter periods of time and for fewer hours.

LOSING SOCIAL RELATIONSHIPS

Much can be understood about the value of social relationships from research that has examined reactions to lost social relationships. Loss of a significant social relationship can affect the structure and dynamics of other relationships (Perkins, 1990). A death in the family, for example, may lead to increased closeness or strain in relationships among surviving family members.

Spouse

In the United States, the marital relationship can be terminated either by death or by divorce. With age, the likelihood of divorce decreases, whereas the likelihood of death of a spouse increases. However, women are more likely to experience divorce and less likely to experience widowhood today than they were 30 years ago.

In 1998, 19.4 million adults—representing 9.8% of the adult population—were divorced (Lugaila, 1998). Divorce is prevalent in the United States, with projections suggesting that almost half of all marriages will end in divorce (Cherlin, 1992; Furstenberg, 1990). Marital disruption is not randomly distributed. The risk of divorce in first marriages is far higher for younger couples than for those marrying after their early twenties (Furstenberg, 1990). Similarly, high-school dropouts have twice the rate of marital breakup as those with at least some college, and the rate of divorce is about 50% higher among African Americans than among European Americans (Castro-Martin & Bumpass, 1989). Second marriages have a higher risk of divorce than do first marriages (McCarthy, 1978).

A great deal of research has addressed the extent to which divorce is predictable. Gottman and Levenson (2000) contend that there are two periods critical to the survival of a marriage: the first 7 years of the marriage, during which half of all divorces occur (Cherlin, 1992); and at midlife, when people often have young teenage children. The set of variables that predicted early divorcing was different from the set that predicted later divorcing. Negative affect during conflict predicted early divorcing, but it did not predict later divorcing. In contrast, the lack of positive affect in events of the day

and conflict discussions predicted later divorcing but not early divorcing.

Research consistently indicates that people who are divorced experience lower levels of psychological well-being than do people who are married (Aseltine & Kessler, 1993; Davies, Avison, & McAlpine, 1997; Marks & Lambert, 1998). Wang and Amato (2000) found that adjustment to divorce was positively associated with income, dating someone steadily, remarriage, having favorable attitudes toward marital dissolution prior to divorce, and being the partner who initiated the divorce. Economically, divorce has more severe implications for women than for men (Furstenberg, 1990).

Divorce has been called a *transitional family status* because eventually nearly 75% of divorced men and 60% of divorced women reenter marriage (Spanier & Furstenberg, 1987). Men remarry more quickly than do women, in large measure due to the greater availability of marriage partners.

When a spouse dies, the survivor must not only adjust to the loss of a close relationship, but also manage the daily decisions and responsibilities that were once shared by both spouses (Wortman, Kessler, & Umberson, 1992). Consistent evidence indicates that widowhood is associated with reduced psychological health (Stroebe & Stroebe, 1987). Most research finds that within the first few months of bereavement, recently widowed people show worse mental health than do married controls (Gallagher-Thompson, Futterman, Farberow, Thompson, & Peterson, 1993; Lund, Caserta, & Dimond, 1993).

It is unclear, however, how long these effects last. Although longitudinal studies typically find that widowed and married people are similar to one another after a year or two (Gallagher-Thompson et al., 1993; Harlow, Goldberg, & Comstock, 1991; Lund et al., 1993; Mendes de Leon, Kasl, & Jacobs, 1994), cross-sectional studies typically find that widowed individuals score higher on depression scales than do married people even 4 years postdeath (Lehman, Wortman, & Williams, 1987; Zisook & Shuchter, 1986).

Using a prospective research design that contrasted the experiences of twins—one who experienced widowhood and one who did not—Lichtenstein, Gatz, Pedersen, Berg, and McClearn (1996) found that widowhood had both short-term and long-term effects on psychosocial health. They found that recently bereaved individuals of both sexes reported more loneliness and depressive symptoms and less satisfaction with life compared to their married twins. These twin control analyses also indicated that among women, the married twin experienced greater well-being than did her long-term bereaved twin, even after 5 years of widowhood. Results from this study show that long-term widowed individuals who have been bereaved an average of 17 years for women and 13 years for men still have lower psychosocial health than do married individuals. These investigators found that widowhood had no effects on self-rated health status.

All losses, however, are not equal. An interesting analysis by Carr et al. (2000) concludes that adjustment to widowhood is most difficult for those experiencing high levels of warmth and instrumental dependence and low levels of conflict in their marriages.

An issue that has been the subject of many studies is whether widowhood is more traumatic for men or for women. Widowhood is a more common experience among women than among men. Although some studies report no gender differences in the psychological consequences of widowhood (Faletti, Gibbs, Clark, Pruchno, & Berman, 1989; Lund, Caserta, & Dimond, 1989), others found widowed women to be more distressed than widowed men (L. W. Thompson, Gallagher, Cover, Galewski, & Peterson, 1989). Most studies, however, have found widowhood to have a more adverse effect on men than on women (G. R. Lee, DeMaris, Bavin, & Sullivan, 2001; Mendes de Leon, Kasl et al., 1994). G. R. Lee et al. (2001) explain that this effect is largely due to the comparatively low levels of depressive symptoms among married men. Although widowed men and women experience similar rates of depressive symptomatology, for men, marriage is such a strong barrier to the symptoms of depression that the end of marriage results in higher rates of depression.

Parent-Adult Child

One of the most common deaths faced by adults is the death of a parent. Demographers report that the death of a mother is most likely to occur when children are between the ages of 45 and 64 and that the death of a father is most likely to occur when children are between the ages of 35 and 54 (Winsborough, Bumpass, & Aquilino, 1991). Annually, approximately 5% of the U.S. population experiences this type of loss (Moss & Moss, 1983).

Researchers have examined the impact of death of a parent on their middle-aged children's emotions (Norris & Murrell, 1990; Scharlach, 1991). Scharlach (1991) found that adult children had a range of persistent emotional responses to their parent's death, including being upset, crying, having painful memories, experiencing loneliness, and being preoccupied with thoughts of their parent. Research by Douglas (1990–1991), Kowalski (1986), Robbins (1990), and Scharlach (1991) examined the extent to which death of a parent affects the sense of self experienced by their middle-aged children.

Another aspect of bereavement that has been examined is family relationships. Umberson (1995), studying a national sample, found that marital quality is negatively affected by the death of a parent. Compared with nonbereaved individuals, individuals who have recently experienced the death of a mother exhibit a greater decline in social support from their partner and an increase in their partner's negative behavior. Compared with nonbereaved individuals, individuals who have recently experienced the death of a father exhibit a greater increase in relationship strain and frequency of conflict, as well as a greater decline in relationship harmony; similar findings are reported by Douglas (1990–1991) and Guttman (1991). Rosenthal (1985) found that if the deceased parent had a central role in the family, that person's death caused a ripple effect in the same and younger generations. Fuller-Thomson (2000) reports that people who have experienced the death of at least one parent and those who have a parent in ill health are more likely to report that they do not get along well with a sibling.

A number of background characteristics of adult children and their parents have been associated with bereavement. Scharlach (1991) and Moss, Moss, Rubinstein, and Resch (1993) found that younger adult children were more affected by grief than were older adult children. Scharlach found that children with higher levels of income and education were more affected by a parent's death than were those with lower socioeconomic status. Moss, Resch, and Moss (1997) report that daughters expressed more emotional upset, somatic response, and continuing ties with their deceased parent than did sons, whereas sons reported more acceptance of their parent's death than did daughters.

Sibling

Adults generally have siblings throughout their lives. When an adult dies there is often a surviving sibling to grieve over the loss. Moss and Moss (1986, 1989) identified three intertwined themes experienced by adults who lose a sibling to death: impact on the personal meaning of death, threat to self, and shifts in family alignments. They contend that when a sibling dies, the survivor often experiences feelings of personal vulnerability to death. Because siblings are members of the same generation, sibling deaths—except among those who are extremely old—are perceived as "off time." The sense of vulnerability may be especially strong for the last surviving sibling. Death of a sibling has the potential to require a shift in the expectations and goals that the survivor has for him- or herself. It can also alter the unity of the family and realign family relationships. It can lead to a redistribution of roles and a shift in family expectations as family members renegotiate relationships with one another.

Friends

Death of a friend has received very little research attention. Sklar and Hartley (1990) used the term *hidden grief* to describe friends who silently grieve the death of close friends. They suggest that these forgotten mourners are at increased risk for complications of bereavement because they may experience the social and emotional transformations of bereavement while they are forced to suffer the lack of institutional outlets that act as supports for the transformations. The degree of grief and mourning that follow the death of a friend varies as a function of the age of the friends and the intensity and centrality of the friendship (Kemp, 1999).

NEXT STEPS

Although a great deal is known about social relationships between adults, scientists have only begun to scratch the surface regarding our understanding of these relationships and the effects that they can have. Conceptual thinking about social relationships has been anchored in descriptions of how social relationships change over time. The concept of a convoy of supportive people—some of whom change over time, others who remain stable, surrounding an individual as he or she ages—is compelling. That reduced rates of social interaction in later life are the result of a lifelong selection process by which people strategically use these convoys to maximize rewards and minimize risk suggests the active role that people take in making and breaking social relationships.

Relationships with close family members and with friends are different. They have different functions and different effects on people. Yet little is known about the processes through which these relationships affect psychological well-being. Future studies examining this issue are needed.

One of the striking conclusions about the current state of the art regarding social relationships in adulthood and aging is the extent to which there is consistency in findings across the empirical studies. Although on the one hand this similarity is reassuring, one wonders whether it represents a true picture of social relationships or whether it is a function of the homogeneity of people who have participated in the research. There has been very little attention to diversity in studies of social relationships in adulthood. As a result, it is unclear whether these findings can be generalized to people of different races, socioeconomic classes, and ethnic backgrounds. One very exciting area for future research is exploration of the extent to which these findings generalize to diverse populations.

One of the most compelling aspects of research about social relationships in adulthood and aging is that these relationships can have negative as well as positive effects on people. The tendency for too much support to be as detrimental as too little is intriguing and begs for further research. Questions such as *How much support is too much?* await future study. More research is needed to understand how negative social relationships develop, how people cope with them, and how they change over time.

Despite the overwhelming number of research studies that have examined social relationships in adulthood and aging, the current knowledge base is marked by its uneven understanding of these primary associations. Not surprisingly, relationships between spouses and those between parents and children have received the greatest attention. However, our understanding of the importance of sibling relationships and of relationships between friends is in its infancy. Questions about the role of lifelong friends and of relatively newfound friends abound, as do questions about the ways in which brothers and sisters affect the lives of one another. As research begins to unravel more about these relationships, it will be critical to do so with an understanding of the other significant social relationships in which individuals are entwined. The importance of friends and siblings for unmarried people has been hinted at. These relationships will be especially important to study in the future.

Certainly a great deal remains to be learned about the endings and loss of social relationships. Although much is known about the effects of divorce, death of a spouse, and death of a parent, little is known about the end of sibling and friend relationships.

Research about social relationships in health and research about these relationships in illness have developed relatively independently of one another. Yet, it is important to understand how relationships change as health changes. In order to better understand these transitions, prospective studies of social relationships are needed. By studying the social relationships of people who have illnesses that have different trajectories and different effects on patients, greater understanding of how illnesses create changes in social relationships will ensue.

Finally, it is interesting that although by definition, social relationships include multiple actors, the overwhelming majority of research about social relationships has relied on data collected from individuals. A more comprehensive understanding of social relationships in adulthood and aging requires that data be collected from multiple perspectives and analyzed from a group—rather than an individual—perspective. For example, a more complete picture of the effects of illness on the marital dyad would collect and analyze data from both the patient and the spouse, and greater understanding of parent-child relationships would derive from studies that collect and analyze data from both generations.

A number of unresolved issues remain regarding adult social relationships. Their significance to the psychological and physical well-being of individuals has been documented, but we have only begun to scratch the surface regarding our understanding of the processes by which these effects ensue. Whereas the focus of the previous several decades of research has been on identifying the importance of social relationships to individuals, the challenge for the next generation of research is to examine how these intricate associations develop and why they have such powerful and intricate effects.

REFERENCES

Adams, R. G., & Blieszner, R. (1989). *Perspectives on later life friendship.* Newbury, CA: Sage.

Adams, R. G., & Blieszner, R. (1994). An integrative conceptual framework for friendship research. *Journal of Social and Personal Relationships, 11,* 163–184.

Adams, R. G., & Blieszner, R. (1995). Aging well with friends and family. *American Behavioral Scientist, 39,* 209–224.

Allan, G., & Adams, R. G. (1989). Aging and the structure of friendship. In R. G. Adams & R. Blieszner (Eds.), *Older adult friendship: Structure and processes* (pp. 45–65). Newbury Park, CA: Sage.

Andersen, B. L., Anderson, B., & DeProsse, C. (1989). Controlled prospective longitudinal study of women with cancer I: Sexual functioning outcomes. *Journal of Consulting and Clinical Psychology, 57,* 683–691.

Antonucci, T. C. (1985). Personal characteristics, social support, and social behavior. In R. H. Binstock & E. Shanas (Eds.), *Handbook on aging and the social sciences* (2nd ed., pp. 94–128). New York: Van Nostrand Reinhold.

Antonucci, T. C. (1990). Social supports and social relationships. In R. H. Binstock & L. K. George (Eds.), *Handbook of aging and the social sciences* (3rd ed., pp. 205–227). San Diego, CA: Academic Press.

Antonucci, T. C., & Akiyama, H. (1987). Social networks in adult life and a preliminary examination of the convoy model. *Journal of Gerontology, 42,* 519–527.

Antonucci, T. C., & Akiyama, H. (1995). Convoys of social relations: Family and friendships within a lifespan context. In R. Blieszner & V. H. Bedford (Eds.), *Handbook of aging and the family* (pp. 355–371). Westport, CT: Greenwood Press.

Antonucci, T. C., Akiyama, H., & Lansford, J. E. (1998). Negative effects of close social relations. *Family Relations, 47,* 379–384.

Antonucci, T. C., & Jackson, J. S. (1987). Social support, interpersonal efficacy, and health. In L. L. Carstensen & B. A. Edelstein (Eds.), *Handbook of clinical gerontology* (pp. 291–311). New York: Pergamon Press.

Aquilino, W. S. (1990). The likelihood of parent-adult child coresidence: Effects of family structure and parental characteristics. *Journal of Marriage and the Family, 52,* 405–419.

Aseltine, R. H., & Kessler, R. C. (1993). Marital disruption and depression in a community sample. *Journal of Health and Social Behavior, 34,* 237–251.

Atchley, R. C. (1992). Retirement and marital satisfaction. In M. Szinovacz, D. J. Ekerdt, & B. H. Vinick (Eds.), *Families and retirement* (pp. 145–158). Newbury Park, CA: Sage.

Avioli, P. S. (1989). The social support functions of siblings in later life: A theoretical model. *American Behavioral Scientist, 33,* 45–57.

Bedford, V. H. (1992). Memories of parental favoritism and the quality of parent-child ties. *Journal of Gerontology: Social Sciences, 47,* S149–S155.

Bedford, V. H. (1995). Sibling relationships in middle and old age. In R. Blieszner & V. H. Bedford (Eds.), *Handbook of aging and the family* (pp. 201–222). Westport, CT: Greenwood Press.

Bedford, V. H. (1996a). Relationships between adult siblings. In A. E. Auhagen & M. von Salisch (Eds.), *The diversity of human relationships* (pp. 120–140). New York: Cambridge University Press.

Bedford, V. H. (1996b). Sibling interdependence in adulthood and old age. In T. Brubaker (Ed.), *Vision 2010: Families and aging* (pp. 18–19). Minneapolis, MN: National Conference on Family Relations Press.

Bengtson, V. L., & Kuypers, J. A. (1971). Generational difference and the developmental stake. *Aging and Human Development, 2,* 249–260.

Bengtson, V. L., & Roberts, R. E. L. (1991). Intergenerational solidarity in aging families: An example of formal theory construction. *Journal of Marriage and the Family, 53,* 856–870.

Berkman, L. F. (1995). The role of social relations in health promotion. *Psychosomatic Medicine, 57,* 245–254.

Berkman, L. F., Leo-Summers, L., & Horwitz, R. I. (1992). Emotional support and survival after myocardial infarction. *Annals of Internal Medicine, 117,* 1003–1009.

Berkman, L. F., Seeman, T. E., Albert, M., Blazer, D., Kahn, R., Mohs, R., Finch, C., Schneider, E., Cotman, C., & McClearn, G. (1993). High, usual and impaired functioning in community-dwelling older men and women: Findings from the MacArthur Foundation Research Network on Successful Aging. *Journal of Clinical Epidemiology, 46,* 1129–1140.

Berkman, L. F., & Syme, S. L. (1979). Social networks, host resistance, and mortality: A nine-year follow-up study of Alameda County residents. *American Journal of Epidemiology, 109,* 186–204.

Blieszner, R., & Adams, R. G. (1992). *Adult friendship.* Newbury Park, CA: Sage.

Blieszner, R., & Shifflett, P. A. (1990). The effects of Alzheimer's disease on close relationships between patients and caregivers. *Family Relations, 39,* 57–62.

Bloom, J. R. (1990). The relationship of social support and health. *Social Science & Medicine, 30,* 635–637.

Booth, A., & Johnson, D. R. (1994). Declining health and marital quality. *Journal of Marriage and the Family, 56,* 218–223.

Bovbjerg, V. E., McCann, B. S., Brief, D. J., Follette, W. C., Retzlaff, B. M., Dowdy, A. A., Walden, C. E., & Knopp, R. H. (1995). Spouse support and long-term adherence to lipid-lowering diets. *American Journal of Epidemiology, 141,* 451–460.

Brody, E., Johnsen, P. T., & Fulcomer, M. C. (1984). What should adult children do for elderly parents? Opinions and preferences of three generations of women. *Journal of Gerontology, 39,* 736–746.

Brown, B. B. (1991). A life-span approach to friendship choices. In H. Z. Lopata & D. R. Maines (Eds.), *Friendship in context* (pp. 23–50). Greenwich, CT: JAI Press.

Burman, B., & Margolin, G. (1992). Analysis of the association between marital relationships and health problems: An interactional perspective. *Psychological Bulletin, 112,* 39–63.

Buunk, B., & Hoorens, V. (1992). Social support and stress: The role of social comparison and social exchange processes. *British Journal of Clinical Psychology, 31,* 445–457.

Campbell, L. D., Connidis, I. A., & Davies, L. (1999). Sibling ties in later life: A social network analysis. *Journal of Family Issues, 20,* 114–148.

Cannon, C. A., & Cavanaugh, J. C. (1998). Chronic illness in the context of marriage: A systems perspective of stress and coping in chronic obstructive pulmonary disease. *Families, Systems and Health, 16,* 401–418.

Cantor, M. H. (1979). Neighbors and friends: An overlooked resource in the informal support system. *Research on Aging, 1,* 434–463.

Carr, D., House, J. S., Kessler, R. C., Nesse, R. M., Sonnega, J., & Wortman, C. (2000). Marital quality and psychological adjustment to widowhood among older adults: A longitudinal analysis. *Journal of Gerontology: Social Sciences, 55B,* S197–S207.

Carstensen, L. L. (1991). Socioemotional selectivity theory: Social activity in life-span context. *Annual Review of Gerontology and Geriatrics, 11,* 195–217.

Carstensen, L. L. (1992). Social and emotional patterns in adulthood: Support for socioemotional selectivity theory. *Psychology and Aging, 7,* 331–338.

Castro-Martin, T., & Bumpass, L. (1989). Recent trends and differentials in marital disruption. *Demography, 26,* 37–51.

Chappell, N. L., & Badger, M. (1989). Social isolation and well-being. *Journal of Gerontology: Social Sciences, 44,* S169–S176.

Cherlin, A. J., & Furstenberg, F. F., Jr. (1994). Stepfamilies in the United States: A reconsideration. *Annual Review of Sociology, 20,* 359–381.

Cherlin, A. J. (1992). *Marriage, divorce, remarriage.* Cambridge, MA: Harvard University Press.

Cicirelli, V. G. (1985). Sibling relationships throughout the life cycle. In L. L'Abate (Ed.), *The handbook of family psychology and therapy* (1st ed., pp. 177–214). Homewood, IL: Dorsey Press.

Cicirelli, V. G. (1988). Interpersonal relationships among elderly siblings: Implications for clinical practice. In M. D. Kahn & K. G. Lewis (Eds.), *Siblings in therapy* (pp. 435–456). New York: W.W. Norton.

Cicirelli, V. G. (1991). Sibling relationships in adulthood. *Marriage and Family Review, 16,* 291–310.

Cicirelli, V. G. (1992). *Family caregiving: Autonomous and paternalistic decision making.* Newbury, CA: Sage.

Cicirelli, V. G. (1995). *Sibling relationships across the life span.* New York: Plenum Press.

Cicirelli, V. G. (1996). Sibling relationships in middle and old age. In G. H. Brody (Ed.), *Sibling relationships: Their causes and consequences* (pp. 47–73). Norwood, NJ: Ablex.

Connidis, I. A. (1989). Siblings as friends in later life. *American Behavioral Scientist, 33,* 81–93.

Connidis, I. A. (1994). Sibling support in older age. *Journal of Gerontology: Social Sciences, 49,* S309–S317.

Connidis, I. A., & Davies, L. (1990). Confidants and companions in later life. *Journal of Gerontology: Social Sciences, 45,* S141–S149.

Corbin, J. M., & Strauss, A. L. (1984). Collaboration: Couples working together to manage chronic illness. *Image, 16,* 109–115.

Coward, R. T., & Dwyer, J. W. (1990). The association of gender, sibling network composition, and patterns of parent care by adult children. *Research on Aging, 12,* 158–181.

Coyne, J. C., Ellard, J. H., & Smith, D. A. F. (1990). Social support, interdependence, and the dilemmas of helping. In B. R. Sarason, I. G. Sarason, & G. R. Pierce (Eds.), *Social support: An interactional view* (pp. 129–149). New York: Wiley.

Coyne, J. C., & Smith, D. A. F. (1991). Couples coping with a myocardial infarction: A perspective on wives distress. *Journal of Personality and Social Psychology, 61,* 404–412.

Crimmins, E. M., & Ingegneri, D. G. (1990). Interaction and living arrangements of older parents and their children: Past trends, present determinants, future implications. *Research on Aging, 12,* 3–35.

Cutrona, C. E., & Russell, D. W. (1987). The provisions of social relationships and adaptation to stress. In W. H. Jones & D. Perlman (Eds.), *Advances in personal relationships* (Vol. 1, pp. 37–67). Greenwich, CT: JAI Press.

Davies, L., Avison, W. R., & McAlpine, D. D. (1997). Significant life experiences and depression among single and married mothers. *Journal of Marriage and the Family, 59,* 294–308.

Davis, K. E., & Todd, M. J. (1985). Assessing friendship: Prototypes, paradigm cases and relationship description. In S. Duck & D. Perlman (Eds.), *Understanding personal relationships* (pp. 17–37). London: Sage.

Dean, A., Matt, G. E., & Wood, P. (1992). The effects of widowhood on social support from significant others. *Journal of Community Psychology, 20,* 309–325.

Dewit, D. J., Wister, A. V., & Burch, T. K. (1988). Physical distance and social contact between elders and their adult children. *Research on Aging, 10,* 56–80.

Dorfman, L. T. (1992). Couples in retirement: Division of household work. In M. Szinovacz, D. J. Ekerdt, & B. H. Vinick (Eds.), *Families and retirement* (pp. 159–173). Newbury Park, CA: Sage.

Dorfman, L. T., & Hill, E. A. (1986). Rural housewives and retirement: Joint decision-making matters. *Family Relations, 35,* 507–514.

Douglas, J. D. (1990–1991). Patterns of change following parent death in midlife adults. *Omega, 22,* 123–137.

Dwyer, J. W., & Coward, R. T. (1991). A multivariate comparison of the involvement of adult sons versus daughters in the care of impaired parents. *Journal of Gerontology, 46,* S259–S269.

Dwyer, J. W., Henretta, J. C., Coward, R. T., & Barton, A. J. (1992). Changes in the helping behaviors of adult children as caregivers. *Research on Aging, 14,* 351–375.

Elliot, D. J., Trief, P. M., & Stein, N. (1986). Mastery, stress, and coping in marriage among chronic pain patients. *Journal of Behavioral Medicine, 9,* 549–558.

Faletti, M. V., Gibbs, J. H., Clark, M. C., Pruchno, R. A., & Berman, E. A. (1989). Longitudinal course of bereavement in older adults. In D. A. Lund (Ed.), *Older bereaved spouses: Research with practical applications* (pp. 37–51). New York: Hemisphere.

Felton, B. J., & Berry, C. A. (1992). Do the sources of the urban elderly's social support determine its psychological consequences? *Psychology and Aging, 7,* 89–97.

Field, D., Minkler, M., Falk, R. F., & Leino, E. V. (1993). The influence of health on family contacts and family feelings in advanced old age: A longitudinal study. *Journal of Gerontology: Psychological Sciences, 48,* P18–P28.

Fischer, C. S. (1982). *To dwell among friends.* Chicago: University of Chicago Press.

Fischer, C. S., & Oliker, S. J. (1983). A research note on friendship, gender, and the life cycle. *Social Forces, 62,* 124–133.

Frederickson, B. L., & Carstensen, L. L. (1990). Choosing social partners: How old age and anticipated endings make people more selective. *Psychology and Aging, 5,* 163–171.

Fujiura, G. T., & Braddock, D. (1992). Fiscal and demographic trends in mental retardation services: The emergence of the family. In L. Rowitz (Ed.), *Mental retardation in the year 2000* (pp. 203–217). New York: Springer.

Fuller, S., & Swensen, C. H. (1992). Marital quality and quality of life among cancer patients and their spouses. *Journal of Psychosocial Oncology, 10,* 41–56.

Fuller-Thomson, E. (2000). Loss of kin-keeper? Sibling conflict following parental death. *Omega, 40,* 547–559.

Furstenberg, F. F. (1990). Divorce and the American family. *Annual Review of Sociology, 16,* 379–403.

Gallagher-Thompson, D., Futterman, A., Farberow, N., Thompson, L. W., & Peterson, J. (1993). The impact of spousal bereavement on older widows and widowers. In M. S. Stroebe, W. Stroebe, & R. O. Hansson (Eds.), *Handbook of bereavement: Theory, research, and intervention* (pp. 227–239). New York: Cambridge University Press.

Giarrusso, R., Stallings, M., & Bengtson, V. L. (1995). The "Intergenerational Stake" hypothesis revisited. In V. L. Bengtson, K. W. Schaie, & L. M. Burton (Eds.), *Adult intergenerational relations* (pp. 227–263). New York: Springer.

Glass, T. A., Matchar, D. B., Belyea, M., & Feussner, J. R. (1993). Impact of social support on outcome in first stroke. *Stroke, 24,* 64–70.

Glenn, N. D. (1998). The course of marital success and failure in five American 10-year marriage cohorts. *Journal of Marriage and the Family, 60,* 569–576.

Goetting, A. (1986). The developmental tasks of siblingship over the life cycle. *Journal of Marriage and the Family, 48,* 703–714.

Gold, D. T. (1989). Generational solidarity: Conceptual antecedents and consequences. *American Behavioral Scientist, 33,* 19–32.

Goodman, C. C. (1999a). Intimacy and autonomy in long term marriage. *Journal of Gerontological Social Work, 32,* 83–97.

Goodman, C. C. (1999b). Reciprocity of social support in long-term marriage. *Journal of Mental Health & Aging, 5,* 341–357.

Gottman, J. M., & Levenson, R. W. (2000). The timing of divorce: Predicting when a couple will divorce over a 14-year period. *Journal of Marriage and the Family, 62,* 737–745.

Gove, W. R., Style, C. B., & Hughes, M. (1990). The effect of marriage on the well-being of adults. *Journal of Family Issues, 11,* 4–35.

Greenberg, J. S., Seltzer, M. M., & Greenley, J. R. (1993). Aging parents of adults with disabilities: The gratifications and frustrations of later-life caregiving. *Gerontologist, 33,* 542–550.

Gupta, V., & Korte, C. (1994). The effects of a confidant and a peer group on the well-being of single elders. *International Journal of Aging and Human Development, 39,* 293–302.

Guttman, H. A. (1991). Parental death as a precipitant of marital conflict. *Journal of Marital and Family Therapy, 17,* 81–87.

Harlow, S. D., Goldberg, E. L., & Comstock, G. W. (1991). A longitudinal study of the prevalence of depressive symptomatology in elderly widowed and married women. *Archives of General Psychiatry, 48,* 1065–1068.

Hatch, L. R., & Thompson, A. (1992). Family responsibilities and women's retirement. In M. Szinovacz, D. J. Ekerdt, & B. H. Vinick (Eds.), *Families and retirement* (pp. 99–113). Newbury Park, CA: Sage.

Hays, J. C., Landerman, L. R., George, L. K., Flint, E. P., Koenig, H. G., Land, K. C., & Blazer, D. G. (1998). Social correlates of the dimensions of depression in the elderly. *Journal of Gerontology: Psychological Sciences, 53B,* P31–P39.

Hess, B., & Soldo, B. J. (1985). Husband and wife networks. In W. J. Sauer & R. T. Coward (Eds.), *Social support networks and the care of the elderly: Theory, research, and practice* (pp. 67–92). New York: Springer.

Hill, E. A., & Dorfman, L. T. (1982). Reactions of housewives to the retirement of their husbands. *Family Relations, 31,* 195–200.

Himes, C. L., & Reidy, E. B. (2000). The role of friends in caregiving. *Research on Aging, 22,* 315–336.

Horowitz, A. (1985a). Family caregiving to the frail elderly. In C. Eisdorfer (Ed.), *Annual review of gerontology and geriatrics* (Vol. 5, pp. 194–246). New York: Springer.

Horowitz, A. (1985b). Sons and daughters as caregivers to older parents: Differences in role performance and consequences. *Gerontologist, 25,* 612–617.

House, J. S., Landis, K. R., & Umberson, D. (1988). Social relationships and health. *Science, 241,* 540–544.

Hurd, M. D. (1990). The joint retirement decision of husbands and wives. In D. A. Wise (Ed.), *Issues in the economics of aging* (pp. 231–258). Chicago: University of Chicago Press.

Huyck, M. H. (1995). Marriage and close relationships of the marital kind. In R. Blieszner & V. H. Bedford (Eds.), *Handbook of aging and the family* (pp. 181–200). Westport, CT: Greenwood Press.

Ingersoll-Dayton, B., Morgan, D., & Antonucci, T. (1997). The effects of positive and negative social exchanges on aging adults. *Journal of Gerontology: Social Sciences, 52B,* S190–S199.

Jenkins, C. D., Stanton, B. A., & Jono, R. T. (1994). Quantifying and predicting recovery after heart surgery. *Psychosomatic Medicine, 56,* 203–212.

Johnson, C. L., & Catalano, D. J. (1981). Childless elderly and their family supports. *Gerontologist, 21,* 610–618.

Johnson, C. L., & Catalano, D. J. (1983). A longitudinal study of family supports to impaired elderly. *Gerontologist, 23,* 612–618.

Kahn, R. L., & Antonucci, T. C. (1980). Convoys over the life course. In P. B. Baltes & O. Brim (Eds.), *Life span development and behavior* (Vol. 3, pp. 254–286). New York: Academic Press.

Kaufman, G., & Uhlenberg, P. (1998). Effects of life course transitions on the quality of relationships between adult children and their parents. *Journal of Marriage and the Family, 60,* 924–938.

Keith, P. M., & Schafer, R. B. (1986). Housework, disagreement, and depression among younger and older couples. *American Behavioral Scientist, 29,* 405–422.

Keith, P. M., & Schafer, R. B. (1991). *Relationships and well-being over the life stages.* New York: Praeger.

Kemp, H. V. (1999). Grieving the death of a sibling or the death of a friend. *Journal of Psychology and Christianity, 18,* 354–366.

Kiecolt-Glaser, J. K., Glaser, R., Shuttleworth, E., Dyer, C., Ogrocki, P., & Speicher, C. (1987). Chronic stress and immunity in family caregivers of Alzheimer's disease victims. *Psychosomatic Medicine, 49,* 523–535.

Knakal, J. (1988). A couples group in oncology social work practice: An innovative modality. *Dynamic Psychotherapy, 6,* 153–156.

Kowalski, N. C. (1986). Anticipating the death of an elderly parent. In T. A. Rando (Ed.), *Loss and anticipatory grief* (pp. 187–199). Lexington, MA: Lexington Books.

Krause, N., & Borawski-Clark, E. (1994). Clarifying the functions of social support in later life. *Research on Aging, 16,* 251–279.

Lansford, J. E., Sherman, A. M., & Antonucci, T. C. (1998). Satisfaction with social networks: An examination of socioemotional selectivity theory across cohorts. *Psychology and Aging, 13,* 544–552.

Larson, R., Mannell, R., & Zuzanek, J. (1986). Daily well-being of older adults with friends and family. *Psychology and Aging, 1,* 117–126.

Lauer, R. H., Lauer, J. C., & Kerr, S. T. (1990). The long-term marriage: Perceptions of stability and satisfaction. *International Journal on Aging and Human Development, 31,* 189–195.

Laumann, E. O. (1973). *Bonds of pluralism: The form and substance of urban social networks.* New York: Wiley.

Lawrence, R. H., Tennstedt, S. L., & Assmann, S. F. (1998). Quality of the caregiver-care recipient relationship: Does it offset negative consequences of caregiving for family caregivers? *Psychology and Aging, 13,* 150–158.

Lee, G. R., DeMaris, A., Bavin, S., & Sullivan, R. (2001). Gender differences in the depressive effect of widowhood in later life. *Journal of Gerontology: Social Sciences, 56B,* S56–S62.

Lee, G. R., & Dwyer, J. W. (1996). Aging parent-adult child coresidence. *Journal of Family Issues, 17,* 46–59.

Lee, G. R., & Ellithorpe, E. (1982). Intergenerational exchange and subjective well-being among the elderly. *Journal of Marriage and the Family, 44,* 217–224.

Lee, G. R., Seccombe, K., & Shehan, C. (1991). Marital status and personal happiness: An analysis of trend data. *Journal of Marriage and the Family, 53,* 839–844.

Lee, G. R., & Shehan, C. L. (1989). Retirement and marital satisfaction. *Journal of Gerontology: Social Sciences, 44,* S226–S230.

Lee, T. R., Mancini, J. A., & Maxwell, J. W. (1990). Sibling relationships in adulthood: Contact patterns and motivations. *Journal of Marriage and the Family, 52,* 431–440.

Lefley, H. P. (1987). Aging parents as caregivers of mentally ill adult children: An emerging social problem. *Hospital and Community Psychiatry, 38,* 1063–1070.

Lehman, D. R., Wortman, C. B., & Williams, A. F. (1987). Long-term effects of losing a spouse or child in a motor vehicle crash. *Journal of Personality and Social Psychology, 52,* 218–231.

Levenson, R. W., Carstensen, L. L., & Gottman, J. M. (1993). Long-term marriage: Age, gender, and satisfaction. *Psychology and Aging, 8,* 301–313.

Lichtenstein, P., Gatz, M., Pedersen, N. L., Berg, S., & McClearn, G. E. (1996). A co-twin-control study of response to widowhood. *Journal of Gerontology: Psychological Sciences, 51B,* P279–P289.

Litman, T. J. (1979). The family in health and health care: A sociobehavioral overview. In E. G. Jaco (Ed.), *Patients, physicians, and illness* (pp. 69–101). New York: Free Press.

Lowenthal, M. F., & Haven, C. (1968). Interaction and adaptation: Intimacy as a critical variable. *American Sociological Review, 33,* 20–30.

Lugaila, T. (1998). *Marital status and living arrangements: March 1998 (Update).* Washington, DC: U.S. Bureau of the Census.

Lund, D. A., Caserta, M. S., & Dimond, M. F. (1989). Impact of spousal bereavement on the subjective well-being of older adults. In D. A. Lund (Ed.), *Older bereaved spouses: Research with practical applications* (pp. 3–15). New York: Hemisphere.

Lund, D. A., Caserta, M. S., & Dimond, M. F. (1993). The course of spousal bereavement in later life. In M. S. Stroebe, W. Stroebe, & R. O. Hanssen (Eds.), *Handbook of bereavement: Theory, research, and intervention* (pp. 240–254). New York: Cambridge University Press.

Lynch, S. A. (1998). Who supports whom? How age and gender affect the perceived quality of support from family and friends. *Gerontologist, 38,* 231–238.

Lynott, P. P., & Roberts, R. E. L. (1997). The developmental stake hypothesis and changing perceptions of intergenerational relations, 1971–1985. *Gerontologist, 37,* 394–405.

Mancini, J. A., & Simon, J. (1984). Older adults expectations of support from family and friends. *Journal of Applied Gerontology, 3,* 150–160.

Marks, N. F. (1996). Flying solo at midlife: Gender, marital status, and psychological well-being. *Journal of Marriage and the Family, 58,* 917–932.

Marks, N. F., & Lambert, J. D. (1998). Marital status continuity and change among young and midlife adults. *Journal of Family Issues, 19,* 652–686.

Matthews, S. H., Delaney, P. J., & Adamek, M. E. (1989). Male kinship ties: Bonds between adult brothers. *American Behavioral Scientist, 33,* 58–69.

Matthews, S. H., & Rosner, T. T. (1988). Shared filial responsibility: The family as the primary caregiver. *Journal of Marriage and the Family, 50,* 185–195.

McCarthy, J. F. (1978). A comparison of the probability of dissolution of the first and second marriages. *Demography, 15,* 345–359.

Mendes de Leon, C. F., Glass, T. A., Beckett, L. A., Seeman, T. E., Evans, D. A., & Berkman, L. F. (1999). Social networks and disability transitions across eight intervals of yearly data in the New Haven EPESE. *Journal of Gerontology: Social Sciences, 54B,* S162–S172.

Mendes de Leon, C. F., Kasl, S. V., & Jacobs, S. (1994). A prospective study of widowhood and changes in symptoms of depression in a community sample of the elderly. *Psychological Medicine, 24,* 613–624.

Mermelstein, R., Cohen, S., Lichtenstein, E., Kanmark, T., & Baer, J. S. (1986). Social support and smoking cessation and maintenance. *Journal of Consulting and Clinical Psychology, 54,* 447–453.

Michael, Y. L., Colditz, G. A., Coakley, E., & Kawachi, I. (1999). Health behaviors, social networks, and healthy aging: Cross-sectional evidence from the Nurses' Health Study. *Quality of Life Research, 8,* 711–722.

Michela, J. L. (1987). Interpersonal and individual impacts of a husband's heart attack. In A. Baum & J. E. Singer (Eds.), *Handbook on psychology and health* (Vol. 5, pp. 255–301). Hillsdale, NJ: Erlbaum.

Miner, S., & Uhlenberg, P. (1997). Intragenerational proximity and the social role of sibling neighbors after midlife. *Family Relations, 46,* 145–153.

Morgan, L. A. (1992). Marital status and retirement plans: Do widowhood and divorce make a difference? In M. Szinovacz, D. J. Ekerdt, & B. H. Vinick (Eds.), *Families and retirement* (pp. 114–126). Newbury Park, CA: Sage.

Morris, L. W., Morris, R. G., & Britton, P. G. (1988). The relationship between marital intimacy, perceived strain, and depression in spouse caregivers of dementia sufferers. *British Journal of Medical Psychology, 61,* 231–236.

Moss, M. S., & Moss, S. Z. (1983). The impact of parental death on middle aged children. *Omega Journal of Death and Dying, 14,* 65–75.

Moss, M. S., & Moss, S. Z. (1986). Death of an adult sibling. *International Journal of Family Psychiatry, 7,* 397–418.

Moss, M. S., & Moss, S. Z. (1989). Death of an elderly sibling. *American Behavioral Scientist, 33,* 94–106.

Moss, M. S., Moss, S. Z., Rubinstein, R., & Resch, N. (1993). Impact of elderly mother's death on middle age daughters. *International Journal on Aging and Human Development, 37,* 1–22.

Moss, M. S., Resch, N., & Moss, S. Z. (1997). The role of gender in middle-age children's responses to parent death. *Omega, 35,* 43–65.

Newman, S., & Revenson, T. A. (1993). Coping with rheumatoid arthritis. In S. Newman & M. Shipley (Eds.), *Balliere's clinical rheumatology: Vol. 7. Psychological aspects of rheumatic disease* (pp. 259–280). London: Bailliere Tindal.

Norris, F. H., & Murrell, S. A. (1990). Social support, life events and stress as modifiers of adjustment to bereavement by older adults. *Psychology and Aging, 5,* 429–436.

Okun, M. A., & Keith, V. M. (1998). Effects of positive and negative social exchanges with various sources on depressive symptoms in younger and older adults. *Journal of Gerontology: Psychological Sciences, 53B,* P4–P20.

O'Rand, A. M., Henretta, J. C., & Krecker, M. L. (1992). Family pathways to retirement. In M. Szinovacz, D. J. Ekerdt, & B. H. Vinick (Eds.), *Families and retirement* (pp. 81–98). Newbury Park, CA: Sage.

Orbuch, T. L., House, J. S., Mero, R. P., & Webster, P. S. (1996). Marital quality over the life course. *Social Psychology Quarterly, 59,* 162–171.

Oxman, T. C., Berkman, L. F., Kasl, S., Freeman, D. H., & Barrett, J. (1992). Social support and depressive symptoms in the elderly. *American Journal of Epidemiology, 135,* 356–368.

Parrott, T. M., & Bengtson, V. L. (1999). The effects of earlier intergenerational affection, normative expectations, and family conflict on contemporary exchanges of help and support. *Research on Aging, 21,* 73–105.

Pederson, L. M., & Valanis, B. G. (1988). The effects of breast cancer on the family: A review of the literature. *Journal of Psychosocial Oncology, 6,* 95–118.

Perkins, H. W. (1990). Familial bereavement and health in adult life course perspective. *Journal of Marriage and the Family, 52,* 233–241.

Pinquart, M., & Sorensen, S. (2000). Influences of socioeconomic status, social network, and competence on subjective well-being in later life: A meta-analysis. *Psychology and Aging, 15,* 187–224.

Pruchno, R. A., Patrick, J. M. H., & Burant, C. J. (1996). Mental health of aging women with children who are chronically disabled: Examination of a two-factor model. *Journal of Gerontology: Social Sciences, 51B,* S284–S296.

Rait, D., & Lederberg, M. (1989). The family of the cancer patient. In J. C. Holland & H. Rowland (Eds.), *Handbook of psychooncology* (pp. 585–597). New York: Oxford University Press.

Reinhardt, J. P. (1996). The importance of friendship and family support in adaptation to chronic vision impairment. *Journal of Gerontology: Psychological Sciences, 51B,* P268–P278.

Revenson, T. A. (1994). Social support and marital coping with chronic illness. *Annals of Behavioral Medicine, 16,* 122–130.

Riley, M. W., & Foner, A. (1968). *Aging and society: An inventory of research findings* (Vol. 1). New York: Russell Sage.

Robbins, M. A. (1990). *Midlife women and death of mother.* New York: Peter Lang.

Roberto, K. A. (1996). Friendships between older women: Interactions and reactions. *Journal of Women and Aging, 8,* 55–73.

Roberto, K. A., & Scott, J. P. (1984). Friendship patterns among older women. *Journal of Aging and Human Development, 19,* 1–10.

Roberts, W. L. (1979). Significant elements in the relationship of long-married couples. *International Journal of Aging and Human Development, 10,* 265–271.

Rolland, J. S. (1994). In sickness and in health: The impact of illness on couples' relationships. *Journal of Marital and Family Therapy, 20,* 327–347.

Rook, K. S. (1984). The negative side of social interaction: Impact on psychological well-being. *Journal of Personality and Social Psychology, 46,* 1097–1108.

Rook, K. S. (1990). Stressful aspects of older adults' social relationships: Current theory and research. In M. A. P. Stephens, J. H. Crowther, S. E. Hobfoll, & D. L. Tennenbaum (Eds.), *Stress and coping in later life* (pp. 173–192). Washington, DC: Hemisphere.

Rook, K. S. (1994). Assessing the health-related dimensions of older adults' social relationships. In M. P. Lawton & J. A. Teresi (Eds.), *Annual review of gerontology and geriatrics* (pp. 142–181). New York: Springer.

Rook, K. S. (1997). Positive and negative social exchanges: Weighing their effects in later life. *Journal of Gerontology: Social Sciences, 52,* S167–S169.

Rosenthal, C. J. (1985). Kinkeeping in the familial division of labor. *Journal of Marriage and the Family, 47,* 965–974.

Ross, H. R., & Milgram, J. I. (1982). Important variables in adult sibling relationships: A qualitative study. In M. E. Lamb & B. Sutton-Smith (Eds.), *Sibling relationships: Their nature and significance across the lifespan* (pp. 225–250). Hillsdale, NJ: Erlbaum.

Russo, J., & Vitaliano, P. P. (1995). Life events as correlates of burden in spouse caregivers of persons with Alzheimer's disease. *Experimental Aging Research, 21,* 273–294.

Ryff, C. D., Schmutte, P. S., & Lee, Y. H. (1996). How children turn out: Implications for parental self-evaluation. In C. D. Ryff & M. M. Seltzer (Eds.), *The parental experience in midlife* (pp. 383–422). Chicago: University of Chicago Press.

Scharlach, A. E. (1991). Factors associated with filial grief following the death of an elderly parent. *American Journal of Orthopsychiatry, 61,* 307–313.

Schulz, R., O'Brien, A. T., Bookwala, J., & Fleissner, K. (1995). Psychiatric and physical morbidity effects of dementia caregiving: Prevalence, correlates, and causes. *Gerontologist, 35,* 771–791.

Scott, J. P. (1990). Sibling interaction in later life. In T. H. Brubaker (Ed.), *Family relationships in later life* (2nd ed., pp. 86–89). Beverly Hills, CA: Sage.

Seccombe, K., & Lee, G. R. (1986). Gender differences in retirement satisfaction and its antecedents. *Research on Aging, 8,* 426–440.

Seelbach, W. C. (1984). Filial responsibility and the care of aging family members. In W. H. Quinn & G. A. Hughston (Eds.), *Independent aging: Family and social system perspectives* (pp. 92–109). Rockville, MD: Aspen.

Seeman, T. E. (1996). Social ties and health. *Annals of Epidemiology, 6,* 442–451.

Seeman, T. E., Charpentier, P. A., Berkman, L. F., Tinetti, M. E., Guralnik, J. M., Albert, M., Blazer, D., & Rowe, J. W. (1994). Predicting changes in physical performance in a high-functioning elderly cohort: MacArthur Studies of Successful Aging. *Journal of Gerontology: Medical Sciences, 49,* M97–M108.

Shanas, E. (1979). The family as a social support system in old age. *Gerontologist, 19,* 169–174.

Sklar, F., & Hartley, S. F. (1990). Close friends as survivors: Bereavement patterns in a "hidden" population. *Omega, 21,* 103–112.

Slater, R. (1995). *The psychology of growing old: Looking forward.* Buckingham, UK: Open University Press.

Soldo, B. J., Wolf, D. A., & Agree, E. M. (1990). Family, households, and care arrangements of frail older women: A structural analysis. *Journal of Gerontology: Social Sciences, 45,* S238– S249.

Spanier, G., & Furstenberg, F. F., Jr. (1987). Remarriage and reconstituted families. In M. B. Sussman & S. K. Steinmetz (Eds.), *Handbook of marriage and the family* (pp. 419–434). New York: Plenum.

Starrels, M. E., Ingersoll-Dayton, B., & Neal, M. B. (1995). Intergenerational solidarity and the workplace: Employees caregiving for their parents. *Journal of Marriage and the Family, 57,* 751– 762.

Stroebe, W., & Stroebe, M. S. (1987). *Bereavement and health: The psychological and physical consequences of partner loss.* New York: Cambridge University Press.

Swensen, C. H., & Fuller, S. R. (1992). Expression of love, marriage problems, commitment and anticipatory grief in the marriages of cancer patients. *Journal of Marriage and the Family, 54,* 191–196.

Szinovacz, M. (1989). Retirement, couples, and household work. In S. J. Bahr & E. T. Peterson (Eds.), *Aging and the family* (pp. 33–58). Lexington, MA: Lexington Books.

Szinovacz, M. (1992). Social activities and retirement adaptation: Gender and family variations. In M. Szinovacz, D. J. Ekerdt, & B. H. Vinick (Eds.), *Families and retirement* (pp. 236–253). Newbury Park, CA: Sage.

Szinovacz, M., & Ekerdt, D. J. (1995). Families and retirement. In R. Blieszner & V. H. Bedford (Eds.), *Handbook of aging and the family* (pp. 375–400). Westport, CT: Greenwood Press.

Szinovacz, M., Ekerdt, D. J., & Vinick, B. H. (1992). Families and retirement: Conceptual and methodological issues. In M. Szinovacz, D. J. Ekerdt, & B. H. Vinick (Eds.), *Families and retirement* (pp. 1–19). Newbury Park, CA: Sage.

Thoits, P. A. (1995). Stress, coping, and social support processes: Where are we? What next? *Journal of Health and Social Behavior, 36,* 53–79.

Thompson, L. W., Gallagher, D., Cover, H., Galewski, M., & Peterson, J. (1989). Effects of bereavement on symptoms of psychopathology in older men and women. In D. A. Lund (Ed.), *Older bereaved spouses: Research with practical applications* (pp. 17–24). New York: Hemisphere.

Thompson, M. G., & Heller, K. (1990). Facets of support related to well-being: Quantitative social isolation and perceived family support in a sample of elderly women. *Psychology and Aging, 5,* 535–544.

Thompson, S. C., & Pitts, J. S. (1991). In sickness and in health: Chronic illness, marriage, and spousal caregiving. In S. Spacapan & S. Oskamp (Eds.), *Helping and being helped: Naturalistic studies* (pp. 115–151). Newbury Park, CA: Sage.

Tower, R. B., & Kasl, S.V. (1996). Depressive symptoms across older spouses: Longitudinal influences. *Psychology and Aging, 11,* 683–697.

Tower, R. B., Kasl, S. V., & Moritz, D. J. (1997). The influence of spouse cognitive impairment on respondents' depressive symptoms: The moderating role of marital closeness. *Journal of Gerontology: Social Sciences, 52B,* S270–S278.

Townsend, A. L., & Franks, M. M. (1995). Binding ties: Closeness and conflict in adult children's caregiving relationships. *Psychology and Aging, 10,* 343–351.

Townsend, A. L., & Franks, M. M. (1997). Quality of the relationship between elderly spouses: Influence on spouse caregivers' subjective effectiveness. *Family Relations, 46,* 33–39.

Troll, L. E., Miller, S. J., & Atchley, R. C. (1979). *Families in later life.* Belmont, CA: Wadsworth.

Turner, B. F., & Troll, L. E. (1994). *Women growing older: Psychological perspectives.* Thousand Oaks, CA: Sage.

Uchino, B. N., Cacioppo, J. T., & Kiecolt-Glaser, J. K. (1996). The relationship between social support and physiological processes: A review with emphasis on underlying mechanisms and implications for health. *Psychological Bulletin, 119,* 488–531.

Umberson, D. (1992). Relationships between adult children and their parents: Psychological consequences for both generations. *Journal of Marriage and the Family, 54,* 664–674.

Umberson, D. (1995). Marriage as support or strain? Marital quality following the death of a parent. *Journal of Marriage and the Family, 57,* 709–723.

Unger, J. B., McAvay, G., Bruce, M. L., Berkman, L., & Seeman, T. (1999). Variation in the impact of social network characteristics on physical functioning in elderly persons: MacArthur Studies of Successful Aging. *Journal of Gerontology: Social Sciences, 54B,* S245–S251.

van der Does, J. V. S., & Duyvis, D. J. (1989). Psychosocial adjustment of spouses of cervical carcinoma patients. *Journal of Psychosomatics in Obstetrics Gynecology, 10,* 163–171.

Vinick, B. H., & Ekerdt, D. J. (1991). The transition to retirement: Responses of husbands and wives. In B. B. Hess & E. Markson (Eds.), *Growing old in America* (4th ed., pp. 305–317). New Brunswick, NJ: Transaction.

Wallerstein, J. S., & Blakeslee, S. (1995). *The good marriage: How and why love lasts.* Boston: Houghton Mifflin.

Wang, H., & Amato, P. R. (2000). Predictors of divorce adjustment: Stressors, resources, and definitions. *Journal of Marriage and the Family, 62,* 655–668.

Ward, R., Logan, J., & Spitze, G. (1992). The influence of parent and child needs on coresidence in middle and later life. *Journal of Marriage and the Family, 54,* 209–221.

Weiss, L., & Lowenthal, M. F. (1975). Life-course perspectives on friendship. In M. E. Lowenthal, M. Thurnher, & D. Chiriboga (Eds.), *Four stages of life* (pp. 48–61). San Francisco, CA: Jossey-Bass.

Weiss, R. (1974). The provisions of social relationships. In Z. Rubin (Ed.), *Doing unto others* (pp. 17–26). Englewood Cliffs, NJ: Prentice Hall.

Wellman, B., & Wortley, S. (1989). Brothers' keepers: Situating kinship relations in broader networks of social support. *Sociological Perspectives, 32,* 273–306.

Wenger, G. C., Davies, R., & Shahtahmasebi, S. (1995). Morale in old age: Refining the model. *International Journal of Geriatric Psychiatry, 10,* 933–943.

Wenger, G. C., & Jerrome, D. (1999). Change and stability in confidant relationships: Findings from the Bangor Longitudinal Study of Aging. *Journal of Aging Studies, 13,* 269–294.

Whitbeck, L., Hoyt, D. R., & Huck, S. M. (1994). Early family relationships, intergenerational solidarity, and support provided to parents by their adult children. *Journal of Gerontology: Social Sciences, 49,* S85–S94.

Wilcox. V. L., Kasl, S., & Berkman, L. F. (1994). Social support and physical disability in older people after hospitalization: A prospective study. *Health Psychology, 13,* 170–179.

Winsborough, H. H., Bumpass, L. L., & Aquilino, W. S. (1991). The death of parents and the transition to old age (Working Paper NSFH-39). Madison, WI: University of Wisconsin Center for Demography and Ecology.

Wortman, C. B., Kessler, R. C., & Umberson, D. (1992). Widowhood and depression: Explaining long-term gender differences in vulnerability. *Journal of Health and Social Behavior, 33,* 10–24.

Wright, L. K. (1991). The impact of Alzheimer's disease on the marital relationship. *Gerontologist, 31,* 224–237.

Wright, L. K., Clipp, E. C., & George, L. K. (1993). Health consequences of caregiver stress. *Medicine, Exercise, Nutrition and Health, 2,* 181–195.

Wright, P. H. (1989). Gender differences in adults' same- and cross-gender friendships. In R. G. Adams & R. Blieszner (Eds.), *Older adult friendship: Structure and process* (pp. 197–221). Newbury Park, CA: Sage.

Zisook, S., & Shuchter, S. R. (1986). The first four years of widowhood. *Psychiatric Annals, 15,* 288–294.

PART SIX

APPLIED DEVELOPMENTAL PSYCHOLOGY ACROSS THE LIFE SPAN

CHAPTER 21

Disabilities and Development

PENNY HAUSER-CRAM AND ANGELA HOWELL

Children often exhibit individual profiles of strengths and weaknesses as they develop. Some children walk at a young age but learn language slowly; others draw elaborate pictures but struggle to ride a bicycle. Such profiles indicate that children display developmental discrepancies, sometimes delayed in one domain of development in relation to others. For many children, delays are modest and temporary. For other children, however, delays are extensive and pervasive. How are children with slow or unusual patterns of development viewed from the perspective of developmental psychology? Are the mechanisms of development the same for children with and without disabilities? Are family processes similar in families in which a child has a developmental disability as for other families? How can developmental psychology as a field benefit from studies of children with developmental disabilities?

According to current estimates, 12.3% of children in the United States who are not in residential care have difficulty

performing one or more everyday activities, including learning, communication, mobility, and self-care (Forum on Child and Family Statistics, 1999). Both historically and currently, Western psychologists have tended to assign pejorative words like imbecile, feebleminded, backwards, moron, and idiot to children who do not accomplish the developmental milestones within specified age limits (Jordan, 2000). The current term, *developmental disabilities,* which is used to refer to children whose development deviates from expectations, is also potentially stigmatizing. In the United Kingdom the term *mental retardation* is no longer accepted; instead, *learning disabilities* is used to refer to all individuals who have difficulty learning or exhibit below-average intelligence (Baron-Cohen, 1998). Concerns about nomenclature continue to plague those who study or work with individuals who deviate from normative development.

In this chapter we focus on theoretical approaches and empirical investigations that have examined evidence about the development of young children with biologically based developmental disabilities. We begin with a discussion of the difficulties in constructing definitional and diagnostic criteria of children with developmental disabilities. Next, we offer a perspective on how the study of developmental disabilities fits into the history of developmental psychology. Then we

Preparation of this chapter was partially supported by grant R40 MC 00177 from the Maternal and Child Health Bureau (Title V, Social Security Act), Health Resources and Services Administration, Department of Health and Human Services and by a grant from the Argyelan Family Education Research Fund.

consider current theoretical perspectives and empirical work on children with developmental disabilities and their families emanating from various perspectives. We conclude with implications for application and reflections on potential directions for future work.

DEVELOPMENTAL DISABILITIES AND DEFINITIONAL DILEMMAS

Developmental disabilities is a general term that describes a wide range of disabilities that occur prenatally or during childhood. This heterogeneous category includes global mental retardation, distinct syndromes (e.g., Down syndrome, Fragile X syndrome), autism and related communication disorders, motor impairment such as cerebral palsy, and developmental delays of unknown etiology. Indeed, the term is rarely defined but generally refers to those individuals who are not exhibiting typical developmental patterns.

Definitional quagmires persist, as even the term *mentally retarded* is difficult to define. From its earliest conception until the present day, debate has existed about the criterion and terminology used in the definition of mental retardation (Baumeister, 1987; MacMillan, Gresham, & Siperstein, 1993). Predominant classification schemes from 1973 to 1992 defined individuals as mentally retarded if they scored 70 or less on standard intelligence tests. This cutoff point reflects scores that lie 2 standard deviations below the mean of the population.

The *Diagnostic and Statistical Manual of Mental Disorder* also included levels of severity based on IQ (e.g., borderline, mild, moderate, severe, and profound mental retardation; e.g., American Psychiatric Association, 1968, 1994). Many individuals raised concerns about definitional criteria based solely on intelligence tests. Some argued that standardized intelligence tests are culturally and linguistically biased and discriminate against members of minority groups (Hawkins & Cooper, 1990), resulting in an overrepresentation of minorities labeled with mental retardation. Others noted that children with mental retardation often display markedly different performance within and between testing sessions, demonstrating avoidance behaviors and inconsistent motivation (Wishart & Duffy, 1990). These behaviors tend to make scores on any one assessment unreliable.

Current definitions of mental retardation have moved away from singular reliance on intelligence testing and instead incorporate knowledge of the individual's adaptive functioning (Luckasson et al., 1992). The latest definition of mental retardation endorsed by the American Association on Mental Retardation (AAMR) and by the American Psychological Association is

> substantial limitations in present functioning . . . characterized by significantly subaverage intellectual functioning, existing concurrently with related limitations in two or more of the following applicable adaptive skill areas: communication, self-care, home living, social skills, community use, self-direction, health and safety, functional academics, leisure and work. Mental retardation manifests before age 18. (AAMR, 1992, p. 1)

This definition also replaces earlier classification schemes that emphasized the severity of retardation (i.e., mild, moderate, severe, profound) with an approach that describes the amount of support needed by the individual in the various adaptive skill areas. Four levels of support are delineated: intermittent, limited, extensive, and pervasive. Although this definition represents a move away from determining mental retardation based on cognitive deficit alone, it raises questions about appropriate methods of assessment. For example, many of the skill areas (e.g., community use, work) are not applicable at all ages, and none of the skill areas are useful in assessing newborns (MacMillan et al., 1993). Indeed, some claim that mental retardation (and by extension, developmental disabilities, more broadly) is, in fact, a socially constructed term (Blatt, 1985), as the delineation of normality and abnormality are based on culturally constructed ideals of age-appropriate behaviors and skills.

A BRIEF HISTORY OF ATTITUDES ABOUT CHILDREN WITH DEVELOPMENTAL DISABILITIES

Philosophical constructs have often served to guide the way psychologists think about phenomena, such as the processes and mechanisms of development (Overton, 1998). Current perspectives on individuals with "slower than expected" development have been shaped historically by philosophical and ideological views. Much of that history reveals exclusionary attitudes and practices toward those with developmental disabilities. Even Aristotle, who viewed humans as unique in comparison to other species because of their rationality, claimed in *Politics* that "as to the exposure and rearing of children, let there be a law that no deformed child shall live" (Aristotle, n.d., p. 315). In the Middle Ages, individuals with developmental disabilities were seen as products of "sin" (Szymanski & Wilska, 1997). During the Inquisition, those with mental retardation were viewed as witches, and their "disease" caused by the devil (Scheerenberger, 1983).

The Reformation brought little enlightenment to public attitudes toward those with disabilities. Martin Luther claimed that a child with mental retardation had no soul and therefore should be drowned (Scheerenberger, 1983). Thus, throughout Western history, children with developmental disabilities often were considered defective and not worthy of care. This historical perspective is important because it has shaped current thinking, even if the current view is one of reacting against the past.

A change in societal perspective first occurred at the end of the eighteenth century in Paris when Philipe Pinel developed an approach to caring for individuals with developmental disabilities employing "moral management." He advocated gentle and humane care, education, and recreation in contrast to former approaches that focused on obedience. Pinel's student, Edouard Seguin, developed educational systems, especially based on physical therapies, which he believed would improve the skills of individuals with mental retardation. Seguin maintained that education of the muscular system would lead to development of the nervous system (Connell, 1980). In the mid-nineteenth century Seguin's ideas flowed to the United States and formed the foundation of the first schools for individuals with developmental disabilities. Seguin himself immigrated to the United States and in 1876 founded the American Institutions for the Feeble Minded with several other physicians (now called the American Association on Mental Retardation).

Around the turn of the last century, however, the treatment of individuals with developmental disabilities in the United States changed and became far less humane. Custodial care, instead of education, became the norm in overcrowded state institutions where those with developmental disabilities were often isolated (Meisels & Shonkoff, 2000). This deleterious change occurred in a sociopolitical context in which the science of human development was emerging. Several ideological movements fused in ways that ultimately were detrimental for the nurturing and education of children with developmental disabilities.

First, G. Stanley Hall's initiation of the child study movement stimulated beliefs about the possibility of collecting scientific information on children's development (Cairns, 1998). Through extensive questionnaires, Hall attempted to gather information with the goal of constructing norms of development against which all children could be measured. Several of Hall's students, notably Goddard, Kuhlmann, and Terman, developed intelligence tests that, in time, were used to segregate individuals with developmental disabilities. Terman, in particular, argued against the malleability of intelligence (Minton, 1984); without belief in malleability, the hope of productively educating those with developmental disabilities was diminished.

Second, in England at the turn of the last century, Frances Galton, a cousin of Charles Darwin, advocated the use of eugenics principles to promote social policies. Galton argued that the only way to improve the human race was through breeding "better people" (Degler, 1991). The eugenics movement became a strong force in American social science, and its proponents maintained that they had an obligation to prevent the reproduction of those with mental retardation (Degler, 1991). The Nazi regime justified "mercy killing" of children with disabilities or deformities with a similar rationale combined with a view that such children met the principle of "life unworthy of life" (Lifton, 1986, p. 46). Finally, genealogical studies led to the belief that mental retardation was associated with criminality (Szmanski & Wilska, 1997). In fact, the term *feebleminded*, which was often used at the turn of the twentieth century to describe those with mental retardation, implied both cognitive impairment and moral decay (Winship, 1900). The combination of these social forces resulted in societal attitudes such as those exemplified by Goddard (1914):

> The feeble-minded person is not desirable, he is a social encumbrance, often a burden to himself. In short it were better both for him and for society had he never been born. Should we not then, in our attempt to improve the race, begin by preventing the birth of more feeble-minded? (p. 558)

Several decades later changes in the treatment of individuals with developmental disabilities were again brought about by the confluence of public ideology and advances in developmental science. Stimulated at least in part by the civil rights movement in the 1950s and 1960s, support for the human rights of all citizens and optimism about the potential benefits of publicly supported programs grew. The contributions of developmental psychologists D. O. Hebb (1949), followed by that of J. McVicker Hunt (1961) and Benjamin Bloom (1964), on the malleability of intelligence during the first few years of life, added scholarly support for the ideological shift away from genetic determinism of intelligence.

During the last decades of the twentieth century several important policy changes were made in the United States in support of the normalization of the lives of individuals with developmental disabilities. One of these movements is deinstitutionalization, which has resulted in more families raising children with disabilities at home and thus normalizing children's daily experiences (Lakin, Bruininks, & Larson, 1992). Educational initiatives have been a second force. Beginning in 1975 with Public Law 94-142, legislation has focused on educating children with disabilities in the "least restricted

environment" and including them in general education programs. Other important legislation followed, including Public Law 99-47, the Education for All Handicapped Children
Act Amendments of 1986, which encouraged states to provide services for children with disabilities younger than
school age. This law which was reauthorized in 1997–1998
and titled Public Law 105-17, the Individuals with Disabilities Education Act (IDEA) requires states to provide free and
appropriate public education for children as young as age 3.
As a consequence, children with disabilities are now entitled
to publicly supported services before school age and are
included in general education (with or without support
services) to the extent deemed advantageous to their learning
(Meisels & Shonkoff, 2000).

In this brief summary, it is apparent that public views
about those with developmental disabilities have changed
enormously. Caldwell (1973) summarized these views in the
United States as representing three phases: (a) forget and
hide, (b) screen and segregate, and (c) identify and help. A
fourth phase could be added today: educate and include
(Meisels & Shonkoff, 2000). At all points, the dual forces of
psychological science and public ideology have exerted
influence on the treatment of children with disabilities.

SCHOLARSHIP ON DISABILITIES BY DEVELOPMENTAL THEORISTS

Based on a view that all children have the potential for change,
several child development theorists conducted studies on
children with developmental disabilities. A small but instructive history exists about the questions they examined and
the findings they published. We discuss these in terms of
three of the major metatheories evident in developmental psychology today: mechanistic, organismic, and developmental
contextualist perspectives (Lerner, 1986; Overton & Reese,
1973).

The Mechanistic Perspective

The mechanistic perspective emphasizes quantitative change
and the role of external activity that impinges on the individual (Dixon & Lerner, 1992). It is best exemplified by behaviorism or learning theory as first described by B. F. Skinner
(1953) and later by Sidney Bijou and Donald Baer (1961),
who applied the principles of learning theory to child development. They maintained that the child differs from the
adult only as a consequence of having a more limited set of
responses and contingencies. Bijou (1966) asserted that

children with retardation differ from other children primarily
by their more constrained set of responses. Thus, "a retarded
individual is one who has a limited repertory of behavior
shaped by events that constitute his history" (Bijou, 1966,
p. 2). According to Bijou, despite having a more constricted
repertoire, children with mental retardation learn according
to the same principles as other children do.

Prior to Bijou's work, behaviorists had applied principles
of operant conditioning to individuals with mental retardation.
Fuller (1949) based an empirical investigation on prior work
that indicated that children with mental retardation could form
conditioned responses to shock faster than other children did.
He reported that after withholding food, he could condition a
"vegetative idiot" to learn to move his right hand when reinforced with sweetened milk. This led to Fuller's claim that
behavioristic principles, especially operant conditioning,
could be used to improve learning in individuals with developmental disabilities.

As the number of studies using operant conditioning
with individuals with mental retardation grew, behaviorists
showed increasing interest in the applications of this approach,
primarily to replace undesirable behaviors with socially
acceptable ones (Spradlin & Girardeau, 1966). Applied behavior analysis and behavior modification techniques were
used frequently in institutions for individuals with developmental disabilities during the 1960s and 1970s (Ellis, 1979).
Indeed, although much of developmental psychology has
moved away from the mechanistic perspective, behavioral
approaches are still active models in many classrooms and
institutional settings. Applied behavioral analysis remains a
recommended intervention for individuals with certain disabilities, particularly autism (Rush & Frances, 2000). In general, the principles of behaviorism are believed to apply to all
individuals, including those with developmental disabilities
(Glenn, 1997).

The Organismic Perspective

In contrast to mechanistic approaches, the organismic
perspective stresses qualitative aspects of change and agency
of the organism in bringing about change (Dixon & Lerner,
1992). Heinz Werner, one of the first psychologists to operate
from this perspective, applied this theoretical approach to
individuals who have mental retardation. In studies on
children with mental retardation, H. Werner and Strauss
(1939) emphasized the importance of a functional analysis of
the *processes* involved in children's learning over data gathered from objective outcome-based assessments like achievement tests. They further maintained that the sequence in which

children with mental retardation learn constructs is similar to that of other children, though delayed chronologically. Finally, H. Werner (1957) reported that in contrast to expectation, children with mental retardation sometimes had greater success with tasks (e.g., completing a puzzle) than their peers because they were using more basic, rather than analytical, processes (such as focusing on individual pieces rather than the puzzle as a whole). These studies have the seeds of H. Werner's (1957) classic work in which he constructed the orthogenetic principle that "development proceeds from a state of relative globality and lack of differentiation to a state of differentiation, articulation, and hierarchical integration" (p. 126). H. Werner's study of children with developmental disabilities served as a catalyst in constructing principles that apply to the development of all children.

Piaget's studies also emanate from the organismic perspective. Piaget himself, however, seldom wrote about developmental disabilities, although his colleague, Barbel Inhelder (1966), conducted several studies with children who were mentally retarded. The purpose of those investigations was twofold: to determine whether children with mental retardation demonstrated the same sequence of stage-related changes as hypothesized by Piaget and to demonstrate the diagnostic value of Piagetian approaches to child assessment. Inhelder (1966) reasoned that through the study of operative and symbolic processes of children with mental retardation, children's fixations at particular stages could be understood. In general, her empirical studies support the hypothesis that children with mental retardation develop through the same sequence of stages as do other children but at a slower pace. She also reported, however, that children with mental retardation reached a type of "false equilibrium" and concluded that "access to certain structures seems to be an end in itself, without hope of subsequent evolution" (Inhelder, 1966, p. 313). Inhelder further indicated that children with mental retardation made regressions to earlier substages under conditions of cognitive challenge. Thus, she found general support for Piaget's model and also raised questions about discrepancies in the cognitive development of children with mental retardation. Nevertheless, Inhelder did not regard these discrepancies as a threat to the principle of similar sequence.

The Developmental Contextualist Perspective

From the developmental contextualist (or more generally, the developmental systems) perspective, children are participants in many intersecting interacting systems (Bronfenbrenner, 1979; Ford & Lerner, 1992; Thelen & Smith, 1998). Those systems generate and are affected by sociocultural ideologies.

Vygotsky's work regarding individuals with developmental disabilities takes a developmental systems approach. In contrast to Skinner and Piaget, Vygotsky wrote extensively about the development of children with disabilities, a field that was termed *defectology* in Russia. Like those working from either the mechanistic or the organismic perspective, Vygotsky maintained that the principles of development do not differ for those with mental retardation or other disabilities. This claim is apparent in his statement that "the difference in the intellect of a retarded and a normal child appears insignificant; the nature of the intellectual process appears identical for both" (Rieber & Carton, 1993, p. 222; Vygotsky, 1929/1931/1993).

Vygotsky viewed the primary difficulty for the child with developmental disabilities as the lack of acceptance within the sociocultural milieu. In emphasizing the importance of the effect of social attitudes on the child over the specific effects of the disability per se, he claimed that the

> immediate consequences of the defect is to diminish the child's social standing; the defect manifests itself as a social aberration. All contact with people, all situations which define a person's place in the social sphere, his role and fate as a participant in life, all the social functions of daily life are reordered. (Rieber & Carton, 1993, p. 35; Vygotsky, 1929/1931/1993)

Vygotsky considered collaboration as essential for the development of higher psychological processes, and he emphasized the importance of children collaborating in a diverse group. Foreshadowing current views about inclusion, he argued that when children with mental retardation are isolated from other children, their development becomes impaired. According to him, a

> one-sided collective, composed entirely of mentally retarded children who are absolutely identical in level of development, is a false pedagogical ideal. It contradicts the basic law of development of higher psychological processes and conflicts with the general notion of the diversity and dynamics of psychological functions in any child, and particularly in a retarded child. (Rieber & Carton, 1993, p. 130; Vygotsky, 1929/1931/1993)

Vygotsky's view was that children compensate for their disabilities. The task of the collaborative community, then, is to aid in that compensation. He considered the compensations to be "round about developmental processes" (Rieber & Carton, 1993, p. 34; Vygotsky, 1929/1931/1993) that restructure and stabilize psychological functioning. Thus, although Vygotsky considered the fundamental processes of development to be the same for children with developmental disabilities, he maintained that support from the sociocultural superstructure was essential for optimal development.

Summary

Though not well known, the scholarship of many of the giants of developmental psychology considered children with developmental disabilities. Vygotsky concentrated directly and extensively on children with disabilities, but his work in this arena is only beginning to be recognized. The scholarship of individuals representing all three major metatheories, however, is similar in the conclusion that the principles of development apply to children with developmental disabilities as they do to other children. The deviance perspective that historically has been prevalent in public attitudes toward disabilities, then, is inconsistent with the significant scholarship in psychology that indicates that general developmental principles apply broadly.

RESEARCH ON CHILDREN WITH DEVELOPMENTAL DISABILITIES

Contemporary psychological investigations of young children with developmental disabilities tend to be based on current views of children as part of complex interacting systems (Lerner, 1998) in which the transactions between individuals are important mechanisms of development (Sameroff & Fiese, 2000). In this section we first review the few longitudinal studies of children with disabilities and then consider contemporary perspectives on the developmental role of the most proximal system in which young children are nurtured, namely, the family.

Longitudinal Studies

Development is about change (Overton, 1998), and one of the most productive ways to study change is through empirical longitudinal investigations. Though less frequently undertaken than cross-sectional examinations, longitudinal studies offer distinct advantages. They allow us to (a) map pathways of development, (b) study emerging processes, (c) understand the relations among reciprocal changes, (d) examine the plasticity of developmental processes, and (e) test theoretically constructed hypotheses about development (Lerner, Hauser-Cram, & Miller, 1998).

Classic longitudinal studies (e.g., Elder, 1974; E. Werner & Smith, 1992) in developmental psychology have led to important knowledge about developmental processes. Longitudinal studies of children with developmental disabilities, though sparse, also have yielded valuable findings. In general, these studies have occurred in two phases. During the first phase children's development (usually IQ) was mapped over

time to provide knowledge about developmental trajectories of children with specific disabilities. In the second phase researchers used theoretical models to study features and predictors of developmental change. Examples of the major studies in each of these phases are described next.

The First Phase: Developmental Mapping

The longitudinal studies in which children's development has been charted over time focus primarily on children with Down syndrome. Perhaps this is because a definite diagnosis can be made based on karyotype and because of a belief that children with a similar genetic syndrome might develop in a similar way. Evidence indicates that this is true to an extent.

In England, Carr (1988, 1995) conducted the most extensive study of children with Down syndrome. She followed 45 children born in 1963 or 1964 from age 6 weeks to 21 years. Because children with Down syndrome were often institutionalized at the time of that study, she included a home-reared and a non-home-reared group. She conducted interviews with mothers and extensive psychological and achievement tests with the children. In mapping the IQ score for children in both groups over the entire study period, Carr found the groups to differ during the early years of life, with differences favoring the home-reared children. The groups did not differ subsequently, and both showed a declining trajectory in IQ during middle childhood followed by stability in IQ during the early adult years. Individual variation was similar to that expected of any sample of children taking an IQ test (i.e., approximately 15 points). In relation to family adaptation, Carr found that although mothers of children with Down syndrome reported more malaise and poorer health than mothers of typically developing children, their malaise scores were not related to their child's level of disability or to social restrictions due to their child's disability (Carr, 1988). Carr's study is remarkable for its longevity and its contributions in charting changes in IQ over time.

Reed, Pueschel, Schnell, and Cronk (1980) also studied children with Down syndrome but only for the first three years of life. Their study began as an assessment of the treatment of 89 children with medical interventions thought to improve serotonin levels (i.e., 5-hydroxytryptophan, 5-hydroxytryptophan/pyridoxine, pridoxine; Pueschel, 1980). They found no effect of the treatment but reported data on developmental change in all samples, including a placebo group. In terms of psychomotor cognitive assessments, they found that children performed at mental age equivalents of about half their chronological age and exhibited relatively greater delays in language development and lesser delays in adaptive behavior (Schnell, 1984). Individual variation appeared to be slightly less than that reported by Carr, but in general, they found similar patterns of change in cognitive performance.

In a longitudinal investigation of children with mild to moderate delays of unknown etiology, Bernheimer and Keogh (1988) investigated a sample of 44 children for 6 years beginning in the preschool years. In analyses of data on children's cognitive performance scores over four time points, they reported strong and consistent stability of scores over the 76-month period; only 4 children demonstrated improvement of more than 1 standard deviation. They concluded that children who were cognitively delayed during the preschool years had a strong probability of continuing to exhibit delays during the early school years (Keogh, Bernheimer, Gallimore, & Weisner, 1998). Their study is unique because of its emphasis on children with delays rather than those with distinct disabilities.

The Second Phase: Theoretically Guided Longitudinal Studies

One would expect theoretically guided longitudinal studies of children with developmental disabilities to appear chronologically after some baseline studies have yielded data on developmental milestones. This appears to be the case. Those investigating the mechanisms of change in the development of children with disabilities have taken a range of theoretical perspectives, however.

The work of Cicchetti and Beeghly represents a clear departure from earlier studies of children with Down syndrome because of its examination of system organization. Operating from an organismic perspective, Cicchetti and Beeghly (1990) tested hypotheses about the extent to which hierarchical organization of behavior applies to children with Down syndrome. They conducted a short-term longitudinal study (i.e., 18 months) of 41 children with Down syndrome ranging in age from 20 to 76 months. Beeghly and Cicchetti (1987) focused on children's representational abilities, especially in communication and symbolic play, and found the development of children with Down syndrome to be delayed but organized in ways similar to their typically developing peers. They concluded that despite the slower rate of skill acquisition, the patterns of development in the social-communication systems are as organized and coherent for children with Down syndrome as they are for other children.

Understanding the complex relation between children's development and family processes has been the focus of the investigators of the Early Intervention Collaborative Study, an ongoing longitudinal study of children with Down syndrome, motor impairment, or developmental delays of unknown etiology (Shonkoff, Hauser-Cram, Krauss, & Upshur, 1992). That study also has been guided by a transactional-ecological model of development (Bronfenbrenner, 1979; Sameroff & Chandler, 1975) and by a developmental-contextual perspective (Lerner, 1991). In accordance with these approaches, children are viewed as agents of development and as participants in multiple interacting systems that have bidirectional relations that change over time.

Based on an investigation of the subsample of children with Down syndrome, Hauser-Cram, Warfield, Shonkoff, Krauss, Upshur, and Sayer (1999) reported that features of the family system, notably mother-child interaction and family cohesiveness, were significant predictors of children's developmental trajectories in social, communication, and daily life skills over the first five years of life. Employing growth analyses of children's development and changes in parental well-being for the full sample of 183 children over a 10-year period, Hauser-Cram, Warfield, Shonkoff, and Krauss (2001) found that children's self-regulatory mastery skills (i.e., their ability to persist with problem-posing tasks) were key predictors of children's developmental change in cognitive and daily living skills. Thus, to some extent children act as agents of their own development. Family dynamics, however, contributed additional predictive power in children's outcomes. Children whose mothers had more positive styles of interaction displayed greater growth in cognitive performance, communication, and social skills. Children from families with more positive relationships among family members had more growth in the development of social skills. Children's emotional self-regulatory skills also were found to influence parental well-being. Children who displayed more behavior problems had parents whose trajectory of stress showed dramatic increases over the 10-year period of study. These results point to the bidirectional influences of the parent-child relationship and highlight the importance that family processes have in predicting developmental change in children with disabilities.

The investigations just described represent an important advance in longitudinal research on children with developmental disabilities. Although each set of investigators operated from a different theoretical perspective and thus posed different questions, the investigations are similar in their focus on the interrelation among developmental processes and systems.

Contextually Based Studies

Given the nature of the difficulty of conducting longitudinal investigations, much of the work on developmental disabilities has remained cross-sectional or focused on a brief time span. The bulk of contemporary psychological research studies on children with disabilities have emanated from a contextual perspective in which the family is considered the primary context in which young children learn and are nurtured (Bronfenbrenner, 1986). In considering children with developmental disabilities, Guralnick (1997) proposed a model that identifies key predictors of children's development based on family factors. He delineated three proximal patterns of family interactions that influence children's development: (a) quality of parent-child interaction; (b) family-orchestrated child experiences; and (c) health and safety provided by the family. Of the three, only the quality of parent-child interaction has received substantial research attention.

Mother-Child Interaction

Studies of dyadic relationships within families in which a child has a disability have focused primarily on the mother-child dyad. Based on much research that indicates that the quality of the mother-child relationship has consequences for the cognitive and socioemotional development of typical children (e.g., Bornstein, 1989; Sroufe, 1996), several researchers have focused on this relationship in dyads where the child has a disability. A transactional approach (Sameroff & Chandler, 1975) has guided most empirical studies of mother-child dyads. This theoretical framework describes a transactional process in which mothers and infants influence each other's behaviors in concert, through reciprocal interaction that continues to regulate more complex behaviors over time and across contexts (Sameroff & Fiese, 2000). Those operating from a transactional approach emphasize that characteristics of both mothers and children must be considered as a dynamic interactive system.

Consistent with R. Q. Bell's (1968) theory of bidirectional interaction, early social signals of infants and mothers, such as eye contact, smiles, and vocal turn taking enable mothers to understand their child's general temperament and become proficient at responding to their child's needs. The contingency of a mother's response to her child then regulates the child's future behaviors as infants begin to recognize the relationship between their actions and responses from the environment (Goldberg, 1977). A mother's sensitivity and contingent responsiveness to her child's social signals are essential for the infant's development of security and attachment, which supports the child's exploration of the environment and development of autonomy (S. M. Bell & Ainsworth, 1972). Alternatively, high levels of control or parental intrusion into the child's play and exploration can diminish the child's motivation to explore objects in the environment independently and

thus reduce the child's opportunities to develop self-efficacy (Heckhausen, 1993).

Barnard et al. (1989) referred to the rhythmic interactive pattern between mother and child as a mutually adaptive dance. The more contingent the responsiveness between mother and child, the more enjoyable the dance is for both partners. When one partner does not have the adequate steps, the dance will be less satisfying, however. Similarly, when one partner leads before the other is ready to follow, the tempo will be disrupted (Barnard et al., 1989). Several studies on the mother-child interactive pattern conclude that such disruption often occurs when the child has a developmental disability (Kelly & Barnard, 2000).

Empirical observations of mother-child dyads engaged in teaching interactions have found that mothers of children with disabilities tend to be highly directive and controlling of their child's behaviors. These mothers also provide more supportive and helping behaviors than mothers of typically developing children (Mahoney, Fors, & Wood, 1990). Even during free play interactions, mothers of preschool children with Down syndrome tend to instruct their children in the appropriate use of toys, displaying more instrumental teaching in comparison to mothers of children without a disability (Eheart, 1982).

Most studies of mother-child dyads have involved children with Down syndrome because this form of mental retardation is prevalent, and often identified prenatally or at birth. During observations of mother-child dyadic interaction, children with Down syndrome often display social signals that are labile (Kasari, Mundy, Yirmiya, & Sigman, 1999) and more delayed (Berger, 1990) compared to those of typically developing children of the same mental age. The social cues of children with Down syndrome are difficult to predict because they often do not match with characteristics of the ongoing interaction. For example, Knieps, Walden and Baxter (1994) found that toddlers with Down syndrome responded with positive affect to their mother's signals of fear during a social referencing task, unlike typically developing children who tended to match their mother's facial expressions. Some investigators suggest that such unusual social interaction patterns of children with Down syndrome may be due to difficulty in shifting attention, especially under situations of high cognitive load (Kasari, Freeman, Mundy, & Sigman, 1995).

Some delayed behaviors of children with developmental disabilities may be related to sensory impairments or health problems. For example, children with Down syndrome often experience transient hearing loss due to middle ear infections or more permanent hearing loss (Cunningham & McArthur, 1981) which can diminish responsiveness to their mother's vocal cues. Neuropsychological development related to sensory-tactile and attentional processes is impaired in children who have autism, limiting their ability to understand social information (Resch, Grand, & May, 1988). As infants, they demonstrate minimal interest in people, rarely displaying eye contact or responding to parents' attempts to engage them in play (Hoppes & Harris, 1990). These behaviors may reduce the opportunities of infants with autism to engage their caregivers in *joint attention,* necessary for the development of language (Sigman & Ruskin, 1999). The diminished responsiveness of children who exhibit autism has been reported by parents to violate their expectations and reduce their perception of attachment to their child (Hoppes & Harris, 1990).

Some researchers suggest that maternal directiveness represents diminished sensitivity and responsiveness of mothers to their children's abilities as a consequence of the unclear social cues of their infants with Down syndrome (Berger, 1990). During observations of free play, mothers of children with Down syndrome directed their child's attention away from objects that the child was playing with and instead directed the child toward tasks that were too difficult (Mahoney et al., 1990). These findings suggested that mothers were not always able to assess the developmental competence of their child appropriately. Thus, the degree of scaffolding necessitated by children with developmental disabilities may be difficult for their mothers to judge. Other researchers maintain that the high level of directiveness observed in mothers of children with Down syndrome reflects an adaptive response by mothers to counter their children's lower competence (e.g., Marfo, 1990). Mothers of children with Down syndrome have been found to vary their directive behavior according to their perception of their child's needs and the demands of the context (Landry, Garner, Pirie, & Swank, 1994). For example, they use fewer directives when their child is engaged in developmentally appropriate play (Maurer & Sherrod, 1987) and use more directives as a task becomes more structured (Landry et al., 1994). This may be especially true in observational settings where mothers are aware that their behavior and the competence of their child is being assessed.

Various researchers have found that directive behaviors are multidimensional and often distinct from the supportive strategies that mothers use to facilitate their child's efforts to master challenging tasks (Roach, Barratt, Miller, & Leavitt, 1998). Maternal directives may benefit children with mental retardation when combined with supportive behaviors (Landry et al., 1994). For example, greater maternal support of children's use of objects has been associated with more object play and greater vocalization in children with Down

syndrome (Roach et al., 1998). Directive behavior of mothers of toddlers with Down syndrome may be especially important in facilitating the complexity of children's play (Landry et al., 1994).

Significant interindividual variation in the interactional styles of mothers of children with developmental disabilities and changes in these styles over time have been observed. For example, McCubbin and Patterson (1982) emphasized that a mother's perception of her child and her role as a parent change over time, affecting her parenting style. The delayed social cues and responsiveness of children with disabilities to their mother's initiatives may affect mothers' perceptions of their children and reduce responsiveness to their children's changing abilities (Zirpoli & Bell, 1987). The ongoing transactional processes between mothers and infants with disabilities may then influence the parenting style that the mother adapts. The dominant and supportive behavior observed in mother-child dyads during teaching tasks may be a reflection of a mother's lower expectation of her child's ability to act independently (Kelly & Barnard, 2000). Others have found that parental beliefs about their child's competence become increasingly dependent on characteristics of the child over time (Clare, Garnier, & Gallimore, 1998).

In summary, the research on mother-child interactions indicates that when children have disabilities, the mother-child dyad tends to develop different patterns of interaction than those noted when children are developing typically. Children often provide less clarity in their social cues, and mothers tend to be more directive, providing more instrumental teaching while often supporting their child's successes. Debates exist, however, about the extent to which maternal directiveness and supportiveness extend or undermine children's optimal development. Nevertheless, current research indicates that maternal interaction is a key predictor of the cognitive, communicative, and social development of children with disabilities over time (Hauser-Cram et al., 2001).

Children affect the interactions and ongoing relationship with their mothers, but they also influence other aspects of their mothers' lives. Moreover, children influence the lives of all members of the family system, including fathers and siblings. In the next section we consider research on families of children with developmental disabilities.

RESEARCH ON FAMILIES OF CHILDREN WITH DEVELOPMENTAL DISABILITIES

Historically, research on the effects that a child with a developmental disability has on the family has been based on an assumption that children with disabilities disturb and distort typical family life (Gallimore, Bernheimer, & Weisner, 1999). Therefore, most research on this topic is based on documenting deleterious outcomes, usually of mothers. Many investigators searched for pathology in mothers, such as depression, whereas others focused on adaptive, but still progressively negative, outcomes such as chronic sorrow (Wikler, 1981). Even recently, when psychiatrists were provided with guidance about not regarding parents of children with disabilities as patients, they were alerted to the need to recognize parents' ongoing sadness (Szymanski & Wilska, 1997).

Theoretically Based Research

Four theoretical perspectives have guided the predominant empirical work on family adaptation to children with disabilities: stage theory models, stress and coping models, family systems models, and social-ecology models. Historically, a stage theory model (i.e., a sequenced pattern of change) was used to explain the patterns of adjustment that parents pass through when coping with the birth or diagnosis of a child with a disability (e.g., Parks, 1977). The exact number of stages and their nomenclature vary with investigators, but in general three stages have been delineated (Blacher, 1984). In the first stage parents cope with the initial crisis of the diagnosis, often by shopping for physicians and treatments. In the next stage parents experience guilt, anger, and disappointment. In the third stage parents reorient themselves toward adjustment and acceptance. The empirical evidence for these stages has been mixed (Blacher, 1984), however, and scholarly work has turned away from attempts to document stages and moved toward developing a deeper understanding of variations among families and across the family life cycle (Krauss, 1997).

Beliefs that having a child diagnosed with a disability precipitates a crisis or creates undue stress on the family continue to dominate theoretical and empirical work on families of children with disabilities. Costigan, Floyd, Harter, and McClintock (1997) proposed that at the time of the birth of a child with a disability families often experience *resilient disruption*. Even though family patterns and routines may be disrupted at the time of a child's birth, families adapt, and relationships and patterns often regain equilibrium.

Over the last two decades much research has been stimulated by the *ABCX model* of family adaptation (Hill, 1949). In this model the family's adaptation to an atypical event, or crisis, is explained by several factors, including the nature of the crisis, the internal and external resources of the family, and the meaning ascribed to the event. The birth or diagnosis of a child with disabilities is considered to be a crisis warranting adaptation. An expanded version, termed the *Double ABCX model,* includes developmental processes believed to relate to family adaptation to chronic stress. This new model also allows for changes in stressors, resources, and the meaning ascribed to the crisis over time (McCubbin & Patterson, 1982).

One set of resources that individuals bring to the parenting experience is their skill in coping with stress. Stress-and-coping models have generated much research in psychology (Somerfield & McCrae, 2000), as well as guided studies of parents who have a child with a disability. Stress is often differentiated into two domains: stress related to the characteristics of the child, often related to the child's temperament and self-regulatory skills (e.g., demandingness, adaptability, and distractibility), and stress related to the demands of the parenting role (e.g., social isolation and sense of competence as a parent; Abidin, 1995).

Several investigators have compared stress in parents of children with disabilities with that reported by other parents. Innocenti, Huh, and Boyce (1992) found that during the early childhood years parents of children with disabilities had greater than normative stress in the child domain after the infant period. They did not differ from the normative sample, however, with respect to stress related to the parenting role. Thus, the more stressful challenges for parents emerged around children's self-regulatory behaviors and temperament than in parenting tasks per se.

Orr, Cameron, Dobson, and Day (1993) examined age-related differences in stress among mothers of children with developmental delays during the preschool, middle childhood, and adolescent periods. They found relatively high stress scores on the child-related domain but primarily normative scores on the parenting domain. They also indicated that the highest levels of stress were reported by mothers during the middle childhood period, a finding replicated in other samples (Warfield, Krauss, Hauser-Cram, Upshur, & Shonkoff, 1999). Thus, like Innocenti et al. (1992), they concluded that for mothers of children with disabilities, stress is related to children's self-regulatory behaviors and temperament; they further added, however, that age-related differences occur and that the middle childhood period is an especially vulnerable time.

Others have looked at parenting stress in relation to children with specific disabilities. For example, Duis, Summers, and Summers (1997) found that parents of children with Down syndrome in dual-parent families reported similar stress levels to their counterparts who had typically developing children but lower stress levels than parents of children with hearing impairments or developmental delay. Different aspects of the family ecological system, however, predicted different aspects of stress. Child-related stress was best predicted by general family resources, whereas parent-related stress was best predicted by the level of external support and the quality of the sibling relationship.

Thus, in comparison to prior studies that focused on parental stages of acceptance and adaptability, the studies on parenting stress indicate that parents' reactions to the parenting demands of raising a child with a disability are somewhat similar to parents' reactions to raising any child. More volatile patterns of stress, however, are evident in relation to the child's self-regulation, mood, and temperament. Children with specific disabilities that tend to have higher rates of behavior problems or greater difficulties with mood may be more taxing for parents. It appears that such stress becomes accentuated during the middle childhood period, when children's behaviors are typically expected to demonstrate increasing levels of self-regulation.

Stress and coping are particular processes that parents activate as they raise a child, but they are only one part of the family dynamic. Family systems theory incorporates a broader conceptual model of family processes. From the family systems perspective the family is considered to be an open, interactive system that operates according to a generalized set of principles (Walsh, 1980). Changes in one family member affect changes in other members, producing multiple iterative responses. Thus, rather than focusing on unidirectional effects of a particular child on the family, those operating from the family systems model consider simultaneous multiple effects of family members on each other (Lewis & Lee-Painter, 1974; Minuchin, 1988).

Several aspects of the family system have been studied in relation to parenting a child with a disability. Mink, Nihira, and colleagues conducted a series of investigations in which they developed family typologies based on the psychosocial environment of the home. They studied the homes of children with mild retardation (Mink, Nihira, & Meyers, 1983), children who are "slow learning" (Mink, Meyers, & Nihira, 1984), and children with severe mental retardation (Mink, Blacher, & Nihira, 1988). Through employing cluster analysis on measures of the home environment, they described seven distinct family types: cohesive, control oriented, responsive to child, moral-religious oriented, achievement oriented, conflictual, and low disclosure. Cohesive families are highly accepting of the child and provide a safe and organized home environment. Control-oriented families focus on children's safety and physical needs but place less emphasis on emotional and verbal expressiveness. In contrast, the responsive-to-child family has members who are verbally and emotionally responsive to each other but offer little intellectual stimulation or concern with routines and organization. Moral-religious-oriented families focus on religious expression, often at the expense of emotional

expression. Achievement-oriented families also offer little emphasis on emotional expression but instead focus on offering a variety of activities and experiences. As might be expected, conflictual families have high rates of disagreements, whereas low-disclosure families are ones in which members reveal little of themselves.

The family typologies were used to analyze the relation between family types and children's development. For example, in a sample of children with mild mental retardation, Mink and Nihira (1986) found that children from cohesive families had more positive self-esteem and social adjustment than did children in other family types. Although the investigators suggested that effects are most likely bidirectional—the child affects the family and the family influences the child (Mink et al., 1988)—the bidirectional process has rarely been captured in empirical studies.

Mink and Nihira's work served the important function of helping researchers and service providers recognize that children live and are cared for in a variety of family systems. Their typology moved the field of family research beyond unidimensional questions about whether having a child with a disability affects the family to broader questions about the fit between the ways a child and family function.

Investigators operating from the perspective of ecocultural theory have broadened the field of family research even further. From this perspective, the family environment is embedded in multiple interacting systems (Bronfenbrenner, 1979), and adaptation is a continuing activity for all families (Weisner, 1993). Gallimore, Coots, Weisner, Garnier, and Guthrie (1996) investigated the functional adjustments that families make to sustain daily routines when raising a child with a disability. The types of accommodations parents make include arranging for suitable child care, making decisions about employment based on their child's needs, and home adaptations based on their child's motor abilities. Although parents make a wide range of accommodations during all phases of childhood, more accommodations tend to be made during middle childhood in comparison to earlier periods (Gallimore et al., 1996). Gallimore et al. (1999) maintained that understanding the many ways families organize their lives, the sources of their daily activities, and the meaning that they attribute to their family patterns of living are critical for the development of a fuller understanding of family functioning.

Both intrafamilial and extrafamilial components of families are critical aspects of the family system. With respect to intrafamilial influences, although the bulk of research has focused on mothers, knowledge is expanding on the well-being of fathers and siblings. Family members often provide support to each other, but they also receive support from those outside of the family (e.g., neighbors, friends, and professionals). Considering extrafamilial influences, the role of social support in parental (and by extension, familial) well-being is an area of rich research on families with a child with disabilities. In the following sections we review the research on fathers, siblings, and the role of social support in family functioning.

Fathers of Children With Developmental Disabilities

Mothers are often the primary caregivers of children and have been the focus of most research on children with disabilities. Indeed, mothers are often asked to be the spokesperson for the family. Although fathers often also have a central role in the life of the family, they have been studied less extensively than mothers, especially in families in which a child has a disability (Lamb & Billings, 1997). Early investigations focused on the extent to which fathers' supportiveness to their wives related to maternal well-being (Bristol, Gallagher, & Schopler, 1988). Thus, fathers were included in investigations as adjuncts to their wives.

In subsequent studies, however, paternal well-being has been investigated as an outcome in addition to being a mediator of maternal outcome. In a study of 30 couples of school-aged children with developmental disabilities, Dyson (1997) reported that fathers and mothers did not differ in their level of parenting stress, social support, or family functioning. Parenting stress was related, however, to problems encountered due to the child's needs and to parents' pessimism about the child's future. For both parents, stress was related to the family environment in terms of nurturance, facilitation of personal growth, and system maintenance.

In a comparison study of parents of children with Down syndrome and parents of children developing typically, Roach, Orsmond, and Barratt (1999) found that although parents of children with Down syndrome reported higher levels of caregiving difficulties, paternal and maternal ratings did not differ. Further, even though parents of children with Down syndrome reported higher rates of parenting stress than did comparison parents, mothers and fathers had similar levels of parenting stress.

In contrast, Scott, Atkinson, Minton, and Bowman (1997) found that mothers, in comparison to fathers, of young children with Down syndrome reported more psychological stress. Krauss (1993) compared the parenting stress of mothers and fathers of toddlers participating in the Early Intervention Collaborative Study (described earlier; Shonkoff et al., 1992). She reported that although levels of stress were quite similar for mothers and fathers (mainly within normative ranges), fathers reported more stress related to

their child's temperament and to their relationship with the child whereas mothers' stress derived from the demands of the parenting role. In longitudinal analyses of the same sample, Hauser-Cram et al. (2001) reported that although both mothers and fathers had increasing levels of stress related to their child with a disability from the early through middle childhood years, fathers showed greater increases in stress than mothers during the early childhood period. Further, trajectories of both maternal and paternal stress were predicted by children's self-regulatory behaviors, especially behavior problems. In addition, increasing patterns of stress were found for mothers with less helpful social support networks and for fathers with fewer problem-focused coping skills. The relation between changes in maternal and paternal well-being is an important area for researchers to address in the future.

Siblings of Children With Developmental Disabilities

Sibling relationships often provide the longest lasting intimate family bond. When reared together, siblings share numerous experiences and know intimate details of each other's history, forming a relationship that is distinct from any other. The familiarity and frequent interaction between siblings provides a context for children to develop perspective taking skills and the management of emotions and behavior (Dunn, 1999).

Similar to other families, siblings of children with developmental disabilities assume multiple roles such as companion, teacher, confidante, and friend (Stoneman, Brody, Davis, & Crapps, 1987). To accommodate the needs and abilities of their siblings with disabilities, they often provide instrumental teaching, behavioral management, and emotional support (Brody, Stoneman, Davis, & Crapps, 1991). Siblings of children with developmental disabilities are also more likely to perform these teaching roles for a longer period of time. Further, roles may be reversed at times when the older sibling has a developmental disability and the younger sibling becomes more advanced developmentally (Stoneman, Brody, Davis, Crapps, & Malone, 1991).

Zetlin (1986) emphasized that all family relationships, including the sibling dyad, change throughout the life span. In a longitudinal study of young children with Down syndrome and their siblings, differences between the cognitive and social abilities of children with developmental disabilities and their siblings affected the relationship less when children were younger (Abramovitch, Stanhope, Pepler, & Corter, 1987). As differences in language and adaptive skills increase, siblings tend to spend less time engaged in reciprocal interactions such as play or conversation (Wilson,

McGillivray, & Zetlin, 1992). School-aged children and their siblings with mental retardation have been observed to play together as frequently as matched comparison groups (Abramovitch et al., 1987). Nondisabled siblings often learn to accommodate to their sibling's lower cognitive abilities by playing less competitively and choosing appropriate toys that interest their siblings (Stoneman et al., 1987). As the reciprocity and equality between siblings decrease, roles can become asymmetric, with the typically developing sibling becoming more dominant and directive during interactions (Wilson et al., 1992).

Many adolescent siblings of individuals with mental retardation report a strong attachment to their brothers and sisters along with significant worries and concerns about the future care of their siblings (Eisenberg, Baker, & Blacher, 1998). In a study of adolescent and adult siblings, the majority indicated a willingness to be responsible for their brothers or sisters with disabilities in the future (Greenberg, Seltzer, Orsmond, & Krauss, 1999). Similar to siblings of typically developing children, more opportunities for interaction between siblings is related to the greater likelihood of stronger feelings, both positive and negative, reported by siblings (Bank & Kahn, 1982).

Much of the research on typically developing siblings indicates age and gender differences. Females who are older than their sibling with a disability have been found to assume a greater proportion of caregiving and household responsibilities than male siblings do (e.g., McHale & Gamble, 1989). Brody et al. (1991) found that greater responsibility of older school-aged siblings was associated with less time spent in leisure activities outside the home and, in some cases, more conflictual sibling interaction. In contrast, younger siblings (ranging in age from 4 to 20 years) who provided significant caregiving for an older sibling with a disability did not reveal negative adjustment but rather displayed a high degree of warmth and closeness to their brother or sister (Stoneman et al., 1991). Sibling outcomes appear to be dependent on multiple factors involving characteristics of the child with a disability, the sibling, as well as the adaptive functioning of the family as a unit.

Just as studies on parents of children with developmental disabilities often assumed pathology, early studies of siblings of children with disabilities assumed disadvantageous outcomes. Typically developing siblings were considered to be at risk for maladjustment as a consequence of the chronic stress, stigma, and responsibilities associated with the care of a sibling with disabilities (e.g., Farber, 1959). Some siblings reported lower self-concepts, anger, and subsequent guilt from perceptions that they received less attention from parents in comparison to their brother or sister with a disability (McHale & Gamble, 1989). Observations of families of children with disabilities have found that siblings of children with disabilities often receive significantly less parental attention than do siblings of typically developing children (Corter, Pepler, Stanhope, & Abramovitch, 1992).

As a consequence of greater time spent caring for their brother or sister with a disability, some typically developing siblings report loneliness due to having fewer opportunities to play outside the home or engage in normative sibling interactions (McHale & Gamble, 1989). Other siblings report feeling pressure to achieve to compensate their parents for the lower skills of their brother or sister with a disability (Seligman, 1983). In some studies, high rates of depression and conduct problems were reported, especially among sisters (Cuskelly & Gunn, 1993; McHale & Gamble, 1989).

In contrast, other researchers found positive adjustment among siblings and the provision of valuable experiences in sibling relationships (e.g., Eisenberg et al., 1998). Indeed, most recent reviews of sibling relationships indicate mixed support for the hypothesis that siblings of children with disabilities assume greater caregiving or are at greater risk for psychopathology (Damiani, 1999; Stoneman, 1998). Dyson (1989) reported that male siblings of children with mental retardation compared to male siblings of typically developing children demonstrated fewer behavior problems. Some adolescent and adult siblings have reported that the experience of living with a brother or sister with mental retardation helped them to develop greater empathy, as well as increased patience and acceptance of differences (Eisenberg et al., 1998). Among adult siblings of children with mental retardation, greater psychological adjustment was positively related to the degree of emotional intimacy between siblings (Seltzer, Greenberg, Krauss, & Gordon, 1997).

The adjustment of siblings is affected by multiple factors including the severity of their brother's or sister's disability and related needs, the temperament of each sibling, and behavioral, psychological, or health problems related to the sibling's disability (Stoneman, 1998). The most consistent finding in studies on sibling relationships is that problematic behaviors of the child with a disability are associated with higher conflict among siblings and less time engaged in activities together (Brody, Stoneman, & Burke, 1987).

Children with certain disabilities are more likely to exhibit problem behaviors. For example, children with Fragile X syndrome tend to exhibit behaviors that are less prosocial and more emotionally volatile than those of same-age children (Kerby & Dawson, 1994). Although children with Williams syndrome display high verbal skills and friendliness, they often exhibit attention-seeking and deficient social skills (Einfeld, Tonge, & Florio, 1997). These maladaptive behaviors have the potential of leading to conflictual relationships between siblings, as well as negatively affecting family functioning (Stoneman, 1998).

Many of the studies on sibling relationships focus on that relationship in the absence of knowledge about the overall functioning of the family system and the broader social-ecological settings in which families are embedded. The findings of several recent studies, however, indicate that sibling adjustment often parallels that of parents. Parents who perceive their child with a disability and the functioning of their family more positively tend to have siblings who have more positive feelings about their family and better psychological adjustment (e.g., Weinger, 1999). Similarly, Dyson, Edgar and Crnic (1989) reported that siblings from families who were less argumentative and more supportive toward family members were rated as more socially competent.

Open communication and responsiveness of family members to each other may be especially important for the positive adjustment of siblings of children with disabilities. Lynch, Fay, Funk, and Nagel (1993) found that conflict between parents and disorganized family functioning was associated with poor outcomes for siblings of children with mental retardation. The degree of cohesive, communicative functioning within the parent-child dyad as well as qualities of the sibling temperament predict fewer behavior problems and more positive adjustment in siblings (Dyson et al., 1989). Self-reports from adolescent siblings of children with mental retardation revealed that adolescents wished that their families would discuss issues concerning their sibling more often. These siblings reported that greater openness and expressiveness between family members would reduce their anxiety and strengthen their relationship with other family members (Eisenberg et al., 1998). Thus, future understanding of sibling relationships will benefit by considering the family context in which such relationships develop.

The Role of Social Support to Families of Children With Developmental Disabilities

Although many factors are hypothesized to explain why some families adjust positively and others experience dysfunction when raising a child with disabilities, social support is a factor that has received much attention from researchers. Social networks supply emotional and instrumental support to individuals and are composed of formally constructed (e.g., professionals and service providers) and informally constructed (e.g., friends, neighbors) groups (Dunst, Trivette, & Jodry, 1997). Thus, support networks are both an intrafamilial and an extrafamilial factor. The construct of support includes objective and subjective perspectives (Crnic & Stormshak, 1997). Support can be measured objectively by the size of support networks, and subjectively by the extent to which network members are appraised as helpful. Measures of helpfulness and satisfaction with one's support network, rather than network size, have generally been more useful indicators of the utility of support (Crnic & Stormshak, 1997).

Although Cochran and Brassard (1979) maintained that support networks could have both direct and indirect effects on children's development, most studies have indicated that social support serves to assist parents in their parenting role. Parental functioning, then, influences children's development. In studies of families with children with disabilities, social support has been found to relate to several parent and family outcomes. Crnic, Greenberg, Ragozin, Robinson, and Basham (1983) found that support from a spouse or partner and others in personal networks was related to maternal satisfaction with parenting and to general life satisfaction. Support has been found to interact with family characteristics, however. For example, in a study of families of children with or at risk for disabilities, Dunst, Trivette, and Cross (1986) reported that child progress was greatest for families with higher socioeconomic status and whose parents reported greater satisfaction with their support networks.

Investigations into the role of social support in the functioning of families of children with disabilities have been extensive because social support is often considered to be an intervention (Dunst et al., 1997). As an intervention, social support functions to assist families when it responds to the explicit needs of family members. Researchers have found that for parents with young children with developmental disabilities, hours of early intervention service are related to positive changes in perceived helpfulness of support (Warfield, Hauser-Cram, Krauss, Shonkoff, & Upshur, 2000). By providing increasing links with other families of young children with disabilities and creating access to knowledgeable service providers, programs like early intervention enhance the helpfulness of maternal support networks. This, in turn, makes it possible for families to mobilize the resources necessary to meet their needs. Social support is not a panacea, however, and increases in social support are only effective in influencing parental well-being and family functioning when parents' current support networks are inadequate to meet their needs. Some investigators have found that program-developed sources of support (i.e., formal support) provided to families who did not perceive a need for additional support resulted in deleterious parental outcomes (Affleck, Tennen, Rowe, Roscher, & Walker, 1989). Nevertheless, social support is recognized as an important factor in the ecology and functioning of the family system.

IMPLICATIONS AND FUTURE DIRECTIONS

The perspective of deviance that has dominated the history of public ideology and attitudes toward individuals with developmental disabilities is also somewhat reflected in the field of developmental psychology. To a large extent, the study of children with disabilities has been relegated to investigators in the fields of medicine, psychopathology, and special education. Indeed, very few, if any, prior handbooks in child psychology or developmental psychology include sections or chapters on children with disabilities. The relative neglect of investigations of children with disabilities in developmental psychology has led to a constricted view of normal development. In this way, developmental psychology remains an incomplete science.

Some have conceptualized the study of developmental delay as an experiment in nature because it creates a natural context in which to examine developmental processes and mechanisms in populations that exist at the extreme of the normal distribution (Hodapp & Burack, 1990). For example, Zigler (1969) studied children with mental retardation to understand if they evidenced a functional delay (and thus behaved like chronologically younger children) or a deficit (and thus behaved differently from other children). Zigler and Balla (1982) posed a question of whether children with mental retardation develop in ways similar to other children in terms of sequence and structure; this question is of central importance to those interested in understanding the process of human development. Other scholars have studied atypical populations to elucidate the extent to which specific developmental principles, such as orthogenesis and structural wholeness, generalize to all individuals (Cicchetti & Beeghly, 1990; H. Werner, 1957). An understanding of the way in which such principles apply to *all* individuals is critical to the growth of developmental psychology as a field in which the full spectrum of human development is studied and the role of individual regulation in the development of plasticity is investigated. Moreover, such understanding is also essential for the promotion of optimal functioning of individuals with developmental disabilities.

Within the past "Decade of the Brain" (Carnegie Task Force on Meeting the Needs of Young Children, 1994; Shore, 1997), advances in neurophysiology have increased knowledge about genetic disorders associated with developmental disabilities. For example, more than 750 genetic disorders have been associated with developmental disabilities, and 350 are related to mental retardation specifically (Matalainen, Airaksinen, Mononen, Launiala, & Kaariainen, 1995; Opitz, 1996). Diverse etiology and an array of behavioral phenotypes also have been specified (Dykens, 1995). The significant interindividual variability in the behavioral phenotypes of individuals with developmental delay demonstrates the numerous ways that typical development can be compromised by the multiple interactions of genetic, neurological, and environmental factors. In particular, a host of environmental teratogens have been identified that can modulate prenatal and postnatal neurological and behavioral development (e.g., Omaye, 1993). The differential probability of these effects, however, reflects the multiple risk or promotive factors that contribute to individual differences in the child's constitutional resilience (Shonkoff & Marshall, 2000; Volpe, 1995).

Developmental delay exemplifies the developmental principles of *equifinality* and *multifinality* (Cicchetti & Rogosch, 1996; Bertalanffy, 1968). In the former a variety of developmental processes can lead to a similar outcome, whereas in the latter a singular process or mechanism can lead to a range of outcomes. Outcomes are highly dependent on the organization and functioning of the systems in which development occurs. For example, equifinality is demonstrated by individuals with developmental disabilities of different etiologies who demonstrate similar levels of cognitive and adaptive functioning. Likewise, individuals who evidence the same chromosomal anomaly may develop very different outcomes depending on the support or organization of the family and related interacting systems in which they live.

The psychological research on the development of children with disabilities highlights the value of understanding the family and multiple systems in which children learn and are nurtured. The patterns found across empirical studies have implications for those developing programs or providing services to families of children with disabilities. Positive relationships within families (regardless of the composition of the family) are central to the optimal development of children with disabilities, their typically developing siblings, and parental well-being. Services during a child's early years typically focus on the child as a member of a family (Meisels & Shonkoff, 2000). Research findings suggest that such a focus is justified. In particular, synchronous styles of mother-child interaction relate to children's development and to the well-being of other family members. School-age services, however, typically focus on the child rather than on the child and family (McWilliam, Maxwell, & Sloper, 1999). Findings from empirical studies indicate, however, that parents are reporting higher levels of stress during the middle childhood period and may benefit from additional support during this time. Siblings' relationships also appear to reflect the relationships within the family system. Thus, school-age services may be more beneficial to children with disabilities if they become more family focused and family friendly.

We are only beginning to construct an understanding of the complex interrelation between the development of children with disabilities and the adaptations and accommodations of their families. For example, despite the growing recognition that culture provides the frame in which children develop, few have investigated how cultural conceptions of development relate to parenting a child with a disability (Garcia Coll & Magnuson, 2000). We also know little about the way families negotiate the multiple systems (e.g., health, education, and therapeutic services) in which they function and how that negotiation influences children's outcomes and family well-being. Aside from a comparatively large set of studies on mother-child interaction, bidirectional relations between children and other family members or among the various systems in which children develop remain unstudied. It is essential that such investigations be undertaken because children with developmental disabilities, like all children, deserve to be nurtured in ways that will optimize their development and help them to lead meaningful lives.

REFERENCES

Abidin, R. (1995). *Parenting Stress Index: Manual* (3rd ed.). Odessa, FL: Psychological Assessment Resources.

Abramovitch, R., Stanhope, L., Pepler, D., & Corter, C. (1987). The influence of Down's syndrome in sibling interaction. *Journal of Child Psychology and Psychiatry, 28,* 865–879.

Affleck, G., Tennen, H., Rowe, J., Roscher, B., & Walker, L. (1989). Effects of formal support on mothers' adaptation to the hospital-to-home transition of high-risk infants: The benefits and costs of helping. *Child Development, 60,* 488–501.

American Association on Mental Retardation (AAMR). (1992). *Mental retardation: Definition, classification, and systems of supports* (9th ed.) Washington, DC: American Association on Mental Retardation.

American Psychiatric Association. (1968). *Diagnostic and statistical manual of mental disorders* (2nd ed.). Washington, DC: Author.

American Psychiatric Association. (1994). *Diagnostic and statistical manual of mental disorders* (4th ed.). Washington, DC: Author.

Aristotle (n.d.). *The politics and the constitution of Athens.* Cambridge, UK: Cambridge University Press.

Bank, S., & Kahn, M. D. (1982). *The sibling bond.* New York: Basic Books.

Barnard, K. E., Hammond, M. A., Booth, C. L., Bee, H. L., Mitchell, S. K., & Spieker, S. J. (1989). Measurement and meaning of parent-child interaction. In F. Morrison, C. Lord, & D. Keating (Eds.), *Applied developmental psychology* (Vol. 3). New York: Academic Press.

Baron-Cohen, S. (1998). Modularity in developmental cognitive neuropsychology: Evidence from autism and Gilles de la Tourette syndrome. In J. A. Burack, R. M. Hodapp, & E. Zigler (Eds.), *Handbook of mental retardation and development* (pp. 334–348). New York: Cambridge University Press.

Baumeister, A. A. (1987). Mental retardation: Some conceptions and dilemmas. *American Psychologist, 52,* 796–800.

Beeghly, M., & Cicchetti, D. (1987). An organizational approach to symbolic development in children with Down syndrome. In D. Cicchetti & M. Beeghly (Eds.), *Symbolic development in atypical children* (pp. 5–30). San Francisco: Jossey-Bass.

Bell, R. Q. (1968). A reinterpretation of effects in studies of socialization. *Psychological Review, 75,* 81–95.

Bell, S. M., & Ainsworth, M. D. S. (1972). Infant crying and maternal responsiveness. *Child Development, 43,* 1171–1190.

Berger, J. (1990). Interactions between parents and their infants with Down syndrome. In D. Cicchetti & M. Beeghly (Eds.), *Children with Down syndrome: A developmental perspective* (pp. 101–146). New York: Cambridge University Press.

Bernheimer, L. P., & Keogh, B. K. (1988). Stability of cognitive performance of children with developmental delays. *American Journal on Mental Retardation, 92,* 539–542.

Bertalanffy, L., von (1968). *General systems theory: Foundation, development, and applications.* New York: Braziller.

Bijou, S. W. (1966). A functional analysis of retarded development. In N. R. Ellis (Ed.), *International review of research in mental retardation* (pp. 1–19). New York: Academic Press.

Bijou, S. W., & Baer, D. M. (1961). *Child development: A systematic and empirical theory.* New York: Appelton.

Blacher, J. (1984). Sequential stages of parental adjustment to the birth of a child with handicaps: Fact or artifact? *Mental Retardation, 22,* 55–68.

Blatt, B. (1985). The implications of the language of mental retardation for LD. *Journal of Learning Disabilities, 18,* 625–626.

Bloom, B. (1964). *Stability and change in human characteristics.* New York: Wiley.

Bornstein, M. H. (1989). Between caretakers and their young: Two modes of interaction and their consequences for cognitive growth. In M. H. Bornstein & J. S. Bruner (Eds.), *Interaction in human development* (pp. 197–214). Hillsdale, NJ: Erlbaum.

Bristol, M. M., Gallagher, J. J., & Schopler, E. (1988). Mothers and fathers of young developmentally disabled and nondisabled boys: Adaptation and spousal support. *Developmental Psychology, 24,* 441–451.

Brody, G. H., Stoneman, Z., & Burke, M. (1987). Child temperaments, maternal differential behavior, and sibling relations. *Developmental Psychology, 23,* 354–362.

Brody, G. H., Stoneman, Z., Davis, C. H., & Crapps, J. M. (1991). Observations of the role relations and behavior between older children with mental retardation and their younger siblings. *American Journal on Mental Retardation, 95,* 527–536.

Bronfenbrenner, U. (1979). *The ecology of human development.* Cambridge, MA: Harvard University Press.

Bronfenbrenner, U. (1986). Ecology of the family as a context for human development: Research perspectives. *Developmental Psychology, 22,* 723–742.

Cairns, R. B. (1998). The making of developmental psychology. In W. Damon (Series Ed.) & R. M. Lerner (Vol. Ed.), *Theoretical models of human development: Vol. 1. Handbook of child psychology* (5th ed., pp. 25–105). New York: Wiley.

Caldwell, B. M. (1973). The importance of beginning early. In M. B. Karnes (Ed.), *Not all little wagons are red: The exceptional child's early years* (pp. 2–10). Arlington, VA: Council for Exceptional Children.

Carnegie Task Force on Meeting the Needs of Young Children. (1994). *Starting points: Meeting the needs of our youngest children.* New York: Carnegie Corporation of New York.

Carr, J. (1988). Six months to twenty-one years old: A longitudinal study of children with Down's syndrome and their families. *Journal of Child Psychology and Psychiatry and Allied Disciplines, 29,* 407–431.

Carr, J. (1995). *Down's syndrome: Children growing up.* Cambridge, UK: Cambridge University Press.

Cicchetti, D., & Beeghly, M. (1990). *Children with Down syndrome: A developmental perspective.* New York: Cambridge University Press.

Cicchetti, R., & Rogosch, F. A. (1996). Equifinality and multifinality in developmental psychopathology. *Development and Psychopathology, 8,* 597–600.

Clare, L., Garnier, H., & Gallimore, R. (1998). Parents' developmental expectations and child characteristics: Longitudinal study of children with developmental delays and their families. *American Journal on Mental Retardation, 103,* 117–129.

Cochran, M. M., & Brassard, J. A. (1979). Child development and personal social networks. *Child Development, 50,* 601–615.

Connell, W. F. (1980). *A history of education in the twentieth century.* New York: Teachers College Press.

Corter, C., Pepler, D., Stanhope, L., & Abramovitch, R. (1992). Home observations of mothers and sibling dyads comprised of Down's syndrome and non-handicapped children. *Canadian Journal of Behavioural Science, 24,* 1–13.

Costigan, C. L., Floyd, F. J., Harter, K. S., & McClintock, J. C. (1997). Family process and adaptation to children with mental retardation: Disruption and resilience in family problem-solving interactions. *Journal of Family Psychology, 11,* 515–529.

Crnic, K., Greenberg, M. T., Ragozin, A. S., Robinson, N. M., & Basham, R. B. (1983). Effects of stress and social support on mothers and premature and full-term infants. *Child Development, 54,* 209–217.

Crnic, K., & Stormshak, E. (1997). The effectiveness of providing social support for families of children at risk. In M. J. Guralnick (Ed.), *The effectiveness of early intervention* (pp. 209–225). Baltimore: Paul H. Brookes.

Cunningham, C., & McArthur, K. (1981). Hearing loss and treatment in young Down syndrome children. *Child: Health, Care, and Development, 7,* 357–374.

Cuskelly, M., & Gunn, P. (1993). Maternal reports of the behavior of siblings of children with Down syndrome. *American Journal on Mental Retardation, 97,* 521–529.

Damiani, V. B. (1999). Responsibility and adjustment in siblings of children with disabilities: Update and review. *Families in Society, 80,* 34–40.

Degler, C. (1991). *In search of human nature: The decline and revival of Darwinism in American social thought.* New York: Oxford University Press.

Dixon, R. A., & Lerner, R. M. (1992). History of systems in developmental psychology. In M. H. Bornstein & M. E. Lamb (Eds.), *Developmental psychology: An advanced textbook* (3rd ed., pp. 3–58). Hillsdale, NJ: Erlbaum.

Duis, S., Summers, M., & Summers, C. R. (1997). Parent versus child stress in diverse family types: An ecological approach. *Topics in Early Childhood Special Education, 17,* 53–73.

Dunn, J. (1999). Siblings, friends, and the development of social understanding. In A. W. Collins & B. Laursen (Eds.), *Relationships as developmental contexts: The Minnesota symposia on child psychology* (Vol. 30, pp. 263–279). Mahwah, NJ: Erlbaum.

Dunst, C. J., Trivette, C. M., & Cross, A. (1986). Mediating influences of social support: Personal, family, and child outcomes. *American Journal of Mental Deficiency, 90,* 403–417.

Dunst, C. J., Trivette, C. M., & Jodry, W. (1997). Influences of social support on children with disabilities and their families. In M. Guralnick (Ed.), *The effectiveness of early intervention* (pp. 499–522). Baltimore: Paul H. Brookes.

Dykens, E. M. (1995). Measuring behavioral phenotypes: Provocations from the "New Genetics." *American Journal on Mental Retardation, 99,* 522–532.

Dyson, L. L. (1989). Adjustment of siblings of handicapped children: A comparison. *Journal of Pediatric Psychology, 14,* 215–229.

Dyson, L. L. (1997). Fathers and mothers of school-age children with developmental disabilities: Parental stress, family functioning, and social support. *American Journal on Mental Retardation, 102,* 267–279.

Dyson, L. L., Edgar, E., & Crnic, K. (1989). Psychological predictors of adjustment of siblings of developmentally disabled children. *American Journal on Mental Retardation, 94,* 292–302.

Eheart, B. K. (1982). Mother-child interactions with non-retarded and mentally retarded preschoolers. *American Journal of Mental Deficiency, 87,* 20–25.

Einfeld, S. L., Tonge, B. J., & Florio, T. (1997). Behavioral and emotional disturbance in individuals with Williams syndrome. *American Journal on Mental Retardation, 102,* 45–53.

Eisenberg, L., Baker, B. L., & Blacher, J. (1998). Siblings of children with mental retardation living at home or in residential placement. *Journal of Child Psychology and Psychiatry and Allied Disciplines, 39,* 355–363.

Elder, G. H., Jr. (1974). *Children of the Great Depression: Social change in life experience.* Chicago: University of Chicago Press.

Ellis, N. R. (1979). Introduction. In N. R. Ellis (Ed.), *Handbook of mental deficiency, psychological theory and research* (2nd ed., pp. xxv–xxix). Hillsdale, NJ: Erlbaum.

Farber, B. (1959). The effects of the severely retarded child on the family system. *Monographs of the Society for Research in Child Development, 24*(Serial No. 2).

Ford, D. L., & Lerner, R. M. (1992). *Developmental systems theory: An integrative approach.* Newbury Park, CA: Sage.

Forum on Child and Family Statistics. (1999). *America's children 1999.* Retrieved April 26, 2002, from www.childstats.gov/AC1999/spectxt.asp

Fuller, P. (1949). Operant conditioning of a vegetative human organism. *American Journal of Psychology, 62,* 587–590.

Gallimore, R., Bernheimer, L. P., & Weisner, T. S. (1999). Family life is more than managing crisis: Broadening the agenda of research on families adapting to childhood disability. In R. Gallimore, L. P. Bernheimer, D. L. MacMillan, D. L. Speece, & S. Vaughn (Eds.), *Developmental perspectives on children with high-incidence disabilities* (pp. 55–80). Mahwah, NJ: Erlbaum.

Gallimore, R., Coots, J., Weisner, T., Garnier, H., & Guthrie, D. (1996). Family responses to children with early developmental delays: II. Accommodation intensity and activity in early and middle childhood. *American Journal on Mental Retardation, 101,* 215–232.

Garcia Coll, C., & Magnuson, K. (2000). Cultural differences as sources of developmental vulnerabilities and resources. In J. P. Shonkoff & S. J. Meisles (Eds.), *Handbook of early childhood intervention* (2nd ed., pp. 94–114). New York: Cambridge University Press.

Glenn, S. S. (1997). Understanding human behavior: A key to solving social problems. In D. M. Baer & E. M. Pinkston (Eds.), *Environment and behavior* (pp. 13–14). Boulder, CO: Westview press.

Goddard, H. H. (1914). *Feeblemindedness: Its causes and consequences.* New York: MacMillan.

Goldberg, S. (1977). Social competence in infancy: A model of parent-infant interaction. *Merrill-Palmer Quarterly, 29,* 163–177.

Greenberg, J. S., Seltzer, M. M., Orsmond, G. I., & Krauss, M. W. (1999). Siblings of adults with mental illness or mental retardation: Current involvement and expectation of future caregiving. *Psychiatric Services, 50,* 1214–1219.

Guralnick, M. J. (1997). Second-generation research in the field of early intervention. In M. J. Guralnick (Ed.), *The effectiveness of early intervention* (pp. 3–20). Baltimore: Paul H. Brookes.

Hauser-Cram, P., Warfield, M. E., Shonkoff, J. P., & Krauss, M. W. (2001). Children with disabilities: A longitudinal study of child development and parent well-being. *Monographs of the Society for Research in Child Development, 66*(3, Serial No. 266).

Hauser-Cram, P., Warfield, M. E., Shonkoff, J. P., Krauss, M. W., Upshur, C. C., & Sayer, A. (1999). Family influences on adaptive development in young children with Down syndrome. *Child Development, 70,* 979–989.

Hawkins, G. D., & Cooper, D. H. (1990). Adaptive behavior measures in mental retardation research: Subject description in AJMD/AJMR articles (1979–1987). *American Journal on Mental Retardation, 94,* 654–660.

Hebb, D. O. (1949). *The organization of behavior: A neuropsychological theory.* New York: Wiley.

Heckhausen, J. (1993). The development of mastery and its perception within caretaker-child dyads. In D. J. Messer (Ed.), *Mastery motivation in early childhood: Development, measurement, and social processes* (pp. 55–79). London: Routledge.

Hill, R. (1949). *Families under stress.* New York: Harper & Row.

Hodapp, R. M., & Burack, J. A. (1990). What mental retardation tells us about typical development: The examples of sequences, rates, and cross-domain relations. *Development and Psychopathology, 2,* 213–225.

Hoppes, K., & Harris, S. L. (1990). Perceptions of child attachment and maternal gratification in mothers of children with autism and Down syndrome. *Journal of Clinical Child Psychology, 19,* 365–370.

Hunt, J. M. (1961). *Intelligence and experience.* New York: Ronald Press.

Inhelder, B. (1966). Cognitive development and its contribution to the diagnosis of some phenomena of mental deficiency. *Merrill-Palmer Quarterly, 11,* 299–319.

Innocenti, M. S., Huh, K., & Boyce, G. (1992). Families of children with disabilities: Normative data and other considerations on parenting stress. *Topics in Early Childhood Special Education, 12,* 403–427.

Jordan, T. E. (2000). Down's (1866) essay and its sociomedical context. *Mental Retardation, 38,* 322–329.

Kasari, C., Freeman, S., Mundy, P., & Sigman, M. D. (1995). Attention regulation by children with Down syndrome: Coordinated joint attention and social referencing looks. *American Journal on Mental Retardation, 100,* 128–136.

Kasari, C., Mundy, P., Yirmiya, N., & Sigman, M. (1991). Affect and attention in children with Down syndrome. *American Journal on Mental Retardation, 95,* 55–67.

Kelly, J. F., & Barnard, K. E. (2000). Assessment of parent-child interaction: Implications for early intervention. In J. Shonkoff & S. Meisels (Eds.), *Handbook of early childhood intervention* (2nd ed., pp. 258–289). New York: Cambridge University Press.

Keogh, B. K., Bernheimer, L. P., Gallimore, R., & Weisner, T. S. (1998). Child and family outcomes over time: A longitudinal perspective on developmental delays. In M. Lewis & C. Feiring (Eds.), *Families, risk, and competence* (pp. 269–287). Mahwah, NJ: Erlbaum.

Kerby, D. S., & Dawson, R. L. (1994). Autistic features, personality and adaptive behavior in males with Fragile X syndrome and no autism. *American Journal on Mental Retardation, 98,* 455–462.

Knieps, L. J., Walden, T. A., & Baxter, A. (1994). Affective expressions of toddlers with and without Down syndrome in a social referencing context. *American Journal on Mental Retardation, 99,* 301–312.

Krauss, M. W. (1993). Child-related and parenting stress: Similarities and differences between mothers and fathers of children with disabilities. *American Journal on Mental Retardation, 97,* 393–404.

Krauss, M. W. (1997). Two generations of family research in early intervention. In M. J. Guralnick (Ed.), *The effectiveness of early intervention* (pp. 611–624). Baltimore: Paul H. Brookes.

Lakin, K. C., Bruininks, R. H., & Larson, S. A. (1992). The changing face of residential services. In L. Rowitz (Ed.), *Mental retardation in the year 2000* (pp. 197–247). New York: Springer-Verlag.

Lamb, M. E., & Billings, L. A. (1997). Fathers of children with special needs. In M. E. Lamb (Ed.), *The role of the father in child development* (pp. 179–190). New York: Wiley.

Landry, S. H., Garner, P. W., Pirie, D., & Swank, P. R. (1994). Effects of social context and mothers' requesting strategies on Down's syndrome children's social responsiveness. *Developmental Psychology, 30,* 293–302.

Lerner, R. M. (1986). *Concepts and theories of human development* (2nd ed.). New York: Random House.

Lerner, R. M. (1991). Changing organism-context relations as the basic process of development: A developmental contextual perspective. *Developmental Psychology, 27,* 27–32.

Lerner, R. M. (1998). Theories of human development: Contemporary perspectives. In W. Damon (Series Ed.) & R. M. Lerner (Vol. Ed.), *Handbook of child psychology: Vol. 1. Theoretical models of development* (5th ed., pp. 1–24). New York: Wiley.

Lerner, R. M., Hauser-Cram, P., & Miller, E. (1998). Assumptions and features of longitudinal designs: Implications for early childhood education. In B. Spodek, O. N. Saracho, & A. Pellegrini (Eds.), *Yearbook in early education: Issues in early childhood educational research* (pp. 113–138). New York: Teachers College Press.

Lewis, M., & Lee-Painter, S. (1974). An interactional approach to the mother-child dyad. In M. Lewis & L. A. Rosenblum (Eds.), *The effect of the infant on its caregiver* (pp. 21–48). New York: Wiley.

Lifton, R. J. (1986). *The Nazi doctors.* New York: Basic Books.

Luckasson, R., Coulter, D. L., Polloway, E. A., Reiss, S., Schalock, R. L., Snell, M. E., Spitalnik, D. M., & Stark, J. A. (1992). *Mental retardation: Definition, classification, and systems of support.* Washington, DC: American Association on Mental Retardation.

Lynch, D. J., Fay, L., Funk, J., & Nagel, R. (1993). Siblings of children with mental retardation: Family characteristics and adjustment. *Journal of Child and Family Studies, 2,* 87–96.

MacMillan, D. L., Gresham, F. M., & Siperstein, G. N. (1993). Conceptual and psychometric concerns over the 1992 AAMR definition of mental retardation. *American Journal on Mental Retardation, 98,* 325–335.

Mahoney, G., Fors, S., & Wood, S. (1990). Maternal directive behavior revisited. *American Journal on Mental Retardation, 94,* 398–406.

Marfo, K. (1990). Maternal directiveness in interactions with mentally handicapped children: An analytical commentary. *Journal of Child Psychology and Psychiatry, 31,* 531–549.

Matalainen, R., Airaksinen, E., Mononen, T., Launiala, K., & Kaariainen, R. (1995). A population-based study on the causes of severe and profound mental retardation. *Acta Pediatrica, 84,* 261–266.

Maurer, H., & Sherrod, K. B. (1987). Context of directives given to young children with Down syndrome and nonretarded children: Development over two years. *American Journal of Mental Deficiency, 91,* 579–590.

McCubbin, H. I., & Patterson, J. M. (1982). Family adaptation to crises. In H. I. McCubbin & J. M. Patterson (Eds.), *Family stress, coping, and social support* (pp. 26–47). Springfield, IL: Charles C. Thomas.

McHale, S. M., & Gamble, W. C. (1989). Sibling relationships of children with disabled and nondisabled brothers and sisters. *Developmental Psychology, 25,* 421–429.

McWilliam, R. A., Maxwell, K. L., & Sloper, K. M. (1999). Beyond "involvement:" Are elementary schools ready to be family-centered? *School Psychology Review, 28,* 378–394.

Meisels, S. J., & Shonkoff, J. P. (2000). Early childhood intervention: A continuing evolution. In J. P. Shonkoff & S. J. Meisels (Eds.), *Handbook of early childhood intervention* (2nd ed., pp. 3–34). New York: Cambridge University Press.

Mink, I. T., Blacher, J., & Nihira, K. (1988). Taxonomy of family life styles: III. Replication with families with severely mentally retarded children. *American Journal on Mental Retardation, 93,* 250–264.

Mink, I. T., Meyers, C. E., & Nihira, K. (1984). Taxonomy of family life styles: II. Homes with slow-learning children. *American Journal of Mental Deficiency, 89,* 111–123.

Mink, I. T., & Nihira, K. (1986). Family life-styles and child behaviors: A study of direction of effects. *Developmental Psychology, 22,* 610–616.

Mink, I. T., Nihira, K., & Meyers, C. E. (1983). Taxonomy of family life styles: I. Homes with TMR children. *American Journal of Mental Deficiency, 87,* 484–497.

Minton, H. L. (1984). The Iowa Child Welfare Research Station and the 1940 debate on intelligence: Carrying on the legacy of a concerned mother. *Journal of the History of the Behavioral Sciences, 20,* 160–176.

Minuchin, P. P. (1988). Relationships within the family: A systems perspective on development. In R. A. Hinde & J. Stevenson-Hinde (Eds.), *Relationships within families: Mutual influences* (pp. 7–26). New York: Oxford University Press.

Omaye, S. T. (1993). Nutrient deficiencies and pregnancy outcome. In R. P. Sharma (Ed.), *Dietary factors and birth defects* (pp. 12–41). San Francisco: Pacific Division, AAAS.

Opitz, J. M. (1996, March). *Histiography of the causal analysis of mental retardation.* Paper presented at the 29th annual Gatlinburg Conference on Research and Theory in Mental Retardation and Developmental Disabilities, Gatlinburg, TN.

Orr, R. R., Cameron, S. J., Dobson, L. A., & Day, D. M. (1993). Age-related changes in stress experienced by families with a child who has developmental delays. *Mental Retardation, 31,* 171–176.

Overton, W. F. (1998). Developmental psychology: Philosophy, concepts, and methodology. In W. Damon (Series Ed.) & R. M. Lerner (Vol. Ed.), *Theoretical models of human development: Vol. 1. Handbook of child psychology* (5th ed., pp. 107–188). New York: Wiley.

Overton, W. F., & Reese, H. W. (1973). Models of development: Methodological implications. In J. R. Nesselroade & H. W. Reese (Eds.), *Life-span developmental psychology: Methodological issues* (pp. 65–86). New York: Academic Press.

Parks, R. (1977). Parental reactions to the birth of a handicapped child. *Health and Social Work, 2,* 52–66.

Pueschel, S. M. (1980). Description of the Down syndrome program. In S. M. Pueschel (Ed.), *The young child with Down syndrome* (pp. 27–37). New York: Human Sciences Press.

Reed, R. B., Pueschel, S. M., Schnell, R. R., & Cronk, C. E. (1980). Interrelationships of biological, environmental, and competency variables. In S. M. Pueschel (Ed.), *The young child with Down syndrome* (pp. 285–299). New York: Human Sciences Press.

Resch, R. C., Grand, S., & May, M. (1988). Eye, hand, and the mother: The mother's role in neuromaturation and development of an autistic child. *Bulletin of the Menninger Clinic, 52,* 304–320.

Roach, M. A., & Barratt, M., Miller, J. F., & Leavitt, L. A. (1998). The structure of mother-child play: Young children with Down syndrome and typically developing children. *Developmental Psychology, 34,* 77–87.

Roach, M. A., Orsmond, G. I., & Barratt, M. (1999). Mothers and fathers of children with Down syndrome: Parental stress and involvement in child care. *American Journal on Mental Retardation, 104,* 422–436.

Rush, J., & Frances, A. (Eds.). (2000). Expert consensus guideline series: Treatment of psychiatric and behavioral problems in mental retardation. *American Journal on Mental Retardation, 105,* 159–226.

Sameroff, A. J., & Chandler, M. J. (1975). Reproductive risk and the continuum of caretaking casualty. In F. D. Horowitz, M. Hetherington, S. Scarr-Salapatek, & G. Siegel (Eds.), *Review of child development research* (Vol. 4., pp. 187–244). Chicago: University of Chicago Press.

Sameroff, A. J., & Fiese, B. H. (2000). Transactional regulation: The developmental ecology of early intervention. In J. P. Shonkoff &

S. J. Meisels (Eds.), *Handbook of early childhood intervention* (2nd ed., pp.135–159). New York: Cambridge University Press.

Scheerenberger, R. C. (1983). *A history of mental retardation.* Baltimore: Paul H. Brookes.

Schnell, R. R. (1984). Psychomotor development. In S. M. Pueschel (Ed.), *The young child with Down syndrome* (pp. 207–226). New York: Human Sciences Press.

Scott, B. S., Atkinson, L., Minton, H., & Bowman, T. (1997). Psychological distress of parents of infants with Down syndrome. *American Journal on Mental Retardation, 102,* 161–171.

Seligman, M. (1983). Sources of psychological disturbance among siblings of handicapped children. *Personnel and Guidance Journal, 67,* 529–531.

Seltzer, M. M., Greenberg, J. S., Krauss, M. W., & Gordon, R. M. (1997). Siblings of adults with mental retardation or mental illness: Effects of lifestyle and psychological well-being. *Family Relations: Interdisciplinary Journal of Applied Family Studies, 46,* 395–405.

Shonkoff, J. P., Hauser-Cram, P., Krauss, M. W., & Upshur, C. C. (1992). Development of infants with disabilities and their families. *Monographs of the Society for Research in Child Development, 57*(6, Serial No. 230).

Shonkoff, J. P., & Marshall, P. C. (2000). The biology of developmental vulnerability. In J. P. Shonkoff & S. J. Meisels (Eds.), *Handbook of early childhood intervention* (2nd ed., pp. 35–53). New York: Cambridge University Press.

Shore, R. (1997). *Rethinking the brain: New insights into early development.* New York: Families and Work Institute.

Sigman, M., & Ruskin, E. (1999). Continuity and change in the social competence of children with autism, Down syndrome, and developmental delays. *Monographs of the Society for Research in Child Development, 64*(Serial No. 256).

Skinner, B. F. (1953). *Science and human behavior.* New York: Macmillan.

Somerfield, M. R., & McCrae, R. R. (2000). Stress and coping research: methodological challenges, theoretical advances, and clinical applications. *American Psychologist, 55,* 620–625.

Spradlin, J. E., & Girardeau, F. L. (1966). The behavior of moderately and severely retarded persons. In N. R. Ellis (Ed.), *International review of research in mental retardation* (pp. 257–298). New York: Academic Press.

Sroufe, L. A. (1996). *Emotional development: The organization of emotional life in the early years.* New York: Cambridge University Press.

Stoneman, Z. (1998). Research on siblings of children with mental retardation: Contributions of developmental theory and etiology. In J. A. Burack, R. M. Hodapp, & E. Zigler (Eds.), *Handbook of mental retardation and development* (pp. 669–692). New York: Cambridge University Press.

Stoneman, Z., Brody, G. H., Davis, C. H., Crapps, J. M. (1987). Mentally retarded children and their older same-sex siblings:

Naturalistic in-home observations. *American Journal on Mental Retardation, 92,* 290–298.

Stoneman, Z., Brody, G. H., Davis, C. H., Crapps, J. M., & Malone, D. M. (1991). Ascribed role relations between children with mental retardation and their younger siblings. *American Journal on Mental Retardation, 95,* 537–550.

Szymanski, L. S., & Wilska, M. (1997). Mental retardation. In A. Tasman, J. King, & J. A. Lieberman (Eds.), *Psychiatry* (pp. 605–635). Philadelphia: W. B. Saunders.

Thelen, E., & Smith, L. B. (1998). Dynamic systems theories. In W. Damon (Series Ed.) & R. M. Lerner (Vol. Ed.), *Handbook of child psychology: Vol. 1. Theoretical models of human development* (5th ed., pp. 563–633). New York: Wiley.

Volpe, J. J. (1995). *Neurology of the newborn.* Philadelphia: W. B. Saunders.

Vygotsky, L. S. (1993). In R. W. Rieber & A. S. Carton (Eds.), *The collected works of L. S. Vygotsky: Vol. 2. The fundamentals of defectology.* New York: Plenum. (Original work published in 1924–1931)

Walsh, F. (Ed.). (1980). *Normal family processes.* New York: Guilford Press.

Warfield, M. E., Hauser-Cram, P., Krauss, M. W., Shonkoff, J. P., & Upshur, C. C. (2000). The effect of early intervention services on maternal well-being. *Early Education and Development, 11,* 499–517.

Warfield, M. E., Krauss, M. W., Hauser-Cram, P., Upshur, C. C., & Shonkoff, J. P. (1999). Adaptation during early childhood among mothers of children with disabilities. *Journal of Developmental and Behavioral Pediatrics, 20,* 9–16.

Weinger, S. (1999). Views of the child with mental retardation: Relationship to family functioning. *Family Therapy, 26,* 63–79.

Weisner, T. S. (1993). Siblings in cultural place: Ethnographic and ecocultural perspectives on siblings of developmentally delayed children. In Z. Stoneman & P. Berman (Eds.), *Siblings of individuals with mental retardation, physical disabilities, and chronic illness* (pp. 51–83). Baltimore: Paul H. Brookes.

Werner, E., & Smith, R. S. (1992). *Overcoming the odds: High risk children from birth to adulthood.* Ithaca, NY: Cornell University Press.

Werner, H. (1957). The concept of development from a comparative and organismic point of view. In D. B. Harris (Ed.), *The concept of development* (pp. 125–148). Minneapolis: University of Minnesota Press.

Werner, H., & Strauss, A. (1939). Problems and methods of functional analysis in mentally deficient children. *Journal of Abnormal and Social Psychology, 34,* 37–62.

Wikler, L. (1981). Chronic stresses of families of mentally retarded children. *Family Relations, 30,* 281–288.

Wilson, C. J., McGillivray, J. A., & Zetlin, A. G. (1992). The relationship between attitude to disabled siblings and ratings of behavioural competency. *Journal of Intellectual Disability Research, 36,* 325–336.

Winship, A. E. (1900). *Jukes—Edwards: A study in education and heredity.* Harrisburg, PA: R. L. Myers.

Wishart, J. G., & Duffy, L. (1990). Instability of performance on cognitive tests in infants and young children with Down's syndrome. *British Journal of Educational Psychology, 60,* 10–22.

Zetlin, A. (1986). Mentally retarded adults and their siblings. *American Journal of Mental Deficiency, 91,* 217–225.

Zigler, E. (1969). Developmental versus difference theories of retardation and the problem of motivation. *American Journal of Mental Deficiency, 73,* 536–556.

Zigler, E., & Balla, D. (1982). Motivational and personality factors in the performance of the retarded. In E. Zigler & D. Balla (Eds.), *Mental retardation: The developmental-difference controversy* (pp. 9–26). Hillsdale, NJ: Erlbaum.

Zirpoli, T. J., & Bell, R. Q. (1987). Unresponsiveness in children with severe disabilities: Potential effects on parent-child interactions. *Exceptional Child, 34,* 31–40.

CHAPTER 22

Applied Developmental Science of Positive Human Development

RICHARD M. LERNER, PAMELA M. ANDERSON, AIDA BILALBEGOVIĆ BALSANO, ELIZABETH M. DOWLING, AND DEBORAH L. BOBEK

The latter part of the twentieth century was marked by public anxiety about a myriad of social problems—some old, some new, but all affecting the lives of vulnerable children, adolescents, adults, families, and communities (Fisher & Murray, 1996; R. M. Lerner & Galambos, 1998; R. M. Lerner, Sparks, & McCubbin, 1999). In America, for instance, a set of problems of historically unprecedented scope and severity involved interrelated issues of economic development, environmental quality, health and health care delivery, poverty, crime, violence, drug and alcohol use and abuse, unsafe sex, and school failure.

Indeed, in the latter portion of the twentieth century and into the present one, and across the United States and in other nations, infants, children, adolescents, and the adults who care for them continued to die from the effects of these social problems (Dryfoos, 1990; Hamburg, 1992; Hernandez, 1993; Huston, 1991; R. M. Lerner, 1995; Schorr, 1988, 1997). If people were not dying, their prospects for future success were being reduced by civil unrest and ethnic conflict, by famine, by environmental challenges (e.g., involving water quality and solid waste management), by school underachievement and dropout, by teenage pregnancy and parenting, by lack of job opportunities and preparedness, by prolonged welfare dependency, by challenges to their health (e.g., lack of immunization, inadequate screening for disabil-

ities, insufficient prenatal care, and lack of sufficient infant and childhood medical services), and by the sequelae of persistent and pervasive poverty (Huston, McLoyd, & Garcia Coll, 1994; R. M. Lerner & Fisher, 1994). These issues challenge the resources and the future viability of civil society in America and throughout the world (R. M. Lerner, Fisher, & Weinberg, 2000a, 2000b).

The potential role of scientific knowledge about human development in addressing these issues of individuals, families, communities, and civil society resulted in growing interest and activity in what has been termed *applied developmental science* (ADS). As explained by Wertlieb (this volume), scholars such as Celia B. Fisher (Fisher & Lerner, 1994; Fisher et al., 1993), Richard A. Weinberg (e.g., R. M. Lerner, Fisher, & Weinberg, 1997, 2000a, 2000b), Lonnie R. Sherrod (e.g., 1999a, 1999b), Jacquelynne Eccles (Eccles, Lord, & Buchanan, 1996), Ruby Takanishi (1993), and Richard M. Lerner (1998b, 2002a, 2002b) specify that ADS is scholarship that is predicated on a developmental systems theoretical perspective. This theoretical approach sees the multiple levels of organizations involved in human development—including biology, psychology, social relations, group/institutions, culture, physical environment, and history—as existing in an integrated, fused system. The perspective stresses that *relations* among components of the system are the appropriate units of developmental analysis (R. M. Lerner, 1998b, 2002a; chapter by Wertlieb in this volume). This approach also views individuals as active producers of their own development through the relationships they have with their contexts (R. M. Lerner, 1982; R. M. Lerner & Walls, 1999). Given that development occurs through the changing relations that individuals have with their contexts, there is an opportunity for plasticity, for systematically changing the course of human development by altering the trajectory of these relations (Fisher & Lerner, 1994; chapter by Wertlieb in this volume).

Consistent with its emphasis on integrated systems, ADS seeks to synthesize developmental research with community outreach in order to describe, explain, and enhance the life chances of vulnerable children, adolescents, young and old adults, and their families across the life span (Fisher & Lerner, 1994; chapter by Wertlieb in this volume). Given its roots in developmental systems theory, ADS challenges the usefulness of decontextualized knowledge and, as a consequence, the legitimacy of isolating scholarship from the pressing human problems of our world.

In this chapter we discuss key facets of the theoretical bases for the integrated approach taken by ADS to knowledge generation and knowledge application. We emphasize the central role of fused relations between individuals and contexts (or, more generally, among levels of organization in the developmental system) in the theoretical and empirical work legitimating the ADS approach to knowledge. To advance our argument we first review the key conceptual principles associated with ADS and the relational foci of ADS scholarship. We emphasize the synthetic view of basic, explanatory research and applied research that is brought to the fore by the developmental systems thinking that frames ADS, and we explain why person-context relations constitute the core focus of research designed to study the basic process of human development envisioned within ADS. Several lines of research that model such person-context relations are reviewed, including those associated with the goodness-of-fit model (e.g., Chess & Thomas, 1999), the stage-environment fit model (e.g., Eccles, Midgley, et al., 1993), and models integrating individual and community assets in the promotion of positive youth development (Benson, 1997; Damon, 1997).

The Principles of Applied Developmental Science

As explained in detail in Wertlieb (this volume), Fisher and her colleagues (Fisher et al., 1993) delineated five conceptual components that characterize the principles or core substantive features of ADS. Taken together, these conceptual features make ADS a unique approach to understanding and promoting positive development.

The first conceptual component of ADS is the notion of the temporality, or historical embeddedness, of change pertinent to individuals, families, institutions, and communities. Some components of the context or of individuals remain stable over time, and other components may change historically. Because phenomena of human behavior and development vary historically, one must assess whether generalizations across time periods are legitimate. Thus, temporality has important implications for research design, service provision, and program evaluation.

Interventions are aimed at altering the developmental trajectory of within-person changes. To accomplish this aim, the second conceptual feature of ADS is that applied developmental scientists take into account interindividual differences (diversity) among, for instance, racial, ethnic, social class, and gender groups, as well as intra-individual changes, such as those associated with puberty.

The third conceptual feature of ADS places an emphasis on the centrality of context. There is a focus on the relations among all levels of organization within the ecology of human development. These levels involve biology, families, peer groups, schools, businesses, neighborhoods and communities, physical-ecological settings, and the sociocultural, political, legal-moral, and economic institutions of society. Together, bidirectional relations among these levels of the developmental system necessitate systemic approaches to research, program and policy design, and program and policy implementation.

The fourth principle of ADS emphasizes descriptively normative developmental processes and primary prevention and optimization rather than remediation. Applied developmental scientists emphasize healthy and normative developmental processes and seek to identify the strengths and assets of individual groups and settings, rather than focusing on deficits, weaknesses, or problems of individuals, families, or communities. Instead of dwelling on the problems faced by people, applied developmental scientists aim to find combinations of individual and ecological assets associated with thriving among people (e.g., Benson, 1997; Benson, Leffert, Scales, & Blyth, 1998; Leffert et al., 1998; Scales, Benson, Leffert, & Blyth, 2000) and with the *five Cs* of positive individual development: competence, confidence, connection, character, and caring/compassion (Hamilton & Hamilton, 1999; R. M. Lerner, 2002b; Little, 1993; Pittman, 1996).

The final principle of ADS is the appreciation of the bidirectional relationship between knowledge generation and knowledge application. By acknowledging bidirectionality, applied developmental scientists recognize the importance of knowledge about life and development that exists among the individuals, families, and communities being served by

ADS. For applied developmental scientists, collaboration and colearning between researchers/universities and communities are essential features of the scholarly enterprise (R. M. Lerner, 1998a, 1998b). Such community-collaborative efforts are termed *outreach scholarship* (R. M. Lerner & Miller, 1998).

In other words, given the developmental systems perspective that ADS is predicated on, applied developmental scientists assume that

> there is an interactive relationship between science and application. Accordingly, the work of those who generate empirically based knowledge about development and those who provide professional services or construct policies affecting individuals and families is seen as reciprocal in that research and theory guide intervention strategies and the evaluation of interventions and policies provides the bases for reformulating theory and future research. . . . As a result, applied developmental [scientists] not only disseminate information about development to parents, professionals, and policy makers working to enhance the development of others, they also integrate the perspectives and experiences of these members of the community into the reformulation of theory and the design of research and interventions. (Fisher & Lerner, 1994, p. 7)

Foci of Applied Developmental Science

The National Task Force on Applied Developmental Science (Fisher et al., 1993) indicated that the activities of ADS span a continuum from knowledge generation to knowledge application (see also chapter by Wertlieb in this volume). These activities include, but are not limited to, research on the applicability of scientific theory to growth and development in natural, ecologically valid contexts; the study of developmental correlates of phenomena of social import; the construction and utilization of developmentally and contextually sensitive assessment instruments; the design and evaluation of developmental interventions and enhancement programs; and the dissemination of developmental knowledge to individuals, families, communities, practitioners, and policy makers through developmental education, printed and electronic materials, the mass media, expert testimony, and community collaborations.

Given their belief in the importance for developmental analysis of systemically integrating all components within the ecology of human development, and their stress on integrating through collaboration and colearning the expertise of the researcher with the expertise of the community, proponents of ADS believe that researchers and the institutions within which they work are part of the developmental system that ADS tries to understand and enhance. ADS emphasizes

that the scholar/university-community partnerships that they seek to enact are an essential means of contextualizing knowledge. By embedding scholarship about human development within the diverse ecological settings within which people develop, applied developmental scientists foster bidirectional relationships between research and practice. Within such relationships developmental research both guides and is guided by the outcomes of community-based interventions, for example, public policies or programs aimed at enhancing human development.

The growth of such outreach scholarship has fostered a scholarly challenge to prior conceptions of the nature of the world (Cairns, Bergman, & Kagan, 1998; R. M. Lerner & Miller, 1998; W. Overton, 1998; Valsiner, 1998). The idea that all knowledge is related to its context has promoted a change in the typical ontology within current scholarship. This change has emerged as a focus on relationism and an avoidance of split conceptions of reality, such as nature versus nurture (W. Overton, 1998). This ontological change has helped advance the view that all existence is contingent on the specifics of the physical and social-cultural conditions that exist at a particular moment of history (W. Overton, 1998; Pepper, 1942). Changes in epistemology that have been associated with this revision in ontology and contingent knowledge can be understood only if relationships are studied.

Accordingly, any instance of knowledge (e.g., the core knowledge of a given discipline) must be integrated with knowledge of (a) the context surrounding it and (b) the relation between knowledge and context. Thus, knowledge that is disembedded from the context is not basic knowledge. Rather, knowledge that is relational to its context, for example, to the community, as it exists in its ecologically valid setting (Trickett, Barone, & Buchanan, 1996), is basic knowledge. Having an ontology of knowledge as ecologically embedded and contingent rationalizes the interest of ADS scholars in learning to integrate what they know with what is known of and by the context (Fisher, 1997). It thus underscores the importance of colearning collaborations between scholars and community members as a key part of the knowledge-generation process (Higgins-D'Alessandro, Fisher, & Hamilton, 1998; R. M. Lerner & Simon, 1998a, 1998b). In sum, significant changes that have occurred in the way in which social and behavioral scientists (and human developmentalists more specifically) have begun to reconceptualize their roles and responsibilities to society is in no greater evidence than in the field of ADS (Fisher & Murray, 1996; R. M. Lerner, 2002a, 2002b; R. M. Lerner et al., 2000a, 2000b).

Human developmental science has long been associated with laboratory-based scholarship devoted to uncovering universal aspects of development by stripping away contextual influences (Cairns et al., 1998; Hagen, 1996; Youniss, 1990). However, the mission and methods of human development are being transformed into an ADS devoted to discovering diverse developmental patterns by examining the dynamic relations between individuals within the multiple, embedded contexts of the integrated developmental systems in which they live (Fisher & Brennan, 1992; Horowitz, 2000; Horowitz & O'Brien, 1989; Morrison, Lord, & Keating, 1984; Power, Higgins, & Kohlberg, 1989; Sigel, 1985). This theoretical revision of the target of developmental analysis from the elements of relations to interlevel relations has significant implications for applications of developmental science to policies and programs aimed at promoting positive human development. Arguably the most radical feature of the theoretical, research, and applied agenda of applied developmental scientists is the idea that research about basic relational processes of development and applications focused on enhancing person-context relations across ontogeny are one and the same. To explain this fusion, it is important to discuss in some detail the link between developmental systems theory and ADS.

FROM DEVELOPMENTAL SYSTEMS THEORIES TO APPLIED DEVELOPMENTAL SCIENCE

Paul Mussen, the editor of the third edition of the *Handbook of Child Psychology,* presaged what today is abundantly clear about the contemporary stress on systems theories of human development. Mussen (1970, p. vii) said, "The major contemporary empirical and theoretical emphases in the field of developmental psychology . . . seem to be on *explanations* of the psychological changes that occur, the mechanisms and processes accounting for growth and development." This vision alerted developmental scientists to a burgeoning interest not in structure, function, or content per se, but in change, in the processes through which change occurs, and in the means through which structures transform and functions evolve over the course of human life.

Today, Mussen's (1970) vision has been crystallized. The cutting edge of contemporary developmental theory is represented by systems conceptions of process, of how structures function and how functions are structured over time. Thus, developmental systems theories of human development are not tied necessarily to a particular content domain, although particular empirical issues or substantive foci (e.g., motor development, successful aging, wisdom, extraordinary cognitive achievements, language acquisition, the self, psychological complexity, or concept formation) may lend

themselves readily as exemplary sample cases of the processes depicted in a given theory (see R. M. Lerner, 1998a).

The power of developmental systems theories lies in their ability not to be limited or confounded by an inextricable association with a unidimensional portrayal of the developing person. In developmental systems theories the person is neither biologized, psychologized, nor sociologized. Rather, the individual is systemized. A person's development is embedded within an integrated matrix of variables derived from multiple levels of organization. Development is conceptualized as deriving from the dynamic relations among the variables within this multitiered matrix.

Developmental systems theories use the polarities that engaged developmental theory in the past (e.g., nature/nurture, individual/society, biology culture; R. M. Lerner, 1976, 1986, 2002a), not to split depictions of developmental processes along conceptually implausible and empirically counterfactual lines (Gollin, 1981; W. Overton, 1998) or to force counterproductive choices between false opposites (e.g., heredity or environment, continuity or discontinuity, constancy or change; R. M. Lerner, 2002a), but to gain insight into the integrations that exist among the multiple levels of organization involved in human development. These theories are certainly more complex than their one-sided predecessors. They are also more nuanced, more flexible, more balanced, and less susceptible to extravagant or even absurd claims (e.g., that nature split from nurture can shape the course of human development; that there is a gene for altruism, militarism, or intelligence; or that when the social context is demonstrated to affect development the influence can be reduced to a genetic one; e.g., Hamburger, 1957; Lorenz, 1966; Plomin, 1986, 2000; Plomin, Corley, DeFries, & Faulker, 1990; Rowe, 1994; Rushton, 1987, 1988a, 1988b, 1997, 1999).

These mechanistic and atomistic views of the past have been replaced, then, by theoretical models that stress the dynamic synthesis of multiple levels of analysis, a perspective having its roots in systems theories of biological development (Cairns, 1998; Gottlieb, 1992; Kuo, 1930, 1967, 1976; T. C. Schneirla, 1956; T. C. Schneirla, 1957; von Bertalanffy, 1933). In other words, development, understood as a property of systemic change in the multiple and integrated levels of organization (ranging from biology to culture and history) comprising human life and its ecology, is an overarching conceptual frame associated with developmental systems models of human development.

Explanation and Application: A Synthesis

This stress on the dynamic relation between the individual and his or her context results in the recognition that a synthesis of perspectives from multiple disciplines is needed to understand the multilevel integrations involved in human development. In addition, to understand the basic process of human development both descriptive and explanatory research must be conducted within the actual ecology of people's lives.

Explanatory studies, by their very nature, constitute intervention research. The role of the developmental researcher conducting explanatory research is to understand the ways in which variations in person-context relations account for the character of human developmental trajectories, life paths that are enacted in the natural laboratory of the real world. To gain an understanding of how theoretically relevant variations in person-context relations may influence developmental trajectories, the researcher may introduce policies or programs as experimental manipulations of the proximal or distal natural ecology. Evaluations of the outcomes of such interventions become a means to bring data to bear on theoretical issues pertinent to person-context relations. More specifically, these interventions have helped applied developmental scientists to understand the plasticity in human development that may exist and that may be capitalized on to enhance human life (Csikszentmihalyi & Rathunde, 1998; R. M. Lerner, 1984).

The interindividual differences in intra-individual change that exist as a consequence of these naturally occurring interventions attest to the magnitude of the systematic changes in structure and function—the plasticity—that characterize human life. Explanatory research is necessary, however, to understand what variables, from what levels of organization, are involved in particular instances of plasticity that have been seen to exist. In addition, such research is necessary to determine what instances of plasticity may be created by science or society. In other words, explanatory research is needed to ascertain the extent of human plasticity or, in turn, to test the limits of plasticity (Baltes, Lindenberger, & Staudinger, 1998; R. M. Lerner, 1984).

From a developmental systems perspective, the conduct of such research may lead the scientist to alter the natural ecology of the person or group he or she is studying. Such research may involve either proximal or distal variations in the context of human development (R. M. Lerner & Ryff, 1978); in any case, these manipulations constitute theoretically guided alterations of the roles and events a person or group experiences at, or over, a portion of the life span.

These alterations are indeed, then, interventions: They are planned attempts to alter the system of person-context relations that constitute the basic process of change; they are conducted in order to ascertain the specific bases of, or to test the limits of, particular instances of human plasticity (Baltes, 1987; Baltes & Baltes, 1980). These interventions are a

researcher's attempt to substitute designed person-context relations for naturally occurring ones in an attempt to understand the process of changing person-context relations that provides the basis of human development. In short, basic research in human development is intervention research (R. M. Lerner et al., 1994).

Accordingly, the cutting edge of theory and research in human development lies in the application of the conceptual and methodological expertise of human developmental scientists to the natural ontogenetic laboratory of the real world. This placement into the actual ecology of human development of explanatory research about the basic, relational process of development involves the fusion of application with basic developmental science. To pursue the study of ontogeny from a developmental systems perspective, a research-application agenda that is focused on the relations between diverse individuals and their similarly diverse contexts is brought to the fore (R. M. Lerner, 2002a). In addition, however, scholars involved in such research must have at least two other concerns, ones deriving from the view that basic, explanatory research in human development is, in its essence, intervention research.

Research in human development that is concerned with one or even a few instances of individual and contextual diversity cannot be assumed to be useful for understanding the life course of all people. Similarly, policies and programs derived from such research, or associated with it in the context of a researcher's tests of ideas pertinent to human plasticity, cannot hope to be applicable, or equally appropriate and useful, in all contexts or for all individuals. Accordingly, developmental and individual differences–oriented policy development and program (intervention) design and delivery must be a key part of the approach to applied developmental research for which we are calling.

The variation in settings within which people live means that studying development in a standard (e.g., a controlled) environment does not provide information pertinent to the actual (ecologically valid) developing relations between individually distinct people and their specific contexts (e.g., their particular families, schools, or communities). This point underscores the need to conduct research in real-world settings (Bronfenbrenner, 1974; Zigler, 1998) and highlights the ideas that (a) policies and programs constitute natural experiments (i.e., planned interventions for people and institutions) and (b) the evaluation of such activities becomes a central focus in the developmental systems research agenda we have described (R. M. Lerner, 1995; R. M. Lerner, Ostrom, & Freel, 1995).

In this view, then, policy and program endeavors do not constitute secondary work, or derivative applications, conducted after research evidence has been complied. Quite to the contrary, policy development and implementation, as well as program design and delivery, become integral components of the ADS approach to research; the evaluation component of such policy and intervention work provides critical feedback about the adequacy of the conceptual frame from which this research agenda should derive (Zigler, 1998; Zigler & Finn-Stevenson, 1992).

In essence, a developmental systems perspective leads us to recognize that if we are to have an adequate and sufficient science of human development, we must integratively study individual and contextual levels of organization in a relational and temporal manner (Bronfenbrenner, 1974; Zigler, 1998). And if we are to serve America's citizens and families through our science, and if we are to help develop successful policies and programs through our scholarly efforts—efforts that result in the promotion of positive human development—then we may make great use of the integrative, temporal, and relational model of the person and of his or her context that is embodied in the developmental systems perspective forwarded in developmental system theories of human development.

Toward the Testing of a Developmental Systems Approach to Applied Developmental Science

The key test of the usefulness of the integrative, relational ideas of applied developmental scientists lies in a demonstration of the greater advantages for understanding and applying a synthetic focus on person-context relations—as compared to an approach to developmental analysis predicated on splitting individual from context or on splitting any level within the developmental system from another (e.g., through genetic reductionism, splitting biological from individual-psychological or social levels; e.g., as in Rowe, 1994, or Rushton, 1999, 2000). In other words, can we improve understanding of human development, and can we enhance our ability to promote positive outcomes of changes across life by adopting the relational approach of an ADS predicated on developmental systems thinking?

We believe the answer to this question is yes, and to support our position we consider scholarship that illustrates how a focus on the person-context relation may enhance understanding of the character of human development and, as well, of the ways in which applications linking person and context in positive ways can enhance human development across the life span. The scholarship we review considers the importance of understanding the match, congruence, quality of fit, or integration between attributes of individuals and characteristics of their contexts for understanding and promoting healthy, positive human development.

Although there are numerous ways in which the literature pertinent to person-context relations may be partitioned in order to ascertain the nature of the support that exists for the developmental systems approach to ADS, we have elected to concentrate on models of person-context relations focused primarily on families, schools, and communities. We believe the literatures associated with these instances of the context afford an assessment of three settings integral to the lives of people across much of the life span. As well, these three foci provide a means to consider integrated issues of research, policies, and programs pertinent to the promotion of positive development across much of ontogeny.

MODELS OF PERSON-CONTEXT RELATION

Biological (organismic) characteristics of the individual affect the context; for example, adolescents who look different as a consequence of contrasting rates of biological growth associated for instance with earlier versus later maturation elicit different social behaviors from peers and adults (Brooks-Gunn, 1987; R. M. Lerner, 1987a, 1987b; Petersen, 1988). At the same time, contextual variables in the organism's world affect its biological characteristics (e.g., girls growing up in nations or at times in history with better health care and nutritional resources reach puberty earlier than do girls developing in less advantaged contexts; Katchadourian, 1977; Tanner, 1991).

Accordingly, scholars using developmental systems thinking to frame their work seek to identify how variables from the levels involved in person-context relations fit together dynamically (i.e., in a reciprocally interactive way) to provide bases for behavior and development. For instance, the goodness-of-fit model (Chess & Thomas, 1984; Thomas & Chess, 1977) and the stage-environment fit model (Eccles, 1991; Eccles & Midgley, 1989), both of which are discussed in greater detail later, represent two important ways in which scholars interested in developmental systems have explored the import of dynamic person-context relations for positive development.

Capitalizing on the tradition of person-context scholarship embodied in such models, other scholars, interested in applying developmental science to promote positive youth development by improving person-context relations, have attempted to understand and enhance the integration of individual and ecological characteristics in the service of fostering healthier developmental trajectories. This scholarship expands the focus of person-context relations beyond child-parent, person-family, or student-teacher (classroom, school) foci to include community-level variables; as such, it includes an explicit recognition of the ethos and values of a community for marshalling its strengths or assets around a vision of improved, healthy trajectories of person-context relations for young people.

The idea involved in all of these variants of person-context relational conceptions is the same. Just as a person brings his or her characteristics of individuality to a particular social setting, there are characteristics of the context (e.g., social demands placed on the person) that exist by virtue of the social and physical components of the setting. These ecological characteristics may take the form of (a) attitudes, values, or stereotypes that are held by others in the context regarding the person's attributes (either physical or behavioral characteristics); (b) the attributes (usually behavioral) of others in the context with whom the individual must coordinate, or fit, his or her attributes (also, in this case, usually behavioral) for adaptive interactions to exist; (c) the physical characteristics of a setting (e.g., the presence or absence of access ramps for those with motor handicaps) that require the person to possess certain attributes (again, usually behavioral abilities) for the most efficient interaction within the setting to occur; or (d) the social assets, resources, or strengths of a neighborhood or community (e.g., mentoring programs for students, community policing programs, or educationally enriching after-school programs for young children).

A congruence, match, or goodness of fit between a person's attributes of individuality (e.g., her/his temperamental characteristics, developmental level) and the features of his or her social and physical ecology (e.g., the demands placed on her/him for particular behaviors by parents, classroom teachers, school peer groups, or other significant people in her/his life) may be established because the individual has characteristics that act on the environment and, at the same time, because the environment acts on her or his characteristics (Chess & Thomas, 1984, 1999; J. V. Lerner & Lerner, 1983; R. M. Lerner & Lerner, 1989; Thomas & Chess, 1977). These two components of the developmental system— individual attributes and ecological characteristics (such as demands and resources)—may interact to promote either adaptive or unhealthy outcomes.

Of course, *any* instance of match, congruence, positive integration, or fit may result in either positive or negative outcomes, depending on the characteristics extant across the other levels of the developmental system at a given point in time (Bronfenbrenner & Morris, 1998; Elder, 1998). However, given that the individual is at the center of these reciprocal actions (or dynamic interactions), individuals, through their own actions, are a source of their own development (R. M. Lerner & Busch-Rossnagel, 1981; R. M. Lerner & Walls, 1999). In short, within developmental systems theo-

ries there is a third source of development—the individual (see, e.g., Schneirla, 1957).

The basis of the specifications provided by these models of person-context relations for positive development lies in this third source of development. Given the influences of the individual (e.g., the child) on his or her context, and thus as a producer of her or his own development, one implication of developmental systems thinking for the understanding of human development is through the creation of *person effects*.

To illustrate, consider the person during his or her childhood (and thus consider child effects on the developmental process; R. M. Lerner & Busch-Rossnagel, 1981; R. M. Lerner & Walls, 1999). How we behave and think as adults— and especially as parents—is very much influenced by our experiences with our children. Our children rear us as much as we do them (R. M. Lerner, Rothbaum, Boulos, & Castellino, in press). The very fact that we are parents makes us different adults than we would be if we were childless. But, more importantly, the specific and often special characteristics of a particular child influence us in very unique ways. How we behave toward our children depends quite a lot on how they have influenced us to behave. Such child influences are the basis of child effects.

Child effects emerge largely as a consequence of a child's individual distinctiveness. All children, with the exception of genetically identical (monozygotic) twins, have a unique genotype, that is, a unique genetic inheritance. Similarly, no two children, including monozygotic twins, experience precisely the same environment. As such, because of person-context fusions, all individuals have systematic characteristics of individuality, distinct features that arise from a probabilistic epigenetic interrelation of genes and environment (Gottlieb, 1970, 1983, 1991, 1992, 1997).

Child effects elicit a "circular function" (Schneirla, 1957) in individual development: Children stimulate differential reactions in their parents, and these reactions provide the basis of feedback to the child; that is, return stimulation influences children's further individual development. The bidirectional child-parent relationships involved in these circular functions underscore the point that children (and adolescents and adults) are producers of their own development and that individuals' relations to their contexts involve bidirectional exchanges (R. M. Lerner, 1982). The parent shapes the child, but part of what determines the way in which parents do this is children themselves.

In short, children shape their parents—as adults, as spouses, and of course as parents per se—and in so doing children help organize feedback to themselves, feedback that contributes further to their individuality and thus starts the circular function all over again (i.e., returns the child effects process to its first component). Characteristics of behavioral or personality individuality allow the child to contribute to this circular function. However, this idea of circular functions needs to be extended; that is, in and of itself the notion is mute regarding the specific characteristics of the feedback (e.g., its positive or negative valence) that children will receive as a consequence of their individuality. In other words, to account for the specific character of child-family relations, the circular functions model needs to be supplemented. The first model of person-context relations we shall consider—the goodness-of-fit model—makes this contribution to the understanding of circular functions within the family.

The Goodness-of-Fit Model of Person-Context Relations in Families

The goodness-of-fit model specifies that a person's characteristics differentially meet the demands of his or her setting, providing a basis for the specific feedback attained from the socializing environment. Although the goodness-of-fit model is put forward as a general model to assist in understanding the valence of the feedback associated with circular functions within and across all instances of person-context relations (Chess & Thomas, 1999; Thomas & Chess, 1970, 1977, 1981), much of the literature involving tests of this model have been linked either to understanding family relations or to the differences between interactions in the family and other key contexts of child development (e.g., the school).

For example, teachers and parents may have relatively individual and distinct expectations about behaviors desired of their students and children; these different expectations typically derive from contrasting attitudes, values, or stereotypes associated with the school versus the home. For instance, teachers may prefer students who show little distractibility, whereas parents might prefer their children to be moderately distractible, for example, when they require their children to move from watching television to the dinner table and then on to bed. Children whose behavioral individuality is either generally distractible or generally not distractible would differentially meet the demands of these two contexts. Problems of adjustment to school or to home might thus develop as a consequence of a child's lack of match (or goodness of fit) in either or both settings. By this analysis, distractible children should, therefore, never be blamed for a poor fit. It is, rather, the dynamic relationship between the child and his or her context(s) that determines the adaptability of the fit (i.e., the functional significance of the fit, e.g., for positive social relations in the context).

When looking specifically at the child's contribution to fit, one may specify different competencies that a child might possess to attain a good fit within and across time within given contexts. These competencies include appropriately evaluating (a) the demands of a particular context, (b) the individual's psychological and behavioral characteristics, and (c) the degree of match that exists between the two. In addition, other cognitive and behavioral skills are necessary. The child must have the ability to select and gain access to those contexts with which there is a high probability of match and to avoid those contexts where poor fit is likely. In contexts that are assigned rather than selected—for example, family of origin or assigned elementary school class—the child must have the knowledge and skills necessary either to change him- or herself to fit the demands of the setting or to alter the context to better fit his or her attributes (Mischel, 1977; Snyder, 1981). In most contexts multiple types of demands will impinge on the person, each with distinct pressures on the individual. The child needs to be able to detect and evaluate such complexity and judge which demand it is best to adapt to when all cannot be met. In these instances, as the child develops competency in self-regulation (Brandtstädter, 1998, 1999; Eccles, Early, Frasier, Belansky, & McCarthy, 1997; Heckhausen, 1999), the child will be able to become an active selector and shaper of the contexts within which he or she develops. Thus, as the child's agency (Bakan, 1966) develops, it will become increasingly true that he or she rears his or her parents as much as they do him or her.

Alexander Thomas and Stella Chess (1977, 1980, 1981; Chess & Thomas, 1984, 1999) asserted that if a child's characteristics of individuality provide a good fit (or match) with the demands of a particular setting, adaptive outcomes will accrue in that setting. Those children whose characteristics match most of the settings within which they exist should receive supportive or positive feedback from the contexts and should show evidence of the most adaptive behavioral development. In turn, of course, poorly fit or mismatched children should show alternative developmental outcomes. The characteristics of individuality through which children may differentially fit their contexts involve what children do, why children show a given behavior, and how children do whatever they do.

Temperament and Tests of the Goodness-of-Fit Model

Much of the initial evidence supporting the use of the goodness-of-fit model is derived from the Thomas and Chess (1977; Chess & Thomas, 1996, 1999) New York Longitudinal Study (NYLS). For instance, information relevant to the goodness-of-fit model exists as a consequence of the multiple samples present in the project. The core NYLS sample was composed of 133 middle-class, mostly European American children of professional parents who were followed from infancy through young adulthood. In addition, a sample of 98 Puerto Rican children of working-class parents was followed for about seven years. The children from both samples were studied from at least the first month of life onward. Although the distribution of temperamental attributes was not different in the two samples, the import of the attributes for psychosocial adjustment was quite disparate.

Two examples that relate to the concept of "easy" versus "difficult" temperament (Chess & Thomas, 1984, 1999; Thomas & Chess, 1977) may suffice to illustrate this distinction. Chess and Thomas (1984, 1999) explained that the fit between the child's temperament and the caregiver's demands may be associated with distinct types of parental or family relations. For instance, temperamentally difficult children may be moody or biologically arrhythmic and, as a result, may not fit with the preferences, expectations, or schedules of caregivers. By contrast, children with easy temperaments may be rhythmic children and have a positive mood and, as a result, have a better fit with the preferences, expectations, or schedules of the caregivers. However, a child's temperamental ease or difficulty does not reside in the child but in the dynamic relations involving the child, the parent, and the larger ecology of human development. What may be difficult in one setting, or a predictor of negative developmental outcomes, may be irrelevant or, instead, a predictor of positive outcomes under different conditions of the developmental system.

To illustrate the significance of individual temperament on the goodness of fit between person and context, the impact of low regularity or rhythmicity of behavior, particularly in regard to sleep-wake cycles, may be considered. Of the two samples of families in the NYLS, the Puerto Rican parents studied by Thomas and Chess (1977; Thomas, Chess, Sillen, & Mendez, 1974) placed no demands in regard to rhythmicity of sleep on the infant or child during at least the first five years of live. In fact, Puerto Rican parents allowed their child during the first five years of life to go to sleep and wake up at any time. These parents molded their schedule around their children. Because this sample of parents was so accommodating, there were no problems of fit associated with an arrhythmic infant or child. In addition, neither within the infancy period nor throughout the first five years of life did arrhythmicity predict adjustment problems in the Puerto Rican children. In this sample arrhythmicity remained continuous and independent of adaptive implications for the child. In turn, in the predominantly European American, middle-class families, strong demands for rhythmic sleep patterns were maintained. Most of the mothers and fathers in this sample worked outside the home (Korn, 1978), and sleep

arrhythmicity in the child interfered with parents' getting sufficient rest at night to perform optimally at work the next day. Thus, an arrhythmic child did not fit with parental demands, and consistent with the goodness of fit model, arrhythmicity was a major predictor of problem behaviors both within the infancy years and through the first five years of life (Korn, 1978; Thomas et al., 1974).

There are at least two ways of viewing this finding. First, consistent with the idea that children influence their parents, it is significant to note that sleep arrhythmicity in the European American sample resulted in parental reports of fatigue, stress, anxiety, and anger (Chess & Thomas, 1984, 1996, 1999; Thomas et al., 1974). It is possible that the presence of arrhythmicity altered previous parenting styles in this NYLS sample in a way that constituted negative feedback (negative parenting) directed to the child—feedback that was then associated with the development of problem behaviors in the child.

A second interpretation of this finding arises from the fact that problem behaviors in the children were identified initially on the basis of parental report. Regardless of problem behaviors evoked in the parent by the child or of any altered parent-child interactions that thereby ensued, one effect of the child on the parent was to increase the probability of the parent labeling the child's temperamental style as problematic and so reporting it to the NYLS staff psychiatrist. The current analyses of the NYLS data do not allow for a discrimination between these two possibilities.

The data in the NYLS do indicate that the European American sample took steps to change their arrhythmic children's sleep patterns. Because temperament may be modified by person-context interactions, low rhythmicity tended to be discontinuous for most of these children. That these parents modified their children's arrhythmicity is an instance of a child effect on its psychosocial context. That is, the child produced alterations in parental caregiving behaviors regarding sleep. That these child effects on the parental context fed back to the child and influenced her or his further development is consistent with the finding that sleep arrhythmicity was discontinuous among these children.

Thus, in the predominantly European American, middle-class sample, early infant arrhythmicity tended to be a problem during this time of life but proved to be neither continuous nor predictive of later adjustment problems. In turn, in the Puerto Rican sample, arrhythmicity, though continuous, was not a poor fit with the context of the child during infancy or within the first five years of life. This is not to say that the parents in the Puerto Rican families were not affected by their children's sleep arrhythmicity. As with the European American parents, it may be that the Puerto Rican parents had problems of fatigue or suffered family or work-related problems due to irregular sleep patterns produced in them as a consequence of their child's sleep arrhythmicity. Again, the data analyses in the NYLS do not indicate this possible child effect on the Puerto Rican parents.

The data do underscore the importance of considering the fit between the individual and the demands of the psychosocial context of development, in that it indicates that arrhythmicity did begin to predict adjustment problems for the Puerto Rican children when they entered the school system. Their lack of a regular sleep pattern interfered with their getting sufficient sleep to perform well in school and often caused them to be late to school (Korn, 1978; Thomas et al., 1974). Thus, although before the age of 5 years only one Puerto Rican child presented a clinical problem diagnosed as a sleep disorder, between ages 5 and 9 years almost 50% of the Puerto Rican children who developed clinically identifiable problems were diagnosed as having sleep problems.

Another example of how the different demands of the two family contexts studied in the NYLS provide different presses for adaptation relates to differences in the demands of the families' physical contexts. As noted by Thomas et al. (1974), as well as Korn (1978), there was a very low overall incidence of behavior problems in the Puerto Rican sample of children in their first five years of life, especially when compared to the corresponding incidence among the European American sample of children. If a problem did arise during this time among the Puerto Rican sample, it was most likely to be a problem of motor activity. Across the first 9 years of their lives, of those Puerto Rican children who developed clinical problems, 53% presented symptoms diagnosed as involving problematic motor activity. The parents of these children complained of excessive and uncontrollable motor activity. However, in the European American sample, only one child (a child with brain damage) was characterized in this way.

The Puerto Rican parents' reports of "excessive and uncontrollable" activity in their children do constitute an example of a child effect on the parents. That is, a major value of the Puerto Rican parents in the NYLS was child obedience to authority (Korn, 1978). The type of motor activity shown by the highly active children of these Puerto Rican parents was inconsistent with parental perceptions of an obedient child (Korn, 1978).

Moreover, the Puerto Rican children's activity-level characteristics serve as an illustration of the embeddedness of the child temperament home-context relation in the broader community context. The Puerto Rican families usually had several children and lived in small apartments, where even average motor activity tended to impinge on others in the setting. At the same time, Puerto Rican parents were reluctant to let their children out of the apartment because of the actual dangers of playing on the streets of their (East Harlem) neighborhood—perhaps especially for children with high activity levels.

In the predominantly European American, middle-class sample, the parents had the financial resources to provide large apartments or houses for their families. There were typically suitable play areas for the children both inside and outside the home. As a consequence, the presence of high activity levels in the home of the European American sample did not cause the problems for interaction that they did in the Puerto Rican group. Thus, as Thomas, Chess, and Birch (1968; Thomas et al., 1974) emphasized, the mismatch between temperamental attribute and physical environmental demand accounted for the group difference in the import of high activity level for the development of reported behavioral problems in the children.

Chess and Thomas (1999) reviewed other data from the NYLS, and from independent data sets, that tested their temperament-context, goodness-of-fit model. One very important study they discussed was conducted by de Vries (1984), who assessed the Masai tribe living in the sub-Sahara region of Kenya at a time when a severe drought was beginning. After obtaining temperament ratings on 47 infants, aged 2 to 4 months, de Vries identified from within his sample the 10 infants with the easiest temperaments and the 10 with the most difficult temperaments. Five months later, at a time when 97% of the cattle herd had died from the drought, he returned to the tribal area. Given that the basic food supply was milk and meat, both derived from the tribe's cattle, the level of starvation and death experienced by the tribe was enormous. De Vries located the families of seven of the easy babies and six of the difficult ones. The families of the other infants had moved to try to escape the drought. Of the seven easy babies, five had died. All of the difficult babies had survived.

Chess and Thomas (1999) suggested two reasons for this dramatic finding. First, difficult infants cried louder and more frequently than did the easy babies. Parents fed the difficult babies either to stop their excessive crying or because they interpreted the cries as signals of extreme hunger. Alternatively, there may be a cultural reason for the survival of the difficult infants, one that would not have emerged to affect behavior during a time of plentiful food, when both easy and difficult babies could have been soothed easily when crying due to hunger. Chess and Thomas suggested that the parents, under the nonnormative historical conditions of the drought, saw the difficult babies not as a problem to be managed but as an asset to the survival of the tribe. As a consequence, the parents might have actually chosen "for survival these lusty expressive babies who have more desirable characteristics according to the tribe's cultural standards" (Chess & Thomas, 1999, p. 111).

In the de Vries (1984) study, the parent-child relation, embedded in the developmental system at a time of non-normative natural environment disaster, led to a switch in the valence, or meaning, of "difficulty" and resulted in a dramatic difference in adaptive developmental outcome (survival or death). Among the core NYLS sample, living under "privileged" conditions in New York City, difficult babies comprised 23% of the clinical behavior problem group (10 babies) but only 4% (4 cases) of the nonclinical sample (Thomas et al., 1968, p. 78). From these collective findings, Chess and Thomas (1999) stressed that the relationship between child and parent—a relation interactive with the multiple levels of the developmental system, including the physical ecology, culture, and history—must be the frame of reference for understanding the role of temperament in parent-child relationships and in the enactment and outcomes of parenting.

A similar conclusion may be derived from the research of Super and Harkness (1981). Studying the Kipsigis tribe in either the rural village of Kokwet, Kenya, or in the urban setting of Nairobi, Kenya, Super and Harkness found that sleep arrhythmicity had different implications for mother-infant interactions. Rural Kipsigis is an agricultural community, and the tribe assigns primary (and in fact virtually exclusive) caregiving duties to the mother, who keeps the infant in close proximity to her (either on her shoulder or within a few feet of her), even if she is working in the fields (or is socializing, sleeping, or the like). Sleep arrhythmicity in such a context is not a dimension of difficulty for the mother because whenever the infant awakes, she or he can be fed or soothed by the mother with little disruption of her other activities. By contrast, however, Kipsigis living in Nairobi are not farmers but office workers, professionals, and the like. In this context, they cannot keep the infant close to them at all times and, as a consequence, Super and Harkness found that sleep arrhythmicity is a sign of difficulty and is associated with problems for the mother and for her interactions with the infant.

Still other studies support the idea that the goodness of fit between parent and child influences the quality of interrelations between these individuals and is associated with the nature of the developmental outcomes for youth. Galambos and Turner (1999) examined adolescent and parent temperaments as predictors of the quality of parent-adolescent relationships. They reported that both parent and adolescent temperament explain unique portions of the variance in parent-adolescent relationships. Adaptable adolescents are more likely to have accepting mothers who tend not to rely on the induction of guilt as a means of control as well as more accepting fathers than other, less adaptable adolescents. Mothers' level of adaptability was also found to contribute uniquely and additively to the parent-adolescent relationship, in that mothers who were more highly adaptable were more accepting of their adolescents. The level of acceptance by mothers was highest when both mother and adolescent adaptability were high.

Moreover, Galambos and Turner (1999) found that adolescent and parent temperaments interact to affect the quality of the parent-adolescent relationship. For instance, conflict between mothers and sons was highest in relationships where the mothers were less adaptable and sons were less active. Conflict between mothers and daughters was highest in relationships where the mother was less adaptable and the daughter was more active. Similarly, as level of activity in female adolescents increased, more conflicts with parents were reported. This result was not found with male adolescents. In turn, when both fathers and female adolescents were low in adaptability, fathers used more psychological control and female adolescents reported more conflicts with parents.

Similarly, using parental stress as a measure of goodness of fit between parent and adolescent characteristics, Bogenschneider, Small, and Tsay (1997) found that, within a study of 8th- to 12th-graders and their parents, a mismatch between a parent and adolescent led to levels of stress that interfered with competent parenting. Schraeder, Heverly, and O'Brien (1996) reported comparable findings. Assessing the later-life effects of low birth weight on child adjustment in the home and in the school, Schraeder et al. noted that features of the social environment, as well as the fit between the child and the social environment, played a greater role in shaping the behavior of the child than did an initial biological risk of very low birth weight. Underscoring the idea that fit involves multiple instances or levels of the context of human development, Flanagan and Eccles (1993) reported that developmental difficulties associated with school may be amplified by parental work status. A decline in parental work status coupled with students' transition to junior high school were associated with an increase in school adjustment problems, as indicated by teachers' assessments of disruptive behavior (Flanagan & Eccles, 1993).

Thus, data pertinent to the goodness-of-fit model underscore the idea that fit involves several levels of the developmental system, that is, the developing individual and multiple contexts—family, school, and culture in the literature just reviewed. Scholarship by Jacquelynne Eccles, Allan Wigfield, and James Byrnes (this volume) extends significantly the idea that the congruence between the person and context is dependent on the child's developmental level and the appropriateness of the context to that level. Her concept of stage-environment fit serves as an important and relevant supplement to the goodness-of-fit model.

The Stage-Environment Fit Model of Adolescent-School Relations

Through a focus on young adolescents and their transition from elementary school to either junior high or middle school, Jacquelynne Eccles and her colleagues (e.g., Eccles & Harold, 1996; Eccles et al., 1996; Fuligni, Eccles, & Barber, 1995; Midgley, Feldlaufer, & Eccles, 1989a, 1989b) have offered a theoretically nuanced and empirically highly productive approach to understanding the significance of person-context relations for healthy development. Eccles and her colleagues argue that there is a connection between a child's developmental level and the developmental appropriateness of the characteristics of the child's social context. Eccles, Midgley, et al. (1993) labeled this type of person-context fit *stage-environment fit*. This model has been used to explore the nature of developmental outcomes that children obtain in their environments, such as school. As Eccles (1997) points out,

> Exposure to the developmentally appropriate environment facilitate[s] both motivation and continued growth; in contrast, exposure to developmentally inappropriate environments, especially developmentally regressive environments, creates a particularly poor person-environment fit, which lead[s] to declines in motivation as well as detachment from the goals of the institution. (p. 531)

Using the stage-environment fit model to study adolescent-school relations, Eccles and her colleagues have noted that changes that young adolescents experience during their transition from elementary school to junior high school (e.g., changes in self-esteem, motivation, and academic achievement) have the potential to negatively affect the adolescents' positive development when junior high schools do not provide developmentally adequate contexts (Eccles, Lord, & Midgley, 1991; Eccles & Midgley, 1989; Eccles & Roeser, 1999; Wigfield, Eccles, Mac Iver, Reumann, & Midgley, 1991). Contrary to students' developmental needs, the school environments that young adolescents encounter on their transfer from elementary to junior high school tend to emphasize

> competition, social comparison, and ability self-assessment at a time of heightened self-focus; decrease[d] decision making and choices at a time when the desire for control is growing up; . . . lower level cognitive strategies at a time when the ability to use higher level strategies is increasing; and . . . [disruption of] social

networks at a time when adolescents are especially concerned with peer relationships. (Eccles & Roeser, 1999, p. 533)

There may be several instances of this mismatch between young adolescents' developmental needs at their specific developmental stage and the demands of their school context. For instance, characteristics of middle schools or junior high schools, such as size and departmentalization, may negatively effect early adolescents' development, particularly by lowering self-esteem (Simmons & Blyth, 1987; Simmons, Carlton-Ford, & Blyth, 1987). Even though junior high schools afford an opportunity to meet many new peers, they are much larger in size than elementary schools and may therefore foster alienation, isolation, and difficulties with intimacy (Simmons et al., 1987). Similarly, Eccles and Midgley (1989) noted that classrooms in junior high schools are characterized by greater teacher control and emphasis on discipline; less positive student-teacher relationships; and decreased opportunities for students to make their own decisions, choose among different options, and exercise self-management skills. Junior high school teachers foster class practices that encourage the use of social comparison, ability self-assessment, and higher standards for judging students' performance than do teachers in elementary schools (Eccles & Midgley, 1989). Moreover, teachers in junior high schools, compared to teachers in elementary schools, have been found to be stronger proponents of students' needing discipline and control, to consider their students to be less trustworthy, and to feel less effective in their work with young adolescent students (Eccles et al., 1991). In addition, young adolescents who had high-efficacy teachers in elementary school but then moved to a low-efficacy teacher in junior high school had lower expectations and perceptions of their own academic performance in their first year of junior high than did students who came from low-efficacy teachers or, once in junior high, were paired with a high-efficacy teacher (Eccles et al., 1991). Wigfield et al. (1991) found that less positive student-teacher relationships and (mathematics) teachers' feeling less efficacious could be partly responsible for early adolescents' decline in confidence in social skills on their transition to junior high school.

In turn, Roeser, Eccles, and Sameroff (1998, 2000) found that academic motivation, achievement, and emotional well-being are promoted when the school environment supports the development of competence, autonomy, and positive relationships with teachers. To the extent that the school environment inhibits the development of feelings of competence, autonomy, and positive relationships, students will feel alienated academically, emotionally, and behaviorally. As such, Roeser et al. (1998, 2000) encouraged educators and school counselors to examine school environments through a "developmental lens" (Roeser et al., 1998, p. 345). Adolescents who report positive academic motivation and emotional well-being perceive their schools as "more developmentally appropriate in terms of norms, practices, and teacher-student interactions, whereas those manifesting poorer functioning reported less developmentally appropriate school environments" (Roeser et al., 1998, p. 345).

To support the development of a sense of competence in early adolescence, through building a better fit between the developing adolescent and the school context, Roeser et al. recommended that middle schools focus on and promote positive teacher regard for students and implement instructional practices that enable students to view self-improvement, effort, and mastery of tasks as the "hallmarks of competence and academic success" (Roeser et al., 1998, p. 346) rather than competition, ability relative to peers, and the rewarding of high achievers. Roeser et al. cautioned that focusing on ability rather than effort during the stage of early adolescence is an inappropriate goal for schools, as all young adolescents are self-conscious and susceptible to social comparisons. A focus on school ability is a particularly detrimental goal for adolescents having academic and/or emotional difficulties.

Similarly, to support the need for autonomy in middle school, and thereby enhancing the development of positive academic and emotional functioning in early adolescence, Roeser et al. (1998, 2000) suggested that middle schools provide students with opportunities to make choices (e.g., in relation to class seating, topics of discussion, and curricula development). In addition, middle schools should create and nurture opportunities for teachers to design curricula that fit the needs and interests of their students so that students can become more involved and invested in their own learning (Roeser et al., 1998, 2000). Moreover, because adolescents who perceive their teachers as providers of both emotional and academic support are less likely to feel alienated from the school environment or to experience emotional distress, Roeser et al. suggested that middle schools provide smaller communities of learning.

The changes in the school context that Roeser et al. (1998, 2000) indicated are needed to promote or better fit with the developmental characteristics of adolescents may be especially important for youth who have expressed academic difficulties prior to a transition to a new school setting. These adolescents are particularly vulnerable to developing the negative developmental outcomes as a consequence of poorness of fit (Eccles et al., 1991; Eccles et al., 1996).

In short, negative developmental outcomes may derive from a poorness of fit between a student's orientation to learning and the curriculum; between the student and the teaching style or the instructional focus at the junior high or middle school; or between the availability in the classroom of sufficient decision-making opportunities for students and their needs to feel effective in class and to have more autonomy and opportunities in their learning environment (Eccles, 1997; Eccles et al., 1996). Moreover, adolescents' perceptions of stage-environment fit can predict also motivation, achievement, and emotional functioning (Roeser et al., 1998).

For young adolescents making a transition into middle or junior high school, changes in classroom environment and teacher-student relations can impact the stage-environment fit (i.e., the balance between students' developmental stage and characteristics of their context). A poor fit may have a negative impact on student motivation and performance (Eccles et al., 1991).

Eccles (1997) concluded that if we want to ensure that adolescents' experiences of the transition are positive and that the match between the adolescents' developmental needs and the school context is a good one, developmentally appropriate educational environments for young adolescents need to be provided. An instance of a developmentally appropriate environment for early adolescent girls, for example, would be classrooms sensitive to gender-bound learning styles, that is, classrooms in which instructions are taught in more cooperative and person-centered ways (Eccles, 1997), to which girls may find it easier to relate. Classrooms such as these are likely to be more motivating as well as better equipped to support students' developmental needs, therefore contributing to students' healthy developmental outcomes.

In sum, by introducing to school environments changes that will ensure better fit between children's developmental needs and characteristics of the school environment, one can create a balanced stage-environment fit, one that will contribute to the promotion of positive youth development. As such, the utility of the student-school relational ideas that Eccles and her colleagues have introduced could possibly be extended to further our understanding of other instances of person-context relations. In addition, the idea of fit may apply to other levels within the developmental system; if so, the relational ideas of Eccles and colleagues and of Thomas and Chess can provide guidance for program innovations or policy engagement aimed at influencing changes in the developmental system in a manner that would continue to promote positive development in young people.

That is, the work of Thomas and Chess (e.g., 1977; Chess & Thomas, 1999) and Eccles (e.g., 1991; Eccles, Lord et al., 1997) supports the idea that by enhancing the fit between individuals and their contexts, positive development may be promoted. It may be possible, then, through the ideas embodied in this work, to extend the utility of person-context relations into more macro instances of individual-context relations. One may ask if it is possible whether, through program innovations at the level of communities, one can simultaneously understand the efficacy of relational analyses of human development and influence changes in the developmental system that promote the positive development of people. One way to address this issue is to explore work on the links between individuals and community settings, which have been studied by applied developmental scientists trying to promote positive youth development among adolescents.

The Integration of Individual and Community Assets in the Promotion of Positive Youth Development

What is required at levels beyond the family or school—for instance, at the level of an entire community—to promote healthy, positive development among young people? Building on developmental systems ideas pertinent to positive person-context relations as integral to healthy development, Damon (1997) envisioned the creation of a youth charter in each community in the United States and in the world. The charter consists of a set of rules, guidelines, and plans of action that each community can adopt to provide its youth with a framework for development in a healthy manner, that is, to build positive relations with other individuals and institutions in their community.

The youth charter reflects "a consensus of clear expectations shared among the important people in a young person's life and communicated to the young person in multiple ways" (Damon & Gregory, in press, p. 10). Damon and Gregory explained that their approach constitutes a shift along four dimensions in the study of youth:

> a positive vision of youth strengths, a use of community as the locus of developmental action, an emphasis on expectations for service and social responsibility, and a recognition of the role of moral values and religious or spiritual faith. (p. 7)

Consistent with the relational emphasis in developmental systems theory, Damon and Gregory (in press) emphasize that

> in a whole community, it is possible to find many people who can introduce young people into the positive, inspirational possibilities of moral commitment. Similarly, an entire community affords many opportunities for authentic service activities, such as helping those in need, that can provide young people with a chance to experience the psychological rewards of moral commitment. . . . In places that operate like true communities, there are many ways in which families, schools, workplaces, agencies, and peer groups connect with one another through their contact with youth. For example, schools are influenced by the values and attitudes that students pick up in their families. Students'

family lives are in turn influenced by their quest for academic achievement, which fills their after school time with homework—and which in turn is supported on the home front. A young person's identity formation, rooted initially in the family, is shaped by a sense of belonging in the community, including sports teams, media, clubs, religious institutions, and jobs. In such communities, there also is concordance between the norms of the peer culture and those of adults. . . . A well-integrated and consciously developed pattern of relationships can provide a stabilizing transformational structure that produces equally integrated identities as workers and citizens and parents; no single institution has the resources to develop all of these roles alone (Ianni, 1989, p. 279). Ianni's name for this stabilizing structure is a "youth charter." (pp. 10–12)

Damon (1997) described how youth and significant adults in their community (e.g., parents, teachers, clergy, coaches, police, and government and business leaders) can create youth partnerships to pursue a common ideal of positive moral development and intellectual achievement:

> To build a youth charter, community members go through a process of discussion, a movement towards agreement, and the development and implementation of action plans. Elements of the process include special town meetings sponsored by local institutions; constructive media coverage on a periodic basis; and the formation of standing committees that open new lines of communication among parents, teachers, and neighbors. (Damon & Gregory, in press, p. 13)

For example, Damon (1997) explained how a youth charter can be developed to maximize the positive person-context experiences and long-term desired developmental outcomes of youth in community sports activities. For instance, he noted that participation in sports is a significant part of the lives of many contemporary adolescents, and he pointed out that there may be important benefits of such participation. Young people enhance their physical fitness, learn athletic and physical skills, and, through sports, experience lessons pertinent to the development of their character (e.g., they learn about the importance of diligence, motivation, teamwork, balancing cooperation versus competition, balancing winning and losing, and the importance of fair play; Damon, 1997). Moreover, sports can be a context for positive parent-child relations, and such interactions can further the adolescent's successful involvement in sports. For example, parental support of their male and female adolescents' participation in tennis is associated with the enjoyment of the sport by the youth and with an objective measure of their performance (Hoyle & Leff, 1997).

However, Damon (1997) noted as well that organized and even informal opportunities for sports participation for youth, ranging from Little League, soccer, or pickup games in school yards, often fall short of providing these relational benefits for young people. He pointed out that in modern American society sports participation is often imbued with a "win at any cost" orientation among coaches and, in turn, their young players. In addition, parents may also have this attitude. Together, a value is conveyed that winning is not just the main goal of competition, but the only thing (Damon, 1997, p. 210).

Damon believes that this orientation to youth sports corrupts the purposes of youth participation in sports. Parents and coaches often forget that most of the young people on these teams will not make sports a life career and, even if they do, they—as well as the majority of young people involved in sports—need moral modeling and guidance about sportsmanship and the significance of representing, through sports, not only physically but also psychologically and socially healthy behaviors (Damon, 1997).

In order to enable youth sports to make these contributions to positive adolescent development, Damon (1997) proposed a youth charter that constitutes guidelines for the design and conduct of youth sports programs. Adherence to the principles of the charter will enable communities to realize the several assets for young people that can be provided by the participation of youth in sports. Components of the charter include the following commitments to

1. Make youth sports a priority for public funding and provide other forms of community support (space, facilities, volunteer coaches);
2. Parents and coaches should emphasize standards of conduct as a primary goal of youth sports;
3. Young people should be provided opportunities to participate in individual as well as team sports;
4. Youth sports programs should encourage broad participation by ordinary players as well as stars; and
5. Sports programs for youth must be carefully coordinated with other community events for young people. (Damon, 1997, pp. 123–125).

In sum, then, Damon and Gregory (in press) note that

The essential requirements of a youth charter are that 1) it must address the core matters of morality and achievement necessary for becoming a responsible citizen; and 2) it must focus on areas of common agreement rather than on doctrinaire squabbles or polarizing issues of controversy. A youth charter guides the younger generation towards fundamental moral virtues such as honesty, civility, decency, and the pursuit of benevolent purposes beyond the self. A youth charter is a moral and spiritual rather than a political document. (p. 13)

Consistent with the ideas of stage-environment fit discussed by Eccles and her colleagues (e.g., Eccles et al., 1991; chapter by Eccles, Wigfield, & Byrnes in this volume), Damon (1997) noted that embedding youth in a caring and developmentally facilitative community can promote their ability to develop morally and to contribute to civil society. For instance, in a study of about 130 African American parochial high school juniors, working at a soup kitchen for the homeless as part of a school-based community service program was associated with identity development and with the ability to reflect on society's political organization and moral order (Yates & Youniss, 1996).

In a study of over 3,100 high school seniors (Youniss, Yates, & Su, 1997), the activities engaged in by youth were categorized into (a) school-based, adult-endorsed norms or (b) engagement in peer fun activities that excluded adults. Youth were then placed into groups that reflected orientations to (a) school-adult norms, but not peer fun (the "School" group); (b) peer fun but not school-adult norms (the "Party" group); or (c) both (a) and (c) (the "All-around" group). The School and the All-around seniors were both high in community service, religious orientation, and political awareness. In turn, the Party group seniors were more likely to use marijuana than were the School group (but not the All-around group) seniors (Youniss et al., 1997).

Furthermore, African American and Latino adolescents who were nominated by community leaders for having shown unusual commitments to caring for others or for contributions to the community were labeled "care exemplars" and compared to a matched group of youth not committed to the community (Hart & Fegley, 1995). The care exemplars were more likely than the comparison youth to describe themselves in terms reflective of moral characteristics, to show commitment to both their heritage and to the future of their community, to see themselves as reflecting the ideals of both themselves and their parents, and to stress the importance of personal philosophies and beliefs for their self-definitions (Hart & Fegley, 1995).

Damon (1997) envisioned that by embedding youth in a community where service and responsible leadership are possible, the creation of community-specific youth charters can enable adolescents and adults together to systematically promote positive youth development. Youth charters can create opportunities to actualize both individual and community goals to eliminate risk behaviors among adolescents and promote in them the ability to contribute to high-quality individual and community life. Through community youth charters, youth and adults may together engage in relationships that serve to create a system wherein civil society is maintained and perpetuated (Damon, 1997).

What sort of person-context relations must be brought together by such charters to ensure the promotion of such positive youth development? Benson and his colleagues at Search Institute in Minneapolis, Minnesota, believe that what is needed is the integration of individual and ecological assets (Benson, 1997; Benson et al., 1998; Leffert et al., 1998; Scales & Leffert, 1999). They noted that "*developmental assets* represent a theoretical construct identifying a set of environmental and intrapersonal strengths known to enhance educational and health outcomes for children and adolescents" (Benson, in press, p. 1). Benson and his colleagues stressed that positive youth development is furthered when actions are taken to enhance the strengths of a person (e.g., a commitment to learning, a healthy sense of identity), a family (e.g., caring attitudes toward children, rearing styles that both empower youth and set boundaries and provide expectations for positive growth), and a community (e.g., social support, programs that provide access to the resources for education, safety, and mentorship available in a community; Benson, 1997).

Consistent with the relational focus of developmental systems theory, Benson (in press) explained that

> the asset framework is intended to speak to and elicit the engagement of multiple sources of asset building energy. These include informal, non-programmatic relationships between adults and youth; traditional socializing systems such as families, neighborhoods, schools, congregations, and youth organizations; and the governmental, economic, and policy infrastructures which inform those socializing systems. (p. 10)
>
> . . . five sources of asset-building potential are hypothesized to exist within all communities, each of which can be marshaled via a multiplicity of community mobilization strategies. These sources of potential asset-building influence include: (1) sustained relationships with adults, both within and beyond family; (2) peer group influence (when peers choose to activate their asset-building capacity); (3) socializing systems; (4) community-level social norms, ceremony, ritual, policy and resource allocation; and (5) programs, including school-based and community-based efforts to nurture and build skills and competencies. (p. 16)

In short, Benson (in press) underscored that "asset-building communities are distinguished as relational and intergenerational places" (p. 16).

Benson and colleagues believe that both internal (individual) and external (contextual, ecological) attributes comprise the developmental assets needed by youth. Benson explained that

> The *human development infrastructure* has to do with the patterns, rhythms, and flow of community attentiveness to essential developmental needs and milestones. In essence, we are speaking here of the constancy and equity of core developmental experiences such as support, engagement, empowerment, belonging, affirmation, boundary-setting, structure, and connectedness, all of which are grounded less in program and policy and more in how citizens and socializing systems identify and utilize their inherent, relational capacities. (Benson & Saito, 2000, p. 5)

Through the research of Search Institute, 40 developmental assets, 20 internal ones, and 20 external ones have been identified. These attributes are presented in Table 22.1.

Benson and his colleagues found that the more developmental assets possessed by an adolescent, the greater is his or her likelihood of positive, healthy development. For instance, in a study of 99,462 youth in Grades 6 through 12 in public and alternative schools from 213 U.S. cities and towns who were assessed during the 1996–1997 academic year for their possession of the 40 assets presented in Table 22.1, Leffert et al. (1998) found that the more assets present among youth, the lower was the likelihood of alcohol use, depression and suicide risk, and violence.

For instance, the level of alcohol use risk for youth in Grades 6 through 8 combined, and for youth in Grades 9 through 12 combined, decreases with the possession of more assets. Youth with 0 to 10 assets have the highest risk, followed by youth with 11 to 20 assets, youth with 21 to 30 assets, and youth with 31 to 40 assets. Thus, consistent with Benson's (1997) view of the salience of developmental assets for promoting healthy behavior among young people, the fact that the group with the most assets has the lowest level of risk shows the importance of the asset approach in work aimed at promoting positive development in children and adolescents. Moreover, other data presented by Leffert et al. (1998) replicated these trends for males and females in regard to depression and suicide risk and for combinations of males and females in different grade groupings in regard to violence risk. In both cases, higher levels of assets were linked with lower levels of risk. This congruence strengthens the argument for the critical significance of a focus on developmental assets in the promotion of positive youth development and, as such, in the enhancement of the capacity and commitment of young people to contribute to civil society.

Other data by Benson and his colleagues provide direct support for this argument. Scales et al. (2000) measured a concept termed *thriving* among 6,000 youth in Grades 6 through 12 evenly divided across six ethnic groups (American Indian, African American, Asian American, Latino, European American, and multiracial). Thriving was defined as involving seven attributes: school success, leadership, valuing diversity, physical health, helping others, delay of gratification,

TABLE 22.1 The 40 Developmental Assets Specified by Search Institute

Asset Type	Asset and Description
External Support	1. Family Support: Family life provides high levels of love and support.
	2. Positive Family Communication: Young person and her or his parent(s) communicate positively, and young person is willing to seek advice and counsel from parents.
	3. Other Adult Relationships: Young person receives support from three or more nonparent adults.
	4. Caring Neighborhood: Young person experiences caring neighbors.
	5. Caring School Climate: School provides a caring, encouraging environment.
	6. Parent Involvement in Schooling: Parents are actively involved in helping young person succeed in school.
Empowerment	7. Community Values Youth: Young person perceives that adults in the community value youth.
	8. Youth as Resources: Young people are given useful roles in the community.
	9. Service to Others: Young person serves in the community one hour or more per week.
	10. Safety: Young person feels safe at home, at school, and in the neighborhood.
Boundaries and Expectations	11. Family Boundaries: Family has clear rules and consequences and monitors the young person's whereabouts.
	12. School Boundaries: School provides clear rules and consequences.
	13. Neighborhood Boundaries: Neighbors take responsibility for monitoring young people's behavior.
	14. Adult Role Models: Parents and other adults model positive, responsible behavior.
	15. Positive Peer Influence: Young person's best friends model responsible behavior.
	16. High Expectations: Both parent(s) and teachers encourage the young person to do well.
Constructive Use of Time	17. Creative Activities: Young person spends three or more hours per week in lessons or practice in music, theater, or other arts.
	18. Youth Programs: Young person spends three or more hours per week in sports, clubs, or organizations at school and/or in the community.
	19. Religious Community: Young person spends one or more hours per week in activities in a religious institution.
	20. Time at Home: Young person is out with friends "with nothing special to do" two or fewer nights per week.
Commitment to Learning	21. Achievement Motivation: Young person is motivated to do well in school.
	22. School Engagement: Young person is actively engaged in learning.
	23. Homework: Young person reports doing at least one or more hour of homework every school day.
	24. Bonding to School: Young person cares about her or his school.
	25. Reading for Pleasure: Young person reads for pleasure three or more hours per week.
Positive Values	26. Caring: Young person places high value on helping other people.
	27. Equality and Social Justice: Young person places high value on promoting equality and reducing hunger and poverty.
	28. Integrity: Young person acts on convictions and stands up for her or his beliefs.
	29. Honesty: Young person "tells the truth even when it is not easy."
	30. Responsibility: Young person accepts and takes personal responsibility.
	31. Restraint: Young person believes it is important not to be sexually active or to use alcohol or other drugs.
Social Competencies	32. Planning and Decision Making: Young person knows how to plan ahead and make choices.
	33. Interpersonal Competence: Young person has empathy, sensitivity, and friendship skills.
	34. Cultural Competence: Young person has knowledge of and comfort with people of different cultural/racial/ethnic backgrounds.
	35. Resistance Skills: Young person can resist negative peer pressure and dangerous situations.
	36. Peaceful Conflict Resolution: Young person seeks to resolve conflict nonviolently.
Positive Identity	37. Personal Power: Young person feels he or she has control over "things that happen to me."
	38. Self-Esteem: Young person reports having a high self-esteem.
	39. Sense of Purpose: Young person reports that "my life has a purpose."
	40. Positive View of Personal Future: Young person is optimistic about her or his personal future.

Source. Reprinted with permission from P. L. Benson, N. Leffert, P. C. Scales, & D. A. Blyth, "Beyond the 'village' rhetoric: Creating healthy communities for children and adolescents," *Applied Developmental Science, 2*(3), 138–159 (Minneapolis, MN: Search Institute). © Search Institute, 1998. www.search-institute.org.

and overcoming adversity. Most, if not all, of these attributes are linked to the presence of prosocial behavior (e.g., helping others, delay of gratification) and to the behaviors requisite for competently contributing to civil society (e.g., valuing diversity, leadership, overcoming adversity). The greater the number of developmental assets possessed by youth, the more likely they were to possess the attributes of thriving. For instance, as developmental assets increased, thriving in regard to helping others, valuing diversity, and possessing leadership qualities increased.

It is important to note that Benson and his colleagues (e.g., Scales et al., 2000) linked these assets for healthy youth development to community-based programs that involve the facilitation of positive person-context relations. That is, in their research, Benson and his colleagues found that time spent in youth programs was the developmental asset that seemed to best predict thriving. Scales et al. interpreted this finding to derive from the fact that youth programs provide young people with access to social networks with caring adults and with responsible peers.

Other data support the importance of focusing on person-context relational and developmental assets in understanding the bases of positive youth development. Luster and McAdoo (1994) sought to identify the factors that contribute to individual differences in the cognitive competence of African American children in early elementary grades. Consistent with an asset-based approach to promoting the positive development of youth (Benson, 1997; Scales & Leffert, 1999), they found that favorable outcomes in cognitive and socio-emotional development were associated with high scores on an *advantage index*. This index was formed by scoring children on the basis of the absence of risk factors (e.g., pertaining to poverty or to relationship problems that affected the quality of the home environment) and of the presence of more favorable economic and family-relationship circumstances in their lives.

Luster and McAdoo (1994) reported that whereas only 4% of the children in their sample who scored low on the advantage index had high scores on a measure of vocabulary, 44% of the children who had high scores on the advantage index had high vocabulary scores. Similar contrasts between low and high scores on the advantage index were found regarding measures of math achievement (14% vs. 37%, respectively), word recognition (0% vs. 35%, respectively) and word meaning (7% vs. 46%, respectively).

Luster and McAdoo (1996) extended the findings of their 1994 research. Seeking to identify the factors that contribute to individual differences in the educational attainment of African American young adults from low socioeconomic status, Luster and McAdoo (1996) found that assets linked with the individual (cognitive competence, academic achievement, and personal adjustment in kindergarten) and the context (parental involvement in schools) were associated longitudinally with academic achievement and educational attainment.

Other research points to the variation in the outcomes of developing in socioeconomically poor settings that exist in relation to different arrays of person-context assets. For instance, and consistent with the findings of Luster and McAdoo (1994, 1996), Leventhal and Brooks-Gunn (in press) noted that the pathway between poverty and child development (e.g., achievement) is moderated by the quality of the home learning environment. Similarly, during young childhood the presence in the community of high-quality child care and early intervention programs has immediate and longer term benefits for poor children's academic and social development (Leventhal & Brooks-Gunn, 2000). For instance, when poor neighborhoods are characterized by crime, underemployment, lack of resources, few role models, and absence of adult supervision of children and youth, children's emotional and social well-being may be adversely

effected (Leventhal & Brooks-Gunn, in press). In turn, affluence in high socioeconomic neighborhoods in comparison to middle-income neighborhoods has assets linked to beneficial influences on children's school readiness and achievement (Leventhal & Brooks-Gunn, in press).

In sum, consistent with the perspective forwarded by Benson (1997) and with the data provided by Benson et al. (1998), Leffert et al. (1998), Scales et al. (2000), Luster and McAdoo (1994, 1996), and Leventhal and Brooks-Gunn (2000, in press), the individual and contextual assets of youth are linked to their positive development. These data underscore the value of integrating the strengths of young people, their families, and their communities in the service of such development. As suggested by the developmental systems perspective that frames our orientation to ADS, such a synthetic approach to positive development seems both to have substantial empirical validity and, as a consequence, to be an optimally productive frame for policy and program innovations aimed at increasing the probability of healthy development across the life span of current and future generations. We believe that the benefit of such applications of developmental science will accrue not only for today's young people but also, because contemporary youth are the future stewards of our democracy, for civil society in our nation.

CONCLUSIONS

Represented by the literature pertinent to the goodness-of-fit model, the stage-environment fit model, and the individual and ecological asset approach to community resources for youth, a focus on person-context relations underscores the key implications of developmental systems models for research and applications pertinent to promoting positive human development. At any given point in ontogenetic and historical time, neither individual's attributes nor the features of their context (e.g., the demands of their parents regarding temperamental style) per se are the foremost predictors of their healthy functioning. Instead, the *relations* between the child, the parent, the school, the community, and the other levels of organization within the developmental system are most important in understanding the character of human development and of the role of the ecology of human development in a person's ontogeny.

Essentially, the developmental systems model specifies that applied developmental scholarship pertinent to understanding and enhancing the life course should focus on the relational process of human development by longitudinally integrating the study of the actions of both the individual and the parents, peers, teachers, neighbors, and the broader institutional context within which the individual is embedded. Bearing in mind the centrality of this complex relational system, the synthetic research and application agenda seems clear. Applied developmental scientists must continue to educate themselves about the best means available to promote (through integrating the developmental system) enhanced life chances among all individuals and families, but especially among those whose potential for positive contributions to civil society is most in danger of being wasted (Dryfoos, 1998; Hamburg, 1992; R. M. Lerner, 2002a; Schorr, 1997).

The collaborative expertise of the research and program delivery communities can provide much of this information, especially if it is obtained in partnership with strong, empowered communities. Such coalitions could become an integral component of an integrated child, family, and human development policy aimed at creating caring communities with the capacity to further the healthy development of children, adolescents, adults, and families (Jensen, Hoagwood, & Trickett, 1999; Kennedy, 1999; B. J. Overton & Burkhardt, 1999; Sherrod, 1999a; Spanier, 1999; Thompson, 1999).

Given the enormous and historically unprecedented challenges facing the youth and families of America ·and the world, there is no time to lose in the development of such collaborations if there is the aspiration to raise healthy and successful children capable of leading civil society productively, responsibly, and morally across the twenty-first century (Benson, 1997; Damon, 1997; R. M. Lerner, 1995). The field of human development has an opportunity through the publication of its ADS research to serve our world's citizens and demonstrate that there is nothing of greater value to civil society than a science devoted to using its scholarship to improve the life chances of all people.

REFERENCES

Bakan, D. (1966). *The duality of human existence.* Chicago: Rand-McNally.

Baltes, P. B. (1987). Theoretical propositions of life-span developmental psychology: On the dynamics between growth and decline. *Developmental Psychology, 23,* 611–626.

Baltes, P. B., & Baltes, M. M. (1980). Plasticity and variability in psychological aging: Methodological and theoretical issues. In G. E. Gurski (Ed.), *Determining the effects of aging on the central nervous system* (pp. 41–66). Berlin: Schering AG (Oraniendruck).

Baltes, P. B., Lindenberger, U., & Staudinger, U. M. (1998). Life-span theory in developmental psychology. In W. Damon (Series Ed.) & R. M. Lerner (Vol. Ed.), *Handbook of child psychology: Vol. 1. Theoretical models of human development* (5th ed., pp. 1029–1144). New York: Wiley.

Benson, P. L. (1997). *All kids are our kids: What communities must do to raise caring and responsible children and adolescents.* San Francisco: Jossey-Bass.

Benson, P. L. (in press). Developmental assets and asset-building communities: Implications for research, policy, and practice. In R. M. Lerner & P. Benson (Eds.), *Developmental assets and asset-building communities: Implications for research, policy, and programs.* Norwell, MA: Kluwer.

Benson, P. L., Leffert, N., Scales, P. C., & Blyth, D. A. (1998). Beyond the "village" rhetoric: Creating healthy communities for children and adolescents. *Applied Developmental Science, 2*(3), 138–159.

Benson, P. L., & Saito, R. N. (2000). The scientific foundations of youth development. In *Youth development: Issues, challenges, and directions* (pp. 125–147). Philadelphia: Public/Private Ventures.

Bogenschneider, K., Small, S. A., & Tsay, J. C. (1997). Child, parent, and contextual influences on perceived parenting competence among parents of adolescents. *Journal of Marriage and the Family, 59,* 345–362.

Brandtstädter, J. (1998). Action perspectives on human development. In W. Damon (Series Ed.) & R. M. Lerner (Vol. Ed.), *Handbook of child psychology: Vol. 1. Theoretical models of human development* (5th ed., pp. 807–863). New York: Wiley.

Brandtstädter, J. (1999). The self in action and development: Cultural, biosocial, and ontogenetic bases of intentional self-development. In J. Brandtstädter & R. M. Lerner (Eds.), *Action and self-development: Theory and research through the life-span* (pp. 37–65). Thousand Oaks, CA: Sage.

Bronfenbrenner, U. (1974). Developmental research, public policy, and the ecology of childhood. *Child Development, 45,* 1–5.

Bronfenbrenner, U., & Morris, P. A. (1998). The ecology of developmental process. In W. Damon (Series Ed.) & R. M. Lerner (Vol. Ed.), *Handbook of child psychology: Vol. 1. Theoretical models of human development* (5th ed., pp. 993–1028). New York: Wiley.

Brooks-Gunn, J. (1987). Pubertal processes in girls' psychological adaptation. In R. M. Lerner & T. T. Foch (Eds.), *Biological-psychosocial interactions in early adolescence: A life-span perspective* (pp. 123–153). Hillsdale, NJ: Erlbaum.

Cairns, R. B. (1998). Intellectual, cultural, and scientific foundations of human development. In W. Damon (Series Ed.) & R. M. Lerner (Vol. Ed.), *Handbook of child psychology: Vol. 1. Theoretical models of human development* (5th ed., pp. 25–106). Editor in Chief: William Damon. New York: Wiley.

Cairns, R. B., Bergman, L. R., & Kagan, J. (1998). *Methods and models for studying the individual: Essays in honor of Marian Radke-Yarrow.* Thousand Oaks, CA: Sage.

Chess, S., & Thomas, A. (1984). *The origins and evolution of behavior disorders: Infancy to early adult life.* New York: Brunner/Mazel.

Chess, S., & Thomas, A. (1996). *Temperament: Theory and practice.* New York: Brunner/Mazel.

Chess, S., & Thomas, A. (1999). *Goodness of fit: Clinical applications from infancy through adult life.* Philadelphia: Brunner/ Mazel.

Csikszentmihalyi, M., & Rathunde, K. (1998). The development of the person: An experiential perspective on the ontogenesis of psychological complexity. In W. Damon (Series Ed.) & R. M. Lerner (Vol. Ed.), *Handbook of child psychology: Vol. 1. Theoretical models of human development* (5th ed., pp. 635–684). New York: Wiley.

Damon, W. (1997). *The youth charter: How communities can work together to raise standards for all our children.* New York: Free Press.

Damon, W., & Gregory, A. (in press). Bringing in a new era in the field of youth development. In R. M. Lerner & P. Benson (Eds.), *Developmental assets and asset-building communities: Implications for research, policy, and programs.* Norwell, MA: Kluwer.

de Vries, M. W. (1984). Temperament and infant mortality among the Masai of East Africa. *American Journal of Psychiatry, 141,* 1189–1194.

Dryfoos, J. G. (1990). *Adolescents at risk: Prevalence and prevention.* New York: Oxford University Press.

Dryfoos, J. G. (1998). *Safe passage: Making it through adolescence in a risky society.* New York: Oxford University Press.

Eccles, J. S. (1991). Academic achievement. In R. M. Lerner, A. C. Petersen, & J. Brooks-Gunn (Eds.), *Encyclopedia of adolescence* (Vol. 1, pp. 1–9). New York: Garland.

Eccles, J. S. (1997). User-friendly science and mathematics: Can it interest girls and minorities in breaking through the middle school wall? In D. Johnson (Ed.), *Minorities and girls in school: Effects on achievement and performance: Vol. 1. Leaders in psychology* (pp. 65–104). Thousand Oaks, CA: Sage.

Eccles, J. S., Early, D., Frasier, K., Belansky, E., & McCarthy, K. (1997). The relation of connection, regulation, and support for autonomy to adolescents' functioning. *Journal of Adolescent Research, 12*(2), 263–286.

Eccles, J. S., & Harold, R. D. (1996). Family involvement in children's and adolescents' schooling. In A. Booth & J. F. Dunn (Eds.), *Family-school links: How do they affect educational outcomes?* (pp. 3–34). Mahwah, NJ: Erlbaum.

Eccles, J. S., Lord, S., & Buchanan, C. M. (1996). School transitions in early adolescence: What are we doing to your young people? In J. A. Graber, J. Brooks-Gunn, & A. C. Petersen (Eds.), *Transitions through adolescence* (pp. 251–284). Mahwah, NJ: Erlbaum.

Eccles, J. S., Lord, S., & Midgley, C. (1991). What are we doing to early adolescents? The impact of educational contexts on early adolescents. *American Journal of Education, 99*(4), 521–542.

Eccles, J. S., Lord, S. E., Roeser, R. W., Barber, B. L., & Jozefowicz, D. M. H. (1997). The association of school transitions in early adolescence with developmental trajectories through high school. In J. Schulenberg, J. L. Maggs, & K. Hurrelmann (Eds.), *Health risks and developmental transitions during adolescence* (pp. 283–320). Cambridge, UK: Cambridge University Press.

Eccles, J. S., & Midgley, C. (1989). Stage-environment fit: Developmentally appropriate classrooms for young adolescents. In C. Ames & R. Ames (Eds.), *Research on motivation in education: Goals and cognitions* (pp. 139–186). New York: Academic Press.

Eccles, J. S., Midgley, C., Wigfield, A., Buchanan, C. M., Reuman, D., Flanagan, C., & Mac Iver, D. (1993). Development during adolescence: The impact of stage-environment fit on young adolescents' experiences in schools and in families. *American Psychologist, 48,* 90–101.

Eccles, J. S., & Roeser, R. W. (1999). School and community influences on human development. In M. H. Bornstein & M. E. Lamb (Eds.), *Developmental psychology: An advanced textbook* (4th ed., pp. 503–554). Mahwah, NJ: Erlbaum.

Elder, G. H., Jr. (1998). The life course and human development. In W. Damon (Series Ed.) & R. M. Lerner (Vol. Ed.), *Handbook of child psychology: Vol. 1. Theoretical models of human development* (5th ed., pp. 939–991). New York: Wiley.

Fisher, C. B. (1997). A relational perspective on ethics-in-science decision-making for research with vulnerable populations. *IRB: A Review of Human Subjects Research, 19,* 1–4.

Fisher, C. B., & Brennan, M. (1992). Application and ethics in developmental psychology. In D. L. Featherman, R. M. Lerner, & M. Perlmutter (Eds.), *Life-span development and behavior* (pp. 189–219). Hillsdale, NJ: Erlbaum.

Fisher, C. B., & Lerner, R. M. (1994). Foundations of applied developmental psychology. In C. B. Fisher & R. M. Lerner (Eds.), *Applied developmental psychology* (pp. 3–20). New York: McGraw-Hill.

Fisher, C. B., & Murray, J. P. (1996). Applied developmental science comes of age. In C. B. Fisher, J. P. Murray, & I. E. Sigel (Eds.), *Applied developmental science: Graduate training for diverse disciplines and educational settings* (pp. 1–22). Norwood, NJ: Ablex.

Fisher, C. B., Murray, J. P., Dill, J. R., Hagen, J. W., Hogan, M. J., Lerner, R. M., Rebok, G. W., Sigel, I., Sostek, A. M., Smyer, M. A., Spencer, M. B., & Wilcox, B. (1993). The national conference on graduate education in the applications of developmental science across the life span. *Journal of Applied Developmental Psychology, 14,* 1–10.

Flanagan, C. A., & Eccles, J. S. (1993). Changes in parents' work status and adolescents' adjustment at school. *Child Development, 64,* 246–257.

Fuligni, A. J., Eccles, J. S., & Barber, B. L. (1995). The long-term effects of seventh-grade ability grouping in mathematics. *Journal of Early Adolescence, 15*(1), 58–89.

Galambos, N. L., & Turner, P. K. (1999). Parent and adolescent temperaments and the quality of parent-adolescent relations. *Merrill-Palmer Quarterly, 45*(3), 493–511.

Gollin, E. S. (1981). Development and plasticity. In E. S. Gollin (Ed.), *Developmental plasticity: Behavioral and biological aspects of variations in development* (pp. 231–251). New York: Academic Press.

Gottlieb, G. (1970). Conceptions of prenatal behavior. In L. R. Aronson, E. Tobach, D. S. Lehrman, & J. S. Rosenblatt (Eds.), *Development and evolution of behavior: Essays in memory of T. C. Schneirla* (pp. 111–137). San Francisco: W. H. Freeman.

Gottlieb, G. (1983). Development of species identification in ducklings: Perceptual specificity in the wood duck embryo requires sib stimulation for maintenance. *Developmental Psychobiology, 16,* 323–333.

Gottlieb, G. (1991). Experiential canalization of behavioral development: Theory. *Developmental Psychology, 27*(1), 4–13.

Gottlieb, G. (1992). *The genesis of novel behavior: Individual development and evolution.* New York: Oxford University Press.

Gottlieb, G. (1997). *Synthesizing nature-nurture: Prenatal roots of instinctive behavior.* Mahwah, NJ: Erlbaum.

Hagen, J. W. (1996). Graduate education in the applied developmental sciences: History and background. In C. B. Fisher & J. P. Murray (Eds.), *Applied developmental science: Graduate training for diverse disciplines and educational settings: Advances in applied developmental psychology* (pp. 45–51). Norwood, NJ: Ablex.

Hamburg, D. A. (1992). *Today's children: Creating a future for a generation in crisis.* New York: Time Books.

Hamburger, V. (1957). The concept of development in biology. In D. B. Harris (Ed.), *The concept of development* (pp. 49–58). Minneapolis: University of Minnesota Press.

Hamilton, S. F., & Hamilton, M. (1999). Creating new pathways to adulthood by adapting German apprenticeship in the United States. In W. R. Heinz (Ed.), *From education to work: Cross-national perspectives* (pp. 194–213). New York: Cambridge University Press.

Hart, D., & Fegley, S. (1995). Prosocial behavior and caring in adolescence: Relations to self-understanding and social judgment. *Child Development, 66,* 1346–1359.

Heckhausen, J. (1999). *Developmental regulation in adulthood: Age-normative and sociocultural constraints as adaptive challenges.* New York: Cambridge University Press.

Hernandez, D. J. (1993). *America's children: Resources for family, government, and the economy.* New York: Russell Sage Foundation.

Higgins-D'Alessandro, A., Fisher, C. B., & Hamilton, M. G. (1998). Educating the applied developmental psychologist for university-community partnerships. In R. M. Lerner & L. A. K. Simon (Eds.), *University-community collaborations for the twenty-first century: Outreach scholarship for youth and families* (pp. 157–183). New York: Garland.

Horowitz, F. D. (2000). Child development and the PITS: Simple questions, complex answers, and developmental theory. *Child Development, 71,* 1–10.

Horowitz, F. D., & O'Brien, M. (1989). In the interest of the nature: A reflective essay on the state of our knowledge and challenges before us. *American Psychologist, 44,* 441–445.

Hoyle, R. H., & Leff, S. S. (1997). The role of parental involvement in youth sport participation and performance. *Adolescence, 32*(125), 233–243.

Huston, A. C. (1991). *Children in poverty: Child development and public policy.* Cambridge, UK: Cambridge University Press.

Huston, A. C., McLoyd, V. C., & Garcia Coll, C. (1994). Children and poverty: Issues in contemporary research. *Child Development, 65,* 275–282.

Ianni, F. (1989). *The search for structure: A report on American youth today.* New York: Free Press.

Jensen, P., Hoagwood, K., & Trickett, E. (1999). Ivory towers or earthen trenches? Community collaborations to foster "real world" research. *Applied Developmental Science, 3*(4), 206–212.

Katchadourian, H. (1977). Temperament and infant mortality among the Masai of East Africa. *American Journal of Psychiatry, 141,* 1189–1194.

Kennedy, E. M. (1999). University-community partnerships: A mutually beneficial effort to aid community development and improve academic learning opportunities. *Applied Developmental Science, 3*(4), 197–198.

Korn, S. J. (1978, September). *Temperament, vulnerability, and behavior.* Paper presented at the Louisville Temperament Conference, Louisville, KY.

Kuo, Z. Y. (1930). The genesis of the cat's response to the rat. *Journal of Comparative Psychology, 11,* 1–35.

Kuo, Z. Y. (1967). *The dynamics of behavior development.* New York: Random House.

Kuo, Z. Y. (1976). *The dynamics of behavior development: An epigenetic view.* New York: Plenum Press.

Leffert, N., Benson, P., Scales, P., Sharma, A., Drake, D., & Blyth, D. (1998). Developmental assets: Measurement and prediction of risk behaviors among adolescents. *Applied Developmental Science, 2,* 209–230.

Lerner, J. V., & Lerner, R. M. (1983). Temperament and adaptation across life: Theoretical and empirical issues. In P. B. Baltes & O. G. Brim, Jr. (Eds.), *Life-span development and behavior* (pp. 197–231). New York: Academic Press.

Lerner, R. M. (1976). *Concepts and theories of human development.* Reading, MA: Addison-Wesley.

Lerner, R. M. (1982). Children and adolescents as producers of their own development. *Developmental Review, 2,* 342–370.

Lerner, R. M. (1984). *On the nature of human plasticity.* New York: Cambridge University Press.

Lerner, R. M. (1986). *Concepts and theories of human development* (2nd ed.). New York: Random House.

Lerner, R. M. (1987a). The concept of plasticity in development. In J. Gallagher & C. T. Ramey (Eds.), *The malleability of children* (pp. 3–14). Baltimore: Paul H. Brooks.

Lerner, R. M. (1987b). A life-span perspective for early adolescence. In R. M. Lerner & T. T. Foch (Eds.), *Biological-psychosocial interactions in early adolescence* (pp. 9–34). Hillsdale, NJ: Erlbaum.

Lerner, R. M. (1995). *America's youth in crisis: Challenges and options for programs and policies*. Thousand Oaks, CA: Sage.

Lerner, R. M. (Ed.). (1998a). *The handbook of child psychology: Theoretical models of human development*. (5th ed., Vol. 1). Editor in Chief: William Damon. New York: Wiley.

Lerner, R. M. (1998b). Theories of human development: Contemporary perspectives. In W. Damon (Series Ed.) & R. M. Lerner (Vol. Ed.), *Handbook of child psychology: Vol. 1. Theoretical models of human development* (pp. 1–24). New York: Wiley.

Lerner, R. M. (2002a). *Concepts and theories of human development* (3rd ed.). Mahwah, NJ: Erlbaum.

Lerner, R. M. (2002b). *Adolescence: Development, diversity, context, and application*. Upper Saddle River, NJ: Prentice Hall.

Lerner, R. M., & Busch-Rossnagel, N. (1981). Individuals as producers of their development: Conceptual and empirical bases. In R. M. Lerner & N. A. Busch-Rossnagel (Eds.), *Individuals as producers of their development: A life-span perspective* (pp. 1–36). New York: Academic Press.

Lerner, R. M., & Fisher, C. B. (1994). From applied developmental psychology to applied developmental science: Community coalitions and collaborative careers. In C. B. Fisher & R. M. Lerner (Eds.), *Applied developmental psychology* (pp. 505–522). New York: McGraw-Hill.

Lerner, R. M., Fisher, C. B., & Weinberg, R. A. (1997). Applied developmental science: Scholarship for our times [Editorial]. *Applied Developmental Science, 1*(1), 2–3.

Lerner, R. M., Fisher, C. B., & Weinberg, R. A. (2000a). Applying developmental science in the twenty-first century: International scholarship for our times. *International Journal of Behavioral Development, 24*, 24–29.

Lerner, R. M., Fisher, C. B., & Weinberg, R. A. (2000b). Toward a science for and of the people: Promoting civil society through the application of developmental science. *Child Development, 71*, 11–20.

Lerner, R. M., & Galambos, N. (1998). Adolescent development: Challenges and opportunities for research, programs, and policies. In J. T. Spence (Ed.), *Annual review of psychology* (pp. 413–446). Palo Alto, CA: Annual Reviews.

Lerner, R. M., & Lerner, J. V. (1983). Temperament-intelligence reciprocities in early childhood: A contextual model. In M. Lewis (Ed.), *Origins of intelligence: Infancy and early childhood* (pp. 399–421). New York: Plenum Press.

Lerner, R. M., & Lerner, J. V. (1989). Organismic and social-contextual bases of development: The sample case of adolescence. In W. Damon (Ed.), *Child development today and tomorrow: The Jossey-Bass social and behavioral science series* (pp. 69–85). San Francisco: Jossey-Bass.

Lerner, R. M., & Miller, J. R. (1998). Developing multidisciplinary institutes to enhance the lives of individuals and families: Academic potentials and pitfalls. *Journal of Public Service and Outreach, 3*(1), 64–73.

Lerner, R. M., Miller, J. R., Knott, J. H., Corey, K. E., Bynum, T. S., Hoopfer, L. C., McKinney, M. H., Abrams, L. A., Hula, R. C., & Terry, P. A. (1994). Integrating scholarship and outreach in human development research, policy, and service: A developmental contextual perspective. In D. L. Featherman, R. M. Lerner, & M. Perlmutter (Eds.), *Life-span development and behavior* (pp. 249–273). Hillsdale, NJ: Erlbaum.

Lerner, R. M., Ostrom C. W., & Freel, M. A. (1995). Promoting positive youth and community development through outreach scholarship: Comments on Zeldin and Peterson. *Journal of Adolescent Research, 10*, 486–502.

Lerner, R. M., Rothbaum, F., Boulos, S., & Castellino, D. R. (2002). A developmental systems perspective on parenting. In M. H. Bornstein (Ed.), *Handbook of parenting* (2nd ed., pp. 315–344). Mahwah, NJ: Erlbaum.

Lerner, R. M., & Ryff, C. (1978). Implementation of the life-span view of human development: The sample case of attachment. In P. B. Baltes (Ed.), *Life-span development and behavior* (pp. 1–44). New York: Academic Press.

Lerner, R. M., & Simon, L. A. K. (1998a). *University-community collaborations for the twenty-first century: Outreach scholarship for youth and families*. New York: Garland.

Lerner, R. M., & Simon, L. A. K. (1998b). Directions for the American outreach university in the twenty-first century. In R. M. Lerner & L. A. K. Simon (Eds.), *University-community collaborations for the twenty-first century: Outreach scholarship for youth and families* (pp. 463–481). New York: Garland.

Lerner, R. M., Sparks, E. S., & McCubbin, L. (1999). *Family diversity and family policy: Strengthening families for America's children*. Norwell, MA: Kluwer.

Lerner, R. M., & Walls, T. (1999). Revisiting individuals as producers of their development: From dynamic interactionism to developmental systems. In J. Brandtstädter & R. M. Lerner (Eds.), *Action and self-development: Theory and research through the life-span* (pp. 3–36). Thousand Oaks, CA: Sage.

Leventhal, T., & Brooks-Gunn, J. (2000). The neighborhoods they live in: The effects of neighborhood residence on child and adolescent outcomes. *Psychological Bulletin, 126*(2), 309–337.

Leventhal, T., & Brooks-Gunn, J. (2001). Poverty and child development. In N. J. Smelser & P. B. Baltes (Eds.), *The international encyclopedia of the social and behavioral sciences* (pp. 11889–11894). Oxford: Elsevier.

Little, R. R. (1993, April). *What's working for today's youth: The issues, the programs, and the learnings*. Paper presented at the ICYF Fellows Colloquium, Michigan State University. East Lansing, Michigan.

Lorenz, K. (1966). *On aggression*. New York: Harcourt Brace & World.

Luster, T., & McAdoo, H. (1994). Factors related to the achievement and adjustment of young African American children. *Child Development, 65,* 1080–1094.

Luster, T., & McAdoo, H. (1996). Family and child influences on educational attainment: A secondary analysis of the High/Scope Perry Preschool data. *Developmental Psychology, 32*(1), 26–39.

Midgley, C., Feldlaufer, H., & Eccles, J. S. (1989a). Changes in teacher efficacy and student self- and task-related beliefs in mathematics during the transition to junior high school. *Journal of Educational Psychology, 81,* 247–258.

Midgley, C., Feldlaufer, H., & Eccles, J. S. (1989b). Student/teacher relations and attitudes toward mathematics before and after the transition to junior high school. *Child Development, 60,* 981–992.

Mischel, W. (1977). On the future of personality measurement. *American Psychologist, 32,* 246–254.

Morrison, F. J., Lord, C., & Keating, D. P. (1984). Applied developmental psychology. In F. J. Morrison, C. Lord, & D. P. Keating (Eds.), *Applied developmental psychology* (pp. 4–20). New York: Academic Press.

Mussen, P. H. (1970). *Carmichael's manual of child psychology* (3rd ed.). New York: Wiley.

Overton, W. (1998). Developmental psychology: Philosophy, concepts, and methodology. In W. Damon (Series Ed.) & R. M. Lerner (Vol. Ed.), *Handbook of child psychology: Vol. 1. Theoretical models of human development* (pp. 107–187). New York: Wiley.

Overton, B. J., & Burkhardt, J. C. (1999). Drucker could be right, but. . . : New leadership models for institutional-community partnerships. *Applied Developmental Science, 3*(4), 217–227.

Pepper, S. C. (1942). *World hypotheses: A study in evidence.* Berkeley: University of California Press.

Petersen, A. C. (1988). Adolescent development. In M. R. Rosenzweig (Ed.), *Annual review of psychology* (Vol. 39, pp. 583–607). Palo Alto, CA: Annual Reviews.

Pittman, K. (1996). Community, youth, development: Three goals in search of connection. *New Designs for Youth Development, Winter,* 4–8.

Plomin, R. (1986). *Development, genetics, and psychology.* Hillsdale, NJ: Erlbaum.

Plomin, R. (2000). Behavioral genetics in the 21st century. *International Journal of Behavioral Development, 24,* 30–34.

Plomin, R., Corley, R., DeFries, J. C., & Faulker, D. W. (1990). Individual differences in television viewing in early childhood: Nature as well as nurture. *Psychological Science, 1,* 371–377.

Power, F. C., Higgins, A., & Kohlberg, L. (1989). *Lawrence Kohlberg's approach to moral education.* New York: Columbia University Press.

Roeser, R. W., Eccles, J. S., & Sameroff, A. J. (1998). Academic and emotional functioning in early adolescence: Longitudinal relations, patterns, and prediction by experience in middle school. *Development and Psychopathology, 10,* 321–352.

Roeser, R. W., Eccles, J. S., & Sameroff, A. J. (2000). School as a context of early adolescents' academic and social-emotional development: A summary of research findings. *The Elementary School Journal, 100,* 443–472.

Rowe, D. (1994). *The limits of family influence: Genes, experience, and behavior.* New York: Guilford Press.

Rushton, J. P. (1987). An evolutionary theory of health, longevity, and personality: Sociobiology, and r/K reproductive strategies. *Psychological Reports, 60,* 539–549.

Rushton, J. P. (1988a). Do r/K reproductive strategies apply to human differences? *Social Biology, 35,* 337–340.

Rushton, J. P. (1988b). Race differences in behavior: A review and evolutionary analysis. *Personality and Individual Differences, 9,* 1009–1024.

Rushton, J. P. (1997). More on political correctness and race differences. *Journal of Social Distress and the Homeless, 6,* 195–198.

Rushton, J. P. (1999). *Race, evolution, and behavior* (Special Abridged ed.). New Brunswick, NJ: Transaction.

Rushton, J. P. (2000). *Race, evolution, and behavior* (2nd Special Abridged ed.). New Brunswick, NJ: Transaction.

Scales, P., & Leffert, N. (1999). *Developmental assets: A synthesis of the scientific research on adolescent development.* Minneapolis, MN: Search Institute.

Scales, P., Benson, P., Leffert, N., & Blyth, D. A. (2000). The contribution of developmental assets to the prediction of thriving among adolescents. *Applied Developmental Science, 4*(1), 27–46.

Schneirla, T. C. (1956). Interrelationships of the innate and the acquired in instinctive behavior. In P. P. Grassé (Ed.), *L'instinct dans le comportement des animaux et de l'homme* (pp. 387–452). Paris: Mason et Cie.

Schneirla, T. C. (1957). The concept of development in comparative psychology. In D. B. Harris (Ed.), *The concept of development: An issue in the study of human behavior* (pp. 78–108). Minneapolis: University of Minnesota Press.

Schorr, L. B. (1988). *Within our reach: Breaking the cycle of disadvantage.* New York: Doubleday.

Schorr, L. B. (1997). *Common purpose: Strengthening families and neighborhoods to rebuild America.* New York: Doubleday.

Schraeder, B. D., Heverly, M. A., & O'Brien, C. M. (1996). Home and classroom behavioral adjustment in very low birthweight children: The influence of caregiver stress and goodness of fit. *Children's Health Care, 25*(2), 117–131.

Sherrod, L. R. (1999a). Funding opportunities for applied developmental science. In P. Ralston, R. M. Lerner, A. K. Mullis, C. Simerly, & J. Murray (Eds.), *Social change, public policy, and community collaboration: Training human development professionals for the twenty-first century* (pp. 121–129). Norwell, MA: Kluwer.

Sherrod, L. R. (1999b). Giving child development knowledge away: Using university-community partnerships to disseminate research on children, youth, and families. *Applied Developmental Science, 3*(4), 228–234.

Sigel, I. E. (1985). *Parental belief systems: The psychological consequences for children.* Hillsdale, NJ: Erlbaum.

Simmons, R. G., & Blyth, D. A. (1987). *Moving into adolescence: The impact of pubertal change and school context.* Hawthorne, NJ: Aldine.

Simmons, R. G., Carlton-Ford, S. L., & Blyth, D. A. (1987). Predicting how a child will cope with the transition to junior high school. In R. M. Lerner & T. T. Foch (Eds.), *Biological-psychosocial interactions in early adolescence* (pp. 325–375). Hillsdale, NJ: Erlbaum.

Snyder, M. (1981). On the influence of individuals on situations. In N. Cantor & J. F. Kihlstorm (Eds.), *Cognition, social interaction, and personality* (pp. 309–329). Hillsdale, NJ: Erlbaum.

Spanier, G. B. (1999). Enhancing the quality of life: A model for the 21st century land-grant university. *Applied Developmental Science, 3*(4), 199–205.

Super, C. M., & Harkness, S. (1981). Figure, ground, and gestalt: The cultural context of the active individual. In R. M. Lerner & N. A. Busch-Rossnagel (Eds.), *Individuals as producers of their own development: A life-span perspective* (pp. 69–86). New York: Academic Press.

Takanishi, R. (1993). An agenda for the integration of research and policy during early adolescence. In R. M. Lerner (Ed.), *Early adolescence: Perspectives on research, policy, and intervention* (pp. 457–470). Hillsdale, NJ: Erlbaum.

Tanner, J. (1991). Menarche, secular trend in age of. In R. M. Lerner, A. C. Petersen, & J. Brooks-Gunn (Eds.), *Encyclopedia of adolescence* (pp. 637–641). New York: Garland.

Thomas, A., & Chess, S. (1970). Behavioral individuality in childhood. In L. R. Aronson, E. Tobach, D. Lehrman, & J. S. Rosenblatt (Eds.), *Development and evolution of behavior* (pp. 529–541). San Francisco: W. H. Freeman.

Thomas, A., & Chess, S. (1977). *Temperament and development.* New York: Brunner/Mazel.

Thomas, A., & Chess, S. (1980). *The dynamics of psychological development.* New York: Brunner/Mazel.

Thomas, A., & Chess, S. (1981). The role of temperament in the contributions of individuals to their development. In R. M. Lerner & N. A. Busch-Rossnagel (Eds.), *Individuals as producers of their own development: A life-span perspective.* New York: Academic Press.

Thomas, A., Chess, S., & Birch, H. (1968). *Temperament and behavioral disorders in childhood.* New York: New York University.

Thomas, A., Chess, S., Sillen, J., & Mendez, O. (1974). Cross-cultural study of behavior in children with special vulnerabilities to stress. In D. F. Ricks, A. Thomas, & M. Roff (Eds.), *Life history research in psychopathology* (pp. 53–63). Minneapolis: University of Minnesota.

Thompson, L. (1999). Creating partnerships with government, communities, and universities to achieve results for children. *Applied Developmental Science, 3*(4), 213–216.

Trickett, E. J., Barone, C., & Buchanan, R. M. (1996). Elaborating developmental contextualism in adolescent research and intervention: Paradigm contributions from community psychology. *Journal of Research on Adolescence, 6*(3), 245–269.

Valsiner, J. (1998). The development of the concept of development: Historical and epistemological perspectives. In W. Damon (Series Ed.) & R. M. Lerner (Vol. Ed.), *Handbook of child psychology: Vol. 1. Theoretical models of human* (5th ed., pp. 189–232). New York: Wiley.

von Bertalanffy, L. (1933). *Modern theories of development.* London: Oxford University Press.

Wigfield, A., Eccles, J. S., MacIver, D., Reumann, D. A., & Midgley, C. (1991). Transitions during early adolescence: Changes in children's domain-specific self-perceptions and general self-esteem across the transition to junior high. *Developmental Psychology, 27,* 552–565.

Yates, M., & Youniss, J. (1996). Community service and political-moral identity in adolescents. *Journal of Research on Adolescence, 6*(3), 271–284.

Youniss, J. (1990). Cultural forces leading to scientific developmental psychology. In C. B. Fisher & W. W. Tryon (Eds.), *Ethics in applied developmental psychology: Emerging issues in an emerging field: Vol. 4. Annual advances in applied developmental psychology* (pp. 285–300). Stamford, CT: Ablex.

Youniss, J., Yates, M., & Su, Y. (1997). Social integration: Community service and Marijuana use in high school seniors. *Journal of Adolescent Research, 12*(2), 245–262.

Zigler, E. (1998). A place of value for applied and policy studies. *Child Development, 69,* 532–542.

Zigler, E., & Finn-Stevenson, M. (1992). Applied developmental psychology. In M. H. Bornstein & M. E. Lamb (Eds.), *Developmental psychology: An advanced textbook* (pp. 677–729). Hillsdale, NJ: Erlbaum.

CHAPTER 23

Child Development and the Law

MICHAEL E. LAMB

The law, broadly conceived, touches the lives of increasing numbers of children in a variety of different ways. For example, legal authorities intervene when parents appear incapable of caring for their children appropriately, when parents are required to work or are incarcerated and thus must place their children in the care of others, when parents cannot agree with one another regarding the custody and care of their children following divorce, and when children have been victimized. Although legal intervention in these cases is often justified by reference to children's best interests, the interventions themselves are seldom informed by reference to developmental theory or the results of scientific research. Indeed, political ideology and cultural values, rather than scientific knowledge, tend to guide the development of policies like those requiring parents to seek employment or job training in exchange for public support, those that emphasize family preservation rather than the removal and adoption of children who have not received adequate care from their parents, or even those that permit the prosecution of juvenile offenders as though they were adults.

That policy makers and enforcers fail to take advantage of a burgeoning and increasingly sophisticated understanding of child development is unfortunate because superior public policy and law would surely emerge if they were better informed. Researchers actually know a great deal about young children's ability to tolerate separations or be influenced by variations in the quality of their parents' and care providers' behavior (R. A. Thompson, 1998). They are increasingly aware of the variability among children with respect to their vulnerability and resilience (Masten & Garmezy, 1985; Rolf,

Masten, Cicchetti, Naechterlein, & Weintraub, 1990), and they have documented age-related changes in children's awareness of their responsibility for the consequences of their actions as well as the inconsistency and fallibility of their moral and causal reasoning (Levesque, 2001; Schwartz, 2001). All of this information could be of value to policy makers and jurists.

In at least two areas, however, legal practice has been at least somewhat responsive to scientific input. I examine these two topics closely in this chapter because they illustrate both (a) how applied research and basic research by developmentalists have combined to offer compelling recommendations to those practitioners whose efforts can have crucial implications for the lives and futures of vulnerable children and (b) how slowly the insights gleaned from scientific research affect first the letter of the law and then, much later, practices in the field. In the first half of the chapter I review research on the extent to which children of different ages are capable of providing detailed information about their experiences—particularly their experiences of child abuse—and the ways in which interview procedures informed by developmental research improve the quality of information provided by children about their alleged abuse. In the second half I discuss the ways in which research on parent-child relationships and on the effects of divorce create a knowledge base that can be used to guide those professionals who must make decisions about children's living arrangements when their parents no longer live together. In both cases, we see how scholarly research can indeed inform practice in the real world, promoting children's welfare and best interests in the process. In both cases, furthermore, close study of children's actual experiences and performance in real-world settings (the court room, the forensic interview, the disintegrating family) has enhanced our cumulative understanding of developmental processes, often in unique ways. This point deserves emphasis because academic psychologists too often view applied research as intellectually and methodologically inferior, unlikely to enhance our broader understanding. I hope to demonstrate in this chapter how basic research and applied research can complement one another and thus that a complete understanding of developmental processes may only be obtained when we are able to learn from the close study of children in experimental, analog, and real-world contexts.

MAXIMIZING THE INFORMATIVENESS OF CHILD SEX ABUSE VICTIMS

Although sex crimes against children are alleged with some—albeit declining—frequency (L. Jones & Finkelhor, 2001; Sedlak & Broadhurst, 1996), such crimes are extremely difficult to investigate because corroborative physical or medical evidence is rarely available, leaving contradictory accounts by the alleged victims and suspects as the only available evidence. This difficulty has increased the importance of obtaining and evaluating information provided by children, and as a result many researchers have studied the capacity of young children to provide reliable and valid information about their experiences (for recent reviews, see Kuehnle, 1996; Lamb, Sternberg, Orbach, Hershkowitz, & Esplin, 1999; Memon & Bull, 1999; Milne & Bull, 1999; Poole & Lamb, 1998; Westcott, Davies, & Bull, 2002). The research summarized in this section has helped identify children's strengths, weaknesses, and characteristics, thereby facilitating improvements in the quality of forensic interviewing and our evaluation of the information elicited from children in this way.

Factors Influencing Children's Informativeness

Language Development

Linguistic and communicative immaturity clearly make it difficult for children to describe their experiences intelligibly, especially because so many interviewers fail to recognize the gradual pace of communicative development and thus overestimate children's linguistic capacities. The more impoverished the children's language, the greater is the likelihood that their statements will be misinterpreted or that children will misinterpret the interviewers' questions and purposes (King &

Yuille, 1987; Perry & Wrightsman, 1991; Walker, 1999). Most children say their first word by early in the second year of life, begin to create two-word sentences by 20 months, and can draw upon an average vocabulary of 8,000 to 14,000 words by the time they are 6 years old (Carey, 1978). The vocabularies of young children are often much more limited and less descriptive than those of adults, however (Brown, 1973; Dale, 1976; de Villiers & de Villiers, 1999). Adjectival and adverbial modifiers are especially likely to be absent in their accounts, which tend to be extremely brief and sparse (Marin, Holmes, Guth, & Kovac, 1979), perhaps in part because syntactical development is so slow. Unlike adults and older children, furthermore, young children cannot draw on an array of past experiences to enrich and clarify their descriptive accounts (Johnson & Foley, 1984). In addition, children do not articulate individual sounds consistently even after they seem to have mastered them (Reich, 1986), and thus it is not uncommon for interviewers to misunderstand children's speech. Misunderstandings occur also because children's rapid vocabulary growth often leads adults to overestimate their linguistic capacities. Despite their apparent maturity, young children—especially preschoolers—frequently use words before they know their conventional adult meaning, use words that they do not understand, and often misunderstand some apparently simple concepts, such as "any," "some," "touch," "yesterday," and "before" (Harner, 1975; Walker, 1999).

The informativeness of conversations with children is greatly influenced by the linguistic style and the complexity of the language addressed to them by investigators. A particularly widespread problem involves compound questions, responses to which are inherently uninterpretable (Walker & Hunt, 1998), but other poorly worded questions pose problems as well. Mismatches between children's abilities and the language addressed to them are not limited to preschoolers, furthermore. Brennan and Brennan (1988) showed that fewer than two thirds of the questions addressed to 6- to 15-year-old children during cross-examination in court were comprehensible to their peers, and lawyers seemed especially likely to overestimate the abilities of 10- to 15-year-olds. Similarly, inappropriate questioning strategies also characterize the vast majority of forensic interviews, as shown later. To make matters worse, Roberts and Lamb (1999) showed that when interviewers misrepresent what children say, they are seldom corrected, and thus the mistakes, rather than the correct information, are recalled later in the interview. Overall, as Poole and Lamb (1998, p. 155) warned, "we cannot assume that the question the child 'heard' was the one the adult asked. Consequently, if the child later answered a similar question differently, we could not assume that the event had not really happened or that the child was an unreliable witness."

Children's accounts of abusive experiences are also influenced by social or pragmatic aspects of communication, particularly their expectations regarding the goals of the forensic interview. In the process of learning words and the rules for combining words into sentences, children learn how to participate in conversations and how to structure story narratives (Warren & McCloskey, 1997). Children's conversations often lack the logical structure that adults expect, with many loose association and digressions, but individual differences are large and developmental changes rapid. Like adults, furthermore, young witnesses are typically unaware of the amount and type of information being sought by forensic investigators and are most likely to be guided by the everyday experience of conversing with adults who already know answers to the questions they ask (e.g., "What color are daddy's shoes?") or are interested in rather brief responses ("What did you do at the playground?"). As a result, interviewers need to communicate their needs and expectations clearly, motivating children to provide as much information as they can, and it is often valuable to train young witnesses explicitly to provide detailed narrative responses before starting to discuss the substantive issues under investigation (Saywitz, Snyder, & Nathanson, 1999; Sternberg et al., 1997). The fact that communicative clarity and careful explanation of the alleged victim's role as a potential source of unique information can affect children's informativeness illustrates that children can indeed remember details of their experiences, although the interviewer's inability to *elicit* information and the child's unwillingness or inability to *express* it may obscure the child's ability to *remember* it.

Memory

Nevertheless, most doubts about the informative capacities of young witnesses focus on the presumed fallibility of their memories, although both their capacities and their weaknesses are frequently misunderstood and misrepresented.

Research on memory development suggests that as children grow older, the length, informativeness, and complexity of their recall memories increase, but the basic structure remains the same (Schneider & Bjorklund, 1998; Davies, Tarrant & Flin, 1989; Flin, Boon, Knox, & Bull, 1992; Nelson & Gruendel, 1981; Saywitz, 1988). Flin and her colleagues (1992) reported that 6-year-old children reported less information than did 9-year-old children and adults and that, like adults, 6- and 9-year-olds reported less information five months after the event. Of particular note is that the amount of incorrect information provided did not increase over time. Memory is a reconstructive process, however: Like adults, children actively work on memory traces in order to understand and organize them. Thus when children are repeatedly interviewed, as is often the case when sexual abuse has been alleged, this is likely not only to consolidate the memory (facilitating subsequent recall) but also to shape it (Ornstein, Larus, & Clubb, 1992). In a recent field study of investigative interviews, Lamb, Sternberg, and Esplin (2000) found that both delay and age affected the amount of information recalled, although in this study it was of course impossible to assess the accuracy of the children's accounts.

In general, young children tend to provide briefer accounts of their experiences than do older children and adults, but their accounts are equivalently accurate (e.g., Goodman & Reed, 1986; Johnson & Foley, 1984; Marin et al., 1979; Oates & Shrimpton, 1991). As time passes, information is forgotten by children just as it is forgotten by adults (Flin et al., 1992). Errors of omission are much more common than errors of commission among both adults and children (Oates & Shrimpton, 1991; Steward, 1993), but the former are a special problem where children are concerned because their accounts—especially their recall narratives—are often so brief.

It is important to distinguish between memory performance and memory capacity, however. Young children's accounts may be brief not only because their memories are poor or because their limited experiences do not provide a rich network of associations from which to draw analogies or metaphors but also because their vocabularies are much more limited and less elaborate than those of adults and because they may not be motivated to reveal what they do remember.

Whenever events recur with any regularity, both children and adults tend to blur distinctions among incidents and establish script memories (representations of averaged or typical events rather than particular incidents). Accounts based on script memories are likely to contain fewer distinctive details than are memories of discrete incidents (Nelson & Gruendel, 1981), and the passage of time between experience and recall increases the tendency to rely on scripts (Myles-Worsley, Cromer, & Dodd, 1986). Scripts are useful because they help individuals to focus on and remember the important features of repetitive events or sequences while enabling them to ignore less central or repetitious elements (Nelson, 1986; Shank & Abelson, 1977). In addition, scripts may provide the temporal sequence or structure that makes the accounts of specific experiences more comprehensible.

However, scripts lead reporters to use general knowledge about a class of events to describe specific events incorrectly. For example, Ornstein, Staneck, Agosto, and Baker-Ward (2001) reported that after a 12-week delay 6-year-olds incorporated into their memory details that were typical of medical checkups but had not actually been experienced during a specific checkup. The tendency to embellish restatements of stories with items and events that were part of the children's scripts generally declines with age (Collins, 1970; Collins & Wellman, 1982; Collins, Wellman, Keniston, & Westby, 1978), and script-based errors can be reduced by preinterview counseling or instruction (Saywitz & Snyder, 1993). Children also tend to remember unusual specific events better than specific events that are congruent with their general or script memories (Davidson, 1991).

Experimental research in the last two decades makes clear that the distinction between recall and recognition testing is crucial when evaluating children's memory capacities and the ways in which memories are accessed (Dale, Loftus, & Rathbun, 1978; Dent, 1982, 1986; Dent & Stephenson, 1979; Goodman & Aman, 1990; Goodman, Hirschman, Hepps, & Rudy, 1991; Hutcheson, Baxter, Telfer, & Warden, 1995; Oates & Shrimpton, 1991; Peterson & Bell, 1996). These researchers have shown that when adults and children are asked to describe events from free recall ("Tell me everything you remember . . . "), their accounts tend to be incomplete and sketchy but are likely to be very accurate. When prompted for more details using open-ended prompts like "Tell me more about that" or "And then what happened?" children often recall additional details, and their accuracy remains high. However, when interviewers prompt with focused questions—especially option-posing questions such as "Did he have a beard?" "Did he touch you with his private?" or "Did this happen in the day or in the night?"—they shift from recall to recognition testing, and the probability of error rises dramatically. Open-ended prompts encourage respondents to provide as much relevant information as they remember, whereas recognition probes focus the child on categories of information or topics of interest to the investigator and exert greater pressure to respond, whether or not the child is sure of the response, often by confirming or rejecting information provided by the interviewer. Such probes are also more likely to elicit erroneous responses from respondents who recognize details that are not remembered from the actual incident but were mentioned in previous conversations (or interviews) or are inferred from the gist of the experienced events (Brainerd & Reyna, 1996). Effective interviewers must thus maximize the opportunities for recall by offering open-ended prompts to minimize the risk of eliciting erroneous information. Recall memories are not always accurate, of course, especially when the events occurred long before the interview or when there have been opportunities for contamination (Leichtman & Ceci, 1995; Poole & Lindsay, 1995, 1996; Poole & White, 1993; Warren & Lane, 1995), but accounts based on recall memory are much more likely to be accurate than those elicited using recognition cues or prompts, regardless of the informants' ages.

Forensic investigators often dismiss the relevance of experimental research on children's memory by arguing that the stressful nature of sexual abuse makes memories of abuse distinctly different. In fact, considerable controversy persists in the experimental literature concerning the effects of increased arousal or stress on the accuracy of children's memory. Some researchers argue that stress improves children's accuracy (Goodman, Bottoms, Schwartz-Kenney, & Rudy, 1991; Goodman, Hirschman, et al., 1991; Ochsner & Zaragoza, 1988; Steward & Steward, 1996). Steward and Steward (1996), for example, reported that children's ratings of distress were correlated with the completeness and accuracy of their descriptions of medical examinations that they had experienced. Other researchers (Oates & Shrimpton, 1991; Ornstein, Gordon, & Larus, 1992; D. P. Peters, 1987, 1991; D. P. Peters & Hagan, 1989; Peterson & Bell, 1996; Vandermaas, 1991) reported that arousal either reduces accuracy or has no effect. In most of these studies, unfortunately, the children experienced low levels of stress, and the ability to recall central elements of experienced events was not assessed. In addition, researchers have not yet studied the effects of social support, which presumably reduces stress (Greenstock & Pipe, 1996; Moston & Engelberg, 1992).

Children are certainly more likely to remember personally meaningful and salient as opposed to meaningless items and events (see Ornstein, Gordon, et al., 1992, for a review) but this does not mean that incidents of maltreatment will necessarily be recalled better. First of all, not all incidents of sexual abuse are distinctive or traumatic, and thus the potentially facilitative effects of arousal on the process of encoding information cannot be assumed. Second, the context in which the child is asked to retrieve information about the experienced event—during interviews with a child protection service worker, a police officer, an attorney, or a judge—may be stressful regardless of whether the target event itself was (Goodman et al., 1992). Third, stress may affect memory encoding, processing, and retrieval in different ways.

Suggestibility

Most researchers agree that the manner in which children are questioned can have profound implications for what is "remembered," and this increases the importance of careful interviewing, particularly in light of studies demonstrating the deleterious (and sometimes devastating) effects of suggestion (Ceci & Bruck, 1993, 1995). Misleading or suggestive questioning can manipulate both young and old witnesses, but the very young are especially vulnerable (Ceci & Bruck, 1993). Suggestibility is a multifaceted concept that involves social, communicative, and memory processes. Children may respond inaccurately because they (a) infer that the interviewer would prefer a particular response (Ceci & Bruck, 1993), (b) do not understand the questions but are eager to be cooperative (e.g. Hughes & Grieve, 1980), (c) retrieve the most recently acquired information about the event in question although they might be able to retrieve information about the actual event if prompted to do so (Newcombe & Siegal, 1996, 1997), or (d) suffer from genuine source-monitoring confusion that prevents them from discriminating between the original event and misinformation about it (Poole & Lindsay, 1997).

Because so many processes underlie suggestibility, it is not surprising that, at first glance, research on children's suggestibility appears to reveal a mixed and confusing picture. These apparently contradictory findings are not difficult to reconcile, however. In the studies documenting the resistance to suggestion by 3- to 4-year-olds (Goodman & Aman, 1990; Goodman, Aman, & Hirschman, 1987; Goodman, Bottoms, et al., 1991; Goodman, Wilson, Hazan, & Reed, 1989), researchers have not repeated misleading questions over a short period of time, exposed children to misleading stereotypes about target individuals, provided incentives to respond falsely, or instructed children to think about nonevents, pretend, or guess. All of these conditions increase the susceptibility to suggestion (e.g. Bruck, Ceci, Francouer, & Barr, 1995; Bruck, Ceci, Francouer, & Renick, 1995; Cassel, Roebers, & Bjorklund, 1996; Ceci, Huffman, Smith, & Loftus, 1994; Ceci, Ross, & Toglia, 1987a, 1987b; Garven, Wood, Malpass, & Shaw; 1998; King & Yuille, 1987; Leichtman & Ceci, 1995; W. C. Thompson, Clarke-Stewart, & Lepore, 1997; Toglia, Ceci, & Ross, 1989). Likewise, suggestive interviewing is most likely to be influential when the memory is not rich or recent, when the content was imagined rather than experienced, when the questions themselves are so complicated that the witness is confused, and when the interviewer appears to have such authority or status that the witness feels compelled to accept his or her implied construction of the events. By contrast, suggestions are less likely to affect children's accounts when they pertain to central or salient details (Dent & Stephenson, 1979; Dodd & Bradshaw, 1980; King & Yuille, 1987) and when interviewers counsel children to report personally experienced events only (Poole & Lindsay, 1997). Unfortunately, little research has been conducted on suggestibility regarding memories of incidents that traumatized or affected individuals profoundly, although Goodman, Hirschman, et al. (1991) found that

children who were more distressed by inoculations were less suggestible than were children who appeared less stressed by the inoculations.

Implications for Practice

As evidence regarding children's linguistic, communicative, social, and memorial capacities and tendencies has accumulated, a surprisingly coherent international consensus has emerged concerning the ways in which children should be interviewed forensically (e.g., American Professional Society on the Abuse of Children [APSAC], 1990/1997; Bull, 1992, 1995, 1996; Fisher & Geiselman, 1992; D. P. H. Jones, 1992; Lamb, Sternberg, & Esplin, 1994, 1995, 1998; Lamb, Sternberg, et al., 1999; Memorandum of Good Practice, 1992; Poole & Lamb, 1998; Raskin & Esplin, 1991; Raskin & Yuille, 1989; Sattler, 1998). Clearly, it is possible to obtain valuable information from children, but doing so requires careful investigative procedures as well as a realistic awareness of their capacities and tendencies. In particular, experts recommend that questions and statements be worded carefully, with due consideration for the child's age and communicative abilities. They further recommend that as much information as possible should be obtained using broad open-ended prompts, like the invitations defined in the next section.

When recall memory is probed using open-ended prompts, respondents attempt to provide as much relevant information as they remember; whereas when recognition is probed using focused questions, children may have to confirm or reject information or options provided by the interviewer. Such probes refocus the child on domains of interest to the investigator and exert greater pressure to respond, whether or not the respondent is sure of the response. Recognition probes are more likely to elicit erroneous responses in eyewitness contexts because of response biases (e.g., tendencies to say "yes" or "no" without reflection) and false recognition of details that were only mentioned in previous interviews or are inferred from the gist of the experienced events (Brainerd & Reyna, 1996). For these reasons, open-ended questions are assumed to yield the most information and the fewest errors in forensic contexts as well. When more focused questions, especially option-posing questions, are necessary, they should be used as sparingly as possible, and only after open-ended prompts have been exhausted. Suggestive and coercive questions and practices should be avoided completely. As we have just seen, all of these recommendations flow directly from the accumulating body of research—most of it conducted in laboratory analog experiments—on children's capacities and tendencies.

Research on Investigative Interviews

Of course, consensus among experts about the manner in which interviews should be conducted does not mean that interviews are typically conducted in accordance with these recommendations, and thus my colleagues and I have undertaken a series of studies designed to determine how forensic interviews are actually conducted by social workers, investigators, and police officers in the everyday course of their work. Our research in this area has all been conducted using verbatim transcriptions of forensic interviews conducted in Israel, the United States, the United Kingdom, and Sweden by social workers, sheriffs, or police officers. For purposes of the analyses summarized here, we focused on the portion of each interview concerned with substantive issues by having coders review the transcripts and tabulate the number of new details identifying and describing individuals, objects, or actions relevant to the alleged incident. Coders also categorized each interviewer utterance, focusing particularly on four common types of utterances:

1. *Invitations* request an open-ended response from the child. Such utterances do not delimit the child's focus except in the most general way (e.g., "And then what happened?").

2. *Directive utterances* focus the child's attention on details or aspects of the event that the child had previously mentioned. Most of these are *wh*-questions (e.g., "What color was that shirt?").

3. *Option-posing utterances* focus the child's attention on aspects of the event that the child had not previously mentioned and prompt the child to choose among two or more possible answers (e.g., "Did you see a knife?" or "Were his clothes on or off?").

4. *Suggestive utterances* are stated in such a way that the interviewer strongly communicates what response is expected ("It hurt, didn't it?") or assumes details that have not been revealed by the child (e.g., "Did he touch your breasts or your vagina?" when the child has not mentioned being touched). Most of these utterances would be called leading by lawyers, jurists, and researchers.

Directive, option-posing, and suggestive utterances are sometimes grouped as focused questions, although they lie along a continuum of risk, varying with respect to the degree of suggestive influence they exert on children's responses.

When used in forensic interviews, invitations consistently yield responses that are three to four times longer and three times richer in relevant details than responses to focused interviewer utterances (e.g., Lamb, Hershkowitz, Sternberg, Boat, & Everson, 1996; Lamb, Hershkowitz, Sternberg,

Esplin, et al., 1996; Orbach et al., 2000; Sternberg et al., 1996). The superiority of open-ended utterances is apparent regardless of the age of the children being interviewed; unfortunately, however, focused utterances are much more common in the field than are open-ended questions. In the field sites we studied initially, for example, around 80% of the interviewer utterances were focused, whereas fewer than 6% were invitations, and the overreliance on focused questions was evident regardless of the children's age, the nature of the offenses, the professional background of the interviewers, or the utilization of props such as anatomical dolls (Craig, Sheibe, Kircher, Raskin, & Dodd, 1999; Davies, Westcott, & Horan, 2000; Lamb, Hershkowitz, Sternberg, Boat, et al., 1996; Lamb, Hershkowitz, Sternberg, Esplin, et al., 1996; Sternberg et al., 1996; Walker & Hunt, 1998). Similar findings were obtained in diverse sites across the United States, the United Kingdom, Sweden, and Israel.

Furthermore, despite research-based warnings concerning the risks of asking option-posing and suggestive questions, analyses of investigative interviews conducted at sites in the United States, the United Kingdom, Sweden, and Israel all reveal that the majority of the information obtained from child victim-witnesses is typically elicited using focused questions (e.g., Aldridge & Cameron, 1999; Cederborg, Orbach, Sternberg, & Lamb, 2000; Craig et al., 1999; Davies et al., 2000; Davies & Wilson, 1997; Lamb, Hershkowitz, Sternberg, Boat, et al., 1996; Lamb, Hershkowitz, Sternberg, Esplin, et al., 1996; Lamb et al., 2000; Sternberg et al., 1996; Sternberg, Lamb, Davies, & Westcott, 2001; Walker & Hunt, 1998; Warren, Woodall, Hunt, & Perry, 1996). These descriptive data are noteworthy because they reveal widespread similarities in forensic interview practices across countries and cultures. Interview practices are at considerable variance with the practices recommended by experts and professional advisory groups from around the world. In other words, despite consistent research documenting the superiority of certain ways of obtaining information from children about their experiences, forensic interviewers continue to employ inferior and potentially dangerous practices when they interview alleged victims.

Enhancing Children's Informativeness

Fortunately, forensic interviewers can be trained to conduct better interviews—interviews in which fewer suggestive questions are asked and in which greater proportions of the information are elicited using open-ended prompts, ideally before any focused or leading questions are asked. In one early study, Sternberg et al. (1997) had forensic interviewers train Israeli children to give narrative responses by asking them a series of open-ended questions about recent neutral events. When later questioned about alleged incidents of abuse, these children provided responses that were 2.5 times more detailed than did children who were (like children in most forensic interviews) trained to respond to focused questions in earlier discussions of neutral events. Comparable findings were obtained when similar training was given by police investigators to alleged victims in the United States (Sternberg, Lamb, Esplin, & Baradaran, 1999).

These findings prompted the development of a fully structured investigative interview protocol designed to translate empirically based research guidelines into a practical tool to be used by investigators conducting forensic interviews (Orbach et al., 2000). The National Institute of Child Health and Human Development's (NICHD) investigative interview protocol covers all phases of the investigative interview and is designed to translate research-based recommendations into operational guidelines in order to enhance the retrieval of informative, complete, and accurate accounts of alleged incidents of abuse by young victim-witnesses. This is accomplished by creating a supportive interview environment (before substantive rapport building), adapting interview practices to children's developmental levels and capabilities (e.g., minimizing linguistic complexity and avoiding interruptions), preparing children for their tasks as information providers (by clarifying the rules of communication and training children to report event-specific episodic memories), and maximizing the interviewers' reliance on utterance types (e.g., invitations) that tap children's free recall memory. When following the protocol, interviewers maximize the use of open-ended questions and probes, introduce focused questions only after exhausting open-ended questioning modes, use option-posing questions only to obtain essential information later in the interview, and eliminate suggestive practices. Interviewers are also encouraged to use information provided by the children themselves as cues to promote further free-recall retrieval. In essence, the protocol is thus designed to maximize the amount of information elicited using recall memory prompts because information elicited in this way is more likely to be accurate. In addition, the structured interview protocol minimizes opportunities for contamination of the children's accounts.

Analyses revealed dramatic improvements in the organization of interviews, the quality of questions asked by interviewers, and the quality of information provided by children when Israeli youth investigators followed the protocol when interviewing 50 4- to 13-year-old alleged victims of sexual abuse (Orbach et al., 2000). Almost all of the children interviewed using the structured protocol made a disclosure and

provided a narrative account of the alleged abuse in response to the first invitation, and the interviewers offered more than five times as many open-ended invitations as they did in comparable interviews conducted before the structured protocol was introduced. The number of option-posing questions dropped by almost 50% as well, and much more of the information was obtained using free recall rather than investigator-directed recognition probes in the protocol-guided interviews. Children in the protocol condition provided proportionally more of the total number of details in their first narrative response than did children in the nonprotocol condition, and they also provided significantly more information before being asked the first option-posing question. More of the details they provided were elicited by open-ended prompts, whereas fewer were elicited by directive, option-posing, and suggestive utterances. Although this was not studied systematically, the interviewers using the NICHD interview protocol also became better critics of their own and of their colleagues' interviews.

Similar results were obtained when investigative interviews conducted by police officers in the western United States were studied (Sternberg, Lamb, Esplin, Orbach, & Hershkowitz, 2002; Sternberg, Lamb, Orbach, Esplin, & Mitchell, 2001). In addition to being better organized, interviewers using the structured protocol used more open-ended prompts and fewer option-posing and suggestive questions than in the comparison (baseline) interviews. In the baseline condition, only 10% of the interviewers' questions were invitations, whereas in the protocol interviews a third of the interviewers' questions were invitations. The total amount of information elicited from free recall memory also increased dramatically; whereas only 16% of the information was elicited using free recall in the preprotocol interviews, about half of the information was obtained using free recall in the protocol interviews. The protocol also reduced the use of directive, option-posing, and suggestive prompts. In the baseline interviews, 41% of the information was obtained using option-posing and suggestive questions compared with 24% in the protocol interviews. Furthermore, this pattern of results was similar regardless of the children's age. Although younger children provided shorter and less detailed responses than did older children, analyses of interviews with 4- to 6-year-old children revealed that the interviewers relied heavily on invitations (34% of their questions) and succeeded in eliciting a substantial amount of information (49% of the total) using free-recall prompts.

To further clarify the ability of preschoolers to address open-ended questions, Lamb et al. (2002) studied forensic interviews of 130 4- to 8-year-olds. Like Sternberg et al. (2001), they showed clearly that children as young as 4 years of age can indeed provide substantial amounts of information about alleged abuse in response to open-ended questions included in well-structured and planned forensic interviews. On average, one half of the information provided by the children came in response to open-ended utterances. Even though the older children reported more details in total and in response to the average invitation than the younger children did, furthermore, the proportion of invitations eliciting new details did not change, suggesting that preschoolers are not uniquely incapable of responding to open-ended prompts. As in other studies, more forensically relevant details were elicited by individual invitations than by other types of utterances at all ages. Because both laboratory analog and field studies consistently show that the information provided in response to invitations is more likely to be accurate, these results suggested that open-ended invitations are superior investigative tools regardless of the interviewees' ages.

Lamb et al. (2002) found that many interviewers made effective use of cued invitations (e.g., "You said that he touched your vagina; tell me more about that") rather than risky focused questions ("So did he put his finger *in* your vagina?"). An interesting point is that action-based cues ("Tell me more about him touching you") were consistently more effective than were time-segmenting cues (e.g., "Tell me more about what happened after he came into the room") at all ages. Developmental improvements were especially dramatic with respect to time-segmenting cues, however, and these were extremely effective when addressed to 8-year-olds. With younger children, by contrast, references to actions already mentioned by the child proved more effective, presumably because such cues are less cognitively demanding than cues that required awareness of temporal sequences. At all ages, furthermore, more information would likely have been elicited if the interviewers had made greater use of cued invitations.

Clearly, forensic interviewers need to provide children of all ages with opportunities to recall information in response to open-ended prompts before assuming that special (i.e., more risky) interview techniques are needed. This admonition is important especially in light of repeated demonstrations that younger children are more likely than older children to give inaccurate responses to yes-no questions (Brady, Poole, Warren, & Jones, 1999), to respond affirmatively to misleading questions about nonexperienced events (Poole & Lindsay, 1998), and to acquiesce to suggestions (e.g., Cassel et al., 1996; Ceci & Huffman, 1997; Ceci et al., 1987b; Robinson & Briggs, 1997). Risky questions are even riskier when addressed to children aged 6 and under, and forensic investigators must thus make special efforts to

maximize the amounts of information elicited from such children using less risky, open-ended prompts.

Conclusion

These findings are particularly encouraging in light of the difficulties that interviewers frequently encounter when interviewing young children, and they illustrate the ways in which applied research can sometimes raise doubts about the interpretation and generalization of the results obtained in experimental laboratory analog settings. In this instance, students of memory and communicative development had long believed that preschoolers were incapable of providing narrative responses to invitations (Bourg et al., 1996; Hewitt, 1999; Kuehnle, 1996). The field research has demonstrated, however, that when invitations are carefully formulated and children are appropriately prepared for their role as informants, even very young children are capable of providing detailed responses to narrative questions. Through a combination of applied and basic research, it has thus been possible to enhance our understanding both of normative developmental processes and of the forensic interview process. In addition, careful research has made it possible to enhance the value of children's testimony in ways that should enable law enforcement, child protection, and judicial agencies to protect children better from further maltreatment.

Studies demonstrating that children can be much more useful informants when they are effectively interviewed have also documented how difficult it is to alter the ways in which forensic interviewers typically perform. As noted earlier, professional consensus regarding the ways in which children should be interviewed did not translate into changes in interviewers' behavior even when they knew what they should do and believed that they were following these recommendations (Aldridge & Cameron, 1999; Warren et al., 1999). My colleagues and I have demonstrated that improvements occurred only when forensic interviewers reviewed transcripts of their interviews and received critical feedback from expert consultants and fellow interviewers (Lamb, Sternberg, Orbach, Hershkowitz, et al., 2002). Somewhat disconcertingly, furthermore, improvements derived from this close monitoring and feedback rapidly diminished when the interviewers stopped attending regular feedback sessions (Lamb, Sternberg, Orbach, Esplin, & Mitchell, 2002). Within six months after the training/supervision ended, police officers in the United States were conducting forensic interviews that resembled their original interviews more than the interviews conducted with the assistance of the NICHD interview protocol and the expert feedback.

PROTECTING THE CHILDREN OF DIVORCE

Researchers can also offer scientific advice to legal practitioners grappling with complex issues while attempting to ensure that children are protected and well cared for when their parents divorce. Although the rates of divorce have leveled recently, about half of the children in America are still likely to experience the separation of their parents before they reach adulthood, and most of them will experience the loss of meaningful contact with their fathers. Common sense and scientific research tell us that these experiences are likely to have psychological costs.

There is substantial consensus that children are better off psychologically and developmentally in two- rather than one-parent families (see reviews by Amato, 2000; Hetherington & Stanley-Hagan, 1997, 1999; Lamb, 1999; McLanahan & Sandefur, 1994; McLanahan & Teitler, 1999). As these reviewers have shown, children growing up in fatherless families are disadvantaged relative to peers growing up in two-parent families with respect to psychosocial adjustment, behavior and achievement at school, educational attainment, employment trajectories, income generation, involvement in antisocial and even criminal behavior, and the ability to establish and maintain intimate relationships. For researchers, of course, it is important to determine why these differences emerge.

The Development of Infant-Parent Attachments

The effects are best understood in the context of normative developmental processes. Scholars have long recognized that the attachments formed to parents are among the most critical achievements of the first year of life (Bowlby, 1969). Bowlby (1969) proposed that there is a sensitive period during which attachments are most easily formed, and early research on adoptions lent support to this belief (Yarrow & Goodwin, 1973) even though scholars have come to believe that the sensitive period is actually quite extensive (Rutter, 1972).

Attachment formation depends on reciprocal interactive processes that foster the infants' ability to discriminate their parents from others and to develop emotional relationships with their parents. These relationships or attachments are consolidated by the middle of the first year of life and are characterized by the onset of separation anxiety and separation protest (Ainsworth, 1969). Infants who receive sensitive, responsive care from familiar adults in the course of feeding, holding, talking, playing, soothing, and being physically close become securely attached to them (Ainsworth, Blehar, Waters, & Wall, 1978; DeWolff & van IJzendoorn, 1997;

R. A. Thompson, 1998). Even adequate levels of responsive parenting foster the formation of infant-parent attachments, although some of these relationships may be insecure. Children are nonetheless better off with insecure attachments than without attachment relationships because these enduring ties play essential formative roles in later social and emotional functioning. Infant-parent attachments promote a sense of security, the beginnings of self-confidence, and the development of trust in other human beings (Ainsworth et al., 1978; Lamb, 1981).

Most infants form meaningful attachments to both of their parents at roughly the same age (6 to 7 months; see Lamb, 1997a, in press a, for reviews) even though most fathers in our culture spend less time with their infants than mothers do (Pleck, 1997). This indicates that the amount of time spent together is not the only factor affecting the development of attachments, although some threshold level of interaction is necessary. Rather, opportunities for regular interaction, even when the bouts themselves are brief, appear sufficient. Most infants come to prefer the parents who take primary responsibility for their care (typically their mothers), but this does not mean that relationships with their fathers are unimportant. The preference for primary caretakers appears to diminish with age and by 18 months has often disappeared. After this age, in fact, many infants seem to prefer their fathers, especially in emotionally undemanding situations. There is no evidence that the amount of time infants spend with their two parents affects the security of either attachment relationship.

Although some studies of both infant-mother and infant-father attachment fail to reveal significant associations between the quality of parental behaviors and the security of infant-parent attachment, meta-analyses reveal that in both cases the quality of parental behavior is reliably associated with the security of infant-parent attachment (DeWolff & Van IJzendoorn, 1997; Van IJzendoorn & DeWolff, 1997). The association between the quality of paternal behavior and the quality of infant-father attachment appears to be weaker than the parallel association between maternal behavior and the security of infant-mother attachment, however. In neither case does the quality of parental behavior explain more than a small proportion of the variance in the security of attachment, although the quality of maternal and paternal behavior and of both mother- and father-child interaction remains the most reliable correlate of individual differences in psychological, social, and cognitive adjustment in infancy, as well as in later childhood (R. A. Thompson, 1998). Not surprisingly, therefore, children in both two- and one-parent families appear better adjusted when they enjoy warm positive relationships with two actively involved parents (Amato &

Gilbreth, 1999; Hetherington & Stanley-Hagan, 1999; Lamb, 1999b, 2002b; R. A. Thompson & Laible, 1999).

The empirical literature also shows that infants and toddlers need regular interaction with their attachment figures in order to foster and maintain the relationships (Lamb, 2002a; Lamb, Bornstein, & Teti, 2002). Extended separations from either parent are undesirable because they unduly stress developing attachment relationships (Bowlby, 1973). In addition, infants need to interact with both parents in a variety of contexts (feeding, playing, diapering, soothing, putting to bed, etc.) to ensure that the relationships are consolidated and strengthened. In the absence of such opportunities for regular interaction across a broad range of contexts, infant-parent relationships fail to develop and may instead weaken. For the same reason, it is extremely difficult to reestablish relationships between infants or young children and their parents when these have been disrupted. Instead, it is considerably better to avoid such disruptions in the first place.

In general, relationships with parents play a crucial role in shaping children's social, emotional, personal, and cognitive development (Lamb, Hwang, Ketterlinus, & Fracasso, 1999), and there is a substantial literature documenting the adverse effects of disrupted parent-child relationships on children's development and adjustment. Children who are deprived of meaningful relationships with one of their parents are at greater risk psychosocially, even when they are able to maintain relationships with their other parents (Amato, 2000; Hetherington & Stanley-Hagan, 1997, 1999; Lamb, 1999; McLanahan & Sandefur, 1994; McLanahan & Teitler, 1999). Stated differently, there is substantial evidence that children are more likely to attain their psychological potential when they are able to develop and maintain meaningful relationships with both of their parents, whether or not the two parents live together. If the parents lived together prior to the separation and the relationships with both parents were of at least adequate quality and supportiveness, the central challenge is to maintain both infant-parent attachments after separation or divorce.

Maintaining Relationships With Parents Who Live Apart

Influenced by Freud (e.g., 1954) and others following in his tradition (e.g., Spitz, 1965), developmental psychologists initially focused exclusively on mothers and infants, presuming fathers to be quite peripheral and unnecessary to children's development and psychological adjustment. When parents separated, therefore, neoanalysts emphasized the importance of continuity in the relationships between infants and

mothers, with children living with their mothers and having limited contact with their fathers (Goldstein, Freud, & Solnit, 1973). When such recommendations were implemented, infants or toddlers who were accustomed to seeing both parents each day abruptly began seeing one parent, usually their fathers, only once every week (or two weeks) for a few hours. Such arrangements were often represented by professionals as being "in the best interests" of the child due to the mistaken belief, based on Freud's (1948) and Bowlby's (1969) speculation, that infants had only one significant or primary attachment. The resulting custody arrangements sacrificed continuity in infant-father relationships, with long-term socioemotional and economic consequences for children.

Very large research literatures now document the adverse effects of severed father-child relationships as well as the positive contributions that nonresidential fathers can make to their children's development (see Lamb, 1999, 2002b, for reviews). It is thus preferable to seek arrangements that preserve the continuity of relationships with both parents. The quality of the relationships between both parents and their children remains important in the majority of divorcing families, just as in the majority of two-parent families. Unfortunately, however, most contemporary custody and visitation decrees do not foster the maintenance of relationships between children and their noncustodial parents (e.g., Maccoby & Mnookin, 1992; H. E. Peters, 1997). Furthermore, initially restrictive awards are typically followed by declining levels of paternal involvement over time, with increasing numbers of children having less and less contact with their noncustodial parents as time goes by (Furstenberg & Cherlin, 1991; Furstenberg, Nord, Peterson, & Zill, 1983). To the extent that contact is beneficial, of course, such data suggest that many children are placed at risk by the withdrawal or apparent disappearance of their noncustodial fathers. Many fathers drift away from their children after divorce, perhaps because they are deprived of the opportunity to be parents rather than visitors. Most noncustodial parents are awarded visitation, and they function as visitors, taking their children to the zoo, to movies, to dinner, and to other special activities in much the same way that grandparents or uncles and aunts behave. Children may well enjoy these excursions and may not regret the respite from arguments about getting homework done, getting their rooms cleaned up, behaving politely, going to bed on time, and getting ready for school, but the exclusion of fathers from these everyday tribulations is crucial, ultimately transforming the fathers' roles and making these men increasingly irrelevant to their children's lives, socialization, and development. Many men describe this as a sufficiently painful experience that they feel excluded from and pushed out of their children's lives (Clark & McKenry, 1997). Among the experts who drafted a recent consensus statement on the effects of divorce and custody arrangements on children's welfare and adjustment, there was agreement that parents not only need to spend adequate amounts of time with their children, but also need to be involved in a diverse array of activities with their children:

> To maintain high-quality relationships with their children, parents need to have sufficiently extensive and regular interactions with them, but the amount of time involved is usually less important than the quality of the interaction that it fosters. Time distribution arrangements that ensure the involvement of both parents in important aspects of their children's everyday lives and routines . . . are likely to keep nonresidential parents playing psychologically important and central roles in the lives of their children. (Lamb, Sternberg, & Thompson, 1997, p. 400)

The ideal situation is one in which children have opportunities to interact with both parents every day or every other day in a variety of functional contexts (feeding, play, discipline, basic care, limit setting, putting to bed, etc.). The evening and overnight periods (like extended days with naptimes) with nonresidential parents are especially important psychologically for infants, toddlers, and young children. They provide opportunities for crucial social interactions and nurturing activities, including bathing, soothing hurts and anxieties, bedtime rituals, comforting in the middle of the night, and the reassurance and security of snuggling in the morning that one- to two-hour-long visits cannot provide. These everyday activities promote and maintain trust and confidence in the parents while deepening and strengthening child-parent attachments, and thus they need to be both encouraged when decisions about custody and access are made.

One implication is that even young children should spend overnight periods with both parents, even though neoanalysts have long counseled against this. As Warshak (2000) pointed out, the prohibition of overnight "visitation" has been justified by prejudices and beliefs rather than by any empirical evidence. As noted here, however, parents who are not allowed overnight periods with their children are excluded from an important array of activities, and the strength or depth of their relationships suffer as a result. Again, empirical research on normative child development can guide the design of policies that promote better child adjustment, even in the face of the stresses imposed by parental separation and divorce. To minimize the deleterious impact of extended separations from either parent, furthermore, attachment theory tells us there should be more frequent transitions than would perhaps be desirable with older children. To be responsive to the infant's

psychological needs, in other words, the parenting schedules adopted for children under age 2 or 3 years should actually involve more transitions, rather than fewer, to ensure the continuity of both relationships and to promote the child's security and comfort during a potentially stressful period. From the third year of life, the ability to tolerate longer separations begins to increase, so most toddlers can manage two consecutive overnights with each parent without stress. Schedules involving separations spanning longer blocks of time, such as 5 to 7 days, should be avoided, as children this age may still become upset when separated from either parent for too long.

Interestingly, psychologists have long recognized the need to minimize the length of separations from attachment figures when devising parenting plans, but they have typically focused only on separations from mothers, thereby revealing their presumption that young children are not meaningfully attached to their fathers. To the extent that children are attached to both of their parents, however, separations from both parents are stressful and at minimum generate psychic pain. As a result, parenting plans that allow children to see their fathers "every Wednesday evening and every other weekend" clearly fail to recognize the adverse consequences of weeklong separations from noncustodial parents. It is little wonder that such arrangements lead to attenuation of the relationships between noncustodial parents and their children.

The adverse long-term effects of divorce on children appear to be associated with the disruption of one or both of the child-parent relationships, typically the father-child relationship, and it is important to recognize that divorce is associated with a number of other adverse circumstances as well. First, the family's financial status is adversely affected by the loss of a major source of income, usually the principal breadwinner. Even in the best of circumstances, furthermore, it is more expensive to maintain two households than one, and the standards of living thus tend to decline. Second, because mothers need to work more extensively outside the home when their partners leave, adults are less likely to be present, and the supervision and guidance of children becomes less intensive and reliable in one- than in two-parent families. Fourth, conflict between the parents commonly precedes or emerges during the divorce process. Fifth, single parenthood is associated with a variety of social and financial stresses with which individuals must cope, largely on their own.

Researchers have shown that all of these factors have adverse effects on children's adjustment, and it is thus not surprising to find that the co-occurrence of these factors at the time of divorce has adverse consequences for children (Amato, 2000; Hetherington & Stanley-Hagan, 1997, 1999;

Lamb, 2002b; McLanahan & Teitler, 1999). Less clear are the specific processes by which these effects are mediated, yet an understanding of how divorce and custody arrangements affect child development is absolutely crucial if we as a society are to minimize or reverse the adverse effects of divorce on children. Stepparenthood and remarriage further complicate efforts to understand the effects of diverse postdivorce custody arrangements on child well-being because these shape family dynamics and child adjustment in complex ways (Hanson, McLanahan, & Thomson, 1996; Hetherington & Henderson, 1997).

As Amato (1993, 2000; Amato & Gilbreth, 1997) showed with particular clarity, the associations between father absence or postdivorce father-child contact and their contrasting effects on child adjustment after divorce are much weaker than one might expect. In part this may well reflect variation in the exposure to the other pathogenic circumstances described earlier, but it likely reflects the diverse types of father-child relationships represented in the samples studied, with abusive, incompetent, or disinterested fathers likely to have much different effects than devoted, committed, and sensitive fathers. In addition, high-quality contacts between fathers and children are surely more beneficial than encounters that lack breadth and intensity. Consistent with this, Amato and Gilbreth (1997) reported following a meta-analysis that children's well-being was significantly enhanced when their relationships with nonresidential fathers were positive and when the nonresidential fathers engaged in active parenting. As explained earlier, most children do not simply need more contact, but rather contact of an extent and type sufficient to potentiate rich and multifaceted parent-child relationships. Clearly, then, postdivorce arrangements should specifically seek to maximize positive and meaningful paternal involvement because regular but superficial contact appears unlikely to promote either the maintenance of relationships between noncustodial fathers and their children or the children's psychological adjustment and well-being.

Of course, several factors affect the development of children when parents divorce, including the level of involvement and quality of relationships between residential or custodial parents and their children, the level of involvement and quality of the relationships between nonresidential parents and their children, the amount of conflict between the two parents, the amount of conflict between the children and their parents, and the socioeconomic circumstances in which the children reside. These factors are interrelated, however, and in the absence of intensive and reliable longitudinal data, it is difficult either to discern casual relationships unambiguously or to establish the relative importance of different factors. In addition, these factors may operate together

in complex ways, such that, for example, contact with noncustodial parents may not have the same positive effect on children when there is substantial conflict between the parents that it is does when levels of conflict are lower (Johnston, Kline, & Tschann, 1989).

Because high conflict is associated with poorer child outcomes following divorce (Johnston, 1994; Kelly, 2000; Maccoby & Mnookin, 1992), it is preferable that interparental conflict be avoided, but it is important to understand how high conflict is conceptualized in the relevant research because the findings are often misunderstood. Almost by definition, of course, custody and access disputes involve conflict, but it is clear that such conflict in and of itself is not necessarily harmful. Conflict localized around the time of divorce is regrettable but is unlikely to have adverse effects on the children, and its occurrence should not be used to justify restrictions on the children's access to either of the parents. The high conflict found harmful by researchers such as Johnston (1994) typically involved repeated incidents of spousal violence and verbal aggression and continued at intense levels for extended periods of time, often in front of the children. As a result, Johnston emphasized the importance of continued relationships with both parents except in those relatively uncommon circumstances in which intense, protracted conflict occurs and persists.

Conclusions

If noncustodial parents are to maintain and strengthen relationships with their children, they need to participate in a range of everyday activities that allow them to function as parents rather than simply as regular, genial visitors. Unfortunately, those constructing custody and visitation awards do not always appear to understand what sort of interaction is needed to consolidate and maintain parent-child relationships; as a result, their decisions seldom ensure either sufficient amounts of time or adequate distributions of that time (overnight and across both school and nonschool days) to promote healthy parent-child relationships. The statistics popularized by Furstenberg and Cherlin (1991) may show fathers drifting away largely because they no longer have the opportunities to function as fathers in relation to their children and because decision makers have failed to recognize the knowledge of children's needs and developmental trajectories that has been compiled over the last few decades of intensive research. In this case, research on normative developmental processes, supplemented by the results of descriptive studies designed to elucidate the effects of divorce and various access arrangements on child development, have combined to identify the deficiencies of common practices and to articulate ways in which child adjustment could be promoted.

CONCLUSIONS AND RECOMMENDATIONS FOR RESEARCH, POLICY, AND PRACTICE

When developmental psychology emerged as a distinct sub-discipline about a century ago, it focused very heavily on applied issues, with prominent scholars offering generous and often definitive advice to parents, pediatricians, and teachers (Clarke-Stewart, 1998; Sears, 1975). By the middle of the century, however, many psychologists shifted their focus to basic research questions, often implying in the process that the concern with applied issues made developmental psychology less credible as a science. Today, we see a new appreciation of applied research, which may provide a forum for meaningful contributions to children's welfare and at the same time permit insight into normative developmental processes that could not be obtained by conducting basic research alone.

Both of the topics discussed in this chapter illustrate well the multifaceted value of applied developmental science. In one instance, basic research on the development of memory, communication, and social perceptions allowed researchers to devise and implement forensic interview processes that greatly improved the informativeness of child witnesses. Research on investigative interviews in turn fostered an enhanced understanding of basic developmental processes, such as the richness and reliability of children's memories, and we can expect these lessons to affect many aspects of research in the years ahead.

Developmental psychologists have learned a great deal about memory development from experimental research, and many of those findings (e.g., those concerning the superior accuracy of information obtained using recall rather than recognition prompts) clearly apply outside the experimental laboratory. There are limitations to the validity and generalizability of experimental research, however. The memorableness of experiences varies depending on the salience and meaningfulness of those experiences: Experienced events are not the same as nonsense syllables or tokens, and the motivation to remember or recall information or events clearly influences the amount of information retrieved. Only through field studies of forensic interviews have researchers come to recognize how much young children can recall when the importance of complete reporting is stressed and when they are urged in diverse ways to recount detailed episodic information, not simply asked a single question ("Can you tell me what happened?"). Both laboratory analog and field studies of these processes have clearly advanced our understanding of memory development more generally (Lamb & Thierry, in press).

Meanwhile, basic research on early social development and descriptive research on the multifaceted correlates of divorce have together yielded a clearer understanding of the ways in which divorce affects children. This has in turn helped us to understand better the multidetermined complexity of socialization processes while offering legal practitioners practical advice regarding ways in which they can minimize the adverse effects of divorce on child development. In particular, psychologists have been reminded how complex the socialization process really is. In order to make their studies interpretable and manageable, researchers have tended to oversimplify, typically focusing on single issues, such as early experiences or mother-child relationships. The literature reviewed in this chapter makes clear not only that children are shaped by relationships with both of their parents (and others) but also that these are dynamic relationships that must be nourished through continuing interactions in order to ensure that the benefits continue to flow. Many other social relationships, as well as many other social, emotional, and cognitive experiences, shape development as well. Furthermore, children are not inoculated from psychological harm by positive early experiences—their susceptibility to influence and change continues throughout the life span. This fact notwithstanding, the burgeoning literature on divorce and its effects underscores the resilience of many children and the fact that children can thrive in diverse contexts, some of which would appear pathogenic.

The research on forensic interviews of alleged abuse victims has clear implications for policy and practice. In particular, researchers have shown that children are capable of providing considerable amounts of forensically valuable information about their experiences, provided that they are carefully interviewed by investigators who explain the importance of the interviews, empower the children to correct them or admit ignorance, motivate the children to be as informative as possible, use age-appropriate terms, and help children to recall information rather than to select from among options generated by the interviewers. Such practices have been incorporated into the NICHD Investigative Interview Protocol, which increases the quality of information provided by alleged victims when implemented in the field. Unfortunately, simply understanding the components of an effective interview does not guarantee that interviewers will continue to interview effectively. Clearly, then, investment in intensive training and ongoing supervision can permit practitioners to benefit from the fruits of many years of research. This, in turn, can permit the legal system to intervene more judiciously on behalf of children.

Similarly, research on the effects of divorce, viewed in the context of research on socialization, also has implications for policy and practice. The most important fact we have learned is that children benefit from supportive relationships with both of their parents, whether or not those parents live together. We also know that relationships are dynamic and are thus dependent on continued opportunities for interaction. In order to ensure that both adults become or remain *parents* to their children, postdivorce parenting plans need to encourage participation by both parents in as broad as possible an array of social contexts on a regular basis. Brief dinners and occasional weekend visits do not provide a broad enough or extensive enough basis for such relationships to be fostered, whereas weekday and weekend daytime and nighttime activities are important for children of all ages. In the absence of sufficiently broad and extensive interactions, many fathers drift out of their children's lives. Their children are thereby placed at risk psychologically and materially, because involved fathers are much more likely to contribute financially to the costs of raising their children.

REFERENCES

Ainsworth, M. D. S. (1969). Object relations, dependency and attachment: A theoretical review of the infant-mother relationship. *Child Development, 40,* 969–1025.

Ainsworth, M. D. S., Blehar, M., Waters, E., & Wall, S. (1978). *Patterns of attachment.* Hillsdale, NJ: Erlbaum.

Amato, P. R. (1993). Children's adjustment to divorce: Theories, hypotheses, and empirical support. *Journal of Marriage and the Family, 55,* 23–38.

Amato, P. R. (2000). The consequences of divorce for adults and children. *Journal of Marriage and the Family, 62,* 1269–1287.

Amato, P. R., & Gilbreth, J. G. (1999). Nonresident fathers and children's well-being: A meta-analysis. *Journal of Marriage and the Family, 61,* 557–573.

American Professional Society on the Abuse of Children. (1997). *Guidelines for psychosocial evaluation of suspected sexual abuse in young children.* Chicago, IL: Author. (Original work published 1990)

Bourg, W., Broderick, R., Flagor, R., Kelly, D. M., Ervin, D. L., & Butler, J. (1996). *A child interviewer's guidebook.* Thousand Oaks, CA: Sage.

Bowlby, J. (1969). *Attachment and loss: Vol. 1. Attachment.* New York: Basic Books.

Bowlby, J. (1973). *Attachment and loss: Vol. 2. Separation: Anxiety and anger.* New York: Basic Books.

Brady, M. S., Poole, D. A., Warren, A. R., & Jones, H. R. (1999). Young children's responses to yes-or-no questions: Patterns and problems. *Applied Developmental Science, 3,* 47–57.

Brainerd, C. J., & Reyna, V. F. (1996). Mere memory testing creates false memories in children. *Developmental Psychology, 32,* 467–476.

Brennan, M., & Brennan, R. E. (1988). *Strange language: Child victims under cross-examination* (3rd ed.). Wagga Wagga, NSW, Australia: Riverina Literacy Centre.

Brown, R. (1973). *A first language.* Cambridge, MA: Harvard University Press.

Bruck, M., Ceci, S. J., Francouer, E., & Barr, R. (1995). "I hardly cried when I got my shot!" Influencing children's reports about a visit to their pediatrician. *Child Development, 66,* 193–208.

Bruck, M., Ceci, S. J., Francouer, E., & Renick, A. (1995). Anatomically detailed dolls do not facilitate preschoolers' reports of a pediatric examination involving genital touching. *Journal of Experimental Psychology: Applied, 1,* 95–109.

Bull, R. (1992). Obtaining evidence expertly: The reliability of interviews with child witnesses. *Expert Evidence, 1,* 5–12.

Bull, R. (1995). Innovative techniques for the questioning of child witnesses, especially those who are young and those with learning disability. In M. S. Zaragoza, J. R. Graham, G. C. N. Hall, R. Hirschman, & Y. S. Ben-Porath (Eds.), *Memory and testimony in the child witness* (pp. 179–194). Thousand Oaks, CA: Sage.

Bull, R. (1996). Good practice for video-recorded interviews with child witnesses for use in criminal proceedings. In G. Davies, S. Lloyd-Bostock, M. McMarran, & C. Wilson (Eds.), *Psychology, law, and criminal justice: International developments in research and practice* (pp. 100–117). Berlin: Walter de Gruyter.

Carey, S. (1978). The child as word learner. In M. Halle, J. Bresnan, & G. A. Miller (Eds.), *Linguistic theory and psychological reality* (pp. 264–293). Cambridge, MA: MIT Press.

Cassel, W. S, Roebers, C. E. M., & Bjorklund, D. F. (1996). Developmental patterns of eyewitness responses to repeated and increasingly suggestive questions. *Journal of Experimental Child Psychology, 61,* 116–133.

Ceci, S. J., & Bruck, M. (1993). Suggestibility of the child witness: A historical review and synthesis. *Psychological Bulletin, 113,* 403–439.

Ceci, S. J., & Bruck, M. (1995). *Jeopardy in the courtroom: A scientific analysis of children's testimony.* Washington, DC: American Psychological Association.

Ceci, S. J., & Huffman, M. L. C. (1997). How suggestible are preschool children: Cognitive and social factors. *Journal of the American Academy of Child Psychiatry, 36,* 948–958.

Ceci, S. J., Huffman, M. L. C., Smith, E., & Loftus, E. F. (1994). Repeatedly thinking about a non-event: Source misattributions among preschoolers. *Consciousness and Cognition, 3,* 388–407.

Ceci, S. J., Ross, D. F., & Toglia, M. P. (1987a). Suggestibility of children's memory: Psycholegal issues. *Journal of Experimental Psychology: General, 116,* 38–49.

Ceci, S. J., Ross, D. F., & Toglia, M. P. (1987b). Age differences in suggestibility: Narrowing the uncertainties. In S. J. Ceci, M. P. Toglia, & D. F. Ross (Eds.), *Children's eyewitness memory* (pp. 79–91). New York: Springer-Verlag.

Cederborg, A., Orbach, Y., Sternberg, K. J., & Lamb, M. E. (2000). Investigative interviews of child witnesses in Sweden. *Child Abuse and Neglect, 24,* 1355–1361.

Clark, K., & McKenry, P. C. (1997). *Unheard voices: Divorced fathers without custody*. Unpublished manuscript, Department of Family Relations and Human Development, Ohio State University, Columbus.

Clarke-Stewart, K. A. (1998). Historical shifts and underlying themes in ideas about rearing young children in the United States. Where have we been? Where are we going? *Early Development and Parenting, 7,* 101–117.

Collins, W. A. (1970). Learning of media content: A developmental study. *Child Development, 41,* 1113–1142.

Collins, W. A., & Wellman, H. (1982). Social scripts and development patterns in comprehension of televised narratives. *Communication Research, 9,* 380–398.

Collins, W. A., Wellman, H., Keniston, A., & Westby, S. (1978). Age-related aspects of comprehension and inference from a televised dramatic narrative. *Child Development, 49,* 389–399.

Craig, R. A, Sheibe, R., Raskin, D. C., Kircher, J., & Dodd, D. (1999). Interviewer questions and content analysis of children's statements of sexual abuse. *Applied Developmental Science, 3,* 77–85.

Dale, P. S. (1976). *Language development: Structure and function*. New York: Holt, Rinehart, and Winston.

Dale, P. S., Loftus, E. F., & Rathbun, L. (1978). The influence of the form of the question on the eyewitness testimony of preschool children. *Journal of Psycholinguistic Research, 74,* 269–277.

Davidson, D. (1991, April). *Children's recognition and recall memory for typical and atypical actions in script-based stories*. Paper presented to the meeting of the Society for Research in Child Development, Seattle, WA.

Davies, G. M., Tarrant, A., & Flin, R. (1989). Close encounters of the witness kind: Children's memory for a simulated health inspection. *British Journal of Psychology, 80,* 415–429.

Davies, G. M., Westcott, H. L., & Horan, N. (2000). The impact of questioning style on the content of investigative interviews with suspected child abuse victims. *Psychology, Crime and Law, 6,* 81–97.

Davies, G., & Wilson, C. (1997). Implementation of the Memorandum: An overview. In H. Westcott & J. Jones (Eds.), *Perspectives on the Memorandum: Policy, practice and research in investigative interviewing* (pp. 1–12). Aldershot, UK: Arena.

Dent, H. R. (1982). The effects of interviewing strategies on the results of interviews with child witnesses. In A. Trankell (Ed.), *Reconstructing the past: The role of psychologists in criminal trials* (pp. 279–297). Stockholm: Norstedt.

Dent, H. R. (1986). An experimental study of the effectiveness of different techniques of questioning mentally-handicapped child witnesses. *British Journal of Clinical Psychology, 25,* 13–17.

Dent, H. R., & Stephenson, G. M. (1979). An experimental study of the effectiveness of different techniques of questioning child witnesses. *British Journal of Social and Clinical Psychology, 25,* 13–17.

de Villiers, J., & de Villiers, P. (1999). Language development. In M. H. Bornstein & M. E. Lamb (Eds.), *Developmental psychology: An advanced textbook* (4th ed., pp. 313–376). Mahwah, NJ: Erlbaum.

DeWolff, M. S., & van IJzendoorn, M. H. (1997). Sensitivity and attachment: A meta-analysis on parental antecedents of infant attachment. *Child Development, 68,* 571–591.

Dodd, D. H., & Bradshaw, J. M. (1980). Leading questions and memory: Pragmatic constraints. *Journal of Verbal Learning and Verbal Behavior, 19,* 695–704.

Fisher, R. P., & Geiselman, R. E. (1992). *Memory-enhancing techniques for investigative interviewing: The cognitive interview*. Springfield, IL: Charles C. Thomas.

Flin, R., Boon, J., Knox, A., & Bull, R. (1992). The effect of a five month delay on children's and adults' eyewitness memory. *British Journal of Psychology, 83,* 323–336.

Freud, S. (1948). *An outline of psychoanalysis*. New York: W. W. Norton.

Freud, S. (1954). *Collected works, standard edition*. London: Hogarth Press.

Furstenberg, F. F., Jr., & Cherlin, A. J. (1991). *Divided families: What happens to children when parents part*. Cambridge, MA: Harvard University Press.

Furstenberg, F. F., Jr., Nord, C. W., Peterson, J. L., & Zill, N. (1983). The life course of children of divorce. *American Psychological Review, 48,* 656–668.

Garven, S., Wood, J. M., Malpass, R. S., & Shaw, J. S. (1998). More than suggestion: The effect of interviewing techniques from the McMartin Preschool case. *Journal of Applied Psychology, 83,* 347–359.

Goldstein, J., Freud, A., & Solnit, A. (1973). *Beyond the best interests of the child*. New York: Free Press.

Goodman, G. S., & Aman, C. (1990). Children's use of anatomically detailed dolls to recount an event. *Child Development, 61,* 1859–1871.

Goodman, G. S., Aman, C., & Hirschman, J. E. (1987). Child sexual and physical abuse: Children's testimony. In S. J. Ceci, M. P. Toglia, & D. P. Ross (Eds.), *Children's eyewitness memory* (pp. 1–23). New York: Springer-Verlag.

Goodman, G. S., Bottoms, B., Schwartz-Kenney, B., & Rudy, L. (1991). Children's testimony about a stressful event: Improving children's reports. *Journal of Narrative and Life History, 1,* 69–99.

Goodman, G. S., Hirschman, J. E., Hepps, D., & Rudy, L. (1991). Children's memory for stressful events. *Merrill-Palmer Quarterly, 37,* 109–158.

Goodman, G. S., & Reed, R. S. (1986). Age differences in eyewitness testimony. *Law and Human Behavior, 10,* 317–332.

Goodman, G. S., Taub, E. P., Jones, D. P. H., England, P., Port, L. K., Rudy, L., & Prado, L. (1992). Testifying in criminal court. *Monographs of the Society for Research in Child Development, 57*(5, Serial No. 229).

Goodman, G. S., Wilson, M. E., Hazan, C., & Reed, R. S. (1989, April). *Children's testimony nearly four years after an event.* Paper presented to the Eastern Psychological Association, Boston, MA.

Greenstock, J., & Pipe, M.-E. (1996). Interviewing children about past events: The influence of peer support and misleading questions. *Child Abuse and Neglect, 20,* 69–80.

Hanson, T. L., McLanahan, S. S., & Thomson, E. (1996). Double jeopardy: Parental conflict and step-family outcomes for children. *Journal of Marriage and the Family, 58,* 141–154.

Harner, L. (1975). Yesterday and tomorrow: Development of early understanding of the terms. *Developmental Psychology, 11,* 864–865.

Hetherington, E. M., & Henderson, S. H. (1997). Fathers in stepfamilies. In M. E. Lamb (Ed.), *The role of the father in child development* (3rd ed., pp. 212–226, 369–373). New York: Wiley.

Hetherington, E. M., & Stanley-Hagan, M. M. (1997). The effects of divorce on fathers and their children. In M. E. Lamb (Ed.), *The role of the father in child development* (3rd ed., pp. 191–211). New York: Wiley.

Hetherington, E. M., & Stanley-Hagan, M. M. (1999). The adjustment of children with divorced parents: A risk and resiliency perspective. *Journal of Child Psychology and Psychiatry and Allied Disciplines, 40,* 129–140.

Hewitt, S. K. (1999). *Assessing allegations of sexual abuse in preschool children: Understanding small voices.* Thousand Oaks, CA: Sage.

Hutcheson, G. D., Baxter, J. S., Telfer, K., & Warden, D. (1995). Child witness statement quality: Question type and errors of omission. *Law and Human Behavior, 19,* 631–648.

Hughes, M., & Grieve, R. (1980). On asking children bizarre questions. *First Language, 1,* 149–160.

Johnson, M. M., & Foley, M. A. (1984). Differentiating fact from fantasy: The reliability of children's memory. *Journal of Social Issues, 40,* 33–50.

Johnston, J. R. (1994). High-conflict divorce. *The Future of Children, 4,* 165–182.

Johnston, J. R., Kline, M., & Tschann, J. (1989). Ongoing postdivorce conflict in families contesting custody: Effects on children of joint custody and frequent access. *American Journal of Orthopsychiatry, 59,* 576–592.

Jones, D. P. H. (1992). *Interviewing the sexually abused child: Investigation of suspected abuse* (4th ed.). London: Gaskell.

Jones, L., & Finkelhor, D. (2001). *The decline in child sexual abuse cases.* Juvenile Justice Bulletin (NCJ184741). Washington, DC: U.S. Department of Justice.

Kelly, J. B. (2000). Children's adjustment in conflicted marriage and divorce: A decade review of research. *Journal of the America Academy of Child and Adolescent Psychiatry, 39,* 963–973.

King, M. A., & Yuille, J. C. (1987). Suggestibility and the child witness. In S. J. Ceci, D. F. Ross, & M. P. Toglia (Eds.), *Children's eyewitness memory* (pp. 24–35). New York: Springer-Verlag.

Kuehnle, K. (1996). *Assessing allegations of child sexual abuse.* Sarasota, FL: Professional Resource Press.

Lamb, M. E. (1981). The development of social expectations in the first year of life. In M. E. Lamb & L. R. Sherrod (Eds.), *Infant social cognition: Empirical and theoretical considerations* (pp. 155–175). Hillsdale, NJ: Erlbaum.

Lamb, M. E. (1997a). The development of infant-father attachments. In M. E. Lamb (Ed.), *The role of the father in child development* (3rd ed., pp. 104–120, 332–342). New York: Wiley.

Lamb, M. E. (Ed.). (1997b). *The role of the father in child development* (3rd ed.). New York: Wiley.

Lamb, M. E. (1999). Non-custodial fathers and their impact on the children of divorce. In R. A. Thompson & P. R. Amato (Eds.), *The post-divorce family: Research and policy issues* (pp. 105–125). Thousand Oaks, CA: Sage.

Lamb, M. E. (2002a). Infant-father attachments and their impact on child development. In C. S. Tamis-LeMonda & N. Cabrera (Eds.), *Handbook of father involvement: Multidisciplinary perspectives* (pp. 93–117). Mahwah, NJ: Erlbaum.

Lamb, M. E. (2002b). Noncustodial fathers and their children. In C. S. Tamis-LeMonda & N. Cabrera (Eds.), *Handbook of father involvement: Multidisciplinary perspectives* (pp. 169–184). Mahwah, NJ: Erlbaum.

Lamb, M. E., Bornstein, M. H., & Teti, D. M. (2002). *Development in infancy* (4th ed.). Mahwah, NJ: Erlbaum.

Lamb, M. E., Hershkowitz, I., Sternberg, K. J., Boat, B., & Everson, M. D. (1996). Investigative interviews of alleged sexual abuse victims with and without anatomical dolls. *Child Abuse and Neglect, 20,* 1251–1259.

Lamb, M. E., Hershkowitz, I., Sternberg, K. J., Esplin, P. W., Hovav, M., Manor, T., & Yudilevitch, L. (1996). Effects of investigative utterance types on Israeli children's responses. *International Journal of Behavioral Development, 19,* 627–637.

Lamb, M. E., Hwang, C. P., Ketterlinus, R., & Fracasso, M. P. (1999). Parent-child relationships. In M. H. Bornstein & M. E. Lamb (Eds.), *Developmental psychology: An advanced textbook* (4th ed., pp. 411–450). Mahwah, NJ: Erlbaum.

Lamb, M. E., Sternberg, K. J., & Esplin, P. W. (1994). Factors influencing the reliability and validity of statements made by young victims of sexual maltreatment. *Journal of Applied Developmental Psychology, 15,* 255–280.

Lamb, M. E., Sternberg, K. J., & Esplin, P. W. (1995). Making children into competent witnesses: Reactions to the amicus brief *In re Michaels. Psychology, Public Policy, and Law, 1,* 438–449.

Lamb, M. E., Sternberg, K. J., & Esplin, P. W. (1998). Conducting investigative interviews of alleged sexual abuse victims. *Child Abuse and Neglect, 22,* 813–823.

Lamb, M. E., Sternberg, K. J., & Esplin, P. W. (2000). Effects of age and delay on the amount of information provided by alleged sex abuse victims in investigative interviews. *Child Development, 71,* 1586–1596.

Lamb, M. E., Sternberg, K. J., Orbach, Y., Esplin, P. W., & Mitchell, S. (2002). Is ongoing feedback necessary to maintain the quality of investigative interviews with allegedly abused children? *Applied Developmental Science, 6,* 35–41.

Lamb, M. E., Sternberg, K. J., Orbach, Y., Esplin, P. W., Stewart, H., & Mitchell, S. (2002, March 9). *Age differences in young children's responses to open-ended invitations in the course of forensic interviews.* Paper presented to the American Psychology—Law Society Biennial Conference, Austin, TX.

Lamb, M. E., Sternberg, K. J., Orbach, Y., Hershkowitz, I., & Esplin, P. W. (1999). Forensic interviews of children. In A. Memon & R. Bull (Eds.), *Handbook of the psychology of interviewing* (pp. 253–277). New York: Wiley.

Lamb, M. E., Sternberg, K. J., Orbach, Y., Hershkowitz, I., Horowitz, D., & Esplin, P. W. (2002). The effects of intensive training and ongoing supervision on the quality of investigative interviews with alleged sex abuse victims. *Applied Developmental Science, 6,* 114–125.

Lamb, M. E., Sternberg, K. J., & Thompson, R. A. (1997). The effects of divorce and custody arrangements on children's behavior, development, and adjustment. *Family and Conciliation Courts Review, 35,* 393–404.

Lamb, M. E., & Thierry, K. L. (in press). Understanding children's testimony regarding their alleged abuse: Contributions of field and laboratory analog research. In D. M. Teti (Ed.), *Handbook of research methods in developmental psychology.* Malden, MA: Blackwell.

Leichtman, M. D., & Ceci, S. J. (1995). The effects of stereotypes and suggestions on preschoolers' reports. *Developmental Psychology, 31,* 568–578.

Levesque, R. A. (2001). *Adolescents, sex and the law.* Washington, DC: American Psychological Association.

Maccoby, E. E., & Mnookin, R. H. (1992). *Dividing the child: Social and legal dilemmas of custody.* Cambridge, MA: Harvard University Press.

Marin, B. V., Holmes, D. L., Guth, M., & Kovac, P. (1979). The potential of children as eyewitnesses. *Law and Human Behavior, 3,* 295–305.

Masten, A. S., & Garmezy, N. (1985). Risk, vulnerability, and protective factors in developmental psychology. *Advances in Clinical Child Psychology, 8,* 1–52.

McLanahan, S. S., & Sandefur, G. (1994). *Growing up with a single parent: What hurts, what helps.* Cambridge, MA: Harvard University Press.

McLanahan, S. S., & Teitler, J. (1999). The consequences of father absence. In M. E. Lamb (Ed.), *Parenting and child development in "nontraditional" families* (pp. 83–102). Mahwah, NJ: Erlbaum.

Memon, A., & Bull, R. (Eds.). (1999). *Handbook of the psychology of interviewing.* New York: Wiley.

Memorandum of Good Practice. (1992). London: Her Majesty's Stationery Office.

Milne, R., & Bull, R. (1999). *Investigative interviewing: Psychology and practice.* Chichester, UK: Wiley.

Moston, S., & Engelberg, T. (1992). The effects of social support on children's eyewitness testimony. *Applied Cognitive Psychology, 6,* 61–75.

Myles-Worsley, M., Cromer, C., & Dodd, D. (1986). Children's preschool script reconstruction: Reliance on general knowledge as memory fades. *Developmental Psychology, 22,* 2–30.

Nelson, K. (1986). *Event knowledge: A functional approach to cognitive development.* Hillsdale, NJ: Erlbaum.

Nelson, K., & Gruendel, J. (1981). Generalized event representations: Basic building blocks of cognitive development. In M. E. Lamb & A. L. Brown (Eds.), *Advances in development psychology* (Vol. 1, pp. 131–158). Hillsdale, NJ: Erlbaum.

Newcombe, P. A., & Siegal, M. (1996). Where to look first for suggestibility in your children. *Cognition, 59,* 337–356.

Newcombe, P. A., & Siegal, M. (1997). Explicitly questioning the nature of suggestibility in preschoolers' memory and retention. *Journal of Experimental Child Psychology,* 185–203.

Oates, K., & Shrimpton, S. (1991). Children's memories for stressful and non-stressful events. *Medical Science and the Law, 31,* 4–10.

Ochsner, J. E., & Zaragoza, M. S. (1988, March). *The accuracy and suggestibility of children's memory of neutral and criminal eyewitness events.* Paper presented to the American Psychology and Law Association, Miami, FL.

Orbach, Y., Hershkowitz, I., Lamb, M. E., Sternberg, K. J., Esplin, P. W., & Horowitz, D. (2000). Assessing the value of structured protocols for forensic interviews of alleged child abuse victims. *Child Abuse and Neglect, 24,* 733–752.

Ornstein, P. A., Gordon, B. N., & Larus, D. M. (1992a). Children's memory for a personally experienced event: Implications for testimony. *Applied Cognitive Psychology, 6,* 49–60.

Ornstein, P. A., Larus, D. M., & Clubb, P. A. (1992b). Understanding children's testimony: Implications of the research on children's memory. In R. Vasta (Ed.), *Annals of child development* (Vol. 8, pp. 147–176). London: Jessica Kingsley.

Ornstein, P. A., Staneck, C. H., Agosto, C. D., & Baker-Ward, L. (2001, April). *Differentiating between what happened and what might have happened: The impact of knowledge and expectations on children's memory.* Paper presented to the Society for Research in Child Development, Minneapolis, MN.

Perry, N. W., & Wrightsman, L. S. (1991). *The child witness: Legal issues and dilemmas.* Newbury Park, CA: Sage.

Peters, D. P. (1987). The impact of naturally occurring stress on children's memory. In S. J. Ceci, M. P. Toglia, & D. F. Ross (Eds.), *Children's eyewitness testimony* (pp. 122–141). New York: Springer-Verlag.

Peters, D. P. (1991). The influence of stress and arousal on the child witness. In J. Doris (Ed.), *The suggestibility of children's recollections* (pp. 60–76). Washington, DC: American Psychological Association.

Peters, D. P., & Hagan, S. (1989, April). *Stress and arousal effects on the child's eyewitness testimony*. Paper presented to the Society for Research in Child Development, Kansas City, MO.

Peters, H. E. (1997). *Child custody and monetary transfers in divorce negotiations: Reduced form and simulation results.* Unpublished manuscript, Department of Economics, Cornell University, Ithaca, NY.

Peterson, C., & Bell, M. (1996). Children's memory for traumatic injury. *Child Development, 67,* 3045–3070.

Pleck, J. H. (1997). Paternal involvement: Levels, sources, and consequences. In M. E. Lamb (Ed.), *The role of the father in child development* (3rd ed., pp. 66–103). New York: Wiley.

Poole, D. A., & Lamb, M. E. (1998). *Investigative interviews of children: A guide for helping professionals.* Washington, DC: American Psychological Association.

Poole, D. A., & Lindsay, D. S. (1995). Interviewing preschoolers: Effects of nonsuggestive techniques, parental coaching, and leading questions on reports of nonexperienced events. *Journal of Experimental Child Psychology, 60,* 129–154.

Poole, D. A., & Lindsay, D. S. (1996, June). *Effects of parental suggestions, interviewing techniques, and age on young children's event reports.* Paper presented at the NATO Advanced Study Institute on Recollections of Trauma, Port de Bourgenay, France.

Poole, D. A., & Lindsay, D. S. (1997, April). *Misinformation from parents and children's source monitoring: Implications for testimony.* Paper presented to the Society for Research in Child Development, Washington, DC.

Poole, D. A., & Lindsay, D. S. (1998). Assessing the accuracy of young children's reports: Lessons from the investigation of child sexual abuse. *Applied and Preventive Psychology, 7,* 1–26.

Poole, D. A., & White, L. T. (1993). Two years later: Effects of question repetition and retention interval on the eyewitness testimony of children and adults. *Developmental Psychology, 29,* 844–853.

Raskin D., & Esplin, P. W. (1991). Statement validity assessments: Interview procedures and content analyses of children's statements of sexual abuse. *Behavioral Assessment, 13,* 265–291.

Raskin, D., & Yuille, J. (1989). Problems in evaluating interviews of children in sexual abuse cases. In S. J. Ceci, M. P. Toglia, & D. F. Ross (Eds.), *Adults' perceptions of children's testimony* (pp. 184–207). New York: Springer-Verlag.

Reich, P. A. (1986). *Language development.* Englewood Cliffs, NJ: Prentice-Hall.

Roberts, K. P., & Lamb, M. E. (1999). Children's responses when interviewers distort details during investigative interviews. *Legal and Criminological Psychology, 4,* 23–31.

Robinson, J., & Briggs, P. (1997). Age trends and eye-witness suggestibility and compliance. *Psychology Crime and Law, 3,* 187–202.

Rolf, J., Masten, A. S., Cicchetti, D., Nuerchterlein, D. H., & Weintraub, S. (Eds.). (1990). *Risk and protective factors in the development of psychopathology.* New York: Cambridge University Press.

Rutter, M. (1972). *Maternal deprivation reassessed.* London: Penguin.

Sattler, J. (1998). *Clinical and forensic interviewing of children and families.* San Diego, CA: Author.

Saywitz, K. J. (1988). The credibility of the child witness. *Family Advocate, 10,* 38.

Saywitz, K. J., & Snyder, L. (1993). Improving children's testimony with preparation. In G. S. Goodman & B. L. Bottoms (Eds.), *Child victims, child witnesses: Understanding and improving testimony* (pp. 117–146). New York: Guilford Press.

Saywitz, K. J., Snyder, L., & Nathanson, R. (1999). Facilitating the communicative competence of the child witness. *Applied Developmental Science, 3,* 58–68.

Schwartz, R. (2001). *Youth and the criminal justice system.* Washington, DC: American Bar Association.

Schneider, W., & Bjorklund, D. F. (1998). Memory. In W. Damon, D. Kuhn, & R. S. Siegler (Eds.), *Handbook of child psychology: Vol. 2. Cognition, perception, and language* (5th ed., pp. 467–521). New York: Wiley.

Sears, R. R. (1975). Your ancients revisited: A history of child development. In E. M. Hetherington (Ed.), *Review of child development research* (Vol. 5, pp. 7–73). Chicago: University of Chicago Press.

Sedlak, A. J., & Broadhurst, D. D. (1996). *Third national incidence study of child abuse and neglect: Final report.* Washington, DC: U.S. Department of Health and Human Resources, Administration for Children and Families.

Shank, R., & Abelson, R. (1977). *Scripts, plans, goals, and understanding.* Hillsdale, NJ: Erlbaum.

Spitz, R. A. (1965). *The first year of life.* New York: International Universities Press.

Sternberg, K. J., Lamb, M. E., Davies, G. M., & Westcott, H. L. (2001). The Memorandum of Good Practice: Theory versus application. *Child Abuse and Neglect, 25,* 669–681.

Sternberg, K. J., Lamb, M. E., Esplin, P. W., & Baradaran, L. B. (1999). Using a scripted protocol in investigative interviews: A pilot study. *Applied Developmental Science, 3,* 70–76.

Sternberg, K. J., Lamb, M. E., Esplin, P. W., Orbach, Y., & Hershkowitz, I. (2002). Using a structured protocol to improve the quality of investigative interviews. In M. L. Eisen, J. A. Quas, & G. S. Goodman (Eds.), *Memory and suggestibility in the forensic interview* (pp. 409–436). Mahwah, NJ: Erlbaum.

Sternberg, K. J., Lamb, M. E., Hershkowitz, I., Esplin, P. W., Redlich, A., & Sunshine, N. (1996). The relation between investigative utterance types and the informativeness of child witnesses. *Journal of Applied Developmental Psychology, 17,* 439–451.

Sternberg, K. J., Lamb, M. E., Hershkowitz, I., Yudilevitch, L., Orbach, Y., Esplin, P. W., & Hovav, M. (1997). Effects of introductory style on children's ability to describe experiences of sexual abuse. *Child Abuse and Neglect, 21,* 1133–1146.

Sternberg, K. J., Lamb, M. E., Orbach, Y., Esplin, P. W., & Mitchell, S. (2001). Use of a structured investigative protocol enhances young children's responses to free recall prompts in the course of forensic interviews. *Journal of Applied Psychology, 86,* 997–1005.

Steward, M. S. (1993). Understanding children's memories of medical procedures: "He didn't touch me and it didn't hurt!" In C. A. Nelson (Eds.), *Memory and affect in development* (pp. 171–225). Hillsdale, NJ: Erlbaum.

Steward, M. S., & Steward, D. S. (with L. Farquhar, J. E. B. Myers, M. Reinhart, J. Welker, N. Joye, J. Driskill, & J. Morgan). (1996). Interviewing young children about body touch and handling. *Monographs of the Society for Research in Child Development, 61*(4–5, Serial No. 248).

Toglia, M. P., Ceci, S. J., & Ross, D. F. (1989, April). *Prestige vs. source monitoring in children's suggestibility.* Paper presented to the Society for Research in Child Development, Kansas City, MO.

Thompson, R. A. (1998). Early sociopersonality development. In W. Damon & N. Eisenberg (Eds.), *Handbook of child development: Vol. 3. Social, emotional, and personality development* (5th ed., pp. 25–104). New York: Wiley.

Thompson, R. A., & Laible, D. J. (1999). Noncustodial parents. In M. E. Lamb (Ed.), *Parenting and child development in "nontraditional" families* (pp. 103–123). Mahwah, NJ: Erlbaum.

Thompson, W. C., Clarke-Stewart, K. A., & Lepore, S. J. (1997). What did the janitor do? Suggestive interviewing and the accuracy of children's accounts. *Law and Human Behavior, 21,* 405–426.

Vandermaas, M. (1991, April). *Does anxiety affect children's event reports?* Paper presented to the Society for Research in Child Development, Seattle, WA.

Van IJzendoorn, M. H., & DeWolff, M. S. (1997). In search of the absent father—Meta-analyses of infant-father attachment: A rejoinder to our discussants. *Child Development, 68,* 604–609.

Walker, A. G. (1999). *Handbook on questioning children: A linguistic perspective* (2nd ed.). Washington, DC: ABA Center on Children and the Law.

Walker, N., & Hunt, J. S. (1998). Interviewing child victim-witnesses: How you ask is what you get. In C. P. Thompson, D. J. Herrman, J. D. Read, D. Bruce, D. Payne, & M. P. Toglia (Eds.), *Eyewitness memory: Theoretical and applied perspectives* (pp. 55–87). Mahwah, NJ: Erlbaum.

Warren, A. R., & Lane, P. (1995). Effects of timing and type of questioning on eyewitness accuracy and suggestibility. In M. S. Zaragoza, J. R. Graham, G. C. N. Hall, R. Hirschman, & Y. S. Ben-Porath (Eds.), *Memory and testimony in the child witness* (pp. 44–60). Thousand Oaks, CA: Sage.

Warren, A. R., & McCloskey, L. A. (1997). Language in social contexts. In S. B. Gleason (Ed.), *The development of language* (4th ed., pp. 210–258). New York: Allyn & Bacon.

Warren, A. R., Woodall, C. E., Hunt, J. S., & Perry, N. W. (1996). "It sounds good in theory, but . . .": Do investigative interviewers follow guidelines based on memory research? *Child Maltreatment, 1,* 231–245.

Warren, A. R., Woodall, C. E., Thomas, M., Nunno, M., Keeney, J. M., Larson, S. M., & Stadfeld, J. A. (1999). Assessing the effectiveness of a training program for interviewing child witnesses. *Applied Developmental Science, 3,* 128–135.

Warshak, R. A. (2000). Blanket restrictions: Overnight contact between parents and young children. *Family and Conciliation Courts Review, 38,* 422–445.

Westcott, H. L., Davies, G. M., & Bull, R. (Eds.). (2002). *Children's testimony: Psychological research and forensic practice.* Chichester, UK: Wiley.

Yarrow, L. J., & Goodwin, M. (1973). The immediate impact of separation: Reactions of infants to a change in mother figures. In L. J. Stone, H. T. Smith, & L. B. Murphy (Eds.), *The competent infant* (pp. 1032–1040). New York: Basic Books.

CHAPTER 24

Health and Human Development

CATHLEEN M. CONNELL AND MARY R. JANEVIC

Examining health and health-related factors within a life-span developmental framework is important for several reasons. First, health and development share many important characteristics—both are lifelong processes that involve gains (growth) and losses (decline), are multidimensional, and change as a function of adaptation to changing biological, psychological, social, environmental, and cultural conditions (Baltes, Staudinger, & Lindenberger, 1999; Whitman, 1999). Second, developmental processes influence health and illness behavior, the experience of illness, illness prevention and health promotion, and the assessment and treatment of disease (Penny, Bennett, & Herbert, 1994). An understanding of how these processes operate to affect health outcomes can help to optimize the effectiveness of interventions and determine when they are most appropriately offered (Peterson, 1996; Roberts, Maddux, & Wright, 1984). Third, a life-span developmental framework can aid in the understanding of health by identifying unique patterns of risk and protective factors that vary predictably by developmental stage (Baltes

et al., 1999; Whitman, 1999). Finally, attention to developmental factors fosters an appreciation of how health-related experiences at earlier stages can affect health and health behaviors at later stages of the life-span. To date, little attention has been given to the ways in which development as a dynamic force shapes health and health behaviors (Peterson, 1996), although there are several notable exceptions (e.g., Schulenberg, Maggs, & Hurrelmann, 1997a). In fact, most models of health and illness ignore developmental factors, limiting their external validity beyond the age group for which they were developed (Whitman, 1999).

The goals of this chapter are (a) to elaborate on the utility of a life-span developmental approach to health; and (b) to discuss how biological, cognitive, and social development influences health and health behavior in each of five life stages—infancy, childhood, adolescence, midlife, and older adulthood. The fact that extrinsic factors such as social class and gender interact with these processes should be kept in mind throughout this discussion. Findings from empirical literature on physical activity and diabetes self-care are used to illustrate the role of these factors in each of the selected life stages.

Biological Development

The ways in which biological systems change with development influence an individual's risk of morbidity and mortality across the life span (Kolberg, 1999). Kolberg (1999) classifies diseases and conditions according to their incidence across the life span: diseases of childhood, which decrease with age; diseases of aging, which increase with age; diseases of adulthood; diseases that are most frequent in infants and the elderly; and diseases that affect all age groups consistently. As an individual moves from infancy to older adulthood, biological systems change in ways that can either protect health or increase risk for morbidity and mortality (Kolberg, 1999). Biological development follows a sequential pattern: physical (and cognitive) abilities resemble an inverted U shape such that they are at their lowest levels of efficacy in very early and very late life (Schulz & Heckhausen, 1996); correspondingly, individuals are at greatest risk for medical problems in very early life and older adulthood (Kolberg, 1999). Some diseases (e.g., coronary artery disease or lung cancer) are most associated with older adulthood because of cumulative insult, or "wear and tear" (Kolberg, 1999), highlighting the need for considering the impact of risk factors and stressors across the life course.

Characterizing health status by age group, however, is a complex process (Whitman, 1999) because it depends to a great extent on external factors—for example, the health of midlife adults with low socioeconomic status (SES) tends to be inferior to that of high-SES older adults (House et al., 1990). In addition to the direct effects of age-related changes in biological systems on health status, the likelihood of illness at any given stage may also be an important determinant of health behaviors. For example, in late midlife and older adulthood, a greater propensity toward chronic illness may make the likely consequences of risky health behaviors seem particularly salient. Among adolescents and young adults, current good health may increase the likelihood of engaging in health-risk behaviors because the perceived threat of future illnesses is relatively remote.

Cognitive Development

Cognitive abilities such as intellectual functioning and feelings of control also vary over the course of the life span and have implications for making decisions about health-related behavior. At the beginning of the life span, increases in cognitive sophistication enable children to become better able to understand concepts of health and illness (Bibace & Walsh, 1980). At the end of the life span, decrements in mechanical (or *fluid*) intelligence and—to a lesser extent—pragmatic (or *crystallized*) intelligence have been found among the old and very old (Baltes, Lindenberger, & Staudinger, 1998; Lindenberger & Baltes, 1997); however, some older adults also exhibit high levels of *wisdom,* or knowledge about the meaning and conduct of life (Baltes et al., 1998). Heckhausen and Schulz (1995) describe shifts in the use of control strategies—either *primary control* (i.e., over the external world) or *secondary control* (i.e., cognitive or internally directed processes) in accordance with differing developmental needs over the life span. All such changes in cognitive processes may affect both the nature of health-related decisions and the extent to which individuals are able to make autonomous choices over the life course regarding their own health behavior.

The implications of developmental differences in cognitive factors, however, are rarely considered in theories that address health decision making. Theories that predict and explain health decision making in adults, for example, might not be appropriate for children and adolescents (Sturges & Rogers, 1996). Prohaska and Clark (1997) note that the Health Belief Model (HBM; Janz & Becker, 1984), one of the most widely used theories to predict health-related behavior, may not adequately predict behavior across age groups. This model assumes that perceived health threat is a strong motivator for engaging in preventive health behaviors; yet adolescents may be more motivated by social pressures than by personal health beliefs (Prohaska & Clark, 1997) or may use health behaviors as a way of accomplishing developmental tasks (Schulenberg, Maggs, Steinman, & Zucker, 2001). Developmental stages may also influence the relative importance of HBM components in predicting health outcomes (i.e., perceived susceptibility to and severity of a health threat and perceived benefits and barriers of taking action to reduce the threat) in midlife (Merluzzi & Nairn, 1999).

The components of Social Cognitive Theory (Bandura, 1986, 2001; N. M. Clark & Zimmerman, 1990), another widely used model to explain health behavior change, can also be affected by age and developmental stage. *Self-efficacy*—the belief of an individual that he or she can successfully perform a certain behavior and one of the central constructs of this theory—may be affected either positively (through experience) or negatively (by repeated failures) by age. Another SCT construct, outcome expectancy—that is, the belief that a behavior will lead to a positive result—may also vary with age, in part because health behaviors will not bring about the same positive results equally across the life span (Prohaska & Clark, 1997).

Social Development

Several theories of health behavior include social factors. For example, the Theory of Planned Behavior (Ajzen, 1991; Montano, Kasprzyk, & Taplin, 1997) includes a component that assesses how an individual perceives important others to think about health and health behavior choices. SCT (Bandura, 1986, 2001) includes the role of others as behavioral models affecting health decision making. These social influences, however, vary by developmental period (Prohaska & Clark, 1997). For example, peer models may be particularly influential during adolescence. In addition, because the primary sources (e.g., friends, parents, spouses) of informational, tangible, and emotional social support are likely to vary predictably throughout the life span (Schulz & Rau, 1985), the way this support shapes health decisions is also likely to vary over the life course. Kahn and Antonucci (1980), for example, propose that an individual's social network is a dynamic convoy that changes in structure and composition throughout the life course in response to changing situational factors of the individual. These changes are likely to affect the amount and type of influence that network members have on an individual's health behaviors.

Structural Influences on Development and Health

Developmental influences on health operate concurrently with external factors that affect health and health behaviors both directly and indirectly. Murphy and Bennett (1994) suggest that health behavior may be best understood as "an interaction between individual features, the micro- and macro-social environment, and different stages in the life cycle." SES is a prominent example of a structural variable that influences development, health, health behavior, and their interaction. Across the life span, health risks and conditions can be traced directly to poverty (e.g., violence in adolescence and young adulthood; mental health problems and lack of insurance in adulthood)—demonstrating that the health profiles of the poor across the life span are marked by risk and prevalence of disease greater at every point than those of their economically better-off counterparts (Bolig, Borkowski, & Brandenberger, 1999). Moreover, malnutrition early in life can affect the cognitive, behavioral, and social development of children, and prolonged exposure to poverty can affect the beliefs, attitudes, and cognitions of adolescents (Bolig et al., 1999). It should also be noted that economic poverty, particularly when combined with discrimination or racism from the society at large, may be associated with the development and maintenance of resources such as social networks and religiosity (McAdoo, 1995) that ultimately affect developmental trajectories, health, and health behavior choices.

SES may also affect the timing of health-related life transitions (e.g., earlier marriage and widowhood among those of low SES). This is exemplified in the *weathering hypothesis* (Geronimus, 1996), which explains high rates of teenage childbearing among the African American population as an adaptive response to impoverished circumstances that foster cumulative health risks in early adulthood (i.e., a weathering effect) that contribute to infant mortality. SES also determines the point in the life span at which the onset of chronic illness is likely to occur; this onset is more likely to take place in midlife for individuals of low SES than it is for their high-SES counterparts (House et al., 1990).

Race and ethnicity, due to their association with SES, discrimination, cultural practices, and health beliefs, are also important structural factors that influence the impact of development on health and health behaviors. For example, the relative importance of family and peers during adolescence in shaping health-related decisions may vary with differences in cultural beliefs such as familism. Race may also affect the timing of developmental stages in ways that have implications for health and health behaviors; for example, poorer health among midlife and older African American males is associated with earlier exit from the labor force relative to Whites (Bound, Schoenbaum, & Waidman, 1996). Race also influences the length of the life span itself—for example, White males and females have a longer life expectancy than their African American counterparts do (R. N. Anderson, 1999)—which may in turn have an impact on health attitudes and practices throughout the life course.

The remaining sections of this chapter are devoted to a stage-specific look at developmental and life span influences on health behavior. A rationale for selecting physical activity and diabetes self-management behaviors to illustrate how these influences operate at each stage is provided first.

Physical Activity Across the Life Span

Physical activity is an "independent risk factor or potential treatment for most of the major causes of morbidity and mortality in western societies" and has been associated with positive physical and mental health across the life span (Singh, 2000, p. 6). For example, physical activity is associated with lower blood pressure, reduced risk of heart disease and cancer, improved cognitive functioning and mood, maintenance of functional independence, higher self-esteem, lower levels of stress, and improved well-being (DiLorenzo, Stucky-Ropp, Vander Wal, & Gotham, 1998; National Center for Chronic Disease Prevention and Health Promotion, Centers for Disease Control and Prevention, 1997). Physical activity is also an important component of self-management regimens for many prevalent chronic illnesses, including diabetes, heart disease, hypertension, arthritis, and stroke (Singh, 2000).

In addition to the general benefits of physical activity, there are unique reasons for exploring the determinants of physical activity during each of the developmental periods highlighted in this chapter. For example, several risk factors for chronic diseases (e.g., hypertension) are associated with health practices, such as sedentary behavior, that originate during childhood (DiLorenzo et al., 1998). In addition, life-long physical activity patterns may be established early. For example, adolescents who engage in regular physical activity are more likely to be active in adulthood than are sedentary adolescents (Telama, Yang, Laakso, & Viikari, 1997). Among midlife and older adults, regular physical activity is considered an integral part of preventive gerontology (Hazzard, 1995). Examining the developmental factors that influence physical activity will assist in the identification of age- and stage-appropriate interventions to foster regular exercise habits across the life span.

Diabetes Across the Life Span

Diabetes is one of the most prevalent chronic health conditions that is diagnosed across the life span. More than 15 million Americans have been diagnosed with this condition, and it is estimated that 5.4 million remain undiagnosed (Centers for Disease Control and Prevention, 1998). In general, children and adolescents are affected by Type 1 diabetes, also known as insulin-dependent diabetes mellitus (IDDM). The vast majority of cases of diabetes diagnosed in adulthood are referred to as Type 2 or non–insulin-dependent diabetes (NIDDM). The prevalence of this condition increases with age, as does the prevalence of diabetes-related complications (Centers for Disease Control and Prevention, 1998).

Diabetes serves as a useful model for self-care, or *self-management* behavior, because it requires the coordination of several behaviors on a daily basis, including diet, exercise, insulin administration, and blood glucose testing (Delamater, 1993). Adherence to a complex behavioral regimen is important for maintaining optimal blood glucose levels and decreasing the risk of complications, including heart disease, stroke, and kidney disease (The Diabetes Control and Complications Trial Research Group, 1993).

Normal developmental processes among children and adolescents may both affect and be affected by diabetes self-care behaviors. For example, diabetes self-management behaviors (e.g., adherence to a strict diet) may interfere with normal striving for independence as children mature and the desire for independence may in turn interfere with regimen adherence. The need to adhere to a complex behavioral regimen presents unique challenges for people with diabetes in midlife and older adulthood, who may be managing other chronic health conditions and may lack appropriate education, support, and motivation to engage in appropriate self-care behaviors (Glasgow et al., 1992). Throughout this chapter, examples from the empirical literature on diabetes self-management are used to illustrate the importance of considering a life-span developmental approach.

INFANCY AND CHILDHOOD

A great deal of attention has been afforded to the influence of developmental processes on health issues during the early stages of life, particularly infancy, childhood, and adolescence. From a life-span perspective, studying health behaviors during these periods is critical, as this may be the time at which the stage is set for health attitudes and behaviors that will persist into adulthood (O'Brien & Bush, 1997; Roberts et al., 1984). The following sections summarize the influence of biological, cognitive, and social developmental factors on health behaviors in childhood (Tinsley, 1992). Although several examples from the infancy period are used, the primary focus of this section is on children, who are able—at least to a limited extent—to perform health-related behaviors and make health-related decisions. The reciprocal effects of health behavior on developmental processes and tasks are also considered in this section.

Biological Development and the Health Behavior of Children

Biological development during infancy and childhood affects health behavior in several ways. First, as children move from infancy to preadolescence, the diseases, conditions, and injuries for which they are at highest risk change. For example, infants, especially newborns, may be at highest risk for infectious disease, and young adolescents are at greater risk for morbidity associated with sexual behavior or substance abuse (Kolberg, 1999; Millstein et al., 1992). The importance of specific preventive health behaviors, therefore, also changes along with these risk profiles. For example, the risk of sudden infant death syndrome (SIDS) in infancy requires appropriate preventive behaviors on the part of parents—for example, placing the infant on his or her back when sleeping (Whitman, White, O'Mara, & Goeke-Morey, 1999). Second, children's motoric and physical maturation and growth allow them ever greater independence in interacting with the physical environment, making them more likely to encounter certain health hazards (Roberts et al., 1984)—for example, bike-related injuries, necessitating instruction in appropriate use of a bike helmet, or infant exploration that necessitates "baby-proofing" by parents (Kolberg, 1999).

Third, as children grow and mature, they become able to perform preventive and self-management behaviors on their own, such as wearing a seatbelt, brushing their teeth, or injecting insulin (Roberts et al., 1984). Fourth, favorable biological conditions during childhood make chronic illnesses such as diabetes relatively rare. Thus, for children with chronic illness, the nonnormative nature of its occurrence has implications for adjustment and regimen adherence. For example, Delamater (1993) reports that adherence with diabetic regimens may be compromised when children are with their peers, suggesting that the fear of appearing different inhibits the practice of self-management behaviors.

Cognitive Development and the Health Behavior of Children

Children's beliefs about health and illness and their implications for preventive and self-care behaviors have been the focus of a sizable body of research. Children make health decisions very differently from the way adults do, given qualitative differences in reasoning and logical thinking skills (O'Brien & Bush, 1997). It is therefore essential to consider cognitive development when attempting to understand the determinants of health behavior in children and when designing effective ways to educate children about health and illness. In general, improvements over time in the ability to think, reason, and understand allow children to make increasingly thoughtful and independent decisions about their health-related behavior (Roberts et al., 1984). However, by the time children reach adolescence, the so-called egocentrism (Elkind, 1967) that is typical of this period—along with social pressures—may actually increase the likelihood of engaging in health risk behaviors or of nonadherence to medical regimens (but see Beyth-Marom & Fischhoff, 1997). Indeed, in spite of increased cognitive sophistication, compliance with diabetic regimens is more of a problem among older children and adolescents who are beginning to test limits and authority than it is among younger children (Delamater, 1993; Kreipe & Strauss, 1989).

Cognitive Development and Health: Theories and Models

Several theories and models offer insight into how cognitive development affects health behavior. Tinsley (1992)

distinguishes between (a) *developmental* models that emphasize similarities in how children progress through stages in their conceptualizations of health and illness; and (b) *individual differences* models that consider personality, social, and cultural variables in explaining health behaviors in children. An example of each of these two types of models is described next.

Bibace and Walsh's model (1980; Thompson & Gustafson, 1996) is one of the most frequently cited cognitive development models of health- and illness-related behavior for children. This model posits six stages—*phenomenism, contagion, contamination, internalization, physiological,* and *psychophysiological*—that closely parallel Piaget's preoperational, concrete, and formal operational stages. These stages are characterized by increasing logic, complexity of thought, ability to think abstractly, and sophistication regarding the causes of health and the relationships between behavior and illness. For example, in the early stages, children conceive of the causes of illness as being spatially proximate to the body and may confuse symptoms and causes of disease. Later, children begin to realize a degree of control over causes or cures of illness by avoiding or performing certain behaviors. Roberts et al. (1984) discuss the implications of this stage-based model for guiding health behavior interventions. For example, programs designed to teach children about health-promoting behaviors should be sensitive to cognitive developmental stages. Efforts that are too sophisticated may be confusing, and those that are too simplistic may be ignored or discounted, although individual differences certainly need to be considered.

The Children's Health Belief Model (CHBM; Iannotti & Bush, 1993), adapted from the widely used Health Belief Model (HBM; Janz & Becker, 1984), examines how individual beliefs inform children's health behavior choices. The HBM posits that the likelihood that an individual will perform a given health behavior depends on (a) the threat an individual perceives from a given health risk, (b) the perceived severity of this risk, (c) the benefits of taking action to counteract the threat relative to the barriers associated with this action, (d) the presence of a cue to action, and (e) the individual's level of self-efficacy for taking action. Similarly, the CHBM considers several *readiness factors:* motivation, perceived vulnerability to the health threat, perceived severity of the threat, and perceived benefits and barriers to taking action to avoid the threat. Unlike the HBM, however, the CHBM posits that these readiness factors are affected by *modifying factors* that are influenced by developmental stage. These modifying factors are classified as *cognitive-affective* (e.g., health locus of control, knowledge), *enabling* (e.g., autonomy), and *environmental* (e.g., attitudes and motivations of the child's caregiver).

Cognitive Development and Illness Self-Care Behaviors

In addition to general cognitive developmental theories and models of health behavior, research has also provided insight into how cognitive development affects self-management behaviors among chronically ill children. Changes in memory, perception of time, and an understanding of causality and consequences all influence children's ability to carry out complex behavioral regimens and to understand and communicate with health care providers (Iannotti & Bush, 1993; Johnson, 1993). Cognitive development—in particular, social reasoning and the ability to regulate emotions—may also influence the types of coping strategies used by chronically ill children. For example, younger children may be less able to engage in cognitive distraction or emotion-focused coping than are older children (Thompson & Gustafson, 1996). Chronic illness may also have an indirect impact on cognitive development among children to the extent that it limits active exploration of the environment or results in school absences (Patterson, 1988).

The effect of cognitive development on self-management behaviors can be clearly illustrated in the case of childhood diabetes. Savinetti-Rose (1994) notes that children who have diabetes and who are in the early stages of cognitive development may not be able to conceive of a connection between their treatment regimen and their illness. She describes how more advanced cognitive development enables children with diabetes to better understand the rationale behind the treatment plan and also to take greater responsibility for carrying it out. For example, after a child is able to understand number concepts and seriation and when memory skills improve, he or she can better plan the timing of insulin doses, meals, and physical activity.

Social Development and the Health Behavior of Children

Two important social influences—parents and peers—on health behaviors during childhood are considered briefly in this section. Special attention is given to the way in which the relative importance of these social influences changes as a child develops. Also highlighted is the increasing autonomy a child experiences in health decision making and health behavior choices. Indeed, the increasing responsibility children assume for their own behavior is one of the most important effects of social development at this stage (Roberts et al., 1984).

Parental Influence

The primary role of parents in shaping health behavior choices among children has been highlighted by a number of researchers (e.g., O'Brien & Bush, 1997; Tinsley, 1992).

DiLorenzo et al. (1998) discuss the importance of socialization within the family and of parental modeling of health behaviors through "patterns of interaction, imposition of opportunities and restraints, and reinforcement of health-related activities" (p. 471).

Empirical evidence, however, for similarities in preventive health behaviors between parents and children has been mixed (O'Brien & Bush, 1997; Tinsley, 1992). DiLorenzo et al. (1998) examined the influence of parental beliefs, attitudes, and behaviors about physical activity on the exercise habits of fifth and sixth graders. Results of this longitudinal study demonstrate that parental influence may vary by age and gender, change over time, and operate in conjunction with other social, cognitive, and environmental variables. For boys, encouragement and modeling of physical activity by friends and family were important determinants of physical activity. For girls, both peer support and family support of physical activity were important, along with exercise knowledge and mother's physical activity level.

Kimiecik, Horn, and Shurin (1996) also examined the impact of the family on children's (ages 11–15) moderate-to-vigorous physical activity. Results indicate that children's beliefs about physical activity were strongly related to their perceptions of their parents' beliefs (in terms of the value placed on physical activity and the child's physical activity competence), although these perceptions were not related to actual physical activity levels. Despite the lack of relationship in this case between beliefs and behavior, this study highlights the congruence between children's and parent's beliefs regarding physical activity and the potential for parental attitudes to shape health behavior-related cognitions in children.

Peer Influence

As children grow and develop, the role of peers in influencing health attitudes and behaviors increases (Tinsley, 1992). General research on peer influences suggests that this influence might vary a great deal depending on individual factors among children (e.g., self-esteem; Tinsley, 1992). In a qualitative analysis of the personal illness models of children with diabetes, Standiford, Turner, Allen, Drozda, and McCain (1997) found that both preadolescents (ages 10–12) and adolescents (ages 13–17) relied strongly on their families for help with diabetes treatment regimens, but that families were mentioned more often by the younger group. More respondents in the older group mentioned support from friends as being important.

As with cognitive development, there may also be a reciprocal effect of illness on social development. This effect may be especially salient in the case of peer relationships. Responses to illness by peers (Thompson & Gustafson, 1996), absences from school, or feelings of being different may impede friendships and make acceptance by peers more difficult (Miceli, Rowland, & Whitman, 1999). In general, chronic illness during childhood poses challenges to the normative transition to greater involvement with a peer group as childhood progresses.

Finally, it is important to keep in mind that developmental variations in the sources of influence on health behavior decision making are likely to be more complex and involve more factors than a simple peer-versus-parent model would suggest. For example, Tinsley, Holtgrave, Reise, Erdley, and Cupp (1995) found that habit and enjoyment (personal factors) were better predictors of preventive (e.g., seat belt use) and risky (e.g., cigarette use) health behaviors than was the perceived influence of parents, teachers, friends, and various media sources across elementary and high school students. They also discovered that personal factors played a larger role in the health behavior decisions of older compared to younger students (Tinsley et al., 1995).

Autonomy in Diabetes Self-Care

Another important transition for children is the gradual process of assuming responsibility for their own health-related decisions and behaviors. Autonomy in health decision making during childhood can be defined as "those behaviors indicating that the child cooperates in, takes the initiative for, has the capability for, or has responsibility for health promotion or treatment" (Iannotti & Bush, 1993, p. 64). The issue of when children are ready to make their own health decisions—and when they actually do so—has increased in importance over the last couple of decades, a development particularly evident in the increased attention to the self-management of childhood chronic illness.

Issues associated with autonomy can be clearly illustrated in the case of diabetes self-care. For example, if too much responsibility is placed on children who are not cognitively ready, they may be inadvertently noncompliant because of knowledge absences or skill deficits (Johnson, 1993). This notion is supported by a study by Wysocki et al. (1996), who found that high levels of self-care autonomy for diabetes (defined by the ratio of diabetes self-management autonomy to intellectual, social-cognitive, and academic maturity) was associated with poorer treatment adherence, poorer diabetes control, lower levels of diabetes knowledge, and increased hospitalizations. These results, however, do not suggest that children are unable to engage in self-care; rather that the expectation for their self-care must be informed by developmental issues.

In fact, research suggests that relatively few self-care responsibilities are perceived as appropriate for preadolescent children by diabetes professionals. Wysocki, Meinhold, Cox, and Clark (1990) asked 229 health professionals to estimate the age at which children typically are able to master 38 diabetes-related skills. Recognizing and reporting hypoglycemia was thought to be appropriate for children at 6.5 years. On the other end of the age continuum, planning an exercise routine and taking into account insulin schedule and diet were thought to be inappropriate until age 14. An interesting result was that the estimates given varied greatly according to profession, with physicians tending to give the highest age estimates for each of the tasks.

This section has highlighted how biological, cognitive, and social development influences health-related behaviors during childhood. Adolescence is associated with a host of developmental transitions that are likely to have a strong impact on the behavioral choices—and ultimately the health status—of members of this age group. These factors are presented in the following section.

ADOLESCENCE

This section focuses on the effects of biological development (i.e., physiological changes associated with puberty), cognitive development (i.e., increasing cognitive sophistication and egocentric beliefs), and social development (i.e., the increasing importance of peers) on health behaviors during adolescence. As noted earlier, environmental, contextual, and structural factors may influence adolescent health behaviors directly and may also shape the way in which developmental factors affect health behavior choices (Brooks-Gunn, 1993; Cowell & Marks, 1997; Lerner, Ostrom, & Freel, 1999; Schulenberg, Maggs, & Hurrelmann, 1997a). Such factors include—but are not limited to—gender, race-ethnicity, social class, culture, religion, social environment, and access to health care services. Thus, the reader is cautioned that the developmental influences as described in subsequent sections are only main effects that must eventually be embedded in a much broader context that includes both structural and demographic factors. Consequently, developmental variables inevitably explain only a limited amount of the variance in health behavior choices among adolescents. Nonetheless, understanding the potential effects on health behavior of the "fundamental and nearly universal transitions" that characterize adolescence is an essential starting point when planning interventions to affect adolescent health (Maggs, Schulenberg, & Hurrelmann, 1997).

Health behaviors take on particular importance in adolescence for two primary reasons. First, several of the leading causes of morbidity and mortality in this age group are related to behavior (Cowell & Marks, 1997). Second, adolescence marks an important period of transition from parental control to self-determination of behavior (Brooks-Gunn, 1993). Although a number of factors suggest that this developmental period should be characterized by optimal health (e.g., increased strength and stamina, a lack of vulnerability to the major health threats of adulthood), many adolescents face significant health risks, particularly those related to accidents (e.g., motor vehicle injuries) and lifestyle choices (e.g., sexually transmitted diseases, substance abuse; Gondoli, 1999). Moreover, these health risks may be increasing with subsequent cohorts of adolescents, lending urgency to the study of adolescent health behaviors and their determinants (Lerner et al., 1999).

Because adolescence is a time of biological, cognitive, emotional, and social transitions (Cowell & Marks, 1997; Gondoli, 1999), it provides a unique context for examining health behavior choices. Although adolescence is most frequently associated with problem health behaviors (e.g., tobacco and alcohol use; Petersen, 1988), this developmental period may have both positive and negative effects on health-related behaviors (Schulenberg et al., 1997b). For example, health risk behaviors may play a constructive role in negotiating developmental transitions (e.g., binge drinking may ease the transition to the college social environment by increasing acceptance by peer groups), while at the same time posing serious health risks (Maggs et al., 1997; Schulenberg et al., 1997b). The impact of adolescent development on preventive health behaviors has received limited attention in the empirical literature, despite the potential for establishing positive lifelong habits at this stage (Maggs et al., 1997). Among adolescents with a chronic illness, health behaviors take on special importance because they face the usual developmental risks for suboptimal health, as well as additional risks related to illness self-management.

Biological Development and the Health Behavior of Adolescents

Puberty has been defined as "a series of hormonal and somatic changes that adolescents experience as they attain reproductive capacity" (Gondoli, 1999, p. 149); it includes development of the adrenal glands, gonads, and secondary sex characteristics (Cowell & Marks, 1997). Although there is a great deal of individual variation in the timing of these changes, they generally take place between 8 and 13 years of age in girls and between 9.5 and 13.5 years of age in boys (Gondoli, 1999).

Gondoli (1999) has identified three themes emerging from research on puberty and health. First, puberty affects how adolescents perceive themselves and how they are

perceived by others. These perceptions in turn may affect health behavior. Among adolescent girls, for example, the increase in body fat associated with puberty may increase their susceptibility to eating disorders (Brooks-Gunn, 1993). Second, the timing of puberty appears to carry a great deal of significance when it comes to health behavior decisions. For example, early or precocious puberty appears to be associated with greater prevalence of risk behaviors such as alcohol and tobacco use in both genders; moreover, in girls, off-time puberty—whether precocious or delayed—might pose a greater risk for low self-esteem (Silbereisen & Kracke, 1999), which might ultimately influence health behavior. Third, the social context in which puberty occurs determines in large part its effects on behavioral choices.

In addition to affecting health risk behaviors, pubertal status may also affect the practice of preventive health behaviors. Lindquist, Reynolds, and Goran (1999) found independent effects of pubertal development and age on physical activity among children ages 6–13 years. Specifically, they found that although older children were more likely than were younger children to participate in organized sports, children in a higher stage of pubertal development were less likely to do so than were children with less advanced development. They conclude that the social, psychological, and behavioral consequences of pubertal development have a negative impact on physical activity levels, and that the apparent effect of age in previous studies on decreases in physical activity may actually be due to physical maturation. Goran, Gower, Nagy, and Johnson (1998) found evidence for a sharp reduction in girls' physical activity preceding pubertal changes that may be related to biological development or to behavioral or environmental changes accompanying puberty.

Hartman-Stein and Reuter (1988) have discussed the potential effects of pubertal status on diabetes self-care behaviors. After puberty, for example, in an effort to maintain or lose weight, adolescent girls with diabetes may be more likely to develop disordered eating patterns that jeopardize blood glucose control. In addition, there may be a reciprocal effect of self-care behaviors on pubertal markers; for example, poor diabetic control in adolescent girls may lead to missed or light menstrual periods.

Cognitive Development and the Health Behavior of Adolescents

Increasing cognitive sophistication among adolescents has important implications for health decision making. Most adolescents have entered the formal operations stage of cognitive development, marked by the ability to engage in abstract thought and to understand the psychological and physiological causes of illness (Schulz & Rau, 1985). In addition, by adolescence, the knowledge base regarding health and illness is much larger than that in childhood (Cowell & Marks, 1997). One result of these changes may be a heightened belief by adolescents in their ability to affect symptoms and health outcomes (Patterson, 1988).

Brooks-Gunn (1993) highlights three additional cognitive processes that may influence adolescent health behavior: perceptions of costs and benefits, perceptions of risk, and understanding of future consequences of health-related actions. The costs and benefits of health-related actions may be evaluated by adolescents differently from the way those in other age groups evaluate them; for example, among adolescents, the social benefits of engaging in a particular risk behavior such as smoking may be more likely to outweigh the known negative consequences.

Although teenagers may be increasingly able to understand concepts of probability and risk, other factors associated with adolescence may foster risk-taking behaviors. For example, perceptions of good health and lack of experience with poor health may lead to feelings of invulnerability. Indeed, one manifestation of so-called adolescent egocentrism is said to be belief in a "personal fable" in which adolescents imagine themselves to be invincible (Elkind, 1967). Such feelings are often assumed to contribute to a propensity for risk behaviors, although it has been argued that there is little empirical evidence to support this notion (Gondoli, 1999). Moreover, later scholars have suggested that the creation of personal fables is adaptive and contributes to resilience and coping (Lapsley, 1993); hence, the influence of such fables might be expected to ultimately have positive influences on health behaviors. Therefore, the precise ways in which adolescent perceptions of invulnerability affect health behavior choices remain unclear.

Other factors that foster health-risk behavior in adolescents may include lack of experience with the consequences of risk, lack of information, or denial (Brooks-Gunn, 1993). Researchers have also suggested that adolescent's risk perceptions reflect their behavioral experiences, instead of the other way around. For example, Halpern-Felsher et al. (2001) found that adolescents and young adults who had engaged in particular health risk behaviors (e.g., related to sexual activity and alcohol use) judged the risks of negative outcomes from those behaviors as less likely than did nonengagers. Such findings have implications for attempts to modify behavior-specific risk perceptions among adolescents and may underscore the importance of preventing initiation of risk behaviors in late childhood or early adolescence.

Finally, the ability of adolescents to consider long-term consequences of health-related actions (Brooks-Gunn, 1993) may have special relevance when it comes to decision making about preventive health behaviors with long-term benefits, such as diet or physical activity. However, the extent to which adolescents consider the proximal versus long-term benefits when it comes to making decisions about these behaviors has not been well established.

Explaining Physical Activity Patterns in Adolescence

In general, levels of physical activity decline between childhood and adolescence (National Center for Chronic Disease Prevention and Health Promotion, Centers for Disease Control and Prevention, 1997), challenging health researchers and professionals to identify the developmental and contextual factors that contribute to this decrease. Much of the research on the determinants of physical activity among adolescents considers cognitive and social-cognitive factors in tandem, along with demographic and social-structural factors. Variables such as SES, ethnicity, gender, and the physical environment all predict patterns of activity in this age group; for example, female adolescents and those of lower SES engage in less activity—as do adolescents living in high-crime areas (Gordon-Larsen, McMurray, & Popkin, 2000); these factors and their interaction with psychosocial factors therefore are an important focus of current research in this area.

Garcia, Pender, Antonakos, and Ronis (1998) conducted a study that explores changes in cognitive and social factors related to physical activity during the transition to adolescence. Their sample (n = 132) was tracked from elementary to junior high school. Results indicate that when girls reached junior high school, they were less likely to report that the benefits of exercise outweighed the barriers, and they had fewer physically active role models than they had at younger ages. Boys making the transition had less self-efficacy for physical activity and were less likely to perceive social expectations that they would be active compared to when they were in elementary school. Both boys and girls were less likely to report social support for exercise from family and friends following the transition to junior high school. In other words, positive beliefs about physical activity declined for both boys and girls.

Allison, Dwyer, and Makin (1999) examined the impact of self-efficacy, perceived barriers, and life strain on the physical activity of 1,041 students in Grades 9 and 11. Results indicated that one component of self-efficacy (i.e., confidence despite external barriers) was positively associated with physical activity participation. Life strain and perceived barriers were not strongly related to physical activity. These findings suggest that efficacy-enhancing strategies may present one way to offset a decline in physical activity as children mature.

Cognitive Development and Diabetes Self-Care in Adolescence

Cognitive changes during adolescence are likely to affect diabetes self-care behaviors in several ways. During early adolescence, children in the concrete operational stage may be unable to consider the potential future complications resulting from noncompliance and may focus instead on more immediate concerns (e.g., inconvenience of blood glucose monitoring, embarrassment of eating a snack during class; Kreipe & Strauss, 1989). By middle adolescence—with the advent of formal operational thinking and an increasing sense of personal control—children may be better able to understand the role of self-care behaviors in preventing long-term complications (Hartman-Stein & Reuter, 1988). Despite this new level of cognitive sophistication, adherence to strict behavioral regimens may be compromised by the fact that adolescents at this stage are striving for independence, identity, and autonomy and are testing limits and authority (Kreipe & Strauss, 1989). Kriepe and Strauss (1989) suggest that at this stage, treatment options should be structured to maximize the adolescent's sense of control and independence. For example, adolescents could be offered the option of using an insulin pump in an effort to avoid regular insulin injections that may interrupt valued social activities.

A study by Ingersoll, Orr, Herrold, and Golden (1986) provides evidence that cognitive development affects diabetes self-care behavior. Among adolescents aged 12–21, Ingersoll et al. (1986) found that those who practiced anticipatory glucose control (i.e., adjusting an insulin dose according to anticipated changes in exercise and diet) had a level of conceptual maturity higher than the conceptual maturity level of those who did not. These results suggest that health care professionals should consider the extent to which an adolescent is able to make the complex decisions involved in diabetes management; they should then work with parents to ensure that the degree of autonomy given to an adolescent to manage his or her treatment plan is developmentally appropriate.

Social Development and the Health Behavior of Adolescents

The increased importance of peer influence is an accepted hallmark of adolescence (Brooks-Gunn, 1993). Adolescents have larger networks of peers than do children, as well as more stable, intimate, and supportive friendships that occupy more time and have more influence over attitudes and behaviors (Brown, Dolcini, & Leventhal, 1997; Petersen, 1988). Despite the central role of peers, research has also demonstrated the ongoing influence of parents on health behavior choices. For example, Lau, Quadrel, and Hartman

(1990) found in a longitudinal study that although peers had a strong effect on the extent to which adolescents experienced changes in health behaviors such as drinking and exercise during the first 3 years of college, the effect of parental influence (particularly via modeling) on these behaviors also remained strong throughout the study period.

Several transformations in peer relationships during the adolescent years may have an impact on health behaviors. These transformations include (a) the development of emotionally supportive friendships, (b) the initiation of romantic relationships, and (c) the emergence of peer crowds (Brown et al., 1997; Gondoli, 1999). Each of these changes may have either a positive or negative influence on health behavior. For example, research has demonstrated both positive and negative associations between the intimacy and level of support from friendships and the practice of health risk (Brown et al., 1997). For example, becoming part of a romantic relationship may increase the probability that an adolescent will engage in sexual risk-taking, but such relationships may also be associated with decreases in risk behaviors more common in same-sex cliques (e.g., alcohol use; Brown et al., 1997). The relationship between peer crowd membership and health behaviors is complex, because peers are often defined (both by researchers and by youth themselves) in terms of the types of health behaviors in which their members engage (e.g., druggies, jocks). Thus, individual differences in the practice of health behaviors may channel youth into certain peer crowds, and peer crowd norms may reinforce positive and negative health behaviors (Brown et al., 1997).

Social Development and Diabetes Self-Care

Adolescent social transitions—in particular, the increase in the importance and influence of peer relationships—are commonly seen as a barrier to effective diabetes self-management. Compared to children, adolescents have been shown to have poorer adherence to diabetic regimens, and older adolescents may be less adherent than younger adolescents (Kovacs, Goldston, Obrosky, & Iyengar, 1992; La Greca et al., 1995). Attaining optimal adherence and metabolic control has been called "more problematic" for adolescents than for any other age group (La Greca et al., 1995). Researchers have noted that adolescents with diabetes experience conflicts between the drive to attain independence and gain peer acceptance on one hand and adherence to their diabetes regimen on the other (Anderson, Wolf, Burkhart, Cornell, & Bacon, 1989; Hartman-Stein & Reuter, 1988). Moreover, barriers to adherence are present at precisely a time when parents and providers begin to expect adolescents to assume a greater degree of independence and autonomy in their self-care (Anderson et al., 1989; Wysocki et al., 1996).

The influence of peer relationships on diabetes self-care behavior, however, is not uniformly negative. As demonstrated by LaGreca et al. (1995), the friendships of adolescents with diabetes can be an important source of support by providing assistance with insulin administration, blood glucose monitoring, following a meal plan, exercising, and "feeling good about diabetes." Although family members provided more tangible support such as preparing meals and helping with blood glucose monitoring, friends offered companionship and emotional support and encouraged physical activity. LaGreca's (1995) study underscores the value of considering the important role of friends in addition to family members in the design of educational interventions for adolescents with diabetes.

MIDLIFE

Compared to early and late in the life span (i.e., infancy, childhood, adolescence, older adulthood), relatively little is known about health and development during midlife (Lachman & James, 1997; Merluzzi & Nairn, 1999; Willis & Reid, 1999). In fact, the middle years are often depicted as little more than a "staging area on the way to old age" (Baruch & Brooks-Gunn, 1984, p. 1). Several factors, however, will result in increased emphasis on midlife in the scholarly literature in the decades ahead; such factors include the movement of the largest cohorts in U.S. history through this developmental period and an accompanying increase in the median age of the U.S. population (Willis & Reid, 1999).

A life-span perspective on health during midlife is important because this transition is influenced by the health behavior choices and patterns of young adulthood and sets the stage for older adulthood. As stated by Willis and Reid (1999), "optimal physical and psychological development in late life will depend largely on the experiences of baby boomers during middle age" (p. xv). Despite the fact that midlife is a period of relatively good health for most people, the frequency of chronic illnesses, persistent symptoms, disability, and mortality rates accelerate during this period (Merrill & Verbrugge, 1999). Thus, middle age represents a shift in how people view their health—in part due to their increased sense of vulnerability to health threats (Hooker & Kaus, 1994; Merluzzi & Nairn, 1999). It should be noted, however, that perceptions of health in middle age are embedded in existing social structures that present both opportunities and constraints (Elder, 1998), including social class, education, gender, and race (Moen & Wethington, 1999).

Although chronological age is an imperfect proxy for marking developmental periods, it provides a starting point for purposes of discussion. Despite the popular view that midlife begins at age 35 (Moen & Wethington, 1999), other conceptualizations of this period have been more refined. For example, Merluzzi and Narin (1999) describe early adulthood as the period from age 22–34 years; early middle age as between 35 and 44 years of age, and late middle age as between 45 and 64 years of age. Age 45 has been viewed as marking the beginning of the period of midlife in the U.S. census as well as by researchers (Merrill & Verbrugge, 1999). Rather than rely on chronological age, several markers of midlife boundaries have been examined in research on this period, including transitions in employment (e.g., career peaking and early retirement; Moen & Wethington, 1999) and parenting (i.e., the period when children move into school age, adolescence, and early adulthood; Brooks-Gunn & Kirsh, 1984).

In midlife, there are few markers of physical change as dramatic as those that occur in childhood and adolescence (e.g., walking, puberty) or in old age (e.g., rapid decline in health, death; Merrill & Verbrugge, 1999). Most physical changes are very gradual, and individual differences greatly affect the rate of physiological change.

As summarized by Merrill and Verbrugge (1999), signs of physiological change include alterations in physical appearance (e.g., wrinkles, age spots, gray hair), losing height and gaining weight, decreased muscle strength, loss of bone density, lower basal metabolic rate, weaker immune response, diminished sense of smell and taste, gradual hearing loss, decline in eyesight, and poorer sleep habits. The extent to which these age-related processes—particularly weight gain and changes in appearance—provide an incentive to engage in health-promoting behaviors and limit health-damaging behaviors has not been explored to any great extent in the literature. Extensive research evidence, however, supports the link between health habits and chronic illnesses and conditions, and it suggests that engaging in health-promoting behaviors can prevent or delay disease and some of the aging changes that occur in midlife (Merrill & Verbrugge, 1999).

In keeping with the general framework established for this chapter, this section highlights how specific aspects of biological (i.e., menopause), cognitive (i.e., personal control, self-efficacy), and social (i.e., social support) development affect health and self-management behaviors during the middle years.

Biological Development and the Health Behavior of Adults in Midlife

Menopause is thought to represent a major cultural, psychological, and physiological milestone for women during the middle years (Avis, 1999), and it represents one of the few distinct health events of midlife. In fact, most of the health-related research among women at midlife focuses on experiences of menopause and the management of its symptoms (Woods & Mitchell, 1997). Although there is wide variability among women in the age of menopause, the median age of last menstrual period is between 50 and 52 years of age (Brambilla & McKinlay, 1989), and 80% of women experience their last menstrual period between 45 and 55 (Avis, 1999). The hormonal changes associated with menopause affect the musculoskeletal, cardiovascular, and urogenital systems, precipitating increases in heart disease, hypertension, osteoporosis, urinary incontinence, autoimmune disease, and diabetes (Avis, 1999). Although menopause represents a significant life event, few empirical studies have examined the impact of this milestone on health behaviors.

Menopause and Physical Activity

One qualitative study of 17 women in middle age lends insight into how menopause might influence women's decisions about health behaviors such as physical activity. Jones (1997) discovered that women perceive menopause as a marker or symbol of more general life-stage developmental issues and respond with lifestyle adjustments, including changes in physical activity (i.e., exercising more regularly and vigorously) and diet (i.e., eating more low-fat foods, introducing or increasing calcium supplements). The women who participated in the study all reported engaging in high levels of exercise and being healthy eaters before menopause; these behaviors increased or became more disciplined with the onset of negative health-related changes associated with menopause (Jones, 1997). Additional research is needed to reveal the specific ways in which attitudes and beliefs about physical activity are affected by this important transition (see Avis & McKinlay, 1995; Pinto, Marcus, & Clark, 1996; Scharff, Homan, Kreuter, & Brennan, 1999).

Menopause and Diabetes Self-Care

More research attention is also needed to determine how the physical transitions experienced in midlife may affect diabetes self-management behavior. According to the HBM, individuals are more likely to engage in preventive and self-management behaviors if they perceive a significant health threat. Perceived threat derives from perceptions of the severity of the health condition and of susceptibility to negative health outcomes attributed to behavior. Thus, to the extent that menopause heightens perceptions of threat, women in midlife may engage in high levels of regimen adherence.

Although empirical evidence of the possible impact of menopause on self-management behaviors is limited, a small body of research addresses the impact of menopause on a variety of diabetes-related and psychosocial outcomes. In a review of the literature, Javanovic (1997, 1998) concludes that menopause decreases the insulin requirement in women with Type 1 diabetes, increases the risk of depression and cardiovascular disease, and increases percentage of body fat, resulting in increased insulin resistance in women with Type 2 diabetes. In her discussion of diabetes among women, Poirier and Coburn (2000) suggest that menopause results in extreme swings in blood glucose levels, which can complicate self-management efforts. She also describes how women with diabetes may not be able to distinguish between episodes of hypoglycemia and hot flashes. Additional research is needed to determine how changes related to menopause affect the experience of diabetes, diabetes-related outcomes, and—ultimately—self-management behaviors.

Cognitive Development and the Health Behavior of Adults in Midlife

As discussed by Merluzzi and Nairn (1999), one of the overarching themes in the transition from perceived invulnerability and risk taking in the early part of the life span to substantial vulnerability to health threats toward the end is a sense of personal control. The middle years have been described as a time of "settling down" (Levinson, 1977), marked by the perception of increased control and feelings of security and stability that are greater than those at other developmental periods (Lachman, Lewkowicz, Marcus, & Peng, 1994; Wallston & Smith, 1994). Thus, the role played by cognitive phenomena—including perceptions of control—in the health behavior decisions of adults at midlife is of particular interest.

Although several conceptualizations of control have been advanced in the literature, self-efficacy is one of the most frequently used measures of this construct. Self-efficacy is defined as the belief that an individual can successfully engage in a particular behavior (Bandura, 1997). This construct is used often in the empirical literature on the determinants and effects of health behaviors, such as physical activity and disease self-management.

Self-Efficacy and Physical Activity in Midlife

In an empirical study of factors associated with physical activity in 653 women across the life span, Scharff et al. (1999) discovered that women in midlife reported having higher levels of self-efficacy for physical activity than did older women; however, women in midlife also reported much lower levels of self-efficacy than did younger women. In fact, the authors report that women in midlife (aged 40–49) were more than twice as likely as the younger women (18–39 years of age) to be unsure of their ability to meet their physical activity goals (Scharff et al., 1999). In terms of their current levels of physical activity, older women were the least likely to be physically active.

Other findings from this study are also of interest. Family characteristics associated with midlife—particularly having children at home—were consistently related to patterns of physical activity. For example, women at midlife with children at home reported significantly higher levels of physical activities of daily living (e.g., house and yard work) than did women without children at home (Scharff et al., 1999). This study represents one of the few examples of research that acknowledges the possible impact of developmental milestones (e.g., menarche, having children, menopause, career choices) on self-efficacy related to the initiation and maintenance of physical activity in women.

Self-Efficacy and Diabetes Self-Care in Midlife

The role of personal control and self-efficacy in diabetes self management has been the focus of a great deal of empirical research across life stages. Adherence to challenging medical regimens like those required for the successful self-management of diabetes is thought to be more consistent and longer lasting among people with strong beliefs in their abilities to affect their health (O'Leary, 1985). In a recent study of 296 adults with diabetes (with a mean age of 52 years), Watkins et al. (2000) discovered that perceived control of diabetes was a significant predictor of diabetes-specific health behaviors, including following a diet and engaging in regular exercise.

In terms of our understanding of how personal control affects diabetes self-management at midlife, additional research is needed to answer such questions as (a) *Does the overall increase in general perceptions of control in midlife translate into higher levels of self-efficacy for self management behaviors;* (b) *Are levels of control and self-efficacy for managing illness relatively stable over the life span, or are they affected significantly by the developmental context;* and (c) *How might control and self-efficacy work differently for people who are diagnosed with diabetes in midlife compared to those who have lived with the disease since adolescence?* Such research could help to identify strategies used to maintain high levels of control and self-efficacy for self-management tasks across the life span, including adopting age-related performance standards, engaging in social comparison with same-age peers, and optimizing skills in selected areas such as health beliefs and physical-capacity change over time (Merluzzi & Nairn, 1999).

Social Development and the Health Behavior of Adults in Midlife

Two aspects of the social environment take on particular importance at midlife—social support and social roles (Antonucci & Akiyama, 1997). A vast empirical literature examines the impact of social support on a variety of mental and physical health outcomes, including morbidity and mortality (for a review, see Berkman & Glass, 2000). A smaller body of literature examines the impact of social support on self-management behaviors during adulthood (for a review, see Gallant, in press). For example, family members and friends may facilitate or impede health and self-management behaviors by offering information, advice, and encouragement, and by providing emotional and tangible support (Lewis & Rook, 1999).

Although the general social support literature is very compelling in its quantity and overall quality, it rarely incorporates specific discussion of the unique developmental context of the middle years (for an exception, see Connell & D'Augelli, 1988). Kahn and Antonucci (1980) argue that there are four major reasons for considering the changing nature of social support over an individual's life: (a) role entries and exits create changing needs and circumstances for support; (b) the forms and amount of support appropriate for a given time and place depend on these changing life stations; (c) individual differences among adults in the need and desire for social support must be understood via reference to earlier life experiences; and (d) age, period cohort, and history effects may be discerned by a reference to individual experiences.

In addition to the changing patterns of social support over the life span, the pattern and types of social roles held during adulthood—particularly work and family—are critical to an understanding of health behavior choices during midlife (Moen & Wethington, 1999). Studies of the interplay of social support, role trajectories, and health in midlife that reflect a developmental perspective, however, are uncommon (Moen & Wethington, 1999).

Social Factors and Physical Activity in Midlife

It is generally assumed that both general and exercise-specific social support factors are positively associated with physical activity. Eyler et al. (1999) conducted one of the few empirical studies to examine the relationship between social support and physical activity levels of women in midlife and older adulthood. Using a national sample of minority women aged 40 and older, results indicate that women with low levels of social support for physical activity were more likely to be sedentary than were women with high levels of such support. The authors suggest that interventions designed to increase physical activity should incorporate the social networks of potential participants to increase the likelihood that women will initiate and maintain an exercise program (Eyler et al., 1999). The authors did not specifically address issues of midlife, however, despite having a large sample size ($n = 2,912$) that would lend itself to comparisons in study outcomes across the life span and contribute to the discussion of how social roles associated with midlife might increase or inhibit physical activity.

Social Factors and Diabetes Self-Care in Midlife

Because diabetes is a psychologically and behaviorally demanding illness, psychosocial factors are particularly relevant to the process of self-management (Delamater et al., 2001). In fact, the psychosocial impact of diabetes has been recognized as a predictor of mortality in people with diabetes that is stronger than many clinical and physiological variables (Davis, Hess, & Hiss, 1988).

In general, the empirical research suggests that higher levels of social support—especially diabetes-related support from spouses and other family members—is associated with better regimen adherence, including diet, exercise, and weight management (Glasgow & Toobert, 1988; Wilson et al., 1986). This research, typically conducted with samples of adults spanning a large age range and based on cross-sectional designs, provides a snapshot of the relationships among social factors and diabetes self-management behaviors. Additional research, however, is needed to determine how the key social roles of midlife (e.g., parent, spouse, employee) affect the relationship between social support and self-management behavior during this period.

OLDER ADULTHOOD

Although a great deal of attention has been afforded to the general area of health and aging, a relatively small subset of this work overtly incorporates a life-span developmental perspective. Because a life-span view of development is dynamic and marked by the continuous interplay between growth and decline, research guided by this perspective is more likely to include a focus on positive (rather than only negative) age-related changes and gains (rather than only losses; Baltes & Baltes, 1990; Lachman, Ziff, & Spiro, 1994). In addition, a life-span developmental perspective emphasizes intra-individual variability; thus, this view recognizes that people—even in later life—have the potential to improve their adaptive capacity and to experience unique developmental trajectories (Baltes, Reese, & Nesselroade, 1988).

In light of this potential, it is apparent that older adults should be a major focus of the growing body of research on the determinants of health behavior and interventions to shape this behavior (Schulz & Martire, 1999). A selected review of the health behavior literature, however, suggests that older adults are not well represented (Connell, 1999). Specifically, only 15% of articles published in two leading health behavior journals (i.e., *Health Education and Behavior,* formerly entitled *Health Education Quarterly;* and *Health Education Research: Theory and Practice*) over a 10-year period included older adults in the sample. In the majority of the articles that included older adults, age was not examined in the data analysis, and the context of older adulthood was not considered in the discussion of findings. A similar finding is reported by Peterson (1996), who found that less than one quarter of the studies published in the journal *Health Psychology* over a 3-year period dealt with older adults. Of the few studies that included adults in more than one period (e.g., midlife and older adulthood), the influence of development was rarely addressed (Peterson, 1996). Thus, despite the vast literature on issues related to health and aging, much remains to be learned about the health behaviors of older adults, particularly from a life-span developmental perspective.

The final section of this chapter focuses on how specific aspects of biological (i.e., functional capacity), cognitive (i.e., personal control, self-efficacy), and social (i.e., social support, social roles) development affect health and self-management behaviors during older adulthood. As with other periods of the life span, the importance of structural factors such as gender, class, race, and ethnicity should be considered throughout this discussion because they are likely to have both independent effects on the health behaviors of older adults (Markides, 1989) and interactive effects with development-related factors discussed here.

Biological Development and the Health Behavior of Older Adults

Normal aging has been described as the time-dependent, irreversible changes that lead to progressive loss of functional capacity (i.e., respiratory function) after the point of maturity (Moody, 1998). Age-related physical changes include sensory declines, loss of muscle mass and bone density, increased risk of fractures, wrinkled skin, and short-term memory lapses. About 80% of people over the age of 65 have one or more chronic conditions. Three quarters of all deaths of people over the age of 65 are due to heart disease, cancer, and stroke (National Center for Health Statistics, 1996).

Despite the health declines that are typically associated with aging, older adults may be more likely than their younger counterparts to engage in positive health behaviors.

For example, results from the National Health Interview Survey suggest that older adults are more likely than younger adults to report *never* having smoked cigarettes, abstaining from alcohol, drinking in moderation, eating breakfast regularly, and obtaining general medical exams (Thornberry, Wilson, & Golden, 1986). Older adults, however, are much less likely than are young and middle-aged adults to be physically active (Healthy People, 2000, 1991; U.S. Department of Health and Human Services, 1996).

Biological Aging and Physical Activity

The bidirectional relationship between physical activity and the declines in functioning associated with aging has not been fully explored. Although it has been established that physical activity is an important avenue for delaying the negative health consequences of aging (e.g., risk of physical decline, chronic disease, and mortality) and promoting a variety of positive psychological and physical outcomes among older adults (for a review, see McAuley & Katula, 1999), little is known about how physiological changes associated with aging affect attitudes and beliefs about physical activity.

Just as during midlife, negative age-related health changes in older adulthood may affect health behaviors such as physical activity in a variety of ways. For example, the onset of illness or a perceived decline in physical ability may provide incentive for people who have engaged in physical activity throughout their adult years to maintain and even increase their patterns of exercise. Alternatively, some adults may feel resentful when confronted with the need to adapt their lifelong exercise routines to their gradually diminishing physical capacity. Age-associated health changes can also mean that individuals who have never engaged in regular exercise may find this period a particularly daunting time to begin a routine of regular physical activity.

Because exercise is a cornerstone of many self-management regimens, older adults who are diagnosed with a chronic illness may be motivated to increase their level of physical activity, even if they had been sedentary earlier in life. This motivation may be bolstered by advice from a health care professional to initiate or maintain physical activity (Russell & Roter, 1993). Additional research is needed to assess how attitudes and beliefs about physical activity may evolve as a result of biological changes—both normal and pathological—associated with older adulthood.

Cognitive Development and the Health Behavior of Older Adults

Perceptions of control may be particularly important for the health of older adults (Mirowsky, 1995; Rodin, 1986).

Empirical evidence, however, suggests that older adults report a decrease in objective and subjective control (Bandura, 1997), and this loss is related to functional impairment, cardiovascular disease, cancer, deterioration of the immune system, and mortality (as summarized in Bergeman & Wallace, 1999). As described in an earlier section, the concept of self-efficacy (i.e., belief that an individual can successfully engage in a particular behavior) is one aspect of perceived control that has demonstrated a strong association with health behavior.

Self-Efficacy and Physical Activity in Older Adulthood

Of the considerable literature that has identified self-efficacy as an important predictor of exercise behavior and vice versa (McAuley, 1992; O'Leary, 1985), several empirical studies have included or focused exclusively on older adults (D. O. Clark, 1996). For example, Resnick (2001) found that among a sample of 175 older adults in a retirement community, self-efficacy for exercise significantly predicted moderate exercise. In another empirical study, McAuley, Lox, and Duncan (1993) examined the extent to which physical activity facilitates self-efficacy over time. Results from a sample of 44 older adults who completed a 20-week exercise program indicated that self-efficacy was the only significant predictor of exercise behavior at 9 months postintervention. Among 225 community-dwelling older adults aged 65–92, Conn (1997) demonstrated that self-efficacy was a strong predictor of physical activity. Finally, in a study of 327 women aged 70–98 years living in Vancouver, British Columbia, self-efficacy for physical activity later in life was found to be associated with recollections of specific childhood physical activity competencies from decades earlier (Cousins, 1997). This study is important because it is one of the few that examines how health-related experiences at earlier stages can affect specific health behaviors at later stages.

Kaplan and his colleagues have conducted several studies to examine the physical and psychosocial responses to physical activity in older adults with chronic obstructive pulmonary disorder (Kaplan, Reis, Prewitt, & Eakin, 1994; Ries, Kaplan, Limberg, & Prewitt, 1995; Toshima, Kaplan, & Ries, 1990). In one such study, Toshima et al. (1990) report that an 8-week exercise training intervention conducted with 119 older adults resulted in higher levels of self-efficacy for exercise and exercise tolerance compared to a comparison group. Thus, the available evidence suggests that enhancing self-efficacy may be one important means of increasing exercise levels among older adults.

Despite evidence that engaging in exercise increases levels of self-efficacy and that self-efficacy for exercise predicts exercise behavior, few studies have examined the extent to which the decline in physical activity that is commonly associated with older adulthood is related to more global decreases in perceived control. Obviously, a longitudinal design is best suited to address this issue. Similarly, we know little about how increasing physical activity levels via interventions may offset age-related declines in control.

In an ongoing study, Connell and colleagues are assessing the impact of a telephone-based physical activity intervention on psychosocial and physical outcomes among women who are providing full-time care to a spouse with a dementing illness. A primary goal of the study is to examine whether women who set and achieve realistic goals for increasing physical activity also experience a heightened sense of self-efficacy in several key domains (e.g., physical activity and self-care) and demonstrate subsequent improvement in indicators of physical and psychological health. Positive findings in this regard would suggest a potentially valuable means of enhancing control among a vulnerable older population.

Additional research is also needed to examine how the developmental context of older adulthood affects the four types of influence on efficacy expectations—*primary experience, secondary experience, verbal persuasion,* and *physiological states* (Bandura, 1986). Older adults may have less direct experience with physical activity as a function of their birth cohort; less secondary experience because there are fewer opportunities to observe exercise behavior in general and among peers; and fewer sources of verbal persuasion to exercise among the media, supportive others, and health care professionals (D. O. Clark, 1996). Physiological states may play a particularly important role in shaping efficacy expectations among older adults. Older adults are more likely than younger and middle-aged adults to experience poorer overall health; more past failures at behavior change; and—regarding physical activity—difficulty with balance, a fear of falling, and complications from comorbidities (D. O. Clark, 1996). Future research should address the specific mechanisms whereby self-efficacy affects exercise behavior and exercise affects self-efficacy among older adults; how the conceptualization and measurement of self-efficacy are shaped by the context of older adulthood; and how contextual variables such as SES, gender, and race affect self-efficacy expectations.

Self-Efficacy and Diabetes Self-Care in Older Adulthood

Although research has demonstrated that self-efficacy is a predictor of diabetes self-management among adults, older adults have not been included in much of this work. An exception is the development and evaluation of a self-management training program designed specifically for people 60 years of age

and over with Type 2 diabetes (Glasgow et al., 1992). Results indicate that the program was effective in improving dietary intake and glucose testing and resulting in weight loss among the participants in the intervention group. Contrary to expectations, however, behavior change was not attributed to increases in diabetes-specific self-efficacy. The authors contend that this surprising finding may be attributed to ceiling effects, given that levels of self-efficacy were high at baseline (Glasgow et al., 1992).

Although this study makes an important contribution to the literature because it describes one of the few published interventions designed exclusively for older adults with diabetes, the authors provide little information about how the program was tailored to the needs of the target audience, whether the process (e.g., self-efficacy) and outcome (e.g., self-care behaviors, glycosylated hemoglobin, quality of life) measures used in the study were appropriate for use with older adults, and how the developmental context of older adulthood may have affected the study findings.

To best examine changes in the relationship between self-efficacy and self-care behavior over the life span, longitudinal research is needed. A case could be made that as people age, they become more experienced at illness self-management, resulting in increasing levels of self-efficacy. Alternatively, it is equally possible that the challenges of older adulthood could erode self-efficacy for illness management. The reciprocal and dynamic nature of these relationships needs to be acknowledged and investigated in future research.

Social Development and the Health Behavior of Older Adults

Social factors are central to the maintenance of health and functioning in older adulthood. For some older adults, aging is associated with good health and fulfillment, whereas for others, aging brings chronic illness, disability, and disengagement (Riley & Bond, 1987). As stated by Riley and Bond (1987), such differences in how people age are influenced not only by biology, but also by the social environments in which they grow old—by the work they do, the people with whom they interact, and the community in which they live. Social factors also influence individuals' perceptions of health and illness and their behavioral responses (Riley & Bond, 1987).

A small body of research examines the impact of life transitions during older adulthood on health behaviors and self-care practices. Many of these life transitions have a direct effect on the quality and quantity of social support available to older adults. For example, dietary changes among older adults may be a result of the loss of a spouse rather than an age-associated change (Prohaska & Clark, 1997). In an empirical study by Rosenbloom and Whittington (1993), married older adults were compared to same-aged adults who were recently widowed. Compared to those whose spouses were still living, widows reported a loss of appetite, a high level of unintentional weight loss, and a lack of enjoyment for eating meals.

Assuming the role of caregiver for an ill spouse is another common life transition among older adults. The responsibilities of caregiving may limit opportunities to engage in positive health behaviors and may promote reliance on negative health behaviors. In an empirical study, Gallant and Connell (1997) discovered that almost half of a sample of 233 spouse caregivers reported being less physically active than they were before they began providing care to their spouse. In addition, almost half of the women in the sample reported gaining weight since caregiving began. The caregivers' attributed these negative health behaviors in part to their changing relationship with their husbands. Specifically, many study participants reported that their patterns of exercise and meal preparation had changed dramatically because they could no longer count on the positive social influence that their husband had provided (e.g., serving as an exercise buddy, having someone with whom to prepare and enjoy healthy meals). Thus, periods of life transition (e.g., widowhood, caregiving, retirement, change in residence) may be viewed as an ideal time to promote and support positive changes in health behaviors, including physical activity (King, 2001).

Social Development and Diabetes Self-Care in Older Adulthood

The social context of older adulthood also affects self-management behaviors of people with chronic illnesses. Continuing with the example of diabetes self-management, Connell, Fisher, and Houston (1992) examined the relationships among both general and diabetes-specific measures of social support and self-care in a sample of 191 older adults with Type 2 diabetes. For men, results from this study support the contention that social support specific to one's diabetes regimen increases self-care behavior. For women, neither diabetes-specific nor general support was related to self-care behavior. Men and women did not differ, however, in the amount of assistance with their diabetes regimen that they receive or desire from their family and friends (e.g., help with following a meal plan). These findings point to the complexity of the relationship between support and self-management behaviors and the importance of considering multiple conceptualizations of support, demographic, and other contextual factors (e.g., gender).

In a related study, Connell (1991) reported that a sample of older adults with diabetes perceived high levels of emotional support related to their diabetes self-care—encouragement, reassurance, and someone to listen to their problems and concerns. In terms of tangible support, however, the majority of older adults reported that they did not want a lot of help from their family and friends related to the self-management. More older adults reported receiving help than reported wanting help with their regimen. Providing support that is not desired, even when offered with good intentions, may be perceived as nagging or as interference (Connell, 1991). As suggested in other research, the characteristics of and the relationship between potential support providers and recipients may determine whether support has a beneficial impact on self-management behavior. Additional research that considers the developmental context of older adulthood is needed to deepen current understanding of the changing role of support over the life span and how it affects both health behaviors and diabetes self-care.

DIRECTIONS FOR FUTURE RESEARCH

The goal of this chapter was to adopt a life-span developmental perspective to guide a discussion of the determinants of health behaviors during five stages—infancy, childhood, adolescence, midlife, and older adulthood. Obviously, the published literature relevant to this topic is voluminous and presented quite a challenge in terms of selecting the best possible examples to illustrate the major themes of the chapter. Despite the impressive quantity and overall high quality of the available research, a great deal of additional work needs to be completed to better address how biological, cognitive, and social development influences health behavior across the life span.

The vast majority of relevant studies are based on cross-sectional designs, which present implicit difficulties when the goal is to assess change over time and the dynamic and reciprocal influences of development on health behaviors. For example, little is known about the effect of health behaviors at one life stage on health behaviors at subsequent stages—in part because of the relatively few longitudinal studies that have been conducted in this area. Additional research is also critical to increase our understanding of the developmental context of health behaviors during midlife. Although great strides have been made in recent research (e.g., Willis & Reid, 1999), much remains to be done.

Discussion of how best to adapt existing health behavior theories (e.g., health belief model, social cognitive theory,

theory of planned behavior) to better address research questions based on a life-span developmental perspective is needed. Similarly, a careful analysis of whether commonly used conceptualizations of relevant concepts (e.g., self-efficacy, personal control, social support) are appropriate for various life stages would be of great value to those conducting research in this area. Finally, in order to better account for the complexity of the determinants of health behavior and to acknowledge the broader context in which health decisions are made, there is a critical need to examine the interaction between developmental phenomena and such extrinsic factors as SES, race, culture, and gender.

REFERENCES

Ajzen, I. (1991). The theory of planned behavior. *Organizational Behavior and Human Decision Processes, 50,* 179–211.

Allison, K. R., Dwyer, J. J. M., & Makin, S. (1999). Self-efficacy and participation in vigorous physical activity by high school students. *Health Education and Behavior, 26*(1), 12–24.

Anderson, B. J., Wolf, F. M., Burkhart, M. T., Cornell, R. G., & Bacon, G. E. (1989). Effects of peer-group intervention on metabolic control of adolescents with IDDM: Randomized outpatient study. *Diabetes Care, 12*(3), 179–183.

Anderson, R. N. (1999). *National Vital Statistics Report, 47*(28). Hyattsville, MD: National Center for Health Statistics.

Antonucci, T. C., & Akiyama, H. (1997). Concern with others at midlife: Care, comfort, or compromise? In M. E. Lachman & J. B. James (Eds.), *Multiple paths of midlife development* (pp. 147–169). Chicago: University of Chicago Press.

Avis, N. E. (1999). Women's health at midlife. In S. L. Willis & J. D. Reid (Eds.), *Life in the middle: Psychological and social development in middle age* (pp. 105–137). San Diego, CA: Academic Press.

Avis, N. E., & McKinlay, S. M. (1995). The Massachusetts women's health study: An epidemiologic investigation of the menopause. *Journal of the Medical Women's Association, 50*(2), 45–49.

Baltes, P. P., & Baltes, M. M. (1990). Psychological perspectives on successful aging: The model of selective optimization with compensation. In P. B. Baltes & M. M. Baltes (Eds.), *Successful aging: Perspectives from the behavioral sciences* (pp. 1–34). New York: Cambridge University Press.

Baltes, P. B., Lindenberger, U., & Staudinger, U. M. (1998). Life-span theory in developmental psychology. In R. M. Lerner (Ed.), *Handbook of child psychology: Vol. 1. Theoretical models of human development* (5th ed., pp. 1029–1111). New York: Wiley.

Baltes, P. B., Reese, H. W., & Nesselroade, J. R. (1988). *Life-span developmental psychology: Introduction to research methods.* Mahwah, NJ: Erlbaum.

Baltes, P. B., Staudinger, U. M., & Lindenberger, U. (1999). Life-span psychology: Theory and application to intellectual functioning. *Annual Review of Psychology, 59,* 471–507.

Bandura, A. (1986). *Social foundations of thought and action: A social cognitive theory.* Englewood Cliffs, NJ: Prentice Hall.

Bandura, A. (1997). *Self-efficacy: The exercise of control.* New York: W. H. Freeman.

Bandura, A. (2001). Social cognitive theory: An agentic perspective. *Annual Review of Psychology, 52,* 1–26.

Baruch, G., & Brooks-Gunn, J. (Eds.). (1984). *Women in midlife.* New York: Plenum Press.

Bergeman, C. S., & Wallace, K. A. (1999). Resiliency in later life. In T. L. Whitman, T. L. Merluzzi, & R. D. White (Eds.), *Life-span perspectives on health and illness* (pp. 207–225). Mahwah, NJ: Erlbaum.

Berkman, L. F., & Glass, T. (2000). Social integration, social networks, and health. In L. F. Berkman & I. Kawachi (Eds.), *Social epidemiology* (pp. 137–173). New York: Oxford University Press.

Beyth-Marom, R., & Fischhoff, B. (1997). Adolescents' decisions about risks: A cognitive perspective. In J. Schulenberg, J. L. Maggs, & K. Hurrelmann (Eds.), *Health risks and developmental transitions during adolescence* (pp. 110–135). Cambridge, UK: Cambridge University Press.

Bibace, R., & Walsh, M. E. (1980). Development of children's concepts of illness. *Pediatrics, 66*(6), 912–917.

Bolig, E. E., Borkowski, J., & Brandenberger, J. (1999). Poverty and health across the life span. In T. L. Whitman, T. L. Merluzzi, & R. D. White (Eds.), *Life-span perspectives on health and illness* (pp. 67–84). Mahwah, NJ: Erlbaum.

Bound, J., Schoenbaum, M., & Waidman, T. (1996). Race differences in labor force attachment and disability status. *Gerontologist, 36*(3), 311–321.

Brambilla, D. J., & McKinlay, S. M. (1989). A prospective study of factors affecting age at menopause. *Journal of Clinical Epidemiology, 42,* 1031–1039.

Brooks-Gunn, J. (1993). Why do adolescents have difficulty adhering to health regimes? In N. A. Krasnegor, L. Epstein, S. B. Johnson, & S. J. Yaffe (Eds.), *Developmental aspects of health compliance behavior* (pp. 125–152). Hillsdale, NJ: Erlbaum.

Brooks-Gunn, J., & Kirsh, B. (1984). Life events and the boundaries of midlife for women. In G. K. Baruch & J. Brooks-Gunn (Eds.), *Women in midlife* (pp. 11–30). New York: Plenum Press.

Brown, B. B., Dolcini, M. M., & Leventhal, A. (1997). Transformations in peer relationships at adolescence: Implications for health-related behavior. In J. Schulenberg, J. L. Maggs, & K. Hurrelmann (Eds.), *Health risks and developmental transitions during adolescence* (pp. 161–189). Cambridge, UK: Cambridge University Press.

Centers for Disease Control and Prevention. (1998). *National diabetes fact sheet: National estimates and general information on diabetes in the United States* (Rev. ed.). Atlanta, GA: U.S.

Department of Health and Human Services, Centers for Disease Control and Prevention.

Clark, D. O. (1996). Age, socioeconomic status, and exercise self-efficacy. *Gerontologist, 36*(2), 157–164.

Clark, N. M., & Zimmerman, B. J. (1990). A social cognitive view of self-regulated learning about health. *Health Education Quarterly, 5*(3), 371–379.

Conn, V. S. (1997). Older women: Social cognitive theory correlates of health behavior. *Women and Health, 26*(3), 71–85.

Connell, C. M. (1991). Psychosocial contexts of diabetes and older adulthood: Reciprocal effects. *Diabetes Educator, 17*(5), 364–371.

Connell, C. M. (1999). Older adults in health education research: Some recommendations. *Health Education Research, 14*(3), 427–431.

Connell, C. M., & D'Augelli, A. R. (1988). Social support and human development: Issues in theory, research, and practice. *Journal of Community Health, 13*(2), 104–114.

Connell, C. M., Fisher, E. B., & Houston, C. A. (1992). Relationships among social support, diabetes outcomes, and morale for older men and women. *Journal of Aging and Health, 4*(1), 77–100.

Cousins, S. O. (1997). Elderly tomboys? Sources of self-efficacy for physical activity in later life. *Journal of Aging and Physical Activity, 5,* 229–243.

Cowell, J. M., & Marks, B. A. (1997). Health behavior in adolescents. In D. S. Gochman (Ed.), *Handbook of health behavior research: Vol. 3. Demography, development, and diversity* (pp. 73–96). New York: Plenum Press.

Davis, W. K., Hess, G. E., & Hiss, R. G. (1988). Psychosocial correlates of survival in diabetes. *Diabetes Care, 11*(7), 538–545.

Delamater, A. M. (1993). Compliance interventions for children with diabetes and other chronic diseases. In N. A. Krasnegor, L. Epstein, S. B. Johnson, & S. Yaffe (Eds.), *Developmental aspects of health compliance behavior* (pp. 335–354). Hillsdale, NJ: Erlbaum.

Delamater, A. M., Jacobson, A. M., Anderson, B., Cox, D., Fisher, L., Lustman, P., Rubin, R., & Wysocki, T. (2001). Psychosocial therapies in diabetes: Report of the Psychosocial Therapies Working Group. *Diabetes Care, 24*(7), 1286–1292.

The Diabetes Control and Complications Trial Research Group. (1993). The effect of intensive treatment of diabetes on the development and progression of long-term complications in insulin-dependent diabetes mellitus. *New England Journal of Medicine, 329*(14), 977–986.

DiLorenzo, T. M., Stucky-Ropp, R. C., Vander Wal, J. S., & Gotham, H. J. (1998). Determinants of exercise among children: Pt. II. A longitudinal analysis. *Preventive Medicine, 27*(3), 470–477.

Elder, G. H., Jr. (1998). The life course as developmental theory. *Child Development, 69*(1), 1–12.

Elkind, D. (1967). Egocentrism in adolescence. *Child Development, 38,* 1025–1034.

Eyler, A. A., Brownson, R. C., Donatelle, R. J., King, A. C., Brown, D., & Sallis, J. F. (1999). Physical activity social support and middle- and older-aged minority women: Results from a US survey. *Social Science and Medicine, 49*(6), 781–789.

Gallant, M. P. (in press). The influence of social support on chronic illness self-management: A review and directions for research. *Health Education and Behavior.*

Gallant, M. P., & Connell, C. M. (1997). Predictors of decreased self-care among spouse caregivers of older adults with dementing illnesses. *Journal of Aging and Health, 9*(3), 373–395.

Garcia, A. W., Pender, N. J., Antonakos, C. L., & Ronis, D. L. (1998). Changes in physical activity beliefs and behaviors of boys and girls across the transition to junior high school. *Journal of Adolescent Health, 22,* 394–402.

Geronimus, A. T. (1996). Black/White differences in the relationship of maternal age to birthweight: A population-based test of the weathering hypothesis. *Social Science and Medicine, 42*(4), 589–597.

Glasgow, R. E., & Toobert, D. J. (1988). Social environment and regimen adherence among type II diabetic patients. *Diabetes Care, 11*(5), 377–386.

Glasgow, R. E., Toobert, D. J., Hampson, S. E., Brown, J. E., Lewinsohn, P. M., & Donnelly, J. (1992). Improving self-care among older patients with Type II Diabetes: The "Sixty Something . . ." Study. *Patient Education and Counseling, 19,* 61–74.

Gondoli, D. M. (1999). Adolescent development and health. In T. L. Whitman, T. L. Merluzzi, & R. D. White (Eds.), *Life-span perspectives on health and illness* (pp. 147–164). Mahwah, NJ: Erlbaum.

Goran, M. I., Gower, B. A., Nagy, T. R., & Johnson, R. K. (1998). Developmental chances in energy expenditure and physical activity in children: Evidence for a decline in physical activity in girls before puberty. *Pediatrics, 101*(5), 887–891.

Gordon-Larsen, P., McMurray, R. G., & Popkin, B. M. (2000). Determinants of adolescent physical activity and inactivity patterns (Electronic article). *Pediatrics, 105*(6), e83–e90.

Halpern-Felsher, B., Millstein, S. G., Ellen, J. M., Adler, N. E., Tschann, J. M., & Biehl, M. (2001). The role of behavioral experience in judging risks. *Health Psychology, 20*(2), 120–126.

Hartman-Stein, P., & Reuter, J. M. (1988). Developmental issues in the treatment of diabetic women. *Psychology of Women Quarterly, 12,* 417–428.

Hazzard, W. R. (1995). Weight control and exercise: Cardinal features of successful preventive gerontology [Editorial]. *Journal of the American Medical Association, 274,* 1964–1965.

Healthy People, 2000. (1991). *National health promotion and disease prevention objectives.* (DHHS Publication No. PHS 91-51213). Washington, DC: U.S. Government Printing Office.

Heckhausen, J., & Schulz, R. (1995). A life-span theory of control. *Psychological Review, 102*(2), 284–304.

Hooker, K., & Kaus, C. R. (1994). Health-related possible selves in young and middle adulthood. *Psychology and Aging, 9*(1), 126–133.

House, J. S., Kessler, R. C., Herzog, A. R., Mero, R. P., Kinney, A. M., & Breslow, M. J. (1990). Age, socioeconomic status, and health. *Milbank Quarterly, 68*(3), 383–411.

Iannotti, R. J., & Bush, P. J. (1993). Toward a developmental theory of compliance. In N. A. Krasnegor, L. Epstein, S. B. Johnson, & S. J. Yaffe (Eds.), *Developmental aspects of health compliance behavior* (pp. 59–76). Hillsdale, NJ: Erlbaum.

Ingersoll, G. M., Orr, D. P., Herrold, A. J., & Golden, M. P. (1986). Cognitive maturity and self-management among adolescents with insulin-dependent diabetes mellitus. *Journal of Pediatrics, 108*(4), 620–623.

Janz, N. K., & Becker, M. H. (1984). The Health Belief Model: A decade later. *Health Education Quarterly, 11*(1), 1–47.

Johnson, S. B. (1993). Chronic diseases of childhood: Assessing compliance with complex medical regimens. In N. A. Krasnegor, L. Epstein, S. B. Johnson, & S. J. Yaffe (Eds.), *Developmental aspects of health compliance behavior* (pp. 157–184). Hillsdale, NJ: Erlbaum.

Jones, J. B. (1997). Representations of menopause and their health care implications: A qualitative study. *American Journal of Preventive Medicine, 13*(1), 58–65.

Jovanovic, L. (1998). Sex and the diabetic woman: Desire versus dysfunction. *Diabetes Reviews, 6,* 65–72.

Jovanovic, L. et al. (1997). Diabetes mellitus in women over the life phases and in pregnancy. In Lila Wallis (Ed.), *In textbook of women's health* (pp. 533–543). Philadelphia: Lippincott Raven.

Kahn, R. L., & Antonucci, T. C. (1980). Convoys over the life course: Attachment, roles, and social support. In P. B. Baltes & O. Brim (Eds.), *Life-span development and behavior* (Vol. 3, pp. 253–286). New York: Academic Press.

Kaplan, R., Reis, A., Prewitt, L., & Eakin, E. (1994). Self-efficacy expectations predict survival for patients with chronic obstructive pulmonary disease. *Health Psychology, 13,* 366–368.

Kimiecik, J. C., Horn, T. S., & Shurin, C. S. (1996). Relationships among children's beliefs, perceptions of their parents' beliefs, and their moderate-to-vigorous physical activity. *Research Quarterly for Exercise and Sport, 67*(3), 324–336.

King, A. C. (2001). Interventions to promote physical activity by older adults. *Journal of Gerontology, 56A*(Special Issue II), 36–46.

Kolberg, K. J. S. (1999). Biological development and health risk. In T. L. Whitman, T. L. Merluzzi, & R. D. White (Eds.), *Life-span perspectives on health and illness* (pp. 23–45). Mahwah, NJ: Erlbaum.

Kovacs, M., Goldston, D., Obrosky, D. S., & Iyengar, S. (1992). Prevalence and predictors of pervasive noncompliance with medical treatment among youths with insulin-dependent diabetes. *Journal of the American Academy of Child and Adolescent Psychiatry, 31*(6), 1112–1119.

Kreipe, R. E., & Strauss, J. (1989). Adolescent medical disorders, behavior, and development. In G. R. Adams, R. Montemayor, & T. P. Gullotta (Eds.), *Biology of adolescent behavior and development* (pp. 98–140). Newbury Park, CA: Sage.

La Greca, A. M., Auslander, W. F., Greco, P., Spetter, D., Fisher, E. B., & Santiago, J. V. (1995). I get by with a little help from my family and friends: Adolescents' support for diabetes care. *Journal of Pediatric Psychology, 20*(4), 449–476.

Lachman, M. E., & James, J. B. (1997). Charting the course of midlife development: An overview. In M. E. Lachman & J. B. James (Eds.), *Multiple paths of midlife development* (pp. 1–17). Chicago: University of Chicago Press.

Lachman, M. E., Lewkowicz, C., Marcus, A., & Peng, Y. (1994). Images of midlife development among young, middle-aged, and elderly adults. *Journal of Adult Development, 1,* 201–211.

Lachman, M. E., Ziff, M. A., & Spiro, R. (1994). Maintaining a sense of control in later life. In R. P. Abeles, H. C. Gift, & M. G. Ory (Eds.), *Aging and quality of life* (pp. 216–232). New York: Springer.

Lapsley, D. K. (1993). Toward an integrated theory of adolescent ego development: The "new look" at adolescent egocentrism. *American Journal of Orthopsychiatry, 63*(4), 562–571.

Lau, R. R., Quadrel, M. J., & Hartman, K. A. (1990). Development and change of young adults' preventive health beliefs and behavior: Influence from parents and peers. *Journal of Health and Social Behavior, 31,* 240–259.

Lerner, R. M., Ostrom, C. W., & Freel, M. A. (1999). Preventing health-compromising behaviors among youth and promoting their positive development: A developmental contextual perspective. In J. Schulenberg, J. L. Maggs, & K. Hurrelmann (Eds.), *Health risks and developmental transitions during adolescence* (pp. 498–521). Cambridge, UK: Cambridge University Press.

Levinson, D. J. (1977). The mid-life transition: A period in adult psychosocial development. *Psychiatry, 40*(2), 99–112.

Lewis, M. A., & Rook, K. S. (1999). Social control in personal relationships: Impact on health behaviors and psychological distress. *Health Psychology, 18*(1), 63–71.

Lindenberger, U., & Baltes, P. B. (1997). Intellectual functioning in old and very old age: Cross-sectional results from the Berlin Aging Study. *Psychology and Aging, 12*(3), 410–432.

Lindquist, C. H., Reynolds, K. D., & Goran, M. I. (1999). Sociocultural determinants of physical activity among children. *Preventive Medicine, 29*(4), 305–312.

Maggs, J. L., Schulenberg, J., & Hurrelmann, K. (1997). Developmental transitions during adolescence: Health promotion opportunities. In J. Schulenberg, J. L. Maggs, & K. Hurrelmann (Eds.), *Health risks and developmental transitions during adolescence* (pp. 522–546). Cambridge, UK: Cambridge University Press.

Markides, K. S. (1989). *Aging and health: Perspectives on gender, race, ethnicity, and class.* Newbury Park, CA: Sage.

McAdoo, H. P. (1995). Stress levels, family help patterns, and religiosity in middle- and working-class African American single mothers. *Journal of Black Psychology, 21*(4), 424–449.

McAuley, E. (1992). The role of efficacy cognitions in the prediction of exercise behavior in middle-aged adults. *Journal of Behavioral Medicine, 15*(1), 65–88.

McAuley, E., & Katula, J. (1999). Physical activity interventions in the elderly: Influence on physical health and psychological function. In R. Schulz, G. Maddox, & M. P. Lawton (Volume Eds.), *Annual review of gerontology and geriatrics* (Vol. 18, pp. 111–153). New York: Springer.

McAuley, E., Lox, C., & Duncan, T. E. (1993). Long-term maintenance of exercise, self-efficacy, and physiological change in older adults. *Journal of Gerontology: Psychological Sciences, 48*(4), 218–224.

Merrill, S. S., & Verbrugge, L. M. (1999). Health and disease in midlife. In S. L. Willis & J. D. Reid (Eds.), *Life in the middle: Psychological and social development in middle age* (pp. 77–103). San Diego, CA: Academic Press.

Merluzzi, T. V., & Nairn, R. C. (1999). Adulthood and aging: Transitions in health and health cognition. In T. L. Whitman, T. L. Merluzzi, & R. D. White (Eds.), *Life-span perspectives on health and illness* (pp. 189–206). Mahwah, NJ: Erlbaum.

Miceli, P. J., Rowland, J. F., & Whitman, T. L. (1999). Chronic illnesses in childhood. In T. L. Whitman, T. L. Merluzzi, & R. D. White (Eds.), *Life-span perspectives on health and illness* (pp. 165–186). Mahwah, NJ: Erlbaum.

Millstein, S. G., Irwin, C. E., Adler, N. E., Cohn, L. D., Kegeles, S. M., & Dolcini, M. M. (1992). Health risk behaviors and health concerns among young adolescents. *Pediatrics, 89,* 422–428.

Mirowsky, J. (1995). Age and the sense of control. *Social Psychology Quarterly, 58,* 31–43.

Moen, P., & Wethington, E. (1999). Midlife development in a life course context. In S. L. Willis & J. D. Reid (Eds.), *Life in the middle: Psychological and social development in middle age* (pp. 3–23). San Diego, CA: Academic Press.

Montano, D. E., Kasprzyk, D., & Taplin, S. H. (1997). The theory of reasoned action and the theory of planned behavior. In K. Glanz, F. M. Lewis, & B. K. Rimer (Eds.), *Health behavior and health education: Theory, research and practice* (2nd ed., pp. 85–112). San Francisco: Jossey-Bass.

Moody, H. R. (1998). *Aging: Concepts and controversies* (2nd ed.). Thousand Oaks, CA: Pine Forge Press.

Murphy, R., & Bennett, P. (1994). Psychological perspectives on young adults' health behavior: Implications for health promotion. In G. N. Penny, P. Bennett, & M. Herbert (Eds.), *Health psychology: A lifespan perspective*. Philadelphia: Harwood.

National Center for Chronic Disease Prevention and Health Promotion, Centers for Disease Control and Prevention. (1997). Guidelines for school and community programs to promote lifelong physical activity among young people. *Journal of School Health, 67*(6), 202–219.

O'Brien, R. W., & Bush, P. J. (1997). Health behavior in children. In D. S. Gochman (Ed.), *Handbook of health behavior research: Vol. 3. Demography, development, and diversity* (pp. 49–71). New York: Plenum Press.

O'Leary, A. (1985). Self-efficacy and health. *Behaviour Research and Therapy, 23*(4), 437–451.

Patterson, J. M. (1988). Chronic illness in children and the impact on families. In C. S. Chilman, E. W. Nunnally, & F. M. Cox (Eds.), *Chronic illness and disability* (Vol. 2, pp. 69–107). Thousand Oaks, CA: Sage.

Penny, G. N., Bennett, P., & Herbert, M. (1994). Health psychology: A lifespan perspective, an introduction. In G. N. Penny, P. Bennett, & M. Herbert (Eds.), *Health psychology: A lifespan perspective* (pp. 1–9). Langhorne, PA: Harwood.

Petersen, A. C. (1988). Adolescent development. *Annual Review of Psychology, 39,* 583–607.

Peterson, L. (1996). Establishing the study of development as a dynamic force in health psychology. *Health Psychology, 15*(3), 155–157.

Pinto, B. M., Marcus, B. H., & Clark, M. M. (1996). Promoting physical activity in women: The new challenges. *American Journal of Preventive Medicine, 12*(5), 395–400.

Poirier, L. M., & Coburn, K. M. (2000). *Women and diabetes: Staying healthy in body, mind, and spirit* (2nd ed.). Alexandria, VA: American Diabetes Association.

Prohaska, T. R., & Clark, M. A. (1997). Health behavior and the human life cycle. In D. S. Gochman (Ed.), *Handbook of health behavior research: Vol. 3. Demography, development, and diversity* (pp. 29–48). New York: Plenum Press.

Resnick, B. (2001). Testing a model of exercise behavior in older adults. *Reasearch in Nursing and Health, 24,* 83–92.

Ries, A. L., Kaplan, R. M., Limberg, T. M., & Prewitt, L. M. (1995). Effects of pulmonary rehabilitation on physiologic and psychosocial outcomes in patients with chronic obstructive pulmonary disease. *Annals of Internal Medicine, 122*(11), 823–832.

Riley, M. W., & Bond, K. (1987). Foreword. In R. A. Ward & S. S. Tobin (Eds.), *Health in aging: Sociological issues and policy directions* (pp. vii–ix). New York: Springer.

Roberts, M. C., Maddux, J. E., & Wright, L. (1984). Developmental perspectives in behavioral health. In J. D. Matarazzo, S. M. Weiss, J. A. Herd, N. E. Miller, & S. M. Weiss (Eds.), *Behavioral health* (pp. 56–68). New York: Wiley.

Rodin, J. (1986). Aging and health: Effects of the sense of control. *Science, 233,* 1271–1276.

Rosenbloom, C. A., & Whittington, F. J. (1993). The effects of bereavement on eating behaviors and nutrient intakes in elderly widowed persons. *Journal of Gerontology, 48*(4), S223–S229.

Russell, N. K., & Roter, D. L. (1993). Health promotion counseling of chronic-disease patients during primary care visits. *American Journal of Public Health, 83*(7), 979–982.

Savinetti-Rose, B. (1994). Developmental issues in managing children with diabetes. *Pediatric Nursing, 20*(1), 11–15.

Scharff, D. P., Homan, S., Kreuter, M., & Brennan, L. (1999). Factors associated with physical activity in women across the life span: Implications for program development. *Women Health, 29*(2), 115–134.

Schulenberg, J., Maggs, J. L., & Hurrelmann, K. (1997a). *Health risks and developmental transitions during adolescence.* Cambridge, UK: Cambridge University Press.

Schulenberg, J., Maggs, J. L., & Hurrelmann, K. (1997b). Negotiating developmental transitions during adolescence and young adulthood: Health risks and opportunities. In J. Schulenberg, J. L. Maggs, & K. Hurrelmann (Eds.), *Health risks and developmental transitions during adolescence* (pp. 1–19). Cambridge, UK: Cambridge University Press.

Schulenberg, J., Maggs, J. L., Steinman, K., & Zucker, R. A. (2001). Development matters: Taking the long view on substance abuse etiology and intervention during adolescence. In P. M. Monti, S. M. Colby, & T. A. O'Leary (Eds.), *Adolescents, alcohol, and substance abuse: Reaching teens through brief intervention* (pp. 19–57). New York: Guilford Press.

Schulz, R., & Heckhausen, J. (1996). A life span model of successful aging. *American Psychologist, 51*(7), 702–714.

Schulz, R., & Martire, L. A. (1999). Intervention research with older adults: Introduction, overview, and future directions. In R. Schulz, G. Maddox, & M. P. Lawton (Eds.), *Annual Review of Gerontology and Geriatrics* (Vol. 18, pp. 1–16). New York: Springer.

Schulz, R., & Rau, M. T. (1985). Social support through the life course. In S. Cohen & S. L. Syme (Eds.), *Social support and health* (pp. 129–149). New York: Academic Press.

Silbereisen, R. K., & Kracke, B. (1999). Self-reported maturational timing and adaptation in adolescence. In T. L. Whitman, T. L. Merluzzi, & R. D. White (Eds.), *Life-span perspectives on health and illness* (pp. 85–109). Mahwah, NJ: Erlbaum.

Singh, M. A. F. (2000). Exercise and aging. In M. A. F. Singh (Ed.), *Exercise, nutrition, and the older woman: Wellness for women over fifty* (pp. 3–36). New York: CRC Press.

Standiford, D. A., Turner, A. M., Allen, S. R., Drozda, D. J., & McCain, G. C. (1997). Personal illness models of diabetes: Preadolescents and adolescents. *Diabetes Educator, 23*(2), 147–151.

Sturges, J. W., & Rogers, R. W. (1996). Preventive psychology from a developmental perspective: An extension of protection motivation theory. *Health Psychology, 15*(3), 158–166.

Telama, R., Yang, X., Laakso, L., & Viikari, J. (1997). Physical activity in childhood and adolescence as predictor of physical activity in young adulthood. *American Journal of Preventive Medicine, 13*(4), 317–323.

Thompson, R. J., & Gustafson, K. E. (1996). *Adaptation to chronic childhood illness.* Washington, DC: American Psychological Association.

Thornberry, R., Wilson, W., & Golden, P. (1986). Health promotion and disease prevention: Provisional data from the National Health Interview Survey: United States, Jan.-June 1985. In *Advance data from vital and health statistics* (DHHS Publication No. PHS 86-1250). Hyattsville, MD: National Center for Health Statistics.

Tinsley, B. J. (1992). Multiple influences on the acquisition and socialization of children's health attitudes and behavior: An integrative review. *Child Development, 63,* 1043–1069.

Tinsley, B. J., Holtgrave, D. R., Reise, S. P., Erdley, C., & Cupp, R. G. (1995). Developmental status, gender, age, and self-reported decision-making influences on students' risky and preventive health behaviors. *Health Education Quarterly, 22*(2), 244–259.

Toshima, M. T., Kaplan, R. M., & Ries, A. L. (1990). Experimental evaluation of rehabilitation in chronic obstructive pulmonary disease: Short-term effects on exercise endurance and health status. *Health Psychology, 9*(3), 237–252.

Wallston, K. A., & Smith, M. S. (1994). Issues of control and health: The action is in the interaction. In G. N. Penny, P. Bennett, & M. Herbert (Eds.), *Health psychology: A lifespan perspective* (pp. 153–168). Langhorne, PA: Harwood.

Watkins, K. W., Connell, C. M., Fitzgerald, J. T., Klem, L., Hickey, T., & Ingersoll-Dayton, B. (2000). Effect of adults' self-regulation of diabetes on quality-of-life outcomes. *Diabetes Care, 23*(10), 1511–1515.

Whitman, T. L. (1999). Conceptual frameworks for viewing health and illness. In T. L. Whitman, T. L. Merluzzi, & R. D. White (Eds.), *Life-span perspectives on health and illness* (pp. 3–21). Mahwah, NJ: Erlbaum.

Whitman, T. L., White, R. D., O'Mara, K. M., & Goeke-Morey, M. C. (1999). Environmental aspects of infant health and illness. In T. L. Whitman, T. L. Merluzzi, & R. D. White (Eds.), *Life-span perspectives on health and illness* (pp. 105–124). Mahwah, NJ: Erlbaum.

Willis, S. L., & Reid, J. D. (1999). *Life in the middle : Psychological and social development in middle age.* San Diego, CA: Academic Press.

Wilson, W., Ary, D. V., Biglan, A., Glasgow, R. E., Toobert, D. J., & Campbell, D. R. (1986). Psychosocial predictors of self-care behaviors (compliance) and glycemic control in non-insulin-dependent diabetes mellitus. *Diabetes Care, 9*(6), 614–622.

Woods, N. F., & Mitchell, E. S. (1997). Women's images of midlife: Observations from the Seattle midlife women's health study. *Health Care for Women International, 18,* 439–453.

Wysocki, T., Meinhold, P., Cox, D. J., & Clarke, W. L. (1990). Survey of diabetes professionals regarding developmental changes in diabetes self-care. *Diabetes Care, 13*(1), 65–68.

Wysocki, T., Taylor, A., Hough, B. S., Linscheid, T. R., Yeates, K. O., & Naglieri, J. A. (1996). Deviation from developmentally appropriate self-care autonomy. Association with diabetes outcomes. *Diabetes Care, 19*(2), 119–125.

CHAPTER 25

Successful Aging

ALEXANDRA M. FREUND AND MICHAELA RIEDIGER

What is successful aging? At first glance, this seems like an easy enough question. After all, don't all humans want to be happy, healthy, wealthy, and beloved well into old age? However, considering that older people are very likely to face health-related problems, maybe *healthy* should be skipped from the list. Similarly, when people advance into very old age, the loss of their spouse or partner and of close friends is the norm rather than the exception. Considering this, *beloved* might take on a meaning in old age that is different from that in younger age groups. Finally, happiness seems such an elusive state that we might not want to make this the criterion for successful aging. Maybe it is not so easy to answer the question of what successful aging is after all.

In this chapter, we approach the concept of successful aging from three different perspectives:

1. We first focus on the context of old age. What are the external and internal changes that distinguish old age from younger age groups? What are the characteristics that might render old age a time in life that is feared rather than hoped for? Why is it (as the saying goes) that everybody wants to *get* old but nobody wants to actually *be* old?

2. We then address the issue of how to define *successful aging*. The term *success* implies some sort of normative judgement on desirable and undesirable end states. This

raises two questions: What can be considered as a meaningful end state of development? And which criteria should be employed to evaluate the desirability of those end states? We review the state of research on these questions and existing attempts to define successful aging in the second part of this chapter.

3. In the final part of this chapter, we discuss some of the current models of developmental regulation in old and very old age. These models shift the focus from a criteria-oriented approach addressing the question *What is successful aging?* to a more process-oriented approach addressing the question *How do people age successfully?* These models underscore that motivational processes of setting, pursuing, and maintaining personal goals are of central importance for understanding how individuals manage to age well.

CHARACTERISTICS OF OLD AGE

When is a person considered to be old? *Old age,* the final phase in life, is commonly thought to begin somewhere between the ages of 60 and 70. An often cited (somewhat arbitrary) threshold is the age of 65. For employees, retirement represents a cultural marker of entering old age. Many people in their 60s, however, appear still young, whereas others have apparently been old for quite some time. Chronological age does not tell much about a person's *biological* (e.g., functional capacity), *psychological* (e.g., feelings, attitudes, interests, future perspectives), or *social* age (e.g., life activities, occupied roles; see Aiken, 1989).

Even within a given person, aging is no uniform process. Different organs, organ systems, and capacities in various functional and psychological domains show differential patterns and rates of aging (P. B. Baltes, 1989). For example, the reproductive system usually ages more rapidly than the nervous system. Furthermore, other variables—such as poor nutrition, illness, or disuse of abilities—affect the rate and degree of aging-related decline (e.g., Aiken, 1989; Krauss Whitbourne, 1985).

In other words, old age—like any other phase in life—is characterized by tremendous inter- and intraindividual variability. In the subsequent sections we delineate some developments that represent *general* characteristics of old age. Aging is a very complex process, and it is beyond the scope of this chapter to attempt a comprehensive characterization of that life phase (for a recent overview, see P. B. Baltes, Staudinger, & Lindenberger, 1999). After characterizing aging as a young phenomenon, so to speak, we restrict our discussion to four domains of functioning in which age-related changes are partly considered losses threatening positive functioning in old age: (a) physiological and health-related changes, (b) cognitive abilities, (c) social relationships, and (d) everyday competence.

Old Age Is Still Young

Until relatively recently in human history, only a small proportion of people survived long enough to become old in today's sense (see Vaupel, 1995): Throughout human history up to about the beginning of the nineteenth century, life expectancy at birth (i.e., the average life span of persons born in a given year) was low for most populations—namely, only between 20 and 30 years. This was largely so because a large proportion of newborns (about one third to one half) died before reaching the age of 5 years. Even for children surviving to age 5, the expected remaining lifetime was only 30–40 years. Only a small minority of people survived diseases, wars, and other life-threatening dangers to become 50. Even for them, the remaining life expectancy was only about 10–15 years.

During the 19th century, life expectancy slowly began to increase. In Finland, for example, where reliable statistics on mortality going back to that time are available (Kannisto, Turpeinen, & Nieminen, 1999), life expectancy at birth increased from 30.4 years for men and 33.2 years for women born between 1801 and 1810 to 45.3 years for men and 48.2 years for women born 100 years later (i.e., between 1901 and 1910). Because of technological advances coupled with improvements in nutrition, sanitation, public health care, and so on, this increase in life expectancy further accelerated during the twentieth century. Men and women born in Finland between 1946 and 1950, for example, had a life expectancy of 58.4 years and 65.8 years, respectively. Estimated life expectancy for children born in Finland another 50 years later (between 1991 and 1995) further increased to 72.1 years (male) and 79.7 (female).

Prior to 1950, the increase in life expectancy largely resulted from reductions in death rates at younger ages—particularly reductions in infant mortality (i.e., from the fact that more people survived to older ages; Vaupel, 1995). The continuing growth of life expectancy since 1950, in contrast, is attributable to the fact that older people live longer. In most modern industrialized countries, death rates above the age of 60 have substantially declined since 1950. This decline has even accelerated—especially since 1970. For example, in modern industrialized countries in 1990, there were about twice as many people in their 90s and four to five times as many centenarians as there would have been if mortality rates after age 80 had stayed the same as in 1960 (Vaupel et al., 1998). To date, the lengthening of the human life span is no longer restricted to modern industrialized countries. More recently, developing countries have started to show similar increases in life expectancy (Meeks, Nickols, & Sweaney, 1999; World Health Organization, 1998). It has been estimated that by the year 2025, 72% of the world's population aged 60 years and above will be living in developing countries (United Nations, 1996).

In most (particularly in industrialized) countries, the increase in life expectancy has been co-occurring with a decline in fertility rates (i.e., a decrease in the average number of children per woman in childbearing age). Both trends together (i.e., declining mortality *and* fertility rates) have drastically altered the population's composition—with the growth of the older population outpacing the total population's growth. This trend is expected to continue in the future, with the fastest expanding group being the oldest old (Dinkel, 1994). Prognoses of the World Health Organization (1998), for example, predict that in Europe's population, the proportion of people older than 60 will increase from about 20% at the end of the twentieth century to about 25% by the year 2020. Estimates indicate that by 2020, the proportion of people older than 80 years in the age group above 60 will make up 22% in Greece and Italy; 21% in Japan, France, and Spain; and 20% in Germany (World Health Organization, 1998).

This lengthening of the average human life might be viewed by many as one of the most precious achievements in recent human history. It does, however, also pose new challenges to cultural and societal developments. Societies need to develop policies that ensure—despite declining proportions of working-age people—adequate income, housing, health care, and other living conditions that provide opportunities for an independent, integrated life for the growing number of older people (United Nations, 1996). To meet this challenge, gerontology needs to seek knowledge about conditions promoting positive aging and to give answers to such questions as what represents adequate housing for the elderly and how to support independent living in old age. This is one of the reasons that the topic of successful aging is not only of scientific but also of social and political importance.

Paradoxically, in one sense old age is a young phenomenon. To date, not much is known about this life phase in general or about processes and conditions that promote successful aging in particular. As a first step in approaching the topic of successful aging, we briefly outline the specific conditions of old age. We start by giving a very short overview of the physiological and health-related changes in old age.

Physiological and Health-Related Changes in Old Age

Aging is characterized by physiological changes that lead to progressive structural and functional decrements in all tissues and organs (for overviews, see Aiken, 1989; Whitbourne, 1985; Medina, 1996). Most obvious to the lay observer are typical changes in appearance—for example, aging skin; graying or whitening hair; changes in body shape and stature; decreased muscular strength and endurance; increased stiffness in the joints; and a general slowing, increased sway, and insecurity while walking or performing motor tasks. Aging is also accompanied by impairments in the functioning of all the sense organs—vision, hearing, taste, smell, vestibular senses (necessary for the maintenance of posture and balance), and sensitivity to touch, pain, and temperature (i.e., cutaneous senses). Sensations become increasingly dull, and responses to sensory stimuli slow down with age. Physiological aging is also characterized by a gradual deterioration of internal organs, leading to a reduced efficiency of the body's vital systems. Age-associated changes in the various systems generally interact. Cardiovascular functions, for example, are influenced by age-associated changes in respiratory function, which in turn are influenced by changes in the musculoskeletal system (Steinhagen-Thiessen, Gerok, & Borchelt, 1994).

Overall, the physiological changes accompanying aging result in reduced functional capacity, impaired biological resilience in the face of stress, lessened ability to physiologically adapt to environmental changes, prolonged phases necessary to physically recuperate from strenuous effort, and—most important—increased susceptibility to acute and chronic diseases (Aiken, 1989; Steinhagen-Thiessen et al., 1994). It is therefore not always possible to clearly delineate normal *physiological* aging and *pathological* changes.

Although age-associated physiological changes are inevitable, they represent no uniform biological process. The kind and magnitude of age-related changes vary greatly from individual to individual. Furthermore, physiological changes interact, for example, with psychological, social, environmental, and lifestyle factors to determine the course and rapidity of aging (Fries, 1990; Rowe & Kahn, 1987; Siegler & Costa, 1985). For example, attitudes and personality characteristics may influence the degree to which an old person seeks intellectual stimulation or engages in physical or social activities, which in turn decelerate and attenuate decline in relevant functional domains. On the other hand, reduced mobility due to physiological impairment might obstruct such activities, precipitating further decline (Bortz, 1982). In this sense, physiological decline associated with aging is not entirely uncontrollable. Particularly lifestyle habits, such as regular exercise, balanced nutrition, and social and intellectual stimulation through active participation might at least temporarily postpone or attenuate physiological decrements associated with aging (Fries, 1990).

In short, physiological changes accompanying aging result in a reduction of the organism's functional capacity and an increased vulnerability to chronic and acute illnesses. These detrimental effects of physiological aging become particularly pronounced in very old age (85 years and beyond). Although it is unavoidable, physiological aging is no uniform progress. It is in part determined by lifestyle factors and thus—particularly in young-old age—temporarily and within boundaries modifiable.

Cognitive Abilities in Old Age

A popular view on aging is that cognitive abilities drastically decline with age (e.g., Heckhausen, Dixon, & Baltes, 1989). Old people are expected to become more and more forgetful, to have large difficulties understanding new things, and to not think as clearly as younger persons. On the other hand, wisdom, life experience, or professional expertise in their commonsensical understanding are clearly positively associated with old age (Clayton & Birren, 1980; Sternberg, 1990). What has science revealed about cognitive aging?

Building on the recognition that cognitive functioning is influenced by biological as well as cultural processes, research has distinguished two main categories of intellectual abilities—the mechanics and pragmatics of cognition (P. B. Baltes, 1987; P. B. Baltes, Lindenberger, & Staudinger, 1998; P. B. Baltes et al., 1999). This distinction draws on and extends earlier conceptualizations, such as the theory of fluid and crystallized intelligence by Cattell and Horn (Cattell, 1971; Horn, 1982). The *mechanics* of cognition stand as metaphor for the largely neurophysiological basis of cognition as it evolved during biological evolution. They represent the hardware of the mind, so to speak, and become evident in the speed, accuracy, and coordination of basic information-processing operations. The *pragmatics* of cognition, in contrast, comprise the culturally transmitted bodies of knowledge individuals acquire in the course of their socialization. They stand for the software of the mind. Typical examples of pragmatic abilities include reading, writing, language, or professional skills. Delineating mechanics and pragmatics of cognitive functioning does not imply that these represent abilities independent of or exclusive from each other. Rather, mechanics and pragmatics are assumed to determine intellectual functioning in their *interaction:* There would not be pragmatics without mechanics and vice versa—mechanics without pragmatics would lack the very medium in which to unfold.

How do these two components of intellectual functioning develop across the life span into old age? Empirical evidence shows that the cognitive *mechanics* (e.g., memory, processing speed) show a pattern of rapid growth during infancy and childhood into adolescence, a monotonic and roughly linear decline during adulthood, and a further acceleration of decline in very old age (e.g., Case, 1985; Kail, 1991; Kail & Salthouse, 1994; Lindenberger & Reischies, 1999; Schaie, 1994, 1996).

This trajectory of loss in the cognitive mechanics can be counteracted to some degree by specific training. Training studies have shown that the majority of healthy older adults are able to improve their performance in tasks reflecting mechanic abilities during training (e.g., P. B. Baltes, Sowarka, & Kliegl, 1989; P. B. Baltes & Willis, 1982; Hayslip, 1989; Kliegl, Smith, & Baltes, 1990; Schaie & Willis, 1986; Verhaegen, Marcoen, & Goossens, 1992). Those training gains, however, are highly task-specific. Transfer to related abilities or generalization to everyday functioning is unlikely (P. B. Baltes, Dittmann-Kohli, & Kliegl, 1986; P. B. Baltes & Lindenberger, 1988). Moreover, the amount of plasticity (i.e., the range of potential change) in the cognitive mechanics clearly decreases with age (e.g., P. B. Baltes & Kliegl, 1992; Singer, 2000).

Pragmatic abilities show a more favorable life-span trajectory than the mechanics do. They remain stable or increase well into young old age (i.e., up to about 75 years of age), and

only after that show some decline, which is much less pronounced than the decline in the cognitive mechanics (e.g., skill-specific expertise: Bosman & Charness, 1996; Charness, 1981a, 1983; Knopf, Kolodziej, & Preussler, 1990; wisdom: P. B. Baltes, Staudinger, Maercker, & Smith, 1995; Clayton & Birren, 1980; Staudinger, 1996; complexity and differentiation of self-representation: Labouvie-Vief, Chiodo, Goguen, Diehl, & Orwoll, 1995).

As mentioned before, mechanics and pragmatics *conjointly* influence cognitive performance in all age groups. Particularly important for understanding the development of cognitive abilities in *old* age are two observations:

- Up to a certain threshold in impairment of the cognitive mechanics, pragmatic knowledge can be efficiently utilized to *compensate* for age-based losses in mechanics. Evidence for this has been provided by quasi-experimental studies on age- and skill-related differences in chess (e.g., Charness, 1981a, 1981b), bridge (e.g., Charness, 1983, 1987), and transcription typing (e.g., Bosman, 1993; Salthouse, 1984; Salthouse & Saults, 1987). A classic illustration is a study on aging typists (Salthouse, 1984); in this study, age was negatively related to typing speed but positively related to eye-hand span. Older typists might have compensated the slowing of their typing (as an expression of cognitive mechanics) by looking further ahead in the to-be-typed text (i.e., a strategy pertaining to knowledge-based pragmatics). The idea that the knowledge-based pragmatics efficiently compensate mechanic decline in older adulthood is further supported by the finding that compared to standard psychometric assessments using artificial and isolated cognitive tasks, negative age trajectories tend to be attenuated in familiar (i.e., knowledge-relevant) domains with everyday relevance, such as everyday problem solving (e.g., Berg & Klaszynski, 1996; Willis, 1996) or memory in context (e.g., Hess & Pullen, 1996).

- If, however, the mechanic information-processing capabilities fall *below* some critical threshold, they delimit the overall capability of cognitive integrity and consequently also impair intellectual functioning in the pragmatic domain (P. B. Baltes, 1997). Individuals reaching a very advanced age are therefore particularly vulnerable to reach such levels of impairment in mechanic abilities that intellectual functioning in a more global manner is substantially impaired. Indeed, correlations among abilities both between and within the cognitive pragmatics and mechanics are higher in very old adults than in younger or middle-aged adults (for an overview, see Li & Lindenberger, 1999). This dedifferentiation in very old age appears to transcend the cognitive domain and to also affect sensory and sensorimotor functioning (e.g., Anstey, Lord, & Williams, 1997; Lindenberger & Reischies, 1999; Salthouse, Hancock, Meinz, & Hambrick, 1996). These findings point to the impact of domain-general processing constraints in very old age, which is further illustrated by the empirical observation that in very old age, the differences in the directionality of the development of pragmatic and mechanic abilities seem to disappear and to give way to negative age-gradients in *both* domains (Lindenberger & Reischies, 1999).

In sum, there is evidence for age-related decline in the biologically based cognitive mechanics. At least up to a certain point, this development can be compensated by culturally determined, knowledge-based cognitive pragmatics. Most older adults are cognitively well able to manage everyday life problems. In very advanced old age, however, a somewhat different picture emerges. Here, the cognitive mechanics might reach a level of impairment that the efficiency of intellectual functioning declines in a more global manner. This development is also reflected if we take a look at *pathological* cognitive changes in old age. The prevalence of dementias increases steeply with age. Several studies have observed that in adults above the age of 60, age-specific prevalence rates of dementias almost double with each additional 5 years of age, leading to prevalence estimates of more than 40% in the population aged 90 years and beyond (e.g., Cooper, 1997; Hofman et al., 1991; Jorm, Korten, & Henderson, 1987).

Social Relationships in Old Age

Kahn and Antonucci (Antonucci, 1985, 1990, 1991; Kahn & Antonucci, 1980) coined the metaphor of *social convoys* to express the idea that throughout their lives, people are surrounded by significant other persons who have a critical influence on their lives. Social integration has been shown to have a significant beneficial impact upon a person's well-being (e.g., Antonucci & Akiyama, 1995; Bowling, 1994; Brubaker, 1990; Kessler & McLeod, 1985), health (e.g., Antonucci & Jackson, 1987; Lang & Carstensen, 1998; Schwarzer & Leppin, 1991), and even mortality (e.g., Seeman, 1996; Tucker, Schwartz, Clark, & Friedman, 1999). Social contact, however, may also have its negative sides. Such experiences include undesirable, ineffective, or excessive support; unpleasant or overly demanding social contact; violence or neglect; and anticipated or experienced loss of social partners (Lang & Carstensen, 1998; Smith & Goodnow, 1999).

As people grow older, their relationships and social networks undergo considerable change not only as a result of changing contexts (e.g., retirement, one's own or others' disease and frailty, grandparenthood, relocation, deaths of significant others) but also as a result of changes in the individual's behaviors and preferences (Lang & Carstensen, 1998). In any event, interpersonal contexts in old age remain multifaceted and heterogeneous. Social networks of older people who are widowed, have never married, or are childless, for example, differ in many respects from those who are living with their partner or are highly involved in the families of their children.

Typically, the number of social contacts declines with advancing age (e.g., Heller & Mansbach, 1984; Lang & Carstensen, 1994; Palmore, 1981). Investigations in the United States and Europe indicate that older people above age 65 typically report having between 5 and 15 close social partners in their social networks compared to a range from 15 to 35 network members in the social networks reported by younger and middle-aged adults (e.g., Antonucci & Akiyama, 1994, 1995; Dykstra, 1993; Lang & Carstensen, 1994, 1998; van Sonderen, Ormel, Brilman, & van Linden van den Heuvell, 1990). As we elaborate when discussing socioemotional selectivity theory later in this chapter, it is questionable whether this decline indeed constitutes a developmental loss as it might appear at first glance (Carstensen, 1993).

Functions of social relationships can be characterized by three main themes—support, affectionate exchanges, and socializing (i.e., interacting with visitors and engaging in shared activities; e.g., Antonucci & Akiyama, 1995; Wagner, Schütze, & Lang, 1999). Generally, the proportion of network partners from whom emotional or instrumental help is *received* increases with age because of aging-related increases in frailty (e.g., Mares, 1995; Zarit & Eggebeen, 1995). Old and even very old persons, however, typically also *give* support, but not to the same degree (e.g., Antonucci, 1991; Zarit & Eggebeen, 1995). Although social support relationships gain in significance with advancing age, socializing and affect exchange remain important functions of social contact. In a sample of German older persons, for example, the number of people with whom participants socialized and with whom they were affectionate decreased into very old age; yet the proportions within the network (around 30% and 20% of the social partners, respectively) did not (Wagner et al., 1999).

Historical increases in life expectancy have led to an increase in the length of marital relationships among those who do not divorce. These demographic developments have also increased the average duration that is spent in illness or caregiving before the relationship is eventually ended by the death of one partner. Because women at any given age have a longer life expectancy than men have and also tend to marry men who are somewhat older, they are more likely to be caretakers of ailing husbands, are more likely to survive husbands than to be survived, and tend to spend a larger proportion of their life spans following the death of a spouse (Bradsher, 1997).

The death of one's partner is undoubtedly one of the most disruptive losses that an individual can be confronted with in life. In addition to the immense grief over the loss of a loved person, bereavement often brings with it significant changes and losses in everyday tasks and routines, economic or social status, and even personal self-identity (Bradsher, 1997). The most impressive evidence of the extreme mental and physical suffering associated with losing a loved one is the well-replicated observation that bereaved persons (particularly men) have a higher mortality risk than do matched samples of nonbereaved controls, especially in the weeks and months immediately following the loss (Stroebe & Stroebe, 1993). The vast majority of elderly people, however, eventually adapt to their dramatically changed life situation within the first few years, as indicated by significant reductions of psychological distress and improvements of mental health and well-being back to levels comparable to those before the loss (e.g., Gallagher-Thompson, Futterman, Farberow, Thompson, & Peterson, 1993; Lund, Caserta, & Dimond, 1993).

Particularly after the loss or in the absence of other relationships, contact between *siblings* often gains in closeness in late life (Cicirelli, 1985; Connidis, 1989; Scott, 1983). As people grow old, their family of origin gradually disintegrates because its older members die. Sibling relations represent the most enduring ties of the original nuclear family (Cicirelli, 1985). Their most significant function in late life seems to be reminiscence about shared experiences in "good old times." It has been argued that the validation of positive feelings in previous family interactions may be related to positive feelings about the family in later life (Brubaker, 1990). The role of siblings in providing instrumental support is comparatively less important (Goetting, 1986)—especially when sibling support is compared to assistance provided by adult *children* (Cicirelli, 1982; Ross & Milgram, 1982; Scott, 1983), who are frequently important sources of emotional and instrumental support in old age (for overviews, see Antonucci & Akiyama, 1995; Brubaker, 1990; Lang & Carstensen, 1998; Mares, 1995; Zarit & Eggebeen, 1995).

Friends also often play a central role in older people's social lives (Field, 1999; Wagner et al., 1999). They are, however, typically less important than family to old persons. De Vries (1996) argued that later life is a phase with a particularly high likelihood of life events that might influence the maintenance of friendships—for example, retirement, relocation, or illness. Particularly for men, *retirement* often is associated with a relatively high risk of erosion of work-based friendships. Female friendships that originated in work contexts are typically more broadly based and thus less prone to dissolution after retirement. *Relocation* (e.g., moving closer to one's children or into a nursing home) may also affect the maintenance of later life friendships. At the same time, it might provide opportunities for forming new friendships, an ability that is preserved well into old age (M. M. Baltes, Wahl, & Reichert, 1991; Field, 1999). The most important barriers to friendship contact in late life, at least for older persons living in private households, are one's own or the friend's *illness* and *frailty*. Furthermore, the likelihood of outliving one's friends increases with age; this is reflected by observations in a sample of German older persons. Sixty-nine percent of the 70- to 84-year-old participants reported having at least one friend, compared to 43% of the (more frail) participants aged 85 years and over (Wagner et al., 1999).

To summarize, the majority of old people are well integrated into their family and friendship networks. Overall, the size of social networks declines with advancing age. The decline in network size is typically due to a decrease in social contact with emotionally not-very-close network partners. Contact with emotionally close persons—particularly with family, but also with some close friends—stays relatively stable. With increasing frailty or disability, support provided by network partners gains in importance. Even in very old age, however, support is not only received but also (at least to some degree) given. Socializing and exchange of affection also remain important into very old age. Social contact with same-aged persons in old age is characterized by an increasing likelihood that one's own or the other's frailty obstructs possibilities for maintaining the relationship in habitual ways. Also, the risk increases that relationships are ended through the deaths of social partners, one of the most hurtful experiences in the social lives of human beings. Most old adults, however, are able to successfully cope with the experience of outliving peers.

Everyday Competence in Old Age

So far we have discussed characteristics of aging pertaining to a selected number of clearly circumscribed functional domains—health-related and physiological changes, cognitive abilities, and social relationships. Those and other domain-specific characteristics of old age converge in an overarching question: How well are old adults able to care for themselves, manage their affairs, and live an autonomous life?

The ability to perform activities essential for the effective mastery of independent living has been referred to as *everyday competence* (e.g., M. M. Baltes, Mayr, Borchelt, Maas, & Wilms, 1993; Diehl, 1998; Schaie & Willis, 1999). M. M. Baltes and colleagues (M. M. Baltes, Maas, Wilms, Borchelt, & Little, 1999; M. M. Baltes et al., 1993; M. M. Baltes & Wilms, 1995) distinguished two components—a *basic* and an *expanded* level of competence. According to M. M. Baltes and colleagues, the interplay of both components makes up the ability to lead an autonomous and satisfying life. The basic level of everyday competence reflects the ability to independently execute personal maintenance activities, such as toileting, grooming, dressing, walking, or shopping; these are highly routinized activities necessary for survival. The expanded level of everyday competence comprises activities that reflect people's active construction of their lives, their preferences and motivations, and their engagement with the world around them. Examples are engaging in leisure, out-of-house, or social activities; helping others; and working. Whereas the basic level of competence guarantees survival, it is the expanded level that turns mere existence into meaningful living.

The Basic Level of Everyday Competence in Old Age

In clinical terms, the basic level of competence reflects an individual's functional health or disability, which is typically assessed by evaluating the degree of help needed for the execution of basic and instrumental activities of daily living (referred to as ADL and IADL; Katz, Ford, Moskowitz, Jackson, & Jaffe, 1963; Lawton & Brody, 1969). The need for assistance in the management of everyday life has been shown to be determined primarily by impairments in the sensory, sensorimotor, and motor domains (e.g., M. M. Baltes et al., 1999; Steinhagen-Thiessen & Borchelt, 1999; see also Diehl, 1998), as well as by functional impairment in the cognitive domain (for summaries, see Diehl, 1998; Willis, 1996). The main risk factor for such functional impairments is somatic morbidity. Different illnesses, however, differentially influence a person's ability to engage in independent living (Furner, Rudberg, & Cassel, 1995). Boult, Kane, Louis, Boult, and McCaffrey (1994), for example, reported that the chronic conditions best predicting the development of dependence in ADL and IADL were cerebrovascular disease, arthritis, and coronary artery disease.

Several studies in modern, industrialized countries have observed that the ongoing decrease in mortality rates in old and very old age coincides with a decline in chronic disability prevalence in that age group (i.e., a decline in the proportion of elderly people with long-term dependence on help for the execution of at least one ADL or IADL; e.g., Bebbington, 1988; Jagger, Clarke, & Clarke, 1991; Manton, Corder, & Stallard, 1993). Manton et al. (1993), for example, reported that whereas the total U.S. population above age 65 grew 14.7% between the years 1982 and 1989, the respective proportion of chronically disabled community-dwelling and institutionalized persons only grew 9.2%. Consequently, the overall prevalence (i.e., relative proportion) of chronic disability or institutionalization dropped from 23.7% in 1982 to 22.6% in 1989. The decrease in chronic disability prevalence in developed countries has been attributed primarily to advances in medical treatments and—to some degree—to increases of the average education and income in elderly cohorts, which are typically associated with an increased self-awareness of health-related lifestyle factors and an early use of professional prevention and therapy (Manton et al., 1993).

Originally developed in the context of mortality developments in old age, the concept of active life expectancy addresses the basic level of everyday competence in the temporal dimension of an individual's expected remaining lifetime. *Active life expectancy* represents the period of life an individual is expected to be able to perform functions necessary for personal care and independent living. *Inactive life expectancy,* in contrast, represents the remaining lifetime when one is unable to perform these functions or would be dependent upon others to perform them (Crimmins, Hayward, & Saito, 1996).

Significant differences in active life expectancy exist with respect to *gender, age,* and *socioeconomic status* (SES). A well-known paradox of the aging process is that women tend to live longer, yet they have a higher prevalence of disability (i.e., dependence) than do men (Verbrugge, 1989). Crimmins et al. (1996), for example, reported the *total* remaining life expectancy for U.S. females at age 70 to be 13.9 years and for same-aged U.S. males to be 10.3 years. The expected length of life in an *inactive* state, however, was twice as high for 70-year-old women (2.8 years or 20.1% of remaining expected lifetime) as that for same-aged men (1.4 years or 13.6% of remaining expected lifetime). Gender differences in the diseases that cause disability play a role in the explanation of this paradox. Women have a higher prevalence of more slowly evolving degenerative processes (e.g., arthritis, skeletal problems, diabetes), whereas men are more at risk to suffer (and die) from more rapidly developing lethal diseases (e.g., cancer, heart attack; Manton, 1990). Overall, women have a higher risk of experiencing longer phases of inactive life, a greater likelihood of experiencing disabling events (i.e., the transition from independent to dependent life), and a greater likelihood of dying from a disabled state (Crimmins et al., 1996).

The percentage of remaining life time expected to be spent in dependent states is higher at any age above 70 for women, but for both sexes it increases rapidly with *age*. Crimmins et al. (1996), for example, reported for U.S. women an increase from 20.1% at age 70 to 60.4% at age 90. The corresponding estimates for U.S. males increased from 13.6% at age 70 to 54.5% at age 90. On the other hand, there is a great variability regarding independent living among old adults. Even in very old age, quite a few individuals exhibit a high degree of independence. In a study of 109 Italian centenarians (aged 100–108 years), for example, 26% of the participants (34.6% of the male and 24.0% of the female centenarians) were classified as completely independent in basic activities of daily living (Bauco et al., 1996).

In addition to gender and age, SES also is associated with basic levels of everyday competence. Those of higher SES are not only more likely to survive to old age, but they are also more likely to live through old age in better functional health (e.g., Feldman, Makuc, Kleinman, & Huntley, 1989; Maddox & Clark, 1992; Matthews, Kelsey, Meilahn, Kuller, & Wing, 1989). In the representative sample of U.S. older persons investigated by Crimmins et al. (1996), active life expectancy for persons with at least 12 years of education was about 1 year longer than that of persons of same age, race, and sex with less education.

The Expanded Level of Everyday Competence in Old Age

How do older adults structure their daily lives above and beyond activities necessary for self-maintenance and survival? Detailed reconstructions of a complete day in the lives of older Germans (M. M. Baltes et al., 1999; Horgas, Wilms, & Baltes, 1998) indicated that on average, 60% of the waking day was spent on activities that were not resting and not self-care. Although there was a substantial amount of variability in the amount of time spent with discretionary activities (Horgas et al., 1998), it appeared that a large amount of time was typically spent on leisure activities (mostly watching TV; about 38%) and on instrumental activities (e.g., housework, dealing with authorities, banking; about 15%). Only 7% of the waking day were on average spent on social activities. The oldest old (aged 85 years and above) as well as institutionalized participants tended to spend less time with instrumental and leisure activities and more time resting compared to young old (aged 70–84 years) and noninstitutionalized participants. Women tended to spend more of their waking time on instrumental activities and less time on leisure activities than did men, which reflects the culturally typical housework distribution in that age group.

M. M. Baltes and colleagues (M. M. Baltes et al., 1999) observed that the level of expanded everyday competence (i.e., the degree of engagement in activities other than self-care and resting) was substantially negatively related to chronological age and substantially positively related to SES. Both relationships were completely mediated by personality characteristics, fluid intelligence, and mobility. Thus, age differences in expanded levels of everyday competence seem to be due to associated differences in health and psychosocial factors. Furthermore, psychosocial resources such as education, financial security, and openness to experience appear to be necessary to guarantee high levels of involvement in discretionary activities. They are, however, not sufficient. Activities indicative of expanded everyday competence also require a critical level of physiological functioning.

In sum, there is great variability in old adults' abilities to lead independent, meaningful, and satisfying lives. Basic levels of everyday competence (i.e., the ability to independently execute activities necessary for self-maintenance and survival) largely depend on the level of functional impairment in sensory, sensorimotor, motor, and cognitive domains. In contrast, the expanded level of competence (i.e., the degree of involvement in discretionary activities that make a life meaningful) is largely determined by psychosocial variables—particularly personality characteristics and cognitive abilities, but it also requires a minimum level of functional health. With advancing age, levels of basic and expanded everyday competence tend to decline, which is due to age-associated changes in physical morbidity and psychosocial variables.

Conclusions: What Characterizes Old Age?

We have characterized the life phase of old age in four relatively well-specified life domains—physiological changes, cognitive functioning, social relations, and everyday competence. On a more abstract level, three central characteristics of old adulthood can be inferred from this discussion:

- With advancing old age, the likelihood of developmental losses increases (e.g., development of chronic and acute illnesses, impairment in the cognitive mechanics, deaths of social partners, loss of the ability to lead an independent life). Overall, the ratio of developmental gains and losses becomes increasingly negative in old age.

- Aging is no uniform process. A large degree of heterogeneity exists both among and within persons. Different functional domains are differentially affected by aging processes.

- Old adults in their 60s and 70s typically exhibit relatively high levels of functioning in different life domains. In very old age (85 years and older), however, detrimental effects of aging become more pronounced. It is therefore necessary to differentiate between a young-old and an older- or oldest-old age.

After having portrayed characteristics of old age in general, we next turn to the question of if and how one can characterize successful aging. Following that discussion, we review a number of theoretical approaches to developmental regulatory processes in old age.

SUCCESSFUL AGING: DEFINITION AND CRITERIA

For several decades, gerontology has struggled to understand and define what successful aging is. As of yet, however, no commonly accepted set of criteria characterizing successful aging exists. In general, there has been a shift away from defining successful aging solely in terms of adaptation to age-related changes in a given context (e.g., Havighurst, 1963) toward emphasizing the balance between a person's needs and competence on the one hand and environmental demands and opportunity structures on the other hand (Lawton & Nahemow, 1973; Thomae, 1976). In accordance with life-span developmental approaches (e.g., P. B. Baltes et al., 1998; Brandtstädter, 1998; Lerner, 1998; Lerner & Busch-Rossnagel, 1981; Magnusson, 1996), these newer conceptualizations of successful aging assume that development is best described as an ongoing and dynamic interaction of a person with his or her environment. This implies that criteria of successful aging should not exclusively comprise factors within the person (e.g., happiness), but should also consider how well a person is doing in a given context (e.g., living in a nursing home).

Attempts to define criteria of how well a person is aging have—at least on a theoretical level—also shifted from a one-criterion approach (mostly using subjective well-being as the only criterion signaling successful aging) to a multicriteria approach. The multiple criteria that have been proposed as characterizing successful aging comprise objective and subjective, short-term and long-term, domain-specific and general, and static and dynamic criteria (M. M. Baltes & Carstensen, 1996; P. B. Baltes & Baltes, 1990). Thus far, however, no consensus has been reached on the questions of which of these criteria have to be met and what their relative importance for determining successful aging is.

Based on the assumption that adaptation to challenges specific to old age and a successful person-environment interaction results in subjective well-being (e.g., Havighurst, 1963; Lawton, 1989), most research on successful aging has employed subjective well-being as a single criterion for successful aging. Next, we provide a brief overview of the empirical evidence available on subjective well-being in old age. Then we turn to a discussion of more comprehensive conceptualizations proposing multiple criteria for the characterization of successful aging.

Is Subjective Well-Being a Sufficient Criterion for Successful Aging?

The most prominent single criterion that has been used for studying successful aging has been subjective well-being. In this line of research, subjective well-being is viewed as a person's global evaluation of the quality of his or her life. High subjective well-being is regarded as indicating that the person successfully manages his or her life and ages well.

Subjective well-being is operationalized most often in terms of life satisfaction, the presence of positive affect, and the absence of negative affect (e.g., Diener, Suh, Lucas, & Smith, 1999). Bradburn (1969) limited subjective well-being to the *affective* reactions towards one's life experiences. More specifically, he defined happiness as a preponderance of positive over negative affect. Life satisfaction, on the other hand, focuses on the *cognitive* assessment of progress towards or achievement of one's goals (Campbell, Converse, & Rodgers, 1976; George, 1981; Lawton, 1985).

Both the cognitive and affective aspects of subjective well-being have been widely studied in gerontology. The central question motivating this line of gerontological research is *Does subjective well-being decline with age?* An assumption underlying this question is that subjective well-being is threatened in old age (e.g., Brandtstädter & Greve, 1994). The expectation of an age-related decline in subjective well-being is based on the observation that old age is a period in life when one is more likely than in earlier phases to experience severe losses: Most old people are excluded from productive employment, almost everybody in this age-group experiences a decline in physical capacity and health (e.g., Steinhagen-Thiessen & Borchelt, 1999), and old people are likely to lose close social partners (e.g., Lang & Carstensen, 1994). We have described a number of these developmental losses associated with aging in more detail in the first part of this chapter. There also is much consensus in social expectations that old age is related to losses rather than gains (Heckhausen et al., 1989). Wouldn't one then expect older people to be dissatisfied with their lives and unhappy? In the following section, we briefly review the literature on emotional well-being and life satisfaction in old age.

With regard to age-related changes in the experience of emotions, Schulz (1986) suggested that because of lifelong experiences, older persons should be habituated to emotions and hence have a higher threshold for experiencing both positive and negative affect. This should lead to less frequent but more intense emotions. Emotions might also linger for a longer time because autonomous activation takes longer to go back to baseline. Contrary to these expectations, Levenson, Carstensen, Friesen, and Ekman (1991) found that the physiological arousal pattern of older adults is comparable to that of younger adult but of less intensity. These results have recently been replicated in a sample of young and older European and Chinese Americans (Tsai, Levenson, & Carstensen, 2000). In this study, older adults showed smaller changes in cardiovascular responding to positive (amusement) and negative (sadness) emotions than did younger adults. Young and old adults did not, however, differ in their self-reported and behavioral expression of emotions during standardized situations (watching film clips). Using a different methodology—namely, self-reported intensity of emotions—Ferring and Filipp (1995) found that the self-rated intensity of general positive emotions seems to decline with age, whereas the intensity of general negative emotions did not appear to be age-related.

With regard to old and very old age, findings from the cross-sectional data set of the Berlin Aging Study (Smith, Fleeson, Geiselmann, Settersten, & Kunzmann, 1999) suggest that within the three decades from 70 to 100+ years, chronological age is not or is only weakly associated with the self-reported frequency of affect. Although with increasing age, self-rated frequency of positive affect tended to decrease somewhat ($r = -.22$), there was no significant correlation of age with frequency of negative affect. In a longitudinal study, Ferring and Filipp (1995) found that with increasing age, older adults reported less frequent positive and more frequent negative emotions. Lawton, Kleban, and Dean (1993), on the other hand, showed that older people reported less frequent depression, anxiety, hostility, and shyness than did younger adults, and—with the exception of contentment—did not differ from younger adults with regard to positive affect frequency.

Evidence from the Duke Longitudinal Study suggests that there are neither cross-sectional nor longitudinal age-related differences in the level of self-reported life satisfaction in middle-aged and older adults (Palmore & Kivett, 1985); this appears to be also true in very old age. Data from the Berlin Aging Study showed only a small negative correlation of age and satisfaction with aging and no significant correlation of age with life satisfaction (Smith et al., 1999).

The differences in some of the findings reviewed previously (e.g., regarding intensity of emotions) might be due partly to methodological differences (questionnaires vs. physiological assessment), partly to the specific age range of the samples under study, and partly to differences between longitudinal and cross-sectional findings. Although some studies suggest that the frequency of positive emotions might decline in old age (Smith et al., 1999; Ferring & Filipp, 1995), the age-related effects are small and the findings are not consistent (e.g., Lawton et al., 1993). Overall, the empirical evidence suggests stability rather than decline in subjective well-being in old age.

This phenomenon—average stability of subjective indicators of well-being in a life phase when people are confronted with loss and decline in both external and internal resources—has been labeled a paradox (e.g., Brandtstädter & Greve, 1994; Staudinger, Marsiske, & Baltes, 1995) and has called for explanations. Labeling this finding a paradox reflects the assumption that age-related losses are detrimental to a person's well-being; yet research on subjective well-being shows that the presence or absence of favorable living conditions such as wealth or health does not have a strong or long-lasting impact on people's subjective well-being (see Diener et al., 1999, for a comprehensive review of the literature).

One of the explanations for this counterintuitive finding is that it is *change* in living conditions rather than their absolute quality that affects a person's well-being (Hobfoll, 2001). According to models of hedonic adaptation (e.g., Frederick & Loewenstein, 1999), persons emotionally adapt very quickly to changes in their lives by setting new standards. Even when drastic changes in living conditions occur, such as winning a lottery or encountering an accident causing paraplegia, individuals seem to adapt astonishingly fast when subjective well-being is used as a criterion (Brickman, Coates, & Janoff-Bulman, 1978).

Consequently, there is no reason to expect that the losses occurring in old age should have a long-term negative effect on older persons' subjective well-being (Carstensen & Freund, 1994). Overall, then, subjective well-being does not appear to be a sufficient criterion signaling successful aging. Newer conceptualizations, therefore, go beyond a single-criterion approach and propose multiple criteria to define successful aging. In the subsequent section, we review the most prominent of these multiple-criteria definitions.

Beyond Well-Being: Other Criteria for Successful Aging

One of the recent attempts to take a more comprehensive approach to characterizing well-being is Ryff's (1989, 1995) model of positive psychological functioning. Ryff differentiates between six dimensions of positive psychological functioning: *autonomy, environmental mastery, personal growth, positive relations, purpose in life,* and *self-acceptance.* Ryff's model is partly based on subjective conceptions of positive functioning in middle-aged and older adults. Ryff (1989) found that older adults define fulfillment not primarily in terms of positive emotions, but rather as a sense of accomplishment, enjoyment of life, and caring for others.

Ryff's approach to defining positive psychological functioning, although it is more comprehensive than focusing exclusively on emotional well-being and life satisfaction, is also a *subjective* approach because it exclusively relies on older persons' self-reports. Going even further, P. B. Baltes and Baltes (1990) argued for *integrating* objective (i.e., observable) and subjective (i.e., self-reported) criteria for defining successful aging. They provided a list of objective and subjective criteria that are most often considered in the literature on successful aging: *longevity, physical and mental health, cognitive functioning, social competence, productivity, perceived personal control,* and *life satisfaction.* According to P. B. Baltes and Baltes (1990), integrating objective and subjective criteria is important because on the one hand, considering exclusively subjective criteria (such as self-reported well-being) might lead to a neglect of optimizing environmental conditions that support successful aging. A prescriptive definition specifying exclusively objective criteria for successful aging, on the other hand, is based on the scientific community's specific value system, which might not be shared by the elderly person. Should an elderly person who encounters health-related problems—as elaborated previously, an almost normative event in old and very old age (e.g., Manton, 1990)—not be considered as aging successfully even if happy and satisfied with his or her life?

Addressing the high prevalence of health-related problems in old age, Rowe and Kahn (1987, 1998) distinguished between successful aging and usual aging. *Usual aging* refers to being able to function well but also being at risk for disease or disability. Successful aging, on the other hand, denotes "the ability to maintain three key behaviors or characteristics:

(i)   low risk of disease and disease-related disability;

(ii) high mental and physical function; and

(iii) active engagement with life" (Rowe & Kahn, 1998; p. 38).

Rowe and Kahn pointed out that only the *combination* of these three characteristics represents successful aging. Riley (1998) criticized this approach by arguing that it neglects social structures as an important aspect supporting successful aging: "Successful aging involves the interplay between lives and the complementary dynamic of structural change ... What Drs. Rowe and Kahn neglect is the dependence of successful aging upon structural opportunities in schools,

offices, nursing homes, families, communities, social networks, and society at large" (p. 151).

Similar criticism was raised against early conceptions of successful aging by Havighurst (1963; Havighurst & Albrecht, 1953), who defined successful aging as the adaptation to the specific conditions of old age. Thomae (1976), for instance, stressed the role of the environment when he conceptualized successful aging as the balance between an individual's needs and competence and the demands of the environment.

The previously discussed approaches do not pay attention to the *proactive* and *agentic* role of the older person in interacting with his or her environment. According to Lawton (1989), a person does not simply passively adapt to environmental conditions, but rather proactively shapes his or her environment. Proactive choices (such as moving to planned housing) can have long-term consequences on how well the environment fits personal demands. One of the consequences of a good person-environment fit, according to Lawton, is subjective well-being and life satisfaction. Accordingly, Lawton (1983) proposed to define "the good life" (or in a gerontological context, successful aging) along four independent dimensions, including both subjective and objective criteria in different life domains:

1. Perceived life quality (subjective satisfaction with various life domains such as family, friends, housing, etc.).

2. Psychological well-being (happiness, optimism, congruence between desired and attained goals).

3. Behavioral competence (health, motor behavior, cognition).

4. Objective environment (income, living conditions, etc.).

Several aspects in this definition of successful aging are worth pointing out. Note first that perceived life quality is not conceptualized as a global evaluation of one's life as a whole but rather as a multifaceted concept comprising satisfaction with various life domains. As has been shown, for instance, by Diener (1999), global life satisfaction is not simply the average of one's satisfaction with different life domains. Global life satisfaction seems to be more of a holistic impression of how well one is doing (maybe taking the current mood as an indicator, as suggested by Schwarz and Strack, 1999) than it is the result of a computation of an aggregate score across several life domains. To propose satisfaction with specific life domains as indicators of successful aging is particularly useful if one is interested in how well an aging person is doing in a specific life domain.

Second, note that psychological well-being in Lawton's sense is a concept broader than emotional well-being. It includes not only positive emotions (happiness), but also optimism—that is to say, "the global expectation that good things will be plentiful in the future and bad things, scarce" (Peterson, 2000, p. 47). Optimism has been repeatedly shown to be positively associated with a number of variables such as positive emotions, high performance, and health (see Peterson, 2000, for an overview). According to Seligman (1991), optimism is a generalized expectancy of the controllability of outcomes. Feeling in control of events might lead elderly persons to actually take more control over their lives and proactively shape their environments in a way that matches their needs. In this way, one might say that optimism is a factor contributing to processes promoting successful aging rather than a criterion for defining successful aging.

Third, note that—as in the definition of Rowe and Kahn—health is one of the criteria that Lawton lists for identifying successful aging. Because Lawton, however, considers the interaction of a person with his or her environment as crucial for determining successful aging, impaired or sick older persons nevertheless have the potential to age well. Even sick or impaired older persons can successfully interact with their environment by modifying their environment, their activities, or both (i.e., environmental proactivity), thereby enhancing the person-environment fit. Lawton introduces the notion of "control centers," denoting that disabled older persons may maintain a sense of control by creating an immediate environment in which they can maximize stimulation, knowledge, and security (e.g., by locating a chair in the living room from which they can oversee the street, reach for medicine and books, and keep in contact with the outside by telephone, radio, and TV (Lawton, 1985). In this way, although listing criteria that might imply a static view on successful aging, Lawton's model of successful aging represents a perspective that focuses on the person-environment interaction.

Taking a similar approach, M. M. Baltes and Carstensen (1996) suggested addressing the problem of defining successful aging by going away from a criteria-oriented approach (which implies the assessment of an end state) to a *process-oriented* approach. Focusing, for instance, on the achievement of long-term goals as a criterion for successful aging as proposed by Lawton, might neglect to consider that goals—whether they will be achieved or not—have a positive function for individuals by organizing and guiding behavior over time and across situations (e.g., Emmons, 1996) and by giving life a purpose (e.g., Klinger, 1977). Because of their function to organize behavior and to contribute to a sense of purpose in life, the very process of having and pursuing personal goals can be viewed as one aspect of successful aging, regardless of the actual achievement of the respective goals.

This perspective adds a new dimension in defining criteria for successful aging—namely, the dimension of a static

versus a dynamic approach. According to M. M. Baltes and Carstensen, it is important to assess not only whether an elderly person has achieved positive outcomes (e.g., health, good living conditions, personal goals) but also whether the ongoing process of getting there is one that maximizes gains and minimizes losses—that is, the gains associated with achieving desired outcomes have to be balanced with the costs associated with the outcomes' attainment (Freund, Li, & Baltes, 1999). Thus, the concept of successful development does not denote a specific end point or state that can be reached but has to take the process of how people achieve desirable states into account. If meeting a certain criterion (e.g., financial security) can only be achieved at high costs (e.g., suffering a number of years in an unfulfilling, boring job), this way of goal pursuit cannot be regarded as being successful (Freund et al., 1999).

A *dynamic* approach to successful aging also points to another difficult question that has not yet been resolved in the literature—namely, the time window one should best consider when evaluating how successfully an individual is aging. Usually, snapshots of living conditions and well-being of older persons are taken with one-time assessments (cf. Diener et al., 1999). According to a static view on successful aging, such snapshots are sufficient to determine how well older people are doing and what the relationship between living conditions and subjective well-being in older people is at a given point in time. According to a dynamic view on successful aging, however, only multiple assessments in various life domains over time can reveal whether a person interacts with his or her environment in a manner that promotes successful aging in the long run (Freund et al., 1999). For instance, drinking a bottle of wine might help one to relax and feel good in the short run. If continued daily over years, however, the costs of such drinking behavior for physical and mental health are likely to outweigh the short-term gains.

On a very abstract and general level, successful aging can be defined as the simultaneous maximization of gains and minimization of losses. When it comes to differentiating concrete criteria indicating how well a person is aging, however, no generally accepted definition is available. As Pulkkinen (2000, p. 278) stated, "successful development is not uniform but polyform." Because successful development can take many different expressions, it seems more appropriate to specify criteria depending on the specific research question at hand than to propose a single—necessarily abstract—definition of successful aging. These specific criteria can vary along several dimensions such as objective versus subjective, short-term versus long-term, domain-specific versus general, and static versus dynamic. In Table 25.1, we have summarized these dimensions of criteria for successful aging, giving examples

TABLE 25.1   Central Dimensions of Criteria for Successful Aging: Examples From Two Domains of Functioning Considered Important for Successful Aging

Dimensions	Domains of Functioning	
	Well-Being	Health
Objective	Household income.	Number of medical diagnoses.
Subjective	Satisfaction with financial situation.	Subjective physical health.
Short-term	Last week's happiness.	Recovery from hip surgery.
Long-term	Meaning in life.	Progression of multiple sclerosis.
General	Life satisfaction.	General functional capacity.
Specific	Marital satisfaction.	Blood pressure.
Static	One-time assessment of life satisfaction.	Health status at a given point in time.
Dynamic	Change in life satisfaction over time.	Healthy lifestyle (e.g., exercising, balanced diet).

for two life domains that are frequently considered as central to successful aging—namely, well-being and health.

PROCESSES RELATED TO SUCCESSFUL AGING

An alternative route to studying successful aging is to shift the focus away from attempting to define criteria as end points of successful aging to identifying *processes* of developmental regulation in old age. Although such a process-oriented approach does not resolve the question of criteria of successful aging, it redirects the attention to the psychologically interesting question of which developmental processes are central in the interaction of an aging person with his or her environment (M. M. Baltes & Carstensen, 1996). This approach is in line with E. Kahana and B. Kahana's (1996, p. 25) observation: "The conceptual framework of successful aging is based on the assumption that the aged face unique stresses and challenges. Successful aging requires preventive actions that help delay or minimize normative stresses of aging prior to their occurrence. It also calls for effective corrective actions after older adults encounter normative stresses." The central question, then, is what processes are involved in minimizing the "normative stresses of aging." This question lies at the heart of different models of developmental regulation in old age that we discuss next.

We begin by giving some historical background in the form of two models that inspired a lot of theoretical and empirical research activity—namely disengagement theory (Cumming & Henry, 1961) and activity theory (e.g., Maddox, 1963). The debate over whether disengagement is the central process promoting successful aging or whether only those who continue to be actively involved in life are to be considered successfully aging has been largely resolved in newer models (discussed in more detail later in this section), such as socioemotional selectivity theory by Carstensen and colleagues (e.g., 1993, 1995; Carstensen, Isaacowitz, & Charles, 1999).

Successful aging does not appear to be a question of *either* engagement *or* disengagement; rather, it is a question of specifying the conditions under which disengagement is more adaptive and the conditions under which activity promotes successful aging. We review three models addressing this question: First, we present a metamodel of successful aging—the model of selection, optimization, and compensation by P. B. Baltes, M. M. Baltes, and colleagues (SOC; e.g., M. M. Baltes & Carstensen, 1996, 1998; P. B. Baltes & Baltes, 1990; P. B. Baltes, 1997; Freund & Baltes, 2000; Freund et al., 1999; Marsiske, Lang, Baltes, & Baltes, 1995). Then we present two models of successful aging that center around the notion of control—namely, the model of primary and secondary control by Heckhausen and Schulz (e.g., 1995) and the model of assimilative and accommodative coping by Brandtstädter and colleagues (e.g., Brandtstädter & Greve, 1994; Brandtstädter & Renner, 1990).

Despite differences among these models, they converge in emphasizing the central role of motivational processes for successful aging. Based on the assumption that a person can take an active part in shaping his or her own development, personal goals (i.e., future states a person desires to attain or wishes to avoid) are seen as playing an important role in a person's aging process. Personal goals motivate and organize behavior over time and across situations, giving directionality to development. For instance, a person who pursues primarily achievement-related goals might put many hours into practicing golf in order to improve his or her handicap, whereas a person who places more emphasis on affiliation-related goals might try to spend as much time as possible with his or her friends and family.

Personal goals also serve as a standard of comparison, determining how well a person feels he or she is doing (e.g., Carver & Scheier, 1995). In this sense, the level of aspiration is also associated with subjective well-being—a fact that should be of particular relevance to aging when the likelihood of being confronted with unobtainable or permanently blocked goals is increased. Here, as particularly Brandtstädter and Greve (1994) and Schulz and Heckhausen (1996) argue, adjustment of goal standards should help to protect older persons' well-being. However, as we elaborate in the following discussion, the SOC model, the model of primary and secondary control, and the model of assimilative and accommodative coping do not focus exclusively on how older people deal with losses; they also take the continued possibilities for growth and gains into account (Carstensen & Freund, 1994).

Successful Aging: A Matter of Disengagement or Continued Activity?

For a long time, the investigation of processes related to successful aging was dominated by two opposed conceptions: disengagement theory (Cumming & Henry, 1961) and activity theory (e.g., Lemon, Bengtson, & Peterson, 1971; Maddox, 1963, 1965, 1985).

Disengagement theory posits that the psychological energy of a person declines with age. Coinciding with a decrease in social roles in old age (e.g., because of retirement) and the anticipation of one's death, the diminished energy was assumed to lead to a change in orientation away from activity towards preoccupation with inner aspects of oneself, life review, and one's death (Cumming & Henry, 1961). According to disengagement theory, the most important task of old age is to disengage from involvement with society and to orient oneself towards inner aspects of the self, accepting age-related changes and the impending death. As Cumming and Henry (1961, p. 226) put it, "the apprehension of death as a not-so-distant goal may be a time of redefinition of the self as less bound to the surrounding network of interaction. The anticipation of being apart from those nearby may accelerate withdrawal of cathexis from them, and hasten the turning of all cathexis inward—to the self for its own sake and the past for its memories."

Disengagement theory has been criticized primarily for two reasons. First, interindividual differences in the level of activity that are apparent in middle adulthood continue to be present in old age. Disengagement can therefore not be viewed as a universal process of old age (e.g., Reichard, Livson & Peterson, 1962). Second, the loss of social roles (e.g., professional occupation) can be substituted by other activities (e.g., volunteer work) and hence does not inevitably lead to a decreased level of activity (e.g., Atchley, 1982).

In contrast to disengagement theory, *activity theory* posits that the maintenance of social roles and activities is crucial for successful aging. According to activity theory, the loss of social roles in old age threatens the self-definition of older people and leads to a loss of orientation and guidance for behavior in everyday life (Blau, 1981; Lemon et al., 1971; Maddox, 1963, 1965, 1985; Rosow, 1973). Hence, activity theory views the maintenance of self-defining roles through active involvement in life as one of the central processes of successful aging.

Taking a similar view, Rowe and Kahn (1998, p. 40) stressed the role of active engagement when elaborating on the difference between (merely) usual and (outstanding) successful aging: "Successful aging goes beyond potential; it involves activity, which we have labeled 'engagement with life.' Active engagement with life takes many forms, but successful aging is most concerned with two—relationships with other people, and behavior that is productive."

One of the more recent theories dealing with the phenomenon of *reduced social contacts* in old age—a phenomenon that disengagement theory claims is a sign of withdrawal from society towards life review and preparation for death, and that activity theory views as problematic for the elderly—is *socioemotional selectivity theory* (SST) by Carstensen and her colleagues (e.g., 1993, 1995; Carstensen, Isaacowitz, & Charles, 1999). Similar to disengagement theory, SST posits that reduced social contacts in old age are due to a limited time perspective—that is, due to the fact that older people tend to perceive their remaining time to death as relatively limited. In contrast to disengagement theory, however, SST postulates that the reduced network size does not result primarily from a deliberate withdrawal from society, but rather from the specific motivation for particular types of social relations in situations in which time perspectives are limited.

According to SST, there are two primary motivations for social interactions—emotion regulation and knowledge acquisition. Emotion regulation is best achieved with familiar and close social partners. Knowledge acquisition, on the other hand, often requires one to meet and interact with new people or with people who are emotionally not very close (namely, those who have or can give access to desired knowledge). The basic tenet of SST is that the perceived time expansion determines the relative importance of these two basic motivations for social interaction. An *extended* future time perspective is more strongly associated with knowledge-related goals for social interactions. A *limited* time perspective, in contrast, brings about a stronger presence-orientation involving goals related to feeling states, emotional meaning, and satisfaction. Emotional meaning and satisfaction as well as emotion regulation are more easily established with familiar and close social partners than with unfamiliar or less important persons.

According to SST, the driving force behind reducing the number of social partners in old age, therefore, is a predominance of the motivation for emotion regulation over knowledge acquisition because of the older adults' limited future time perspective. Older persons choose to be with a smaller circle of familiar social partners with whom they can have emotionally meaningful interactions. The decline in the number of social partners in old age, accordingly, does not result from withdrawing from social goals but instead reflects a stronger focus on emotion regulation.

Several empirical studies have demonstrated that the reduction of social network size in old age is primarily due to focusing on the closest social partners such as family and confidants (e.g., Field & Minkler, 1988; Lang & Carstensen, 1994; Lang, Staudinger, & Carstensen, 1998). The change in the ranking of knowledge-related and emotional goals in social relations, however, is only related to age, caused by age. When younger people are faced with time limitations and when future social opportunities are perceived as constrained, the salience of emotion goals also increases; this has been shown in studies in which younger adults were asked to imagine a limited future and older adults were asked to imagine an expansive future (e.g., Fredrickson & Carstensen, 1990), as well as in field studies with younger samples who actually experienced a very limited future time expansion, such as HIV-infected persons (Carstensen & Fredrickson, 1998) or residents of Hong Kong 2 months before the city would be handed over to the People's Republic of China (Fung, Carstensen, & Lutz, 1999).

SST suggests that there is no universal process of continued activity or disengagement in old age, but that it is perceived time expansion that best explains whether older people prefer to focus on close, familiar social partners or are motivated to gain knowledge through knowledgeable novel social partners. This view is also consistent with the finding that activity level per se does not seem to be related to well-being and life satisfaction in old age. An early study by Havighurst, Neugarten, and Tobin (1968) suggests that interindividual differences in personality styles might moderate the relationship between activity and well-being. Similarly, results from the Bonn Longitudinal Study (BOLSA) show that the relationship between level of activity and well-being depends on the specific life domains or role contents under study (Thomae, 1987). Taken together, these results suggest that depending on personality, lifestyle, and life domain, high or low levels of activity can be associated with well-being in old age.

Another factor determining the relationship between activity and well-being might be how much control a person has over whether to engage in an activity. Whereas disengagement theory seems to imply that role losses are inevitable in old age, activity theory works on the assumption that older people have control over finding alternative activities in which to engage. Two important theories of successful development and aging center around the notion of control: the theory of primary and secondary control by Heckhausen

and Schulz (1995) and the model of assimilative and accommodative coping by Brandtstädter and his colleagues (Brandtstädter & Greve, 1994; Brandtstädter & Renner, 1990; Brandtstädter & Wentura, 1995). Both models suggest that under conditions of reduced controllability—such as those that occur in old age because of health-related reductions in functional capacity and activity radius (Manton, 1990; Krauss Whitbourne, 1985)—disengagement from rather than persistence in the pursuit of desired activities promotes well-being. These two models are discussed in more detail later in this chapter. First, however, we present a metatheoretical framework of successful development—the model of selection, optimization, and compensation (SOC), which was first formulated by P. B. Baltes and Baltes (1980, 1990).

Selection, Optimization, and Compensation (SOC): A Metamodel of Successful Aging

The model of selection, optimization, and compensation (SOC) provides a general framework for conceptualizing processes of successful aging (P. B. Baltes & Baltes, 1990). The SOC model is based on the assumption that throughout the lifespan, individuals continually seek to successfully manage their lives through the orchestration of three processes of developmental regulation: selection, optimization, and compensation.

As a metamodel, the SOC theory (M. M. Baltes, 1987; M. M. Baltes & Carstensen, 1996, 1998; M. M. Baltes & Lang, 1997; P. B. Baltes, 1997; P. B. Baltes, & Baltes, 1990; P. B. Baltes, Dittmann-Kohli, & Dixon, 1984; Freund & Baltes, 1998, 2000; Lerner, Freund, DeStefanis, & Habermas, 2001; Marsiske et al., 1995; Wiese, Freund, & Baltes, 2000) represents a framework for the understanding of developmental continuity and change across different periods of the life span (e.g., early and late adulthood), across different levels of analysis (e.g., individual, group), and across different domains of functioning (e.g., social, cognitive, physical).

Selection, optimization, and compensation, which we define in more detail later in this section, are proposed to be universal processes of developmental regulation that can vary greatly in their phenotypic expression, depending on the sociohistorical and cultural context, the domain of functioning, and the unit of analysis at hand (P. B. Baltes, 1997). The SOC model in its general formulation therefore does not designate any *specific* content or mechanisms to its proposed developmental regulatory principles. In this sense, the model represents a relativistic heuristic framework. In order to understand specific manifestations of the SOC processes in particular developmental domains, it is necessary to specify the SOC processes by linking the metamodel with more specific theories pertaining to the phenomena of interest.

Taking an action-theoretical approach (e.g., Brandtstädter, 1999), one such content-driven specification of the SOC model conceptualizes expressions of selection, optimization, and compensation in the context of goal-related action (Freund & Baltes, 2000; Freund et al., 1999). This approach integrates motivational processes into a life-span perspective by considering processes of goal setting and goal pursuit within a long-term temporal perspective. In our discussion of the processes of selection, optimization, and compensation in this section, we use this action-theoretical specification of the model to illustrate specific expressions of the general-purpose processes in the domain of personal goals.

Selection

Throughout the life span, biological, social, and individual opportunities and constraints both provide and delimit the variety of developmental pathways a person can potentially take. The number of those options, however, is usually larger than the amount of resources available to the individual. Selection—that is, focusing one's resources on a subset of potentially available options—thus functions as a precondition for canalization and developmental specialization. One of the central functions of selection is to efficiently utilize the limited amount of available resources. In old and very old age, when resources become more constrained, selection should hence be of particular importance. Consistent with this view, Staudinger and Freund (1998) found that selecting few life domains on which to focus was particularly adaptive for older people with highly constrained resources.

In an action-theoretical framework, selection can be defined as developing, elaborating, and committing oneself to personal goals. On this level of analysis, selection directs development because personal goals guide and organize behavior across situations and time (e.g., Emmons, 1996). Successful goal selection requires developing and setting goals in domains for which resources are available or can be acquired and in domains that match a person's needs and environmental demands (Freund, 1997; Heckhausen, 1999).

The SOC model distinguishes between two kinds of selection, *elective selection* and *loss-based selection*. Both aspects of selection differ in their specific developmental regulatory function. *Elective selection* denotes the delineation of goals in order to advance the match of a person's needs and motives with the given or attainable resources and opportunity structures. It aims at achieving higher levels of functioning.

In contrast, *loss-based selection* occurs as a response to losses in previously available goal-relevant means threatening the maintenance of a goal. Loss-based selection involves changes in goals or the goal system, such as reconstructing one's goal hierarchy by focusing on the most important goal(s), adapting standards, or substituting for goals that are no longer achievable (see also our discussion of assimilative coping, Brandtstädter & Wentura, 1995, and our discussion of compensatory secondary control, Heckhausen, 1999). The SOC model posits that loss-based selection is an important process of life mastery. Throughout the life span, individuals encounter losses in goal-relevant resources affecting their positive functioning. Loss-based selection allows focusing or redirecting resources adaptively when other means for the maintenance of positive functioning substituting the loss (compensation) are either not available or would be invested at the expense of other, more promising goals (M. M. Baltes, 1996; Heckhausen, 1999).

Selection promotes positive development in a number of ways. To hold and feel committed to goals contributes to feeling that one's life has a purpose, thereby giving meaning to life (e.g., Klinger, 1977; Little, 1989). Furthermore, goals organize behavior into action sequences. They reduce the complexity of any given situation as they guide attention and behavior. In other words, goals can also be seen as chronically available decision rules (*implemental mind-set;* Gollwitzer, 1996) for directing attention and behavior to those of the numerous stimuli and behavioral options in a given situation that are goal-relevant. In this sense, goals help one to efficiently interact with one's environment. Instead of deliberating about all of the possible alternatives one has in any given situation, people scan their environment for possibilities to pursue their goals.

Goals do not necessarily need to be conscious in order to function as guides for attention and behavior. According to the auto-motive model by Bargh and Gollwitzer (1994), the repeated activation of a goal in a certain situation leads to an association of the respective goal and situational cues. Such situational features can then automatically trigger a goal and activate goal-relevant actions. In this sense, goals that are very frequently and consistently activated can initiate and guide behavior particularly efficiently.

Optimization

Whereas selection is the first step towards positive functioning, the SOC model posits that for achieving desired outcomes in selected domains, it is crucial to acquire, apply, and refine goal-relevant means, a process that is referred to as *optimization*. Which means are best suited for achieving one's goals varies according to the specific goal domain (e.g., achievement vs. social domain), personal characteristics (e.g., gender), and the sociocultural context (e.g., institutional support systems). It is possible, however, to identify a number of general processes involved in the acquisition, application, and refinement of goal-relevant means (see P. B. Baltes, 1997; Freund & Baltes, 2000; Freund et al., 1999). Later in this section, we briefly discuss some prototypical instances.

On the most general level, some sort of monitoring of the discrepancy between the actual and the desired state (goal) needs to take place (Carver & Scheier, 1995; Miller, Galanter, & Pribram, 1960). This continuous monitoring, which might occur outside of conscious awareness (Wegner, 1992), allows a constant adaptation of goal-related action. Progress toward the goal motivates the continuation of the invested goal-relevant means, whereas lack of progress or even an increase in the distance to the goal indicates that other means might be better suited for achieving the respective goal.

Another example for a general process related to optimization is the delay of immediate gratification for the sake of a more long-term payoff (e.g., Mischel, 1996). Long-term goals often require investing resources without immediate gains. Not giving in to temptations that offer short-term gratifications is thus a precondition for the persistent pursuit of a goal over an extended period of time.

One of the most important general processes of optimization is practice. As has been shown in the expertise literature, deliberate practice is a key factor for acquiring new skills and reaching peak performance (Ericsson, 1996). Repeated practice leads to the refinement of skill components, to their integration and automatization that thereby become less resource-demanding, and to free resources that can be devoted to other goal-related means. Although the role of practice might be most obvious in domains with a clear achievement aspect such as academic achievement, sports, or music (Ericsson, 1996), practice may also be important in domains with less clearly defined skills and success criteria, such as interpersonal relationships.

In old age, optimization continues to be of great importance for life management because engaging in growth-related goals generally has positive regulative functions. A number of studies with younger adults (e.g., Coats, Janoff-Bulman, & Alpert, 1996; Elliot & Church, 1997; Elliot & Sheldon, 1997; Elliot, Sheldon, & Church, 1997; Emmons, 1996) have shown that trying to achieve gain- or growth-oriented goals (optimization) is associated with a higher degree of self-efficacy and leads to positive emotions and well-being, whereas trying to avoid losses and functional decline is related to negative emo-

tions and distress. In old age, when losses are prevalent and expected, it might be of particular importance for promoting well-being and a sense of self-efficacy to sustain growth- or gain-related goals and not to focus only on losses. In fact, data from the Berlin Aging Study support the positive function of optimization in old age: Older people who reported to engage in optimization also reported more positive emotions and higher satisfaction with aging (Freund & Baltes, 1998).

Compensation

How do older people manage to maintain positive functioning in the face of health-related constraints and other losses in plasticity and reserve capacity that we discussed in the first part of this chapter? One relevant strategy for the regulation of losses has already been mentioned—loss-based selection. This strategy denotes the restructuring of one's goal system—for example, by giving up unattainable goals and developing new ones. Even in the face of losses, however, when losses are not too pervasive, goals can often be maintained by using alternative means. This process is referred to as *compensation*.

Compensation denotes the acquisition and use of means to counteract loss or decline in goal-related means. Typical instances are the substitution of previously available goal-relevant means by acquiring new or activating unused internal or external resources (Bäckman & Dixon, 1992; Carstensen, Hanson, & Freund, 1995; Marsiske et al., 1995). As we discussed in the context of optimization, which means are best suited for maintaining a given level of functioning in the face of loss or decline depends on the domain of functioning. Once again, such aspects of self-regulation as delay of gratification, control beliefs, and practice generally play an important role in the acquisition and investment of compensatory means. In contrast to optimization, compensation aims at counteracting or avoiding losses rather than at approaching positive states. Because of the losses associated with increasing age, aging individuals have to allocate more and more of their resources into the maintenance of functioning and the resilience against losses rather than into processes of growth (Staudinger et al., 1995). The negative effects of avoidance goals for younger age groups that were mentioned above (e.g., Coats et al., 1996; Elliot, & Church, 1997; Emmons, 1996) might be less pronounced or even absent in old age, when a focus on maintenance might be experienced as something positive (Freund & Baltes, 2000; Heckhausen, 1999). Again, data from the Berlin Aging Study (Freund & Baltes, 1998) support the positive effect of compensation, showing that self-reported compensation was associated with subjective indicators of successful aging (i.e., emotional well-being, satisfaction with aging, and life satisfaction).

SOC and Age

Although selection, optimization, and compensation are conceptualized as general processes of developmental regulation that function throughout the life span, these processes also undergo developmental changes. Regarding old age, two predictions seem plausible (Freund & Baltes, 2000): On the one hand, older adults might become better at the use of SOC strategies because of their increasing life experience. On the other hand, the use of SOC strategies itself is resource dependent and effortful. As the resources available to older persons decrease, the engagement in SOC-related behaviors might become more difficult. In old age, SOC-related behaviors might therefore decline. Consistent with the latter argument, cross-sectional data revealed a decrease in self-reported SOC with increasing age (Freund & Baltes, 1998, 2000). Despite such a decline in self-reported SOC behaviors, however, selection, optimization, and compensation continued to have positive associations to well-being (Freund & Baltes, 1998, 1999, 2000) and to everyday functioning (M. M. Baltes & Lang, 1997) well into old age.

In sum, the SOC model conceptualizes successful aging as the interplay of three processes:

- Developing, elaborating, and committing to those goals of functioning that promote a fit between personal needs or preferences, environmental, societal, or biological demands and actual or acquirable resources (*selection*). In old age, when an individual is confronted with changes in personal needs or preferences, demands, and resources, selection of goals in which all three of these factors converge should be of particular importance for positive functioning.

- Acquiring, refining, and investing (internal or external) resources into the pursuit of the selected goals (*optimization*). To promote gains and growth in old age—a life phase in which developmental losses outweigh developmental gains—it is important to acquire new or activate previously unused goal-relevant external or internal means (e.g., social support).

- Acquiring and investing resources into selected domains of functioning in order to counteract losses of previously available goal-relevant means (*compensation*). Given the inevitable losses of old age, an important facet of successful aging is the management of losses and the maintenance of functioning. Because compensatory efforts also require resources, careful selection of goals on which to focus in

the face of loss (i.e., loss-based selection) is essential for successful aging.

In the following discussion, we present two models of successful aging that are compatible with the SOC metamodel but that put a particular emphasis on the controllability of events: the model of primary and secondary control by Heckhausen and Schulz (1995) and the model of assimilative and accommodative coping by Brandtstädter and colleagues (e.g., Brandtstädter & Renner, 1990).

The Model of Optimization in Primary and Secondary Control (OPS)

Converging with the SOC model, the model of optimization in primary and secondary control (OPS model) by Heckhausen and Schulz stresses the importance of selectivity and compensation for developmental regulation and successful aging (Heckhausen, 1999; Heckhausen & Schulz, 1995, 1999; Schulz, 1986; Schulz & Heckhausen, 1996). Unlike the developers of the SOC model, Heckhausen and Schulz (1998, pp. 55–56) "conceptualize optimization as a higher order regulatory process" that balances and maintains selectivity and compensation. In the OPS model, selectivity denotes the focused investment of resources into selected goals, whereas compensation refers to strategies helping to attain a selected goal when internal resources are insufficient or when faced with failure or losses.

Heckhausen and Schulz propose that the challenges of life can be mastered by jointly employing two modes of control: primary and secondary control. According to their model, humans have an innate need to control their world. The primary way to achieve control is by employing instrumental efforts to modify the environment according to one's goals (i.e., primary control). If such control strategies directed at the external world are not available or if they fail, an internal focus on changing one's goals and standards or engaging in self-protective attributions or social comparisons takes over (i.e., secondary control). The main function of secondary control is to focus and protect motivational resources for primary control. In general, Heckhausen and Schulz propose that the maximization of primary control potential is the criterion of adaptive functioning across the life span. This is particularly difficult in old age, when losses become more prominent and less controllable, thereby depleting the potential for primary control (Schulz, 1986). Thus, in old age, secondary control strategies should gain more and more in importance for successful developmental regulation.

Heckhausen and Schulz distinguish two forms of primary and secondary control strategies—namely selective and compensatory forms. *Selective primary control* denotes actions that are directly aimed at goal achievement, such as investing time, effort, and skills into the pursuit of goals. *Compensatory primary control*—that is, the investment of external resources (e.g., help of others) or the acquisition of alternative resources takes place when available internal resources are not sufficient for achieving one's goals. This process is particularly important in old age when internal resources are subject to decline and losses. *Selective secondary control* refers to enhanced selectivity of resource investment into already existing goals through motivational processes such as enhancing commitment to a given goal. Finally, *compensatory secondary control* buffers negative effects of failure in primary control strivings through cognitive reframing of goals, such as decreasing the desirability of unobtainable goals or favorable social comparisons. These strategies—again of particular importance in old age when resource-intensive goals might become increasingly difficult to achieve due to loss and decline in relevant resources—should contribute to the long-term primary control potential because they work against the negative motivational effects of failure experience and contribute to the maintenance of self-efficacy and well-being.

According to Heckhausen and Schulz, none of these four types of control strategies alone is sufficient to bring about successful development. Instead, the four types of control have to be orchestrated according to the opportunity structure and constraints of an individual's developmental ecology. For instance, Wrosch and Heckhausen (1999) showed that control strategies differ systematically between younger and older adults who encounter the same situation—namely, separation or divorce from a long-term partner. Based on demographic data, they assumed that these two age groups differ in their opportunities for finding a new partner, such that younger adults have much better chances than do older adults. In accordance with propositions of the OPS model, younger separated adults reported more primary control strivings for attaining partnership goals, whereas older separated adults reported higher levels of goal deactivation (compensatory secondary control). Moreover, Wrosch and Heckhausen could show that goal disengagement was positively related to change in positive affect over time in older adults but negatively related in younger adults.

With regard to aging, Heckhausen, Schulz, and Wrosch (1998) found that in general, endorsement of control strategies increases from young to old adulthood. The one exception to this age pattern pertained to compensatory secondary control, which was reported least in all age groups. The authors interpreted this finding as supporting their notion of the primacy of primary control. Moreover, they concluded that "overall, with increasing age adults appear to know about, appreciate, and maybe rely more on strategies of developmental regulation"

(Heckhausen & Schulz, 1998, p. 70). All four types of control strategies were shown to be positively related to self-esteem, which further supports the importance of primary and secondary control strategies for successful aging.

The Model of Assimilative and Accommodative Coping

Brandtstädter and his colleagues (Brandtstädter & Greve, 1994; Brandtstädter & Renner, 1990; Brandtstädter & Wentura, 1995; Brandtstädter, Wentura, & Rothermund, 1999) proposed a model that addresses the question what processes can explain the so-called paradox of stability in well-being despite the many losses and constraints older persons encounter. According to their model, people use primarily two distinct, complementary forms of coping to achieve "a match between actual developmental outcomes or prospects and personal goals and ambitions" (Brandtstädter et al., 1999, pp. 375–376)—namely, assimilation and accommodation. *Assimilation* refers to tenacious goal pursuit by modifying the environment or the circumstances so that they fit personal goals. It involves actional (i.e., intentional) neutralization of a mismatch between the current and the desired states. In contrast, *accommodation* denotes processes of flexible goal adjustment by changing, downgrading, or discarding personal goals or lowering one's level of aspirations so that they fit the circumstances. It is characterized by mental neutralizations of a mismatch between the actual and the desired state that work primarily on a nonintentional, unconscious level.

Brandtstädter and colleagues (e.g., Brandtstädter et al., 1999) posit that people first use assimilative strategies to cope with loss—that is, they first try to overcome obstacles blocking their goals by actional neutralizations. If goals remain blocked despite assimilative attempts, a gradual shift to the accommodative mode occurs. The gradual shift from the assimilative to the accommodative mode is theorized to occur in the following order: When attempts at altering the situation do not succeed, auxiliary activities will be activated or acquired. When these auxiliary attempts do not lead to the desired outcomes, external aids or support systems might be engaged (cf. the concept of proxy control by Bandura, 1982). When all of these instrumental actions do not help to alter the situation in the desired way, people, according to Brandtstädter, feel helpless and depressed. This state, however, is only temporary and marks the shift to accommodative processes such as disengagement from goals or adjustment of standards take place.

Brandtstädter et al. (1999), however, also point out that the shift from assimilative to accommodative coping does not always follow this fixed temporal pattern; rather, it depends on personal and situational factors. Brandtstädter and Wentura (1995) list three key factors affecting assimilative and accommodative tendencies in opposite directions: (a) importance of the goal—when a goal is of great personal importance, assimilative tendencies are activated, whereas accommodative tendencies are inhibited; (b) probability of success—if there is a sufficient probability of success in achieving a goal, assimilative coping prevails over accommodative coping; and (c) accessibility of palliative information—contextual or chronically available palliative information (e.g., social norms, personal attitudes) that eases the acceptance of a previously aversive situation fosters a shift to the accommodative mode.

Brandtstädter and colleagues predict a general shift during aging from assimilative to accommodative coping. When losses begin to occur, people should first respond with assimilative coping directed at actively counteracting losses. When with increasing age, losses begin to become more widespread and hence both the probability of success and the resources to engage in assimilative actions decline, accommodative coping should gain in importance. This theoretically expected pattern, which has been empirically confirmed (Brandtstädter & Renner, 1990; Brandtstädter, Rothermund, & Schmitz, 1997), is seen as important for successful aging because Brandtstädter et al. (1999, p. 391) "consider the process of continuously readjusting goals and preferences to action reserves as crucial to the maintenance of self-esteem and even efficacy in later life." Again, empirical evidence supports this hypothesis. Brandtstädter and Renner (1990) could show that accommodative tendencies such as flexible goal adjustment buffer the negative association between perceived developmental deficits and life satisfaction as well as buffer the negative effect of health-related problems on subjective well-being (Brandtstädter, Wentura, & Greve, 1993).

According to this model, successful aging can be characterized primarily as a coping process that shifts from actively counteracting beginning age-related losses to cognitively restructuring personal goals or standards: "A comprehensive theoretical view [of successful aging] . . . must also account for the fact that to maintain a sense of efficacy and self-esteem, personal goals and self-evaluative standards have to be continually revised and adjusted to the changes that characterize the processes of physical, psychological, and social aging" (Brandtstädter et al., 1999, p. 382).

SUMMARY

Old age is a relatively new phenomenon because life expectancy has only relatively recently extended into old age. In many modern countries, this increase in life expectancy has been co-occurring with a decline in fertility rates. This has drastically altered the population's composition. Declining proportions of working-age people have to ensure adequate living conditions for a growing number of old people. To meet this challenge, gerontology needs to provide knowledge about positive or successful aging and the conditions that foster it. In this chapter, we reviewed current knowledge and theory on this topic.

In the first part of the chapter, we elaborated the specific context of old age in four life domains: physiological changes, cognitive functioning, social relations, and everyday competence. From this discussion, we inferred (a) that with advancing age, the ratio of developmental gains and losses becomes increasingly negative; (b) that old age, like any other phase in life, is characterized by tremendous intra- and interindividual heterogeneity; and (c) that it is necessary to distinguish between young-old and old-old age. Many individuals in their 60s and 70s exhibit relatively high levels of functioning, whereas in very old age (85 years and older) the detrimental effects of aging become more pronounced.

Given the unfavorable ratio of developmental gains to losses in older adulthood, the term *successful aging* sounds like an oxymoron. This lead us to the question of how to best define successful aging. We discussed the current state of research on this question in the second part of this chapter. On an abstract level, researchers typically agree that successful aging can be defined as the simultaneous maximization of gains and minimization of losses. What exactly constitute gains and losses, however, must be specified depending on the specific research question at hand. Presumably because of the inherent value-judgement required for delineating criteria for successful aging, no generally accepted set of criteria characterizing successful aging exists. It is, however, generally acknowledged that an encompassing characterization of how well a person is aging should comprise objective as well as subjective, short-term as well as long-term, general as well as domain-specific, and static as well as dynamic indicators.

In the third part of this chapter, we shifted the focus away from discussing criterion-centered approaches to defining successful aging to reviewing theories that address the question of processes underlying successful aging. Recently, the role of proactive processes in aging has been increasingly recognized. A basic assumption underlying this notion is that development is a dynamic process of both reacting to and proactively shaping one's environment as well as oneself (e.g., Lawton, 1989; Lerner & Busch-Rossnagel, 1981). According to this view, individuals continuously adapt to their changing environment, act upon their environment, and actively create environments that fit their needs (e.g., move to a ground-floor apartment in which a wheelchair can be used when mobility is impaired).

Recent models of successful aging stress the role of motivational processes in understanding developmental regulation in old age, such as the model of selection, optimization, and compensation (P. B. Baltes, 1997; P. B. Baltes & Baltes, 1990; Freund et al., 1999; Marsiske et al., 1995), the model of assimilative and accommodative coping (e.g., Brandtstädter & Greve, 1994; Brandtstädter & Renner, 1990), and the model of primary and secondary control (e.g., Heckhausen & Schulz, 1995). According to these models, an important way in which individuals play an active role in their development is by choosing, committing to, and pursuing personal goals. By adapting goals and standards to the increasingly constrained resources (e.g., health-related decline), older people can maintain their well-being and a certain degree of control.

At this point, most of the research on processes of developmental regulation in old age is primarily concerned with understanding how and under what conditions these processes contribute to successful aging. We hope, however, that identifying the central processes of successful aging will help to develop prevention or intervention programs to enhance the quality of older persons' lives in the not-so-distant future.

REFERENCES

Aiken, L. R. (1989). *Later life* (3rd ed.). Hillsdale, NJ: Erlbaum.

Anstey, K. J., Lord, S. R., & Williams, P. (1997). Strength in the lower limbs, visual contrast, and simple reaction time predict cognition in older women. *Psychology and Aging, 12,* 137–144.

Antonucci, T. C. (1985). Personal characteristics, social support, and social behavior. In R. H. Binstock & E. Shanas (Eds.), *Handbook of aging and the social sciences* (2nd ed., pp. 94–128). New York: Van Nostrand Reinhold.

Antonucci, T. C. (1990). Social supports and social relationships. In R. H. Binstock & L. K. George (Eds.), *Handbook of aging and the social sciences* (3rd ed., pp. 205–226). San Diego, CA: Academic Press.

Antonucci, T. C. (1991). Attachment, social support, and coping with negative life events in mature adulthood. In E. M. Cummings, A. L. Greene, & K. H. Karraker (Eds.), *Life-span developmental psychology: Perspectives on stress and coping* (pp. 261–276). Hillsdale, NJ: Erlbaum.

Antonucci, T. C., & Akiyama, H. (1994). Convoys of attachment and social relations in children, adolescents, and adults. In F. Nestmann & K. Hurrelmann (Eds.), *Social networks and social support in childhood and adolescence* (pp. 37–52). Berlin: de Gruyter.

Antonucci, T. C., & Akiyama, H. (1995). Convoys of social relations: Family and friendship within a lifespan context. In

R. Blieszner & V. H. Bedford (Eds.), *Handbook of aging and the family* (pp. 355–371). Westport, CT: Greenwood Press.

Antonucci, T. C., & Jackson, J. S. (1987). Social support, interpersonal efficacy, and health: A life course perspective. In L. L. Carstensen & B. A. Edelstein (Eds.), *Handbook of clinical gerontology* (pp. 291–311). New York: Pergamon Press.

Atchley, R. C. (1982). The aging self. *Psychotherapy: Theory, Research and Practice, 19,* 388–396.

Bäckman, L., & Dixon, R. A. (1992). Psychological compensation: A theoretical framework. *Psychological Bulletin, 112,* 1–25.

Baltes, M. M. (1987). Erfolgreiches Altern als Ausdruck von Verhaltenskompetenz und Umweltqualität [Successful aging as expression of behavioral competence and environmental quality]. In C. Niemitz (Ed.), *Der Mensch im Zusammenspiel von Anlage und Umwelt [The human being in the interaction of nature and nature]* (pp. 353–376). Frankfurt, Germany: Suhrkamp.

Baltes, M. M. (1996). *The many faces of dependency in old age.* New York: Cambridge University Press.

Baltes, M. M., & Carstensen, L. L. (1996). The process of successful ageing. *Ageing and Society, 16,* 397–422.

Baltes, M. M., & Carstensen, L. L. (1998). Social psychological theories and their applications to aging: From individual to collective. In V. L. Bengtson & K. W. Schaie (Eds.), *Handbook of theories of aging* (pp. 209–226). New York: Springer.

Baltes, M. M., & Lang, F. R. (1997). Everyday functioning and successful aging: The impact of resources. *Psychology and Aging, 12,* 433–443.

Baltes, M. M., Maas, I., Wilms, H.-U., Borchelt, M., & Little, T. D. (1999). Everyday competence in old and very old age: Theoretical considerations and empirical findings. In P. B. Baltes & K. U. Mayer (Eds.), *The Berlin Aging Study. Aging from 70 to 100* (pp. 384–402). New York: Cambridge University Press.

Baltes, M. M., Mayr, U., Borchelt, M., Maas, I., & Wilms, H.-U. (1993). Everyday competence in old and very old age: An interdisciplinary perspective. *Ageing and Society, 13,* 657–680.

Baltes, M. M., Wahl, H.-W., & Reichert, M. (1991). Successful aging in long-term care institutions? In K. W. Schaie & M. P. Lawton (Eds.), *Annual review of gerontology and geriatrics* (Vol. 11, pp: 311–337). New York: Springer.

Baltes, M. M., & Wilms, H.-U. (1995). Alltagskompetenz im Alter [Everyday competence in old age]. In R. Oerter & L. Montada (Eds.), *Entwicklungspsychologie [Developmental psychology]* (pp. 1127–1136). Weinheim, Germany: Psychologie Verlags Union.

Baltes, P. B. (1987). Theoretical propositions of life-span developmental psychology: On the dynamics between growth and decline. *Developmental Psychology, 23,* 611–626.

Baltes, P. B. (1989). The dynamics between growth and decline. *Contemporary Psychology, 34,* 983–984.

Baltes, P. B. (1997). On the incomplete architecture of human ontogeny: Selection, optimization, and compensation as foundation of developmental theory. *American Psychologist, 52,* 366–380.

Baltes, P. B., & Baltes, M. M. (1980). Plasticity and variability in psychological aging: Methodological and theoretical issues. In G. Gurski (Ed.), *Determining the effects of aging on the central nervous system* (pp. 41–60). Berlin: Schering.

Baltes, P. B., & Baltes, M. M. (1990). Psychological perspectives on successful aging: The model of selective optimization with compensation. In P. B. Baltes & M. M. Baltes (Eds.), *Successful aging: Perspectives from the behavioral sciences* (pp. 1–34). New York: Cambridge University Press.

Baltes, P. B., Dittmann-Kohli, F., & Dixon, R. A. (1984). New perspectives on the development of intelligence in adulthood: Toward a dual-process conception. In P. B. Baltes & J. O. G. Brim (Eds.), *Life-span development and behavior* (Vol. 6, pp. 33–76). New York: Academic Press.

Baltes, P. B., Dittmann-Kohli, F., & Kliegl, R. (1986). Reserve capacity of the elderly in aging-sensitive tests of fluid intelligence: Replication and extension. *Psychology and Aging, 1,* 172–177.

Baltes, P. B., & Kliegl, R. (1992). Further testing of limits of cognitive plasticity: Negative age differences in a mnemonic skill are robust. *Developmental Psychology, 28,* 121–125.

Baltes, P. B., & Lindenberger, U. (1988). On the range of cognitive plasticity in old age as a function of experience: 15 years of intervention research. *Behavior Therapy, 19,* 283–300.

Baltes, P. B., Lindenberger, U., & Staudinger, U. M. (1998). Life-span theory in developmental psychology. In R. M. Lerner (Ed.), *Handbook of child psychology: Vol. 1. Theoretical models of human development* (5th ed., pp. 1029–1143). New York: Wiley.

Baltes, P. B., Sowarka, D., & Kliegl, R. (1989). Cognitive training research on fluid intelligence in old age: What can older adults achieve by themselves? *Psychology and Aging, 4,* 217–221.

Baltes, P. B., Staudinger, U. M., & Lindenberger, U. (1999). Life-span psychology: Theory and application to intellectual functioning. *Annual Review of Psychology, 50,* 471–507.

Baltes, P. B., Staudinger, U. M., Maercker, U. M., & Smith, J. (1995). People nominated as wise: A comparative study of wisdom-related knowledge. *Psychology and Aging, 10,* 155–166.

Baltes, P. B., & Willis, S. L. (1982). Enhancement (plasticity) of intellectual functioning in old age: Penn State's Adult Development and Enrichment Project (ADEPT). In F. I. M. Craik & S. Trehub (Eds.), *Aging and cognitive processes* (pp. 353–389). New York: Plenum Press.

Bandura, A. (1982). Self-efficacy mechanism in human agency. *American Psychologist, 37,* 122–147.

Bargh, J. A., & Gollwitzer, P. M. (1994). Environmental control of goal-directed action: Automatic and strategic contingencies between situations and behavior. In W. D. Spaulding (Ed.), *Nebraska Symposium on Motivation: Vol. 41. Integrative views of motivation, cognition, and emotion* (pp. 71–124). Lincoln: University of Nebraska Press.

Bauco, C., Golosio, F., Cinti, A. M., Borriello, C., Raganato, P., Cicconetti, P., Cacciafesta, M., & Marigliano, V. (1996). Functional status and well-being of centenarians. *Archives of Gerontology and Geriatry, 5,* 363–366.

Bebbington, A. C. (1988). The expectation of life without disability in England and Wales. *Social Science Medicine, 27,* 321–326.

Berg, C. A., & Klaszynski, P. A. (1996). Practical intelligence and problem solving: Searching for perspectives. In F. Blanchard-Fields & T. M. Hess (Eds.), *Perspectives on cognitive change in adulthood and aging* (pp. 323–357). New York: McGraw-Hill.

Blau, Z. S. (1981). *Aging in a changing society* (2nd ed.). New York: Franklin Watts.

Bortz, W. M. (1982). Disuse and aging. *Journal of the American Medical Association, 248,* 1203–1208.

Bosman, E. A. (1993). Age-related differences in the motoric aspects of transcription typing skill. *Psychology and Aging, 8,* 87–102.

Bosman, E. A., & Charness, N. (1996). Age-related differences in skilled performance and skill acquisition. In F. Blanchard-Fields & T. M. Hess (Eds.), *Perspectives on cognitive change in adulthood and aging* (pp. 428–453). New York: McGraw-Hill.

Boult, C., Kane, R. L., Louis, T. A., Boult, L., & McCaffrey, D. (1994). Chronic conditions that lead to functional limitations in the elderly. *Journal of Gerontology: Medical Sciences, 49,* M28–M36.

Bowling, A. (1994). Social networks and social support among older people and implications for emotional well-being and psychiatric morbidity. *International Review of Psychiatry, 6,* 41–58.

Bradburn, N. M. (1969). *The structure of psychological wellbeing.* Chicago: Aldine.

Bradsher, J. E. (1997). Older women and widowhood. In J. M. Coyle (Ed.), *Handbook on women and aging* (pp. 418–429). Westport, CT: Greenwood Press.

Brandtstädter, J. (1998). Action perspectives on human development. In R. M. Lerner (Ed.), *Handbook of child psychology: Vol. 1. Theoretical models of human development* (5th ed., pp. 807–866). New York: Wiley.

Brandtstädter, J. (1999). The self in action and development: Cultural, biosocial, and ontogenetic bases of intentional self-development. In J. Brandtstädter & R. M. Lerner (Eds.), *Action and self-development: Theory and research through the life span* (pp. 37–65). Thousand Oaks, CA: Sage.

Brandtstädter, J., & Greve, W. (1994). The aging self: Stabilizing and protective processes. *Developmental Review, 14,* 52–80.

Brandtstädter, J., & Renner, G. (1990). Tenacious goal pursuit and flexible goal adjustment: Explication and age-related analysis of assimilative and accommodative strategies of coping. *Psychology and Aging, 5,* 58–67.

Brandtstädter, J., Rothermund, K., & Schmitz, U. (1997). Coping resources in later life. *European Review of Applied Psychology, 47,* 107–114.

Brandtstädter, J., & Wentura, D. (1995). Adjustment to shifting possibility frontiers in later life: Complementary adaptive modes. In R. A. Dixon & L. Bäckman (Eds.), *Compensating for psychological deficits and declines: Managing losses and promoting gains* (pp. 83–106). Hillsdale, NJ: Erlbaum.

Brandtstädter, J., Wentura, D., & Greve, W. (1993). Adaptive resources of the aging self: Outlines of an emergent perspective. *Journal of Behavioral Development, 16,* 323–349.

Brandtstädter, J., Wentura, D., & Rothermund, K. (1999). Intentional self-development through adulthood and later life: Tenacious pursuit and flexible adjustment of goals. In J. Brandtstädter & R. M. Lerner (Eds.), *Action and self-development: Theory and research through the life span* (pp. 373–400). Thousand Oaks, CA: Sage.

Brickman, P., Coates, D., & Janoff-Bulman, R. (1978). Lottery winners and accident victims: Is happiness relative? *Journal of Personality and Social Psychology, 37,* 917–927.

Brubaker, T. H. (1990). Families in later life: A burgeoning research area. *Journal of Marriage and the Family, 52,* 959–981.

Campbell, A., Converse, P. E., & Rodgers, W. L. (1976). *The quality of American life: Perceptions, evaluations, and satisfaction.* New York: Russell Sage Foundation.

Carstensen, L. L. (1993). Motivation for social contact across the life-span: A theory of socioemotional selectivity. In J. E. Jacobs et al. (Ed.), *Nebraska Symposium on Motivation, 1992: Developmental perspectives on motivation. Current theory and research in motivation* (Vol. 40, pp. 209–254). Lincoln: University of Nebraska Press.

Carstensen, L. L. (1995). Evidence for a life-span theory of socioemotional selectivity. *Current Directions in Psychological Science, 4,* 151–156.

Carstensen, L. L., & Fredrickson, B. F. (1998). Socioemotional selectivity in healthy older people and younger people living with the human inmmunodeficiency virus: The centrality of emotion when the future is constrained. *Health Psychology, 17,* 1–10.

Carstensen, L. L., & Freund, A. M. (1994). The resilience of the self. *Developmental Review, 14,* 81–92.

Carstensen, L. L., Hanson, K. A., & Freund, A. M. (1995). Selection and compensation in adulthood. In R. A. Dixon & L. Bäckman (Eds.), *Compensating for psychological deficits and declines: Managing losses and promoting gains* (pp. 107–126). Mahwah, NJ: Erlbaum.

Carstensen, L. L., Isaacowitz, D. M., & Charles, S. T. (1999). Taking time seriously: A theory of socioemotional selectivity. *American Psychologist, 54,* 165–181.

Carver, C. S., & Scheier, M. F. (1995). *On the self-regulation of behavior.* Cambridge, UK: Cambridge University Press.

Case, R. (1985). *Intellectual development: From birth to adulthood.* New York: Academic Press.

Cattell, R. B. (1971). *Abilities: Their structure, growth, and action.* Boston: Houghton Mifflin.

Charness, N. (1981a). Search in chess: Age and skill differences. *Journal of Experimental Psychology: Human Perception and Performance, 7,* 467–476.

Charness, N. (1981b). Visual short-term memory and aging in chess players. *Journals of Gerontology, 36,* 615–619.

Charness, N. (1983). Age, skill, and bridge bidding: A chronometric analysis. *Journal of Verbal Learning and Verbal Behavior, 22,* 406–416.

Charness, N. (1987). Component processes in bridge bidding and novel problem solving tasks. *Canadian Journal of Psychology, 41,* 223–243.

Cicirelli, V. G. (1982). Sibling influence throughout the life span. In M. E. Lamb & B. Sutton-Smith (Eds.), *Sibling relationships: Their nature and significance across the lifespan* (pp. 267–284). Hillsdale, NJ: Erlbaum.

Cicirelli, V. G. (1985). The role of siblings as family caregivers. In W. J. Sauer & R. T. Coward (Eds.), *Social support networks and the care of the elderly* (pp. 93–107). New York: Springer.

Clayton, V. P., & Birren, J. E. (1980). The development of wisdom across the life span: A reexamination of an ancient topic. In P. B. Baltes & J. O. G. Brim (Eds.), *Life-span development and behavior* (Vol. 3, pp. 103–135). New York: Academic Press.

Coats, E. J., Janoff-Bulman, R., & Alpert, N. (1996). Approach versus avoidance goals: Differences in self-evaluation and well-being. *Personality and Social Psychology Bulletin, 22,* 1057–1067.

Connidis, I. A. (1989). Siblings as friends in later life. *American Behavioral Scientist, 33,* 81–93.

Cooper, B. (1997). Epidemiology of the dementias in late life. In R. Jacoby & C. Oppenheimer (Eds.), *Psychiatry in the elderly* (pp. 439–453). Oxford, UK: Oxford University Press.

Crimmins, E. M., Hayward, M. D., & Saito, Y. (1996). Differentials in active life expectancy in the older population of the United States. *Journals of Gerontology: Social Sciences, 51B,* S111–S120.

Cumming, E., & Henry, W. E. (1961). *Growing old.* New York: Basic Books.

Diehl, M. (1998). Everyday competence in later life: Current status and future directions. *Gerontologist, 38*(4), 422–433.

Diener, E. (1999, November). *Measurement and findings on subjective well-being.* Distinguished Lecture presented at the Max Planck Institute for Human Development, Berlin, Germany.

Diener, E., Suh, E. K., Lucas, R. E., & Smith, H. L. (1999). Subjective well-being: Three decades of progress. *Psychological Bulletin, 125,* 276–302.

Dinkel, R. H. (1994). Demographische Alterung: Ein Überblick unter besonderer Berücksichtigung der Mortalitätsentwicklung [Demographic aging: An overview with special consideration of the development of mortality]. In P. B. Baltes, J. Mittelstraß, & U. M. Staudinger (Eds.), *Alter und Altern: Ein interdisziplinärer Studientext zur Gerontologie [Age and Aging: An interdisciplinary textbook on gerontology]* (pp. 62–93). Berlin: de Gruyter.

Dykstra, P. A. (1993). The differential availability of relationships and the provision and effectiveness of support to older adults. *Journal of Social and Personal Relationships, 10,* 355–370.

Elliot, A. J., & Church, M. A. (1997). A hierarchical model of approach and avoidance motivation. *Journal of Personality and Social Psychology, 72,* 218–232.

Elliot, A. J., & Sheldon, K. M. (1997). Avoidance achievement motivation: A personal goal analysis. *Journal of Personality and Social Psychology, 73,* 171–185.

Elliot, A. J., Sheldon, K. M., & Church, M. A. (1997). Avoidance personal goals and subjective well-being. *Personality and Social Psychology Bulletin, 23,* 915–927.

Emmons, R. A. (1996). Striving and feeling: Personal goals and subjective well-being. In P. M. Gollwitzer & J. A. Bargh (Eds.), *The psychology of action: Linking cognition and motivation to behavior* (pp. 313–337). New York: Guilford Press.

Ericsson, K. A. (1996). *The road to excellence: The acquisition of expert performance in the arts and sciences, sports and games.* Mahwah, NJ: Erlbaum.

Feldman, J. J., Makuc, D. M., Kleinman, J. C., & Huntley, J. C. (1989). National trends in educational differences in mortality. *American Journal of Epidemiology, 129,* 919–933.

Ferring, D., & Filipp, S.-H. (1995). The structure of subjective well-being in the elderly: A test of different models by structural equation modeling. *European Journal of Psychological Assessment, 11,* 32.

Field, D. (1999). Continuity and change in friendships in advanced old age: Findings from the Berkeley Older Generations Study. *International Journal of Aging and Human Development, 48,* 325–346.

Field, D., & Minkler, M. (1988). Continuity and change in social support between young-old and old-old or very-old age. *Journal of Gerontology: Psychological Sciences, 43,* P100–P106.

Frederick, S., & Loewenstein, G. (1999). Hedonic adaptation. In D. Kahneman, E. Diener, & N. Schwarz (Eds.), *Well-being: The foundations of hedonic psychology* (pp. 302–329). New York: Russell Sage Foundation.

Fredrickson, B. C., & Carstensen, L. L. (1990). Choosing social partners: How old age and anticipated endings make people more selective. *Psychology and Aging, 5,* 163–171.

Freund, A. M. (1997). Individuating age-salience: A psychological perspective on the salience of age in the life course. *Human Development, 40,* 287–292.

Freund, A. M., & Baltes, P. B. (1998). Selection, optimization, and compensation as strategies of life-management: Correlations with subjective indicators of successful aging. *Psychology and Aging, 13,* 531–543.

Freund, A. M., & Baltes, P. B. (1999). Selection, optimization, and compensation as strategies of life management: Correction to Freund and Baltes (1998). *Psychology and Aging, 14,* 700–702.

Freund, A. M., & Baltes, P. B. (2000). The orchestration of selection, optimization, and compensation: An action-theoretical conceptualization of a theory of developmental regulation. In W. J. Perrig & A. Grob (Eds.), *Control of human behavior, mental processes and consciousness* (pp. 35–58). Mahwah, NJ: Erlbaum.

Freund, A. M., Li, K. Z. H., & Baltes, P. B. (1999). Successful development and aging: The role of selection, optimization, and compensation. In J. Brandtstädter & R. M. Lerner (Eds.), *Action and self-development: Theory and research through the life span* (pp. 401–434). Thousand Oaks, CA: Sage.

Fries, J. F. (1990). Medical perspectives upon successful aging. In P. B. Baltes & M. M. Baltes (Eds.), *Successful aging: Perspectives from the behavioral sciences* (pp. 35–49). Cambridge, UK: Cambridge University Press.

Fung, H., Carstensen, L. L., & Lutz, A. (1999). Influence of time on social preferences: Implications for life-span development. *Psychology and Aging, 14,* 595–604.

Furner, S. E., Rudberg, M. A., & Cassel, C. K. (1995). Medical conditions differentially affect the development of IADL disability: Implications for medical care and research. *Gerontologist, 35,* 444–450.

Gallagher-Thompson, D., Futterman, A., Farberow, N., Thompson, L. W., & Peterson, J. (1993). The impact of spousal bereavement on older widows and widowers. In M. S. Stroebe, W. Stroebe, & R. O. Hansson (Eds.), *Handbook of bereavement: Theory, research, and intervention* (pp. 227–239). Cambridge, UK: Cambridge University Press.

George, L. K. (1981). Subjective well-being: Conceptual and methodological issues. In C. Eisdorfer (Ed.), *Annual review of gerontology and geriatrics* (Vol. 2). New York: Springer.

Goetting, A. (1986). The developmental tasks of siblingship over the life cycle. *Journal of Marriage and the Family, 48,* 703–714.

Gollwitzer, P. M. (1996). Das Rubikonmodell der Handlungsphasen [The rubicon model of action phases]. In J. Kuhl & H. Heckhausen (Eds.), *Motivation, Volition, und Handlung* [*Motivation, volition, action*] (Vol. 4, pp. 531–582). Göttingen, Germany: Hogrefe.

Havighurst, R. J. (1963). Successful aging. In R. H. Williams, C. Tibbitts, & W. Donahue (Eds.), *The process of aging: Social and psychological perspectives* (Vol. 1, pp. 299–320). New York: Atherton Press.

Havighurst, R. J., & Albrecht, R. (1953). *Older people.* New York: Longmans Green.

Havighurst, R. J., Neugarten, B. L., & Tobin, S. S. (1968). Disengagement and patterns of aging. *Gerontologist, 4,* 24.

Hayslip, B. (1989). Alternative mechanisms for improvements in fluid ability performance among older adults. *Psychology and Aging, 4,* 122–124.

Heckhausen, J. (1999). *Developmental regulation in adulthood: Age-normative and sociostructural constraints as adaptive challenges.* New York: Cambridge University Press.

Heckhausen, J., Dixon, R. A., & Baltes, P. B. (1989). Gains and losses in development throughout adulthood as perceived by different adult age groups. *Developmental Psychology, 25,* 109–121.

Heckhausen, J., & Schulz, R. (1995). A life-span theory of control. *Psychological Review, 102,* 284–304.

Heckhausen, J., & Schulz, R. (1998). Developmental regulation in adulthood: Selection and compensation via primary and secondary control. In J. Heckhausen & C. S. Dweck (Eds.), *Motivation and self-regulation across the life span* (pp. 50–77). New York: Cambridge University Press.

Heckhausen, J., & Schulz, R. (1999). Biological and societal canalizations and individuals' developmental goals. In J. Brandtstädter & R. Lerner (Eds.), *Action and self-development: Theory and research through the life span* (pp. 67–103). London, UK: Sage.

Heckhausen, J., Schulz, R., & Wrosch, C. (1998). *Developmental regulation in adulthood: Optimization in primary and secondary control.* Berlin: Max Planck Institute for Human Development.

Heller, K., & Mansbach, W. E. (1984). The multifaceted nature of social support in a community sample of elderly women. *Journal of Social Issues, 40,* 99–113.

Hess, T. M., & Pullen, S. M. (1996). Memory in context. In F. Blanchard-Fields & T. M. Hess (Eds.), *Perspectives on cognitive change in adulthood and aging* (pp. 387–427). New York: McGraw-Hill.

Hobfoll, S. E. (2001). The influence of culture, community, and the nested-self in the stress process: Advancing conservation of resources theory. *Applied Psychology: An International Review, 50,* 337–421.

Hofman, A., Rocca, W., Brayne, C., Breteler, M. B. B., Clarke, M., Cooper, B., Copeland, J. R., Dartigues, J. F., da Silva Droux, A., & Hagnell, O. (1991). The prevalence of dementia in Europe: A collaborative study of 1980–1990 findings. *International Journal of Epidemiology, 20,* 736–748.

Horgas, A. L., Wilms, H.-U., & Baltes, M. M. (1998). Daily life in very old age: Everyday activities as expression of successful living. *Gerontologist, 38,* 556–568.

Horn, J. L. (1982). The theory of fluid and crystallized intelligence in relation to concepts of cognitive psychology and aging in adulthood. In F. I. M. Craik & S. Trehub (Eds.), *Aging and cognitive processes* (pp. 237–278). New York: Plenum Press.

Jagger, C., Clarke, M., & Clarke, S. J. (1991). Getting older—feeling younger: The changing health profile of the elderly. *International Journal of Epidemiology, 20,* 234–238.

Jorm, A. F., Korten, A. E., & Henderson, A. S. (1987). The prevalence of dementia: A quantitative integration of the literature. *Acta Psychiatrica Scandinavica, 76,* 465–479.

Kahana, E., & Kahana, B. (1996). Conceptual and empirical advances in understanding aging well through proactive adaptation. In V. L. Bengtson (Ed.), *Adulthood and aging: Research on continuities and discontinuities* (pp. 18–40). New York: Springer.

Kahn, R. L., & Antonucci, T. C. (1980). Convoys over the life course. Attachment, roles, and social support. In P. B. Baltes & O. G. Brim (Eds.), *Life-span development and behavior* (pp. 254–283). New York: Academic Press.

Kail, R. (1991). Developmental change in speed of processing during childhood and adolescence. *Psychological Bulletin, 109,* 490–501.

Kail, R., & Salthouse, T. A. (1994). Processing speed as a mental capacity. *Acta Psychologica, 86,* 199–225.

Kannisto, V., Turpeinen, O., & Nieminen, M. (1999). *Finnish life tables since 1751.* Rostock, Germany: Max Planck Institute for Demographic Research. Retrieved from www.demographic-research.org/Volumes/Vol1/1 (August 2000).

Katz, S., Ford, A. B., Moskowitz, R. W., Jackson, B. A., & Jaffe, M. W. (1963). Studies of illness in the aged. The index of ADL: A standardized measure of biological and psychosocial function. *Journal of the American Medical Association, 185,* 914–919.

Kessler, R. C., & McLeod, J. D. (1985). Social support and mental health in community samples. In S. Cohen & S. L. Syme (Eds.), *Social support and health* (pp. 219–240). New York: Academic Press.

Kliegl, R., Smith, J., & Baltes, P. B. (1990). On the locus and process of magnification of age differences during mnemonic training. *Developmental Psychology, 26,* 894–904.

Klinger, E. (1977). *Meaning and void: Inner experience and the incentives in people's lives.* Minneapolis: University of Minnesota Press.

Knopf, M., Kolodziej, P., & Preussler, W. (1990). Der ältere Mensch als Experte: Literaturübersicht über die Rolle von Expertenwissen für die kognitive Leistungsfähigkeit im höheren Alter [The elderly person as expert: Literature review on the role of expert knowledge for cognitive performance in older age]. *Zeitschrift für Gerontopsychologie und -psychiatrie, 4,* 233–248.

Labouvie-Vief, G., Chiodo, L. M., Goguen, L. A., Diehl, M., & Orwoll, L. (1995). Representations of self across the life span. *Psychology and Aging, 10,* 404–415.

Lang, F. R., & Carstensen, L. L. (1994). Close emotional relationships in late life: Further support for proactive aging in the social domain. *Psychology and Aging, 2,* 315–324.

Lang, F. R., & Carstensen, L. L. (1998). Social relationships and adaptation in later life. In A. S. Bellack & M. Hersen (Ed.), *Comprehensive clinical psychology: Vol. 7. Clinical geropsychology* (pp. 55–72). Oxford, UK: Elsevier Science.

Lang, F. R., Staudinger, U. M., & Carstensen, L. L. (1998). Perspectives on socioemotional selectivity in late life: How personality and social context do (and do not) make a difference. *Journal of Gerontology: Psychological Sciences, 53B,* 21–30.

Lawton, M. P. (1983). Environment and other determinants of well-being in older people. *Gerontologist, 23,* 349–357.

Lawton, M. P. (1985). The elderly in context: Perspectives from environmental psychology and gerontology. *Environment and Behavior, 17,* 501–519.

Lawton, M. P. (1989). Environmental proactivity in older people. In V. L. Bengston & K. W. Schaie (Eds.), *The course of later life: Research and reflections* (pp. 15–23). New York: Springer.

Lawton, M. P., & Brody, E. M. (1969). Assessment of older people: Self-maintaining and instrumental activities of daily living. *Gerontologist, 9,* 179–186.

Lawton, M. P., Kleban, M. H., & Dean, J. (1993). Affect and age: Cross-sectional comparisons of structure and prevalence. *Psychology and Aging, 8,* 165–175.

Lawton, M. P., & Nahemow, L. (1973). Ecology and the aging process. In C. Eisdorfer & M. P. Lawton (Eds.), *The psychology of adult development and aging* (pp. 619–674). Washington, DC: American Psychological Association.

Lemon, B. W., Bengtson, V. L., & Peterson, J. A. (1971). An exploration of the activity theory of aging: Activity types and life satisfactions among in-movers to a retirement community. *Journal of Gerontology, 27,* 511–523.

Lerner, R. M. (Ed.). (1998). *The handbook of child psychology: Theoretical models of human development* (5th ed., Vol. 1). New York: Wiley.

Lerner, R. M., & Busch-Rossnagel, N. A. (1981). Individuals as producers of their development: Conceptual and empirical bases. In R. M. Lerner & N. A. Busch-Rossnagel (Eds.), *Individuals as producers of their development: A life-span perspective* (pp. 1–36). New York: Academic Press.

Lerner, R. M., Freund, A. M., DeStefanis, I., & Habermas, T. (2001). Understanding Developmental Regulation in Adolescence: The use of the selection, optimization, and compensation model. *Human Development, 44*(1), 29–50.

Levenson, R. W., Carstensen, L. L., Friesen, W. V., & Ekman, P. (1991). The influence of age and gender on affect, physiology, and their interrelations: A study of long-term marriages. *Journal of Personality and Social Psychology, 67,* 56–68.

Li, S.-C., & Lindenberger, U. (1999). Cross-level unification: A computational exploration of the link between deterioration of neurotransmitter systems and dedifferentiation of cognitive abilities in old age. In L. G. Nilsson & H. Markowitsch (Eds.), *Cognitive neuroscience of memory* (pp. 104–146). Toronto, Canada: Hogrefe & Huber.

Lindenberger, U., & Reischies, F. M. (1999). Limits and potentials of intellectual functioning in old age. In P. B. Baltes & K. U. Mayer (Eds.), *The Berlin Aging Study: Aging from 70 to 100* (Vol. 12, pp. 329–359). New York: Cambridge University Press.

Little, B. R. (1989). *Personal projects analysis: Trivial pursuits, magnificent obsessions, and the search for coherence.* New York: Springer.

Lund, D. A., Caserta, M. S., & Dimond, M. F. (1993). The course of spousal bereavement in later life. In M. S. Stroebe, W. Stroebe, & R. O. Hansson (Eds.), *Handbook of bereavement: Theory, research, and intervention* (pp. 240–254). Cambridge, UK: Cambridge University Press.

Maddox, G. L. (1963). Activity and morale: A longitudinal study of selected elderly subjects. *Social Forces, 42,* 195–204.

Maddox, G. L. (1965). Fact and artefact: Evidence bearing on disengagement theory. *Human Development, 8,* 117–130.

Maddox, G. L. (1985). The process of disengagement: Unfalsifiable theories never die [Special Issue]. *Gerontologist, 25,* 27.

Maddox, G. L., & Clark, D. O. (1992). Trajectories of functional impairment in later life. *Journal of Health and Social Behavior, 33,* 114–125.

Magnusson, D. (Ed.). (1996). *The life-span development of individuals: Behavioural, neurobiological and psychosocial perspectives.* Cambridge, UK: Cambridge University Press.

Manton, K. G. (1990). Mortality and morbidity. In R. Binstock & L. George (Eds.), *Handbook of aging and social sciences* (3rd ed., pp. 64–89). San Diego, CA: Academic Press.

Manton, K. G., Corder, L. S., & Stallard, E. (1993). Estimates of change in chronic disability and institutional incidence and prevalence rates in the U.S. elderly population from the 1982, 1984, and 1989 National Long Term Care Survey. *Journal of Gerontology: Social Sciences, 48,* S153–S166.

Mares, M.-L. (1995). The aging family. In M. A. Fitzpatrick & A. L. Vangelisti (Eds.), *Explaining family interactions* (pp. 344–374). Thousand Oaks, CA: Sage.

Marsiske, M., Lang, F. R., Baltes, P. B., & Baltes, M. M. (1995). Selective optimization with compensation: Life-span perspectives on successful human development. In R. A. Dixon & L. Bäckman (Eds.), *Compensating for psychological deficits and declines: Managing losses and promoting gains* (pp. 35–79). Mahwah, NJ: Erlbaum.

Matthews, K. A., Kelsey, S. F., Meilahn, E. N., Kuller, L. H., & Wing, R. R. (1989). Educational attainment and behavioral and biological risk factors for coronary heart disease in middle-aged women. *American Journal of Epidemiology, 129,* 1132–1144.

Medina, J. J. (1996). *The clock of ages. Why we age—how we age—winding back the clock.* Cambridge, UK: Cambridge University Press.

Meeks, C. B., Nickols, S. Y., & Sweaney, A. L. (1999). Demographic comparisons of aging in five selected countries. *Journal of Family and Economic Issues, 20,* 223–250.

Miller, G. A., Galanter, E., & Pribram, K.-H. (1960). *Plans of structure of behavior.* New York: Holt, Rinehart, and Winston.

Mischel, W. (1996). From good intentions to willpower. In P. M. Gollwitzer & J. A. Bargh (Eds.), *The psychology of action* (pp. 197–218). New York: Guilford Press.

Palmore, E. (1981). *Social patterns in normal aging: Findings from the Duke Longitudinal Study.* Durham, NC: Duke University Press.

Palmore, E. B., & Kivett, V. R. (1985). Change in life satisfaction. In E. B. Balmore, E. W. Busse, G. L. Maddox, J. B. Nowline, & I. C. Siegler (Eds.), *Normal aging: Vol. 3. Reports from the Duke Longitudinal Studies, 1975–1984* (pp. 373–380). Durham, NC: Duke University Press.

Peterson, C. (2000). The future of optimism. *American Psychologist, 55,* 44–55.

Pulkkinen, L. (2000). Developmental psychology. In K. Pawlik & M. R. Rosenzweig (Eds.), *International handbook of psychology: Vol. 2. Adulthood and aging* (pp. 261–282). Thousand Oaks, CA: Sage.

Reichard, S., Livson, F., & Peterson, P. G. (1962). *Aging and personality. A study of eighty-seven older men.* New York: Arno Press.

Riley, M. W. (1998). Letters to the editor. *Gerontologist, 38,* 151.

Rosow, I. (1973). The social context of the aging self. *Gerontologist, 13,* 82–87.

Ross, H. G., & Milgram, J. I. (1982). Important variables in adult sibling relationships: A qualitative analysis. In M. E. Lamb & B. Sutton-Smith (Eds.), *Sibling relationships: Their nature and significance across the lifespan* (pp. 225–266). Hillsdale, NJ: Erlbaum.

Rowe, J. W., & Kahn, R. L. (1987). Human aging: Usual and successful. *Science, 237,* 143–149.

Rowe, J. W., & Kahn, R. L. (1998). *Successful aging.* New York: Pantheon Books.

Ryff, C. D. (1989). Happiness is everything, or is it? Explorations on the meaning of psychological well-being. *Journal of Personality and Social Psychology, 57,* 1069–1081.

Ryff, C. D. (1995). Psychological well-being in adult life. *Current Directions in Psychological Science, 4,* 99–104.

Salthouse, T. A. (1984). Effects of age and skill in typing. *Journal of Experimental Psychology: General, 113,* 345–371.

Salthouse, T. A., Hancock, H. E., Meinz, E. J., & Hambrick, D. Z. (1996). Interrelations of age, visual acuity, and cognitive functioning. *Journal of Gerontology: Psychological Sciences, 51B,* P317–P330.

Salthouse, T. A., & Saults, J. S. (1987). Multiple spans in transcription typing. *Journal of Applied Psychology, 72,* 187–196.

Schaie, K. W. (1994). The course of adult intellectual development. *American Psychologist, 49,* 304–313.

Schaie, K. W. (1996). *Intellectual development in adulthood: The Seattle Longitudinal Study.* New York: Cambridge University Press.

Schaie, K. W., & Willis, S. L. (1986). Can intellectual decline in the elderly be reversed? *Developmental Psychology, 22,* 223–232.

Schaie, K. W., & Willis, S. L. (1999). Theories of everyday competence and aging. In V. L. Bengtson & K. W. Schaie (Eds.), *Handbook of theories of aging* (pp. 174–195). New York: Springer.

Schulz, R. (1986). Successful aging: Balancing primary and secondary control. *Adult Development and Aging News, 13,* 2–4.

Schulz, R., & Heckhausen, J. (1996). A life-span model of successful aging. *American Psychologist, 51,* 702–714.

Schwarz, N., & Strack, F. (1999). Reports of subjective well-being: Judgmental processes and their methodological implications. In D. Kahneman, E. Diener, & N. Schwarz (Eds.), *Well-being: The foundations of hedonic psychology* (pp. 61–84). New York: Russell Sage Foundation.

Schwarzer, R., & Leppin, A. (1991). Social support and health: A theoretical and empirical overview. *Journal of Social and Personal Relationships, 8,* 99–127.

Scott, J. P. (1983). Siblings and other kin. In T. H. Brubaker (Ed.), *Family relationships in later life* (pp. 47–62). Beverly Hills, CA: Sage.

Seeman, T. E. (1996). Social ties and health: The benefits of social integration. *Annals of Epidemiology, 6,* 442–451.

Seligman, M. E. P. (1991). *Learned optimism.* New York: Knopf.

Siegler, I. C., & Costa, P. T., Jr. (1985). Health behavior relationships. In J. E. Birren & K. W. Schaie (Eds.), *Handbook of the psychology of aging* (2nd ed., pp. 144–166). New York: Van Nostrand Reinhold.

Singer, T. (2000). *Testing-the-Limits in einer mnemonischen Fähigkeit: Eine Studie zur kognitiven Plastizität im hohen Alter* [*Testing-the-Limits in a mnemonic technique: A study of cognitive plasticity in very old age*]. Berlin, Germany: Free University. Retrieved 2001, from www.Diss.FU-Berlin.de/2000/78/index. html

Smith, J., Fleeson, W., Geiselmann, B., Settersten, R. A., Jr., & Kunzmann, U. (1999). Well-being in very old age: Predictions from objective life conditions and subjective experience. In P. B. Baltes & K. U. Mayer (Eds.), *The Berlin Aging Study: Aging from 70 to 100* (pp. 450–471). New York: Cambridge University Press.

Smith, J., & Goodnow J. J. (1999). Unasked-for support and unsolicited advice: Age and the quality of social experience. *Psychology and Aging, 14,* 108– 121.

Staudinger, U. M. (1996). Wisdom and the social-interactive foundation of the mind. In P. B. Baltes & U. M. Staudinger (Eds.), *Interactive minds: Life-span perspectives on the social foundation of cognition* (pp. 276–318). New York: Cambridge University Press.

Staudinger, U. M., & Freund, A. M. (1998). Krank und "arm" im hohen Alter und trotzdem guten Mutes? Untersuchungen im Rahmen eines Modells psychologischer Widerstandsfähigkeit [Sick and "poor" in old age and still in good spirits? A study of psychological resilience]. *Zeitschrift für Klinische Psychologie, 27,* 78–85.

Staudinger, U. M., Marsiske, M., & Baltes, P.B. (1995). Resilience and reserve capacity in later adulthood: Potentials and limits of development across the life span. In D. Cicchetti & D. J. Cohen (Eds.), *Developmental psychopathology: Vol. 2. Risk, disorder, and adaptation* (pp. 801–847). New York: Wiley.

Steinhagen-Thiessen, E., & Borchelt, M. (1999). Morbidity, medication, and functional limitations in very old age. In P. B. Baltes & K. U. Mayer (Eds.), *The Berlin Aging Study: Aging from 70 to 100* (pp. 131–166). New York: Cambridge University Press.

Steinhagen-Thiessen, E., Gerok, W., & Borchelt, M. (1994). Innere Medizin und Geriatrie [Internal medicine and geriatrics]. In P. B. Baltes, J. Mittelstraß, & U. M. Staudinger (Eds.), *Alter und Altern: Ein interdisziplinärer Studientext zur Gerontologie [Age and aging: An interdisciplinary textbook on gerontology]* (pp. 124–150). Berlin: de Gruyter.

Sternberg, R. J. (1990). Wisdom and its relations to intelligence and creativity. In R. J. Sternberg (Ed.), *Wisdom: Its nature, origins, and development* (pp. 142–149). New York: Cambridge University Press.

Stroebe, M. S., & Stroebe, W. (1993). The mortality of bereavement: A review. In M. S. Stroebe, W. Stroebe, & R. O. Hansson (Eds.), *Handbook of bereavement: Theory, research, and intervention* (pp. 175–226). Cambridge, UK: Cambridge University Press.

Thomae, H. E. (1976). *Patterns of aging*. Basel, Switzerland: Karger.

Thomae, H. E. (1987). Alternsformen: Wege zu ihrer methodischen und begrifflichen Erfassung [Forms of aging: Approaches for their methodological and conceptual assessment]. In U. Lehr & H. Thomae (Eds.), *Formen seelischen Alterns [Forms of mental aging]* (pp. 173–195). Stuttgart, Germany: Enke.

Tsai, J. L., Levenson, R. W., & Carstensen, L. L. (2000). Autonomic, subjective, and expressive responses to emotional films in older and younger Chinese Americans and European Americans. *Psychology and Aging, 15,* 684–693.

Tucker, J. S., Schwartz, J. E., Clark, K. M., & Friedman, H. S. (1999). Age-related changes in the associations of social network ties with mortality risk. *Psychology and Aging, 14,* 564–571.

United Nations. (1996). *The ageing of the world's population.* Retrieved August 2000, from http://www.un.org/ecosocdev/geninfo/ageing/ageing-e.htm

van Sonderen, E., Ormel, J., Brilman, E., & van Linden van den Heuvell, C.-M. (1990). Personal network delineation: A comparison of the exchange, affective and role-relation approach. In K. C. P. M. Knipscheer & T. C. Antonucci (Eds.), *Social network research* (pp. 101–120). Amsterdam: Swets & Zeitlinger.

Vaupel, J. (1995). Life expectancy. In G. L. Maddox (Ed.), *The encyclopedia of aging* (pp. 559–560). New York: Springer.

Vaupel, J. W., Carey, J. R., Christensen, K., Johnson, T. E., Yashin, A. I., Holm, N. V., Iachine, I. A., Kannisto, V., Khazaeli, A. A., Liedo, P., Longo, V. D., Zeng, Y., Manton, K. G., & Curtsinger, J. W. (1998). Biodemographic trajectories of longevity. *Science, 280,* 855–860.

Verbrugge, L. M. (1989). The twain meet: Empirical explanation of sex differences in health and mortality. *Journal of Health and Social Behavior, 30,* 282–304.

Verhaegen, P., Marcoen, A., & Goossens, L. (1992). Improving memory performance in the aged through mnemonic training: A metaanalytic study. *Psychology and Aging, 7,* 242–251.

Wagner, M., Schütze, Y., & Lang, F. R. (1999). Social relationships in old age. In P. B. Baltes & K. U. Mayer (Eds.), *The Berlin Aging Study: Aging from 70 to 100* (pp. 282–301). New York: Cambridge University Press.

Wegner, D. M. (1992). You can't always think what you want: Problems in the suppression of unwanted thoughts. In M. Zanna (Ed.), *Advances in experimental social psychology* (Vol. 25, pp. 193–225). San Diego, CA: Academic Press.

Whitbourne, S. K. (1985). *The aging body.* New York: Springer.

Wiese, B. S., Freund, A. M., & Baltes, P. B. (2000). Selection, optimization, and compensation: An action-related approach to work and partnership. *Journal of Vocational Behavior, 57,* 273–300.

Willis, S. L. (1996). Everyday problem solving. In J. E. Birren & K. W. Schaie (Eds.), *Handbook of the psychology of aging* (4th ed., pp. 287–307). San Diego, CA: Academic Press.

World Health Organization. (1998). *Fact Sheet Nr 135. Population aging: A public health challenge.* Retrieved August 2000, from http://www.who.int/inf-fs/fact135.html

Wrosch, C., & Heckhausen, J. (1999). Control processes before and after passing a developmental deadline: Activation and deactivation of intimate relationship goals. *Journal of Personality and Social Psychology, 77,* 415–427.

Zarit, S. H., & Eggebeen, D. J. (1995). Parent-child relationships in adulthood and old age. In M. H. Bornstein (Ed.), *Handbook of parenting: Vol. 1. Children and parenting* (pp. 119–140). Mahwah, NJ: Erlbaum.

Author Index

Aaronson, D., 177
Abbott, R. D., 378, 379, 380, 381
Abbott, R., 380
Abe, J. A., 213, 480
Abeles, R., 103
Abelson, R., 561
Aber, J. L., 152, 345
Aber, L., 376, 380
Aber, L., 400
Abidin, R., 522
Abramovitch, R., 524, 525
Abrams, L. A., 539
Abramson, L. Y., 355, 356
Achenbach, T. M., 303
Achenbaum, W. A., 454
Ackerman, B. P., 50, 213
Ackermann, C., 128
Acredolo, L. P., 38
Adair, V., 362
Adamek, M. E., 497
Adami, H. O., 309, 313
Adams, G., 155
Adams, G. R., 353
Adams, M. J., 48
Adams, R. G., 489, 495, 498
Adams, R. J., 72
Adamson, L., 96
Adelman, H. S., 48
Adler, N. E., 305, 582, 587
Adler, P., 255, 256, 404
Adler, P. A., 255, 256, 404
Adler, T. F., 337, 338, 340, 341
Administration on Children, Youth,
    and Families, 378
Adolfsson, R., 448, 458
Adolph, K. E., 69
Affleck, G., 526
Ageton, S. S., 408
Agnew, R., 406
Agosto, C. D., 561
Agree, E. M., 493
Ahadi, S. A., 358
Ahmed, M. L., 300
Aiken, L. R., 602, 603
Ainsworth, M., 253
Ainsworth, M. D., 196
Ainsworth, M. D. S., 100, 101, 136, 217, 223,
    224, 400, 520, 567
Airaksinen, E., 527
Ajzen, I., 581
Akana, S. F., 115
Akhtar, N., 183, 188
Akiyama, H., 488, 489, 491, 591, 605, 606
Aksan, N., 217, 218

Alansky, J. A., 128, 401
Albert, M., 491
Albrecht, H. T., 306
Albrecht, R., 611
Albus, K. E., 101
Aldwin, C., 481
Aldwin, C. M., 52, 426
Alessandri, S. M., 214
Alfredson, B., 428
Alkon, A., 127
Allan, G., 495, 498
Allard, M., 429
Allen, J. P., 353, 356, 400, 405, 406
Allen, K., 357
Allen, K. R., 252
Allen, S. R., 584
Allen, V., 296, 306
Allensworth, E., 380
Allhusen, V. D., 135
Allison, K. R., 587
Allport, G. W., 148
Almeida, D. M., 358
Alpert, A., 226
Alpert, N., 617
Altaribba, J., 282
Altham, P. M., 304
Alwin, A., 126
Amadio, L., 428
Aman, C., 562, 563
Amaral, D. G., 118
Amato, P. R., 499, 567–568, 569, 570
American Association of University Women, 335
American Association on Mental Retardation
    (AAMR), 514
American Professional Society on the Abuse of
    Children, 563
American Psychiatric Association, 514
American Psychological Association, 43, 55
American Psychological Society, 43
Ames, C., 333
Ames, E. W., 67
Amling, C. L., 435
Ammons, C., 200, 202
Ampos, J. J., 149
Amsel, G., 77
Anastasi, A., 23
Anderman, E., 333
Anderman, E. M., 330
Anders, T., 121
Andersen, B. L., 496
Andersen, C., 19, 329
Andersen-Ranberg, K., 428
Anderson, B., 496, 592
Anderson, B.-E., 156, 157

Anderson, B. J., 588
Anderson, C., 128
Anderson, D. I., 98, 99, 104
Anderson, K. E., 398
Anderson, L. P., 362
Anderson, N. A., 433
Anderson, P. M., 94
Anderson, R. N., 424, 581
Andersson, T., 306
Andres, D., 445, 476, 477
Andrews, D. W., 257, 411
Aneshensel, C. S., 306
Angell, K. E., 355, 356
Angleitner, A., 357
Angold, A., 302–303, 306
Ansbacher, H. L., 258, 259
Ansbacher, R. R., 258, 259
Anstey, K. J., 605
Anthony, E. J., 384
Antonakos, C. L., 587
Antonova, T. G., 66
Antonucci, T. C., 488, 489, 490, 491, 581, 591,
    605, 606
Antonucci, T., 490
Appelbaum, M., 83
Appelbaum, M. I., 98
Applebaum, J. C., 159
Apter, D., 309
Apter, D. L., 309
Aquilino, W. S., 493, 500
Arbreton, A. J., 340
Arbuckle, T., 445
Arbuckle, T. Y., 476, 477
Arbuthnot, J., 379
Archer, J., 301, 302
Arcus, D., 94, 128
Arias, R. M., 434
Aristotle, 514
Armstead, C. A., 433
Arnett, J., 156
Arnett, J. J., 330, 354, 355
Arnold, G. S., 302, 303, 304
Arnold, K. D., 337
Arny, L., 384
Aronson, J., 344
Arseneault, L., 302
Arsenio, W. F., 247
Arterberry, M. E., 72
Arunkumar, R., 385, 386
Ary, D., 401
Ary, D. V., 304, 401
Asamen, J. K., 343
Asarnow, J. R., 48, 315
Aseltine, R. H., 499

629

Subject Index